Maat F19 LtS

D0339789

GENDER THROUGH THE PRISM OF DIFFERENCE

FIFTH EDITION

Edited by

Maxine Baca Zinn
Michigan State University

Pierrette Hondagneu-Sotelo
University of Southern California

Michael A. Messner
University of Southern California

Amy M. Denissen
California State University Northridge

New York   Oxford
OXFORD UNIVERSITY PRESS

Oxford University Press is a department of the University of Oxford.
It furthers the University's objective of excellence in research,
scholarship, and education by publishing worldwide.

Oxford   New York
Auckland   Cape Town   Dar es Salaam   Hong Kong   Karachi
Kuala Lumpur   Madrid   Melbourne   Mexico City   Nairobi
New Delhi   Shanghai   Taipei   Toronto

With offices in
Argentina   Austria   Brazil   Chile   Czech Republic   France   Greece
Guatemala   Hungary   Italy   Japan   Poland   Portugal   Singapore
South Korea   Switzerland   Thailand   Turkey   Ukraine   Vietnam

Copyright © 2016, 2011, 2005 by Oxford University Press

For titles covered by Section 112 of the US Higher Education
Opportunity Act, please visit www.oup.com/us/he for the
latest information about pricing and alternate formats.

Published by Oxford University Press
198 Madison Avenue, New York, New York 10016
http://www.oup.com

Oxford is a registered trademark of Oxford University Press.

All rights reserved. No part of this publication may be reproduced,
stored in a retrieval system, or transmitted, in any form or by any means,
electronic, mechanical, photocopying, recording, or otherwise,
without the prior permission of Oxford University Press.

Library of Congress Cataloging-in-Publication Data
Gender through the prism of difference / edited by Maxine Baca Zinn,
Michigan State University, Pierrette Hondagneu-Sotelo, University of
Southern California, Michael A. Messner, University of Southern California,
Amy M. Denissen, California State University Northridge,
New York Oxford. -- Fifth Edition.
      pages cm
   Revised edition of Gender through the prism of difference, 2011.
   Includes bibliographical references.
   ISBN 978-0-19-020004-6
 1. Sex role. I. Zinn, Maxine Baca, 1942- editor. II. Hondagneu-Sotelo,
Pierrette, editor. III. Messner, Michael A., editor.
   HQ1075.G4666 2015
   305.3--dc23
                                                                2015006108

Printing number: 9 8 7 6 5 4 3 2

Printed in the United States of America
on acid-free paper

CONTENTS

---

*Denotes a reading new to this edition.

PREFACE

Over the past 40 years, texts and readers intended for use in women's studies and gender studies courses have changed and developed in important ways. In the 1970s and into the early 1980s, many courses and texts focused almost exclusively on women as a relatively undifferentiated category. Two developments have broadened the study of women. First, in response to criticisms by women of color and by lesbians that heterosexual, white, middle-class feminists had tended to "falsely universalize" their own experiences and issues, courses and texts on gender began in the 1980s to systematically incorporate race and class diversity. And simultaneously, as a result of feminist scholars' insistence that gender be studied as a relational construct, more concrete studies of men and masculinity began to emerge in the 1980s.

This book reflects this belief that race, class, and sexual diversity among women and men should be central to the study of gender. But this collection adds an important new dimension that will broaden the frame of gender studies. By including some articles that are based on research in nations connected to the United States through globalization, tourism, and labor migrations, we hope that *Gender through the Prism of Difference* will contribute to a transcendence of the often myopic, U.S.-based, and Eurocentric focus on the study of sex and gender. The inclusion of these perspectives is not simply useful for illuminating our own cultural blind spots; it also begins to demonstrate how, early in the twenty-first century, gender relations are increasingly centrally implicated in current processes of globalization.

NEW TO THIS EDITION

Because the amount of high-quality research on gender has expanded so dramatically in the past decade, the most difficult task in assembling this collection was deciding *what* to include. The fifth edition, while retaining the structure of the previous edition, is different and improved. This edition includes 26 new articles and discusses material on gender issues relevant to the college-age generation, including gender and popular culture. We have also included articles on Occupy Wall Street, transgender identities and public policies, high-stakes testing and academic profiling, policing and incarceration, the intersection of gender and immigration, and gender and disabilities.

ACKNOWLEDGMENTS

We thank faculty and staff colleagues in the Department of Sociology and the Gender Studies program at the University of Southern California, the Department of Sociology at Michigan State University, and the Department of Sociology at California State University Northridge for their generous support and assistance. Other people contributed their labor to the development of this book. We are grateful to Amy Holzgang, Cerritos College; Lauren McDonald, California State University Northridge; and Linda Shaw, California State University San Marcos, for their invaluable feedback and advice. We thank Heidi R. Lewis of Colorado College for her contributions to the book's ancillary program, available at www.oup-arc.com/bacazinn.

We acknowledge the helpful criticism and suggestions made by the following reviewers: Tennille Allen, Lewis University; Ellen Arnold, Coastal Carolina University; Colleen Bell, Hamline University; Sarah E. Cribbs, Georgetown College; Robert Jenkot, Coastal Carolina University; Heidi R. Lewis, Colorado College; Amanda Moras, Sacred Heart University; Teal Rothschild, Roger Williams University; Maura Ryan, Georgia State University; and Deborah Woodman, Algoma University. We also thank our editor at Oxford University Press, Sherith Pankratz, who has been encouraging, helpful, and patient, and Katy Albis for her assistance throughout the process. We also thank Roxanne Klaas and Tony Mathias for their editorial and marketing assistance with the book.

Finally, we thank our families for their love and support as we worked on this book. Alan Zinn, Prentice Zinn, Gabrielle Cobbs, and Edan Zinn provide inspiration through their work for progressive social change. Miles Hondagneu-Messner and Sasha Hondagneu-Messner continually challenge the neatness of Mike and Pierrette's image of social life. Kari Denissen Cunnien and Isaiah Cunnien instill a commitment to living gently and responsibly on this earth. We do hope, however, that the kind of work that is collected in this book will eventually help them and their generation make sense of the world and move that world into more peaceful, humane, and just directions.

Introduction

Sex and Gender Through the Prism of Difference

"Men can't cry." "Women are victims of patriarchal oppression." "After divorces, single mothers are downwardly mobile, often moving into poverty." "Men don't do their share of housework and child care." "Professional women face barriers such as sexual harassment and a 'glass ceiling' that prevent them from competing equally with men for high-status positions and high salaries." "Heterosexual intercourse is an expression of men's power over women." Sometimes, the students in our sociology and gender studies courses balk at these kinds of generalizations. And they are right to do so. After all, some men are more emotionally expressive than some women, some women have more power and success than some men, some men do their share—or more—of housework and child care, and some women experience sex with men as both pleasurable and empowering. Indeed, contemporary gender relations are complex and changing in various directions, and as such, we need to be wary of simplistic, if handy, slogans that seem to sum up the essence of relations between women and men.

On the other hand, we think it is a tremendous mistake to conclude that "all individuals are totally unique and different," and that therefore all generalizations about social groups are impossible or inherently oppressive. In fact, we are convinced that it is this very complexity, this multifaceted nature of contemporary gender relations, that fairly begs for a sociological analysis of gender. In the title of this book, we use the image of "**the prism of difference**" to illustrate our approach to developing this sociological perspective on contemporary gender relations. The *American Heritage Dictionary* defines "prism," in part, as "a homogeneous transparent solid, usually with triangular bases and rectangular sides, used to produce or analyze a continuous spectrum." Imagine a ray of light—which to the naked eye appears to be only one color—refracted through a prism onto a white wall. To the eye, the result is not an infinite, disorganized scatter of individual colors. Rather, the refracted light displays an order, a structure of relationships among the different colors—a rainbow. Similarly, we propose to use the prism of difference in this book to analyze a continuous spectrum of people to show how gender is organized and experienced differently when refracted through the prism of sexual, racial-ethnic, social class, abilities, age, and national citizenship differences.

EARLY WOMEN'S STUDIES: CATEGORICAL VIEWS OF
"WOMEN" AND "MEN"

Taken together, the articles in this book make the case that it is possible to make good generalizations about women and men. But these generalizations should be drawn carefully, by always asking the questions *"which* women?" and *"which* men?" Scholars of sex and gender have not always done this. In the 1960s and 1970s, women's studies focused on the differences *between* women and men rather than *among* women and men. The very concept of gender, women's studies scholars demonstrated, is based on socially defined difference between women and men. From the macro level of social institutions such as the economy, politics, and religion to the micro level of interpersonal relations, distinctions between women and men structure social relations. Making men and women *different* from one another is the essence of gender. It is also the basis of men's power and domination. Understanding this was profoundly illuminating. Knowing that difference produced domination enabled women to name, analyze, and set about changing their victimization.

In the 1970s, riding the wave of a resurgent feminist movement, colleges and universities began to develop women's studies courses that aimed first and foremost to make women's lives visible. The texts that were developed for these courses tended to stress the things that women shared under **patriarchy**—having the responsibility for housework and child care, the experience or fear of men's sexual violence, a lack of formal or informal access to education, and exclusion from high-status professional and managerial jobs, political office, and religious leadership positions (Brownmiller, 1975; Kanter, 1977).

The study of women in society offered new ways of seeing the world. But the 1970s approach was limited in several ways. Thinking of gender primarily in terms of differences *between* women and men led scholars to overgeneralize about both. The concept of patriarchy led to a dualistic perspective of male privilege and female subordination. Women and men were cast as opposites. Each was treated as a homogeneous category with common characteristics and experiences. This approach *essentialized* women and men. **Essentialism**, simply put, is the notion that women's and men's attributes and indeed women and men themselves are categorically different. From this perspective, male control and coercion of women produced conflict between the sexes. The feminist insight originally introduced by Simone de Beauvoir in 1953— that women, as a group, had been socially defined as the "other" and that men had constructed themselves as the subjects of history, while constructing women as their objects—fueled an energizing sense of togetherness among many women. As college students read books such as *Sisterhood Is Powerful* (Morgan, 1970), many of them joined organizations that fought—with some success—for equality and justice for women.

THE VOICES OF "OTHER" WOMEN

Although this view of women as an oppressed "other" was empowering for certain groups of women, some women began to claim that the feminist view of universal sisterhood ignored and marginalized their major concerns. It soon became apparent that treating women as a group united in its victimization by patriarchy was biased by too narrow a focus on the experiences and perspectives of women from more privileged social groups. "Gender" was treated as a generic category, uncritically applied to women. Ironically, this analysis, which was meant to unify women, instead produced divisions between and among them. The concerns projected as "universal" were removed from the realities of many women's lives. For example, it became a matter of faith in second-wave **feminism** that women's liberation would be accomplished by breaking down the "gendered public-domestic split." Indeed, the feminist call for women to move out of the kitchen and into the workplace resonated in the experiences of many of the college-educated white women who were inspired by Betty Friedan's 1963 book, *The Feminine Mystique*. But the idea that women's movement into workplaces was itself empowering or liberating seemed absurd or irrelevant to many working-class women and women of color. They were already working for wages, as had many of their mothers and grandmothers, and did not consider access to jobs and public life "liberating." For many of these women, liberation had more to do with organizing in communities and workplaces—often alongside men—for better schools, better pay, decent benefits, and other policies to benefit their neighborhoods, jobs, and families. The feminism of the 1970s did not seem to address these issues.

As more and more women analyzed their own experiences, they began to address the power relations that created differences among women and the part that privileged women played in the oppression of others. For many women of color, working-class women, lesbians, and women in contexts outside the United States (especially women in non-Western societies), the focus on male domination was a distraction from other oppressions. Their lived experiences could support neither a unitary theory of gender nor an ideology of universal sisterhood. As a result, finding common ground in a universal female victimization was never a priority for many groups of women.

Challenges to gender stereotypes soon emerged. Women of varied races, classes, national origins, and sexualities insisted that the concept of gender be broadened to take their differences into account (Baca Zinn et al., 1986; Hartmann, 1976; Rich, 1980; Smith, 1977). Many women began to argue that their lives were affected by their location in a number of different hierarchies: as African Americans, Latinas, Native Americans, or Asian Americans in the race hierarchy; as young or old in the age hierarchy; as heterosexual, lesbian, or bisexual in the sexual orientation hierarchy; and as women outside the Western industrialized nations, in subordinated geopolitical contexts. These arguments made it clear that women were not victimized by gender alone but by the historical and systematic denial of rights and privileges based on other differences as well.

MEN AS GENDERED BEINGS

As the voices of "other" women in the mid- to late 1970s began to challenge and expand the parameters of women's studies, a new area of scholarly inquiry was beginning to stir—a critical examination of men and masculinity. To be sure, in those early years of gender studies, the major task was to conduct studies and develop courses about the lives of women to begin to correct centuries of scholarship that rendered invisible women's lives, problems, and accomplishments. But the core idea of feminism—that "femininity" and women's subordination is a social construction—logically led to an examination of the social construction of "masculinity" and men's power. Many of the first scholars to take on this task were psychologists who were concerned with looking at the social construction of "the male sex role" (e.g., Pleck, 1976). By the late 1980s, there was a growing interdisciplinary collection of studies of men and masculinity, much of it by social scientists (Brod, 1987; Kaufman, 1987; Kimmel, 1987; Kimmel & Messner, 1989).

Reflecting developments in women's studies, the scholarship on men's lives tended to develop three themes: First, what we think of as "masculinity" is not a fixed, biological essence of men, but rather is a **social construction** that shifts and changes over time as well as between and among various national and cultural contexts. Second, power is central to understanding gender as a relational construct, and the dominant definition of masculinity is largely about expressing difference from—and superiority over—anything considered "feminine." And third, there is no singular "male sex role." Rather, at any given time there are various masculinities. R. W. Connell (1987, 1995, 2002) has been among the most articulate advocates of this perspective. Connell argues that **hegemonic masculinity** (the dominant and most privileged form of masculinity at any given moment) is constructed in relation to femininities *as well as* in relation to various subordinated or marginalized masculinities. For example, in the United States, various racialized masculinities (e.g., as represented by African American men, Latino immigrant men, etc.) have been central to the construction of hegemonic (white middle-class) masculinity. This "othering" of racialized masculinities, as well as their selective incorporation by dominant groups (Bridges and Pascoe in this volume), helps to shore up the privileges that have been historically connected to hegemonic masculinity. When viewed this way, we can better understand hegemonic masculinity as part of a system that includes gender as well as racial, class, sexual, and other relations of power.

The new literature on men and masculinities also begins to move us beyond the simplistic, falsely categorical, and pessimistic view of men simply as a privileged sex class. When race, social class, sexual orientation, physical abilities, immigrant, or national status are taken into account, we can see that in some circumstances, "male **privilege**" is partly—sometimes substantially—muted (Kimmel & Messner, 2010, Kimmel in this volume). Although it is unlikely that we will soon see a "men's movement" that aims to undermine the power and privileges that are connected with hegemonic masculinity, when we begin to look at "masculinities" through the prism of difference, we can begin to see similarities and possible points of coalition between and among certain groups of women and men (Messner, 1998). Certain kinds of changes in gender relations—for instance, a national family leave policy for working parents—might serve as a means of uniting particular groups of women and men.

GENDER IN GLOBAL CONTEXTS

It is an increasingly accepted truism that late twentieth-century increases in transnational trade, international migration, and global systems of production and communication have diminished both the power of nation-states and the significance of national borders. A much more ignored issue is the extent to which gender relations—in the United States and elsewhere in the world—are increasingly linked to patterns of global economic restructuring. Decisions made in corporate headquarters located in Los Angeles, Tokyo, or London may have immediate repercussions on how women and men thousands of miles away organize their work, community, and family lives (Sassen, 1991). It is no longer possible to study gender relations without giving attention to global processes and inequalities. Scholarship on women in third world contexts has moved from liberal concerns for the impact of development policies on women (Boserup, 1970) to more critical perspectives that acknowledge how international labor and capital mobility are transforming gender and family relations (Hondagneu-Sotelo and Avila; and Mojola, this volume). The transformation of international relations from a 1990s "post–Cold War" environment to an expansion of militarism and warfare in recent years has realigned international gender relations in key ways that call for new examinations of gender, violence, militarism, and culture (Enloe, 1993, 2000; Okin, 1999). The now extended U.S. military presence in the Middle East has brought with it increasing numbers of female troops and, with that, growing awareness of gender and sexual violence both by and within the military.

Around the world, women's paid and unpaid labor is key to global development strategies. Yet it would be a mistake to conclude that gender is molded from the "top down." What happens on a daily basis in families and workplaces simultaneously constitutes and is constrained by structural transnational institutions. For instance, in the second half of the twentieth century young, single women, many of them from poor rural areas, were (and continue to be) recruited for work in export assembly plants along the U.S.–Mexico border, in East and Southeast Asia, in Silicon Valley, in the Caribbean, and in Central America. Although the profitability of these multinational factories depends, in part, on management's ability to manipulate the young women's ideologies of gender, the women do not respond passively or uniformly, but actively resist, challenge, and accommodate. At the same time, the global dispersion of the assembly line has concentrated corporate facilities in many U.S. cities, making available myriad managerial, administrative, and clerical jobs for college-educated women. Women's paid labor is used at various points along this international system of production. Not only employment but also consumption embodies global interdependencies. There is a high probability that the clothing you are wearing and the computer you use originated in multinational corporate headquarters and in assembly plants scattered around third world nations. And if these items were actually manufactured in the United States, they were probably assembled by Latin American and Asian-born women.

Worldwide, international labor migration and refugee movements are creating new types of multiracial societies. Although these developments are often discussed and analyzed with respect to racial differences, gender typically remains absent. As several commentators have noted, the white feminist movement in the United States has not addressed issues of immigration and nationality. Gender, however, has been fundamental in shaping immigration policies (Chang, 1994; Hondagneu-Sotelo, 1994). Direct labor recruitment programs generally solicit either male or female labor (e.g., Filipina nurses and Mexican male farm workers), national disenfranchisement has particular repercussions for women and men, and current immigrant laws are based on very gendered notions of what constitutes "family unification." As Chandra Mohanty suggests, "analytically these issues are the contemporary metropolitan counterpart of women's struggles against colonial occupation in the geographical third world" (1991:23). Moreover, immigrant and refugee women's daily lives often challenge familiar feminist paradigms. The occupations in which immigrant and refugee women concentrate—paid domestic work, informal sector street vending, assembly or industrial piecework performed in the home—often blur the ideological distinction between work and family and between public and private spheres (Hondagneu-Sotelo, 2001; Parreñas, 2001). As the Hondagneu-Sotelo & Avila and the Parreñas articles (this volume) show, immigrant women creatively respond to changes in work and family brought about through migration, innovating changes in what were once thought to be stable, fixed sexuality practices and mores.

FROM PATCHWORK QUILT TO PRISM

All of these developments—the voices of "other" women, the study of men and masculinities, and the examination of gender in transnational contexts—have helped redefine the study of gender. By working to develop knowledge that is inclusive of the experiences of all groups, new insights about gender have begun to emerge. Examining gender in the context of other differences makes it clear that nobody experiences themselves as solely gendered. Instead, gender is configured through cross-cutting forms of difference that carry deep social and economic consequences.

By the mid-1980s, thinking about gender had entered a new stage, which was more carefully grounded in the experiences of diverse groups of women and men. This perspective is a general way of looking at women and men and understanding their relationships to the structure of society. Gender is no longer viewed simply as a matter of two opposite categories of people, males and females, but as a range of social relations among differently situated people. Because centering on difference is a radical challenge to the conventional gender framework, it raises several concerns. If we think of all the systems that converge to simultaneously influence the lives of women and men, we can imagine an infinite number of effects these interconnected systems have on different women and men. Does the recognition that gender can be understood only contextually (meaning that there is no singular "gender" per se) make women's studies and men's studies newly vulnerable to critics in the academy? Does the immersion in difference throw us into a whirlwind of "spiraling diversity" (Hewitt, 1992:316) whereby multiple identities and locations shatter the categories "women" and "men"?

Throughout the book, we take a position directly opposed to an empty pluralism. Although the categories "woman" and "man" have multiple meanings, this does not reduce gender to a "postmodern kaleidoscope of lifestyles. Rather, it points to the *relational* character of gender" (Connell, 1992:736). Not only are masculinity and femininity relational, but different *masculinities* and *femininities* are interconnected through other social structures such as race, class, and nation. The concept of relationality suggests that "the lives of different groups are interconnected even without face-to-face relations (Glenn, 2002:14). The meaning of "woman" is defined by the existence of women of different races and classes. Being a white woman in the United States is meaningful only insofar as it is set apart from and in contradistinction to women of color.

Just as masculinity and femininity each depend on the definition of the other to produce domination, differences *among* women and *among* men are also created in the context of structured relations between dominant and subordinate groups. Situating women's lives in the context of other forms of inequality makes it clear that the privileges of some groups are directly tied to the oppression of others. "Powerful groups gain and maintain power by exploiting the labor and lives of others" (Weber, 2010:6). They may even use their race and class advantage to minimize some of the consequences of patriarchy and/or to oppose other women. Similarly, one can become a man in opposition to other men. For example, "the relation between heterosexual and homosexual men is central, carrying heavy symbolic freight. To many people, homosexuality is the *negation* of masculinity. . . . Given that assumption, antagonism toward homosexual men may be used to define masculinity" (Connell, 1992:736). This relationship is revealed in Jane Ward's study of straight identified men who engage in "dude sex," or sex with other straight identified men (this volume).

In the past two decades, viewing gender through the prism of difference has profoundly reoriented the field (Acker, 1999, 2006; Andersen, 2005; Glenn, 1999, 2002; Messner, 1996; West & Fenstermaker, 1995). Yet analyzing the multiple constructions of gender does not just mean studying groups of women and groups of men as different. It is clearly time to go beyond what we call the "patchwork quilt" phase in the study of women and men—that is, the phase in which we have acknowledged the importance of examining differences within constructions of gender, but to do so largely by collecting together a study here on African American women, a study there on gay men, a study on working-class Chicanas, and so on. This patchwork quilt approach too often amounts to no more than "adding difference and stirring." The result may be a lovely mosaic, but like a patchwork quilt, it still tends to overemphasize boundaries rather than highlight bridges of interdependency. In addition, this approach too often does not explore the ways that social constructions of femininities and masculinities are based on and reproduce relations of power. In short, we think that the substantial quantity of research that has now been done on various groups and subgroups needs to be analyzed within a framework that emphasizes differences and inequalities not as discrete areas of separation, but as interrelated bands of color that together make up a spectrum.

A recent spate of sophisticated sociological theorizing along these lines has introduced some useful ways to think about difference in relational terms. Patricia Hill Collins (1990, 1998, 2004) has suggested that we think of race, class, and gender as a socially structured "matrix of domination"; Raewyn Connell has pressed us to think of multiple differences not in simple additive ways, but rather as they "abrade, inflame, amplify, twist, negate, dampen, and complicate each other" (Kessler et al., 1985). Similarly, Maxine Baca Zinn and Bonnie Thornton Dill (this volume) have suggested that we consider a body of theory and practice they call "multiracial feminism" as a means of coming to grips with the relations between various systems of inequality. Scholarship linking the interactive effects of race, class, gender, and sexuality has emerged into a new feminist paradigm (Andersen, 2005:443). Today, "**intersectional**" frameworks foster a more complete view of the different experiences of women and men across and within varied groups.

These are the kinds of concerns that we had in mind in putting together this collection. We sought individual articles that explored intersections or axes in the matrix of domination by comparing different groups. We brought together articles that explored the lives of people who experience the daily challenges of multiple marginality (e.g., black lesbians, immigrant women) or the often paradoxical realities of those who may identify simultaneously with a socially marginalized or subordinated identity (e.g., gay, poor, physically disabled, Latino) along with a socially dominant identity (e.g., man, white, professional class). When we could not find articles that directly compared or juxtaposed categories or groups, we attempted to juxtapose two or three articles that, together, explored differences and similarities between groups.

To this end, we added a fifth dimension to the now commonly accepted "race/class/gender/sexuality" matrix: national origin. Reflecting a tendency in U.S. sociology in general, courses on sex and gender have been far too U.S. focused and Eurocentric. Focusing on the construction of gender in industrializing societies or the shifting relations of gender among transnational immigrant groups challenges and broadens our otherwise narrow assumptions about the constraints and possibilities facing contemporary women and men. But it is not enough to remain within the patchwork quilt framework, to simply focus on women and men in other nations as though they were somehow separate from processes occurring in the United States. Again, the metaphor of the prism better illustrates the dual challenges we face in integrating analyses of national inequalities. A central challenge facing scholars today is to understand how constructions of masculinities and femininities move across national borders. In this regard, we need to acknowledge two distinct but interrelated outcomes. In the process of moving across national boundaries—through media images, immigration, or global systems of production—gender inequalities are reconstructed and take new shape. At the same time, global movements of gender transform the gendered institutions with which they come into contact. Although it may seem ironic to focus on the nation in this era that some commentators have termed "postnational," we believe that we need to focus more on national difference precisely because of the increasing number and intensity of global connections and interdependencies.

The fifth edition of this book continues with all of these themes, strengthening them with new articles on age/generation, popular culture, challenges to binary thinking, constructing gender in the workplace, and social movements and social change. In this edition we've also added a new theme on *gender and disabilities* as well as a glossary where readers may find key definitions for concepts that appear in **bold type**.

One of the areas we've strengthened is Prism's attention to differences of age and generation. Pundits have employed the terms *Generation X* and *Generation Y* (or Millennials) to refer to the vast and diverse group of "thirty-something" and "twenty-something" populations. Although celebrated by some as a new market for new products and condemned as spoiled slackers (Gen X) or as entitled and lazy (Gen Y) by others, Generations X and Y are, in fact, more heterogeneous than the pundits would allow. In addition, boys, girls, and young women and men tend to relate to gender and sexuality issues in somewhat different ways than did the older generation of writers and activists who made up the "second wave" of **feminism**. "Third-wave" feminism is a generational sensibility that is beginning to have an impact on college campuses and in popular culture in recent years (Snyder, 2008). The articles on youth culture and generational differences are sprinkled throughout the various sections of this volume including two new readings by Heather R. Hlavka and Lorena Garcia on sexual violence and sexual respectability among girls and young women as well as research by Victor Rios on young black and Latino men. The gendered character of these generational communities is, in many instances, defined by differences of race, class, sexuality, and nation. Yet these constituencies are also deliberately constructed by young people in ways that underline their distinctiveness, and sometimes oppositional stances, to other groups and older generations. The structuring of youth culture—and the agency of youth groups—can be seen in various contexts.

The fifth edition also strengthens the focus on popular culture and ideology. In recent years, the flourishing scholarship in cultural studies has shown that our experiences of gender are strongly shaped by mass media, advertisements, consumption, and leisure activities. Music, sports, and the marketing of difference through consumer goods, to cite a few examples, convey particular embodiments of gender. And yet, as much of the new scholarship on consumption suggests, people situated differently in a matrix of difference and inequality tend to interpret, use, and respond to popular culture and marketing messages in quite different ways. New articles in this section examine antifeminist messages in American television programming for young girls (Kristen Myers) and the role of conservative talk programs, such as Michael Savage and Rush Limbaugh, in shaping the anger and sense of "aggrieved entitlement" felt by many downwardly mobile white men (Michael Kimmel).

In recent years, an emergent trend in gender studies questions the limits of simplistic binary thinking: male–female, masculinity–femininity, gay–straight, etc. As many of today's college students point out to their professors, people do not neatly fit into these binary boxes. Instead, people's gender and sexual performances and identities vary across a wide-ranging spectrum. In the fifth edition of the book, we continue to emphasize this refracting prism of sexual and gender differences with articles that touch on gender and biology (Lisa Wade), transgender prisoners (Valeria Jenness and Sarah Fenstermaker), and transgender policies (Laurel Westbrook and Kristen Schilt), in addition to two articles on **intersexuality** from the last edition.

The fifth edition also introduces a new theme on gender and disabilities. By the 1980s and 1990s, studies examining the gender dynamics of disability had criticized the "dual discrimination" of women with disabilities and the conflict between masculinity and disability for men (the former associated with strength and independence and the later with weakness and dependence) (Shuttleworth et al., 2012). Since then, disability studies have expanded, particularly in the area of intersectionality and the relationship between disabilities and other marginalized categories. A number of significant contributions have emerged, including a critique of the ability/ disability binary (since everyone has abilities and everyone experiences disabilities and impairments), recognition of differences *among* people with disabilities (such as differences in the experience of early and late onset disabilities), and attention to the **agency** of people with disabilities (Shuttleworth et al., 2012).

In this volume, Liddiard examines the unique forms of gender and emotion work that people with disabilities perform in their sexual and intimate lives. She argues that this work is significantly shaped by **disablism**, a social oppression that restricts people with impairments and undermines their well-being (Thomas, 1999). A second article, "Ageism and Feminism: From 'Et Cetera' to Center" (this volume), discusses disabilities within the context of changes that occur with aging, two areas that are often neglected. Last, Roberts and Jesudason examine the different and conflicting views of genetic reproductive technologies (such as the right to abortion in cases of genetic abnormalities) among a diverse group of women, including women of color, lesbians, and disabled women. Although these differences had previously divided the women's rights, disability rights, and racial justice movements, Roberts and Jesudason show how an intersectional approach led to shared policy priorities regarding genetic technologies. Thus, **intersectional theory** and praxis has transformative potential to use understandings of difference as the basis for developing shared political and social actions.

We hope this book contributes to a new generation of scholarship in the study of sex and gender—one that moves beyond the patchwork quilt approach, which lists or catalogs difference, to an approach that takes up the challenge to explore the relations of power that structure these differences and identify sources of solidarity. The late Gloria Anzaldúa (1990), a Chicana lesbian and feminist, used the border as a metaphor to capture the spatial, ethnic, class, and sexual transitions traversed in one's lifetime. She states in a poem that "To survive the borderlands you must live *sin fronteras*" (without borders). Breaking down, reassessing, and crossing the borders that divide the patches on the quilt—both experientially and analytically—is key to the difficult task of transforming knowledge about gender. Looking at the various prisms that organize gender relations, we think, will contribute to the kind of bridge building that will be needed for constructing broad-based coalitions to push for equality and social justice in the twenty-first century.

REFERENCES

Acker, Joan. 1999. "Rewriting Class, Race and Gender: Problems in Feminist Rethinking." Pp. 44–69 in Myra Marx Ferree, Judith Lorber, & Beth B. Hess (eds.), *Revisioning Gender*. Thousand Oaks, CA: Sage.

Acker, Joan. 2006. "Inequality Regimes, Gender, Class, and Race in Organizations," *Gender & Society* 20: (4): 441–464.

Andersen, Margaret L. 2005. "Thinking about Women: A Quarter Century's View," *Gender & Society* 19: (4): 437–455.

Anzaldúa, Gloria. 1990. "To Live in the Borderlands Means You." Pp. 194–195 in Gloria Anzaldúa, *Borderlands La Frontera: The New Mestiza*. San Francisco: Spinsters/Aunt Lute.

Baca Zinn, M., L. Weber Cannon, E. Higginbotham, & B. Thornton Dill. 1986. "The Costs of Exclusionary Practices in Women's Studies," *Signs: Journal of Women in Culture and Society 11*: 290–303.

Boserup, Ester. 1970. *Woman's Role in Economic Development*. London: Allen & Unwin.

Brod, Harry (ed.). 1987. *The Making of Masculinities: The New Men's Studies*. Boston: Allen & Unwin.

Brownmiller, Susan. 1975. *Against Our Will: Men, Women, and Rape*. New York: Simon & Schuster.

Chang, Grace. 1994. "Undocumented Latinas: The New 'Employable Mothers.'" Pp. 259–285 in Evelyn Nakano Glenn, Grace Chang, & Linda Rennie Forcey (eds.), *Mothering, Ideology, Experience, and Agency*. New York and London: Routledge.

Collins, Patricia Hill. 1990. *Black Feminist Thought: Knowledge, Consciousness, and the Politics of Empowerment*. Boston: Unwin Hyman.

Collins, Patricia Hill. 1998. *Fighting Words: Black Women and the Search for Justice*. Minneapolis: University of Minnesota Press.

Collins, Patricia Hill. 2004. *Black Sexual Politics: African Americans, Gender and the New Racism*. New York and London: Routledge.

Connell, Raewyn 1987. *Gender and Power*. Stanford, CA: Stanford University Press.

Connell, Raewyn 1992. "A Very Straight Gay: Masculinity, Homosexual Experience, and the Dynamics of Gender," *American Sociological Review 57*: 735–751.

Connell, Raewyn 1995. *Masculinities*. Berkeley: University of California Press.

Connell, Raewyn 2002. *Gender*. Cambridge, UK: Polity.

De Beauvoir, Simone. 1953. *The Second Sex*. New York: Knopf.

Enloe, Cynthia. 1993. *The Morning After: Sexual Politics at the End of the Cold War*. Berkeley: University of California Press.

Enloe, Cynthia. 2000. *Maneuvers: The International Politics of Militarizing Women's Lives*. Berkeley: University of California Press

Glenn, Evelyn Nakano. 1999. "The Social Construction and Institutionalization of Gender and Race: An Integrative Framework." Pp. 3–43 in Myra Marx Ferree, Judith Lorber, & Beth B. Hess (eds.), *Revisioning Gender*. Thousand Oaks, CA: Sage.

Glenn, Evelyn Nakano. 2002. *Unequal Freedom: How Race and Gender Shaped American Citizenship and Labor*. Cambridge, MA: Harvard University Press.

Hartmann, Heidi. 1976. "Capitalism, Patriarchy, and Job Segregation by Sex," *Signs: Journal of Women in Culture and Society 1:* (3), part 2, Spring: 137–167.

Hewitt, Nancy A. 1992. "Compounding Differences," *Feminist Studies 18:* 313–326.

Hondagneu-Sotelo, Pierrette. 1994. *Gendered Transitions: Mexican Experiences of Immigration*. Berkeley: University of California Press.

Hondagneu-Sotelo, Pierrette. 2001. *Domestica: Immigrant Workers Cleaning and Caring in the Shadows of Affluence*. Berkeley: University of California Press.

Kanter, Rosabeth Moss. 1977. *Men and Women of the Corporation*. New York: Basic Books.

Kaufman, Michael. 1987. *Beyond Patriarchy: Essays by Men on Pleasure, Power, and Change*. Toronto and New York: Oxford University Press.

Kessler, Sandra, Dean J. Ashendon, R. W. Connell, & Gary W. Dowsett. 1985. "Gender Relations in Secondary Schooling," *Sociology of Education 58:* 34–48.

Kimmel, Michael S. (ed.). 1987. *Changing Men: New Directions in Research on Men and Masculinity*. Newbury Park, CA: Sage.

Kimmel, Michael S., & Michael A. Messner (eds.). 1989. *Men's Lives*. New York: Macmillan.

Kimmel, Michael S., & Michael A. Messner (eds.). 2010. *Men's Lives*, 9th ed. Boston: Pearson Allyn & Bacon.

Messner, Michael A. 1996. "Studying Up on Sex," *Sociology of Sport Journal 13:* 221–237.

Messner, Michael A. 1998. *Politics of Masculinities: Men in Movements*. Thousand Oaks, CA: Sage.

Mohanty, Chandra Talpade. 1991. "Cartographies of Struggle: Third World Women and the Politics of Feminism." Pp. 51–80 in Chandra Talpade Mohanty, Ann Russo, and Lourdes Torres (eds.), *Third World Women and the Politics of Feminism*. Bloomington: Indiana University Press.

Morgan, Robin. 1970. *Sisterhood Is Powerful: An Anthology of Writing from the Women's Liberation Movement*. New York: Vintage Books.

Okin, Susan Moller. 1999. *Is Multiculturalism Bad for Women?* Princeton, NJ: Princeton University Press.

Parreñas, Rhacel Salazar. 2001. *Servants of Globalization: Women, Migration and Domestic Work*. Stanford, CA: Stanford University Press.

Pleck, J. H. 1976. "The Male Sex Role: Definitions, Problems, and Sources of Change," *Journal of Social Issues 32:* 155–164.

Rich, Adrienne. 1980. "Compulsory Heterosexuality and the Lesbian Experience," *Signs: Journal of Women in Culture and Society 5:* 631–660.

Sassen, Saskia. 1991. *The Global City: New York, London, Tokyo.* Princeton, NJ: Princeton University Press.

Shuttleworth, Russell, Nikki Wedgwood, & Nathan J. Wilson. 2012. "The Dilemma of Disabled Masculinity." *Men and Masculinities* 15: 174.

Smith, Barbara. 1977. *Toward a Black Feminist Criticism.* Freedom, CA: Crossing Press.

Snyder, R. Claire. 2008. "What Is Third-Wave Feminism? A New Directions Essay," *Signs: Journal of Women in Culture and Society 34*: (1): 175–196.

Weber, Lynn. 2010. *Understanding Race, Class, Gender, and Sexuality: A Conceptual Framework*, 2nd ed. New York: Oxford University Press.

West, Candace, & Sarah Fenstermaker. 1995. "Doing Difference," *Gender & Society 9:* 8–37.

PART I

PERSPECTIVES ON SEX, GENDER, AND DIFFERENCE

Are women and men or boys and girls really different, or do we just think and act as though they are different? In other words, are gender differences and inequalities rooted in biology or are they socially constructed? This is a key question that has occupied much of the scholarly debate on gender and gender relations. Today, these questions are rarely answered with simplistic, pat answers. And the questions that gender scholars are asking have also grown more complex. Are these differences constant over time, and under what social conditions do they vary and how? If women and men are different, then are women—as a group—similar to one another? Do white women share experiences similar to those of women of color? To what extent do women in various parts of the world share commonalities, or are their differences more important? What are the consequences of a scholarly focus on gender differences? For example, could the very focus on difference inadvertently reinforce and naturalize commonly held perceptions rather than problematize the very notion of gender differences? The chapters in this opening section reflect a sampling of gender scholarship on the remarkable variability of gender. They tackle tricky questions related to differences between women and men, as well as issues of difference among groups of women and among groups of men.

Difference has always preoccupied feminist thought. Not long ago, difference *between* women and men was a primary concern. "Difference feminism" rested on the notion that women's distinctive characteristics required a special approach to overcome discrimination. Unlike feminist demands that women and men receive "the same" treatment, difference feminists sought women's equality by appealing to the logic of a gender dichotomy. By acknowledging and sometimes even underscoring biological, emotional, and social differences between women and men, they argued that women should rely on women's, rather than men's, strategies to achieve equality. In the context of patriarchal societies, where women's experiences are overlooked and suppressed, difference feminists argued that a reassertion of women's perspectives is central to combating oppression.

SEXES, GENDERS, AND DIMENSIONS OF DIFFERENCE

Today, scholars have transformed perspectives on gender difference. It is clear that although women and men everywhere are constructed in opposition to each other, the categories "women" and "men" have wide-ranging meanings. Gender is always complicated by the complex stratification of intersecting power systems. More important, gender operates with and through other systems of opportunity and oppression, which give rise to a variety of different, yet sometimes overlapping, gender experiences among women and among men. The chapters in this section move beyond dichotomous simplifications of women and men and show how gender differences are contingent on other dimensions of difference. Collectively, the chapters provide a foundation for seeing gender through a prism of difference.

In the first reading, Ann Fausto-Sterling takes up a subject of much current debate—the relationship between sex and gender. By deconstructing the "making" of the **two-sex system** of male and female, she disputes the division of the world into only two genders based simply on genital differences. This raises provocative questions about gender and about sex and whether the relationship between them is a given. Our conceptions of gender begin to look very different, and our assumptions about gender differences begin to break down, if the human sexes are viewed as multiple.

In the next reading, Lisa Wade deepens our understanding of the making of gender difference. She reviews recent research from the biological sciences on genetics, hormones, and brains. Her analysis moves far beyond the **nature/nurture dichotomy** (a long-standing debate over the relative importance of biology and innate traits versus environment and social learning in explaining human behavior) to explore the complex interactions between our biology and our sociocultural environment. She argues that biological research is a powerful tool for examining how social inequalities impact our bodies in ways that limit, suppress, or exploit our human potential. Further, new research on the body's ability to adapt to changing circumstances serves as a powerful critique of **naturalization**, or the claim that inequalities based in biology are natural, irreversible, or difficult to change. Instead, Wade encourages us to "reimagine biology" as "the very substance through which social forces exert an influence." Thus, she explains that many biological gender differences, such as mental rotational ability and bone density, are caused by social inequalities that can be remedied.

Continuing our exploration of gender difference, Maxine Baca Zinn and Bonnie Thornton Dill argue that a focus on race and class makes it clear that there can be no unitary analysis of women as a category. They analyze the development of multiracial feminism, noting both the tensions and the benefits, as they explore the theories and concepts in the growing body of scholarship on the intersections of race, class, and gender. In particular, they identify six themes that distinguish and guide multiracial feminist work. A key insight here is recognition of the ways in which the differences among women are historically and socially constructed and grounded in diverse locations and interconnected inequalities.

GENDER, DIFFERENCE, AND GLOBALIZATION

The next three readings consider issues of gender and difference in relation to **globalization**. Exactly how is global restructuring affecting gender, and how is gender affecting global restructuring? In contrast to the common image of a homogenizing process sweeping the globe to make gender more uniform, global forces are, in fact, creating new gender hierarchies.

Raewyn Connell untangles key strands in the **world gender order** to reveal how masculinities are reconfigured by transnational power relations. Connell begins by introducing a relatively new area of gender scholarship on men and masculinities and its central concept, **hegemonic masculinity**, which refers to the dominant form of masculinity in any sociohistorical context. The article traces the development of hegemonic masculinity across three time periods: the early colonialism of conquest and settlement, the late colonialism of empire, and the current period of postcolonialism and neoliberalism. Connell concludes with a discussion of **transnational business masculinity**, the hegemonic masculinity of our time, and its relationship to subordinate masculinities. In particular, she considers the development of fundamentalist masculinities as contenders for hegemony and gay masculinities as potential forms of opposition to hegemonic masculinity.

Barbara Ehrenreich and Arlie Hochschild expose some of the contradictory demands that globalization places on women in different parts of the world. They describe the **globalization of women's work** or the global labor market in which much of the work associated with women's traditional roles in poor countries—child care, homemaking, and sex—is transferred as women move from poor countries to rich ones. Much of **the second shift** or **care work** in the United States is becoming the domain of immigrant women of color who are driven from their countries only to remain disenfranchised in the receiving country. This global transfer of services benefits many professional women and their careers as well as many men who can continue to avoid the second shift. Yet, this resolution rests on both global and intimate relations of dominance and subordination.

Finally, in reminding us to avoid essentialist images of local women in different parts of the world, Chandra Mohanty shifts our focus from "gender" or "gender difference," which may be static categories that carry essentialist implications, to a consideration of "gender relations," which emphasizes the dynamic, shifting, and contingent nature of the status of women and men in society. Her review of three strategies currently used to globalize or internationalize the women's studies curriculum also calls for a **comparative feminist studies model** that bridges the histories, experiences, and struggles of women in local communities and the effects of globalization on their differences, commonalities, and interconnections.

1

The Five Sexes, Revisited

ANNE FAUSTO-STERLING

As Cheryl Chase stepped to the front of the packed meeting room in the Sheraton Boston Hotel, nervous coughs made the tension audible. Chase, an activist for intersexual rights, had been invited to address the May 2000 meeting of the Lawson Wilkins Pediatric Endocrine Society (LWPES), the largest organization in the United States for specialists in children's hormones. Her talk would be the grand finale to a four-hour symposium on the treatment of genital ambiguity in newborns, infants born with a mixture of both male and female anatomy, or genitals that appear to differ from their chromosomal sex. The topic was hardly a novel one to the assembled physicians.

Yet Chase's appearance before the group was remarkable. Three and a half years earlier, the American Academy of Pediatrics had refused her request for a chance to present the patients' viewpoint on the treatment of genital ambiguity, dismissing Chase and her supporters as "zealots." About two dozen intersex people had responded by throwing up a picket line. The Intersex Society of North America (ISNA) even issued a press release: "Hermaphrodites Target Kiddie Docs."

It had done my 1960s street-activist heart good. In the short run, I said to Chase at the time, the picketing would make people angry. But eventually, I assured her, the doors then closed would open. Now, as Chase began to address the physicians at their own convention, that

prediction was coming true. Her talk, titled "Sexual Ambiguity: The Patient-Centered Approach," was a measured critique of the near-universal practice of performing immediate, "corrective" surgery on thousands of infants born each year with ambiguous genitalia. Chase herself lives with the consequences of such surgery. Yet her audience, the very endocrinologists and surgeons Chase was accusing of reacting with "surgery and shame," received her with respect. Even more remarkably, many of the speakers who preceded her at the session had already spoken of the need to scrap current practices in favor of treatments more centered on psychological counseling.

What led to such a dramatic reversal of fortune? Certainly, Chase's talk at the LWPES symposium was a vindication of her persistence in seeking attention for her cause. But her invitation to speak was also a watershed in the evolving discussion about how to treat children with ambiguous genitalia. And that discussion, in turn, is the tip of a biocultural iceberg—the gender iceberg—that continues to rock both medicine and our culture at large.

Chase made her first national appearance in 1993, in these very pages, announcing the formation of ISNA in a letter responding to an essay I had written for *The Sciences,* titled "The Five Sexes" [March/April 1993]. In that article I argued that the two-sex system embedded

Ann Fausto-Sterling, "The Five Sexes, Revisited," from *The Sciences,* July/August, 2000, Volume 40, Issue 4, pp. 18–24.

17

in our society is not adequate to encompass the full spectrum of human sexuality. In its place, I suggested a five-sex system. In addition to males and females, I included "herms" (named after true hermaphrodites, people born with both a testis and an ovary); "merms" (male pseudohermaphrodites, who are born with testes and some aspect of female genitalia); and "ferms" (female pseudohermaphrodites, who have ovaries combined with some aspect of male genitalia).

I had intended to be provocative, but I had also written with tongue firmly in cheek. So I was surprised by the extent of the controversy the article unleashed. Right-wing Christians were outraged, and connected my idea of five sexes with the United Nations–sponsored Fourth World Conference on Women, held in Beijing in September 1995. At the same time, the article delighted others who felt constrained by the current sex and gender system.

Clearly, I had struck a nerve. The fact that so many people could get riled up by my proposal to revamp our sex and gender system suggested that change—as well as resistance to it—might be in the offing. Indeed, a lot has changed since 1993, and I like to think that my article was an important stimulus. As if from nowhere, intersexuals are materializing before our very eyes. Like Chase, many have become political organizers, who lobby physicians and politicians to change current treatment practices. But more generally, though perhaps no less provocatively, the boundaries separating masculine and feminine seem harder than ever to define.

Some find the changes underway deeply disturbing. Others find them liberating.

Who is an intersexual—and how many intersexuals are there? The concept of intersexuality is rooted in the very ideas of male and female. In the idealized, Platonic, biological world, human beings are divided into two kinds: a perfectly dimorphic species. Males have an X and a Y chromosome, testes, a penis and all of the appropriate internal plumbing for delivering urine and semen to the outside world. They also have well-known secondary sexual characteristics including a muscular build and facial hair. Women have two X chromosomes, ovaries, all of the internal plumbing to transport urine and ova to the outside world, a system to support pregnancy and fetal development, as well as a variety of recognizable secondary sexual characteristics.

That idealized story papers over many obvious caveats: some women have facial hair, some men have none; some women speak with deep voices, some men veritably squeak. Less well known is the fact that, on close inspection, absolute dimorphism disintegrates even at the level of basic biology. Chromosomes, hormones, the internal sex structures, the gonads and the external genitalia all vary more than most people realize. Those born outside of the Platonic dimorphic mold are called intersexuals.

In "The Five Sexes" I reported an estimate by a psychologist expert in the treatment of intersexuals, suggesting that some 4 percent of all live births are intersexual. Then, together with a group of Brown University undergraduates, I set out to conduct the first systematic assessment of the available data on intersexual birthrates. We scoured the medical literature for estimates of the frequency of various categories of intersexuality, from additional chromosomes to mixed gonads, hormones and genitalia. For some conditions we could find only anecdotal evidence; for most, however numbers exist. On the basis of that evidence, we calculated that for every 1,000 children born, seventeen are intersexual in some form. That number—1.7 percent—is a ballpark estimate, not a precise count, though we believe it is more accurate than the 4 percent I reported.

Our figure represents all chromosomal, anatomical and hormonal exceptions to the dimorphic ideal; the number of intersexuals who might, potentially, be subject to surgery as infants is smaller—probably between one in 1,000 and one in 2,000 live births. Furthermore, because some populations possess the relevant genes at high frequency, the intersexual birthrate is not uniform throughout the world.

Consider, for instance, the gene for congenital adrenal hyperplasia (CAH). When the CAH gene is inherited from both parents, it leads to a baby with masculinized external genitalia who possesses two X chromosomes and the internal reproductive organs of a potentially fertile woman. The frequency of the gene varies widely around the world: in New Zealand it occurs in only forty-three children per million; among the Yupik Eskimos of southwestern Alaska, its frequency is 3,500 per million.

Intersexuality has always been to some extent a matter of definition. And in the past century physicians have been the ones who defined children as intersexual—and provided the remedies. When only the chromosomes are unusual, but the external genitalia and gonads clearly indicate either a male or a female, physicians do not advocate intervention. Indeed, it is not clear what kind of intervention could be advocated in such cases. But the story is quite different when infants are born with mixed genitalia, or with external genitals that seem at odds with the baby's gonads.

Most clinics now specializing in the treatment of intersex babies rely on case-management principles developed in the 1950s by the psychologist John Money and the psychiatrists Joan G. Hampson and John L. Hampson, all of Johns Hopkins University in Baltimore, Maryland. Money believed that gender identity is completely malleable for about eighteen months after birth. Thus, he argued, when a treatment team is presented with an infant who has ambiguous genitalia, the team could make a gender assignment solely on the basis of what made the best surgical sense. The physicians could then simply encourage the parents to raise the child according to the surgically assigned gender. Following that course, most physicians maintained, would eliminate psychological distress for both the patient and the parents. Indeed, treatment teams were never to use such words as "intersex" or "hermaphrodite"; instead, they were to tell parents that nature intended the baby to be the boy or the girl that the physicians had determined it was. Through surgery, the physicians were merely completing nature's intention.

Although Money and the Hampsons published detailed case studies of intersex children who they said had adjusted well to their gender assignments, Money thought one case in particular proved his theory. It was a dramatic example, inasmuch as it did not involve intersexuality at all: one of a pair of identical twin boys lost his penis as a result of a circumcision accident. Money recommended that "John" (as he came to be known in a later case study) be surgically turned into "Joan" and raised as a girl. In time, Joan grew to love wearing dresses and having her hair done. Money proudly proclaimed the sex reassignment a success.

But as recently chronicled by John Colapinto, in his book *As Nature Made Him,* Joan—now known to be an adult male named David Reimer—eventually rejected his female assignment. Even without a functioning penis and testes (which had been removed as part of the reassignment) John/Joan sought masculinizing medication, and married a woman with children (whom he adopted).

Since the full conclusion to the John/Joan story came to light, other individuals who were reassigned as males or females shortly after birth but who later rejected their early assignments have come forward. So, too, have cases in which the reassignment has worked—at least into the subject's mid-twenties. But even then the aftermath of the surgery can be problematic. Genital surgery often leaves scars that reduce sexual sensitivity. Chase herself had a complete clitoridectomy, a procedure that is less frequently performed on intersexuals today. But the newer surgeries, which reduce the size of the clitoral shaft, still greatly reduce sensitivity.

The revelation of cases of failed reassignments and the emergence of intersex activism have led an increasing number of pediatric endocrinologists, urologists and psychologists to reexamine the wisdom of early genital surgery. For example, in a talk that preceded Chase's at the LWPES meeting, the medical ethicist Laurence B. McCullough of the Center for Medical Ethics and Health Policy at Baylor College of Medicine in Houston, Texas, introduced an ethical framework for the treatment of children with ambiguous genitalia. Because sex phenotype (the manifestation of genetically and embryologically determined sexual characteristics) and gender presentation (the sex role projected by the individual in society) are highly variable, McCullough argues, the various forms of intersexuality should be defined as normal. All of them fall within the statistically expected variability of sex and gender. Furthermore, though certain disease states may accompany some forms of intersexuality, and may require medical intervention, intersexual conditions are not themselves diseases.

McCullough also contends that in the process of assigning gender, physicians should minimize what he calls irreversible assignments: taking steps such as the surgical removal or modification of gonads or genitalia that the patient may one day want to have reversed. Finally, McCullough urges physicians to abandon their practice of treating the birth of a child with genital ambiguity as a medical or social emergency. Instead, they should take the time to perform a thorough medical workup and should disclose everything to the parents, including the uncertainties about the final outcome.

The treatment mantra, in other words, should be therapy, not surgery.

I believe a new treatment protocol for intersex infants, similar to the one outlined by McCullough, is close at hand. Treatment should combine some basic medical and ethical principles with a practical but less drastic approach to the birth of a mixed-sex child. As a first step, surgery on infants should be performed only to save the child's life or to substantially improve the child's physical well-being. Physicians may assign a sex—male or female—to an intersex infant on the basis of the probability that the child's particular condition will lead to the formation of a particular gender identity. At the same time, though, practitioners ought to be humble enough to recognize that as the child grows, he or she may reject the assignment—and they should be wise enough to listen to what the child has to say. Most important, parents should have access to the full range of information and options available to them.

Sex assignments made shortly after birth are only the beginning of a long journey. Consider, for instance, the life of Max Beck: Born intersexual, Max was surgically assigned as a female and consistently raised as such. Had her medical team followed her into her early twenties, they would have deemed her assignment a success because she was married to a man. (It should be noted that success in gender assignment has traditionally been defined as living in that gender as a heterosexual.) Within a few years, however, Beck had come out as a butch lesbian; now in her mid-thirties, Beck has become a man and married his lesbian partner, who (through the miracles of modern reproductive technology) recently gave birth to a girl.

Transsexuals, people who have an emotional gender at odds with their physical sex, once described themselves in terms of dimorphic absolutes—males trapped in female bodies, or vice versa. As such, they sought psychological relief through surgery. Although many still do, some so-called transgendered people today are content to inhabit a more ambiguous zone. A male-to-female transsexual, for instance, may come out as a lesbian. Jane, born a physiological male, is now in her late thirties and living with her wife, whom she married when her name was still John. Jane takes hormones to feminize herself, but they have not yet interfered with her ability to engage in intercourse as a man. In her mind Jane has a lesbian relationship with her wife, though she views their intimate moments as a cross between lesbian and heterosexual sex.

It might seem natural to regard intersexuals and transgendered people as living midway between the poles of male and female. But male and female, masculine and feminine, cannot be parsed as some kind of continuum. Rather, sex and gender are best conceptualized as points in a multidimensional space. For some time, experts on gender development have distinguished between sex at the genetic level and at the cellular level (sex-specific gene expression, X and Y chromosomes); at the hormonal level (in the fetus, during childhood and after puberty); and at the anatomical level (genitals and secondary sexual characteristics). Gender identity presumably emerges from all of those corporeal aspects via some poorly understood interaction with environment and experience. What has become increasingly clear is that one can find levels of masculinity and femininity in almost every possible permutation. A chromosomal, hormonal and genital male (or female) may emerge with a female (or male) gender identity. Or a chromosomal female with male fetal hormones and masculinized genitalia—but with female pubertal hormones—may develop a female gender identity.

The medical and scientific communities have yet to adopt a language that is capable of describing such diversity. In her book *Hermaphrodites and the Medical Invention of Sex,* the historian and medical ethicist Alice Domurat Dreger of Michigan State University in East Lansing documents the emergence of current medical systems for classifying gender ambiguity. The current usage remains rooted in the Victorian approach to sex. The logical structure of the commonly used terms "true hermaphrodite," "male pseudohermaphrodite" and "female pseudohermaphrodite" indicates that only the so-called true hermaphrodite is a genuine mix of male and female. The others, no matter how confusing their body parts, are really hidden males or females. Because true hermaphrodites are rare—possibly only one in 100,000—such a classification system supports the idea that human beings are an absolutely dimorphic species.

At the dawn of the twenty-first century, when the variability of gender seems so visible, such a position is hard to maintain. And here, too, the old medical consensus has begun to crumble. Last fall the pediatric urologist Ian A. Aaronson of the Medical University of South Carolina in Charleston organized the North American Task Force on Intersexuality (NATFI) to review the clinical responses to genital ambiguity in infants. Key medical associations, such as the American Academy of Pediatrics, have endorsed NATFI. Specialists in surgery, endocrinology, psychology, ethics, psychiatry, genetics and public health, as well as intersex patient-advocate groups, have joined its ranks.

One of the goals of NATFI is to establish a new sex nomenclature. One proposal under consideration replaces the current system with emotionally neutral terminology that emphasizes developmental processes rather than preconceived gender categories. For example, Type I intersexes develop out of anomalous virilizing influences; Type II result from some interruption of virilization; and in Type III intersexes the gonads themselves may not have developed in the expected fashion.

What is clear is that since 1993, modern society has moved beyond five sexes to a recognition that gender variation is normal and, for some people, an arena for playful exploration. Discussing my "five sexes" proposal in her book *Lessons from the Intersexed,* the psychologist Suzanne J. Kessler of the State University of New York at Purchase drives this point home with great effect:

> The limitation with Fausto-Sterling's proposal is that . . . [it] still gives genitals . . . primary signifying status and ignores the fact that in the everyday world gender attributions are made without access to genital inspection. . . . What has primacy in everyday life is the gender that is performed, regardless of the flesh's configuration under the clothes.

I now agree with Kessler's assessment. It would be better for intersexuals and their supporters to turn everyone's focus away from genitals. Instead, as she suggests, one should acknowledge that people come in an even wider assortment of sexual identities and characteristics than mere genitals can distinguish. Some women may have "large clitorises or fused labia," whereas some men may have "small penises or misshapen scrota," as Kessler puts it, "phenotypes with no particular clinical or identity meaning."

As clearheaded as Kessler's program is—and despite the progress made in the 1990s—our society is still far from that ideal. The intersexual or transgendered person who projects a social gender—what Kessler calls "cultural genitals"—that conflicts with his or her physical genitals still may die for the transgression. Hence legal protection for people whose cultural and physical genitals do not match is needed during the current transition to a more gender-diverse world. One easy step would be to eliminate the category of "gender" from official documents, such as driver's licenses and passports. Surely attributes both more visible (such as height, build and eye color) and less visible (fingerprints and genetic profiles) would be more expedient.

A more far-ranging agenda is presented in the International Bill of Gender Rights, adopted in 1995 at the fourth annual International Conference on Transgender Law and Employment Policy in Houston, Texas. It lists ten "gender rights," including the right to define one's own gender, the right to change one's physical gender if one so chooses and the right to marry whomever one wishes. The legal bases for such rights are being hammered out in the courts as I write and, most recently, through the establishment, in the state of Vermont, of legal same-sex domestic partnerships.

No one could have foreseen such changes in 1993. And the idea that I played some role, however small, in reducing the pressure—from the medical community as well as from society at large—to flatten the diversity of human sexes into two diametrically opposed camps gives me pleasure.

Sometimes people suggest to me, with not a little horror, that I am arguing for a pastel world in which androgyny reigns and men and women are boringly the same. In my vision, however, strong colors coexist with pastels. There are and will continue to be highly masculine people out there; it's just that some of them are women. And some of the most feminine people I know happen to be men.

2

The New Science of Sex Difference

LISA WADE

... any living cell carries with it the experience of a billion years of experimentation by its ancestors. You cannot expect to explain so wise an old bird in a few simple words.

—*Max Delbrück (1949a,b)*

In the early 1800s a French biologist named Jean-Baptiste Lamarck, working on the question of what would someday be called "evolution," proposed that individual animals could pass on acquired as well as inherited traits to their offspring (Bowler 2003). That is, adjustments an organism made to its environment during its life could somehow appear in the biological building blocks of the next generation. His most famous example involved the neck of the giraffe, a feature that bewildered early scientists. Lamarck theorized that each generation of giraffes stretched their neck to reach higher and higher leaves, passing on a slightly longer neck than they had inherited themselves. Likewise, Lamarck speculated, the traits that humans developed over the course of their lives could be inherited by their children. For example, if a man became strong, his children would be born with a greater predisposition for large muscles; if a woman became educated, she would pass onto her children heightened intellectual potential.

After Darwin, this model of evolution fell out of favor. In its place was the theory of natural selection: evolution works not through organisms actively responding to the environment, but through random genetic variation and the failure of the maladapted to reproduce. The idea that we could change our genes during our lives and pass on a different genome than the one we inherited came to seem laughably naïve.

Emerging research now suggests that Lamarck was onto something. Indeed, our understanding of biology and its relationship to the phenomena of interest to sociologists—cultural ideas, social interaction, and social structures—is undergoing a paradigmatic change (Silverman 2004; Strohman 1997). In this essay I review three biological bases of sex difference and similarity—genes, hormones, and brains—and explore the new research that shows how each mechanism interacts with the socio-cultural context. I conclude by joining the call to reorient our relationship to the life sciences (e.g., Bearman 2008; Franks 2010; Freese et al. 2003; Mazur 2005; Udry 1995). These developments should inspire us to further develop research programs that take advantage of the interaction of biology and society. Engaging with the biological sciences in this way need not naturalize inequality, though this is an outcome against which we must be vigilant, but rather can offer social scientists stronger tools with which to identify, criticize, and eliminate mechanisms of oppression. . . .

Lisa Wade, "The New Science of Sex Difference," *Sociology Compass* 7 (4): 278–293. Copyright © 2013 Blackwell Publishing. Reproduced with permission of Blackwell Publishing Ltd.

GENES AND GENDER

Overview

Scientists divide the genetic contribution to sex differences into three types of influences: sex-linked, sex-limited, and sex-influenced. Sex-linked traits refer to those that are influenced by the fact that genetic males and females have different sex chromosomes (XY and XX, respectively). Although the fact that men, but not women have a Y chromosome seems a likely candidate for a cause of difference, scholars largely agree that the Y chromosome does little other than give XY fetuses testes and facilitate the adult male's fertility (Craig et al. 2004; Hawley and Mori 1999).

Women's two X chromosomes are a more significant contributor to sex difference, primarily by making females less vulnerable to chromosomal conditions. Since people (e.g., men) need only one X to survive, most cells in a genetic female will include one deactivated X (in about 50 percent of the cells it is the maternal X, the other 50 percent, the paternal). In this sense women are similar to men—they both have only one functioning X chromosome in each cell—but women have the advantage of having a "back up" in the case of a defective gene on the X chromosome. If one fails, the other mediates or eliminates the negative effect. Genetic men, then, are more vulnerable to problems caused by defective Xs. Relatedly, if a trait carried on the X chromosome is recessive, then men will be more likely to show it, since they only need to inherit one recessive gene to express the trait, whereas women need to inherit two. Color blindness and hemophilia are examples of X-linked recessive traits seen more commonly in men.

Sex-linked traits are the most obvious source of sex differences because men and women have different sex chromosomes, but genes on other chromosomal pairs are relevant too. Some are sex-limited, meaning they are only expressed if they are in a male or female body. The genes governing lactation, allowing a woman to produce milk for an infant, are carried by both men and women, but they are usually expressed only in mothers. Likewise, a common developmental problem, undescended testes, is genetic, but does not cause trouble for women.

A final set of genes, called sex-influenced, do different things in male and female bodies. It is this type of gene that explains why men are more likely to go bald. The baldness gene only has a strong influence on phenotype in the presence of high levels of testosterone, so most women who carry the gene do not show signs of baldness. Another example involves our singing voices. The same genes that produce an especially high voice in women cause a particularly deep voice in men.

Genetic influences, then, set us on paths to have male or female bodies and contribute to some differences between men and women. The new science of genetics, however, has revealed that the "blueprint" metaphor in which genotypes dictate phenotypes has turned out to be wholly insufficient for understanding how genes work, and this has significant implications for thinking about the relationship between genes and gender.

GENE/ENVIRONMENT INTERACTIONS

Anticipating the mapping of the human genome, entrepreneurs in the late 1990s and early 2000s devised businesses that would capitalize on the linking of genes to desirable and undesirable traits. Upon completion of the project, however, these entrepreneurs would find themselves largely stymied (Silverman 2004). The one-gene/one-outcome mechanism that applies to certain diseases turns out to be the exception, not the rule.

For one, we have learned that our developmental processes are replete with redundancies. "Knock-out" studies, in which seemingly-essential genes are removed in order to discern their impact, often result in no developmental difference at all (Keller 2000). Instead, genetic harm usually has to be widespread or present in several different parts of the genome simultaneously in order to have an impact on phenotype. Explained geneticist Mario Capecchi: ". . . the organism has choices. . . . If a problem is encountered, the thing has to figure out a solution. Sometimes the solution is fantastic, other times it is less so. . . . If we didn't have extensive overlap and redundancy in our genome, we wouldn't be here at all" (quoted in Keller 2000, 112).

Genes are also dynamic in that they shape our development in response to information. Both the immediate biochemical environment of our cells and the environment outside our bodies are important determining factors. In other words, what our genes do is heavily influenced by what happens to and around us.

As Rebecca Jordan-Young (2010, 271) explains: what is "written in our genes" is a "very open-ended story." In fact, 95 percent of our genes do not encode for proteins at all. Instead, our genes are about 5 percent story (genes that actively code for proteins) and 95 percent storyteller (chemical molecules put on our DNA that influence how genes will be used) (see also Meaney 2001). Because a single gene can encode for up to tens of thousands of different proteins, genes do not lead unidirectionally and deterministically to straightforward outcomes.

The instructions communicated to our "story" genes from our "storyteller" markers are called epigenetic tags. These change our expressed genome over the course of our lives. Even genetically-identical twins become both genotypically and phenotypically different over time; they do not necessarily develop the same diseases or continue to look alike (Fraga et al. 2005; Poulsen et al. 2007; Wong Albert and Petronis 2005). If one twin is schizophrenic, for example, a condition shown to be strongly related to genetics, the other twin is diagnosed with the mental illness only 50 percent of the time (Gottesman 1991).

These developments in research on genetics have implications for both individual and group level phenomena. Some genetic profiles, for example, increase the risk that a child will be a violent adult, but only if that child is exposed to violence when they are young (Jacobson 2009). Living in a happy home with loving parents decreases the likelihood that a person genetically predisposed to aggression will become aggressive. In contrast, poverty, a dysfunctional family life, and suffering child abuse all increase the chances that the genes for aggression will be "turned on" and lead to violent behavior. Genes matter: a person without a genetic predisposition for violence probably will not grow up to be violent, even if they suffer trauma (Cadoret et al. 1995). A person with the genetic predisposition may or may not; it all depends on the quality of her life.

If poor, urban, racial minorities disproportionately find themselves in violent neighborhoods, we should expect them to exhibit more violence than they otherwise would and more violence than genetically-similar youth who are not exposed to violence. Boys and men, insofar as they are more likely to experience or be recruited into violent activities, may end up more violent than girls. In other words, even if the genetic predisposition for violence is equally prevalent across two groups, we may see higher rates of violence in one because of asymmetries in the social structure. Meanwhile, generations of exposure may exacerbate the relationship between biology and society as violent adults are more and more likely to expose their own children to violence, with no underlying change in the population genome. Genetic similarities, then, can nevertheless result in group-level behavioral differences.

While most of the epigenetic tags that change our genome over the course of our lives are erased in the early development of our offspring, some are not (Reik and Walter 2001). This is where Lamarck's giraffe hits close to the mark. Parents can pass on to their descendants some of the changes to their genomes caused by the environments in which they lived. Genes silenced in response to limited food supply, for example, have been found in the grandchildren of men and women who suffered through famine, contributing to higher rates of death from cardiovascular disease and diabetes (Pembrey et al. 2006). Adding another layer of complexity, there is some evidence that erasure and maintenance of imprinted genes works differently in chromosomes inherited from the mother versus the father, a phenomenon called parental imprinting.

In sum, our genome is designed to dynamically respond to life events. The geneticist Richard Strohman (1997) warns us not to underestimate this flexibility. The role of epigenetics in multiplying the sheer possibility of outcomes is, he writes, "transcalculational, a mathematical term for mind boggling" (p. 197). A single gene can do many (unpredictable) things at different times during development or may control multiple different phenotypical phenomena (called pleiotropy). Different genes can produce similar outcomes (phenogenetic equivalence) and no one gene is necessarily required for any given outcome (due to genetic redundancy). Evelyn Fox Keller (2000, 137–8) goes so far as to say: ". . . our new understandings of the complexity of developmental dynamics have critically undermined the conceptual adequacy of genes as causes of development." Even "the question of what genes are for," Keller continues, "has become increasingly difficult to answer."

HORMONES AND GENDER

Overview

Hormones are messengers in our chemical communication system. Released by glands or cells in one part of the body, they carry instructions to the rest of our body. All human hormones circulate in both men's and women's bodies, but some of them do so in different proportions. Men tend to have higher levels of androgens and women higher levels of estrogens. The relationship between hormone level and observed difference, however, is not straightforward; men seem to be insensitive to wide variations in testosterone levels (between 20 percent and 200 percent of normal), while women have been shown to be sensitive to smaller changes, making it possible for women to experience an equivalent effect with a smaller amount of hormone (Archer 2006; Sapolsky 1997; Wood and Eagly 2012; Yates et al. 1999). In short, the colloquial terms "male hormones" and "female hormones" are misnomers.

It is equally incorrect to say that androgens and estrogens are masculinizing and feminizing hormones. Research on animals shows, for example, that estrogen and testosterone sometimes perform identical functions and estrogens can have masculinizing effects (Hines 2009). So, just as we are not "opposite sexes," our hormones are far from opposite in their chemical structure, presence, or function. Still, men and women do vary in their hormonal profiles and these differences have different effects at different stages of development.

Scientists divide the influences of hormones into organizational and activational effects. Organizational effects are those that occur early in life: before or shortly after birth. These are generally more permanent than the activational effects of hormones. They include, for example, the development of masculine and feminine internal and external genitalia during fetal growth and they may have an organizational effect on the brain, producing some of the differences reviewed in the next section (for a measured review, see Jordan-Young 2010). The remainder of this section will focus on activational effects.

Activational effects occur throughout life, producing changes that often last only so long as the hormone is present. The common phrase "adrenaline rush" suggests that experience can invoke a hormonal response. In fact, our bodies can be flooded with adrenaline in a mere instant, a physical change that can be entirely reversed in the space of two minutes. Similarly, estrogens and androgens have been shown to have several differential activational influences on men and women. I offer three examples below.

First, research shows that testosterone, an androgen, is strongly related to sex drive in both women and men and may be weakly related to physical aggression in men (Book et al. 2001; Hines 2009; Mazur and Booth 1998). Since men have more free testosterone than women, this might have some influence on why men, on average, have higher levels of aggression and sex drive than women (Baumeister et al. 2001). Notably, higher levels of estrogen are also associated with dominant behavior in women, a reminder that so-called "female hormones" can have masculinizing effects (Stanton and Edelstein 2009).

Second, testosterone levels correlate with visual-spatial ability, a cognitive skill that shows a robust sex difference (Halpern 2012). Very high and very low levels of testosterone are correlated with poor ability, so high-testosterone women and low-testosterone men do best on visual-spatial tests because they both fall into the middle range. As men's and women's hormones fluctuate, their performance on tests fluctuates as well; women score better right before ovulation (when their testosterone levels are highest) and men in the Western hemisphere score better in the spring (when their levels are lowest). All of these differences are quite small, however, and have not been shown to have consequences outside of the laboratory (Hines 2009; Klebanov and Ruble 1994).

Third, there is good evidence that the hormone cycles that regulate women's menstrual cycles correspond to mild changes in libido, partner choice, interest in extra-pair copulation, and mood, with a decrease in positive feelings just prior to menstruation (Halpern 2012; Oinonen and Mazmanian 2001). Men experience hormone fluctuations as well, on both daily and seasonal cycles. Interestingly, in relation to mood, studies of mood fluctuations in men find that they are just as emotionally "unstable" as women (McFarlane and Williams 1994; McFarlane et al. 1988). These mood swings are small in both men and women. Hormones are a relatively minor force in determining our mood compared to even mundane life events (e.g., whether it is Monday morning or Friday afternoon) (Fausto-Sterling 1992).

We have good data, then, that levels of circulating hormones correlate with sex differences, but it is a mistake to divide hormones and mood or behavior into independent and dependent variables. Instead, the production of hormones in our bodies is closely tied to the real and imagined experiences we have with others. That is, hormones are one way that society "gets under the skin" (Taylor et al. 1997).

HORMONE/ENVIRONMENT INTERACTIONS

Hormones can be thought of, in part, as mechanisms of social interaction. They enable us to respond emotionally to interactions, contributing to feelings of love, the desire to nurture, stress, happiness, and the flight or fight reaction. To illustrate our chemical response to social interaction, I will use the example of testosterone, primarily in men.

Like other hormones, testosterone rises and falls in response to our experiences. Levels in men rise in anticipation of playing competitive sports; they rise further in men who win and decline in men who lose (Booth et al. 1989, 1999; Nisbett and Cohen 1996; Sapolsky 1997). This is not only true for physical activity, but also primarily mental games like chess, symbolic activities like video games, and vicarious competitive experiences such as watching sports on television (Bernhardt et al. 1998; Mazur et al. 1992, 1997; van der Meij et al. 2012). Testosterone increases, as well, in response to status acquisition and display. Driving a sports car produces an increase in testosterone; driving a sports car in front of other people produces a greater increase (Saad and Vongas 2009).

Men's testosterone levels also respond to life changes. They decline, for example, when they are in close relationships with women and if they become parents, but only if they are actively involved with their children (Alvergne et al. 2009; van Anders and Watson 2007; Booth et al. 2006; Gettler et al. 2011; Mazur and Michalek 1998; Storey et al. 2000). This phenomenon has been found at the group as well as the individual level. The average testosterone levels of fathers in societies that normalize involved parenting is lower than the average testosterone levels in societies that do not (Muller et al. 2009).

In addition to shaping our responses to social interaction, hormones are impacted by our place in the social structure. Being suddenly positioned below others in a social or organizational hierarchy, such as starting boot camp, correlates with a drop in testosterone that can last a few weeks (Kreuz and Rose 1972; Thompson et al. 1990). Likewise, correlations of testosterone with the emergence of conduct disorders in boys are much stronger when their friends regularly engage in deviant behavior (Rowe et al. 2004). This may be because, while testosterone facilitates an aggressive response when aggression is called for, it facilitates other types of responses, such as sociality, when threat is low (Booth et al. 2006; Bos et al. 2012). In all cases, interpersonal and social structural factors, such as marriage, employment, and middle- or upper-class status, mediate the role of testosterone in antisocial behavior (Booth and Wayne Osgood 1993; Dabbs and Morris 1990).

Importantly, many of the phenomena that cause a change in testosterone levels are not, in themselves, biologically rewarding or punishing. Instead, they are socially constructed "wins" that affect our bodies because we have collectively decided that they are important. We are thus designed to respond chemically not only to objective things in the world, but to anything we make meaningful. In other words, social constructions are embodied through the chemicals our glands produce, which in turn influence our moods and behaviors.

Hormones, then, are not part of a biological program that influences us to act out the desires of our ancestors. They are a dynamic part of our biology designed to give us the ability to respond to the physical, social, and cultural environment.

BRAINS AND GENDER

Overview

The idea that male and female brains may have different strengths and weaknesses is part of brain organization theory. Scientists have documented quite a few small average sex differences in brain anatomy (e.g., the size and shape of its parts), composition (e.g., characteristics of the tissue), and function (e.g., rate of blood flow, metabolism of glucose, and neurotransmitter levels) (Halpern 2012; Hines 2009). Scientists have also discovered differences in size and tissue ratios. Women have smaller brains (largely explained by their overall smaller size) and men and women have different ratios of white matter (brain tissue responsible for sending and receiving information) to gray matter (brain tissue responsible for information processing) in some regions. New meta-analyses find no evidence for a difference in lateralization, whether a person uses one side of their brain more than the other; both men and women are "whole-brained," though they both tend to be left dominant (Pfannkuche et al. 2009; Sommer et al. 2008).

Sex differences in the brain may be initially and partially caused by the different hormone profiles of developing fetuses and elevated levels of hormones during the first 6–12 months of life, but the source and meaning of these average differences between male and female brains is still uncertain (Halpern 2012; Hines 2009, 2011; Jordan-Young 2010). In other words, scientists have largely failed to connect these differences to any observed strengths and weaknesses in men and women. Even establishing simple correlations between brain differences and differences in behavior, skills, or interests has been largely unsuccessful. This is likely explained, in part, by brain plasticity, our brain's ability to respond to the environment.

BRAIN/ENVIRONMENT INTERACTIONS

Newborns do not immediately have the neural capacity to make sense of their environment. We are not, for example, born with the ability to process sight, sound, and touch. Instead, our brain has to learn how to interpret data from our senses. Because of this, even when we have technologies that substitute for sensory dysfunction, like the cochlear implant, individuals must train their brains to be able to use them (Moore and Shannon 2009).

Brain plasticity means, however, that a person with a sensory deficit may learn to use the part of the brain originally allocated for that task to do something else. They sometimes take stronger advantage of other brain functions and senses that they do have. In some instances, people can teach the brain to do remarkable

things. A boy named Ben Underwood, for example, who lost his sight at the age of three, trained his brain to echolocate, allowing him to deftly skateboard through crowded streets (Rigby 2006).

Brain plasticity has taught us that the brain requires input for it to organize itself in a useful manner, but also that it can be organized in many different ways. Further, we now know that the brain can adopt a sort of functional plasticity by which it can produce the same outcome via different strategies (Halpern 2012). Studies of brain function, for example, have found gender differences in the cognitive strategies used by men and women matched for mental rotation ability (Jaušovec and Jaušovec 2012) as well as sex differences in the brain regions used to retrieve emotional memories, but no sex difference in the quality of men's and women's memories or the degree of emotion expressed (Piefke et al. 2005). Likewise, neither brain size nor the gray/white ratio differences have yet to correlate with any observed difference in intelligence (Halpern 2012).

So, differences in the brain may not produce differences in traits or abilities. Instead, the brain may have multiple strategies for achieving the same outcome (De Vries and Södersten 2009; McCarthy et al. 2009). Alternatively, one difference in the brain (such as neurotransmitter function) might exist specifically to compensate for another difference (such as proportion of gray to white matter). In regard to gender, neuroendocrinologist Geert De Vries (2004, 1064) writes that differences between men's and women's brains might produce male- and female-typical outcomes, but they may "just as well do the exact opposite, that is, they may prevent sex differences in overt functions and behaviors by compensating for sex differences in physiology."

While our brains are most plastic during development and early childhood, they continue to change over the entire lifespan in response to whatever challenges and opportunities we give them (Halpern 2012; Jordan-Young 2010). Neural re-organization has been documented in response to engaging in activities such as juggling, dancing, singing, meditating, and even driving a taxi (Taubert et al. 2010). Even our most reliable differences in cognitive skills respond to training. Consider the example of mental rotation, the ability to imagine an object turning in your mind (Geiser et al. 2008). This sex difference is a large one; in any given experiment, the average man does better than 72–75 percent of women (Hyde 2005; University of Medicine and Dentistry of New Jersey nd). Mental rotation is also one of the few observed sex differences for which we have some evidence of a biological foundation (Jordan-Young 2010; Puts et al. 2008) and it has been demonstrated in infants (Moore and Johnson 2008; Quinn and Liben 2008).

Despite the robust nature of this finding, the difference between men's and women's mental rotations can be significantly diminished or even erased with simple interventions (for a summary, see Cherney 2008). One study found that assigning women to a semester of Tetris (a simple video game that involves rotating and fitting various geometric shapes into one another) almost closed the gap between men's and women's scores (Terlecki et al. 2008). In another study, just 10 hours of video game play reduced the gap to statistical insignificance (Feng et al. 2007). In a third study, 5½ hours of video game play erased the sex difference (De Lisi and Wolford 2002). In a fourth, just two minutes of practice before the test erased the different performance levels of men and women (Cherney et al. 2003).

Consistent with what we know about brain plasticity, the change in ability manifests itself in our neuro-anatomy. In one study the brains of 12- to 15-year-old girls were measured before and after a three month period during which they played Tetris for an hour and a half each week (Haier et al. 2009). At the end, their brains showed enhanced cortical thickness, heightened blood flow to the area, and increased mass. Thus, whatever our natural predispositions or prior experience, training and practice are key (Baenninger and Newcombe 1995). Both men and women benefit from interventions, suggesting that the natural ability in question is not men's advantage over women, but both men's and women's ability to improve their mental rotation ability (Cherney 2008). Indeed, the difference between the scores of people with training and people without training is larger than the difference between men and women (Newcombe 2007). Those who have undergone training, on average, perform better than 66–79 percent of those who have not (Hyde 2007).

If this process applies to an individual measure, we may well expect it to apply to cognitive ability more generally. Shifting demands on the brain operating at more macro levels (e.g., economic and technological change and corresponding increases in educational demands)

may account for the Flynn Effect, a surprisingly strong and consistent rise in IQ scores all over the world (Flynn 1984; Neisser 1998). Research suggests that the rise may be due primarily to a lifting of the lowest scores instead of an increase in the highest ones, suggesting that societies may be increasingly less likely to let their weakest members languish (Teasdale and Owen 1989; Colom et al. 2005; but see Kaufman 2009).

In short, the brilliance of the human brain lies in its ability to adjust to a wide range of demands. In this way, writes sociologist David Franks (2010, 17), "the brain is basically a social organ."

LESSONS FOR SOCIOLOGISTS

While feminists in the social sciences, among others, have long argued that sex difference and inequality is embodied, biologists have now discovered many of the mechanisms by which this occurs. As our genes, hormones, and brains respond to the environment, we become materially different. The evidence in support of this is so overwhelming that scientists now agree that it makes no sense to talk about "human nature," except insofar as ". . . the social is the natural" and vice versa (Lorber 1993, 36). Biology is, literally, the flesh and blood of society.

Given this, sociologists now have powerful arguments against the naturalization of biological states. Finding evidence of a biological dimension to social stratification can no longer be used to argue that this is an inevitable or neutral state of affairs. Nor can it be used to argue that it is irreversible, even within a single generation. The idea that some features of our biology are overwhelmingly immutable, difficult or impossible to change, is no longer a tenable position.

Sociologists who embrace this have a new tool in their tool kit. Methodologically, this means using biological measures to make sociological arguments. For example, using functional MRI scans that observe the brain in action, Mina Cikara et al. (2010) found that, among men who scored high on tests of hostile sexism, viewing images of sexually objectified women was negatively correlated with activity in the parts of the brain that recognize others' mental state. In a similar study, Lasana Harris and Fiske (2006) found that observing images of addicts and the homeless activated parts of the brain associated with disgust. Dehuman-ization and sexual objectification are neurological processes, not the fantasies of scholars who study in-equality. Hormones, too, which can often be measured with samples of saliva, can be integrated into socio-logical research. Scholars have used levels of cortisol, a "stress hormone" implicated in elevated rates of morbidity and mortality, to show the harm of persistent economic strain and prejudice (Adam 2005; Adam and Kumari 2009; Chen et al. 2010; Dickerson and Kemeny 2004; Friedman et al. 2012; Pollard 1997; see Taylor 2012 for a review). Likewise, Peter Bearman (2008, vi) argues that the research on population genetics offers sociologists a "new archive to dig around in" given that social structural change is a central trigger for changes in genetic expression.

Theoretically, these new developments in the bio-logical sciences means reimagining biology not as a limit on culture, but the very substance through which social forces exert an influence. Omar Lizardo (2007), for example, uses the concept of mirror neurons—brain cells that fire in response to observations of others as if the observer were doing the action—to explain how ideas and practices become collective attributes. Will Kalkhoff et al. (2011) use mirror neurons as well, argu-ing that they help account for social solidarity. Turning to genetics, Jeremy Freese (2008) argues that social scientists should be on the forefront in theorizing the relationship between genes and society. Some genetic predispositions, he argues, ". . . may matter much more in some originating environments than others," as the relationship between genetics and aggression reveals (p. S7). Likewise, the same genome can be maladaptive in one context and adaptive in another. A genetic pro-pensity for obesity, for example, is problematic in a so-ciety with plentiful food in a way that it is not where food is scarce (Bearman 2008). To paraphrase C. Wright Mills (1959), our lives are deeply tied to the interaction of our genetic biographies with history.

For sociologists of gender, as well as other scholars who are interested in the production of social hierar-chies, these tools promise to enhance our understanding of how difference and inequality emerge, persist, and are interrupted. We now know, for example, that we can build cognitive prisons. The intellectually impoverished environments disproportionately inhabited by the poor and racial minorities interfere with the ability of residents to reach their genetic potential for intelligence (Guo and Stearns 2002; Turkheimer and Halpern 2009). Similarly, but in relation to brain plasticity, neuroscien-tist Lise Eliot (2009) argues that sex differences in mental rotation ability are probably the result of the fact that we fail to teach mental rotation in school and boys have a greater likelihood of learning it elsewhere through activities like building toys, video games, and sports (Cherney and London 2006; Kersh et al. 2008). If women have weaker mental rotation skills than men on average, it may be because we fail to provide op-portunities for both girls and boys to learn these skills. The same argument can be applied to boys from low income backgrounds who do not have as much access to cognitive-building toys and activities and, accordingly, score worse on mental rotation tests than boys from middle and high income backgrounds (Levine et al. 2005; Noble et al. 2005). Uneven social structures, then, likely create populations that reflect them. Social depriva-tion can become a biological deficit, in true Bourdieuian fashion (1990).

As these examples illustrate, the sociology of em-bodiment has a lot to gain from this sort of inquiry. Adding an intersectional analysis promises to further develop our understanding (Crenshaw 1991). What be-comes embodied in each of us is the interaction of our material selves with the sum total of our life experiences. Gender is just one piece of a much more complicated puzzle. Anne Fausto-Sterling (2005), for example, has shown how genes, hormones, and gendered rules that depress girls' bone-building activities all contribute to the fact that men have 20–30 percent greater bone mass and strength than women. This sex difference is re-versed, however, among Ultra-Orthodox Jewish ado-lescents. Boys in these communities are tasked with intense study of religious documents from a young age, so they spend much less time exercising than otherwise similar boys. As a result, their bones never grow as strong as those of their sisters, who have lighter study loads and more sunshine and activity.

This inherent complexity—in our biological and social systems as well as in their interaction—likely explains why the tens of thousands of studies aimed at under-standing the biological bases of gender in humans have not, on the whole, offered many clear conclusions (Eliot 2009; Halpern 2012; Hines 2004; Jordan-Young 2010). Just as dividing causes of social patterns into nature and nurture fails spectacularly to account for the complexity of our bodies, dividing humans into male and female fails spectacularly to account for the diversity of human existence and our evolved ability to respond to that diversity. This is not to say that research into the biological bases of gender is useless, but to point out that we are mistaken if we think that such research is going to offer us a bright, bold line between the two categories. In other words, we should not expect to find clear cut sex differences in our biologies, even if some differences exist.

Ultimately, while many feminists have eyed the biological sciences with skepticism, the developments reviewed here may be useful for drawing attention and opposition to inequality. If we can show that biology is neither the source of inequality nor neutral in its effects but is, instead, harnessed by the forces of inequality and exploited by the powerful to their own advantage, then oppression is not just an abstract force—whether ideological, economic, or structural—but one that imposes cognitive limitations, manipulates our chemistries, and activates or suppresses our genetic potential. What is new here is not the observation that bodies have been interpreted in ways that serve the interests of elites—of this we have long been aware (e.g., Bordo 1993; Fausto-Sterling 1992, 2005; Gilman 1991; Gould 1981; Haraway 1989; Lorber 1993)—but that the oppression goes far beyond interpretation; it violates our bodily boundaries in something more akin to occupation. When control of our societies are in the hands of the few, so are our bodies.

REFERENCES

Adam, Emma K. 2005. "Momentary Emotion and Cortisol Levels in the Everyday Lives of Working Parents." Pp. 105–33 in *Being Together, Working Apart: Dual Career Families and the Work–Life Balance*, edited by Barbara Schneider and Linda J. Waite. Cambridge, UK: Cambridge University Press.

Adam, Emma K. and Meena Kumari. 2009. "Assessing Salivary Cortisol in Large-Scale Epidemiological Research." *Psychoneuroendocrinology* 34: 1423–1436.

Alvergne, Alexandra, Charlotte Faurie and Michel Raymond. 2009. "Variation in Testosterone Levels and Male Reproductive Effort: Insight from a Polygynous Human Population." *Hormones and Behavior* 56: 491–7.

Archer, John. 2006. "Testosterone and Human Aggression: An Evaluation of the Challenge Hypothesis." *Neuroscience and Biobehavioral Review* 30: 319–45.

Baenninger, Maryann and Nora Newcombe. 1995. "Environmental Input to the Development of Sex-Related Differences in Spatial and Mathematical Ability." *Learning and Individual Differences* 7: 363–79.

Baumeister, Roy, Kathleen Catanese and Kathleen Vohs. 2001. "Is There a Gender Difference in Strength of Sex Drive? Theoretical Views, Conceptual Distinctions, and a Review of Relevant Evidence." *Personality and Social Psychology Review* 5: 242–73.

Bearman, Peter. 2008. "Exploring Genetics and Social Structure." *American Journal of Sociology* 114: v–x.

Bernhardt, Paul, James Dabbs Jr., Julie Fielden and Candice Lutter. 1998. "Testosterone Changes During Vicarious Experiences of Winning and Losing Among Fans at Sporting Events." *Physiology & Behavior* 65: 59–62.

Book, Angela, Katherine Starzyk and Vernon Quinsey. 2001. "The Relationship Between Testosterone and Aggression: A Meta-Analysis." *Aggression and Violent Behavior* 6: 579–99.

Booth, Alan, Douglas Granger, Allan Mazur and Katie Kivlighan. 2006. "Testosterone and Social Behavior." *Social Forces* 85: 167–91.

Booth, Alan, David Johnson and Douglas Granger. 1999. "Testosterone and Men's Depression: The Role of Social Behavior." *Journal of Health and Social Behavior* 40: 130–40.

Booth, Alan, Greg Shelley, Allan Mazur, Gerry Tharp and Roger Kittok. 1989. "Testosterone, and Winning and Losing in Human Competition." *Hormones and Behavior* 23: 556–71.

Booth, Alan and D. Wayne Osgood. 1993. "The Influence of Testosterone on Deviance in Adulthood: Assessing and Explaining the Relationship." *Criminology* 31: 93–117.

Bordo, Susan. 1993. Unbearable Weight: Feminism, Western Culture, and the Body. Berkeley and Los Angeles: University of California Press.

Bos, Peter, Jaak Panksepp, Rose-Marie Bluthé and Jack van Honk. 2012. "Acute Effects of Steroid Hormones and Neuropeptides on Human Social-Emotional Behavior: A Review of Single Administration Studies." *Frontiers in Neuroendocrinology* 33: 17–35.

Bourdieu, Pierre. 1990. The Logic of Practice. Cambridge: Polity Press.

Bowler, Peter. 2003. Evolution: The History of an Idea. Berkeley and Los Angeles: University of California Press.

Cadoret, Remi, William Yates, Ed Troughton, George Woodworth and Mark Stewart. 1995. "Genetic–Environmental Interaction in the Genesis of Aggressivity and Conduct Disorders." *Archives of General Psychiatry* 52: 916–24.

Chen, Edith, Sheldon Cohen and Gregory E. Miller. 2010. "How Low Socioeconomic Status Affects 2-Year Hormonal Trajectories in Children." *Psychological Science* 21: 31–7.

Cherney, Isabelle D. 2008. "Mom, Let Me Play More Computer Games: They Improve My Mental Rotation Skills." *Sex Roles* 59: 776–86.

Cherney, Isabelle D., Kavita Jagarlamudi, Erika Lawrence and Nicole Shimabuku. 2003. "Experiential Factors on Sex Differences in Mental Rotation." *Perceptual and Motor Skills* 96: 1062–70.

Cherney, Isabelle D. and Kamala London. 2006. "Gender-Linked Differences in the Toys, Television Shows, Computer Games, and Outdoor Activities of 5- to 13-year-old Children." *Sex Roles* 54: 717–26.

Cikara, Mina, Jennifer Eberhardt and Susan Fiske. 2010. "From Agents to Objects: Sexist Attitudes and Neural Responses to Sexualized Targets." *Journal of Cognitive Neuroscience* 23: 540–51.

Colom, Roberto, Josep Luis-Font and Antonio Andrés-Pueyo. 2005. "The Generational Intelligence Gains Are Caused by Decreasing Variance in the Lower Half of the Distribution: Supporting Evidence for the Nutrition Hypothesis." *Intelligence* 33: 83–91.

Craig, Ian, Emma Harper and Caroline Loat. 2004. "The Genetic Basis for Sex Differences in Human Behaviour: Role of the Sex Chromosomes." *Annals of Human Genetics* 68: 269–84.

Crenshaw, Kimberlé W. 1991. "Mapping the Margins: Intersectionality, Identity Politics, and Violence Against Women of Color." *Stanford Law Review* 43: 1241–99.

Dabbs Jr, James and Robin Morris. 1990. "Testosterone, Social Class, and Antisocial Behavior in a Sample of 4,462 Men." *Psychological Science* 1: 209–11.

De Lisi, Richard and Jennifer Wolford. 2002. "Improving Children's Mental Rotation Accuracy with Computer Game Playing." *The Journal of Genetic Psychology* 163: 272–82.

De Vries, Geert. 2004. "Sex Differences in Adult and Developing Brains: Compensation, Compensation, Compensation." *Endocrinology* 145: 1063–8.

De Vries, Geert and Per Södersten. 2009. "Sex Differences in the Brain: The Relation Between Structure and Function." *Hormones and Behavior* 55: 589–96.

Delbrück, Max. 1949a. "A Physicist Looks at Biology." Pp. 9–22 in *Phage and the Origins of Molecular Biology*, edited by John Cairns, Gunther Stent and James Watson. New York: Cold Spring Harbor Laboratory Press.

Delbrück, Max. 1949b. "A Physicist Looks at Biology." *Transactions of the Connecticut Academy of Arts and Sciences* 38: 173–90.

Dickerson, Sally and Margaret Kemeny. 2004. "Acute Stressors and Cortisol Responses: A Theoretical Integration and Synthesis of Laboratory Research." *Psychological Bulletin* 130: 355–91.

Eliot, Lise. 2009. Pink Brain, Blue Brain. New York: Houghton Mifflin Harcourt Publishing Company.

Else-Quest, Nicole, Janet Hyde, H. Hill Goldsmith and Carol Van Hulle. 2006. "Gender Differences in Temperament: A Meta-Analysis." *Psychological Bulletin* 132: 33–72.

Else-Quest, Nicole, Janet Hyde and Marcia Linn. 2010. "Cross-National Patterns of Gender Differences in Mathematics: A Meta-Analysis." *Psychological Bulletin* 136: 103–27.

Fausto-Sterling, Anne. 1992. Myths of Gender: Biological Theories about Women and Men. New York: Basic Books.

Fausto-Sterling, Anne. 2005. "The Bare Bones of Sex: Part 1—Sex and Gender." *Signs* 30: 1491–527.

Feng, Jing, Ian Spence and Jay Pratt. 2007. "Playing an Action Video Game Reduces Gender Differences in Spatial Cognition." *Psychological Science* 18: 850–5.

Fine, Cordelia. 2010. Delusions of Gender: How Our Minds, Society, and Neurosexism Create Difference. New York and London: W. W. Norton and Company.

Flynn, James. 1984. "The Mean IQ of Americans: Massive Gains 1932 to 1978." *Psychological Bulletin* 95: 29–51.

Fraga, Mario, Esteban Ballestar, Maria Paz, Santiago Ropero, Fernando Setien, Maria Ballestar, Damia Heine-Suñer, Juan Cigudosa, Miguel Urioste, Javier Benitez, Manuel Boix-Chornet, Abel Sanchez-Aguilera, Charlotte Ling, Emma Carlsson, Pernille Poulson, Allan Vaag, Zarko Stephan, Tim Spector, Yue-Zhong Wu, Christoph Plass and Manual Esteller. 2005. "Epigenetic Differences Arise During the Lifetime of Monozygotic Twins." *PNAS* 102: 10604–9.

Franks, David. 2010. Neurosociology: The Nexus Between Neuroscience and Social Psychology. New York: Springer.

Freese, Jeremy. 2008. "Genetics and the Social Science Explanation of Individual Outcomes." *American Journal of Sociology* 114: S1–35.

Freese, Jeremy, Allen Li and Lisa Wade. 2003. "The Potential Relevances of Biology to Social Inquiry." *Annual Review of Sociology* 29: 233–56.

Friedman, Esther, Arun Karlamangla, David Almeida and Teresa Seeman. 2012. "Social Strain and Cortisol

Regulation in Midlife in the US." *Social Science and Medicine* 74: 607–15.

Geiser, Christian, Wolfgang Lehmann and Michael Eid. 2008. "A Note on Sex Differences in Mental Rotation in Different Age Groups." *Intelligence* 36: 556–63.

Gettler, Lee, Thomas McDade, Alan Feranil and Christopher Kuzawa. 2011. "Longitudinal Evidence that Fatherhood Decreases Testosterone in Human Males." *PNAS* 108: 16194–9.

Gilman, Sander. 1991. The Jew's Body. New York: Routledge.

Gottesman, Irving. 1991. Schizophrenia Genesis: The Origin of Madness. New York: Freeman.

Gould, Stephen Jay. 1981. The Mismeasure of Man. New York: W. W. Norton.

Guo, Guang and Elizabeth Stearns. 2002. "The Social Influences on the Realization of Genetic Potential for Intellectual Development." *Social Forces* 80: 881–910.

Haier, Richard, Sherif Karama, Leonard Leyba and Rex Jung. 2009. "MRI Assessment of Cortical Thickness and Functional Activity Changes in Adolescent Girls Following Three Months of Practice on a Visual-Spatial Task." *BioMed Central Research Notes* 2: 174.

Halpern, Diane. 2012. Sex Differences in Cognitive Abilities (4th ed.). New York: Psychology Press.

Haraway, Donna. 1989. Primate Visions: Gender, Race, and Nature in the World of Modern Science. New York: Routledge.

Harris, Lasana and Susan Fiske. 2006. "Dehumanizing the Lowest of the Low." *Psychological Science* 17: 847–53.

Hawley, R. Scott and Catherine Mori. 1999. The Human Genome: A User's Guide. San Diego, CA: Academic Press.

Hines, Melissa. 2004. Brain Gender. New York: Oxford University Press.

Hines, Melissa. 2009. "Gonadal Hormones and Sexual Differentiation of Human Brain and Behavior." Pp. 1869–909 in *Hormones, Brain, and Behavior* (2nd ed.), edited by Donald Pfaff, Arthur Arnold, Susan Fahrbach, Anne Etgen and Robert Rubin. Amsterdam, Netherlands: Elsevier/Academic Press.

Hines, Melissa. 2011. "Gender Development and the Human Brain." *Annual Review of Neuroscience* 34: 69–88.

Hyde, Janet. 2005. "The Gender Similarities Hypothesis." *American Psychologist* 60: 581–92.

Hyde, Janet. 2007. "Women in Science: Gender Similarities in Abilities and Sociocultural Forces." Pp. 131–45 in *Why Aren't More Women in Science? Top Researchers Debate the Evidence*, edited by Stephen Ceci and Wendy Williams. Washington DC: American Psychological Association.

Jacobson, Kristen. 2009. "Considering Interactions Between Genes, Environment, Biology, and Social Context." Psychological Science Agenda. [Online]. Retrieved on 13 August 2012 from: http://www.apa.org/science/about/psa/2009/04/sci-brief.aspx

Jaušovec, Norbert and Ksenija Jaušovec. 2012. "Sex Differences in Mental Rotation and Cortical Activation Patterns: Can Training Change Them?" *Intelligence* 40: 151–62.

Jordan-Young, Rebecca. 2010. Brain Storm: The Flaws in the Science of Sex Differences. Harvard, Mass: Harvard University Press.

Kalkhoff, Will, Joseph Dippong and Stanford Gregory Jr. 2011. "The Biosociology of Solidarity." *Sociology Compass* 5: 936–48.

Kaufman, Alan. 2009. IQ Testing 101. New York: Springer Publishing Company.

Keller, Evelyn Fox. 2000. The Century of the Gene. Cambridge, Mass: Harvard University Press.

Kersh, Joanne, Beth Casey and Jessica Mercer Young. 2008. "Research on Spatial Skills and Block Building in Girls and Boys: The Relationship to Later Mathematics Learning." Pp. 233–53 in *Mathematics, Science and Technology in Early Childhood Education: Contemporary Perspectives on Mathematics in Early Childhood Education*, edited by Bernard Spodak and Olivia Saracho. Charlotte, NC: Information Age.

Klebanov, Pamela and Diane Ruble. 1994. "Toward an Understanding of Women's Experience of Menstrual Cycle Symptoms." Pp. 183–222 in *Psychological Perspectives on Women's Health*, edited by Vincent Adesso. Washington DC: Taylor & Francis.

Kreuz, Leo and Robert Rose. 1972. "Suppression of Plasma Testosterone Levels and Psychological Stress." *Archives of General Psychiatry* 26: 479–82.

Levine, Susan, Marina Vasilyeva, Stella Lourenco, Nora Newcombe and Janellen Huttenlocher. 2005. "Socioeconomic Status Modifies the Sex Difference in Spatial Skill." *Psychological Science* 16: 841–5.

Lizardo, Omar. 2007. "'Mirror Neurons,' Collective Objects and the Problem of Transmission: Reconsidering Stephen Turner's Critique of Practice Theory." *Journal for the Theory of Social Behaviour* 37: 319–50.

Lorber, Judith. 1993. Paradoxes of Gender. New Haven, CT: Yale University Press.

Mazur, Allan. 2005. The Biosociology of Dominance and Deference. Lanham, MD: Rowman & Littlefield Publishers.

Mazur, Allan and Alan Booth. 1998. "Testosterone and Dominance in Men." *Behavioral and Brain Sciences* 21: 353–97.

Mazur, Allan, Alan Booth and James Dabbs Jr. 1992. "Testosterone and Chess Competition." *Social Psychology Quarterly* 55: 70–7.

Mazur, Allan and Joel Michalek. 1998. "Marriage, Divorce, and Male Testosterone." *Social Forces* 77: 315–30.

Mazur, Allan, Elizabeth Susman, and Sandy Edelbrock. 1997. "Sex Difference in Testosterone Response to a Video Game Contest." *Evolution and Human Behavior* 18: 317–26.

McCarthy, Margaret, Geert de Vries and Nancy Forger. 2009. "Sexual Differentiation of the Brain: Mode, Mechanisms, and Meaning." Pp. 1707–44 in *Hormones, Brain, and Behavior*, edited by Donald Pfaff, Arthur Arnold, Susan Fahrbach, Anne Etgen and Robert Rubin. Amsterdam: Elsevier.

McFarlane, Jessica, Carol Martin and Tannis Williams. 1988. "Mood Fluctuations: Women versus Men and Menstrual versus other Cycles." *Psychology of Women Quarterly* 12: 201–24.

McFarlane, Jessica and Tannis Williams. 1994. "Placing Premenstrual Syndrome in Perspective." *Psychology of Women Quarterly* 18: 339–74.

Meaney, Michael. 2001. "Nature, Nurture, and the Disunity of Knowledge." *Annals New York Academy of Sciences* 935: 50–61.

Mills, C. Wright. 1959. The Sociological Imagination. London: Oxford University Press.

Moore, David and S. Johnson. 2008. "Mental Rotation in Human Infants: A Sex Difference." *Psychological Science* 19: 1063–6.

Moore, David and Robert Shannon. 2009. "Beyond Cochlear Implants: Awakening the Deafened Brain." *Nature Neuroscience* 12: 686–91.

Muller, Martin, Frank Marlowe, Revocatus Bugumba and Peter Ellison. 2009. "Testosterone and Paternal Care in East African Foragers and Pastoralists." *Proceedings of the Royal Society B: Biological Sciences* 276: 347–54.

Neisser, Ulric (ed.). 1998. The Rising Curve: Long-Term Gains in IQ and Related Measures. Washington, DC: American Psychological Association.

Newcombe, Nora. 2007. "Science Seriously: Straight Thinking About Spatial Sex Differences." Pp. 69–77 in *Why Aren't More Women in Science? Top Researchers Debate the Evidence*, edited by Stephen Ceci and Wendy Williams. Washington DC: American Psychological Association.

Nisbett, Richard and Dov Cohen. 1996. Culture of Honor: The Psychology of Violence in the South. Boulder, CO: Westview.

Noble, Kimberly, M. Frank Norman and Martha Farah. 2005. "Neurocognitive Correlates of Socioeconomic Status in Kindergarten Children." *Developmental Science* 8: 74–87.

Oinonen, Kirsten and Dwight Mazmanian. 2001. "Effects of Oral Contraceptives on Daily Self-Ratings of Positive and Negative Affect." *Journal of Psychosomatic Research* 51: 647–58.

Pembrey, Marcus, Lars Bygren, Gunnar Kaati, Sören Edvinsson, Kate Northstone, Michael Sjöström, Jean Golding, and The ALSPAC Study Team. 2006. "Sex-Specific, Male-Line Transgenerational Responses in Humans." *European Journal of Human Genetics* 14: 159–66.

Petersen, Jennifer and Janet Hyde. 2010. "A Meta-Analytic Review of Research on Gender Differences in Sexuality, 1993–2007." *Psychological Bulletin* 136: 21–38.

Pfannkuche, Kristina, Anke Bouma and Ton Groothuis. 2009. "Does Testosterone Affect Lateralization of Brain and Behaviour? A Meta-Analysis in Humans and Other Animal Species." *Philosophical Transactions of the Royal Society* 364: 929–42.

Piefke, Martina, Peter Weiss, Hans Markowitsch and Gereon Fink. 2005. "Gender Differences in the Functional Neuroanatomy of Emotional Episodic Autobiographical Memory." *Human Brain Mapping* 24: 313–24.

Pollard, Tessa. 1997. "Physiological Consequences of Everyday Psychosocial Stress." *Collegium Antropologicum* 21: 17–28.

Poulsen, Pernille, Manel Esteller, Allan Vaag and Mario Fraga. 2007. "The Epigenetic Basis of Twin Discordance in Age-Related Diseases." *Pediatric Research* 61: 38R–42R.

Puts, David, Michael McDaniel, Cynthia Jordan and S. Marc Breedlove. 2008. "Spatial Ability and Prenatal Androgens: Meta-Analyses of Congenital Adrenal Hyperplasia and Digit Ratio (2D:4D) Studies." *Archives of Sexual Behavior* 37: 100–11.

Quinn, Paul and Lynn Liben. 2008. "A Sex Difference in Mental Rotation in Young Infants." *Psychological Science* 19: 1067–70.

Reik, Wolf and Jörn Walter. 2001. "Genomic Imprinting: Parental Influence on the Genome." *Nature Review Genetics* 2: 21–32.

Rigby, Theo. 2006. "The Boy Who Sees with Sound." People. [Online]. Retrieved on 10 June 2012 from: http://www.people.com/people/article/0,26334,1212568,00.html

Rowe, Richard, Barbara Maughan, Carol Worthman, Jane Costello and Adrian Angold. 2004. "Testosterone, Antisocial Behavior, and Social Dominance in Boys:

Pubertal Development and Biosocial Interaction." *Biological Psychiatry* 55: 546–52.

Saad, Gad and John Vongas. 2009. "The Effect of Conspicuous Consumption on Men's Testosterone Levels." *Organizational Behavior and Human Decision Processes* 110: 80–92.

Sapolsky, Robert. 1997. The Trouble with Testosterone and Other Essays on the Biology of the Human Predicament. New York: Simon and Schuster.

Silverman, Paul. 2004. "Rethinking Genetic Determinism." *The Scientist* 18: 32.

Sommer, Iris, André Aleman, Metten Somers, Marco Boks and René Kahn. 2008. "Sex Differences in Handedness, Asymmetry of the Planum Temporale and Functional Language Lateralization." *Brain Research* 1206: 76–88.

Stanton, Steven and Robin Edelstein. 2009. "The Physiology of Women's Power Motive: Implicit Power Motivation Is Positively Associated with Estradiol Levels in Women." *Journal of Research in Personality* 43: 1109–13.

Storey, Anne, Carolyn Walsh, Roma Quinton and Katherine Wynne-Edwards. 2000. "Hormonal Correlates of Paternal Responsiveness in New and Expectant Fathers." *Evolution and Human Behavior* 21: 79–95.

Strohman, Richard. 1997. "The Coming Kuhnian Revolution in Biology." *Nature Biotechnology* 15: 194–200.

Taubert, Marco, Bogdan Draganski, Alfred Anwander, Karsten Müller, Annette Horstmann, Arno Villringer and Patrick Ragert. 2010. "Dynamic Properties of Human Brain Structure: Learning-Related Changes in Cortical Areas and Associated Fiber Connections." *The Journal of Neuroscience* 30: 11670–7.

Taylor, Catherine. 2012. "A Sociological Overview of Cortisol as a Biomarker of Response to the Social Environment." *Sociology Compass* 6(5): 434–44.

Taylor, Shelley, Rena Repetti and Teresa Seeman. 1997. "Health Psychology: What Is an Unhealthy Environment and How Does It Get Under the Skin?" *Annual Review of Psychology* 48: 411–47.

Teasdale, T. W. and David Owen. 1989. "Continuing Secular Increases in Intelligence and a Stable Prevalence of High Intelligence Levels." *Intelligence* 13: 255–62.

Terlecki, Melissa, Nora Newcombe and Michelle Little. 2008. "Durable and Generalized Effects of Spatial Experience on Mental Rotation: Gender Differences in Growth Patterns." *Applied Cognitive Psychology* 22: 996–1013.

Thompson, Wendy, James Dabbs Jr., and Robert Frady. 1990. "Changes in Saliva Testosterone Levels During a 90-day Shock Incarceration Program." *Criminal Justice and Behavior* 17: 246–52.

Turkheimer, Eric and Diane Halpern. 2009. "Sex Differences in Variability for Cognitive Measures: Do the Ends Justify the Genes?" *Perspectives on Psychological Science* 4: 612–4.

Udry, Richard. 1995. "Sociology and Biology: What Biology Do Sociologists Need to Know?" *Social Forces* 73: 1267–78.

University of Medicine and Dentistry of New Jersey. nd. Effect Size and Clinical/Practical Significance. [Online]. Retrieved on 15 August 2012 from: http://www.umdnj.edu/idsweb/shared/effect_size.htm

van Anders, Sari and Neil Watson. 2007. "Testosterone Levels in Women and Men who are Single, in Long-Distance Relationships, or Same-City Relationships." *Hormones and Behavior* 51: 820–6.

van der Meij, Leander, Mercedes Almela, Vanesa Hidalgo, Carolina Villada, Hans Ijzerman, Paul van Lange and Alicia Salvador. 2012. "Testosterone and Cortisol Release among Spanish Soccer Fans Watching the 2010 World Cup Final." *PLoS One* 7: 1–7.

Wallentin, Mikkel. 2009. "Putative Sex Differences in Verbal Abilities and Language Cortex: A Critical Review." *Brain and Language* 108: 175–83.

Wong Albert, Irving Gottesman and Arturas Petronis. 2005. "Phenotypic Differences in Genetically Identical Organisms: The Epigenetic Perspective." *Human Molecular Genetics* 14: R11–8.

Wood, Wendy and Alice Eagly. 2012. "Biosocial Construction of Sex Differences and Similarities in Behavior." Pp. 55–123 in *Advances in Experimental Social Psychology* (vol. 46), edited by J. M. Olson and M. P. Zanna. London, UK: Elsevier.

Yates, William, Paul Perry, John Macindoe, Tim Holman and Vicki Ellingrod. 1999. "Psychosexual Effects of Three Doses of Testosterone Cycling in Normal Men." *Biological Psychiatry* 45: 254–60.

3

Theorizing Difference from Multiracial Feminism

Maxine Baca Zinn

Bonnie Thornton Dill

Women of color have long challenged the hegemony of feminisms constructed primarily around the lives of white middle-class women. Since the late 1960s, U.S. women of color have taken issue with unitary theories of gender. Our critiques grew out of the widespread concern about the exclusion of women of color from feminist scholarship and the misinterpretation of our experiences,[1] and ultimately "out of the very discourses, denying, permitting, and producing difference."[2] Speaking simultaneously from "within and against" *both* women's liberation and antiracist movements, we have insisted on the need to challenge systems of domination,[3] not merely as gendered subjects but as women whose lives are affected by our location in multiple hierarchies.

Recently, and largely in response to these challenges, work that links gender to other forms of domination is increasing. In this article, we examine this connection further as well as the ways in which difference and diversity infuse contemporary feminist studies. Our analysis draws on a conceptual framework that we refer to as "multiracial feminism."[4] This perspective is an attempt to go beyond a mere recognition of diversity and difference among women to examine structures of domination, specifically the importance of race in understanding the social construction of gender. Despite the varied concerns and multiple intellectual stances which

characterize the feminisms of women of color, they share an emphasis on race as a primary force situating genders differently. It is the centrality of race, of institutionalized racism, and of struggles against racial oppression that link the various feminist perspectives within this framework. Together, they demonstrate that racial meanings offer new theoretical directions for feminist thought.

TENSIONS IN CONTEMPORARY DIFFERENCE FEMINISM

Objections to the false universalism embedded in the concept "woman" emerged within other discourses as well as those of women of color.[5] Lesbian feminists and postmodern feminists put forth their own versions of what Susan Bordo has called "gender skepticism."[6]

Many thinkers within mainstream feminism have responded to these critiques with efforts to contextualize gender. The search for women's "universal" or "essential" characteristics is being abandoned. By examining gender in the context of other social divisions and perspectives, difference has gradually become important—even problematizing the universal categories, "women" and "men." Sandra G. Harding expresses the shift best

This article is reprinted from *Feminist Studies,* Volume 22, Number 2 (Summer 1996), pp. 321–331, by permission of the publisher, Feminist Studies, Inc.

in her claim that "there are no gender relations *per se,* but only gender relations as constructed by and between classes, races, and cultures."[7]

Many feminists now contend that difference occupies center stage as *the* project of women studies today.[8] According to one scholar, "difference has replaced equality as the central concern of feminist theory."[9] Many have welcomed the change, hailing it as a major revitalizing force in U.S. feminist theory.[10] But if *some* priorities within mainstream feminist thought have been refocused by attention to difference, there remains an "uneasy alliance"[11] between women of color and other feminists.

If difference has helped revitalize academic feminisms, it has also "upset the apple cart," and introduced new conflicts into feminist studies.[12] For example, in a recent and widely discussed essay, Jane Rowland Martin argues that the current preoccupation with difference is leading feminism into dangerous traps. She fears that in giving privileged status to a predetermined set of analytic categories (race, ethnicity, and class), "we affirm the existence of nothing but difference." She asks, "How do we know that for us, difference does not turn on being fat, or religious, or in an abusive relationship?"[13]

We, too, see pitfalls in some strands of the difference project. However, our perspectives take their bearings from social relations. Race and class difference are crucial, we argue, not as individual characteristics (such as being fat) but insofar as they are primary organizing principles of a society which locates and positions groups within that society's opportunity structures.

Despite the much-heralded diversity trend within feminist studies, difference is often reduced to mere pluralism; a "live and let live" approach where principles of relativism generate a long list of diversities which begin with gender, class, and race and continue through a range of social structural as well as personal characteristics.[14] Another disturbing pattern, which bell hooks refers to as "the commodification of difference," is the representation of diversity as a form of exotica, "a spice, seasoning that livens up the dull dish that is mainstream white culture."[15] The major limitation of these approaches is the failure to attend to the power relations that accompany difference. Moreover, these approaches ignore the inequalities that cause some characteristics to be seen as "normal" while others are seen as "different" and thus, deviant.

Maria C. Lugones expresses irritation at those feminists who see only the *problem* of difference without recognizing *difference.*[16] Increasingly, we find that difference *is* recognized. But this in no way means that difference occupies a "privileged" theoretical status. Instead of using difference to rethink the category of women, difference is often a euphemism for women who differ from the traditional norm. Even in purporting to accept difference, feminist pluralism often creates a social reality that reverts to universalizing women:

> So much feminist scholarship assumes that when we cut through all of the diversity among women created by differences of racial classification, ethnicity, social class, and sexual orientation, a "universal truth" concerning women and gender lies buried underneath. But if we can face the scary possibility that no such certainty exists and that persisting in such a search will always distort or omit someone's experiences, with what do we replace this old way of thinking? Gender differences and gender politics begin to look very different if there is no essential woman at the core.[17]

WHAT IS MULTIRACIAL FEMINISM?

A new set of feminist theories have emerged from the challenges put forth by women of color. Multiracial feminism is an evolving body of theory and practice informed by wide-ranging intellectual traditions. This framework does not offer a singular or unified feminism but a body of knowledge situating women and men in multiple systems of domination. U.S. multiracial feminism encompasses several emergent perspectives developed primarily by women of color: African Americans, Latinas, Asian Americans, and Native Americans, women whose analyses are shaped by their unique perspectives as "outsiders within"— marginal intellectuals whose social locations provide them a particular perspective on self and society.[18] Although U.S. women of color represent many races and ethnic backgrounds—with different histories and cultures—our feminisms cohere in their treatment of race as a basic social division, a structure of power, a focus of political struggle and hence a fundamental force in shaping women's and men's lives.

This evolving intellectual and political perspective uses several terms. While we adopt the label "multiracial," other terms have been used to describe this broad framework. For example, Chela Sandoval refers to "U.S. Third World feminisms,"[19] while other scholars refer to "indigenous feminisms." In their theory text-reader, Alison M. Jagger and Paula M. Rothenberg adopt the label "multicultural feminism."[20]

We use "multiracial" rather than "multicultural" as a way of underscoring race as a power system that interacts with other structured inequalities to shape genders. Within the U.S. context, race, and the system of meanings and ideologies which accompany it, is a fundamental organizing principle of social relationships.[21] Race affects all women and men, although in different ways. Even cultural and group differences among women are produced through interaction within a racially stratified social order. Therefore, although we do not discount the importance of culture, we caution that cultural analytic frameworks that ignore race tend to view women's differences as the product of group-specific values and practices that often result in the marginalization of cultural groups which are then perceived as exotic expressions of a normative center. Our focus on race stresses the social construction of differently situated social groups and their varying degrees of advantage and power. Additionally, this emphasis on race takes on increasing political importance in an era where discourse about race is governed by color-evasive language[22] and a preference for individual rather than group remedies for social inequalities. Our analyses insist upon the primary and pervasive nature of race in contemporary U.S. society while at the same time acknowledging how race both shapes and is shaped by a variety of other social relations.

In the social sciences, multiracial feminism grew out of socialist feminist thinking. Theories about how political economic forces shape women's lives were influential as we began to uncover the social causes of racial ethnic women's subordination. But socialist feminism's concept of capitalist patriarchy, with its focus on women's unpaid (reproductive) labor in the home, failed to address racial differences in the organization of reproductive labor. As feminists of color have argued, "reproductive labor has divided along racial as well as gender lines, and the specific characteristics have varied regionally and changed over time as capitalism has reorganized."[23] Despite the limitations of socialist feminism, this body of literature has been especially useful

in pursuing questions about the interconnections among systems of domination.[24]

Race and ethnic studies was the other major social scientific source of multiracial feminism. It provided a basis for comparative analyses of groups that are socially and legally subordinated and remain culturally distinct within U.S. society. This includes the systematic discrimination of socially constructed racial groups and their distinctive cultural arrangements. Historically, the categories of African American, Latino, Asian American, and Native American were constructed as both racially and culturally distinct. Each group has a distinctive culture, shares a common heritage, and has developed a common identity within a larger society that subordinates them.[25]

We recognize, of course, certain pitfalls inherent in an uncritical use of the multiracial label. First, the perspective can be hampered by a biracial model in which only African Americans and whites are seen as racial categories and all other groups are viewed through the prism of cultural differences. Latinos and Asians have always occupied distinctive places within the racial hierarchy, and current shifts in the composition of the U.S. population are racializing these groups anew.[26]

A second problem lies in treating multiracial feminism as a single analytical framework, and its principle architects, women of color, as an undifferentiated category. The concepts "multiracial feminism," "racial ethnic women," and "women of color" homogenize quite different experiences and can falsely universalize experiences across race, ethnicity, sexual orientation, and age.[27] The feminisms created by women of color exhibit a plurality of intellectual and political positions. We speak in many voices, with inconsistencies that are born of our different social locations. Multiracial feminism embodies this plurality and richness. Our intent is not to falsely universalize women of color. Nor do we wish to promote a new racial essentialism in place of the old gender essentialism. Instead, we use these concepts to examine the structures and experiences produced by intersecting forms of race and gender.

It is also essential to acknowledge that race itself is a shifting and contested category whose meanings construct definitions of all aspects of social life.[28] In the United States it helped define citizenship by excluding everyone who was not a white, male property owner. It defined labor as slave or free, coolie or contract, and family as available only to those men whose marriages were recognized or whose wives could immigrate with them. Additionally, racial meanings are contested both within groups and between them.[29]

Although definitions of race are at once historically and geographically specific, they are also transnational, encompassing diasporic groups and crossing traditional geographic boundaries. Thus, while U.S. multiracial feminism calls attention to the fundamental importance of race, it must also locate the meaning of race within specific national traditions.

THE DISTINGUISHING FEATURES OF MULTIRACIAL FEMINISM

By attending to these problems, multiracial feminism offers a set of analytic premises for thinking about and theorizing gender. The following themes distinguish this branch of feminist inquiry.

First, multiracial feminism asserts that gender is constructed by a range of interlocking inequalities, what Patricia Hill Collins calls a "matrix of domination."[30] The idea of a matrix is that several fundamental systems work with and through each other. People experience race, class, gender, and sexuality differently depending upon their social location in the structures of race, class, gender, and sexuality. For example, people of the same race will experience race differently depending upon their location in the class structure as working class, professional managerial class, or unemployed; in the gender structure as female or male; and in structures of sexuality as heterosexual, homosexual, or bisexual.

Multiracial feminism also examines the simultaneity of systems in shaping women's experience and identity. Race, class, gender, and sexuality are not reducible to individual attributes to be measured and assessed for their separate contribution in explaining given social outcomes, an approach that Elizabeth Spelman calls "pop-bead metaphysics," where a woman's identity consists of the sum of parts neatly divisible from one another.[31] The matrix of domination seeks to account for the multiple ways that women experience themselves as gendered, raced, classed, and sexualized.

Second, multiracial feminism emphasizes the intersectional nature of hierarchies at all levels of social life. Class, race, gender, and sexuality are components of both social structure and social interaction. Women and men are differently embedded in locations created by these cross-cutting hierarchies. As a result, women and men throughout the social order experience different forms of privilege and subordination, depending on their race, class, gender, and sexuality. In other words, intersecting forms of domination produce *both* oppression *and* opportunity. At the same time that structures of race, class, and gender create disadvantages for women of color, they provide unacknowledged benefits for those who are at the top of these hierarchies—whites, members of the upper classes, and males. Therefore, multiracial feminism applies not only to racial ethnic women but also to women and men of all races, classes, and genders.

Third, multiracial feminism highlights the relational nature of dominance and subordination. Power is the cornerstone of women's differences.[32] This means that women's differences are *connected* in systematic ways.[33] Race is a vital element in the pattern of relations among minority and white women. As Linda Gordon argues, the very meanings of being a white woman in the United States have been affected by the existence of subordinated women of color; "They intersect in conflict and in occasional cooperation, but always in mutual influence."[34]

Fourth, multiracial feminism explores the interplay of social structure and women's agency. Within the constraints of race, class, and gender oppression, women create viable lives for themselves, their families, and their communities. Women of color have resisted and often undermined the forces of power that control them. From acts of quiet dignity and steadfast determination to involvement in revolt and rebellion, women struggle to shape their own lives. Racial oppression has been a common focus of the "dynamic of oppositional agency" of women of color. As Chandra Talpade Mohanty points out, it is the nature and organization of women's opposition which mediates and differentiates the impact of structures of domination.[35]

Fifth, multiracial feminism encompasses wide-ranging methodological approaches, and like other branches of feminist thought, relies on varied theoretical tools as well. Ruth Frankenberg and Lata Mani identify three guiding principles of inclusive feminist inquiry: "building complex analyses, avoiding erasure, specifying location."[36] In the last decade, the opening up of academic feminism has focused attention on social location in the production of knowledge. Most basically, research by and about marginalized women has destabilized what used to be universal categories of gender. Marginalized locations are well-suited for grasping social relations that remained obscure from more privileged vantage points. Lived experience, in other words, creates alternative ways of understanding the social world and the experience of different groups of women within it. Racially informed standpoint epistemologies have provided new topics, fresh questions, and new understandings of women and men. Women of color have, as Norma Alarcon argues, asserted ourselves as subjects, using our voices to challenge dominant conceptions of truth.[37]

Sixth, multiracial feminism brings together understandings drawn from the lived experiences of diverse and continuously changing groups of women. Among Asian Americans, Native Americans, Latinas, and blacks are many different national cultural and ethnic groups. Each one is engaged in the process of testing, refining, and reshaping these broader categories in its own image. Such internal differences heighten awareness of and sensitivity to both commonalities and differences, serving as a constant reminder of the importance of comparative study and maintaining a creative tension between diversity and universalization.

DIFFERENCE AND TRANSFORMATION

Efforts to make women's studies less partial and less distorted have produced important changes in academic feminism. Inclusive thinking has provided a way to build multiplicity and difference into our analyses. This has led to the discovery that race matters for everyone. White women, too, must be reconceptualized as a category that is multiply defined by race, class, and other differences. As Ruth Frankenberg demonstrates in a study of whiteness among contemporary women, all kinds of social relations, even those that appear neutral, are, in fact, racialized. Frankenberg further complicates the very notion of a unified white identity by introducing issues of Jewish identity.[38] Therefore, the lives of women of color cannot be seen as a *variation* on a more general model of white American womanhood. The model of womanhood that feminist social science once held as "universal" is also a product of race and class.

When we analyze the power relations constituting all social arrangements and shaping women's lives in distinctive ways, we can begin to grapple with core feminist issues about how genders are socially constructed and constructed differently. Women's difference is built into our study of gender. Yet this perspective is quite far removed from the atheoretical pluralism implied in much contemporary thinking about gender.

Multiracial feminism, in our view, focuses not just on differences but also on the way in which differences and domination intersect and are historically and socially constituted. It challenges feminist scholars to go beyond the mere recognition and inclusion of difference to reshape the basic concepts and theories of our disciplines. By attending to women's social location based on race, class, and gender, multiracial feminism seeks to clarify the structural sources of diversity. Ultimately, multiracial feminism forces us to see privilege and subordination as interrelated and to pose such questions as, How do the existences and experiences of all people—women and men, different racial-ethnic groups, and different classes—shape the experiences of each other? How are those relationships defined and enforced through social institutions that are the primary sites for negotiating power within society? How do these differences contribute to the construction of both individual and group identity? Once we acknowledge that all women are affected by the racial order of society, then it becomes clear that the insights of multiracial feminism provide an analytical framework, not solely for understanding the experiences of women of color but for understanding *all* women, and men, as well.

NOTES

1. Maxine Baca Zinn, Lynn Weber Cannon, Elizabeth Higginbotham, and Bonnie Thornton Dill, "The Costs of Exclusionary Practices in Women's Studies," *Signs* 11 (winter, 1986): 290–303.

2. Chela Sandoval, "U.S. Third World Feminism: The Theory and Method of Oppositional Consciousness in the Postmodern World," *Genders* (spring, 1991): 1–24.

3. Ruth Frankenberg and Lata Mani, "Cross Currents, Crosstalk: Race, 'Postcoloniality' and the Politics of Location," *Cultural Studies* 7 (May, 1993): 292–310.

4. We use the term "multiracial feminism" to convey the multiplicity of racial groups and feminist perspectives.

5. A growing body of works on difference in feminist thought now exists. Although we cannot cite all of the current work,

the following are representative: Michèle Barrett, "The Concept of Difference," *Feminist Review* 26 (July, 1987): 29–42; Christina Crosby, "Dealing With Difference," in *Feminists Theorize the Political,* ed. Judith Butler and Joan W. Scott (New York: Routledge, 1992): 130–43; Elizabeth Fox-Genovese, "Difference, Diversity, and Divisions in an Agenda for the Women's Movement" in *Color, Class, and Country: Experiences of Gender,* ed. Gay Young and Bette J. Dickerson (London: Zed Books, 1994): 232–48; Nancy A. Hewitt, "Compounding Differences," *Feminist Studies* 18 (summer, 1992): 313–26; Maria C. Lugones, "On the Logic of Feminist Pluralism," in *Feminist Ethics,* ed. Claudia Card (Lawrence: University of Kansas Press, 1991), 35–44; Rita S. Gallin and Anne Ferguson, "The Plurality of Feminism: Rethinking 'Difference,'" in *The Woman and International Development Annual* (Boulder: Westview Press, 1993), 3: 1–16; and Linda Gordon, "On Difference," *Genders* 10 (spring, 1991): 91–111.

6. Susan Bordo, "Feminism, Postmodernism, and Gender Skepticism," in *Feminism/Postmodernism,* ed. Linda J. Nicholson (London: Routledge, 1990), 133–56.

7. Sandra G. Harding, *Whose Science? Whose Knowledge? Thinking from Women's Lives* (Ithaca: Cornell University Press, 1991), 179.

8. Crosby, 131.

9. Fox-Genovese, 232.

10. Faye Ginsberg and Anna Lowenhaupt Tsing, Introduction to *Uncertain Terms, Negotiating Gender in American Culture,* ed. Faye Ginsberg and Anna Lowenhaupt Tsing (Boston: Beacon Press, 1990), 3.

11. Sandoval, 2.

12. Sandra G. Morgan, "Making Connections: Socialist-Feminist Challenges to Marxist Scholarship," in *Women and a New Academy: Gender and Cultural Contexts,* ed. Jean F. O'Barr (Madison: University of Wisconsin Press, 1989), 149.

13. Jane Rowland Martin, "Methodological Essentialism, False Difference, and Other Dangerous Traps," *Signs* 19 (spring, 1994): 647.

14. Barrett, 32.

15. bell hooks, *Black Looks: Race and Representation* (Boston: South End Press, 1992), 21.

16. Lugones, 35–44.

17. Patricia Hill Collins, Foreword to *Women of Color in U.S. Society,* ed. Maxine Baca Zinn and Bonnie Thornton Dill (Philadelphia: Temple University Press, 1994), xv.

18. Patricia Hill Collins, "Learning from the Outsider Within: The Sociological Significance of Black Feminist Thought," *Social Problems* 33 (December, 1986): 514–32.

19. Sandoval, 1.

20. Alison M. Jagger and Paula S. Rothenberg, *Feminist Frameworks: Alternative Theoretical Accounts of the Relations between Women and Men.* 3d ed. (New York: McGraw-Hill, 1993).

21. Michael Omi and Howard Winant, *Racial Formation in the United States: From the 1960s to the 1980s,* 2d ed. (New York: Routledge, 1994).

22. Ruth Frankenberg, *The Social Construction of Whiteness: White Women, Race Matters* (Minneapolis: University of Minnesota Press, 1993).

23. Evelyn Nakano Glenn, "From Servitude to Service Work: Historical Continuities in the Racial Division of Paid Reproductive Labor," *Signs* 18 (autumn, 1992): 3. See also Bonnie Thornton Dill, "Our Mothers' Grief: Racial-Ethnic Women and the Maintenance of Families," *Journal of Family History* 13, no. 4 (1988): 415–31.

24. Morgan, 146.

25. Maxine Baca Zinn and Bonnie Thornton Dill, "Difference and Domination," in *Women of Color in U.S. Society,* 11–12.

26. See Omi and Winant, 53–76, for a discussion of racial formation.

27. Margaret L. Andersen and Patricia Hill Collins, *Race, Class, and Gender: An Anthology* (Belmont, Calif.: Wadsworth, 1992), xvi.

28. Omi and Winant.

29. Nazli Kibria, "Migration and Vietnamese American Women: Remaking Ethnicity," in *Women of Color in U.S. Society,* 247–61.

30. Patricia Hill Collins, *Black Feminist Thought: Knowledge, Consciousness, and the Politics of Empowerment* (Boston: Unwin Hyman, 1990).

31. Elizabeth Spelman, *Inessential Women: Problems of Exclusion in Feminist Thought* (Boston: Beacon Press, 1988).

32. Several discussions of difference make this point. See Baca Zinn and Dill, 10; Gordon, 106; and Lynn Weber, in the "Symposium on West and Fenstermaker's 'Doing Difference,'" *Gender & Society* 9 (August, 1995): 515–19.

33. Glenn, 10.

34. Gordon, 106.

35. Chandra Talpade Mohanty, "Cartographies of Struggle: Third World Women and the Politics of Feminism," in *Third World Women and the Politics of Feminism,* ed. Chandra Talpade Mohanty, Ann Russo, and Lourdes Torres (Bloomington: Indiana University Press, 1991), 13.

36. Frankenberg and Mani, 307.

37. Norma Alarcon, "The Theoretical Subject(s) of *This Bridge Called My Back* and Anglo American Feminism," in *Making Face, Making Soul, Haciendo Caras: Creative and Critical Perspectives by Women of Color,* ed. Gloria Anzaldua (San Francisco: Aunt Lute, 1990), 356.

38. Frankenberg. See also Evelyn Torton Beck, "The Politics of Jewish Invisibility," *NWSA Journal* (fall, 1988): 93–102.

4

Masculinities and Globalization

RAEWYN W. CONNELL

The current wave of research and debate on masculinity stems from the impact of the women's liberation movement on men, but it has taken time for this impact to produce a new intellectual agenda. Most discussions of men's gender in the 1970s and early 1980s centered on an established concept, the male sex role, and an established problem: how men and boys were socialized into this role. There was not much new empirical research. What there was tended to use the more abstracted methods of social psychology (e.g., paper-and-pencil masculinity/femininity scales) to measure generalized attitudes and expectations in ill-defined populations. The largest body of empirical research was the continuing stream of quantitative studies of sex differences—which continued to be disappointingly slight (Carrigan, Connell, and Lee 1985).

The concept of a unitary male sex role, however, came under increasing criticism for its multiple oversimplifications and its incapacity to handle issues about power (Kimmel 1987; Connell 1987). New conceptual frameworks were proposed that linked feminist work on institutionalized patriarchy, gay theoretical work on homophobia, and psychoanalytic ideas about the person (Carrigan, Connell, and Lee 1985; Hearn 1987). Increasing attention was given to certain studies that located issues about masculinity in a fully described local context, whether a British printing shop (Cockburn 1983) or a Papuan mountain community (Herdt 1981). By the late 1980s, a genre of empirical research based on these ideas was developing, most clearly in sociology but also in anthropology, history, organization studies, and cultural studies. This has borne fruit in the 1990s in what is now widely recognized as a new generation of social research on masculinity and men in gender relations (Connell 1995; *Widersprueche* 1995; Segal 1997).

Although the recent research has been diverse in subject matter and social location, its characteristic focus is the construction of masculinity in a particular milieu or moment—a clergyman's family (Tosh 1991), a professional sports career (Messner 1992), a small group of gay men (Connell 1992), a bodybuilding gym (Klein 1993), a group of colonial schools (Morrell 1994), an urban police force (McElhinny 1994), drinking groups in bars (Tomsen 1997), a corporate office on the verge of a decision (Messerschmidt 1997). Accordingly, we might think of this as the "ethnographic moment" in masculinity research, in which the specific and the local are in focus. (This is not to deny that this work *deploys* broader structural concepts simply to note the characteristic focus of the empirical work and its analysis.)

The ethnographic moment brought a much-needed gust of realism to debates on men and masculinity, a corrective to the simplifications of role theory. It also provided a corrective to the trend in popular culture where

R. W. Connell, "Masculinities and Globalization," from *Men and Masculinities,* Volume 1/1999, pp. 3–23. Copyright © 1999 Sage Publications, Inc. Reprinted by permission.

vague discussions of men's sex roles were giving way to the mystical generalities of the mythopoetic movement and the extreme simplifications of religious revivalism.

Although the rich detail of the historical and field studies defies easy summary, certain conclusions emerge from this body of research as a whole. In short form, they are the following.

Plural Masculinities   A theme of theoretical work in the 1980s, the multiplicity of masculinities has now been very fully documented by descriptive research. Different cultures and different periods of history construct gender differently. Striking differences exist, for instance, in the relationship of homosexual practice to dominant forms of masculinity (Herdt 1984). In multicultural societies, there are varying definitions and enactments of masculinity, for instance, between Anglo and Latino communities in the United States (Hondagneu-Sotelo and Messner 1994). Equally important, more than one kind of masculinity can be found within a given cultural setting or institution. This is particularly well documented in school studies (Foley 1990) but can also be observed in workplaces (Messerschmidt 1997) and the military (Barrett 1996).

Hierarchy and Hegemony   These plural masculinities exist in definite social relations, often relations of hierarchy and exclusion. This was recognized early, in gay theorists' discussions of homophobia; it has become clear that the implications are far-reaching. There is generally a hegemonic form of masculinity, the most honored or desired in a particular context. For Western popular culture, this is extensively documented in research on media representations of masculinity (McKay and Huber 1992). The hegemonic form need not be the most common form of masculinity. Many men live in a state of some tension with, or distance from, hegemonic masculinity; others (such as sporting heroes) are taken as exemplars of hegemonic masculinity and are required to live up to it strenuously (Connell 1990a). The dominance of hegemonic masculinity over other forms may be quiet and implicit, but it may also be vehement and violent, as in the important case of homophobic violence.

Collective Masculinities   Masculinities, as patterns of gender practice, are sustained and enacted not only by individuals but also by groups and institutions. This fact was visible in Cockburn's (1983) pioneering research on informal workplace culture, and it has been confirmed over and over: in workplaces (Donaldson 1991), in organized sport (Whitson 1990; Messner 1992), in schools (Connell 1996), and so on. This point must be taken with the previous two: institutions may construct multiple masculinities and define relationships between them. Barrett's (1996) illuminating study of hegemonic masculinity in the U.S. Navy shows how this takes different forms in the different subbranches of the one military organization.

Bodies as Arenas   Men's bodies do not determine the patterns of masculinity, but they are still of great importance in masculinity. Men's bodies are addressed, defined, and disciplined (as in sport; see Theberge 1991), and given outlets and pleasures by the gender order of society. But men's bodies are not blank slates. The enactment of masculinity reaches certain limits, for instance, in the destruction of the industrial worker's body (Donaldson 1991). Masculine conduct with a female body is felt to be anomalous or transgressive, like feminine conduct with a male body; research on gender crossing (Bolin 1988) shows the work that must be done to sustain an anomalous gender.

Active Construction   Masculinities do not exist prior to social interaction, but come into existence as people act. They are actively produced, using the resources and strategies available in a given milieu. Thus the exemplary masculinities of sports professionals are not a product of passive disciplining, but as Messner (1992) shows, result from a sustained, active engagement with the demands of the institutional setting, even to the point of serious bodily damage from "playing hurt" and accumulated stress. With boys learning masculinities, much of what was previously taken as socialization appears, in close-focus studies of schools (Walker 1988; Thorne 1993), as the outcome of intricate and intense maneuvering in peer groups, classes, and adult–child relationships.

Contradiction   Masculinities are not homogeneous, simple states of being. Close-focus research on masculinities commonly identifies contradictory desires and conduct; for instance, in Klein's (1993) study of bodybuilders, the contradiction between the heterosexual definition of hegemonic masculinity and the homosexual practice by which some of the bodybuilders finance the making of an exemplary body. Psychoanalysis provides the classic evidence of conflicts within personality, and recent psychoanalytic writing (Chodorow 1994; Lewes 1988) has laid some emphasis on the conflicts and emotional compromises within both hegemonic and subordinated forms of masculinity. Life-history research influenced by existential psychoanalysis (Connell 1995) has similarly traced contradictory projects and commitments within particular forms of masculinity.

Dynamics   Masculinities created in specific historical circumstances are liable to reconstruction, and any pattern of hegemony is subject to contestation, in which a dominant masculinity may be displaced. Heward (1988) shows the changing gender regime of a boys' school responding to the changed strategies of the families in its clientele. Roper (1991) shows the displacement of a production-oriented masculinity among engineering managers by new financially oriented generic managers. Since the 1970s, the reconstruction of masculinities has been pursued as a conscious politics. Schwalbe's (1996) close examination of one mythopoetic group shows the complexity of the practice and the limits of the reconstruction.

If we compare this picture of masculinity with earlier understandings of the male sex role, it is clear that the ethnographic moment in research has already had important intellectual fruits.

Nevertheless, it has always been recognized that some issues go beyond the local. For instance, mythopoetic movements such as the highly visible Promise Keepers are part of a spectrum of masculinity politics; Messner (1997) shows for the United States that this spectrum involves at least eight conflicting agendas for the remaking of masculinity. Historical studies such as Phillips (1987) on New Zealand and Kimmel (1996) on the United States have traced the changing public constructions of masculinity for whole countries over long periods; ultimately, such historical reconstructions are essential for understanding the meaning of ethnographic details.

I consider that this logic must now be taken a step further, and in taking this step, we will move toward a new agenda for the whole field. What happens in localities is affected by the history of whole countries, but what happens in countries is affected by the history of the world. Locally situated lives are now (indeed, have long been) powerfully influenced by geopolitical struggles, global markets, multinational corporations, labor migration, transnational media. It is time for this fundamental fact to be built into our analysis of men and masculinities.

To understand local masculinities, we must think in global terms. But how? That is the problem pursued in this article. I will offer a framework for thinking about masculinities as a feature of world society and for thinking about men's gender practices in terms of the global structure and dynamics of gender. This is by no means to reject the ethnographic moment in masculinity research. It is, rather, to think how we can use its findings more adequately.

THE WORLD GENDER ORDER

Masculinities do not first exist and then come into contact with femininities; they are produced together, in the process that constitutes a gender order. Accordingly, to understand the masculinities on a world scale, we must first have a concept of the globalization of gender.

This is one of the most difficult points in current gender analysis because the very conception is counterintuitive. We are so accustomed to thinking of gender as the attribute of an individual, even as an unusually intimate attribute, that it requires a considerable wrench to think of gender on the vast scale of global society. Most relevant discussions, such as the literature on women and development, fudge the issue. They treat the entities that extend internationally (markets, corporations, intergovernmental programs, etc.) as ungendered in principle—but affecting unequally gendered recipients of aid in practice, because of bad policies. Such conceptions reproduce the familiar liberal-feminist view of the state as in principle gender-neutral, though empirically dominated by men.

But if we recognize that very large scale institutions such as the state are themselves gendered, in quite precise and specifiable ways (Connell 1990b), and if we recognize that international relations, international trade, and global markets are inherently an arena of gender formation and gender politics (Enloe 1990), then we can recognize the existence of a world gender order. The term can be defined as the structure of relationships that interconnect the gender regimes of institutions, and the gender orders of local society, on a world scale. That is, however, only a definition. The substantive questions remain: what is the shape of that structure, how tightly are its elements linked, how has it arisen historically, what is its trajectory into the future?

Current business and media talk about globalization pictures a homogenizing process sweeping across the world, driven by new technologies, producing vast unfettered global markets in which all participate on equal terms. This is a misleading image. As Hirst and Thompson (1996) show, the global economy is highly unequal and the current degree of homogenization is often overestimated. Multinational corporations based in the three major economic powers (the United States, European Union, and Japan) are the major economic actors worldwide.

The structure bears the marks of its history. Modern global society was historically produced as Wallerstein (1974) argued, by the economic and political expansion of European states from the fifteenth century on and by the creation of colonial empires. It is in this process that we find the roots of the modern world gender order. Imperialism was, from the start, a gendered process. Its first phase, colonial conquest and settlement, was carried out by gender-segregated forces, and it resulted in massive disruption of indigenous gender orders. In its second phase, the stabilization of colonial societies, new gender divisions of labor were produced in plantation economies and colonial cities, while gender ideologies were linked with racial hierarchies and the cultural defense of empire. The third phase, marked by political decolonization, economic neocolonialism, and the current growth of world markets and structures of financial control, has seen gender divisions of labor remade on a massive scale in the "global factory" (Fuentes and Ehrenreich 1983), as well as the spread of gendered violence alongside Western military technology.

The result of this history is a partially integrated, highly unequal, and turbulent world society, in which gender relations are partly but unevenly linked on a global scale. The unevenness becomes clear when different substructures of gender (Connell 1987; Walby 1990) are examined separately.

The Division of Labor   A characteristic feature of colonial and neocolonial economies was the restructuring of local production systems to produce a male wage worker–female domestic worker couple (Mies 1986). This need not produce a "housewife" in the Western suburban sense, for instance, where the wage work involved migration to plantations or mines (Moodie 1994). But it has generally produced the identification of masculinity with the public realm and the money economy and of femininity with domesticity, which is a core feature of the modern European gender system (Holter 1997).

Power Relations   The colonial and postcolonial world has tended to break down purdah systems of patriarchy in the name of modernization, if not of women's emancipation (Kandiyoti 1994). At the same time, the creation of a westernized public realm has seen the growth of large-scale organizations in the form of the state and corporations, which in the great majority of cases are culturally masculinized and controlled by men. In *comprador* capitalism, however, the power of local elites depends on their relations with the metropolitan powers, so the hegemonic masculinities of neocolonial societies are uneasily poised between local and global cultures.

Emotional Relations   Both religious and cultural missionary activity has corroded indigenous homosexual and cross-gender practice, such as the native American *berdache* and the Chinese "passion of the cut sleeve" (Hinsch 1990). Recently developed Western models of romantic heterosexual love as the basis for marriage and of gay identity as the main alternative have now circulated globally—though as Altman (1996) observes, they do not simply displace indigenous models, but interact with them in extremely complex ways.

Symbolization   Mass media, especially electronic media, in most parts of the world follow North American and European models and relay a great deal of metropolitan content; gender imagery is an important part of what is circulated. A striking example is the reproduction of a North American imagery of femininity by Xuxa, the blonde television superstar in Brazil (Simpson 1993). In counterpoint, exotic gender imagery has been used in the marketing strategies of newly industrializing countries (e.g., airline advertising from Southeast Asia)—a tactic based on the long-standing combination of the exotic and the erotic in the colonial imagination (Jolly 1997).

Clearly, the world gender order is not simply an extension of a traditional European-American gender order. That gender order was changed by colonialism, and elements from other cultures now circulate globally. Yet in no sense do they mix on equal terms, to produce a United Colours of Benetton gender order. The culture and institutions of the North Atlantic countries are hegemonic within the emergent world system. This is crucial for understanding the kinds of masculinities produced within it.

THE REPOSITIONING OF MEN AND THE RECONSTITUTION OF MASCULINITIES

The positioning of men and the constitution of masculinities may be analyzed at any of the levels at which gender practice is configured: in relation to the body, in personal life, and in collective social practice. At each level, we need to consider how the processes of globalization influence configurations of gender.

Men's bodies are positioned in the gender order, and enter the gender process, through body-reflexive practices in which bodies are both objects and agents (Connell 1995)—including sexuality, violence, and labor. The conditions of such practice include where one is and who is available for interaction. So it is a fact of considerable importance for gender relations that the global social order distributes and redistributes bodies, through migration, and through political controls over movement and interaction.

The creation of empire was the original "elite migration," though in certain cases mass migration followed. Through settler colonialism, something close to the gender order of Western Europe was reassembled in North America and in Australia. Labor migration within the colonial systems was a means by which gender practices were spread, but also a means by which they were reconstructed, since labor migration was itself a gendered process—as we have seen in relation to the gender division of labor. Migration from the colonized world to the metropole became (except for Japan) a mass process in the decades after World War II. There is also migration within the periphery, such as the creation of a very large immigrant labor force, mostly from other Muslim countries, in the oil-producing Gulf states.

These relocations of bodies create the possibility of hybridization in gender imagery, sexuality, and other forms of practice. The movement is not always toward synthesis, however, as the race/ethnic hierarchies of colonialism have been re-created in new contexts, including the politics of the metropole. Ethnic and racial conflict has been growing in importance in recent years, and as Klein (1997) and Tillner (1997) argue, this is a fruitful context for the production of masculinities oriented toward domination and violence. Even without the context of violence, there can be an intimate interweaving of the formation of masculinity with the formation of ethnic identity, as seen in the study by Poynting, Noble, and Tabar (1997) of Lebanese youths in the Anglo-dominant culture of Australia.

At the level of personal life as well as in relation to bodies, the making of masculinities is shaped by global forces. In some cases, the link is indirect, such as the working-class Australian men caught in a situation of structural unemployment (Connell 1995), which arises from Australia's changing position in the global economy. In other cases, the link is obvious, such as the executives of multinational corporations and the financial sector servicing international trade. The requirements of a career in international business set up strong pressures on domestic life: almost all multinational executives are men, and the assumption in business magazines and advertising directed toward them is that they will have dependent wives running their homes and bringing up their children.

At the level of collective practice, masculinities are reconstituted by the remaking of gender meanings and the reshaping of the institutional contexts of practice. Let us consider each in turn.

The growth of global mass media, especially electronic media, is an obvious "vector" for the globalization of gender. Popular entertainment circulates stereotyped gender images, deliberately made attractive for marketing purposes. The example of Xuxa in Brazil has already been mentioned. International news media are also controlled or strongly influenced from the metropole and circulate Western definitions of authoritative masculinity, criminality, desirable femininity, and so on. But there are limits to the power of global mass communications.

Some local centers of mass entertainment differ from the Hollywood model, such as the Indian popular film industry centered in Bombay. Further, media research emphasizes that audiences are highly selective in their reception of media messages, and we must allow for popular recognition of the fantasy in mass entertainment. Just as economic globalization can be exaggerated, the creation of a global culture is a more turbulent and uneven process than is often assumed (Featherstone 1995).

More important, I would argue, is a process that began long before electronic media existed, the export of institutions. Gendered institutions not only circulate definitions of masculinity (and femininity), as sex role theory notes. The functioning of gendered institutions, creating specific conditions for social practice, calls into existence specific patterns of practice. Thus, certain patterns of collective violence are embedded in the organization and culture of a Western-style army, which are different from the patterns of precolonial violence. Certain patterns of calculative egocentrism are embedded in the working of a stock market; certain patterns of rule following and domination are embedded in a bureaucracy.

Now, the colonial and postcolonial world saw the installation in the periphery, on a very large scale, of a range of institutions on the North Atlantic model: armies, states, bureaucracies, corporations, capital markets, labor markets, schools, law courts, transport systems. These are gendered institutions and their functioning has directly reconstituted masculinities in the periphery. This has not necessarily meant photocopies of European masculinities. Rather, pressures for change are set up that are inherent in the institutional form.

To the extent that particular institutions become dominant in world society, the patterns of masculinity embedded in them may become global standards. Masculine dress is an interesting indicator: almost every political leader in the world now wears the uniform of the Western business executive. The more common pattern, however, is not the complete displacement of local patterns but the articulation of the local gender order with the gender regime of global-model institutions. Case studies such as Hollway's (1994) account of bureaucracy in Tanzania illustrate the point; there, domestic patriarchy articulated with masculine authority in the state in ways that subverted the government's formal commitment to equal opportunity for women.

We should not expect the overall structure of gender relations on a world scale simply to mirror patterns known on the smaller scale. In the most vital of respects, there is continuity. The world gender order is unquestionably patriarchal, in the sense that it privileges men over women. There is a patriarchal dividend for men arising from unequal wages, unequal labor force participation, and a highly unequal structure of ownership, as well as cultural and sexual privileging. This has been extensively documented by feminist work on women's situation globally (e.g., Taylor 1985), though its implications for masculinity have mostly been ignored. The conditions thus exist for the production of a hegemonic masculinity on a world scale, that is to say, a dominant form of masculinity that embodies, organizes, and legitimates men's domination in the gender order as a whole.

The conditions of globalization, which involve the interaction of many local gender orders, certainly multiply the forms of masculinity in the global gender order. At the same time, the specific shape of globalization, concentrating economic and cultural power on an unprecedented scale, provides new resources for dominance by particular groups of men. This dominance may become institutionalized in a pattern of masculinity that becomes, to some degree, standardized across localities. I will call such patterns *globalizing masculinities,* and it is among them, rather than narrowly within the metropole, that we are likely to find candidates for hegemony in the world gender order.

GLOBALIZING MASCULINITIES

In this section, I will offer a sketch of major forms of globalizing masculinity in the three historical phases identified above in the discussion of globalization.

Masculinities of Conquest and Settlement

The creation of the imperial social order involved peculiar conditions for the gender practices of men. Colonial conquest itself was mainly carried out by segregated groups of men—soldiers, sailors, traders, administrators, and a good many who were all these by turn (such as the Rum Corps in early New South Wales, Australia). They were drawn from the more segregated occupations and milieu in the metropole, and it is likely that the men drawn into colonization tended to be the more rootless. Certainly the process of conquest could produce frontier masculinities that combined the occupational culture of these groups with an unusual level of violence and egocentric individualism. The vehement contemporary debate about the genocidal violence of the Spanish conquistadors—who in fifty years completely exterminated the population of Hispaniola—points to this pattern (Bitterli 1989).

The political history of empire is full of evidence of the tenuous control over the frontier exercised by the state—the Spanish monarchs unable to rein in the conquistadors, the governors in Sydney unable to hold back the squatters and in Capetown unable to hold back the Boers, gold rushes breaking boundaries everywhere, even an independent republic set up by escaped slaves in Brazil. The point probably applies to other forms of social control too, such as customary controls on men's sexuality. Extensive sexual exploitation of indigenous women was a common feature of conquest. In certain circumstances, frontier masculinities might be reproduced as a local cultural tradition long after the frontier had passed, such as the gauchos of southern South America and the cowboys of the western United States.

In other circumstances, however, the frontier of conquest and exploitation was replaced by a frontier of settlement. Sex ratios in the colonizing population changed, as women arrived and locally born generations succeeded. A shift back toward the family patterns of the metropole was likely. As Cain and Hopkins (1993) have shown for the British empire, the ruling group in the colonial world as a whole was an extension of the dominant class in the metropole, the landed gentry, and tended to reproduce its social customs and ideology. The creation of a settler masculinity might be the goal of state policy, as it seems to have been in late-nineteenth-century New Zealand, as part of a general process of pacification and the creation of an agricultural social order (Phillips 1987). Or it might be undertaken through institutions created by settler groups, such as the elite schools in Natal studied by Morrell (1994).

The impact of colonialism on the construction of masculinity among the colonized is much less documented, but there is every reason to think it was severe. Conquest and settlement disrupted all the structures of indigenous society, whether or not this was intended

by the colonizing powers (Bitterli 1989). Indigenous gender orders were no exception. Their disruption could result from the pulverization of indigenous communities (as in the seizure of land in eastern North America and southeastern Australia), through gendered labor migration (as in gold mining with Black labor in South Africa; see Moodie 1994), to ideological attacks on local gender arrangements (as in the missionary assault on the *berdache* tradition in North America; see Williams 1986). The varied course of resistance to colonization is also likely to have affected the making of masculinities. This is clear in the region of Natal in South Africa, where sustained resistance to colonization by the Zulu kingdom was a key to the mobilization of ethnic-national masculine identities in the twentieth century (Morrell 1996).

Masculinities of Empire

The imperial social order created a hierarchy of masculinities, as it created a hierarchy of communities and races. The colonizers distinguished "more manly" from "less manly" groups among their subjects. In British India, for instance, Bengali men were supposed effeminate while Pathans and Sikhs were regarded as strong and warlike. Similar distinctions were made in South Africa between Hottentots and Zulus, in North America between Iroquois, Sioux, and Cheyenne on one side, and southern and southwestern tribes on the other.

At the same time, the emerging imagery of gender difference in European culture provided general symbols of superiority and inferiority. Within the imperial "poetics of war" (MacDonald 1994), the conqueror was virile, while the colonized were dirty, sexualized, and effeminate or childlike. In many colonial situations, indigenous men were called "boys" by the colonizers (e.g., in Zimbabwe; see Shire 1994). Sinha's (1995) interesting study of the language of political controversy in India in the 1880s and 1890s shows how the images of "manly Englishman" and "effeminate Bengali" were deployed to uphold colonial privilege and contain movements for change. In the late nineteenth century, racial barriers in colonial societies were hardening rather than weakening, and gender ideology tended to fuse with racism in forms that the twentieth century has never untangled.

The power relations of empire meant that indigenous gender orders were generally under pressure from the colonizers, rather than the other way around. But the colonizers too might change. The barriers of late colonial racism were not only to prevent pollution from below but also to forestall "going native," a well-recognized possibility—the starting point, for instance, of Kipling's famous novel *Kim* ([1901] 1987). The pressures, opportunities, and profits of empire might also work changes in gender arrangements among the colonizers, for instance, the division of labor in households with a large supply of indigenous workers as domestic servants (Bulbeck 1992). Empire might also affect the gender order of the metropole itself by changing gender ideologies, divisions of labor, and the nature of the metropolitan state. For instance, empire figured prominently as a source of masculine imagery in Britain, in the Boy Scouts, and in the cult of Lawrence of Arabia (Dawson 1991). Here we see examples of an important principle: the interplay of gender dynamics between different parts of the world order.

The world of empire created two very different settings for the modernization of masculinities. In the periphery, the forcible restructuring of economics and workforces tended to individualize, on one hand, and rationalize, on the other. A widespread result was masculinities in which the rational calculation of self-interest was the key to action, emphasizing the European gender contrast of rational man/irrational woman. The specific form might be local—for instance, the Japanese "salaryman," a type first recognized in the 1910s, was specific to the Japanese context of large, stable industrial conglomerates (Kinmonth 1981). But the result generally was masculinities defined around economic action, with both workers and entrepreneurs increasingly adapted to emerging market economies.

In the metropole, the accumulation of wealth made possible a specialization of leadership in the dominant classes, and struggles for hegemony in which masculinities organized around domination or violence were split from masculinities organized around expertise. The class compromises that allowed the development of the welfare state in Europe and North America were paralleled by gender compromises—gender reform movements (most notably the women's suffrage movement) contesting the legal privileges of men and forcing concessions from the state. In this context, agendas of reform in masculinity emerged: the temperance movement, compassionate marriage, homosexual rights movements, leading eventually

to the pursuit of androgyny in "men's liberation" in the 1970s (Kimmel and Mosmiller 1992). Not all reconstructions of masculinity, however, emphasized tolerance or moved toward androgyny. The vehement masculinity politics of fascism, for instance, emphasized dominance and difference and glorified violence, a pattern still found in contemporary racist movements (Tillner 1997).

Masculinities of Postcolonialism and Neoliberalism

The process of decolonization disrupted the gender hierarchies of the colonial order and, where armed struggle was involved, might have involved a deliberate cultivation of masculine hardness and violence (as in South Africa; see Xaba 1997). Some activists and theorists of liberation struggles celebrated this, as a necessary response to colonial violence and emasculation; women in liberation struggles were perhaps less impressed. However one evaluates the process, one of the consequences of decolonization was another round of disruptions of community-based gender orders and another step in the reorientation of masculinities toward national and international contexts.

Nearly half a century after the main wave of decolonization, the old hierarchies persist in new shapes. With the collapse of Soviet communism, the decline of postcolonial socialism, and the ascendancy of the new right in Europe and North America, world politics is more and more organized around the needs of transnational capital and the creation of global markets.

The neoliberal agenda has little to say, explicitly, about gender: it speaks a gender-neutral language of "markets," "individuals," and "choice." But the world in which neoliberalism is ascendant is still a gendered world, and neoliberalism has an implicit gender politics. The "individual" of neoliberal theory has in general the attributes and interests of a male entrepreneur, the attack on the welfare state generally weakens the position of women, while the increasingly unregulated power of transnational corporations places strategic power in the hands of particular groups of men. It is not surprising, then, that the installation of capitalism in Eastern Europe and the former Soviet Union has been accompanied by a reassertion of dominating masculinities and, in some situations, a sharp worsening in the social position of women.

We might propose, then, that the hegemonic form of masculinity in the current world gender order is the masculinity associated with those who control its dominant institutions: the business executives who operate in global markets, and the political executives who interact (and in many contexts, merge) with them. I will call this *transnational business masculinity*. This is not readily available for ethnographic study, but we can get some clues to its character from its reflections in management literature, business journalism, and corporate self-promotion, and from studies of local business elites (e.g., Donaldson 1997).

As a first approximation, I would suggest this is a masculinity marked by increasing egocentrism, very conditional loyalties (even to the corporation), and a declining sense of responsibility for others (except for purposes of image making). Gee, Hall, and Lankshear (1996), studying recent management textbooks, note the peculiar construction of the executive in "fast capitalism" as a person with no permanent commitments, except (in effect) to the idea of accumulation itself. Transnational business masculinity is characterized by a limited technical rationality (management theory), which is increasingly separate from science.

Transnational business masculinity differs from traditional bourgeois masculinity by its increasingly libertarian sexuality, with a growing tendency to commodify relations with women. Hotels catering to businessmen in most parts of the world now routinely offer pornographic videos, and in some parts of the world, there is a well-developed prostitution industry catering for international businessmen. Transnational business masculinity does not require bodily force, since the patriarchal dividend on which it rests is accumulated by impersonal, institutional means. But corporations increasingly use the exemplary bodies of elite sportsmen as a marketing tool (note the phenomenal growth of corporate "sponsorship" of sport in the last generation) and indirectly as a means of legitimation for the whole gender order.

MASCULINITY POLITICS
ON A WORLD SCALE

Recognizing global society as an arena of masculinity formation allows us to pose new questions about masculinity politics. What social dynamics in the global arena give rise to masculinity politics, and what shape does global masculinity politics take?

The gradual creation of a world gender order has meant many local instabilities of gender. Gender instability is a familiar theme of poststructuralist theory, but this school of thought takes as a universal condition a situation that is historically specific. Instabilities range from the disruption of men's local cultural dominance as women move into the public realm and higher education, through the disruption of sexual identities that produced "queer" politics in the metropole, to the shifts in the urban intelligentsia that produced "the new sensitive man" and other images of gender change.

One response to such instabilities, on the part of groups whose power is challenged but still dominant, is to reaffirm *local* gender orthodoxies and hierarchies. A masculine fundamentalism is, accordingly, a common response in gender politics at present. A soft version, searching for an essential masculinity among myths and symbols, is offered by the mythopoetic men's movement in the United States and by the religious revivalists of the Promise Keepers (Messner 1997). A much harder version is found, in that country, in the right-wing militia movement brought to world attention by the Oklahoma City bombing (Gibson 1994), and in contemporary Afghanistan, if we can trust Western media reports, in the militant misogyny of the Taliban. It is no coincidence that in the two latter cases, hardline masculine fundamentalism goes together with a marked anti-internationalism. The world system—rightly enough—is seen as the source of pollution and disruption.

Not that the emerging global order is a hotbed of gender progressivism. Indeed, the neoliberal agenda for the reform of national and international economics involves closing down historic possibilities for gender reform. I have noted how it subverts the gender compromise represented by the metropolitan welfare state. It has also undermined the progressive-liberal agendas of sex role reform represented by affirmative action programs, anti-discrimination provisions, child care services, and the like. Right-wing parties and governments have been persistently cutting such programs, in the name of either individual liberties or global competitiveness. Through these means, the patriarchal dividend to men is defended or restored, without an *explicit* masculinity politics in the form of a mobilization of men.

Within the arenas of international relations, the international state, multinational corporations, and global markets, there is nevertheless a deployment of masculinities and a reasonably clear hegemony. The transnational business masculinity described above has had only one major competitor for hegemony in recent decades, the rigid, control-oriented masculinity of the military, and the military-style bureaucratic dictatorships of Stalinism. With the collapse of Stalinism and the end of the cold war, Big Brother (Orwell's famous parody of this form of masculinity) is a fading threat, and the more flexible, calculative, egocentric masculinity of the fast capitalist entrepreneur holds the world stage.

We must, however, recall two important conclusions of the ethnographic moment in masculinity research: that different forms of masculinity exist together and that hegemony is constantly subject to challenge. These are possibilities in the global arena too. Transnational business masculinity is not completely homogeneous; variations of it are embedded in different parts of the world system, which may not be completely compatible. We may distinguish a Confucian variant, based in East Asia, with a stronger commitment to hierarchy and social consensus, from a secularized Christian variant, based in North America, with more hedonism and individualism and greater tolerance for social conflict. In certain arenas, there is already conflict between the business and political leaderships embodying these forms of masculinity: initially over human rights versus Asian values, and more recently over the extent of trade and investment liberalization.

If these are contenders for hegemony, there is also the possibility of opposition to hegemony. The global circulation of "gay" identity (Altman 1996) is an important indication that nonhegemonic masculinities may operate in global arenas, and may even find a certain political articulation, in this case around human rights and AIDS prevention.

REFERENCES

Altman, Dennis. 1996. Rupture or continuity? The internationalisation of gay identities. *Social Text* 48 (3): 77–94.

Barrett, Frank J. 1996. The organizational construction of hegemonic masculinity: The case of the U.S. Navy. *Gender Work and Organization* 3 (3): 129–42.

BauSteineMaenner, ed. 1996. *Kritische Maennerforschung* [Critical research on men]. Berlin: Argument.

Bitterli, Urs. 1989. *Cultures in conflict: Encounters between European and non-European cultures, 1492–1800.* Stanford, CA: Stanford University Press.

Bolin, Anne. 1988. *In search of Eve: Transexual rites of passage.* Westport, CT: Bergin & Garvey.

Bulbeck, Chilla. 1992. *Australian women in Papua New Guinea: Colonial passages 1920–1960.* Cambridge, U.K.: Cambridge University Press.

Cain, P. J., and A. G. Hopkins. 1993. *British Imperialism: Innovation and expansion, 1688–1914.* New York: Longman.

Carrigan, Tim, Bob Connell, and John Lee. 1985. Toward a new sociology of masculinity. *Theory and Society* 14 (5): 551–604.

Chodorow, Nancy. 1994. *Femininities, masculinities, sexualities: Freud and beyond.* Lexington: University Press of Kentucky.

Cockburn, Cynthia. 1983. *Brothers: Male dominance and technological change.* London: Pluto.

Cohen, Jon. 1991. NOMAS: Challenging male supremacy. *Changing Men* (Winter/Spring): 45–46.

Connell, R. W. 1987. *Gender and power.* Cambridge, MA: Polity.

Connell, R. W. 1990a. An iron man: The body and some contradictions of hegemonic masculinity. In *Sport, men and the gender order: Critical feminist perspectives,* edited by Michael A. Messner and Donald F. Sabo, 83–95. Champaign. IL: Human Kinetics Books.

Connell, R. W. 1990b. The state, gender and sexual politics: Theory and appraisal. *Theory and Society* 19: 507–44.

Connell, R. W. 1992. A very straight gay: Masculinity, homosexual experience and the dynamics of gender. *American Sociological Review* 57 (6): 735–51.

Connell, R. W. 1995. *Masculinities.* Cambridge, MA: Polity.

Connell, R. W. 1996. Teaching the boys: New research on masculinity, and gender strategies for schools. *Teachers College Record* 98 (2): 206–35.

Cornwall, Andrea, and Nancy Lindisfarne, eds. 1994. *Dislocating masculinity: Comparative ethnographies.* London: Routledge.

Dawson, Graham. 1991. The blond Bedouin: Lawrence of Arabia, imperial adventure and the imagining of English–British masculinity. In *Manful assertions: Masculinities in Britain since 1800,* edited by Michael Roper and John Tosh, 113–44. London: Routledge.

Donaldson, Mike. 1991. *Time of our lives: Labour and love in the working class.* Sydney: Allen & Unwin.

Donaldson, Mike. 1997. Growing up very rich: The masculinity of the hegemonic. Paper presented at the conference

Masculinities: Renegotiating Genders, June, University of Wollongong, Australia.

Enloe, Cynthia. 1990. *Bananas, beaches and bases: Making feminist sense of international politics*. Berkeley: University of California Press.

Featherstone, Mike. 1995. *Undoing culture: Globalization, postmodernism and identity*. London: Sage.

Foley, Douglas E. 1990. *Learning capitalist culture: Deep in the heart of Tejas*. Philadelphia: University of Pennsylvania Press.

Fuentes, Annette, and Barbara Ehrenreich. 1983. *Women in the global factory*. Boston: South End.

Gee, James Paul, Glynda Hall, and Colin Lankshear. 1996. *The new work order: Behind the language of the new capitalism*. Sydney: Allen & Unwin.

Gender Equality Ombudsman. 1997. *The father's quota*. Information sheet on parental leave entitlements, Oslo.

Gibson, J. William. 1994. *Warrior dreams: Paramilitary culture in post-Vietnam America*. New York: Hill and Wang.

Hagemann-White, Carol, and Maria S. Rerrich, eds. 1988. *FrauenMaennerBilder* (Women, Imaging, Men). Bielefeld: AJZ-Verlag.

Hearn, Jeff. 1987. *The gender of oppression: Men, masculinity and the critique of Marxism*. Brighton, U.K.: Wheatsheaf.

Herdt, Gilbert H. 1981. *Guardians of the flutes: Idioms of masculinity*. New York: McGraw-Hill.

Herdt, Gilbert H. ed. 1984. *Ritualized homosexuality in Melanesia*. Berkeley: University of California Press.

Heward, Christine. 1988. *Making a man of him: Parents and their sons' education at an English public school 1929–1950*. London: Routledge.

Hinsch, Bret. 1990. *Passions of the cut sleeve: The male homosexual tradition in China*. Berkeley: University of California Press.

Hirst, Paul, and Grahame Thompson. 1996. *Globalization in question: The international economy and the possibilities of governance*. Cambridge, MA: Polity.

Hollstein, Walter. 1992. *Machen Sie Platz, mein Herr! Teilen statt Herrschen* [Sharing instead of dominating]. Hamburg: Rowohlt.

Hollway, Wendy. 1994. Separation, integration and difference: Contradictions in a gender regime. In *Power/gender: Social relations in theory and practice*, edited by H. Lorraine Radtke and Henderikus Stam, 247–69. London: Sage.

Holter, Oystein Gullvag. 1997. Gender, patriarchy and capitalism: A social forms analysis. Ph.D. diss., University of Oslo, Faculty of Social Science.

Hondagneu-Sotelo, Pierrette, and Michael A. Messner. 1994. Gender displays and men's power: The "new man" and the Mexican immigrant man. In *Theorizing masculinities*, edited by Harry Brod and Michael Kaufman, 200–218. Twin Oaks, CA: Sage.

Ito Kimio. 1993. *Otokorashisa-no-yukue* [Directions for masculinities]. Tokyo: Shinyo-sha.

Jolly, Margaret. 1997. From point Venus to Bali Ha'i: Eroticism and exoticism in representations of the Pacific. In *Sites of desire, economies of pleasure: Sexualities in Asia and the Pacific*, edited by Lenore Manderson and Margaret Jolly, 99–122. Chicago: University of Chicago Press.

Kandiyoti, Deniz. 1994. The paradoxes of masculinity: Some thoughts on segregated societies. In *Dislocating masculinity: Comparative ethnographies*, edited by Andrea Cornwall and Nancy Lindisfarne, 197–213. London: Routledge.

Kaufman, Michael. 1997. Working with men and boys to challenge sexism and end men's violence. Paper presented at UNESCO expert group meeting on Male Roles and Masculinities in the Perspective of a Culture of Peace, September, Oslo.

Kimmel, Michael S. 1987. Rethinking "masculinity": New directions in research. In *Changing men: New directions in research on men and masculinity*, edited by Michael S. Kimmel, 9–24. Newbury Park, CA: Sage.

Kimmel, Michael S. 1996. *Manhood in America: A cultural history*. New York: Free Press.

Kimmel, Michael S., and Thomas P. Mosmiller, eds. 1992. *Against the tide: Pro-feminist men in the United States, 1776–1990, a documentary history*. Boston: Beacon.

Kindler, Heinz. 1993. *Maske(r)ade: Jungen- und Maennerarbeit fuer die Pratis* [Work with youth and men]. Neuling: Schwaebisch Gmuend und Tuebingen.

Kinmonth, Earl H. 1981. *The self-made man in Meiji Japanese thought: From Samurai to salary man*. Berkeley: University of California Press.

Kipling, Rudyard. [1901] 1987. *Kim*. London: Penguin.

Klein, Alan M. 1993. *Little big men: Bodybuilding subculture and gender construction*. Albany: State University of New York Press.

Klein, Uta. 1997. Our best boys: The making of masculinity in Israeli society. Paper presented at UNESCO expert group meeting on Male Roles and Masculinities in the Perspectives of a Culture of Peace, September, Oslo.

Lewes, Kenneth. 1988. *The psychoanalytic theory of male homosexuality*. New York: Simon & Schuster.

MacDonald, Robert H. 1994. *The language of empire: Myths and metaphors of popular imperialism, 1880–1918*. Manchester, U.K.: Manchester University Press.

McElhinny, Bonnie. 1994. An economy of affect: Objectivity, masculinity and the gendering of police work. In *Dislocating masculinity: Comparative ethnographies*, edited by Andrea Cornwall and Nancy Lindisfarne, 159–71. London: Routledge.

McKay, Jim, and Debbie Huber. 1992. Anchoring media images of technology and sport. *Women's Studies International Forum* 15 (2): 205–18.

Messerschmidt, James W. 1997. *Crime as structured action: Gender, race, class, and crime in the making.* Thousand Oaks, CA: Sage.

Messner, Michael A. 1992. *Power at play: Sports and the problem of masculinity.* Boston: Beacon.

Messner, Michael A. 1997. *The politics of masculinities: Men in movements.* Thousand Oaks, CA: Sage.

Metz-Goeckel, Sigrid, and Ursula Mueller. 1986. *Der Mann: Die Brigitte-Studie* [The male]. Beltz: Weinheim & Basel.

Mies, Maria. 1986. *Patriarchy and accumulation on a world scale: Women in the international division of labour.* London: Zed.

Moodie, T. Dunbar. 1994. *Going for gold: Men, mines, and migration.* Johannesburg: Witwatersand University Press.

Morrell, Robert. 1994. Boys, gangs, and the making of masculinity in the White secondary schools of Natal, 1880–1930. *Masculinities* 2 (2): 56–82.

Morrell, Robert ed. 1996. *Political economy and identities in KwaZulu-Natal: Historical and social perspectives.* Durban, Natal: Indicator Press.

Nakamura, Akira. 1994. *Watashi-no Danseigaku* [My men's studies]. Tokyo: Kindaibugei-sha.

Oftung, Knut, ed. 1994. *Menns bilder og bilder av menn* [Images of men]. Oslo: Likestillingsradet.

Phillips, Jock. 1987. *A man's country? The image of the Pakeha male, a history.* Auckland: Penguin.

Poynting, S., G. Noble, and P. Tabar. 1997. "Intersections" of masculinity and ethnicity: A study of male Lebanese immigrant youth in Western Sydney. Paper presented at the conference Masculinities: Renegotiating Genders, June, University of Wollongong, Australia.

Roper, Michael. 1991. Yesterday's model: Product fetishism and the British company man, 1945–85. In *Manful assertions: Masculinities in Britain since 1800,* edited by Michael Roper and John Tosh, 190–211. London: Routledge.

Schwalbe, Michael. 1996. *Unlocking the iron cage: The men's movement gender politics, and the American culture.* New York: Oxford University Press.

Segal, Lynne. 1997. *Slow motion: Changing masculinities, changing men.* 2d ed. London: Virago.

Seidler, Victor J. 1991. *Achilles heel reader: Men, sexual politics and socialism.* London: Routledge.

Shire, Chenjerai. 1994. Men don't go to the moon: Language, space and masculinities in Zimbabwe. In *Dislocating masculinity: Comparative ethnographies,* edited by Andrea

Cornwall and Nancy Lindisfarne, 147–58. London: Routledge.

Simpson, Amelia. 1993. *Xuxa: The mega-marketing of a gender, race and modernity.* Philadelphia: Temple University Press.

Sinha, Mrinalini. 1995. *Colonial masculinity: The manly Englishman and the effeminate Bengali in the late nineteenth century.* Manchester, U.K.: Manchester University Press.

Taylor, Debbie. 1985. Women: An analysis. In *Women: A world report,* 1–98. London: Methuen.

Theberge, Nancy. 1991. Reflections on the body in the sociology of sport. *Quest* 43:123–34.

Thorne, Barrie. 1993. *Gender play: Girls and boys in school.* New Brunswick. NJ: Rutgers University Press.

Tillner, Georg. 1997. Masculinity and xenophobia. Paper presented at UNESCO meeting on Male Roles and Masculinities in the Perspective of a Culture of Peace, September, Oslo.

Tomsen, Stephen. 1997. A top night: Social protest, masculinity and the culture of drinking violence. *British Journal of Criminology* 37 (1): 90–103.

Tosh, John. 1991. Domesticity and manliness in the Victorian middle class: The family of Edward White Benson. In *Manful assertions: Masculinities in Britain since 1800,* edited by Michael Roper and John Tosh, 44–73. London: Routledge.

United Nations Educational, Scientific and Cultural Organization (UNESCO). 1997. *Male roles and masculinities in the perspective of a culture of peace: Report of expert group meeting, Oslo, 24–28 September 1997.* Paris: Women and a Culture of Peace Programme, Culture of Peace Unit, UNESCO.

Walby, Sylvia. 1990. *Theorizing patriarchy.* Oxford, U.K.: Blackwell.

Walker, James C. 1988. *Louts and legends: Male youth culture in an inner-city school.* Sydney: Allen & Unwin.

Wallerstein, Immanuel. 1974. *The modern world-system: Capitalist agriculture and the origins of the European world-economy in the sixteenth century.* New York: Academic Press.

Whitson, David. 1990. Sport in the social construction of masculinity. In *Sport, men, and the gender order: Critical feminist perspectives,* edited by Michael A. Messner and Donald F. Sabo, 19–29. Champaign, IL: Human Kinetics Books.

Widersprueche. 1995. Special Issue: Maennlichkeiten. Vol. 56/57.

Williams, Walter L. 1986. *The spirit and the flesh: Sexual diversity in American Indian culture.* Boston: Beacon.

Xaba, Thokozani. 1997. Masculinity in a transitional society: The rise and fall of the "young lions." Paper presented at the conference Masculinities in Southern Africa, June, University of Natal-Durban, Durban.

5

Global Woman

BARBARA EHRENREICH

ARLIE RUSSELL HOCHSCHILD

"Whose baby are you?" Josephine Perera, a nanny from Sri Lanka, asks Isadora, her pudgy two-year-old charge in Athens, Greece.

Thoughtful for a moment, the child glances toward the closed door of the next room, in which her mother is working, as if to say, "That's my mother in there."

"No, you're *my* baby," Josephine teases, tickling Isadora lightly. Then, to settle the issue, Isadora answers, "Together!" She has two mommies—her mother and Josephine. And surely a child loved by many adults is richly blessed.

In some ways, Josephine's story—which unfolds in an extraordinary documentary film, *When Mother Comes Home for Christmas,* directed by Nilita Vachani—describes an unparalleled success. Josephine has ventured around the world, achieving a degree of independence her mother could not have imagined, and amply supporting her three children with no help from her ex-husband, their father. Each month she mails a remittance check from Athens to Hatton, Sri Lanka, to pay the children's living expenses and school fees. On her Christmas visit home, she bears gifts of pots, pans, and dishes. While she makes payments on a new bus that Suresh, her oldest son, now drives for a living, she is also saving for a modest dowry for her daughter, Norma. She dreams of buying a new house in which the whole family can live. In the meantime, her work as a nanny enables Isadora's parents to devote themselves to their careers and avocations.

But Josephine's story is also one of wrenching global inequality. While Isadora enjoys the attention of three adults, Josephine's three children in Sri Lanka have been far less lucky. According to Vachani, Josephine's youngest child, Suminda, was two—Isadora's age—when his mother first left home to work in Saudi Arabia. Her middle child, Norma, was nine; her oldest son, Suresh, thirteen. From Saudi Arabia, Josephine found her way first to Kuwait, then to Greece. Except for one two-month trip home, she has lived apart from her children for ten years. She writes them weekly letters, seeking news of relatives, asking about school, and complaining that Norma doesn't write back.

Although Josephine left the children under her sister's supervision, the two youngest have shown signs of real distress. Norma has attempted suicide three times. Suminda, who was twelve when the film was made, boards in a grim, Dickensian orphanage that forbids talk during meals and showers. He visits his aunt on holidays. Although the oldest, Suresh, seems to be on good terms with his mother, Norma is tearful and sullen, and Suminda does poorly in school, picks quarrels, and otherwise seems withdrawn from the world.

"Global Woman" from *Global Woman,* by Barbara Ehrenreich and Arlie Russell Hochschild. Copyright © 2002 by Barbara Ehrenreich and Arlie Russell Hochschild. Reprinted by permission of Henry Holt and Company, LLC.

Still, at the end of the film, we see Josephine once again leave her three children in Sri Lanka to return to Isadora in Athens. For Josephine can either live with her children in desperate poverty or make money by living apart from them. Unlike her affluent First World employers, she cannot both live with her family and support it.

Thanks to the process we loosely call "globalization," women are on the move as never before in history. In images familiar to the West from television commercials for credit cards, cell phones, and airlines, female executives jet about the world, phoning home from luxury hotels and reuniting with eager children in airports. But we hear much less about a far more prodigious flow of female labor and energy: the increasing migration of millions of women from poor countries to rich ones, where they serve as nannies, maids, and sometimes sex workers. In the absence of help from male partners, many women have succeeded in tough "male world" careers only by turning over the care of their children, elderly parents, and homes to women from the Third World. This is the female underside of globalization, whereby millions of Josephines from poor countries in the south migrate to do the "women's work" of the north—work that affluent women are no longer able or willing to do. These migrant workers often leave their own children in the care of grandmothers, sisters, and sisters-in-law. Sometimes a young daughter is drawn out of school to care for her younger siblings.

This pattern of female migration reflects what could be called a worldwide gender revolution. In both rich and poor countries, fewer families can rely solely on a male breadwinner. In the United States, the earning power of most men has declined since 1970, and many women have gone out to "make up the difference." By one recent estimate, women were the sole, primary, or coequal earners in more than half of American families (Gallinsky and Friedman 1995). So the question arises: Who will take care of the children, the sick, the elderly? Who will make dinner and clean house?

While the European or American woman commutes to work an average twenty-eight minutes a day, many nannies from the Philippines, Sri Lanka, and India cross the globe to get to their jobs. Some female migrants from the Third World do find something like "liberation," or at least the chance to become independent breadwinners and to improve their children's material lives. Other, less fortunate migrant women end up in the control of criminal employers—their passports stolen, their mobility blocked, forced to work without pay in brothels or to provide sex along with cleaning and childcare services in affluent homes. But even in more typical cases, where benign employers pay wages on time, Third World migrant women achieve their success only by assuming the cast-off domestic roles of middle- and high-income women in the First World—roles that have been previously rejected, of course, by men. And their "commute" entails a cost we have yet to fully comprehend.

The migration of women from the Third World to do "women's work" in affluent countries has so far received little scholarly or media attention—for reasons that are easy enough to guess. First, many, though by no means all, of the new female migrant workers are women of color, and therefore subject to the racial "discounting" routinely experienced by, say, Algerians in France, Mexicans in the United States, and Asians in the United Kingdom. Add to racism the private "indoor" nature of so much of the new migrants' work. Unlike factory workers, who congregate in large numbers, or taxi drivers, who are visible on the street, nannies and maids are often hidden away, one or two at a time, behind closed doors in private homes. Because of the illegal nature of their work, most sex workers are even further concealed from public view.

At least in the case of nannies and maids, another factor contributes to the invisibility of migrant women and their work—one that, for their affluent employers, touches closer to home. The Western culture of individualism, which finds extreme expression in the United States, militates against acknowledging help or human interdependency of nearly any kind. Thus, in the time-pressed upper middle class, servants are no longer displayed as status symbols, decked out in white caps and aprons, but often remain in the background, or disappear when company comes. Furthermore, affluent career women increasingly earn their status not through leisure, as they might have a century ago, but by apparently "doing it all"—producing a full-time career, thriving children, a contented spouse, and a well-managed home. In order to preserve this illusion, domestic workers and nannies make the house hotel-room perfect, feed and bathe the children, cook and clean up—and then magically fade from sight.

The lifestyles of the First World are made possible by a global transfer of the services associated with a wife's traditional role—child care, home-making, and sex—from poor countries to rich ones. To generalize and perhaps oversimplify: in an earlier phase of imperialism, northern countries extracted natural resources and agricultural products—rubber, metals, and sugar, for example—from lands they conquered and colonized. Today, while still relying on Third World countries for agricultural and industrial labor, the wealthy countries also seek to extract something harder to measure and quantify, something that can look very much like love. Nannies like Josephine bring the distant families that employ them real maternal affection, no doubt enhanced by the heartbreaking absence of their own children in the poor countries they leave behind. Similarly, women who migrate from country to country to work as maids bring not only their muscle power but an attentiveness to detail and to the human relationships in the household that might otherwise have been invested in their own families. Sex workers offer the simulation of sexual and romantic love, or at least transient sexual companionship. It is as if the wealthy parts of the world are running short on precious emotional and sexual resources and have had to turn to poorer regions for fresh supplies.

There are plenty of historical precedents for this globalization of traditional female services. In the ancient Middle East, the women of populations defeated in war were routinely enslaved and hauled off to serve as household workers and concubines for the victors. Among the Africans brought to North America as slaves in the sixteenth through nineteenth centuries, about a third were women and children, and many of those women were pressed to be concubines, domestic servants, or both. Nineteenth-century Irishwomen—along with many rural Englishwomen—migrated to English towns and cities to work as domestics in the homes of the growing upper middle class. Services thought to be innately feminine—child care, housework, and sex—often win little recognition or pay. But they have always been sufficiently in demand to transport over long distances if necessary. What is new today is the sheer number of female migrants and the very long distances they travel. Immigration statistics show huge numbers of women in motion, typically from poor countries to rich. Although the gross statistics give little clue as to the jobs women eventually take, there are reasons to infer that much of their work is "caring work,"

performed either in private homes or in institutional settings such as hospitals, hospices, child-care centers, and nursing homes.

The statistics are, in many ways, frustrating. We have information on legal migrants but not on illegal migrants, who, experts tell us, travel in equal if not greater numbers. Furthermore, many Third World countries lack data for past years, which makes it hard to trace trends over time; or they use varying methods of gathering information, which makes it hard to compare one country with another. Nevertheless, the trend is clear enough for some scholars . . . to speak of a "feminization of migration." From 1950 to 1970, for example, men predominated in labor migration to northern Europe from Turkey, Greece, and North Africa. Since then, women have been replacing men. In 1946, women were fewer than 3 percent of the Algerians and Moroccans living in France; by 1990, they were more than 40 percent. Overall, half of the world's 120 million legal and illegal migrants are now believed to be women.

Patterns of international migration vary from region to region, but women migrants from a surprising number of sending countries actually outnumber men, sometimes by a wide margin. For example, in the 1990s, women make up over half of Filipino migrants to all countries and 84 percent of Sri Lankan migrants to the Middle East. Indeed, by 1993 statistics, Sri Lankan women such as Josephine vastly outnumbered Sri Lankan men as migrant workers who'd left for Saudi Arabia, Kuwait, Lebanon, Oman, Bahrain, Jordan, and Qatar, as well as to all countries of the Far East, Africa, and Asia. About half of the migrants leaving Mexico, India, Korea, Malaysia, Cyprus, and Swaziland to work elsewhere are also women. Throughout the 1990s women outnumbered men among migrants to the United States, Canada, Sweden, the United Kingdom, Argentina, and Israel.

Most women, like men, migrate from the south to the north and from poor countries to rich ones. Typically, migrants go to the nearest comparatively rich country, preferably one whose language they speak or whose religion and culture they share. There are also local migratory flows: from northern to southern Thailand, for instance, or from East Germany to West. But of the regional or cross-regional flows, four stand out. One goes from Southeast Asia to the oil-rich Middle and Far East—from Bangladesh, Indonesia, the Philippines, and

Sri Lanka to Bahrain, Oman, Kuwait, Saudi Arabia, Hong Kong, Malaysia, and Singapore. Another stream of migration goes from the former Soviet bloc to western Europe—from Russia, Romania, Bulgaria, and Albania to Scandinavia, Germany, France, Spain, Portugal, and England. A third goes from south to north in the Americas, including the stream from Mexico to the United States, which scholars say is the longest-running labor migration in the world. A fourth stream moves from Africa to various parts of Europe. France receives many female migrants from Morocco, Tunisia, and Algeria. Italy receives female workers from Ethiopia, Eritrea, and Cape Verde.

Female migrants overwhelmingly take up work as maids or domestics. As women have become an ever greater proportion of migrant workers, receiving countries reflect a dramatic influx of foreign-born domestics. In the United States, African-American women, who accounted for 60 percent of domestics in the 1940s, have been largely replaced by Latinas, many of them recent migrants from Mexico and Central America. In England, Asian migrant women have displaced the Irish and Portuguese domestics of the past. In French cities, North African women have replaced rural French girls. In western Germany, Turks and women from the former East Germany have replaced rural native-born women. Foreign females from countries outside the European Union made up only 6 percent of all domestic workers in 1984. By 1987, the percentage had jumped to 52, with most coming from the Philippines, Sri Lanka, Thailand, Argentina, Colombia, Brazil, El Salvador, and Peru.

The governments of some sending countries actively encourage women to migrate in search of domestic jobs, reasoning that migrant women are more likely than their male counterparts to send their hard-earned wages to their families rather than spending the money on themselves. In general, women send home anywhere from half to nearly all of what they earn. These remittances have a significant impact on the lives of children, parents, siblings, and wider networks of kin—as well as on cash-strapped Third World governments. Thus, before Josephine left for Athens, a program sponsored by the Sri Lankan government taught her how to use a microwave oven, a vacuum cleaner, and an electric mixer. As she awaited her flight, a song piped into the airport departure lounge extolled the opportunity to

earn money abroad. The songwriter was in the pay of the Sri Lanka Bureau of Foreign Employment, an office devised to encourage women to migrate. The lyrics say:

> After much hardship, such difficult times,
> How lucky I am to work in a foreign land.
> As the gold gathers so do many greedy flies.
> But our good government protects us from them.
> After much hardship, such difficult times,
> How lucky I am to work in a foreign land.
> I promise to return home with treasures for everyone.

Why this transfer of women's traditional services from poor to rich parts of the world? The reasons are, in a crude way, easy to guess. Women in Western countries have increasingly taken on paid work, and hence need others—paid domestics and caretakers for children and elderly people—to replace them. For their part, women in poor countries have an obvious incentive to migrate: relative and absolute poverty. The "care deficit" that has emerged in the wealthier countries as women enter the workforce *pulls* migrants from the Third World and postcommunist nations; poverty *pushes* them.

In broad outline, this explanation holds true. Throughout western Europe, Taiwan, and Japan, but above all in the United States, England, and Sweden, women's employment has increased dramatically since the 1970s. In the United States, for example, the proportion of women in paid work rose from 15 percent of mothers of children six and under in 1950 to 65 percent today. Women now make up 46 percent of the U.S. labor force. Three-quarters of mothers of children eighteen and under and nearly two-thirds of mothers of children age one and younger now work for pay. Furthermore, according to a recent International Labor Organization study, working Americans averaged longer hours at work in the late 1990s than they did in the 1970s. By some measures, the number of hours spent at work have increased more for women than for men, and especially for women in managerial and professional jobs.

Meanwhile, over the last thirty years, as the rich countries have grown much richer, the poor countries have become—in both absolute and relative terms—poorer. Global inequalities in wages are particularly striking. In Hong Kong, for instance, the wages of a Filipina domestic are about fifteen times the amount she could make as a schoolteacher back in the

Philippines. In addition, poor countries turning to the IMF or World Bank for loans are often forced to undertake measures of so-called structural adjustment, with disastrous results for the poor and especially for poor women and children. To qualify for loans, governments are usually required to devalue their currencies, which turns the hard currencies of rich countries into gold and the soft currencies of poor countries into straw. Structural adjustment programs also call for cuts in support for "noncompetitive industries," and for the reduction of public services such as health care and food subsidies for the poor. Citizens of poor countries, women as well as men, thus have a strong incentive to seek work in more fortunate parts of the world.

But it would be a mistake to attribute the globalization of women's work to a simple synergy of needs among women—one group, in the affluent countries, needing help and the other, in poor countries, needing jobs. For one thing, this formulation fails to account for the marked failure of First World governments to meet the needs created by its women's entry into the workforce. The downsized American—and to a lesser degree, western European—welfare state has become a "deadbeat dad." Unlike the rest of the industrialized world, the United States does not offer public child care for working mothers, nor does it ensure paid family and medical leave. Moreover, a series of state tax revolts in the 1980s reduced the number of hours public libraries were open and slashed school-enrichment and after-school programs. Europe did not experience anything comparable. Still, tens of millions of western European women are in the workforce who were not before—and there has been no proportionate expansion in public services.

Secondly, any view of the globalization of domestic work as simply an arrangement among women completely omits the role of men. Numerous studies, including some of our own, have shown that as American women took on paid employment, the men in their families did little to increase their contribution to the work of the home. For example, only one out of every five men among the working couples whom Hochschild interviewed for *The Second Shift* (Hochschild 1989), in the 1980s shared the work at home, and later studies suggest that while working mothers are doing somewhat less housework than their counterparts twenty years ago, most men are doing only a little more. With divorce, men frequently abdicate their child-care

responsibilities to their ex-wives. In most cultures of the First World outside the United States, powerful traditions even more firmly discourage husbands from doing "women's work." So, strictly speaking, the presence of immigrant nannies does not enable affluent women to enter the workforce; it enables affluent *men* to continue avoiding the second shift.

The men in wealthier countries are also, of course, directly responsible for the demand for immigrant sex workers—as well as for the sexual abuse of many migrant women who work as domestics. Why, we wondered, is there a particular demand for "imported" sexual partners? Part of the answer may lie in the fact that new immigrants often take up the least desirable work, and, thanks to the AIDS epidemic, prostitution has become a job that ever fewer women deliberately choose. But perhaps some of this demand grows out of the erotic lure of the "exotic." Immigrant women may seem desirable sexual partners for the same reason that First World employers believe them to be especially gifted as caregivers: they are thought to embody the traditional feminine qualities of nurturance, docility, and eagerness to please. Some men feel nostalgic for these qualities, which they associate with a bygone way of life. Even as many wage-earning Western women assimilate to the competitive culture of "male" work and ask respect for making it in a man's world, some men seek in the "exotic Orient" or "hot-blooded tropics" a woman from the imagined past.

Of course, not all sex workers migrate voluntarily. An alarming number of women and girls are trafficked by smugglers and sold into bondage. Because trafficking is illegal and secret, the numbers are hard to know with any certainty. Kevin Bales estimates that in Thailand alone, a country of 60 million, half a million to a million women are prostitutes, and one out of every twenty of these is enslaved (Bales 1999). Many of these women are daughters whom northern hill-tribe families have sold to brothels in the cities of the South. Believing the promises of jobs and money, some begin the voyage willingly, only to discover days later that the "arrangers" are traffickers who steal their passports, define them as debtors, and enslave them as prostitutes. Other women and girls are kidnapped, or sold by their impoverished families, and then trafficked to brothels. Even worse fates befall women from neighboring Laos and Burma, who flee crushing poverty and repression at home only to fall into the hands of Thai slave traders.

If the factors that pull migrant women workers to affluent countries are not as simple as they at first appear, neither are the factors that push them. Certainly relative poverty plays a major role, but, interestingly, migrant women often do not come from the poorest classes of their societies. In fact, they are typically more affluent and better educated than male migrants. Many female migrants from the Philippines and Mexico, for example, have high school or college diplomas and have held middle-class—albeit low-paid—jobs back home. One study of Mexican migrants suggests that the trend is toward increasingly better-educated female migrants. Thirty years ago, most Mexican-born maids in the United States had been poorly educated maids in Mexico. Now a majority have high school degrees and have held clerical, retail, or professional jobs before leaving for the United States. Such women are likely to be enterprising and adventurous enough to resist the social pressures to stay home and accept their lot in life.

Noneconomic factors—or at least factors that are not immediately and directly economic—also influence a woman's decision to emigrate. By migrating, a woman may escape the expectation that she care for elderly family members, relinquish her paycheck to a husband or father, or defer to an abusive husband. Migration may also be a practical response to a failed marriage and the need to provide for children without male help. In the Philippines, Rhacel Salazar Parreñas (2002) tells us, migration is sometimes called a "Philippine divorce." And there are forces at work that may be making the men of poor countries less desirable as husbands. Male unemployment runs high in the countries that supply female domestics to the First World. Unable to make a living, these men often grow demoralized and cease contributing to their families in other ways. Many female migrants tell of unemployed husbands who drink or gamble their remittances away. Notes one study of Sri Lankan women working as maids in the Persian Gulf: "It is not unusual . . . for the women to find upon their return that their Gulf wages by and large have been squandered on alcohol, gambling and other dubious undertakings while they were away" (Gamburd 2002).

To an extent then, the globalization of child care and housework brings the ambitious and independent women of the world together: the career-oriented upper-middle-class woman of an affluent nation and the striving woman from a crumbling Third World or postcommunist economy. Only it does not bring them together in the way that second-wave feminists in affluent countries once liked to imagine—as sisters and allies struggling to achieve common goals. Instead, they come together as mistress and maid, employer and employee, across a great divide of privilege and opportunity.

This trend toward global redivision of women's traditional work throws new light on the entire process of globalization. Conventionally, it is the poorer countries that are thought to be dependent on the richer ones—a dependency symbolized by the huge debt they owe to global financial institutions. What we explore, however, is a dependency that works in the other direction, and it is a dependency of a particularly intimate kind. Increasingly often, as affluent and middle-class families in the First World come to depend on migrants from poorer regions to provide child care, homemaking, and sexual services, a global relationship arises that in some ways mirrors the traditional relationship between the sexes. The First World takes on a role like that of the old-fashioned male in the family—pampered, entitled, unable to cook, clean, or find his socks. Poor countries take on a role like that of the traditional woman within the family—patient, nurturing, and self-denying. A division of labor feminists critiqued when it was "local" has now, metaphorically speaking, gone global.

To press this metaphor a bit further, the resulting relationship is by no means a "marriage," in the sense of being openly acknowledged. In fact, it is striking how invisible the globalization of women's work remains, how little it is noted or discussed in the First World. Trend spotters have had almost nothing to say about the fact that increasing numbers of affluent First World children and elderly persons are tended by immigrant care workers or live in homes cleaned by immigrant maids. Even the political groups we might expect to be concerned about this trend—antiglobalization and feminist activists—often seem to have noticed only the most extravagant abuses, such as trafficking and female enslavement. So if a metaphorically gendered relationship has developed between rich and poor countries, it is less like a marriage and more like a secret affair.

But it is a "secret affair" conducted in plain view of the children. Little Isadora and the other children of the First World raised by "two mommies" may be learning more than their ABC's from a loving surrogate parent. In their own living rooms, they are learning a vast and tragic global politics. Children see. But they also learn how to disregard what they see. They learn how adults make the visible invisible. That is their "early childhood education." . . .

The globalization of women's traditional role poses important challenges to anyone concerned about gender and economic inequity. How can we improve the lives and opportunities of migrant women engaged in legal occupations such as nannies and maids? How can we prevent trafficking and enslavement? More basically, can we find a way to counterbalance the systematic transfer of caring work from poor countries to rich, and the inevitable trauma of the children left behind? . . . Before we can hope to find activist solutions, we need to see these women as full human beings. They are strivers as well as victims, wives and mothers as well as workers—sisters, in other words, with whom we in the First World may someday define a common agenda.

REFERENCES

Bales, Kevin. 1999. *Disposable People: New Slavery in the Global Economy*. Berkeley: University of California Press.

Hochschild, Arlie Russell with Anne Machung. 1989. *The Second Shift*. New York: Viking Penguin.

Gallinsky, Ellen, and Dana Friedman. 1995. *Woman: The New Providers*. Whirlpool Foundation Study, Part 1. New York: Families and Work Institute.

Gamburd, Michele. 2002. "Breadwinner No More," In *Global Woman*. Barbara Ehrenreich and Arlie Russell Hochschild (eds.), 190–206. New York: Metropolitan Books.

Parreñas, Rhacel Salazar. 2002. "The Care Crisis in the Philippines: Children and Transnational Families in the New Global Economy," In *Global Woman*. Barbara Ehrenreich and Arlie Russell Hochschild (eds.), 39–54. New York: Metropolitan Books.

6

Antiglobalization Pedagogies and Feminism

CHANDRA TALPADE MOHANTY

ANTIGLOBALIZATION STRUGGLES

. . . What does it mean to make antiglobalization a key factor for feminist theorizing and struggle? To illustrate my thinking about antiglobalization, let me focus on two specific sites where knowledge about globalization is produced. The first site is a pedagogical one and involves an analysis of the various strategies being used to internationalize (or globalize) the women's studies curriculum in U.S. colleges and universities. I argue that this move to internationalize women's studies curricula and the attendant pedagogies that flow from this is one of the main ways we can track a discourse of global feminism in the United States. Other ways of tracking global feminist discourses include analyzing the documents and discussions flowing out of the Beijing United Nations conference on women, and of course popular television and globalization scholarship I focus on is the emerging, notably ungendered and deracialized discourse on activism against globalization.

Antiglobalization Pedagogies

Let me turn to the struggles over the dissemination of a feminist cross-cultural knowledge base through pedagogical strategies "internationalizing" the women's studies curriculum. The problem of "the (gendered) color line" remains, but is more easily seen today as developments of transnational and global capital. While I choose to focus on women's studies curricula, my arguments hold for curricula in any discipline or academic field that seeks to internationalize or globalize its curriculum. I argue that the challenge for "internationalizing" women's studies is no different from the one involved in "racializing" women's studies in the 1980s, for very similar politics of knowledge come into play here.

So the question I want to foreground is the politics of knowledge in bridging the "local" and the "global" in women's studies. How we teach the "new" scholarship in women's studies is at least as important as the scholarship itself in the struggles over knowledge and citizenship in the U.S. academy. . . .

Drawing on my own work with U.S. feminist academic communities, I describe three pedagogical models used in "internationalizing" the women's studies curriculum and analyze the politics of knowledge at work. Each of these perspectives is grounded in particular conceptions of the local and the global, of women's agency, and of national identity, and each curricular model presents different stories and ways of crossing

---

Chandra Talpade Mohanty, "Antiglobalization Pedagogies and Feminism," in *Feminism without Borders: Decolonizing Theory, Practicing Solidarity,* pp. 237–251. Copyright © 2003, Duke University Press. All rights reserved. Used by permission of the publisher.

borders and building bridges. I suggest that a "comparative feminist studies" or "feminist solidarity" model is the most useful and productive pedagogical strategy for feminist cross-cultural work. It is this particular model that provides a way to theorize a complex relational understanding of experience, location, and history such that feminist cross-cultural work moves through the specific context to construct a real notion of universal and of democratization rather than colonization. It is through this model that we can put into practice the idea of "common differences" as the basis for deeper solidarity across differences and unequal power relations.

Feminist-as-Tourist Model   This curricular perspective could also be called the "feminist as international consumer" or, in less charitable terms, the "white women's burden or colonial discourse" model. It involves a pedagogical strategy in which brief forays are made into non–Euro-American cultures, and particular sexist cultural practices addressed from an otherwise Eurocentric women's studies gaze. In other words, the "add women as global victims or powerful women and stir" perspective. This is a perspective in which the primary Euro-American narrative of the syllabus remains untouched, and examples from non-Western or Third World/South cultures are used to supplement and "add" to this narrative. The story here is quite old. The effects of this strategy are that students and teachers are left with a clear sense of the difference and distance between the local (defined as self, nation, and Western) and the global (defined as other, non-Western, and transnational). Thus the local is always grounded in nationalist assumptions—the United States or Western European nation-state provides a normative context. This strategy leaves power relations and hierarchies untouched since ideas about center and margin are reproduced along Eurocentric lines.

For example, in an introductory feminist studies course, one could include the obligatory day or week on dowry deaths in India, women workers in Nike factories in Indonesia, or precolonial matriarchies in West Africa, while leaving the fundamental identity of the Euro-American feminist on her way to liberation untouched. Thus Indonesian workers in Nike factories or dowry deaths in India stand in for the totality of women in these cultures. These women are not seen in their everyday lives (as Euro-American women are)—just in these stereotypical terms. Difference in the case of non–Euro-American women is thus congealed, not seen contextually with all of its contradictions. This pedagogical strategy for crossing cultural and geographical borders is based on a modernist paradigm, and the bridge between the local and the global becomes in fact a predominantly self-interested chasm. This perspective confirms the sense of the "evolved U.S./Euro feminist." While there is now more consciousness about not using an "add and stir" method in teaching about race and U.S. women of color, this does not appear to be the case in "internationalizing" women's studies. Experience in this context is assumed to be static and frozen into U.S.- or Euro-centered categories. Since in this paradigm feminism is always/already constructed as Euro-American in origin and development, women's lives and struggles outside this geographical context only serve to confirm or contradict this originary feminist (master) narrative. This model is the pedagogical counterpart of the orientalizing and colonizing Western feminist scholarship of the past decades. In fact it may remain the predominant model at this time. Thus implicit in this pedagogical strategy is the crafting of the "Third World difference," the creation of monolithic images of Third World/South women. This contrasts with images of Euro-American women who are vital, changing, complex, and central subjects within such a curricular perspective.

Feminist-as-Explorer Model   This particular pedagogical perspective originates in area studies, where the "foreign" woman is the object and subject of knowledge and the larger intellectual project is entirely about countries other than the United States. Thus, here the local and the global are both defined as non–Euro-American. The focus on the international implies that it exists outside the U.S. nation-state. Women's, gender, and feminist issues are based on spatial/geographical and temporal/historical categories located elsewhere. Distance from "home" is fundamental to the definition of international in this framework. This strategy can result in students and teachers being left with a notion of difference and separateness, a sort of "us and them" attitude, but unlike the tourist model, the explorer perspective can provide a deeper, more contextual understanding of feminist issues in discretely defined geographical and cultural spaces. However, unless these discrete spaces are taught in relation to one another, the story told is usually a cultural relativist one, meaning that differences between cultures are discrete and relative with no real connection or common basis for evaluation. The local and the global are here collapsed into the international that by definition excludes the United States. If the dominant discourse is the discourse of cultural relativism, questions of power, agency, justice, and common criteria for critique and evaluation are silenced.

In women's studies curricula this pedagogical strategy is often seen as the most culturally sensitive way to "internationalize" the curriculum. For instance, entire courses on "Women in Latin America" or "Third World Women's Literature" or "Postcolonial Feminism" are added on to the predominantly U.S.-based curriculum as a way to "globalize" the feminist knowledge base. These courses can be quite sophisticated and complex studies, but they are viewed as entirely separate from the intellectual project of U.S. race and ethnic studies. The United States is not seen as part of "area studies," as white is not a color when one speaks of people of color. This is probably related to the particular history of institutionalization of area studies in the U.S. academy and its ties to U.S. imperialism. Thus areas to be studied/conquered "out there," never within the United States. The fact that area studies in U.S. academic settings were federally funded and conceived as having a political project in the service of U.S. geopolitical interests suggests the need to examine the contemporary interests of these fields, especially as they relate to the logic of global capitalism. In addition, as Ella Shohat argues, it is to "reimagine the study of regions and cultures in a way that transcends the conceptual borders inherent in the global cartography of the cold war" (2001, 1271). The field of American studies is an interesting location to examine here, especially since its more recent focus on U.S. imperialism. However, American studies rarely falls under the purview of "area studies."

The problem with the feminist-as-explorer strategy is that globalization is an economic, political, and ideological phenomenon that actively brings the world and its various communities under connected and interdependent discursive and material regimes. The lives of women are connected and interdependent, albeit not the same, no matter which geographical area we happen to live in.

Separating area studies from race and ethnic studies thus leads to understanding or teaching about the global as a way of not addressing internal racism, capitalist hegemony, colonialism, and heterosexualization as central to processes of global domination, exploitation, and resistance. Global or international is thus understood apart from racism—as if racism were not central to processes of globalization and relations of rule at this time. An example of this pedagogical strategy in the context of the larger curriculum is the usual separation of "world cultures" courses from race and ethnic studies courses. Thus identifying the kinds of representations of (non–Euro-American) women mobilized by this pedagogical strategy, and the relation of these representations to implicit images of First World/North women are important foci for analysis. What kind of power is being exercised in this strategy? What kinds of ideas of agency and struggle are being consolidated? What are the potential effects of a kind of cultural relativism on our understandings of the differences and commonalities among communities of women around the world? Thus the feminist-as-explorer model has its own problems, and I believe this is an inadequate way of building a feminist cross-cultural knowledge base because in the context of an interwoven world with clear directionalities of power and domination, cultural relativism serves as an apology for the exercise of power.

The Feminist Solidarity or Comparative Feminist Studies Model   This curricular strategy is based on the premise that the local and the global are not defined in terms of physical geography or territory but exist simultaneously and constitute each other. It is then the links, the relationships, between the local and the global that are foregrounded, and these links are conceptual, material, temporal, contextual, and so on. This framework assumes a comparative focus and analysis of the directionality of power no matter what the subject of the women's studies course is—and it assumes both distance and proximity (specific/universal) as its analytic strategy.

Differences and commonalities thus exist in relation and tension with each other in all contexts. What is emphasized are relations of mutuality, co-responsibility, and common interests, anchoring the idea of feminist solidarity. For example, within this model, one would not teach a U.S. women of color course with additions on Third World/South or white women, but a comparative course that shows the interconnectedness of the histories, experiences, and struggles of U.S. women of color, white women, and women from the Third World/ South. By doing this kind of comparative teaching that is attentive to power, each historical experience illuminates the experiences of the others. Thus, the focus is not just on the intersections of race, class, gender, nation, and sexuality in different communities of women but on mutuality and coimplication, which suggests attentiveness to the interweaving of the histories of these communities. In addition the focus is simultaneously on individual and collective experiences of oppression and exploitation and of struggle and resistance.

Students potentially move away from the "add and stir" and the relativist "separate but equal" (or different) perspective to the coimplication/solidarity one. This solidarity perspective requires understanding the historical and experiential specificities and differences of women's lives as well as the historical and experiential connections between women from different national, racial, and cultural communities. Thus it suggests organizing syllabi around social and economic processes and histories of various communities of women in particular substantive areas like sex work, militarization, environmental justice, the prison/industrial complex, and human rights, and looking for points of contact and connection as well as disjunctures. It is important to always foreground not just the connections of domination but those of struggle and resistance as well.

In the feminist solidarity model the One-Third/ Two-Thirds paradigm makes sense. Rather than Western/ Third World, or North/South, or local/global seen as oppositional and incommensurate categories, the One-Third/Two-Thirds differentiation allows for teaching and learning about points of connection and distance among and between communities of women marginalized and privileged along numerous local and global dimensions. Thus the very notion of inside/ outside necessary to the distance between local/ global is transformed through the use of a One-Third/ Two-Thirds paradigm, as both categories must be understood as containing difference/similarities, inside/ outside, and distance/proximity. Thus sex work, militarization, human rights, and so on can be framed in their multiple local and global dimensions using the One-Third/Two-Thirds, social minority/social majority paradigm. I am suggesting then that we look at the

women's studies curriculum in its entirety and that we attempt to use a comparative feminist studies model wherever possible.

I refer to this model as the feminist solidarity model because, besides its focus on mutuality and common interests, it requires one to formulate questions about connection and disconnection between activist women's movements around the world. Rather than formulating activism and agency in terms of discrete and disconnected cultures and nations, it allows us to frame agency and resistance across the borders of nation and culture. I think feminist pedagogy should not simply expose students to a particularized academic scholarship but that it should also envision the possibility of activism and struggle outside the academy. Political education through feminist pedagogy should teach active citizenship in such struggles for justice.

My recurring question is how pedagogies can supplement, consolidate, or resist the dominant logic of globalization. How do students learn about the inequities among women and men around the world? . . .

After almost two decades of teaching feminist studies in U.S. classrooms, it is clear to me that the way we theorize experience, culture, and subjectivity in relation to histories, institutional practice, and collective struggles determines the kind of stories we tell in the classroom. If these varied stories are to be taught such that students learn to democratize rather than colonize the experiences of different spatially and temporally located communities of women, neither a Eurocentric nor a cultural pluralist curricular practice will do. In fact narratives of historical experience are crucial to political thinking not because they present an unmediated version of the "truth" but because they can destabilize received truths and locate debate in the complexities and contradictions of historical life. . . . These are the kinds of stories we need to weave into a feminist solidarity pedagogical model.

Antiglobalization Scholarship and Movements

Women's and girls' bodies determine democracy: free from violence and sexual abuse, free from malnutrition and environmental degradation, free to plan their families, free to not have families, free to choose their sexual lives and preferences.

—*Zillah Eisenstein*, Global Obscenities, *1998*

There is now an increasing and useful feminist scholarship critical of the practices and effects of globalization. Instead of attempting a comprehensive review of this scholarship, I want to draw attention to some of the most useful kinds of issues it raises. Let me turn, then, to a feminist reading of antiglobalization movements and argue for a more intimate, closer alliance between women's movements, feminist pedagogy, cross-cultural feminist theorizing, and these ongoing anticapitalist movements.

I return to an earlier question: What are the concrete effects of global restructuring on the "real" raced, classed, national, sexual bodies of women in the academy, in workplaces, streets, households, cyberspaces, neighborhoods, prisons, and in social movements? And how do we recognize these gendered effects in movements against globalization? Some of the most complex analyses of the centrality of gender in understanding economic globalization attempt to link questions of subjectivity, agency, and identity with those of political economy and the state. This scholarship argues persuasively for a need to rethink patriarchies and hegemonic masculinities in relation to present-day globalization and nationalisms, and it also attempts to retheorize the gendered aspects of the refigured relations of the state, the market, and civil society by focusing on unexpected and unpredictable sites of resistance to the often devastating effects of global restructuring on women. And it draws on a number of disciplinary paradigms and political perspectives in making the case for the centrality of gender in processes of global restructuring, arguing that the reorganization of gender is part of the global strategy of capitalism.

Women workers of particular caste/class, race, and economic status are necessary to the operation of the capitalist global economy. Women are not only the preferred candidates for particular jobs, but particular kinds of women—poor, Third and Two-Thirds World, working-class, and immigrant/migrant women—are the preferred workers in these global, "flexible" temporary job markets. The documented increase in the migration of poor, One-Third/Two-Thirds World women in search of labor across national borders has led to a rise in the international "maid trade" (Parreñas 2001) and in international sex trafficking and tourism. Many global cities now require and completely depend on the service and domestic labor of immigrant and migrant women. The proliferation of structural adjustment policies around the world has reprivatized women's labor by shifting the responsibility for social welfare from the state to the household and to women located there. The rise of religious fundamentalisms in conjunction with conservative nationalisms, which are also in part reactions to global capital and its cultural demands, has led to the policing of women's bodies in the streets and in the workplaces.

Global capital also reaffirms the color line in its newly articulated class structure evident in the prisons in the One-Third World. The effects of globalization and deindustrialization on the prison industry in the One-Third World leads to a related policing of the bodies of poor, One-Third/Two-Thirds World, immigrant and migrant women behind the concrete spaces and bars of privatized prisons. Angela Davis and Gina Dent (2001) argue that the political economy of U.S. prisons, and the punishment industry in the West/North, brings the intersection of gender, race, colonialism, and capitalism into sharp focus. Just as the factories and workplaces of global corporations seek and discipline the labor of poor, Third World/South, immigrant/migrant women, the prisons of Europe and the United States incarcerate disproportionately large numbers of women of color, immigrants, and noncitizens of African, Asian, and Latin American descent.

Making gender and power visible in the processes of global restructuring demands looking at, naming, and seeing the particular raced, and classed communities of women from poor countries as they are constituted as workers in sexual, domestic, and service industries; as prisoners; and as household managers and nurturers. . . .

While feminist scholarship is moving in important and useful directions in terms of a critique of global restructuring and the culture of globalization, I want to ask some of the same questions I posed in 1986 once again. In spite of the occasional exception, I think that much of present-day scholarship tends to reproduce particular "globalized" representations of women. Just as there is an Anglo-American masculinity produced in and by discourses of globalization, it is important to ask what the corresponding femininities being produced are. Clearly there is the ubiquitous global teenage girl factory worker, the domestic worker, and the sex worker. There is also the migrant/immigrant service worker, the refugee, the victim of war crimes, the woman-of-color prisoner who happens to be a mother and drug user, the consumer-housewife, and so on. There is also the mother-of-the-nation/religious bearer of traditional culture and morality.

Although these representations of women correspond to real people, they also often stand in for the contradictions and complexities of women's lives and roles. Certain images, such as that of the factory or sex worker, are often geographically located in the Third World/South, but many of the representations identified above are dispersed throughout the globe. Most refer to women of the Two-Thirds World, and some to women of the One-Third World. And a woman from the Two-Thirds World can live in the One-Third World. The point I am making here is that women are workers, mothers, or consumers in the global economy, but we are also all those things simultaneously. Singular and monolithic categorizations of women in discourses of globalization circumscribe ideas about experience, agency, and struggle. While there are other, relatively new images of women that also emerge in this discourse—the human rights worker or the NGO advocate, the revolutionary militant and the corporate bureaucrat—there is also a divide between false, overstated images of victimized and empowered womanhood, and they negate each other. We need to further explore how this divide plays itself out in terms of a social majority/minority, One-Third/Two-Thirds World characterization. The concern here is with whose agency is being colonized and who is privileged in these pedagogies and scholarship. These then are my new queries for the twenty-first century.

Because social movements are crucial sites for the construction of knowledge, communities, and identities, it is very important for feminists to direct themselves toward them. The antiglobalization movements of the last five years have proven that one does not have to be a multinational corporation, controller of financial capital, or transnational governing institution to cross national borders. These movements form an important site for examining the construction of transborder democratic citizenship. But first a brief characterization of antiglobalization movements is in order.

Unlike the territorial anchors of the anticolonial movements of the early twentieth century, antiglobalization movements have numerous spatial and social origins. These include anticorporate environmental movements such as the Narmada Bachao Andolan in central India and movements against environmental racism in the U.S. Southwest, as well as the antiagribusiness small-farmer movements around the world. The 1960s consumer movements, people's movements against the IMF and World Bank for debt cancelation and against structural adjustment programs, and the antisweatshop student movements in Japan, Europe, and the United States are also a part of the origins of the antiglobalization movements. In addition, the identity-based social movements of the late twentieth century (feminist, civil rights, indigenous rights, etc.) and the transformed U.S. labor movement of the 1990s also play a significant part in terms of the history of antiglobalization movements.

While women are present as leaders and participants in most of these antiglobalization movements, a feminist agenda only emerges in the post-Beijing "women's rights as human rights" movement and in some peace and environmental justice movements. In other words, while girls and women are central to the labor of global capital, antiglobalization work does not seem to draw on feminist analysis or strategies. Thus, while I have argued that feminists need to be anticapitalists, I would now argue that antiglobalization activists and theorists also need to be feminists. Gender is ignored as a category of analysis and a basis for organizing in most of the antiglobalization movements, and antiglobalization (and anticapitalist critique) does not appear to be central to feminist organizing projects, especially in the First World/North. In terms of women's movements, the earlier "sisterhood is global" form of internationalization of the women's movement has now shifted into the "human rights" arena. This shift in language from "feminism" to "women's rights" has been called the mainstreaming of the feminist movement—a successful attempt to raise the issue of violence against women on to the world stage.

If we look carefully at the focus of the antiglobalization movements, it is the bodies and labor of women and girls that constitute the heart of these struggles. For instance, in the environmental and ecological movements such as Chipko in India and indigenous movements against uranium mining and breast-milk contamination in the United States, women are not only among the leadership: their gendered and racialized bodies are the key to demystifying and combating the processes of recolonization put in place by corporate control of the environment. . . .

Women have been in leadership roles in some of the cross-border alliances against corporate injustice. Thus, making gender, and women's bodies and labor visible, and theorizing this visibility as a process of articulating a more inclusive politics are crucial aspects of feminist anticapitalist critique. Beginning from the social location of poor women of color of the Two-Thirds World is an important, even crucial, place for feminist analysis. . . .

A transnational feminist practice depends on building feminist solidarities across the divisions of place, identity, class, work, belief, and so on. In these very fragmented times it is both very difficult to build these alliances and also never more important to do so. Global capitalism both destroys the possibilities and also offers up new ones. . . .

REFERENCES

Davis, Angela, and Gina Dent. 2001. "Prison as a Border: A Conversation on Gender, Globalization, and Punishment." *Signs* 26, no. 4 (summer): 1235–42.

Elsenstein, Zillah R. 1998. *Global Obscenities: Patriarchy, Capitalism, and the Lure of Cyberfantasy.* New York: New York University Press.

Parreñas, Rhacel Salazar. 2001. "Transgressing the Nation-State: The Partial Citizenship and 'Imagined (Global) Community' of Migrant Filipina Domestic Workers." *Signs* 26, no. 4 (summer): 1129–54.

Shohat, Ella. 2001. "Area Studies, Transnationalism, and the Feminist Production of Knowledge." *Signs* 26, no. 4 (summer): 1269–72.

PART II

BODIES

In Part I, we learned that the **essentialist** dictum, "biology is destiny," is rather simplistic and deterministic. Women's and men's different social positions and practices are not simply reflections of "natural" differences between the sexes. The articles in this section further demonstrate that such **naturalizing** beliefs do not stand up to critical scrutiny. First, even when we acknowledge the fact that there are some average differences between women's and men's bodies (for instance, on average, men are taller than women), average differences are not categorical differences (e.g., some women are taller than some men). Second, average bodily differences between women and men do not necessarily translate into particular social relations, structures, or practices.

In fact, recent research in the sociology of the body shows a dynamic, reciprocal relationship between bodies and their social environments. For example, boys and men have been encouraged and rewarded for "building" muscular bodies, whereas girls and women have been discouraged or punished for this. Even among today's fitness-conscious young women, most feel that "too much muscle" is antithetical to feminine attractiveness. All kinds of food products and dietary supplements, from high-protein "muscle milk" to low-calorie diet foods, are marketed in gendered ways. These social beliefs, practices, and products result in more muscular male bodies and "slimmed and toned" female bodies that appear to reflect natural differences.

CONTROL AND RESISTANCE

Part II examines the relationship between the body and the larger social context that our bodies inhabit. The articles in this first section complicate the idea of women as uniformly disempowered body objects and men as empowered body subjects. They show how the reality of gendered embodiment, as a site for social control and as a resource for resistance, is more complicated and nuanced.

In the first article, Laurel Westbrook and Kristen Schilt provide an intersectional analysis of how gender is determined for trans-people. They refer to the practice of placing others into gender categories as **determining gender**. One fascinating element of this practice is that the criteria for determining gender vary across social situations. Thus, Westbrook and Schilt describe practices that appear to be contradictory, such as the rule that "no athlete with a penis can compete as a woman, [but] athletes are not required to have a penis to compete as a man." In addition, Westbrook and Schilt consider the relationship between how we determine other people's gender and how the sex/gender/sexuality system is changed or maintained. Although we might assume that official recognition of transgender people challenges a dichotomous sex/gender/sexuality binary, Westbrook and Schilt show the surprising ways that the sex/gender/sexuality system is able "to adapt to and re-absorb trans-people."

The second article also focuses on the topic of cultural norms and expectations for binary gendered bodies, as Betsy Lucal offers a fascinating glimpse into her lived experiences with gender bending. What is it like, Lucal asks, to be a person whose physical appearance does not neatly "fit" into one of U.S. culture's two acceptable sex categories? Lucal is a woman who is regularly mistaken as a man, yet she chooses nonparticipation in the accoutrements of femininity, in part, to begin to dismantle patriarchal culture. Taken together, it is interesting to reflect on the similarities and differences between Lucal's experiences as a gender bender and Westbrook and Schilt's description of the experiences of trans-people.

The next three articles consider different aspects of the body—weight, skin color, and age. The articles explore how the meaning of these physical characteristics, and how individual or institutional attempts to control them, are shaped by gender and other social factors. In the article on body weight, Abigail Saguy and Kjerstin Gruys compare how the media *frames* or promotes different perceptions of anorexia/bulimia, binge eating, and obesity. Specifically, they examine how the stigmatization of heavier bodies in the United States leads to strikingly different representations of eating disorders in the media. Although some disorders are portrayed as beyond individual control and deserving of serious medical attention, others are blamed on individual gluttony and poor self-control. Further, eating disorders and their meanings are associated with specific racial-ethnic and social class groups in ways that reinforce group-based stereotypes. Thus, the portrayal of eating disorders in the media works to justify providing help for some and punishing others.

The article by Evelyn Nakano Glenn shifts the focus to skin bleaching and beauty. Around the globe, but particularly in the global South, the consumption of skin-lightening products is growing among young, urban, and educated women. Rather than focusing only on individual consciousness, Nakano Glenn shows the role of transnational pharmaceutical and cosmetics companies in fueling the desire for lighter skin and the association of light skin with feminine beauty.

The last chapter in this section addresses how age intersects with gender and other inequalities in the marginalization of old bodies. Toni Calasanti, Kathleen Slevin, and Neal King argue that not only are old people oppressed, but also age relations represent a political location that should be addressed in its own right. They show how a focus on old people would change feminist theories and activism by taking account, for example, of how some women's bodies are desexualized and cast aside.

VIOLENCE

When we think about violence, the image that often comes to mind is one of direct interpersonal violence, where one person does physical harm to another. The first article in this section seeks to broaden our vision of violence by describing five different, but related, forms of violence: structural violence, political violence, interpersonal violence, symbolic violence, and gender and gendered violence. Cecilia Menjívar examines each of these through the lives of Ladina women in Guatemala. In doing so, she shows how different forms of violence are mutually constituted and reinforced within larger power structures and how violence impacts people differently based on their positions in society. Menjívar also shows how violence comes to be "ideologically legitimized," so that it appears normal and acceptable, or how it is made invisible, despite the oppressive nature of violence on people's lives.

Victor Rios's article examines how enhanced police surveillance in the criminal justice system affects black and Latino male teenagers in Oakland, California. As a former gang member who grew up in the same neighborhood as the teenagers he studied, Rios actually became a target of police harassment and brutality while conducting his research. He describes how police and correctional officers use **gender violence** to teach young black and Latino men "lessons" by feminizing them in humiliating ways or holding them to unobtainable standards of masculinity. In response, the black and Latino youths embrace **hypermasculinity**, overemphasizing masculine aggression to protect themselves from the police and from violence in the street. Yet, the pursuit of hypermasculinity has negative effects: not only did it lead to violence against women and other men, it was used within the criminal justice system as justification for the incarceration and brutal treatment of black and Latino youth. Thus, Rios's research shows how institutionalized gender practices in the criminal justice system perpetuate racial-ethnic inequality.

The last article in this section focuses on sexual violence against girls. It provides further clues to solving perplexing problems such as: (1) why rates of sexual and gender violence remain high despite decades of attempts to combat it and (2) why so few victims of sexual and gender violence report these incidents despite high rates of abuse. To answer these questions, Heather Hlavka describes how girls (ages 3–17) make sense of their experiences of sexual violence. She explains that girls learn cultural messages about sex, or **sexual scripts**, that normalize men's heterosexual aggression as natural, while holding women responsible as the "gatekeepers of male desire." As a consequence, girls learn to hold themselves and each other accountable for their own victimization. Taken together, the readings in this section show how gendered violence protects and enforces patriarchal power for some but at great cost for the majority of women, men, and children. As you read the articles in this section, think about possible ways to address gendered violence. In Part IX, we return to this challenge.

7

Doing Gender, Determining Gender

Transgender People, Gender Panics, and the Maintenance of the Sex/Gender/Sexuality System

LAUREL WESTBROOK

KRISTEN SCHILT

In 1989, Christie Lee Cavazos married Jonathon Littleton, a marriage that lasted until Jonathon's untimely death in 1996. Christie filed a medical malpractice suit against the Texas doctor she alleged had misdiagnosed her husband. What might have been an open-and-shut case, however, was complicated by her biography: In the 1970s she had undergone what was then termed a surgical "sex change" operation. Before considering her case, the court first examined the validity of her marriage as a transgender woman to a cis-gender man. At the center of this case was the determination of her gender. Christie had undergone genital surgery, legally amended all of her government documents to categorize her as "female," had a legal marriage, lived as a woman for 20 years, and had medical experts who testified that she was, physically and psychologically, a woman. Yet, the court ruled that she was, and would always be, chromosomally male and, therefore, could not file a malpractice suit as a spouse. Musing about the nature of gender in his ruling, Chief Justice Hardberger wrote, "There are some things you cannot will into being. They just are" (*Littleton v. Prange* 1999).

The Littleton case illustrates two competing cultural ideologies about how a person's gender[1] is to be authenticated by other people. The judge's ruling that gender is an unchangeable, innate fact illustrates what we term a "biology-based determination of gender." In contrast, the validation of Littleton's identity as a woman by others highlights what we term an "identity-based determination of gender." Such a premise does not mean seeing gender identity as fluid, or as an "anything goes" proposition. Rather, under an identity-based gender ideology, people can be recognized as a member of the gender category with which they identify if their identity claim is accepted as legitimate by other people determining their gender—in the Littleton case, her husband, friends, and medical experts.

We term this social process of authenticating another person's gender identity "determining gender." In face-to-face interactions, determining gender is the response to doing gender. When people do gender in interactions, they present information about their gender. Others then interpret this information, placing them in gender categories and determining their gender. Yet,

Westbrook, L., and K. Schilt. "Doing Gender, Determining Gender: Transgender People, Gender Panics, and the Maintenance of the Sex/Gender/Sexuality System." *Gender & Society* 28 (1): 32–57, copyright © 2014 by SAGE Publications Ltd. Reprinted by Permission of SAGE Publications.

the process of gender determination does not always rely on visual and behavioral cues. Expanding upon interactional theories of gender attribution (Kessler and McKenna 1978; West and Zimmerman 1987), we examine gender determination criteria in policy and court cases, where a great deal of biographical and bodily knowledge is known about the person whose gender is in question, as well as how gender is determined in imagined interactions—namely, cis-people's imagined interactions with trans-people, where the knowledge about the person's body and identity are hypothetical. We use "determining gender" as an umbrella term for these diverse practices of placing a person in a gender category. Additionally, we explore the consequences of gender determination, an exploration that goes beyond "How is gender socially attributed?" to an analysis of "How does gender attribution challenge or maintain the sex/gender/sexuality system?"

We examine the criteria for gender determination in moments of ideological collision. As we have previously argued (Schilt and Westbrook 2009; Westbrook 2009), many people use genitalia (biological criteria) to determine another person's gender in (hetero)sexual[2] and sexualized interactions. Yet, since the advent of the "liberal moment" (Meyerowitz 2002), a cultural turn in the 1960s toward values of autonomy and equality, there has been more acceptance of a person's gender self-identity in spaces defined as nonsexual,[3] such as many workplaces (Schilt 2010). When questions of access to gender-segregated locations arise, however, identity-based and biology-based determinations clash. We center our analysis on three such moments: (1) federal and state proposals made between 2009 and 2011 to prohibit discrimination based on gender identity and expression in the arena of employment, housing, and public accommodations (often called "transgender rights bills"); (2) a 2006 proposed policy in New York City to remove the genital surgery requirement for a change of sex marker on birth certificates; and (3) controversies over trans-people participating in competitive sports.

Our cases address different social milieu: sports, employment, and government documents. Yet, each case is, at its core, about upholding the logic of gender segregation. In these ideological collisions, social actors struggle with where actual and imagined trans-people fit in gender-segregated spaces, such as public restrooms. These struggles provoke what we term "gender panics,"

situations where people react to disruptions to biology-based gender ideology by frantically reasserting the naturalness of a male–female binary. When successful, this labor, which we term "gender naturalization work," quells the panics. In our cases, enacting policies requiring surgical and hormonal criteria for admission into gender-segregated spaces ends the panic. As in sexual and sexualized interactions, genitals determine gender in gender-segregated spaces, as it is often fear of unwanted (hetero)sexuality that motivates gender identity policing.

These cases demonstrate that criteria for determining gender vary across social situations. In gender-integrated public settings, such as the workplace, identity-based criteria can suffice to determine a person's gender. However, in interactional situations that derive their form and logic from gender oppositeness, such as heterosexual acts and gender-segregated sports competitions, social actors tend to enforce more rigid, biology-based criteria. Yet, gender-segregated spaces are not evenly policed, as the criteria for access are heavily interrogated only for women's spaces. Exploring the implications of this difference, we posit that bodies (mainly the presence or absence of the penis) matter for determining gender in women's spaces because of cultural ideologies of women as inherently vulnerable and in need of protection (Hollander 2001) that reproduce gender inequality under the guise of protecting women. We argue that, in the liberal moment of gender, access to gender-segregated spaces is not determined by unchangeable measures such as chromosomes but, instead, by genitals—a move that suggests a greater acceptance of an identity-based determination of gender. However, as we show, by using changeable bodily aspects to determine gender, the basic premises of the "sex/gender/sexuality system" (Seidman 1995) are maintained, as the system repatriates those whose existence potentially calls it into question, thereby naturalizing gender difference and gender inequality.

CONCEPTUAL FRAMEWORK

Sociologists of gender emphasize the social, rather than biological, processes that produce a person's gender. Focused on the interactional level, such theories illustrate how people sort each other into the category of "male" or "female" in social situations on the basis of visual information cues (such as facial hair) and implicit rules for assigning characteristics to particular genders (women wear skirts; men do not). Such visual cues act as proxies for biological criteria invisible in many interactions. This categorization process, termed "gender attribution" (Kessler and McKenna 1978, 2) or "sex categorization" (West and Zimmerman 1987, 127), is theorized as an inescapable but typically unremarkable hallmark of everyday social interactions—except in instances of ambiguity, which can create an interactional breakdown, generating anxiety, concern, and even anger (Schilt 2010; West and Zimmerman 1987).

This theory is a useful counterpoint to essentialism. Yet, the focus on face-to-face interactions can be analytically limiting. Kessler and McKenna note, "The only physical characteristics that can play a role in gender attribution in everyday life are those that are visible" (Kessler and McKenna 1978, 76). West and Zimmerman, too, see characteristics that are visible in interaction as paramount to sex categorization, arguing, "Neither initial sex assignment (pronouncement at birth as female or male) nor the actual existence of essential criteria for that assignment (possession of a clitoris and vagina or penis and testicles) has much—if anything—to do with the identification of sex category in everyday life" (West and Zimmerman 1987, 132). While such propositions may hold in many nonsexual interactions, genitals play a much more key role in gender determination in sexual and sexualized interactions (Schilt and Westbrook 2009). In addition, as the Littleton case demonstrates, invisible characteristics, such as chromosomes, can override visual cues as the appropriate criteria for determining gender when legal rights are at stake.

We seek to expand these theories beyond face-to-face interactions by proposing a broader conceptualization, offering "determining gender" as an umbrella term for the different subprocesses of attributing or, in some cases, officially deciding another person's gender. Gender determination does occur at the level of *everyday interaction*, a process already well documented in the literature. Both cis- and trans-women, for instance, may find their biological claim to use a public women's restroom challenged by other women if they do not present the expected visual cues warranted for access (Cavanagh 2010), while both groups may have their gender self-identity affirmed in gender-integrated

interactions. Gender determination also occurs at the level of *legal cases* and *policy decisions*, where social actors with organizational power devise criteria for who counts as a man or a woman (and therefore who gains or is denied access to gender-specific rights and social settings) (Meadow 2010). In addition, gender determinations occur at the level of the *imaginary*. Illustrating this point, as trans-inclusive policies and laws are discussed in the media, opponents and supporters often draw on hypothetical interactions with trans-people in gender-segregated spaces, such as bathrooms. In these imagined interactions, hypothetical knowledge of the person's genitals or their self-identity, rather than visible gender cues, is used to determine their gender.

When social actors officially or unofficially determine another person's gender, accepted criteria differ across contexts. Face-to-face interactions rely mostly on implicit, culturally agreed on criteria. Imagined interactions and legal or policy decisions, in contrast, often demand more explicit, officially defined criteria. Such a focus on developing explicit criteria for determining gender has grown alongside new surgical possibilities for gender transitions (Meyerowitz 2002). To receive legal and medical gender validation, trans-people have had to follow particular protocols, such as genital reconstructive surgery, that symbolically repatriate them from one side of the gender binary to the other. These criteria, which reflect dominant understandings of sex/gender/sexuality, allowed liberal values of self-determination to co-exist with beliefs about the innateness of the gender binary (Meyerowitz 2002).

This co-existence faced greater challenges in the 1990s when the hegemony of the "stealth model" of transitioning (Schilt 2010) began to dissipate, and transsexual, intersex, and transgender groups organized in an effort to gain greater cultural recognition and civil rights (Stryker 2008). With this push came wider coverage of trans-people in the media, including debates about where trans-men and trans-women fit in institutions, such as legal marriage, and in public gender-segregated spaces, such as bathrooms, prisons, and sports competitions. Policy and lawmakers began to grapple with how to balance trans-inclusivity in a social system predicated on clear, fixed distinctions between men and women, and how to address some cis-gender concerns that the cultural validation of trans-people was a direct challenge to a biologically-determined and/or God-given gender binary.

Cultural beliefs about the sanctity of gender binarism naturalize a sex/gender/sexuality system in which heterosexuality is positioned as the only natural and desirable sexual form. Showing the interrelatedness of ideas about (hetero)sexuality and gender difference, men and women's assumed psychological and embodied distinctions are widely held to be complementary and to require particular relationships with one another (Connell 1995). In nonsexual interactions, in contrast, men and women sometimes are physically segregated on the basis of those same assumed differences in their bodies, capabilities, and interests (Fausto-Sterling 2000; Goffman 1977; Lorber 1993), as well as widely shared beliefs about what activities are normal and appropriate for each gender. While men and women freely interact in many social settings, such as the workplace, the creation of "men's space" and "women's space" "ensure[s] that subcultural differences can be reaffirmed and reestablished in the face of contact between the sexes" (Goffman 1977, 314). In these spaces, gender differences are highlighted, though the same differences are minimized in other settings.

Media coverage of transgender people in the late 2000s provides a useful case study for how gender is determined in various social spaces, what larger cultural beliefs motivate deployment of biology-based and identity-based criteria, and how such criteria are forged in moments of gender ideology collision. We develop the concept of gender determination beyond face-to-face interactions through an analysis of policy and law debates and imagined interactions, situations that often display a call for explicit criteria for deciding who counts as a man or as a woman. At stake in such determinations are the criteria by which trans-people's gender identities are recognized and their rights defined and protected.

METHODS

Our data come from a textual analysis of newspaper coverage gathered from LexisNexis. Such a focus is warranted, as the media tend to both reflect and shape prevailing understandings (Gamson et al. 1992; Macdonald 2003). Investigating beliefs about an issue presented in the news media allows researchers to map out the existing dominant viewpoints within the marketplace of ideas, as news is a commodity for attracting audiences who can then be sold to advertisers (Gamson et al. 1992), and, as such, it has to make cultural sense to its audience (Best 2008). Mainstream journalists write stories that reflect commonsense understandings held by (college educated, middle-class, usually white and heterosexual) journalists and their similarly socially situated audience. While there is no single understanding of gender in our society, the dominant views are visible in the mainstream news.

Media scholars have demonstrated that the media do not only represent reality, they also participate in constructing it (Berns 2004; Gamson et al. 1992; Jansen 2002; Macdonald 2003). The mainstream news media do this by providing audiences with narratives, frames, and belief systems that shape interpretations of the world as well as actions within it. While media do not determine the audience viewpoint (Gamson et al. 1992), they greatly influence it, particularly for people with little preexisting knowledge of an issue (Berns 2004). Examining news coverage allows us to see what ideas might be disseminated to readers who had never before thought about transgender people changing their birth certificates, competing in sports, or seeking protection from employment discrimination.

To explore the criteria for determining gender in nonsexual contexts, we sought out instances in which biology-based and identity-based gender ideologies collided. As the visibility of transgender lives increased broadly in the 2000s, we centered our search in that decade. We looked for moments where who counts as a man or a woman was openly discussed, thus making the process of determining gender more visible. We identified five possible moments of ideological collision surrounding trans-people: sports inclusion, prison housing, inclusion of transgender children in schools, employment rights, and altering of government documents. All of these cases provided instances of cis-people grappling with how trans-people "fit" into previously unquestioned systems and locations. We chose not to examine schools or prisons because we wanted, respectively, all cases to have a comparative focus on adults and to not involve penal settings. Our three remaining cases generated substantial public debate and represented, on our initial selection, different issues: employment nondiscrimination laws, birth certificate alteration policies, and sports participation. We did not focus solely on cases of gender-segregated spaces; however, it is these locales that emerged as salient points of focus.

Birth certificate laws usually get amended with little fanfare. By contrast, a New York City proposal allowing people to change sex markers on their birth certificates without requiring genital surgery generated extensive media coverage. We gathered all the available stories that mentioned "New York" and "birth certificate" and included coverage of the proposed change in policy during 2006–2007, the time period when the amendment was proposed, discussed, and abandoned (a total of 42 articles).

Transgender employment nondiscrimination laws have been debated since the 1990s. Because we were interested in analyzing current criteria for determining gender, we limited our focus to a two-year period (January 1, 2009, to December 31, 2010). We searched for articles that mentioned "transgender" and "nondiscrimination" and were about trans-rights legislation. After a preliminary analysis of the articles, we also searched "bathroom bills," an often applied moniker. We compiled all news stories on the three bills proposed during this time: a federal bill and state-level bills in New Hampshire and Massachusetts (a total of 57 articles).

Since scholars have extensively analyzed most of the major controversies over trans-people in sports, we employ this literature in our analysis. Because this scholarship focuses almost exclusively on transwomen, we supplemented it with media coverage of two cases about transmen from 2009 to 2011: Kye Allums, a transman who played women's basketball, and "Will," a transman who played Australian men's football (a combined total of 92 articles).

We thematically coded each of the 191 articles for beliefs about gender, with a focus on gender determination criteria (such as chromosomes, genitals, or self-identity), and the types of spaces that generated panic (gender-integrated or gender-segregated). We each coded articles from all three of the cases, ensuring intercoder reliability through extensive discussions about themes. Through this preliminary analysis, we recognized the importance of gender-segregated social spaces to each of our three cases. Upon this analytic shift, we further coded the rationales offered in these moments of gender panic for blocking trans-people's access to gender-segregated spaces (such as safety, privacy, and fairness), the final

criteria adopted for determining gender (biology-based, identity-based, none), and the gender of the trans-people at the center of these panics. This second wave of analysis revealed the greater policing of transwomen's access to women-only spaces, and the greater ability of biology-based criteria, rather than identity-based criteria, to quell gender panics.

FINDINGS

Messages in news stories are rarely homogeneous (Gamson et al. 1992). To avoid accusations of biased coverage, journalists typically try to provide at least two sides to a story (Best 2008) that typically represent dominant understandings of a particular topic. In our cases, reporters regularly presented the perspectives of people who supported identity-based determination of gender as well as the views of people who positioned biological criteria as essential for determining gender. These inclusions suggest that, in the late 2000s, the identity-based model and the biology-based model represent the two most dominant and competing understandings of gender. An examination of these ideologies provides a deeper understanding of the sex/gender/sexuality system in the liberal moment of gender, the criteria for determining gender, and how gender determination (re)produces inequality.

Ideology Collision, Gender Panics, and Gender Naturalization Work

Modern athletic competition, like all gender-segregated spaces, rests on and reproduces an idea of two opposite genders (Lorber 1993). Because of its influence on other athletic organizations, we focus here on policies enacted by the International Olympic Committee (IOC) that determine under what circumstances and in what categories transgender and intersex athletes can compete. In the modern Olympics, almost all events are gender-segregated (Tucker and Collins 2009). To maintain this segregation, IOC officials have devised policies on coping with athletes who do not fit easily into this binary. This question of where to place transgender athletes first gained national attention in 1977, when the New York Supreme Court ruled that Dr. Renee Richards, a postoperative transsexual woman, could participate in the U.S. Women's Open Tennis Tournament because her testes had been removed and her body was physically "weakened" by the resulting loss of testosterone (Birrell and Cole 1990; Shy 2007). Following similar logic, in 2003 the IOC adopted the Stockholm Consensus, which allows trans-athletes to compete as the gender they identify as if they have undergone bodily modifications that "minimize gender related advantages" (Ljungqvist and Genel 2005). According to the IOC Medical Commission (2003), the criteria for appropriate transgender bodies are:

> Surgical anatomical changes have been completed, including external genitalia changes and gonadectomy.
> Legal recognition of their assigned sex has been conferred by the appropriate official authorities.
> Hormonal therapy appropriate for the assigned sex has been administered in a verifiable manner and for a sufficient length of time to minimize gender-related advantages in sport competitions.

In June 2012, the IOC added an additional set of criteria, stating that athletes competing as women cannot have a testosterone level "within the male range" unless it "does not confer a competitive advantage because it is non-functional" (IOC Medical and Scientific Department 2012), thus minimizing what is viewed as an unfair hormonal advantage. These explicit criteria allow the IOC to incorporate trans and intersex athletes, and thus to validate the liberal moment of gender, without challenging the premise that modern competitive athletics rests on: the presumption that there are two genders and all athletes must be put into one of those two categories for competition.

These biology-based criteria quieted a slow-burning gender panic that resurfaced with each new case of a trans or intersex athlete (for discussion of intersex athletes, see Buzuvis 2010; Dreger 2010; Fausto-Sterling 2000; Nyong'o 2010). These cases raised questions about whether or not it is fair for cis- and trans-people to compete against one another (Cavanagh and Sykes 2006). The answer hinged on which gender ideology is given primacy (i.e., fair to whom?). While transwomen might self-identify as women, people who subscribed to biology-based ideologies of gender view these athletes as males who carry a size and strength advantage over females. The official goal of the IOC policies is to be fair to all athletes, which means that trans-athletes

could compete as the gender with which they identify, but only if they met the aforementioned criteria. With such explicit criteria, cis-gender people could have confidence that only transwomen who were as "weak" as cis-women were able to compete, a move that diffused gender panic and upheld the logic of gender segregation in the arena of sports.

In the New York birth certificate case, a policy proposal intended to improve the lives of transgender people set off a rapid gender panic. Since many trans-people do not have genital surgery, they are often unable to have a sex marker that reflects their self-identity and gender presentation on their official documents (Currah and Moore 2009). In 2006, the City of New York proposed legislation that validated identity-based determination of gender by removing the genital surgical requirement for a change of sex marker on the birth certificate if applicants were over 18 years of age, had lived as their desired gender for at least two years, and had documentation from medical and mental health professionals stating that their transitions were intended to be permanent. Under this amendment, trans-people were still regulated by the medical institution but their genital configurations would not determine their gender. The New York City Board of Health worked closely with other officials and trans-rights advocates in writing the new policy, and politicians and transgender activists lauded the amendment, which was, by all accounts, expected to pass (Caruso 2006b; Cave 2006a).

Journalists initially presented the amendment in positive terms (e.g., Caruso 2006a; Colangelo 2006; Finn 2006). However, the proposed policy resulted in an intensely negative public reaction. The Board of Health was inundated with calls and emails from people asking how this policy change would affect access to gender-segregated spaces, such as restrooms, hospital rooms, and prison blocks (Currah and Moore 2009). To quell the panic, the Board of Health withdrew the proposal and quickly amended it to maintain emphasis on genitals as the criteria for determining gender. Transgender people in New York could change their sex marker, but like the requirement to compete in the Olympics, they would have to provide proof of genital surgery. In this way, the Board of Health attempted to balance biology-based and identity-based gender models that had come into collision, doing the gender naturalization work of symbolically restoring the primacy of bodies (here, genitals) for determining gender while still validating the possibility for gender transitions.

The "transgender rights" bills we analyzed also resulted in gender panics by embracing identity-based determination of gender. At both the federal and state level, these bills typically offer protections for "gender identity and gender expression" or "transgender expression" in the realms of employment, housing, and public accommodations. In an attempt to make such protections widely inclusive, there is no definition of "expressions" or explicit bodily criteria for transpeople. The resulting gender panics center on this lack of definitional criteria. In response to the proposed bill in New Hampshire, some opponents worried that the bill "did not adequately define transgender individuals" (*The Lowell Sun* 2009). A similar argument was raised about the Massachusetts bill, with concerned citizens worrying that "transgender identity and expression" was too vague (Letter to the Editor 2009a) and created "dangerous ambiguity" over who was legally transgender (Prunier 2009) and therefore had access to men's or women's bathrooms. Highlighting this concern about bathroom access, one opponent in Massachusetts noted, "This bill opens the barn door to everybody. There is no way to know who of the opposite sex is using the [bathroom] facility for the right purposes" (Ring 2009). In these cases, what appears to critics as too much validation of identity-based determination of gender sets off panic, panic that is quelled if the bills do not pass into law. When the bills do pass, opponents continue to raise concerns about the potential for danger to women and children in public restrooms, a point we return to in the following sections.

By enforcing explicit bodily criteria for determining gender, the IOC and New York City policies shore up the fissures created in the strict two-category model of gender by the visibility of trans-people while also allowing for some degree of identity-based determination of gender. Similar to judicial rulings permitting name and sex marker changes on government documents (Meyerowitz 2002), policies about birth certificates and athletes work to balance liberal values of autonomy with the belief that there are two genders and that all people (trans or cis) can be put into one category or the other. A lack of bodily criteria, in contrast, appears as a threat to the gender binary. An editorial opposing federal protections for trans-people highlights this fear clearly: "The Left seeks to obliterate the distinction between men and women. This distinction is considered to be a social construct. . . . For those of us who believe that the male–female distinction is vital to civilization, the Left's attempt to erase this distinction is worth fighting against" (Prager 2010). Similarly, Shannon McGinley, of the conservative Cornerstone Policy Research group, worried that the goal of transgender rights bills was "to create a genderless society" (Distaso 2009). These concerns illustrate our concept of "gender panic," as public debate centers on the necessity of culturally defending a rigid male–female binary that is simultaneously framed as stable and innate. These concerns further underscore the extensive naturalization work that goes into legitimating the current sex/gender/sexuality system. Yet, this work did not evenly center on gender-segregated spaces, or on all biological characteristics that could be used as criteria for determining gender. Rather, opposition gathered around "people with penises" in spaces designated as women-only.

Genitals = Gender: Determining Gender in Women-Only Spaces

In our three cases, concerned citizens and journalists posed many questions about what genitals would be allowed in which gender-segregated spaces. This overwhelming focus on genitalia as the determinant of gender is interesting when considered against other possible criteria. Within biology-based gender ideology, gender is determined at birth by doctors on the visible recognition of genitalia. However, such gender categorization is assumed by many to be the result of other, less visible, biological forces, namely, chromosomes and hormones. While genitalia and hormones can be modified, chromosomes are static—meaning, on some level, XY and XX could be the best criteria for maintaining a binary gender system. Within the transgender rights case, opponents to such bills occasionally drew on chromosomes to further their case for why such bills would be problematic. As one man wrote to a newspaper in Michigan: "Your DNA is proof of your genetic code and determines race [and] sex. . . . There is also one fact that transgender individuals cannot deny: your DNA proves if you are a man or a woman. It does not matter what changes you have made to your sexual organs" (Letter to the Editor 2009b). Yet, such responses comprise a very small part of the discourse in our cases.

That less weight is given to chromosomes in these cases of gender determination is interesting. In everyday interactions, chromosomes are poor criteria for gender attribution, because they are not visible (Kessler and McKenna 1978). Athletes can be tested for chromosomal makeup. Yet, the IOC did not include chromosomes as part of the criteria for competition, as such a requirement would bar trans-athletes from competition. Similarly, our other cases do not use chromosomes as gender determination criteria, because such rigid genetic criteria would effectively invalidate the possibility of gender transitions. Where we saw a call for chromosomal criteria was in cis-people's imagined interactions with trans-people, scenarios that sought to delegitimize calls for identity-based determination of gender. That chromosomes did not figure widely in policy decisions, in contrast, suggests that identity-based gender ideologies have gained some degree of cultural legitimacy. To balance both ideologies, institutions cannot use unchangeable criteria, such as chromosomes, to determine a person's gender.

Genitalia are the primary determiner of gender in all of our cases. Starting with the sports case, which has the most clearly defined criteria for determining gender, the IOC permits transwomen (who are assumed to have XY chromosomes) to compete as women as long as they undergo the removal of the testes and the penis.[4] While testes are a source of testosterone, which is a central concern in sports competition,[5] the IOC does not state why transwomen athletes must undergo a penectomy to compete as women, since penises themselves do not provide advantages in sports. Such a requirement may be partially due to deep cultural beliefs that a person with a penis cannot be a woman (Kessler and McKenna 1978), and so they cannot compete with women in athletics. Moreover, this requirement may be a result of a widely held belief that people with penises present a danger to women, a question we take up later in this article.

This emphasis on determining gender through hormone levels and genitalia is applied only to athletes attempting to compete as women. If an athlete competing as a woman has her gender called into question (usually for performing "too well" for a woman), her hormone levels are tested for "irregularities." In contrast, people who want to compete as men (cis or trans) are allowed to inject testosterone if their levels are seen as lower than "those naturally occurring in eugonadal men" (Gooren and Bunck 2004, 151). Thus, in this sex/gender/sexuality system, testosterone is a right of people claiming the category of "men." Further, while no athlete with a penis can compete as a woman, athletes are not required to have a penis to compete as men. Highlighting this point, "Will," an Australian transman who played football on a men's team, was required to undergo a hysterectomy in order to change his sex marker, but he was not required to have phalloplasty (Stark 2009). Moreover, his use of testosterone was not seen as an unfair advantage because his levels did not exceed those of an average cis-gender man.

The heightened attention to the presence or absence of a penis in spaces marked as "women only" was reflected in all of our cases. In news stories about the New York City birth certificate policy and the transgender rights bills, opponents frequently hinged their concerns on "male anatomies" (Cave 2006b) or "male genitalia" (Kwok 2006) in women's spaces. A common imagined interaction that generated gender panic was transwomen with "male anatomies" being housed with female prisoners (Cave 2006b; Staff 2006; Weiss 2006; Yoshino 2006), or transwomen "who still have male genitalia" using women's bathrooms (Kwok 2006; Yoshino 2006). While several articles included interviews with transmen activists who emphasized how hard it would be for them as people with facial hair to be forced to use a women's restroom on the basis of the sex marker on their birth certificates, only one opponent cited in the same articles used the example of transmen in the bathroom rather than transwomen.[6] Thus, biology-based gender ideologies were more likely to be deployed when debating transgender access to women's spaces. Those debates suggest that it is penises rather than other potential biological criteria that are the primary determiner of gender because male anatomies are framed as sexual threats toward women in gender-segregated spaces.

Separate and Unequal: Reproducing Gender Inequality in Gender-Segregated Spaces

Women-only spaces generate the most concern in these moments of gender ideology collision. In the resulting gender panics, ideas about "fairness" and "safety" work to naturalize gender difference and to maintain unequal gender relations. In these moments of ideological collision, two persistent ideologies about womanhood are deployed to counter identity-based determination of gender: Women are weaker than men, and, as a result, women are always at (hetero)sexual risk. This construction produces "woman" as a "vulnerable subjecthood" (Westbrook 2008), an idea that what it is to be part of the category of woman is to be always in danger and defenseless.[7] Conversely, men, or more specifically, penises, are imagined as sources of constant threat to women and children, an idea that reinforces a construction of heterosexual male desire as natural and uncontrollable. Women-only spaces, then, can be framed as androphobic and, as a result, heterophobic, due to the assumed inability of women to protect themselves from men combined with the assumption that all men are potential rapists. These ideas carry enough cultural power to temper institutional validation of identity-based determination of gender. What people are attempting to protect in these moments of ideological collision, we suggest, is not just women, but also the binary logic that gender-segregated spaces are predicated on and (re)produce.

Within the sports case, the IOC focused on the issue of fairness when determining when a transwoman can compete against cis-women. Attempting to maintain both the values of identity-based determination and the logic of gender difference that justifies gender-segregated athletic competitions, sports officials put transwomen athletes into a peculiar situation: In order to gain access to the chance to compete in tests of strength and endurance, they must first prove their weakness (Buzuvis 2010; Shy 2007). This equation of women with weakness also accounts for the regulation of women's, but not men's, sports: If women are inherently weak, they must be protected from competing with stronger bodies (e.g., men). Cis-men, in contrast, should not need such protection from people with XX chromosomes.

Gender panics around the issue of trans-athletes also focus on the question of safety. The United Kingdom's 2004 Gender Recognition Act, a law intended to grant more rights to transgender people, includes a provision that prohibits trans-athletes' competition in cases that endanger the "safety of competitors" (Cavanagh and Sykes 2006). Discussion of safety in this case revolved around regulating access to contact sports. Yet, during debate around this act, another meaning of safety surfaced. Lord Moynihan is reported as saying that "many people will be greatly concerned at the idea of themselves or their children being forced to share a changing room with a transsexual person" (Mcardle 2008, 46). The allusion is that transgender people present a sexual danger to vulnerable others, conflating transgenderism and sexual deviance.

This portrayal of transgender people as potential sexual dangers in gender-segregated spaces appeared repeatedly in our other two cases. People advocating biology-based determination of gender worried about protecting women and children, another group generally vested with vulnerable subjecthood, from sexual risk from people with penises who would, with the new policies, be legally able to enter women-only spaces. When opponents to the New York City birth certificate policy worried about "male anatomies" in women's prisons (Cave 2006b), they were hinting at the possibility that those "male anatomies" would sexually assault the women with whom they shared prison space. While most articles about the New York City proposal merely suggested this possibility, some were more explicit. An opinion piece argued that one of the dangers of the proposed law was "personal safety: Many communal spaces, like prison cells and public bathrooms, are segregated by sex to protect women, who are generally physically weaker than men, from assault or rape" (Yoshino 2006). Explaining his opposition to the transgender rights bill, New Hampshire Representative Robert Fesh similarly noted, "Parents are worried about their kids and sexual abuse" (Macarchuk 2009). In these imagined interactions, opponents to identity-based criteria for determining gender both rely upon and shore up an idea that women are uniquely susceptible to assault. Moreover, they position transwomen as dangerous, a perspective that is often used in other contexts to justify violence against them (Westbrook 2009).

Since the panics produced in these moments of ideology collision focus on the penis as uniquely terrifying, "gender panics" might more accurately be termed "penis panics." In these hypothetical interactions, opponents give penises the power to destroy the sanctity of women's spaces through their (presumed natural) propensity to rape. The imagined sexual threat takes three forms in the news stories we examined. Most commonly, the threat is stated in general terms, such as opponents claiming that passage of transgender rights bills in New Hampshire and Massachusetts would put "women and children at risk" (Love 2009) in public restrooms. Second, some opponents imagined cis-men pretending to be transwomen in order to gain access to women's restrooms for sexually nefarious purposes. Contesting the vague criteria of who counts as transgender, Representative Peyton Hinkle of New Hampshire stated his opposition to the bill by calling it an "invitation . . . to people with predatory tendencies to come and hide behind the fact that they are having a transgender experience" (Fahey 2009). A spokesperson for the Massachusetts Family Institute told a reporter that the anti-discrimination bill allowed sexual predators to enter women's restrooms under the "guise of gender confusion" (Nicas 2009). Finally, transwomen themselves (not cis-men pretending to be trans) are imagined as the potential threat. Dr. Paul McHugh, chair of the psychiatry department at Johns Hopkins University, is reported to have written an email protesting the proposed New York City policy that stated: "I've already heard of a 'transgendered' man who claimed at work to be 'a woman in a man's body but is a lesbian' and who had to be expelled from the ladies' restroom because he was propositioning women there" (Cave 2006b). In these imagined interactions, transwomen have legal permission to enter gender-segregated spaces without the proper biological credentials. As such, their presence transforms a nonsexual space into a dangerously (hetero)sexual one. Within this heteronormative logic, all bodies with male anatomies, regardless of gender identity, desire female bodies, and many of them (enough to elicit concern from the public) are willing to use force to get access to those bodies.[8]

That these imagined sexual assaults occur only in women-only spaces is worth further analysis, as women share space with men daily without similar concerns. We suggest that women-only spaces generate intense androphobia because, by definition, these spaces should not contain bodies with penises. If women are inherently unable to protect themselves, and men (or, more specifically, penises) are inherently dangerous (Hollander 2001), the entrance of a penis into women's space becomes terrifying because there are no other men there to protect the women. The "safe" (read: gender-segregated) space is transformed into a dangerous, sexual situation by the entrance of an "improper body." These fears rely

on and reproduce gender binarism, specifically the assumption of strong/weak difference in male/female bodies, as opponents assume that people who could be gaining access to women's space (people with penises) are inherently stronger than cis-women and easily able to overpower them.

This emphasis on the sexual threat of penises in women-only spaces shows that gender panics are not just about gender, but also about sexuality. In the sex/gender/sexuality system, all bodies are presumed heterosexual. This assumption makes gender-segregated spaces seem safe because they are then "sexuality-free zones." Because there are only two gender categories, gay men and lesbians must share gender-segregated spaces with heterosexual men and women, respectively, an entrance that is tolerated as long as such entrants demonstrate the appropriate visual cues for admittance and use the bathroom for the "right" purpose (waste elimination). The use of public restrooms for homosexual sex acts can, of course, create a panic (Cavanagh 2010). Gender-segregated spaces, then, can be conceived of as both homophobic and heterophobic, as the fear is about unwanted sexual acts in supposedly sex-neutral spaces. Unlike normative sexual interactions, where gender difference is required to make the interaction acceptable (Schilt and Westbrook 2009), in gender-segregated spaces, gender difference is a source of discomfort and potential sexual threat and danger. Rhetoric about women and children as inherently vulnerable to sexual threats taps into cultural anxieties about sexual predators and pedophiles, who are always imagined to be men (Levine 2002); such fears have been repeatedly successful in generating sex panics. Because unwanted sexual attention is seen as a danger to women and children, but rarely, if ever, as a danger to adult men (Vance 1984), men's spaces are not policed. This differential policing of gender-segregated spaces illustrates the cultural logics that uphold gender inequality and heteronormativity—two systems whose underlying logic necessitates male–female oppositeness.

CONCLUSION

In this article, we examine the process of determining gender. We argue that collisions of biology-based and identity-based ideologies in the liberal moment have produced a sex/gender/sexuality system where the criteria for determining gender vary across social spaces. Many people have long assumed that biological factors, such as chromosomes, are always the ultimate determiner of gender. Contrary to the dominant assumption, we suggest that the sex/gender/sexuality system is slowly changing. As it has encountered liberal values of self-determinism, the criteria for determining gender have shifted away from pure biological determinism. In nonsexual gender-integrated spaces, identity can be used to determine gender, as long as that identity is as a man or a woman (Schilt and Westbrook 2009). By contrast, in gender-segregated spaces, a combination of identity and body-based criteria is used, allowing someone to receive cultural and institutional support for a change of gender only if they undergo genital surgery. Finally, in heterosexual interactions, biology-based criteria (particularly genitals) are used to determine gender (Schilt and Westbrook 2009).

While most cis-gender people keep the same classification in all spaces, transgender people may be given different gender classifications by social actors depending on the type of interaction occurring in the space. Thus, one could speak of a trans-person's "social gender," "sexual gender," and "sports (or other gender-segregated space) gender." To illustrate this point, Kye Allums, a trans-man who played college basketball on a woman's team, has a social gender of "man" and a sports gender of "woman." Within the criteria for trans-athletes, he can continue to play basketball with women as long as he does not take testosterone or have genital surgery (Thomas 2010), a modification that would change his sports gender from "woman" to "man." Another way to conceptualize this point is to say that access to gender-integrated social spaces is determined by identity while access to gender-segregated spaces is mostly determined by biology, a point we summarize in Table 1.

The criteria for gender determination vary across social spaces because of the different imagined purposes of interactions that should occur in these settings. Heterosexual encounters and gender-segregated spaces both justify and reproduce an idea of two opposite genders. In spaces in which a higher level of oppositeness is required from participants, visual and behavioral gender cues often are not considered sufficient for determining gender and, instead, the participants must also demonstrate bodily oppositeness. Because heterosexual interactions and gender-segregated spaces rely on (and reproduce) gender binarism, it is these spaces where validation of identity-based determination of gender produces panics and biology-based gender ideologies reign. In contrast, validation of identity-based determination of gender is more likely to occur when it cannot be framed as endangering other people, particularly others seen as more worthy of protection than trans-people (cis-women and children). In gender-integrated workplaces, for example, coworkers may not feel endangered by working with a trans-man who has the "cultural genitals" to support his social identity as a man, such as facial hair, particularly if he identified himself as crossing from one side of the gender binary to the other (Schilt and Westbrook 2009). It is important to add, however, that, in these spaces, identity-based determination of gender is more likely to be accepted by others when the person in question is, in the social imagination, "penis free" (all trans-men as well as "post-op" trans-women), as the penis is culturally associated with power and danger. These attitudes have profound consequences for transgender rights.

Table 1 Criteria for Determining Gender across Contexts

	Nonsexual, gender-integrated	Nonsexual, gender-segregated	Heterosexual
Trans-men	Identity-based criteria determine gender. Changes to genitalia are not typically required to establish legitimacy of their gender.	Identity-based criteria determine gender. Changes to genitalia are not typically required to gain access to men's spaces.	Biology-based criteria determine gender. Changes to genitalia required. This criterion is not typically enforced in a violent way.
Trans-women	Identity-based criteria determine gender. Changes to genitalia are more typically required to establish legitimacy of their gender.	A combination of identity-based and biology-based criteria determine gender. Changes to genitalia are required to gain access to women's spaces.	Biology-based criteria determine gender. Changes to genitalia required. This criterion is often enforced in a violent way.

The criteria for determining gender also differ for placement in the category of "man" or "woman." Here, we have focused on the criteria for accessing women-only spaces because it is those spaces that produced the most panic in our media sources and that have the clearest criteria for admission. This focus of cultural anxiety on trans-women is unsurprising. We have detailed how the mainstream media portrayed trans-women as dangerous to heterosexual men because they use their feminine appearance to trick men into homosexual encounters (Schilt and Westbrook 2009; Westbrook 2009). In these cases, it is again trans-women who are portrayed as dangerous, yet this time they are positioned as endangering women and children.

We do not take the lack of attention to trans-men in men-only spaces to mean that trans-men are more accepted by people who vocally oppose trans-women. In contrast, we suggest that trans-men and trans-women are policed differently. Trans-men's perceived lack of a natural penis renders them, under the logic of vulnerable subjecthood, unable to be threatening (and, therefore, unlikely to generate public outcry). Cis-gender men, the group who would share a bathroom or locker room with trans-men, also are not seen in the public imagination as potential victims of sexual threat, as such an image is contradictory to cultural constructions of maleness and masculinity (Lucal 1995). Trans-men enter a liminal state, in some ways, as they cannot hurt men (making them women), but are not seen as needing protection from men (making them part of a "pariah femininity" [Schippers 2007] that no longer warrants protection). Thus, because of gender inequality, the criteria for the category "man" are much less strict than those for the category "woman," at least for access to gender-segregated spaces.

But why do genitals carry more weight in determining gender in these segregated spaces? Our research hints at three possible answers for further exploration. First, genitals are changeable criteria, unlike chromosomes, which allows for some validation of liberal values of self-determination. Second, male and female genitals are imagined to be opposite, so using them as the criteria for determining gender maintains a binaristic gender system. Finally, genitals play a central role in gender panics because gender and sexuality are inextricably intertwined. The social actors opposed to identity-based determination of gender assume that all bodies, regardless of gender identity, are heterosexual. Although genitals are not supposed to be used in interactions in gender-segregated spaces, a fear of their (mis)use drives the policing of bodies in those spaces, making sexuality a central force in deciding which criteria will be used to determine gender.

By using genitals as the criteria for determining gender, the sex/gender/sexuality system is able to adapt to new liberal ideals of self-determination and to withstand the threat that trans-people might pose to a rigid binary system of gender. Although the existence of transgender and genderqueer people is seen as capable of "undoing gender" (Deutsch 2007; Risman 2009), the binaristic gender system tends to adapt to and reabsorb trans-people (Schilt and Westbrook 2009; Westbrook 2010).

Rather than being undone, gender is constantly "redone" (Connell 2010; West and Zimmerman 2009). Like all other norms and social systems, people create gender. Challenges to the gender system modify rather than break it. Gender crossing can receive some validation in the liberal moment, but only when a binary remains unquestioned. By providing criteria for who can transition and how they can do it, the sex/gender/sexuality system is both altered and maintained.

NOTES

1. Following Kessler and McKenna (1978), we highlight the social construction of both "sex" and "gender" by using the term "gender" throughout this article, even in moments where most people use the term "sex" (e.g., "gender-segregated" rather than "sex-segregated"). We reserve "sex" for references to intercourse, unless using a specific term such as "sex marker".

2. We use the term "(hetero)sexuality" to highlight that when many social actors speak of "sexuality" they are inferring heterosexuality.

3. As sexuality and sexualization are social processes, it is difficult to draw a conceptual line between a sexual and nonsexual space. Workplaces, for example, can contain sexualized interactions, though the dominant understanding of a workplace might be nonsexual. We use this term to refer to settings in which the commonly agreed on purpose is nonsexual. Sexual interactions do, of course, occur in these settings, but many see such interactions as a violation of the expected purpose of these spaces.

4. It is notable that women athletes do not have to possess what would be considered female genitals in order to compete. The criteria for determining gender in sports are thus very similar to Kessler and McKenna's findings that "penis equals male but vagina does not equal female" (1978, 151) when determining gender.

5. This use of "sex hormones"—mainly the levels of testosterone—to determine gender emerged only in the sports case because of the belief that testosterone provides a competitive advantage.

6. The image of a trans-man in men-only spaces was referenced by opponents only once in our analysis. A conservative activist told a reporter that allowing "men" to go into women's bathrooms legally would create discomfort for women and put them at sexual risk. The reporter asked what bathroom transgender men should use, as their male appearance could also make cis-women uncomfortable in the bathroom. The activist replied, "They [trans-men] should use the women's bathroom, regardless of whom it makes uncomfortable because that's where they are supposed to go" (Ball 2009).

7. Often, it is actors with good intentions, such as antiviolence activists, who, in their attempt to protect a particular group, unintentionally (re)produce an idea that the group is constantly prone to attack and unable to protect themselves (Westbrook 2008).

8. The ability to harm others attributed to trans-people in these narratives should be problematized. The trans-people described by biological determiners function as monstrous specters, so there is often little nuance in these portrayals of trans lives. By contrast, arguments made for trans rights bills and for access to gender-segregated spaces often include descriptions of trans-people as victims of violence and harassment rather than as perpetrators.

REFERENCES

Ball, Molly. 2009. Robocall distorts record. *Las Vegas Review–Journal*, 6 April.

Berns, Nancy. 2004. *Framing the victim: Domestic violence, media, and social problems.* Somerset, NJ: Transaction.

Best, Joel. 2008. *Social problems*, 1st edition. New York: Norton.

Birrell, Susan, and Cheryl L. Cole. 1990. Double fault: Renee Richards and the construction and naturalization of difference. *Sociology of Sport Journal* 7:1–21.

Buzuvis, Erin. 2010. Caster Semenya and the myth of a level playing field. *The Modern American* 6:36–42.

Caruso, David. 2006a. New York City to ease rules for records reflecting gender change. *The Associated Press*, 6 October.

Caruso, David. 2006b. New York City seeks to ease rules for official documents reflecting gender change. *The Associated Press*, 7 November.

Cavanagh, Sheila. 2010. *Queering bathrooms: Gender, sexuality, and the hygienic imagination.* Toronto, Ontario, Canada: University of Toronto Press.

Cavanagh, Sheila L., and Heather Sykes. 2006. Transsexual bodies at the Olympics: The International Olympic Committee's policy on transsexual athletes at the 2004 Athens Summer Games. *Body & Society* 12:75–102.

Cave, Damien. 2006a. New York plans to make gender personal choice. *The New York Times*, 7 November.

Cave, Damien. 2006b. No change in definition of gender. *The New York Times*, 6 December.

Colangelo, Lisa. 2006. Change of sex IDs on city docket. *New York Daily News*, 25 September.

Connell, Catherine. 2010. Doing, undoing, or redoing gender? Learning from the workplace experiences of trans-people. *Gender & Society* 24:31–55.

Connell, Raewyn. 1995. *Masculinities.* Berkeley: University of California Press.

Currah, Paisley, and Lisa Jean Moore. 2009. We won't know who you are: Contesting sex designations in New York City birth certificates. *Hypatia* 24:113–35.

Deutsch, Francine M. 2007. Undoing gender. *Gender & Society* 21:106–27.

Distaso, John. 2009. No to marriage, "bathroom bills." *New Hampshire Union Leader*, 24 April.

Dreger, Alice. 2010. Sex typing for sport. *Hastings Center Report* 40:22–24.

Fahey, Tom. 2009. Transgender rights in "bathroom bill." *New Hampshire Union Leader*, 15 March.

Fausto-Sterling, Anne. 2000. *Sexing the body: Gender politics and the construction of sexuality.* New York: Basic Books.

Finn, Robin. 2006. Battling for one's true sexual identity. *The New York Times*, 10 November.

Gamson, William A., David Croteau, William Hoynes, and Theodore Sasson. 1992. Media images and the social construction of reality. *Annual Review of Sociology* 18:373–93.

Goffman, Erving. 1977. The arrangement between the sexes. *Theory and Society* 4:301–31.

Gooren, Louis, and Mathijs Bunck. 2004. Transsexuals and competitive sports. *European Journal of Endocrinology* 151:425–29.

Hollander, Jocelyn A. 2001. Vulnerability and dangerousness: The construction of gender through conversation about violence. *Gender & Society* 15:83–109.

International Olympic Committee Medical Commission. 2003. Statement of the Stockholm Consensus on sex reassignment in sports. http://www.olympic.org/Assets/ImportedNews/Documents/en_report_905.pdf.

International Olympic Committee Medical and Scientific Department. 2012. IOC regulations on female hyperandrogenism. http://www.olympic.org/Documents/Commissions_PDFfiles/Medical_commission/2012-06-22-IOC-Regulationson-Female-Hyperandrogenism-eng.pdf.

Jansen, Sue Curry. 2002. When the center no longer holds: Rupture and repair. In *Critical communication theory: Power, media, gender, and technology*, edited by Nick Couldry and James Curran. Lanham, MD: Rowman & Littlefield.

Kessler, Suzanne, and Wendy McKenna. 1978. *Gender: An ethnomethodological approach.* Chicago: University of Chicago Press.

Kwok, Stephan. 2006. N.Y. gender law not realistic. *Daily Trojan*, 10 November.

Letter to the Editor. 2009a. Seeking support against vaguely defined identities. *Sentinel & Enterprise*, 13 July.

Letter to the Editor. 2009b. Anti-discrimination ordinance would harm Kalamazoo County. *Kalamazoo Gazette*, 9 October.

Levine, Judith. 2002. *Harmful to minors*. Minneapolis: University of Minnesota Press.

Littleton v. Prange. 1999. No. 99-1214 (Tex. 18).

Ljungqvist, Arne, and Myron Genel. 2005. Transsexual athletes: When is competition fair? *Medicine and Sport* 366:S42–S43.

Lorber, Judith. 1993. Believing is seeing: Biology as ideology. *Gender & Society* 7:568–81.

Love, Norma. 2009. NH Senate committee rejects transgender plan. *The Associated Press*, 23 April.

Lowell Sun, The. 2009. Transgender rights bill passes in N.H. House. 8 April.

Lucal, Betsy. 1995. The problem with "battered husbands." *Deviant Behavior* 16:95–112.

Macarchuk, Alexis. 2009. N.H. transgender bill aims to extend protections. *University Wire*, 10 April.

Macdonald, Myra. 2003. *Exploring media discourse*. London: Arnold.

Mcardle, D. 2008. Swallows and amazons, or the sporting exception to the Gender Recognition Act. *Social & Legal Studies* 17:39–57.

Meadow, Tey. 2010. A rose is a rose: On producing legal gender classifications. *Gender & Society* 24:814–37.

Meyerowitz, Joanne. 2002. *How sex changed: A history of transsexuality in the United States*. Cambridge, MA: Harvard University Press.

Nicas, Jack. 2009. Downing backs transgender bill. *The Berkshire Eagle*, 20 February.

Nyong'o, Tavia. 2010. The unforgivable transgression of being Caster Semenya. *Women & Performance: A Journal of Feminist Theory* 20:95–100.

Prager, Dennis. 2010. Why activists connect men in dresses to same-sex marriage. *Creators Syndicate*, 31 May.

Prunier, Chanel. 2009. Transgender bill is misguided. *Telegram & Gazette*, 14 July.

Ring, Dan. 2009. Transgenders fighting for protection. *The Republican*, 15 July.

Risman, Barbara J. 2009. From doing to undoing: Gender as we know it. *Gender & Society* 23:81–84.

Schilt, Kristen. 2010. *Just one of the guys? Transgender men and the persistence of gender inequality*. Chicago: University of Chicago Press.

Schilt, Kristen, and Laurel Westbrook. 2009. Doing gender, doing heteronormativity: "Gender normals," transgender people, and the social maintenance of heterosexuality. *Gender & Society* 23:440–64.

Schippers, Mimi. 2007. Recovering the feminine other: Masculinity, femininity, and gender hegemony. *Theory & Society* 36:85–102.

Seidman, Steven. 1995. Deconstructing queer theory or the under-theorization of the social and the ethical. In *Social postmodernism: Beyond identity politics*, edited by Linda J. Nicholson and Steven Seidman. Cambridge, UK: Cambridge University Press.

Shy, Yael Lee Aura. 2007. Like any other girl: Male-to-female transsexuals and professional sports. *Sports Lawyers Journal* 14:95.

Staff. 2006. Facing facts Dec. 3–Dec. 9. *The New York Times*, 10 December.

Stark, Jill. 2009. I'm just an ordinary guy who wants to play footy. *Sunday Age*, 7 June.

Stryker, Susan. 2008. *Transgender history*. Seattle, WA: Seal Press.

Thomas, Katie. 2010. Transgender man is on women's team. *The New York Times*, 1 November.

Tucker, Ross, and Malcolm Collins. 2009. The science and management of sex verification in sport. *South African Journal of Sports Medicine* 21 (4):147–50.

Vance, Carol. 1984. *Pleasure and danger: Exploring female sexuality*. New York: Routledge.

Weiss, Jillian Todd. 2006. NYC rejects birth certificate change regs. Transgender Workplace Diversity (blog), 5 December, 2006, http://transworkplace.blogspot.com.

West, Candace, and Don Zimmerman. 1987. Doing gender. *Gender & Society* 1:125–51.

West, Candace, and Don H. Zimmerman. 2009. Accounting for doing gender. *Gender & Society* 23:112–22.

Westbrook, Laurel. 2008. Vulnerable subjecthood: The risks and benefits of the struggle for hate crime legislation. *Berkeley Journal of Sociology* 52:3–24.

Westbrook, Laurel. 2009. Violence matters: Producing gender, violence, and identity through accounts of murder. Ph.D. diss., University of California, Berkeley, CA.

Westbrook, Laurel. 2010. Becoming knowably gendered: The production of transgender possibilities in the mass and alternative press. In *Transgender identities: Towards a social analysis of gender diversity*, edited by Sally Hines and Tam Sanger. London: Routledge.

Yoshino, Kenji. 2006. Sex and the city. *Slate Magazine*, 11 December.

8

What It Means to Be Gendered Me

Life on the Boundaries of a Dichotomous Gender System

BETSY LUCAL

I understood the concept of "doing gender" (West and Zimmerman 1987) long before I became a sociologist. I have been living with the consequences of inappropriate "gender display" (Goffman 1976; West and Zimmerman 1987) for as long as I can remember.

My daily experiences are a testament to the rigidity of gender in our society, to the real implications of "two and only two" when it comes to sex and gender categories (Garfinkel 1967; Kessler and McKenna 1978). Each day, I experience the consequences that our gender system has for my identity and interactions. I am a woman who has been called "Sir" so many times that I no longer even hesitate to assume that it is being directed at me. I am a woman whose use of public rest rooms regularly causes reactions ranging from confused stares to confrontations over what a man is doing in the women's room. I regularly enact a variety of practices either to minimize the need for others to know my gender or to deal with their misattributions.

I am the embodiment of Lorber's (1994) ostensibly paradoxical assertion that the "gender bending" I engage in actually might serve to preserve and perpetuate gender categories. As a feminist who sees gender rebellion as a significant part of her contribution to the dismantling of sexism, I find this possibility disheartening.

In this article, I examine how my experiences both support and contradict Lorber's (1994) argument using my own experiences to illustrate and reflect on the social construction of gender. My analysis offers a discussion of the consequences of gender for people who do not follow the rules as well as an examination of the possible implications of the existence of people like me for the gender system itself. Ultimately, I show how life on the boundaries of gender affects me and how my life, and the lives of others who make similar decisions about their participation in the gender system, has the potential to subvert gender.

Because this article analyzes my experiences as a woman who often is mistaken for a man, my focus is on the social construction of gender for women. My assumption is that, given the gendered nature of the gendering process itself, men's experiences of this phenomenon might well be different from women's.

THE SOCIAL CONSTRUCTION OF GENDER

. . . We apply gender labels for a variety of reasons; for example, an individual's gender cues our interactions

Betsy Lucal, "What It Means to Be Gendered Me: Life on the Boundaries of a Dichotomous Gender System," from *Gender & Society,* Volume 13/1999, pp. 781–797. Copyright © 1999 Sage Publications, Inc. Reprinted by permission of SAGE Publications.

with her or him. Successful social relations require all participants to present, monitor, and interpret gender displays (Martin 1998; West and Zimmerman 1987). We have, according to Lorber, "no social place for a person who is neither woman nor man" (1994, 96); that is, we do not know how to interact with such a person. There is, for example, no way of addressing such a person that does not rely on making an assumption about the person's gender ("Sir" or "Ma'am"). In this context, gender is "omnirelevant" (West and Zimmerman 1987). Also, given the sometimes fractious nature of interactions between men and women, it might be particularly important for women to know the gender of the strangers they encounter, do the women need to be wary, or can they relax (Devor 1989)?

According to Kessler and McKenna (1978), each time we encounter a new person, we make a gender attribution. In most cases, this is not difficult. We learn how to read people's genders by learning which traits culturally signify each gender and by learning rules that enable us to classify individuals with a wide range of gender presentations into two and only two gender categories. As Weston observed, "Gendered traits are called attributes for a reason: People attribute traits to others. No one possesses them. Traits are the product of evaluation" (1996, 21). The fact that most people use the same traits and rules in presenting genders makes it easier for us to attribute genders to them.

We also assume that we can place each individual into one of two mutually exclusive categories in this binary system. As Bem (1993) notes, we have a polarized view of gender; there are two groups that are seen as polar opposites. Although there is "no rule for deciding 'male' or 'female' that will always work" and no attributes "that always and without exception are true of only one gender" (Kessler and McKenna 1978, 158), we operate under the assumption that there are such rules and attributes. . . .

Not only do we rely on our social skills in attributing genders to others, but we also use our skills to present our own genders to them. The roots of this understanding of how gender operates lie in Goffman's (1959) analysis of the "presentation of self in everyday life," elaborated later in his work on "gender display" (Goffman 1976). From this perspective, gender is a performance, "a stylized repetition of acts" (Butler 1990, 140, emphasis removed). Gender display refers to "conventionalized portrayals" of social correlates of gender (Goffman 1976). These displays are culturally established sets of behaviors, appearances, mannerisms, and other cues that we have learned to associate with members of a particular gender. . . .

A person who fails to establish a gendered appearance that corresponds to the person's gender faces challenges to her or his identity and status. First, the gender nonconformist must find a way in which to construct an identity in a society that denies her or him any legitimacy (Bem 1993). A person is likely to want to define herself or himself as "normal" in the face of cultural evidence to the contrary. Second, the individual also must deal with other people's challenges to identity and status—deciding how to respond, what such reactions to their appearance mean, and so forth.

Because our appearances, mannerisms, and so forth constantly are being read as part of our gender display, we do gender whether we intend to or not. For example, a woman athlete, particularly one participating in a nonfeminine sport such as basketball, might deliberately keep her hair long to show that, despite actions that suggest otherwise, she is a "real" (i.e., feminine) woman. But we also do gender in less conscious ways such as when a man takes up more space when sitting than a woman does. In fact, in a society so clearly organized around gender, as ours is, there is no way in which to not do gender (Lorber 1994).

Given our cultural rules for identifying gender (i.e., that there are only two and that masculinity is assumed in the absence of evidence to the contrary), a person who does not do gender appropriately is placed not into a third category but rather into the one with which her or his gender display seems most closely to fit; that is, if a man appears to be a woman, then he will be categorized as "woman," not as something else. Even if a person does not want to do gender or would like to do a gender other than the two recognized by our society, other people will, in effect, do gender for that person by placing her or him in one and only one of the two available categories. We cannot escape doing gender or, more specifically, doing one of two genders. (There are exceptions in limited contexts such as people doing "drag" [Butler 1990; Lorber 1994].)

People who follow the norms of gender can take their genders for granted. Kessler and McKenna asserted,

"Few people besides transsexuals think of their gender as anything other than 'naturally' obvious"; they believe that the risks of not being taken for the gender intended "are minimal for nontranssexuals" (1978, 126). However, such an assertion overlooks the experiences of people such as those women Devor (1989) calls "gender blenders" and those people Lorber (1994) refers to as "gender benders." As West and Zimmerman (1987) pointed out, we all are held accountable for, and might be called on to account for, our genders.

People who, for whatever reasons, do not adhere to the rules, risk gender misattribution and any interactional consequences that might result from this misidentification. What are the consequences of misattribution for social interaction? When must misattribution be minimized? What will one do to minimize such mistakes? In this article, I explore these and related questions using my biography.

For me, the social processes and structures of gender mean that, in the context of our culture, my appearance will be read as masculine. Given the common conflation of sex and gender, I will be assumed to be a male. Because of the two-and-only-two genders rule, I will be classified, perhaps more often than not, as a man—not as an atypical woman, not as a genderless person. I must be one gender or the other; I cannot be neither, nor can I be both. This norm has a variety of mundane and serious consequences for my everyday existence. Like Myhre (1995), I have found that the choice not to participate in femininity is not one made frivolously.

My experiences as a woman who does not do femininity illustrate a paradox of our two-and-only-two gender system. Lorber argued that "bending gender rules and passing between genders does not erode but rather preserves gender boundaries" (1994, 21). Although people who engage in these behaviors and appearances do "demonstrate the social constructedness of sex, sexuality, and gender" (Lorber 1994, 96), they do not actually disrupt gender. Devor made a similar point: "When gender blending females refused to mark themselves by publicly displaying sufficient femininity to be recognized as women, they were in no way challenging patriarchal gender assumptions" (1989, 142). As the following discussion shows, I have found that my own experiences both support and challenge this argument. . . .

GENDERED ME

Each day, I negotiate the boundaries of gender. Each day, I face the possibility that someone will attribute the "wrong" gender to me based on my physical appearance.

I am six feet tall and large-boned. I have had short hair for most of my life. For the past several years, I have worn a crew cut or flat top. I do not shave or otherwise remove hair from my body (e.g., no eyebrow plucking). I do not wear dresses, skirts, high heels, or makeup. My only jewelry is a class ring, a "men's" watch (my wrists are too large for a "women's" watch), two small earrings (gold hoops, both in my left ear), and (occasionally) a necklace. I wear jeans or shorts, T-shirts, sweaters, polo/golf shirts, button-down collar shirts, and tennis shoes or boots. The jeans are "women's" (I do have hips) but do not look particularly "feminine." The rest of the outer garments are from men's departments. I prefer baggy clothes, so the fact that I have "womanly" breasts often is not obvious (I do not wear a bra). Sometimes, I wear a baseball cap or some other type of hat. I also am white and relatively young (30 years old).[1]

My gender display—what others interpret as my presented identity—regularly leads to the misattribution of my gender. An incongruity exists between my gender self-identity and the gender that others perceive. In my encounters with people I do not know, I sometimes conclude, based on our interactions, that they think I am a man. This does not mean that other people do not think I am a man, just that I have no way of knowing what they think without interacting with them.

Living with It

I have no illusions or delusions about my appearance. I know that my appearance is likely to be read as "masculine" (and male) and that how I see myself is socially irrelevant. Given our two-and-only-two gender structure, I must live with the consequences of my appearance. These consequences fall into two categories: issues of identity and issues of interaction.

My most common experience is being called "Sir" or being referred to by some other masculine linguistic marker (e.g., "he," "man"). This has happened for years for as long as I can remember, when having encounters with people I do not know.[2] Once, in fact, the same worker at a fast-food restaurant called me "Ma'am" when she took my order and "Sir" when she gave it to me.

Using my credit cards sometimes is a challenge. Some clerks subtly indicate their disbelief, looking from the card to me and back at the card and checking my signature carefully. Others challenge my use of the card, asking whose it is or demanding identification. One cashier asked to see my driver's license and then asked me whether I was the son of the cardholder. Another clerk told me that my signature on the receipt "had better match" the one on the card. Presumably, this was her way of letting me know that she was not convinced it was my credit card.

My identity as a woman also is called into question when I try to use women-only spaces. Encounters in public rest rooms are an adventure. I have been told countless times that "This is the ladies' room." Other women say nothing to me, but their stares and conversations with others let me know what they think. I will hear them say, for example, "There was a man in there." I also get stares when I enter a locker room. However, it seems that women are less concerned about my presence there, perhaps because, given that it is a space for changing clothes, showering, and so forth, they will be able to make sure that I am really a woman. Dressing rooms in department stores also are problematic spaces. I remember shopping with my sister once and being offered a chair outside the room when I began to accompany her into the dressing room.

Women who believe that I am a man do not want me in women-only spaces. For example, one woman would not enter the rest room until I came out, and others have told me that I am in the wrong place. They also might not want to encounter me while they are alone. For example, seeing me walking at night when they are alone might be scary.[3]

I, on the other hand, am not afraid to walk alone, day or night. I do not worry that I will be subjected to the public harassment that many women endure (Gardner 1995). I am not a clear target for a potential rapist. I rely on the fact that a potential attacker would not want to attack a big man by mistake. This is not to say that men never are attacked, just that they are not viewed, and often do not view themselves, as being vulnerable to attack.

Being perceived as a man has made me privy to male–male interactional styles of which most women

are not aware. I found out, quite by accident, that many men greet, or acknowledge, people (mostly other men) who make eye contact with them with a single nod. For example, I found that when I walked down the halls of my brother's all-male dormitory making eye contact, men nodded their greetings at me. Oddly enough, these same men did not greet my brother; I had to tell him about making eye contact and nodding as a greeting ritual. Apparently, in this case I was doing masculinity better than he was!

I also believe that I am treated differently, for example, in auto parts stores (staffed almost exclusively by men in most cases) because of the assumption that I am a man. Workers there assume that I know what I need and that my questions are legitimate requests for information. I suspect that I am treated more fairly than a feminine-appearing woman would be. I have not been able to test this proposition. However, Devor's participants did report "being treated more respectfully" (1989, 132) in such situations.

There is, however, a negative side to being assumed to be a man by other men. Once, a friend and I were driving in her car when a man failed to stop at an intersection and nearly crashed into us. As we drove away, I mouthed "stop sign" to him. When we both stopped our cars at the next intersection, he got out of his car and came up to the passenger side of the car, where I was sitting. He yelled obscenities at us and pounded and spit on the car window. Luckily, the windows were closed. I do not think he would have done that if he thought I was a woman. This was the first time I realized that one of the implications of being seen as a man was that I might be called on to defend myself from physical aggression from other men who felt challenged by me. This was a sobering and somewhat frightening thought.

Recently, I was verbally accosted by an older man who did not like where I had parked my car. As I walked down the street to work, he shouted that I should park at the university rather than on a side street nearby. I responded that it was a public street and that I could park there if I chose. He continued to yell, but the only thing I caught was the last part of what he said: "Your tires are going to get cut!" Based on my appearance that day—I was dressed casually and carrying a backpack, and I had my hat on backward—I believe he thought that I was a young male student rather than a female professor. I do not think he would have yelled at a person he thought to be a woman—and perhaps especially not a woman professor.

Given the presumption of heterosexuality that is part of our system of gender, my interactions with women who assume that I am a man also can be viewed from that perspective. For example, once my brother and I were shopping when we were "hit on" by two young women. The encounter ended before I realized what had happened. It was only when we walked away that I told him that I was pretty certain that they had thought both of us were men. A more common experience is realizing that when I am seen in public with one of my women friends, we are likely to be read as a heterosexual dyad. It is likely that if I were to walk through a shopping mall holding hands with a woman, no one would look twice, not because of their open-mindedness toward lesbian couples but rather because of their assumption that I was the male half of a straight couple. Recently, when walking through a mall with a friend and her infant, my observations of others' responses to us led me to believe that many of them assumed that we were a family on an outing, that is, that I was her partner and the father of the child.

Dealing with It

Although I now accept that being mistaken for a man will be a part of my life so long as I choose not to participate in femininity, there have been times when I consciously have tried to appear more feminine. I did this for a while when I was an undergraduate and again recently when I was on the academic job market. The first time, I let my hair grow nearly down to my shoulders and had it permed. I also grew long fingernails and wore nail polish. Much to my chagrin, even then one of my professors, who did not know my name, insistently referred to me in his kinship examples as "the son." Perhaps my first act on the way to my current stance was to point out to this man, politely and after class, that I was a woman.

More recently, I again let my hair grow out for several months, although I did not alter other aspects of my appearance. Once my hair was about two and a half inches long (from its original quarter inch), I realized, based on my encounters with strangers, that I had more or less passed back into the category of "woman."

Then, when I returned to wearing a flat top, people again responded to me as if I were a man.

Because of my appearance, much of my negotiation of interactions with strangers involves attempts to anticipate their reactions to me. I need to assess whether they will be likely to assume that I am a man and whether that actually matters in the context of our encounters. Many times, my gender really is irrelevant, and it is just annoying to be misidentified. Other times, particularly when my appearance is coupled with something that identifies me by name (e.g., a check or credit card) without a photo, I might need to do something to ensure that my identity is not questioned. As a result of my experiences, I have developed some techniques to deal with gender misattribution.

In general, in unfamiliar public places, I avoid using the rest room because I know that it is a place where there is a high likelihood of misattribution and where misattribution is socially important. If I must use a public rest room, I try to make myself look as non-threatening as possible. I do not wear a hat, and I try to rearrange my clothing to make my breasts more obvious. Here, I am trying to use my secondary sex characteristics to make my gender more obvious rather than the usual use of gender to make sex obvious. While in the rest room, I never make eye contact, and I get in and out as quickly as possible. Going in with a woman friend also is helpful; her presence legitimizes my own. People are less likely to think I am entering a space where I do not belong when I am with someone who looks like she does belong.[4]

To those women who verbally challenge my presence in the rest room, I reply, "I know," usually in an annoyed tone. When they stare or talk about me to the women they are with, I simply get out as quickly as possible. In general, I do not wait for someone I am with because there is too much chance of an unpleasant encounter.

I stopped trying on clothes before purchasing them a few years ago because my presence in the changing areas was met with stares and whispers. Exceptions are stores where the dressing rooms are completely private, where there are individual stalls rather than a room with stalls separated by curtains, or where business is slow and no one else is trying on clothes. If I am trying on a garment clearly intended for a woman, then I usually can do so without hassle. I guess the attendants assume that I must be a woman if I have, for example, a women's bathing suit in my hand. But usually, I think it is easier for me to try the clothes on at home and return them, if necessary, rather than risk creating a scene. Similarly, when I am with another woman who is trying on clothes, I just wait outside.

My strategy with credit cards and checks is to anticipate wariness on a clerk's part. When I sense that there is some doubt or when they challenge me, I say, "It's my card." I generally respond courteously to requests for photo ID, realizing that these might be routine checks because of concerns about increasingly widespread fraud. But for the clerk who asked for ID and still did not think it was my card, I had a stronger reaction. When she said that she was sorry for embarrassing me, I told her that I was not embarrassed but that she should be. I also am particularly careful to make sure that my signature is consistent with the back of the card. Faced with such situations, I feel somewhat nervous about signing my name—which, of course, makes me worry that my signature will look different from how it should.

Another strategy I have been experimenting with is wearing nail polish in the dark bright colors currently fashionable. I try to do this when I travel by plane. Given more stringent travel regulations, one always must present a photo ID. But my experiences have shown that my driver's license is not necessarily convincing. Nail polish might be. I also flash my polished nails when I enter airport rest rooms, hoping that they will provide a clue that I am indeed in the right place.

There are other cases in which the issues are less those of identity than of all the norms of interaction that, in our society, are gendered. My most common response to misattribution actually is to appear to ignore it, that is, to go on with the interaction as if nothing out of the ordinary has happened. Unless I feel that there is a good reason to establish my correct gender, I assume the identity others impose on me for the sake of smooth interaction. For example, if someone is selling me a movie ticket, then there is no reason to make sure that the person has accurately discerned my gender. Similarly, if it is clear that the person using "Sir" is talking to me, then I simply respond as appropriate. I accept the designation because it is irrelevant to the situation. It takes enough effort to be alert for misattributions and to decide which of them matter;

responding to each one would take more energy than it is worth.

Sometimes, if our interaction involves conversation, my first verbal response is enough to let the other person know that I am actually a woman and not a man. My voice apparently is "feminine" enough to shift people's attributions to the other category. I know when this has happened by the apologies that usually accompany the mistake. I usually respond to the apologies by saying something like "No problem" and/or "It happens all the time." Sometimes, a misattributor will offer an account for the mistake, for example, saying that it was my hair or that they were not being very observant.

These experiences with gender and misattribution provide some theoretical insights into contemporary Western understandings of gender and into the social structure of gender in contemporary society. Although there are a number of ways in which my experiences confirm the work of others, there also are some ways in which my experiences suggest other interpretations and conclusions.

WHAT DOES IT MEAN?

Gender is pervasive in our society. I cannot choose not to participate in it. Even if I try not to do gender, other people will do it for me. That is, given our two-and-only-two rule, they must attribute one of two genders to me. Still, although I cannot choose not to participate in gender, I can choose not to participate in femininity (as I have), at least with respect to physical appearance.

That is where the problems begin. Without the decorations of femininity, I do not look like a woman. That is, I do not look like what many people's commonsense understanding of gender tells them a woman looks like. How I see myself, even how I might wish others would see me, is socially irrelevant. It is the gender that I *appear* to be (my "perceived gender") that is most relevant to my social identity and interactions with others. The major consequence of this fact is that I must be continually aware of which gender I "give off" as well as which gender I "give" (Goffman 1959).

Because my gender self-identity is "not displayed obviously, immediately, and consistently" (Devor 1989, 58), I am somewhat of a failure in social terms with respect to gender. Causing people to be uncertain or wrong about one's gender is a violation of taken-for-granted rules that leads to embarrassment and discomfort; it means that something has gone wrong with the interaction (Garfinkel 1967; Kessler and McKenna 1978). This means that my nonresponse to misattribution is the more socially appropriate response; I am allowing others to maintain face (Goffman 1959, 1967). By not calling attention to their mistakes, I uphold their images of themselves as competent social actors. I also maintain my own image as competent by letting them assume that I am the gender I appear to them to be.

But I still have discreditable status; I carry a stigma (Goffman 1963). Because I have failed to participate appropriately in the creation of meaning with respect to gender (Devor 1989), I can be called on to account for my appearance. If discredited, I show myself to be an incompetent social actor. I am the one not following the rules, and I will pay the price for not providing people with the appropriate cues for placing me in the gender category to which I really belong.

I do think that it is, in many cases, safer to be read as a man than as some sort of deviant woman. "Man" is an acceptable category; it fits properly into people's gender worldview. Passing as a man often is the "path of least resistance" (Devor 1989; Johnson 1997). For example, in situations where gender does not matter, letting people take me as a man is easier than correcting them.

Conversely, as Butler noted, "We regularly punish those who fail to do their gender right" (1990, 140). Feinberg maintained, "Masculine girls and women face terrible condemnation and brutality—including sexual violence—for crossing the boundary of what is 'acceptable' female expression" (1996, 114). People are more likely to harass me when they perceive me to be a woman who looks like a man. For example, when a group of teenagers realized that I was not a man because one of their mothers identified me correctly, they began to make derogatory comments when I passed them. One asked, for example, "Does she have a penis?"

Because of the assumption that a "masculine" woman is a lesbian, there is the risk of homophobic reactions (Gardner 1995; Lucal 1997). Perhaps surprisingly, I find that I am much more likely to be taken for a man than for a lesbian, at least based on my interactions with people and their reactions to me. This might be because people are less likely to reveal that they

have taken me for a lesbian because it is less relevant to an encounter or because they believe this would be unacceptable. But I think it is more likely a product of the strength of our two-and-only-two system. I give enough masculine cues that I am seen not as a deviant woman but rather as a man, at least in most cases. The problem seems not to be that people are uncertain about my gender, which might lead them to conclude that I was a lesbian once they realized I was a woman. Rather, I seem to fit easily into a gender category—just not the one with which I identify.

In fact, because men represent the dominant gender in our society, being mistaken for a man can protect me from other types of gendered harassment. Because men can move around in public spaces safely (at least relative to women), a "masculine" woman also can enjoy this freedom (Devor 1989).

On the other hand, my use of particular spaces—those designated as for women only—may be challenged. Feinberg provided an intriguing analysis of the public restroom experience. She characterized women's reactions to a masculine person in a public restroom as "an example of genderphobia" (1996, 117), viewing such women as policing gender boundaries rather than believing that there really is a man in the women's restroom. She argued that women who truly believed that there was a man in their midst would react differently. Although this is an interesting perspective on her experiences, my experiences do not lead to the same conclusion.[5] Enough people have said to me that "This is the ladies' room" or have said to their companions that "There was a man in there" that I take their reactions at face value.

Still, if the two-and-only-two gender system is to be maintained, participants must be involved in policing the categories and their attendant identities and spaces. Even if policing boundaries is not explicitly intended, boundary maintenance is the effect of such responses to people's gender displays.

Boundaries and margins are an important component of both my experiences of gender and our theoretical understanding of gendering processes. I am, in effect, both woman and not-woman. As a woman who often is a social man but who also is a woman living in a patriarchal society, I am in a unique position to see and act. I sometimes receive privileges usually limited to men, and I sometimes am oppressed by my status as a deviant woman. I am, in a sense, an outsider-within (Collins 1991). Positioned on the boundaries of gender categories, I have developed a consciousness that I hope will prove transformative (Anzaldua 1987).

In fact, one of the reasons why I decided to continue my nonparticipation in femininity was that my sociological training suggested that this could be one of my contributions to the eventual dismantling of patriarchal gender constructs. It would be my way of making the personal political. I accepted being taken for a man as the price I would pay to help subvert patriarchy. I believed that all of the inconveniences I was enduring meant that I actually was doing something to bring down the gender structures that entangled all of us.

Then, I read Lorber's (1994) *Paradoxes of Gender* and found out, much to my dismay, that I might not actually be challenging gender after all. Because of the way in which doing gender works in our two-and-only-two system, gender displays are simply read as evidence of one of the two categories. Therefore, gender bending, blending, and passing between the categories do not question the categories themselves. If one's social gender and personal (true) gender do not correspond, then this is irrelevant unless someone notices the lack of congruence.

This reality brings me to a paradox of my experiences. First, not only do others assume that I am one gender or the other, but I also insist that I *really am* a member of one of the two gender categories. That is, I am female; I self-identify as a woman. I do not claim to be some other gender or to have no gender at all. I simply place myself in the wrong category according to stereotypes and cultural standards; the gender I present, or that some people perceive me to be presenting, is inconsistent with the gender with which I identify myself as well as with the gender I could be "proven" to be. Socially, I display the wrong gender; personally, I identify as the proper gender.

Second, although I ultimately would like to see the destruction of our current gender structure, I am not to the point of personally abandoning gender. Right now, I do not want people to see me as genderless as much as I want them to see me as a woman. That is, I would like to expand the category of "woman" to include people like me. I, too, am deeply embedded in our gender system, even though I do not play by many of its rules. For me, as for most people in our society, gender is a

substantial part of my personal identity (Howard and Hollander 1997). Socially, the problem is that I do not present a gender display that is consistently read as feminine. In fact, I consciously do not participate in the trappings of femininity. However, I do identify myself as a woman, not as a man or as someone outside of the two-and-only-two categories.

Yet, I do believe, as Lorber (1994) does, that the purpose of gender, as it currently is constructed, is to oppress women. Lorber analyzed gender as a "process of creating distinguishable social statuses for the assignment of rights and responsibilities" that ends up putting women in a devalued and oppressed position (1994, 32). As Martin put it, "Bodies that clearly delineate gender status facilitate the maintenance of the gender hierarchy" (1998, 495).

For society, gender means difference (Lorber 1994). The erosion of the boundaries would problematize that structure. Therefore, for gender to operate as it currently does, the category "woman" *cannot* be expanded to include people like me. The maintenance of the gender structure is dependent on the creation of a few categories that are mutually exclusive, the members of which are as different as possible (Lorber 1994). It is the clarity of the boundaries between the categories that allows gender to be used to assign rights and responsibilities as well as resources and rewards.

It is that part of gender—what it is used for—that is most problematic. Indeed, is it not *patriarchal*—or, even more specifically, *heteropatriarchal*—constructions of gender that are actually the problem? It is not the differences between men and women, or the categories themselves, so much as the meanings ascribed to the categories and, even more important, the hierarchical nature of gender under patriarchy that is the problem (Johnson 1997). Therefore, I am rebelling not against my femaleness or even my womanhood; instead, I am protesting contemporary constructions of femininity and, at least indirectly, masculinity under patriarchy. We do not, in fact, know what gender would look like if it were not constructed around heterosexuality in the context of patriarchy.

Although it is possible that the end of patriarchy would mean the end of gender, it is at least conceivable that something like what we now call gender could exist in a postpatriarchal future. The two-and-only-two categorization might well disappear, there being no hierarchy for it to justify. But I do not think that we should make the assumption that gender and patriarchy are synonymous. . . .

. . . In a recent book, *The Gender Knot,* Johnson (1997) argued that when it comes to gender and patriarchy, most of us follow the paths of least resistance; we "go along to get along," allowing our actions to be shaped by the gender system. Collectively, our actions help patriarchy maintain and perpetuate a system of oppression and privilege. Thus, by withdrawing our support from this system by choosing paths of greater resistance, we can start to chip away at it. Many people participate in gender because they cannot imagine any alternatives. In my classroom, and in my interactions and encounters with strangers, my presence can make it difficult for people not to see that there *are* other paths. In other words, following from West and Zimmerman (1987), I can subvert gender by doing it differently. . . .

NOTES

1. I obviously have left much out by not examining my gendered experiences in the context of race, age, class, sexuality, region, and so forth. Such a project clearly is more complex. As Weston pointed out, gender presentations are complicated by other statuses of their presenters: "What it takes to kick a person over into another gendered category can differ with race, class, religion, and time" (1996, 168). Furthermore, I am well aware that my whiteness allows me to assume that my experiences are simply a product of gender. For now, suffice it to say that it is my privileged position on some of these axes and my more disadvantaged position on others that combine to delineate my overall experience.

2. In fact, such experiences are not always limited to encounters with strangers. My grandmother, who does not see me often, twice has mistaken me for either my brother-in-law or some unknown man.

3. My experiences in rest rooms and other public spaces might be very different if I were, say, African American rather than white. Given the stereotypes of African American men, I think that white women would react very differently to encountering me.

4. I also have noticed that there are certain types of rest rooms in which I will not be verbally challenged; the higher the social status of the place, the less likely I will be harassed. For example, when I go to the theater, I might get stared at, but my presence never has been challenged.

5. An anonymous reviewer offered one possible explanation for this. Women see women's rest rooms as their space; they feel safe, and even empowered, there. Instead of fearing men in such space, they might instead pose a threat to any man who might intrude. Their invulnerability in this situation is, of course, not physically based but rather socially constructed. I thank the reviewer for this suggestion.

REFERENCES

Anzaldua, G. 1987. *Borderlands/La Frontera.* San Francisco: Aunt Lute Books.

Bem, S. L. 1993. *The lenses of gender.* New Haven, CT: Yale University Press.

Butler, J. 1990. *Gender trouble.* New York: Routledge.

Collins, P. H. 1991. *Black feminist thought.* New York: Routledge.

Devor, H. 1989. *Gender blending: Confronting the limits of duality.* Bloomington: Indiana University Press.

Feinberg, L. 1996. *Transgender warriors.* Boston: Beacon.

Gardner, C. B. 1995. *Passing by: Gender and public harassment.* Berkeley: University of California.

Garfinkel, H. 1967. *Studies in ethnomethodology.* Englewood Cliffs, NJ: Prentice Hall.

Goffman, E. 1959. *The presentation of self in everyday life.* Garden City, NY: Doubleday.

Goffman, E. 1963. *Stigma.* Englewood Cliffs, NJ: Prentice Hall.

Goffman, E. 1967. *Interaction ritual.* New York: Anchor/ Doubleday.

Goffman, E. 1976. Gender display. *Studies in the Anthropology of Visual Communication* 3:69–77.

Howard, J. A., and J. Hollander. 1997. *Gendered situations, gendered selves.* Thousand Oaks, CA: Sage.

Kessler, S. J., and W. McKenna. 1978. *Gender: An ethnomethodological approach.* New York: John Wiley.

Johnson, A. G. 1997. *The gender knot: Unraveling our patriarchal legacy.* Philadelphia: Temple University Press.

Lorber, J. 1996. Beyond the binaries: Depolarizing the categories of sex, sexuality, and gender. *Sociological Inquiry* 66:143–59.

Lucal, B. 1997. "Hey, this is the ladies' room!": Gender misattribution and public harassment. *Perspectives on Social Problems* 9:43–57.

Martin, K. A. 1998. Becoming a gendered body: Practices of preschools. *American Sociological Review* 63:494–511.

Myhre, J. R. M. 1995. One bad hair day too many, or the hairstory of an androgynous young feminist. In *Listen up: Voices from the next feminist generation,* edited by B. Findlen. Seattle, WA: Seal Press.

West, C., and D. H. Zimmerman. 1987. Doing gender. *Gender & Society* 1:125–51.

Weston, K. 1996. *Render me, gender me.* New York: Columbia University Press.

9

Morality and Health: News Media Constructions of Overweight and Eating Disorders

Abigail C. Saguy

Kjerstin Gruys

In 2005, in the wealthy suburbs of Richmond, Virginia, Emily and Mark Krudys' ten-year-old daughter, Katherine, was diagnosed with anorexia, and her parents were desperate for a cure. "Emily and Mark tried everything. They were firm. Then they begged their daughter to eat. Then they bribed her. We'll buy you a pony, they told her. But nothing worked" (Tyre 2005). Finally, Katherine was admitted for inpatient treatment at a children's hospital in another town. During the two months of her daughter's treatment, Emily stayed nearby so that she could attend family-therapy sessions. After Katherine was released, Emily homeschooled her while Katherine regained strength. Considered a success story, *Newsweek* reported that Katherine entered sixth grade in fall of 2005: "She's got the pony, and she's become an avid horsewoman, sometimes riding five or six times a week . . . But the anxiety still lingers. When Katherine says she's hungry, Emily has been known to drop everything and whip up a three-course meal" (Tyre 2005).

Only a short drive away, in Washington, DC, Leslie Abbott, a black single mother, was dealing with a very different food battle. She had lost custody of her son Terrell after months of fighting neglect charges related to his body weight. Known to his friends as "Heavy-T," Terrell had recently been released from an inpatient weight-loss program, but—once at home—had gained weight. Leslie explained to a reporter why it was unfair for public authorities to blame her for Terrell's backslide: "This boy is 15, going to be 16 years old. I can't watch him 24 hours a day. They want me to hold his hand, take him to the Y, make him eat salad" (Eaton 2007). Leslie said she would have had to quit her minimum-wage job in order to follow the health regimen suggested by Terrell's doctors. But, as noted by the journalist, "How could she afford that? To her thinking, the healthy food Terrell needed meant she needed more money, not less" (Eaton 2007).

These two news articles discuss topics—anorexia and obesity—in which body size (too thin or too heavy) and eating (too little or too much) are treated as medical risks and/or diseases. The American Psychiatric Association (APA) defines anorexia as the refusal to maintain body weight at or above a minimally "normal weight" for age and height, fear of gaining weight or becoming "fat," and denial of the gravity of one's low body weight. The Centers for Disease Control and Prevention (CDC)

Saguy, Abigail C., and Kjerstin Gruys, "Morality and Health: News Media Constructions of Overweight and Eating Disorders" (abridged), *Social Problems 57* (2): 231–50, copyright © 2010 Oxford University Press. Reprinted by permission of Oxford University Press.

defines "obesity" among adults as having a body mass index (BMI) (weight in kilograms divided by height in meters squared) equal to or greater than 30, and "overweight" as having a BMI equal or greater than 25 but less than 30.[1] Different measures are used for children and teenagers under 18-years old, which adjust for age.

While anorexia and overweight/obesity are both medical categories related to body weight and eating, they have strikingly different social and moral connotations. In the contemporary United States, being heavy is seen as the embodiment of gluttony, sloth, and/or stupidity (Crandall and Eshleman 2003; Latner and Stunkard 2003), while slenderness is taken as the embodiment of virtue (Bordo 1993). A deep-seated cultural belief in self-reliance makes body size—like wealth—especially likely to be regarded as being under personal control and as reflecting one's moral fiber (Stearns 1997).

To what extent does the contemporary American social and moral valence of body size shape how the news media report on overweight/obesity and eating disorders as medical issues? Comparing only the two news media articles above suggests that the news media treats anorexics as *victims* of a terrible illness beyond their and their parents' control, while obesity is caused by bad individual behavior, including, in the case of children, parental neglect. Second, the difference in class and racial profile of these two families is striking. A young white girl from a well-to-do family provides "the face" of anorexia, while a young boy and his low-earning, black single mother are discussed in an article on obesity. If these reflect typical patterns in reporting, then news reports on eating disorders and obesity may reinforce moral hierarchies based on body size, race, and class. That is, they may reproduce stereotypes of young white female victims and irresponsible, out-of-control lower class minorities. Moreover, articles may represent the issues of eating disorders and overweight differently depending on which demographic groups are the focus of the discussion.

To investigate this issue more systematically, we draw on content analyses of 332 articles published between 1995 and 2005 in *The New York Times* and *Newsweek* on the topic of eating disorders or overweight/obesity. We also draw on qualitative analyses of five additional articles published in these publications in 2006 and 2007 that specifically discuss binge eating disorder and were not included in our larger sample. We examine how news reports on these issues assign blame and responsibility as well as how they discuss gender, race, and class. In so doing, we contribute to sociological understandings of how cultural values shape the construction of social problems and, in turn, reproduce social inequalities.

THEORETICAL PERSPECTIVE

Body weight has long been a marker of social status. However, at most times and in most places, where food is scarce, corpulence signals *high* rather than low status. In these cultures, plumpness in women is especially prized. Among elite Nigerian Arabs, for instance, girls are fattened up in early childhood (Popenoe 2005). A young girl's girth is physical evidence of her father's—and later her husband's—wealth. Being so fat that she is immobile signifies that her labor is not needed, making fat women the ultimate "trophy wives." Similarly, up until the early twentieth century, women in the United States and Europe strived to be fat, not thin. There too, food was scarce and plumpness signaled wealth, while thinness suggested illness (Klein 1996; Stearns 1997). Yet, while thinness was regarded as ungainly in these contexts, especially in women, it did not reflect on one's *moral* character (Stearns 1997), nor have individual women been personally blamed for being too thin (Popenoe 2005).

As the agricultural and industrial revolutions reduced food shortages, fatness was no longer a reliable sign of wealth and, as the poor got fatter, the symbolic meaning of body size flipped. As corpulence increasingly became a marker for *lower* prestige and status, those with greater resources had more ability and motivation to avoid the stigma of fatness (Aronowitz 2008). Moreover, as moral condemnation of consumerism lessened, maintaining a slender body became the new way for Americans to demonstrate their moral virtue. As Historian Peter Stearns (1997) argues, beginning in the late nineteenth and early twentieth century:

> People could indulge their taste for fashion and other products with a realization that, if they disciplined their bodies through an attack on fat, they could preserve or even enhance their health and also establish their moral credentials. . . . An appropriately slender figure could denote the kind of firm character, capable of self-control, that one would seek in a good worker in an age of growing indulgence; ready employability and weight management could be conflated. (pp. 59–60)

This moral association of slenderness with "firm character" and heaviness as the embodiment of gluttony, sloth, and stupidity is still with us today (Bordo 1993; Crandall and Eshleman 2003; Latner and Stunkard 2003). In the United States, where there is a deep-seated cultural belief in self-reliance, body size is especially likely to be regarded as under personal control and reflecting moral fiber (Stearns 1997), despite research suggesting that much of the variation in body size is biologically determined (Kolata 2007). Thinness is a *cultural value* in the contemporary United States—it is a quality that is widely prized by members of this society.

In the contemporary United States, body size intersects with other dimensions of inequality. Stereotypes of fat people as gluttonous and undisciplined echo similar stereotypes of the working classes as "the archetypal 'uncontrolled' body in public health discourse, as lazy, dirty, immoral, incapable of resisting their urges" (Lupton 1995:75). Compared to men, women are held to higher standards of thinness and suffer greater penalties if they fall short, in terms of marriage prospects as well as employment (Conley and Glauber 2007; Puhl, Andreyeva, and Brownell 2008). On average, wealthier white people—especially women—tend to be thinner than poorer people of color (Flegal et al. 1998; Flegal et al. 2002; Sobal and Stunkard 1989). This is, in part, because having a thin and toned body is expensive in contemporary Western contexts, where fresh fruits and vegetables are more expensive than higher calorie processed foods and where physical activity requires leisure time (Drewnowski and Barratt-Fornell 2004). Heavier women are also poorer, however, because of weight-based stigma. For women, higher body mass *predicts* lower personal and spousal earnings (Puhl et al. 2008).

Negative stereotypes of fatness and ethnic minority status often reinforce each other, such that a fat black woman is stigmatized for both her body size and race. However, these stigmas can also be disassociated with various consequences. Thus, a white middle class woman will lose some of her class and racial privilege if she is heavy, while a woman of color can gain status by being thin. Realizing this, some black and Latino families pressure their daughters to be thin as part of a strategy of upward mobility (Thompson 1994).

Yet, white middle class women and girls are more likely than poorer women and girls, women and girls of color, and boys or men to be diagnosed with anorexia or bulimia, also referred to as "thinness-oriented eating disorders" (Bruch 1978; Striegel-Moore et al. 2003).[2] In contrast, rates of binge eating disorder, which are often associated with higher body weight, are similar among black women, white women, and white men (Smith et al. 1998). Indeed, some scholars have found recurrent binge eating to be *more* common among black women than among white women (Striegel-Moore et al. 2000). This makes news media discussions of binge eating disorder important for understanding how discussions of eating and body weight are racialized and gendered.

Anorexia is listed in the *Diagnostic and Statistical Manual of Mental Disorders* (DSM-IV) as an eating disorder, along with bulimia, which is defined as recurrent episodes of binge eating (eating extremely large amounts of food in one sitting) followed by "inappropriate compensatory" purging (i.e., by vomiting and/or talking laxatives) and an undue influence of body shape in self-evaluation. Binge eating disorder is categorized in the DSM-IV as an "Eating Disorder—Not Otherwise Specified," an umbrella category for various eating disorders that do not meet the precise criteria for either anorexia or bulimia. The APA provides a "provisional diagnosis" of binge eating disorder as bingeing without compensatory purging and/or extreme dietary constraint (APA 1994). This provisional diagnosis signals that binge eating disorder is being seriously considered for its own diagnostic category in the DSM-V (expected in 2012), while also providing clinical researchers with shared criteria for studying the disorder. Binge eating is likely to be the object of more public discussions as it gains more attention from clinicians.

The mass media offer important primary sources for cultural and social research. Television, radio, magazines, newspapers, and Internet content provide a sensitive barometer of social process and change. Once created, these texts remain unchanged and available for analysis, making them ideal for the study of attitudes, concerns, ideologies, and power relations, and how they shift over time (Lupton 1994). Aware of these strengths, early feminist work examined the fashion media, demonstrating how fashion magazines and advertisements convey to readers the importance of slenderness and the shame of fatness for women (Bordo 1993). Anthropologist Mimi Nichter (2000) has argued that such images contribute to negative body image and eating problems among young girls; however, she finds that African American girls are buffered from fashion pressures to be thin by a vibrant ethnic culture that values personal style as well as "thicker" body types.

News accounts of health and illness differ from other media texts in that they have the weight of "expert" opinion, making them especially important to study (Lupton 1994; Nelkin 1987). In recent years, a few scholars have begun examining media reporting on the so-called "obesity epidemic" (Boero 2007; Lawrence 2004; Saguy and Almeling 2008). Natalie Boero (2007) finds that news reporting has largely framed obesity as a moral problem of gluttony and sloth. Abigail C. Saguy and Rene Almeling (2008) find that body size is predominantly blamed on individual choices rather than social or biological factors, while Regina Lawrence (2004) shows that there is increasing discussion of social-structural factors over time. Saguy and Almeling (2008) find that news reports on scientific findings are more likely than the original research on which they report to focus on individual blame and to describe obesity as a public health crisis and/or epidemic. They further find that articles discussing the poor, blacks, or Latinos are more likely than articles not discussing these groups to blame body size on individual choices (Saguy and Almeling 2008). Similarly, previous research has shown that news reports are more likely to portray welfare recipients as dependent (and thus unworthy) when they are unmarried or black, compared to when they are widowed or white (Misra, Moller, and Karides 2003). These studies suggest that news reports will blame individuals for overweight and obesity, especially when such individuals are poor and/or from minority ethnic groups, thus reflecting and reinforcing negative stereotypes of fat people, the poor, and ethnic minorities.

While important, extant studies have methodological and conceptual limitations. For instance, Lawrence (2004) does not examine how views about gender, race, or class inform news media reports of obesity, while Boero (2007) draws heavily on qualitative analysis of seven articles published in the fall of 2000 as part of a series on the "Fat Epidemic," thereby limiting the generalizability of her findings. Saguy and Almeling's (2008) analysis of news reporting on two special issues on obesity published in the *Journal of the American Medical Association (JAMA)* in 1999 and 2003 allows for a systematic examination of how scientific research is

popularized by the news media, but does not constitute a representative sample of reporting on the topic of overweight/obesity. Moreover, because all of these studies lack a comparative case, it is impossible to know the extent to which these patterns are simply a product of generic news media routines that favor sensationalism and morality tales (Schudson 2003), combined perhaps with health policy tendencies to emphasize individual blame and responsibility (Fitzpatrick 2000; Lupton 1995; Tesh 1988).

Motivated by research on social problem construction (Best 2008; Gusfield 1981; Kitsuse and Spector 1973) and news media framing research (e.g., Benson and Saguy 2005; Entman 1993; Gamson 1992), this article examines how news reports *frame* overweight/obesity and eating disorders in particular ways by drawing attention to some aspects of these issues while obscuring others. It draws on quantitative and qualitative analyses of a random sample of news reports on overweight/obesity or eating disorders published between 1995 and 2005 in *The New York Times* and *Newsweek*. The comparative case study allows us to disentangle general aspects of news reporting from the specific cases at hand. In that anorexics and bulimics are seen as pursuing a culturally valued ideal (slenderness), we expect that the news media will be less likely to blame them—compared to the overweight or obese—for their malady. Rather, we expect anorexics and bulimics to be portrayed as victims of a host of complex factors beyond their control. To the extent that the news media focuses on cases of young, white middle class anorexics and bulimics, they risk reproducing cultural stereotypes of young, white female victims. In contrast, in that the news media frame overweight/obesity as a public health crisis produced by irresponsible individuals, while focusing on cases of overweight among the poor and minorities, they are likely to reinforce negative stereotypes based on body size, ethnicity, and class.

. . .

FINDINGS

Our news sample typically attributes anorexia and bulimia to a host of complex and interrelated factors, thus mitigating individual blame while representing anorexics and bulimics as victims. In contrast, it predominantly blames overweight exclusively on bad individual choices and emphasizes individual-level weight loss solutions. News reports emphasize medical intervention when it comes to anorexia and bulimia *but not* when discussing binge eating disorder, which they tend to deny the status of a real eating disorder and frame instead as *ordinary* overeating caused by lack of self-control and requiring greater personal discipline.

After reviewing the quantitative patterns, we examine each case qualitatively.

As shown in Figure 1, news reports on both eating disorders and overweight invoke personal choices, with over 40 percent of articles in both categories mentioning personal choices as contributors. However, several factors are described as equally contributing to eating disorders, while individual choice is the *predominant* explanation offered for overweight. Articles about eating disorders discuss structural causes at the same rate as individual choices (47 percent for both), while 19 percent of eating disorder articles cite biological causes. In contrast, 41 percent of articles about overweight mention individual choices, with socio-structural and biological causes mentioned in 29 and 16 percent of articles, respectively. Press reports are more likely to describe eating disorders, compared to overweight, as a disease (29 percent versus 4 percent) and/or as a psychological problem (27 percent versus 3 percent) triggered by cultural messages (30 percent versus 8 percent).

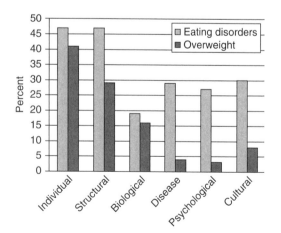

Figure 1. Percentage of Articles Discussing Specific Causes
Note: With the exception of individual and biological causes, all cross-issue differences are statistically significant ($p < .05$, one-tailed tests).

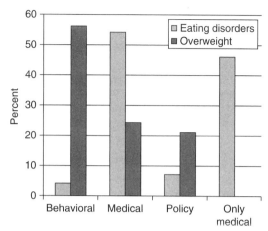

Figure 2. Percentage of Articles Discussing Specific Solutions
Note: All cross-issue differences are statistically significant ($p < .05$, one-tailed tests).

Even more strikingly, as shown in Figure 2, the articles were much less likely to hold individuals responsible for curing eating disorders (4 percent of eating disorder sample) than for fixing overweight (56 percent of overweight sample). Articles in the eating disorders sample discuss medical interventions at least *seven times* more frequently than they mention either policy or behavioral solutions (54 percent versus 7 percent and 4 percent, respectively). In contrast, articles on overweight/obesity are over twice as likely to discuss behavioral modification than either medical interventions (24 percent) or policy solutions (21 percent). Forty-six percent of articles on eating disorders, but no articles on overweight, discuss *only* medical solutions.

As is shown in Figure 3, 94 percent of eating disorder articles discuss women or girls, compared to 47 percent that mention men or boys. By contrast, articles on overweight mention women/girls and men/boys at similar rates (47 percent compared to 42 percent). Thirteen percent of articles on eating disorders discuss people from the upper or middle class, compared to the 4 percent that discuss poor people, and 17 percent mention whites, compared to 13 percent that discuss minority races, despite the tendency for "white" to function as an unmarked category.[3] In contrast, articles on overweight discuss nonwhites (including blacks, Latino, Asian, and other race) more often than whites (13 percent versus 8 percent) and discuss the poor as

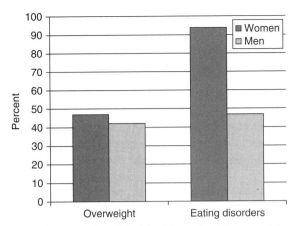

Figure 3. Proportion of Articles Discussing Women or Men
Note: Frequencies of specific themes *within the same sample* are *not* independent of each other and are therefore unsuitable for a chi-square test of statistical significance.

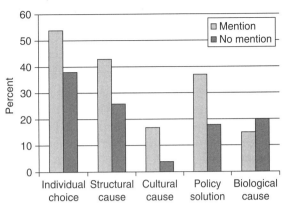

Figure 5. Percentage of Overweight Articles Evoking Specific Frames, by Whether or Not They Discuss Blacks, Latinos, or the Poor
Notes: With the exception of biological cause and individual choice, all differences are statistically significant ($p < .05$, one-tailed tests). Thirty-five articles mention blacks, Latinos, or the poor whereas 227 articles do not explicitly mention these groups.

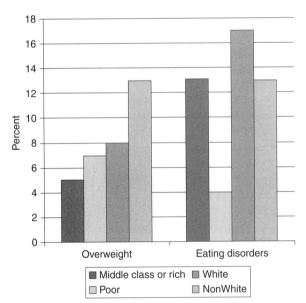

Figure 4. Proportion of Articles Discussing Specific Demographic Groups
Note: Frequencies of specific themes within the same sample are not independent of each other and are therefore unsuitable for a chi-square test of statistical significance.

frequently as the middle class or rich (7 percent versus 5 percent).

Moreover, as shown in Figure 5, we find that news reports mentioning blacks, Latinos, or the poor are more likely to blame social structural factors, but not

biological factors, for overweight/obesity. Forty-three percent of articles mentioning these groups, compared to 26 percent of articles that do not mention these groups, cite social structural contributors to obesity, a difference that is statistically significant. Coded as a subset of social-structural factors, cultural causes for overweight/obesity are also significantly more likely to be mentioned when blacks, Latinos, or the poor are cited (17 percent versus 4 percent), often because—as we discuss below—*minority culture* is being blamed. Articles that mention blacks, Latinos, or the poor are also more likely than those that do not mention these groups to discuss obesity policy solutions (37 percent versus 18 percent). As we discuss below, many of these not only address social-structural problems, such as access to affordable fresh fruits and vegetables, but also seek to educate people considered unable to make good food and exercise choices, and to change minority ethnic *cultural attitudes* about food and eating.[4] Fifty-four percent of articles that mention blacks, Latinos, or the poor, compared to 38 percent that do not, discuss how individual choices lead to overweight, but this difference is just shy of statistical significance at $p < .05$ ($p = .055$). Fifteen percent of articles mentioning blacks, Latinos, or the poor discuss biological causes of overweight, compared to 20 percent of articles not mentioning these groups, a difference that is not statistically significant.

Note that the number of articles that *explicitly* mentions blacks, Latinos, or the poor are relatively small, so that most articles that frame obesity as an individual, social-structural, cultural, or biological issue or mention policy solutions do *not* explicitly mention these groups. However, the fact that certain kinds of frames are more or less prevalent depending on the groups being discussed suggests that these news publications may be reproducing common social assumptions about these groups. Below, we flesh out these quantitative patterns with details from the qualitative analyses. We discuss news reporting on (thinness-oriented) eating disorders, overweight, and binge eating disorder, respectively, in three separate sections.

Anorexia and Bulimia: No-One to Blame

A typical article on anorexia evokes "complex webs of cultural factors and psychological processes" (Isherwood 2005), serving to diffuse responsibility amongst several factors. Similarly, a *Newsweek* editorial proclaims: "Good news: scientists are developing a better sense of how genetic and social triggers interact" (Whitaker 2005). In such articles, genetic factors and social constraints are said to work in tandem, jointly diffusing focus away from individual blame. In contrast to how parents are frequently blamed for their children's (over)weight problems, the article cited in the introduction to this article concludes: "Parents do play a role, but most often it's a genetic one. In the last 10 years, studies of anorexics have shown that the disease often runs in families" (Tyre 2005). In other words, when it comes to anorexia there is, as the title of this article proclaims, "no-one to blame" (Tyre 2005). Contemporary reports on anorexia tend to portray parents as part of the solution, rather than as part of the problem. For instance, an article on anorexia describes how parents of anorexics "are encouraged to think of the disorder as an outside force that has taken over their daughter's life. And they are exhorted to be unwavering in finding ways to feed their child" (Goode 2002).

Even when an eating disorder is described as beginning with a choice (i.e., to start a diet), the choice is depicted as a "normal" response to cultural pressures, rather than as an irresponsible or self-indulgent behavior. For instance, an article entitled "When Weight Loss Goes Awry" describes a teenager's anorexia as

beginning with an innocent diet: "last summer, as friends started dieting, she decided to lose five to 10 pounds. Within a few months Amelia, now 15, was on the death-march called anorexia nervosa" (Kalb 2000). Of course, in a society where watching one's weight is a moral obligation, it makes sense that Amelia would not be faulted for beginning a diet. Rather, anorexia is viewed as a case in which good intentions go too far. Amelia is described as "a straight-A student and cheerleader" who says "in a weak but determined voice from her bed at the Children's Hospital in Denver" that she "would never want this to happen to anybody else" (Kalb 2000). The article thus describes anorexia as something that "happens to" people, even model teenagers, rather than something people bring upon themselves. The article states, "there's no simple explanation for why intelligent, often highly accomplished kids spiral into such destructive behavior." It considers a host of factors from "obsessive-compulsive disorder, depression, low self-esteem and anxiety" to the "'reduce fat in your diet' drumbeat, which can haunt children who already feel pressure—from gaunt models or each other—to be thin" (Kalb 2000). Similarly, absolving anorexics from blame, the article cited at the start of this article explains that "For some kids, *innocent*-seeming behavior carries enormous risks" (Tyre 2005, emphasis added).

Despite wide acceptance of dieting as normal and desirable, many news articles point the finger at the narrow beauty standards of popular culture. For instance, discussing anorexia and bulimia, one article declares that "the apparent precipitant of these [eating] disorders seems to be an overwhelming desire to be thin, thin enough to walk down a Paris fashion runway, to act in a Hollywood movie, or to dance with a leading ballet company" (Brody 2000). In these discussions, African American subculture, and specifically an alleged preference for larger female bodies among black Americans, is cast in a positive light, as protecting minority girls from internalizing mainstream pressures to be thin. Quoting a medical doctor, one article reads:

> Dr. Brooks said experts traditionally had thought that "anorexia and bulimia didn't happen to black, Asian or Hispanic women, that they were somehow immune." . . . "Curvy African-American women were celebrated," Dr. Brooks said. "These girls didn't experience anxiety and shame about their bodies. Being curvy or large was

a source of pride within the African-American community." (Brodey 2005)

Those black (and sometimes Latina) girls who do develop eating disorders are often seen as being especially vulnerable to "white" pressures. The article quoted above, for instance, describes how one black teenage girl developed bulimia because, as one of nine black students in a high school of 3,000, she was "struggling simply to be accepted. [In her words:] 'When it came to body image, my perception of beauty was based on my white peers and images of white celebrities in the media'" (Brodey 2005). Thus a mainstream diet culture is implicated in (thinness-oriented) eating disorders, while African American culture is praised as offering some cultural buffering.

Yet, even such blaming of mainstream cultural pressures is tempered by arguing that they only result in eating disorders among people with a biological or psychological predisposition. For example, after noting that doctors have observed a "disturbing trend: a growing group of women in their 30s, 40s and 50s who have eating disorders," one article reassures readers that many of these newly diagnosed older women have actually had lifelong psychological problems and that "lots of people in our culture diet, [but] relatively few end up with an eating disorder" (Rothman Morris 2004). Here, not only are individual dieters not blamed for their behavior but the *culture of dieting* is normalized. Another similar article writes that:

> While everyone is exposed to similar societal pressures to be thin, only a small percentage develop eating disorders. Those who succumb typically are prompted by extreme career pressures, as often happens to ballerinas, models, actresses, and jockeys, or they have some underlying emotional and/or physical vulnerability (Brody 2000).

Similarly, the article cited in the introduction to this article compares anorexia to alcoholism and depression, "potentially fatal diseases that may be set off by environmental factors such as stress or trauma, but have their roots in a complex combination of genes and brain chemistry" (Tyre 2005). It continues:

> Many kids are affected by pressure-cooker school environments and a culture of thinness promoted by magazines and music videos, but most of them don't secretly scrape their dinner into the garbage. The

environment "pulls the trigger," . . . but it's a child's latent vulnerabilities that "load the gun."

By stressing the complex interplay between individual factors, biological predisposition, and macro-level environmental factors, this type of reporting mitigates blame of individual anorexics and their parents.

As victims of a complex illness, sufferers of eating disorders are not expected to "pull themselves up by their bootstraps." Rather, they are depicted as needing medical intervention. For example, one article describes an anorexic 14-year old who, despite wanting "to improve," had failed to recover when going it alone: "It took a second hospitalization at Schneider, the following spring, before Molly could maintain a healthy weight" (Hochman 1996). The article cited at the start of this article similarly describes how young Katherine was only able to recover after *repeated* hospitalizations, because she frequently relapsed when not under direct medical supervision (Tyre 2005). Such failures are not seen as evidence of weak-will, as failed diet attempts are, nor are they blamed on their parents. Rather, they are used to underscore the seriousness of anorexia as a medical illness that requires medical intervention.

Even when eating disorder articles explicitly state that individuals can cure themselves, it is almost always under the guidance of a doctor. Thus, we read about new therapies for bulimia in which specially trained nurses coach bulimics to help themselves: "Many bulimics do not need traditional psychiatric therapy. Instead, he said, patients will learn to help themselves. 'What we've done is change the treatment into a self-help format,' said Dr. Fairburn" (Liotta 1999). Yet, when "self-help" for eating disorders is enacted under medical supervision, curing disordered individuals is still presented as the responsibility of an expert physician.

Obesity: No-One to Blame but Yourself (and Your Parents)

In contrast to reporting on eating disorders, even when articles mention more than one cause for overweight, individual blame usually predominates. For instance, a *Newsweek* article explains that "you can't pick your parents, but you can pick what you eat and how often you exercise" (Barrett Ozols 2005). Thus, genetics does not provide an excuse for body weight. Rather, the article emphasizes people's ability (and, seemingly, their obligation) to make *choices* regarding diet and exercise. Similarly, another article cites new research on "race and weight," explaining that "on average, black women burn nearly 100 fewer calories a day than white women do when their bodies are at rest" but cautions that "the new findings do not mean that controlling and losing weight is a hopeless task for people with lower metabolic rates, just that it may require *more attention to diet and exercise*" (Brody 1997, emphasis added). Again, the reader is reminded that managing her weight is her responsibility. In that pursuing health has become a moral obligation (Edgley and Brissett 1990), this responsibility carries moral connotations.

Moreover, while heaping the blame on individuals, news reports also draw upon and reproduce stereotypes of fat people as gluttonous, slothful, and ignorant, and of parents of fat children as neglectful and irresponsible. Thus, such reports reproduce the negative moral valence of fatness. For instance, one *Newsweek* article writes:

> Bruce and Lisa Smith never skimped much on food. Chips, fried chicken, canned fruit, sodas—they ate as much as they wanted, whenever they wanted. Exercise? Pretty much nonexistent, unless you count working the TV remote or the computer mouse. "We were out of control," says Bruce, 42. And so was their son, Jarvae, who is 5 feet 4 and weighs 176 pounds (Springen 2007).

The Smiths' obesity is portrayed as the direct consequence of a lifestyle of sloth and gluttony. Few readers would consider working a TV remote or a computer mouse physical exercise. Rather, sarcasm is employed to convey disdain and contempt for the Smiths, who are portrayed as lazy and irresponsible individuals and parents. This same article is unrepentant in its blaming of parents for an alleged impending crisis of global proportions. It continues: "The problem [of childhood obesity] is so grave that some researchers predict that the life expectancy of today's children could shrink by as much as five years. The key to reversing the trend? Parents" (Kalb and Springen 2005). Thus, individuals and parents are not only blamed for the onset of obesity, they are held responsible for "reversing the trend."

The fix is presented as a matter of common sense: "One simple way to get the entire family fit is to turn off the television and shut down the computer" (Kalb and Springen 2005). By describing solutions as "simple,"

the authors imply a logic under which those who have fat children must be stupid, ignorant, or willfully disobedient. Indeed, in the context of childhood obesity, parents (and especially mothers, who are mentioned over twice as often as fathers)[5] are sometimes described as legally unfit to care for their offspring. This was the context in which Heavy-T, discussed in the introduction, was removed from his mother's custody. This type of reporting reproduces negative stereotypes. Likewise, from another *New York Times* article:

> [It] is the confounding truth that parents—whether distracted, oblivious or both—are ultimately to blame for what their children eat. "Parents were created for that function," said Dan Jaffe, executive vice president for government relations at the Association of National Advertisers, an organization based in Washington whose members include food companies. "I don't know of any little child who jumps in the car and drives to a supermarket and buys their own food." (Buss 2004)

Again, this article portrays obesity as the product of parental neglect, heaping moral blame on the parents of heavy children. Another article portrays a lawsuit against McDonald's as absurd, arguing that it was the plaintiffs own fault for "gorging themselves so wantonly" on fast food, whether ignorant of, or indifferent to, the likely consequences:

> The [two black-girl plaintiffs from the Bronx] in the McDonald's lawsuit use their ignorance as an argument, claiming that if they'd only known about the nutritional shortcomings of fast food, they certainly would not have gorged themselves so wantonly. (If that's really true, they should consider a lawsuit against their parents for endangering the welfare of their children rather than a suit against McDonald's). (Kuntzman 2002)

The word *wanton* is often used to indicate lewd or bawdy behavior and is clearly moralizing. Similarly, to *gorge* is to consume greedily, thus conjuring up gluttony. Thus, these girls are represented as immorally stuffing themselves with food. That they did not know any better is mentioned as grounds for a lawsuit for neglect against their parents. Also evoking parental responsibility, a letter to the editor in *Newsweek* (2000) asks "Are adults who permit their children to eat as they please (meaning anything and everything) supremely ignorant or genuinely abusive?"

In that heavier body weight is negatively associated with socioeconomic status and given that blacks and Latinos tend to have higher body mass than whites, any discourse that blames people for weighing too much risks reinforcing class and racial stigma. This is even more true when news reports focus on cases of overweight among blacks, Latinos, or the poor. Moreover, many news articles *explicitly* blame ethnic communities for contributing to higher rates of obesity amongst their own. For instance, an article reporting on a women's health study states that "more subtle societal influences, like differences in acceptable body images among different ethnic groups, all contributed to greater obesity among women with lower incomes and those in certain ethnic groups" (Santora 2005). Ethnic culinary practices are also blamed for the alleged obesity epidemic. For instance, a 2003 *New York Times* article discusses how Latino culinary preferences contribute to overweight among Latino children: "[Mr. Batista] says some cultural habits are simply getting the best of his people. Latinos eating vegetables? Come on, he says, raising his hands in frustration. 'We don't eat vegetables. It's rice and beans and meat. It's very natural'" (Richardson 2003).

Another article, discussing the higher rate of overweight among minorities in inner cities, quotes a news source who acknowledges that "it is easier and less expensive to eat fast food and very difficult to find, in some of these neighborhoods, appropriate foods, fruits, and vegetables at a reasonable price" (Braiker 2003). But the article then shifts to a focus on ethnic culture:

> In the end, she says, "it will take a culture change" to reverse the trend. . . . "Eating healthy is synonymous with whiteness for some of these kids," [an activist] says. They'll be like, "Salmon? That's white people food." There are ways to make it more accessible; the first part is about education. (Braiker 2003)

Thus, ethnic minorities are depicted as backward or ignorant and needing to be educated in proper food choices and preparation, thus reproducing stereotypes based on race as well as body size.

Consistent with such stereotypes, many of the policy interventions discussed seek to educate people—and especially ethnic minorities—to make better choices. For instance, an article chronicling a public health intervention in a southern black community describes a recipe for "low-fat catfish" developed by nutritionists as "one of a series [of new recipes] showcasing revered family recipes purged of their sins by two Auburn University nutritionists" and notes how a leader of a public health intervention "recited a litany of virtuous eating for her largely female audience" (Markus 1998). The moral associations with food and eating in this article are striking. As with articles on eating disorders, this article identifies mothers as a crucial part of the solution, recounting how these interventions recruit minority mothers as "cheerleaders for good health" (Markus 1998) and target them as the preparers of food for their families: "We're building on community talent with women who are cooking for their children and passing on behavior patterns to their children and their children's children" (Markus 1998).

Binge Eating Disorder: A Need for Self-Control

Articles that discuss binge eating disorder in detail draw upon frames typical of *both* thinness-oriented eating disorders articles and of articles on overweight, underscoring the extent to which this condition straddles the symbolic space between usually polarized conceptions of body size. Ultimately, however, binge eating disorder is more firmly situated within an "overeating" frame, depicting sufferers as needing "self-control" more than medical assistance. For instance, in an account of her personal struggle with binge eating disorder, reporter Jane Brody (2007) writes: "My despair was profound, and one night in the midst of a binge I became suicidal. I had lost control of my eating; it was controlling me, and I couldn't go on living that way." A psychologist helped Brody resist suicide but "was not able to help me stop binging. That was something I would have to do on my own." As with eating disorder victims in other accounts, this binge eater is presented as needing help from a doctor or therapist, but ultimately, as with overweight, it is suggested that she needs to control overeating on her own.

Two articles that discuss binge eating disorder argue that the most important reason binge eating disorder needs to be taken seriously is because it makes it more difficult to *succeed at weight-loss*. In other words, the concern with achieving a "normal" weight, which also dominates discussions of overweight, seems to trump more general concerns about eating disorders as psychological problems. One article explains: "The importance of binge eating disorder is that people who fit these criteria do worse than others in weight management programs" (Alter Hubel 1997). By focusing on the importance of weight loss, these articles obscure or downplay the psychiatric symptoms experienced by binge eaters, which have been shown to have negative health effects independent of body size (Telch and Agras 1994). Another article draws upon binge eating disorder's relationship to overweight in order to depict it as a *public* health risk: "Because of the disorder's close link with obesity . . . it's a major public-health burden" (Springen 2007), a theme that we *never* encountered in discussions of anorexia or bulimia.

Further, while feminist authors have identified binge eating and compulsive overeating as serious "eating problems," which—like anorexia and bulimia—often "begin as ways women numb pain and cope with violations of their bodies" and are "a logical response to injustices" (Thompson 1994:26), our news sample describes individuals with binge eating disorder as "overeaters" who have an "ordinary, if unfortunate, human behavior" (Bakalar 2007), and a few articles express concern that binge eating disorder has been "invented" by greedy drug companies. For instance, another article quotes an eating disorders researcher who says, "Outside North America, it's basically a laugh. . . . No one thinks it's a serious condition. . . . These are overeaters" (Goode 2000). In other words, there is resistance to giving binge eating disorder the status of a full-fledged eating disorder like anorexia or bulimia, for which outside forces of biology or culture—rather than individual choices—are to blame.

DISCUSSION AND CONCLUSION

Previous research has shown that the news media frame obesity as a moral problem of gluttony and sloth (Boero 2007) and overwhelmingly blame bad individual choices (Saguy and Almeling 2008), despite increasing discussion of social-structural factors over time (Lawrence 2004). Extant work, however, has been limited either analytically—by, for instance, not examining the role of gender, class, or race (Lawrence 2004)—or methodologically, by relying heavily on a small (Boero 2007) or nonrepresentative sample (Saguy and Almeling 2008). In contrast, the current study draws on a relatively large and representative sample of news reports in the *New*

York Times and *Newsweek*, while harnessing the analytical power of both quantitative and qualitative analysis. Moreover, the systematic comparison of reporting of overweight/obesity with reporting on eating disorders—a first of its kind—allows us to tease out the effects of negative attitudes about fatness from generic media routines that favor morality tales and the tendency in the United States to individualize responsibility for health (Fitzpatrick 2000; Lupton 1995; Tesh 1988). We find that, in the contemporary U.S. society where thinness is highly prized, news articles are less likely to blame individuals for being (or trying to be) *too thin* than they are to blame them for being *too fat*. This suggests that, more generally, cultural values shape how the news media assign blame and responsibility. In turn, such reporting is likely to reinforce and naturalize such values. This article further suggests that, depending on how they report on the demographics of a given condition, the news media may reinforce group-based stereotypes.

Specifically, the association of heavier bodies with gluttony and sloth and thinner bodies with discipline and responsibility leads our news sample to frame anorexics as victims of cultural and biological forces beyond their control, while blaming the obese for their weight, which, in turn, reinforces these original associations. Our sample of news articles tends to deny binge eating disorder, in which sufferers eat large quantities of food and tend to be heavier, the status of a "real" eating disorder, reframing it instead as ordinary and blameworthy overeating. Moreover, because anorexia and bulimia are described as more often affecting middle class white girls and women, the analyzed news reports on these disorders reinforce the image of white middle class girls and women as victims. Since overweight/obesity is described as a problem most common among the poor and minorities, such news reporting on obesity reinforces stereotypes of poor minorities as ignorant or willfully defiant of health guidelines. While articles discussing blacks, Latinos, or the poor are more likely to blame weight on social-structural factors, they are also more likely to blame ethnic preferences for larger women or ethnic cuisine.

These findings have important substantive implications. To the extent that reporting on bigger bodies as a health problem reinforces the negative stigma associated with being heavier, women—who suffer more from weight-based discrimination (Puhl et al. 2008)—will bear the brunt of this stigma. Women, the greater consumers of medical weight-loss interventions, including weight-loss diets, drugs, and surgery (Bish et al. 2005; Santry, Gillen, and Lauderdale 2005), are also likely to increase their use of these costly and often risky interventions. As higher body weight is increasingly discussed as a medical and public health crisis, men may increase their consumption of these products as well. Moreover, characterization of obesity as an "epidemic"—warranted or not—creates a sense of urgency and potentially justifies forms of regulatory intervention that would otherwise appear excessive (Lupton 1995). Given the greater vulnerability of the poor and ethnic minorities to surveillance, we can expect regulatory intervention to target these groups.

Demand for increasingly punitive measures may come in response to images of fat populations as "wantonly gorging" themselves and allowing their children to do the same, thereby bringing diabetes and heart disease upon themselves, their families, and their communities. Removing children from their homes, like Heavy T, discussed in the introduction, is the most chilling example of such punitive measures. Anamarie Regino is another such child who was wrested from her parents by state officials, in her case at the age of four years (Belkin 2001). The state of New Mexico justified putting her in foster care on the grounds that her weight was both life threatening and her parents' fault (Belkin 2001). In Anamarie's case, her family's Latino ethnicity was taken as further evidence of her parents' ignorance and inability to care for her. Despite the fact that Anamarie's mother was born in the United States and spoke fluent English, the social worker's affidavit stated that, "the family does not fully understand the threat to their daughter's safety and welfare due to language or cultural barriers" (Belkin 2001).

As these examples show, the way in which body size and eating are framed in public discourse has far-reaching consequences for individual behavior, public policy, and social control. Because of their visibility and cultural authority, the news media are important sites of meaning making and merit serious attention from sociologists. We hope that others will join us in investigating, not only the content of news reporting on eating and body size, but also its ramifications for individual behavior, interpersonal relations, public policy, and personal freedoms.

NOTES

1. The definition of "overweight" and "obesity," and even these terms themselves, are contested. Fat acceptance activists, who advocate for civil rights on the basis of body size, argue that these terms pathologize normal biological variation and reclaim the word "fat" as a neutral descriptor like "tall" or "short" (Cooper 1998; Wann 1999). Similarly, many feminist scholars have avoided the term "eating disorder" because it situates "disorder" within individuals rather than in complex social structures. We do not use "overweight," "obesity," or "eating disorders" because we endorse a medical or public health framing, but because we seek to establish how *these particular terms* have been constructed in the news media. We note that a search for articles using the term "fat" produced very few relevant articles, which is not surprising given that this word is still taboo in most social circles in the contemporary United States. An article search using the term "eating problems" was similarly unproductive. For stylistic reasons we do not place the terms "overweight," "obesity," or "eating disorder" in quotations throughout the article, but we wish to be clear that this is the spirit in which we use them.

2. However, new evidence suggests that bulimia—but not anorexia—may be more *prevalent* among poor minority, compared to middle class white women and girls (Goeree, Ham, and Iorio 2009).

3. Note however, that, following research trends, there is increased discussion of nonwhites with eating disorders in our sample over time, with 29 percent of the 2002–2005 sample mentioning nonwhites, compared to 8 percent of the 1995–2001 sample.

4. Race and class are often conflated in news media discussions of obesity, by, for instance, discussing "the poor and minorities" as a group or by using examples of poor members of ethnic minorities to illustrate larger discussions of, say, "black" or "Latino" culture.

5. On mother blame, see the work of McGuffy (2005).

REFERENCES

Alter Hubel, Joy. 1997. "Studies Under Way in Fight against Binging Disorder." *The New York Times*, August 3, p. LI13.
American Psychiatric Association (APA). 1994. *Diagnostic and Statistical Manual of Mental Disorders (DSM-IV)*. Washington, DC: American Psychiatric Association.
Aronowitz, Robert. 2008. "Framing Disease: An Underappreciated Mechanism for the Social Patterning of Health." *Social Science & Medicine* 67:1–9.
Bakalar, Nicholas. 2007. "Survey Puts New Focus on Binge Eating as a Diagnosis." *The New York Times*, February 13, p. F5.
Barrett Ozols, Jennifer. 2005. "Generation XL." *Newsweek*, January 6. Retrieved February 12, 2010 (www.newsweek.com/id/47977).
Belkin, Lisa. 2001. "Watching Her Weight." *The New York Times*, July 8, p. 630.

Benson, Rodney and Abigail C. Saguy. 2005. "Constructing Social Problems in an Age of Globalization: A French-American Comparison." *American Sociological Review* 70:233–59.

Best, Joel. 2008. *Social Problems*. New York: Norton.

Bish, Connie L., Heidi Michels Blanck, Mary K. Serdula, Michele Marcus, Harold W. Kohl, and Laura Kettel Khan. 2005. "Diet and Physical Activity Behaviors among Americans Trying to Lose Weight: 2000 Behavioral Risk Factor Surveillance System." *Obesity Research* 13:596–607.

Boero, Natalie. 2007. "All the News That's Fat to Print: The American 'Obesity Epidemic' and the Media." *Qualitative Sociology* 30:41–60.

Bordo, Susan. 1993. *Unbearable Weight: Feminism, Western Culture, and the Body*. Berkeley: University of California Press.

Braiker, Brian. 2003. "Beets, Not Burgers." *Newsweek*, June 25. Retrieved February 12, 2010 (www.newsweek.com/id/58541).

Brodey, Denise. 2005. "Blacks Join the Eating-Disorder Mainstream." *The New York Times,* September 20, p. F5.

Brody, Jane E. 1997. "Health Watch." *New York Times,* March 26, p. C8.

Brody, Jane E. 2000. "Exposing the Perils of Eating Disorders." *New York Times,* December 12, p. F8.

Brody, Jane E. 2007. "Out of Control: A True Story of Binge Eating." *New York Times,* p. F7.

Bruch, Hilde. 1978. *The Golden Cage: The Enigma of Anorexia Nervosa*. Cambridge, MA: Harvard University Press.

Buss, Dale. 2004. "Is the Food Industry the Problem or the Solution?" *New York Times,* August 29, p. 35.

Conley, Dalton and Rebecca Glauber. 2007. "Gender, Body Mass, and Economic Status: New Evidence from the PSID." *Advances in Health Economics and Health Services Research* 17:253–75.

Cooper, Charlotte. 1998. *Fat and Proud: The Politics of Size*. London, UK: Women's Press.

Crandall, Chris S. and Amy Eshleman. 2003. "A Justification–Suppression Model of the Expression and Experience of Prejudice." *Psychological Bulletin* 129:414–46.

Drewnowski, Adam and Anne Barratt-Fornell. 2004. "Do Healthier Diets Cost More?" *Nutrition Today* 39:161–68.

Eaton, Joe. 2007. "The Battle over Heavy T." *Washington City Paper*, September 26. Retrieved January 22, 2010 (www.washingtoncitypaper.com/display.php?id=8136).

Edgley, Charles and Dennis Brissett. 1990. "Health Nazis and the Cult of the Perfect Body: Some Polemic Observations." *Symbolic Interaction* 13:257–79.

Entman, Robert M. 1993. "Framing: Toward Clarification of a Fractured Paradigm." *Journal of Communication* 43:51–58.

Feder, Barnaby J. 2005. "One Alternative: A Ring That Squeezes the Stomach." *The New York Times,* May 27, p. C2.

Fitzpatrick, Michael. 2000. *The Tyranny of Health: Doctors and the Regulation of Lifestyle*. New York: Routledge.

Flegal, K. M., M. D. Carroll, R. J. Kuczmarski, and C. L. Johnson. 1998. "Overweight and Obesity in the United States: Prevalence and Trends, 1960–1994." *International Journal of Obesity* 22:39–47.

Flegal, Katherine M., Margaret D. Carroll, Cynthia L. Ogden, and Clifford L. Johnson. 2002. "Prevalence and Trends in Obesity among U.S. Adults, 1999–2000." *JAMA* 288:1723–27.

Gamson, William. 1992. *Talking Politics*. Cambridge, UK: Cambridge University Press.

Gans, Herbert. 1979. *Deciding What's News*. New York: Pantheon.

Goeree, Michele Sovinky, John C. Ham, and Daniela Iorio. 2009. "Caught in the Bulimic Trap? Socioeconomic Status, State Dependence, and Unobserved Heterogeneity." Pp. 1–41 in *Working Paper Series*. Zurich, Switzerland: Institute for Empirical Research in Economics.

Goode, Erica. 2000. "Watching Volunteers, Experts Seek Clues to Eating Disorders." *The New York Times,* October 24, p. F1.

Goode, Erica. 2002. "Anorexia Strategy: Family as Doctor." *The New York Times,* June 11, p. F1.

Gusfield, Joseph R. 1981. *The Culture of Public Problems: Drinking-Driving and the Symbolic Order*. Chicago: University of Chicago Press.

Hochman, Nancy S. 1996. "Eating Disorders Strike Younger Girls and Men." *The New York Times,* April 28, p. LI1.

Hof, Sonja van't and Malcolm Nicolson. 1996. "The Rise and Fall of a Fact: The Increase in Anorexia Nervosa." *Sociology of Health and Illness* 18:581–608.

Holsti, Ole R. 1969. *Content Analysis for the Social Sciences and Humanities*. Reading, MA: Addison–Wesley Publishing Co.

Isherwood, Charles. 2005. "A Happy Family Is Stalked by Heartbreak as a Daughter Wastes Herself Away." *The New York Times,* November 1, p. E5.

Kalb, Claudia. 2000. "When Weight Loss Goes Awry." *Newsweek*, July 3, p. 46.

Kalb, Claudia and Karen Springen. 2005. "Pump up the Family." *Newsweek*, p. 62.

Kitsuse, John L. and Malcolm Spector. 1973. "Toward a Sociology of Social Problems: Social Conditions, Value Judgments, and Social Problems." *Social Problems* 20:407–19.

Klein, Richard. 1996. *Eat Fat*. New York: Pantheon.

Kolata, Gina. 2007. *Rethinking Thin: The New Science of Weight Loss—And the Myths and Realities about Dieting.* New York: Farrar, Straus and Giroux.

Kuntzman, Gersh. 2002. "American Beat: Food Fight." *Newsweek*, December 9. Retrieved February 12, 2010 (www.newsweek.com/id/66569).

Latner, Janet D. and Albert J. Stunkard. 2003. "Getting Worse: The Stigmatization of Obese Children." *Obesity Research* 11:452–56.

Lawrence, Regina G. 2004. "Framing Obesity: The Evolution of News Discourse on a Public Health Issue." *Press/Politics* 9:56–75.

Liotta, Jarret. 1999. "Searching for a New Way to Treat Bulimia." *The New York Times,* June 6, p. CN3.

Lupton, Deborah. 1994. *Moral Threats and Dangerous Desires: AIDS in the News Media.* Taylor and Francis.

Lupton, Deborah. 1995. *The Imperative of Health: Public Health and the Regulated Body.* London, UK: Sage Publications.

Markus, Frances Frank. 1998. "Why Baked Catfish Holds Lessons for Their Hearts." *The New York Times,* June 21, p. 1524.

McGuffey, C. Shawn. 2005. "Engendering Trauma: Race, Class, and Gender Reaffirmation after Child Sexual Abuse." *Gender & Society* 19:621–43.

Misra, Joya, Stephanie Moller, and Marina Karides. 2003. "Envisioning Dependency: Changing Media Depictions of Welfare in the 20th Century." *Social Problems* 50:482–504.

Nelkin, Dorothy. 1987. *Selling Science: How the Press Covers Science and Technology.* New York: Freeman.

New York Times. 2002. "America's Epidemic of Youth Obesity." *The New York Times,* November 29, p. A38.

Newsweek. 2000. "Mail Call." *Newsweek*, July 24, p. 14.

Nichter, Mimi. 2000. *Fat Talk: What Girls and the Parents Say About Dieting.* Cambridge, MA: Harvard University Press.

Popenoe, Rebecca. 2005. "Ideal." Pp. 9–28 in *Fat: The Anthropology of an Obsession*, edited by D. Kulick and A. Meneley. New York: Tarcher/Penguin.

Puhl, R. M., T. Andreyeva, and K. D. Brownell. 2008. "Perceptions of Weight Discrimination: Prevalence and Comparison to Race and Gender Discrimination in America." *International Journal of Obesity* 32:992–1000.

Richardson, Lynda. 2003. "Telling Children Not to Inhale Junk Food, Either." *The New York Times,* July 24, p. B2.

Rohlinger, Deana A. 2007. "American Media and Deliberative Democratic Processes." *Sociological Theory* 25:122–48.

Rothman Morris, Bonnie. 2004. "Older Women, Too, Struggle with a Dangerous Secret." *The New York Times,* July 6, p. F5.

Saguy, Abigail C. and Rene Almeling. 2008. "Fat in the Fire? Science, the News Media, and the 'Obesity Epidemic.'" *Sociological Forum* 23:53–83.

Santora, Marc. 2005. "Study Finds More Obesity and Less Exercising among New York City's Women Than Its Men." *The New York Times,* March 8, p. B3.

Santry, Heena P., Daniel L. Gillen, and Diane S. Lauderdale. 2005. "Trends in Bariatric Surgical Procedures." *JAMA* 294:1909–17.

Schlesinger, Mark. 2005. "Editor's Note: Weighting for Godot." *Journal of Health Politics, Policy, and Law* 30:785–801.

Schudson, Michael. 2003. *The Sociology of the News.* New York: W. W. Norton & Company.

Smith, Delia E., Marsha D. Marcus, Cora Lewis, Marian Fitzgibbon, and Pamela Schreiner. 1998. "Prevalence of Binge Eating Disorder, Obesity, and Depression in a Biracial Cohort of Young Adults." *Annals of Behavioral Medicine* 20:227–32.

Sobal, Jeffery and Albert J. Stunkard. 1989. "Socioeconomic Status and Obesity: A Review of the Literature." *Psychological Bulletin* 105:260–75.

Springen, Karen. 2007. "Health: Battle of the Binge." *Newsweek*, February 19, p. 62.

Stearns, Peter N. 1997. *Fat History: Bodies and Beauty in the Modern West.* New York and London: New York University Press.

Striegel-Moore, Ruth H., Denise E. Wilfley, Kathleen M. Pike, Faith-Anne Dohm, and Christopher G. Fairburn. 2000. "Recurrent Binge Eating in Black American Women." *Archives of Family Medicine* 9:83–87.

Striegel-Moore, Ruth H., Faith A. Dohm, Helena C. Kraemer, C. Barr Taylor, Stephen Daniels, Patricia B. Crawford, and George B. Schrieber. 2003. "Eating Disorders in White and Black Women." *American Journal of Psychiatry* 160:1326–31.

Telch, Christy F. and W. Stewart Agras. 1994. "Obesity, Binge Eating, and Psychopathology: Are They Related?" *International Journal of Eating Disorders* 15:53–61.

Tesh, Sylvia Noble. 1988. *Hidden Arguments: Political Ideology and Disease Prevention Policy.* New Brunswick, NJ: Rutgers University Press.

Thompson, Becky W. 1994. *A Hunger So Wide and So Deep: A Multiracial View of Women's Eating Problems.* Minneapolis: University of Minnesota Press.

Tyre, Peg. 2005. "Fighting Anorexia: No-One to Blame." *Newsweek*, December 5, p. 50.

Wann, Marilyn. 1999. *Fat!So?: Because You Don't Have to Apologize for Your Size.* Berkeley, CA: Ten Speed Press.

Whitaker, Mark. 2005. "The Editor's Desk." *Newsweek*, December 5, p. 4.

10

Yearning for Lightness

Transnational Circuits in the Marketing and Consumption of Skin Lighteners

Evelyn Nakano Glenn

With the breakdown of traditional racial categories in many areas of the world, colorism, by which I mean the preference for and privileging of lighter skin and discrimination against those with darker skin, remains a persisting frontier of intergroup and intragroup relations in the twenty-first century. Sociologists and anthropologists have documented discrimination against darker-skinned persons and correlations between skin tone and socioeconomic status and achievement in Brazil and the United States (Hunter 2005; Sheriff 2001; Telles 2004). Other researchers have revealed that people's judgments about other people are literally colored by skin tone, so that darker-skinned individuals are viewed as less intelligent, trustworthy, and attractive than their lighter-skinned counterparts (Herring, Keith, and Horton 2003; Hunter 2005; Maddox 2004).

One way of conceptualizing skin color, then, is as a form of symbolic capital that affects, if not determines, one's life chances. The relation between skin color and judgments about attractiveness affect women most acutely, since women's worth is judged heavily on the basis of appearance. For example, men who have wealth, education, and other forms of human capital are considered "good catches," while women who are physically attractive may be considered desirable despite the lack of other capital. Although skin tone is usually seen as a

form of fixed or unchangeable capital, in fact, men and women may attempt to acquire light-skinned privilege. Sometimes this search takes the form of seeking light-skinned marital partners to raise one's status and to achieve intergenerational mobility by increasing the likelihood of having light-skinned children. Often, especially for women, this search takes the form of using cosmetics or other treatments to change the appearance of one's skin to make it look lighter.

This article focuses on the practice of skin lightening, the marketing of skin lighteners in various societies around the world, and the multinational corporations that are involved in the global skin-lightening trade. An analysis of this complex topic calls for a multilevel approach. First, we need to place the production, marketing, and consumption of skin lighteners into a global political–economic context. I ask, How is skin lightening interwoven into the world economic system and its transnational circuits of products, capital, culture, and people? Second, we need to examine the mediating entities and processes by which skin lighteners reach specific national/ethnic/racial/class consumers. I ask, What are the media and messages, cultural themes and symbols, used to create the desire for skin-lightening products among particular groups? Finally, we need to examine the meaning and significance of skin color for

Evelyn Nakano Glenn, *Gender & Society* (Vol. 22, Issue 3) 22 pp. Copyright © 2008 Sage Publications. Reprinted by permission of Sage Publications.

consumers of skin lighteners. I ask, How do consumers learn about, test, and compare skin-lightening products, and what do they seek to achieve through their use?

The issue of skin lightening may seem trivial at first glance. However, it is my contention that a close examination of the global circuits of skin lightening provides a unique lens through which to view the workings of the Western-dominated global system as it simultaneously promulgates a "white is right" ideology while also promoting the desire for and consumption of Western culture and products.

SKIN LIGHTENING AND GLOBAL CAPITAL

Skin lightening has long been practiced in many parts of the world. Women concocted their own treatments or purchased products from self-styled beauty experts offering special creams, soaps, or lotions, which were either ineffective sham products or else effective but containing highly toxic materials such as mercury or lead. From the perspective of the supposedly enlightened present, skin lightening might be viewed as a form of vanity or a misguided and dangerous relic of the past.

However, at the beginning of the twenty-first century, the search for light skin, free of imperfections such as freckles and age spots, has actually accelerated, and the market for skin-lightening products has mushroomed in all parts of the world. The production and marketing of products that offer the prospect of lighter, brighter, whiter skin has become a multi-billion-dollar global industry. Skin lightening has been incorporated into transnational flows of capital, goods, people, and culture. It is implicated in both the formal global economy and various informal economies. It is integrated into both legal and extralegal transnational circuits of goods. Certain large multinational corporations have become major players, spending vast sums on research and development and on advertising and marketing to reach both mass and specialized markets. Simultaneously, actors in informal or underground economies, including smugglers, transnational migrants, and petty traders, are finding unprecedented opportunities in producing, transporting, and selling unregulated lightening products.

One reason for this complex multifaceted structure is that the market for skin lighteners, although global in scope, is also highly decentralized and segmented along socioeconomic, age, national, ethnic, racial, and cultural lines. Whether the manufacturers are multi-billion-dollar corporations or small entrepreneurs, they make separate product lines and use distinct marketing strategies to reach specific segments of consumers. Ethnic companies and entrepreneurs may be best positioned to draw on local cultural themes, but large multinationals can draw on local experts to tailor advertising images and messages to appeal to particular audiences.

The Internet has become a major tool/highway/ engine for the globalized, segmented, lightening market. It is the site where all of the players in the global lightening market meet. Large multinationals, small local firms, individual entrepreneurs, skin doctors, direct sales merchants, and even eBay sellers use the Internet to disseminate the ideal of light skin and to advertise and sell their products. Consumers go on the Internet to do research on products and shop. Some also participate in Internet message boards and forums to seek advice and to discuss, debate, and rate skin lighteners. There are many such forums, often as part of transnational ethnic Web sites. For example, IndiaParenting .com and sukh-dukh.com, designed for South Asians in India and other parts of the world, have chat rooms on skin care and lightening, and Rexinteractive.com, a Filipino site, and Candymag.com, a site sponsored by a magazine for Filipina teens, have extensive forums on skin lightening. The discussions on these forums provide a window through which to view the meaning of skin color to consumers, their desires and anxieties, doubts and aspirations. The Internet is thus an important site from which one can gain a multilevel perspective on skin lightening.

CONSUMER GROUPS AND MARKET NICHES

Africa and African Diaspora

In Southern Africa, colorism is just one of the negative inheritances of European colonialism. The ideology of white supremacy that European colonists brought included the association of Blackness with primitiveness, lack of civilization, unrestrained sexuality, pollution, and dirt. The association of Blackness with dirt can be seen in a 1930 French advertising poster for Dirtoff. The poster shows a drawing of a dark African man washing his hands, which have become white, as he declares, "Le Savon Dirtoff me blanchit!" The soap was designed not for use by Africans but, as the poster notes, *pour mechanciens automobilises et menagers*—French auto mechanics and housewives. Such images showing Black people "dramatically losing their pigmentation as a result of the cleansing process," were common in late nineteenth- and early twentieth-century soap advertisements, according to art historian Jean Michel Massing (1995, 180).

Some historians and anthropologists have argued that precolonial African conceptions of female beauty favored women with light brown, yellow, or reddish tints. If so, the racial hierarchies established in areas colonized by Europeans cemented and generalized the privilege attached to light skin (Burke 1996; Ribane 2006, 12). In both South Africa and Rhodesia/Zimbabwe, an intermediate category of those considered to be racially mixed was classified as "coloured" and subjected to fewer legislative restrictions than those classified as "native." Assignment to the coloured category was based on ill-defined criteria, and on arrival in urban areas, people found themselves classified as native or coloured on the basis of skin tone and other phenotypic characteristics. Indians arriving in Rhodesia from Goa, for example, were variously classified as "Portuguese Mulatto" or coloured. The multiplication of discriminatory laws targeting natives led to a growing number of Blacks claiming to be coloured in both societies (Muzondidya 2005, 23–24).

The use of skin lighteners has a long history in Southern Africa, which is described by Lynn Thomas and which I will not recount here (in press). Rather, I will discuss the current picture, which shows both a rise in the consumption of skin-lightening products and concerted efforts to curtail the trade of such products. Despite bans on the importation of skin lighteners, the widespread use of these products currently constitutes a serious health issue in Southern Africa because the products often contain mercury, corticosteroids, or high doses of hydroquinone. Mercury of course is highly toxic, and sustained exposure can lead to neurological damage and kidney disease. Hydroquinone (originally an industrial chemical) is effective in suppressing melanin production, but exposure to the sun—hard to avoid in Africa—damages skin that has been treated. Furthermore, in dark-skinned people, long-term hydroquinone use can lead to ochronosis, a disfiguring condition involving gray and blue-black discoloration of the skin (Mahe, Ly, and Dangou 2003). The overuse of topical steroids can lead to contact eczema, bacterial and fungal infection, Cushing's syndrome, and skin atrophy (Margulies n.d.; Ntambwe 2004).

Perhaps the most disturbing fact is that mercury soaps used by Africans are manufactured in the European Union (EU), with Ireland and Italy leading in the production of mercury soap. One company that has been the target of activists is Killarney Enterprises, Ltd., in County Wicklow, Ireland. Formerly known as W&E Products and located in Lancashire, England, the company was forced to close following out-of-court settlements of suits filed by two former employers who had given birth to stillborn or severely malformed infants due to exposure to mercury. However, W&E Products then secured a 750,000-pound grant from the Irish Industrial Development Authority to relocate to Ireland, where it changed its name to Killarney Enterprises, Ltd. The company remained in business until April 17, 2007, producing soaps under the popular names Tura, Arut, Swan, Sukisa Bango, Meriko, and Jeraboo (which contained up to 3 percent mercuric iodide). Distribution of mercury soap has been illegal in the EU since 1989, but its manufacture has remained legal as long as the product is exported (Chadwick 2001; Earth Summit 2002, 13–14). These soaps are labeled for use as antiseptics and to prevent body odor; however, they are understood to be and are used as skin bleaches. To complete the circuit, EU-manufactured mercury soaps are smuggled back into the EU to sell in shops catering to African immigrant communities. An Irish journalist noted that the very same brands made by Killarney Enterprises, including Meriko and Tura (banned in both the EU and South Africa) could easily be found in African shops in Dublin (De Faoite 2001; O'Farrell 2002).

As a result of the serious health effects, medical researchers have conducted interview studies to determine how prevalent the practice of skin lightening is among African women. They estimate that 25 percent of women in Bamaki, Mali; 35 percent in Pretoria, South Africa; and 52 percent in Dakar, Senegal, use skin lighteners, as do an astonishing 77 percent of women traders in Lagos, Nigeria (Adebajo 2002; del Guidice and Yves 2002; Mahe, Ly, and Dangou 2003; Malangu and Ogubanjo 2006).

There have been local and transnational campaigns to stop the manufacture of products containing mercury in the EU and efforts to inform African consumers of the dangers of their use and to foster the idea of Black pride. Governments in South Africa, Zimbabwe, Nigeria, and Kenya have banned the import and sale of mercury and hydroquinone products, but they continue to be smuggled in from other African nations (Dooley 2001; Thomas 2004).

Despite these efforts, the use of skin lighteners has been increasing among modernized and cosmopolitan African women. A South African newspaper reported that whereas in the 1970s, typical skin lightener users in South Africa were rural and poor, currently, it is upwardly mobile Black women, those with technical diplomas or university degrees and well-paid jobs, who are driving the market in skin lighteners. A recent study by Mictert Marketing Research found that 1 in 13 upwardly mobile Black women aged 25 to 35 used skin lighteners. It is possible that this is an underestimation, since there is some shame attached to admitting to using skin lighteners (Ntshingila 2005).

These upwardly mobile women turn to expensive imported products from India and Europe rather than cheaper, locally made products. They also go to doctors to get prescriptions for imported lighteners containing corticosteroids, which are intended for short-term use to treat blemishes. They continue using them for long periods beyond the prescribed duration, thus risking damage (Ntshingila 2005). This recent rise in the use of skin lighteners cannot be seen as simply a legacy of colonialism but rather is a consequence of the penetration of multinational capital and Western consumer culture. The practice therefore is likely to continue to increase as the influence of these forces grows.

African America

Color consciousness in the African American community has generally been viewed as a legacy of slavery, under which mulattos, the offspring of white men and slave women, were accorded better treatment than "pure" Africans. While slave owners considered dark-skinned Africans suited to fieldwork, lighter-skinned mulattos were thought to be more intelligent and better suited for indoor work as servants and artisans. Mulattos were also more likely to receive at least rudimentary education and to be manumitted. They went on to form the nucleus of many nineteenth-century free Black communities. After the civil war, light-skinned mulattos tried to distance themselves from their darker-skinned brothers and sisters, forming exclusive civic and cultural organizations, fraternities, sororities, schools, and universities (Russell, Wilson, and Hall 1992, 24–40). According to Audrey Elisa Kerr, common folklore in the African American community holds that elite African Americans used a "paper bag" test to screen guests at social events and to determine eligibility for membership in their organizations: anyone whose skin was darker than the color of the bag was excluded. Although perhaps apocryphal, the widespread acceptance of the story as historical fact is significant. It has been credible to African Americans because it was consonant with their observations of the skin tone of elite African American society (Kerr 2005).

The preference and desire for light skin can also be detected in the longtime practice of skin lightening. References to African American women using powders and skin bleaches appeared in the Black press as early as the 1850s, according to historian Kathy Peiss. She notes that *American Magazine* criticized African Americans who tried to emulate white beauty standards: "Beautiful black and brown faces by application of rouge and lily white are made to assume unnatural tints, like the vivid hue of painted corpses" (Peiss 1998, 41). How common such practices were is unknown. However, by the 1880s and 1890s, dealers in skin bleaches were widely advertising their wares in the African American press. A Crane and Company ad in the *Colored American Magazine* (1903) promised that use of the company's "wonderful Face Bleach" would result in a "peach-like complexion" and "turn the skin of a black or brown person five or six shades lighter and of a mulatto person perfectly white" (Peiss 1998, 41, 42).

Throughout the twentieth century, many African American leaders spoke out against skin bleaching, as well as hair straightening, and the African American press published articles decrying these practices. However, such articles were far outnumbered by advertisements for skin bleaches in prominent outlets such as the *Crusader, Negro World,* and the *Chicago Defender.*

An estimated 30 to 40 percent of advertisements in these outlets were for cosmetics and toiletries including skin bleaches. Many of the advertised lighteners were produced by white manufacturers; for example, Black and White Cream was made by Plough Chemicals (which later became Plough-Shearing), and Nadolina was made by the National Toilet Company. A chemical analysis of Nadolina Bleach conducted in 1930 found it contained 10 percent ammoniated mercury, a concentration high enough to pose a serious health risk. Both brands are still marketed in African American outlets, although with changed ingredients (Peiss 1998, 210, 212).[1]

The manufacture and marketing of Black beauty products, including skin lighteners, provided opportunities for Black entrepreneurs. Annie Turnbo Malone, who founded the Poro brand, and Sara Breedlove, later known as Madam C. J. Walker, who formulated and marketed the Wonder Hair Grower, were two of the most successful Black entrepreneurs of the late nineteenth and early twentieth centuries. Malone and Walker championed African American causes and were benefactors of various institutions (Peiss 1998, 67–70; see also Bundles 2001). Significantly, both refused to sell skin bleaches or to describe their hair care products as hair straighteners. After Walker died in 1919, her successor, F. B. Ransom, introduced Tan-Off, which became one of the company's best sellers in the 1920s and 1930s. Other Black-owned companies, such as Kashmir (which produced Nile Queen), Poro, Overton, and Dr. Palmer, advertised and sold skin lighteners. Unlike some white-produced products, they did not contain mercury but relied on such ingredients as borax and hydrogen peroxide (Peiss 1998, 205, 212, 213).

Currently, a plethora of brands is marketed especially to African Americans, including Black and White Cream, Nadolina (sans mercury), Ambi, Palmer's, DR Daggett and Remsdell (fade cream and facial brightening cream), Swiss Whitening Pills, Ultra Glow, Skin Success, Avre (which produces the Pallid Skin Lightening System and B-Lite Fade Cream), and Clear Essence (which targets women of color more generally). Some of these products contain hydroquinone, while others claim to use natural ingredients.

Discussions of skin lightening on African American Internet forums indicate that the participants seek not white skin but "light" skin like that of African American celebrities such as film actress Halle Berry and

singer Beyonce Knowles. Most women say they want to be two or three shades lighter or to get rid of dark spots and freckles to even out their skin tones, something that many skin lighteners claim to do. Some of the writers believe that Halle Berry and other African American celebrities have achieved their luminescent appearance through skin bleaching, skillful use of cosmetics, and artful lighting. Thus, some skin-lightening products, such as the Pallid Skin Lightening System, purport to offer the "secret" of the stars. A Web site for Swiss Lightening Pills claims that "for many years Hollywood has been keeping the secret of whitening pills" and asks, rhetorically, "Have you wondered why early childhood photos of many top celebs show a much darker skin colour than they have now?"[2]

India and Indian Diaspora

As in the case of Africa, the origins of colorism in India are obscure, and the issue of whether there was a privileging of light skin in precolonial Indian societies is far from settled. Colonial-era and postcolonial Indian writings on the issue may themselves have been influenced by European notions of caste, culture, and race. Many of these writings expound on a racial distinction between lighter-skinned Aryans, who migrated into India from the North and darker-skinned "indigenous" Dravidians of the South. The wide range of skin color from North to South and the variation in skin tone within castes make it hard to correlate light skin with high caste. The most direct connection between skin color and social status could be found in the paler hue of those whose position and wealth enabled them to spend their lives sheltered indoors, compared to the darker hue of those who toiled outdoors in the sun (Khan 2008).

British racial concepts evolved over the course of its colonial history as colonial administrators and settlers attempted to make sense of the variety of cultural and language groups and to justify British rule in India. British observers attributed group differences variously to culture, language, climate, or biological race. However, they viewed the English as representing the highest culture and embodying the optimum physical type; they made invidious comparisons between lighter-skinned groups, whose men they viewed as more intelligent and marital and whose women they considered more attractive, and darker-skinned groups, whose men they viewed as lacking intelligence and masculinity, and whose women they considered to be lacking in beauty (Arnold 2004).

Regardless of the origins of color consciousness in India, the preference for light skin seems almost universal today, and in terms of sheer numbers, India and Indian diasporic communities around the world constitute the largest market for skin lighteners. The major consumers of these products in South Asian communities are women between the ages of 16 and 35. On transnational South Asian blog sites, women describing themselves as "dark" or "wheatish" in color state a desire to be "fair." Somewhat older women seek to reclaim their youthful skin color, describing themselves as having gotten darker over time. Younger women tend to be concerned about looking light to make a good marital match or to appear lighter for large family events, including their own weddings. These women recognize the reality that light skin constitutes valuable symbolic capital in the marriage market (Views on Article n.d.).

Contemporary notions of feminine beauty are shaped by the Indian mass media. Since the 1970s, beauty pageants such as Miss World–India have been exceedingly popular viewer spectacles; they are a source of nationalist pride since India has been highly successful in international pageants such as Miss World. As might be expected, the competitors, although varying in skin tone, tend to be lighter than average. The other main avatars of feminine allure are Bollywood actresses, such as Isha Koopikari and Aiswarya Rai, who also tend to be light skinned or, if slightly darker, green eyed (see http://www.indianindustry.com/herbalcosmetics/10275.htm).

Many Indian women use traditional homemade preparations made of plant and fruit products. On various blog sites for Indians both in South Asia and diasporic communities in North America, the Caribbean, and the United Kingdom, women seek advice about "natural" preparations and trade recipes. Many commercial products are made by Indian companies and marketed to Indians around the globe under such names as "fairness cream," "herbal bleach cream," "whitening cream," and "fairness cold cream." Many of these products claim to be based on ayurvedic medicine and contain herbal and fruit extracts such as saffron, papaya, almonds, and lentils (Runkle 2004).

With economic liberalization in 1991, the number of products available on the Indian market, including cosmetics and skin care products, has mushroomed. Whereas prior to 1991, Indian consumers had the choice of two brands of cold cream and moisturizers, today, they have scores of products from which to select. With deregulation of imports, the rise of the Indian economy, and growth of the urban middle class, multinational companies see India as a prime target for expansion, especially in the area of personal care products. The multinationals, through regional subsidiaries, have developed many whitening product lines in various price ranges that target markets ranging from rural villagers to white-collar urban dwellers and affluent professionals and managers (Runkle 2005).

Southeast Asia: The Philippines

Because of its history as a colonial dependency first of Spain and then of the United States, the Philippines has been particularly affected by Western ideology and culture, both of which valorize whiteness. Moreover, frequent intermarriage among indigenous populations, Spanish colonists, and Chinese settlers has resulted in a substantially mestizo population that ranges widely on the skin color spectrum. The business and political elites have tended to be disproportionately light skinned with visible Hispanic and/or Chinese appearance. In the contemporary period, economic integration has led to the collapse of traditional means of livelihood, resulting in large-scale emigration by both working-class and middle-class Filipinos to seek better-paying jobs in the Middle East, Asia, Europe, and North America. An estimated 10 million Filipinos were working abroad as of 2004, with more than a million departing each year. Because of the demand for domestic workers, nannies, and care workers in the global North, women make up more than half of those working abroad (Tabbada 2006). Many, if not most, of these migrants remit money and send Western consumer goods to their families in the Philippines. They also maintain transnational ties with their families at home and across the diaspora through print media, phone, and the Internet. All of these factors contribute to an interest in and fascination with Western consumer culture, including fashion and cosmetics in the Philippines and in Filipino diasporic communities (Parrenas 2001).

Perhaps not surprising, interest in skin lightening seems to be huge and growing in the Philippines, especially among younger urban women. Synovate, a market research firm, reported that in 2004, 50 percent of respondents in the Philippines reported currently using skin lightener (Synovate 2004). Young Filipinas participate in several Internet sites seeking advice on lightening products. They seek not only to lighten their skin overall but also to deal with dark underarms, elbows, and knees. Judging by their entries in Internet discussion sites, many teens are quite obsessed with finding "the secret" to lighter skin and have purchased and tried scores of different brands of creams and pills. They are disappointed to find that these products may have some temporary effects but do not lead to permanent change. They discuss products made in the Philippines but are most interested in products made by large European and American multinational cosmetic firms and Japanese and Korean companies. Clearly, these young Filipinas associate light skin with modernity and social mobility. Interesting to note, the young Filipinas do not refer to Americans or Europeans as having the most desirable skin color. They are more apt to look to Japanese and Koreans or to Spanish- or Chinese-appearing (and light-skinned) Filipina celebrities, such as Michelle Reis, Sharon Kuneta, or Claudine Baretto, as their ideals.[3]

The notion that Japanese and Korean women represent ideal Asian beauty has fostered a brisk market in skin lighteners that are formulated by Korean and Japanese companies. Asian White Skin and its sister company Yumei Misei, headquartered in Korea, sell Japanese and Korean skin care products in the Philippines both in retail outlets and online. Products include Asianwhiteskin Underarm Whitening Kit, Japanese Whitening Cream Enzyme Q-10, Japan Whitening Fruit Cream, Kang Tian Sheep Placenta Whitening Capsules, and Kyusoku Bhaku Lightening Pills (see http://yumeimise.com/store/index).

East Asia: Japan, China, and Korea

East Asian societies have historically idealized light or even white skin for women. Intage (2001), a market research firm in Japan, puts it, "Japan has long idolized ivory-like skin that is 'like a boiled egg'—soft, white and smooth on the surface." Indeed, prior to the Meiji Period (starting in the 1860s), men and women of the higher classes wore white-lead powder makeup (along with blackened teeth and shaved eyebrows). With modernization, according to Mikiko Ashikari, men completely abandoned makeup, but middle- and upper-class women continued to wear traditional white-lead powder when dressed in formal kimonos for ceremonial occasions, such as marriages, and adopted light-colored modern face powder to wear with Western clothes. Ashikari finds through observations of 777 women at several sites in Osaka during 1996–1997 that 97.4 percent of women in public wore what she calls "white face," that is, makeup that "makes their faces look whiter than they really are" (2003, 3).

Intage (2001) reports that skin care products, moisturizers, face masks, and skin lighteners account for 66 percent of the cosmetics market in Japan. A perusal of displays of Japanese cosmetics and skin care products shows that most, even those not explicitly stated to be whitening products, carry names that contain the word "white," for example, facial masks labeled "Clear Turn White" or "Pure White." In addition, numerous products are marketed specifically as whiteners. All of the leading Japanese firms in the cosmetics field, Shiseido, Kosa, Kanebo, and Pola, offer multiproduct skin-whitening lines, with names such as "White Lucent" and "Whitissimo." Fytokem, a Canadian company that produces ingredients used in skin-whitening products, reports that Japan's market in skin lighteners topped $5 billion in 1999 (Saskatchewan Business Unlimited 2005). With deregulation of imports, leading multinational firms, such as L'Oreal, have also made large inroads in the Japanese market. French products have a special cachet (Exhibitor Info 2006).

While the Japanese market has been the largest, its growth rate is much lower than those of Korea and China. Korea's cosmetic market has been growing at a 10 percent rate per year while that of China has been growing by 20 percent. Fytokem estimates that the market for skin whiteners in China was worth $1 billion in 2002 and was projected to grow tremendously. A 2007 Nielsen global survey found that 46 percent of Chinese, 47 percent of people in Hong Kong, 46 percent of Taiwanese, 29 percent of Koreans, and 24 percent of Japanese had used a skin lightener in the past year. As to regular users, 30 percent of Chinese, 20 percent of Taiwanese, 18 percent of Japanese and Hong Kongers, and 8 percent of Koreans used them weekly or daily.

However, if money were no object, 52 percent of Koreans said they would spend more on skin lightening, compared to 26 percent of Chinese, 23 percent of Hong Kongers and Taiwanese, and 21 percent of Japanese (Nielsen 2007).

Latin America: Mexico and the Mexican Diaspora

Throughout Latin America, skin tone is a major marker of status and a form of symbolic capital, despite national ideologies of racial democracy. In some countries, such as Brazil, where there was African chattel slavery and extensive miscegenation, there is considerable color consciousness along with an elaborate vocabulary to refer to varying shades of skin. In other countries, such as Mexico, the main intermixture was between Spanish colonists and indigenous peoples, along with an unacknowledged admixture with African slaves. *Mestizaje* is the official national ideal. The Mexican concept of mestizaje meant that through racial and ethnic mixture, Mexico would gradually be peopled by a whiter "cosmic race" that surpassed its initial ingredients. Nonetheless, skin tone, along with other phenotypical traits, is a significant marker of social status, with lightness signifying purity and beauty and darkness signifying contamination and ugliness (Stepan 1991, 135). The elite has remained overwhelmingly light skinned and European appearing while rural poor are predominantly dark skinned and Indigenous appearing.

Ethnographic studies of Mexican communities in Mexico City and Michoacan found residents to be highly color conscious, with darker-skinned family members likely to be ridiculed or teased. The first question that a relative often poses about a newborn is about his or her color (Farr 2006, chap. 5; Guttman 1996, 40; Martinez 2001). Thus, it should not be a surprise that individuals pursue various strategies to attain light-skinned identity and privileges. Migration from rural areas to the city or to the United States has been one route to transformation from an Indian to a mestizo identity or from a mestizo to a more cosmopolitan urban identity; another strategy has been lightening one's family line through marriage with a lighter-skinned partner. A third strategy has been to use lighteners to change the appearance of one's skin (Winders, Jones, and Higgins 2005, 77–78).

In one of the few references to skin whitening in Mexico, Alan Knight claims that it was "an ancient practice . . . reinforced by film, television, and advertising stereotypes" (1990, 100). As in Africa, consumers seeking low-cost lighteners can easily purchase mercury-laden creams that are still manufactured and used in parts of Latin America (e.g., Recetas de la Farmacia–Crema Blanqueadora, manufactured in the Dominican Republic, contains 6000 ppm of mercury) (NYC Health Dept. 2005). The use of these products has come to public attention because of their use by Latino immigrants in the United States. Outbreaks of mercury poisoning have been reported in Texas, New Mexico, Arizona, and California among immigrants who used Mexican-manufactured creams such as Crema de Belleza–Manning. The cream is manufactured in Mexico by Laboratories Vide Natural SA de CV., Tampico, Tamaulipas, and is distributed primarily in Mexico. However, it has been found for sale in shops and flea markets in the United States in areas located along the U.S.–Mexican border in Arizona, California, New Mexico, and Texas. The label lists the ingredient calomel, which is mercurous chloride (a salt of mercury). Product samples have been found to contain 6 to 10 percent mercury by weight (Centers for Disease Control 1996; U.S. Food and Drug Administration 1996).

For high-end products, hydroquinone is the chemical of choice. White Secret is one of the most visible products since it is advertised in a 30-minute, late-night television infomercial that is broadcast nationally almost nightly.[4] Jamie Winders and colleagues (2005), who analyze the commercial, note that the commercial continually stresses that White Secret is "una formula Americana." According to Winders, Jones, and Higgins, the American pedigree and English-language name endow White Secret with a cosmopolitan cachet and "a first worldliness." The infomercial follows the daily lives of several young urban women, one of whom narrates and explains how White Secret cream forms a barrier against the darkening rays of the sun while a sister product transforms the color of the skin itself. The infomercial conjures the power of science, showing cross sections of skin cells. By showing women applying White Secret in modern, well-lit bathrooms, relaxing in well-appointed apartments, and protected from damaging effects of the sun while walking around the city, the program connects skin lightening with cleanliness, modernity, and mobility (Winders, Jones, and Higgins 2005, 80–84).

Large multinational firms are expanding the marketing of skin care products, including skin lighteners, in Mexico and other parts of Latin America. For example, Stiefel Laboratories, the world's largest privately held pharmaceutical company, which specializes in dermatology products, targets Latin America for skin-lightening products. Six of its 28 wholly owned subsidiaries are located in Latin America. It offers Clariderm, an over-the-counter hydroquinone cream and gel (2 percent), in Brazil, as well as Clasifel, a prescription-strength hydroquinone cream (4 percent), in Mexico, Peru, Bolivia, Venezuela, and other Latin American countries. It also sells Claripel, a 4 percent hydroquinone cream, in the United States.[5]

Middle-Aged and Older White Women in North America and Europe

Historically, at least in the United States, the vast majority of skin lightener users have been so-called white women. Throughout the nineteenth and early twentieth centuries, European American women, especially those of Southern and Eastern European origins, sought to achieve whiter and brighter skin through use of the many whitening powders and bleaches on the market. In 1930, J. Walter Thomson conducted a survey and found 232 brands of skin lighteners and bleaches for sale. Advertisements for these products appealed to the association of white skin with gentility, social mobility, Anglo-Saxon superiority, and youth. In large cities, such as New York and Chicago, some Jewish women used skin lighteners and hair straighteners produced by Black companies and frequented Black beauty parlors (Peiss 1998, 85, 149, 224).

By the mid-1920s, tanning became acceptable for white women, and in the 1930s and 1940s, it became a craze. A year-round tan came to symbolize high social status since it indicated that a person could afford to travel and spend time at tropical resorts and beaches. In addition, there was a fad for "exotic" Mediterranean and Latin types, with cosmetics designed to enhance "olive" complexions and brunette hair (Peiss 1998, 148–49, 150–51).

However, in the 1980s, as the damaging effects of overexposure to sun rays became known, skin lightening among whites reemerged as a major growth market. Part of this growth was fueled by the aging baby boom generation determined to stave off signs of aging. Many sought not only toned bodies and uplifted faces but also youthful skin—that is, smooth, unblemished, glowing skin without telltale age spots. Age spots are a form of hyperpigmentation that results from exposure to the sun over many years. The treatment is the same as that for overall dark skin: hydroquinone, along with skin peeling, exfoliants, and sunscreen.[6]

MULTINATIONAL COSMETIC AND PHARMACEUTICAL FIRMS AND THEIR TARGETING STRATEGIES

Although there are many small local manufacturers and merchants involved in the skin-lightening game, I want to focus on the giant multinationals, which are fueling the desire for light skin through their advertisement and marketing strategies. The accounts of the skin-lightening markets have shown that the desire for lighter skin and the use of skin bleaches is accelerating in places where modernization and the influence of Western capitalism and culture are most prominent. Multinational biotechnology, cosmetic, and pharmaceutical corporations have coalesced through mergers and acquisitions to create and market personal care products that blur the lines between cosmetics and pharmaceuticals. They have jumped into the field of skin lighteners and correctors, developing many product lines to advertise and sell in Europe, North America, South Asia, East and Southeast Asia, and the Middle East (Wong 2004).

Three of the largest corporations involved in developing the skin-lightening market are L'Oreal, Shiseido, and Unilever. The French-based L'Oreal, with €15.8 billion in sales in 2006, is the largest cosmetics company in the world. It consists of 21 major subsidiaries including Lancome; Vichy Laboratories; La Roche-Posay Laboratoire Pharmaceutique; Biotherm; Garnier; Giorgio Armani Perfumes; Maybelline, New York; Ralph Lauren Fragrances; Skinceuticals; Shu Uemura; Matrix; Redken; and SoftSheen Carlson. L'Oreal is also a 20 percent shareholder of Sanofi-Synthelabo, a major France-based pharmaceutical firm. Three L'Oreal subsidiaries produce the best-known skin-lightening lines marketed around the world (which are especially big in Asia): Lancome Blanc Expert with Melo-No Complex, LaRoche-Posay Mela-D White skin lightening daily lotion with a triple-action formula, and Vichy Biwhite, containing procystein and vitamin C.

A second major player in the skin-lightening market is Shiseido, the largest and best-known Japanese cosmetics firm, with net sales of $5.7 billion. Shiseido cosmetics are marketed in 65 countries and regions, and it operates factories in Europe, the Americas, and other Asian countries. The Shiseido Group, including affiliates, employs approximately 25,200 people around the globe. Its two main luxury lightening lines are White Lucent (for whitening) and White Lucency (for spots/aging). Each product line consists of seven or eight components, which the consumer is supposed to use as part of a complicated regimen involving applications of specific products several times a day.[7]

The third multinational corporation is Unilever, a diversified Anglo-Dutch company with an annual turnover of more than €40 billion and net profits of €5 billion in 2006 (Unilever 2006). It specializes in so-called fast-moving consumer goods in three areas: food (many familiar brands, including Hellman's Mayonnaise and Lipton Tea), home care (laundry detergents, etc.), and personal care, including deodorants, hair care, oral care, and skin care. Its most famous brand in the skin care line is Ponds, which sells cold creams in Europe and North America and whitening creams in Asia, the Middle East, and Latin America.

Through its Indian subsidiary, Hindustan Lever Limited, Unilever patented Fair & Lovely in 1971 following the patenting of niacinamide, a melanin suppressor, which is its main active ingredient. Test marketed in South India in 1975, it became available throughout India in 1978. Fair & Lovely has become the largest-selling skin cream in India, accounting for 80 percent of the fairness cream market. According to anthropologist Susan Runkle (2005), "Fair and Lovely has an estimated sixty million consumers throughout the Indian subcontinent and exports to thirty-four countries in Southeast and Central Asia as well as the Middle East."

Fair & Lovely ads claim that "with regular daily use, you will be able to unveil your natural radiant fairness in just 6 weeks!" As with other successful brands, Fair & Lovely has periodically added new lines to appeal to special markets. In 2003, it introduced Fair & Lovely, Ayurvedic, which claims to be formulated according to a 4,500-year-old Indian medical system. In 2004, it introduced Fair & Lovely Oil-Control Gel and Fair & Lovely Anti-Marks. In 2004, Fair & Lovely also announced the "unveiling" of a premium line, Perfect Radiance, "a complete range of 12 premium skin care solutions" containing "international formulations from Unilever's Global Skin Technology Center, combined with ingredients best suited for Indian skin types and climates." Its ads say "Experience Perfect Radiance from Fair & Lovely. Unveil Perfect Skin." Intended to compete with expensive European brands, Perfect Radiance is sold only in select stores in major cities, including Delhi, Mumbai, Chennai, and Bangalore.[8]

Unilever is known for promoting its brands by being active and visible in the locales where they are marketed. In India, Ponds sponsors the Femina Miss India pageant, in which aspiring contestants are urged to "be as beautiful as you can be." Judging by photos of past winners, being as beautiful as you can be means being as light as you can be. In 2003, partly in response to criticism by the All India Democratic Women's Association of "racist" advertisement of fairness products, Hindustani Lever launched the Fair & Lovely Foundation, whose mission is to "encourage economic empowerment of women across India" through educational and guidance programs, training courses, and scholarships.[9]

Unilever heavily promotes both Ponds and Fair & Lovely with television and print ads tailored to local cultures. In one commercial shown in India, a young, dark-skinned woman's father laments that he has no son to provide for him and his daughter's salary is not high enough. The suggestion is that she could neither get a better job nor marry because of her dark skin. The young woman then uses Fair & Lovely, becomes fairer, and lands a job as an airline hostess, making her father happy. A Malaysian television spot shows a college student who is dejected because she cannot get the attention of a classmate at the next desk. After using Pond's lightening moisturizer, she appears in class brightly lit and several shades lighter, and the boy says, "Why didn't I notice her before?" (BBC 2003).

Such advertisements can be seen as not simply responding to a preexisting need but actually creating a need by depicting having dark skin as a painful and depressing experience. Before "unveiling" their fairness, dark-skinned women are shown as unhappy, suffering from low self-esteem, ignored by young men, and denigrated by their parents. By using Fair & Lovely or Ponds, a woman undergoes a transformation of not only her complexion but also her personality and her fate. In short, dark skin becomes a burden and handicap that can be overcome only by using the product being advertised.

CONCLUSION

The yearning for lightness evident in the widespread and growing use of skin bleaching around the globe can rightfully be seen as a legacy of colonialism, a manifestation of "false consciousness," and the internalization of "white is right" values by people of color, especially women. Thus, one often-proposed solution to the problem is reeducation that stresses the diversity of types of beauty and desirability and that valorizes darker skin shades, so that lightness/whiteness is dislodged as the dominant standard.

While such efforts are needed, focusing only on individual consciousness and motives distracts attention from the very powerful economic forces that help to create the yearning for lightness and that offer to fulfill the yearning at a steep price. The manufacturing, advertising, and selling of skin lightening is no longer a marginal, underground economic activity. It has become a major growth market for giant multinational corporations with their sophisticated means of creating and manipulating needs.

The multinationals produce separate product lines that appeal to different target audiences. For some lines of products, the corporations harness the prestige of science by showing cross-sectional diagrams of skin cells and by displaying images of doctors in white coats. Dark skin or dark spots become a disease for which skin lighteners offer a cure. For other lines, designed to appeal to those who respond to appeals to naturalness, corporations call up nature by emphasizing the use of plant extracts and by displaying images of light-skinned women against a background of blue skies and fields of flowers. Dark skin becomes a veil that hides one's natural luminescence, which natural skin lighteners will uncover. For all products, dark skin is associated with pain,

rejection, and limited options; achieving light skin is seen as necessary to being youthful, attractive, modern, and affluent—in short, to being "all that you can be."

NOTES

1. Under pressure from African American critics, Nadolina reduced the concentration to 6 percent in 1937 and 1.5 percent in 1941.

2. Discussions on Bright Skin Forum, Skin Lightening Board, are at http://excoboard.com/exco/forum.php?forumid=65288. Pallid Skin Lightening system information is at http://www.avreskincare.com/skin/pallid/index.html. Advertisement for Swiss Whitening Pills is at http://www.skinbleaching.net.

3. Skin whitening forums are at http://www.candymag.com/tcentalk/index.php/topic,131753.0.html and http://www.rexinteractive.com/forum/topic.asp?TOPIC_ID=41.

4. Discussion of the ingredients in White Secret is found at http://www.vsantivirus.com/hoax-white-secret.htm.

5. I say that Stiefel targets Latin America because it markets other dermatology products, but not skin lighteners, in the competitive Asian, Middle Eastern, African, and European countries. Information about Stiefel products is at its corporate Web site, http://www.stiefel.com/why/about.aspx (accessed May 1, 2007).

6. Many of the products used by older white and Asian women to deal with age spots are physician-prescribed pharmaceuticals, including prescription-strength hydroquinone formulas. See information on one widely used system, Obagi, at http://www.obagi.com/article/homepage.html (accessed December 13, 2006).

7. *Shiseido Annual Report 2006,* 34, was downloaded from http://www.shiseido.co.jp/e/annual/html/index.htm. Data on European, American, and Japanese markets are at http://www.shiseido.co.jp/e/story/html/sto40200.htm. World employment figures are at http://www.shiseido.co.jp/e/story/html/sto40200.htm. White Lucent information is at http://www.shiseido.co.jp/e/whitelucent_us/products/product5.htm. White Lucency information is at http://www.shiseido.co.jp/e/whitelucency/ (all accessed May 6, 2007).

8. "Fair & Lovely Launches Oil-Control Fairness Gel" (Press Release, April 27, 2004) is found at http://www.hll.com/mediacentre/release.asp?fl=2004/PR_HLL_042704.htm (accessed May 6, 2007). "Fair & Lovely Unveils Premium Range" (Press Release, May 25, 2004) is available at http://www.hll.com/mediacentre/release.asp?fl=2004/PR_HLL_052104_2.htm (accessed on May 6, 2007).

9. The Pond's Femina Miss World site is http://feminamissindia.indiatimes.com/articleshow/1375041.cms. The All India Democratic Women's Association objects to skin lightening ad is at http://www.aidwa.org/content/issues_of_concern/women_and_media.php. Reference to Fair & Lovely campaign is at http://www.aidwa.org/content/issues_of_concern/women_and_media.php. "Fair & Lovely Launches Foundation to Promote Economic Empowerment of Women" (Press Release, March 11, 2003) is found at http://www.hll.com/mediacentre/release.asp?fl=2003/PR_HLL_031103.htm (all accessed December 2, 2006).

REFERENCES

Adebajo, S. B. 2002. An epidemiological survey of the use of cosmetic skin lightening cosmetics among traders in Lagos, Nigeria. *West African Journal of Medicine* 21 (1): 51–55.

Arnold, David. 2004. Race, place and bodily difference in early nineteenth century India. *Historical Research* 77:162.

Ashikari, Makiko. 2003. Urban middle-class Japanese women and their white faces: Gender, ideology, and representation. *Ethos* 31 (1): 3, 3–4, 9–11.

BBC. 2003. India debates "racist" skin cream ads. *BBC News World Edition,* July 24. http://news.bbc.co.uk/1/hi/world/south_asia/3089495.stm (accessed May 8, 2007).

Bundles, A'Lelia. 2001. *On her own ground: The life and times of Madam C. J. Walker.* New York: Scribner.

Burke, Timothy. 1996. *Lifebuoy men, lux women: Commodification, consumption, and cleanliness in modern Zimbabwe.* Durham, NC: Duke University Press.

Centers for Disease Control and Prevention. 1996. *FDA warns consumers not to use Crema De Belleza.* FDA statement. Rockville, MD: U.S. Food and Drug Administration.

Chadwick, Julia. 2001. Arklow's toxic soap factory. *Wicklow Today,* June. http://www.wicklowtoday.com/features/mercurysoap.htm (accessed April 18, 2007).

De Faoite, Dara. 2001. Investigation into the sale of dangerous mercury soaps in ethnic shops. *The Observer,* May 27. http://observer.guardian.co.uk/uk_news/story/0,6903,497227,00.html (accessed May 1, 2007).

del Guidice, P., and P. Yves. 2002. The widespread use of skin lightening creams in Senegal: A persistent public health problem in West Africa. *International Journal of Dermatology* 41:69–72.

Dooley, Erin. 2001. Sickening soap trade. *Environmental Health Perspectives,* October.

Earth Summit. 2002. *Telling it like it is: 10 years of unsustainable development in Ireland.* Dublin, Ireland: Earth Summit.

Exhibitor info. 2006. http://www.beautyworldjapan.com/en/efirst.html (accessed May 8, 2007).

Farr, Marcia. 2006. *Rancheros in Chicagocan: Language and identity in a transnational community.* Austin: University of Texas Press.

Guttman, Matthew C. 1996. *The meanings of macho: Being a man in Mexico City.* Berkeley: University of California Press.

Herring, Cedric, Verna M. Keith, and Hayward Derrick Horton, eds. 2003. *Skin deep: How race and complexion matter in the "color blind" era.* Chicago: Institute for Research on Race and Public Policy.

Hunter, Margaret. 2005. *Race, gender, and the politics of skin tone.* New York: Routledge.

Intage. 2001. Intelligence on the cosmetic market in Japan. http://www.intage.co.jp/expess/01_08/market/index1.html (accessed November 2005).

Kerr, Audrey Elisa. 2005. The paper bag principle: The myth and the motion of colorism. *Journal of American Folklore* 118:271–89.

Khan, Aisha. 2008. "Caucasian," "coolie," "Black," or "white"? Color and race in the Indo-Caribbean Diaspora. Unpublished paper.

Knight, Alan. 1990. Racism, revolution, and indigenismo: Mexico, 1910–1940. In *The idea of race in Latin America, 1870–1940,* edited by Richard Graham. Austin: University of Texas Press.

Maddox, Keith B. 2004. Perspectives on racial phenotypicality bias. *Personality and Social Psychology Review* 8:383–401.

Mahe, Antoine, Fatimata Ly, and Jean-Marie Dangou. 2003. Skin diseases associated with the cosmetic use of bleaching products in women from Dakar, Senegal. *British Journal of Dermatology* 148 (3): 493–500.

Malangu, N., and G. A. Ogubanjo. 2006. Predictors of tropical steroid misuse among patrons of pharmacies in Pretoria. *South African Family Practices* 48 (1): 14.

Margulies, Paul. n.d. Cushing's syndrome: The facts you need to know. http://www.nadf.us/diseases/cushingsmedhelp.org/www/nadf4.htm (accessed May 1, 2007).

Martinez, Ruben. 2001. *Crossing over: A Mexican family on the migrant trail.* New York: Henry Holt.

Massing, Jean Michel. 1995. From Greek proverb to soap advert: Washing the Ethiopian. *Journal of the Warburg and Courtauld Institutes* 58:180.

Muzondidya, James. 2005. *Walking a tightrope, towards a social history of the coloured community of Zimbabwe.* Trenton, NJ: Africa World Press.

Nielsen. 2007. Prairie plants take root. In *Health, beauty & personal grooming: A global Nielsen consumer report.* http://www.acnielsen.co.in/news/20070402.shtml (accessed May 3, 2007).

Ntambwe, Malangu. 2004. Mirror mirror on the wall, who is the fairest of them all? *Science in Africa, Africa's First On-Line Science Magazine,* March. http://www.scienceinafrica.co.za/2004/march/skinlightening.htm (accessed May 1, 2007).

Ntshingila, Futhi. 2005. Female buppies using harmful skin lighteners. *Sunday Times, South Africa,* November 27. http://www.sundaytimes.co.za (accessed January 25, 2006).

NYC Health Dept. 2005. NYC Health Dept. warns against use of "skin lightening" creams containing mercury or similar products which do not list ingredients. http://www.nyc.gov/html/doh/html/pr/pr008-05.shtml (accessed May 7, 2007).

O'Farrell, Michael. 2002. Pressure mounts to have soap plant shut down. *Irish Examiner,* August 26. http://archives.tcm.ie/irishexaminer/2002/08/26/story510455503.asp (accessed May 1, 2007).

Parrenas, Rhacel. 2001. *Servants of globalization: Women, migration, and domestic work.* Palo Alto, CA: Stanford University Press.

Peiss, Kathy. 1998. *Hope in a jar: The making of America's beauty culture.* New York: Metropolitan Books.

Ribane, Nakedi. 2006. *Beauty: A Black perspective.* Durban, South Africa: University of KwaZulu-Natal Press.

Runkle, Susan. 2004. Making "Miss India": Constructing gender, power and nation. *South Asian Popular Culture* 2 (2): 145–59.

Runkle, Susan. 2005. The beauty obsession. *Manushi* 145 (February). http://www.indiatogether.org/manushi/issue145/lovely.htm (accessed May 5, 2007).

Russell, Kathy, Midge Wilson, and Ronald Hall. 1992. *The color complex: The politics of skin color among African Americans.* New York: Harcourt Brace Jovanovich.

Saskatchewan Business Unlimited. 2005. Prairie plants take root in cosmetics industry. *Saskatchewan Business Unlimited* 10 (1): 1–2.

Sheriff, Robin E. 2001. *Dreaming equality: Color, race and racism in urban Brazil.* New Brunswick, NJ: Rutgers University Press.

Stepan, Nancy Ley. 1991. *The hour of eugenics: Race, gender, and nation in Latin America.* Ithaca, NY: Cornell University Press.

Synovate. 2004. In:fact. http://www.synovate.com/knowledge/infact/issues/200406 (accessed March 21, 2007).

Tabbada, Reyna Mae L. 2006. Trouble in paradise. Press release, September 20. http://www.bulatlat.com/news/6-33/6-33-trouble.htm (accessed May 5, 2007).

Telles, Edward E. 2004. *Race in another America: The significance of skin color in Brazil.* Princeton, NJ: Princeton University Press.

Thomas, Iyamide. 2004. "Yellow fever": The disease that is skin bleaching. *Mano Vision* 33 (October): 32–33. http://www.manovision.com/ISSUES/ISSUE33/33skin.pdf (accessed May 7, 2007).

Thomas, Lynn M. (in press.) Skin lighteners in South Africa: Transnational entanglements and technologies of the self. In *Shades of difference: Why skin color matters,* edited by Evelyn Nakano Glenn. Stanford, CA: Stanford University Press.

Unilever. 2006. Annual report. http://www.unilever.com/ourcompany/investorcentre/annual_reports/archives.asp (accessed May 6, 2007).

U.S. Food and Drug Administration. 1996. *FDA warns consumers not to use Crema De Belleza.* FDA statement, July 23. Rockville, MD: U.S. Food and Drug Administration.

Views on article—Complexion. n.d. http://www.indiaparenting.com/beauty/beauty041book.shtml (accessed November 2005).

Winders, Jamie, John Paul Jones III, and Michael James Higgins. 2005. Making gueras: Selling white identities on late-night Mexican television. *Gender, Place and Culture* 12 (1): 71–93.

Wong, Stephanie. 2004. Whitening cream sales soar as Asia's skin-deep beauties shun Western suntans. *Manila Bulletin.* http://www.mb.com.ph/issues/2004/08/24/SCTY2004082416969.html# (accessed March 24, 2007).

11

Ageism and Feminism

From "Et Cetera" to Center

Toni Calasanti

Kathleen F. Slevin

Neal King

Although women's studies scholars and activists do not deny the reality of ageism, they have relegated it to secondary status, neglecting to theorize age relations or place old age at the center of analysis. After explaining what we mean by age relations and their intersections with other inequalities, we discuss the ways in which old people are oppressed, and why age relations represent a political location that needs to be addressed in its own right. We then demonstrate ways in which feminist theories and activism might change if the focus shifted to old people.

An inadvertent but pernicious ageism burdens much of women's studies scholarship and activism. It stems from failing to study old people on their own terms and from failing to theorize age relations—the system of inequality, based on age, which privileges the not-old at the expense of the old (Calasanti 2003). Some feminists mention age-based oppression but treat it as a given—an "et cetera" on a list of oppressions, as if to indicate that we already know what it is. As a result, feminist work suffers, and we engage in our own oppression. Using scholarship on the body and carework as illustrative,

this article explores both the absence of attention to the old and age relations, and how feminist scholarship can be transformed by the presence of such attention.

NEGLECTING OLD AGE

Feminist scholars have given little attention either to old women or to aging (Arber and Ginn 1991), despite Barbara Macdonald's work in the women's movement in the 1980s and her plea that old age be recognized (Macdonald and Rich 1983); despite the increases in absolute and relative numbers of those over age 65, and the skewed sex ratio among old people in the United States; and despite the shifting age ratios in nations worldwide. The number of women's studies scholars engaged in work on later life is still so small that those with any interest in aging can count them; the rest (probably the majority) may know their names (such as Woodward 1999; Gullette 2004; and Cruikshank 2003) but not their work. The issues go ignored by most scholars, and one must ask why.

Calasanti, Toni M., Kathleen F. Slevin, and Neal King. Ageism and Feminism: From "Et Cetera" to Center. National Women's Studies Association Journal 18:1 (2006), 13–30. Copyright © 2006 NWSA Journal. Reprinted with permission of The Johns Hopkins University Press.

AGE RELATIONS

Scholars, including gerontologists, have scarcely theorized age relations beyond Laws's (1995) important work on age as one of a complex of social relations. As a result, our discussion here represents an early stage in this endeavor. Our notion of age relations comprises three dimensions. First, age serves a social *organizing principle*; second, different age groups gain *identities and power* in relation to one another; and third, age relations *intersect with other power relations*. Together, these have consequences for life chances—for people's abilities to enjoy economic security and good health. The focus on age relations enables us to learn more about how all of our positions and experiences rest upon power relations based on age.

The first assertion, that societies are organized on the basis of age, is widely documented by scholars in aging studies. Age is a master status characteristic that defines individuals as well as groups (Hendricks 2003). Societies proscribe appropriate behaviors and obligations based on age. The second and third aspects of age relations speak more directly to issues of power, and how and why such age-based organization matters for life chances. Old age does not just exacerbate other inequalities but is a social location in its own right, conferring a loss of power for all those designated as "old" regardless of their advantages in other hierarchies.

When feminists explore power relations such as those based on gender, we point to systematic differences between women and men (recognizing that other power relations come into play). In theorizing age relations, then, we also posit systematic differences between being, for instance, an *old* woman and a *young* woman. This position does not deny the importance of life course and aging processes but instead posits discrimination and exclusion based on age—across lines of such inequalities as race, ethnicity, sexuality, class, or gender. The point at which one becomes "old" varies with these other inequalities. Once reached, old age brings losses of authority and status. Old age is a unique time of life and not simply an additive result of events occurring over the life course. Those who are perceived to be old are marginalized and lose power, they are subjected to violence (such as elder abuse) and to exploitation and cultural imperialism (Laws 1995). They suffer inequalities in distributions of authority, status, and money, and

these inequalities are seen to be natural, and thus beyond dispute. Below, we briefly discuss how old people experience these inequalities.

Loss of Power

Old people lose authority and autonomy. For instance, doctors treat old patients differently than younger clients, more often withholding information, services, and treatment of medical problems (Robb, Chen, and Haley 2002). On the one hand, doctors often take the complaints of old people less seriously than younger clients, attributing them to "old age" (Quadagno 1999). On the other hand, old age has been biomedicalized—a process whereby the outcomes of social factors are defined as medical or personal problems to be alleviated by medical intervention. Old people lose their ability to make decisions about their bodies and undergo drug therapies rather than other curative treatments (Wilson 2000; Estes and Binney 1991).

Workplace Issues and Marginalization

Ageism costs old people in the labor market both status and money. Although the attitudes and beliefs of employers are certainly implicated (see Encel 1999), often ageism is more subtly incorporated into staffing and recruitment policies, career structures, and retirement policies (Bytheway 1995). The inability to earn money in later life means that most old people must rely on others—family members or the state. And when we consider the economic dependence and security of old people, the oppressive nature of age relations becomes apparent. The fiscal policies and welfare retrenchment in many Western countries provide one lens on the discrimination faced by old people as they increasingly face cutbacks. As Wilson notes, "Economic policies are often presented as rational and inevitable but, given the power structure of society, these so-called inevitable choices usually end up protecting younger age groups and resulting in unpleasant outcomes for those in later life (cuts in pensions or charges for health care)" (2000, 9). Demographic projections about aging populations are often used to justify such changes, even though relevant evidence is often lacking. Further, neither the public nor decision makers seem willing to consider counterevidence, such as cross-cultural comparisons that reveal little relationship between the percentage of social spending on old persons and their percentage within the overall population (2000). Predictions of dire consequences attendant upon an aging population are similarly unrelated. Indeed, with only 12.4 percent of its population age 65 and over, the United States ranks 37th among countries with at least 10 percent of their population age 65 and over, well below the almost 19 percent of the top three countries, Italy, Japan, and Greece (Federal Interagency Forum on Aging Related Statistics 2004).

Decreases in income, erosion of pensions, and proposals to "reform" Social Security are not the only ways old people are marginalized when they leave the labor market. Laws suggest that labor market participation shapes identity—such that participation in waged labor "is a crucial element of citizenship, in the definition of social worthiness, and in the development of a subject's self-esteem" (1995, 115). In conjunction with the sort of cultural denigration we describe next, the lack of labor market participation encourages young people to see old people as "other" and not fully deserving of citizenship rights (Wilson 2000, 161). Such disenfranchisement may be informal (rather than based in laws), but it is real nonetheless as seen in the previous policy discussion (Laws 1995).

Wealth and Income

In the contemporary United States, many people believe that many old people hold vast economic resources—an assertion that is certainly counter to claims that old people lose status or money in later life. However, the greatest inequalities in terms of income and wealth exist among old people, such that many are quite poor (Pampel 1998). The vast majority that relies on Social Security to stay above the poverty line offsets the small number of old people with tremendous wealth. In concrete terms, Social Security—with monthly payments that averaged $1,013 for men and $764 for women in 2003—provides more than half of all income received for two-thirds of old people in the United States; indeed, it amounts to almost half of all income for four-fifths. Even more, it comprises 90 percent or more of all income for a full one-third of elderly people, and 100 percent of all income for more than one-fifth (22 percent). Reliance on these payments is high for all but the richest quintile

of old people, whose earnings and pensions add more income than does Social Security. Overall economic dependence of old people on this state-administered program is thus quite high, and higher still when we realize that, even with Social Security, about one-fifth of old minority men and more than a fourth of old minority women fall below the age-adjusted poverty line (Social Security Administration 2004; Federal Interagency Forum on Aging Related Statistics 2004).

The poverty line itself provides an example of the differential treatment of old people. The poverty threshold is lower for old people. In 2003, an old person's income had to be below $8,825—compared to $9,573 for those under 65—in order to be officially designated "poor" (DeNavas-Walt, Proctor, and Mills 2004). It's worth noting that most of the public is unaware of this. Poverty thresholds are calculated based on estimates of costs for nutritionally adequate diets, and because of slower metabolism, old people need fewer calories than younger people. Thus, old people are assumed to need less money than those under 65, despite their high medical expenses. As a result, official statistics greatly underestimate the number of old people who are poor.

Cultural Devaluation

Finally, old people are subject to a "cultural imperialism" exemplified by "the emphasis on youth and vitality that undermines the positive contributions of older people" (Laws 1995, 113). The reality that being old, in and of itself, is a position of low status is apparent in the burgeoning anti-aging industry (including the new field of "longevity medicine"), which is estimated to gross between 27 and 43 billion dollars a year (with the expectation of a rise to $64 billion by 2007), depending on how expansive a definition one uses (Mehlman et al. 2004; U.S. Senate, Special Committee on Aging 2001; *Dateline NBC,* March 6, 2001). Besides ingesting nutritional supplements and testosterone or human growth hormones, increasing numbers of people spend hours at the gym, undergo cosmetic surgery, and use lotions, creams, and hair dyes to erase the physical markers of age. The equation of old age with disease and physical and mental decline is so prevalent that visible signs of aging serve to justify the limitation of the rights and authority of old people. Many view old age as a "natural" part of life with unavoidable decrements—an equation apparent in the medical doctors' treatment of symptoms as "just old age" rather than as signs of illness or injury that merit care. The equation of aging with a natural order justifies ageism.

Old people internalize these notions of old age in early life and carry them as they age. Indeed, they may come to see old age as "a social contagion" that compels them to avoid other old people and to seek the company of those younger than themselves (Slevin 2006/in press). Further, to protest ageism would mean acknowledging one's own old age and stigma (Levy 2001; Minichiello, Browne, and Kendig 2000). As a result, and contrary to common belief that old people vote as a bloc, ageism makes it less likely that old people would band together politically to promote age-based power and rights.

Age relations differ from other power relations in that one's group membership shifts over time. As a result, one can experience both aspects of age relations—advantage and disadvantage—over the course of a lifetime. Although other social locations can be malleable, such dramatic shifts in status remain uncommon. Few change racial or gender identities, but we all grow old or die first. Intersecting inequalities affect when this (becoming old) occurs, but the fact remains, where individuals stand in relation to old age *must* change (Calasanti and Slevin 2001).

Next, we explore how placing old age and age relations at the center of our analysis might transform feminist theories and practices. We look at issues of the body and carework as illustrative of how this deliberate shift of focus creates a more inclusive feminist lens—one that can be applied to multiple issues.

CENTERING ON OLD AGE: THE CHALLENGE TO FEMINISMS

Aging Bodies

Because women's studies scholars begin with the experiences of young adults and middle-aged women, much of their argument against cosmetic surgery and the skin-care industry centers on women's relationship to the "male gaze." In this theory, women are styled in visual media to function as erotic spectacle for the pleasure of men (Mulvey 1990, 33). Thus, these critiques

concentrate on the *male-defined* nature of both cosmetic surgery and the skin-care industry. However, when we recognize that an old woman's attractiveness is judged by the disciplining "gaze of youth," then age is revealed as an intersecting axis of inequality (Twigg 2004, 65). Each "gaze" freezes a person as an object defined by subordinate status; and such judgments may be internalized or rejected as foreign by their objects. Yet, the judgments implicit in the male and youthful gazes differ sharply. Twigg describes the power relations between the old care receivers and the younger women who typically bathe them. The naked old people are subjected to the judgmental, always potentially disgusted gaze of youth, indicative of the more subtle stigma attached to old bodies.

Figures of ignorance or scorn, women grow invisible as sexual beings through the aging process—not only in terms of the disappearance of the desirous male gaze, for instance, but also in terms of neglect by younger members of the women's movement and lesbian communities (Holstein 1999; Copper 1986; Macdonald and Rich 1983). Such invisibility calls forth a different set of responses and generates a different form of dependence than those experienced by younger women. In addition, we might ask how putting old women's sexuality at the center of theorizing might change feminist theories. What if we explore the lives of old, heterosexual women who still see themselves as sexual, but feel *cast aside* rather than *objectified*? Neither circumstance amounts to privilege, but they are worth exploring separately. Would the expropriation of women's reproductive labor or exploitation of their bodies still seem like defining moments of women's oppression if we took age relations seriously? And how would our judgments be affected by intersecting inequalities? For instance, many black, retired, professional women express an appreciation for themselves as sexual beings, in contrast to similar white women who feel less desirous or desired (Slevin and Wingrove 1998; Wingrove and Slevin 1991).

Hurtado argues that white, heterosexual women can gain power by aligning as (potential) mates with white men, a possibility from which women of color are typically excluded (1989). White women thus profit from the subordination of racial and ethnic minority women. Furthering Hurtado's argument about relational privilege, we might point to the ways in which younger women benefit from old women's de/sexualization.

That old women are cast aside as sexual partners enhances the abilities of younger women to gain power by partnering with privileged men.

In addition, when we put old women who are lesbian at the center of our analysis, we uncover the ways old age intersects with other social locations in shaping responses to aging and old age. For example, old lesbians may openly reproduce the ageism and age inequality that burdens them in the first place by consciously avoiding other old lesbians and electing to spend time only with younger lesbians (Slevin 2006/in press). Exploring the challenges of being an old lesbian in an ageist and homophobic society enhances a focus on what it means to be a woman in the years when reproduction and heterosexual desirability are no longer privileged.

Carework and Dependence

Centering on old people also would transform our study of carework. Although many feminists have contributed to this research, they have attended to elder care only in relation to the younger women who must balance it with their paid work (and perhaps other forms of care). Research on and interest in old care receivers or spousal caregivers is nonexistent. Yet, spousal caregivers are both preferred and far more like one another than not, exhibiting few gender differences. Spouses engaged in primary care tend to spend similar amounts of time in carework and perform similar tasks, including personal care (Thompson 2000). Understanding how and why spouses provide similar care gives us a different lens on carework, such as men's abilities and structural inducements to give care (Risman 1987). Focusing on caregiving relationships among the old also can point to ways in which gender shapes the meanings of the carework experience and how people negotiate identities in its context. For instance, most people believe that women are natural caregivers. As a result, white, middle-class wives who give care may experience more stress than husbands, despite the fact that husbands are often less prepared to engage in these tasks at the outset. At the same time, men may describe their stress in different terms, or keep it to themselves and use alcohol to cope (Calderon and Tennstedt 1998; Calasanti 2006/in press). Such study can reveal problems for caregivers that result from their being men or

being old, or ways in which frail elders can receive care without feeling dependent (Gibson 1998).

Centering on old careworkers and receivers reveals the power relations embedded in the gaze of youth and the relatively high status given to the care of children. Feminists have long noted that some forms of care work are undervalued, particularly the care of old people (Diamond 1992; Hooyman and Gonyea 1999; Milne and Hazidimitriadou 2002). This is not simply due to the greater value accorded care performed by men. In part, this is so because care for children is more highly valued. To be sure, the carework that men perform for the young is recognized and often lauded, as we see in the esteem accorded the "stay-at-home father" or fathers who share child care. But the carework that old husbands perform for their wives is virtually invisible—from the public eye and from feminist concern.

These discrepant values also should prompt feminists to rethink issues of dependence. Feminists have exposed the gender and race relations underlying "dependence" on the welfare state (see Fraser and Gordon 1994; Estes 2004); but age relations also are implicated. For instance, we noted that projections of age-skewed dependency ratios have been used to promote fiscal retrenchment and cutbacks in old-age policies and programs, including the present call for Social Security "reform" (Estes 2004). Yet, when such skewed ratios reflect a large young population, they do not create the same sort of public outcry, despite the reality that young children are more likely to need care than those, say, ages 65–70 (Gee 2000; Calasanti and Slevin 2001).

Those who are economically active—be they family members or the state—hold economic power over those who are not; and the latter are thus dependent upon them (Bytheway 1995). Women largely depend upon men or the state (Gibson 1998), but in old age, men also become dependents of the state, relying upon the redistribution of economic resources through such policies as public pensions. Although many men are cushioned by multiple privileges when old, they still end up in a position regarded as unmanly (Calasanti and Slevin 2001).

Feminists have demonstrated women's productivity by pointing to their engagement in economic but unpaid activities, such as domestic labor. And gerontologists have followed suit in relation to old people. Still, an unchallenged middle-aged bias guides much of this work, so that arguments assume that "productive" is better than "unproductive." As a result, old people feel compelled to stay active in order to be of worth. Making age-blind arguments to demonstrate that old people also are productive, and hence valuable, can result in a sort of tyranny to prove one's productive value, one that is also shaped by gender relations. For example, grandmothers may be pressed into service caring for grandchildren so that their mothers can pursue paid labor or other activities that carry greater status. In this way, younger women exploit their elders. Grandmothers may enjoy caring for grandchildren, but the role confines them as well, limiting the freedom old women might otherwise enjoy (Browne 1998; Facio 1996). It reinforces women's status as domestic laborers and servers of others, and it exploits women based on their age in that their unpaid labor benefits other family members (Laws 1995, 116).

The feminist silence on policy issues related to old persons, particularly those disadvantaged by other inequalities, is striking. For instance, little discussion among women's studies scholars ensued before or after Medicare "reform," despite old women's greater reliance on this program and the fact that they are further disadvantaged by its focus on acute illnesses (Hendricks, Hatch, and Cutler 1999). More surprising still, given the women's movement's concern for equal economic opportunities, is the quiet surrounding proposals to "reform" Social Security. The multiple relations of oppression embedded in the debates over privatization and concrete proposals have received attention only from those few feminists within aging studies. It seems likely that age relations not only shape Social Security debates but also the lack of concern of the majority of feminist scholars, intentionally or not. This situation may be analogous to the advantages younger women may have in terms of sexual attractiveness such that they do not question this privilege until it is lost. In like manner, it may be that younger women, who have more job opportunities, pension plans, and the like at their disposal, may well favor privatization at the expense of older women. Thus, the fact that schemes touted by politicians will benefit few younger women does not come to light as such plans are not held up to close scrutiny. Cloaked as the debates are in the sort of "voodoo demographics" (Gee 2000) concerning dependence

that we discussed above, much of the public, perhaps including feminist scholars, appear to believe that reform must occur. The ageism and other relations of inequality underlying the privatization movement are palpable. But because feminists focus so closely on earlier ages when they explore dependence, the potentially devastating impact of Social Security reform on disadvantaged groups goes unexplored.

DISCUSSION

In the 1970s, feminists who argued for the inclusion of women were often ignored or treated with hostility. To overcome the apathy of other scholars and activists, they emphasized gender and relationality. They demonstrated that the inclusion of women would broaden understanding and improve the quality of life for both sexes. Likewise, scholars and activists whose work focuses on aging and ageism have been ignored by the mainstream, including those in Women's Studies. They too must argue for inclusion and must demonstrate that old age is a political location, one related to lives of other age groups. But feminists also had other women scholars and advocates with whom they could work, a handful of women in positions of power, and a smattering of profeminist men with whom to ally. Where are the old women in Women's Studies, or their advocates? The age relations that push old women from our professions leave us ignorant of their perspectives as we do our collective work. Perhaps because privilege is often invisible, most women's studies scholars and activists have been blind to age relations and deaf to age studies advocates. As with other systems of oppression, people tend not to see the importance or contours of age relations when they are privileged by youth, even if they are disadvantaged in other ways. Are we to wait, then, until we are old before we will take seriously age relations?

To leave age relations unexplored reinforces the inequality old people face, an inequality that shapes other relations of oppression, and one that we reproduce for ourselves. Unlike other hierarchies, in which the privileged rarely become the oppressed, we all face age oppression if we live long enough. We can envision feminists striving to be empowered and to "age successfully" while overlooking the contradictory nature of this endeavor, embedded as it is in the denial of age.

Yet, we hope that this specter will prompt women's studies scholars and activists to bring age relations to the center of their analyses.

As feminists and people growing old, we need to be smarter about this. We need to recognize that just as gender, race, class, and sexual orientation serve as organizing principles of power, so too does age. We should no longer assume, rather than theorize, these age relations. We cannot continue to write of gender, or generalize about "women," for instance, as if they were all middle aged or younger any more than we can assume they are all white, middle class, or heterosexual. Further, "adding old people in" to theories developed on the basis of younger groups' experiences is just as fraught as was adding women to male models. It renders old people deviant, telling us little beyond the extent to which they conform to middle-aged norms. We learn little of how their daily lives are shaped by broader social currents as well as their own actions, or how age relations privilege their younger counterparts.

As with other systems of inequality, an exploration of age relations must begin by listening to those disadvantaged by them. However, this process can present complications not encountered with the study of other groups. Because old age is a social location into which people grow, admitting that we are "old" is to admit to loss of privilege and membership in a devalued group—a transition that many people will resist (Minichiello, Browne, and Kendig 2000). In theorizing age relations, then, we would worry less about affixing the chronological age at which middle age or old age occur than about the tensions surrounding the designation of age categories, particularly old age. For instance, if an employer or co-workers see a worker as "old," what is the consequence for the individual? How does this vary by gender, race, or other inequalities? Does it matter that women in the workplace are viewed as "old" sooner than men are (Rodeheaver 1990), and if so, how?

Women's studies scholars can explore the process by which old people (and other age groups) "accomplish age" (Laz 2003), an analogous endeavor to doing gender or doing difference (Fenstermaker and West 2002). Of course, our premise is that these are not accomplished alone, but simultaneously. Feminists have given little thought to how age might influence the ways that women and men might do gender. The dubious claim that men and women become more androgynous with age has not been challenged, nor the related claim that they become less sexual. Certainly the way in which 80-year-old women accomplish gender is different from a 20-year-old female; and her race, ethnicity, class, and sexual orientation would shape this process.

Finally, we hope that once women's studies scholars and activists take old age into account, they will work to imbue old age with positive content—a content that reflects the diversity of old people, their lives, and their varied contributions. Rather than having to deny old age, or to strive to look young, old people should be able to be flabby, contemplative, or sexual, or not. In short, the goal of women's studies scholars and activists should be to enhance old people's freedom to choose lifestyles and ways of being old that are suited to them.

REFERENCES

Andrews, M. 1999. "The Seductiveness of Agelessness." *Ageing and Society* 19:301–18.

Arber, Sara, and Jay Ginn. 1991. *Gender and Later Life.* Thousand Oaks, CA: Sage Publications.

Barker, Judith C., Joelle Morrow, and Linda S. Mitteness. 1998. "Gender, Informal Social Support Networks, and Elderly Urban African Americans." *Journal of Aging Studies* 12(2):199–222.

Brook, Barbara. 1999. *Feminist Perspectives on the Body.* London: Longman.

Browne, Colette V. 1998. *Women, Feminism, and Aging.* New York: Springer Publishing Company.

Bytheway, Bill. 1995. *Ageism.* Buckingham, UK: Open University Press.

Calasanti, Toni M. 2006. "Gender and Old Age: Lessons from Spousal Caregivers." In *Age Matters: Re-Aligning Feminist Thinking.* New York: Routledge.

Calasanti, Toni M. 2003. "Theorizing Age Relations." In *The Need for Theory: Critical Approaches to Social Gerontology,* eds. Simon Biggs, Ariela Lowenstein, and Jon Hendricks, 199–218. New York: Baywood Press.

Calasanti, Toni M., and Kathleen F. Selvin. 2001. *Gender, Social Inequalities, and Aging,* Walnut Creek, CA: Alta Mira Press.

Calderon, V., and S. L. Tennstedt, 1998. "Ethnic Differences in the Expression of Caregiver Burden: Results of a Qualitative Study." *Journal of Gerontological Social Work* 30(1–2):162–75.

Carroll, Berenice A. 2001. "Reflections on '2000 Subversions: Women's Studies and the 21st Century.'" *NWSA Journal* 13(1): 139–49.

Copper, Baba. 1986. "Voices: On Becoming Old Women." In *Woman and Aging: An Anthology by Women*, eds. Jo Alexander, Debi Berrow, and Lisa Domitrovich, 46–57. Corvallis, OR: Calyx Books.

Cruikshank, Margaret. 2003. *Learning to Be Old*. New York: Rowman and Littlefield.

Dateline NBC. 2001. 6 March.

DeNavas-Walt, Carmen, Bernadette D. Proctor, and Robert J. Mills. 2004. "Income, Poverty, and Health Insurance Coverage in the United States: 2003." *Current Population Reports, P60–226*. U.S. Census Bureau. Washington, D.C.: U.S. Government Printing Office.

Diamond, Timothy. 1992. *Making Gray Gold: Narratives of Nursing Home Care*. Chicago: University of Chicago Press.

Encel, Sol. 1999. "Age Discrimination in Employment in Australia." *Ageing International* 25:69–84.

Estes, Carroll L. 2004. "Social Security Privatization and Older Women: A Feminist Political Economy Perspective." *Journal of Aging Studies* 18(1):9–26.

Estes, Carroll L., and E. A. Binney. 1991. "The Biomedicalization of Aging: Dangers and Dilemmas." In *Critical Perspectives on Aging: The Political and Moral Economy of Growing Old*, eds. Meredith Minkler and Carroll L. Estes, 117–34. New York: Baywood.

Facio, Elisa. 1996. *Understanding Older Chicanas: Sociological and Policy Perspectives*. Thousand Oaks, CA: Sage Publications.

Federal Interagency Forum on Aging Related Statistics. 2004. *Older Americans 2004: Key Indicators of Well-Being*. Washington, D.C.: U.S. Government Printing Office.

Fenstermaker, Sarah, and Candace West, eds. 2002. *Doing Gender, Doing Difference: Inequality, Power, and Institutional Change*. New York: Routledge.

Fraser, Nancy, and Linda Gordon. 1994. "A Genealogy of Dependency: Tracing a Keyword of the U.S. Welfare State." *Signs* 19:309–36.

Friedan, Betty. 1993. *The Fountain of Age*. New York: Simon and Schuster.

Gee, E. M. 2000. "Population Politics: Voodoo Demography, Population Aging, and Social Policy." In *The Overselling of Population Aging*, eds. Ellen Margaret Gee and Gloria Gutman, 5–25. New York: Oxford University Press.

Gibson, Diane. 1998. *Aged Care: Old Policies, New Problems*. New York: Cambridge University Press.

Gibson, Diane. 1996. "Broken Down by Age and Gender: 'The Problem of Old Women' Redefined." *Gender & Society* 10:433–48.

Gullette, Margaret M. 2004. *Aged by Culture*. Chicago: University of Chicago Press.

Hendricks, Jon. 2003. "Structure and Identity—Mind the Gap: Toward a Personal Resource Model of Successful Aging." In *The Need for Theory; Critical Approaches to Social Gerontology*, eds. Simon Biggs, Ariela Lowenstein, and Jon Hendricks, 63–87. New York: Baywood Press.

Hendricks, Jon, Laurie Russell Hatch, and Stephen J. Cutler. 1999. "Entitlement, Social Compact, and the Trend toward Retrenchment in U.S. Old-Age Programs." *Hallym International Journal of Aging* 1(1):14–32.

Holstein, Martha B. 1999. "Women and Productive Aging: Troubling Implications." In *Critical Gerontology: Perspectives from Political and Moral Economy*, eds. Meredith Minkler and Carroll L. Estes, 359–73. Amityville, NY: Baywood Press.

Holstein, Martha B., and Meredith Minkler. 2003. "Self, Society, and the 'New Gerontology.'" *The Gerontologist* 43(6):787–96.

Hooyman, N. R., and Gonyea, J. G. 1999. "A Feminist Model of Family Care: Practice and Policy Directions." *Journal of Women & Aging* 11(2/3):149–69.

Hurtado, Aida. 1989. "Relating to Privilege: Seduction and Rejection in the Subordination of White Women and Women of Color." *Signs* 14:833–55.

Katz, Stephen. 2001/2002. "Growing Older Without Aging? Positive Aging, Anti-Ageism, and Anti-Aging." *Generations* 25(4):27–32.

Katz, Stephen. 2000. "Busy Bodies: Activity, Aging, and the Management of Everyday Life." *Journal of Aging Studies* 14:135–52.

Laws, Glenda. 1995. "Understanding Ageism: Lessons from Feminism and Postmodernism." *The Gerontologist* 35(1):112–8.

Laz, Cheryl. 2003. "Age Embodied." *Journal of Aging Studies* 17:503–19.

Levy, Becca R. 2001. "Eradication of Ageism Requires Addressing the Enemy Within." *The Gerontologist* 41(5):578–9.

Macdonald, Barbara, and Cynthia Rich. 1983. *Look Me in the Eye: Old Women, Aging and Ageism*. San Francisco: Spinsters Ink.

McHugh, K. 2000. "The 'Ageless Self'? Emplacement of Identities in Sun-Belt Retirement Communities." *Journal of Aging Studies* 14:103–15.

Mehlman, Maxwell J., Robert H. Binstock, Eric T. Juengst, Roseel S. Ponsaran, and Peter J. Whitehouse. 2004. "Anti-Aging Medicine: Can Consumers Be Better Protected?" *The Gerontologist* 44(3):304–10.

Milne, A., and E. Hatzidimitriadou. 2002. "Isn't He Wonderful? Exploring the Contribution and Conceptualisation of Older Husbands as Carers." Paper presented at the

Reconceptualising Gender and Ageing Conference, University of Surrey, UK, June 2002:25–7.

Minichiello, Victor, Jan Browne, and Hal Kendig. 2000. "Perceptions and Consequences of Ageism: Views of Older People." *Ageing and Society* 20(3): 253–78.

Mulvey, Laura. 1990. "Visual Pleasure and Narrative Cinema." In *Issues in Feminist Film Criticism,* ed. Paula Erens, 28–40. Bloomington: Indiana University Press.

Pampel, Fred C. 1998. *Aging, Social Inequality, and Public Policy.* Thousand Oaks, CA: Pine Forge Press.

Quadagno, Jill S. 1999. *Aging, and the Life Course.* Boston: McGraw-Hill.

Risman, B. J. 1987. "Intimate Relationships from a Micro-structural Perspective: Men Who Mother." *Gender & Society* 1(1): 6–32.

Robb, Claire, Hongbin Chen, and William E. Haley. 2002. "Ageism in Mental Health Care: A Critical Review." *Journal of Clinical Geropsychology* 8(1):1–2.

Rodeheaver, Dean. 1990. "Labor Market Progeria." *Generations* 14(3):53–8.

Rowe, John W., and Robert L. Kahn. 1998. *Successful Aging.* New York: Pantheon Books.

Ruddick, Sara. 1999. "Virtues and Age." In *Mother Time Women, Aging and Ethics,* ed. Margaret U. Walker, 45–60. Lanham, MD: Rowman and Littlefield.

Slevin, Kathleen F. 2006. "Lesbians Inhabiting Ageing Bodies." In *Age Matters: Re-Aligning Feminist Thinking,* eds. Toni Calasanti and Kathleen F. Slevin. New York: Routledge.

Slevin, Kathleen F., and C. Ray Wingrove. 1998. *From Stumbling Blocks to Stepping Stones: The Life Experiences of Fifty Professional African American Women.* New York: New York University Press.

Social Security Administration. 2004. *Fast Facts & Figures about Social Security, 2004.* Washington, D.C.: U.S. Government Printing Office.

Sontag, Susan. 1972. "The Double Standard of Aging." In *Saturday Review of the Society* 55: 29–38. Rpt. in *On the Contrary: Essays by Men and Women,* eds. Martha Rainbolt and Janet Fleetwood, 1983, 99–112. Albany: State University of New York Press.

Thompson, Edward H., Jr. 2000. "Gendered Caregiving of Husbands and Sons." In *Intersections of Aging: Readings in Social Gerontology,* eds. Elisabeth W. Markson and Lisa A. Hollis-Sawyer, 333–4. Los Angeles: Roxbury Publishing Company.

Thompson, Edward H., Jr. 1994. "Older Men as Invisible in Contemporary Society." In *Older Men's Lives,* ed. Edward H. Thompson, Jr., 197–219. Thousand Oaks, CA: Sage Publications.

Twigg, Julia. 2004. "The Body, Gender, and Age: Feminist Insights in Social Gerontology." *Journal of Aging Studies* 18(1):59–73.

U.S. Senate, Special Committee on Aging. 2001. *Swindlers, Hucksters and Snake Oil Salesmen: Hype and Hope Marketing Anti-Aging Products to Seniors.* (Serial No. 107–14), Washington, DC: U.S. Government Printing Office.

Wallace, Claire, and Pamela Abbott. 1999. "Series Editors' Preface." In *Feminist Perspectives on the Body,* ed. Barbara Brook, vii. London: Longman.

Wilson, Gail. 2000. *Understanding Old Age.* Thousand Oaks, CA: Sage Publications.

Wingrove, C. Ray, and Kathleen F. Slevin. 1991. "A Sample of Professional and Managerial Women's Success in Work and Retirement." *Journal of Women & Aging* 3:95–117.

Woodward, Kathleen, ed. 1999. *Figuring Age: Women, Bodies, Generations.* Bloomington: Indiana University Press.

12

A Framework for Examining Violence

CECILIA MENJÍVAR

People say that before the fighting we had peace. But what do you call peace? The war begins at the psychological level, in the plantations, where every day we were dying a little bit, every day we were consuming ourselves.

—Guatemalan peasant, quoted in Daniel Wilkinson,
Silence on the Mountain

Es que la vida de una mujer es dura, Usted, Los hijos sirven de consuelo. A veces uno dice, "¡Ay Diosito, no me olvides, por favor ten piedad!" ¿Pero es que así es la vida de uno, no?

[A woman's life is tough. Children are the consolation. Sometimes one says, "Oh, my little God, don't forget me, please have mercy!" But that's our life, no?]

—Woman in San Alejo

The first epigraph above points to the usefulness of opening up the analytic lens to examine instances of violence beyond those embodied in physical pain and injury, and the second brings up reflections on everyday violence in the world of the women I came to know. Both express the enduring reality of violence that crosses multiple spaces and spheres of life, and they elucidate the two aspects of violence I wish to examine in this book: the multifaceted character of violence and its expression in the quotidian lives of ladina women that contributes to its normalization. Raka Ray and Seemin Qayum's (2009: 4) conceptualization of "normalized" as "legitimized ideologically such that domination,

dependency, and inequality are not only tolerated but accepted" is useful here to convey what I mean by the normalization of violence. Although a neat compartmentalization of the multiple sources of suffering is rarely found in practice, here I disaggregate them for the purpose of presenting my analytic framework. Taken individually, the structural, symbolic, or gender forms of violence can be so general as to be visible anywhere, and they can be interpreted differently (e.g., structural violence can be taken as poverty); and each can arise in any number of situations. However, taking these forms of violence *as a whole,* in this context and from the angle I propose, allows us to see that they are mutually constituted. Paraphrasing James Gilligan (1996), the question of whether to disentangle the different forms to see which one is more dangerous is moot, as they are all related to one another. The approach I lay out also permits me to unveil a context of violence that shapes the lives of women in gender-specific ways and in a manner that exposes deep power inequalities. This approach reveals the systematic patterns of disadvantage that are neither natural nor necessary (cf. Kent 2006); or in Gilligan's (1996: 196) words, "not acts of God."

In establishing the links between violence at the interpersonal level with that which originates in broader structures, I seek analytic distance from individual-focused explanations or those that focus on "tradition" to elucidate the roots of violence in structures of power,

Cecilia Menjívar, *Enduring Violence: Ladina Women's Lives in Guatemala,* © 2011 by the Regents of the University of California. Published by the University of California Press.

away from personal circumstances. Farmer (2003, 2004) warns against conflating poverty and cultural difference, for example; in his view, the linkage of assaults on human dignity to the cultural institutions of a particular society constitutes an abuse of cultural concepts. He (2004) then cautions that such an approach is especially insidious because cultural difference as a form of essentialism is used to explain suffering and assaults on dignity. Thus although it is important to interpret particular situations as forms of violence, it is equally significant to trace links to broader structures, lest we inflict even more harm on the vulnerable.

There are three considerations regarding my discussion of violence. First, the political economy of violence does not affect everyone in the same manner; violence weighs differently for those in dissimilar social positions. Women and men from different social classes and ethnic and racial backgrounds face dissimilar forms of violence and may experience the same violence in different ways. Thus class violence parallels sexual and ethnic violence, and these are often conflated in real life (Forster 1999: 59). Second, following the scholars on whose work I have built this framework, I argue that violence is not always an event, a palpable outcome that can be observed, reported, and measured. From the angle I propose, violence constitutes a *process,* one that is embedded in the everyday lives of those who experience it. Third, as Torres-Rivas (1998: 48) observes, not all societies recognize the same things as violent, either in their origins or in their effects. Torres-Rivas's observation can be extended to researchers, for scholars often make use of different theoretical repertoires and frameworks to examine the same cases and thus do not assess them in the same manner. In Rashomonesque fashion, the same situation may be interpreted in a different light according to the lens used to examine it. In the rest of this chapter, I present one lens, one in which violence emerges as fundamental. I present each of the components and end with a discussion of how they intertwine to affect life in a gender-specific fashion. As Martín-Baró (1991b: 334) noted, considering forms of social violence other than the political–military helps us to "arrive at a picture that is more complex but also more distressing." My portrayal of the lives of Guatemalan ladinas in this book, therefore, is not sanitized and should not be taken as culturally accusatory or as a careless characterization of an overly objectivized world.

STRUCTURAL VIOLENCE

Torres-Rivas (1998: 49) notes that structural violence (or structural repression) "is rooted in the uncertainty of everyday life caused by the insecurity of wages or income, a chronic deficit in food, dress, housing, and health care, and uncertainty about the future which is translated into hunger and delinquency, and a barely conscious feeling of failure. . . . It is often referred to as structural violence because it is reproduced in the context of the market, in exploitative labor relations, when income is precarious and it is concealed as underemployment, or is the result of educational segmentation and of multiple inequalities that block access to success." And for Farmer (2003: 40), "the term is apt because such suffering is 'structured' by historically given (and often economically driven) processes and forces that conspire . . . to constrain agency."

An important feature of structural violence, Kent (2006: 55) observes, is that "it is not visible in specific events." Structural violence is "exerted systematically, that is, indirectly by everyone who belongs to a certain social order" (Farmer 2004: 307). Indeed, in Johan Galtung's (1969) classic work, the differentiating aspect between direct and structural violence is that in the second there is no identifiable actor who does the harming, so that "violence is built into the structure and shows up as unequal power and consequently as unequal life chances" (171). For him, direct violence comes from harmful acts of individuals that leave physical scars, whereas structural violence is not observable and is the result of a process. Thus, in contrast to direct, physical violence, structural violence causes people to suffer harm indirectly, often through a slow and steady process. But it is easier to see direct violence (Kent 2006); and when violence is a by-product of our social and economic structure, and it is invisible, it is hard to care about it (Gilligan 1996). As Galtung (1990) observed, for some people, malnutrition and lack of access to goods and services do not amount to violence because they do not result in killings, but for the weakest in society, such shortfalls amount to a slow death. An examination of the ills that afflict the poor from this vantage point highlights how a political economy of inequality under neoliberal capitalism promotes social suffering. As Miguel Ángel Vite Pérez (2005) observes, when trying to understand how individuals become unemployed one must focus on how neoliberal economic regimes have led to labor instability, to the commodification of public services, and to a precarious situation that engenders poverty rather than focus just on someone's inability to keep a job.

Structural violence as expressed in unemployment, layoffs, unequal access to goods and services, and exploitation has an impact on a range of social relations in multiple forms, including those that lead to the formation of social capital, a point I developed in fieldwork among Salvadoran immigrants in San Francisco (Menjívar 2000). Kleinman (2000: 238) argues, "Through violence in social experience, as mediated by cultural representations, . . . the ordinary lives of individuals are also shaped, and all too often twisted, bent, even broken." And as Bourdieu (1998: 40) noted, "The structural violence exerted by financial markets, in the form of layoffs, loss of security, etc., is matched sooner or later in the form of suicides, crime and delinquency, drug addiction, alcoholism, a whole host of minor and major everyday acts of violence." The broader political economy does not *cause* violence directly, but one must understand the extent to which it conditions structures within which people suffer and end up inflicting harm on one another and distorting social relations (see also Bourgois 2004a).

While it is crucial to acknowledge the devastating effects of neoliberal structural adjustment policies initiated by the International Monetary Fund (IMF) in Latin America that have resulted in sharp and unprecedented levels of poverty (see Auyero 2000; Auyero and Swistun 2009), it must be noted that what the region is experiencing is the cumulative effects of disadvantage in a much longer historical process. Economic vulnerability is a part of this process rather than a condition or state, and this process is cumulative, dynamic, and relational (see Auyero 2000). Thus Guatemalans' current living conditions are hardly the result of a few decades of neoliberal reforms.

Latin America historically has exhibited a high degree of income inequality relative to other regions; it has the most unbalanced distribution of resources of all regions in the world (Hoffman and Centeno 2003). And Guatemala has consistently ranked among the most unequal, even by Latin American standards. The richest 10 percent of Guatemalans earn 43.5 percent of the country's total income, whereas the poorest 30 percent

earn 3.8 percent (World Bank 2006). In 1998 Guatemala's Gini Index was 55.8, five years later it was 58, and in 2002 it was 55.1, which indicates that inequality rates remained stable over time. As an aggregate measure of inequality, the Gini Index does not detect levels of absolute poverty. For instance, between 1990 and 2001, 16 percent of Guatemalans lived on less than $1 per day and approximately 37.4 percent on less than $2 per day (UNDP 2003), meaning that about half of Guatemalans live under $2 a day. Guatemala also holds the dubious distinction of having one of the two most exploitative and coercive rural class structures in Central America (the other one is El Salvador), with high rural poverty and inequality and high levels of unequal landownership (Brockett 1991: 62–70). Whereas 3 percent of landholdings control 65 percent of the agricultural surface, close to 90 percent of the landholdings are too small for peasant subsistence (Manz 2004: 16). Such disparities vary by ethnicity and location. Thus 58 percent of Guatemalans nationally lived in poverty in 1989, while 72 percent did so in rural areas, a proportion that dropped to 56 percent nationally in 2002 but rose to 75 percent in rural areas the same year (World Bank 2006). And although the majority of ladinos are poor and lack access to basic services, the Maya are even poorer and disproportionately disadvantaged. And in spite of development programs aimed at reducing the poverty gap, inequality has increased in Guatemala.

Structural violence also comes in the form of a sweatshop economy that exacerbates gendered vulnerabilities. In a careful examination of the effects of sweatshop *(maquila)* employment in Guatemala, María José Paz Antolín and Amaia Pérez Orozco (2001) discuss the psychological violence that takes place in the maquila, with serious consequences for the workers, including loss of self-esteem. According to the authors, this situation creates a belief among the women that it is their fault that they do not have more education, and thus they blame themselves for their precarious situation. Indeed, the women with whom I spoke in San Alejo were well aware of the benefits that education can bring, but due to the need for their labor in their families many had been forced to abandon school early or not to attend at all. However, they pointed to themselves or their families as culpable for their lack of education and diminished potential for success in life. The average years of schooling for adults in Guatemala is three and a half years, even though the duration of compulsory education is eleven years, and the literacy rate for men in 2002 was 75 percent and for women 63 percent (World Bank 2006). Education and level of poverty are related; by the Guatemalan government's own estimates, more than 95 percent of the poor have had no secondary education, and 44 percent have never attended school at all (Manz 2004: 16–17).

Nine of the thirty women I interviewed in San Alejo had never attended school. Some had learned how to sign their names or to read simple words, a couple had attended adult literacy classes, and another nine had only attended elementary school. They cited their parents, other relatives, or themselves as the reason they had not acquired more schooling. It is only by tracing the links to the profoundly unequal access to education and resources that one can turn attention to the root of this lack of opportunities. Hortencia, the mother of five whom I mentioned in chapter 1, explained why she never attended school:

> Because my *papa* was a *mujeriego* [womanizer] and a drunk and my *mama* suffered a lot with him so they never sent me to school. I had to help her. I learned in the *alfabetización* [literacy classes] how to read and write, and now I have even written letters to the United States for other people who don't know how to write [she smiles and her eyes light up]! The other day my *compadre* [lit., "co-father"; co-parent] came by so I could help him calculate how old he is because he needed to go get his *cédula* [ID card]. Ay, the shame of having to learn how to read and write as an adult . . . one feels bad, ashamed. I was very embarrassed, but in time I learned.

While Hortencia saw her father as responsible for her illiteracy, one must recognize that access to education in rural Guatemala when she was growing up was a privilege, not a right, especially for poor women. Not everyone could attend school, and since the town had only a primary school, many who did attend stopped at the sixth grade; only the few with more means traveled to the city to continue beyond the sixth grade. Thus blocked educational opportunities and illiteracy are expressions of the structural violence that assaults the lives of the poor. However, some women of more means noted that the poor (or the children of the poor) do not attend school because they are "lured" to work, not forced to work, as women from poor backgrounds explained, Lucía, a teacher, said:

> The children work too much. People cultivate tomatoes in this area, and the kids go to harvest them and then don't go to school. Instead they go to a literacy course in the afternoons. You see lots of patojos, young ones, congregated outside those centers [for literacy classes]. Instead of wanting an education, they want to earn money. Oh yes, they are poor and need money, but they don't want the education. No, really, believe me, they just don't want to be educated, otherwise they would go to school, don't you think? As a teacher, it pains me to see how kids go for money and not their future. But it's all the parents' fault.

Other women were more elaborate in their assessments, but most explanations ended up blaming the poor for their predicament, adding insult to injury. Ofelia, a receptionist, explained, "You see, they [the poor] have many children, so their money is never enough. You know why? Because there is no family planning. Well, there is, but the *gente humilde* [lit. "humble people," meaning the poor] don't accept it, and they prefer to have as many children as God sends them. So it's because of their beliefs that they end up worsening their own situation, right?"

The majority of the women with whom I spoke in San Alejo mentioned situations they faced in their daily lives that highlight structural violence and the normalization of inequality. Several women talked about the effects of the unequal land distribution system, couching their reflections in a framework of the ordinary, explaining multiple forms of exploitation as the way things were. In San Alejo women do not work the land directly (they can participate in the harvest), but the men do, and they do so through an exploitative land tenure system. Many are landless and rent land from landowners through a contract called *medianía,* which implies "half and half" but is hardly that. As it was explained to me, the landowner provides the land and the renter tills it and supplies everything else—seeds, fertilizer, and workers to harvest the crop. Then the landowner and the renter supposedly share the crop. Such a system lends itself to multiple forms of abuse, and it is risky for the renter but not for the landowner.

This system exemplifies what Galtung (1990) conceptualizes as the archetypal structure of violence.

Many women brought up the injurious consequences inherent in the system. Sometimes their partners were hired to work the land but were cheated and not paid after the harvest, losing money that was earmarked for other purposes, including medicine and food. Mirna, twenty-eight years old and the mother of five, complained that the landowner with whom her husband worked would deduct money for everything needed to work the land, leaving them with Q.100 (about $15 in 1997) per month in profits. She had to use some of this money to feed the twelve laborers who helped her husband, even when she was eight months' pregnant. In the case of Leticia, when her partner fell ill from HIV/AIDS they had to sell half of a tiny plot of land so that he could afford his checkups in the capital. After he died, she found out she also was infected, and she sold the other half of the plot to pay for her own checkups. In her last year of life she was tormented about being unable to leave any land, or even a small adobe structure, to her young daughters. When she was already ill, one of the few ways she could make a living was picking tomatoes in the fields, but even this became difficult toward the end because others in town knew of her illness and some potential employers did not want any contact with her. As the women recounted these stories, they presented them as the way things were, normalizing the relationship between those who own the land and those who till it, only occasionally insinuating how exploitative this "natural order of things" was. Not surprisingly, when I spoke with the women whose families owned the land, their stories conveyed the other half of the picture, naturalizing the narratives of exploitation I heard from poor women.

POLITICAL VIOLENCE AND STATE TERROR

For thirty-six years, from 1960 to 1996, political violence and state terror were the order of the day in Guatemalan society. During this time politically motivated violence became an integral part of the functioning, governance, and maintenance of the state (Falla 1994; Jonas 2000; Nelson 1999). Violence and terror, epitomized in public assassinations, ruthless massacres, and

unsolved disappearances, became the favored political tools for Guatemala's military and political elites (McCleary 1999, cited in Torres 2005). Politically motivated violence was so successful during Guatemala's reign of terror that it came to be known as a "cultural fact," as somehow "natural" and "cultural" (Nordstrom 1997; Sluka 2000; Torres 2005). The Guatemalan anthropologist M. Gabriela Torres (2005; 143–44) notes that "the naturalization of political violence into a cultural fact was produced, in part, through the creation and promotion of a language or pattern of political violence that—while it generated terror—at the same time obfuscated the political economy of its own production."

Until 1980 the targets of state terror were primarily ladinos—students, peasants, union organizers, politicians, and revolutionaries—and in the 1960s and 1970s the state-sponsored violence had an urban character (Godoy-Paiz 2008). But in 1981 the army launched its scorched earth campaign against Maya communities. Throughout this period ladinos continued to be killed, but the atrocities committed against the Maya, described as ethnocide or genocide, targeted "Indians as Indians" (Grandin 2000: 16). The widespread and systematic nature of this slaughter arguably reached the threshold of crimes against humanity. As an intricate aspect of a regional political structure in which U.S. political interests have weighed heavily (Menjívar and Rodríguez 2005), in 1954 the U.S. government orchestrated the overthrow of democratically elected Jacob Arbenz Guzmán and installed a military regime that would govern the country, in various guises, for the next several decades. Successive U.S. administrations supported this regime as it engaged in widespread human rights violations, providing training and support for the Guatemalan army's counterinsurgency operations (Manz 2004; Menjívar and Rodríguez 2005). According to the 1999 report of the U.N.-sponsored Truth Commission, formally known as the Comisión para el Esclarecimiento Histórico (CEH; Historical Clarification Commission), the state responded to both the insurgency and the civil movements with unimaginable repression, repression that climaxed in 1981–82 with a bloodbath in which the army committed over six hundred massacres (Sanford 2008: 19). It tortured, murdered, and was responsible for the disappearance of more than 200,000 Guatemalans (mostly Mayas); it destroyed 626 villages, and hundreds of thousands were displaced internally and internationally (Parenti and Muñoz 2007; Sanford 2008).

Although ladino communities were not targeted in the scorched earth campaigns, there are ways in which the general political violence led to the normalization of violence, distorting social relations and affecting life in ladino communities as well. The breadth and depth of state-sponsored terror reached all Guatemalans in one way or another, for one of the most destructive aspects of state terror in Guatemala was the widespread reliance on civilians to kill other civilians (Ball, Kobrak, and Spirer 1999), as well as the strategic dissemination of gruesome killings in the media. Thus the political violence that claimed many lives and destroyed communities in the Altiplano was so pervasive that it engulfed the entire country. Writing about the insidious effects of the militarization of life in El Salvador, Martín-Baró (1991c: 311–12) stated, "The militarization of daily life in the main parts of the social world contributes to the omnipresence of overpowering control and repressive threats. . . . This is how an atmosphere of insecurity is fostered, unpredictable in its consequences, and demanding of people a complete submission to the dictates of power." He referred to this phenomenon as the "militarization of the human mind" (1991b: 341). In such contexts, to paraphrase Cynthia Enloe (2000), lives become militarized not only through direct means and exposure but also when militarized products, views, and attitudes are taken as natural and unproblematic (see also Green 1999). Even if concrete expressions of political violence differ in degree, tactics, and expression, the broad effects cannot be contained or isolated in one geographic area when the state itself is the chief perpetrator. As Galtung (1990: 294) observed, "A violent structure leaves marks not only on the human body but also on the mind and the spirit." It was this kind of political violence, created and spread through state structures, that reached, in one way or another, everyone in Guatemala.

Political violence is linked to other forms of violence, including interpersonal violence in the home (itself linked to symbolic violence) and what is referred to as "common crime." Douglas Hay (1992) notes the reciprocal relationship between violence from the state and violence in private spheres. And referring to a chain of political violence, Jennifer Turpin and Lester Kurtz (1997) note the interrelated causes of violence at the micro- and macrolevels, such that the violence that occurs in intimate relations is connected to the violence that occurs between ethnic groups, which in turn is linked to global patterns of interstate wars, because the same mechanisms sustain them. Understanding the links between the different manifestations of violence, they argue, is a key step toward addressing the causes.

Thus the cruelty with which certain assaults such as robberies and burglaries are sometimes committed in the context of common crime cannot be examined independently of the violence engendered by state terror, as Taussig (2005) has observed for the case of Colombia. Often, acts of common crime are characterized by the same brutality and professionalization with which acts associated with political violence are carried out. Torres-Rivas (1998: 49) notes that the criminogenic conditions of postwar violence can be examined in the context of power and state violence: "The bad example of the use of violence on the part of the state is then imitated by the citizens." "Common criminals" adopt strategies similar to those used by the state (the same individuals may be engaged in both), and, as posited by examinations using brutalization frameworks (see Kil and Menjívar 2006), individuals who commit common crimes mimic the state as it metes out punishments on enemies or dissidents. The violence of common crime therefore is not dissociated from state-sponsored political violence. However, as Snodgrass Godoy (2006:25) notes, "The depoliticization of crime [is] among the hallmarks of neoliberal governance in our insecure world[,] . . .most starkly sketched in settings of extreme marginality."

The effects of political violence, then, are seldom contained in a specific geographic area, among the members of only a targeted group, or in only one aspect of life. It is not surprising therefore that the ladinas with whom I spoke did not openly question the taken-for-granted world of violence that surrounded them, conveyed daily in newspapers, on television, and along the roads. Regular images and stories of gruesome deaths created a climate of insecurity and continuous alert (the "nervous system," in Taussig's [1992] conceptualization) in eastern Guatemala as well, and it was "part of life." Moving the analytic lens from the Altiplano, where political violence has been well documented and acknowledged, to eastern Guatemala, where for the most part it has not, unearths the breadth and depth of the project of state terror that engulfed, with varying degrees of force and visibility, the entire country.

Torres (2005) argues that in the process of making violence quotidian, "natural," and "cultural," the Guatemalan Armed Forces relied on a discourse expressed in the patterned and continuous appearance of cadaver reports and articulated through both the signs of torture left on bodies and the strategy of displaying the reports. Mutilated bodies left on the sides of roads and the unidentifiable victims of torture were meant to send a message to the living. Victims of terror "disappeared" from their normal existence, making the disappearance itself a powerful message of what awaited those who contemplated sympathizing with the opposition (Menjívar and Rodríguez 2005). The innocent bystanders who witnessed abductions or discovered a tortured body on a road got the message, one that was carefully and strategically broadcast in the media (Torres 2005). Although such sightings are associated with the Altiplano, they were not uncommon in other parts of Guatemala.

These observations are not meant to suggest that the entire country experienced state terror in the same way or to lessen the atrocities committed against the Maya in the Altiplano; on the contrary, they underscore the reach of the political violence suffered in Guatemala. As scholars have documented for the Altiplano, relatives of the disappeared who never saw their loved ones again live with the torment of not knowing if these relatives were in fact killed. Rosita, whom I interviewed in the Altiplano, would cry whenever she tried to explain what it meant to have had her husband disappear fourteen years earlier. On one occasion she told me, "I live wondering, will he come back one day? How about for our daughter's fifteen-year celebration? Every Christmas, every New Year's, every birthday, I wonder if he will come back. Sometimes I almost go crazy. Why did they [government army] not return his body to me? Why such cruelty? I think my torture will last all my life." Filita, on the other hand, explained that her father was killed right in front of her and her siblings rather than having disappeared and noted that this had been a consolation to the family because at least they could give him a proper burial. Only in the brutality of Guatemala's reign of terror could the killing of a father in front of his children serve as consolation. The women I interviewed in San Alejo did not have similar experiences, but this kind

of violence often loomed in the background of their assessments and perspectives.

As the project of state violence reached all corners of the country in different ways, the militarization of life was evident beyond the Altiplano; it materialized in soldiers and military vehicles on roads even in areas that were supposed to be far from the "conflict" zones, such as in San Alejo. The military presence there served as an eerie reminder that violence was never far or contained in just one area, and thus everyone could be "at risk." Military violence was not separated in a black-and-white geographic mapping because the repressive state could reach anyone, anywhere, any time, and the reminders of this were ubiquitous. One day as my assistant, our driver, and I were on the main road leading to San Alejo, we saw there was commotion, and traffic was slow in a large town we were supposed to pass through. A crowd was lined up on the sides of a semipaved road; it looked as if they were waiting for a pageant to go by, and I did not want to miss it. To my surprise, I saw a convoy of U.S. military vehicles, Humvees too wide for the narrow roads of the town. People had come out of their homes to look at how these massive vehicles almost touched the houses on both sides of the road as they maneuvered their way through town. The military presence felt as huge as those vehicles in that narrow road, and I wondered about the need to establish such a presence even in this region of Guatemala. I was told that a military presence—both Guatemalan and U.S.—was in fact routine; the reason people were watching that day was out of curiosity. I asked a small group of people what this was all about, and a man said, "It's the gringos. They are on their way to fix the roads around here." "So they have come to help?" I ventured to ask. The man smiled, shrugged his shoulders, shook his head slightly, and simply responded, "Saber" (Who knows). As Linda Green (2004: 187) observes, civic actions mixed with counterinsurgency strategies do "not negate the essential fact that violence is intrinsic to the military's nature and logic. Coercion is the mechanism that the military uses to control citizens even in the absence of war." The scene was troubling to me, but for the town dwellers and everyone in the region, accustomed to such sightings, it was life as usual. As Green (2004: 187) continues, in Guatemala "language and symbols are utilized to normalize a continued army presence."

The end of the armed conflict has not resulted in an absence of violence, and in fact new modalities have emerged. Death threats, attacks, kidnappings, and acts of intimidation are a daily occurrence in "postwar" Guatemala. Mutilated bodies are still found on the sides of roads, kidnappings occur regularly, people live in fear, and there are guns and security forces in places where people conduct their daily lives—challenging conventional assumptions about what it means to live in "peacetime." All this is exacerbated by the impunity that has been the hallmark of the postwar regime; many of those responsible for human rights violations have entered politics and have even been elected to public offices (Menjívar and Rodríguez 2005).

EVERYDAY VIOLENCE, INTERPERSONAL VIOLENCE, AND CRIME

Everyday violence refers to the daily practices and expressions of violence on a micro-interactional level, such as interpersonal, domestic, and delinquent (Bourgois 2004a: 428). I borrow the concept from Philippe Bourgois to focus on the routine practices and expressions of interpersonal aggression that serve to normalize violence at the micro-level. This concept focuses attention on "the individual lived experience that normalizes petty brutalities and terror at the community level and creates a common sense or ethos of violence" (Bourgois 2004a: 426). Analytically, the concept helps to avoid explaining individual-level confrontations and expressions of violence, such as "common" crime and domestic violence, through psychological or individualistic frameworks. Instead, this prism links these acts to broader structures of inequality that promote interpersonal violence. As Alejandro Portes and Bryan Roberts (2005) note, increasing trends of inequality are very much associated with rising crime in Latin America (see also Torres 2008), even if precise causality cannot always be established. Indeed, Portes and Roberts (2005: 76) note, "from a sociological standpoint, the reaction of some of society's most vulnerable members in the form of unorthodox means to escape absolute and relative deprivation is predictable." From this angle one can trace the violence of common crime to structural and political violence, as well as to the creation of a

"culture of terror" that normalizes violence in the private and public spheres, and can begin to understand how those who experience it end up directing their brutality against themselves rather than against the structures that oppress them (see Bourgois 2004a, 2004b).

Thus the most immediate threat in postwar Guatemala in the eyes of Guatemalan women and men is common crime, and today there is gang-related crime everywhere, from the capital to the countryside (see Manz 2004). Guatemala's homicide rate is one of the highest in the hemisphere, and it has escalated annually. In 2001 there were 3,230 homicides; in 2005, 5,338 (Procuraduría de Derechos Humanos [PDH], in Sanford 2008: 24). If the rate continues to increase, Sanford (2008) notes, there will be more deaths in the first twenty-five "postwar" years than in all the thirty-six years of "wartime." In an unsettling situation (also observed in other postconflict societies), street youth in Guatemala, the criminalized young women and men often referred to as *maras* (gangs) because their origins have been traced to a gang bearing that name, are often blamed for the high levels of crime. Public officials and the media offer these gangs as "explanations" for interpersonal violence and crime and make it seem necessary to "eliminate the maras," as a man in San Alejo once told me. Guatemala is not alone in this predicament. In his examination of the *"limpieza"* (cleansing) in Colombia, Michael Taussig (2005) notes the ease with which the seemingly random violence in postconflict societies is attributed to delinquent youth. My point here is that blaming poor young women and men for the postwar violence isolates the issue, a strategy that depoliticizes it (see Godoy-Paiz 2008) and muddles attempts to explain and understand it.

On a return visit three years after I first went to the Altiplano, I happened to see an extraordinary image: two girls, in their traditional traje, writing graffiti on a wall and then walking into a local arcade to play video games with their friends. In my conversations with people in town, I mentioned what I saw, and the talk quickly turned to crime. I was told that all the crime committed these days was the work of the maras, integrated by teenage boys and girls whose "parents don't know what the kids are doing." People were concerned because they used to hear about these activities in the capital but not in their town. Perhaps because of the military attacks this town suffered during the years of the violence, some of the town's residents were quick to link the militarization of life to the emergence of the maras. For example, Lita, a thirty-nine-year-old mother of three, observed, "Thanks to God, my husband didn't want to stay in the army any longer. Maybe he could have had a higher rank by now. But he wouldn't have been content with that and would have become a thief, because the more you have, the more you want. And the longer you stay in the army, the worse a person becomes. You learn how to pressure people to do what you want."

Paralleling Lita's assessment, the emergence of the maras in Guatemala, as well as in the rest of Central America, has been linked to the militarization of life during the years of political violence. However, even if poverty and a recent political conflict are mentioned as factors behind the emergence and expansion of gangs in Central America (and of the violence we see today), it is interesting that it is the countries with a recent history of *state* violence (not just political conflict) that targeted their own people, such as Guatemala, El Salvador, and, to some degree, Honduras, where this seems to be the case. On the other hand, in Nicaragua, where there are similar conditions of poverty and recent political conflict but where the state was not involved in terrorizing its own citizens (in that conflict, the "Contra War," the government fought external aggression), youth gangs have not proliferated, and those that exist do not seem to be as violent as those in the other Central American countries.

Though I did not ask directly about violence in their lives, San Alejo women brought it up in our conversations, often in its direct, physical form, even when we were talking about aspects of their lives that seemed remote from the topic of violence. Sometimes they would mention instances of common crime that their friends and families had experienced; sometimes they would talk about how "easy it is to die" in their town. Yet at other times they would talk about additional sources of fear and suffering. It was surprising to me how easily and often this issue came up. In fact, the topic of direct violence made such an impression on me that in a field note entry in 1995 I wrote, "Almost everyone in this town seems to have had a relative killed. Everyone seems to own and use guns. Is it supposed to be this way here [in San Alejo]?" What I was trying to reconcile was that this was the region of Guatemala considered relatively peaceful, far from the Altiplano,

where overt, direct forms of political violence were more likely to take place. Isabel mentioned that her brother had been shot and was recuperating. The incident reminded her of the time, two years earlier, when her uncle was shot and killed not far from where her brother had just been shot. She also mentioned a series of robberies and assaults on people close to her. She attributed such acts, like others did, to drunkenness, jealousy, and revenge. Similarly, when Teresa and I were talking about her family, she said, "These days my uncle is recuperating from a gunshot wound. Oh, he had a few drinks, you know how it is, then got his gun and shot himself in the leg." And Estrella, with a shrug of the shoulders, said, "There are always people being killed around here. Sometimes you walk around and see a crowd of people, and most of the time it's going to be someone killed in the street. Normally it's a *bolo* [drunk]." Isabel seemed a bit relieved when she said, "These days, it's only my brother"; no one else in her family had been assaulted recently. And Mirna was worried about a brother-in-law who drank too much; in the end, she said, anyone could be killed: "No one is safe. Such is life, one is here today and gone tomorrow, right?" Perhaps what seemed more startling to me was the element of ordinariness in the women's accounts. As Scheper-Hughes (1997: 483) notes, "The routinization of everyday violence against the poor leads them to accept their own violent deaths and those of their children as predictable, natural, cruel, but all too usual."

The topic of direct physical violence came up even when speaking with Lucrecia about the town's fiesta. We were having a lively conversation in the living room of her house about the music, the queens, the three days of festivities, the *bailes* (dances), when suddenly she said:

> Oh yes, for the fiestas *siempre hay muertos* [there are always dead people]. People drink too much. Oh God, there is always a *matazón* [widespread killings] during the fiestas. They kill each other. Well, this time, I don't know, I think there were only three or four dead. Not too many this year. In other years there are more, sometimes eight or nine. There will be at least some dead people during the fiestas. It's what happens during a fiesta, right?

During my last visits to San Alejo in 1999 and 2000, I heard gunshots almost every night. One evening a man brandishing a gun, chasing another man, ran past our street, and I was told to stay inside. I was left shaken, but my reaction made everyone laugh and tease me because I had made a big deal out of a guy running around with a gun. This experience and others corroborated the women's normalized descriptions of direct violence in their town. Again, this was postwar, "non-conflict," eastern Guatemala.

SYMBOLIC VIOLENCE AND THE INTERNALIZATION OF INEQUALITY

Symbolic violence, according to Bourdieu (2004), refers to the internalized humiliations and legitimations of inequality and hierarchy that range from sexism and racism to intimate expressions of class power. As Bourdieu and Loïc Wacquant (2004: 273) put it, "It is the violence which is exercised upon a social agent with his or her complicity." And, according to Bourgois (2004b), this violence is exercised through cognition and misrecognition, with the unwitting consent of the dominated. In this conceptualization, "the dominated apply categories constructed from the point of view of the dominant to the relations of domination, thus making it appear as natural. This can lead to systematic self-depreciation, even self-denigration" (Bourdieu 2004: 339). A key point in Bourdieu's conceptualization that captures a fundamental aspect of the case I examine here is that the everyday, normalized familiarity with violence renders it invisible, power structures are misrecognized, and the mechanisms through which it is exerted do not lie in conscious knowing. According to Bourdieu:

> Symbolic violence is exercised only through an act of knowledge and practical recognition which takes place below the level of consciousness and will and which gives all its manifestations—injunctions, suggestions, seduction, threats, reproaches, orders, or calls to order—their "hypnotic power." But a relation of domination that functions only through the complicity of dispositions depends profoundly, *for its perpetuation or transformation,* on the perpetuation or transformation of the structures of which those dispositions are the product. (2004: 342; original emphasis)

Significantly, symbolic violence in the form of feelings of inadequacy, mutual recrimination, and exploitation of fellow victims diverts attention away from those responsible (e.g., the state and classes in power) for the conditions of violence in the first place (see Bourgois 2004a, 2004b). This theoretical angle allows us to capture how multiple inequalities, power structures, and denigrating social relations become internalized dispositions (Bourdieu's "habitus" [1984]) that organize practices and are unquestioned, misrecognized, accepted, and ultimately reproduced in everyday life. Bourdieu's key conceptualization, as it focuses on gender violence, constitutes my main framework for examining the different aspects of life of the women in San Alejo.

Symbolic violence is exerted in multiple forms of stratification, social exclusion, and oppression in Guatemala; as such, it is constitutive of other forms. I began to reflect on the insidiousness of structural violence and its links to the hidden injuries of symbolic violence when a female street vendor outside the city hall in San Alejo shooed away a barefoot blond boy (his blond hair was the result of extreme malnutrition) wearing a tattered Harvard Alumni T-shirt of undescribable color, because she thought he was bothering me when he asked me for food. He took a couple of steps back and looked afraid. The expression on my face led the woman to explain her actions and she assured me that it was okay to shoo him away, saying, "Ay, estos patojos son peor que animales, son como moscas, Usted" (Ah, these kids are worse than animals; they are like flies). At first I wondered why this woman, who did not look much better off than the patojo in question and had probably experienced hunger herself, could not feel compassion for him. As I thought about the incident I realized that it had more to do with the context of multifaceted violence in which both she and the boy lived than with the woman's lack of compassion. I had mistakenly interpreted this act. In a fashion similar to the initial reaction of Scheper-Hughes (1992) to the seeming indifference of the mothers to their infants' deaths and life chances in Bom Jesus do Alto, I was not initially aware of the inadequacy of my reading. To link this moment to the ravages of violence in the lives of this woman and this child required shifting from a focus on the individual interaction to the structures that give rise to and facilitate these forms of violent relations, and it parallels other examinations of dehumanization and objectification, such as Douglas Massey's (2007) discussion of the dehumanization of undocumented immigrants in the United States that opens up the way for inhumane treatment.

The women I met in the Altiplano had countless stories, many dealing with racism, about their experiences of symbolic violence in its overt forms. For instance, Lita's teenage daughter spoke about her life as a worker in Guatemala City, where ladinos often stare at her, scold her (*regañan*), and speak roughly to her, calling her *india*, just because she is a *"natural"* (the term Maya often use to refer to themselves). Equally important to note is how such expressions of violence are internalized by the dominated and how the self is wounded under these conditions. Ivette, a thirty-year-old ladina in San Alejo, was married to a Maya man from the town in the Altiplano where I did research. Ivette wore fashionable clothes, always had her nails manicured, and had dyed her hair blond. We were talking about what life was like for her, as a ladina, in the Altiplano, and she said:

> Well, I live well here. Everyone speaks Kaqchikel around here and all the women wear traje. But my husband says that that's why he married me; he didn't want a woman with traje. In fact, he never had a girlfriend who wore traje. Yes, on purpose, he didn't want *una de traje* [a woman who wore traje, meaning a Maya]. And he doesn't want me to dress our daughter with traje. My sisters-in-law tell him to, but my husband doesn't like it; he thinks it's not in good taste.

The stories I heard in the Altiplano were disturbing and provided me with a small window onto how racism in Guatemala is experienced. In the Oriente I heard stories that show the other side of racism and support those I heard in the Altiplano. Comments in San Alejo usually came in the form of an outright racist statement about the Maya, or in the form of a joke (see Nelson 1999), or in a naturalized, normalized assertion (I return to this in chapter 7). On one occasion I was chatting with a couple of women in San Alejo on the steps of one of their homes, and the life and accomplishments of Rigoberta Menchú came up. With surprise, one of them explained what she thought about the Nobel Prize winner: "Right, she is not dumb. Because, you know, one thinks that the Indians are dumb, well, that's what one believes, right? But you'd be surprised. Many are not. Look at La Rigo [Rigoberta], *que chispuda salió* [how smart she turned out]."

However, in San Alejo I was stunned by stories of another form of symbolic violence that is also naturalized and misrecognized. I often heard the ladinas talk about their perceived inadequacies, their understanding of being "naturally" unequal to men, and how "as women" they knew "their place." Such expressions were so common that one hardly noticed them. These powerful and insidious forms of symbolic violence encapsulate Bourdieu and Wacquant's (2004: 272) conceptualization that, "being born in a social world, we accept a whole range of postulates, axioms, which go without saying and require no inculcating. . . . Of all the forms of 'hidden persuasion,' the most implacable is the one exerted, quite simply, by the *order of things*" (original emphasis). I discuss this form of violence under gender violence below, because for Bourdieu and Wacquant (2004) gender domination is the paradigmatic form of symbolic violence.

GENDER AND GENDERED VIOLENCE

I examine the different forms of gender violence that assault women's lives in San Alejo by borrowing from Lawrence Hammar (1999), from a Guatemalan team of social scientists who conducted a thorough study of gender and gendered violence in Guatemala (UNICEF-UNIFEM-OPS/OMS-FNUAP 1993), and from Bourdieu's work on gender violence. According to Hammar's (1999: 91) conceptualization, gender differences in a gender-imbalanced political economy that disadvantage women represent *gender* violence, whereas acts of violence, including physical, psychological, and linguistic violence, constitute *gendered* violence. The Guatemalan team differentiates public from domestic violence and notes that the two cannot be isolated from each other; they define violence as "intentional maltreatment of a physical, sexual, or emotional nature, which leads to an environment of fear, miscommunication and silence" (UNICEF-UNIFEM-OPS/OMS-FNUAP 1993: 22). The team notes that all forms of violence are the product of unequal power relations; among these the greatest inequality is that between men and women. And, according to Bourdieu and Wacquant (2004: 273), "the male order is so deeply grounded as to need no justification[,] . . . leading to [a] construct [of relations] from the standpoint of the dominant, i.e., as natural." They argue further: "The case of gender domination shows better than any other that *symbolic violence accomplishes itself through an act of cognition and of misrecognition that lies beyond—or beneath—the controls of consciousness and will*, in the obscurities of the schemata of habitus that are at once gendered and gendering" (original emphasis). Similarly, as Laurel Bossen (1983) observed in her research on Guatemala, an added dimension of systems of gender stratification is the development of ideologies that reinforce and rationalize sexual differentiation and inequality.

Gender and gendered violence and public and domestic violence work in conjunction, and the interlocking of gender violence and gendered violence increasingly hurts women, as new arenas in which gender is a significant axis of stratification multiply. Guatemala's Gender Development Index is 0.63, which places it 119th of 175 ranked countries, below the 0.71 overall rate for Latin America and the Caribbean (UNDP 2003). Education at different levels is unequal by gender, and access to land is equally lopsided. Already 40 percent of rural families do not have access to land, and within this hierarchy women have a much lower rate of direct ownership. A survey found that only 28 percent of 99,000 female agriculturalists in Guatemala had permanent salaried employment; the rest were employed temporarily (Escoto et al. 1993). Disparities by ethnicity further exacerbate gender inequality, as indigenous Maya women fare far worse than ladinas in human development indicators.

The study by the Guatemalan team mentioned above presents a number of insights that show the institutionalization of gender hierarchies and violence, as authorities in the medical and judicial fields frame their actions and decisions in the same "social order of things" that shapes gender and gendered violence. The team interviewed sixteen professionals, including physicians, nurses, policemen, lawyers, gynecologists, a journalist, and a social worker, working in the public and private sectors who, in one way or another, dealt with instances of domestic violence. They were asked about their views of men and women, and overwhelmingly all agreed that "women are weaker," that "women are dependent on men," that "women must obey men," that "men are the ones who hold authority," and that "women are loving and caring." When they were asked under what conditions a man is justified in assaulting a woman, five of the professionals pointed to jealousy, alcoholism, or infidelity on the part of the woman. When they were asked if violence against women affected society in general, they responded negatively, indicating that these are isolated cases that do not have a wider effect. Some of the professionals did say that violent acts against women can have a broad effect when the children imitate the actions of the fathers and become aggressors themselves, when families disintegrate, when women become a public charge if they are left physically unable to work, and when society in general becomes more violent (UNICEF-UNIFEM-OPS/OMS-FNUAP 1993). Therefore, institutions such as the criminal justice system reinforce and formalize violent structures, causing more injury and suffering (often though not solely through neglect).

Gender and gendered violence in Guatemala emerge in quotidian events, and it is precisely these everyday forms, sometimes expressed in seemingly innocuous acts, that contribute to their normalization. Gender ideologies create spheres of social action that contribute not only to normalizing expressions of violence but also to justifying "punishments" for deviations from normative gender role expectations. This is manifested in imposed demarcations of public and private spaces and in the resulting restriction of women's movement in public, as well as in practices that are more directly physically violent, such as abductions of women before they marry *(robadas)*, a point to which I return in chapter 4.

Often the women I spoke with found their self-perceptions corroborated by their partners' threats, assaults, reproaches, and orders, but in some cases it was other women who did the reproaching or contributed to the assault. For instance, Delfina told me that her husband insulted her in front of friends and family, threw food at her when it was not prepared to his taste, and often threatened to leave her for a younger woman. This treatment was routine, though in a moment of reflection that epitomized the normalization of gender violence and gendered violence in San Alejo she somehow considered herself a bit fortunate. In her words, "He's never touched me. Can you believe he's never hit me? Yes, I'm serious. It's true. You'd think, with his character, it could be awful. But he's not like others who hit their wives." Delfina's reflection about physical violence in the lives of women and its absence in her life casts it as normalized for others. Nonetheless, Delfina mentioned that she felt depressed, tense, and unloved; the perverse effects of her husband's behavior also led her to accept her situation as ordinary.

So many other women she knew suffered similar (or worse) assaults routinely that she did not find her own condition "that bad." I am not recounting these comments in an accusatory manner; rather, I want to call attention to the connection between extrapersonal, macrostructures of inequality and the microlevel, everyday world, as it is here that gender-based symbolic violence, the violence found in the social order, is instantiated.

To be sure, gender violence and gendered violence, and their normalization, are not new in Guatemala. In an examination of gender and justice in rural Guatemala, Cindy Forster (1999) notes that between 1936 and 1956 there were several recorded cases involving harmful acts against women (one had been killed) that failed to generate criminal proceedings. Authorities noted "nothing strange" in criminal acts against women; the "business as usual" attitude was especially noticeable in cases in which the women were poor and/or Maya. A justice system that carries inconsequential punishments for crimes against women, Carey and Torres (forthcoming) note, offers no legal sanction against gender-based violence. Carey and Torres, as well as Forster, link all these forms of violence against women. Forster writes:

> In Guatemala as elsewhere, dominant ideologies that justify coercion have shared a common purpose in the routinization of human inequality. Closely linked behaviors and social philosophies have legitimized the extraction of labor and obedience from masses of people across culture, class, or sex divides, sometimes through the use of terror. Abstractions that separate the political from the personal and gender from race or class, often damage the real-life permeability of these various oppressions. . . . Like violence against women, violence against the poor and nonwhite exists as a persistent threat. . . . In Guatemala . . . these oppressions were not necessarily parallel or dual systems. Rather, each was intimately bound up with the others, resting on the same scaffolding of structural inferiority and manifested in daily violence that enforced domination and submission. (1999: 57–58)

Gender violence and gendered violence in Guatemala today have roots in gender ideologies and in the country's history of political violence. Though only one quarter of the 200,000 disappeared and those executed extrajudicially during Guatemala's internal armed conflict were women (CEH 1999; REHMI 1998), Torres (2005: 163) notes that "when women were killed, their cadavers showed evidence of overkill and rape." This point, Torres (2005) argues, suggests that women more often than men were punished for divergence from expected behavioral norms. Indeed, in her meticulous analysis of published records, Torres finds that the victim's gender played a crucial role in determining the type of torture, the way bodies were disposed of, and the extent and type of reporting made on violated cadavers. Thus, Torres (2005) argues, the gender-specific necrographic maps and the significance of their signs point to the role of women in the restructuring of the Guatemalan nation through violence.

As in other politically conflictive societies, therefore, women in Guatemala have been murdered, disappeared, terrorized, and stripped of their dignity, and rape and sexual violence against them have been an integral part of the counterinsurgency strategy (Amnesty International 2005). Susan Blackburn (1999) and Cynthia Enloe (2000) have argued that such treatment can be linked to more obvious forms of state violence against women, as strategies of state terror and as part of a process of intimidation of dissidents or minority groups. In this generalized context of gendered violence, indigenous women were singularly violated (Torres 2005), for this violence was directed at them because they were women and because they were Mayas. As Nelson (1999: 326) notes, the disdain for indigenous life, in particular, indigenous female life, was temporarily extended by the counterinsurgency, which treated all "probable insurgents" "like Indians— expendable, worthless, bereft of civil and human rights." But the real magnitude of the violence women suffered during Guatemala's civil conflict will never be known, in part because many cases were not documented, but also because many women, out of guilt or shame, remained too traumatized to come forward, and afraid of rejection by their communities (Amnesty International 2005). The U.N. Truth Commission report states that rape, especially in indigenous areas, resulted in "breaking marriage and social ties[,] generating social isolation and communal shame[,] and provok[ing] abortions [and] infanticide and obstruct[ing] births and marriages within these groups, thus facilitating the destruction of indigenous groups" (CEH 1999: 14).

Thus Guatemala's regime and militarization of life has made possible multiple acts of gendered violence, reflected in direct political violence against Maya women but also by the encouragement of abduction, torture, rape, and murder of female workers as a lesson to other women who might think of asserting their rights. Direct and indirect forms of violence have coalesced so that Guatemalan women have lived "in a chronic state of emergency," Carey and Torres (forthcoming) note, which has been a *precursor* to the violence we see today. Direct physical violence against women has increased in postwar Guatemala in absolute and relative numbers. Police records indicate that in 2002 women accounted for 4.5 percent of all killings, in 2003 for 11.5 percent, and in 2004 for 12.1 percent; figures compiled by the Policía Nacional Civil (PNC) (cited in Amnesty International 2005) note that the number of women murdered rose from 163 in 2002 to 383 in 2003 to more than 527 in 2004, and according to Oxfam (Oxfam Novib n.d.), in the first half of 2005 there were 239 women killed, including 33 girls under the age of fifteen. The Guatemalan lawyer Claudia Paz y Paz Bailey (quoted in Preston 2009) noted that over 4,000 women had been killed violently in Guatemala in the previous decade, with only 2 percent of the cases solved. In fact, Torres (2008: 6) argues that impunity in Guatemala demonstrates tolerance to multiple forms of violence but also "the extent to which violence has become naturalized in Guatemalan society." In Ciudad Juárez, Mexico, a similar pattern of killings has drawn international attention and condemnation. Aside from reports by Amnesty International and the Inter-American Commission on Human Rights, however, the Guatemalan women's deaths have started to receive international attention only in recent years.

As with the killings during the years of overt political conflict, those in Guatemala today are reported in gruesome detail in the national media, sending a similar message of uncertainty and fear. Only this time the message is directed at women, at *all* women regardless of ethnic background but especially at those from poor backgrounds who work outside the home. And as Godoy-Paiz (2008) notes, not all women in Guatemala experience life and violence in the same ways; social position shapes how women live and how they die. The women in both San Alejo and the Altiplano pay attention to the news; the images and descriptions refresh memories of the insecurity of life, and they often make decisions about travel, study, and work based on this information. For instance, several women in San Alejo mentioned that it was dangerous for women to travel by bus to work or to study, or to walk at certain times, even during the daytime, along roads that were not frequently used. Linking the violence of the past and the dangers of the present, Rosita, in the Altiplano, said that when her daughter informed her that she wanted to go to Guatemala City to study to be a secretary Rosita just about died thinking of the many dangers her daughter might face: "I couldn't sleep that night, just thinking and thinking. How could I live without her by my side? And memories of all the ugly things come to my mind. My hands shake just to think what can happen to her. One hears so much—well, I have seen horrible things. My sister-in-law tells me not to put this fear into the girl's head, to let her do what she wants, go to school, but this is terrible [Rosita is in tears]. Tell me, what if I see her photo in the newspaper [meaning as the victim of a gruesome death]?"

In two instances during my last visits to Guatemala, I had the opportunity to glimpse the feelings of insecurity and fear that women in both San Alejo and the Altiplano experienced every day, though I would not equate my limited experiences with what the women go through. In May 1999, during a conversation with Hortencia in San Alejo, she told me that two women had been found killed, their bodies badly tortured, on a road not far from her house. Then she added a sentence that sent chills down my spine: "Right away, I thought about you two [my assistant and I], since you two walk around town and work, and the two women found were workers. I thought, could it be Cecilia and her friend?" I responded with a nervous laugh that no, thank God, it was not us. In December the same year, during a visit to the Altiplano, the husband of one of the women I was visiting told me he had heard that a young woman was kidnapped and found dead about 30 kilometers away. "She was an anthropologist," he said, "doing the same thing you're doing here." In an instant reaction, not thinking clearly and perhaps seeking distance from the woman found dead, I responded, "But I am not an anthropologist," as if disciplinary training would have mattered. In a fitting comment to my ridiculous response, he added with a shrug of his shoulder and a chuckle, "Oh, maybe she wasn't an anthropologist either, but in any case, she was asking a lot of questions of women just like you do, and she was found dead."

Hortencia's and this man's words were unsettling to me and left me thinking not only about my own safety but also, especially, about what it must be like for many of the women I had met to live every day with the constant threat of a horrific death.

The presence of naked or partially naked bodies in public places, on roadsides and city streets, continues to be an everyday sight in *postwar* Guatemala. One of the most gruesome recent sightings was four human heads and two decapitated bodies found in separate public points of Guatemala City in June 2010 (*El Periódico* 2010). And to be sure, men also have been affected by the violence; in fact, many more men than women have been killed. But the brutality and evidence of sexual violence (in most cases amounting to torture) creates a different context for the deaths of women. Amnesty International (2005) reported that although the murders may be attributed to different motives and may have been committed in different areas of the country, the violence today is overwhelmingly gender based. The murders of students, housewives, professionals, domestic employees, unskilled workers, members or former members of street youth gangs, and sex workers in both urban and rural areas, the overwhelming majority of them uninvestigated, are often attributed to "common" or "organized" crime, drug and arms trafficking, maras, or a jealous boyfriend or husband. In response to increasing demands for action, in 2008 the Guatemalan government enacted a law stipulating special sanctions for these crimes against women (Preston 2009), but only a tiny percentage of cases have been prosecuted.

Many of the women who have been killed in recent years come from poor backgrounds, which signals discrimination on the basis of both class and gender. Whereas the majority of women who were victims of violence during Guatemala's overt civil conflict were indigenous Mayas living in rural areas, the reported murder victims today are both Mayas and ladinas living in urban or semiurban areas. This new violence against women is all-encompassing. However, the brutality of the killings and the signs of sexual violence on women's mutilated bodies today bear many of the hallmarks of the atrocities committed during the political conflict, making the differences between "wartime" and "peacetime" Guatemala imperceptible.

CONCLUSION

I have laid out a conceptual framework that includes structural, political, symbolic, everyday, and gender and gendered violence to examine the lives of the women I came to know in Guatemala. Three points need to be kept in mind. First, the multiple forms of violence I have presented never occur in isolation, though sometimes one form appears to be more salient. Thus in the chapters that follow they appear intertwined in different spheres of the women's lives. Second, violence is normalized in the women's everyday lives. Only when discussed or pointed to do routine practices (sometimes attributed to tradition) become obvious and disturb the normalized gaze. Indeed, it is the insidiousness of this routinized violence in regions that are perceived as "calm" or "peaceful," or in practices that are taken as "part of tradition," to which I call attention. It is through this normalization and misrecognition that dehumanization becomes possible and suffering becomes a part of life. Once violence is unleashed, whether in the form of state violence, domestic abuse, or exploitation, it emerges in different forms and shapes the lives and minds of individuals. In the chapters that follow I examine the women's "private terrors" that encapsulate the multilayered violence I have presented here.

13

The Consequences of the Criminal Justice Pipeline on Black and Latino Masculinity

Victor M. Rios

Black and Latino youth are overrepresented in every major component in the juvenile justice system (Kupchik 2006; Leiber 2002). Some researchers have called this "cumulative disadvantage," as the overrepresentation increases from the time of arrest through the final point in the system, imprisonment (National Council on Crime and Delinquency [NCCD] 2007, 4). It is noteworthy that nearly 75 percent of juveniles admitted to adult state prisons in 2002 were youth of color (Kupchik 2006; NCCD 2007), although only 30 percent of juveniles arrested in this country are persons of color (NCCD 2007).

Mauer and Chesney-Lind (2004) have argued that the disproportionate incarceration of people of color has had unintended consequences in poor communities. They contend that such punishment not only adversely affects confined individuals but also extends to negative effects on families, communities, and the future livelihoods of those who come into contact with the criminal justice system. Among the collateral consequences of punitive criminal justice treatment of young adults in the inner city are constant surveillance and stigma imposed by schools, community centers, and families (Rios 2006); permanent criminal credentials that exclude black males from the labor market

(Pager 2003); and a sense of mistrust and resentment toward police and the rest of the criminal justice system (Brunson and Miller 2006; Fine and Weiss 1998). In this article, I argue that an additional consequence of enhanced policing, surveillance, and punitive treatment of youth of color is the development of a specific set of gendered practices, heavily influenced by interactions with police, detention facilities, and probation officers. This criminal justice pipeline provides young men with meanings of masculinity that ultimately influence their decisions to commit crime and engage in violence. While race affects how a young person is treated in the criminal justice pipeline, masculinity plays a role in how young men desist or recidivate as they pass through the system. One of the outcomes of pervasive criminal justice contact for young black and Latino men is the production of a hypermasculinity that obstructs desistance and social mobility.

Harris (2000, 785) defines hypermasculinity as the "exaggerated exhibition of physical strength and personal aggression" that is often a response to a gender threat "expressed through physical and sexual domination of others." Drawing on this definition, I contend that the criminal justice pipeline encourages expressions of hypermasculinity by threatening and confusing young

Victor Rios, "The Consequences of the Criminal Justice Pipeline on Black and Latino Masculinity," *Annals of the American Academy of Political and Social Science* vol. 623, pp. 150–62, copyright © 2009 SAGE Publications Ltd. Reprinted by permission of SAGE Publications.

men's masculinity. This, in turn, leads the young men to rely on domination through violence, crime, and a school and criminal justice counterculture. Multiple points in the criminal justice pipeline may be salient for producing hypermasculinity, including three that are examined here: policing, incarceration, and probation. Detrimental forms of masculinity are partly developed through a youth's interaction with these institutions of criminal justice.

Messerschmidt (1993, 1997, 2000) has argued that crime is a resource for "doing" race and gender (see also West and Fenstemaker 1995; West and Zimmerman 1987). He contends that "crime is employed to produce and sustain a specific race and class masculine identity" (1997, 41). In other words, crime is one of the avenues that men turn to in developing, demonstrating, and communicating their manhood. Indeed, criminal activity constitutes a gendered practice that can be used to communicate the parameters of manhood. As such, crime is more likely when men need to prove themselves and when they are held accountable to a strict set of expectations (Messerschmidt 1997). Furthermore, West and Fenstemaker (1995) contend that this accountability—the gendered actions that people develop in response to what they perceive others will expect of them—is encountered in interactions between individuals and institutions:

> While individuals are the ones who do gender, the process of rendering something accountable is both interactional and institutional in character. . . . Gender is . . . a mechanism whereby situated social action contributes to the reproduction of social structure. (p. 21)

Here, I expand on Messerschmidt's notion of crime as a masculinity-making resource and on West and Fenstemaker's understanding of gender as a mechanism by which social structure is created and reproduced. Conceptualizing gender as structured action, a social process that changes based on interactions with specific types of institutions, in turn, allows us to explore how the criminal justice system shapes the development of specific forms of masculinity.

MASCULINITY, CRIME, AND CRIME CONTROL

Individuals shape their behavior according to gendered expectations and are subject to a system of accountability that is gendered, raced, and classed (Fenstemaker and

West 2002; West and Fenstemaker 1995). Youth of color are inculcated into a set of hypermasculine expectations that often lead them to behaviors that conflict with the structures of dominant institutions. For example, Ferguson (2000) demonstrated that schools participate in the making of black masculinity in children as young as ten years old. Masculinity-making is heavily responsible for the deviance and punishment that takes place in the classroom and later in the criminal justice system.

To be assigned "real man" status by relevant others and institutions, young men must pass multiple litmus tests among peers, family, and other institutions. These masculinity tests, or codes, were identified by sociologists as early as the 1920s. In 1924, Edwin Sutherland discussed how boys are taught to be rough and tough, rendering them more likely than girls to become delinquent (cited in Sutherland and Cressey 1955). In 1947, Parsons noted that at the very core of American adolescence an aggressive masculinity is at play:

> Western men are peculiarly susceptible to the appeal of an adolescent type of assertively masculine behavior . . . to revolt against the routine aspects of the primary institutionalized masculine role of sober responsibility, meticulous respect for the rights of others, and tender affection towards women. (Quoted in Kimmel 2006, 82)

Contemporary urban ethnographers also emphasize this point. For example, Anderson (1999) describes "young male syndrome" as the perceived, expected, and often necessary pressure to perform a tough, violent, and deviant manhood to receive and maintain respect (see also Dance 2002; Duneier 1999). Pyke (1996) found that masculinity is expressed differently by men of varied class positions. While wealthy men can prove their masculinity through the ability to earn money and consume products that make them manly, poor young men have to use toughness, violence, and survival as the means of proving their masculinity and resilience. Toughness, dominance, and the willingness to resort to violence to resolve interpersonal conflicts are central characteristics of masculine identity (Anderson 1999; Messerschmidt 1993). Such studies also explore how masculinity is central to the perpetuation of crime, but they do not examine how the criminal justice system is involved in the masculinity-making process.

Kimmel and Mahler (2003, 1440) move beyond an emphasis on crime, arguing that violent youth are not psychopaths but, rather, "overconformists to a particular normative construction of masculinity." I contend that these overconforming violent and delinquent youth give us clues as to how masculinity is developed in relation to institutional constructions of manhood. Mainstream society and the criminal justice system expect a masculine conformity that emphasizes hard work, law abidance, and an acceptance of subordinate social positions. Some young men attempt to embrace this masculinity as a means to reform. However, when they attempt to follow these expectations, they come to realize that doing so does not allow for survival on the streets, a place to which they can always expect to return.

In attempts to deal with young men's criminality, institutions develop practices heavily influenced by masculinity. In turn, inner-city males become socialized to specific meanings of manhood that are diametrically opposed to those expected by dominant institutions of control. Thus, gendered interactions with the criminal justice system place young men of color in a double bind. Most buy into the system's ideals of reform by being "hardworking men." However, frustration with the lack of viable employment and guidance opportunities lead many young men to what seems to be the only alternative: hypermasculinity, or the exaggerated exhibition of physical and personal aggression. The stories and actions of young men in this study provide insight into how this double bind is partially generated by the criminal justice system itself.

METHOD

This investigation is based on ethnography involving in-depth interviews with forty black and Latino male adolescents living in Oakland, California. The study was conducted from 2002 to 2005. The sample includes twenty black males and twenty Latino males, ranging from ages fourteen to eighteen. Participants were recruited from two organizations that worked with "at-promise" youth and were selected through convenience and snowball sampling. Interviews were conducted either at the sites of the two community organizations or at a public space where the youth felt comfortable. Throughout this article I use pseudonyms for participants, organizations, schools, and gangs. Thirty of the forty participants had recently been incarcerated. The remaining ten youth had not come into

contact with the criminal justice system. Most of the offenses committed by the delinquent boys were nonviolent. All forty youth reported having persistent contact with police officers while growing up. The thirty formerly arrested youth had all spent at least a week in juvenile facilities, and twenty-four had been assigned a probation officer.

I shadowed these young men, with permission from them and their parents, as they walked the streets, attended court, and participated in community center activities. While ethnographers traditionally study a specific site, I studied a mobile population and followed participants wherever they went, sometimes to a neighboring city, and sometimes to court and juvenile facilities by way of their parents. Shadowing allowed me to see and analyze routine practices and how these fit in with the full range of participants' activities.

My own biographic characteristics contributed to this research approach. I was twenty-five years old when the study began, had grown up in the neighborhood where most of these young men were from, and, like them, was incarcerated as a juvenile. This allowed me to gain the young men's trust and to develop a sense of camaraderie with them. Because of my similar biography, I also was subject to some of the punitive treatment that youth received during my observations. I too was constantly harassed by adults and brutalized by police who associated me with the participants. This gave me a keen insider sense, or what might be called a "carnal sociology" (Wacquant 2004; see also Goffman 1963), of what the young people were experiencing. On the other hand, as an insider, I was aware that I may have adopted some of the bias held by the youth in the study and deliberately tried to remain reflexive throughout the study and data analyses.

MASCULINITY VERSUS CRIMINALIZATION

Junior, a sixteen-year-old Chicano from Oakland, California, attended continuation school, which is a small campus where delinquent, truant, and other problem students are sent to do their course work as a final alternative to expulsion. I often shadowed Junior, walking with him to and from school, places of leisure, and home. One morning, as I walked with him to school, I counted six police cars patrolling his usual route, which is used by most teenagers from the poorer side of the neighborhood to get to school. Each patrol car slowed to stare us down as they spotted him. To buy a snack, Junior had to wait outside the neighborhood store for a few minutes because of store policy clearly stated on a sign reading, "only two kids allowed in store at one time."

Junior's school was located in the middle-class part of town, about five miles uphill from his home. As we approached the school's neighborhood, the residents who had previously called the police on Junior for sitting on their steps stared with suspicion. As he entered the school, he passed by the school-stationed officer. The officer asked him, "What kind of trouble are you going to give me today?" We parted ways as I left him at the foot of the school entrance and watched him enter under the eye of the surveillance camera. He later told me that his teacher reported him to the school-based police officer for sleeping in class. All of this policing happened in a one-hour span, from 7:45 to 8:45 a.m. on a typical Monday morning.

These day-to-day interactions fostered a sense of criminalization, that is, being viewed as a criminal when simply going about routine practices, and they forced Junior to wonder whether he would ever be seen as a normal person or only as a criminal:

> I mean, I mean, you know, I try hard but I get messed with all the time even if I'm trying to keep it cool. It's like when I keep it cool is when they fuck with me the most. . . . I might as well be hard and let them know that they ain't gonna fuck with me.

As a reaction to such treatment, Junior developed a tough front (Dance 2002) that used hypermasculinity as a form of coping, survival, and resistance. Junior's criminalization intensified his conflicts over manhood and ran a collision course with the criminal justice system's demands of passivity, compliance, and conformity to a subjugated racialized social status. Expectations of passivity and compliance, unaccompanied by change in social conditions, engender hopelessness and an inability to function both in mainstream institutions and on the street, where survival skills are intricately connected to hypermasculinity. Criminalization, policing, and the justice system's pressures on young men force them to make a choice: comply or become hard. When they comply, they fail on the street because they have to

become passive and nondeviant, while at the same time they are unable to obtain employment or eliminate the criminal stigma marked on them by the system. On the other hand, when they fail to comply, they are likely to be harassed or arrested. Like Junior, the rest of the young men in this study encountered criminalization through gendered interactions as they entered the system. The first point of contact with hypermasculinity through criminal justice is with the police.

Police

Police officers are themselves embedded in an environment that embraces masculinity. Indeed, academies train officers to practice a rogue and hostile masculinity. Prokos and Padavic (2002, 442) note that male officers "equate men and masculinity with guns, crime-fighting, a combative personality . . . and a desire to work in high crime areas." This positioning reverberates in the inner city as "police officers in poor minority neighborhoods may come to see themselves as law enforcers in a community of savages, as outposts of the law in a jungle" (Harris 2000, 798). In this context, punitive police treatment of men of color is not only racial violence; it is also gender violence: "Violent acts committed by men, whether these acts break the law or are designed to uphold it, are often a way of demonstrating the perpetrator's manhood. I call this kind of violence 'gender violence' and assert that men as well as women may be its victims" (Harris 2000, 783).

Young people in Oakland encounter this gender violence regularly by police on the street, at school, at community centers, and in front of their apartment complexes. The boys often become victims in the course of police officers' attempts to uphold the law. Officers want to "teach" young men lessons by feminizing them. They manhandle them, constantly call them "little bitches," humiliate them in front of female peers, challenge them to fights, and otherwise brutalize them. The following interchange is illustrative of how the young men respond:

CASTRO: Dude [the officer] was pointing his gun. "I give up, I give up." He hit him with a stick and broke his arm and this other fool had his knee on my neck. All 'cause we were smoking some weed . . . they beat us down and call us "little bitches."

RAFA: They kick your ass, pistol whip you even try to kill you . . . them bust'as just trying to prove themselves you feel me? They trying to prove they are more manly than us but if they didn't have guns or jails they would end up being the bitches.

Gendered police interactions and gendered violence begin at an early age (see Brunson and Miller 2006; Ferguson 2000). Slick's story illustrates this phenomenon. He lives in the heart of a neighborhood that is home to one of Oakland's largest gangs, "La Nueve" (the East 9th Street Gang). In his childhood, Slick expected police to protect him from violent gang members. Then one day he realized that police saw him as "the enemy." Slick was eleven years old when he was first brutalized by the police, the same officers who had policed his neighborhood from the time that he was a small child:

> One time we were at St. Anthony's [park] . . . the police out of nowhere started talking shit to me. And I uh, uh I pulled up my pants, I just pulled up my pants and he just grabbed me and slammed me on the ground and hit me with the club. He was like, he was like "Oh you look like you was gonna pull up your pants and do something." I was, I was pullin' up my pants 'cause I be sagging my pants sometimes.

Slick tried to pull up his pants to appear more formal and to signify to the officer that he was complying with the law. He figured if he pulled up his pants, the cop might see him as a "good kid," by explaining, "He tried to tell me not to sag my pants anymore so he wouldn't have to think I was a criminal." Eventually, Slick would develop coping strategies that helped him deal with the animosity he felt around police: he acted tough and put on a menacing performance when police came around. Slick cursed at police and gave them "dirty" looks when they drove by or pulled up next to us; his hypermasculinity became a resource for keeping the police at bay. This strategy often worked, which led officers to call in backup when they decided to approach us. During my shadowing in Oakland, officers often approached preadolescent boys in only one patrol car. However, once the boys reached adolescence and commanded a certain bravado, officers always showed up in at least two patrol cars. The boys' "hardcore" behavior—developed through negative interactions with police officers—may have signaled to officers that they were armed and dangerous, and officers treated them as such.

On various occasions, the boys and I were "roughed up" by groups of police officers who drove up in multiple patrol cars. We were harassed, humiliated, and sometimes beaten. During these dozen or so times over the three years, I learned that officers use a brutal masculinity that inculcates a tough-toughness, a manly-manliness, and a hypermasculinity. This model often leads young men to perpetrate crime and violence, and it may sanction police to brutalize and arrest them, which leads youth to the next gate in the justice pipeline: incarceration. Once in confinement, these young men adopt a masculinity that would protect them not only from the streets and police but also from violence in confinement.

Incarceration

While incarcerated, young men are forced to overemphasize their masculinity. The story of Big Rob, an African American sixteen-year-old from Oakland, illustrates this point. He had been arrested for driving a "G-ride" (i.e., a stolen car). Rob's specialty was stealing cars and selling them to "chop shops," car shops that dismantle the cars and sell them for parts. At the time of the arrest, Rob was driving in a 1987 Buick Grand National. He was stripped and cavity-searched upon arrival at "one-hundred-and-fiftieth," the county's juvenile justice facility. His possessions were confiscated, and he was provided a dark blue jumpsuit with the words "property of Alameda County" printed on it.

> The guard told me "take a shower and make sure you don't drop the soap, boy!" I didn't know what he was talking about. It wasn't until I asked some dude that I figured out what he meant.

"Don't drop the soap" is a reference to rape by other inmates in detention showers. Rob was placed in a cafeteria where about twenty or so youth congregated. They stared Rob down, giving him dirty looks. A few boys walked up to him and asked, "Where you from?" Rob told them, "Dirty thirties." They responded with the names of their turfs. "I had to act hard. I balled up my fist and was ready to knock a nigga' out." Rob eventually got into a fight, protecting himself from an attack. He was sent to "solitary," only allowed outside of his tiny cell with a cement bed to take a shower and call home. The officer who supervised his cell commented "you gonna' learn how to be a man the hard way." Once released, Rob and other young men like him bring this repertoire to the streets. "Man! They think I got better. Mothafucka's just taught me how to be more violent, steal tighter rides [nicer cars]. . . . I even ended up with more bitch-ass enemies."

Probation

Probation practices subject boys' ideas of manhood to strict evaluation. As agents of reform, probation officers attempt to teach young men how to be "real men" by demanding that they work toward a societally acceptable form of masculinity: acquire an education, attain a job, and support a family. They are told to get a job, do well in school, and stay out of trouble. The likelihood of failure is high since most avenues of legitimate success are out of reach. Kimmel (2006) argues that in the contemporary era,

> Deindustrialization made men's hold on the successful demonstration of masculinity increasingly tenuous; there are fewer and fewer self-made successes and far more self-blaming failures. (p. 216)

When these youth fail, they abandon the false expectations of obtaining a job; instead of becoming passive and hopeless, they adopt a hypermasculine ideal of survival.

For example, José, a fifteen-year-old who had been arrested for selling marijuana, lived in a state of confusion when it came to masculinity. His description highlights the contradiction he confronted:

> They [probation officers] tell us to be "real men," to show respect but they don't see that if we show respect we'll get treated like punk . . . being a man out here is different. It means smashing on a scrub [beating an enemy up] if he breaks your respect . . . it means handling your business in order to get paid . . . not being a bitch and shit, it means going to jail if you have to.

From José's perspective, and those of many other youth I interviewed, it was extremely self-defeating for probation officers trying to reform them to attempt to do so by teaching them how a real man should act. These messages did not provide youth with tools to navigate the streets, to do well at home and in school, or to succeed at a job and make an income. Instead, youth saw

two extreme worlds of manhood where only one was accessible—hypermasculinity. It is at this point where male youth made their decisions to affirm, develop, and demonstrate a manhood that appears to offer respect, economic gain, and social status (Anderson 1999; Jones 2004) instead of hopelessness.

The ideal of manhood that probation officers try to inculcate is also one of responsibility. For these officials, the responsibility of a young man is to follow his "program" and not be rearrested. The message becomes, "a real man does not belong in jail." Once a male enters jail or prison, he is at risk of becoming emasculated as his life is run by a system outside of himself. According to José, his probation officer, Mr. Bryan, explained the condition of men in containment through associations with feminization, by playing upon the fear and dread associated with men being treated like women:

> You want to go to prison where everybody is gonna pimp you? The guards are gonna run you like a little bitch. The murderers and rapists [will] make you bend over, they gonna treat you like somebody's wife.

While probation officers, and the community, attempt to instill young men with positive notions of manhood, the street contradicts this masculinity—one demands law abidance, the other contempt for the law. In trying to teach a dominant masculinity as a set of ideals, probation officers unintentionally push young men of color further into hypermasculinity.

DISCUSSION AND CONCLUSION

After being arrested and placed on probation, unable to continue selling drugs or stealing cars for income, and unable to secure a job because of his record, T, a sixteen-year-old African American from Oakland, resorted to using women as a central source of income. When asked, "Where do you get money from?" T replied,

> Pimp a bitch you know, let that bitch come out her pocket . . . act like I like her so she'll give me money and shit . . . most bitches will give me whatever I need . . . shoes, shirts, food, bus pass, whatever . . . or make her sell shit for me.

T made the decision to no longer commit crime. However, his solution was to fully embrace hypermasculinity and dominate women to accomplish what the criminal justice system expected of him—to desist from committing crime.

As a result, inner-city men come to embrace gendered practices that further limit their futures and harm those around them. The youth in this study reported trying to be "good men," following the criminal justice system's ideals of manhood by being passive, trying to do well in school, or looking for work. However, these strategies often placed them in a double bind such that they were unable to succeed both at work and in the streets. When the strategies fail, a seductive alternative surfaces in times of crisis—hypermasculinity.

As the criminal justice system perpetuates gender violence on young men to "teach them a lesson," young men develop a hypermasculinity that symbolically attacks the system. They also embrace domination of others as a way to compensate for having their masculinity threatened. As adolescent boys make masculinity on the street, the institutions of control that manage them also generate meanings of manhood that correlate with the damaging identities these youth form on the street.

Both gender and race simultaneously shape the life course of inner-city men in the criminal justice system. Gender, like race, is always determined by specific contexts. In this case, the criminalization of black and Latino males and the criminal justice system's expectations of masculinity provide young men with gender resources that often limit their life chances and channel them deeper into the racialized and gendered criminal justice system. The gender ideals purveyed by police, probation officers, and others do not translate adequately into the realities of the youth's lives. In this context, hypermasculinity serves both as resistance and as a resource for self-affirmation. The criminal justice pipeline, in its attempt to reform racialized youth, imposes gender practices fraught with failure and insolvable contradictions. Provided with the options of hypermasculinity or hopelessness by the criminal justice system and the streets, marginalized boys end up choosing to become "real men," to embrace hypermasculinity. While hypermasculinity may attract disrepute, it makes its practitioners feel self-fulfilled. This survival strategy, in turn, impedes desistance and social mobility and entitles the system to further punish racialized and gendered youth. In essence, then, gender is one of the processes by which the criminal justice system is involved in the reproduction of racial inequality.

REFERENCES

Anderson, Elijah. 1999. *Code of the street: Decency, violence, and moral life of the inner city.* New York: Norton.

Brunson, Rod K., and Jody Miller. 2006. Gender, race, and urban policing: The experience of African American youth. *Gender & Society* 20:531–52.

Dance, Lory Janelle. 2002. *Tough fronts: The impact of street culture on schooling.* London: Routledge.

Duneier, Mitchell. 1999. *Sidewalk.* New York: Farrar, Straus and Giroux.

Fenstemaker, Sarah, and Candace West. 2002. *Doing gender, doing difference: Inequality, power, and institutional change.* New York: Routledge.

Ferguson, Anne A. 2000. *Bad boys: Public schools in the making of black masculinity.* Ann Arbor: Michigan University Press.

Fine, Michelle, and Lois Weiss. 1998. *The unknown city: Lives of poor and working-class young adults.* Boston: Beacon.

Goffman, Erving. 1963. *Stigma: Notes on the management of spoiled identity.* New York: Simon & Schuster.

Harris, Angela P. 2000. Gender, violence, race, and criminal justice. *Stanford Law Review* 52:777–807.

Jones, Nikki. 2004. "It's not where you live, it's how you live": How young women negotiate conflict and violence in the inner city. *The Annals of the American Academy of Political and Social Science* 595:49–62.

Kimmel, Michael S. 2006. *Manhood in America: A cultural history.* New York: Oxford University Press.

Kimmel, Michael, and Matthew Mahler. 2003. Adolescent masculinity, homophobia, and violence. *American Behavioral Scientist* 46:1439–58.

Kupchik, Aaron. 2006. *Judging juveniles: Prosecuting adolescents in adult and juvenile courts.* New York: New York University Press.

Leiber, Michael J. 2002. Disproportionate minority confinement (DMC) of youth: An analysis of state and federal efforts to address the issue. *Crime and Delinquency* 48:3–45.

Mauer, Marc, and Meda Chesney-Lind, eds. 2004. *Invisible punishment: The collateral consequences of mass imprisonment.* New York: New Press.

Messerschmidt, James W. 1993. *Masculinities and crime: Critique and reconceptualization of theory.* Lanham, MD: Rowman & Littlefield.

Messerschmidt, James W. 1997. *Crime as structured action: Gender, race, class and crime in the making.* Thousand Oaks, CA: Sage.

Messerschmidt, James W. 2000. *Nine lives: Adolescent masculinities, the body, and violence.* Boulder, CO: Westview.

National Council on Crime and Delinquency. 2007. And justice for some: Differential treatment of youth of color in the juvenile system. http://www.nccd-crc.org/nccd/pubs/2007jan_justice_for_some.pdf (accessed April 10, 2008).

Pager, Devah. 2003. The mark of a criminal record. *American Journal of Sociology* 108:937–75.

Prokos, Anastasia, and Irene Padavic. 2002. "There oughtta be a law against bitches": Masculinity lessons in police academy training. *Gender, Work and Organization* 9:439–59.

Pyke, Karen D. 1996. Class-based masculinities: The interdependence of gender, class, and interpersonal power. *Gender & Society* 10:527–49.

Rios, Victor. 2006. The hyper-criminalization of black and Latino male youth in the era of mass incarceration. *Souls* 8:40–54.

Sutherland, Edwin H., and Donald R. Cressey. 1955. *Principles of criminology.* Philadelphia: J. B. Lippincott.

Wacquant, Loic J. D. 2004. *Body and soul: Notebooks of an apprentice boxer.* New York: Oxford University Press.

West, Candace, and Sarah Fenstemaker. 1995. Doing difference. *Gender & Society* 9:8–37.

West, Candace, and Don Zimmerman. 1987. Doing gender. *Gender & Society* 1:125–51.

14

Normalizing Sexual Violence

Young Women Account for Harassment and Abuse

HEATHER R. HLAVKA

Coming up against "the wall of patriarchy" (Gilligan 1990, 503), early adolescence is a defining period for young women. Many regard harassment and violence to be a normal part of everyday life in middle and high schools (Fineran and Bennett 1999), yet most of these crimes go unreported. A 2011 American Association of University Women (AAUW 2011) study found that almost half (48 percent) of the 1,965 students surveyed experienced harassment, but only 9 percent reported the incident to an authority figure. Girls were sexually harassed more than boys (56 percent vs. 40 percent); they were more likely to be pressured for a date, pressured into sexual activity, and verbally harassed (AAUW 2001; Fineran and Bennett 1999).

According to prevalence studies, reported violence in adolescent dating relationships ranges between 8.8 and 40 percent (Sousa 1999). Data from the Youth Risk Behavior Survey (YRBS) show that almost 20 percent of girls experience physical and sexual violence from dating partners (Silverman et al. 2001), and sexual assault accounts for one-third of preteen victimization (Finkelhor and Ormrod 2000). It is tempting to ask: Why do so few young women formally report their victimization experiences? Assuming that peer sexual harassment and assault is an instrument that creates

and maintains gendered and sexed hierarchies (e.g., MacKinnon 1979; Phillips 2000; Tolman et al. 2003), attention instead must turn toward understanding how and why these violent acts are produced, maintained, and normalized in the first place. Despite the considerable body of research that shows high rates of gendered violence among youth, there has been little discussion of its instruments and operations.

This study is concerned with girls' relational experiences of sexuality, harassment and assault, coercion, and consent. With few exceptions, girls' construction of violence has received little attention from victimization scholars and those interested in the gendered power dynamics of adolescent sexual development. The lack of research is clear and a shift in analytical focus toward appraisals of violence is critical. It cannot be assumed that legal definitions of sexual harassment and assault are socially agreed on, understood, or similarly enacted. Research from the vantage point of young women themselves is necessary. How do girls talk about experiences that researchers and the law would label as harassment and rape? In what ways do they account for these experiences?

This study addresses how girls negotiate their lived experiences in ways that are often ignored by law and

Hlavka, H. R., "Normalizing Sexual Violence: Young Women Account for Harassment and Abuse." *Gender & Society* 28 (3): 337–58, copyright © 2014 SAGE Publications. Reprinted by permission of SAGE Publications.

policy. This work aims to re-cast youth as agentic, having intentions, desires, and standpoints (Corsaro 1997; Hlavka 2010; Lee 2001), rather than as passive objects. The study is situated within feminist research and practices that embody the legitimacy of patriarchy, including sexual harassment and violence, sexual subjectivity, and heteronormativity (Gavey 1992). The narrative data come from a larger study on child sexual abuse in which youth were interviewed by specialized forensic interviewers following reports of sexual victimization. I situate the analysis to show how girls make use of culturally available discourses to explain their experiences. The findings complicate studies on the formal underreporting of sexual assault and provide a nuanced understanding of how violence is woven into youths' sexed and gendered relationships from very young ages (Phillips 2000; Tolman et al. 2003).

FEMINIST PERSPECTIVES AND HETERO-RELATIONAL DISCOURSES

Feminist scholarship on compulsory heterosexuality (Connell 1987; Rich 1980; Tolman et al. 2003), heteronormativity (Kitzinger 2005; Martin 2009; Thorne and Luria 1986), and heterogender (Ingraham 1994) consistently finds that traditional gender arrangements, beliefs, and behaviors reinforce women's sexual subordination to men. Heterosexuality is compulsory in that it is an *institution* (Rich 1980) that organizes the conventions by which women and men relate; it is assumed and expected (Jackson 2009) as it is understood as natural and unproblematic (Kitzinger 2005; Schippers 2007). Heteronormative discourses consistently link female sexuality with passivity, vulnerability, and submissiveness, and male sexuality with dominance, aggression, and desire (Butler 1999; Ingraham 1994).

Young people are socialized into a patriarchal culture that normalizes and often encourages male power and aggression, particularly within the context of heterosexual relationships (Fineran and Bennett 1999; Tolman et al. 2003). As men's heterosexual violence is viewed as customary, so too is women's endurance of it (Stanko 1985). For example, Messerschmidt (1986) has argued that "normative heterosexuality" involves a "presumption that men have a special and overwhelming 'urge' or 'drive' toward heterosexual intercourse."

Women come to be justifiable objects of sexual exploitation. These discourses shape embodied experiences (Crawley, Foley, and Shehan 2008; Lorber and Moore 2007), normalizing the presumption that men's sexual aggression is simply "boys being boys" (Connell 1987; French 2003; Messerschmidt 2012). Stanko (1985, 73) argued that "women learn, often at a very early age, that their sexuality is not their own and that maleness can at any point intrude into it." Girls are thus expected to endure aggression by men because that is *part* of man. Coupled with the presumption that women are the gatekeepers of male desire (Fine 1988; Tolman 1991), heteronormative discourses have allowed for men's limited accountability for aggressive, harassing, and criminal sexual conduct. Indeed, dominant notions of gender and heterosexuality underscore much of young people's identity work; they are subject to the pressures of heteronormativity from an early age. Youth negotiate and maintain gendered hierarchies and hegemonies, both within and between genders (Butler 1999). Young women's subjective understandings of gender, sexuality, and violence are thus critical sites for the reproduction of inequality on which feminist scholarship has much to offer.

DISCOURSES OF CHILDREN, SEXUALITY, AND SEXUAL ABUSE

Beginning in the 1970s, rape reformists urged legal change to increase rape reporting to police, encourage prosecution, and increase conviction of sexual offenders in courtrooms across the country. Rape law reforms have not necessarily translated into increased system efficacy or sensitivity toward victims, however (Frohmann and Mertz 1995). Some argue that legal reforms do not address the structures and symbolic constructions through which people make sense of rape (Erlich 2001; Matoesian 1993). Legal reform is limited by the everyday perceptions and cultural constructs that shape individuals' interpretations of coercion and consent.

Children and youth have largely remained exempt from legal and policy discussions of consent to sexual activity, and little scholarly research has taken up the task, perhaps, in part, because Western cultures today often characterize children as innocent, asexual, ignorant, and in need of protection from adult sexual knowledge and practices (Angelides 2004; Best 1990). Adults have historically worked to police the sexual behavior of young people, particularly of girls (Fine 1988; Gilligan 1982). Dominant cultural frameworks perpetuate adult/child, agent/subject, active/passive binaries, and, in this way, law and policy often ignore the subjectivities and experiences of youth. Of course, there are special taboos and tensions surrounding youth sexuality (Thorne and Luria 1986), often making it socially and discursively restricted to adults. Youth learn early that they should not talk about sex (Ryan 2000), often extending to sexual violence and harassment (Gilgun 1986; Phillips 2000; Thompson 1995).

Feminist writings have long documented the public silencing of women and children, especially as it has related to abuse and exploitation. To varying degrees, discursive strategies and ideologies have operated to undermine or dismiss survivors' speech. Alcoff and Gray (1993, 265–66) argue that, through history, survivor speech has been "absolutely prohibited, categorized as mad or untrue, or rendered inconceivable . . . and therefore could not exist within the dominant discourses." Further, feminist theorists argue that "real rape" (Estrich 1987)—or forcible stranger rape—is narrowly defined, largely enforced by law, and reinforced by popular media. Discursively, law and media draw absolutes between healthy heterosexual encounters and dangerous, abusive relationships, creating divisions between what is and what is not violence, between "real rape" and "everyday violence," or what Stanko (1985) termed "little rapes." What counts as sexual violence, then, are the extreme cases "which constrain[s] and construct[s] the framework through which women have to make sense of events" (Kelly and Radford 1990, 41). The struggle to negotiate these tensions has meaningful outcomes, and young people are not exempt.

According to Averill's (1980) social constructivist theory of emotion, an individual must appraise an experience in order to understand and respond to it. Appraisals are based both on dominant discourses and individual desires (Reavey and Gough 2000). Dominant discourses include core cultural beliefs about gender, sex and sexuality, childhood, victimhood, and the like (Ridgeway and Correll 2004). Gagnon and Simon (1973) have termed these discourses "sexual scripts." Like discourses, scripts mediate individuals' relationships and sexual interactions through social context and cultural commitments (Brickell 2006). Dominant notions of heterosexuality underscore much of youths' identity work, and their relationships are subject to the pressures of compulsory heterosexuality (Rich 1980). Certain discourses make available particular subjectivities, and youth must wade through complex and pervasive cultural messages about sexuality, power, and violence. Much has been written on child sexual abuse, but little has come from the perspective of youth. Therefore, research has had little to say about how heteronormative discourses might impact young people's descriptions and interpretations of sexual violence. To speak to the gaps in the literature, I focus on girls' relational experiences and explanations of sexuality, violence, coercion, and consent. Gagnon (1977) suggested that sexual scripts are acquired and practiced during adolescence, and this study aims to contribute to the call for increased research on the "hetero-gendering" and "hetero-sexualising" of children (Angelides 2004; Martin 2009; Myers and Raymond 2010; Renold 2006).

METHODS

The data for this study include audio-videotaped interviews of youths seen by forensic interviewers for reported cases of sexual abuse between 1995 and 2004. The interviews come from the nonprofit Children's Advocacy Center (CAC) located in an urban Midwest community. The CAC provides investigative interviews and medical examinations for youths who may have been sexually or physically assaulted or witnessed a violent crime. Interviews take place between one forensic interviewer and one child referred to the CAC by law enforcement or Child Protection Services (CPS). Youths were brought to the CAC for an interview because they reported sexual abuse to someone, someone else witnessed or reported the abuse to authorities, or the offender confessed to the abuse.

The forensic interview is based on a semi-structured interview protocol designed to maximize youth's ability to communicate their experiences and conforms to standards set by the American Professional Society on the Abuse of Children (APSAC 2002). Protocol components include first establishing rapport and, next, obtaining details about sexual abuse only if the child first verbally discloses victimization to the interviewer. The two then discuss the circumstances surrounding the abuse using nonsuggestive, largely open-ended, questions. So, while the interview is set up to investigate whether or not abuse occurred, youths were consistently allowed to raise and discuss subjects important to them in response to questions such as "What happened? Did you tell anyone? How did they respond? How did you feel about that? Are you worried about anything?" This format allows for rich narrative data that do not rely solely on retrospective reports common in most sexual abuse studies. The interviews were video recorded and varied in length and scope, primarily based on age.

The study sample included 100 interviews of youths between ages three and 17, stratified disproportionately by gender and age and proportionately by race.

The study subsample includes 23 racially diverse young women (13 white girls, six black girls, and four Latina girls) between 11 and 16 years of age. The reported offenders were known to the girls, either as acquaintances or intimate others (intrafamilial abuse was more common in the larger study sample). Accounts were unpacked as everyday violence, instruments of coercion, and accounts of consent. These categories illuminate the heteronormative cultures within which girls accounted for sexual violence and negotiated what happened, how it happened, and why.

FINDINGS

Everyday Violence

Objectification, sexual harassment, and abuse appear to be part of the fabric of young women's lives (Orenstein 1994). They had few available safe spaces; girls were harassed and assaulted at parties, in school, on the playground, on buses, and in cars. Young women overwhelmingly depicted boys and men as *natural* sexual aggressors, pointing to one of the main tenets of compulsory heterosexuality. Incorporating male sexual drive discourse (Phillips 2000), they described men as unable to control their sexual desires. Male power and privilege and female acquiescence were reified in descriptions of "routine" and "normal" sexualized interactions (Fineran and Bennett 1999; French 2003). Assaultive behaviors were often justified, especially

when characterized as indiscriminate. For example, Patricia (age 13, white) told the interviewer: "They grab you, touch your butt and try to, like, touch you in the front, and run away, but it's okay, I mean . . . I never think it's a big thing because they do it to everyone." Referring to boys at school, Patricia described unwelcome touching and grabbing as normal, commonplace behaviors.

Compulsory heterosexuality highlights how conventional norms of heterosexual relations produce and often require male dominance and female subordination (Phillips 2000; Tolman et al. 2003). Young women like Patricia described sexually aggressive behaviors as customary: "It just happens," and "They're boys—that's what they do." Similarly, Kelly (age 13, white) told the forensic interviewer about her experiences with 20-year-old Eric:

> [He] would follow me around all the time, tell me I was beautiful and stuff, that he could have me when he wanted to. He did that all the time, like, would touch me and say, "Am I making you wet, do you want me?" when he wanted. I think that's just . . . like, that's what he does, it's just, like, how it goes on and everyone knows it, no one says nothing.

Kelly trivializes her experiences of sexual harassment by a man seven years older, telling the interviewer of this ordinary and allowable "masculine" practice. Her description of ongoing harassment also confounds romance and aggression, because Eric's harassment was fused with courting, compliments, and sexual desire (Phillips 2000).

Girls' characterizations of everyday violence paralleled both their assessments that "boys will be boys" and their understanding of harassment as a normal adolescent rite of passage. Sexual harassment is an instrument that maintains a gendered hierarchy (MacKinnon 1979), and girls described the many ways they protected themselves against expected sexual aggression, at the expense of their own feelings. Carla (age 14, white), for example, cast assault and threats as expected because they were typical. In this passage, she described chronic harassment by a young man as they rode the school bus. He often threatened to "come over to [her] house and rape [her]":

CARLA: Like, on the bus, like when I'll sit, he'll try and sit next to me and then slide his hand under my butt.

INTERVIEWER: Okay, does he say anything?

CARLA: No, he just kinda has this look on his face. And then I'll, like, shove him out of the seat and then he'll get mad.

INTERVIEWER: What happens when he gets mad?

CARLA: He just kinda doesn't talk. He gets, like, his face gets red and he doesn't talk. And he, I guess he feels rejected, but I don't care. He told me . . . he was like, "I'm gonna come over to your house and rape you."

And then, I know he's just joking, but that can be a little weird to hear.

INTERVIEWER: Yeah, so when did he tell you that?

CARLA: He tells me it all the time, like the last time I talked to him. He just says that he's gonna come to my house and rape me since I won't do anything with him. And, I mean, I think . . . I'm . . . I know he's joking, it's just hard to, like, why would he say that?

Threats were used for compliance, becoming more persistent and coercive over time. Unsure of whether to take the threats seriously, Carla names her experience "weird" while normalizing the young man's behavior as understandable within a male sexual drive discourse ("I guess he feels rejected"), and trivializes his threats twice, saying, "I know he's just joking." Harassment was dangerously constructed as romance and flirting. These discourses often entitle young men to violate the bodies of young women (Connell 1995; Messerschmidt 2012). Prior to the forensic interview, Carla had not told anyone about these experiences, considering them an everyday hazard of riding the bus.

Given expectations of, and experiences with, male aggression, young women were charged with self-protection by reading and responding to potentially dangerous situations. While some girls attempted to "ignore" the behavior, others had to make additional maneuvers. In her interview, Lana (age 15, white) explained how 18-year-old Mike "tries to bring [girls] downstairs in the [school] basement and, like, try and force 'em to like make out with him and stuff." She said Mike tried to force her to go downstairs on numerous occasions and he would "get mad when [she'd] say no." In response, Lana altered her behavior by avoiding being alone in the school hallways, at her locker, or in the bathroom. Young women responded to harassment

with a barrage of maneuvers, like avoidance and diverting attention. These tactics did not always work, however. In Lana's case, Mike was eventually "able to catch [her] off-guard":

> I was going to the bathroom and he wouldn't let me go in. He put his foot in front of [the door], and he's a really strong person, so I didn't really, like, I couldn't open the door. And he said, "I'll let you in if you give me a kiss," and I said, "No." And I was going back to the classroom and he pinned me against the wall and tried to, like, lift up my shirt. And, like, touched me, and then I . . . I got up . . . I started to scream, and I guess someone heard, 'cause then, um, someone started coming. So he got away from me, I just went back in the classroom and forgot about it. I just didn't think it was really anything.

Girls in this study said they did not want to make a "big deal" out of their experiences and rarely reported these incidents to persons in authority. Most questioned whether anyone would care about the behavior; if it was not "rape" it was not serious enough to warrant others' involvement. "Real" assault was narrowly defined and contingent on various conditions that were rarely met (Phillips 2000; Stanko 1985).

Young women constructed classic boundaries between "real rapes" and everyday violence or "little rapes." Terri (age 11, black) was interviewed at the CAC because she told a friend she was forced to perform oral sex on a 17-year-old neighbor boy: "He forced me, he, uh, he grabbed me tighter, and he said if I didn't do it he was gonna rape me." For Terri, rape was only intercourse, as she candidly explained: "They always say they gonna rape you, if you don't do what they want, they say they'll rape you." Terri's mother also cautioned her about male sexual drives, warning her to expect aggression and to protect herself. Sitting in her apartment stairwell alone that day, Terri assumed responsibility for her own assault. Terri's experience demonstrates that if girls do not acquiesce to the pressure to have sex, they risk being raped. She did not tell her mother, because "I shouldn't have been there, my mom said I should've been home anyway, but I didn't want to get raped so I had to."

Instruments of Coercion

The normalization of violence was intensified in peer groups and assault was often perpetrated by one older man. Peers communicated a specialized sense of sexual acceptability largely based on the perception of women as sexual gatekeepers. Gatekeeping occurred in a variety of ways, including allocation of resources, such as food, alcohol, or a space away from adult others. Janice (age 14, white), for example, told the interviewer that 30-something-year-old Matt touched her and four girlfriends on a regular basis:

> He does, like, touch us, you know? Like, he like rubs my leg, the thigh, but none of us told him, told him to stop, you know? But I . . . I always moved away when he did it. He'd just rub my leg and touch my boobs. And one time when I was over at his house, I asked him for something to eat and he goes, "Not unless I can touch your boobs."

Via access to resources, Matt presented Janice with a "gatekeeping choice" that deflected responsibility. Janice later told the interviewer that Matt had also touched her vagina, commenting, "He does it to everyone, you know, it just happens sometimes," and justified Matt's behavior by placing responsibility on the group: "But none of us told him to stop." Matt's actions were minimized because they were customary and something they "just dealt with."

Sexualized bartering or exchange for in/tangible resources (Orenstein 1994; Thompson 1995; Van Roosmalen 2000) was common. Access or restriction to something was a tactic used by men to coerce young women like Natalie (age 16, Latina) into sexual contact. Natalie was sexually assaulted by Jim, a 37-year-old neighbor. She told the interviewer that Jim allowed Natalie and her friends to "hang out," play basketball in his backyard, and drink beer and vodka. During the interview, Natalie described Jim's sexual touching and kissing as typical male behavior:

> He'd just rub his hand across my butt, and then one time I was sitting there and he—I was, like, laying on the couch watching TV—and he came home. He was kinda drunk, then he, like, literally just, like, laid *on* me. That's what he . . . well, guys always try to get up on you, like just normal.

Because both were drinking alcohol, Natalie tolerated his actions: "He would be touching my butt, you know, with this hand, going under my butt, under the blanket. I was, like, oh well, but all this . . . nothing like totally big happened."

Overwhelmingly described as "normal stuff" that "guys do" or tolerating what "just happens," young women's sexual desire and consent are largely absent (Martin 1996; Tolman 1994). Sex was understood as something done to them and agency was discursively attributed only to gatekeeping. Abby (age 12, white) presents an ideal example of the highly prescriptive norms of heterosexual practice. Like others, Abby's peer group normalized the sexual interactions between her and 19-year-old Glen. According to Abby, many of her friends had been "hit on" by Glen, knew about how he "moved from girl to girl" in the group, or were sexually active with him. Abby was referred for a forensic interview after her mother overheard her talking to Glen about "having sex." Abby recounted her experience, making use of particular culturally available discourses of gender, heterosexuality, and power:

INTERVIEWER: What didn't you like about [Glen]?

ABBY: The way he used a lot of people, the way he moved from girl to girl, the way that . . . he thought that he was the ruler of everybody, he was really commanding, he always had to be in control, and he was rough, and just, you know.

INTERVIEWER: What kind of stuff did he do that was rough or commanding?

ABBY: I don't know, he'd just order me around, and be like, "Oh, do this for me," or, I don't know, he'd ask me to do certain things to him and he'd take my hands and put 'em . . . I don't know, he'd just . . . he'd make me do things.

INTERVIEWER: When he would, like, take your hands and make you do things, was it stuff that you didn't want to do?

ABBY: Sometimes, and then I'd stop and he'd be fine with it, but after a while he'd, like, start it up again and he'd keep trying.

INTERVIEWER: You said he was rough—did he ever hurt you?

ABBY: No, but, like, he was just . . . I don't know, he was just . . . I don't know how to explain it, he was just . . . he'd pull my hair [laughs], so I don't know what he did, he'd like, he'd grab my hair and he'd pull me closer and he'd just, like, pull my hair backward, push my head or somethin' like that and it'd be weird. I don't know what he did.

INTERVIEWER: Okay, did he ever hit you or anything?

ABBY: He was very controlling.

INTERVIEWER: Can you give me examples of that?

ABBY: Basically he thought I was his maid, or, like, a toy with him that he could just, like, wind up and use whenever he wanted me to, and then he'd just, like, you know, like you have a Barbie doll and you can, like, use it whenever you want to and then you, like, throw it in the back and then you pick it up, how you have, like, a maid or butler, and you can just order them around if you don't get what you want you get mad at them and then you keep trying, he'd just . . . he'd do that, but I wasn't really . . . I think he thought I wanted it—but part of me did, but I knew it was wrong that he . . . that I didn't really care for it, and I knew that he'd just leave anyways since he was nineteen.

In this powerful sequence, Abby links sex with male power and female passivity. She positions herself as "acted upon" and Glen as the "actor" in sexual encounters. In response to the interviewer, she describes how Glen was controlling and rough and would "make" her do things. Analogous to "working a 'yes' out" (Sanday 1990), Abby twice told the interviewer ". . . he'd, like, start it up again and he'd keep trying" despite her resistance. Juxtaposed with Glen's pulling and pushing of her head, when asked if he ever hurt her, Abby responds, "No . . . I don't know how to explain it. . . . It'd be weird. I don't know what he did." She positions herself within particular social hierarchies, describing feeling like a "Barbie doll," a "maid," or a "toy" that could be used and thrown away. Abby reflexively identified with particular cultural positions, simultaneously perceiving herself as object but also as subject, holding herself responsible for Glen's actions.

With all its complexity, Abby interprets her experience far outside of victim/agent, passive/active dichotomies. Positioned in a social landscape of gendered power and sex, Abby struggles to account for consent and desire ("I think he thought I wanted it—but part of me did . . .") and responsibility ("but I knew it was wrong that he . . . that I didn't really care for it, and I knew that he'd just leave anyways since he was nineteen"). These shifts in blame uncover the power of heteronormative discourses that support a sexually unconstrained, emotionally detached male, but a "relational" female. Embedded in the dilemmas and double standards of heterosexual practice (Phillips 2000), Abby silences her own feelings and desires (Thorne 1993) and questions whether a sexual relationship was acceptable if "he'd just leave anyways."

Accounts of Consent

The links between everyday harassment and violence were further reproduced through attributions of blame. Girls criticized each other for not successfully maneuvering men's normalized aggressive behavior. Even when maneuvers "failed," concessions were made. For example, Lily (age 14, Latina) was raped by a 17-year-old school acquaintance in a park as she walked home from school. The offender quickly spread rumors and she was labeled "sexually active" and a "slut" by her classmates: "There's rumors about me already, that aren't even true . . . that I want, that I want to, and I let him do that . . . and it wasn't even true." Cast as promiscuous, she was deemed complicit in her rape. On the rare occasion that rape was reported to an adult or authority figure, young women described feeling suspect. Kiley (age 14, black) was raped by a 27-year-old family friend at his home. She provided details about the assault, including how he held her down and covered her mouth to muffle her cries:

> I didn't want to but he did, you know, and I don't know, [sex] just happened. I thought he was just a friend and that's it. . . . He was calling me names, he was calling me a "ho" and a "slut" and all this kind of stuff, and that I gave him a lap dance and everything. That I was, I can't . . . I took all my clothes off and that I was, like, asking him for it. That I wanted to be with him, and everyone believed him.

Sexual reputation mattered to girls (Van Roosmalen 2000) and the threat of being labeled a "ho" or a "slut" loomed large. The threat of sexualization and social derogation was often a barrier to rape reporting; it was connected with accusations of exaggeration through which peers decided whether and how to include, label, and ostracize. This finding is consistent with prior studies (Phillips 2000) that find young women are under pressure to manage their sexuality and sexual reputations. This is a confusing endeavor, of course, as girls may gain cultural capital among peers for being desired and pursued but not for sexual agency.

The precarious balancing act of attaining sexual status and avoiding the "slander of the slut" (Schalet 2010) proved powerful. Some girls belittled others' experiences, holding them responsible for their victimizations. Obligated to set limits for sexual behavior (Orenstein 1994), it was girls' duty to be prepared to say "no" (Tolman 1994) and to police each other. When asked about her friend who had reported sexual assault by a mutual acquaintance, Jacki (age 15, white) said, "I don't know why she's making such a big deal out of it anyway. He does it to everyone, so I say, well, 'Just back off,' I say 'No'—so she should if she don't want it, but she probably wants it anyway." Jacki worked to discursively separate herself from her friend as she spoke of sexual desire and exaggeration.

Similarly, 12-year-old Jillian (black) was brought to the forensic interview in relation to reports of her friend's sexual assault. Jillian explained that her 13-year-old friend Rachel said she was raped by 18-year-old Trevor. The interviewer asked her to explain:

> Well, that's what people been saying and I asked her. First she told me that she got raped and I asked her, "Did you really get . . . did you get raped?" and she goes, "Yeah." Then I asked her again, "Why you telling everybody you got raped when you didn't?" and she goes, "I'm not telling everybody I got raped." And I go, "What you telling 'em?" and she goes, "That he forced me into it," forced her into having sex which he, which, I don't know if it's true or not, but as far as I know, it's not true that he forced her because [my friend] was there and she told me that he ask . . . or, this, it all started when Rachel wanted to have sex with Nate and Nate didn't want to so Trevor said he would. And . . . and Rachel wanted to, but see, the reason why she's telling everybody that he forced her into it 'cause she don't want it right there and then. But he did . . . he talked her into it. But Rachel could of said no but she didn't, so how should he know?

Girls were consistently positioned as the gatekeeper of sexual activity; they were disbelieved and policed by their peers, and their words were reconstructed and their actions deemed false. Jillian disbelieved her friend's report of rape and chastised her for not saying "No." Jillian did not hold Trevor accountable for his actions, at least partly because he was characterized as incompetent when it came to communication and consent. Instead, Rachel carried the responsibility and

suffered the consequences for failing to clearly and effectively establish boundaries.

Girls were also aware of double standards and traditional sexual scripts. They claimed "guys get away with everything" and "they can do anything and not get in trouble." This critique stopped short of attributions of sexual responsibility, however; girls self-framed as active subjects by labeling others as passive objects. In this way, the complexities of naming sexual aggression were premised on behavior comparisons. April (age 13, white) reported that her 13-year-old friend "had sex" with Sean, a 22-year-old man. During her interview, she described her friend as passive and naïve:

> I've heard rumors about that he's had sex with girls, and I know Sara has had sex with him, she came out and told me . . . she said that he came over and he was telling her that she was gorgeous and that he loved her and that he wanted to have her baby and all this stuff, and I guess it just happened, and that's what she said, it just happened, and I was like, "Oh, okay" [laughs], you know, which didn't surprise me, 'cause Sara, she'll be mad at him and then she'll go back to him, like, two days later.

April characterized sexual intercourse ("it") as something men do "to" women. She further interpreted Sean's manipulative tactics ("telling her that she was gorgeous and that he loved her and that he wanted to have her baby") as successful because "it [intercourse] just happened." April said similar ploys did not work on her: "First of all, he asked me, 'Would you . . . would you ever go out with me?' and I said, 'No' . . . and he's like, 'Well, would you ever have sex with me?' and I was like, 'No.'"

Despite April's resistance, Sean put his hands under her shirt, and tried to put her hands in his pants and her head on his penis. April told the interviewer: "I told him to stop and he didn't and he got to, like, right here, you know, he was tryin' to lift up my bra and I was like, 'No, stop!'" Further couched in rumors and reputation, April differentiated herself from Sara: "There's rumors going around saying that Sara had sex with him and so did I and that [she's] a slut and all this stuff." April insisted the rumors about her were untrue because, unlike Sara who let "it just happen," she "said no." As Nelson and Oliver (1998, 573) state, "Under these rules, any girl who permits herself to be persuaded into sexual activity is weak and to blame, as is a girl who voluntarily enters a situation where she can be raped."

CONCLUSION

Research on sexual violence has long asked why victims do not report these incidents. Studies with adults have examined how women account for and "name" their experiences, yet adolescents remain largely outside the scope of this work. Exploring sexual violence via the lens of compulsory heterosexuality highlights the relational dynamics at play in this naming process. Unique characteristics emerged through inductive analyses and revealed patterned heterogendered (Martin 2009) and heteronormative scripts appropriated to account for the violence experienced. The current study adds to a significant body of work of girls' sexuality development using different modes of inquiry and method (Martin 1996; Phillips 2000; Thompson 1995).

Descriptions of assault here are concerning, having much to do with heteronormativity and compulsory heterosexuality. Sex was "something they [men and boys] do," or "something he wanted," and sexual assault was a "weird" threat, something "they just say," or "something she let happen." When resistance was voiced, as in April's case, it was couched in sexual refusal and used to establish boundaries. In their policing of each other, young women often held themselves and their peers responsible for acting as gatekeepers of men's behaviors; they were responsible for being coerced, for accepting gifts and other resources, for not fending off or resisting men's sexual advances, for miscommunication, or, in Abby's words, for engaging in sexual activity she "didn't really care for." The discourses offer insight into how some young women talked about their sexual selves and relationships as they navigated a world ordered by gendered binaries and heterosexual frameworks (Butler 1999).

Importantly, the violence described in this study must be situated both by context and as told within an institutionalized, forensic interview setting. Child crime victims are often positioned as passive in exploitative relationships, in reporting practices, and in criminal justice processes. However, the significant research on youth's agency, subjectivity, and desire reviewed here turns our attention toward active negotiations within the interview setting. Foremost, CACs work within criminal justice systems, and youths might rightfully view forensic interviewers as an extension of the system. Girls' narratives in this study are produced

within that system; thus, it is possible that young women's discursive minimizations and justifications of abuse also work to accomplish specific goals. As the findings demonstrate, girls understand their position in a patriarchal sexual system and therefore might assume authority figures of all types will blame them or perceive them as bad girls who "let it happen." Revealing sexual desire or agency in this setting might be perceived risky in the same way involving law enforcement might be; girls may be viewed as blameworthy for putting themselves in a situation where one can be raped (Nelson and Oliver 1998). The fear of revealing one's use of drugs or alcohol could also influence what and how disclosure is made with interviewers. This might be especially true for minority and socioeconomically disadvantaged youths with little trust of criminal justice authorities (Hlavka 2013). Therefore, conclusions offered here must be tempered not only by class and neighborhood context, but also by how the forensic interview is perceived and interpreted differently by young women depending on race, class, and sexuality. In this study, age, type of offender, and peer groups seemed to affect girls' narratives in important ways, whereas race did not. Also, it is not assumed that all the girls in this study identified as heterosexual, but without a measure of sexual orientation, the question remains, "How might lesbian or bisexual girls interact with common heteronormative discourses?" Based on the available data, class and sexuality could not be systematically analyzed in this study, but future work must prioritize intersectional analyses (Tolman 2006). Important implications for young women's relational sexuality and gender ideologies are bound to sociocultural context (Thompson 1995).

While my data cannot speak to variations among girls in terms of desire and agency found in other studies using different methods (e.g., Thompson 1995; Tolman 1994), it is certainly likely that young women both understand and internalize scripts to varying degrees. Appraisals are based both on dominant discourses and individual desires used for self-representation (Reavey and Gough 2000). Whether girls' accounts of violence reflect their subjective understanding of what happened, or are constructed to eliminate or negotiate possibilities of blame by authority figures, the specificity of the appropriated discourses engaged is significant. In the process of appraising and explaining violence, girls drew upon particular macro-understandings of gender and sex to interpret and justify actions that legitimated men's dominance. Specific heteronormative scripts were used to explain and describe, as well as to negotiate, within the forensic interview. These scripts were presented as legitimate, commonplace, and powerful—evident in the co-construction of common knowledge with interviewers ("you know"). These discourses are used to "pass," to "fit in," and to make events believable and understandable to others. To be sure, the absence of oppositional or alternative discourses is as relevant as the presence of dominant discourses. As Connell (1987, 195) points out, agencies of socializing "invite the child to participate in social practice on given terms. The invitation may be, and often is, coercive—accompanied by heavy pressure to accept and no mention of an alternative." Discourses are used to manage young people's place in the social order (Corsaro 1997) as they are encouraged into established hierarchies and compelled into prescribed scripts.

Alternative solutions for the education of young people on sexual relations and abuse are long overdue, and many have called for new sexual paradigms for some time (Fine 1988; Phillips 2000; Tolman 1994; Tolman et al. 2003). The sexual scripts culturally available to girls largely exclude sexual desire and pleasure, representing girls as victims in need of protection against boys' desires (Fine 1988). Placing responsibility on women and girls to "just say no" and excusing boys and men as they "work a 'yes' out" works to erase institutional and structural responsibilities. The lack of safe, supportive space for girls is palpable. We can thus better understand why young women in this study felt they were expected to protect themselves from everyday violence with little help from others, including those in authority positions. The lack of institutional support assumed by girls in this study should be deeply concerning for educators and policy makers. As Stein (1995) has argued, lack of adult interruption or response to sexual harassment and abuse functionally permits and encourages it. It is not enough to establish new policies and practices aimed at increasing reporting; there are larger underlying cultural practices and discourses acting as barriers. By drawing attention to youths' voices, structures of violence, power, and privilege become apparent in their gendered experiences that do not easily translate to law and policy reforms.

Sexual education must be gender equity education (Stein et al. 2002), resistant to troubled, heteronormative binaries and cultural constraints that omit discourses of desire, gender, and sexuality. By treating young people as agents and decision makers, we could create spaces where they can work together with adults to appraise experiences of sex, assault, power, coercion, and consent prevalent in their lives.

REFERENCES

Alcoff, Linda, and Laura Gray. 1993. Survivor discourse: Transgression or recuperation? *Signs: Journal of Women in Culture and Society* 18:260–90.
AAUW (American Association of University Women). 2001. *Hostile hallways II: Bullying, teasing and sexual harassment in school.* Washington, DC: AAUW.
AAUW (American Association of University Women). 2011. *Crossing the line: Sexual harassment at school.* Washington, DC: Catherine Hill and Holly Kearl.
Angelides, Steven. 2004. Feminism, child sexual abuse, and the erasure of child sexuality. *GLQ: A Journal of Lesbian and Gay Studies* 10:141–77.
APSAC (American Professional Society on the Abuse of Children). 2002. *Investigative interviewing in cases of alleged child abuse.* Chicago: APSAC.
Averill, James. 1980. A constructivist view of emotion. In *Theory, research, and experience,* edited by R. Plutchik and H. Kellerman. New York: Academic Press.
Best, Joel. 1990. *Threatened children: Rhetoric and concern about child victims.* Chicago: University of Chicago Press.
Brickell, Christopher. 2006. The sociological construction of gender and sexuality. *The Sociological Review* 54:87–113.
Butler, Judith. 1999. *Gender trouble.* New York: Routledge.
Connell, Raewyn. 1987. *Gender and power.* Cambridge, UK: Polity Press.
Connell, Raewyn. 1995. *Masculinities.* Berkeley: University of California Press.
Corsaro, William. 1997. *The sociology of childhood.* Thousand Oaks, CA: Pine Forge.
Crawley, Sara, Lara Foley, and Constance Shehan. 2008. *Gendering bodies.* Lanham, MD: Rowman & Littlefield.
Erlich, Susan. 2001. *Representing rape: Language and sexual consent.* New York: Routledge.
Estrich, Susan. 1987. *Real rape.* Cambridge, MA: Harvard University Press.
Fine, Michelle. 1982. An injustice by any other name. . . *Victimology* 6:48–58.

Fine, Michelle. 1988. Sexuality, schooling, and adolescent females: The missing discourse of desire. *Harvard Educational Review* 58:29–53.

Fineran, Susan, and Larry Bennett. 1999. Gender and power issues of peer sexual harassment among teenagers. *Journal of Interpersonal Violence* 14:626–41.

Finkelhor, David, and Richard Ormrod. 2000. *Characteristics of crimes against juveniles.* Washington, DC: U.S. Department of Justice, Office of Justice Programs.

French, Sandra L. 2003. Reflections on healing: Framing strategies utilized by acquaintance rape survivors. *Journal of Applied Communication Research* 31:298–319.

Frohmann, Lisa, and Elizabeth Mertz. 1995. Legal reform and social construction: Violence, gender, and the law. *Law & Social Inquiry* 19:829–51.

Gagnon, John. 1977. *Human sexualities.* Glenview, IL: Scott, Foresman.

Gagnon, John, and William Simon. 1973. *Sexual conduct: The social sources of human sexuality.* Chicago: Aldine.

Gavey, Nicola. 1992. Technologies and effects of heterosexual coercion. *Feminism & Psychology* 2:325–51.

Gilgun, Jane. 1986. Sexually abused girls' knowledge about sexual abuse and sexuality. *Journal of Interpersonal Violence* 1:309–25.

Gilligan, Carol. 1982. *In a different voice.* Cambridge, MA: Harvard University Press.

Gilligan, Carol. 1990. Joining the resistance: Psychology, politics, girls and women. *Michigan Quarterly Review* 29:501–26.

Glaser, Barney, and Anselm Strauss. 1967. *The discovery of grounded theory.* Chicago: Aldine.

Gubrium, Jaber, and James Holstein. 1998. Narrative practice and the coherence of personal stories. *Sociological Quarterly* 39:163–87.

Hlavka, Heather. 2010. Child sexual abuse and embodiment. *Sociological Studies of Children and Youth* 13:131–65.

Hlavka, Heather. 2013. Legal subjectivity among youth victims of sexual abuse. *Law & Social Inquiry,* published online July 8, 2013, DOI: 10.1111/lsi.12032.

Ingraham, Chrys. 1994. The heterosexual imaginary. *Sociological Theory* 12:203–19.

Jackson, Stevi. 2009. Sexuality, heterosexuality, and gender hierarchy. In *Sex, gender & sexuality,* edited by Abby Ferber, Kimberly Holcomb, and Tre Wentling. New York: Oxford University Press.

Kelly, Liz, and Jill Radford. 1990. "Nothing really happened": The invalidation of women's experiences of sexual violence. *Critical Social Policy* 10:39–53.

Kitzinger, Celia. 2005. Heteronormativity in action: Reproducing the heterosexual nuclear family in after-hours medical calls. *Social Problems* 52:477–98.

Lee, Nick. 2001. *Children and society: Growing up in an age of uncertainty.* New York: Open University Press.

Lorber, Judith, and Lisa Moore. 2007. *Gendered bodies: Feminist perspectives.* Los Angeles: Roxbury.

MacKinnon, Catherine. 1979. *Sexual harassment of working women.* New Haven, CT: Yale University Press.

Martin, Karin. 1996. *Puberty, sexuality, and the self.* New York: Routledge.

Martin, Karin. 2009. Normalizing heterosexuality. *American Sociological Review* 74:190–207.

Matoesian, Gregory. 1993. *Reproducing rape: Domination through talk in the courtroom.* Chicago: University of Chicago Press.

Messerschmidt, James. 1986. *Capitalism, patriarchy, and crime.* Totowa, NJ: Rowman & Littlefield.

Messerschmidt, James. 2012. *Gender, heterosexuality, and youth violence: The struggle for recognition.* New York: Rowman & Littlefield.

Myers, Kristen, and Laura Raymond. 2010. Elementary school girls and heteronormativity: The girl project. *Gender & Society* 24:167–88.

Nelson, Andrea, and Pamela Oliver. 1998. Gender and the construction of consent in child–adult sexual contact: Beyond gender neutrality and male monopoly. *Gender & Society* 12:554–77.

Orenstein, Peggy. 1994. *Schoolgirls: Young women, self-esteem, and the confidence gap.* New York: Doubleday.

Patton, Michael Quinn. 1990. *Qualitative evaluation and research methods,* 2nd edition. New York: Sage.

Phillips, Lynn M. 2000. *Flirting with danger: Young women's reflections on sexuality and domination.* New York: New York University Press.

Reavey, Paula, and Brenda Gough. 2000. Dis/locating blame: Survivors' constructions of self and sexual abuse. *Sexualities* 3:325–46.

Renold, Emma. 2006. "They won't let us play . . . unless you're going out with one of them": Girls, boys and Butler's heterosexual matrix in the primary years. *British Journal of Sociology of Education* 27:1830–42.

Rich, Adrienne. 1980. Compulsory heterosexuality and lesbian existence. *Signs: Journal of Women in Culture and Society* 5:631–60.

Ridgeway, Cecilia, and Shelley Correll. 2004. Unpacking the gender system: A theoretical perspective on gender beliefs and social relations. *Gender & Society* 18:510–31.

Ryan, Gail. 2000. Childhood sexuality: A decade of study. *Child Abuse & Neglect* 24:33–48.

Sanday, Peggy Reeves. 1990. *Fraternity gang rape: Sex, brotherhood, and privilege on campus.* New York: New York University Press.

Schalet, Amy. 2010. Sexual subjectivity revisited: The significance of relationships in Dutch and American girls' experiences of sexuality. *Gender & Society* 24:304–29.

Schippers, Mimi. 2007. Recovering the feminine other: Masculinity, femininity, and gender hegemony. *Theory & Society* 36:85–102.

Silverman, Jay, Anita Raj, Lorelei Mucci, and Jeanne Hathaway. 2001. Dating violence against adolescent girls and associated substance use, unhealthy weight control, sexual risk behavior, pregnancy, and suicidality. *Journal of the American Medical Association* 286:572–79.

Sousa, Carole A. 1999. Teen dating violence: The hidden epidemic. *Family and Conciliation Courts Review* 37:356–74.

Stanko, Elizabeth. 1985. *Intimate intrusions: Women's experience of male violence.* London: Routledge and Kegan Paul.

Stein, Nan. 1995. Sexual harassment in K-12 schools: The public performance of gendered violence. *Harvard Educational Review* 65:145–62.

Stein, Nan, Deborah Tolman, Michelle Porche, and Renée Spencer. 2002. Gender safety: A new concept for safer and more equitable schools. *Journal of School Violence* 1:35–50.

Strauss, Anselm, and Juliet Corbin. 1998. *Basics of qualitative research: Techniques and procedures for developing grounded theory,* 2nd edition. Thousand Oaks, CA: Sage.

Thompson, Sharon. 1995. *Going all the way: Teenage girls' tales of sex, romance, and pregnancy.* New York: Hill and Wang.

Thorne, Barrie. 1993. *Gender play: Girls and boys in school.* New Brunswick, NJ: Rutgers University Press.

Thorne, Barrie, and Zella Luria. 1986. Sexuality and gender in children's daily worlds. *Social Problems* 33:176–90.

Tolman, Deborah. 1991. Adolescent girls, women and sexuality: Discerning dilemmas of desire. In *Women, girls and psychotherapy: Reframing resistance,* edited by C. Gilligan, A. Rogers, and D. Tolman. New York: Haworth.

Tolman, Deborah. 1994. Doing desire: Adolescent girls' struggles for/with sexuality. *Gender & Society* 8:324–42.

Tolman, Deborah. 2006. In a different position: Conceptualizing female adolescent sexuality development within compulsory heterosexuality. *New Directions for Child and Adolescent Development* 112:71–89.

Tolman, Deborah, Renée Spencer, Myra Rosen-Reynosa, and Michelle Porche. 2003. Sowing the seeds of violence in heterosexual relationships: Early adolescents narrate compulsory heterosexuality. *Journal of Social Issues* 59:159–78.

Van Roosmalen, Erica. 2000. Forces of patriarchy: Adolescent experiences of sexuality and conceptions of relationships. *Youth & Society* 32:202–27.

PART III

SEXUALITIES

Are sexual relations a realm of pleasure, empowerment, danger, or oppression? The women's movement reawakened during the late 1960s and 1970s during a sexual revolution that told youth, "It if feels good, do it!" In this context, an initial impulse of second wave feminism began to argue that "sexual liberation" had simply freed men to objectify and exploit women more completely. As studies began to illuminate the widespread realities of rape, sexual harassment in workplaces, and sexual exploitation of women in sex work, it became clear that for women, sexuality was too often a realm of danger rather than pleasure. As a result, by the mid- to late 1970s, radical feminist activists focused more and more on antirape and antipornography efforts.

By the mid-1980s, other feminists—often younger women, women of color, lesbian, and bisexual women—began to criticize the preoccupation of some radical feminists with the centrality of male heterosexuality and pornography in women's oppression. By the 1990s, many younger feminists sought to reclaim sexual pleasure as a realm of empowerment for women, renewing the efforts of some radical feminists such as Adrienne Rich and Charlotte Bunch who came before them. Today, feminists across the theoretical spectrum tend to see sexuality in complicated ways—as a potential source of both pleasure *and* danger, both empowerment *and* oppression. Moreover, research now indicates that the experience of sexuality is not determined solely by gender; rather, race, age, sexual orientation, religion, culture, and nationality also shape sexual experiences and attitudes.

SEXUAL RELATIONS, INTIMACY, AND POWER

In the first article in this section, Rashawn Ray and Jason A. Rosow analyze the distinctive approaches to sexuality exhibited by white and black fraternity men. Relying on data from interviews and focus groups, they argue that normative institutional arrangements on college campuses shape sexuality in ways that encourage black fraternities to be more gender egalitarian than their white peers. The black men are held more accountable, and the black fraternity system promotes more consciousness of the dangers of objectifying women than does the white fraternity system. What might other college campuses and student organizations learn from this article regarding gender egalitarianism in their own institutions?

The next article describes how young Latinas in Chicago negotiate their sexual health, sexual respectability, and sexual agency in the shadow of the good girl/bad girl dichotomy. According to Lorena Garcia, this was accomplished by "handlin' one's business" as a sign of sexual responsibility. By this she refers to the importance Latina girls assigned to avoiding pregnancy, sexually transmitted infections, and a "bad girl" reputation. Further, by distinguishing themselves from sexually active Latinas and white girls, sexual respectability operated "as a form of gendered sexual and racial-ethnic boundary." Garcia further considers how the young Latinas' attempts to maintain respectable femininity within a racially sexualized context affected their sexual **agency**. Garcia's analysis calls upon us to examine the ways that sexuality is a source of empowerment and a source of oppression for Latinas. What enables and what restricts their sexual agency?

The last two articles examine commodified sex in non-U.S. contexts. Rhacel Parreñas worked alongside Filipina hostesses in the red-light districts of Tokyo. Whereas migrant hostesses are often considered **sex trafficking** victims by the United States, Parreñas describes how immigration and marriage laws impact Filipinas' agency as workers. Specifically, she shows that many of the measures designed to combat sex trafficking have contributed to the Filipina hostesses' vulnerability to exploitation. In the next article, Julia O'Connell Davidson examines the "demand side" of international sex tourism. "Sexpatriots" in the Dominican Republic, Davidson observes, are mostly middle-aged, white heterosexual Euro-American men whose activities simultaneously endanger the health and safety of Dominican women while serving to shore up the fragile identities of these privileged men.

SEXUALITY AND IDENTITY

Are gay men and lesbians clearly and categorically distinguishable from heterosexual men and women? Are Filipina and Mexican immigrant women and girls always objects of the sexual gaze of others, and, if not, how do they negotiate their own sexual identities? The articles in the second part of this section explore the area of sexual identity. Today, most scholars agree that the idea that there are distinct sexual "types" of people such as "the homosexual" and "the heterosexual" is a recent social construction. But they also recognize that social constructions have real consequences. Modern medical and scientific discourse may have created the homosexual with the goal of controlling "deviant" character types and normalizing the heterosexual. But starting mostly in the 1970s, men and women who identified as "gay," "lesbian," and "queer" drew strength from their shared identities. From this strength, they challenged prevailing cultural attitudes, customs, and laws.

As you might imagine, prisons for men are difficult and dangerous places for trans-people. In the next article, Valerie Jenness and Sarah Fenstermaker describe how, despite the risks, transgender inmates try to achieve "the real deal" or recognition as a "real girl" with affection from a "real man." They discuss these efforts in the context of transgender inmates' pursuit of **gender authenticity** and the implications of transgender identity for challenging the larger gender order.

Yet, as Jane Ward shows, not all of those who enjoy sexual relations with same-sex partners identify as homosexual. Ward studied the Craigslist advertisements of "str8 white dudes" (straight white men) who are looking for sexual encounters with other straight men. The ads reveal how these men use elements of white racial identity and gender misogyny to demonstrate their heterosexual identification. Ward argues that rather than defining sexual identities on the basis of sex acts (for example, by claiming that str8 white dudes are, in fact, closeted gay men), it is important to recognize how identities communicate our membership in political and cultural communities. Thus, rather than a challenge, the sexual identities practiced by str8 white dudes reinforce heteronormativity and homophobia.

The next article reveals the nuanced ways in which immigrant women and girls challenge and reinvent sexual identities that are constructed in contexts of unequal power by race, gender, sexuality, and national origin. Yen Le Espiritu's study illustrates the ways that Filipina immigrant girls in the United States often define themselves in opposition to their conception of white women as sexually "immoral." In comparison to Garcia's article on Latina sexual identities, what similarities or differences do you notice?

Finally, Kirsty Liddiard explores the private and emotional dimensions of disability in the intimate lives of couples. She focuses on the **emotion work** that sustains these partnerships despite an ableist culture that treats disabled people as sexually undesirable. Her research shows how the emotion work performed by disabled partners simultaneously benefits the couple while reproducing inequalities.

15

Getting Off and Getting Intimate

How Normative Institutional Arrangements Structure
Black and White Fraternity Men's Approaches toward Women

RASHAWN RAY

JASON A. ROSOW

Despite the proliferation of research on collegiate gender and sexual relations (Martin and Hummer 1989; Boswell and Spade 1996; Armstrong, Hamilton, and Sweeney 2006), we know little about one of the key groups within this institutional arrangement—fraternity men. Meanwhile, we know even less about differences and similarities in Black and White high-status men's relations with women (Brandes 2007; Peralta 2007; Flood 2008). Because fraternity men typically are situated on top of the peer culture hierarchy, a comprehensive understanding of the organization of collegiate social life must take into account how these specific enclaves of men understand and perceive gender relations and sexuality, and whether these understandings and perceptions vary by race.

Scholars have offered three competing explanations regarding racial differences in men's approaches toward women: (a) Black and White men objectify women similarly; (b) Black men objectify women more than White men; (c) White men objectify women more than Black men. The first possibility contends that most men, irregardless of status or race, sexually objectify women in the same manner. Thus, Black and White men's performances in masculinities are expected to be similar. In patriarchal societies, men control sexual and romantic environments by promoting sexually aggressive behavior among men (Clark and Hatfield 1989; Hatfield et al. 1998; Flood 2008). Through the emphasis of the importance of sexual prowess, cultural mandates concerning gender encourage men to "sexually objectify" women and appear "sexual." However, such mandates encourage women to stress relationship viability and appear "romantic" (Hatfield et al. 1998). Hence, men are often authorized to express themselves sexually,

Rashawn Ray and Jason A. Rosow, "Getting Off and Getting Intimate: How Normative Institutional Arrangements Structure Black and White Fraternity Men's Approaches toward Women," *Men and Masculinities* (2009). Copyright © 2009 Sage Publications. Reprinted by permission of Sage Publications.

while women who act this way are shunned. This possibility suggests that gender trumps race and status concerning men's interactions with women.

A second possibility is that Black men exhibit more sexually objectifying approaches toward women than do White men. This explanation is most in line with scholarship on Black men's relations with women. More specifically, cultural motifs like the "cool pose" (Majors and Billson 1992) portray Black men as culprits of sexual violence (Majors and Billson 1992; Anderson 1999). However, this perspective, which is echoed with public discourses and much scholarly research, gives the impression that all Black men are part of the same cultural spaces, thereby neglecting the fact that Black men may be part of different sociocultural[1] spaces that yield distinctly different structural consequences for their treatment of women. It should also be noted that the stereotypical nature of Black men as the Mandingo—overly aggressive, sexually promiscuous, physically superior yet intellectually inferior—has long been purported in mainstream discourses (Hunter and Davis 1992; Collins 2004). Race scholars assert this is a problematized, dramatized, and monolithic perception of Black men that is often exacerbated in the media (Staples 1982; Hoberman 1997).

Finally, the third possibility asserts that White men are more sexually objectifying than Black men. By virtue of their presumed greater status and esteem, White men are more likely to control social environments and accept, and even normalize, sexual objectifications of women (Connell 1987; Kimmel and Messner 1989; Kimmel 2006). This perspective echoes the sentiments of women who claim sexual harassment in high-status institutions such as law, academia, and corporate America where White men are typically the controllers of social environments (Kanter 1977). In contrast to the aforementioned "cool pose," some extant literature finds that Black men's gender attitudes, compared to their White counterparts, are more supportive of gender equality because of a shared oppression and subordination with women (Millham and Smith 1986; Konrad and Harris 2002).

In this article, we assess these three predictions by analyzing 30 in-depth, individual interviews and surveys and two focus group interviews with Black and White high-status fraternity men. We find evidence that White men are more sexually objectifying than their Black

counterparts, in support of the third prediction. However, we also find that the reasons behind this pattern go beyond the explanations typically asserted by this prediction and the first two predictions. Collectively, the three explanations noted above neglect the extent to which cultural and social norms are embedded within and shaped by the structure of institutions, and in turn, how structure shapes men's approaches toward women and the performances of masculinities. Accordingly, we contend that "normative institutional arrangements" are one of the key factors that underlie racial differences regarding how men interact with women romantically and sexually on college campuses.

NORMATIVE INSTITUTIONAL ARRANGEMENTS IN HIGHER EDUCATION

Normative institutional arrangements are boundaries that shape social interactions and establish control over social environments (Gerson and Peiss 1985; Hays 1994; Britton 2003), and one structural mechanism that should be of importance to scholars interested in intersectionality research. Normative institutional arrangements identify social contexts (e.g., social environments in fraternity houses), whereby certain behaviors are more or less acceptable and certain structures hold individuals more or less accountable for their treatment of others. Such arrangements represent taken-for-granted assumptions that are external and exist outside of individuals, "social, durable, and layered" (Hays 1994), and constraining and enabling. Normative institutional arrangements focus on the accepted arrangement of relationships within social institutions. In this article, normative institutional arrangements draw attention to the ways in which performances of masculinities are legitimized across different sociocultural categories of men, and the role structure plays in men's approaches toward women. Here, we showcase the implications of the intersecting forces of race and status by examining two normative institutional arrangements that are common themes in Black and White men's understandings and perceptions of gender and sexual relations: (a) small Black student and Greek communities; (b) living arrangements including a lack of on-campus fraternity houses.

The Black student community at most Predominately White Institutions (PWIs) is small and insular. There is also a limited amount of social interaction between Black and White fraternities and between Black and White students overall (Allen 1992; Massey et al. 2003). Similar to patterns at the societal level, interracial dating is infrequent (Joyner and Kao 2005). As a result, even high-status Black fraternity men are mostly invisible in White social arenas.

In contrast, the relatively small number of Black students and limited interactions with Whites indicate that Black fraternity men are much more visible in the Black community. In fact, this group of Black men aligns with the ideals of what DuBois (1903, 1939) conceptualized as the "Talented Tenth." Such members of the Black elite are expected to sacrifice personal interests and endeavors to provide leadership and guidance to the Black community (Battle and Wright II 2002). However, being part of the Talented Tenth signifies the monitoring of this group's behavior, particularly actions that are inconsistent with a greater good for the Black community. This monitoring by others on Black fraternity men is intensified in a structural setting with a small community size, and in turn, increases the likelihood that their treatment of women will be publicized and scrutinized by members of their own social community and the broader college and off-campus communities. Although White fraternity men may also be visible, the sheer number of White students leads to them being held less accountable, and consequently, able to perform masculinity in a manner that Black fraternity men cannot.

Not only is the Black community relatively small but Black Greeks have very different on-campus living arrangements than White Greeks. There is a historical legacy of racial discrimination, both within and external to the university, that has traditionally precluded Black fraternities and sororities from gaining equal access to economic resources such as Greek houses and large alumni endowments (Kimbrough and Hutcheson 1998). To date, most Black Greek Letter Organizations (BGLOs) do not have fraternity or sorority houses on university property (Harper, Byars, and Jelke 2005). If they do, these houses normally are not the same size or stature of those of their White counterparts. To the extent that the structure of living arrangements facilitates a certain treatment of women, racial differences in access to housing on-campus may have implications in potential racial differences in approaches toward women.

In sum, the claims by masculinities, sexualities, and race scholars suggest that culture provides a portal whereby men view women as physical objects. However, research in this area suffers from three important shortcomings. First, the structural mechanisms by which normative institutional arrangements promote women's subordination have been underemphasized. Most recently, scholars have called for a resurgence of such research and have pointed to the exploration of contextual and structural factors to uncover these mechanisms (Reskin 2003; Epstein 2007). Second, the perspectives of high-status men remain absent in the literature. Hence, this study seeks to understand how elite men decipher their worlds and how privileged statuses influence the processes underlying gender dynamics. Third, research largely has not explored the potential for racial differences in men's gender relations. Consequently, gender and sexuality research has portrayed men as homogenous proponents of gender inequality, irregardless of race and/or social context.

Our work offers an opportunity to address these gaps in the literature by reporting on interviews with Black and White high-status men. Some high-status Black men (e.g., Black fraternity men) may have attitudes and beliefs that are similar to their White male counterparts. However, due in part to a hyper level of visibility and accountability, Black men may be unable to perform hegemonic masculinity similar to their White male counterparts.[2] Actually, because of a relative lack of accountability and visibility afforded to high-status White fraternity men in this structural setting,[3] it is White men's performances of masculinities that may be closer to that of the "cool pose." Therefore, we hypothesize that Black men will exhibit less sexually objectifying approaches toward women than their White counterparts.

Accordingly, we pose two essential questions: (a) Regarding high-status fraternity men's relations with women, are there racial differences in romantic versus sexually objectifying approaches? (b) How do "normative institutional arrangements" structure men's approaches toward women? Because there has been limited empirical research on elite men, we privilege their accounts and voices to gain an insider's perspective into the intersections of masculinities, status, sexuality, and race.

SETTING AND METHOD

We conducted 30 in-depth individual interviews and surveys, along with two focus group interviews, from 15 Black and 15 White fraternity men at a PWI that we call Greek University (GU). Enrolling approximately 30,000 undergraduates, GU is ideal for this study because of its strong academic reputation, vibrant social life, and party scene. GU's emphasis on Greek life facilitates the examination of gender relations among high-status men. About 20% of GU undergraduates are members of Greek letter organizations, which is larger than similar universities.[4] For members, the Greek system normally offers a home away from home, friendships, and social and philanthropic activities. There are approximately 25 White fraternities with memberships around 100, some with on-campus and some with off-campus status, and five Black fraternities with memberships around 10 and all hold off-campus status.[5] Although approximately 25% of White students are members of Greek organizations, less than 10% of Black students are members of Greek organizations.[6] Black and White fraternities are operated by two different governing bodies, the National Pan-Hellenic Council (NPHC)[7] and the Interfraternity Council (IFC), respectively. Although none of these fraternities appear to explicitly discriminate on the basis of race, there is virtually no overlap in race among members of these organizations.

Data Collection

To select our sample, we used a reputational approach (Boswell and Spade 1996) to identify high-status fraternities. Relying on rankings of fraternities by members of sororities and fraternities, students in sociology classes, informants in Greek Affairs, and the Assistant Dean of Students that rank fraternities based on popularity, academic and philanthropic events, and athletic prowess, three White fraternities consistently ranked high on all lists. We include all three in our study. Because only five historically Black fraternities are recognized by the NPHC, membership in any of these fraternities normally conveys a certain high-status, particularly at GU because the Black population is only about 4% (1,524). We interviewed members from four of the five Black fraternities. We attempted to interview all five and gained entry to four. The sampling strategy

enables us to check for commonalities and differences within and between race. Participants were recruited by emailing the fraternity presidents to see if the investigators could attend a chapter meeting to make an announcement about the study, invite members to participate, and leave detailed study flyers.

As a Black and White team of male researchers, we note that gender may elicit certain responses with participants de-emphasizing romanticism. We also conducted interviews with the authors matched with participants by race to elicit candid responses about the other racial group. Based on the data presented throughout this article, we are confident that we limited methodological biases. For example, one White respondent states, "Blacks will fuck anything." Another says, "Yeah, my friends at home are Black. They like to put it in girls' asses." Based on our experiences interacting with these respondents, we believe they would not have made these comments if they were being interviewed by a Black interviewer. (See The Fraternity House section for a Black quotation about Whites.) These quotations show that respondents did not hesitate to make derogatory statements about the other group.

All the men in our study report being family-oriented and having lofty career goals. Most participants are active on campus and have higher GPAs than non-Greeks. However, a substantial class difference exists between Blacks and Whites. The Black men's self-reported family household income is lower middle class, whereas the White men's self-reported family household income is upper-middle class. Many of the Black fraternity men have scholarships, student loans, and/or jobs to pay for tuition and housing costs, whereas most of the White fraternity men have scholarships and/or their parents pay a substantial portion of their tuition and living expenses. All respondents self-identify as heterosexual (see Table 1).

Interview Procedure

Most of the data presented come from the individual interviews. In-depth interviews are useful for developing a broad understanding of students' experiences in various aspects of college life and for exploring the meanings students attach to these experiences (Denzin and Lincoln 1994). Similar to Armstrong, Hamilton, and Sweeney (2006), we used an 8-page, semistructured

Table 1 Descriptive Statistics of Sample by Race

Variable	Range	Variable description	White = 15	Black = 15	Total = 30
Age	18–24	Years	20.11	21.27	20.69
Classification	1–4	1 = Freshman, 2 = Sophomore, 3 = Junior, 4 = Senior	2.22	3.73	2.98
GPA	0–4	Cumulative grade point average	3.31	2.92	3.12
Living situation	0–1	0 = Lives off campus, 1 = Lives in a fraternity house	0.87	0.00	0.45
Years in fraternity	1–5	Years respondent has been a fraternity member	1.94	2.00	1.97
Religiosity	1–4	1 = Not at all, 2 = Slightly, 3 = Moderately, 4 = Very	2.00	3.07	2.54
Family's social class	1–6	1 = Poor, 2 = Working, 3 = Lower-middle, 4 = Middle, 5 = Upper-middle, 6 = Upper	4.56	3.87	4.22
Relationship status	0–1	0 = Single or dating, 1 = Committed relationship	0.33	0.67	0.50

interview guide to ask participants about many topics including the Greek system, race relations, partying, hooking-up, dating, sexual attitudes and experiences, and their goals for the future. With interviews averaging 2 hours, we aimed to obtain a holistic perspective of these men's collegiate lives. All interviews were digitally recorded and transcribed using pseudonyms to ensure personal and organizational anonymity. Following the interviews, we recorded ethnographic field notes to capture aspects of the interview interactions that might not be evident in the transcripts (Emerson, Fretz, and Shaw 1995). At the end of each interview, we asked respondents to complete a paper-and-pencil survey. Data from this survey on sociodemographics, family background, sexual attitudes and experiences, and relationship history provide contextual information about each respondent.

The focus groups were conducted after the individual interviews were completed to support the individual interviews. Most focus group respondents were part of the 30 individual interviews. The focus groups were used to triangulate the data and focused on themes that evolved from the individual interviews. They also allowed us to interrogate emerging propositions. Because shared discourses are documented to occur in peer groups, the unique environment generated in focus groups was well suited to this project (Morgan 1997; Hollander 2004). Although focus groups have been criticized for their lack of ability to elicit truthful views about gender and

sexuality from young men, the interviewers had preexisting knowledge of the men and could question specific accounts and perspectives.

Analytical Strategy

We use deductive and inductive reasoning as analytic approaches to "double fit" the data with emergent theory and literature (Ragin 1994). We initially allowed analytical categories to emerge as we searched for similarities and differences in how Black and White fraternity men interact with women. Guided by these themes and patterns, we then used deductive reasoning to look for evidence and theories to make sense of the data. We used ATLAS.ti, a qualitative data analysis software package, to connect memos, notes, and transcriptions. After establishing patterns in the coding, we searched the interviews thoroughly again looking for examples that both confirmed and contradicted emerging patterns. Our emerging propositions were then refined or eliminated to explain these negative cases (Rizzo, Corsaro, and Bates 1992).

RACIALIZING GENDER RELATIONS ON CAMPUS

The interviews suggest that Black fraternity men exhibit more romantic approaches than White fraternity men.

Although both groups sexually objectify women, Black men emphasize romanticism more than their White counterparts. They indicate that women are physical objects of enjoyment but should also be respected. White fraternity men make few romantic references and primarily view women as sexual objects.

The following quotations exemplify sexually objectifying approaches. This participant suggests that romance is unnecessary in the quest for gratification.

> Pretty much you do not need to do all that wine and dine them and all that. You can skip all that and just bring them back to the house and do what's important to you. (White)

In two different parts of the interview, a participant explains which factors affect how far he will go with a woman.

R: If they [women] were decent or just okay, I'll just mess around with them. . . . Get head.

I: When she gives you head, do you go down on her?

R: Honestly, I don't like that. . . . I do it every once in a while. Honestly depends how hot the girl is. If I'm drunk and into the girl, I probably would. But other girls, I just make out with them for a little bit.

R: We were talking for about a week and we started messing around. She starts giving me head, and when I took her shirt off, I put my hand on her stomach and this girl had abs. I think that's the most disgusting thing. Like, girls with abs, its like . . . too masculine. So that like turned me off and I couldn't get off and I never called her again. (White)

Nine of the 15 White participants report engaging in sexual behavior that they do not prefer including performing oral sex because of a woman's desirable physical characteristics. They also rarely describe "hot girls" in terms of social competence and popularity. Reports from Black men also contain sexually objectifying approaches. While describing what he desires in a woman, a participant compares women to cars as he explains why his standards for sexual encounters are lower than for relationships.

I: Are your standards lower for a hookup than a committed relationship?

R: I use this analogy. Some people say it's corny, but whatever. When you have the title of a car, you want it to be nice, but you'll jump in your friend's car. You'll ride, you'll ride anything because it's not your title. But if I'm going to have the title to you, you've got to be nice because you represent me! But now I'll ride in a pinto, but I just won't buy one. (Black)

Although both groups exhibit sexually objectifying approaches, romantic approaches in quality and content are far more prevalent among Black men. They respond when asked to "describe ways you or your friends respect women on campus."

> I definitely think my fraternity brothers do a lot of stuff that make them [women] feel appreciated like getting them flowers; whether write them a poem, whether it's just tell them they look beautiful. (Black)

> I think you have to treat women with respect. I think because of how society is I think a lot of males have been misshapen to be like the world leader; the dominant figure in the relationship. They wear the pants in the relationship. I feel like I would treat a woman the way that I would want to be treated. (Black)

Conversely, many White men describe a very different notion of respecting women.

> We respect women. We won't take advantage of them if they're wasted. If she's puking in our bathroom, one of the pledges will get her a ride home. (White)

> One way that I respect women? A lot of ways. I'll never ask if she needs a ride home after we hookup. I'll let her bring it up or let her spend the night. You respect a girl more if you let her stay. (White)

Black and White differences are also evident in responses to "what do you consider a serious relationship?" White men understand a serious relationship primarily in terms of physical monogamy, whereas Black men define serious relationships in terms of socioemotional exchanges.

R: If you're in a serious relationship, you shouldn't be making out . . . that's wrong.

I: So serious relationships are when you don't cheat on a girl.

R: No. You shouldn't be making out in front of people. If you have a girlfriend you can't be like all over girls at parties. (White)

> Serious relationship is pretty much a basic understanding that two people are together. You have somebody to talk to; somebody who is going to be there on the

other end of the phone call. When you leave that message they're calling back. Maybe at night you got somebody to cuddle with. Somebody that could possibly cook for you. Somebody that might be taking you out, picking you up. Somebody that is worrying about what you're doing. (Black)

Twelve of the 15 Black fraternity men explain that having someone to "share" and do "special" things with is the best thing about being in a serious relationship.

> I'd say you get the companionship, the love. You've got somebody there in daytime hours, not just in nighttime hours. The nine to five hours they're going to be there to go out with you. They might send you out with some stuff, take you out to eat, go see a movie, and like it's that constant companionship. (Black)

Comparatively, only 7 of the 15 White fraternity men mention that this is a benefit of a committed relationship. Instead, 12 of them explain that having a "regular hookup" is the best thing about being in a relationship.

> Lots of sex. You can have it every day without having to go out and get it. It's a lot easier, but you do have to put up with shit occasionally. (White)

> The best thing is you don't have to use a condom. It feels better and you can go right to it. And you got someone to call that you know what they want and knows what you like. (White)

In contrast, only 3 of the 15 Black men mention sexual convenience as a benefit of being in a committed relationship.

Perhaps most revealing are the responses to "describe a romantic evening." Black men volunteer specific details without hesitation and reveal intimate knowledge of their partners, thoughtful planning, and intricate execution.

> I try to do romantic things on occasion, not just on occasions. On her birthday I surprised her. I told her we were going out to dinner. There is a whole day of events. I left a dozen roses in front of her door. I have a key to her apartment just because she likes to have that kind of security just in case I need to go over there and do something for her. When she came home I had prepared a dinner for her. I cooked her favorite dinner which was spaghetti and she was really surprised. It was a candlelight dinner, lights were off, food all served, salad, and spaghetti. She really liked that and I gave her some more gifts, but the last thing I got her was a ring that she loves. (Black)

Of course, "romantic" does not necessarily imply equitable gender relations. "Romantic" can also have negative connotations for gender relations (e.g., women need to be taken care of, pampered, put on a pedestal). Comparatively, most White men's narratives imply less thought and planning. Only three of them could describe a romantic evening, two of which were descriptions encompassing "dinner and a movie," preferably an "expensive establishment."

> I clean up, shave, put on a nice shirt with a nice pair of pants, you come out of the car, you wait for her, open the door for her. Nice expensive restaurant; something with a good reputation. Maybe somewhere someone's parents would take them, because that lets them know you're dropping some cheddar, you know, you're dropping some money. Have some easy conversation, then come back have a few more drinks, and then, you know, {laughs}. (White)

Another White participant says, "Well, on her birthday I got her an iPod. She loved it. I took her out to dinner, an expensive dinner."

Finally, the language used by White fraternity men to describe women in gender interactions suggests sexually objectifying approaches, whereas the language exhibited most frequently by Black fraternity men implies more romantic approaches. White men commonly refer to women as "chicks," "girls," and other belittling terms. Conversely, Black men generally use more "respectful" terms like "women," "ladies," and "females" or refer to individuals by name.[8] As seen in many quotations throughout the article, the examples below illustrate the role of language regarding gender relations.

> I know this one time I was real drunk, a little too flirtatious with a female who was actually a friend of mine. I did—I was not trying to hook up with her. Actually, she was trying to hook up with me. And when the alcohol mixed with the flirtatious lady, mixing with me not driving having to be at her house that night. I did regret it when I woke up the next morning {laughs}. (Black)

> When the booze settles in you can make mistakes and you'll screw up with a "frat rat" or something. (White)

Collectively, Black excerpts normally acknowledge women's agency, whereas the White accounts typically display the use of the passive voice, whereby a woman is always acted on and never acting. Black men emphasize more romanticism in their accounts regarding experiences with and attitudes about women. However, these differences are not solely related to race.

NORMATIVE INSTITUTIONAL ARRANGEMENTS STRUCTURE APPROACHES TOWARD WOMEN

We find that differences in men's approaches toward women are structured by normative institutional arrangements centering on community size and living arrangements. Participant accounts suggest that the size of their respective racial communities on campus and the presence or absence of a fraternity house underlie racial differences in romantic versus sexually objectifying approaches toward women.

Greek and Racially Based Communities

Fraternity men are concerned about their individual and group reputations when making gender relation choices. Thus, they aim to steer clear of certain social scenes to preserve their status as elite men. In the following accounts, participants indicate that to maintain their reputations they normally will not "hookup" with low-status women. We asked, "Are there any women you wouldn't hookup with?"

> Fat girls. I stay away from them. Sluts too. They're disgusting. I don't need to hookup with that, that's not *our* [his fraternity] style. (White)

> Everyone has the one, two, or three girls that they're like what the hell was I doing? But you don't want to have too many. I mean its good to hookup, but you don't want to do it with a girl that's easy. If it's a girl that every guy wants and you bring her back its like, "Wow! You hooked up with that girl? That's impressive!" It feels good. If you hookup with an ugly girl, you're friends will give you shit for it. (White)

> Yes. They're not attractive, [laughs] That might sound mean, but that's what they are. Not attractive girls. I don't think there's no woman here that's higher than what we think we can reach. And then lower, yes there is a group of people that you should just not touch. I hear a lot of guys in other fraternities say, "Man I wish I could get a girl like that." Instead, we just get the girl like that. (Black)

White fraternity men indicate that the "word" gets around easily within the Greek community regarding

gender interactions. They normally engage in a variety of unspoken rules to preserve their reputations. The following White participant describes the "card" rule.

R: You got one card to play. You can hookup with two girls in the same house [sorority organization] and you might be alright. As long as you don't piss off the first one. If you do, you're done. You won't have a chance with any other girls in that house. But you can't play the card unless some time has passed.

I: How much time do you need?

R: It can't be the same weekend for sure. Probably after a week or so you should be okay. (White)

The Greek community seems to hold White fraternity men accountable to sorority women. As the quotation above alludes, it is only for reasons of saving face that will allow them access to other women in the same sorority. Another White participant describes how cheating could result in a bad reputation if he got caught.

I: What would happen if you got caught cheating?

R: The way I could see it [cheating] affecting something is if it's a sorority girl you fuck over.

I: You can't screw with a sorority sister?

R: You could, but you could get the name, you're an asshole, you're a player, or something like that. I mean it might. It could spread around the [her sorority] house. Then you're Blacklisted. (White)

Although repercussions exist with sorority women, there are an abundance of non-Greek women with no reputational constraints. The large number and high percentage of White students give White fraternity men an ample pool of women not connected to the Greek community. When relating with non-Greek women or GDIs,[9] White fraternity men do not have to worry about "the word" getting around. Moreover, White fraternity men can disassociate from the fraternity, blend into the crowd, and interact as they please.

R: GDIs come here and it's like sensory overload. They are like in awe. If you're in awe, it's like so easy. {laughs} You can say anything to a GDI. Adam makes girls cry.

I: He wouldn't do that to a sorority girl?

R: You make a sorority girl cry she's going to tell all her friends. "I was at XYZ [fraternity] and this guy made me cry and he's such an asshole." If you say it to a GDI, she's going home and you're probably never going to see her again and she's not going to tell all of XYZ [sorority] that you said this and you're not going to have a whole sorority that hates you. (White)

Black fraternity men face a different organizational structure. These men feel that they cannot "do things like other guys."

> Because there's only seven [Black Greek] organizations on campus, we have a huge impact on the Black race here. Where there's like 750 different [White] organizations, their impact is not as severe. It's not as deep, especially cause they have more people than our race. (Black)

> It's kind a like being on the basketball team or being on a football team. You know what I'm saying? Its kinda like "Eta" [his fraternity name] puts you on the next level. Like you're Black Greek but you are like the . . . you are supposed to be representing the Black Greek. It's kinda hard to get that out, but when we do something we are suppose to be setting the bar for everybody else. It's like a known thing that we suppose to be setting a bar. You know what I mean? (Black)

Black fraternity men, and many Black students, cannot overcome the reputational constraints of the small Black population. Black men report being very conscious of their behavior when interacting with women. Although White fraternity men can generally be anonymous and "get off" safely, Black fraternity men perceive themselves to be constantly visible and therefore continuously held accountable for their treatment of women.

The Fraternity House

The organizational structure of "the house" facilitates sex, discourages intimacy, and is used as a resource, which affords White fraternity men control of sexual environments. For instance, these men report that women normally engage in relationships to be associated with a particular fraternity and to have access to fraternity functions and/or alcohol.

> I know I'm Jack "B" ["B" represents his fraternity's name], and there's probably a Jack "C," but I don't care. I know she just wants to come to our parties and know someone there. (White)

College-aged women younger than 21 years old seem to rely on fraternities for basic ingredients of the mainstream version of the college experience—big parties and alcohol. In fact, an interview with a White participant was interrupted twice because of orders for alcohol placed by an ex-girlfriend and another woman from the dorm.

"The house" also facilitates a convenient means of engaging sexual behavior. A participant discusses the difference between living in "the house" and living off-campus.

> You meet a lot more girls in the house. The frat [house] is easier, a lot easier too in that sense cause coming back from the bars, it's not necessarily like "let's go back to my place." Instead it's like, "Let's go back to the frat [house] and have a couple more drinks." It's like you don't sound like you're trying to hook up with them. "Let's go back to my house and just . . . get it on" . . . [laughs] . . . It's easier. (White)

"The house" also constrains men's gender relations. Although the fraternity houses at GU are impressive mansion-like structures, they are chaotic, nonprivate spaces that promote nonromantic activities. Most White fraternities require a "live-in" period. In the first year, members sleep in cold dorms, which are rooms composed of dozens of bunk beds.

> It's like fifty of us sleep together. But you put your beds together and have all these sheets and stuff. It's like a bungalow. But sometimes you can hear other people having sex. (White)

If members earn enough "house points" for representing the fraternity well through activities like philanthropy or sports, they then typically live with three roommates in a tiny bunk-style room.

White fraternity men indicate that they could never "get away" with having romantic time. A White participant says, "There's so many people running around that house, someone's bound to see or hear something." The public nature of fraternity living arrangements is also confirmed in our field notes. While entering a fraternity room to do an interview, the interviewee and interviewer interrupted a roommate who was masturbating. The interviewer reported surprise that the masturbator seemed only slightly uncomfortable with the interruption. This suggests that interruptions like these are commonplace.

Although privacy would intuitively be linked to more sexually objectifying approaches, in the context of Greek social life, a lack of privacy facilitates these approaches by preventing intimacy. While having other people as witnesses should reduce the degree of exploitation, Greek social life is a normative institutional arrangement structured by hegemonic masculinity with sexual prowess as one of its essential ideals. Thus, men who engage in public displays of sexual objectification are applauded. A participant describes one evening in the cold dorm.

> Lunch on Fridays are the best. It's like all the stories from Thursday night. It's pretty funny. It's a good time. For instance, Tom came into the cold dorm and he was with his girlfriend and they were really drunk. And he's like, "We're having sex." I was like, "You should have heard him. He punished her."[10] (White)

Romantic displays, because they are not in concert with hegemonic ideals, are sanctioned. For example, participants indicate that men who make romantic displays like saying "I love you" or opting for alone time with a woman over "hanging with the guys" will quickly be referred to as "pussy-whipped."

> You don't want to be known as pussy-whipped. Guys that are pussy-whipped are wimps. They just let their girl tell them what to do. You can't count on them. They'll tell you one thing, but if the girl says something different, they're doing what she says. (White)

Another White participant characterizes how public displays of romanticism are considered to be uncool by the general Greek community.

> I don't know how romantic it gets. Am I like going to set up a table in my frat room and light a candle? It'd be cool, if I had the balls to do it. (White)

When asked directly "why don't you and your friends have romantic evenings," a White participant explains.

> Frat houses aren't the place for that [romantic behavior]. Have you looked around? The place is filthy and you have no privacy. None. I shower with five guys; people always coming in and out. You're never alone. I used to feel weird about it [sex], but now I don't. Like I used to try to be quiet, but I'm having sex less than four feet from where my roommate, whose having sex with his girlfriend. You're going to hear something. So you don't worry about it. (White)

Conversely, Black fraternity men's off-campus status offers private space for romantic relations. Most members are scattered across two- to four-person apartments and rental houses. Interviews conducted in bedrooms at Black residencies were devoid of interruptions, whereas interviews with Whites had three to four interruptions, on average. Field notes document that Black men's rooms are frequently decorated with expressions of personal achievement and style, whereas White men's rooms are often decorated with mainstream posters and sexually objectifying appeals. Consider the following field notes.

> We conducted the interview in E3's room. He had mafia posters around his room from the movies *Godfather* and *Scarface*. He also had a Dr. Seuss book and a pimp poster in his room as well. E3 is a martial arts champion and has several of his large trophies in his room and around the house. (Black)

> The room was filthy. It felt dirty like it hadn't been disinfected in a while. There were many posters and artifacts on the walls of beer or liquor companies and one wall decoration was of some Dr. Dre records. The coffee table had three Playboy magazines laid out in a fan-like shape and the windows had two suction cup Playboy Bunnies hanging off of them. (White)

A Black participant comments on his interactions with the decoration styles of White men.

> I go through some of these [White] male's rooms and that's all they got—they got posters. I mean I just can't have no posters of naked women just *all* around my room. Like when you walk in you see nothing but nude! (Black)

In sum, normative institutional arrangements—the presence or absence of a fraternity "house" and the size of the Greek and racially based community in the larger student population—afford Blacks and Whites different opportunity structures for romantic and sexual relations. The small, highly visible and insular Black communities normally force Black fraternity men to be conscious about their positions as leaders and role models, thus affecting their experiences with and treatment of women. This consciousness often leads Black fraternity men to conveying more romantic approaches toward women. Because of the size of the White student population, White fraternity men often find relief from reputational constraints. "The house" facilitates White fraternity men's relations with women by putting them in control of sexual environments. At the same time, however, the "public" nature of fraternity houses constrains gender relations by providing only nonprivate and unromantic spaces, thereby promoting more sexually objectifying approaches.

Culture Mediating Normative Institutional Arrangements

Although we have emphasized the importance of structure in approaches toward women, some may assert that maturation or relationship status may be factors. Black fraternity men are one year older and further along in college. Because of different recruitment practices between Black and White fraternities, most Blacks do not become members until their sophomore or junior years, whereas Whites primarily "rush" during their freshman year. Hence, the number of years Blacks and Whites have been fraternity members is roughly the same. So this 1 year age difference should not be overstressed. More importantly, we compared the responses of older White fraternity men with those of their younger counterparts. We find their approaches toward women to be similar. Because Black men tend to be in more committed relationships, it could be argued that higher relationship rates result in more romantic approaches. Our data do not offer much support for this argument. White men in committed relationships still report more sexually objectifying approaches than Black men. Comparatively, Black men who are not in committed relationships report similar romantic approaches to Black men in committed relationships.

Religiosity, however, seems to play a factor in approaches toward women, albeit mediating normative institutional arrangements. A White participant explains why he is still a virgin. He says, "Well, because I'm a Christian. I'm waiting to share that with my wife. It's a faith thing." While explaining how he manages to be a virgin, he explains that "they [women] just have to understand. I don't do that [intercourse]. It's been tough because girls say 'are you serious?'" He continues to explain his frustrations with the Greek community's emphasis on sexuality.

I'm sure you're not going to find too many twenty-two year old virgins around. It's kind of funny too, because it is almost frowned upon around here. It's almost like

you're the Black sheep of the crew, because it's socially acceptable to have sex and stuff like that. You see me, nobody ever believes it. But it's almost like a stigma that you're kind of labeled with people that know. Always when people find out it's a surprise to them. (White)

Another participant explains why he does not hookup as often as his fraternity brothers.

Not as much as some of the guys in this house. I'm not that way. It's a conscious decision. I need to really like the girl and feel comfortable. My parents have been together forever. You don't just do that kind of stuff with just anybody. (White)

Although the two negative cases highlighted above demonstrate the significance of cultural values, they also stress the importance of normative institutional arrangements for approaches toward women. These men feel uncomfortable and are frequently ridiculed and scrutinized by their fraternity brothers and women for not adhering to the hegemonic ideals reinforced by the normative institutional arrangements of Greek social life. Moreover, they are the exceptions that prove the rule.

As an added point of emphasis, focus group and ethnographic field note excerpts highlight participants' own awareness of the importance of normative institutional arrangements. When Black men were asked in a focus group if things would be different if GU was not a PWI, and instead a Historically Black College or University (HBCU), they unanimously responded, "Yes." If Black men had a house, they think their behavior would be similar to their White counterparts. They perceive "the house" as a place to socialize in large groups that is free from police contact and potentially hostile strangers. If they were the "majority," they perceive being free from the incessant scrutiny of the general campus community. Black men explain how "nice it would be" to not have to represent "every Black man on the planet." An ethnographic field note is fitting here.

While attending Etas step practice, the members began discussing their Spring Break plans. They planned to go "road tripping" to Panama City Beach. I asked why Panama City? They replied that it was cheap and a place where they could go and meet new women who do not go to GU. I asked why this was so important. They replied because the new women cannot come back to school and tell everyone else what they did and who they were with. One member replied, "We can just wild out!" (Black)

When White men were asked in a focus group to imagine life without "the house," they replied, "It would be like being a GDI." They further explained that "the house" is "like a face" which enables them to "meet girls." White men also mirror issues of safety indicated by Black men. For instance, they are concerned that if they lose "the house," they would have to go to bars, small house-parties, or third-party vendors and would then have to worry about drinking and driving, public intoxication, and police breaking up parties. In other words, White fraternity men perceive that losing "the house" would make them "just like everybody else."

DISCUSSION AND CONCLUSION

We have explored whether there are racial differences in men's approaches toward women. By characterizing elite Black and White fraternity men's understandings of their sexual and romantic relationships, this research fills three critical empirical gaps. First, we explore the perspectives and insights of a group that is often implicated in mainstream discourses in romantic and sexual relations on college campuses—high-status fraternity men. Second, we explicitly compare Black and White men. Third, we examine how the normative institutional arrangements of institutions shape the performances of masculinities.

Our findings suggest that both Black and White fraternity men sexually objectify women; however, Black fraternity men exhibit more romantic approaches in their perceptions of their relations with women. Black college social scenes, particularly Black Greek scenes, are often more gender egalitarian. Although the small size of the Black community and the organizational structure of the Black Greek system generally force Black men to be more conscious about their treatment of women, the organizational structure of the White Greek community facilitates sexually objectifying approaches toward women. White fraternity men also have a larger pool of non-Greek women to engage; therefore, they are held less accountable for their relations with women because of a hyper level of anonymity. Although the presence of a fraternity house enables White fraternity men to be in control of sexual environments, it also constrains gender relations by offering nonprivate and nonintimate spaces.

Unlike the lower class men in studies by Majors and Billson (1992) and Anderson (1999), Black men in this study are more affiliated with DuBois's (1903, 1939) Talented Tenth and double-consciousness concepts.[11] For Black men who identify as or with this elite group, the racialization of high-status institutions holds them more accountable for their treatment of women and constrains their approaches. As a result, some may assert these Black men's attitudes and values about the treatment of women are different from other Black men and their White fraternity male counterparts. Although there is support for this perspective, particularly because Black fraternity men stress more holistic qualities of women and tend to perceive more aspects of romanticism to be masculine, we argue the influential effects normative institutional arrangements have on shaping racial and status differences in men's gender scripts surfaces in the behavior or at the performance level of these men. To save face and status, Black fraternity men have to be more concerned about how their interactions with women are perceived by others. This leads to a unique set of reputational boundaries and constraints for Black fraternity men not exhibited by White fraternity men.

Our emphasis on normative institutional arrangements does not deny the presence of other factors that may be implicated in racial differences. For example, Black men in this study report being more religious than White men. Therefore, we would still expect for them to have cultural values that buffer sexually objectifying approaches. Less religious Black men, however, still exhibit more romantic approaches than the White men in the sample. Thus, we contend these patterns are an artifact of the racialized level of accountability and visibility within the normative institutional arrangements of campus social life. Our research confirms that when normative institutional arrangements are in concert with mainstream hegemonic ideals, sexual objectifications are more likely to occur.

Our findings offer an interesting parallel to Armstrong, Hamilton, and Sweeney's (2006) ethnographic examination of women who reside on a women's floor in a "party dorm." They find that female college students, especially those in their first year and under the legal drinking age, rely on fraternities for parties and alcohol, and consequently, relinquish power and control of social and sexual environments to these men.

They conclude that individual, organizational, and institutional practices (e.g., prohibiting alcohol in dormitories) contribute to higher levels of sexual assault.

Our research further argues that structural settings shape how actors perceive others (e.g., as sexual, romantic, and/or holistic others) and reflect the racial and gender dynamics of college campuses including racial segregation and skewed gender ratios. Along these lines, hegemonic masculinity is about much more than gender beliefs and masculine performances. Hegemonic masculinity is also about normative accountability structures and the preservation of normative personal, social, and institutional resources. Privileges across gender, race, and status divides afford White fraternity men less accountability when performing a hegemonic masculine self during interactions with women. As shown here, under certain institutional arrangements, racial disadvantage, as with Black fraternity men, can decrease gender inequality and reduce a traditional hegemonic style of engagement toward women. However, race and/or class advantage, as with White fraternity men, and disadvantage, as with the Black men in Majors and Billson's (1992) and Anderson's (1999) studies, can increase gender inequality and propel a hegemonic presentation of self such as the "cool pose."

Now that we have a greater understanding of the importance of not just being a racial/ethnic minority but also being a numerical minority or majority and how these normative institutional arrangements structure the gender relations of high-status men on campus, future research should investigate how common these patterns are among individuals across a range of institutional settings. Specifically, our research has implications for masculinities and its relationships with White men at small colleges, or where they are the minority group, and men of other racial/ethnic groups in institutional settings where they are the majority group. Although these propositions cannot be sufficiently answered in this study, it does provide a blueprint for how scholars should approach research in this area.

Particularly useful in extrapolating the findings presented here is DeLamater's (1987) recreational-centered approach,[12] whereby approaches toward others are facilitated by contextual and structural factors. Applied here, the recreational approach assumes that actors can exhibit both romantic and sexually objectifying approaches based on the dynamics of the structural setting.

Men and women do not fit into monolithic groups. Although the literature has traditionally established a gender dichotomy whereby men exhibit sexual prowess and women cling to romantic ideals, we find men exhibit both sexually objectifying and romantic approaches. By integrating the recreational approach into the discourse on romantic and sexual relations, scholars will be better equipped to extrapolate the interconnections between masculinities, sexualities, gender inequality, and race.

Taken together, our findings suggest that efforts to increase gender equality on college campuses should center on increasing the perceived accountability of men by offering social spaces that enable communicative and intimate gender relations. For example, Boswell and Spade (1996) find that fraternity houses and commercial bars that are low-risk for sexual assault encourage men and women to get acquainted. Although the data implicate the presence of a fraternity house in unequal gender relations, they do not necessarily suggest that the elimination of fraternity houses is required to accomplish gender equality. Many sorority houses do not seem to have these problems because they have strict guidelines regarding gender ratios, parties, alcohol, and overnight guests (Armstrong, Hamilton, and Sweeney 2006). Thus, the normative institutional arrangements that afford men—in this context White fraternity men—a lack of accountability to exploit hegemonic prowess must be restructured to alter the level of accountability that encourages gender inequality. Our study concludes with an optimistic suggestion: by promoting normative institutional arrangements that facilitate accountability structures and romantic and equitable approaches, improvements toward gender equality are possible.

NOTES

1. Allport (1954) uses "sociocultural" to refer to the intersection between class (status) and caste (race).

2. Previous research has suggested that Black men's performances of masculinities are constrained by their marginalized status within the racial paradigm (Connell 1987, 1995; Kimmel 1987, 2006; Kimmel and Messner 1989; Hearn 2004). We advance this thesis by focusing on the intersections of race and status within a specific institutional structure (e.g., fraternity house).

3. Edwards (2008) states, "White structural advantage is Whites' disproportionate control or influence over nearly every social institution in this country. This affords Whites the ability to structure

social life so that it privileges them. White normativity is the normalization of Whites' cultural practices . . . their dominant social location over other racial groups as accepted as just how things are. White normativity also privileges Whites because they, unlike non-whites, do not need to justify their way of being."

4. The statistics concerning GU come from Student Activities and Greek Affairs.

5. On-campus status means the fraternity has a fraternity house on university property, whereas off-campus status means the fraternity does not.

6. Since the founding of Phi Beta Kappa (now an honor society), Greek organizations have been an integral part of colleges and universities for more than 200 years (Brown, Parks, and Phillips 2005). Fraternities are national organizations composed of college students that are men, usually designated by Greek letters. Most fraternities were founded on principles such as scholarship, community service, sound learning, and leadership and are distinguished by highly symbolic and secretive rituals. Greek fraternities and sororities are normally high-status organizations on collegiate campuses. Members of Greek fraternities and sororities are often members of student government and honor societies, are frequently some of the most recognizable student leaders on campus, and have higher grades and graduation rates than other students (Kimbrough and Hutcheson 1998).

7. Some of the most influential and celebrated African American leaders—Martin Luther King, W. E. B. DuBois, Thurgood Marshall, and Maya Angelou—became members of nationally recognized African American fraternities and sororities. Having such a distinguished lineage of past members often makes members of African American fraternities and sororities feel that they must uphold an esteemed legacy (Kimbrough and Hutcheson 1998).

8. Throughout the duration of the project, women were categorized as many sexually objectifying and derogatory terms by Black and White fraternity men including "bitch," "hoe" (whore), "skank," "freak," and "tramp." Most of these names are given to fraternity groupies or women who are perceived to be sexually promiscuous.

9. "GDI" is an acronym for "God Damn Independent," which is a derogatory term used to describe non-Greeks.

10. In this context, the statement "punish her" implies that "Tom" was making his girlfriend moan and that the bed was rocking because of sexual movements.

11. The comparison between this study and the ones by Majors and Billson (1992) and Anderson (1999) should not be overstated. Although the men in all three studies are Black men, they are embedded within different normative institutional arrangements. As asserted in the literature review, minority men exhibit intragroup differences in the performances of masculinities and should be evaluated outside the traditional monolithic box they are often placed within.

12. Although DeLamater (1987) at times interchanges the sexual objectifying approach (which he calls body-centered) with the recreational-centered approach, we choose to distinguish these two approaches. As we have discussed throughout the article, normative institutional arrangements propel more or less sexual objectification and romanticism. The recreational approach allows the researcher the ability to assess complex decisions actors make based on structural settings.

REFERENCES

Allen, Walter R. 1992. The color of success: African-American college student outcomes at predominantly white and historically black public colleges and universities. *Harvard Educational Review* 62:26–44.

Allport, Gordon W. 1954. *The Nature of Prejudice.* Reading, MA: Addison–Wesley.

Anderson, Elijah. 1999. *Code of the street: Decency, violence, and the moral life of the inner city.* New York, NY: W. W. Norton & Company.

Armstrong, Elizabeth, Laura Hamilton, and Brian Sweeney. 2006. Sexual assault on campus: A multilevel explanation of party rape. *Social Problems* 53:483–99.

Battle, Juan, and Earl Wright II. 2002. W.E.B. DuBois's talented tenth: A quantitative assessment. *Journal of Black Studies* 32:654–72.

Boswell, A. A., and J. Z. Spade. 1996. Fraternities and collegiate rape culture: Why are some fraternities more dangerous places for women? *Gender & Society* 10:133–47.

Brandes, Holger. 2007. Hegemonic Masculinities in East and West Germany (German Democratic Republic and Federal Republic of Germany). *Men and Masculinities* 10: 178–96.

Britton, Dana. M. 2003. *At work in the iron cage: The prison as gendered organization.* New York, NY: New York University Press.

Brown, T. L., G. L. Parks, and C. M. Phillips, eds. 2005. *African American fraternities and sororities: The history and the vision.* Lexington, KY: University Press of Kentucky.

Clark, R. D., and E. Hatfield. 1989. Gender differences in receptivity to sexual offers. *Journal of Psychology and Human Sexuality* 2:39–55.

Collins, Patricia Hill. 2004. *Black sexual politics: African Americans, gender, and the new racism.* New York, NY: Routledge.

Connell, R. W. 1987. *Gender and power.* Stanford, CA: Stanford University Press.

Connell, R. W. 1995. *Masculinities.* Second Ed. Berkeley: University of California Press.

DeLamater, J. 1987. Gender differences in sexual scenarios. In *Females, males, and sexuality: Theories and research,* ed. K. Kelley. Albany, NY: SUNY Press.

Denzin, Norman K., and Yvonna S. Lincoln, eds. 1994. *Handbook of qualitative research.* Thousand Oaks, CA: Sage.

DuBois, W. E. B. 1903. *The souls of black folk*. New York, NY: Dover.

DuBois, W. E. B. 1939. *Black folk, then and now: An essay in the history and sociology of the Negro race*. New York: Henry Holt.

Edwards, Korie. 2008. Bringing race to the center: The importance of race in racially diverse religious organizations. *Journal for the Scientific Study of Religion* 47:5–9.

Emerson, Richard, Rachel Fretz, and Linda Shaw. 1995. *Writing ethnographic fieldnotes*. Chicago, IL: University of Chicago Press.

Epstein, Cynthia Fuchs. 2007. Women's subordination in global context. *American Sociological Review* 72:1–2.

Flood, Michael. 2008. How bonds between men shape their sexual relations with women. *Men and Masculinities* 10:339–59.

Gerson, Judith M., and Kathy Peiss. 1985. Boundaries, negotiation, consciousness: Reconceptualizing gender relations. *Social Problems* 32:317–31.

Harper, Shaun R., Byars, L. F., and Jelke, T. B. 2005. How Black Greek-Letter Organization Membership Affects Adjustment and Undergraduate Outcomes. In *African American fraternities and sororities: The legacy and the vision,* ed. T. L. Brown, G. S. Parks, and C. M. Phillips, 393–416. Lexington, KY: University Press of Kentucky.

Hatfield, E., S. Sprecher, J. T. Pillemer, D. Greenberger, and P. Wexler. 1998. Gender differences in what is desired in the sexual relationship. *Journal of Psychology and Human Sexuality* 1:39–52.

Hays, Sharon. 1994. Structure and agency and the sticky problem of culture. *Sociological Theory* 12:57–72.

Hearn, Jeff. 2004. From hegemonic masculinity to the hegemony of men. *Feminist Theory* 5:49–72.

Hoberman, John. 1997. *Darwin's athletes*. New York, NY: Houghton.

Hollander, Jocelyn A. 2004. The social contexts of focus groups. *Journal of Contemporary Ethnography* 33:605–37.

Hunter, Andrea G., and James E. Davis. 1992. Constructing gender: An exploration of Afro-American men's conceptualization of manhood. *Gender and Society* 6:464–79.

Joyner, Kara, and Grace Kao. 2005. Interracial relationships and the transition to adulthood. *American Sociological Review* 70:563–81.

Kanter, Rosenbath Moss. 1977. Some effects of proportions of group life: Skewed sex ratios and responses to token women. *American Journal of Sociology* 5:965–90.

Kimbrough, Walter M., and Philo A. Hutcheson. 1998. The impact of membership in black Greek-letter organizations on black students' involvement in collegiate activities and their development of leadership skills. *The Journal of Negro Education* 67:96–105.

Kimmel, Michael S., ed. 1987. *Changing men: New directions in research on men and masculinity*. Newbury Park, CA. Sage.

Kimmel, Michael S., ed. 2006. Racism as adolescent male rite of passage: Ex-Nazis in Scandinavia. *Journal of Contemporary Ethnography* 36:202–18.

Kimmel Michael S., and Michael A. Messner, eds. 1989. *Men's lives*. New York, NY: Macmillan.

Konrad, A. M., and C. Harris. 2002. Desirability of the Bem sex-role inventory items for women and men: A comparison between African-Americans and European Americans. *Sex Roles* 47:259–72.

Majors, Richard G., and Janet Billson. 1992. *Cool pose: The dilemmas of black manhood in America*. New York, NY: Lexington Books.

Martin, P. Yancey, and R. A. Hummer. 1989. Fraternities and rape on campus. *Gender and Society* 3:457–73.

Massey, Douglas S., Camille Z. Charles, Garvey F. Lundy, and Mary L. Fischer. 2003. *The source of the river: The social origins of freshmen at America's selective colleges and universities*. Princeton, NJ: Princeton University Press.

Millham, J., and L. E. Smith. 1986. Sex Role Differential among Black and White Americans: A Comparative Study. *The Journal of Black Psychology* 7:77–90.

Morgan, David L. 1997. *Focus groups and qualitative research*. Thousand Oaks, CA: Sage.

Peralta, Robert L. 2007. College alcohol use and the embodiment of hegemonic masculinity among European American men. *Sex Roles* 56:741–56.

Ragin, Charles C. 1994. *Constructing social research: The unity and diversity of method*. Thousand Oaks, CA: Sage.

Reskin, Barbara F. 2003. Including mechanisms in our models of ascriptive inequality: 2002 presidential address. *American Sociological Review* 68:1–21.

Rizzo, Thomas A., William A. Corsaro, and John E. Bates. 1992. Ethnographic methods and interpretive analysis: Expanding the methodological options of psychologists. *Developmental Review* 12:101–23.

Staples, R. 1982. *Black masculinity: The black males' role in American society*. San Francisco, CA: Black Scholar.

16

"Handlin' Your Business"

Sexual Respectability and Peers

LORENA GARCIA

The cool air inside Las Palmitas, a small Latino-owned grocery store in the West Town community, offered us a welcome relief from the muggy weather outside. Hearing the bell attached to the door jingle, a middle-aged Latino man near the register looked up from the newspaper he was reading to greet us. Centro Adelante youth often strolled to Las Palmitas, only a couple blocks away, to buy their snacks of choice, a small bag of potato chips and a can of pop. I had joined sixteen-year-old Irene and Asucena and fifteen-year-old Felix that afternoon to buy a snack. As we paid, Magdalena walked into the store; Irene and Asucena immediately greeted her with a hug and kiss. Magdalena, a petite and shy Puerto Rican young woman, had regularly participated in the youth program when I first began my fieldwork but had not been back to Centro Adelante for quite some time. Irene gently touched Magdalena's round belly: "Damn, girl, what you been up to!?" she said jokingly. Her cheeks flushing, Magdalena sheepishly giggled as she looked down at her belly. After talking briefly about Magdalena's due date and the sex of the baby, the girls hugged goodbye, and our group exited the store. We were silent as we opened our ice-cold cans of pop and slowly walked back to the center. Asucena, looking behind us to make sure that Magdalena was not around, broke the silence: "That's crazy, huh?" Tall and lanky, Felix also looked cautiously behind us and replied, "I know . . . she should've used some protection. Too late now." Irene, slightly nodding in agreement, added, "Guess some females just don't know how to handle their business."

I frequently heard the phrase "handle your business" in interviews with Latina girls and in my fieldwork observations. Generally, it was within the context of being challenged to take charge of a specific task or an affair in need of attention, such as confronting someone who had publicly offended you, addressing disagreements with others, or even setting your academic affairs in order. And, although, like many people, I had heard the phrase before, it seemed to take on an especially powerful meaning for the girls I spoke with. When they talked about "handling their business," as Irene did when she considered Magdalena's pregnancy, it was with an understanding that the stakes were especially high in the context of girls' sexual experiences. Sexually handling one's business, according to Irene and other young women, was certainly about safe sex in that it referred to the ability to effectively avoid pregnancy and STDs. They equated safe sex with the prevention of STDs and pregnancy through the use of condoms and/or "protection," a meaning drawn from the widely circulated

"Handlin' Your Business: Sexual Respectability and Peers" in *Respect Yourself, Protect Yourself* by Lorena Garcia. New York University Press 2012. Reprinted with permission.

safe-sex rhetoric available to them. But, as I delved deeper into the safe-sex discourse that they articulated, it became clear that the girls' vigilance against negative sexual outcomes was not just about their reproductive and sexual health. Sexually handling one's business was also about sexual respectability and the formation of one's sexual subjectivities as young urban Latinas. They expressed much anxiety about the implications for their social status if they failed to practice safe sex, pointing to another meaning that they assigned to safe sex. They associated safe sex with the kind of Latina girls they understood themselves to be and wanted others to see them as—sexually responsible girls. The girls I got to know were invested in being the type of young women who knew how to handle their sexual business, resisting being classified as "bad girls" because of their sexual behavior.

All young women are subjected to being placed within the good-girl/ bad-girl dichotomy that is designed to both socially control women's sexuality and to privilege men's sexuality. One significant strategy by which these girls negotiated their sexual subjectivity and their positioning in the good-girl/bad-girl dichotomy was to establish a symbolic boundary of sexuality between themselves and other "sexually active" girls, with the lines drawn around sexual respectability. As the sociologists Michéle Lamont and Virág Molnár explain, symbolic boundaries "conceptualize distinctions made by social actors to categorize objects, people, practices . . . they are an essential medium through which people acquire status and monopolize resources." Sexual respectability among Latina youth operated as a gendered sexual and racial/ethnic boundary formation that distinguished them from other Latina girls and from white young women and affirmed their identities as sexually responsible girls among their peers. It allowed them to participate in sexual activities and still be "good" girls on the basis of their constructions of themselves as sexually "handling their business" and other girls as sexually irresponsible. This symbolic boundary of sexuality was a tool by which they attempted to delineate their identities and status as sexual "good" girls. But this boundary formation process also restricted their ability to fully explore their sexuality, evidenced in their interactions with close friends, to whom they turned in their efforts to enact safe-sex practices and to claim sexual respectability for themselves. Their accounts of these exchanges

with friends point to how their constructions of sexual respectability and safe sex limited their engagement with their sexual desires and pleasures.

AVOIDING UNPLANNED PREGNANCY AND STDs

The majority of girls primarily understood sex as referring to sexual intercourse. Heterosexual-identified girls thought of sex as primarily meaning penile–vaginal intercourse, while lesbian-identified girls understood sex to include both vaginal intercourse and oral sex. And it was upon these comprehensions of sex that they developed their ideas about safe sex. Rolling her neck and pointing to herself with her right index finger, Celia explained, "To me, safe sex is about using protection like condoms 'cause, you know, you gotta take care of yourself." As if they were giving well-memorized answers to a sex education quiz, girls consistently cited the phrases "using protection" and "using condoms" in their interviews when asked what safe sex meant to them. The manner in which they initially responded to my questions about what safe sex meant to them reminded me of how children respond to adults when they are asked to explain what they will do if someone offers them drugs ("say no") or if a stranger approaches them ("don't talk to strangers"). Sixteen-year-old Norma, a thin and light-skinned Puerto Rican with an inviting smile, illustrated this when she asserted that information about safe sex was readily available: "Come on! Everyone knows that safe sex means you gotta use protection!" Asucena, who joined Irene at the store in asking Magdalena about her pregnancy, told me that anyone who did not know what safe sex meant was "ignorant." The devoted soccer fan insisted, "I mean, you gotta be really stupid or not ever seen anything, and I mean *anything,* about sex to at least know that to have safe sex, you should be using condoms or some other kind of protection." Like Celia, Norma, and Asucena, almost all the girls tended to equate safe sex with the use of condoms and/or "protection."

Latina girls were well versed in the ubiquitous rhetoric of safe sex that has unfolded since the 1980s. The safe-sex concept, initially developed in the early 1980s by gay communities as a response to the devastating impact of HIV on this group, began to be applied to HIV-prevention education campaigns directed at heterosexuals by the late 1980s, when it became evident that HIV and AIDS were not just a "gay man's disease." The adoption of the safe-sex concept as a strategy to curb the sexual transmission of HIV among heterosexuals was informed by encouraging evidence of gay men's behavioral changes, particularly the adoption of condom use. The safe-sex concept has been a valuable tool for disseminating information about the transmission and prevention of HIV and has been extended to educate young people on other STDs and on teen pregnancy through school-based sex education and public health campaigns and has even been incorporated into films, TV shows, and music that are produced for a teen audience. In a highly sexualized culture such as ours, the cultural visibility of the concept of safe sex is undeniable. In a sense, safe sex, as an idea and as a practice, is now part of the everyday ways we talk and think about sex. Like the adults around them, young people may not all consistently adopt safe-sex practices, but it certainly is now part of the vocabulary they use to talk about sex and make sense of their sexual experiences.

I often witnessed Latina girls draw on the rhetoric of safe sex in their interactions with peers. Late one afternoon, for example, Stephanie, an athletic Mexican young woman with deep dimples in her cheeks, was in the Hogar del Pueblo computer lab diligently trying to finish writing a paper on teen pregnancy for her English composition class. She wanted to do well on this paper, and I was helping her organize her main points. Her friend surfed the Internet as she waited for Stephanie because they were going to walk home together. As Stephanie tried to wrap up her conclusion, her friend impatiently whined, "Girl, come on! Just write something like, respect yourself, protect yourself, and use a condom, *y punto* [and that's that]!" Stephanie exasperatedly exclaimed, "I can't just end the paper like that!" "Why not?" asked her friend, who then turned to me for affirmation and commented, "It's true, ain't it?" I did not have a chance to reply because Stephanie instantly answered, "Yeah, but it's really more about respecting yourself, though. Just give me five more minutes, I'm almost done." With that, the opinionated high school junior turned her attention back to the computer screen and continued to type. Before printing out her paper, Stephanie asked me to look over her concluding paragraph, in which she stated that the "problem of teen pregnancy" had many causes and that among these was

the "issue" of girls not being taught enough about "respecting themselves." Elaborating on this point within her conclusion, she explained that a girl's self-respect also had to do with the respect she wanted others to show her.

The theme of self-respect surfaced frequently in the girls' talk of safe sex with me. As if reading from a public health poster, they matter-of-factly stated that everyone should have sexual self-respect and use protection. But, like Stephanie, they felt that it was especially critical for young women to be mindful of their self-respect. One key reason that they offered for this was the possible physical consequences of sexual activity, namely an unplanned pregnancy or an STD. Sixteen-year-old Soledad, whose mother, Aracelia, had found a letter she wrote to her boyfriend after searching her personal belongings, explained, "If I didn't respect my body and I didn't care then I would be one of those girls that just had sex with anyone and didn't really care if I got pregnant." Like the other young women, Soledad particularly raised concerns about the implications of an unplanned pregnancy. Adjusting her high pony tail, the soft-spoken young woman with an interest in teaching kindergarten added, "And I don't want to have a kid right now. I gotta do what I gotta for me right now, like finish school and get a good job. No taking care of babies for me right now." An unplanned pregnancy, according to the girls, would interfere with their educational and career ambitions, which, as discussed in chapter 3, were seen as within reach so long as they were sexually responsible and pursued these goals in a prescribed order. However, Latina girls also were concerned that an unplanned pregnancy would more immediately constrain their already limited freedom outside the home, a restriction they witnessed occurring to young moms around them.

Arriving early at Hogar del Pueblo for the weekly tutoring program, Marta and Yvette, both sophomores, were excitedly talking to me about their MySpace pages and trying their best to convince me to join the popular online social networking site. Marta, who regularly wore her long, black, and curly hair in a tight bun to meet JROTC uniform and self-presentation requirements, commented to Yvette, "Oh, I saw a picture of Ruthie's son! He's so cute!" Ruthie was Yvette's cousin, who was only a year older than she. Yvette, whose shoulder-length loose brown hair and hot pink acrylic nails stood in contrast to Marta's hairstyle and short nails, smilingly replied, "He looks just like her, right?" Sighing, she continued, "I feel kinda sorry for her, though." "Why?" I asked Yvette. She explained that Ruthie was pretty much "stuck at home" because her parents babysat her eight-month-old son only when Ruthie went to work at her part-time job at a local shoe store. "I think they're even more strict with her now that she had a baby!" she exclaimed, disapprovingly shaking her head. She added, "My parents would probably put me on lockdown, too, if I had a baby. So not trying to do that . . . they barely let me do anything now! I'm lucky they even let me come here!" Frequently, like Yvette, the young women expressed frustration with the close monitoring they received from their parents. As their developing bodies began to signal their emerging sexualities, the girls found that their parents responded by restricting how much time they could spend outside the home, which many of them already felt was limited because of their responsibility for some household tasks. The gendered division of labor in their households that they described set them up to take responsibility for cooking, cleaning, and/or taking care of younger siblings while their mothers worked outside the home. Many girls noted that male siblings were often exempt from household responsibilities. One significant way in which they carved out freedom for themselves was through their participation in youth activities at community organizations. For more than half of the girls I interviewed, this was the only afterschool activity they were permitted to join; it represented one of the few sanctioned spaces outside the home where they could move about without parental scrutiny and/or criticism that they were *callejeras* (street-roaming girls) or *en la calle* (on the street) too much. Thus, for the young Latinas I spoke with, handling their business, particularly the prevention of an unplanned pregnancy, was also a means by which they protected this small degree of autonomy.

The girls' avoidance of an unplanned pregnancy was also related to their perspective on abortion. Abortion, most of them believed, was not an acceptable way to sexually handle one's business. Dramatically rolling her dark-brown, almond-shaped eyes, eighteen-year-old Fabiola explained, "Girls can't be just like, 'Oh, if I do get pregnant, then I'll just go and have an abortion.' That shouldn't be how you think about safe sex . . . that you always have that resort there." Slightly more than one-third of girls firmly asserted that they were opposed to abortion, citing their Catholic upbringing.

Jocelyn, who had commented that her friend should have "waited" before having a baby, declared, "I couldn't ever have an abortion if I did get pregnant, though," adding, "I don't believe in abortion. That's the worst thing you could do." Other young women, however, talked about abortion without explicitly stating their position on it. Instead, they imagined out loud how those close to them would react if they were to ever consider or have an abortion. Soledad, who stated that she was not ready to have a baby because she wanted to focus on school and a career, speculated, "My parents would be real mad if I got pregnant, but they would be more pissed off at me if they found out that I had an abortion." And Inés, whose mother slapped her during their initial confrontation about Inés's sexual behavior, told me, "I don't know what I'd do if I was pregnant, but my boyfriend would never go for that [abortion] anyway." As evidence of her boyfriend's stance on abortion, she went on to explain that her boyfriend had not spoken to his sister for six months after she had an abortion.

When these young women shared with me their fears of an unplanned pregnancy and having to grapple with abortion as an option, none of them utilized the language of "choice" that has framed mainstream discussions and debates about abortions. But they knew that it would not just be their own perspective on abortion that they would have to contend with if they encountered an unplanned pregnancy. Juanita saw what happened to her older sister, who had a baby girl when she was a senior in high school. Juanita, whose heavily made up face made her look older than her sixteen years, said to me, "I don't know how they [parents] found out she was pregnant and that she was thinking about an abortion . . . they told her not to even bother coming home if she did that. I think she was scared of what they would do, so she just didn't do it." After detailing her sister's experience, Juanita avowed, "I'm just going to keep takin' care of myself 'cause I don't ever want to have to go there and even deal with that kind of drama!" Like Juanita, other girls expressed great concern about the possibility of having to negotiate the outcome of an unplanned pregnancy with those close to them; thus, handling their business meant that they had to work to avoid being placed in such a predicament.

Latinas/os have long been described as being anti-abortion, a stance that has been attributed primarily to their Catholic faith and to familism. However, recent surveys, such as a 2007 joint survey conducted by the Pew Forum on Religion and Public Life and the Pew Hispanic Center, suggest that a shift in attitudes on abortion may be occurring among Latinas/os depending on their generational status. This survey showed that, while 65 percent of first-generation U.S. Latinas/os believed abortion should be illegal, only 48 percent of second-generation U.S. Latinas/os felt the same way. One possible explanation offered for this difference has been the second-generation's movement toward assimilation, given its longer period of residence in the United States. However, these shifts in abortion stance among Latinas/os cannot be interpreted only as a product of assimilation, nor can it be understood solely as a reflection of mainstream pro-life and pro-choice discourses. As reproductive justice activists and scholars have long argued, the reproductive lives of women of color unfold at the intersection of various systems of oppression, such as patriarchy, heteronormativity, and racism. Latina girls' narratives reveal that their viewpoints on abortion are also shaped by their perceived vulnerability and by their ability to enact their agency—not feeling equipped with the skills and resources to negotiate abortion in the face of an unplanned pregnancy, they instead try to claim some control over their sexual and reproductive lives by developing strategies for practicing safe sex, particularly the prevention of an unplanned pregnancy.

Young women's concerns about an unplanned pregnancy, however, did not mean that they were dismissive of their potential risk for contracting an STD and the sexual and reproductive health consequences associated with STDs. Girls cited several different STDs they wanted to avoid in their safe-sex efforts, but they were especially apprehensive about HIV. As an example, Linda, who was the only lesbian-identified young woman who asked a question about same-sex attraction during sex education, said to me, "Supposedly I should be okay and not worry about HIV because I only have sex with girls. But I still worry about that shit and just try to be safe." Celia, who had told me that one needed to use protection because "you gotta take care of yourself," adamantly stated that she would never have sex without a condom, insisting, "I'm scared to get pregnant, but I'm scared to get AIDS, too. It's just not worth it to me . . . it's not worth my life."

The life that Celia pointed to was her physical well-being, but she also placed value on the social dimensions of her life. In other words, Celia, like the other girls, was equally worried about the social consequences associated with STDs, as well as those related to an unplanned pregnancy. This was made evident in the anxiety they expressed over the constant threat that their peers would designate them as "dirty" or "*sucia*." The term "*sucia*" literally means "filthy" or "grimy," such as when one gets dirt or mud on him or her. But the term can mean that one's actions, words, or thoughts are sexually perverse. Young Latinas fiercely sought to avoid this label because it made distinctions between "good" and "bad" girls, specifically marking some girls as infected with a sexually transmitted disease and therefore also as infectious. Lisa, who initially assumed that I was a reporter investigating Latina teen pregnancy, confided in me that she had recently taken an HIV test upon the unrelenting urging of one of her girlfriends. She had discovered that her boyfriend had been "playing her" (seeing another young woman), explaining, "My friend, she told me, 'If he's been with her, imagine who else he's been with?' She got me all paranoid, 'cause, you know, it was true and I know the girl I found he was messin' with!" Pausing for a minute and crinkling her nose in disgust, she continued, "She is nasty 'cause she's been with half the guys on my block. Everyone knows! I didn't want people thinking I was the *sucia* [dirty one] if he ended up giving me something . . . 'cause you know people always think it's the girl who was all out there." Inés, who had stated that her boyfriend was strongly against abortion, also conveyed frustration about what they saw as a double standard: "See, guys, they can get away with a lot of shit when it comes to sex. Not girls, though. We don't only gotta worry about getting pregnant but like other stuff, like people talking shit about us 'cause we have sex." Similarly, Margarita, who self-identified as lesbian, sat forward in her chair and angrily pointed out: "Everyone's always like it ain't no big deal for guys, it's what guys are supposed to do or whatever! But when it comes to girls, people are always trippin' and I hate that!" All of these young women felt especially vulnerable to the possibility of getting a bad reputation because of their sexual behavior.

Girls felt little control over whether others would bad-mouth them because of their sexual behavior and instead tried to manage how their peers interpreted any such attacks. For instance, Stephanie, who wrote the paper on the connections between teen pregnancy and girls' self-respect, asserted, "I don't like that someone can say I'm a ho or something because I'm having sex, but ain't nobody can say I'm dirty or that I have some disease." She believed that she did not deserve this designation because she used condoms. And Miriam insisted, "My boyfriend might tell someone I had sex with him, but he ain't gonna be able to say I let him hit it [have sex with her] without a condom. No one is gonna be thinking I'm a skank who doesn't respect her body." As reflected in Stephanie's and Miriam's comments, the young women anticipated that negative things would be said about them and tried to control what types of things could be said by pointing to their practice of safe sex. They reasoned that they may have engaged in sexual activity, but this did not mean they were "dirty" or "skanks," like some other girls, because, like wearing "badges of dignity," they made it clear that they embodied sexual respectability because they sexually handled their business. This, according to them, set them apart from girls for whom they did not want to be mistaken, namely girls that they saw as sexually irresponsible.

NOT LIKE ONE OF THOSE GIRLS

As a volunteer with the youth program at Hogar del Pueblo, I occasionally joined in on various field trips throughout the city. Field trips typically generated much excitement among the young people, who enjoyed taking excursions together outside the center. On one oppressively humid summer day, I sat in the back of the yellow school bus with Marta and two of her friends. The three girls were attentively looking out the window trying to see if they would spot anyone from the neighborhood as the bus pulled away from the center. Marta suddenly exclaimed in surprise, "Aww, hell no! It's true! She did get pregnant!" The group turned their attention to a young pregnant Latina who was slowly crossing the street. Looking straight ahead, she had not noticed her peers on the bus, or at least she pretended that she did not see them. As Marta continued to observe the young woman, she loudly commented, "And people always thought I would be the first one to get pregnant . . . whatever!" One of her friends quickly chimed in, "People can talk all the shit they want about me, but that ain't gonna be me." When I asked them what they meant, they glanced at one other as they considered how to explain their comments. Marta, who wanted to join the Marines after high

school, responded with frustration: "It's like everyone just thinks we're going to end up pregnant or something. It feels like they are watching and just waiting for us to fuck up . . . not me, I ain't trying to end up like that."

As they had done when they talked to me about their educational aspirations, the young women expressed a keen awareness of the negative perceptions others had of them as they explained how and why they wanted to practice safe sex. They referenced stereotypical notions of urban African American and Latina women and mentioned derogatory slang names such as "baby mommas," "bitches and hos," "skanks," and "hoodrats" when they described how others perceived them and expected of them. And they were resentful that they could so easily be classified in such negative ways, a sentiment that many of them had conveyed in our initial interactions with one another.

Seventeen-year-old Graciela expressed this when I ran into her at a local laundromat on a frigid Saturday morning. As the slim young woman quickly sorted clothes into three large washing machines, she glanced in my direction, rolled her big brown eyes, and explained that she was doing the laundry for her family, asserting, "But it's all right 'cause at least it gets me out the house for a bit, 'cause sometimes they all be getting on my nerves." Prior to this chance meeting, Graciela had never directly spoken to me, although she saw me regularly at Centro Adelante. After she inserted quarters into the washing machines, she walked in my direction to grab a *Sun-Times* newspaper that was on a seat nearby. Plopping down a couple seats away from me, she abruptly asked, "So . . . why do you want to interview Hispanic teenagers about safe sex?" Her question caught me off guard. I began to explain, but Graciela immediately interrupted: "But why? Who wants to know about that? I mean, people think that we should not even be having sex. And if they know we have sex, they think we all don't know what we're doing or that we're just hos." Somewhat satisfied with my explanation that I did not agree with such assumptions, Graciela shifted the rest of our conversation to her curiosity about what exactly sociologists did on a day-to-day basis. While Graciela and I did regularly interact at Centro Adelante after our laundromat exchange, she did not approach me about participating in the study until two months after our initial encounter. When we sat down for her first interview, she began by jokingly warning me, "All right, I'm going to answer some of your questions, but remember, you better not make me look like some of these girls who don't know what they're talking about and being baby mommas and all that." The strong desire that Graciela had to be differentiated from particular girls was echoed by almost all of the young women. Their meanings of sexual respectability and their assertion of their identities as sexually responsible girls were reflected in the way they talked about and categorized other girls.

As feminist scholars and writers have pointed out, girls encounter an omnipresent and powerful good-girl-versus-bad-girl dichotomy that sets limits on their sexual agency. On the basis of gendered expectations surrounding women's expressions of their sexuality, "chaste" women have traditionally been classified as good women, while "sexual" women have been designated as bad women. While the categories of "chaste" and "sexual" remain central elements of this dichotomy, as a socially created way to classify women, this dichotomy sometimes shifts to incorporate certain expressions of women's sexuality that may be more culturally acceptable at a given time. For instance, young women regularly come across both implicit and explicit messages that stress the importance of producing an "emphasized femininity" that is desirable to men, particularly the performance of sexy. Set within a heterosexual erotic system and a larger context of gender inequality, women may produce such a femininity to garner some privilege for themselves. In other words, girls and young women may deploy their femininity, particularly their heterosexuality, as a "gender strategy" to gain power and status among their peers. However, in doing so, they also run the risk of crossing the fine line between being a "sexy good girl" and a "sexy bad girl." Therefore, while there seems to be some room for girls to express aspects of their sexual selves, what marks good and bad girls can seem to change capriciously at any given moment because girls' sexual behavior is scrutinized in ways that boys' sexual behavior is not. One wrong move and a girl can suddenly find herself on the "bad" side of the dichotomy. Furthermore, the categories of race/ethnicity and class serve to differentially position girls within the good-girl/bad-girl dichotomy, in which poor and working-class girls and young women of color are assumed to embody an inappropriate femininity, marked by sexuality that is out of bounds. This becomes especially evident when one considers how we

typically discuss girls' expressions of their sexualities and the "interventions" we think that they need; concerns about white, middle-class young women tend to center on the implications of their behavior for their social and emotional health, whereas concerns about young women of color and poor and working-class girls concentrate on their sexual precociousness and their "culture" of teenage motherhood.

Latina girls were attuned to the good-girl/bad-girl dichotomy and, finding it inescapable, incorporated it into their identity-making repertoires. However, they elaborated on this dichotomy to make room for themselves on the "good" side on the basis of their sexual respectability, which, according to them, was reflected in their self-protective sexual practices. And this meant that there needed to be "bad" sexual girls if they were to be able to define themselves as "good" sexual girls and to be acknowledged as such by their peers. Like Graciela, girls who saw themselves as sexually handling their business set themselves apart from girls who they felt had not been sexually responsible. As they shared their sexual experiences and choices with me, they consistently and resolutely pointed to girls they were not going to be like, establishing boundaries between themselves and two specific types of "bad" girls in their communities: those they described as "hos" and "skanks" (sexually promiscuous girls) and "baby mommas" (teen mothers). They insisted that they did not want to be "one of those girls."

CONFRONTING AND CREATING RACIAL SEXUALIZED REPRESENTATIONS

Girls also moved beyond discussing the implications of these gendered sexual stigmatized identities for individual girls and connected them to larger characterizations of their communities. As I discussed in chapter 3 and earlier in this chapter, Latina girls were cognizant of how they were represented within the larger society. Elvia, who had questioned a sex educator's assumptions about Latina girls, shared how she thought others viewed her and other young women in her community: "I think people just think, 'Oh, she's Puerto Rican or Latina or whatever, she probably just wants to have babies really young or something.' People think that we are all like those girls on them shows, like on *Jerry Springer* or that *Maury* guy, trying to find out who their baby daddy is or talking about how they want to have a baby at fifteen." After a brief pause, the JROTC cadet with plans to join the Navy continued, "And I ain't saying that there ain't girls out there that are like that, but we aren't all like that . . . there are a lot of us who are not like that, who want to do other things with our lives and can take care of ourselves." Elvia, like the other girls, resented the assumption that she was sexually irresponsible because of her racial/ethnic identity.

Despite their recognition that such misconceptions were informed by racism, they still assigned some blame on girls they thought of as sexually irresponsible for these stereotypes. Camila, for instance, told me, "Regardless of what we do, white people are always gonna talk shit about us [Latinas], but people talk about us being ghetto and baby mommas and hos 'cause of some these girls who act like *pendejas* [idiots], too!" Thus, Latina girls also connected their sexual self-respect to the responsibility they felt for contributing to the integrity of their communities, articulating a politics of sexual respectability. That they were expected to do this was also communicated to them by some of the adults around them, as one of the Centro Adelante youth staff members did one muggy summer afternoon after the group returned from a trip to the Art Institute of Chicago. The staff member, a Latina in her mid-thirties, was angrily scolding the young people for their various misbehaviors during this trip. At one point, she turned to a couple of girls who were wearing midriff shirts and "Daisy Duke" shorts and chided them, saying, "And you all should know better than to dress like that. What do you think people think about us when they see you lookin' like that?" Then, addressing the entire group, she continued, "Remember, the young folks of Centro Adelante only look as good as you all make us look!" The girls, feeling embarrassed, just rolled their eyes and crossed their arms over their chests, obviously now self-conscious about their appearance.

The politics of respectability that Latina girls articulated was not grounded in a desire to emulate the sexual behavior of young white women, as was also evidenced in their interactions with their mothers when they were accused of wanting to "act white." In other words, they did not interpret the sexual behavior of young white women as the model of sexual propriety. Latina girls

had limited opportunities to interact with white young women on a regular basis, given that they lived in predominately working-class Latina/o neighborhoods. When they spoke of the sexual behavior of young white women, they relied on the images they encountered through the media, such as the notorious *Girls Gone Wild* videos, talk shows like *Jerry Springer*, and popular films. As Latina girls made sense of how and why they were hypersexualized within the larger society, they resentfully brought up what they perceived to be the invisibility of young white women's sexual behavior. Carla, who vehemently denied wanting to be like white girls when her mother confronted her about her sexual behavior, expressed this to me: "White girls can do whatever they want, hook-up with all kinds of guys, but they ain't hos?! Yeah, right!"

White young women, it is certain, would disagree with Carla's claim that they are free to do as they sexually please without repercussions. Feminist scholars have illustrated that interpretation of white girls' sexual behavior is also shaped by a good-girl/bad-girl dichotomy. But what Carla was also perceptively noting was how race/ethnicity mattered for how different groups of girls were judged within the larger society. Most of the young women I spoke with, like Carla, believed that the sexual behavior of young white women was not scrutinized, criticized, or pathologized to the degree that their own behavior was because of their white racial privilege.

Characterizing some white girls as hos, these young women asserted that they did not want to be described as sexually "acting like a white girl." I witnessed this play out at a Halloween dance hosted by one of the other youth programs in the West Town neighborhood. As they sang along with the lyrics to Lil' Kim's hip-hop song featuring 50 Cent, "Magic Stick," a mixed-gender group of young people, including Isela and Graciela, was dancing in a circle to the popular tune's beat. One of the young men in the group began to slightly push Isela toward Graciela, saying, "Come on, kiss her!" The other two guys in the group began to egg them on as well, chanting, "Go, Isela, go, Isela!" Trying to ignore them, Isela finally spun around and angrily shoved the young man, exclaiming, "What the fuck?! Get off me! Do I look like a white girl to you?!" With that, she walked off the dance floor, with Graciela following her. When I asked Isela about this interaction a few days later, the tan young woman with bright hazel eyes explained to me that she "hated" when guys behaved like that, adding, "They just love to see girls kissing each other, you know, like some white girls be acting, kissing each other, showing their thongs, acting like hos! I ain't no white girl." As a lesbian-identified young woman, Isela distanced herself from white young women as a way to resist her objectification and the commodification of her sexuality for the sexual pleasure of men.

It would be easy to simply interpret or dismiss the remarks of the young women I got to know as judgments or gossip about other girls' sexual behaviors. But an appreciation of the social location from which they attempt to construct their sexual respectability demonstrates that this behavior is more complex than girls just being mean to one another. Feminist scholars have broadened our understanding of girls' antagonistic interactions with one another by laying out the connections between these particular intragender relations and the gender inequality embedded throughout society. On the basis of interviews she conducted with over four hundred girls, the psychologist Lyn Mikel Brown, for instance, argues:

> Simply put, girls' treatment of other girls is too often a reflection and a reaction to the way society sees and treats them. While we may not want to admit or even believe it, girls and women—by their association with conventional understandings of femininity—have less power and garner less respect in our culture. . . . Girls' meanness to other girls is a result of their struggle to make sense of or to reject their secondary status in the world and to find ways to have power and experience feeling powerful.

With very few culturally acceptable ways for girls to claim respect for themselves, sexuality, particularly interpretations of sexual behavior, often becomes a central way for them to do so. Confronting gendered-sexual prescriptions for their behavior and racial sexualized stereotypes about themselves, the Latina girls I spoke with struggled to create respect for themselves among their peers and within the dominant society. They did so by defining themselves as sexual "good" girls, in part through their construction of girls whom they saw as not embodying sexual respectability. Unfortunately, these young women also inadvertently participate in their own subordination by positioning themselves as superior to other young women on the basis of sexual behavior. The

advantaged position in the good-girl/bad-girl dichotomy that they seek, predicated on appropriate gendered sexual behavior and race/ethnicity sexual difference, depends upon and sustains, as the sociologist Amy Wilkins notes, "the maintenance of a gender hierarchy that positions men over women and good women over bad women."

REGULATING SEXUAL DESIRE AND PLEASURE

Through the distinctions that they made between themselves and other "sexually active" young women and the safe-sex resources and skills they gathered through their friendships with other young women, the Latina girls I came to know fashioned their identities as sexually respectable young women. However, this identity-work had implications for their ability to explore their sexual desire and pleasure in their interactions with close friends (and, as I explore in the next chapter, also shaped how they negotiated safe sex with partners). This was particularly so for heterosexual-identified girls. References to sexual desire and pleasure in front of their peers, according to this group of girls, could undermine the credibility of the image for sexual respectability that they were trying to establish for themselves. Fabiola, a high school senior with a two-year university scholarship, expressed this when I asked her whether she discussed what she enjoyed about sex with her friends. She had just finished animatedly describing the condom tips her friends shared with her when I posed this question. Noticeably less enthusiastic, the honor roll student replied:

> No, I can't say we really like talk about de eso [that (referring to pleasure)] too much . . . sometimes we say that it was good, you know, sex. But I don't think we get into details and stuff . . . if I was like, "Oh, I like the way this position feels or this and that," they'd be all weird about it and probably talk about me when I wasn't around.

Yvette, whose aunt had reservations about the amount of time she spent at Hogar del Pueblo, responded to my question in a similar manner:

> We all just kinda keep it at that level where we do talk about sex, but just certain things. Like, I mean, it's okay to talk about having sex, but not what you like to do, 'cause then they might be there listening to you

and thinking you some kind of ho and maybe even talking shit about you behind your back.

Though girls conversed with me at times about desire and pleasure, the subject came up rarely and was even avoided in the conversations they described having with close friends, as indicated by Fabiola's and Yvette's experiences.

Nevertheless, they did not completely avoid the topic of sexual desire or pleasure in their conversations with friends. The majority of the girls wanted to be able to discuss this topic in more detail with their close friends and suspected that their friends also wanted to do this. Graciela, whom I had bumped into at the laundromat, communicated this to me when she discussed her friends:

I think we all kinda think about it, you know, but won't say it. It's there, in the back of our minds when we are talking about sex! Like I could tell we all really do wanna know more about orgasms and stuff like that, but we're either too embarrassed or scared to just bring it up 'cause you don't want your girls to be thinking you're a freak or something like that! We'll talk about this or that, like using condoms, no problem, but when it comes down to other things like that, we get all real quiet.

Finding it too risky to directly divulge their feelings of desire and/or pleasure to their friends, heterosexual-identified Latina girls instead cautiously wove this topic into more acceptable sexual discussions among their peers. Patricia, whose mother, Maria, felt that it was necessary for mothers to openly discuss sexuality with daughters, was one such young woman. Uncertain as to whether she had indeed experienced an orgasm during sexual intercourse with her boyfriend and not wanting to seem either too sexually inexperienced or too sexually eager to her friends, Patricia described how she had indirectly raised this issue by asking them about condoms: "We were talking about how guys sometimes act like condoms don't fit them and I was like, 'Hey, do you think sex feels better with or without a condom?' That's when some of them talked a lil' bit about how they felt when they were doing it, so that kinda helped me a lil' bit." Thus, some girls explored their sexual desire or pleasure in conversations they had with close friends about safe-sex methods, such as the impact of condom use on bodily sensation or decreased sexual drive as a side effect of the birth control pill.

Another key manner in which heterosexual-identified girls touched on their sexual pleasure and desire in these interactions was through the process of demonstrating the solidity of their relationships with their boyfriends, which for some of them was one of the grounds on which they established their sexual respectability. They made references to pleasure and desire to convey their commitment to their partner, most commonly expressed through the touting of the partner's sexual prowess and, occasionally, their own sexual skills. For example, Graciela recounted how she had responded to her friends' inquiries about the possible infidelity of her boyfriend:

I don't let them know all our business, like what he likes to do to me or what I do to him, but they know that it's all good between us. Like, I tell them that he's all good in that department, you know? My man knows how I like it! Or they'll know that I know how to treat him good, that I ain't no little girl.

Likewise, Yvette asserted to her friends the stability of her relationship with her boyfriend: "I ain't gonna be there and be like, okay, I did this and that to him, 'cause they ain't gotta know all that. But if they ask me if I like it, I'll tell them I do, because I do! He ain't got no reason to hook up with anyone else 'cause everything is cool with us when it comes to that." As illustrated by the experiences of Graciela and Yvette, this group of girls relied upon comments about sexual pleasure and desire to lend creditability to their sexual relationships.

Furthermore, rather than highlight their own pleasure and desire in these conversations with friends, they described their focus on their partner's experiences of pleasure and desire. For instance, Stephanie described how she and her friends sometimes disclosed to one another the specific things that sexually excited their partners:

I don't really know how we get to talking about it, but like just the other day, one of my girls was telling us how her man likes her to wear thongs, you know, stuff like that, and then everyone was like, "Oh yeah, well, my man is a freak, he likes this or that or I read in *Cosmopolitan* that guys like it when you do this or that."

In our interviews, almost all of the young women listed the varied sources from which they culled specific knowledge on their own pleasure and desire—the Internet, romance novels, magazines (typically *Cosmopolitan* and *Glamour*), movies, and videos—but this was often undertaken as an individual endeavor, rather than being done in the company of a group of girlfriends.

While many heterosexual-identified girls found it easier to discuss their partners' pleasure and desire rather than their own with their close friends, lesbian-identified girls described feeling less restricted in talking to friends about their sexual pleasure and desire. Lesbian-identified young women were more willing to elicit specific information about enhancing their own pleasure from other young women, mostly other young women who identified as lesbian or bisexual. A self-described "hard-core" salsa fan, Cristina recounted how she approached a close friend to inquire about the subject:

> Each time I get with her [her partner], I feel like I'm just beginning to learn about sex, it's cool, but it also feels so weird. I mean, she's the first girl I've been with, 'cause before her, I had only been with my boyfriend. But, with Melissa, I remember thinking, "Damn, so this is what it's supposed to feel like" . . . 'cause I didn't really have those feelings before. I was talking to my friend, she's been out since she was like fifteen, and I was asking her about different things she likes to do, just to kind of see what I might want to check out for myself.

As Cristina's experience illustrates, she actively sought information about her own pleasure through her conversations with a friend whom she perceived to be more experienced with this issue. Two lesbian-identified girls even recounted how they had tried to introduce the topic of pleasure and desire when hanging out with their heterosexual-identified friends. Linda, who had asked a question about same-sex desire during a sex education lesson, described the reaction she had received from a close circle of girlfriends when she attempted to introduce the topic of sexual desire after they had watched a show about the sexual lives of teenage girls on *Oprah*:

> Of course, it was mostly about white girls from nice suburbs and some black girls . . . but they made it seem as if girls just have sex to fit in and were being used by boys. We were saying that how come they don't ever talk to girls like us, you know, like Latinas from around here . . . then I was like, "And girls like to get their freak on, too, right? It's not just guys." Then they got kinda weird about it, like they didn't know what I was talking about.

Although Linda and her friends were critical about the lack of diverse perspectives on the popular talk show, the conversation focused on race/ethnicity and class, rather than on notions of gendered sexuality, even when Linda attempted to initiate a conversation about girls' sexual desire and pleasure. For many of the young women I spoke to, talking about pleasure and desire with friends was risky because it might invite speculation about the appropriateness of their sexual behavior. Open to her friends about her identity as a lesbian, Linda was already challenging heteronormative prescriptions of gendered sexuality and was more willing to critique such limited representations of girls' sexuality. But her heterosexual-identified friends' silence about pleasure and desire helped to ensure that they themselves would remain within the boundaries of sexual respectability.

CONCLUSION

The Latina girls I came to know made no apologies for their sexual interests and activities. Though they acknowledged that virginity was important to some of their female peers, they did not see themselves as having violated notions of proper femininity because they were no longer virgins. Rather, they believed that sexual respectability, a key element of proper femininity, was something they were still entitled to claim because of their self-protective sexual practices. In other words, Latina girls coupled sexual respectability and safe sex to negotiate their sexual subjectivity in the face of the good-girl/bad-girl dichotomy that, while seemingly increasingly open to women's expression of their sexualities, continues to be characterized by a sexual double standard that privileges men.

The power and pervasiveness of the good-girl/bad-girl dichotomy makes it extremely challenging, if not altogether impossible at this time, for young women to form sexual identities and subjectivities outside that dichotomy. As girls who engaged in sexual behaviors, the young women I spoke with knew that they were perpetually at risk of being defined as bad girls and therefore sought to define themselves and to control where they were situated in this patriarchal gendered sexual construct. They did so by establishing a symbolic boundary of sexuality between themselves and other "sexually active" girls that was predicated on sexual respectability; they set themselves apart from girls in their communities who they believed had not been sexually responsible and from young white women, whom they saw as sexually out of control. Thus, sexual respectability functioned as a gendered sexual and racial/ethnic boundary formation that distanced them from these other young women and affirmed their identities as sexually responsible girls.

Gender scholars have asserted that we cannot currently exist outside the gender order but that we can decide how we are going to participate in it, particularly how we will challenge it. While I agree that this is one promising route by which we can effect positive social change, we cannot lose sight of the constraints under which differently situated groups in our society must do so. For instance, the stories of the lesbian-identified Latina girls in this study provide further evidence of the need to account for the specific conditions under which different groups of queer-identified girls negotiate their sexual identities and, more important, the consequences that process entails for them socially, politically, and economically. The experiences of all of the Latina girls I spoke with provide insight into how they negotiated some of the gendered, sexual, and racial constraints under which they must form their sexual subjectivities. They walked a fine line between being good girls and bad girls, one riddled with gender-sexual and racially sexualized classifications of girls. Latina girls' meanings of safe sex and sexual respectability and the ways they connected them to gender, sexuality, and race illustrate how these categories construct each other and are relied upon to stabilize and destabilize them. With few or no resources and little of the support that would allow them to step back and try to determine alternative ways to proceed with their sexual agency, this group of young women instead attempted to make room for their sexual lives and experiences on the "right" side of the good-girl/bad-girl binary. In a sense, they expanded what it means to be a "good" girl. However, this also legitimated the very dichotomy that restricted their sexuality. Much of their sexual agency was spent on their effort to be able to claim sexual respectability for themselves, particularly by articulating who they were not going to be—those "other" girls. This means that there was little space for them to explore and articulate whom they wanted to be as sexual beings on their own terms and without positioning themselves vis-à-vis other young women, which, as I explore in the next chapter, also had consequences for how they negotiated safe sex with partners.

17

The Migration of Entertainers to Japan

RHACEL PARREÑAS

Amy turned eighteen years old not long after I met her. At the age of seventeen, while many U.S. students are worrying over college applications or drivers' license tests, at an age where anyone is considered "severely trafficked" under U.S. policy guidelines, she chose to leave her home to become a first-time contract worker in Japan. Amy fraudulently entered Japan with the use of another person's passport, but no one coerced her or forced her to do so. Instead, it was Amy who was quite determined to secure a contract as an entertainer and venture to Japan before she turned eighteen years old to help her parents financially. Because all of her older siblings had gotten married quite early, Amy felt that this responsibility was left to her. She wanted to work in Japan for a few years to raise the funds that her parents would need to start a small business to support them in their old age.

Amy grew up as one of the working poor in Manila. Her fifty-six-year-old mother was a homemaker, and her father, whose age she did not know, hardly made ends meet with his daily earnings as a driver of a passenger jeepney. Like Amy, many entertainers are among the poorest of the poor in the Philippines. Many had to drop out of school prior to migration. While some members of the middle class pursue hostess work in Japan because they have a passion for singing and dancing, most enter this line of work to escape their lives of dire poverty.

Many of the entertainers I met grew up having to pick through garbage for food, sell cigarette sticks in bus terminals, and clean car windows in heavy traffic. Amy peddled pastries at the bus stop for a local bakery. She considered migrant hostess work her most viable means of financial mobility. Without financial resources, most other migrant employment opportunities had been closed to her. For instance, she could not afford the US$3,000 to US$5,000 fee that recruiters charge prospective migrant domestic workers in Hong Kong or Taiwan. Yet, even if she could afford the fees imposed on domestic workers, Amy had no desire to become one, seeing their work as more difficult and dangerous than hostess work. For Amy, domestic work was made more perilous by the fact that it isolates the worker in a private home. Hostesses in Japan generally prefer their jobs over domestic work. Rikka, a veteran hostess, explained:

> Well, the salary is higher. In Hong Kong, it is only maids there. The contract workers who come back from Japan wear nice clothes, and the ones who come from Hong Kong have bags made of boxes. The women from Japan wear Louis Vuitton, and they have big earrings. The women from Japan, they have impressive necklaces, as big as dog chains. [We laugh.] The people from Hong Kong and Saudi Arabia, they are callused. The people from Japan, their hands are milky.

From *Illicit Flirtations: Labor, Migration, and Sex Trafficking in Tokyo* by Rhacel Salazar Parreñas. Copyright © 2011 by the Board of Trustees of the Leland Stanford Jr. University. All rights reserved. Used with the permission of Stanford University Press, www.sup.org.

While migrant hostess work is considered desirable, it is not easily accessible.

Prospective migrant hostesses must undergo a highly selective audition in which they have to compete with around 200 other women for a handful of slots to go to Japan. At the audition, which is held at various promotion agencies in Manila, prospective hostesses are not judged on the merits of their talent but instead on their looks. Prospective migrants do not have to sing or dance at an audition but must instead look more attractive than the scores of other women around them. The local staff of the promotion agency, along with a Japanese promoter who has flown to the Philippines for the sole purpose of finding entertainers to place at various clubs in Japan, physically evaluate prospective migrants at an audition, where women parade in front of them as they would in a beauty contest. The women do not have to speak except perhaps to say their name, age, and how many times they have worked in Japan as an entertainer. Return migrants are sometimes tested briefly on their Japanese language skills, but their skills need not be more than rudimentary. For instance, they at most would have to demonstrate that they know how to throw a compliment to a customer in Japanese.

Amy had to undergo an audition at least three times before she was finally chosen to go to Japan. She described her slew of auditions as a disheartening process, one in which she had to undergo a series of rejections that she only managed to survive with the emotional support of the woman who had designated herself as her "talent manager." Amy's manager basically acted as her job coach, teaching her how to dress and apply makeup. In exchange for her services, she would receive at least 50 percent of Amy's salary, evidently not only for Amy's first labor contract but apparently for her next six. On signing a contract to be one of her manager's "talents," Amy agreed to complete six contracts for the next few years; yet securing six job contracts to work as a hostess in Japan is not easy. Unless Amy would be requested at the end of her contract to return to her club of employment, she would have to go through another round of auditions in various promotion agencies in Manila. Amy would have to do so because migrant entertainers cannot work continuously in Japan; instead they must return to the Philippines between contracts.

Refusing to complete six contracts in Japan would incur Amy a sizeable penalty of at least US$3,000.

Amy could avoid this penalty without completing six contracts if she tried but fails to secure a contract at an audition, which is a risk that managers knowingly take when investing on the "training" of prospective migrant entertainers such as Amy. But Amy would probably have to go to at least twenty more auditions and do poorly, for instance not be selected as one of the top twenty candidates in any of them, before her manager would release her from future bookings. The point is that managers do not easily release entertainers such as Amy from their long-term contracts.

It would not only be Amy's manager in the Philippines who would be entitled to a portion of her salary. So would the promotion agency in the Philippines and the promoter in Japan. Between the two of them, they could legally obtain up to 40 percent of Amy's salary. For a number of reasons, a club in Japan technically cannot employ Amy; as I will later explain, the promotion agency in the Philippines and the promoter in Japan were her official employers. In most cases, a club would usually pay the promoter and promotion agency the salary of entertainers such as Amy prior to their arrival in Japan, but they in turn would withhold this salary from the entertainer until her very last day in that country. In fact, Amy had yet to be paid a dime of her earnings after having already worked in Japan for almost four months. Instead, she would not be paid the wages given by the club owner to her promoter until she completed her contract. It is common practice for the promoter to pay entertainers such as Amy at the airport when they are about to depart for the Philippines.

To survive, Amy lived off the tips she receives from customers, the commissions she received every ten days for her sales, and a daily food allowance of 500 yen, or US$5, that she received from the club owner. Some advocacy workers in Manila have said that the practice of withholding wages forces entertainers such as Amy into prostitution. Regardless, the fact that her wages were withheld not only violates Japan's labor laws but technically made her vulnerable to forced labor. Also leaving Amy vulnerable to abusive work conditions was the fact that her promoter had confiscated her passport soon after she arrived in Japan. The promoter told Amy that he would return the passport to her at the airport on the completion of her six-month contract. Having her passport and wages withheld not only discouraged Amy from quitting but technically made her an unfree worker.

Although Amy had not yet been paid her salary, she already knew that she would receive only US$500 on her last day in Japan. The Japanese government stipulates a minimum monthly salary of 200,000 yen (approximately US$2,000) for foreign entertainers, but the middlemen who brokered Amy's migration are entitled to most of her salary. Under the terms and conditions of her migration, Amy agreed to allocate US$1,000 of her monthly salary to the promotion agency and promoter who arranged her migration, while a US$500 monthly stipend was earmarked for her manager in the Philippines. These terms left Amy with a monthly salary of no more than US$500. Yet Amy knew that she was going to return home to the Philippines with a cumulative salary of only US$500 for six months of work in Japan, which is far less than the US$3,000 to which she should have been paid after the completion of her contract. This was the case because Amy had been paid US$500 of her salary prior to migration, and she additionally accrued US$1,000 in debt to her promotion agency, which compounded to US$2,000 due to the 100 percent interest rate the agency placed on it. Amy incurred this debt to cover various migration-related expenses such as the passport fee, medical exam fee, and so on.

Migrating to Japan is not free, as prospective migrants eventually learn they must pay the promotion agency for the dancing or singing lessons they must complete to qualify for an entertainer visa along with the cost of their passport, police clearance, medical examination, and other government requirements. Amy had borrowed money to pay for some of these costs. Most if not all entertainers accrue some debt before they go to Japan for the very first time, but most are not saddled with an interest by promotion agencies or managers, as Amy had been.

Disgruntled by her small salary, Amy admitted to selectively engaging in paid sex with customers. She knows that solely relying on her salary would not get her far. Amy did have certain boundaries. She had sex only with customers whom she found physically attractive. She also never received a direct payment for sex; instead, she received gifts. Amy told me that she engaged in compensated sex so as to guarantee that she would amass some financial gain from her time in Japan. However, still somewhat constrained by the moral stigma attached to prostitution, that is, the direct payment of money for sex, Amy wanted to clarify that she did not

engage in prostitution. Interestingly, some of Amy's co-workers still ostracized her, as most of them would not engage in any form of commercial sex, suggesting that Amy's actions are the exception and not the norm among Filipina hostesses in Japan. The nineteen-year-old Reggie, for instance, was saddled with an even larger debt than her co-worker Amy but could not be tempted to accept the US$100 tip offered to her by a customer in exchange for a French kiss. The third-timer Kay, who also worked with Amy, also could not get herself to go to bed with her frequent customer, despite his threat that he would no longer give her gifts of jewelry from Tiffany's if she did not have sex with him after a month. The actions of Amy raise the question of whether she is a "severely trafficked person," not only because she was under age but also because her salary reductions pushed her into sex work in the first place. Some would say yes, but Amy herself would say no and insist that it had been her choice to engage in sex with some of her customers.

THE PROCESS OF MIGRATION

In the last twenty-five years, a steady stream of migrant women from the Philippines has entered Japan with entertainer visas. These visas allow them to work as professional singers and dancers in Japan for a period of three months up to a maximum stay of six months. Because the government of Japan bans the labor migration of unskilled workers, the visas of entertainers restrict their employment to singing and dancing on stage. Their visas additionally bar them from interacting with customers because doing so would supposedly jeopardize the professional status of their jobs, as government officials fear that interacting with customers would mirror the activities of a waitress. Still, most if not all entertainers closely interact with customers. Most enter Japan knowing that their work will require they do so.

While the government of Japan worries that close interactions between entertainers and customers would threaten the professional status of entertainers as performance artists, the U.S. government argues that such interactions suggest their prostitution. In the 2004 TIP Report, U.S Department of State identified migrant Filipina entertainers as sexually trafficked persons, asserting that the "Abuse of 'Artistic' or 'Entertainer' Visas" is a vehicle "used by traffickers to bring victims to

Japan." Disregarding the factor of consent, the U.S. Trafficking Victims Protection Act of 2000 (TVPA) defines sex trafficking as "the recruitment, harboring, transportation, provision, or obtaining of a person for the purpose of a commercial sex act." This definition automatically renders any migrant sex worker a trafficked person, one who is assumed to be in need of "rescue, rehabilitation, and reintegration," regardless of their volition.

Migrant Filipina entertainers are susceptible to forced labor. Their vulnerability arises primarily from their relation of servitude to middlemen, some of whom have been legally designated to broker the hostesses' migration. These include (1) the labor recruiter from Japan, otherwise known as the promoter, who places the entertainer at a club; (2) the local promotion agency in the Philippines, who makes sure that the terms of employment for hostesses abide by labor standards in the Philippines; and lastly (3) the talent manager, the self-designated job coach of prospective migrants whose responsibility is to increase the marketability and employability of prospective migrant entertainers.

Due to the presence of migrant brokers, going to Japan from the Philippines is not a simple process of moving from A to B for migrant entertainers. It begins with a prospective migrant signing on with a talent manager, who then takes the prospective migrant to an audition at a labor placement agency in the Philippines, otherwise known as a promotion agency, and the subsequent selection of the prospective migrant by what is called a Japanese promoter at the audition. The Japanese promoter then places the prospective migrant in a club in Japan without much input from the club owner. Notably, the club in Japan is *not* the employer of the migrant entertainer, even though the migrant entertainer is technically working for the club owner. Instead, the Japanese promoter and Filipino promotion agency are the employers of the migrant entertainer. What explains this complex migration process? (See Figure 1.) Why the need for brokers such as the promoter or promotion agency? Can migrant entertainers ever circumvent this process and negotiate directly with the club, that is, their workplace, in Japan? In what sort of dependent position vis-à-vis brokers does the current migration process leave migrant entertainers? By addressing these questions, I unravel the relationship of entertainers and migrant brokers, specifically talent managers, promotion agencies,

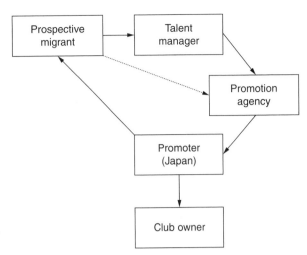

Figure 1. The Migration Process

and promoters, and explicitly describe the legally sanctioned relations of servitude that these brokers maintain with entertainers.

By calling attention to the role of middlemen in the process of migration, I am acknowledging the susceptibility of migrant Filipina entertainers to forced labor. My discussion establishes that a culture of benevolent paternalism shapes the migration of women, resulting in the state's impulse to support their social and moral values with protectionist laws, including minimum age requirements, a stringent professional accreditation system, standards of employment, and broker regulation. Protectionist laws in Japan and the Philippines—laws that emerge from the state's culture of benevolent paternalism—diminish women's capacity to migrate independently because they leave the women dependent on middleman brokers. The word *paternalism* in the most recent *Oxford English Dictionary* (*OED*) refers to "the policy or practice of restricting the freedoms and responsibilities of subordinates or dependants in what is considered or claimed to be their best interests." In the case of migrant entertainers, "their best interests" would refer to the need to protect them not just from unscrupulous club owners but also from the immorality of close sexual interactions with customers, in other words, hostess work. Yet, rather than deter abuse, protectionist laws actually increase the likelihood of forced labor because they diminish women's ability to migrate independently. This tells us that it is the principle of wanting to protect women, including from human trafficking, that likely results in their exploitation.

The History of Government Accreditation

Protective measures engender relations of unequal dependency between brokers and entertainers. The first of these measures is the Japanese government's required professional qualifications for entertainers. Requiring the professional certification of entertainers as singers or dancers supposedly deters the entrance of unskilled workers and reduces the likelihood that entertainers would engage in the unskilled labor of hostess work. For this reason, the Japanese government has imposed strict labor requirements that would ensure that each prospective migrant entertainer meets the highest level of professional skills for a performance artist. As an officer of the Ministry of Justice told me, "Only those without real talent will do hostess work."

Historically, Japan has given the Philippines the leeway to evaluate the professional qualifications of migrant entertainers. In 1981, Japan allowed the entry of Filipina entertainers without any work experience or training on the condition that the Philippine government would certify them to be bona fide performance artists. In contrast, prospective migrants from other countries were required to complete at least two years of training in the performance arts to qualify for an entertainer visa. With the discretion to determine the professional qualifications of their Japan-bound performance artists, Philippine government officials chose not to require them to fulfill two years of training. Instead, they required only that prospective migrants complete a much shorter skills training session at a government-accredited center. These training sessions could be as little as one month for singers and as long as six months for dancers. At the end of their training, prospective overseas performance artists must then be evaluated by a panel of judges and pass a skills-level examination to complete their certification; singers must perform two of five preselected songs in front of a panel of professional judges, and dancers must successfully complete a five-minute dance routine that shows their adeptness in a variety of dances including ballet, modern dance, and, sometimes, traditional folk dances of the Philippines. It is in the prospective migrants' vested interest to pass the accreditation exam. Those who do so qualify for

an entertainer visa. Those who do not must resort to purchasing a visa under the table. Purchasing a visa would likely place an entertainer in debt to her broker, which would only diminish her control over her labor migration. . . .

. . . However, the Japanese government stopped recognizing the accreditation program of the Phillipine government. . . . The Japanese government claims that the Philippine government does not accredit "real entertainers" because they suspect that most deployed migrants from the Philippines still do hostess work. Since March 15, 2005, the government of Japan has required Filipino performance artists to complete two years of either training or work experience in the performance arts outside Japan to qualify for an entertainer visa. Disqualifying most experienced entertainers from reentry to Japan, this new policy does not count the experience of singing or dancing on stage in Japan toward a prospective migrant's qualification for an entertainer visa. What it does do is aggravate the dependence of migrant entertainers on middleman brokers, who now have to train them not for just six months but instead for two years to ensure they qualify for a visa to work in Japan.

Migrant Brokers: Promotion Agencies, Promoters, and Talent Managers

The dependence of migrant entertainers on brokers is not only because of Japanese government accreditation requirements. Philippine labor migration policies also diminish entertainer's ability to act as independent labor migrants, as they require overseas performance artists to work with middleman brokers to secure employment in Japan. Migrant entertainers must work with three groups of middleman brokers: the promotion agency, the promoter, and the talent manager. The Philippine government requires hostesses to work with various brokers to protect them from unscrupulous employers and to ensure that their work conditions in Japan meet labor standards in the Philippines.

The Philippine government displays their protective stance over entertainers by requiring them to sign a contract of employment within five days of their arrival in Japan, after which this contract is registered at the Philippine Embassy in Tokyo. Interestingly, the official employer designated in this contract is not the club owner but instead the Philippine-based promotion agency and its proxy of the Japanese job recruiter, otherwise known as the promoter. By registering the labor contracts of entertainers at the Philippine Embassy in Tokyo, the government makes official that the contract, which is made between two parties under the jurisdiction of the Philippine state, is subject to Philippine law. In actuality, foreign entertainers in Japan are not protected by Japanese labor laws as they are not considered workers but instead performers. In this context, one could argue that establishing employment contracts within the jurisdiction of the Philippines, while providing some protection, only reinforces the lack of entertainers' rights in Japan. Notably, the employment contract could guarantee some protection for migrant entertainers by stipulating that a migrant entertainer could terminate her employment if subjected to "inhuman and/or unbearable treatment accorded to the Performing Artist by the Employer." The glitch, however, is the fact that the "employer" is not the club owner but instead the promoter and promotion agency, who rarely if ever visit the club where the foreign entertainer might face "unbearable treatment" every night.

In recent years, POEA has accredited 322 promotion agencies to not only train and deploy but more importantly employ migrant entertainers in Japan. Accreditation to become a promotion agency requires an initial capital of 2,000,000 pesos (approximately US$40,000), the operation of a TESDA-certified training program, and lastly proof of a special power of attorney granted by a Japanese employer to hire on its behalf a minimum of fifty overseas performance artists from the Philippines per year. In Japan, most clubs employ no more than twenty-five overseas performance artists, which consequently means most clubs *cannot* directly hire prospective migrants even through a promotion agency in Manila. To circumvent the minimum requirement of fifty hires per annum imposed by the Philippine government, hostess clubs in Japan have resourcefully turned to Japanese middlemen, that is, the promoters, who recruit the minimum number of prospective entertainers required of employers by the Philippine government and then assign them to different clubs in Japan, thus operating like the "body shops" that supply Indian information technology workers to businesses in the United States and Australia.

In his book *Global "Body Shopping,"* Biao Xiang describes "body shopping" as a system of subcontracting

in high technology. Body shops function as temporary placement agencies that assign migrant employees to companies on a short-term basis. Under this arrangement, the "body shop" remains the official employer of the worker and as such maintains responsibility for his or her temporary work visa, salary, and accommodations. A similar scenario of subcontracting occurs in the nightlife industry of Japan, where foreign entertainers are employed not by the clubs where they work but technically by the middlemen, that is, the promotion agency and promoter, who place them at a club in Japan. On behalf of the promotion agency in the Philippines, this promoter is responsible for finding an eligible place of employment for the entertainer, providing the entertainer with transportation to and from the airport at the beginning and end of her contract, and escorting her to the club officially listed as her workplace at the Office of Immigration in Japan.

Promoters arguably function like "body shops." Similar to Japanese promoters that supply migrant entertainers to hostess clubs in Japan, "body shops" secure their business by placing workers in multiple job sites. "Body shops" would take a portion of the worker's monthly wages, charge workers a placement fee, and if possible transfer the costs of migration (such as airfare and visa fees) to the prospective migrant worker. Likewise, Japanese promoters receive the salaries of prospective migrant workers from club owners prior to their arrival to Japan. They have also been known to receive a commission from club owners and to incur a portion of the entertainer's salary and charge her for the cost of her travel. No one monitors the activities of promoters. As middleman brokers, they could double dip and charge both the migrant worker and her prospective employer the cost of her airfare. While the handful of club owners I spoke with claim to have prepaid the travel costs of migrant workers prior to their arrival in Japan, many hostesses likewise maintain that they incurred wage deductions from the cost of their airfare and travel documents.

Promoters in Japan as well as their counterpart of the promotion agency in the Philippines ironically emerge from the impulse of the state to protect overseas performance artists from harm. The Philippine government legally requires prospective Japanese employers to guarantee a large volume of placement, that is, fifty individuals per year, so as to protect prospective migrant entertainers from fly-by-night operations or small-scale establishments in Japan, where the Philippine government assumes migrant entertainers would be more vulnerable to unscrupulous labor practices. The state impulse to protect entertainers also results in their dependence on promotion agencies in the Philippines, which must oversee their labor protection and ensure that employment standards in hostess clubs abide by Philippine labor laws. The legal mandate for entertainers to work with middleman brokers unavoidably heightens the culture of benevolent paternalism that shapes their migration. Their presence institutionalizes this paternalistic culture, which in turn justifies the need for talent managers as a third group of brokers to oversee the protection of migrant entertainers.

Although the state does not sanction the brokering of talent managers, the salience of this group of brokers unquestionably emerges from the culture of benevolent paternalism around women's migration and more particularly the migration of entertainers. The cultural assumption of the need of migrant entertainers for protection results in the prominence of talent managers. The primary responsibility of talent managers is to assist prospective migrants through the predeployment process. Although promotion agencies are responsible for ensuring that contract workers meet all the requirements of POEA for prospective migrant entertainers, the talent manager often undertakes this responsibility. Frequently, managers are staff members of promotion agencies, who assist prospective migrants through the migration process by introducing them to representatives of local promotion agencies as well as promoters from Japan, walking them through the training process, and ensuring that they meet all of the predeployment requirements set forth by the government. These include the completion of a medical clearance, a one-day predeployment seminar, singing and dancing lessons (including ballet and modern dance), and finally securing a passport and the required government certification for performance artists.

Entertainers are not legally obligated to work with talent managers, but managers see themselves as necessary to the migration process. First, they claim to give entertainers the "opportunity" to work in Japan under the presumption that entertainers would otherwise have no access to such employment. For instance, an entertainer is unlikely to know about an audition without the help of a talent manager. Secondly, they perceive themselves to be the primary "protectors" of entertainers. For example, they supposedly ensure that promoters do not underpay entertainers. Lastly, they develop the marketability of the entertainer, increasing the likelihood of her selection in an audition by cultivating her artistry and looks. For this reason, talent managers are quite prominent during auditions.

Wage Reductions

Middlemen amass significant profits for brokering the labor and migration of entertainers. Brokering entitles them to a significant portion of the entertainer's salary. Under Philippine law, promoters and promotion agencies are obligated to pay overseas performance artists only 60 percent of their salary. This means that Philippine law denies overseas performance artists the minimum wage stipulated by the government of Japan, which is 200,000 yen (approximately US$2,000) per month. Club owners usually pay middlemen the minimum wage stipulations of the government. If middlemen take no more than a 40 percent commission, then hostesses should earn at least 120,000 yen or US$1,200 per month. However, they do not. In fact, the standard employment contract that overseas performance artists sign at the Philippine Embassy limits their earnings to 100,000 yen per month. According to the standard employment contract, the minimum gross compensation of 200,000 yen per month could be reduced by a 30,000 yen food allowance, a 30,000 yen housing cost, and lastly 20 percent in income tax.

The frustration of seeing various forms of *legalized* deductions is the reason most of my interviewees refused to read the official labor contract that they signed and filed at the Philippine Embassy, claiming that it would only upset them to see their listed salary as more than what they actually receive. These employment contracts seem to be "just for show," many told me. They believed this was the case for many reasons. First, most knew they would receive far less than the stipulated amount of 100,000 yen as a monthly salary. They also knew that promoters do *not* provide entertainers with a food allowance and housing. Club owners provide both, and neither amounts to 30,000 yen. For instance, entertainers receive no more than 15,500 yen in food allowance per month.

In actuality, the earnings of entertainers fall far short of what is designated even in their contracts at the Philippine Embassy. They receive an average wage of only US$500 as first-time contract workers and not much more as experienced entertainers. Second-time contract workers usually earn US$600 per month, while a third-time contract worker could negotiate a salary of US$700 per month. Among my interviewees, a few very experienced entertainers, for instance those who have completed eight or more labor contracts, earned close to US$2,000 per month, but these were rare cases, especially as clubs tend to hire only entertainers with minimal experience.

Most entertainers had only a vague understanding of the distribution of their income. While they knew that middlemen receive a portion of their salary, they usually could not explain why this was the case, for instance often responding to my request for an explanation of the logic behind their income distribution with the comment, "It is just the way it is." This was the case, for instance, with Elizabeth, a former contract worker who first migrated to Japan in the mid-1980s. Explaining her past income distribution, she stated:

> It is just the way it is. See, our *papa* [club owner] cannot pay us directly. He really has to give our salary to our promoter. Then the promoter would give money to the promotion agency. So everyone gets our money. To be honest with you, we really did not know what happened to our salary. Our monthly salary before was $1500, but we know only $500 of that would go to us. We knew that $1000 would go to the promoter and promotion.

When I asked her what she thought of the financial distribution of her income, she gave an ambivalent response: "I think it is OK, because we probably would not be able to come here without them. But I think that they pay us too little. Work is hard." As the employer of entertainers, middleman brokers are entitled to a share of their earnings, a fact that does not always sit well with entertainers but one that entertainers have come to accept as the unquestionable norm and standard of employment for them.

One could conceivably argue that the situation of migrant entertainers does no more than follow the basic tenets of capitalism. After all, middleman brokers—as capitalists—own the labor of migrant entertainers and merely extract profits, or the surplus value, produced by this labor. As such, the relationship among promotion agencies, promoters, and migrant entertainers is sanctioned by the state. Yet the relationship between migrant entertainers and middlemen extends beyond a capitalist relationship and turns to abuse when middlemen fail to fulfill the responsibilities that entitle them to extract profit from the entertainer, which is to protect entertainers from labor violations.

Servitude

Middleman brokers ironically do not protect but instead violate the labor rights and freedom of migrant entertainers. They do this by subjecting them to peonage, that is, by binding them to servitude because of debt, and through indentured servitude, meaning work as "contractual but unfree" workers. First, promoters withhold the salary of entertainers until their very last day in Japan, literally at the airport soon after they check in for their return flight to the Philippines. In other words, promoters do not pay entertainers during the entire time that they are contract workers in Japan. Second, promoters deter entertainers from quitting by withholding their passports and restricting them to alien registration cards as their only proof of legal residency while in Japan. Third, entertainers must sign a legal document with the promotion agency in the Philippines prior to their departure, stipulating that they will incur the severe penalty of 150,000 to 200,000 pesos, approximately US$3,000 to US$4,000, if they quit their job prior to the end of their contract. Fourth, talent managers collect the passports of entertainers on their return to the Philippines and keep them until the entertainer goes back to Japan. None of the above conditions are sanctioned by the state.

Talent managers subject migrant entertainers to a longer period of servitude than other brokers. Prior to escorting an entertainer to her first audition, the talent manager usually binds the prospective migrant to an agreement that earmarks a sizable percentage of the entertainer's earnings to the manager, sometimes as much as 50 percent, in the next three to five years. Talent managers actually require entertainers to pursue and complete a set number of contracts, usually three to five, in the next few years. During this entire time, the manager would receive a percentage of the entertainer's salary. According to my interviewees, unscrupulous managers would demand a 50 percent commission, while "nice" managers would charge only a $200 monthly fee. The relation between talent managers and entertainers would be difficult to justify in court, but talent managers have been able to control the migration of entertainers by requiring them to sign blank checks prior to their departure or blank contracts, which they would later fill in with debt if they ever had a disagreement with the entertainer. As one interviewee told me, "You just sign the form." When I asked what form, she responded, "A blank piece of paper." Reneging on this arrangement with talent managers would usually cost entertainers a penalty of anywhere from US$3,000 to US$5,000.

One could argue that middleman brokers force entertainers to abdicate their freedom when they migrate to Japan. For some, servitude, regardless of context, would constitute unfreedom. This is because servitude binds one to the will of another person. However, servitude may accord material advantages that are otherwise closed to hostesses. Prospective migrant hostesses face two bad options of unfreedom: a life of servitude in Japan or one of abject poverty in the Philippines. Choosing between servitude and poverty, migrant entertainers evaluate their limited choices and make the "autonomous" decision to agree to a relation of servitude with middleman brokers. We should recognize that they do so as thinking persons, who evaluate the risks of staying in the Philippines to those of going to Japan with "critical self-reflection."

While one could argue that servitude indicates the trafficking of migrant entertainers, this assumption would risk the erasure of their will and desires; hence my insistence on viewing their migration as one of indentured mobility. In recognizing the limited choices of migrant Filipina entertainers, we should realize that freedom is more complicated than "the absence of restraints," as reasoned by the liberal thinker John Mill. Freedom is not ontological but procedural. Significant in our conceptualization of freedom is the aim for what philosopher John Christman calls a "content neutral" conception, one that does not judge or dismiss migrant entertainers for making the illiberal choice of servitude. When entertainers choose to be in a relation of servitude to middleman brokers, they take this risk conscious of their means of exit. For instance, many know of their option to escape their club and become undocumented workers. They also know that they can be free of their managers if they use another person's identity when returning to Japan. Amy was one of those who planned to do so.

While unable to stake a claim on her current earnings (hence her reliance on the compensation provided by her customers), Amy knew that she could walk away from her middleman brokers free of penalty because the name they used in her contract was that of someone else, and the passport she used to migrate to Japan also belonged to another person. This means that the person whom her manager could sue for a "breach of contract" was fictive. Amy's situation, and her knowledge of the loophole in her labor agreement with middleman brokers, indicated that servitude had not completely subjected her to the domination of others. Yet her choice to become subjugated did not justify her subjugation. Migrant brokers could choose not to bind entertainers such as Amy to a relationship of servitude, but the fact is that they do.

While promotion agencies and promoters subject entertainers to servitude for six months, talent managers do so for at least three years. While still bound to talent managers, entertainers must continuously pursue contract work in Japan. Pregnancy, marriage, and other such life course events that could prevent a woman from returning to Japan would result in a penalty. Rowena, who first worked in Japan at the age of fifteen, paid her manager US$3,000 to be released from her "contract" to marry a customer who had proposed to her, a man nine years her senior. At that point, she still owed her manager the completion of four more labor contracts. Eleven years later, at the time of our interview, Rowena lived in Tokyo with her husband and two children. Living comfortably as a stay-at-home mother, she justified to herself the payment of US$3,000 she made to her manager by looking at it as a reward, otherwise known as a *balato* (shared winnings), to those who helped her meet her husband. Her logic was that without her manager she probably would never have had the opportunity to go to Japan and meet and marry a Japanese man, escaping her life of poverty in the Philippines.

In general, hostesses suffer from the unfair distribution of their earnings with middleman brokers. Many complained to me that it was they, and not their managers or other staff members of the promotion agency, who were working hard in Japan. Most did accept the need to reward managers with a commission, but they also distinguished between what would be acceptable and non-acceptable commissions. According to most, a fair commission for managers would be no more than $200 per month.

Because most migrant entertainers seem to know little about their rights, it is likely that many just tolerate their work even if they find it almost unbearable. Entertainers, for instance, can circumvent penalties if they can prove to the appropriate Philippine government agency, in this situation the Overseas Worker's Welfare Administration (OWWA), that they had been required by the club to perform illegal activities. However, rarely did the entertainers I met in Japan turn to the government for assistance. An entertainer who was disgruntled about her work would usually escape her club of employment and become an undocumented worker before she would formally complain to the Philippine Embassy.

Talent managers justify the penalties they impose on entertainers as compensation for loss of investment. As one talent manager explained, "We have to feed them and shelter them. So we have to deduct that cost from their wages. . . . *It is not possible for a manager not to get half of your salary. It is because she is the one that struggled and worked hard for you*" (my own emphasis). Surprisingly, brokers generally see their actions as falling within the purview of their legal responsibility to protect migrant workers and for the overall good of these workers. They consider their presence to be necessary to the well-being of entertainers. According to promoters, holding onto the passports of entertainers while they work in Japan assures them that these workers are unlikely to escape and place themselves at risk of becoming undocumented workers. Withholding wages for six months means migrant entertainers are more likely to take back their earnings to the Philippines instead of spending them on frivolous items in Japan, a reasoning that suggests the infantilization of these workers. Talent managers likewise claim that they hold onto passports once migrant entertainers are in the Philippines only to ensure their safekeeping. Replacing a passport stamped with the accreditation of the migrant entertainer supposedly entails an extended process that could delay the return migration of the entertainer. Not many would agree with the logic behind the arguments of middleman brokers. In contrast to their perspective, nongovernmental organizations in the Philippines consider migrant brokers neither as advocates nor as protectors of migrant entertainers. Instead, they consider them to be traffickers who shackle entertainers, perhaps not physically but without doubt mentally, and coerce them to do their job for the purpose of their economic exploitation.

OTHER VULNERABILITIES OF MIGRATION

Protective laws should be in place to ensure the rights of migrant workers. At the same time, the government should also monitor the administration of these protective laws. At the moment, they do not; instead they give migrant brokers free rein to do whatever they deem fit to protect migrant workers. As such, governments are not in a position to prevent migrant brokers from charging exorbitant fees to entertainers and obtaining a disproportionate share of their salaries. Currently, there is no system of checks and balances in the labor migration process of entertainers. Because the current system designates complete control to brokers, entertainers are left vulnerable to exploitation. In addition, brokers abuse their power over entertainers by also subjecting them to debt inflation and "flying bookings," meaning illegal club placements.

According to my interviewees, middlemen regularly inflate their debt. Prior to migration, middleman brokers will make entertainers sign a blank document, referred to as a *listahan* (list) that they will later fill with the expenses the entertainer has incurred. Thinking that this document is conditional to their migration, many entertainers sign it because "the only thing in your head is wanting to be able to leave." Those who abuse the power of having a signed blank piece of paper compound the debt of entertainers by charging them twice for travel documents, imposing large fees for minor services, and overcharging them for the food and housing expenses that they have incurred during their training period.

Most if not all entertainers incur a debt with middleman brokers because middlemen usually bear the cost of various premigration expenses, including the training required of overseas performance artists. Only the expenses of airfare and life insurance policy in Japan are covered by a middleman broker, in this case the promoter, because the Philippine government mandates it. However, promoters can still get away with passing this cost on to the entertainer with salary reductions as they are without government monitoring.

To cover the costs of migration, entertainers usually need to borrow funds from their promotion agency or talent manager because many are members of the working poor in the Philippines. The largest expense incurred by prospective migrants is the cost of training, which is an amount unknown to many of them, and the cost of their accommodation during this period. In interviews, promotion agency representatives and talent managers claim not to charge for food and lodging during the training period of prospective migrants, or, if they do, they claim to charge no more than 2,000 pesos a month (US$40). On the contrary, many entertainers whom I met in Tokyo claim to have paid significantly more for their food and lodging prior to migration. They accumulated debt while training because they were often required to live in the housing provided by either their talent manager or promotion agency. Due to the varied expenses that a woman incurs to secure her labor certification as a migrant entertainer, many do not earn an income during the first contract stint in Japan. As Irene, who has completed eight labor contracts in Japan, states, "The first time you ever travel is payment for your visa."

In addition to lodging, the prospective migrant must pay for the cost of a passport (1,000 pesos); POEA seminar (200 pesos); medical checkup for AIDS, tuberculosis, and other communicable diseases by a government-certified medical agency (800 to 1,000 pesos); TESDA exam (200 pesos); and lastly the certification fee (500 pesos). The largest debt among my interviewees reached 200,000 pesos (US$4,000), but most debts range anywhere from 10,000 to 50,000 pesos (US$200 to US$1,000). According to a broker whom I interviewed in the Philippines, the average debt hostesses owe him is 20,000 pesos (US$400). Those requiring more than a year of training prior to certification amassed greater debt than others. While debts bind entertainers to talent managers and promotion agencies, rarely is the debt compounded with interest. The case of Amy, described earlier, was an exception.

It is not necessarily the accumulation of debt but the practice of debt inflation that bothers entertainers. One way middleman brokers inflate debt is by charging entertainers not once but twice for a service. This happened to many of the entertainers whom I met in Japan. They would pay twice for a passport, a medical exam, a certification exam, and other such expenses. During interviews, entertainers often laughed over this common practice. Rowena could only shake her head when she complained about having to pay twice for her passport. She recalled, "So you come home, and you are surprised that you have a debt. You paid for your passport before you left, and you pay for your passport again when you

come home . . . They charged me 10,000 pesos for a passport." Rowena was not only overcharged US$200 for a passport that should have only cost her US$25, but she also had to pay for this expense twice. However, signing that blank piece of paper made her feel obligated to pay. She explained that, at the age of fifteen, she did not know any better.

Entertainers who migrated with "fake" identities provided by managers and promotion agencies are those most susceptible to debt inflation. Almost all of them incurred a fee of 60,000 pesos (US$1,200) upwards to 100,000 pesos (US$2,000) for the use of another person's identity. To subvert Japanese legal restrictions, for instance age requirements or deportation restrictions, hostesses commonly use others' identity to go to Japan. They use the passport of a relative they know is unlikely to venture abroad to avoid the penalty imposed by middleman brokers. But while entertainers use others' identity to maximize their resources, so do middleman brokers. Many force their clients to use a "fake" identity that they have provided so they can impose fees on them. Promotion agencies would sometimes make it seem that the departure of the entertainer is conditional to her use of another's identity. This happened to Reggie, Amy's co-worker and, like Amy, a first-time contract worker in Japan. Reggie's use of another person's passport landed her a debt of 120,000 pesos (approximately US$2,400), which was slightly less than her projected six-month income of US$2,500. According to Reggie, her debts accumulated because she had used another person's identity. Reggie knew she was charged 60,000 pesos for her certification and 10,000 pesos for her passport, but she was unable to account for the remaining 50,000 pesos of her debt. She could only speculate that it had come from her housing cost; she had to live with the promotion agency for nearly four months while she auditioned in Manila. Reggie's story was complicated. She actually had been selected in two previous auditions, but those bookings got cancelled, holding up the use of her original travel documents.

Reggie desperately wanted to go to Japan and accepted the offer by her promotion agency to use "fake" travel documents when an opportunity to be deployed suddenly came while her other bookings were still pending and were holding up her original passport. Reggie did not mind the added cost of using another person's identity because she thought that her first labor contract would open the door to more contracts in the future. Reggie saw her first contract in Japan as part of a long-term investment. She agreed to the use of a false identity knowing she would earn only US$100 from her first contract stint but with the assumption that she would earn much more, at least US$3,600, from her second time around in Japan. Reggie's situation is a common one among entertainers as many accumulate debt nearly equal to if not more than the sum of their first six months of salary in Japan. They begin to earn from their work in Japan only during their second labor contract. In the past, promotion agencies would allow entertainers to spread the payment of their debt across two or even three work contracts. Reggie, for instance, hoped that her promotion agency would collect only US$1,000 of her debt after her first contract. However, promotion agencies are no longer agreeing to an extended installment plan to cover the debt of entertainers because they are unlikely to return due to the recent crackdown in Filipino migration to Japan. Plenty of first-time contract workers have consequently been returning to the Philippines without pay and without the guarantee that they will have another opportunity to work in Japan as an entertainer.

Entertainers do not always know of their debt prior to migration. In some cases, they accumulate debt unknowingly. This happened to an undocumented worker, Marie, who was shocked to learn during her last day as a first-time contract worker in Japan that she was going to be paid only US$100 for six months of work in Tokyo by the promoter because of the debt she supposedly acquired prior to migration. Marie could not explain to me the source of her debt, but I assume that it must have originated from the cost of her training and housing as she resided at the promotion agency for over a year while preparing to go to Japan. Not wanting to return to the Philippines empty handed, Marie decided to escape her club during her last night of work. She had since been in Japan as a visa overstayer for nearly two decades.

In their quest to protect migrant workers, the governments of both the Philippines and Japan have instituted protectionist laws that give middleman brokers control over the migration of entertainers. This in turn has diminished the capacity of entertainers to migrate independently. Bound to work with middleman brokers, they are unable to choose the club of their employment or directly negotiate the terms of their employment with clubs. Additionally, protectionist laws subject them to servitude. Some would argue that servitude would make all entertainers nothing but trafficked persons who are in need of rescue, while others would argue that it results in their susceptibility to forced labor and calls attention for their need to have greater control over their labor and migration.

THE U.S. ANTITRAFFICKING CAMPAIGN AND ITS UNIVERSAL SOLUTION TO TRAFFICKING

How has migrant Filipina entertainers' identification as trafficked persons shaped their experience of migration? Has it improved the condition of their labor migration? Has it facilitated their greater control over their situation? At the turn of this century, the United States declared war on its two greatest perceived threats to democracy—terrorism and human trafficking. Unlike the war on terrorism, the war on trafficking gained momentum not overnight but slowly through a series of hearings with bipartisan sponsorship, calling attention to the forced labor, debt bondage, and coerced migration of 800,000 individuals, 80 percent of whom supposedly were women and children, throughout the world. In these hearings, which culminated in the passage of the Trafficking Victims Protection Act (TVPA), much emphasis had been placed on the trafficking of individuals in the sex industry, which suggests that the "aspirational morality" of the antiprostitution movement and the quest to ensure the feminine respectability of migrant women had been strong motivations in the passage of this law. As the legal scholar Jennifer Chacon notes, "Stories involving sexual exploitation were, by far, the most common stories invoked during consideration of the Act. Some members of Congress seemed convinced that they were enacting a sex trafficking bill." As one of the bill's primary sponsors, Representative Christopher Smith, exclaimed, "It's time to declare war on sex traffickers."

The U.S. antitrafficking campaign fits a historical continuum in which the migration of women has been subject to moral policing by the state. What is different is that, in the past, the United States monitored the migration of women only within its own borders. Historically, the United States barred the entry of any woman suspected to be in danger of becoming a public charge, transgressing gender boundaries, and living immorally. The protection of women's sexual morality also motivated the antiprostitution and antitrafficking hysteria in the late 1800s and early 1900s, which culminated in the passage of the U.S. White Slave Traffic Act of 1910, otherwise known as the Mann Act. This law banned the interstate transport of females for immoral purposes with the intention of addressing prostitution and human trafficking. Interestingly, the intentions of lawmaker James Robert Mann are reflected a hundred years later in those of Congressman Christopher Hill. The only difference between them is the global scope in Hill's antitrafficking campaign.

Reflecting the global scope of TVPA, this law requires the U.S. Department of State to submit to congress an annual report—the TIP Report—that describes the efforts of foreign governments to eliminate human trafficking. Foreign governments in turn are pressured to submit records and reports on their antitrafficking activities to the United States so it can accordingly monitor and evaluate their antitrafficking efforts. According to the U.S. Department of State,

> [The TIP Report] is intended to raise global awareness and spur foreign governments to take effective actions to counter all forms of trafficking in persons—a form of modern day slavery. . . . A country that fails to take significant actions to bring itself into compliance with the minimum standards for the elimination of trafficking in persons receives a negative "Tier 3" assessment in this Report. Such an assessment could trigger the withholding of non-humanitarian, non-trade-related assistance from the United States to that country. In assessing foreign governments' efforts, the TIP Report highlights the "three P's"—prosecution, protection, and prevention. But a victim-centered approach to trafficking requires us equally to address the "three R's"— rescue, rehabilitation, and reintegration.

In its war on trafficking, the United States pressures other countries politically to implement policies and programs that follow its universal template of the Three *P*s and Three *R*s to avoid receiving a low mark in the annual TIP Report. According to TVPA, foreign countries must prohibit and punish severe forms of trafficking, punish so as to deter trafficking, and demonstrate sustained efforts to eliminate trafficking. To receive a Tier 3 ranking translates to social ostracism in the international community. In 2004, Japan was placed in

the dreaded group of the Tier 2 Watch List, a deeply embarrassing position to be in as one of only two G-8 countries along with Russia to be placed in this low category. One primary factor for the demotion of Japan had been the migration flow of Filipina entertainers, which the United States highly suspected to be a back door to prostitution. As the 2004 TIP Report notes, "It is reported that Japan issued 55,000 entertainer visas to women from the Philippines in 2003, many of whom are suspected of having become trafficking victims." Explaining the low standing of Japan in the TIP Report is the fear of the U.S. Department of State that "women and children are primarily trafficked to Japan from Thailand, the Philippines, Russia, and Eastern Europe for sexual exploitation." They supposedly come seeking "legal work but are deceived or coerced into debt bondage or sexual servitude."

The TIP Report constructs supposed trafficked victims as dupes deceived or coerced into debt bondage. This assertion simplifies their situation and allows the United States to pose the easy solution of rescue. However, the situation of migrant Filipina entertainers, and perhaps also their counterparts from other countries, is much more complicated. First, middleman brokers, including those who have been legally sanctioned to protect Filipina entertainers in the process of migration, and not club owners are the ones who subject them to peonage and indentured servitude. Second, these women do not suddenly find themselves bound to servitude; instead, the legal system of their migration forces them to migrate under this condition. Faced with limited choices for mobility, they agree to servitude prior to migration, as their departure is almost always conditional to it. They see servitude abroad as a much better option than their other choice of immobility in the Philippines. Currently the solution to their human trafficking advocated by the United States, which is their rescue, not only fails to address their condition of servitude but also ignores their preference to be left with the option to work in Japan, albeit free of the control of middleman brokers, and instead forces them to return to their life of immobilized poverty in the Philippines.

Perhaps out of pressure or maybe in agreement with the U.S. government, the government of Japan designed a solution that abided by U.S. government recommendations. As of March 15, 2005, Japan imposed new visa requirements for migrant entertainers from the

Philippines, in response to the recommendation by the U.S. Department of State for the Japanese government to impose the higher scrutiny of visa requirements and implement greater screening procedures "for repeat applicants and sponsors." The most relevant change in policy concerning foreign entertainers involves the evaluation of artistic skills and the disqualification of the Philippine government to evaluate the artistic ability of entertainers they deploy to Japan. Notes the government of Japan:

> It has been recognized that not a few people who have entered Japan with the status of residence as entertainer have become victims of trafficking in persons, in particular those who have entered Japan having fulfilled the criteria for landing permission by holding a certificate issued by the Government of the Philippines, which testifies that the holder is an artist, but as a matter of fact do not have capability as an artist. Given this situation, the paragraph below the description of the activities of entertainers—"The applicant who is qualified by a foreign national or local government agency or an equivalent public or private organization"—will be deleted from the [law].

This change in policy revoked the accreditation power of the Philippines and resulted in more stringent landing and resident examinations for foreign entertainers, with the most striking change being the extension of the training required of "overseas performance artists" to two years. Work experience in Japan does not qualify for training purposes. This means that an experienced migrant entertainer can become ineligible to renew her visa if she had received training to be an overseas performance artist for less than two years outside of Japan. As a reward for its efforts, Japan was taken out of the Tier 2 Watch List and placed back in the Tier 2 category in the 2005 TIP Report. Notably, the U.S. Department of State explicitly lauded Japan for its decision to curtail Filipino migration. As the 2005 TIP Report states: "During the reporting period, the government undertook major reforms to significantly tighten the issuance of entertainer visas to women from the Philippines, a process used by traffickers to enslave thousands of Philippine women in Japan each year."

In its implementation of an antitrafficking platform, the government of Japan directly responded to the accusation that Filipina entertainers are prostitutes by implementing more stringent criteria for evaluating their professional skills as well as those of other foreign entertainers. Increased professionalism, according to Japanese officials, translates to a lower likelihood of prostitution. However, the longer training required of entertainers means not the validity of their professional status (or the combating of prostitution) but instead contributes to a longer duration of training under the control of middleman brokers. Longer training translates to the greater likelihood of larger debts for the few still able to enter Japan and thus peonage. This suggests that the solutions posed by Japan do not necessarily prevent trafficking but instead put prospective migrants at a higher risk of it.

If we look at the solutions implemented by Japan to protect migrant Filipina entertainers from human trafficking, we see that the enforcement of stricter visa regulations has not necessarily decreased migrant entertainers' desire to work in Japan. This means that prospective migrants are likely to seek illegal modes of entry. Nongovernmental organizations speculate that more have done so as a result of the greater scrutiny given to prospective migrant entertainers seeking entry to Japan. Many, for instance, have resorted to buying fake marriage papers as a means of reentry. According to representatives at the Philippine Embassy in Tokyo, migrant entertainers who enter illegally with false visas are those most susceptible to abuse by employers. They note that these workers are more likely to visit the Philippine Embassy to report cases of trafficking. In his autobiographical account of his life as an undocumented worker in Japan, *Underground in Japan*, Ray Ventura similarly observed that those who migrate via illegal brokers are more likely to end up in servitude. Ironically, the new antitrafficking legislation encourages the illegal migration of workers, which in turn does not protect them from but instead leaves them even more susceptible to forced labor.

Across the globe, feminists have long fought for the greater protection of women from various forms of violence, including female genital mutilation, sex trafficking, and domestic violence. From transnational feminist efforts there have emerged particular norms regarding women's rights. In the era that calls for "women's rights as human rights," few would argue against the claim that the need to protect migrant women from abusive work conditions is one such norm. A protectionist culture over the labor and migration of women has consequently emerged and affected the lives of migrant women, including entertainers in Japan. For instance, we see a cultural collusion between the Philippines and Japan over the need to protect migrant entertainers. But these protectionist laws have not necessarily protected entertainers; instead they have diminished these women's capacity to control their labor migration and accordingly have increased migrant brokers' power over them. Protectionist laws have made the entertainers vulnerable to coercion.

The solutions that have been implemented to combat the trafficking of entertainers have also done little to protect them. For instance, the "rescue" of migrant entertainers has simply curtailed their migration, while the increase in their training requirements has only heightened their susceptibility to peonage. Why do the current solutions used to combat trafficking fail to address the needs of migrant entertainers from the Philippines?

Why do they perpetuate or even aggravate the susceptibility to forced labor of migrant entertainers? Current solutions are ineffective because they emerge not from practical design but instead from the passionate zeal of antiprostitution. Increased professionalism is supposed to lead to the less likelihood of sex work, but this comes at the cost of the entertainers' greater dependence on middleman brokers. This also tells us then that current solutions maintain the status quo because they uphold a culture of benevolent paternalism. In so doing, current solutions maintain the system that leaves migrant entertainers susceptible to forced labor. But instead of increasing their professionalism or barring their employment, hostesses such as Amy would like to be independent labor migrants. Only then could they remain gainfully employed, be free of migrant brokers, and be in control of their labor and migration.

18

The Sex Tourist, the Expatriate, His Ex-Wife, and Her "Other"

The Politics of Loss, Difference, and Desire

JULIA O'CONNELL DAVIDSON

The English word "desire" comes from the Latin *desiderare*, literally, to be away from the stars, whence to cease to see, regret the absence of, to seek.
—*Bishop and Robinson, 1998: 114*

[W]e go to the exotic other to lose everything, including ourselves—everything that is but the privilege which enabled us to go in the first place.
—*Dollimore, 1991: 342*

In Western discourses on "racial" Otherness, the notion of "civilization" as the apex of an evolutionary process of social development has often been read as implying a radical separation from and/or a corruption of "nature," and thus involving a kind of loss, even as it confers intellectual supremacy upon the "civilized races." A number of authors have drawn attention to the relationship between this sense of loss and sexual desire for the Other (Bhatacharyya, 1997; Dollimore, 1991; Mercer, 1995; Said, 1978), and it is also highlighted in Bishop and Robinson's (1998) compelling analysis of the sex tourist industry in Thailand. Bishop and Robinson (1998) explore sex tourism in relation to discursive traditions which have constructed "Other cultures as qualitatively and quantitatively different with regard to sexual practices and mores" (1998: 114). One of the things their analysis of 18th-, 19th- and 20th-century western texts that eroticize Other cultures illuminates is the tension surrounding the idea of "civilization." Paying particular attention to the writings of Denis Diderot and, to a lesser extent Jean-Jacques Rousseau, Bishop and Robinson interrogate a discursive tradition wherein a vision of Other cultures as closer to "the state of nature" serves as a foil against which to critique certain aspects of European morality and social development. They show very clearly how contemporary accounts of sex tourism to Thailand (provided by sex tourists themselves as well as other commentators) resonate with these 18th-century representations of Other cultures' sexuality as in tune with "nature" and "untainted by European morality" (p. 114).

Whether and how these accounts of sex tourism resonate with post-Enlightenment representations of European and North American "civilization" is less explicitly addressed in Bishop and Robinson's work, and these questions provide the starting point for this

"The Sex Tourist, the Expatriate, His Ex-Wife, and Her 'Other': The Politics of Loss, Difference, and Desire" in *Sexualities*, Volume 4, Number 1, pp. 5–24. Copyright © 2001 by Sage Publications, Ltd. Reproduced with permission of Sage Publications, Ltd.

article. Drawing on an ethnographic study of sex tourism in the Dominican Republic,[1] this article explores the worldview of a group of white European and North American male heterosexual tourists and expatriates whose sexual desires are immediately and transparently linked to a set of political discontents with contemporary "civilization." Their desire for the Other does not express a wish to lose everything, so much as a wish to reclaim what they feel they have already lost. These are sexually hostile men, and my aim is not to suggest that they are somehow representative of *all* European and North American heterosexual men or even necessarily of *all* male sex tourists. What I do want to argue, however, is that the model of human sociality they use to make sense of their experience is informed by a mainstream political tradition within liberalism. The sense of loss which lies behind their desire is not extraordinary or unique to them as individuals, and an interrogation of that desire therefore sheds light on European/North American constructions of Self as well as of Other. Above all, the moral philosophy of these men reveals something of the whiteness, maleness and heterosexuality of classical liberalism's sovereign self and the tensions generated by its partial and exclusive universalism.

SEX TOURISM AND THE DOMINICAN REPUBLIC

The Dominican Republic, which occupies the eastern two-thirds of the island of Hispaniola, has a population of almost 8 million. Historically, the country's economy has been weakened by colonial neglect, Trujillo's 32-year dictatorship, foreign intervention and, above all in recent decades, by international debt. In the early 1980s, debt crisis and negotiations with the International Monetary Fund (IMF) led to the adoption of structural adjustment measures. These measures did little to improve the lot of the ordinary people (according to World Bank estimates in 1992, 60% of Dominicans were living in poverty, Howard, 1999: 33), but they did stimulate the expansion of tourism, a sector which the Dominican government had been promoting since the 1970s. The country now hosts around 1.8 million tourists annually, most of whom are North American or European (WTO, 1997).

Many, perhaps the majority, of these visitors are "ordinary" tourists seeking a cheap holiday or honeymoon in the Caribbean, but the country does also attract "sex tourists." Defined as those tourists who enter into some form of sexual–economic exchange with women, men or children resident in the host destination, sex tourists are a heterogeneous group. They vary in terms of nationality, gender, age, ethnicity and racialized identity, sexual orientation and socioeconomic background, as well as in terms of their sexual practices whilst abroad and the subjective meanings they attach to their sexual encounters (Clift and Carter, 2000; Kruhse-MountBurton, 1995; O'Connell Davidson, 1995; Pruitt and LaFont, 1995; Sanchez Taylor, 2000). They also differ as regards how central sex is to their travel experience.

For those to whom I shall refer to as "hardcore" sex tourists, however, the desire for particular kinds of sexual experience (generally those which are expensive, scarce or risky at home, such as sex with multiples of prostitute women or men, and/or with children, or transsexuals and/or with racialized Others) is a conscious and explicit part of the motivation to travel. Some hardcore sex tourists find the pleasures associated with a particular destination so great that they eventually decide to migrate and settle permanently in their chosen "sexual paradise." Such expatriates (or "sexpatriates") often play an active role in promoting sex tourism and organizing tourist-related prostitution in a given destination (see Ireland, 1993; O'Connell Davidson and Sanchez Taylor, 1996; Seabrook, 1996; Truong, 1990), and this is certainly the case in the Dominican Republic.

Many of the hotels, restaurants and bars that facilitate prostitute-use by tourists in Boca Chica, Puerto Plata and in Sosua (the country's three main sex tourist destinations) are owned or managed by North American or European expatriates. The more entrepreneurial amongst them have discovered that the internet offers excellent marketing opportunities, and their hotels and bars now featured on several websites that promote sex tourism. For instance, a number of American sexpatriates living in Boca Chica have established strong links with an American-based travel club, Travel and the Single Male (TSM), through which their businesses are advertised. The club, which is one of several similar organizations run by and for male sex tourists, boasts some 5000 members, most of whom are white Americans. TSM publishes a guidebook (Cassirer, 1992) and sells club membership for US$50 per annum. Members receive a quarterly newsletter, discounts in some hotels and brothels, and most importantly, are provided access to the TSM internet site. This provides information on travel and prostitution in various countries around the world, access to softcore pornographic photographs of female sex workers from those countries, two message boards and a chat room for members to swap "sexperiences," views, news and handy travel tips.

As well as drawing on interviews with 31 sexpatriates and 30 hardcore sex tourists in the Dominican Republic, five of whom were members of TSM, this article makes fairly extensive use of materials published by TSM. The worldview of its members typifies that of hardcore male heterosexual sex tourists more generally (O'Connell Davidson, 1995, 1996, 1998), and their attitudes towards gender, "race" and sexuality are consistent with those expressed in other guidebooks and internet sites which promote this form of sex tourism (for instance, "Travel Philippines," "Brothels, Bordellos and Sinbins of the World," and the "World Sex Guide,") (see Bishop and Robinson, 1998; Hughes, 1998/9). The following extract from a posting on TSM's message board captures these attitudes well:

> Boca is a place of [European/North American] men's dreams and [European/North American] women's nightmares. It finds the heart of desire within all of us. Boca . . . is a place where sexual fantasies become commonplace. A place where you can go into your room with a pack of multi-colored girls and no one will blink twice. A place where an older man can convince himself that the young girl rotating on his lap cares for him and understands his needs more than the women from his homeland. It's a place where men come for lust and sometimes end up confusing it for love. It's where a man can be a star in his own adult videos. It's a place where a young pretty girl once offered me sex for a [plate of] lasagna. It's a place where every woman you see whether whore or maid or waitress, young or old, can be bought for a few hundred pesos. It's a place where you can have a girl, her sisters and her cousins. (TSM, posted 19 March 1998)

Though its organizers and members would not describe it as a political organization, the ethos of TSM is aggressively heterosexist, deeply misogynist and profoundly racist, and the club thus expresses and promotes a particular worldview, as well as a particular form of travel. Indeed, it implicitly, and sometimes explicitly, presents travel to "Third World" countries as a means of release from the restraints that are supposedly placed on the white male's self-sovereignty in the "First World." This form of sex tourism reflects a particular political vision of the West, then, as well as of the so-called "Third World." The following section considers this vision in relation to a mainstream discursive tradition of liberal political theory.

"NATURAL RIGHTS" AND SOCIAL CONTRACT

Classical political theory starts from the proposition that human beings are naturally competitive and self-interested and for this reason need safeguarding from each other. Hobbes (1968), for instance, holds that in a state of nature, each man would use all means available to him to possess, use and enjoy all that he would, or could, get. By agreeing (on condition that all men do the same) to a social contract that creates a political society or state, and by transferring rights of law-making and enforcement to that state, individuals can, it is argued, simultaneously retain powers of sovereignty over themselves, and be restrained from invading and destroying others. The legitimacy of the liberal democratic state hinges upon its role as enactor of laws that preserve and protect the "natural rights" of its citizens, "rights" which include possessing property, disposing of their own labour, exercising sovereignty over themselves, their own minds and bodies.

Carole Pateman (1988) has observed that missing from this story that social contract theorists tell about the origins of the liberal democratic state is the tale of the sexual contract. She argues that the pact through which powers of law-making and enforcement are transferred to the state is a pact between men, and is:

> a sexual as well as a social contract: it is sexual in the sense of patriarchal—that is, the contract establishes men's political right over women—and also sexual in the sense of establishing orderly access by men to women's bodies. (Pateman, 1988: 2)

Pateman's thesis thus suggests that the legitimacy of the liberal state actually rests on its role as enactor of laws which preserve and protect the "natural rights" of its *male* citizens, "rights" which are understood to include a right of access to women's bodies. Viewed in this way, it is possible to see how the extent and nature of such rights of access to female bodies, alongside the details of other "natural rights," can become the focus of political dispute. In other words, while in principle happy to enter into a pact with other men as regards access to women's bodies and other social arrangements, men might feel that the particular restraints imposed on male sexuality by a given state conflict with, rather than protect, the "natural rights" of its citizens. This was precisely the nature of Diderot's dispute with European moral and legal regulation of sexuality in the 18th century (for his criticisms of monogamy and the private ownership of women through the institution of marriage, see Bishop and Robinson, 1998: 120).

A similar case can be made in relation to "race," for as Mills (1998) and Puwar (1999) argue, the social contract is "raced" as well as gendered. In the sense that the myth of the original pact is a story about white men agreeing to transfer rights of law-making and enforcement to a political body, we can say that the legitimacy of the liberal democratic state is based upon and reinforces a particular racialized hierarchy. Again, the extent and precise details of white male rights over Others may be subject to dispute, even amongst those who are, in principle, reconciled to the liberal model of political contract.[2]

Here I want to suggest that hardcore sex tourists' political vision is informed by a classical liberal model of self, community and contract, within which naturally brutish men living in a "state of nature" are simultaneously free to conquer and at risk of invasion. They are "suspended between a fantasy of conquest and a dread of engulfment, between rape and emasculation" (McClintock, 1995: 27). The social contract of "civilization" is imagined as a release from this paranoiac paralysis, but only so long as it guarantees each man his "natural rights." If the "civilized" state comes to invade and deny individual men's "natural rights" over themselves, and over women and "racialized" Others, it loses legitimacy. This, I will argue, helps to explain the attraction that sites perceived as closer to "the state of nature" hold for hardcore male heterosexual sex tourists.

Rejecting the Authority of the "Civilized" State

In the course of interview work in the Dominican Republic, we have found that European and North American male sexpatriates and hardcore sex tourists are more than willing to hold forth on what is wrong with European/North American societies. The developments that trouble them most are those which they perceive to undermine a "natural" hierarchy that is classed, gendered and "faced." They rail against taxes, and most especially against tax-payers' money being spent on social welfare programmes for the undeserving poor (and more or less anyone who is poor in the West is deemed to be undeserving); they remonstrate against affirmative action programmes and/or equal opportunities legislation, as well as against divorce laws which empower women in relation to men, against women's entitlement to child support payments, and so on. Without prompting, they also bemoan the state's increasing incursion into spheres of life which they believe should be a matter of individual (white male) conscience, so that, for example, they take great exception to laws which compel them to wear seatbelts in cars and which prohibit drunk-driving.

For all of the sexpatriates we have interviewed, the decision to migrate to the Dominican Republic was at least partially informed by their unwillingness to accept the authority of their home state, and in several cases, their move was urgently precipitated by their active refusal of this authority. Sometimes migration represented an attempt to escape prosecution for drugs or other offences, but more commonly sexpatriates are tax exiles from their own country (indeed, there is a British-based organization called Scope, which provides members with information about tax avoidance schemes and tax havens as well as "sex havens"). A French-Canadian expatriate interviewed in Boca Chica is fairly typical of such men, if perhaps more unashamed than most about his desire to exercise white male privilege.

"Richard" worked as a real estate notary in Montreal until he pulled off a major deal in 1994. The Canadian government presented him with a tax bill for $200,000, so he put his money in a Swiss bank, bought a luxury yacht and left Canada for good. After cruising around the Caribbean for a couple of months, he ended up in the Dominican Republic, where he bought a bar. The bar, he says, does not make money, "but I don't need money. It's just for fun." Richard loves the Dominican Republic:

> Here, the white man is king, everyone treats you like a king. You see, no one has forgotten Trujillo. It was a reign of terror, and everyone here, well, everyone over 60, they still tremble when a white man talks

to them. . . . In Canada, we don't have so many blacks, but the Indians own the place. The whites are the second-class citizens in their own country because the Indians have all the rights now. Things are much better here, much better. This is really a racist country, everyone knows their place.

In his mid-50s, Richard is on his eighth wife, a Dominican woman in her 20s. This marriage will last he believes, because "In the Dominican Republic, women are slaves." They have to keep their husbands happy, or the men will beat them. So Richard is married, but free: "I can do what I want, and she can't say a thing. She doesn't have the right." Richard uses prostitutes and facilitates tourist-related prostitution by encouraging women and teenagers to solicit from his bar. He boasts that he is immune from prosecution by the Dominican authorities because he knows how to "do business" here:

> You have to understand it's corrupt from the top to the bottom. So you have to be in with the Dominicans, get a Dominican wife, make contacts, make some friends in the police and the military. You have to make your own security.

Richard's male bar staff are, he says, "fully armed," and this further adds to the impression that he views his bar as his own private fiefdom.

In interviews, hardcore male heterosexual sex tourists as well as sexpatriates emphasize contrasts between the burdens carried by the white male in "civilized" countries and the freedoms he enjoys in the Dominican Republic. A rather lengthy extract from an interview with an American sexpatriate and two of his sex-tourist friends (one of whom was a New Jersey police officer) shows how deeply disturbed such men are by legal and social changes which undermine what they see as their 'natural rights' in relation to women and racialized minority groups:

SEXPATRIATE: I'm 53 years old. Up in New York I've gotta screw 50-year-old women. Down here, 15 to 20 year olds, gorgeous women. . . . A friend of mine, he just threw out a 13-year-old girlfriend . . . [in the States] they've got laws. . . . I pay $1100 child support a month [to his American ex-wife] . . . 17 percent of your gross income for one child she gets, 25 percent for two, 33 percent for three. I've no idea what happens to men who have four

kids. . . . Women's lib in America in the United States has killed marriage in America for any man who has brains. I wouldn't even marry a rich woman. . . . [Here] they're raised different. Women's lib hasn't hit here. . . .

SEX TOURIST A: In the States, [women] hire folks with cameras. They go to bed with cameras. If they wake up with a bruise, they take a picture of it. Call it abuse. Possible abuse.

SEXPATRIATE: In the United States, if you grab your wife like that, and you yell at her, put a little black blue mark, just a little one, she'll. . . .

SEX TOURIST A: When you've got a goddamn female announcing the NBA basketball game. These females go into the men's locker rooms, but the males cannot go into the ladies locker rooms. Most of these girls are dykes anyways. . . .

SEXPATRIATE: Oh yeah. She can call the police and say "He hit me. Didn't leave a bruise, but he hit me." And he never even punched her and he goes to jail. She can take a knife to him, and nothing.

SEX TOURIST B: Yeah, no marks, nothing. . . .

O'CD: Is it here like it was 40 years ago in the States?

SEX TOURIST A: 50 years ago. The worst thing that ever ever happened in the States was they gave women the right to vote.

SEXPATRIATE: The right to vote and the right to drive. . . .

O'CD: Is this what people mean when they talk about political correctness in America?

SEXPATRIATE: You can't use the N word, nigger. Always when I was raised up, the only thing was the F word, you can't use the F word. Now you can't say cunt, you can't say nigger. . . . There's just so many words I could use against women in the United States. I don't like white women. . . .

O'CD: What about black women in the States?

SEXPATRIATE: They're Americanized. They've all got their lawyer's number tattooed on their wrist just like the white women.

Read as a commentary on the social contract between the state and its citizens, this interview extract, as well as earlier quotes from Richard, suggest that hardcore sex tourists and sexpatriates are only really able to reconcile themselves to the authority of a state which is overtly patriarchal and white supremacist. Legal measures which accord even basic rights of self-sovereignty to women or non-whites are perceived as attacks upon the white male citizen's "natural rights," upon his selfhood, bodily integrity and honour. This response is clearly paranoid, but I do not think it can be dismissed as merely *individual* paranoia. Rather, I would argue that it has its basis in the contradictions of the liberal political theory that informs their worldview.

Bodies, "Natural Rights" and the "State of Nature"

Wellman (1997: 321) has commented on the increasing visibility of whiteness and maleness in the contemporary USA:

> Until recently, the categories "white" and "male" were taken for granted. . . . The taken for granted world of white male Americans, then, was their normalcy, not their whiteness or gender. As a result, the privileges that came with whiteness and masculinity were experienced as "normal," not advantages. But that is no longer possible. The normal has been made problematic by people of color and women, who have, through their visibility, challenged assumptions once taken for granted.

Similar developments are occurring in European societies, and are, at one level, a logical result of liberalism's rhetoric of universalism. Yet these developments also draw attention to the tension between that rhetoric of universal rights and liberalism's basis in a social contract that is gendered, classed and "raced." For many white European/North American men, the extension of universal rights to persons of colour and women is experienced as a loss of male sovereignty and selfhood. The sex tourists and sexpatriates under consideration here are certainly not alone in their disquiet, but they are distinguished by the fact that they attach such an immediate *erotic* significance to this sense of loss. This perhaps reflects their unusually intense anxiety about/fascination with matters corporeal (such as the ageing process, sexual functions and organs, phenotypical characteristics), something which may well be explained as a function of individual psychology and personal history.

At the same time, however, this anxiety/fascination resonates with the post-Enlightenment discourses about "nature" and "civilization" that perpetuated a Cartesian and Christian tradition which views the body as part of the physical world that must be controlled (see Seidler, 1987: 94). Where men are imagined as victims of biologically given heterosexual drives, control over male and female bodies can easily come to seem like a zero-sum game. Men can only control their own bodies if they can command control over women's bodies and access to women's bodies is thus one of the "natural" rights that the liberal state must guarantee men.

Equally, where a "racial" hierarchy is assumed to exist in nature, self-control over the white body entails dominance over Other bodies. The political and social order must ensure that Others pay white men their "natural" dues, not just by suffering themselves to be called "nigger," for example, but also by physically trembling when the white man speaks. Ferber (1999: 40) notes that under the Jim Crow system, it was commonly assumed that "a white boy doesn't become a man until he has had sexual relations with a black girl," and it seems to me that this too can be read as the physical exaction of a "natural" due. It is telling, therefore that the sexpatriate quoted above conjured with an image of equal rights as inscriptions on the body when he stated that black American women have "their lawyer's number tattooed on their wrist just like the white women."[3] Fantasies about the "Third World" as closer to a "state of nature" have to be understood in the context of these anxieties and discontents about the political order in the West. It is not a generalized nostalgia for a mythical past that informs these men's desires, but a wish to reclaim very specific powers. Hardcore sex tourists and sexpatriates see the Dominican Republic as a lawless and corrupt place ("There is no law here," they say), but it is simultaneously described as a place where "natural laws" operate. Thus, white men are feared, revered and obeyed by their "racial" and gender subordinates, while "naturally" promiscuous Dominican women and girls are available to meet the white man's "needs" uninhibited by European/North American codes of sexual morality, Here, then, white men can shed the burdens of First World "civilization," even as they retain all its economic and political privileges and collect their "natural" dues as "civilized" white men.

This leaves them in a position to make almost unlimited choices, and so to exercise quite extraordinary powers of sovereignty (their description of themselves as "kings" is, in this respect, not so very far-fetched). They are relieved of the burdens of civic responsibility beyond those that they choose for themselves. It is down to them to decide whether or not they provide economic support for the children they father, whether or not to beat their wives, or to leave bruises on women they sleep with, whether or not to mete out racist abuse, whether to pay prostitutes for the "services" they have "consumed" or to simply offer them a plate of lasagne, even whether or not to sexually abuse children. It is, in short, down to them to choose whether to harm or help their "natural" subordinates (Brace and O'Connell Davidson, 1996).

For these men, the exercise of power over "natural" subordinates does not appear to be simply an end in itself, however. As the following section will show, they are as concerned to establish and maintain "proper" relations among themselves as they are to reinstate traditional hierarchies of gender and "race." Again it will be argued that their preoccupations are perfectly consistent with traditional liberal discourses about selfhood and sovereignty.

SEX TOURISM AND THE "COMMUNITY"

In Sosua, Puerto Plata and Boca Chica, there are networks of European and North American heterosexual sexpatriates and sex tourists who visit regularly and/or for lengthy periods, whose ties to each other are both economic and social. They variously provide each other with custom, business, employment and/or services and enjoy a hard-drinking social life together. They "hang out" in bars, they gossip, they complain about the petty hardships they encounter in the Dominican Republic, give each other advice, reminisce together and generally enjoy a sense of collective inclusion in what would otherwise be an alien environment. These networks can loosely be termed "communities," and sexuality is pivotal to sex tourists' and sexpatriates' sense of collective inclusion. Rey Chow's (1999) discussion of community formation and the politics of admittance can be usefully applied here:

> As the etymological associations of the word 'community' indicate, community is linked to the articulation of commonality and consensus; a community is always based on a kind of collective inclusion. . . . At

the same time, however, there is no community formation without the implicit understanding of who is and is not to be admitted. As the principle that regulates community formations, admittance operates in several crucial senses. There is first, admittance in the most physical sense of letting enter . . . to "let enter" is . . . closely connected with recognition and acknowledgement, which is the second major connotation of admittance. . . . Third, there is admittance in the sense of a confession—such as the admittance of a crime. Insofar as confession is an act of repentance, a surrender of oneself in reconciliation with the rules of society, it is also related to community. (1999: 35)

In the Dominican Republic, it is sexual contact with local women and teenagers which admits the male expatriate or tourist into the sex tourist "community" in the first two senses of admittance which Chow identifies. Take "Biggles," for example, a 52-year-old white Canadian sexpatriate living in Sosua. He first visited the country for a one-week holiday with a friend in 1990. At this point, he was not a habitual prostitute-user back home in Canada, nor did he travel to the Dominican Republic with the intention of sexually exploiting local women or children. Indeed, he had no particular desire to sexually experience the Other:

> I came down here . . . for a week and I stayed for a month. I came down with this guy, and as soon as we get down to the beach, he's got these two black girls, and I mean black. They weren't Dominican, they were Haitian. The blackest girls on the beach. And I said "no." I wasn't interested, I said I would never do that. . . . I'm not a bigot or anything but I just, I just don't, whatever, whatever. But hell, within the next couple of days I went with this girl and it was fantastic. . . . It was something I'd never done before. I don't know, I just thought, "Give it a try."

Biggles penetrated the "black girl" and entered the sex tourist "scene." So pleasing did he find the subculture of hardcore sex tourism that, over the next six years, he made repeated and regular visits to Sosua, always engaging in prostitute-use. In 1996, he decided to retire there, and his life now revolves entirely around this subculture.

Dominican women and girl's bodies are also often transacted between sexpatriates who own bar-brothels, or who make a living by procuring prostitutes for male tourists, and these exchanges also serve to establish and cement relationships between sexpatriates and sex tourists. Thus, for example, a 63-year-old white American expatriate who owns a beachside bar in Boca Chica explains that he gets "a lot of steady customers, a lot of guys that come here three, four, six, seven times a year." His bar, and photographs of its female bar staff, feature in the information on the Dominican Republic on TSM's website, and the owner is frequently referred to in the "chat" between members. He estimates that between 15 to 20 TSM members arrive at his bar each month and other American sexpatriates and sex tourists interviewed in Boca Chica described him as "the biggest pimp in town." In facilitating tourists' "entry" into Dominican women and teenagers, he simultaneously admits them to the sex tourist "community." They become "one of the guys."

Sexual contact with Dominican women and girls is also central to admittance in the sense that it provides the basis for recognition and acknowledgement between men. As one TSM member explains in a message board posting, he spent a great deal of time in his hotel bar in Boca Chica "bullshitting with guys" and "making friends":

We are all there for the same carnal reason—[the] hotel is probably 95% single men—and a typical opening conversation would be—pointing at one of the girls—"have you been blown by her yet?"—"no, but I hear from so and so that she gives a great one." It makes for great comradery (TSM, posted 26 September 1997).

Another posting reads:

Day 2. . . . I must comment on the fantastic camaraderie that was nurtured between Worm, Omega, Voodoo Chile and yours truly. It was just a whole lot of fun the whole time. And later we ran into Ronnie, Bogey, Pat, Newt, Jann, Digger, Woolf, JD and probably a couple more TSMers I can't remember. A quick breakfast . . . then down to . . . the beach . . . for a day in Paradise. Before I knew it, a large-breasted black woman in tight attire was grinning at me and massaging my back . . . At one point, I headed into the bathroom and before I knew it she was standing behind me at the toilet, trying to grab my dick. She wanted to suckee suckee me right then and there. (TSM, posted 11 January 1999)

And another:

[The taxi] took me to the now infamous Ronnie's, upon entering I met some of the TSM crew. Omega (also known as Obi-wan, for his willingness to provide his invaluable wisdom to TSM newbies such as myself) . . . and of course Ronnie. After speaking to them for perhaps 5 minutes, I notice a cute girl enter the bar. She locked her gaze on me and promptly began to suck a bottle in a way not usually seen. Needless to say she had my undivided attention. I . . . inquire about her and whether Omega had any advice . . . I proceeded to throw her over my shoulder and carry her out of the bar, [back] to the hotel, and . . . the fun was underway. (TSM, posted 10 January 1999)

In these and other similar postings, Boca Chica is constructed as a sexual playground for European/North American men, and Dominican women and girls as play-objects shared amongst them. The hardcore sex tourist's play-*mates,* that is, the subjects who give recognition and acknowledgement, are other European/North American men.

It is also worth noting that because admittance is predicated upon a common European/North American masculine identity and consensus about sexuality, it tends to nullify differences between sex tourists and sexpatriates in terms of age and class identity. Men in their 70s bond with men in their 20s and 30s; wealthier sexpatriates who own businesses socialize with the relatively poor sexpatriates who work for them; sex tourists who are police officers or scaffolders back home "have a whole lot of fun" with those who are senior accountants or company directors. The sense of group belonging comes from sharing the "natural" privileges of masculinity and whiteness, and sex tourists/sexpatriates enjoy the idea that they have secured a competitive advantage not just over local men, but also over the European/North American men who remain at home. As a 71-year-old American sex tourist told us:

We all like to look like heroes. . . . Would I rather have a 70-year-old woman or an 18-year-old or a 25-year-old? Please. . . . You'll find very few men . . . that has done what I've done in the last 50 years. Right now they're all sitting in Hyde Park, feeding the pigeons.

This man is reliant on his sex tourist and sexpatriate friends to affirm this pleasing image. What good is heroically fucking 18-year-olds while your contemporaries feed pigeons in a park if nobody of equal worth recognises this mark of your distinction?

Finally, I would argue that the hardcore sex tourist's impulse to divulge the details of his sexual experience (in conversations with other sex tourists/sexpatriates and in postings on internet sites) can be read as an attempt at group formation through admittance in Chow's third sense, that of confession:

> Little Ingris. . . . She isn't totally pro yet. I had her 3 times—my limit on a girl. . . . She is so tight that I broke 5 condoms on her and she was crying out something I've never heard before "*Tu Lance, ai ai*" over and over. . . . [Another] girl, broke 2 condoms on her. . . . After several screws I got her to do a posing session and used some of my toys with her, thank god 4 KY jelly. . . . I have some good poses of her for TSM.

I do not think such passages can be interpreted as acts of repentance, but they could be read as attempts at reconciliation with the rules of a subculture that bases membership and identity upon a shared willingness to reduce women and girls to sexual objects and to flout what are seen as repressive social strictures on heterosexual male sexuality (hardcore sex tourists fondly describe themselves as "bad boys"). In repeatedly confessing to his sexual transgressions, the sex tourist demonstrates himself to be "one of the guys." Homosexual acts cannot be confessed, of course, and male homosexuals are not admitted to the heterosexual male sex tourist "community." As one interviewee in Boca Chica put it, "Gays do come down here, but we don't have nothing to do with them."[4]

Thus far, I have been emphasizing the fact that "racially" Other female bodies serve as vehicles for relationships between European/North American male heterosexual sex tourists and sexpatriates in the Dominican Republic. Female bodies are exchanged, sometimes for money (as in the case of sexpatriates who organize prostitution), sometimes as free gifts (as in cases where sex tourists or sexpatriates "recommend" or share a woman/girl), and, as Rubin has observed, where "it is women who are being transacted, then it is the men who give and take them who are linked, the woman being a conduit of a relationship rather than a partner to it" (1975: 174).

It should also be clear that a hardcore sex tourist's worldview is nothing if not contradictory. They buy into overtly denigrating racisms, but women of colour are their chosen sexual objects. They say that women are the weaker sex, but berate them for the power they supposedly exercise over men. They are virulent homophobes,

but are endlessly fascinated by the sex of other men. Let me now examine their urge to forge relationships with each other in relation to these contradictions and those implicit in the model of human sociality they accept.

DIFFERENCE AND INVASION

Late-19th-century and early-20th-century scientific discourses on race, gender and sexuality informed and buttressed one another (Somerville, 1997), and their legacy is conspicuous in overtly racist politics, which are invariably also sexist and homophobic politics. To the extent that biologically essentialist models of difference naturalize social and political inequalities based on gender and sexual orientation as well as "race," they can perhaps be said to inform an internally consistent worldview. But this *menage à trois* does not always appear to be a happy one. Indeed, essentialist understandings of gender and sexual difference seemingly pose huge problems for those whose imaginary communities are premised on notions of "race" sameness, problems which can become particularly acute during periods of social upheaval or change.[5]

The contradiction between men's perceived dependency upon women as mothers of "the race" and their dread of women's physical difference may be most visible in "racial" supremacist politics, but similar problems dog any model of community formation within which men establish links with each other through the exchange of women (see Chow, 1999). Wherever the traditional masculinist view that equates women with sex is accepted, women's relation to "the community" is necessarily difficult and ambiguous. Female sexuality and sexual difference is the key to maintaining the boundaries of community, not simply in the sense that women biologically reproduce its members, but also in the sense that, as objects of exchange between men, women serve to reproduce social links between the male members of the community. The ultimate taboo is thus the taboo against the sameness of men and women, for women's difference is vital to community formation (Chow, 1999; Freud, 1985; Rubin, 1975).

At the same time, however, female sexuality poses a profound threat to the boundaries of community. Since women are not actually objects, but only treated as such, their potential sexual agency is extremely dangerous. They could refuse:

> . . . their traditional position as "gifts," as the conduits and vehicles that facilitate social relations and enable group identity, [and] actually *give themselves*. By giving themselves, such women enter social relationships as active partners in the production of meanings rather than simply as the bearers of those meanings. (Chow, 1999:47–8)

If women break the taboo against the sameness of men and women by assuming sexual agency, they "no longer represent reliable conduits for men's relationships with each other and there is further a risk of boundary loss through acts of miscegenation" (Chow, 1999: 49). These anxieties are central to the worldview of hardcore male heterosexual sex tourists and sexpatriates. For these men, the legal construction of women as men's equals, combined with shifts to the traditional gendered division of labour, has broken this ultimate taboo. European/North American women claim male territory (they announce the NBA basketball game, they go into the men's locker rooms) and male rights (they call the police when beaten, they demand child support payments from absent fathers). They can no longer simply be treated as objects of exchange, and this has ramifications not just for European/North American men's relationships with European/North American women, but also for European/North American men's relationships with each other.

Without the certainty of sexual difference, all the laws and bonds of community that were based upon it are in jeopardy. As active agents in the production of community, women cannot be relied upon to reproduce a political order that these men are willing to contract into, indeed, they are likely to push for laws and law enforcement that conflict with, rather than protect, men's "natural rights." For hardcore sex tourists and sexpatriates, European/North American women's transgression of the fundamental taboo against the sameness of men and women also raises the spectre of another disastrous boundary loss, that between heterosexuality and homosexuality. Bishop and Robinson quote from a novel written by a Canadian expatriate who lives in Bangkok—"fucking a white woman is a step away from homosexuality" (Moore, 1993:107, cited in Bishop and Robinson, 1998: 167), and the same sentiment is reproduced in TSM postings on the subject of white women.

This draws attention to the relationship between taboos against the sameness of men and women and against homosexuality, and traditional liberal discourses about selfhood and sovereignty. Brace's (1997) discussion of Hobbes' vision of the "territorial" self is particularly useful here. Hobbes was preoccupied by the idea of a self that is vulnerable to invasion, a self "bounded by a hostile world it must seek to conquer and restrain":

> Hobbes encloses the self, the "rational inside" within a fortress, buttressed by our own sense of esteem and relating to others as outsiders or as absentees. Each person becomes a potential invader and a potential resistance fighter. We understand and experience our selfhood as enclosed, in need of protection against intrusion and invasion. . . . Each person may be a bounded sphere, but the boundary may prove fragile. Hobbes exhorts us to look at fully grown men "and consider how brittle the frame of our humane body is" . . . Hobbes's emphasis on the brittleness, the fragility of the human body is . . . central to male anxiety about boundary loss. (1997: 143–4)

Brace goes on to note that the Hobbesian self, like McClintock's (1995) colonial self, is characterized by "dread of catastrophic boundary *loss* (implosion), associated with fears of impotence and infantilization and attended by an *excess* of boundary order and fantasies of unlimited power" (McClintock, 1995: 26). Imagining the self as territory and relations between selves in terms of invasion or conquest must, in sexual terms, translate into a fear of rape. If sex tourists imagine the Dominican Republic as close to a "state of nature," a space where fragile-bodied men are not constrained by any law, then their fantasies of conquest would simultaneously invoke the spectre of invasion and engulfment by other, stronger-bodied men. As well as shedding light on their obsessive fascination with each other as sexual beings, this, I believe, helps us to understand hardcore sex tourist/sexpatriates' impulse to forge links with each other in the Dominican Republic and other sites of sex tourism. The sexual objectification and exchange of women not only facilitates social relations and group identity, but also diffuses fears about homosexual invasion.

CONCLUSION

The subculture of male heterosexual sex tourism that has been considered in this article has grave consequences for the safety, health and well-being of local women and girl children in the countries it targets. It also reveals something of the extent and chilling human consequences of global inequalities. Individual sexual agency is mediated through institutions of power, and the hardcore sex tourist's capacity to reclaim a particular vision of the European/North American Self through the sexual objectification of Others is predicated upon the existence of an equally particular economic, legal and political world order. And in terms of our understandings of the politics of "race," gender and sexuality in the West, the phenomenon of hardcore male heterosexual sex tourism sounds a warning bell, for the sense of loss which lies behind these sex tourists and sexpatriates' desires is not so very extraordinary. The same regrets, the same sense of being "away from the stars" can be found in speeches by right-wing politicians in North America and Europe and in the works of right-wing "think-tanks," newspaper editors and columnists and academics (for instance, Herrnstein and Murray, 1994; Murray, 1990), as well as in the publications of organizations like the UK Men's Movement (UKMM, 1999).

The men considered in this article are not differentiated from their more conventional right-wing compatriots by their preoccupation with European/North American notions of "civilization" and "nature," whiteness and blackness, maleness and femaleness, heterosexuality and homosexuality, merely by the fact that they seek to diffuse those tensions and reconcile contradictions through very specific sexual practices. Concluding her study of white supremacism in the USA, Ferber observes that "White supremacist discourse rearticulates dominant discourses on race and gender: therefore, any effective political response to the white supremacist movement must also attack these mainstream narratives" (1999: 156). The same point holds good in relation to the subculture of hardcore male heterosexual sex tourism.

NOTES

1. The interview data presented in this article was collected by Jacqueline Sanchez Taylor and the author in the course of ESRC funded research on tourist-related prostitution in the Caribbean.

2. See, for example, Hall's (1992) discussion of the debate between Thomas Carlyle and John Stuart Mill on Governor Eyre's reprisals against black Jamaicans following the 1865 Morant Bay riot, also Parekh (1995).

3. See Elizabeth Grosz's discussion of Nietzsche and "body inscription as the cultural condition for establishing social order and obedience" (1994: 129).

4. Men who seek sexual contact with boy children are the focus of particularly intense hostility from hardcore male heterosexual tourists, but the boundary between "regular guys" and "paedophiles" is less clear cut in relation to girl children.

5. See Theweleit's (1989) analysis of the writings of members of the German *Freikorps* in the 1920s, and Ferber's (1999) discussion of white supremacists in the contemporary USA.

REFERENCES

Bhattacharyya, G. (1997). "The Fabulous Adventures of the Mahogany Princesses," in H. Mirza (ed.) *Black British Feminism*. London: Routledge.

Bishop, R. and Robinson, L. (1998) *Night Market: Sexual Cultures and the Thai Economic Miracle*. London: Routledge.

Brace, L. (1997) "Imagining the Boundaries of a Sovereign Self," in L. Brace and J. Hoffman (eds.) *Reclaiming Sovereignty*, pp. 137–54. London: Cassell.

Brace, L. and O'Connell Davidson, J. (1996) "Desperate Debtors and Counterfeit Love: The Hobbesian World of the Sex Tourist," *Contemporary Politics* 2(3): 55–78.

Cassirer, B. (1992) *Travel & the Single Male*. Channel Island, CA: TSM.

Chow, R. (1999) "The Politics of Admittance: Female Sexual Agency, Miscegenation, and the Formation of Community in Frantz Fanon," in A. Alessandrini (ed.) *Frantz Fanon: Critical Perspectives*, pp. 34–56. London: Routledge.

Clift, S. and Carter, S., eds. (2000) *Tourism and Sex: Culture, Commerce and Coercion*. London: Pinter.

Dollimore, J. (1991) *Sexual Dissidence: Augustine to Wilde, Freud to Foucault*. Oxford: Clarendon Press.

Ferber, A. (1999) *White Man Falling: Race, Gender and White Supremacy*. New York: Rowman and Littlefield.

Freud, S. (1985 [1913]) "Totem and Taboo," in Sigmund Freud *The Origins of Religion*, vol. 13, pp. 43–224. Harmondsworth: Penguin.

Grosz, E. (1994) *Volatile Bodies: Toward a Corporeal Feminism*. Bloomington and Indianapolis: Indiana University Press.

Hall, C. (1992) *White, Male and Middle Class*. Cambridge: Polity.

Herrnstein, R. and Murray, C. (1994) *The Bell Curve: Intelligence and Class Structure in American Life*. New York: The Free Press.

Hobbes, T. (1968) *Leviathan*. Harmondsworth: Penguin.

Howard, D. (1999) *Dominican Republic*. London: Latin America Bureau.

Hughes, D. (1998/9) "men@exploitation.com," *Trouble & Strife* 38: 21–27.

Ireland, K. (1993) *Wish You Weren't Here*. London: Save the Children.

Kruhse-MountBurton, S. (1995) "Sex Tourism and Traditional Australian Male Identity," in M. Lanfant, J. Allcock and E. Bruner (eds.) *International Tourism: Identity and Change*. London: Sage.

McClintock, A. (1995) *Imperial Leather: Race, Gender and Sexuality in the Colonial Contest*. London: Routledge.

Mercer, K. (1995) "Busy in the Ruins of Wretched Phantasia," in R. Farr (ed.) *Mirage: Enigmas of Race, Difference and Desire*. London: ICA/Institute of International Visual Arts.

Mills, C. (1998) *The Racial Contract*. Ithaca: Cornell University Press.

Moore, C. (1993) *A Haunting Smile*. Bangkok: White Lotus Press.

Murray, C. (1990) *The Emerging British Underclass*. London: The IEA Health and Welfare Unit.

O'Connell Davidson, J. (1995) "British Sex Tourists in Thailand," in M. Maynard and J. Purvis (eds.), *(Hetero)-sexual Politics,* pp. 42–64. London: Taylor & Francis.

O'Connell Davidson, J. (1996) "Sex Tourism in Cuba," *Race & Class* 37(3): 39–48.

O'Connell Davidson, J. (1998) *Prostitution, Power and Freedom*. Cambridge: Polity.

O'Connell Davidson, J. and Sanchez Taylor, J. (1996) "Child Prostitution and Sex Tourism," research papers 1–7. Bangkok: ECPAT.

Parekh, B. (1995) "Liberalism and Colonialism: A Critique of Locke and Mill," in J. Nederveen and B. Parekh (eds.) *The Decolonisation of Imagination: Culture, Knowledge and Power,* pp. 81–98. London: Zed.

Pateman, C. (1988) *The Sexual Contract*. Cambridge: Polity.

Pruitt, D. and LaFont, S. (1995) "For Love and Money: Romance Tourism in Jamaica," *Annals of Tourism Research* 22(2): 422–40.

Puwar, N. (1999) "Embodying the Body Politic: Race and Gender in the British State Elite," PhD thesis, University of Essex.

Rubin, G. (1975) "The Traffic in Women: Notes on the "Political Economy" of Sex," in R. Reiter (ed.) *Toward an Anthropology of Women*. New York: Monthly Review Press.

Said, E. (1978) *Orientalism: Western Conceptions of the Orient*. Harmondsworth: Penguin.

Sanchez Taylor, J. (2000) "Tourism and 'Embodied' Commodities: Sex Tourism in the Caribbean," in S. Clift and S. Carter (eds.) *Tourism and Sex: Culture, Commerce and Coercion,* pp. 41–53. London: Pinter.

Seabrook, J. (1996) *Travels in the Skin Trade: Tourism and the Sex Industry*. London: Pluto Press.

Seidler, V. (1987) "Reason, Desire and Male Sexuality," in P. Caplan (ed.) *The Cultural Construction of Sexuality,* pp. 82–112. London: Routledge.

Somerville, S. (1997) "Scientific Racism and the Invention of the Homosexual Body," in R. Lancaster and M. di Leonardo (eds.) *The Gender/Sexuality Reader,* pp. 37–52. London: Routledge.

Theweleit, K. (1987) *Male Fantasies, Volume 1*. Cambridge: Polity.

Truong, T. (1990) *Sex, Money and Morality: Prostitution and Tourism in Southeast Asia*. London: Zed Books.

UKMM (1999) *UK Men's Movement Mission Statement* http://www.ukmm.org.net

Wellman, D. (1997) "Minstrel Shows, Affirmative Action Talk, and Angry White Men: Marking Racial Otherness in the 1990s," in R. Frankenberg (ed.) *Displacing Whiteness,* pp. 311–31. London: Duke University Press.

WTO (World Tourism Organization) (1997) "International Arrivals in the Americas 1996," cited in *Travel Weekly,* November 6.

19

Agnes Goes to Prison

Gender Authenticity, Transgender Inmates in Prisons for Men, and Pursuit of "The Real Deal"

Valerie Jenness

Sarah Fenstermaker

In 2009, Raewyn Connell published a thoughtful consideration of Harold Garfinkel's story of "Agnes" (Garfinkel 1967), a young woman who identified herself to the UCLA Neuropsychiatric Clinic researchers and clinicians studying gender identity disorders and who was seeking a surgical "correction" for the "mistake" that was her penis. Agnes became what Garfinkel (1967, 180) referred to as a "practical methodologist" to deliberately seek acceptance as an unassailably "normal, natural" female, deserving of surgical attention. Agnes's project was to convince Garfinkel and others that she was "naturally" a female, that her "inner" female was adequately reflected in her outward appearance, comportment, and point of view as a woman. From this, West and Zimmerman (1987) concluded: "Her [Agnes's] problem was to produce configurations of behavior that would be by others seen as normative gender behavior" (quoted in R. Connell 2009, 134). Garfinkel's chronicle of this "production" provided what Zimmerman referred to as "an unusually clear vision" (Zimmerman 1992,

197): to wit, the empirical means to decouple the initial outcome of sex assignment and the interactional accomplishment of gender.

The discovery that Agnes was not intersex, as she was asserting, but instead was taking hormones to enhance her feminine appearance, drew attention to the fact that Agnes was passing—conventionally understood as making efforts to successfully hide a stigmatizing secret. Connell argued that this "preoccupation" with Agnes's efforts to pass avoided "important issues of contradictory embodiment" (R. Connell 2009, 107). Without denying the central role of accountability, Connell suggested an alternative: that Agnes was not so much hiding a secret about herself as she was seeking affirmation and an identity within a particular community that sex category might deliver.

Connell reminds us that Agnes's problem was not only one of interaction in the abstract, but *embodied* interaction in the here and now. It requires concerted effort, specific actions, and constant evaluation to ensure that

Jenness, V., and S. Fenstermaker, "Agnes Goes to Prison: Gender Authenticity, Transgender Inmates in Prisons for Men, and Pursuit of 'The Real Deal.'" *Gender & Society* 28 (1): 5–31, copyright © 2014 SAGE Publications. Reprinted by permission of SAGE Publications.

the embodied comportment adequately reflects the ultimate purpose of achieving recognition. Connell (2012) has advanced a consideration of the implications of "contradictory embodiment"—embodiment that is at once unnatural, unpredictable, and unacceptable—as understood through an empirical examination of transsexuality in all its complexity. She calls for a turn away from a preoccupation with matters of individual identity toward the realities of practice and process in the interactional achievement of gender in specific contexts. Referring to transgender as "intransigent" (i.e., demanding recognition), Connell argues: "The contradiction has to be handled, and it has to be handled at the level of the body, since it arises in the process of embodiment" (2012, 868).

The compulsory character and the everyday challenges of such embodied recognition provide a theoretical point of departure for our analysis of transgender women in men's prisons. As an exemplar of Connell's "contradictory embodiment," Agnes—our imagined Agnes—cannot pass in a prison for men. In prison, Agnes and her transgender sisters reside in a setting where "everyone knows" they are biologically male, but where they nevertheless are motivated to seek continuous affirmation of their "natural" female and womanly characters. Under the sometimes brutal, and always difficult, conditions of the prison, transgender prisoners engage in a competitive pursuit of a femininity that does not constitute "passing" but does involve accountability to a normative standard and a "ladylike" ideal. Such practices require an intense preoccupation with bodily adornment and appearance as well as a deferent demeanor and a studied comportment. The result is the achievement of a *recognition* from others that one is close enough to a "real girl" to feel deserving of a kind of privilege.

The unique and often predatory environment of the prison is defined by deprivation, including both loss of freedom and markers of individuality typically used on the outside. In this context, transgender prisoners are distinct from their counterparts on the outside who seek to pass, and often do pass, as women. Precisely because transgender prisoners' lives are so radically unconventional, we use this article as an occasion to give voice to the pursuit of femininity in a men's prison and to reaffirm the value of a theoretical and empirical focus on the actual practices that constitute our gendered lives. To do so, we first turn to the theoretical stakes that motivate

our empirical inquiry, and then we describe the original data employed to understand the lives of transgender prisoners. Thereafter, we offer an empirical analysis of how transgender prisoners orient to and accomplish gender in prisons for men. We conclude with a discussion of the complicated relationship between embodiment and accountability in a context in which doing gender is problematized in consequential ways.

THEORETICAL CONSIDERATIONS

In their classic work "Doing Gender," West and Zimmerman (1987) made problematic the prevailing perspective that the sex categories of female and male are (1) naturally defined and spring from mutually exclusive reproductive functions rooted in an unchanging biological nature; (2) clearly reflected in the myriad differences commonly observed between girls and boys, men and women; and (3) foundational to social inequalities that are commonsensically and adequately rationalized via these apparently intractable differences between males and females.

At the heart of the "doing gender" approach is the idea that individuals and their conduct—in virtually any course of action—can be evaluated in relation to a womanly or manly nature and character. The powerful gender ideals and norms that dominate in popular culture, advertising, and the media serve as cultural resources to guide a normative understanding of a gendered world. However, the doing of gender is far more than stylized performance or a regimented, scripted interaction. Owing to sex category assignment, women and men operate as if they are "naturally" different, and navigate a world that instantiates those differences. This is a cultural constant; how and in what ways those differences are created, granted meaning, and rendered consequential vary by the particulars of social setting and historical period.

This is akin to what Connell refers to as the ontoformative character of gender: "Practice starts from structure, but does not repetitively cite its starting point. Rather, social practice continuously brings social reality into being, and that social reality becomes the ground of new practice through time" (R. Connell 2012, 866; see also Butler 1993). Founded on this very idea, "doing gender" asserted the social mechanisms by which people preoccupy themselves with the gendering of social life, organize their expressions of themselves as competently feminine or masculine, and reaffirm the social structure that lends social life meaning and consequence. Seen in these terms, what animates the sex category/gender system is crucial to understanding both the unshakeable salience of sex category and the workings of gender in social life. For that, we turn briefly to the concept of "accountability."

In a recent reexamination of the concept of accountability as it applies to gender, Jocelyn Hollander (2013) provides a roadmap to disentangling three distinct aspects of accountability: *orientation* to sex category, evaluative *assessment* of oneself and others in relevant accountable conduct, and interactional *enforcement* of expectations associated with categorical membership, with a vast range of consequences for violation. In her discussion of each aspect, Hollander reaffirms what West and Zimmerman (1987) argued over a quarter of a century ago: Orientation to sex category is ubiquitous—and probably inevitable—but what is wholly dependent on context and which can change markedly over time is the particular focus of assessment, enforcement, and that which constitutes accountable conduct.[1]

West and Zimmerman did not concern themselves with the myriad ways in which social life is gendered; they theorized *how* we as members of social worlds make them meaningfully gendered. They did not show us the consequences of a gendered world; they identified and theorized an interactional route to those consequences. Likewise, they did not merely argue that gendered social structures produce inequality; they theorized the mechanisms behind the production of that inequality. By interrogating these mechanisms, they gave us a way to think about social order *and* social change. As Connell explained, "If the situated accomplishment of gender creates the illusion of a hierarchical natural order, this same situated accomplishment is a site where hierarchy can be contested" (R. Connell 2009, 109).

Gender scholars are turning to the experiences of transgender people to reinterrogate the workings of gender in social life (e.g., Gagne, Tewksbury, and McGaughey 1997; Halberstam 2005). These treatments underscore the situated character of gender, resist the impositions of the binary, and raise possibilities for structural disruption and social change. As Susan Stryker explained with regard to transgender studies writ large, a focus on

transgender people and their experiences in specific institutional contexts brings to the fore "myriad specific subcultural expressions of gender atypicality" (Stryker 2006, 3). Also breaking new ground, the interactions of so-called "gender normals" and transgender people were examined by Schilt and Westbrook (2009). They found that the demands of doing gender appropriately varied not only by situation but by how sexualized those situations were. In addition, they found that the policing of gender, and the failure to fulfill gender expectations was itself gendered (see also Catherine Connell's [2010] analysis of the experiences of 19 transgendered people). More recently, Connell directs analytic attention to how a changed embodied position in gender relations grounds new practices. She reminds us that "a transsexual woman must generate a practice" and asks, "What is to be done?" (R. Connell 2012, 868). Taking this call seriously, we turn to the unique data to unearth gender practices occurring within the dual realities of incarceration and contradictory embodiment.

RESEARCH METHODS AND DATA

. . . Inmates in California prisons who met the eligibility criteria described were invited to participate in the study. The field data collection process began in late April 2008 and ended in late June 2008. During this time, a trained interview team of eight interviewers traveled to 27 California prisons for adult men, met face-to-face with more than 500 inmates identified by the California Department of Corrections and Rehabilitation (CDCR) as potentially transgender, and completed interviews with 315 transgender inmates. The interview schedule employed for the larger project from which the data are drawn was designed to capture a wealth of information on inmates' lives inside and outside prison. The mean duration for interviews was slightly less than one hour, the total interview time approached 300 hours, and the response rate was 95 percent. . . .

PURSUIT OF "THE REAL DEAL"

One of the basic underlying assumptions of prison operations is that there are two types of people—males and females—and that fact looms large. Until the latter part of the twentieth century, sex segregation in prison was arguably the least contested prison policy/practice across geographical region, local government, prison level, and inmate population. In short, the institutional manifestation of the prison culture's sex/gender binary is taken for granted and defines prison existence in virtually every aspect (Sumner and Jenness 2014).

It is within this context that we focus on the pursuit of "the real deal" to refer to the complicated dynamic whereby transgender prisoners claim and assert their femininity in prison—a hegemonically defined hyper-masculine and heteronormative environment with an abundance of alpha males, sexism, and violence. By their own account, transgender prisoners assert themselves with well-understood motivations, patterned manifestations, and an understanding of very real consequences for themselves and others. To quote them, they are "the girls among men." For these inmates, their very presence in a men's prison establishes their sex categorization as male; subsequent and ongoing interaction, however, offers the chance to vie for an "authentic" femininity.

We use the term *gender authenticity* to refer to the pursuit of full recognition, or what some transgender prisoners refer to as "the real deal," or being a "real girl." This pursuit begins with an orientation to, and acknowledgement of, the self as male (at least in the first instance) and an awareness of the fact that, as prisoners in a men's prison, transgender prisoners are immediately understood as male in a prison for men (Jenness 2010; Sumner and Jenness 2014). The manifest desire to be taken as feminine, and thus female, prompts and sustains a commitment to "act like a lady." The commitment to, and everyday practice of, acting like a lady sets the stage for a playful *and* serious competition among transgender prisoners for the attention and affection of "real men" in prison. The attention and adoration of "real men," in turn, is taken to be an important measure of gender status among transgender prisoners. These features of the competitive pursuit of gender authenticity are crucial to the social organization of gender in prison.[2] The effort to be recognized as "a lady" is not something one finally achieves, but pursues as an ongoing proposition. The status of lady—as authentically female—is a provisional one deployed in a context in which transgender prisoners are "clocked," a subject to which we now turn.

Being Known as Male: "I'm in Here and I'm Already Clocked"

Transgender prisoners often used the word "clocked" as a way of indicating that their ability to pass as women is effectively denied in a prison built for and inhabited exclusively by males. The institutional context in which they reside determines which side of the sex categorical binary system they are thought to belong. Being clocked, therefore, is not about attempting to pass and being "discovered" so that some are privy to the "truth" and others are not. A sex-segregated prison for men is a unique environment where there is no other truth possible: Every prisoner is male, no matter how they look or act. It is here where the institutionalization of sex category membership interacts so critically with gender practice. Being clocked sets the terms and conditions for doing gender in prison precisely because it precludes passing as it is conventionally understood.

A white[3] transgender prisoner in her mid-twenties reported taking hormones when she was 15 and coming to prison when she was 18 for "an armed robbery and carjacking I did with my boyfriend" (ID no. 35[4]). She explained, "I was stupid, just stupid. But, I've learned the hard way. Twenty-four years of my life! That's the hard way." Comparing her life outside prison to her life in prison, she said, "I lived as a girl in high school, passed on the streets. Now [in prison], everyone knows, so who cares?" She explained that now that she is in prison there is no passing "because I'm in here and I'm already clocked." Elaborating, she described how outside prison she didn't wear shorts because she has "manly legs," but contrasted this to life in prison with "now I'll wear shorts, too, even though I have manly legs." She went on to say "my legs are not manly in a good way—not like Tina Turner's." In this case, even as "clocking" makes one vulnerable to certain dangers, it can also be liberating to be relieved of the need to pass.

Likewise, an African American transgender prisoner in her midthirties who identified herself as a "pre-op transsexual" with "some facial surgery (chin, cheeks, and nose)" reported, "I've never been clocked on the streets" (ID no. 32). However, later in the interview she explained that, while in prison, she is treated by CDCR personnel and other inmates alike as male. When asked how correctional officers treat her, she reported being harassed routinely: "Most of the time, actually. Just today an officer said, 'Your jaw is wired shut,[5] you're out of service.' C'mon, how rude is that? They also call me 'sissy boy.' That gets old." Later in the interview she made it clear how correctional officers and other prisoners reveal that "they think I'm gay or a gay boy."[6]

Other transgender prisoners made explicit connections between being clocked and the many challenges they face being transgender in prison, including the ongoing management of the threat and reality of violence. A biracial transgender prisoner serving time for fraud reported that she came to California from a state in the Midwest because she assumed California would be more tolerant of alternative lifestyles. She described the nature of being transgender in a men's prison this way: "Everyone in prison knows I'm transgender. But outside they don't" (ID no. 34). Later in the interview, she lamented, "Yes, but most people don't know. They think, 'You like men, you're gay.' Most people don't get it— that I'm transgender, not gay." An African American transgender prisoner, who lived as a woman on the streets in Los Angeles and worked as a prostitute for over 20 years, proclaimed, "I know I'm not a girl; I was born a boy. But I have tendencies as a girl" (ID no. 1).

Other transgender prisoners cited anatomical realities (as they existed at the time of the interview) as evidence of their nonnormative status as women, referencing their maleness along the way. An African American transgender inmate who reported removing her own male genitals and being on hormones to enhance her feminine appearance since her teen years made it clear that she has not forgotten how she was born (as a male). She complicated the picture by describing her attributes compared to those of other transgender prisoners:

> I'm 40D. Not many like that in here. And, I have a big ass, we call it "booty." I don't mind being on a yard with other transgenders because they can't match this. And, the hormones shrink your dick and I don't have any testicles. I had them cut off when I was a teenager. . . . When you're in prison, everyone knows who you are—a man. It's not a big secret. Or, at least they think they know who you are. I'm a man. I'm not confused. I'm not a woman. I know I don't bleed. I can't produce children. I don't have a pussy. I have breasts because I grew them with hormones. It's not like you. I just assume your breasts are natural. Anyone who says, "I'm just like you" is full of shit. C'mon. We're women, but not like you. You know the difference. I know the difference. And they know the difference.

Here we see differing theories reflected in inmate accounts for why, if they are embodied males, they are transgender. The prisoner just quoted alludes to "tendencies," suggesting misplacement in sex category. Others bow to the primacy of embodiment and the naturalness of sex category when they say, as they often did, "I'm not like you" (to a female interviewer) or "I'm a woman, but not a female."

Transgender prisoners made reference to women who are "biologics" as compared to themselves, who are not. Consider the description provided by an outspoken white transgender prisoner who self-identifies as "the transgender ring leader" and who "takes care of the girls around here" while serving a life sentence and maintaining a "marriage-like" relationship with another prisoner. During an interview, she asked the lead author, "Val, you're a biologic, right?"[7] After receiving an affirmative response, she went on to say:

> I figured. We have the utmost respect for biologics. You are perfection. I am Memorex. You are what I can never attain. But, like all good Memorexes, I try to get close. Always a copy. Never the real deal. But a damn good copy. People can't tell the difference between the real deal and a damn good copy. You're real. I'll never be the same. Do you know Lt. Commander Data [on Star Trek] looks human and acts human, but will never be human. He's an android, not a human. It's kind of the same. (ID no. 40)

The distinction between a "biologic" and another type of woman is illustrated with reference to anatomy and biological functioning. When a transgender prisoner who proudly revealed she has legal documentation that identifies her as female was asked whether she would prefer to be housed in a men's prison or a women's prison, she immediately replied, "Men's." She added, "That's a hard one. I don't want to be with women because they are vicious. They are worse than men. Their hormones are going all the time. Imagine being around 60 women and two are on their period at the same time! God. Imagine how bad that would be?" (ID no. 34). Likewise, an Asian transgender prisoner who was born outside the United States and expressed concerns about her immigration status reported that she has been transgender since high school, began taking hormones at 14, and earned a good living as a hairdresser before coming to prison. Noting that her family accepts her transgender status, she said, "Before I got into drugs I had a good life. I got into meth—the monster. Everything went downhill" (ID no. 39). She went on to compare herself to other transgender prisoners, as well as other [real] women:

> People on the outside are way different. I came here transgender, but I call them broken souls. A lot of them find themselves here, transition in here. I think it is for affection, the attention, the loneliness. You could be anything in here. You can still find yourself a man. They are gay boys, but men. I came in transgender. I'm different. I knew I was transgender, not a gay boy who became transgender. I would give my soul to be a woman. Who wouldn't want to be nurturant, to be loving, to be kind? Women bring peace to the world. They unite people. A mother is everything.

She made a distinction between "fat men titties" and the breasts of women, and lamented that she can never give birth like other women.

Regardless of whether one believes one is inherently female, the biologic remains a crucial reference point, as transgender prisoners expressed enthusiasm for being as close to the real deal as possible. An Hispanic transgender prisoner with a long history of engaging in sex work, struggling with drug addiction, and enduring imprisonment explained, "They [respect me because they] see that I'm all the way out—that I'm the real deal. I'm going all the way. I'm hoping to have surgery. I'm not a transgender, I'm a woman. I have my breasts from hormones. I'm the real deal. I want Marcy Bowers to do the surgery" (ID no. 4).[8] Expressions such as these are often accompanied by self-assessments regarding how close to the goal—the real deal—one is, and is becoming.

What we might call the "problem of approximation" is an ever-present normative benchmark to separate the biologic from both the real woman and the failed pretender, even when intentions to seek sex reassignment surgery are in play. Therefore, extant theories of passing as a sociological process are inapplicable, and accountability to membership in one's sex category is no longer at issue. However, orienting accountability to a locally defined authenticity puts a premium on the process of pursuing a convincingly feminine appearance and demeanor. The context renders sensible and recognizable the ongoing effort (and its consequence) that seeks to move beyond the (known) biological truth to approach the real deal, even if it is inevitably a "Memorex." Accordingly, passing is less about biological and anatomical secrets to be managed and more about making gender commitments visible.

The prison environment sets the stage for embodiment to be understood as unforgiving ("Everyone knows") *and* eminently deniable ("Who cares?"). Through the pursuit of the real deal, however, gender expectations remain and demand that the transgender prisoner's behavior reflects an inherent femininity—as if one were really and truly female. To do this requires participation in an additional dynamic—acting like a lady in prison—which, as we describe in the next section, reveals the distinct ways in which gender is embedded in individual selves, cultural rules, social interaction, and organizational and institutional arrangements (Lorber 1994).

The Importance of Acting Like a Lady: "It's Being Proper"

To enhance one's feminine appearance and approach the real deal, transgender prisoners emphasized the importance of "acting like a lady." As they did so, particular constructs of classed normative understandings were employed to establish a valued femininity as a route to respect, as revealed in the following exchange:

INTERVIEWER: How do transgender inmates get respect?

PRISONER: Act like a lady.

INTERVIEWER: Why does acting like a lady in a men's prison get you respect?

PRISONER: If a man is a gentleman and they see a queen act that way, it's important for him to trust you because you're showing self-confidence in an environment that is crazy. That's why queens don't get hurt. You being a lady is like a gold credit card.

The dynamic nexus between being transgender in a sex-segregated environment and the centrality of earning respect as a lady is anchored in the embrace of a feminine ideal akin to the iconic Victorian-era normative construct first described by Barbara Welter in "The Cult of True Womanhood, 1820–1860" (Welter 1966).

When asked "What does a 'lady' act like?" transgender prisoners provided illuminating answers. A Mexican transgender prisoner explained that acting like a lady entailed "staying in the women's spot. Don't talk bad. Don't make comments about things that don't concern you. Being a woman is about staying in line" (ID no. 12). Another transgender prisoner, who attributed many of her problems throughout her adult life to methamphetamine use that led to prostitution, went further:

INTERVIEWER: What does a lady act like?

PRISONER: No sleeping with everyone. No going out on the yard with just a sports bra on. C'mon, you know what a lady acts like. It's being proper. (ID no. 35)

Many transgender prisoners were quick to talk about other transgender prisoners as "skanks," a clear reference to sexual promiscuity with connotations of disapproval in a context in which the values of social and sexual restraint are privileged. Jennifer Sumner explained the transgender code of conduct: "Transgender inmates who are seen to be 'messing' with another's man or 'messing' with too many men are labeled as 'slutty' and considered to be 'whores' or 'skanks'" (Sumner 2009, 190).

For transgender prisoners in men's prisons, a commitment to acting like a lady often was revealed in response to questions designed to solicit respondents' sense of what gets them—and other transgender prisoners—respect in prison. When asked "Does appearing more feminine get you respect from other (nontransgender) inmates?" the majority of the respondents (64.3 percent) said "Yes." When asked "Why?" a transgender prisoner in her midthirties serving her third term explained the benefits of acting like a lady in prison this way:

PRISONER: They [other prisoners] give me a different pardon. If I'm going in line to chow, it's likely someone will let me go first.

INTERVIEWER: What exactly is a different pardon?

PRISONER: A pardon is a special consideration. That's what makes me feel respected. It's tasteful, especially if it comes from a regular guy. That's him telling me that I'm carrying myself like a lady. It's about being treated like a lady and made to feel like a lady. That's a special pardon. The more you get special pardons, the more you are being treated like a lady. (ID no. 32)

In a more dramatic illustration, a middle-aged African American transgender prisoner who introduced herself by using a famous model's name and later in the interview called herself a "crack whore" invited the interviewer to see the poster above the toilet in her cell and said, "I act like a lady and I have a poster that says so above the toilet in my cell" (ID no. 3). She explained that she

sits when she pees, and because cells are shared and visible to other prisoners in the cell block, everyone can see that she sits when she pees. For her, this is a sign that indicates she is acting like a lady, and for all to see that she pees accordingly.

Life for transgender prisoners is nothing if not variable and a set of contradictions, and here is where the multiplicities of gender are evident. Transgender prisoners reported circumstances in which the luxury of "acting like a lady" necessarily gave way to expressions of violence. Almost half (44.7 percent) of the transgender prisoners in this study reported being involved in violence while living in their current housing unit, and, on average, they have been in their current housing unit only about a year. Moreover, well over half (89.2 percent) of the transgender prisoners in this study reported being involved in violence while incarcerated in a California prison, with an average sentence in California prisons of 10.9 years.

For some, engagement in physical violence was not at odds with acting like a lady insofar as any woman in a situation that requires violence would behave similarly. A middle-aged African American transgender prisoner convicted of a second strike for "great bodily injury" explained how she initiated a violent confrontation with a group of four men on the yard after they refused to cease making pejorative comments about her husband (who was also her cellmate for over three years) because he was openly involved with her. She approached the men on the yard, confronted them about their harassment, asked them if there was a problem, told them to "cut the comments," and advised them that if the comments continued she would have to "get busy" with them:

INTERVIEWER: What do you mean by "get busy"?

PRISONER: You know, put the cheese on the crackers and make it happen.

INTERVIEWER: And what does that—"put the cheese on the crackers"—mean?

PRISONER: Fight. (ID no. 105)

In response to being asked "Does fighting feel at odds with being a woman?" she said:

Oh, girl, you just don't understand. Let's review. Take a transgender. Take any female. A Black woman. A Latina woman. A Asian woman. *Any* woman. There is no way a woman with a strong will and self-respect is going to let themselves be mistreated. You'd be surprised what women can do. Women will cut you. Women will stab you. Violence is violence. There's no such thing as transgender violence and other women's violence.

It's all the same. People do what they have to do to take care of themselves. The difference with us is, well, violence is ugly. We don't want to be violent. We want to be beautiful. We're on hormones, girl. But hit me or disrespect me and I'll knock you out. I will. You would knock someone out, too. You'd be surprised what you would do if you had to; you just haven't had to—have you?

Others described situations in which they had to "man up," "put on my shoes," and "put down my purse and fight." In many cases, transgender prisoners reported taking a "time out" or a "stop pattern" to acting like a lady, and engaging in physical altercations with other prisoners as a way to protect or marshal respect. An older white transgender prisoner explained:

If you don't respect yourself, no one will. You don't have to be tough. I can fight and lose and get respect. I can run from a fight and get no respect. I'd be a coward. So, it's not about being tough, it's about standing your ground. (ID no. 6)

The use of violence for transgender inmates to gain respect is comparable to Nikki Jones's vivid descriptions of West Philadelphia high school girls crafting a femininity that accommodates periodic violent defense of one's self-respect (Jones 2009; see also Miller 2008).

In more dramatic terms, when asked if there are situations in prison in which violence between inmates is necessary, an HIV-positive transgender prisoner said:

PRISONER: Yes. Gang bangers come in here and say something—like, "Hey, half dead!" [to HIVs] or "You're dying anyway." With me, if it becomes too much I put my purse down and fight. I'll let that part of me come out.

INTERVIEWER: What part is that?

PRISONER: The non-ladylike. The ugly side of me. (ID no. 8)

Here the dual status of clocked as male and feminine like a lady exist in close social proximity. The situatedness of gender in this context allows us to see this dynamic as far more than a choice between absolutes—*either* femininity *or* masculinity. The violence engaged in may draw its content from forms of expression typically

understood as masculine, but such forms are undertaken in the context of a *suspended* ladylike "ideal" or an extension of what a woman has to do to demand and secure respect. In other words, violence represents an "ugly side" of a lady, and not the lady herself. As a consequence, the accomplishment of gender to invoke a normative *feminine* standard rests next to the accomplishment of gender to invoke a normative *masculine* standard. In the context of a prison, there is perhaps no better example of the situated character of gender than when one pees "like a lady" in one moment and "stands her ground" in the next.

For transgender prisoners, however, violence can carry consequences for the successful pursuit of the real deal. Being clocked as male means that any deployment of the "ugly side" constitutes a counter affirmation of a "natural" status as male. Thus, transgender prisoners are motivated to find ways to avoid physical violence. A white transgender prisoner with long flowing hair who has been doing time—off and on—since the late 1980s and is now in her midforties explained this dilemma:

PRISONER: I am a man, but I choose to look like a woman and I want to be treated like a woman. That's what makes me transgender. I recently had an argument with my cellie and he told me to put my shoes on, which means to fight. I wouldn't put them on. I wouldn't fight.

INTERVIEWER: So women don't fight?

PRISONER: Right.

INTERVIEWER: What else makes you feel treated like a woman?

PRISONER: All the courtesies a man would afford a woman, like my trays are cleared by my cellie—he takes my tray in chow line. (ID no. 26)

Whether transgender women actually fight or not—and the data suggest they do—is not the point; the point is the fact that they render fighting sensible through a gendered lens.

Competition among the Ladies: "Fun, Dangerous, and Real"

Ample self-report evidence reveals friendly competition among ladies. For example, when asked "Would you prefer more transgender inmates in your housing unit?"

quite often transgender prisoners expressed ambivalence born of wanting more "girls" in their living environments in the hopes of importing understanding and support, but at the same time expressed reluctance at the prospect of increased competition for social status in the prison order. An African American transgender prisoner said, "It's hard. I want the company of men, but I feel safe around the transgenders, but I like women friends" (ID no. 1). When asked the same question, an Hispanic transgender prisoner replied:

> We call them [other transgender inmates] bitches, but with affection. Because the straights will try to hit on them as much. It's odd. You want friends, but you don't want the hassle, the drama that comes with them. I'm torn. I want them around, but I don't want them around. It's good and bad. (ID no. 2)

Similarly, an HIV-positive transgender prisoner who reported recently breaking up with her cellmate/institutional husband and having "a gentleman on the street who is waiting for me" described her relationship with other transgender prisoners:

> Yes, they flirt, but it's not pressure. That's just play. They know what kind of person I am—monogamous. I don't behave like a slut. Most of the other girls do, but I don't. I respect myself too much. [I] don't want to live with other transgenders—it's like too many women in the kitchen. It sounds so selfish, but less transgender inmates is better; like I said, too many women in the kitchen. Too much promiscuity. I want a relationship that is monogamous. Some of the girls, I don't respect. They are more promiscuous. They are nasty. Skanky. They are. I'm not like that. (ID no. 5)

When asked "Does appearing more feminine get you respect from other transgender inmates?" a white transgender prisoner living among many other transgender prisoners explained, "It tends to get negative. They get jealous. Because I look and act like a woman; they have to try harder [than I do]. They feel threatened by how natural it is for me" (ID no. 8). Similarly, a white transgender prisoner who has served almost 20 years of a life sentence in more than ten different prisons said, "I'm not sure. Sometimes it's jealousy, competition. If people compete with me that means they respect me enough to treat me as a girl—and they do compete" (ID no. 9). An older, more subdued white transgender inmate who explained "I didn't become transgender until I hit [current

housing unit] at [current prison]," and "My morals have come a long way [since being in prison]" also commented on the complexities of femininity and respect:

> Some respect you a lot; some are angered because you do better than they—you look better; some are angry because you're not normal. Lots goes on when you're trying to be fem. It's fun, dangerous, and it's real. All girls learn from other girls. Transgenders learn from other transgenders. It's a way of learning to do things better, to be better women. (ID no. 6)

Finally, a young Hispanic transgender inmate said, "No, they're jealous. It's like a beauty pageant. You're all here and seemingly getting along. But not really. Really, it's a competition. They smile to your face, but not sincerely. There's only one winner and maybe a runner-up" (ID no. 35).

This "pageant" requires other prisoners—the men—to be judges socially positioned to bestow status on transgender prisoners. The accomplishment of gender by transgender prisoners must draw crucial meaning from their primary audience. In various ways, transgender prisoners reported the centrality of securing attention from men (i.e., nontransgender prisoners). An older white transgender prisoner playfully described:

> I was going into chow and a couple of other inmates grabbed my ass and told me how sweet it is. They are males who are here and want sex. It's like a guy who goes to the strip club. I'm the entertainment and the meat. I wasn't offended. Those kinds of comments and gropes—I find it complimentary at my age. I'm [over 50]. I'm glad I can still draw the attention. (ID no. 6)

Moving beyond stories of (seemingly) superficial pleasure, transgender prisoners told touching stories of caretaking from other nontransgender prisoners with whom they formed intimate relationships. In an emotional interview, a very ill transgender prisoner who reported struggling with addiction most of her adult life, living on the streets before coming to prison, engaging in prostitution for many years, and being HIV-positive explained how important her prison husband is to her ability to manage in prison:

PRISONER: We [my husband in prison and I] clicked and we have a lot in common. He's very supportive of me. Because I'm on an HIV regime he does nice things for me.

INTERVIEWER: Like what?

PRISONER: Well, like hold my hair when I vomit in the cell and not get mad at me. (ID no. 8)

This simple consideration took on significant meaning to her because it came at the hands of a man (and a husband, no less) and is easily seen by her as an affirmation of her status as female (i.e., a woman worthy of being cared for by a man and taken care of like a wife). Throughout the interviews, transgender prisoners expressed appreciation for caring interactions with real men that served to recognize them as women. These simple, but much desired, interactions included being walked across the yard, given cuts in the chow line, and having an umbrella held over your head in the rain.

From the point of view of many transgender prisoners, the nontransgender prisoners are seen as protectors as well as providers. When asked "What is the best way for transgender inmates to avoid being victimized?" a white transgender prisoner who worked as a marketing researcher before coming to prison described a familiar gendered reciprocity: "Get someone to protect you. He'll take you under his wing. He'll become protective of you—like men do with women" (ID no. 10). She went on to explain her own relationship situation:

> We're involved, but it's not sexual yet. It's been a month. It's good for us to be in a marriage. We can and we can't fend for ourselves. He's our protector—just like on the streets. If someone did something to you, he would take care of them. If someone were to put his hands on me or degrade me, he would go and tell him, "Don't disrespect her. If you're disrespecting her, you're disrespecting me." See, I can get some respect through him.

She paused and added, "One of the things I have to do as a transgender is to deal with men who always want sex. So, I've found that the best thing to do is to make them give me something. I make them give me things—like take me to the mini canteen. It's like going on a date." She then described the similarities in terms of "give and take" in which "I give them a little flirt—it doesn't take much," concluding, "It's like petting a dog, only the dog pays you. I've found that men need women to be vulnerable. They want to take care of you—almost like a pet. I like it."

When asked about the best way to avoid victimization in prison, another transgender prisoner said, "I've been lucky to have guys who look at me as female and then they want to take care of me. They have that natural instinct—to protect me as a woman—from other men. That's how men are" (ID no. 8). Here, the bargain that results in a borrowing of respect depends on acceptance of the accomplishment of gender as indicative of a "natural" state, whether a male instinct to protect a woman, or the essential female qualities exhibited by transgender prisoners. According to transgender prisoners, nontransgender prisoners may be moved to chivalry, solicitous or protective behavior toward them as "ladies," calling forth a natural response from men. For some, respect is the precursor to love. An African American transgender prisoner said, "It just means getting to be nice, getting to be taken care of, and getting to be, you know, understood and loved" (ID no. 1).

The pursuit of femininity within this particular context illuminates the body's uncanny ability to override the biological convictions that are being imposed on it through institutional conditions. The absence of biologics among the prison population does not undermine gender, nor does the obvious lack of the real deal suspend the pursuit of femininity inside this alpha male space. A Latina transgender woman in her twenties who described herself as a "gay boy" "doing drag outside [of prison]" reported first taking hormones in prison and showcased her breasts during the interview by lifting them while talking about their growing size. She said, "A lot of guys get fed the illusion. I give good illusion. My hair. My ass. The hormones help. I create the package. They buy it—sometimes, anyway" (ID no. 21). She continued, "I'm still male. I know that. I know I'm not a woman. I'm transgender. Everything about me is female. But, my anatomy is male. . . . See, I know I'm an illusion." However, it is not a capricious or arbitrary illusion. A transgender prisoner explained, "It's not something I just made up" (ID no. 27).

Within the institutional context of sex-segregated carceral environments, the "fragile fictions" of personhood (Snorton 2009) and the interactional dynamics we report are informed by a binary logic that supports the "natural" gendering of bodies and, at the same time, serves as a catalyst for a radical rupture of that logic. In the context of prisons for men (and only men), it is not the commitment to biological differences that dictate the gender dynamics among members, but the *commitment of bodies* to act like, and be received as, "ladies" and "men." Though biological considerations are readily available, they are systematically rendered incompatible with the business of upholding categorical distinctions between women and men. In their capacity to engage in social practice, transgender people and bodies triumphantly make use of "natural categories" despite institutional evidence that claims otherwise (Fenstermaker and Budesa 2013). The dynamics reported in this analysis reveal that transgender women in men's prisons are simultaneously positioned as a source of cultural affirmation, intervention, and critique.

DISCUSSION AND CONCLUSION

The empirical analysis we present in this article suggests that under the harsh conditions of the prison, transgender prisoners engage in a set of activities that together constitute what we refer to as a pursuit of gender authenticity, or what they call the real deal. These activities begin with an orientation to sex category through an acknowledgement that prisoners are institutionally understood as male. Transgender prisoners in men's prisons express a desire to secure standing as a "real girl" or the "best girl" possible in a men's prison. This desire translates into expressions of situated gendered practices that embrace male dominance, heteronormativity, classed and raced gender ideals, and a daily acceptance of inequality. To succeed in being "close enough" to the real deal requires a particular type of participation in a male-dominated system that can, under the right conditions, dole out a modicum of perceived privilege.

We argue that orientation to sex category is crucial to understanding the content of specific gender practices that make reference to a "natural" female and that are informed by expectations of what it is to be a "real lady." The playful yet serious competition among transgender prisoners for the attention and affection of "real men" allows the community of prisoners—transgender and nontransgender alike—to participate in a gendered existence that orders everyday expectations and behaviors, as well as the allocation of resources, symbolic and material. The experiences of transgender inmates illustrate that whatever femininity is undertaken, in whatever way, and for whatever ends, it is not done to pass—to mask a secret that, if revealed, could be discrediting (Goffman 1963; see also R. Connell 2012; Snorton 2009). In prison, the pursuit of femininity

involves accountability to a set of normative standards, informed by cultural constructions of a "ladylike" ideal, even when sometimes transgender prisoners engage in a "stop pattern" and allow the "ugly side" to be revealed. What is sought is accountability to a putative sex category: if, through the accomplishment of gender in this setting, one can appear to embody the imagined biologic real deal, then one is close enough—and good enough—to hope for some respect. All gendered practices are undertaken within the context of a powerfully heteronormative masculine environment that privileges males and denigrates females. One pursues a femininity that achieves the real deal in order to manage the inevitable disrespect and violence heaped upon the feminine.

In her recent article, Raewyn Connell writes eloquently of the "multiple narratives of embodiment" (2012, 867), such that we cannot speak meaningfully of *the* transgender or *the* transsexual experience. This should come as no surprise to gender theorists, which is likely why Connell calls for greater empirical and analytic attention to the multiplicities of transsexual lives. Those social scientists who study gender are less likely to be seduced by a unitary construction of transgender or a new binary composed of "us" and "transgender." Attention to both the complexities of transgender and its situated character reveals the myriad ways in which social change is—and is not—made. Transgender women in prison for men are, to borrow the words of Connell one last time, "neither enemies of change nor heralds of a new world" (R. Connell 2012, 872).

Transgender prisoners assessed themselves and other transgender inmates according to a set of normative expectations deftly designed with a sex categorical world in mind. We learn from the Agneses in prison that the accomplishment of gender through the pursuit of the real deal certainly affirms one's elective place in the binary and justifies behavior as if springing "naturally" from it. Moreover, it directs us not only to the agentic power of embodiment that Connell asserts (R. Connell 2012) but also to the likewise powerfully constructed and situated nature of both sex *and* gender. Together they are adapted to and are made meaningful in a real world, including the harsh world of prisons for men.

Transgender inmates exemplify a will to present and live one's "real" self, even under impossible—and sometimes impossibly dangerous—conditions. Future research that includes not only the "real girls" but also the "real men" would be able to contribute to the picture we paint here of how masculinity and femininity are accomplished by transgender prisoners. What are, after all, "real girls" without "real men" and vice versa?

We conclude where we began: in the UCLA clinic long ago when Agnes's behavior was interpreted only as passing. The Agneses in prison do not hide and they cannot deceive. Their gendered behavior in prison can be understood as part of an ongoing, cooperative collusion where their selves are revealed and their relationships with non-transgender prisoners likewise reaffirm an unequal, often violent and always hegemonically male, community. The search for the real deal is fundamentally a pursuit of recognition, respect, and belonging.

NOTES

1. Sex category is not the only categorical membership around which we order social life (see West and Fenstermaker [1995] for a discussion of "doing" race, class, and gender).

2. Not every transgender prisoner was engaged in the quest for "gender authenticity" as we describe it, and therefore any interpretation of the analysis as a unitary one is misplaced. Nevertheless, the transgender prisoners who participated in this study revealed a preponderance of evidence that both the expectations and the practices we describe are an important aspect of daily existence and a salient feature of prison culture.

3. Designations of the race/ethnicity of these prisoners are presented to render visible the diversity of the transgender prisoner population. These designations are based on their self-identification, if given during an interview or on official institutional data. These two sources of designations may differ in interesting ways (Calavita and Jenness 2013) and different classification categories are a function of the fluid and contingent nature of racial identification and larger processes of racialization in a prison context (Saperstein and Penner 2010).

4. The use of interviewee numbers allows us to maintain confidentiality and allows the reader to track particular study participants throughout the article as well as to attribute multiple quotes to the same prisoner. We considered using pseudonyms, but in the interest of not imposing gendered identities on them, we chose the neutrality of interviewee numbers. According to prisoners with whom we have consulted, this practice is not offensive or dehumanizing; some prefer it to the assignment of a false name insofar as that practice seems misleading and falsely intimate. Fortunately, the use of ID numbers is an accepted convention in sociology journals (e.g., Calavita and Jenness 2013).

5. This person had just been discharged from the infirmary after sustaining injuries in a physical altercation with another prisoner. Her jaw was wired shut, but she was able to do the interview, which she wanted to do.

6. Transgender prisoners often distinguish themselves from what they and other prisoners call "gay boys."

7. Being a "biologic" means being born biologically female.

8. Marcy Bowers is a well-known male-to-female transgender surgeon seen on television.

REFERENCES

Brown, George R., and Everett McDuffie. 2009. Health care policies addressing transgender inmates in prison systems in the United States. *Journal of Correctional Health Care* 15:280–91.

Butler, Judith. 1993. *Bodies that matter.* New York: Routledge.

Calavita, Kitty, and Valerie Jenness. 2013. Inside the pyramid of disputes. *Social Problems* 60:50–80.

Connell, Catherine. 2010. Doing, undoing or redoing gender? Learning from the workplace experiences of transpeople. *Gender & Society* 24:31–55.

Connell, Raewyn. 2009. Accountable conduct. *Gender & Society* 23:104–11.

Connell, Raewyn. 2012. Transsexual women and feminist thought. *Signs* 37:857–81.

Donaldson, Stephen. 1993. A million jockers, punks, and queens. *Just Detention International.* http://www.justdetention.org/en/docs/doc_01_lecture.aspx.

Fenstermaker, Sarah, and Joan Budesa. 2013. Contradictory embodiment. Unpublished manuscript.

Gagne, Patricia, Richard Tewksbury, and Deanna McGaughey. 1997. Coming out and crossing over. *Gender & Society* 11:478–508.

Garfinkel, Harold. 1967. *Studies in ethnomethodology.* Englewood Cliffs, NJ: Prentice Hall.

Goffman, Erving. 1963. *Stigma.* Upper Saddle River, NJ: Prentice Hall.

Halberstam, Judith. 2005. *In a queer time and place.* New York: New York University Press.

Hollander, Jocelyn. 2013. Accountability, interaction, and gender changes. *Gender & Society* 27:5–29.

Jenness, Valerie. 2010. From policy to prisoners to people. *Journal of Contemporary Ethnography* 39:517–53.

Jenness, Valerie. 2011. Getting to know "the girls" in an "alpha-male community." In *Sociologists backstage,* edited by Sarah Fenstermaker and Nikki Jones. New York: Routledge.

Jenness, Valerie. 2014. Pesticides, prisoners, and policy. *Sociological Perspectives.*

Jenness, Valerie, Cheryl L. Maxson, Jennifer Macy Sumner, and Kristy N. Matsuda. 2010. Accomplishing the difficult, but not impossible. *Criminal Justice Policy Review* 21:3–30.

Jenness, Valerie, Lori Sexton, and Jennifer Sumner. 2011. Transgender inmates in California prisons. Report to the California Department of Corrections and Rehabilitation. Irvine: University of California.

Jenness, Valerie, Jennifer Sumner, Lori Sexton, and Nikkas Alamillo-Luchese. 2014. Cinderella, Wilma Flintstone, and Xena the Warrior Princess. In *Understanding diversity,* edited by Claire Renzetti, Daniel Curran, and Raquel Kennedy-Bergen. Upper Saddle River, NJ: Allyn & Bacon.

Jones, Nikki. 2009. *Between good and ghetto.* New Brunswick, NJ: Rutgers University Press.

Lorber, Judith. 1994. *Paradoxes of gender.* New Haven, CT: Yale University Press.

Miller, Jody. 2008. *Getting played.* New York: New York University Press.

Petersilia, Joan. 2008. California correctional paradox of excess and deprivation. In *Crime and justice,* edited by Michael Tonry. Chicago: University of Chicago Press.

Saperstein, Aliya, and Andrew M. Penner. 2010. The race of a criminal record. *Social Problems* 57: 92–113.

Schilt, Kristen, and Laurel Westbrook. 2009. Doing gender, doing heteronormativity: "Gender normals," transgender people, and the social maintenance of heterosexuality. *Gender & Society* 23:440–64.

Sexton, Lori, and Valerie Jenness. 2013. We're like community. Paper presented at Annual Meeting, Society for the Study of Social Problems, New York.

Sexton, Lori, Valerie Jenness, and Jennifer Macy Sumner. 2010. Where the margins meet. *Justice Quarterly* 27:835–60.

Snorton, C. Riley. 2009. A new hope. *Hypatia* 24:77–92.

Stryker, Susan. 2006. (De)Subjugated knowledges. In *The transgender studies reader,* edited by Susan Stryker and Stephen Whittle. New York: Routledge.

Sumner, Jennifer. 2009. Keeping house. Ph.D. diss., University of California–Irvine.

Sumner, Jennifer, and Valerie Jenness. 2014. Gender integration in sex-segregated prisons. *The handbook of LGBT communities, crime, and justice.* New York: Springer.

Sumner, Jennifer, Lori Sexton, Valerie Jenness, and Cheryl Maxson. In press. The (Pink) Elephant in the Room: The Structure and Experience of Race and Violence in the Lives of Transgender Inmates in California Prison. The International Handbook of Race, Class, and Gender, edited by Shirley Jackson. London: Routledge.

Tewksbury, Richard, and Roberto H. Potter. 2005. Transgender prisoners—A forgotten group. In *Managing special populations in jails and prisons,* edited by Stan Stojkovic. New York: Civic Research Institute.

Valentine, David. 2007. *Imagining transgender.* Durham, NC: Duke University Press.

Welter, Barbara. 1966. The cult of true womanhood, 1820–1860. *American Quarterly* 18:151–74.

West, Candace, and Sarah Fenstermaker. 1995. Doing difference. *Gender & Society* 9:8–37.

West, Candace, and Don H. Zimmerman. 1987. Doing gender. *Gender & Society* 1:125–51.

Zimmerman, Don H. 1992. They were all doing gender, but they weren't all passing. *Gender & Society* 6:192–98.

20

Dude-Sex: White Masculinities and "Authentic" Heterosexuality among Dudes Who Have Sex with Dudes

JANE WARD

"Closeted" men of color have increasingly become the focus of public health research and media exposés, with these accounts pointing to the likelihood that straight "men who have sex with men" (MSMs)[1] may explain rising rates of HIV infection among heterosexual women of color (Boykin, 2005; Denizet-Lewis, 2003). People of color—and particularly Black men on the "down low" (DL) and Latino MSMs—are newly central figures in discussions regarding internalized homophobia, sexual repression, HIV/AIDS, the betrayal of unsuspecting wives and girlfriends, and the failure to come out of the closet (Boykin, 2005; Hill Collins, 2004; King, 2004; Denizet-Lewis, 2003; Mukherjea and Vidal-Ortiz, 2006). To make sense of the factors that would prevent men of color from being "honest" about their "real" lives and desires, analyses of MSMs have drawn heavily on theories of the closet and its racialized underpinnings (Boykin, 2005; Hill Collins, 2004; King, 2004). Black men on the DL, in particular, have been described as "a new subculture of gay men" for whom "masculinity that is so intertwined with hyper-heterosexuality renders an openly gay identity impossible" (Hill Collins, 2004: 207). Similarly, Latino MSMs have been implicitly characterized as closeted gay or bisexual men for whom

cultural barriers, rigid ideas about gender, and strong ties to family and religion prevent public identification as gay or bisexual (Diaz, 1997).

Critics of these discourses have argued that the lack of discussion about white men on the DL has reinforced stereotypes about Black male sexuality as dangerous and predatory, as well as provided "evidence" that African Americans are more homophobic than other racial groups (Boykin, 2005). Others have shown that the down low has the all too familiar ingredients of moral panic: "concealed non-normative sexualities, a subaltern genre of expressive culture (Hip-Hop), a pandemic caused by a sexually transmitted agent, *innocent victims* (heterosexual women), and a population often accused of misbehavior (men of color)" (González, 2007: 27, emphasis in original). In sum, dominant narratives about the DL reveal a new set of fears about uncontrollable male bodies of color, or the volatile intersections of masculinity, race, and sexuality.

In addition to the racial components of down low rhetoric, the characterization of straight-identified MSMs as closeted also exemplifies the persistent tendency to view sex *acts* as meaningful and objective indicators of a true sexual selfhood and to gloss over larger questions

Reproduced by permission of SAGE Publications Ltd., London, Los Angeles, New Delhi, Singapore, and Washington DC, from Ward, J., "Dude-Sex: White Masculinities and 'Authentic' Heterosexuality among Dudes Who Have Sex with Dudes" *Sexualities* 11(4), Copyright © SAGE Publications 2008.

about the gendered and racialized construction of heterosexual and homosexual categories (Foucault, 1978; Katz, 1996; Sedgwick, 1992). According to the logic of the closet, same-sex sexual practices among heterosexuals signify sexual repression, or a failure to be honest about who one *is*, and the sexual community or culture in which one belongs. The recent insistence that MSMs are actually closeted gay men constrained by racially-specific or culturally-internal forms of homophobia has helped to solidify a narrow and essentialist conceptualization of homophobia. At the individual level, "internalized homophobia" is believed to arise from the unwillingness of MSMs to recognize and/or celebrate their essential nature, or "who they really are." At the cultural level, and akin to "culture of poverty" arguments used to pathologize African Americans, mainstream down low and MSM discourses imply that homophobia stems from essential, ethno-racial cultures of sexual repression.

As I will argue, however, a more productive reading of homophobia views the disavowal of gay identity and culture as one of the constitutive elements of heterosexual subjectivity—or a primary means of expressing heterosexual selfhood in a sexually binary world. While down low discourse implies that same-sex sexuality reveals a homosexual selfhood and that homophobia is an expression of culture, this article explores the theoretical insights that emerge from a reversal of this logic, or from viewing gay and straight as cultural spheres, and homophobia as a subjectifying practice (or a struggle to construct heterosexual selfhood).

Based on examination of an online community in which white "str8"-identified men assert that sex with other white men *bolsters* their heterosexual masculinity, I highlight the heterosexual and racialized meanings that white MSMs attach to their same-sex behaviors. I argue that while some men who have sex with men prefer to do so within gay/queer cultural worlds, others (such as the "straight dudes" described here[2]) indicate a greater sense of belonging or cultural "fit" with heterosexual identity and heteroerotic culture. For the latter group, homophobia, or the need to strongly disidentify with gay men and gay culture, is less a symptom of the *repression* of a "true self," but rather an attempt to *express* a "true self"—or one's strong sense of identification with heteropatriarchal white masculinity—in the context of having sex with men.

More specifically, this study points to the role of whiteness—including white archetypes and images—in the process of establishing heterosexual "realness," or believable straight culture. In contrast with the media's recent efforts to locate tensions between sexual identity and practice within African American and Latino cultures, my findings suggest that whiteness is also a commonly used resource for bridging the gap between heterosexual identification and same-sex desire. Previous research has pointed to various institutional contexts in which straight-identified men have sex with men, such as "tearooms," prisons, and the military (Humphreys, 1978; Kaplan, 2003; Schifter, 1999). These studies have demonstrated how men leverage hyper-masculinity, socioeconomic success, and the "need" for quick and easy sex to preserve heterosexual identity and moral "righteousness" (to use Humphrey's term). Building upon this research, the present study considers how *race* (including racial identification) and *racialized culture* (including racialized images, clothing, language and "style") are also used to bolster claims to heterosexuality and to reframe sex between men as a hetero-masculine and "not-gay" act. Similar to the assertion of feminist theorists that gender is always an intersectional accomplishment—or a construction that takes forms in and through race, class, and sexuality (Bettie, 2002; Hill Collins, 2004; Hull et al., 1982)—I show that the appearance of "authentic" heterosexuality is also accomplished in interaction with race, socioeconomic class, and gender. While recent research has begun to critically explore these intersections for men of color (González, 2007), this article marks the often-invisible significance of race and culture for white dudes who have sex with dudes.

RACE, CULTURE, AND THE SOCIAL CONSTRUCTION OF HETEROSEXUALITY

While other research has examined the historical relationship between racial ideologies and the invention of homosexuality (Ferguson, 2004; Somerville, 2000), limited attention has been given to the role of race in the routine and daily accomplishment of heterosexuality and homosexuality. In this article, I argue that the ongoing construction of authentic or believable male heterosexuality is reliant upon racial codes that signify "normal" straight male bonding, "average" heterosexual masculinity, and lack of interest in gay culture. Whiteness—and more specifically the use of white masculine archetypes for example frat boys, surfers, skaters, jocks, and white "thugs"—can play a central role in the production of an authentic and desirable heterosexual culture distinct from gay male culture.

In this article I do not make claims about the "actual" sexual and racial identities of men who place advertisements for sex online, instead I am interested in the sexualized and racialized *cultures* these advertisements draw upon and reproduce. Indeed, a growing body of queer scholarship has pointed to the significance of *culture* in the construction and regulation of the heterosexual/homosexual binary. Following Foucault's assertion that "homosexuality threatens people as a 'way of life,' rather than a way of having sex," Halberstam (2005) has argued that "queer subjects" might be redefined as those who "live (deliberately, accidentally, or of necessity) during the hours when others sleep and in the spaces (physical, metaphysical, and economic) that others have abandoned," including, "ravers, club kids, HIV-positive barebackers, rent boys, sex workers, homeless people, drug dealers, and the unemployed" (2005: 10). Halberstam expands the boundaries of queerness to include subjects often not thought of as queer, and in a distinct but similarly motivated move, other queer scholars have "disidentified" with mainstream or "homonormative" lesbian and gay politics and its focus on monogamy, domesticity, and prosperity (Duggan, 2003; Muñoz, 1999). Queer, in each of these approaches, is less about sexual practices than about a "way of life" that defies the rules of normative, respectable adult citizenship. Transcending long-held debates about whether to privilege sexual identification or sexual practice in the study of sexuality, this conceptualization of queerness is de-linked from both. Instead, because queer sexual culture or "way of life" is what most violates social norms, *culture* becomes the material of queer resistance.

This article offers support for the argument that the lines between queerness and normativity are marked less by sexual practices and identities than by cultural practices and interpretive frames. In contrast with recent work that has expanded queer subjectivity or disavowed "normal" gays and lesbians, I take a different empirical approach by demonstrating how whiteness and masculinity interact to offer *heterosexual culture* to white

men who have sex with men. At the end of this article, I return to the question of culture and to my own queer disidentification with the hetero-erotic culture produced by str8 dudes online.

METHOD: STUDYING DUDE-SEX

. . . As I will argue, the production of heterosexual culture on Craigslist is accomplished not only through what is arguably a "homophobic" and hyper-masculine rejection of queer culture; it is also dependent upon racial archetypes and images that invoke "real" heterosexual white masculinity. For this study, I collected and analyzed all ads placed on Craigslist Los Angeles by "str8" self-identified men during May through July of 2006.[3] Of the resulting 125 "Casual Encounters" ads collected and analyzed, 71 per cent made reference to race—either the racial identification of the person placing the ad or a specific racial preference for a sex partner. Among the ads that made reference to race, 86 per cent were placed by men who either identified themselves as white, or included a photo of themselves in which they appeared to be white (though I recognize that the latter is a flawed indicator of racial identity and that race itself is socially and historically constructed).[4] In order to capture all ads placed by straight-identified men seeking men, I searched for ads containing either the terms "DL" or "str8," the latter of which was more commonly used on Craigslist. In "Casual Encounters," self-identified white men placed approximately 85 per cent of the ads, regardless of whether the term "str8" or "DL" was used. . . .

REGULAR DUDES,
CASUAL ENCOUNTERS

Before describing how whiteness was deployed in Casual Encounters, I begin with a general description of str8 dudes' heteroerotic culture. In contrast with the logic that gay and straight are at opposite ends of a behavioral and biologically-determined binary, the str8 dudes who post on Craigslist construct "gay" as a chosen identity that is not particularly linked to who is having sex, or what sexual acts are involved. Instead, being gay is about *how* sex is done—the language that is used, the type of "porn" films that are watched, the beverages consumed, and the motivation that drives the sex itself. The following ads, representative of dozens of others, illustrate how str8 dudes lay claim to "straightness" while soliciting sex with other men:

Straight Dude Drunk and Horny . . . Any str8 bud wanna jack?—27. Here's the deal. Went out drinking and clubbing, thought I'd hook up with a chick, but didn't pan out. I'm buzzed, horny, checking out porn. Is there any other straight dude out there who would be into jacking while watching porn? . . . I'd rather hook up with a chick, but none of the CL [Craigslist] chicks ever work out.

What happened to the cool bi/str8 dude circle jerks?— 33. What happened to a group of masc[uline] dudes just sitting around stroking, watching a game, drinking some brews, jerking, showing off, swapping college stories, maybe playing a drinking game and see what comes up?

Str8 guy wants to try BJ tonight—27. Ok, I'll make this short. I'm up late tonight. I have a girlfriend. But I'm at home by myself now. I watch porn and I like when the women suck on big cocks. I've been thinking about it, and I think I'd like to suck one. I'm not attracted to guys so I'd rather not look at you much. Just suck your cock. I have a Polaroid and would like to take a pic with cum on my face. But this is really only for tonight cuz I'm horny! . . . I am Caucasian and prefer Caucasian.

$300 Bucks Cash if You're STR8 & Goodlooking!!—27. Hey, are you str8, goodlooking and broke? Are you Under 30 and hella cool? Like watching porn and talking bout pussy? You're in luck. 300 bucks every time we hangout. Be under 30. Honestly STR8. I'm mostly str8, great looking chill bro.

Str8 jackoff in briefs outside male bonding edging stroke—34. I am a tall blond built packin' jockman with a big bulge in my jockeys. Dig hanging in just our briefs man to man in the hot sun workin' my bulge freely . . . If you are into jackin' and being free to be a man, let's hang. If you have a pool or a yard to layout and jack freely smoke some 420 [marijuana] and just be men, hit me up. No gay sex, I am looking for legit male bonding, masturbating in the hot sun only.

Unlike in similar websites for gay men, women are a central part of str8 dudes' erotic discourse. As these ads illustrate, str8 dudes often describe sex between dudes as a less desirable, but "easy," alternative to sex with women, or suggest that dude-sex is a means of getting the kind of sex that all straight men want from women, but can only get from men—uncomplicated, emotionless,

and guaranteed. Str8 dudes get drunk, watch heterosexual porn, talk about "pussy," and maintain a clear emotional boundary between each other that draws upon the model of adolescent friendship, or the presumably "harmless," "proto-sexual" circle jerk. References to being "chill bros" and "male bonding" help to reframe dude-sex as a kind of sex that bolsters, rather than threatens, the heterosexual masculinity of the participants. Only those who are "man enough" and "chill enough" will want dude-sex or be able to handle it.

In some cases, misogyny and references to violence against women are used to reinforce the link between dude-sex and heterosexual male bonding:

Whackin Off to Porn: STR8 porn. Gang bang. STR8, bi-curious masculine white guy lookin' for a masculine guy. Get into stroking bone with a bud, talkin' bout pussy and bangin' the bitch.

Any Straight/Bi Guys Want to Help Me Fuck My Blow-up Doll???: Come on guys . . . we can't always pick up the chick we want to bone right??? So let's get together and fuck the hell out of my hot blow-up doll. Her mouth, her pussy, and her ass all feel GREAT. Just be cool, uninhibited, horny, and ready to fuck this bitch. It's all good here . . . lates.

Such ads suggest that dude-sex is a sexual and often violent expression of heterosexual masculinity and heterosexual culture, distinct from gay male culture in which misogyny typically manifests as the invisibility, rather than the objectification, of women (Ward, 2000). Marilyn Frye (1983), in her analysis of drag queens, argues "What gay male affectation of femininity seems to be is a serious sport in which men may exercise their power and control over the feminine, much as in other sports . . . But the mastery of the feminine is not feminine. It is masculine." I draw on Frye's analysis to suggest that while dude-sex makes use of and "masters" homosexual or non-normative sex practices, this deployment of non-normative sexuality in the service of "str8" culture is perhaps not best understood as "queer."

WHITE DUDES, RACE, AND CLASS

Str8 dudes draw on the imagery of male bonding and the symbols of straight male culture, including references to sports, beer, fraternity membership, smoking pot and being "chill," "buds," or "bros." Yet "dude speak" and "dude style" is not simply masculine and heterosexual, it is also racialized. Recent studies of Black and Latino men on the down low have emphasized the importance of shared urban culture, and particularly hip hop, to the construction of down-low masculinity and sexuality (González, 2007). González explains that *culture* (and not public or politicized identity) is what is at stake for Latinos on the down low: "gay is not an option; Hip Hop is" (2007). Here I argue that *racial cultures* are also a central player in how white str8 dudes make sense of their str8 sexuality. In some cases, white dudes appropriate the symbols of Black and Latino down-low masculinity; in other cases, they foreground symbols of white masculinity (surfers, frat guys, jocks and so on) or synthesize the former with the latter.

Appropriating Hip Hop Masculinity: White Bros and Thugs on the DL

White str8 dudes—like a growing number of young white men in general—bolster their masculinity through the appropriation of terms and gestures used by Black and Latino men, especially within rap lyrics and culture. Writers critical of the mainstreaming and white ownership of rap have pointed to the ways in which its consumption by white youth has bled into other forms of racial and cultural appropriation (Kitwana, 2005). Young white men, in particular, have turned to rap for a new model of masculinity, male rivalry/violence, and heterosexual male bonding—resulting in white males giving each other "daps," wearing hip hop clothing, and "affectionately" referring to one another using the term "nigga" (Kitwana, 2005). While the appropriation of Black culture is rarely this explicit on Craigslist, str8 dudes nonetheless construct a masculine and heterosexual culture through a complex synthesis of white masculinity (e.g., surfer dudes) and masculinities of color (e.g. bros, thugs, and the DL). Str8 dudes commonly use phrases identified by African American studies scholars as "Black slang," such as "sup?," "hit me up," and "thugged out" (Smitherman, 2000), such as in the following ads:

23 y/o white dude party in Hollywood—Hey guys, I'm partyin right now at home and have plenty of stuff to share. . . . I'm lookin to meet a cool str8 thugged out white dude around my age, who would wanna come over, kick back, watch a lil porn, smoke a lil, and

stroke off together. I might even be down to deep-throat some cock so if you love getting awesome head you should definitely hit me back! I'm lookin for someone chill & masculine so hit me up if this sounds like you . . . LATE

Str8 curious on the DL. Lookin' to chill—23. Sup? Just looking to chill with another str8/bi dude, into young or older bros type . . . to mess around, not into perverted shit. Also not into fatty, femm guys. If you're a guy, please be in shape. I'm sort of skinny, curious here and haven't really acted on it. Just regular sane dude. Discretion a must. Aiite, late.

In an effort to convey that the sexual encounter will be casual, meaningless, and embedded in heterosexual male culture, white str8 dudes rely upon "urban" slang derived from Black culture to represent heterosexuality. However, as with many forms of cultural appropriation, the slang used by str8 dudes is fast becoming associated with whites, and white masculinity in particular. For instance, according to the American Heritage Dictionary, "bro," a term commonly used by str8 dudes, is a slang term for "brother" with etymological roots in African American vernacular English. However, its popular and contemporary usage by young white men in California has transformed its local and contextual meaning. Bloggers on urbandictionary.com, for example, define "bros" as: "white frat guys," "stupid white trash guys," and "usually white young males, found commonly in places like San Bernardino County in California, as well as Orange County."

It may be most accurate to describe the racialized heterosexuality of str8 dudes as a kind of Eminem-inspired white working-class "thuggery," constructed through an in-your-face reclamation of "white trash" and homophobic, or anti-gay, sexuality. While some ads express desire for "average" working-class men (e.g. "carpenters, carpet layers, plumbers, construction workers, mechanics, truckers, cable guys, delivery guys, overall just a hard working guy as I am. NO GAYS sorry"), others eroticize aggressive "white trash" masculinity, such as in the following ad:

Str8 fuck a guy in his briefs, masc(uline) man to man fuck, hiv neg only. Hey fucks. I need to fuckin lay the pipe in some tight manhole today. I am hiv neg fuck with rubbers only. I want to have a hot packin guy in some tighty whities bent over and on all fours takin my dick like a champ. No fems or tweeking pnp ["party and play"] dudes. I hate that shit. Only 420 and a hot packin butt. Hit me up with your pix and your contact info.

Ads such as this amplify the appearance of heterosexuality through a synthesis of working-class culture, whiteness, and what is arguably the subtle appropriation of Black masculinity through hip hop slang ("hit me up") and "thug" masculinity. Other ads produced similar images of "rough" white masculinity through reference to skinheads and other archetypes of white male rebellion historically rooted in white racist, sexist and homophobic violence—"lookin for str8, bi, surfr, sk8r, punk, military, truckers, skinhead, rough trade. . . . I'll give you the best head ever, buddy."

Though being on the DL has been sensationalized in the media as a rejection of white gay culture specific to Black men living "otherwise heterosexual lives" (Denizet-Lewis, 2003), a few white str8 dudes on Craigslist claimed DL identity as their own (though "str8" was used far more commonly):

> *STR8 DUDES . . . White boy lookin for a NO CHAT suck . . . u lemme suck u . . . —29.* Hot dude on ur dick . . . u fuck my throat and bust it . . . we never talk. Come over, kick back, pull ur cock out and get a kick ass wet deepthroat BJ. Love to deepthroat a hot str8 dude on the DL . . . bust ur nut and split. I'm a very goodlooking in shape white dude . . . totally on the DL . . . just wanna suck a hot str8 dude off, take ur nut . . . that's all. My place is kewl.

> *SECRET SERVICE HEAD—28.* Sup? Looking for bi/str8 bud who is just looking to crack a nut. . . . Just walk in kick back watch a porn and get blown. . . . Cum and go. . . . That's all I am looking for . . . Be white, under 30, masculine and discreet. This is on the DL. . . . Have a girlfriend . . . but new to town.

Black gay writer and activist Keith Boykin has argued that there is a racist stigma and double standard associated with the "down low." Referring to the white characters in the hit film *Brokeback Mountain,* Boykin contends,

> the reason why we don't say they're on the down low is simple—they're white. When white men engage in this behavior, we just call it what it is and move on. But when black men do it, then we have to pathologize it into something evil called the "down low." (Boykin, blog on keithboykin.com, May, 2006)

Indeed, the stereotypical image of the DL is that of partnered, heterosexual, masculine Black men having quick and deceitful sexual relations unconnected to mainstream gay culture. As such, the DL is a useful shorthand available to white str8 dudes wishing to affirm their own heterosexuality, as well as to invoke the perhaps fetishized imagery of deceitful, immoral, or "evil" sex (to use Boykin's term).

Surfers, Skaters, and Frat Guys: Archetypes of White Heterosexual Masculinity

Archetypes of youthful, white, heterosexual masculinity are also popular among str8 dudes on Craigslist, who commonly include a list of desired "male types" in their ads. Many str8 dudes express an explicit preference for other white dudes, and this preference is strengthened by naming specific forms of hegemonic masculinity, such as jocks, skaters, surfers and frat dudes (Connell, 2005):

> *Any HOT White jocks lookin to get sucked off???—* 23. Hey guys, I'm just a chill good looking dude heading down to the area for a BBQ and I'm looking for any other HOT Str8 or bi white dudes looking to get sucked off. Just sit back and relax and get drained. I'm especially into sucking off hot jocks, skaters, surfers, and frat dudes. If you're hot and if you're into a hot no strings blow job, then hit me up.

> *Seeking a MASCULINE JACK OFF BUD to STR8 PORN—29.* Hot masculine white dude here . . . looking for another hot white dude to come by my place, and work out a hot load side by side. Straight Porn only. Prefer str8, surfer, etc. Not usually into gay dudes.

In such ads, the heterosexual culture of dude-sex is established by drawing upon available typologies of white heterosexual masculinity. Others make reference to specific white ethnicities, such as one ad seeking "blondes, Italian(s), Jewish types, fat dick heads, hairy, white and/or Latin dudes . . . suit and tie types."[5] Just as the appropriation of Black and white working-class masculinities helps construct an authentic "heteroerotic" culture, so too does the image of a normative middle-class or professional whiteness (i.e. dudes who go to college, participate in sports, wear suit and ties, and so on). In both cases, race and socioeconomic class play a central role in making heterosexuality legible in the context of men's sexual seduction of other men.

In addition to naming racialized archetypes, some ads include long and detailed accounts of the exact clothing, dialogue, sex acts, and erotic mood required to maintain the heteroeroticism of dude-sex. For instance, the following ad was placed by a "str8 guy" who "lives a very str8 life" seeking someone to enact a "role play" in exchange for $400. The ad included a much longer script from which I have excerpted only a small segment:

> . . . You come to the hotel in loose shorts with no underwear on, a tank top and flip flops, and when you get there we just kick back and maybe have a few beers and shoot the shit to get to know each other a little bit and feel more comfortable, then we start talking about our girlfriends and girls that we have fucked before or the best blow jobs we have had, etc., the whole time acting like we are just good friends that are horny. I am kind of dumb and don't have a lot of experience with chicks and you want to teach me and help me learn more. You then tell me that you are getting really horny thinking about all the hot sex you have had and ask me if I have any porn we can watch. I put one on and as we watch the porn, you are constantly grabbing your dick and playing with it as it gets harder and harder. . . . Then you sit down right next to me and you say, "dude, you gotta hear this story about this one chick that I made suck my dick until I blew my load in her," then you tell me the story about it. While you are telling me the story you act it out with me . . .

While whiteness is not explicitly named in the role-play, the script mirrors the white surfer/frat dude fetishism common in the "Casual Encounters" section of Craigslist–Los Angeles. As stated in a web article on "frat fashion" (published by the New York hipster website blacktable.com in 2005): "From out of the shower or off the lacrosse field and right into happy hour, flip-flops take [frat guys] every place they want to go. Flip-flops suggest sand and SoCal-cool [southern-California-cool] . . . !" Thus, some of the ad's references—such as the "costume" of flip flops, shorts and a tank top—possibly hint at white surfer/frat masculinity, exemplifying the ways in which erotic fantasies may be implicitly or unintentionally racialized. Yet the glorification of surfers and frat dudes also illustrates the way in which the racialized construction of heterosexual and homosexual cultures are locally or regionally specific. Many of the references to white masculinity on Craigslist–Los Angeles—surfers, bros, dudes—appear to be rooted in southern California lifestyles, or at least the imagination of them.

Less Str8, More DL: Desiring Black Men?

In addition to self-identifying with the DL, a small number of white str8 dudes expressed desire for "no strings" sex with "hung" Black men on the DL. These ads, in contrast with the ads in which white dudes used Black slang and style to seduce one another, produced a distinct cultural effect. While many "white on white" ads implied sameness, reciprocity or egalitarianism (let's stroke together, watch porn together, "work out a hot load side by side" and so on), "white seeking Black" ads typically emphasized difference, hierarchy, and service. The majority of such ads were placed by white men looking to perform "blow jobs" for big, muscular Black men. Many of the ads in "Casual Encounters" mention the importance of being "hung," but ads seeking Black men placed particular emphasis on the relationship between race and body size (e.g., "big BLACK cock," "nice big meaty Black guys"):

> *Discreet White Deep Throat 4 DL Black—Size Matters—44.* Discreet 44 yr old white guy lookin' to service hot Black guys on the DL. I'm hairy, good shape. I'm lookin' for very hung Black guys who love to kick back, watch porn and get their cocks serviced. I really like to deep throat big BLACK cock. If you are interested, hit me back with your stats and a pic if you have one. . . . I really love very tall skinny men, hung huge.

> *Looking to suck off big black men, on the DL*—White guy here looking to suck off big muscular black guys. I like them big, over 250lbs and muscular. No strings attached. Hoping to meet some men on the DL. Got my own place, it's private and discreet, no strings, no hassles, etc. Just want to suck off some nice big meaty black guys.

Ads placed by white guys seeking Black men on the DL were less likely to focus on authenticating heterosexuality through reference to women, straight porn, and friendship (male bonding, "being buddies") and more likely to focus on "the DL" as pre-formulated code for impersonal sex across racial difference.

White submission and Black dominance was also a central theme in these ads. In the following ad, an image is included that reverses the master/slave relationship (a dominant Black male, and a shackled white male) and has likely been taken from BDSM-themed gay porn:

> *Muscled Guy Looking for Str8 or Bi to Service on the Down Low*—Meet me at the construction site. I will

be there waiting for you [in the?] dark, service you and leave anonymous. . . . Send pic must be hot like me.

While race is not mentioned in the text of this ad, the figure of the dominant Black male (and the submissive white male body) is used to represent the queerer—or less normal and natural—white fantasy of the down low. This and similar ads suggest that in the Black–white encounter, Black men are always dominant; they receive sexual service, but they don't provide it. Friendship, equity, and "normal and natural male bonding" are represented as either undesirable or impossible across racial lines. In some ads, class differences also pervade the encounter. In the foregoing ad, the "construction site"—in contrast to the reference to white "suit and tie types"—invokes manual labor and the type of job more likely to be held by men of color. The DL requires anonymity, discretion, and meeting in "dark" places like the construction site. In the Craigslist representation of the Black–white encounter, cross-racial sex is not an organic expression of "male bonding" or "just being men." Instead, the presence of (or desire for) race and class difference produces a darker, less natural and less straight encounter.

Because of its association with men of color and the closet (or hidden homosexuality), the term "DL" was less likely to be associated with authentic white heterosexuality in "Casual Encounters" ("str8" was preferred by white dudes) and was more likely to be used by men of color in the "Men Seeking Men" section of Craigslist. In fact, though beyond the scope of this study (which focuses on white men), I noticed during data collection that ads placed by men of color appeared more frequently in the "Men Seeking Men" section than in the "Casual Encounters" section. I can only speculate about why men of color would not have chosen to post ads in "Casual Encounters," but it seems likely that they were deterred by the predominance of white dudes seeking other white dudes. Conversely, it makes sense that white dudes uninterested in gay identification would be drawn to "Casual Encounters," given that its moniker makes no reference to gender identity (or identity at all), while "Men Seeking Men" makes gender identity primary.

While reference to the symbols of Black masculinity and style helped in the production of authentic heterosexuality, reference to actual sexual contact with Black men generally did not. Instead, cross-racial sex was permeated with difference and inequality, becoming itself somewhat queer. This finding mirrors the findings of the study more broadly—for straight-identified white men seeking men, maintaining a heteroerotic culture was largely reliant upon specifically white forms of heterosexual masculinity (including those that appropriate some elements of Black culture).

DISCUSSION: DISAVOWING STR8 DUDES

Str8 dudes who seek sex with men draw upon a wide variety of conceptual resources to assert a heterosexual male identity, including the use of racialized archetypes and images intended to signify authentic heterosexuality. While other research has highlighted the ways in which racial binaries were used to construct the heterosexual/homosexual binary in the late 19th century (Somerville, 2000), the ads placed on "Casual Encounters" suggest that race continues to play a central role in the daily accomplishment of heterosexual "realness," particularly when authenticity is likely to be called into question. This deployment of race to signify heterosexuality included both cross-racial identifications and the preservation of white racial boundaries. In some cases, white str8 dudes appropriated the symbols/language of Black heterosexual masculinity to construct a culture of male bonding that is arguably recognizable as the antithesis of gay male culture. In other cases, white str8 dudes invoked the "DL" as a means of eroticizing deceitful and "evil" sex or expressing desire for closeted Black men looking to be "serviced."

However, most commonly, white str8 dudes drew on archetypes of white heterosexual masculinity to provide evidence of being an average, normal dude. The majority of white str8 men who posted in "Casual Encounters" expressed a preference for men like themselves, or men who fit the paradigmatic image of the straight middle-class white male (i.e., frat dudes, suit and tie types, surfers, skaters and so on). While being gay has often been stereotyped as a "white thing" (Muñoz, 1999), the figure of the *straight* white man symbolizes both financial and cultural power as well as the average man, the "everyman," the "regular dude." Given the ways in which systems of white racial dominance construct whiteness as natural, invisible, and non-racialized (Frankenberg,

2001; Lipsitz, 1998), sex between white men is likely to be experienced as deracialized and "natural," possessing none of the "difference" or racial fetishism expressed in cross-racial sexual encounters. Thus, for white str8 dudes, whiteness played a key role in producing evidence of normal/average male heterosexuality. This may be because desire for the ostensibly deracialized (but white) "everyman" is less threatening than the desire for men of color, who are coded as both hypermasculine and hypersexual within US popular culture (Hill Collins, 2004).

However, despite the ways in which the emphasis on whiteness may be experienced as the absence of racial fetish, the erotic culture of "Casual Encounters" was rife with white fetishism. In addition to simply declaring oneself a white str8 dude, detailed descriptions of white male bodies, white male lifestyles ("looking for surfers, [and other] LA-types"), and white male bonding helped to create and maintain the heteroerotic culture of dudesex. Surfers, for example, were a particularly desired type, not because of the importance of surfing skills or the desire to actually surf together, but more likely because of the white, hetero-masculine script associated with southern California surf lifestyle—flip flops, chillin', just being bros and talking about chicks. In sum, racial markers are not used only to identify one's physical "type," they also provide an entire cultural universe from which to draw heterosexual costumes, scripts, and countless other codes for heterosexual masculinity.

At a broader level, this and other studies indicate that racial categories are always already sexualized and that sexuality categories are always already raced (González, 2007; Muñoz-Laboy, 2004; Somerville, 2000). Though I have focused on the intersections of whiteness and heterosexuality, my aim is not to position whiteness simply as one of several possible and equivalent examples of the racialization of heterosexuality. Instead, the ads on Craigslist suggest that in a culture constituted by both a racial and sexual binary (white/other and heterosexual/other), whiteness and heterosexuality become "natural" bedfellows. Both whiteness and heterosexuality simultaneously signify the "really, really normal, nothing out of the ordinary" subject. For the str8 dudes on Craigslist, it appears that the most average and normal of male heterosexualities is white heterosexuality, even when it engages in same-sex practices and appropriates Black culture. In the context of white male bonding, Black bodies disrupt the staging of normalcy

and occupy a distinctly queerer space "down low."[6] Building on sociological analyses of hegemonic and marginalized masculinities (Connell, 2005), future research might also reveal the range and hierarchy of heterosexualities by conceptualizing white heterosexuality as "hegemonic" and heterosexualities of color as "marginalized."

In addition to highlighting the racialization of heterosexuality and heteroerotic culture, the ads placed by str8 dudes also confirm the importance of giving as much consideration to sexual *culture* as has been given to sexual practice. When queer feminist colleagues and I first read an ad placed by a str8 dude in "Casual Encounters"—"nothing gay here at all, just two guys, watching hot porn, stroking until the point of no return"—we marveled at the suggestion that the ad was anything but gay. Later, I marveled that my colleagues and I had been so invested in owning (as queer) a cultural space that is so decidedly intent on identifying with heterosexuality. In Casual Encounters, sex practices are not useful guides for delineating the boundaries of queer and non-queer, or establishing political alliances with queer stakeholders. While the white str8 dudes who post ads in Casual Encounters express their desire for sex with other men, their desire takes form within the context of heterosexual identification and heterosexual erotic culture (in other words, the use of heterosexual pornography, the disavowal of gay culture, misogynistic discussions of women and their bodies, insistence on "normal" heterosexual male bonding as the organizing principle of the sexual encounter).

To de-queer the sex described on Craigslist is to give up the epistemological pleasure of self-righteous knowing, owning, outing and naming. In the face of homophobia and heterosexism, honing one's "gaydar" and revealing that *we are everywhere* have been among few queer luxuries. Yet as others have argued (Halberstam, 2005; Duggan, 2003), political solidarity built primarily around sex acts misrecognizes what is most threatening, and subversive, about queerness. Queer *culture*—including a collective rejection of the rules associated with normal, adult, reproductive sexuality and (nonconsensual) heterosexual power relations—may better help scholars and activists determine the meaning of queer. On the one hand, str8 dudes exemplify sexual rule-breaking and the defiance of respectable sex behavior. On the other hand, their reliance on misogyny and homophobia to interpret and organize their sexual practices suggests a greater degree of cultural alignment with heterosexual traditions of same-sex sexuality, in which male sexual bonding is interconnected with violence against women and gay men. This complexity reveals the permeability of the categories "straight" and "queer," which signify not only the divide between normal and abnormal sexual practices but also the divide between normal and abnormal interpretive frames for understanding these practices. Str8 dudes have abnormal sex, but they invest in ideologies of racial and sexual normalcy. Thus, str8 dudes' "erotic culture of normalcy" also suggests the need to rethink the ways in which repression and "internalized homophobia" are mapped onto all straight-identified same-sex behaviors. Rather than a symptom of repression, passivity, or lack of self-awareness, str8 dudes' rejection of queerness may be more accurately understood as agentic acts of identification with heterosexual culture.

This article has pointed to the value of viewing queer and straight as cultural spheres that people choose to inhabit in large part because they experience a cultural and political fit. Such an approach highlights the *intersections* of queer and straight cultures, identities, and practices, and suggests that some intersections may be formed by queer sexual practices and straight cultural and political investments. Redefining queer and nonqueer as cultural affiliations also implies that queer "rights" serve to protect not everyone who engages in same-sex sexuality, but all those who cannot or will not invest in hegemonic str8 culture—gender freaks, kids in gay–straight alliances, and all people who are or are willing to be part of this thing we call "queer."

NOTES

1. MSM is a term first adopted by epidemiologists to classify men who have sex with men, regardless of whether they identify as gay, bisexual or, heterosexual.

2. "Dude" is a vernacular term used by young white men in the USA to refer to one another. It was originally popularized by young, primarily white, surfers and skaters (or skateboarders) in California, but has since achieved popularity throughout the USA. "Jock" is a slang term used to refer to young male athletes, and "frat" is an abbreviation for a college fraternity.

3. There is disagreement on the web regarding the meaning of the term "str8." In some online communities, "str8" functions simply as internet slang for "straight," and it has also been used as an abbreviation for "straight" in rap lyrics. However, others, such

as contributors to "urbandictionary.com," argue that "str8" is used almost exclusively by gay and bisexual men "in the closet."

4. See González (2007) for a discussion of the distinction between "cyberdata" and real time observations in "cyberethnography."

5. Thank you to Rachel Luft for clarifying this point.

6. I note here that the association between light skin and whiteness is not specific to the research context, but is an aspect of racial hegemony that arguably exists independent of data selection methods and over-determines the analysis of visual images.

REFERENCES

Bettie, Julie (2002) *Women without Class: Girls, Race, and Identity.* Berkeley: University of California Press.

Blacktable.com (2005) "That Was Then, This is Now: Frat Fashions, They Are a Changin", *Black Table* 28 July, URL (accessed 5 May 2008): http://blacktable.com/fratguys050728.htm

Boykin, Keith (2005) *Beyond the Down Low: Sex, Lies, and Denial in Black America.* New York: Carroll & Graf.

Boykin, Keith (2006) "The White Down Low," 23 May, URL (accessed 5 May 2008): http://www.keithboykin.com/arch/2006/05/23/the_white_down

Butler, Judith (1990) *Gender Trouble: Feminism and the Subversion of Identity.* New York: Routledge.

Connell, R. W. (2005) *Masculinities* (2nd edition). Berkeley: University of California Press.

Craigslist.org (2006) "Casual Encounters," ads posted by "str8" self-identified men, May through July 2006 (particular ads no longer available). Home page URL (accessed April 2008): www.craigslist.org

Denizet-Lewis, Benoit (2003) "Double Lives on the Down Low," *The New York Times Sunday Magazine* 3 August, URL (accessed May 2008): http://query.nytimes.com/gst/fullpage.html?res=9F0CE0D61E3FF930A3575BC0A9659C8B63.

Diaz, Rafael (1997) *Latino Gay Men and HIV: Culture, Sexuality, and Risk Behavior.* New York: Routledge.

Duggan, Lisa (2003) *The Twilight of Equality? Neoliberalism, Cultural Politics, and the Attack on Democracy.* New York: Beacon Press.

Ferguson, Roderick (2004) *Aberrations in Black: Toward a Queer of Color Critique.* Minneapolis: University of Minnesota Press.

Foucault, Michel (1978) *The History of Sexuality: An Introduction.* New York: Vintage Books.

Frankenberg, Ruth (2001) "The Mirage of Unmarked Whiteness," in B. B. Rasmussen, E. Klinenberg, I. J. Nexica and M. Wray (eds.) *The Making and Unmaking of Whiteness,* pp. 72–96. Durham, NC: Duke University Press.

Frye, Marilyn (1983) "Lesbian Feminism and the Gay Rights Movement: Another View of Male Supremacy, Another Separatism," in Marilyn Frye *The Politics of Reality: Essays in Feminist Theory,* pp. 128–51. New York: Crossing Press.

González, M. Alfredo (2007) "Latinos on Da Down Low: The Limitations of Sexual Identity in Public Health," *Latino Studies* 5(1): 25–52.

Halberstam, Judith (2005) *In a Queer Time and Place: Transgender Bodies, Subcultural Lives.* New York: New York University Press.

Hill Collins, Patricia (2004) *Black Sexual Politics: African Americans, Gender, and the New Racism.* New York: Routledge.

Hull, Gloria, Bell Scott, Patricia and Smith, Barbara (eds.) (1982) *All the Women Are White, All the Blacks Are Men, But Some of Us Are Brave: Black Women's Studies.* New York: Feminist Press.

Humphreys, Laud (1978) *Tearoom Trade: Impersonal Sex in Public Places* (2nd edition). Chicago, IL: Aldine Transaction.

Kaplan, Danny (2003) *Brothers and Others in Arms: The Making of Love and War in Israeli Combat Units.* New York: Harrington Park Press.

Katz, Jonathan (1996) *The Invention of Heterosexuality.* New York: Plume.

King, J. K. (2004) *On the Down Low: A Journey into the Lives of "Straight" Black Men Who Sleep with Men.* New York: Broadway.

Kitwana, Bakari (2005) *Why White Kids Love Hip Hop: Wangstas, Wiggers, Wannabes, and the New Reality of Race in America.* New York: Basic Civitas Books.

Lipsitz, George (1998) *The Possessive Investment in Whiteness: How White People Profit from Identity Politics.* Philadelphia, PA: Temple University Press.

Mukherjea, Ananya and Vidal-Ortiz, Salvador (2006) "Studying HIV Risk in Vulnerable Communities: Methodological and Reporting Shortcomings in the Young Men's Study in New York City," *The Qualitative Report* 11(2): 393–416, URL (accessed 5 May 2008): http://www.nova.edu/ssss/QR/QR11–2/mukherjea.pdf

Muñoz, Jose (1999) *Disidentifications: Queers of Color and the Performance of Politics.* Minneapolis: University of Minnesota Press.

Muñoz-Laboy, Miguel (2004) "Beyond 'MSM': Sexual Desire among Bisexually-Active Latino Men in New York City." *Sexualities* 7(1): 55–80.

Rodriguez, Juana Maria (2003) *Queer Latinidad: Identity Practices, Discursive Spaces.* New York: New York University Press.

Schifter, Jacobo (1999) *Macho Love: Sex Behind Bars in Central America.* New York: Harrington Park Press.

Sedgwick, Eve Kosofsky (1992) *Epistemology of the Closet.* Berkeley: University of California Press.

Smitherman, Geneva (2000) *Black Talk: Words and Phrases from the Hood to the Amen Corner.* New York: Mariner Books.

Somerville, Siobhan (2000) *Queering the Color Line: Race and the Invention of Homosexuality in American Culture.* Durham, NC: Duke University Press.

Urbandictionary.com (1999–2008) Slang dictionary, URL (accessed April 2008): http://www.urbandictionary.com

Ward, Jane (2000) "Queer Sexism: Rethinking Gay Men and Masculinity," in Peter Nardi (ed.) *Gay Masculinities,* pp. 152–75. Thousand Oaks: SAGE Publications.

Ward, Jane (2007) "Straight Dude Seeks Same: Mapping the Relationship between Sexual Identities, Practices, and Cultures," in Mindy Stombler, Dawn M. Baunauch, Elisabeth O. Burgess and Denise Donnelly (eds.) *Sex Matters: The Sexuality and Society Reader* (second edition), pp. 31–7. New York: Allyn & Bacon.

West, Candace and Zimmerman, Don (1987) "Doing Gender," *Gender & Society* 1(2): 125–51.

21

"Americans Have a Different Attitude"

Family, Sexuality, and Gender in Filipina American Lives

YEN LE ESPIRITU

I want my daughters to be Filipino especially on sex. I always emphasize to them that they should not participate in sex if they are not married. We are also Catholic. We are raised so that we don't engage in going out with men while we are not married. And I don't like it to happen to my daughters as if they have no values. I don't like them to grow up that way, like the American girls.

—Filipina immigrant mother

I found that a lot of the Asian American friends of mine, we don't date like White girls date. We don't sleep around like White girls do. Everyone is really mellow at dating because your parents were constraining and restrictive.

—Second generation Filipina daughter

Drawing from my research on Filipino American families in San Diego, California, this paper explores the ways in which racialized immigrants claim through gender the power denied them through racism. Gender shapes immigrant identity and allows racialized immigrants to assert cultural superiority over the dominant group. For Filipino immigrants who come from a homeland that was once a U.S. colony, cultural reconstruction has been a way to counter the cultural Americanization of the Philippines, to resist the assimilative and alienating demands of U.S. society, and to reaffirm to themselves their self-worth in the face of colonial, racial, and gendered subordination.

The opening narratives above, made by a Filipina immigrant mother and a second generation Filipina daughter, suggest that the virtuous Filipina daughter is partially constructed on the conceptualization of white women as sexually immoral. They also reveal the ways in which women's sexuality—and their enforced "morality"—is fundamental to the structuring of social inequalities. Historically, the sexuality of racialized women has been systematically demonized and denigrated by dominant or oppressor groups to justify and bolster nationalist movements, colonialism, and/or racism. But as the above narratives indicate, racialized groups also castigate the morality of white women as a strategy of resistance—a means to assert a morally superior public face to the dominant society. But this strategy is not without costs. The elevation of Filipina chastity (particularly that of young women) has the effect of reinforcing masculinist and patriarchal power in the name of a greater ideal of national/ethnic self-respect. Because the control of women is one of the principal means of asserting moral superiority, young women in immigrant families face

Reprinted by permission of the author.

numerous restrictions on their autonomy, mobility, and personal decision making.

STUDYING FILIPINOS IN SAN DIEGO

The information on which this article is based comes mostly from original research: in-depth interviews that I conducted with about one hundred Filipinos in San Diego. As in other Filipino communities along the Pacific Coast, the San Diego community grew dramatically in the twenty-five years following passage of the 1965 Immigration Act. In 1990, there were close to 96,000 Filipinos in San Diego County. Although they comprised only 4 percent of the county's general population, they constituted close to 50 percent of the Asian American population (Espiritu 1995). Many post-1965 Filipinos have come to San Diego as professionals— most conspicuously as health care workers. A 1992 analysis of the socio-economic characteristics of recent Filipino immigrants in San Diego indicated that they were predominantly middle class, college-educated, and English-speaking professionals who were much more likely to own rather than rent their homes (Rumbaut 1994).

Using the "snowball" sampling technique, I started by interviewing Filipino Americans whom I knew and then asking them to refer me to others who might be willing to be interviewed. In other words, I chose participants not randomly but rather through a network of Filipino American contacts whom the first group of respondents trusted. To capture as much as possible the diversity within the Filipino American community, I sought and selected respondents of different backgrounds and with diverse viewpoints. The interviews, tape-recorded in English, ranged from three to ten hours each and took place in offices, coffee shops, and homes. My questions were open-ended and covered three general areas: family and immigration history, ethnic identity and practices, and community development among San Diego's Filipinos. The interviewing process varied widely: some respondents needed to be prompted with specific questions, while others spoke at great length on their own. Some chose to cover the span of their lives; others focused on specific events that were particularly important to them.

CONSTRUCTING THE DOMINANT GROUP: THE MORAL FLAWS OF WHITE AMERICANS

In this section, I argue that female morality—defined as women's dedication to their families and sexual restraints—is one of the few sites where economically and politically dominated groups can construct the dominant group as "other" and themselves as superior. Because womanhood is idealized as the repository of tradition, the norms which regulate women's behaviors become a means of determining and defining group status and boundaries. As a consequence, the burdens and complexities of cultural (re)presentation fall most heavily on immigrant women and their daughters. Below, I show that Filipino immigrants claim moral distinctiveness for their community by (re)presenting "Americans" as morally flawed and themselves as family-oriented model minorities and their wives and daughters as paragons of morality.

Family-Oriented Model Minorities: "White Women Will Leave You . . ."

Many of my respondents constructed their "ethnic" culture as principled and the "American" culture as deviant. Most often, this morality narrative revolves around family life and family relations. When asked what set Filipinos apart from other Americans, my respondents—of all ages and class backgrounds— repeatedly contrasted the close-knit Filipino families to what they perceived to be the more impersonal quality of U.S. family relations. In the following narratives, "Americans" are characterized as lacking in strong family ties and collective identity, less willing to do the work of family and cultural maintenance, and less willing to abide by patriarchal norms in husband/wife relations:

> Our [Filipino] culture is different. We are more close-knit. We tend to help one another. Americans, ya know, they are all right, but they don't help each other that much. As a matter of fact, if the parents are old, they take them to a convalescent home and let them rot there. We would never do that in our culture. We would nurse them; we would help them until the very end. (Filipino immigrant, 60 years old)

Our (Filipino) culture is very communal. You know that your family will always be there, that you don't have to work when you turn 18, you don't have to pay rent when you are 18, which is the American way of thinking. You also know that if things don't work out in the outside world, you can always come home and mommy and daddy will always take you and your children in. (second generation Filipina, 33 years old)

Asian parents take care of their children. Americans have a different attitude. They leave their children to their own resources. They get baby sitters to take care of their children or leave them in day care. That's why when they get old, their children don't even care about them. (Filipina immigrant, 46 years old)

Implicit in the negative depiction of U.S. families—as uncaring, selfish, and distant—is the allegation that White women are not as dedicated to their families as Filipina women. Several Filipino men who married White women recalled being warned by their parents and relatives that "White women will leave you." As one man related, "My mother said to me, 'Well, you know, don't marry a White person because they would take everything that you own and leave you.'" For some Filipino men, perceived differences in attitudes about women's roles between Filipina and non-Filipina women influenced their marital choice. A Filipino American navy man explained why he went back to the Philippines to look for a wife:

My goal was to marry a Filipina. I requested to be stationed in the Philippines to get married to a Filipina. I'd seen the women here and basically they are spoiled. They have a tendency of not going along together with their husband. They behave differently. They chase the male, instead of the male, the normal way of the traditional way is for the male to go after the female. They have sex without marrying. They want to do their own things. So my idea was to go back home and marry somebody who has never been here. I tell my son the same thing: if he does what I did and finds himself a good lady there, he will be in good hands.

Another man who had dated mostly White women in high school recounted that when it came time for him to marry, he "looked for the kind of women that I'd met in the Philippines."

It is important to note the gender implications of these claims. That is, while both men and women identify the family system as a tremendous source of cultural pride, it is women—through their unpaid housework and kin work—who shoulder the primary responsibility for maintaining family closeness. Because the moral status of the community rests on women's labor, women, as wives and daughters, are not only applauded for but are expected to dedicate themselves to the family. Writing on the constructed image of ethnic family and gender, di Leonardo (1984) reminds us that "a large part of stressing ethnic identity amounts to burdening women with increased responsibilities for preparing special foods, planning rituals, and enforcing 'ethnic' socialization of children" (p. 222). A twenty-three-year-old Filipina spoke about the reproductive work that her mother performed and expected her to learn:

In my family, I was the only girl, so my mom expected a lot from me. She wanted me to help her to take care of the household. I felt like there was a lot of pressure on me. It's very important to my mom to have the house in order: to wash the dishes, to keep the kitchen in order, vacuuming, and dusting and things like that. She wants me to be a perfect housewife. It's difficult. I have been married now for about four months and my mother asks me every now and then what have I cooked for my husband. My mom is also very strict about families getting together on holidays and I would always help her to organize that. Each holiday, I would try to decorate the house for her, to make it more special.

The burden of unpaid reproductive and kin work is particularly stressful for women who work outside the home. In the following narrative, a Filipina wife and mother described the pulls of family and work that she experienced when she went back to school to pursue a doctoral degree in nursing:

The Filipinos, we are very collective, very connected. Going through the doctoral program, sometimes I think it is better just to forget about my relatives and just concentrate on school. All that connectedness, it steals parts of myself because all of my energies are devoted to my family. And that is the reason why I think Americans are successful. The majority of the American people they can do what they want. They don't feel guilty because they only have a few people to relate to. For us Filipinos, it's like roots under the tree, you have all these connections. The Americans are more like the trunk. I am still trying to go up to the trunk of the tree but it is too hard. I want to be more independent, more like the Americans.

It is important to note that this Filipina interprets her exclusion and added responsibilities as only racial when they are largely gendered. For example, when she says, "the American people they can do what they want," she ignores the differences in the lives of white men and white women—the fact that most white women experience similar pulls of family, education, and work.

Racialized Sexuality and (Im)morality: "In America . . . Sex Is Nothing"

Sexuality, as a core aspect of social identity, is fundamental to the structuring of gender inequality (Millett 1970). Sexuality is also a salient marker of Otherness and has figured prominently in racist and imperialist ideologies (Gilman 1985; Stoler 1991). Filipinas—both in the Philippines and in the United States—have been marked as desirable but dangerous "prostitutes" and/or submissive "mail order brides" (Halualani 1995; Egan 1996). These stereotypes emerged out of the colonial process, especially the extensive U.S. military presence in the Philippines. Until the early 1990s, the Philippines housed—at times unwillingly—some of the United States' largest overseas airforce and naval bases (Espiritu 1995, 14). Many Filipino nationalists have charged that "the prostitution problem" in the Philippines stemmed from U.S. and Philippine government policies that promoted a sex industry—brothels, bars, massage parlors—for servicemen stationed or on leave in the Philippines (Coronel and Rosca 1993; Warren 1993). In this context, *all* Filipinas were racialized to be sexual commodities, usable and expendable. The sexualized racialization of Filipina women is captured in Marianne Villanueva's short story "Opportunity" (1991). As the protagonist Nina, a "mail order bride" from the Philippines, enters the lobby to meet her American fiancé, the bellboys snicker and whisper *puta,* whore: a reminder that U.S. economic and cultural colonization of the Philippines always forms a backdrop to any relations between Filipinos and Americans (Wong 1993, 53).

In an effort to counter the pervasive hypersexualization of Filipina women, many of my respondents constructed American society—and White American women in particular—to be much more sexually promiscuous than Filipino. In the following narrative, a mother who came to the United States in her thirties contrasted the controlled sexuality of Filipinas in the Philippines with the perceived promiscuity of White women in the United States:

> In the Philippines, we always have chaperons when we go out. When we go to dances, we have our uncle, our grandfather, and auntie all behind us to make sure that we behave in the dance hall. Nobody goes necking outside. You don't even let a man put his hand on your shoulders. When you were brought up in a conservative country, it is hard to come here and see that it is all freedom of speech and freedom of action. Sex was never mentioned in our generation. I was thirty already when I learned about sex. But to the young generation in America, sex is nothing.

Similarly, another immigrant woman criticized the way young American women are raised, "Americans are so liberated. They allow their children, their girls, to go out even when they are still so young." In contrast, she stated that "the Filipino way, it is very important, the value of the woman, that she is a virgin when she gets married."

In this section on the "moral flaws of White Americans," I have suggested that the ideal "Filipina" is partially constructed on the community's conceptualization of White women. The former was everything which the latter was not: the one was sexually modest and dedicated to her family; the other sexually promiscuous and uncaring. Embodying the moral integrity of the idealized ethnic community, immigrant women, particularly young daughters, are expected to comply with male-defined criteria of what constitutes "ideal" feminine virtues. While the sexual behavior of adult women is confined to a monogamous and heterosexual context, that of young women is denied completely (c.f. Dasgupta and DasGupta 1996, 229–231). In the next section, I detail the ways in which Filipino immigrant parents, under the rubric of "cultural preservation," police their daughters' behaviors in order to safeguard their sexual innocence and virginity.

THE CONSTRUCTION(S) OF THE "IDEAL" FILIPINA: "BOYS ARE BOYS AND GIRLS ARE DIFFERENT . . ."

As the designated "keepers of the culture" (Billson 1995), the behaviors of immigrant women come under intensive scrutiny from both women and men of their own groups and from U.S.-born Americans (Gabbacia

1994, xi). In a study of the Italian Harlem community, 1880–1950, Robert Anthony Orsi (1985, 135) reports that "all the community's fears for the reputation and integrity of the domus came to focus on the behavior of young women." Because women's moral and sexual loyalties were deemed central to the maintenance of group status, changes in female behavior, especially of growing daughters, were interpreted as signs of moral decay and ethnic suicide, and were carefully monitored and sanctioned (Gabbacia 1994, 113).

Although immigrant families have always been preoccupied with passing on culture, language, and traditions to both male and female children, it is daughters who have the unequal burden of protecting and preserving the family name. Because sons do not have to conform to the image of an "ideal" ethnic subject as daughters do, they often receive special day-to-day privileges denied to daughters (Waters 1996, 75–76; Haddad and Smith 1996, 22–24). This is not to say that immigrant parents do not place undue expectations on their sons; it is rather that these expectations do not pivot around the sons' sexuality or dating choices. In contrast, parental control over the movement and action of daughters begins the moment she is perceived as a young adult and sexually vulnerable. It regularly consists of monitoring her whereabouts and rejecting dating (Wolf 1997). For example, the immigrant parents I interviewed seldom allowed their daughters to date, to stay out late, to spend the night at a friend's house, or to take an out-of-town trip.

Many of the second generation women I spoke to complained bitterly about these parental restrictions. They particularly resent what they see as gender inequity in their families: the fact that their parents place far more restrictions on their activities and movements than on their brothers. Some decried the fact that even their *younger* brothers had more freedom than they did. "It was really hard growing up because my parents would let my younger brothers do what they wanted but I didn't get to do what I wanted even though I was the oldest. I had a curfew and my brothers didn't. I had to ask if I could go places and they didn't. My parents never even asked my brothers when they were coming home."

When questioned about this "double standard," parents responded by pointing to the fact that "girls are different:"

I have that Filipino mentality that boys are boys and girls are different. Girls are supposed to be protected,

to be clean. In the early years, my daughters have to have chaperons and curfews. And they know that they have to be virgins until they get married. The girls always say that is not fair. What is the difference between their brothers and them? And my answer always is, "In the Philippines, you know, we don't do that. The girls stay home. The boys go out." It was the way that I was raised. I still want to have part of that culture instilled in my children. And I want them to have that to pass on to their children.

Even among self-described western-educated and "tolerant" parents, many continue to ascribe to "the Filipino way" when it comes to raising daughters. As one college-educated father explains:

Because of my Western education, I don't raise my children the way my parents raised me. I tended to be a little more tolerant. But at times, especially in certain issues like dating, I find myself more towards the Filipino way in the sense that I have only one daughter so I tended to be a little bit stricter. So the double standard kind of operates: it's alright for the boys to explore the field but I tended to be overly protective of my daughter. My wife feels the same way because the boys will not lose anything, but the daughter will lose something, their virginity, and it can be also a question of losing face, that kind of thing.

Although many parents generally discourage dating or forbid their daughters to date, they still fully expect these young women to fulfill their traditional roles as women: to get married and have children. A young Filipina recounted the mixed messages she received from her parents:

This is the way it is supposed to work. Okay, you go to school. You go to college. You graduate. You find a job. Then you find your husband, and you have children. That's the whole time line. But my question is, if you are not allowed to date, how are you supposed to find your husband? They say "no" to the whole dating scene because that is secondary to your education, secondary to your family. They do push marriage, but at a later date. So basically my parents are telling me that I should get married and I should have children but that I should not date.

The restrictions on girls' movement sometimes spill over to the realms of academics. Dasgupta and DasGupta (1996, 230) recount that in the Indian American community, while young men were expected to attend faraway competitive colleges, many of their female peers were encouraged by their parents to go to the local colleges so that they could live at or close to home. Similarly, Wolf (1997, 467) reports that some Filipino parents pursued contradictory tactics with their children's, particularly their daughters', education by pushing them to achieve academic excellence in high school, but then "pulling the emergency brake" when they contemplated college by expecting them to stay at home, even if it means going to a less competitive college, if at all.

The above narratives suggest that the process of parenting is gendered in that immigrant parents tend to restrict the autonomy, mobility, and personal decision making of their daughters more so than of their sons. I argue that these parental restrictions are attempts to construct a model of Filipina womanhood that is chaste, modest, nurturing, and family-oriented. This is not to say that parent–daughter conflicts exist in all Filipino immigrant families. Certainly, Filipino parents do not respond in a uniform way to the challenges of being racial-ethnic minorities. I met parents who have had to change some of their ideas and practices in response to their inability to control their children's movements and choices:

> I have three girls and one boy. I used to think that I wouldn't allow my daughters to go dating and things like that, but there is no way I could do that. I can't stop it. It's the way of life here in America. Sometimes you kind of question yourself, if you are doing what is right. It is hard to accept but you got to accept it. That's the way they are here.

> My children are born and raised here, so they do pretty much what they want. They think they know everything. I can only do so much as a parent. . . . When I try to teach my kids things, they tell me that I sound like an old record. They even talk back to me sometimes. . . .

These narratives, made by a professional Filipino immigrant father and a working-class Filipino immigrant mother, respectively, call attention to the shifts in the generational power caused by the migration process and to the possible gap between what parents say they want for their children and their ability to control the young. On the other hand, the interview data do suggest that intergenerational conflicts are socially recognized occurrences in the Filipino community(ies). Even when

respondents themselves had not experienced intergenerational tensions, they could always recall a cousin, a girlfriend, or a friend's daughter who had.

SANCTIONS AND REACTIONS: "THAT IS NOT WHAT A DECENT FILIPINO GIRL SHOULD DO . . ."

I do not wish to suggest that immigrant communities are the only ones who regulate their daughters' mobility and sexuality. Feminist scholars have long documented the construction, containment, and exploitation of women's sexuality in various societies (Maglin and Perry 1996). We also know that the cultural anxiety over unbounded female sexuality is most apparent with regard to adolescent girls (Tolman and Higgins 1996, 206). The difference, I believe, is in the ways that immigrant and non-immigrant families sanction girls' sexuality. Non-immigrant parents rely on the gender-based good girl/bad girl dichotomy to control sexually assertive girls (Tolman and Higgins 1996, 206). In the dominant cultural accounts of women's sexuality, "good girls" are passive, threatened sexual objects while "bad girls" are active, desiring sexual agents (Tolman and Higgins 1996). As Dasgupta and DasGupta write (1996, 236), "the two most pervasive images of women across cultures are the goddess and whore, the good and bad women." This good girl/bad girl cultural story conflates femininity with sexuality, increases women's vulnerability to sexual coercion, and justifies women's containment in the domestic sphere.

Immigrant families, on the other hand, have an extra disciplining mechanism: they can discipline their daughters as racial/national subjects as well as gendered ones. That is, as self-appointed guardians of "authentic" cultural memory, immigrant parents can opt to regulate their daughters' independent choices by linking them to cultural ignorance or betrayal. As both parents and children recounted, young women who disobeyed parental strictures were often branded "non-ethnic," "untraditional," "radical," "selfish," and not "caring about the family." Parents were also quick to warn their daughters about "bad" Filipinas who had gotten pregnant outside of marriage. Filipina Americans who veered from acceptable behaviors were deemed "Americanized"—women who have adopted the sexual mores and practices of

White women. As one Filipino immigrant father described the "Americanized" Filipinas: "They are spoiled because they have seen the American way. They go out at night. Late at night. They go out on dates. Smoking. They have sex without marrying."

From the perspective of the second generation daughters, these charges are stinging. Largely unacquainted with the "home" country, U.S.-born children depend on their parents' tutelage to craft and affirm their ethnic self and thus are particularly vulnerable to charges of cultural ignorance or betrayal (Espiritu 1994). The young women I interviewed were visibly pained—with many breaking down and crying—when they recounted their parents' charges. This deep pain—stemming in part from their desire to be validated as Filipina—existed even among the more "rebellious" daughters. As a 24-year-old daughter explained:

> My mom is very traditional. She wants to follow the Filipino customs, just really adhere to them, like what is proper for a girl, what she can and can't do, and what other people are going to think of her if she doesn't follow that way. When I pushed these restrictions, when I rebelled and stayed out later than allowed, my mom would always say, "That is not what a decent Filipino girl should do. You should come home at a decent hour. What are people going to think of you?" And that would get me really upset, you know, because I think that my character is very much the way it should be for a Filipina. I wear my hair long, I wear decent make-up. I dress properly, conservative. I am family oriented. It hurts me that she doesn't see that I am decent, that I am proper and that I am not going to bring shame to the family or anything like that.

This narrative suggests that even when parents are unable to control the behaviors of their children, their (dis)approval remained strong and powerful in shaping the emotional lives of their daughters (see Wolf 1997). Although better-off parents can and do exert greater controls over their children's behaviors than poorer parents (Wolf 1992; Kibria 1993), I would argue that *all* immigrant parents—regardless of class backgrounds—possess this emotional hold on their children. Therein lies the source of their power.

These emotional pains withstanding, many young Filipinas I interviewed contest and negotiate parental restrictions in their daily lives. Faced with parental restrictions on their mobility, young Filipinas struggle to gain some control over their own social lives, particularly over dating. In many cases, daughters simply misinform their parents of their whereabouts or date without their parents' knowledge. They also rebel by vowing to create more egalitarian relationships with their own husbands and children. A thirty-year-old Filipina who is married to a White American explained why she chose to marry outside her culture:

> In high school, I dated mostly Mexican and Filipino. It never occurred to me to date a white or black guy. I was not attracted to them. But as I kept growing up and my father and I were having all these conflicts, I knew that if I married a Mexican or a Filipino, they would be exactly like my father. And so I tried to date anyone that would not remind me of my dad. A lot of my Filipina friends that I grew up with had similar experiences. So I knew that it wasn't only me. I was determined to marry a white person because he would treat me as an individual.

Another Filipina who was labeled "radical" by her parents indicated that she would be more open-minded in raising her own children: "I see myself as very traditional in upbringing but I don't see myself as constricting on my children one day and I wouldn't put the gender roles on them. I wouldn't lock them into any particular way of behaving." It is important to note that even as these Filipinas desired new gender norms and practices for their own families, the majority hoped that their children would remain connected to the Filipino culture. My respondents also reported more serious reactions to parental restrictions, recalling incidents of someone they knew who had run away, joined gangs, or attempted suicide.

CONCLUSION

In this paper, I have shown that many Filipino immigrants use the largely gendered discourse of morality as one strategy to decenter Whiteness and to locate themselves above the dominant group, demonizing it in the process. Like other immigrant groups, Filipinos praise the United States as a land of significant economic opportunity but simultaneously denounce it as a country inhabited by corrupted and individualistic people of questionable morals. In particular, they criticize American family life, American individualism, and American women (cf. Gabbacia, 1994, 113). Enforced by distorting powers of memory and nostalgia, this rhetoric of moral superiority often leads to patriarchal calls for cultural "authenticity" which locates family honor and national integrity in its female members. Because the policing of women's bodies is one of the main means of asserting moral superiority, young women face numerous restrictions on their autonomy, mobility, and personal decision making. This practice of cultural (re)construction reveals how deeply the conduct of private life can be tied to larger social structures.

The construction of White Americans as the "other" and American culture as deviant serves a dual purpose: It allows immigrant communities to reinforce patriarchy through the sanctioning of women's (mis)behavior *and* to present an unblemished, if not morally superior, public face to the dominant society. Strong in family values, heterosexual morality, and a hierarchical family structure, this public face erases the Filipina "bad girl" and ignores competing (im)moral practices in the Filipino communities. Through the oppression of Filipina women and the castigation of White women's morality, the immigrant community attempts to exert its moral superiority over the dominant Western culture and to reaffirm to itself its self-worth in the face of economic, social, political, and legal subordination. In other words, the immigrant community uses restrictions on women's lives as one form of resistance to racism. Though significant, this form of cultural resistance severely restricts women's lives, particularly those of the second generation, and casts the family as a site of potentially the most intense conflict and oppressive demands in immigrant lives.

REFERENCES

Billson, Janet Mancini. 1995. *Keepers of the Culture: The Power of Tradition in Women's Lives.* New York: Lexington Books.

Coronel, Sheila and Ninotchka Rosca. 1993. "For the Boys: Filipinas Expose Years of Sexual Slavery by the U.S. and Japan." *Ms.,* November/December p. 11+.

Dasgupta, Shamita Das and DasGupta, Sayantani. 1996. "Public Face, Private Face: Asian Indian Women and Sexuality." Pp. 226–243 in *Women, Sex, and Power in the Nineties,* edited by Nan Bauer Maglin and Donna Perry. New Brunswick, NJ: Rutgers University Press.

di Leonardo, Micaela. 1984. *The Varieties of Ethnic Experience: Kinship, Class, and Gender among California Italian-Americans.* Ithaca and London: Cornell University Press.

Eastmond, Marita. 1993. "Reconstructing Life: Chilean Refugee Women and the Dilemmas of Exile." Pp. 35–53 in *Migrant Women: Crossing Boundaries and Changing Identities,* edited by Gina Buijs. Oxford: Berg.

Egan, Timothy. 1996. "Mail-Order Marriage, Immigrant Dreams and Death." *New York Times,* 26 May, p. 12+.

Espiritu, Yen Le. 1994. "The Intersection of Race, Ethnicity, and Class: The Multiple Identities of Second Generation Filipinos." *Identities* 1(2–3):249–273.

Espiritu, Yen Le. 1995. *Filipino American Lives.* Philadelphia: Temple University Press.

Gabbacia, Donna. 1994. *From the Other Side: Women, Gender, and Immigrant Life in the U.S., 1820–1990.* Bloomington and Indianapolis: Indiana University Press.

Gilman, Sander L. 1985. *Difference and Pathology: Stereotypes of Sexuality, Race, and Madness.* Ithaca: Cornell University Press.

Haddad Yvonne Y. and Jane I. Smith. 1996. "Islamic Values among American Muslims." Pp. 19–40 in *Family and Gender among American Muslims: Issues Facing Middle Eastern Immigrants and Their Descendants,* edited by Barbara C. Aswad and Barbara Bilge. Philadelphia: Temple University Press.

Halualani, Rona Tamiko. 1995. "The Intersecting Hegemonic Discourses of an Asian Mail-Order Bride Catalog: Philipina 'Oriental Butterfly' Dolls for Sale." *Women's Studies in Communication* 18(1):45–64.

Kibria, Nazli. 1993. *Family Tightrope: The Changing Lives of Vietnamese Americans.* Princeton, NJ: Princeton University Press.

Maglin, Nan Bauer and Donna Perry. 1996. "Introduction." Pp. xiii–xxvi in *"Bad Girls/Good Girls": Women, Sex, and Power in the Nineties,* edited by Nan Bauer Maglin and Donna Perry. New Brunswick, NJ: Rutgers University Press.

Millet, Kate. 1970. *Sexual Politics.* Garden City, NY: Doubleday.

Rumbaut, Ruben. 1994. "The Crucible within: Ethnic Identity, Self-Esteem, and Segmented Assimilation among Children of Immigrants." *International Migration Review,* 28(4):748–794.

Stoler, Ann Laura. 1991. "Carnal Knowledge and Imperial Power: Gender, Race, and Morality in Colonial Asia." Pp. 51–101 in *Gender at the Crossroads of Knowledge: Feminist Anthropology in the Postmodern Era,* edited by Micaela di Leonardo. Berkeley: University of California Press.

Tolman, Deborah L. and Tracy E. Higgins. 1996. "How Being a Good Girl Can Be Bad for Girls." Pp. 205–225 in *"Bad Girls/Good Girls": Women, Sex, and Power in the Nineties,* edited by Nan Bauer Maglin and Donna Perry. New Brunswick, NJ: Rutgers University Press.

Villanueva, Marianne. 1991. *Ginseng and Other Tales from Manila.* Corvallis, OR: Calyx.

Warren, Jenifer. 1993. "Suit Asks Navy to Aid Children Left in Philippines." *Los Angeles Times,* 5 March, p. A3+.

Waters, Mary C. 1996. "The Intersection of Gender, Race, and Ethnicity in Identity Development of Caribbean American Teens." Pp. 65–81 in *Urban Girls: Resisting Stereotypes, Creating Identities,* edited by Bonnie J. Ross Leadbeater and Niobe Way. New York and London: New York University Press.

Wolf, Diane L. 1992. *Factory Daughters: Gender, Household Dynamics, and Rural Industrialization in Java.* Berkeley: University of California Press.

Wolf, Diane L. 1997. "Family Secrets: Transnational Struggles among Children of Filipino Immigrants." *Sociological Perspectives* 40(3):457–482.

Wong, Sau-ling. 1993. *Reading Asian American Literature: From Necessity to Extravagance.* Princeton, NJ: Princeton.

22

The Work of Disabled Identities in Intimate Relationships

Kirsty Liddiard

INTRODUCTION

The oppressions experienced by disabled people in their sexual and intimate lives have long been overshadowed by wider rights for their rightful place within civil and public life (Shakespeare, Gillespie-Sells, and Davies 1996). The consequences of this, Shakespeare (1999, 54) argues, have been the marginalisation of disabled people's sexual politics and the omission of the "personal and individual dimensions of oppression." Feminist authors within disability studies have challenged these important omissions, and have at the same time located gender and other social categories within analyses of disability (Baron 1997; Thomas 1999). Much of this critical scholarship has been through writing openly about their own embodiment, intersectional identities, and lived experiences of impairment (see Morris 1989; Wendell 1996; Thomas 1999), causing what Sherry (2004, 776) called a crucial "deconstruction of the public/private divide."

While social model orthodoxy holds the psychological "as epiphenomenal, diversionary, and potentially misappropriated in the buttressing of pathologising accounts of disablement" (Watermeyer 2009, iii), feminist authors—markedly Thomas (1999), and later Reeve (2002)—have argued for the inclusion of the psychological and emotional dimensions of disability and impairment within disability studies (see also Goodley

2011). For example, in her social relational model of disability, Thomas (1999, 60; emphasis added) redefines disability as "a form of social oppression involving the social imposition of restrictions of activity on people with impairments *and* the socially engendered undermining of their psycho-emotional well-being." Thus, "disability" is reimagined to have political, material, economic, structural, emotional, intimate, and personal dimensions. Redefining disability along these lines contextualises that "the oppression disabled people can experience operates on the 'inside' as well as on the 'outside'" (Thomas 2004, 40); or, as Reeve (2004, 84; original emphasis) articulates, "operates at both the public and personal levels, affecting what people can *do,* as well as what they can *be.*"

Psycho-emotional disablism is defined by Thomas (1999, 60) as "the socially engendered undermining of emotional well-being." Reeve (2004, 86) proposes that this form of social oppression occurs through "the experience of being excluded from physical environments" (which, she argues, instigates a feeling of not belonging); through routine objectification and voyeurism perpetrated by (but not exclusive to) non-disabled others; and through internalised oppression, which she defines as when "individuals in a marginalised group in society internalise the prejudices held by the dominant group" (Reeve 2004, 91). Thus, psycho-emotional disablism is

Kirsty Liddiard, "The work of disabled identities in intimate relationships," *Disability & Society* Vol. 29, No. 1, 115–128, © 2014 Routledge. Reprinted by permission of the publisher Taylor & Francis Ltd, www.tandfonline.com.

a relational form of disablism embodied through experiences of "hostility or pitying stares, dismissive rejection, infantilisation, patronising attitudes, altruism, help and care on the part of non-disabled people" (Goodley 2010, 96), which "frequently results in disabled people being made to feel worthless, useless, of lesser value, unattractive, a burden" (Thomas 2006, 182).

Building upon existing knowledge of psycho-emotional disablism, particularly its potential impact within the personal, intimate and sexual spaces of disabled people's lives, I present findings from a relevant empirical study that explored disabled men and women's lived experiences of sexuality and intimate relationships. To clarify, my use of the term "intimate relationship" refers to a (non-commercial) shared intimacy with another person, which my informants identified as significant and a source of sexual, physical and/or emotional intimacy. The doctoral research, which took place in England between 2008 and 2011, examined disabled people's management and negotiation of their sexual and intimate lives, selves and bodies in the context of ableist cultures where they are, as Brown (1994, 125) states, assigned the paradoxical social categories of "asexual, oversexed, innocents, or perverts." This article draws upon the sexual stories of 25 disabled people, detailing a thematic analysis of their accounts of intimate relationships that reveal the—often routine—carrying out of considerable emotional work (Hochschild 1983), as well as other forms of (gendered) work, such as sex work (Cacchioni 2007). By making visible their work of "telling, hiding, keeping up, waiting, teaching, networking and negotiating" (Church et al. 2007, 10), I explore the ways in which informants' work was shaped by their lived experiences of gender, sexuality, impairment and disability. Crucially, I critically question such work, suggesting that, while it was often strategically and consciously employed to manage competing intimate oppressions, for the most part, the requirement of informants to carry out forms of work within their sexual and intimate lives constituted a form of psycho-emotional disablism (Thomas 1999).

Learning to Labour: Emotional Work and Disability Performance

Church et al. (2007, 1) state that "complex invisible work is performed by disabled people in every day/night life."

In their research on disabled employees' experiences of corporate settings, Church et al. (2007, 1) uncovered multiple kinds of work that employees routinely utilised within the workplace in order to "stay corporately viable." Types of work included hiding impairment and its effects; being extra productive to counter employers' negative assumptions; and carrying out informal teaching around disability issues for co-workers and managers (Church et al. 2007). Similarly, Wong (2000) has documented the multiple forms of (emotion and other) work employed by disabled women in reproductive and sexual health care; she states that "work has become an umbrella code that encompasses both the barriers women face and the agency they exercise in dealing with them" (2000, 303). Likewise, Goodley (2010, 92) has identified the *performances* disabled people are expected to give: "disabled people learn to respond to the expectations of non-disabled culture—the demanding public—in ways that range from acting the passive disabled bystander, the grateful recipient of others' support, the non-problematic receiver of others' disabling attitudes."

However, while the psycho-emotional dimensions (Reeve 2002; Thomas 1999) and "work" and "performances" of the "disabled" identity have been explored within disability studies (Church et al. 2007; Goodley 2010), the concepts of "emotional work" and "emotional labour" have seldom been applied to disabled people's experiences (Wilton 2008). The little empirical work that has taken place has related to work settings and public spaces and systems (see Church et al. 2007; Wilton 2008; Bolton and Boyd 2003; Wong 2000). To clarify, "emotional work" and "emotional labour" are terms coined by Arlie Hochschild (1983, 7) to represent the "labour [which] one is required to induce or suppress feeling in order to sustain the outward countenance that produces the proper state of mind to others." Emotional labour is mostly required within employment settings and refers to the "management of feeling to create a publicly observable facial and bodily display . . . [that] is sold for a wage and therefore has *exchange value*" (Hochschild 1983, 7; original emphasis). In contrast, "emotional work" or "management" are forms of work that are required in private settings, such as the family or home, and which have "*use value*" (Hochschild 1983, 7; original emphasis). "Emotional work," then, is a better-fitting conceptual framework for explorations of disabled people's lived experiences of their intimate relationships.

My definition of the term follows that of Exley and Letherby (2001, 115; emphasis added) and refers to the "effort and skill required to deal with one's own feelings and those of others within the *private* sphere."

Emotional work takes many forms and serves a variety of functions; for example, work can be on or for the self (Hochschild 1983); on or for others (Exley and Letherby 2001); have both positive and negative consequences (Wilton 2008); and be both a collective and individual labour (see Korczynski 2003). Predominantly, women, "as traditionally more accomplished managers of feeling" (Hochschild 1983, 11), have been found to carry out the majority of emotional work in the private sphere (Strazdins 2000)—largely because they take prime responsibility for the emotional well-being of other family members (Devault 1999). Identifying this work serves important functions. Early work by Blumer (1969, 148) argues that identifying the "invisible" work carried out as part of our daily lives can act as a "sensitising concept," in that it can thrust previously neglected activities (e.g. childcare, caring for relatives) onto the public agenda. Furthermore, Devault (1999, 62) suggests that identifying the customary emotional work that takes place within family life is invaluable towards providing "fuller, more accurate accounts of how family members work at sustaining themselves as individuals and collectivities," an understanding that, she argues, provides "an essential foundation for equitable policy aimed at enhancing the well-being of all citizens."

Before outlining the research methodology, I must stress that by utilising the concept of emotional work (Hochschild 1983), I am not individualising, pathologising or psychologising disabled informants' emotional experiences. The psycho-emotional, psychological and now psychoanalytic (see Goodley 2011) aspects of disability remain contentious within disability studies for fear that they encompass a return to early "individual, medical, bio-psychological, traditional, charity and moral models of disability" (Goodley 2011, 716), which "locate social problems in the head and bodies—the psyches—of disabled people" (Goodley 2011, 716). On the contrary, through deconstructing informants' work I highlight the very social, cultural, political and material processes through which their work is produced.

RESEARCH FINDINGS AND DISCUSSION

The Strategic Work of Staying

In keeping with western conceptualisations of coupledom, all informants who had been in an intimate relationship before ($n = 21$) reported it as having considerable *benefits*. For example, the intimate relationship was narrated as a "safe space" from a range of oppressions, discrimination and prejudices experienced in the "outside world," and as a powerful means to challenge ableist discourses of disabled people as sexless and as not being "prospective" partners (Gillespie-Sells, Hill, and Robbins 1998). It was further described as a space where gender and sexual selves could be confirmed and (re)built. For example, Rhona,[1] a 21-year-old recently-single woman with a congenital impairment, said: "being in a relationship is a constant reassurance in my worth as a person and a woman." Therefore, the intimate relationship could serve as a space to embody (gendered) desirability, contradicting dominant cultural representations of disability and the impaired body as both degendered (Shakespeare 1999) and monstrous (Shildrick 2002).

However, a common theme centred on informants residing in intimate relationships for reasons beyond (romantic) feelings for a partner, and exacerbated by a disabled identity within an ableist heteronormative sexual culture. For example, Robert, a 26-year-old wheelchair user with congenital impairment, said that "having" or "being with" an intimate partner was an important symbol to *others*:

> I've discussed with my [disabled] best friend, how we need a girlfriend to show "Look a real girl likes me, I have sex with her and we are in love—I must be ok, world." (Robert)

Robert's strategy openly acclaims a sexual identity and thus, he feels, "puts right" the dominant ableist assumptions of asexuality and sexual inadequacy cast upon impaired male bodies (Shakespeare, Gillespie-Sells, and Davies 1996). This indicates that, as DeVault (1999) suggests, merely surviving oppression is a form of work in itself.

However, for others, residing in intimate relationships, even where informants had expressed they were often unfulfilled and/or unhappy, was a means through which to avoid oppressive dimensions of dominant sexual cultures; for example, "being single" once again (and thus losing many of the benefits listed above); being rejected on the "dating scene" (because of disability and impairment); and negotiating the (often risky) disclosure of disability and impairment to prospective partners. Notably, this strategy required the employment of considerable emotional work (Hochschild 1983):

> Because of my disability I thought "oh well, I need to stick with this because I might not find anybody else." . . . (Shaun)

> Because I am disabled, it gives you the worry about getting a girlfriend, you hold onto it for dear life, until it's like flogging a dead horse and that's no good for anybody. (Tom)

The accounts of Shaun, a married man who acquired spinal injury at the age of 11, and Tom, a single man with congenital physical impairment, show how their choices to stay in (former) unfulfilling intimate relationships were shaped by the potential difficulties of finding a partner as physically impaired men within a gendered sexual culture that privileges hegemonic masculinities—from which disabled men are largely excluded (Shakespeare 1999). Further, I suggest that phrases like "sticking with it" and "flogging a dead horse" emphasise their *emotional* efforts. For example, Shaun said that in previous intimate relationships with (non-disabled) women he had painfully and silently worked past partners' infidelities because he desperately "wanted to be in a relationship and wanted to have a partner." Therefore, Shaun had to employ an acute form of what Hochschild (1983, 33) calls (emotional) "mental work," whereby he not only had to perform the appropriate "display work" of a contented partner (Hochschild 1983, 10), but carry out significant "mental work" on his emotional self to really *feel* like—or *become*—a contented partner (Hochschild 1983, 6).

Another common chapter in many informants' stories (n = 23) related to the way that they felt that a relationship, love and sex were "out of reach" as a disabled person—a form of sexual oppression internalised through ableist constructions of disabled people as lacking sexual agency and opportunity (Siebers 2008). For those with congenital impairments, such thoughts were reported as having been internalised from a young age and had often been confirmed by (usually, well-meaning) family

members; for example, telling them "not to get their hopes up." This was narrated to have substantial impact upon sexual self-confidence and esteem (and thus constituted significant sexual oppression) and supports the notion that psycho-emotional disablism can be at its most acute when carried out by known agents (Reeve 2002). Graham, a 52-year-old single male who acquired physical impairment at age 20, told of how he had been in intimate relationships with women to whom he was not attracted and did not like because he saw them as the "only opportunity" to have a relationship; but also because these relationships provided an (albeit, temporary) solution to his isolation and loneliness:

> I didn't like her . . . my attitude was entirely "I've got no choice . . . she likes me for some reason and it's her or nothing." . . . Never liked her; never fancied her. I didn't like her touching me. . . . It's horrible but there's no other option. You either just spend your life entirely alone or try and be with someone who's willing to be with you. (Graham)

Graham spoke at length of the multiple emotional performances that such relationships required. For example, he talked about performing emotional displays of sincerity, honesty and authenticity when "pretending" to like these intimate partners. The abhorrence Graham reveals in the above account shows that these situations required routine surface acting (Hochschild 1983). Rather than *becoming* an intimate partner through what Hochschild (1983, 33) defines as "deep acting" or "mental work," the emphasis for Graham was upon imitating the "correct" emotional behaviours synonymous with love, intimacy and affection. To add context, Graham reported experiencing significant marginalisation and isolation, which many disabled people experience: he lived alone, said he had no real friends or family, and rarely went out. Using Thomas' (1999) social relational model of disability, Graham's marginalisation and feelings of loneliness sit at the nexus of structural, psycho-emotional and material dimensions of disability: he dropped out of university upon acquiring impairment because, he said, his institution could not cater adequately for a disabled student; a lack of qualifications combined with having to negotiate a disabled identity within an ableist labour market and capitalist economy led to both long-term underemployment and unemployment, which has in turn impacted upon his social mobility and his access to material resources (see Oliver 1990). Graham described these structural oppressions, then, as having significant impact upon his self-esteem and confidence (especially with women), denoting to him the feeling that he did not belong in, or did not have the attributes to attain, a meaningful intimate relationship (see Reeve 2004).

"Women's Work"

The carrying out of emotional work could also be couched within particular forms of gendered work, most notably "sex work" (Cacchioni 2007, 299). In her exploration of heterosexual women's perceptions of their sexual problems, Cacchioni (2007, 301) found that women carried out "sex work," which she defines as "the unacknowledged effort and the continuing monitoring which women are expected to devote to managing theirs and their partners' sexual desires and activities." Of my informants, while it was not uncommon for both men and women to openly question their role as a sexual partner, particularly their ability to sexually "fulfil" partners (in ways fitting with heteronormative sexual practices), three women (of 10 in total) in the sample took it further and were explicit about the ways in which they consciously (sex) "worked" to "compensate" non-disabled male partners in order to "make up" for having an impaired body.

For example, Jenny, aged 64, who acquired spinal injury at the age of 11, talked about how she would "get involved in every aspect of sex you could think of, any way that was pleasurable to him [her ex-husband]." She said: "I would put myself out to give him that pleasure even if I wasn't getting any that particular time." Jenny carried out this sex work in order to not be perceived as "sexually inadequate" by her husband in comparison with his non-disabled ex-wife. The sacrificing of her own sexual pleasure shows the "entwined nature of embodied and emotional performance work" (Wilton 2008, 367). Similarly, Lucille, 36, who became tetraplegic at age 23 (when she was already married), told how following her injury she had offered her non-disabled husband multiple chances to be unfaithful: "I felt so bad about not wanting sex that I kept telling him to have an affair." Lucille and Jenny's actions cannot be separated from their identities as disabled women; their sex work is indicative of the low sexual self-esteem that is widespread

among disabled women generally (Gillespie-Sells, Hill, and Robbins 1998), and more likely to occur in women with severe impairment who "tend to be furthest away from cultural constructions of ideal feminine beauty" (Hassouneh-Phillips and McNeff 2005, 228).

However, while Jenny and Lucille talked very matter of factly about their sex work, acknowledging that their labour was *conscious* towards embodying desirability for their non-disabled male partners, most women in the sample spoke about hiding bodily difference during sexual encounters—but seldom questioned such practices. Hiding was described by women to take place through a complex (yet remarkably routine) organisation of duvets, bed sheets, clothing, and lighting in a bid to both perform and embody the highly gendered role of the seductress. I suggest that this hiding can be seen as a *private* form of "aesthetic labour," which Wolkowitz (2006, 86) defines as "employers' attempts to make the body more visible in customer service work through a focus on the body's aesthetic qualities." Carrying out some form of aesthetic labour, whether private or public, is, undoubtedly, a likely reality for *all* women due to the ways in which heterosexist and patriarchal constructions of femininity instil, as Bartky (1990, 40) suggests, an "infatuation with an inferiorised body" against which women will always feel inadequate. However, for the disabled women in my research this was undoubtedly compounded by (impaired) bodily difference being wholly intolerable within the rubric of the normative body. Actively hiding the body in this way affirms that disabled informants fear that their departure from bodily normalcy can be a basis for rejection (even from intimate partners), and thus the need to "pass" (and all of the work that goes with this) remains.

The Emotional Work of the Care Receiver

Emotional work through surface acting (Hochschild 1983) took place most explicitly when informants received care from partners within intimate relationships. Of 10 informants who said they regularly received care and assistance from a partner, all said that this arrangement could be a site of tension that required emotional management (see Morris 1989). Many narrated care from partners as something they had to "put up with," in that partners did not carry out tasks correctly or in preferred ways. Even though this could be a central source of frustration—and often anger—it was a situation where the disabled partner had to show incredible tolerance and grace, and be grateful through surface acting (Hochschild 1983), often when they fervently felt the opposite. Thus, in order to manage the "feeling rules" present within the caring relationship (Hochschild 1979, 552), rules that "govern how people try or try not to feel in ways appropriate to the situation," disabled informants had to show emotions that were "appropriate" for those receiving care (see Morris 1989). Importantly, this extensive emotional work was crucial towards simultaneously maintaining functioning care relationships alongside intimate partnerships.

For example, Helen, who is 21 years old and has a congenital and progressive impairment, emphasised the extensive emotional work required in having to "teach" her new partner how to care, which involved "smiling through" what she called "bad care" while he learned her preferred way of doing particular caring tasks. She warned that this meant always appearing "tolerant" and "grateful," for fear that "he could just tell me to get stuffed!" Often these difficult dynamics increased when the disabled partner had an increasing level of need; for example, on becoming ill or through impairment progression. Gemma, a 42-year-old lesbian who has immunity impairment, told how a cancer diagnosis meant she had to be cared for full-time by her then-partner. Gemma spoke of the ways in which she had to manage her partner's anxiety around her cancer, even when she was the one who had it. Notably, this emotional work had to be carried out at a time of significant personal emotional anxiety, emphasising the ways that emotional work is often on or for others (Exley and Letherby 2001). Some informants ($n = 4$) said that receiving care from a partner affected the way in which they dealt with conflict within their intimate relationship. Thus, caring was often conceptualised as something a non-disabled partner could offer, rather than a requirement. As such, it was also something that could be denied. For example, Robert, age 26, and Terry, age 20, who both have a congenital physical impairment, said that they avoided conflict or arguments with a partner, as a strategy to ensure continued care:

> If an argument arose, could I really defend my point even if I'm right, but then ask for help knowing they're annoyed with me? (Robert)

> With a girlfriend, I know that I can't be easily irritated by things they do, because I've got to rely on them to help. In the past I haven't had an argument with a girlfriend unless it's been at a time where I don't need them for any help. (Terry)

Robert and Terry's actions to purposefully avoid conflict are evidence that receiving care from an intimate partner can mean having to consciously mediate and manage these complex relationships through very careful strategies. Such strategies undeniably required various forms of emotional work, management and performance—notably, tolerance; "submission"; graciousness; the assessment of when and when not to assert oneself; and the general management of a very problematic set of power relations, in order to continue to receive the required care or assistance from intimate partners.

DRAWING SOME CONCLUSIONS

The stories (re)told throughout this article have uncovered the work and labours of disabled men and women within multiple locations of their intimate relationships. Throughout their stories, informants cast *themselves* as active subjects, revealing their diverse roles as teacher, sex worker, negotiator, manager, mediator, performer and educator. Paradoxically, much of the skilled emotional work disabled informants carried out is highly valued within western labour markets (Hochschild 1983), from which they are largely excluded. Irrespective, recognising and labelling the work of disabled people within their sexual and intimate lives is important. Firstly, doing so provides fuller, more accurate and inclusive descriptions of the complex ways that disability, impairment, gender and sexuality interact within sexual and intimate life—as well as of the potential psycho-emotional dimensions of such interactions. Secondly, by identifying informants as skilful managers of their intimate and sexual lives—regardless of the outcome or efficacy of their work—their labour challenges dominant ableist constructions of the disabled sexual identity and subjectivity as passive and lacking agency (Siebers 2008).

However, clearly evident within informants' stories and in the analysis of their feelings was the extent to which they devalued their (sexual) selves, revealing the ways in which low sexual self-esteem and self-worth, feelings of inadequacy (in relation to heteronormative discourse), and low body confidence can be common parts of the disabled (sexual) psyche in ableist heteronormative sexual cultures. Despite exercising a form of sexual agency as active "emotional workers," then, the requirement of informants to carry out forms of work within their sexual and intimate lives, I argue, constituted a form of psycho-emotional disablism (Thomas 1999). For example, rather than overt transgressive resistance, much of the (invisible) work uncovered in this research was carried out largely through *necessity*—in order to survive; to be loved; to be human; to be included; to be "normal"; to be sexual; and to be valued. Thus, it is crucial not to underestimate the sizeable extent to which work was rooted in and thus indicative of the oppressive and inherent inequalities of ableist culture.

Further, analysis has shown that informants' work was both located and produced at the intersections of disability, gendered and sexual identities, emphasising the value of appreciating relational and psycho-emotional dimensions of disability (Reeve 2002, 2004; Thomas 1999) when exploring the sexual lives of disabled people. The fact that much of informants' work was routinely employed for the benefit of *others* supports Goodley's (2010, 92) notion of disability performances that fit with "expectations of non-disabled culture." Significantly, where emotional and other work did take place on or for the self, it extended only to emotional and/or bodily management; typically, either through a conscious and rigid policing (or hiding) of emotional responses or bodily difference—forms of work that seldom bought informants *pleasure* or personal fulfilment. For example, surface and "deep" acting within intimate relationships; engaging in forms of sex work; and providing "appropriate" performances of gratitude and gratefulness when receiving care, were markedly detrimental to a positive sense of (sexual) self in most cases and constituted a distinct form of psycho-emotional disablism that operated at a level which required informants' complicity.

In certain spaces, typically gendered performances that affirmed dominant constructions of masculinity and femininity were offered; notably seen within the different strategies men and women employed to sexualise themselves, either in their own eyes or in the eyes of others. Thus, disabled male informants' employment of forms of emotional work within intimate spaces challenges the idea of the male identity as privileged within emotional working (Hochschild 1983) and sheds

light on the ways in which alternative (non-hegemonic) masculinities interact with emotional work and labours. Moreover, women's employment of normatively gendered labours such as sex work (Cacchioni 2007) and "private" aesthetic labour (Wolkowitz 2006) reveals how emotional work is rooted in their social and political positioning as disabled people and—as with the motivations of non-disabled heterosexual women—by normative notions of womanhood, femininity and (hetero)sexuality. This emphasises the similarities between the experiences of disabled and non-disabled women, who occupy analogous subordinate positions within heteronormativity and heterosexuality. It also illustrates—as other disabled feminists already have (Morris 1989; Wendell 1996; Thomas 1999)—the need for mainstream hegemonic feminism to be more inclusive of all types of women and thus broaden its contextualisation of the female experience that, while diverse, is unified by women's suppression under patriarchy and male (sexual) power.

In sum, the analysis detailed in this article supports feminist contributions to disability studies—particularly those that have called for inclusion of the gendered and psycho-emotional dimensions of disability (Thomas 1999; Reeve 2004). Crudely, a "pure" social model analysis would simply not have bared the intimate, personal and gendered oppressions central to informants' lived experiences. As Thomas (1999, 74) points out, rather than psychologising disabled people's emotions, applying a (feminist) disability studies or social relational lens to disabled people's emotional lives removes these from being "'open season' to psychologists and others who would not hesitate to apply the individualistic/personal tragedy model to these issues." In this vein, then, revealing linkages between structural and psycho-emotional forms of disablism can actually serve to de-pathologise disabled people's experiences in ways advocated by social model politic, at the same time as theorising and reframing disability in ways that best attends—most importantly—to the emotional well-being of disabled people.

NOTE

1. All informant names used within this article are pseudonyms.

REFERENCES

Barron, K. 1997. "The Bumpy Road to Womanhood." *Disability & Society* 12 (2): 223–240.

Bartky, S. L. 1990. *Femininity and Domination: Studies in the Phenomenology of Oppression.* New York: Routledge.

Blumer, H. 1969. *Symbolic Interactionism: Perspective and Method.* Englewood Cliffs, NJ: Prentice Hall.

Bolton, S., and C. Boyd. 2003. "Trolley Dolly or Skilled Emotion Manager? Moving on from Hochschild's Managed Heart." *Work, Employment & Society* 17 (2): 289–308.

Brown, H. 1994. "'An Ordinary Sexual Life?': A Review of the Normalisation Principle as It Applies to the Sexual Options of People with Learning Disabilities." *Disability & Society* 9 (2): 123–144.

Cacchioni, T. 2007. "Heterosexuality and 'the Labour of Love': A Contribution to Recent Debates on Female Sexual Dysfunction." *Sexualities* 10 (3): 299–320.

Church, K., C. Frazee, M. Panitch, T. Luciani, and V. Bowman. 2007. *Doing Disability at the Bank: Discovering the Work of Learning/Teaching Done by Disabled Bank Employees Public Report.* Toronto: Ryerson RBC Foundation Institute for Disability Studies Research and Education.

Clarke, H., and S. McKay. 2008. *Exploring Disability, Family Formation and Break-Up: Reviewing the Evidence.* Norwich: Department for Work and Pensions.

Davies, D. 2000. "Sharing Our Stories, Empowering Our Lives: Don't Dis Me!" *Sexuality and Disability* 18 (3): 179–186.

Dei, G. J. S., and G. S. Johal. 2005. *Critical Issues in Anti-Racist Research Methodologies.* New York: Lang.

DeVault, M. L. 1999. "Comfort and Struggle: Emotion Work in Family Life." *The Annals of the American Academy of Political and Social Science* 561 (1): 52–63.

Exley, C., and G. Letherby. 2001. "Managing a Disrupted Life Course: Issues of Identity and Emotion Work." *Health* 5 (1): 112–132.

Gillespie-Sells, K., M. Hill, and B. Robbins. 1998. *She Dances to Different Drums.* London: King's Fund.

Goodley, D. 2010. *Disability Studies: An Interdisciplinary Introduction.* London: Sage.

Goodley, D. 2011. "Social Psychoanalytic Disability Studies." *Disability & Society* 26 (6): 715–728.

Hassouneh-Phillips, D., and E. McNeff. 2005. "'I Thought I Was Less Worthy': Low Sexual and Body Esteem and Increased Vulnerability to Intimate Partner Abuse in Women with Physical Disabilities." *Sexuality and Disability* 23 (4): 227–240.

Hochschild, A. R. 1979. "Emotion Work, Feeling Rules, and Social Structure." *The American Journal of Sociology* 85 (3): 551–575.

Hochschild, A. R. 1983. *The Managed Heart: Commercialization of Human Feeling.* Berkeley, CA: University of California Press.

Kitchen, R. 2000. "The Researched Opinions on Research: Disabled People and Disability Research." *Disability and Society* 15 (1): 25–47.

Korczynski, M. 2003. "Communities of Coping: Collective Emotional Labour in Service Work." *Organization* 10 (1): 55–79.

Langellier, K. 2001. "'You're Marked': Breast Cancer, Tattoo and the Narrative Performance of Identity." In *Narrative and Identity: Studies in Autobiography, Self, and Culture,* edited by J. Brockmeier and D. Carbaugh, 145–184. Amsterdam: John Benjamins.

Leibowitz, R. Q. 2005. "Sexual Rehabilitation Services after Spinal Cord Injury: What Do Women Want?" *Sexuality and Disability* 23 (2): 81–107.

Morris, J. 1989. *Able Lives: Women's Experience of Paralysis.* London: The Women's Press.

Oliver, M. 1990. *The Politics of Disablement.* Basingstoke: Macmillian.

Oliver, M. 1992. "Changing the Social Relations of Research Production." *Disability and Society* 7 (2): 115–120.

Oliver, M. 1997. "Emancipatory Research: Realistic Goal or Impossible Dream?" In *Doing Disability Research,* edited by C. Barnes and G. Mercer, 15–31. Leeds: The Disability Press.

Reeve, D. 2002. "Negotiating Psycho-emotional Dimensions of Disability and Their Influence on Identity Constructions." *Disability and Society* 17 (5): 493–508.

Reeve, D. 2004. "Psycho-emotional Dimensions of Disability and the Social Model." In *Implementing the Social Model of Disability: Theory and Research,* edited by C. Barnes and G. Mercer, 83–100. Leeds: The Disability Press.

Sandahl, C. 2003. "Queering the Crip or Cripping the Queer? Intersections of Queer and Crip Identities in Solo Autobiographical Performance." *GLQ: A Journal of Lesbian and Gay Studies* 9 (1): 25–56.

Shakespeare, T. 1999. "The Sexual Politics of Disabled Masculinity." *Sex and Disability* 17 (1): 53–64.

Shakespeare, T., K. Gillespie-Sells, and D. Davies. 1996. *Untold Desires: The Sexual Politics of Disability.* London and New York: Cassell.

Sherry, M. 2004. "Overlaps and Contradictions between Queer Theory and Disability Studies." *Disability & Society* 19 (7): 769–783.

Shildrick, M. 2002. *Embodying the Monster: Encounters with the Vulnerable Self.* London: Sage.

Siebers, T. 2008. *Disability Theory.* Michigan, MI: University of Michigan Press.

Strazdins, L. 2000. "Integrating Emotions: Multiple Role Measurement of Emotional Work." *Australian Journal of Psychology* 52 (1): 41–50.

Thomas, C. 1999. *Female Forms: Experiencing and Understanding Disability*. Buckingham: Open University Press.

Thomas, C. 2004. "Developing the Social Relational in the Social Model of Disability: A Theoretical Agenda." In *Implementing the Social Model of Disability: Theory and Research*, edited by C. Barnes and G. Mercer, 32–47. Leeds: The Disability Press.

Thomas, C. 2006. "Disability and Gender: Reflections on Theory and Research." *Scandinavian Journal of Disability Research* 8 (2–3): 177–185.

Watermeyer, B. P. 2009. Conceptualising Psycho-Emotional Aspects of Disablist Discrimination and Impairment: Towards a Psychoanalytically Informed Disability Studies. PhD diss., Stellenbosch University.

Wendell, S. 1996. *The Rejected Body: Feminist Philosophical Reflections on Disability*. London: Routledge and Kegan Paul.

Whitaker, D. S., and L. Archer. 1994. "Partnership Research and Its Contributions to Learning and to Team-Building." *Social Work Education* 13 (3): 39–60.

Wilton, R. D. 2008. "Workers with Disabilities and the Challenges of Emotional Labour." *Disability and Society* 23 (4): 361–373.

Wolkowitz, C. 2006. *Bodies at Work*. London: Sage.

Wong, A. 2000. "The Work of Disabled Women Seeking Reproductive Health Care." *Sexuality and Disability* 18 (4): 301–306.

PART IV

IDENTITIES

Our sense of who we are as women and men is not likely to remain the same over the span of our lives, but how are our identities formed and contested? How do our gendered identities change as they feed into our identities as members of religious groups, nations, or social movements? There is nothing automatic about identities. Identities are fluid rather than primordial, socially constructed rather than inherited, and they shift with changing social contexts. As the world grows more complex and interconnected, our identities, or self-definitions, respond to diverse and oftentimes competing pulls and tugs.

Identities are both intensely private and vociferously public. Identities are also fundamentally about power and alliances. Racial-ethnic, religious, national, and sexual identities are at the core of many of today's social movements and political conflicts. Intertwined with these emergent and contested identities are strong ideas—stated or implicit—of what it is to be feminine and masculine. The articles in this section examine how gender interacts with the creation and contestation of multifaceted identities. Together, the authors suggest some of the ways that identities are actively shaped and defined in contradistinction to other identities and the ways in which identities are sometimes imposed from above or resisted. In this view, identities involve a process of simultaneously defining and erasing difference and of claiming and constructing spheres of autonomy.

This section opens with a spin-off inspired by a classic article on white privilege by Peggy McIntosh. In the original, McIntosh suggests that **privileged identities**—white, male, heterosexual, middle or upper class—are often invisible *as* identities. This is a key way in which power operates, by rendering invisible the very mechanisms that create and perpetuate group-based inequities. McIntosh created the first "privilege checklist" that helped readers become aware of the many manifestations of white privilege. In this section, we include Deutsch's "Male Privilege Checklist." Perhaps after completing the male privilege checklist you will be inspired to create an intersectional "Privilege through the Prism of Difference" checklist.

The second article is another classic. Here, the poet and lesbian activist Audre Lorde draws on her own experience to argue that age, race, class, and sex are all simultaneous aspects of one's identity that cannot be easily separated out. Lorde argues that embracing these intertwined differences can offer opportunities for personal and collective growth and can point the way toward peaceful and just changes in the world.

In the next chapter, Jen'nan Ghazal Read and John Bartkowski examine the ways that young Muslim women shape unique femininities as they negotiate the tensions between dominant forms of femininity in "mainstream white America," with their experience of gender in their more gender-dichotomous families and communities. Relying on in-depth interviews, they examine what veiling means to these largely middle-class women, exploring how agency and identity are negotiated within systems of gender, religion, and culture.

The next article reviews recent developments in the growing research on men and masculinities. Tristan Bridges and C. J. Pascoe focus on **hybrid masculinities**, a contemporary form of masculinity among privileged men who incorporate selective elements from subordinate masculinities and femininities into their gender identity. The central question of their article asks whether these hybrid masculinities are simply new ways of concealing power and inequality or whether they are taking gender in a more liberating direction.

In the final article in this section, Sanyu Mojola shows how the HIV/AIDS pandemic has upended gender relations in Africa in ways that appear to challenge patriarchal masculinities, but that ultimately fail to improve conditions for women. Mojola's fieldwork in Western Kenya examines a new gender relationship between older women who become "providers" for younger men who have few employment options. Mojola shows that despite taking on the traditionally feminine practice of being "kept" or provided for, these young men refashion "provider" masculinities for themselves, and also maintain the larger patriarchal system, through co-optation of the older women's inheritance money. Importantly, Mojola's analysis shows how women's and men's efforts to create valued identities and relationships for themselves, within a changing and uncertain patriarchal system, reproduce the patriarchal system in new ways.

23

The Male Privilege Checklist

An Unabashed Imitation of an Article by Peggy McIntosh

B. DEUTSCH

In 1990, Wellesley College professor Peggy McIntosh wrote an essay called "White Privilege: Unpacking the Invisible Knapsack." McIntosh observes that whites in the U.S. are "taught to see racism only in individual acts of meanness, not in invisible systems conferring dominance on my group." To illustrate these invisible systems, McIntosh wrote a list of 26 invisible privileges whites benefit from.

As McIntosh points out, men also tend to be unaware of their own privileges as men. In the spirit of McIntosh's essay, I thought I'd compile a list similar to McIntosh's, focusing on the invisible privileges benefiting men.

Due to my own limitations, this list is unavoidably U.S. centric. I hope that writers from other cultures will create new lists, or modify this one, to reflect their own experiences.

Since I first compiled it, the list has been posted many times on internet discussion groups. Very helpfully, many people have suggested additions to the checklist. More commonly, of course, critics (usually, but not exclusively, male) have pointed out men have disadvantages too—being drafted into the army, being expected to suppress emotions, and so on. These are indeed bad things—but I never claimed that life for men is all ice cream sundaes.

Obviously, there are individual exceptions to most problems discussed on the list. The existence of individual exceptions does not mean that general problems are not a concern.

Pointing out that men are privileged *in no way denies that bad things happen to men*. Being privileged does not mean men are given everything in life for free; being privileged does not mean that men do not work hard, do not suffer. In many cases—from a boy being bullied in school, to soldiers selecting male civilians to be executed, to male workers dying of exposure to unsafe chemicals—the sexist society that maintains male privilege also immeasurably harms boys and men.

However, although I don't deny that men suffer, *this* post is focused on advantages men experience.

Several critics have also argued that the list somehow victimizes women. I disagree; pointing out problems is not the same as perpetuating them. It is not a "victimizing" position to acknowledge that injustice exists; on the contrary, without that acknowledgment it isn't possible to fight injustice.

"The Male Privilege Checklist" was inspired by "White Privilege: Unpacking the Invisible Knapsack" by Peggy MacIntosh (1990). Updated versions of the checklist at amptoons.com/blog/the-male-privilege-checklist. Reprinted with permission per author statement.

An internet acquaintance of mine once wrote, "The first big privilege which whites, males, people in upper economic classes, the able bodied, the straight (I think one or two of those will cover most of us) can work to alleviate is the privilege to be oblivious to privilege." This checklist is, I hope, a step towards helping men to give up the "first big privilege."

THE MALE PRIVILEGE CHECKLIST

1. My odds of being hired for a job, when competing against female applicants, are probably skewed in my favor. The more prestigious the job, the larger the odds are skewed.
2. I can be confident that my co-workers won't think I got my job because of my sex—even though that might be true. . . .
3. If I am never promoted, it's not because of my sex.
4. If I fail in my job or career, I can feel sure this won't be seen as a black mark against my entire sex's capabilities.
5. I am far less likely to face sexual harassment at work than my female co-workers are. . . .
6. If I do the same task as a woman, and if the measurement is at all subjective, chances are people will think I did a better job.
7. If I'm a teen or adult, and if I can stay out of prison, my odds of being raped are relatively low. . . .
8. On average, I am taught to fear walking alone after dark in average public spaces much less than my female counterparts are.
9. If I choose not to have children, my masculinity will not be called into question.
10. If I have children but do not provide primary care for them, my masculinity will not be called into question.
11. If I have children and provide primary care for them, I'll be praised for extraordinary parenting if I'm even marginally competent. . . .
12. If I have children and a career, no one will think I'm selfish for not staying at home.
13. If I seek political office, my relationship with my children, or who I hire to take care of them, will probably not be scrutinized by the press.
14. My elected representatives are mostly people of my own sex. The more prestigious and powerful the elected position, the more this is true.
15. When I ask to see "the person in charge," odds are I will face a person of my own sex. The higher-up in the organization the person is, the surer I can be.
16. As a child, chances are I was encouraged to be more active and outgoing than my sisters. . . .
17. As a child, I could choose from an almost infinite variety of children's media featuring positive, active, non-stereotyped heroes of my own sex. I never had to look for it; male protagonists were (and are) the default.
18. As a child, chances are I got more teacher attention than girls who raised their hands just as often. . . .
19. If my day, week or year is going badly, I need not ask of each negative episode or situation whether or not it has sexist overtones.
20. I can turn on the television or glance at the front page of the newspaper and see people of my own sex widely represented.
21. If I'm careless with my financial affairs it won't be attributed to my sex.
22. If I'm careless with my driving it won't be attributed to my sex.
23. I can speak in public to a large group without putting my sex on trial.
24. Even if I sleep with a lot of women, there is no chance that I will be seriously labeled a "slut," nor is there any male counterpart to "slut-bashing." . . .
25. I do not have to worry about the message my wardrobe sends about my sexual availability. . . .
26. My clothing is typically less expensive and better-constructed than women's clothing for the same social status. While I have fewer options, my clothes will probably fit better than a woman's without tailoring. . . .
27. The grooming regimen expected of me is relatively cheap and consumes little time. . . .
28. If I buy a new car, chances are I'll be offered a better price than a woman buying the same car. . . .
29. If I'm not conventionally attractive, the disadvantages are relatively small and easy to ignore.

30. I can be loud with no fear of being called a shrew. I can be aggressive with no fear of being called a bitch.

31. I can ask for legal protection from violence that happens mostly to men without being seen as a selfish special interest, since that kind of violence is called "crime" and is a general social concern. (Violence that happens mostly to women is usually called "domestic violence" or "acquaintance rape," and is seen as a special interest issue.)

32. I can be confident that the ordinary language of day-to-day existence will always include my sex. "All men are created equal," mailman, chairman, freshman, he.

33. My ability to make important decisions and my capability in general will never be questioned depending on what time of the month it is.

34. I will never be expected to change my name upon marriage or questioned if I don't change my name.

35. The decision to hire me will not be based on assumptions about whether or not I might choose to have a family sometime soon.

36. Every major religion in the world is led primarily by people of my own sex. Even God, in most major religions, is pictured as male.

37. Most major religions argue that I should be the head of my household, while my wife and children should be subservient to me.

38. If I have a wife or live-in girlfriend, chances are we'll divide up household chores so that she does most of the labor, and in particular the most repetitive and unrewarding tasks. . . .

39. If I have children with my girlfriend or wife, I can expect her to do most of the basic childcare such as changing diapers and feeding.

40. If I have children with my wife or girlfriend, and it turns out that one of us needs to make career sacrifices to raise the kids, chances are we'll both assume the career sacrificed should be hers.

41. Assuming I am heterosexual, magazines, billboards, television, movies, pornography, and virtually all of media is filled with images of scantily-clad women intended to appeal to me sexually. Such images of men exist, but are rarer.

42. In general, I am under much less pressure to be thin than my female counterparts are. . . . If I am fat, I probably suffer fewer social and economic consequences for being fat than fat women do. . . .

43. If I am heterosexual, it's incredibly unlikely that I'll ever be beaten up by a spouse or lover. . . .

44. Complete strangers generally do not walk up to me on the street and tell me to "smile." . . .

45. Sexual harassment on the street virtually never happens to me. I do not need to plot my movements through public space in order to avoid being sexually harassed, or to mitigate sexual harassment. . . .

46. On average, I am not interrupted by women as often as women are interrupted by men. . . .

47. I have the privilege of being unaware of my male privilege.

24

Age, Race, Class, and Sex

Women Redefining Difference

AUDRE LORDE

Much of western European history conditions us to see human differences in simplistic opposition to each other: dominant/subordinate, good/bad, up/down, superior/inferior. In a society where the good is defined in terms of profit rather than in terms of human need, there must always be some group of people who, through systematized oppression, can be made to feel surplus, to occupy the place of the dehumanized inferior. Within this society, that group is made up of Black and Third World people, working-class people, older people, and women.

As a forty-nine-year-old Black lesbian feminist socialist mother of two, including one boy, and a member of an interracial couple, I usually find myself a part of some group defined as other, deviant, inferior, or just plain wrong. Traditionally, in American society, it is the members of oppressed, objectified groups who are expected to stretch out and bridge the gap between the actualities of our lives and the consciousness of our oppressor. For in order to survive, those of us for whom oppression is as American as apple pie have always had to be watchers, to become familiar with the language and manners of the oppressor, even sometimes adopting them for some illusion of protection. Whenever the need for some pretense of communication arises, those who profit from our oppression call upon us to share our knowledge with them. In other words, it is the responsibility of the oppressed to teach the oppressors their mistakes. I am responsible for educating teachers who dismiss my children's culture in school. Black and Third World people are expected to educate White people as to our humanity. Women are expected to educate men. Lesbians and gay men are expected to educate the heterosexual world. The oppressors maintain their position and evade responsibility for their own actions. There is a constant drain of energy which might be better used in redefining ourselves and devising realistic scenarios for altering the present and constructing the future.

Institutionalized rejection of difference is an absolute necessity in a profit economy which needs outsiders as surplus people. As members of such an economy, we have all been programmed to respond to the human differences between us with fear and loathing and to handle that difference in one of three ways: ignore it, and if that is not possible, copy it if we think it is dominant, or destroy it if we think it is subordinate. But we have no patterns for relating across our human differences as equals. As a result, those differences have been misnamed and misused in the service of separation and confusion.

Audre Lorde, "Age, Race, Class, and Sex: Women Redefining Difference," from *Sister Outsider*. Copyright © 1984 Crossing Press.

Certainly there are very real differences between us of race, age, and sex. But it is not those differences between us that are separating us. It is rather our refusal to recognize those differences, and to examine the distortions which result from our misnaming them and their effects upon human behavior and expectation.

Racism, the belief in the inherent superiority of one race over all others and thereby the right to dominance. Sexism, the belief in the inherent superiority of one sex over the other and thereby the right to dominance. Ageism. Heterosexism. Elitism. Classism.

It is a lifetime pursuit for each one of us to extract these distortions from our living at the same time as we recognize, reclaim, and define those differences upon which they are imposed. For we have all been raised in a society where those distortions were endemic within our living. Too often, we pour the energy needed for recognizing and exploring difference into pretending those differences are insurmountable barriers, or that they do not exist at all. This results in a voluntary isolation, or false and treacherous connections. Either way, we do not develop tools for using human difference as a springboard for creative change within our lives. We speak not of human difference, but of human deviance.

Somewhere, on the edge of consciousness, there is what I call a *mythical norm,* which each one of us within our hearts knows "that is not me." In America, this norm is usually defined as White, thin, male, young, heterosexual, Christian, and financially secure. It is with this mythical norm that the trappings of power reside within this society. Those of us who stand outside that power often identify one way in which we are different, and we assume that to be the primary cause of all oppression, forgetting other distortions around difference, some of which we ourselves may be practicing. By and large within the women's movement today, White women focus upon their oppression as women and ignore differences of race, sexual preference, class, and age. There is a pretense to a homogeneity of experience covered by the word *sisterhood* that does not in fact exist.

Unacknowledged class differences rob women of each others' energy and creative insight. Recently a women's magazine collective made the decision for one issue to print only prose, saying poetry was a less "rigorous" or "serious" art form. Yet even the form our creativity takes is often a class issue. Of all the art

forms, poetry is the most economical. It is the one which is the most secret, which requires the least physical labor, the least material, and the one which can be done between shifts, in the hospital pantry, on the subway, and on scraps of surplus paper. Over the last few years, writing a novel on tight finances, I came to appreciate the enormous differences in the material demands between poetry and prose. As we reclaim our literature, poetry has been the major voice of poor, working-class, and Colored women. A room of one's own may be a necessity for writing prose, but so are reams of paper, a typewriter, and plenty of time. The actual requirements to produce the visual arts also help determine, along class lines, whose art is whose. In this day of inflated prices for material, who are our sculptors, our painters, our photographers? When we speak of a broadly based women's culture, we need to be aware of the effect of class and economic differences on the supplies available for producing art.

As we move toward creating a society within which we can each flourish, ageism is another distortion of relationship which interferes without vision. By ignoring the past, we are encouraged to repeat its mistakes. The "generation gap" is an important social tool for any repressive society. If the younger members of a community view the older members as contemptible or suspect or excess, they will never be able to join hands and examine the living memories of the community, nor ask the all important question, "Why?" This gives rise to a historical amnesia that keeps us working to invent the wheel every time we have to go to the store for bread.

We find ourselves having to repeat and relearn the same old lessons over and over that our mothers did because we do not pass on what we have learned, or because we are unable to listen. For instance, how many times has this all been said before? For another, who would have believed that once again our daughters are allowing their bodies to be hampered and purgatoried by girdles and high heels and hobble skirts?

Ignoring the differences of race between women and the implications of those differences presents the most serious threat to the mobilization of women's joint power.

As White women ignore their built-in privilege of Whiteness and define *woman* in terms of their own experience alone, then women of Color become "other," the outsider whose experience and tradition is too "alien" to comprehend. An example of this is the signal absence of the experience of women of Color as a resource for women's studies courses. The literature of women of Color is seldom included in women's literature courses and almost never in other literature courses, nor in women's studies as a whole. All too often, the excuse given is that the literatures of women of Color can only be taught by Colored women, or that they are too difficult to understand, or that classes cannot "get into" them because they come out of experiences that are "too different." I have heard this argument presented by White women of otherwise quite clear intelligence, women who seem to have no trouble at all teaching and reviewing work that comes out of the vastly different experiences of Shakespeare, Molière, Dostoyefsky, and Aristophanes. Surely there must be some other explanation.

This is a very complex question, but I believe one of the reasons White women have such difficulty reading Black women's work is because of their reluctance to see Black women as women and different from themselves. To examine Black women's literature effectively requires that we be seen as whole people in our actual complexities—as individuals, as women, as human—rather than as one of those problematic but familiar stereotypes provided in this society in place of genuine images of Black women. And I believe this holds true for the literatures of other women of Color who are not Black.

The literatures of all women of Color re-create the textures of our lives, and many White women are heavily invested in ignoring the real differences. For as long as any difference between us means one of us must be inferior, then the recognition of any difference must be fraught with guilt. To allow women of Color to step out of stereotypes is too guilt provoking, for it threatens the complacency of those women who view oppression only in terms of sex.

Refusing to recognize difference makes it impossible to see the different problems and pitfalls facing us as women.

Thus, in a patriarchal power system where White-skin privilege is a major prop, the entrapments used to neutralize Black women and White women are not the same. For example, it is easy for Black women to be used by the power structure against Black men, not because they are men, but because they are Black. Therefore, for Black women, it is necessary at all times to separate the needs of the oppressor from our own legitimate conflicts within our communities. This same problem does not exist for White women. Black women and men have shared racist oppression and still share it, although in different ways. Out of that shared oppression we have developed joint defenses and joint vulnerabilities to each other that are not duplicated in the White community, with the exception of the relationship between Jewish women and Jewish men.

On the other hand, White women face the pitfall of being seduced into joining the oppressor under the pretense of sharing power. This possibility does not exist in the same way for women of Color. The tokenism that is sometimes extended to us is not an invitation to join power; our racial "otherness" is a visible reality that makes that quite clear. For White women there is a wider range of pretended choices and rewards for identifying with patriarchal power and its tools.

Today, with the defeat of ERA, the tightening economy, and increased conservatism, it is easier once again for White women to believe the dangerous fantasy that if you are good enough, pretty enough, sweet enough, quiet enough, teach the children to behave, hate the right people, and marry the right men, then you will be allowed to co-exist with patriarchy in relative peace, at least until a man needs your job or the neighborhood rapist happens along. And true, unless one lives and loves in the trenches it is difficult to remember that the war against dehumanization is ceaseless.

But Black women and our children know the fabric of our lives is stitched with violence and with hatred, that there is no rest. We do not deal with it only on the picket lines, or in dark midnight alleys, or in the places where we dare to verbalize our resistance. For us, increasingly, violence weaves through the daily tissues of our living—in the supermarket, in the classroom, in the elevator, in the clinic and the schoolyard, from the plumber, the baker, the saleswoman, the bus driver, the bank teller, the waitress who does not serve us.

Some problems we share as women, some we do not. You fear your children will grow up to join the patriarchy and testify against you, we fear our children will be dragged from a car and shot down in the street, and you will turn your backs upon the reasons they are dying.

The threat of difference has been no less blinding to people of Color. Those of us who are Black must see that the reality of our lives and our struggle does not make us immune to the errors of ignoring and misnaming difference. Within Black communities where racism is a living reality, differences among us often seem dangerous and suspect. The need for unity is often misnamed as a need for homogeneity, and a Black feminist vision mistaken for betrayal of our common interests as a people. Because of the continuous battle against racial erasure that Black women and Black men share, some Black women still refuse to recognize that we are also oppressed as women, and that sexual hostility against Black women is practiced not only by the White racist society, but implemented within our Black communities as well. It is a disease striking the heart of Black nationhood, and silence will not make it disappear. Exacerbated by racism and the pressures of powerlessness, violence against Black women and children often becomes a standard within our communities, one by which manliness can be measured. But these woman-hating acts are rarely discussed as crimes against Black women.

As a group, women of Color are the lowest paid wage earners in America. We are the primary targets of abortion and sterilization abuse, here and abroad. In certain parts of Africa, small girls are still being sewed shut between their legs to keep them docile and for men's pleasure. This is known as female circumcision, and it is not a cultural affair as the late Jomo Kenyatta insisted, it is a crime against Black women.

Black women's literature is full of the pain of frequent assault, not only by a racist patriarchy, but also by Black men. Yet the necessity for and history of shared battle have made us, Black women, particularly vulnerable to the false accusation that anti-sexist is anti-Black. Meanwhile, womanhating as a recourse of the powerless is sapping strength from Black communities, and our very lives. Rape is on the increase, reported and unreported, and rape is not aggressive sexuality, it is sexualized aggression. As Kalamu ya Salaam, a Black male writer points out, "As long as male domination exists, rape will exist. Only women revolting and men made conscious of their responsibility to fight sexism can collectively stop rape."[1]

Differences between ourselves as Black women are also being misnamed and used to separate us from one another. As a Black lesbian feminist comfortable with the many different ingredients of my identity, and a woman committed to racial and sexual freedom from oppression, I find I am constantly being encouraged to pluck out some one aspect of myself and present this as the meaningful whole, eclipsing or denying the other parts of self. But this is a destructive and fragmenting way to live. My fullest concentration of energy is available to me only when I integrate all the parts of who I am, openly, allowing power from particular sources of my living to flow back and forth freely through all my different selves, without the restrictions of externally imposed definition. Only then can I bring myself and my energies as a whole to the service of those struggles which I embrace as part of my living.

A fear of lesbians, or of being accused of being a lesbian, has led many Black women into testifying against themselves. It has led some of us into destructive alliances, and others into despair and isolation. In the White women's communities, heterosexism is sometimes a result of identifying with the White patriarchy, a rejection of that interdependence between women-identified women which allows the self to be, rather than to be used in the service of men. Sometimes it reflects a die-hard belief in the protective coloration of heterosexual relationships, sometimes a self-hate which all women have to fight against, taught us from birth.

Although elements of these attitudes exist for all women, there are particular resonances of heterosexism and homophobia among Black women. Despite the fact that woman-bonding has a long and honorable history in the African and African-American communities, and despite the knowledge and accomplishments of many strong and creative women-identified Black women in the political, social and cultural fields, heterosexual Black women often tend to ignore or discount the existence and work of Black lesbians. Part of this attitude has come from an understandable terror of Black male attack within the close confines of Black society, where the punishment for any female self-assertion is still to be accused of being a lesbian and therefore unworthy of the attention or support of the scarce Black male. But part of this need to misname and ignore Black lesbians comes from a very real fear that openly women-identified Black women who are no longer dependent upon men for their self-definition may well reorder our whole concept of social relationships.

Black women who once insisted that lesbianism was a White woman's problem now insist that Black lesbians are a threat to Black nationhood, are consorting with the enemy, are basically un-Black. These accusations, coming from the very women to whom we look for deep and real understanding, have served to keep many Black lesbians in hiding, caught between the racism of White women and the homophobia of their sisters. Often, their work has been ignored, trivialized, or misnamed, as with the work of Angelina Grimke, Alice Dunbar-Nelson, and Lorraine Hansberry. Yet women-bonded women have always been some part of the power of Black communities, from our unmarried aunts to the amazons of Dahomey.

And it is certainly not Black lesbians who are assaulting women and raping children and grandmothers on the streets of our communities.

Across this country, as in Boston during the spring of 1979 following the unsolved murders of twelve Black women, Black lesbians are spear-heading movements against violence against Black women.

What are the particular details within each of our lives that can be scrutinized and altered to help bring about change? How do we redefine difference for all women? It is not our differences which separate women, but our reluctance to recognize those differences and to deal effectively with the distortions which have resulted from the ignoring and misnaming of those differences.

As a tool of social control, women have been encouraged to recognize only one area of human difference as legitimate, those differences which exist between women and men. And we have learned to deal across those differences with the urgency of all oppressed subordinates. All of us have had to learn to live or work or coexist with men, from our fathers on. We have recognized and negotiated these differences, even when this recognition only continued the old dominant/subordinate mode of human relationship, where the oppressed must recognize the masters' difference in order to survive.

But our future survival is predicated upon our ability to relate within equality. As women, we must root out internalized patterns of oppression within ourselves if we are to move beyond the most superficial aspects of social change. Now we must recognize differences among women who are our equals, neither inferior nor superior, and devise ways to use each others' difference to enrich our visions and our joint struggles.

The future of our earth may depend upon the ability of all women to identify and develop new definitions of power and new patterns of relating across difference. The old definitions have not served us, nor the earth that supports us. The old patterns, no matter how cleverly rearranged to imitate progress, still condemn us to cosmetically altered repetitions of the same old exchanges, the same old guilt, hatred, recrimination, lamentation, and suspicion.

For we have, built into all of us, old blueprints of expectation and response, old structures of oppression, and these must be altered at the same time as we alter the living conditions which are a result of those structures. For the master's tools will never dismantle the master's house.

As Paulo Freire shows so well in *The Pedagogy of the Oppressed*,[2] the true focus of revolutionary change is never merely the oppressive situations which we seek to escape, but that piece of the oppressor which is planted deep within each of us, and which knows only the oppressors' tactics, the oppressors' relationships.

Change means growth, and growth can be painful. But we sharpen self-definition by exposing the self in work and struggle together with those whom we define as different from ourselves although sharing the same goals. For Black and White, old and young, lesbian and heterosexual women alike, this can mean new paths to our survival.

We have chosen each other
and the edge of each others battles
the war is the same
if we lose
someday women's blood will congeal
upon a dead planet
if we win
there is no telling
we seek beyond history
for a new and more possible meeting.[3]

NOTES

1. From "Rape: A Radical Analysis, an African-American Perspective" by Kalamu ya Salaam in *Black Books Bulletin,* vol. 6, no. 4 (1980).

2. Seabury Press, New York, 1970.

3. From "Outlines," unpublished poem.

25

To Veil or Not To Veil?

A Case Study of Identity Negotiation among Muslim Women in Austin, Texas

Jen'nan Ghazal Read

John P. Bartkowski

In light of expanded social opportunities for women in Western industrialized countries, scholars have turned their attention to the status of women in other parts of the world. This burgeoning research literature has given rise to a debate concerning the social standing of Muslim women in the Middle East. On one hand, some scholars contend that Muslim women occupy a subordinate status within many Middle Eastern countries. Some empirical evidence lends support to this view, as many researchers have highlighted the traditional and gendered customs prescribed by Islam—most notably, the veiling and shrouding of Muslim women (Afshar 1985; Fox 1977; Odeh 1993; Papanek 1973; see Dragadze 1994 for review).

On the other hand, a growing number of scholars now argue that claims about the oppression and subjugation of veiled Muslim women may, in many regards, be overstated (Brenner 1996; El-Guindi 1981, 1983; El-Solh and Mabro 1994; Fernea 1993, 1998; Gocek and Balaghi 1994; Hessini 1994; Kadioglu 1994; Kandiyoti 1991, 1992; Webster 1984). Scholars who have

generated insider portraits[1] of Islamic gender relations have revealed that Muslim women's motivations for veiling can vary dramatically. Some Muslim women veil to express their strongly held convictions about gender difference, others are motivated to do so more as a means of critiquing Western colonialism in the Middle East. It is this complexity surrounding the veil that leads Elizabeth Fernea (1993, 122) to conclude that the veil (or *hijab*) "means different things to different people within [Muslim] society, and it means different things to Westerners than it does to Middle Easterners" (see also Abu-Lughod 1986; Walbridge 1997).

Our study takes as its point of departure the conflicting meanings of the veil among both Muslim religious elites and rank-and-file Islamic women currently living in the United States. In undertaking this investigation, we supplement the lone study (published in Arabic) that compares the gender attitudes of veiled and unveiled women (see L. Ahmed 1992 for review). That study, based largely on survey data collected from university women living in the Middle East,

---

Jen'nan Ghazal Read and John P. Bartkowski, "To Veil or Not to Veil? A Case Study of Identity Negotiation among Muslim Women in Austin, Texas," from *Gender & Society,* Volume 14/2000, pp. 395–417. Copyright © 2000, Sage Publications, Inc. Reprinted by permission.

demonstrates that while veiled women evince somewhat conservative gender attitudes, the vast majority of them support women's rights in public life and a substantial proportion subscribe to marital equality. We seek to extend these suggestive findings by using in-depth, personal interviews, because data from such interviews are more able to capture the negotiation of cultural meanings by veiled and unveiled respondents, as well as the nuances of these women's gender identities (Mishler 1986). . . .

THE LANDSCAPE OF ISLAM

. . . The most germane aspects of Muslim theology for this study concern two sets of Islamic sacred texts, the Qur'an and the hadiths (e.g., Munson 1988). The Qur'an is held in high esteem by virtually all Muslims. Not unlike the "high view" of the Bible embraced by various conservative Christian groups, many contemporary Muslims believe that the Qur'an is the actual Word of God that was ably recorded by Muhammad during the early portion of the seventh century. In addition to the Qur'an, many Muslims also look to the hadiths for moral and spiritual guidance in their daily lives. The hadiths, second-hand reports of Muhammad's personal traditions and lifestyle, began to be collected shortly after his death because of the difficulty associated with applying the dictates of the Qur'an to changing historical circumstances. The full collection of these hadiths has come to be known as the *sunna.* Along with the Qur'an, the hadiths constitute the source of law that has shaped the ethics and values of many Muslims.

Within Islam, the all-male Islamic clergy (variously called *faghihs, imams, muftis, mullahs,* or *ulumas*) often act as interpretive authorities who are formally charged with distilling insights from the Qur'an or hadiths and with disseminating these scriptural interpretations to the Muslim laity (Munson 1988). Given that such positions of structural privilege are set aside for Muslim men, Islam is a patriarchal religious institution. Yet, patriarchal institutions do not necessarily produce homogeneous gender ideologies, a fact underscored by the discursive fissures that divide Muslim religious authorities and elite commentators concerning the veil.

COMPETING DISCOURSES OF THE VEIL IN CONTEMPORARY ISLAM

Many Muslim clergy and Islamic elites currently prescribe veiling as a custom in which "good" Muslim women should engage (Afshar 1985; Al-Swailem 1995; Philips and Jones 1985; Siddiqi 1983). Proponents of veiling often begin their defense of this cultural practice by arguing that men are particularly vulnerable to corruption through unregulated sexual contact with women (Al-Swailem 1995, 27–29; Philips and Jones 1985, 39–46; Siddiqi 1983). These experts contend that the purpose of the hijab or veil is the regulation of such contact:

> The society that Islam wants to establish is not a sensate, sex-ridden society. . . . The Islamic system of *Hijab* is a wide-ranging system which protects the family and closes those avenues that lead toward illicit sex relations or even indiscriminate contact between the sexes in society. . . . To protect her virtue and to safeguard her chastity from lustful eyes and covetous hands, Islam has provided for purdah which sets norms of dress, social get-together . . . and going out of the four walls of one's house in hours of need. (Siddiqi 1983, vii–viii)

Many expositors of the pro-veiling discourse call attention to the uniquely masculine penchant for untamed sexual activity and construe the veil as a God-ordained solution to the apparent disparities in men's and women's sexual appetites. Women are therefore deemed responsible for the management of men's sexuality (Al-Swailem 1995, 29). Some contend that the Muslim woman who veils should be sure that the hijab covers her whole body (including the palms of her hands), should be monotone in color ("so as not to be attractive to draw the attentions to"), and should be opaque and loose so as not to reveal "the woman's shape or what she is wearing underneath" (Al-Swailem 1995, 24–25).

Pro-veiling Muslim luminaries also defend veiling on a number of nonsexual grounds. The veil, according to these commentators, serves as (1) a demonstration of the Muslim woman's unwavering obedience to the tenets of Islam; (2) a clear indication of the essential differences distinguishing men from women; (3) a reminder to women that their proper place is in the home rather than in pursuing public-sphere activities; and (4) a sign of the devout Muslim woman's disdain for the profane, immodest, and consumerist cultural customs of the West (e.g., Al-Swailem 1995, 27–29; Siddiqi 1983, 140, 156). In this last regard, veiling is legitimated as an anti-imperialist statement of ethnic and cultural distinctiveness.

Nevertheless, the most prominent justifications for veiling entail, quite simply, the idea that veiling is prescribed in the Qur'an (see Arat 1994; Dragadze 1994; Hessini 1994; Sherif 1987; Shirazi-Mahajan 1995 for reviews). Several Muslim clergy place a strong interpretive emphasis on a Qur'anic passage (S. 24:31) that urges women "not [to] display their beauty and adornments" but rather to "draw their head cover over their bosoms and not display their ornament." Many of these same defenders of the veil marshal other Qur'anic passages that bolster their pro-veiling stance: "And when you ask them [the Prophet's wives] for anything you want ask them from before a screen (hijab); that makes for greater purity for your hearts and for them" (S. 33:53); "O Prophet! Tell your wives and daughters and the believing women that they should cast their outer garments over themselves, that is more convenient that they should be known and not molested" (S. 33:59).

In addition to these Qur'anic references, pro-veiling Muslim clergy highlight hadiths intended to support the practice of veiling (see Sherif 1987 for review). Many pro-veiling Muslim clergy maintain that the veil verse was revealed to Muhammad at a wedding five years before the Prophet's death. As the story goes, three tactless guests overstayed their welcome after the wedding and continued to chat despite the Prophet's desire to be alone with his new wife. To encourage their departure, Muhammad drew a curtain between the nuptial chamber and one of his inconsiderate companions while ostensibly uttering "the verse of the hijab" (S. 33:53, cited above). A second set of hadiths claim that the verse of hijab was prompted when one of the Prophet's companions accidentally touched the hand of one of Muhammad's wives while eating dinner. Yet a third set of hadiths suggests that the verse's objective was to stop the visits of an unidentified man who tarried with the wives of the Prophet, promising them marriage after Muhammad's death.

In stark contrast to the pro-veiling apologias discussed above, an oppositional discourse against veiling has emerged within Islamic circles in recent years. Most prominent among these opponents of veiling are Islamic feminists (Al-Marayati 1995; Mernissi 1991; Shaheed 1994, 1995; see contributions in Al-Hibri 1982; Gocek and Balaghi 1994; see AbuKhalil 1993; An-Na'im 1987; Anees 1989; Arat 1994; Badran 1991; Fernea 1998 for treatments of Islamic feminism and related issues). Although Islamic feminists are marginalized from many of the institutional apparatuses available to the all-male Muslim clergy, they nevertheless exercise considerable influence via the dissemination of dissident publications targeted at Islamic women and through grassroots social movements (Fernea 1998; Shaheed 1994). Fatima Mernissi (1987, 1991), arguably the most prominent Muslim feminist, is highly critical of dominant gender conceptualizations that construe veiling as the ultimate standard by which the spiritual welfare and religious devoutness of Muslim women should be judged. In *The Veil and the Male Elite: A Feminist Interpretation of Women's Rights in Islam,* Mernissi (1991, 194) queries her readers:

> What a strange fate for Muslim memory, to be called upon in order to censure and punish [Islamic women]! What a strange memory, where even dead men and women do not escape attempts at assassination, if by chance they threaten to raise the hijab [veil] that covers the mediocrity and servility that is presented to us [Muslim women] as tradition. How did the tradition succeed in transforming the Muslim woman into that submissive, marginal creature who buries herself and only goes out into the world timidly and huddled in her veils? Why does the Muslim man need such a mutilated companion?

Mernissi and other Muslim commentators who oppose veiling do so on a number of grounds. First, Mernissi seeks to reverse the sacralization of the veil by linking the hijab with oppressive social hierarchies and male domination. She argues that the veil represents a tradition of "mediocrity and servility" rather than a sacred standard against which to judge Muslim women's devotion to Allah. Second, antiveiling Muslim commentators are quick to highlight the historical fact that veiling is a cultural practice that originated from outside of Islamic circles (see Schmidt 1989). Although commonly assumed to be of Muslim origin, historical evidence reveals that veiling was actually practiced in the ancient Near East and Arabia long before the rise of Islam (Esposito 1995; Sherif 1987; Webster 1984). Using this historical evidence to bolster their antiveiling stance, some Muslim feminists conclude that because the veil is not a Muslim invention, it cannot be held up as the standard against which Muslim women's religiosity is to be gauged.

Finally, Islamic feminists such as Mernissi (1991, chap. 5) point to the highly questionable scriptural interpretations on which Muslim clergy often base their pro-veiling edicts (see Hessini 1994; Shirazi-Mahajan 1995). Dissident Islamic commentators call attention to the fact that the Qur'an refers cryptically to a "curtain" and never directly instructs women to wear a veil. Although proponents of veiling interpret Qur'anic edicts as Allah's directive to all Muslim women for all time, Islamic critics of veiling counter this interpretive strategy by placing relatively greater weight on the "occasions of revelation" (*asbab nuzul al-Qur'an*)— that is, the specific social circumstances under which key Qur'anic passages were revealed (Mernissi 1991, 87–88, 92–93; see Sherif 1987). It is with this interpretive posture that many Islamic feminists believe the veil verse (S. 33:53) to be intended solely for the wives of Muhammad (Mernissi 1991, 92; see Sherif 1987). Muslim critics of veiling further counter many of the pro-veiling hadith citations by arguing that they are interpretations of extrascriptural texts whose authenticity is highly questionable (Mernissi 1991, 42–48; see Sherif 1987; Shirazi-Mahajan 1995). Finally, critics of hijab point to select verses in the Qur'an that invoke images of gender egalitarianism, including one passage that refers to the "vast reward" Allah has prepared for both "men who guard their modesty and women who guard their modesty" (S. 33:35).

THE VEIL AND GENDER IDENTITY NEGOTIATION AMONG MUSLIM WOMEN IN AUSTIN

To this point, we have drawn comparisons between pro-veiling edicts that link devout, desexualized Muslim womanhood to the practice of veiling and antiveiling discourses that reject this conflation of hijab and women's religious devotion. We now attempt to

gauge the impact of these debates on the gender identities of a sample of 24 Muslim women—12 of whom veil, 12 of whom do not. All women in our sample define themselves as devout Muslims (i.e., devoted followers of Muhammad who actively practice their faith). These women were recruited through a combination of snowball and purposive sampling. Taken together, the respondents identify with a range of different nationalities (e.g., Iranian, Pakistani, Kuwaiti) and Muslim sects (e.g., Sunni, Shi'i, Ahmadia). Nineteen women have lived 10 or more years in the United States, while five women in our sample have immigrated in the past 5 years. Their ages range from 21 to 55 years old, and they occupy a range of social roles (e.g., college students, professional women, homemakers). Consistent with the demographic characteristics of U.S. Muslim immigrants at large (Haddad 1991b), our sample is composed of middle-class women with some postsecondary education (either a college degree or currently attending college). Class homogeneity among the respondents is also partly a product of the locale from which the sample was drawn, namely, a university town. Consequently, this study extends cross-cultural scholarship on the intersection of veiling, ethnicity, and nationality for middle-class Muslim women living in Western and largely modernized societies (e.g., Bloul 1997; Brenner 1996; Hatem 1994). . . .

Interview data collected from these women, identified below by pseudonyms, are designed to address several interrelated issues: What does the veil itself and the practice of veiling mean to these women? Among the women who veil, why do they do so? Among the women who do not veil, how have they arrived at the decision to remain unveiled? Finally, how does each group of our respondents feel about women who engage in the "opposite" cultural practice?

VEILED CONTRADICTIONS: PERCEPTIONS OF HIJAB AND GENDER PRACTICES AMONG VEILED MUSLIM WOMEN

Religious Edicts and Social Bonds

In several respects, the veiled respondents' accounts of wearing hijab conform to the pro-veiling gender discourse explicated above. Many of the veiled women invoke various sorts of religious imagery and theological edicts when asked about their motivations for veiling. One respondent in her early twenties, Huneeya, states flatly: "I wear the hijab because the Qur'an says it's better [for women to be veiled]." Yet another veiled woman, Najette, indicates that hijab "makes [her] more special" because it symbolizes her commitment to Islam. Mona says outright: "The veil represents submission to God," and Masouda construes the veil as a "symbol of worship" on the part of devout Muslim women to Allah and the teachings of the Prophet Muhammad. Not surprisingly, many veiled women contend that veiling is commanded in the Qur'an.

Of course, this abundance of theological rationales is not the only set of motivations that the veiled women use to justify this cultural practice. For many of the veiled respondents, the scriptural edicts and the religious symbolism surrounding the veil are given palpable force through their everyday gender practices and the close-knit social networks that grow out of this distinctive cultural practice. Indeed, narratives about some women's deliberate choice to begin veiling at a particular point in their lives underscore how religious edicts stand in tension with the women's strategic motivations. Several women recount that they began to veil because they had friends who did so or because they felt more closely connected to significant others through this cultural practice. Aisha, for example, longed to wear the veil while she attended high school in the Middle East approximately three decades ago. Reminiscent of issues faced by her teen counterparts in the United States, Aisha's account suggests that high school was a crucial time for identity formation and the cultivation of peer group relationships. The veil served Aisha as a valuable resource in resolving many of the dilemmas she faced 30 years ago as a maturing high school student. She decided to begin veiling at that time after hearing several prominent Muslim speakers at her school "talk[ing] about how good veiling is." The veil helped Aisha not only to form meaningful peer relationships at that pivotal time in her life (i.e., adolescence) but also continues to facilitate for her a feeling of connectedness with a broader religious community of other veiled Muslim women. During her recent trip to Egypt during the summer, Aisha says that the veil helped her "to fit in" there in a way that she would not have if she were unveiled.

Several other respondents also underscore the significance of Islamic women's friendship networks that form around the veil, which are particularly indispensable because they live in a non-Muslim country (i.e., the United States). In recounting these friendship circles that are cultivated around hijab in a "foreign" land, our veiled respondents point to an important overlay between their gender identities (i.e., good Muslim women veil) and their ethnic identities (i.e., as Middle Easterners). The common foundation on which these twin identities are negotiated is distinctively religious in nature. Hannan touts the personal benefits of veiling both as a *woman*—"the veil serves as an identity for [Islamic] women"—and as a *Muslim*: "[Because I veil,] Muslim people know I am Muslim, and they greet me in Arabic." This interface between gender and ethnicity is also given voice by Aisha, whose initial experiences with the veil were noted above. Aisha maintains, "The veil differentiates Muslim women from other women. When you see a woman in hijab, you know she's a Muslim." Much like the leading Muslim commentators who encourage Islamic women to "wear" their religious convictions (literally, via the veil) for all to see, these veiled respondents find comfort in the cultural and ethnic distinctiveness that the veil affords them. In this way, hijab is closely connected with their overlapping religious–gender–ethnic identities and links them to the broader community (*ummah*) of Islamic believers and Muslim women.

Gender Difference and Women's "Emancipation"

In addition to providing religious rationales for wearing the veil, many of the women who wear hijab also invoke the discourse of masculine–feminine difference to defend the merits of veiling. For several women, the idea of masculine hyper-sexuality and feminine vulnerability to the male sex drive is crucial to this essentialist rationale for veiling. Despite the fact that veiled women were rather guarded in their references to sex, their nods in that direction are difficult to interpret in any other fashion. In describing the veil's role in Islam and in the lives of Muslim men and women (such as herself), Sharadda states, "Islam is natural and men need some things naturally. If we abide by these needs [and veil accordingly], we will all be happy." She continues, "If the veil did not exist, many evil things would happen. Boys would mix with girls, which will result in evil things."

Similarly, Hannan describes what she perceives to be women's distinctive attributes and their connection to the veil: "Women are like diamonds; they are so precious. They should not be revealed to everyone—just to their husbands and close kin." Like Qur'anic references to women's "ornaments," Hannan is contrasting the "precious" diamond-like feminine character to the ostensibly less refined, less distinctive masculine persona. Interestingly, it is by likening women to diamonds that Hannan rhetorically inverts traditional gender hierarchies that privilege "masculine" traits over their "feminine" counterparts. In the face of those who would denigrate feminine qualities, Hannan reinterprets the distinctiveness of womanhood as more "precious" (i.e., more rare and valuable) than masculine qualities. Women's inherent difference from men, then, is perceived to be a source of esteem rather than denigration.

It is important to recognize, however, that the respondents who invoke this rhetoric of gender difference are not simply reproducing the pro-veiling discourse advanced by Muslim elites. Despite their essentialist convictions, many of the veiled respondents argue that the practice of wearing hijab actually liberates them from men's untamed, potentially explosive sexuality and makes possible for them various sorts of public-sphere pursuits. So, whereas pro-veiling Islamic elites often reason that women's sexual vulnerability (and, literally, their fragile bodily "ornaments") should restrict them to the domestic sphere, many of the veiled women in this study simply do not support this view of domesticized femininity. To the contrary, these women—many of whom are themselves involved in occupational or educational pursuits—argue that the veil is a great equalizer that enables women to work alongside of men. In the eyes of Hannan, women's "preciousness" should not be used to cajole them to remain in the home: "Women who wear the hijab are not excluded from society. They are freer to move around in society because of it."

Rabbab, who attends to various public-sphere pursuits, offers a similar appraisal. She argues that the face veil (hijab) is an invaluable aid for Muslim women who engage in extradomestic pursuits. In advancing this claim, Rabbab uses women who veil their whole bodies (such body garments are called *abaya*) as a counterpoint of excessive traditionalism. When asked what the veil means to her personally, as well as to Muslim women and Islamic culture at large, she says,

> It depends on the extent of the hijab [that is worn]. . . . Women who wear face veils and cover their whole bodies [with abaya] are limited to the home. They are too dependent on their husbands. How can they interact when they are so secluded? . . . [However,] taking away the hijab [i.e., face veil] would make women have to fight to be taken seriously [in public settings]. . . . With hijab, men take us more seriously.

This hijab-as-liberator rationale for veiling was repeated by many of the veiled women who pursued educational degrees in schools and on college campuses where young predatorial men ostensibly rove in abundance. Aisha, a 41-year-old former student, recounts how the veil emancipated her from the male gaze during her school years:

> There was a boy who attended my university. He was very rude to all of the girls, always whistling and staring at them. One day, I found myself alone in the hallway with him. I was very nervous because I had to walk by him. But because I was wearing the hijab, he looked down when I walked past. He did not show that respect to the unveiled girls.

Drawing on experiences such as these, Aisha concludes succinctly: "The veil gives women advantages. . . . They can go to coeducational schools and feel safe." A current student, Najette, says that the veil helps her to "feel secure" in going about her daily activities. Finally, the account of a young female student who is 22 years of age sheds further light on the hijab's perceived benefits in the face of men's apparent propensity to objectify women: "If you're in hijab, then someone sees you and treats you accordingly. I feel more free. Especially men, they don't look at your appearance—they appreciate your intellectual abilities. They respect you." For many of the veiled women in this study, the respect and protection afforded them by the hijab enables them to engage in extradomestic pursuits that would ironically generate sharp criticism from many pro-veiling Muslim elites.

The Discontents of Hijab and Tolerance for the Unveiled

While the foregoing statements provide clear evidence of these women's favorable feelings about hijab, many of the veiled women also express mixed feelings about this controversial cultural symbol. It was not uncommon for the veiled respondents to recount personal difficulties that they have faced because of their decision to wear hijab. Some dilemmas associated with the veil emanate from the fact that these women live in a secular society inhabited predominantly by Christians rather than Muslims. Najette, the same respondent who argued that veiling makes her feel "special," was quick to recognize that this esteem is purchased at the price of being considered "weird" by some Americans who do not understand her motivations for veiling. For women like her, engaging in a dissident cultural practice underscores Najette's cultural distinctiveness in a way that some people find refreshing and others find threatening.

Such points of tension surrounding the veil are evident not only in cross-cultural encounters such as that mentioned above. Even within Muslim circles, the practice of veiling has generated enough controversy to produce rifts among relatives and friends when some of the veiled respondents appear publicly in hijab. Huneeya, a student who veils because she wishes to follow Qur'anic edicts and enjoys being treated as an intellectual equal by her male peers, highlighted just this point of friction with her family members, all of whom except her are "against hijab. [My family members] think it is against modernity."

For some women, the tensions produced within intimate relationships by the veil move beyond the realm of intermittent family squabbles. One veiled respondent, Asma, revealed that extended family difficulties surrounding the veil have caused her to alter the practice of veiling itself, if only temporarily. Her recent experiences underscore the complex machinations of power involved in the contested arenas of family relations and friendships where veiling is concerned. Asma moved to the United States with her husband only two years ago. Asma was quite conscientious about veiling. She relished the sense of uniqueness and cultural distinctiveness afforded to her by the hijab while living in a non-Muslim country. Yet, recent summer-long visits

from her mother-in-law presented her with a dilemma. Asma's mother-in-law had arranged the marriage between her son and daughter-in-law. At the time, the mother-in-law greatly appreciated the conservative religious values embraced by her future daughter-in-law, evidenced in Asma's attentiveness to wearing the veil. Yet, since that time, Asma's mother-in-law had undergone a conversion of sorts concerning the practice of veiling. Quite recently, Asma's mother-in-law stopped wearing the veil and wanted her daughter-in-law to follow suit by discarding the veil as well. Indeed, this mother-in-law felt that Asma was trying to upstage her by using the veil to appear more religiously devout than her elder. Asma's short-term solution to this dilemma is to submit to the wishes of her mother-in-law during her summer visits to the United States. Consequently, for two months each summer, Asma discards her veil. Yet, this solution is hardly satisfactory to her and does not placate Asma's veiled friends who think less of her for unveiling:

> I feel very uncomfortable without the veil. The veil keeps us [Muslim women] from getting mixed up in American culture. But I don't want to make my mother-in-law feel inferior, so I take it off while she is here. I know my friends think I am a hypocrite.

Although Asma is sanctioned by her friends for unveiling temporarily during her mother-in-law's visit, our interview data suggest that the preponderance of veiled women in this study harbor no ill will toward their Muslim sisters who choose not to veil. Despite these veiled women's enthusiastic defenses of hijab, they are willing to define what it means to be a good Muslim broadly enough to include Islamic women who do not veil. When asked, for instance, what she thought being a good Muslim entails, one of our veiled respondents (Najette) states simply: "You must be a good person and always be honest." Echoing these sentiments, Masouda suggests, "Your attitude towards God is most important for being a good Muslim—your personality. You must be patient, honest, giving." Even when asked point-blank if veiling makes a woman a good Muslim, another veiled respondent answers, "Hijab is not so important for being a good Muslim. Other things are more important, like having a good character and being honest." One respondent even took on a decidedly ecumenical tone in detaching veiling from Islamic devotion: "Being a good Muslim is the same as being a good Christian or a good Jew—treat others with respect and dignity. Be considerate and open-minded." In the end, then, these women in hijab are able to distinguish between what veiling means to them at a personal level (i.e., a sign of religious devotion) versus what the veil says about Muslim women in general (i.e., a voluntary cultural practice bereft of devotional significance). These veiled women's heterogeneous lived experiences with the hijab—both comforting and uncomfortable, affirming and tension producing, positive and negative—seem to provide them with a sensitivity to cultural differences that often seems lacking in the vitriolic debates about veiling currently waged by leading Muslims.

ISLAMIC FEMINISM MODIFIED: PERCEPTIONS OF HIJAB AND GENDER PRACTICES AMONG THE UNVEILED

Patriarchal Oppression and Religious Fanaticism

Just as veiled women draw on the pro-veiling discourse to defend the wearing of hijab, the unveiled women in this study often justify their abstention from this cultural practice by invoking themes from the antiveiling discourse. Several of these unveiled women argue quite straightforwardly that the veil reinforces gender distinctions that work to Muslim women's collective disadvantage. According to many of the unveiled women, the veil was imposed on Muslim women because of Middle Eastern men's unwillingness to tame their sexual caprice and because of their desire to dominate women. Rabeeya, for example, contends that Muslim women are expected to veil because "Middle Eastern men get caught up in beauty. The veil helps men control themselves." Offering a strikingly similar response, Najwa argues that "men can't control themselves, so they make women veil." Using the same critical terminology—that is, *control*—to make her point, Fozia has an even less sanguine view of the veil's role in Islam. When asked about the significance of the veil in Muslim societies, she states flatly: "The veil is used to control women." In short, many of the unveiled

respondents view hijab in much the same way as elite Islamic feminists; that is, as a mechanism of patriarchal control.

Comments such as these suggest points of congruence between the veiled and unveiled respondents' understandings of hijab. Both groups of women seem to agree that hijab is closely related to men's sexuality. Recall that some of the veiled women contrast masculine hypersexuality to a desexualized view of femininity. Such women conclude that the veil is the God-ordained corrective for men's inability to control their own sexual impulses. Likewise, as evidenced in several statements from unveiled women, they link the veil to men's apparent inability (or, better, unwillingness) to contain their sexual desires. However, whereas several of the veiled women see masculine hypersexuality as natural and view the veil as a divine remedy for such sexual differences, many of the unveiled women reject these views. The unveiled respondents seem less willing to accept the notion that categorical gender differences should translate into a cultural practice that (literally and figuratively) falls on the shoulders of women. In a key point of departure from their sisters who wear hijab, the unveiled women in this study trace the origin of the veil not to God but rather to men's difficulties in managing their sexuality (again, "men can't control themselves, so they make women veil"). In men's attempt to manage their sexual impulses, so the account goes, they have foisted the veil on women. Very much in keeping with feminist discourses that take issue with such gendered double standards, the unveiled women conclude that it is unfair to charge women with taming men's sexuality.

Apart from these issues of social control and sexuality, several of the unveiled respondents also invoke themes of religious devotion and ethnic identity when discussing the significance of the veil for Muslims in general and for themselves (as unveiled Islamic women) in particular. Recall that leading Muslims who support veiling often highlight the religious and ethnic distinctiveness of hijab; however, prominent Muslim feminists counter that veiling did not originate with Islam and should not be understood as central to women's religious devoutness or ethnic identities (as non-Westerners). Echoing these Muslim feminist themes, several of the unveiled respondents seek to sever the veil from its religious and ethnic moorings. Fozia says that Muslim "women are made to believe that the veil is religious. In reality, it's all political," while Fatima asserts, "The veil is definitely political. It is used by men as a weapon to differentiate us from Westerners." Yet another respondent, Mah'ha, argues that it is only "fanatical" and "strict" Muslims who use the veil to draw sharp distinctions between Middle Easterners and Westerners. These remarks and others like them are designed to problematize the conflation of religious devotion, ethnic distinctiveness, and hijab evidenced in the pro-veiling discourse. Whereas the dominant discourse of veiling measures women's devotion to Islamic culture against hijab, many of the unveiled respondents imply—again, via strategic terms such as *political, fanatical,* and *strict*—that religious devotion and ethnic identification are good only in proper measure.

This rhetorical strategy allows these unveiled women to claim more moderate (and modern) convictions over and against those whose devotion to Allah has in their view been transmogrified into political dogmatism, religious extremism, and racial separatism. The unveiled women in our study do not eschew religious commitment altogether, nor are they in any way ashamed of their ethnic heritage. To the contrary, the unveiled respondents champion religious commitment (again, in good measure) and are proud to count themselves among the followers of Muhammad. Yet, they are quick to illustrate that their devotion to Allah and their appreciation of their cultural heritage are manifested through means that do not include the practice of veiling. Amna, for example, says, "Religious education makes me feel like a more pious Muslim. I read the Qur'an weekly and attend Friday prayer sermons," while Rabeeya states, "Being a good Muslim means believing in one God; no idolatry; following the five pillars of Islam; and believing in Muhammad." Concerning the issue of ethnoreligious identity, the basic message articulated by many of the unveiled women can be stated quite succinctly: A Muslim woman can be true to her cultural and religious heritage without the veil. Samiya, a 38-year-old unveiled woman, says as much: "Muslim society doesn't exist on the veil. Without the veil, you would still be Muslim." Therefore, many of the unveiled women believe that the veil is of human (actually, male) origin rather than of divine making. And it is this very belief

about the veil's this-worldly origins that enables many of the unveiled women to characterize themselves as devout followers of Muhammad who honor their cultural heritage even though they have opted not to veil.

Standing on Common Ground: Tolerance for the Other among Unveiled Women

Finally, we turn our attention to the subjective contradictions that belie the prima facie critical reactions of our unveiled respondents toward the veil. Interestingly, just as the veiled women are reluctant to judge harshly their unveiled counterparts, these unveiled women who eschew hijab at a personal level nevertheless express understanding and empathy toward their Middle Eastern sisters who veil. At several points during interview encounters, the unveiled respondents escape the polemical hold of the antiveiling discourse by building bridges to their sisters who engage in a cultural practice that they themselves eschew.

First, several respondents imply that it would be wrong to criticize veiled women for wearing hijab when it is men—specifically, male Muslim elites—who are to blame for the existence and pervasiveness of the veil in Islamic culture. Amna, who does not veil, takes on a conciliatory tone toward women who do so by conceding that "the veil helps women in societies where they want to be judged solely on their character and not on their appearances." How is it that such statements, which sound so similar to the justifications for wearing hijab invoked by veiled women, emanate from the unveiled respondents? The strongly antipatriarchal sentiments of the unveiled women (described in the preceding section) seem to exonerate veiled women from charges of gender traitorism. Recall that many of the unveiled respondents, in fact, locate the origin of the veil in *men's* sexual indiscretion and in *men's* desire to control women: "Middle Eastern *men* get caught up in beauty. The veil helps *men* control *themselves*" (Rabeeya); "*Men* can't control *themselves, so they* make women veil" (Najwa); "The veil is *used to control women*. The women are *made to believe* that the veil is religious" (Fozia) (emphasis added). Ironically, it is the very antipatriarchal character of these statements that simultaneously enables the unveiled women to express their stinging criticism of the veil itself while proclaiming tolerance and respect for Islamic women who wear the veil. Indeed, since many of the unveiled respondents construe hijab to be a product of *patriarchal* oppression and assorted *masculine* hang-ups (e.g., struggles with sexuality, a preoccupation with domination and control), veiled women cannot legitimately be impugned for wearing hijab.

Second, many of the unveiled respondents are willing to concede that despite their own critical views of the veil, hijab serves as an important cultural marker for Islamic women other than themselves. When asked about the role of the veil among Muslim women she knows in the United States, Rabeeya recognizes that many of her veiled Islamic sisters who currently live in America remain "very, very tied to their culture. Or they are trying to be. They [veil because they] want to feel tied to their culture even when they are far away from home." Because she herself is a devout Islamic woman living in a religiously pluralistic and publicly secularized society, Rabeeya is able to empathize with other Muslim women residing in the United States who veil in order to shore up their cultural identity. Similarly, Sonya draws noteworthy distinctions between her personal antipathy toward veiling and veiled women's attraction to hijab: "Some Muslim women need the veil to identify themselves with the Muslim culture. I don't feel that way."

Finally, several of the unveiled women in our study seem to express tolerance and empathy for their sisters in hijab because, at one time or another in the past, they themselves have donned the veil. Two of the unveiled respondents, for example, are native Iranians who are currently living in the United States. When these women return to Iran, they temporarily don the veil. Najwa, one of these women, explains, "As soon as we cross the Iranian border, I go to the bathroom on the airplane and put on the hijab." The experiences of our other native-born Iranian woman, Fatima, speak even more directly to the practical nuances that undergird unveiled women's tolerance for their veiled counterparts. On one hand, Fatima is highly critical of the veil, which has been the legally required dress for women in Iran during the past two decades. Referring to this fact, she impugns the veil as a "political . . . weapon" used by religious elites to reinforce invidious distinctions between Westerners and Middle Easterners. Yet, on the other hand, her personal experiences with hijab lead her to reject the stereotype that women who veil are "backward": "Progress has nothing to do with veiling. Countries without veiling can be very

backwards . . . I have nothing against veiling. I feel very modern [in not veiling], but I respect those who veil." Like so many of her unveiled sisters, then, Rabeeya is critical of the veil as a religious icon but is unwilling to look down on Islamic women who wear hijab.

CONCLUSION AND DISCUSSION

This study has examined how a sample of Muslim women living in Austin, Texas, negotiate their gender identities in light of ongoing Islamic disputes about the propriety of veiling. Interview data with 12 veiled and 12 unveiled women reveal that many of them draw upon the pro-veiling and antiveiling discourses of Muslim elites, respectively, to justify their decisions about the veil. At the same time, the women highlight various subjective contradictions manifested in many of their accounts of veiling. Women who veil are not typically disdainful toward their unveiled Muslim sisters, and unveiled women in our sample seem similarly reluctant to impugn their veiled counterparts. Such findings were unanticipated in light of elite Muslim debates about the propriety of veiling.

What are we to make of the fact that the acrimony manifested between elite Muslim proponents and opponents of veiling is largely absent from these women's accounts of the veil? Several possible answers to this question emerge from our investigation. First, both the veiled and unveiled women in our study clearly exercise agency in crafting their gender identities. Drawing on themes of individualism and tolerance for diversity, the women are able to counterpose their own "choice" to veil or to remain unveiled on one hand with the personal inclinations of their sisters who might choose a path that diverges from their own. In this way, the respondents fashion gender identities that are malleable and inclusive enough to navigate through the controversy surrounding the veil. Second, the social context within which the women are situated seems to provide them with resources that facilitate these gender innovations. As noted above, our sample is composed of middle-class, well-educated Muslim women. We suspect that the progressive, multicultural climate of Austin and the human capital enjoyed by the women foster greater empathy between the veiled respondents and their unveiled counterparts. This degree of tolerance between veiled and unveiled Muslim women evinced in our study may be decidedly different for Islamic women living in other parts of the United States, other Western nations, or particular countries in the Middle East where the veil is a more publicly contested symbol.

Consequently, this study lends further credence to the insight that culture is not simply produced from "above" through the rhetoric of elites to be consumed untransformed by social actors who are little more than judgmental dopes. While the pro-veiling and antiveiling discourses have carved out distinctive positions for veiled Muslim women and their unveiled counterparts within the late twentieth century, the respondents in our study are unique and indispensable contributors to contemporary Islamic culture. It is these women, rather than the often combative elite voices within Islamic circles, who creatively build bridges across the contested cultural terrain of veiling; who forge ties of tolerance with their sisters, veiled and unveiled; and who help foster the sense of community (*ummah*) that is so esteemed by Muslims around the world. Convictions about Islamic culture and community take on new meaning as they are tested in the crucible of Muslim women's everyday experiences. . . .

NOTE

1. The merits of this insider or "emic" perspective are also clearly evidenced by a growing body of research that highlights the heterogeneous and contested character of gender relations among conservative Protestants (e.g., Bartkowski 1997a, 1997b, 1998, 1999, 2000; Gallagher and Smith 1999; Griffith 1997; Stacey 1990) and Orthodox Jews (Davidman 1993), an issue to which we return in the final section of this article.

REFERENCES

AbuKhalil, As'ad. 1993. Toward the study of women and politics in the Arab world: The debate and the reality. *Feminist Issues* 13:3–23.

Abu-Lughod, Lila. 1986. *Veiled sentiments.* Berkeley: University of California Press.

Acker, Joan. 1990. Hierarchies, jobs, bodies: A theory of gendered organizations. *Gender & Society* 4:139–58.

Afshar, Haleh. 1985. The legal, social and political position of women in Iran. *International Journal of the Sociology of Law* 13:47–60.

Ahmed, Gutbi Mahdi. 1991. Muslim organizations in the United States. In *The Muslims of America,* edited by Y. Y. Haddad. Oxford, UK: Oxford University Press.

Ahmed, Leila. 1992. *Women and gender in Islam: Historical roots of a modern debate.* New Haven, CT: Yale University Press.

Al-Hibri, Azizah, ed. 1982. *Women and Islam.* Oxford, UK: Pergamon.

Al-Marayati, Laila. 1995. Voices of women unsilenced— Beijing 1995 focus on women's health and issues of concern for Muslim women. *UCLA Women's Law Journal* 6:167.

Al-Swailem, Sheikh Abdullah Ahmed. 1995. Introduction. In *A comparison between veiling and unveiling,* by Halah bint Abdullah. Riyadh, Saudi Arabia: Dar-es-Salam.

Anees, Munawar Ahmad. 1989. Study of Muslim women and family: A bibliography. *Journal of Comparative Family Studies* 20:263–74.

An-Na'im, Abdullahi. 1987. The rights of women and international law in the Muslim context. *Whittier Law Review* 9:491.

Arat, Yesim. 1994. Women's movement of the 1980s in Turkey: Radical outcome of liberal Kemalism? In *Reconstructing gender in the Middle East: Tradition, identity, and power,* edited by F. M. Gocek and S. Balaghi. New York: Columbia University Press.

Badran, Margot. 1991. Competing agendas: Feminists, Islam and the state in 19th and 20th century Egypt. In *Women, Islam & the state,* edited by D. Kandiyoti. Philadelphia: Temple University Press.

Bartkowski, John P. 1997a. Debating patriarchy: Discursive disputes over spousal authority among evangelical family commentators. *Journal for the Scientific Study of Religion* 36:393–410.

Bartkowski, John P. 1997b. Gender reinvented, gender reproduced: The discourse and negotiation of spousal relations within contemporary Evangelicalism. Ph.D. diss., University of Texas, Austin.

Bartkowski, John P. 1998. Changing of the gods: The gender and family discourse of American Evangelicalism in historical perspective. *The History of the Family* 3:97–117.

Bartkowski, John P. 1999. One step forward, one step back: "Progressive traditionalism" and the negotiation of domestic labor within Evangelical families. *Gender Issues* 17:40–64.

Bartkowski, John P. 2000. Breaking walls, raising fences: Masculinity, intimacy, and accountability among the promise keepers. *Sociology of Religion* 61:33–53.

Bloul, Rachel A. 1997. Victims or offenders? "Other" women French sexual politics. In *Embodied practices: Feminist perspectives on the body,* edited by K. Davis. Thousand Oaks, CA: Sage.

Bozorgmehr, Mehdi, Claudia Der-Martirosian, and Georges Sabagh. 1996. Middle Easterners: A new kind of immigrant. In *Ethnic Los Angeles,* edited by R. Waldinger and M. Bozorgmehr. New York: Russell Sage Foundation.

Brasher, Brenda E. 1998. *Godly women: Fundamentalism and female power.* New Brunswick, NJ: Rutgers University Press.

Brenner, Suzanne. 1996. Reconstructing self and society: Javanese Muslim women and the veil. *American Ethnologist* 23:673–97.

Britton, Dana M. 1997. Gendered organizational logic: Policy and practice in men's and women's prisons. *Gender & Society* 11:796–818.

Currie, Dawn H. 1997. Decoding femininity: Advertisements and their teenage readers. *Gender & Society* 11:453–57.

Davidman, Lynn. 1993. *Tradition in a rootless world: Women turn to Orthodox Judaism.* Berkeley: University of California Press.

Davis, Kathy, ed. 1997. *Embodied practices: Feminist perspectives on the body.* Thousand Oaks, CA: Sage.

Dellinger, Kirsten, and Christine L. Williams. 1997. Makeup at work: Negotiating appearance rules in the workplace. *Gender & Society* 11:151–77.

Dragadze, Tamara. 1994. Islam in Azerbaijan: The position of women. In *Muslim women's choices: Religious belief and social reality,* edited by C. F. El-Solh and J. Mabro. New York: Berg.

El-Guindi, Fadwa. 1981. Veiling Infitah with Muslim ethic: Egypt's contemporary Islamic movement. *Social Problems* 28:465–85.

El-Guindi, Fadwa. 1983. Veiled activism: Egyptian women in the contemporary Islamic movement. *Mediterranean Peoples* 22/23:79–89.

El-Solh, Camillia Fawzi, and Judy Mabro, eds. 1994. *Muslim women's choices: Religious belief and social reality.* New York: Berg.

Esposito, John L., ed. 1995. *The Oxford encyclopedia of the modern Islamic world.* New York: Oxford University Press.

Esposito, John L., ed. 1998. Women in Islam and Muslim societies. In *Islam, gender, and social change,* edited by Y. Y. Haddad and J. L. Esposito. New York: Oxford University Press.

Fernea, Elizabeth W. 1993. The veiled revolution. In *Everyday life in the Muslim Middle East,* edited by D. L. Bowen and E. A. Early. Bloomington: Indiana University Press.

Fernea, Elizabeth W. 1998. *In search of Islamic feminism: One woman's journey.* New York: Doubleday.

Fox, Greer L. 1977. "Nice girl": Social control of women through a value construct. *Signs: Journal of Women in Culture and Society* 2:805–17.

Gallagher, Sally K., and Christian Smith. 1999. Symbolic traditionalism and pragmatic egalitarianism: Contemporary Evangelicals, families, and gender. *Gender & Society* 13:211–233.

Gerami, Shahin. 1996. *Women and fundamentalism: Islam and Christianity.* New York: Garland.

Ghanea Bassiri, Kambiz. 1997. *Competing visions of Islam in the United States: A study of Los Angeles.* London: Greenwood.

Gocek, Fatma M., and Shiva Balaghi, eds. 1994. *Reconstructing gender in the Middle East: Tradition, identity, and power.* New York: Columbia University Press.

Griffith, R. Marie. 1997. *God's daughters: Evangelical women and the power of submission.* Berkeley: University of California Press.

Haddad, Yvonne Yazbeck. 1991a. American foreign policy in the Middle East and its impact on the identity of Arab Muslims in the United States. In *The Muslims of America,* edited by Y. Y. Haddad. Oxford, UK: Oxford University Press.

Haddad, Yvonne Yazbeck. 1991b. Introduction. In *The Muslims of America,* edited by Y. Y. Haddad. Oxford, UK: Oxford University Press.

Hatem, Mervat F. 1994. Egyptian discourses on gender and political liberalization: Do secularist and Islamist views really differ? *Middle East Journal* 48:661–76.

Hermansen, Marcia K. 1991. Two-way acculturation: Muslim women in America between individual choice (liminality) and community affiliation (communitas). In *The Muslims of America,* edited by Y. Y. Haddad. Oxford, UK: Oxford University Press.

Hessini, Leila. 1994. Wearing the hijab in contemporary Morocco: Choice and identity. In *Reconstructing gender in the Middle East: Tradition, identity, and power,* edited by F. M. Gocek and S. Balaghi. New York: Columbia University Press.

Hollway, Wendy. 1995. Feminist discourses and women's heterosexual desire. In *Feminism and discourse,* edited by S. Wilkinson and C. Kitzinger. London: Sage.

Hunter, James Davison. 1994. *Before the shooting begins: Searching for democracy in America's culture war.* New York: Free Press.

Johnson, Steven A. 1991. Political activity of Muslims in America. In *The Muslims of America,* edited by Y. Y. Haddad. Oxford, UK: Oxford University Press.

Kadioglu, Ayse. 1994. Women's subordination in Turkey: Is Islam really the villain? *Middle East Journal* 48:645–60.

Kandiyoti, Deniz. 1988. Bargaining with patriarchy. *Gender & Society* 2:274–90.

Kandiyoti, Deniz, ed. 1991. *Women, Islam & the state.* Philadelphia: Temple University Press.

Kandiyoti, Deniz. 1992. Islam and patriarchy: A comparative perspective. In *Women in Middle Eastern history: Shifting boundaries in sex and gender,* edited by N. R. Keddie and B. Baron. New Haven, CT: Yale University Press.

Mahoney, Maureen A., and Barbara Yngvesson. 1992. The construction of subjectivity and the paradox of resistance: Reintegrating feminist anthropology and psychology. *Signs: Journal of Women in Culture and Society* 18:44–73.

Mann, Susan A., and Lori R. Kelley. 1997. Standing at the crossroads of modernist thought: Collins, Smith, and the new feminist epistemologies. *Gender & Society* 11:391–408.

Manning, Cristel. 1999. *God gave us the right: Conservative Catholic, Evangelical Protestant, and Orthodox Jewish women grapple with feminism.* New Brunswick, NJ: Rutgers University Press.

Mernissi, Fatima. 1987. *Beyond the veil.* Rev. ed. Bloomington: Indiana University Press.

Mernissi, Fatima. 1991. *The veil and the male elite: A feminist interpretation of women's rights in Islam.* Translated by Mary Jo Lakeland. New York: Addison–Wesley.

Mishler, Elliot G. 1986. *Research interviewing: Context and narrative.* Cambridge, MA: Harvard University Press.

Munson, Henry Jr. 1988. *Islam and revolution in the Middle East.* New Haven, CT: Yale University Press.

Odeh, Lama Abu. 1993. Post-colonial feminism and the veil: Thinking the difference. *Feminist Review* 43:26–37.

Papanek, Hanna. 1973. Purdah: Separate worlds and symbolic shelter. *Comparative Studies in Society and History* 15:289–325.

Philips, Abu Ameenah Bilal, and Jameelah Jones. 1985. *Polygamy in Islam.* Riyadh, Saudi Arabia: International Islamic Publishing House.

Schmidt, Alvin J. 1989. *Veiled and silenced: How culture shaped sexist theology.* Macon, GA: Mercer University Press.

Shaheed, Farida. 1994. Controlled or autonomous: Identity and the experience of the network, women living under Muslim laws. *Signs: Journal of Women in Culture and Society* 19:997–1019.

Shaheed, Farida. 1995. Networking for change: The role of women's groups in initiating dialogue on women's issues. In *Faith and freedom: Women's human rights in the Muslim world,* edited by M. Afkhami. New York: Syracuse University Press.

Sherif, Mostafa H. 1987. What is hijab? *The Muslim World* 77:151–63.

Shirazi-Mahajan, Faegheh. 1995. A dramaturgical approach to hijab in post-revolutionary Iran. *Journal of Critical Studies of the Middle East* 7 (fall): 35–51.

Siddiqi, Muhammad Iqbal. 1983. *Islam forbids free mixing of men and women.* Lahore, Pakistan: Kazi.

Smith, Dorothy E. 1987. *The everyday world as problematic: A feminist sociology.* Boston: Northeastern University Press.

Stacey, Judith, 1990. *Brave new families.* New York: Basic Books.

Stombler, Mindy, and Irene Padavic. 1997. Sister acts: Resisting men's domination in Black and white fraternity little sister programs. *Social Problems* 44:257–75.

Stone, Carol L. 1991. Estimate of Muslims living in America. In *The Muslims of America,* edited by Y. Y. Haddad. Oxford, UK: Oxford University Press.

Todd, Alexandra Dundas, and Sue Fisher, eds. 1988. *Gender and discourse: The power of talk.* Norwood, NJ: Ablex.

Walbridge, Linda S. 1997. *Without forgetting the imam: Lebanese Shi'ism in an American community.* Detroit, MI: Wayne State University Press.

Webster, Sheila K. 1984. Harim and hijab: Seclusive and exclusive aspects of traditional Muslim dwelling and dress. *Women's Studies International Forum* 7:251–57.

West, Candace, and Sarah Fenstermaker. 1995. Doing difference. *Gender & Society* 9:8–37.

Wodak, Ruth, ed. 1997. *Discourse and gender.* Thousand Oaks, CA: Sage.

26

Hybrid Masculinities: New Directions in the Sociology of Men and Masculinities

TRISTAN BRIDGES
C. J. PASCOE

INTRODUCTION

A growing body of sociological theory and research on men and masculinities addresses recent transformations in men's behaviors, appearances, opinions, and more. While historical research has shown masculinities to be in a continuous state of change (e.g., Kimmel 1996; Segal 1990), the extent of contemporary transformations as well as their impact and meaning is the source of a great deal of theory, research, and debate. While not a term universally adopted among masculinities scholars, the concept of "hybrid masculinities" is a useful way to make sense of this growing body of scholarship. It critically highlights this body of work that seeks to account for the emergence and consequences of recent transformations in masculinities.

The term "hybrid" was coined in the natural sciences during the 19th century. Initially used to refer to species produced through the mixing of two separate species, by the 20th century, it was applied to people and social groups to address popular concern with miscegenation. Today, scholars in the social sciences and humanities use "hybrid" to address cultural miscegenation—processes and practices of cultural interpenetration (Burke 2009). "Hybrid masculinities" refers to the selective incorporation of elements of identity typically associated with various marginalized and subordinated masculinities and—at times—femininities into privileged men's gender performances and identities (e.g., Arxer 2011; Demetriou 2001; Messerschmidt 2010; Messner 2007). Work on hybrid masculinities has primarily, though not universally, focused on young, White, heterosexual-identified men. This research is centrally concerned with the ways that men are increasingly incorporating elements of various "Others" into their identity projects. While it is true that gendered meanings change historically and geographically, research and theory addressing hybrid masculinities are beginning to ask whether recent transformations point in a new, more liberating direction.

The transformations addressed by this literature include men's assimilation of "bits and pieces" (Demetriou 2001: 350) of identity projects coded as "gay" (e.g., Bridges, forthcoming; Heasley 2005; Hennessy 1995) "Black" (e.g., Hughey 2012; Ward 2008), or "feminine" (e.g., Arxer 2011; Messerschmidt 2010; Schippers 2000; Wilkins 2009) among others. A central research question in this literature considers the extent and meaning of these practices in terms of gender, sexual, and racial inequality. More specifically, this field of inquiry asks: are hybrid masculinities

---

Bridges, Tristan, and C. J. Pascoe,"Hybrid Masculinities: New Directions in the Sociology of Men and Masculinities" (abridged), *Sociology Compass* 8 (3), © 2014 John Wiley and Sons. Reprinted by permission of the publisher.

widespread and do they represent a significant change in gendered inequality?

In reviewing contemporary theorizing and empirical research on masculinity, we suggest that hybrid masculinities work in ways that not only reproduce contemporary systems of gendered, raced, and sexual inequalities but also obscure this process as it is happening. We argue that hybrid masculinities have at least three distinct consequences that shape, reflect, and mask inequalities. Hybrid masculinities may place discursive (though not meaningful) distance between certain groups of men and hegemonic masculinity, are often undertaken with an understanding of White, heterosexual masculinity as less meaningful than other (more marginalized or subordinated) forms of masculinity, and fortify social and symbolic boundaries and inequalities. As Coston and Kimmel write, "The idealized notion of masculinity operates as both an ideology and a set of normative constraints" (2012: 98). We argue that the emergence of hybrid masculinities indicates that normative constraints are shifting but that these shifts have largely taken place in ways that have sustained existing ideologies and systems of power and inequality. Each of the consequences of contemporary hybrid masculinities we address here represents elaborations on the processes by which meanings and practices of hegemonic masculinity change over time in ways that nonetheless maintain the structure of institutionalized gender regimes to advantage men collectively over women and some men over other men. Indeed, hybrid masculinities may be best thought of as contemporary expressions of gender and sexual inequality.

THEORIZING CHANGES IN MASCULINITY

The question driving the bulk of the literature on hybrid masculinities[1] is whether (and how) they are perpetuating and/or challenging systems of gender and sexual inequality. Scholars answer the question in three ways. (i) Some are skeptical of whether hybrid masculinities represent anything beyond local variation (e.g., Connell and Messerschmidt 2005). (ii) Others argue that hybrid masculinities are both culturally pervasive and indicate that inequality is lessening and possibly no longer structures men's identities and relationships

(e.g., Anderson 2009; McCormack 2012). (iii) The majority of the research and theory supports the notion that hybrid masculinities are widespread. But, rather than suggesting that they are signs of increasing levels of gender and sexual equality, these scholars argue that hybrid masculine forms illustrate the flexibility of systems of inequality. Thus, they argue that hybrid masculinities represent significant changes in the expression of systems of power and inequality, though fall short of challenging them (e.g., Demetriou 2001; Messerschmidt 2010; Messner 1993, 2007).

While not necessarily challenging the notion that hybrid masculinities exist, Connell and Messerschmidt (2005)—in their analysis of "hegemonic masculinity"—question the extent of hybrid masculine practices, their meaning, and influence. "Clearly, specific masculine practices may be appropriated into other masculinities, creating a hybrid (such as the hip-hop style and language adopted by some working-class White teenage boys and the unique composite style of gay 'clones'). Yet we are not convinced that the hybridization . . . is hegemonic, at least beyond a local sense" (2005: 845). Here, Connell and Messerschmidt (2005) suggest that while hybrid masculine forms may exist and might promote inequality in new ways, they are unconvinced that hybrid masculinities are illustrative of a transformation in hegemonic masculinity beyond local subcultural variation. Thus, they argue that hybrid masculine forms have not significantly affected the meanings of masculinity at regional or global levels.[2] Significantly, while Connell and Messerschmidt (2005) are critical of the extent and reach of hybrid masculinities, they agree that, while these new identities and practices blur social and symbolic boundaries, they are not necessarily undermining systems of dominance or hegemonic masculinity in any fundamental way.

Anderson's (2009) theory of the rise of "inclusive masculinities" challenges Connell and Messerschmidt's (2005) perspective. He argues that contemporary transformations in men's behaviors and beliefs are widespread *and* are best understood as challenging systems of gender and sexual inequality. Studying a variety of young, primarily heterosexual-identified, White men, Anderson finds that masculinity among these groups is characterized by "inclusivity" rather than exclusivity (what Anderson terms "orthodoxy"). In this model masculinities are organized horizontally, rather than hierarchically. As such, men are increasingly adopting practices characterized by acceptance of diverse masculinities, opening up the contemporary meanings of "masculinity" in ways that allow a more varied selection of performances to "count" as masculine. This "inclusivity"—like hybridity—is part of a process of incorporating performances that are culturally coded as "Other." Anderson argues that these practices indicate "decreased sexism" and "the erosion of patriarchy" (2009: 9). Thus, Anderson theorizes hybrid masculinities (which he calls "inclusive masculinities") as endemic and as a fundamental challenge to existing systems of power and inequality.

To account for this transformation, Anderson (2009) argues that what he calls "homohysteria" is decreasing (see also McCormack 2012). Broadly described as a "fear of being homosexualized" (2009: 7), the term considers three issues: popular awareness of gay identity, cultural disapproval of homosexuality, and the cultural association of masculinity with heterosexuality. While awareness of gay identity has increased, Anderson argues that disapproval of homosexuality is diminishing[3] as is the cultural association of masculinity with heterosexuality. Unyoked from compulsory heterosexuality, he argues that contemporary masculinities are characterized by increasing levels of equality and less hierarchy.

The majority of the research concerning hybrid masculinities supports Anderson's (2009) claim that hybrid masculinities are extensive but frames the meanings and consequences of hybrid masculine practices and identities differently. Rather than illustrating a decline in gender and sexual inequality, scholars suggest that hybrid masculinities work in ways that perpetuate existing systems of power and inequality in historically new ways (e.g., Demetriou 2001; Messner 1993, 2007). Thus, this body of research is at odds with Connell and Messerschmidt's (2005) analysis of the significance of hybrid masculinities and with Anderson's (2009) consideration of the consequences.

Messner (1993) analyzes transformations among American men toward more "emotionally expressive" performances of masculinity and critiques scholarly investigations of these transformations precisely because they tended to focus primarily on "*styles* of masculinity, rather than the institutional *position of power* that men still enjoy" (732). Messner examines the cultural impact of these shifts in men's behavior by analyzing the mythopoetic men's movement, men's increasing involvement as parents, and an increase in the number of high-status men crying in public.

Messner's framing of hybrid masculinities as "more style than substance" (1993: 724) represents a dominant approach in scholarship discussing the meanings and consequences of hybrid masculinities. This body of work discusses hybrid masculinities as

represent[ing] highly significant (but exaggerated) shifts in the cultural and personal styles of hegemonic masculinity, but these changes do not necessarily contribute to the undermining of conventional structures of men's power over women. Although "softer" and more "sensitive" styles of masculinity are developing among some privileged groups of men, this does not necessarily contribute to the emancipation of women; in fact, quite the contrary may be true. (Messner 1993: 725)

This shift is complex and not unidirectional. In fact, new gendered practices and identities often work in ways that either produce new forms of inequality or conceal existing inequalities in new ways.

Messner's (2007) analysis of changes in the public image of Arnold Schwarzenegger, e.g., illustrates what he calls an "ascendant hybrid masculinity" combining toughness with tenderness in ways that work to obscure—rather than challenge—systems of power and inequality (Messner 2007). Similar phenomena have been documented within various "men's movements" like the Promise Keepers and the Ex-gay Movement (e.g., Donovan 1998; Gerber 2008; Heath 2003; Wolkomir 2001), new ways of performing heterosexuality while engaging in "gay" styles, practices, and sex (e.g., Bridges forthcoming; Pascoe 2007; Schippers 2000; Ward 2008; Wilkins 2009), the masculinization of concerns with hygiene and appearance (e.g., Barber 2008), presidential discourses surrounding militarism (Messerschmidt 2010), and throughout popular culture more generally (e.g., Carroll 2011; Jeffords 1994; Pfeil 1995; Savran 1998).

Contemporary transformations in masculinity have primarily been documented among groups of young, heterosexual-identified, White men. This fact evidences the flexibility of identity afforded privileged groups. Indeed, ignoring intersectional distinctions that inequitably distribute access to specific hybrid masculine forms risks presenting contemporary changes as indicative of transformations in systems of inequality that may still exist—albeit in new forms. Messner (1993) argues that, "framing shifts in styles of hegemonic masculinity as indicative of the arrival of a New Man [often situates] marginalized men (especially poor black men, in the United States) as Other" (1993: 733). Men of color, working-class men, immigrant men, among others, are often (in)directly cast as the possessors of regressive masculinities in the context of these emergent hybrid masculinities. That said, young, straight, White men are not the only ones with hybrid masculinities. Research also illustrates the ways that groups of marginalized and subordinated Others craft hybrid gender identities—though often with very different consequences and concerns.

Demetriou (2001) coins the term "dialectical pragmatism" to theorize the consequences of the changes Messner (1993) described. Dialectical pragmatism refers to the ability of hegemonic masculinities to appropriate elements of subordinated and marginalized "Others" in ways that work to recuperate existing systems of power and inequality. Dialectical pragmatism speaks to the transformative capacities of systems of power inequality. Demetriou suggests that what makes hegemonic masculinities so powerful is precisely their ability to adapt. He suggests that hegemonic masculinity is better understood as a "hegemonic masculine bloc" capable of appropriating "what appears pragmatically useful and constructive for the project of domination at a particular historical moment" (2001: 345). Demetriou argues that Connell's initial conceptualization of hegemonic masculinity fails to account for the ways that subordinated and marginalized masculinities affect the formation, style, look, and feel of hegemonic masculinity. Thus, Demetriou's framework illustrates how the meanings and consequences of hybrid masculinities are much more complicated than they might initially appear.

Demetriou focuses primarily on one example of hybridity: the assimilation of elements of "gay male culture" into heterosexual masculinities. He illustrates how this hybrid masculinity might be better understood as a contemporary expression of—rather than challenge to—existing forms of gender and sexual inequality. Demetriou shows how heterosexual men incorporate "bits and pieces [of gay male culture,] . . .

[producing] new, hybrid configurations of gender practice that enable them to reproduce their dominance over women [and other men] in historically novel ways" (2001: 350–351). Like Messner (1993, 2007), Demetriou shows how hybrid masculinities blur gender differences and boundaries in ways that present no real challenge to existing systems of power and inequality.

The theorizing of hybrid masculinities as illustrated by Demetriou (2001) and Messner (1993, 2007) challenges the analyses set forth by Anderson (2009) and Connell and Messerschmidt (2005). Anderson's (2009) theory of "inclusive masculinity" argues that these new configurations of identity and practice are best understood as resistance to gender and sexual inequality, while Connell and Messerschmidt (2005) argue that these challenges to hegemonic masculinity have not been significant. The research in the following section, however, broadly supports Demetriou's (2001) conceptualization of "dialectical pragmatism" and Messner's (1993, 2007) analysis of transformations in masculine *style* but not substance of contemporary masculinities. This work illustrates how contemporary performances of masculinity are part of a transformation in the practices, identities, and discourses through which contemporary inequalities are being perpetuated and expressed. In connecting with a much more diverse body of literature than existing work on "hybrid masculinities," we illustrate the depth and breadth of the meanings and consequences of gendered hybridization and comment on the origins of contemporary transformations.

RESEARCH ON HYBRID MASCULINITIES

Research on hybrid masculinities highlights several consequences associated with these gender projects and performances. First, hybrid masculine practices often work in ways that create some discursive distance between young, White, straight men and hegemonic masculinity, enabling some to frame themselves as outside of existing systems of privilege and inequality. Second, hybrid masculinities are often premised on the notion that the masculinities available to young, White, straight men are somehow less meaningful than the masculinities of various marginalized and subordinated Others, whose identities were at least partially produced by collective struggles for rights and recognition. Third, hybrid masculinities work to fortify symbolic and social boundaries between (racial, gender, sexual) groups—further entrenching, and often concealing, inequality in new ways.

Discursive Distancing

The gender flexibility of postmodern patriarchy is pernicious because it casts the illusion that patriarchy has disappeared. (Hennessy, 1995:172)

Hybrid masculine practices often work in ways that create some discursive distance between White, straight men and "hegemonic masculinity." However, as men are distanced from hegemonic masculinity, they also (often more subtly) align themselves with it. Research on men's pro-feminist, political, and grooming activities illustrates how hybrid masculinities can work in ways that discursively distance men from hegemonic masculinity.

Bridges (2010) highlights this distancing in his documentation of men's participation in Walk a Mile in Her Shoes marches—an event to raise awareness about domestic violence. In it, men wear high-heeled shoes and walk one mile. This practice of standing with women and wearing women's clothing seemingly distances them from the sexism and gendered dominance that partially constitutes hegemonic masculinity. As Bridges points out, however, the men in this march can reproduce gender inequality even as they actively work against it. The way men interact during this march reiterates forms of gender inequality that undergird domestic violence. The male participants joke about wearing women's clothing, about their ability to walk in heels, and about same-sex sexual desire. These jokes discursively align participants with hegemonic masculinity even as their practices might seem to distance them from it.

The "My Strength Is Not for Hurting" campaign—one of the few anti-rape campaigns directed at men—also acts to distance men from hegemonic masculinity by framing men "as a unitary group" made to look bad by rapists (Masters 2010). Non-rapist men are simultaneously aligned with hegemonic masculinity through framing "real" and "strong" men as fundamentally different from (presumably weak and unmanly) rapists. Campaigns like this discursively separate "good" from

"bad" men and fail to account for the ways that presenting strength and power as natural resources for men perpetuates gender and sexual inequality even as they are called into question (see also Murphy 2009). Both Walk a Mile in Her Shoes marches and the My Strength Is Not for Hurting campaign create some distance between these (good) men and (bad) hegemonic masculinity. Yet, in challenging men's violence against women, they simultaneously reaffirm many qualities that typify hegemonic masculine forms and dominance.

Similarly, men can embrace political stances that seem to distance them from hegemonic masculinity. Such stances allow public male figures to disguise toughness with tenderness. For instance, Arnold Schwarzenegger forged an identity that Messner (2007) refers to as the "kindergarten commando," representing a masculinity "foregrounding muscle, toughness and the threat of violence" followed with "situationally appropriate symbolic displays of compassion" (Messner 2007: 461). Schwarzenegger's "sexy, hybrid mix of hardness and compassion" is a "configuration of symbols that forge a masculinity that is useful for securing power among men who already have it" (Messner 2007: 473). This same shift is reflected in mediated depictions of idealized masculinities in action films of the 1980s and 90s (Jeffords 1994) and more recently as well (Carroll 2011). For instance, while action films in the 90s seem to implicitly critique or satirize the masculine "hard bodies" of the 80s, they do so in ways that Jeffords suggests "[do not reject] that body so much as [refigure] it" (1994: 191).

Messerschmidt (2010) illustrates a similar dynamic at work in international arenas. Analyzing speeches surrounding the "War on Terror" spanning the presidencies of George Bush and George W. Bush, he finds that both presidents mobilized discourses of rescue to justify military action. As Messerschmidt argues, "Bush Senior's and Bush Junior's inclusion of humane, sensitive, and empathic aspects in their masculine rhetoric shows how hegemonic masculinity at the regional and global levels is fluid and flexible . . . Such an appropriation of traditionally defined 'feminine' traits blurs gender difference but does not undermine gender dominance" (2010: 161). Messerschmidt illustrates the fluid properties of hegemonic masculinities and the ways in which masculinities are capable of incorporating elements of "femininity" to obscure gender boundaries, while reproducing existing systems of power and authority. These masculinized strategies allow trust to be gained "in times of fear and insecurity" and "[project] a veiled feminized stigma onto more liberal candidates" (Messner 2007: 461). Messerschmidt's findings also imply that hybrid masculinities have attained ideological power and influence on a global stage, suggesting—contrary to Connell and Messerschmidt's (2005) earlier assessment—that they are implicated in global-level processes and relations.

This kind of "feminization" has been documented in very different locations as well. For instance, Kristen Barber's (2008) study of White, middle-class, heterosexual men in professional men's hair salons illustrates one way that some men engage in beauty work formerly coded "feminine." Barber finds that these men rely on a rhetoric of expectations associated with professional-class masculinities to justify their participation in the beauty industry while simultaneously naturalizing distinctions between themselves and working-class men, framing the latter as misogynistic and reproducing gender inequality. While these men are engaging in a practice that might be labeled "feminine," Barber highlights the ways they avoid feminization and create some distance between themselves and masculinities they associate with reproducing gender and sexual inequality. Similarly, Wilkins (2009) addresses the ways that both goth and young Christian men engage in boundary-blurring gender projects that ultimately work to recuperate existing systems of power and privilege. Navigating "masculine" norms surrounding heterosexual interest and participation in different ways, Wilkins finds that both groups reiterate existing structures of gender power and authority much more than challenge them.

As this research illustrates, contemporary hybrid masculinities create space between men and hegemonic masculinity while reiterating gendered relations of power and inequality. While this process is happening in diverse ways, this research shows it is occurring at local, regional, national, and international levels.

Strategic Borrowing

If there is one aspect that separates the current crisis of masculinity from those that have come before, it is

white masculinity's turn to the representational politics of identity . . . [W]hite masculinity places itself in other identity locations (white trash, queer, blue-collar, Irish) in order to disavow that it is normative . . . [O]nce it has become visible . . . it reworks the meaning of that visibility by locating itself elsewhere. (Carroll 2011:6–7)

Hybrid masculinities are often premised on the notion that the masculinities available to young, White, straight men are meaningless when compared with various "Others," whose identities were forged in struggles for rights and recognition. Indeed, cultural appropriation is a defining characteristic of hybrid identities. Research on hybrid masculinities documents the way that men who occupy privileged social categories strategically borrow from Others in ways that work to reframe themselves as symbolically part of socially subordinated groups. Through this process, White men frame themselves as victims (Messner 1993: 77) and inequality becomes less easily identified. Like Waters' (1990) research documenting White people's relative ignorance of the ethnic flexibility they are afforded, the hybrid identities available to young, straight, White men may be very different from those available to marginalized and subordinated groups. As Patricia Hill Collins argues, "Authentic Black people must be contained—their authentic culture can enter White controlled spaces, but they cannot" (Collins 2004: 177). By strategically borrowing elements of the performative "styles" associated with various marginalized and subordinated "Others," research has documented the more pernicious consequences of these hybrid practices.

Demetriou (2001) charts this process by examining the incorporation of elements of gay culture by heterosexual-identified men. Rather than illustrating a fundamental challenge to systems of inequality, Demetriou theorizes the ways that culturally dominant models of masculinity assimilate elements from subordinated "Others" in ways that fundamentally alter the shape (but not structural position of power) of contemporary performances of gender and gender relations. Similarly, by theorizing the aesthetic elements of sexuality, Bridges (forthcoming) analyzes the causes and consequences of heterosexual men subjectively identifying aspects of themselves as "gay" in ways that preserve their heterosexuality and simultaneously reinforce existing boundaries between gay and straight individuals and cultures.

Arxer's (2011) study of interactions between heterosexual men at a college bar documents an analogous practice. Extremely different from the competitive, emotionally detached, sexually objectifying performances of masculinity that characterize straight men's interactions with each other in Bird's (1996) or Grazian's (2007) research, Arxer (2011) examines these men's assimilation of aspects of gay masculinity, but simultaneous maintenance of existing systems of power and dominance.

> These men seem to perceive a sense of intersectional deprivation wherein heterosexual masculinity (as defined traditionally to be aggressive and emotionally detached) is *devalued* relative to gay masculinities. In response to this "crisis" in hegemonic capital, the men agree to a hybridized model of masculinity that affords them a new framework to assess *who* ("gay people") has profited from being labeled as "sensitive" and *how* they can claim a slice of the dividend. (Arxer 2011: 408)

Yet, in the process of drawing on the emotionality presumably displayed by gay men, these men reassert gender inequality by using it to increase their chances of sexually "scoring" with women (Arxer 2011: 409). Thus, while a dramatically different collective performance of masculinity from "the girl hunt" that Grazian (2007) documents or Bird's (1996) "men's club," the consequences of these performances are strikingly similar in terms of sustaining existing systems of power and inequality.

Research has also analyzed racialized strategic borrowing—a process which works in similar ways. Similar to the research on men's appropriation of elements of gay culture, research on the cultural appropriation of and identification with hip-hop music among young White men finds that their incorporation of elements of "black culture" is often not associated with recognition of the consequences of this practice (e.g., Hess 2005; Hughey 2012; Rodriquez 2006). Rodriquez's (2006) research on young White hip-hop music fans documents these men justifying their interest in and identification with hip-hop utilizing "colorblind" discourses (e.g., Bonilla-Silva 2001) that enable them to conceal race (and racial inequality) as a significant element of this cultural form.

White appropriation of cultural forms is certainly not a new cultural phenomenon (e.g., Lott 1993; Deloria 1998) nor is the appropriation necessarily confined to boys and young men (e.g., Wilkins 2004, 2008) or the United States (Garner 2009). Yet, reasons

behind and consequences of contemporary men's "borrowings" are historically novel. As Cutler points out with respect to White appropriation of African-American linguistic patterns and style, "Its origins are complex, its consequences can be serious, and although its representativeness can't be stated systematically, it is not an isolated instance" (1999:439).

Hughey's (2012) research with anti-racist and White nationalist groups composed primarily of men places these practices in a larger cultural perspective. Hughey refers to this appropriation as a reliance on what he terms "color capital" by Whites. He argues that Whites engage in these practices in an effort to assuage feelings of "culturelessness" associated with White identity (see also Perry 2001 and Wilkins 2004). In very different ways, the two groups in Hughey's study struggled to both relate to and distance themselves from color capital in ways that illustrated their cultural affiliation with racialized identities that they saw as bloated with meaning when situated alongside their own racial identities—which most understood as devoid of "culture." Yet, while working to alleviate feelings of meaninglessness associated with White identity, Hughey finds that these practices simultaneously promote more destructive racial consequences.

Messner (1993) argues that when we frame young, straight, White men's new performances of masculinity solely as indicators of a decline in gender and sexual inequality, already marginalized groups of men often end up situated as playing a greater role in perpetuating inequality. By framing middle-class, young, straight, White men as both the embodiment and harbinger of feminist change in masculinities, social scientists participate in further marginalizing poor men, working-class men, religious men, undereducated men, rural men, and men of color (among others) as the bearers of uneducated, backwards, toxic, patriarchal masculinities. Even as young White men borrow practices and identities from young, gay, Black, or urban men in order to boost their masculine capital, research shows that these practices often work simultaneously to reaffirm these subordinated groups as deviant, thus supporting existing systems of power and dominance.

Fortifying Boundaries

The outward styles of masculinity may appear to be more enlightened and egalitarian while the underlying basis of male privilege and power remains fundamentally unquestioned, reminding us that "softer" forms of masculinity are not inherently emancipatory for women and can, in fact, mask usurpation of women's rights. (Donovan 1998:837)

By co-opting elements of style and performance from less powerful masculinities, young straight, White men's hybridizations often obscure the symbolic and social boundaries between groups upon which such practices rely. Through this process, systems of inequality are further entrenched and concealed in historically new ways, often along lines of race, gender, sexuality, and class.

Hybrid masculinities may, for instance, complicate claims about and understandings of relationships between normative masculinity and homophobia. In recent history, homophobia has been a hallmark of adolescent masculinity (Kehler 2007; Levy et al. 2012; Pascoe 2007; Poteat et al. 2010). However, research indicates that such sentiments are on the decline among young men (McCormack 2012). While fear or dislike of actual gay people may be declining, what Pascoe (2007) calls a "fag discourse" continues to structure the socialization practices of boys and young men. Simply put, boys socialize each other into normatively masculine behaviors, practices, attitudes, and dispositions in a way that has little relationship with boys' fear of actual gay men (Corbett 2001; Kimmel 1994). Indeed, many boys who would never insult a gay person by calling him "gay" do not hesitate to use these words to tease each other (McCormack 2012; Pascoe 2007). While McCormack argues that homophobic jokes—when not directed at gay boys—have been stripped of their discriminatory meanings, Pascoe's work illustrates that "fag discourse" is a potent form of gender policing for contemporary young men. Thus, while seemingly non-homophobic masculinities are proliferating (Anderson 2009, McCormack 2012), a closer look at the gendered meanings of homophobia complicates these claims (Bridges forthcoming; Pascoe 2007).

Even when men engage in sexual practices that challenge the relationship between normative masculinity and homophobia, they may reify inequality. Jane Ward's (2008) research on White straight-identifying men who have sex with men illustrates how their sexual practices may initially seem to transgress traditional notions of heterosexual masculinity but simultaneously work to reify gendered, sexual, and raced boundaries.

Ward documents the ways that, in their search for sexual partners, these men objectify women, reject effeminacy among men, and hyper-eroticize men of color. They talk about hooking up with other men while watching "pussy porn," say they do not want to have sex with men who are feminine "sissy la las," and use exotic and stigmatizing language to describe their ideal men of color sex partners. Ward calls this particular configuration of practices "dude sex." Though violating the "one-act rule" (Schilt and Westbrook 2009) of male homosexuality by participating in same-sex sex, these men simultaneously reinforce gendered and raced inequality. Their identity projects consist of presenting themselves as having a better "cultural fit" with heterosexuality, relying on stereotypes and gendered and racialized performances of masculinity as proof of heterosexual masculine identities.

Ward's participants in some ways both reflect and invert Connell's (1992) and Levine's (1998) analysis of gay men's assimilation of elements of straight masculinities into some gay men's identity projects. Connell's discussion of gay Australian men who identify with elements of "straight" masculine performances and identities finds that the practices ultimately shore up gender and sexual boundaries. Connell (1992) argues that these performances are primarily undertaken out of an interest in gender identification (as "masculine" men) and concerns with safety (due to the threat of violence against men performing effeminate gay identities). Ward's participants take this a step further. Not only do they perform heterosexual masculinities—often relying on racialized performances associated with hip-hop and/or surfer culture—they also identify as "straight" because of their affiliation with straight culture, in spite of their participation in same-sex sexual behavior. In some ways, this research is also an example of "strategic borrowing," illustrating how, in practice, the three consequences of hybrid masculinities we address here often work in congress and overlap.

Men's practices that initially appear to be feminist can also reify gender inequality even as they obscure it. Recent changes in the ideologies and practices of fathering may seem progressive—such as increasing levels of emotionality and time spent with children. But upon closer investigation they also entrench gender inequality. Messner (1993) makes clear that the new fathering movement was not necessarily about challenging gender inequality in the family, but about a particular *style* of male parenting, that, as Stein (2005) indicates, may draw boundaries around male heterosexuality. In her study of the Promise Keeper movement, Melanie Heath (2003) examines the ways that men embody "new fathering" by playing larger roles in their children's lives and being more emotionally available while simultaneously enforcing gender inequality by espousing a "biblical" notion of "the family" in which women are instructed to submit to their husbands. Donovan (1998) refers to this process as "masculine rescripting," and also argues that such a process does not necessarily challenge existing systems of power and inequality. Schwalbe (1996) discusses similar ideological shifts as "loose essentialism"—a process that acknowledges and supports change in men and allows them to redefine traits formerly associated with femininity as "masculine."[4]

Groups of evangelical Christian men may be the quintessential example of "loose essentialism" as research has documented their engagement in "masculine rescripting" practices when talking about sex in ways that are seemingly progressive, but simultaneously homophobic and working to reify gender inequality (Gerber 2008; Wilkins 2009). Gerber's (2008) analysis of the Ex-Gay Movement highlights some of the ways that ex-gay identities and performances of masculinity are often non-normative. In the interest of creating "a livable space" for Christian men grappling with same-sex desires, hybrid masculine options offer resources for alternative masculinities that illustrate a great transformation in *styles* of masculinity, but do little to challenge the boundaries between "gay" and "straight," or "masculine" and "feminine."

While all of this work illustrates the diverse ways in which contemporary performances of masculinity are playing with social and symbolic boundaries (gendered, raced, sexual, etc.), this body of scholarship also illustrates the ways that much of this play is best understood as superficial. While the young White men participating in "dude sex" (Ward 2008) are certainly blurring gender and sexual boundaries by discursively playing with the qualities that "count" when identifying sexualities, they are also reestablishing boundaries between gay and straight and gendered, racialized, and sexual systems of power and inequality. Similarly, Heath's (2003) study of Promise Keeper masculinities

finds significant changes in masculine norms surrounding parenting, but—like Messner's (1993) analysis of the fathers' rights movement more generally—argues that these changes have done little to disrupt existing gendered power relations in the family. Thus, a great deal of research finds that hybrid masculine practices often work in ways that fortify symbolic and social boundaries, perpetuating social hierarchies in new (and "softer") ways.

CONCLUSION

Connell (1995:84) argued that the gender order continually tends toward crisis, but also suggests that such "crisis tendencies" have intensified recently. "They have resulted, clearly enough, in a major loss of legitimacy for patriarchy, and different groups of men are now negotiating this loss in very different ways" (1995:202). Hybrid masculinities research has primarily examined this process of transformation among groups of men who hold concentrated constellations of power and authority in the current gender order (young, White, heterosexual, etc.).

Privilege works best when it goes unrecognized. Indeed, as Johnson notes, "Perhaps the most efficient way to keep patriarchy going is to promote the idea that it doesn't exist . . . Or, if it does exist, it's by reputation only, a shadow of its former self that no longer amounts to much in people's lives" (2005:154). Research on hybrid masculinities suggests that recent changes—sparked by feminist critique and reform—have shed light upon masculinity and masculine privilege in historically unprecedented ways. When privilege becomes visible, however, this research illustrates how it does not necessarily cease to exist. But, the experiences of privilege by privileged groups do change, as do the "legitimating stories" or justifications for existing systems of power and inequality. Hybrid masculinities are one illustration of what Johnson (2005) refers to as the "flexibility of patriarchy." This is not to say that men's awareness of privileges associated with masculinity causes their privileges to cease to exist. Rather, research on hybrid masculinities illustrates another possibility—experiences and justifications of privilege have transformed. And this transformation has led to a host of new identity projects as different groups of men negotiate this change in different ways.

Hybridization is a cultural process with incredible potential for change. Research on hybrid masculinities has primarily documented shifts in—rather than challenges to—systems of power and inequality. The question that remains concerns how we can recognize meaningful change in systems of gender inequality when we see it. Questions about how and when real—not just stylistic—change happens in the gender order remain to be answered by gender scholarship.

NOTES

1. It should be noted that while we refer to what these authors are writing about as "hybrid masculinities," the term is not used by all of these scholars. Demetriou (2001); Connell and Messerschmidt (2005); Messner (2007); Arxer (2011); Messerschmidt (2010), and Bridges (forthcoming) all explicitly use the term. But, the identity projects, practices, and discourses to which they refer are present in a great deal of scholarship that does not explicitly use "hybrid masculinity" to make sense of ideas and findings. We use the term to bring together lines of theorizing and claims-making that have not, historically, been in dialog with one another.

2. Importantly, Messerschmidt's (2010) more recent analysis of US presidential discourses mobilized during the "War on Terror" indicates that hybrid masculinities may increasingly exist on a global scale.

3. Indeed, public opinions in the United States concerning homosexuality have taken a marked turn in recent history—particularly those of younger men (Loftus 2001; Saad 2010). What these changes mean is more difficult to assess, as other data illustrates the continuance of harassment and bullying utilizing derogatory epithets for homosexuality and gender expression among US boys (Kosciw et al. 2012). Opinion polls are also at odds with a great deal of qualitative research among US boys and young men. So, there is some disagreement concerning how we can interpret the meanings of this change.

4. Messner (2011) theorizes a similar transformation in discourse through which youth sports leagues are gendered in ways that maintain a separation between boys and girls. He refers to this discourse as "soft essentialism." Messner argues that the notion that boys are *better than* girls (more athletic, intelligent, rational, etc.) has been successfully challenged, while the idea that boys are *different from* girls persists. Because gender inequality is institutionalized, ideologies of difference are sometimes all that is necessary to perpetuate existing inequalities.

REFERENCES

Anderson, Eric. 2009. *Inclusive Masculinity*. New York: Routledge.

Arxer, Steven. 2011. "Hybrid Masculine Power." *Humanity & Society* 35(4): 390–422.

Barber, Kristen. 2008. "The Well-Coiffed Man." *Gender & Society* 22(4): 455–76.

Bird, Sharon. 1996. "Welcome to the Men's Club." *Gender & Society* 10(2): 120–32.

Bonilla-Silva, Eduardo. 2001. *White Supremacy and Racism in the Post–Civil Rights Era*. Boulder: Lynne Rienner.

Bridges, Tristan. 2010. "Men Just Weren't Made To Do This." *Gender & Society* 24(1): 5–30.

Bridges, Tristan. Forthcoming. "A Very 'Gay' Straight?" *Gender & Society*.

Burke, Peter. 2009. *Cultural Hybridity*. New York: Polity.

Carroll, Hamilton. 2011. *Affirmative Reaction*. Durham: Duke University Press.

Collins, Patricia Hill. 2004. *Black Sexual Politics*. New York: Routledge.

Connell, R. W. 1992. "A Very Straight Gay." *American Sociological Review* 57(6): 735–51.

Connell, R. W. 1995. *Masculinities*. Stanford: Stanford University Press.

Connell, R. W. and James Messerschmidt. 2005. "Hegemonic Masculinity: Rethinking the Concept." *Gender & Society* 19(6): 829–59.

Corbett, Ken. 2001. "Faggot = Loser." *Studies in Gender and Sexuality* 2 (1): 3–28.

Coston, Bethany and Michael Kimmel. 2012. "Seeing Privilege Where It Isn't." *Journal of Social Issues* 68(1): 97–111.

Cutler, Cecilia. 1999. "Yorkville Crossing: White Teens, Hip Hop and African American English." *Journal of Sociolinguistics* 3(4): 428–42.

Demetriou, Demetrakis. 2001. "Connell's Concept of Hegemonic Masculinity: A Critique." *Theory and Society* 30(3): 337–61.

Donovan, Brian. 1998. "Political Consequences of Private Authority." *Theory and Society* 27(6): 817–43.

Garner, Steve. 2009. "Empirical Research into White Racialized Identities in Britain." *Sociology Compass* 3(5): 789–802.

Gerber, Lynne. 2008. "The Opposite of Gay." *Nova Religio* 11(4): 8–30.

Grazian, David. 2007. "The Girl Hunt." *Symbolic Interaction* 30(2): 221–43.

Heasley, Robert. 2005. "Crossing the Borders of Gendered Sexuality." pp. 109–30 in *Thinking Straight*, edited by Chrys Ingraham. New York: Routledge.

Heath, Melanie. 2003. "Soft-Boiled Masculinity." *Gender & Society* 17(3): 423–44.

Hennessy, Rosemary. 1995. "Queer Visibility in Commodity Culture." pp. 142–83 in *Social Postmodernism*, edited by Linda Nicholson and Steven Seidman. New York: Cambridge University Press.

Hess, Mickey. 2005. "Hip-hop Realness and the White Performer." *Critical Studies in Media Communication* 22(5): 372–89.

Hughey, Matthew. 2012. *White Bound.* Stanford: Stanford University Press.

Jeffords, Susan. 1994. *Hard Bodies.* New Brunswick: Rutgers University Press.

Johnson, Allan. 2005. *The Gender Knot* (revised and updated edition). Philadelphia: Temple University Press.

Kehler, Michael. 2007. "Hallway Fears and High School Friendships." *Discourse* 28(2): 259–77.

Kimmel, Michael. 1994. "Masculinity as Homophobia." Pp. 119–41 in *Theorizing Masculinities*, edited by Harry Brod and Michael Kaufman. Thousand Oaks, CA: Sage.

Kimmel, Michael. 1996. *Manhood in America.* New York: The Free Press.

Kosciw, Joseph G., Emily A. Greytak, Mark J. Bartkiewicz, Madelyn J. Boesen and Neal A. Palmer. 2012. *The 2011 National School Climate Survey: The Experiences of Lesbian, Gay, Bisexual and Transgender Youth in Our Nation's Schools.* New York: GLSEN.

Levy, Nathaniel, Sandra Cortesi, Urs Gasser, Edward Crowley, Meredith Beaton, June Casey and Caroline Nolan. 2012. *Bullying in a Networked Era.* Cambridge: Berkman Center for Internet & Society Research Publication Series.

Loftus, Jeni. 2001. "America's Liberalization in Attitudes toward Homosexuality, 1973 to 1998." *American Sociological Review* 66(5): 762–82.

Lott, Eric. 1993. *Love and Theft: Blackface Minstrelsy and the American Working Class.* New York: Oxford University Press.

Masters, N. Tatiana. 2010. "'My Strength Is Not for Hurting': Men's Anti-Rape Websites and Their Construction of Masculinity and Male Sexuality." *Sexualities* 13(1): 33–46.

McCormack, Mark. 2012. *The Declining Significance of Homophobia.* New York: Oxford University Press.

Messerschmidt, James. 2010. *Hegemonic Masculinities and Camouflaged Politics.* Boulder: Paradigm Publishers.

Messner, Michael. 1993. "'Changing Men' and Feminist Politics in the United States." *Theory and Society* 22(5): 723–37.

Messner, Michael. 2007. "The Masculinity of the Governator." *Gender & Society* 21(4): 461–80.

Messner, Michael. 2011. "Gender Ideologies, Youth Sports, and the Production of Soft Essentialism." *Sociology of Sport Journal* 28(2): 151–70.

Murphy, Michael. 2009. "Can 'Men' Stop Rape? Visualizing Gender in the 'My Strength Is Not for Hurting' Rape Prevention Campaign." *Men and Masculinities* 12(1): 113–30.

Pascoe, C. J. 2007. *Dude, You're a Fag.* Berkeley: University of California Press.

Perry, Amanda. 2001. "White Means Never Having to Say You're Ethnic." *Journal of Contemporary Ethnography* 30(1): 56–91.

Pfeil, Fred. 1995. *White Guys.* New York: Verso.

Poteat, V. Paul, Michael Kimmel and Riki Wilchins. 2010. "The Moderating Effects of Support for Violence." *Journal of Research on Adolescence* 21(2): 434–47.

Rodriquez, Jason. 2006. "Color-Blind Ideology and the Cultural Appropriation of Hip-Hop." *Contemporary Ethnography* 35(6): 645–68.

Saad, Lydia. 2010. Gallup Report: Americans' Acceptance of Gay Relations Crosses 50% Threshold. In *Gallup Politics.* Retrieved July 18, 2013, from http://www.gallup.com/poll/135764/americans-acceptance-gay-relations-crosses-threshold.aspx.

Savran, David. 1998. *Taking It Like a Man.* Princeton: Princeton University Press.

Schilt, Kristen and Laurel Westbrook. 2009. "Doing Gender, Doing Heteronormativity." *Gender & Society* 23(4): 440–64.

Schippers, Mimi. 2000. "The Social Organization of Sexuality and Gender in Alternative Hard Rock." *Gender & Society* 14(6): 747–64.

Schwalbe, Michael. 1996. *Unlocking the Iron Cage.* New York: Oxford University Press.

Segal, Lynne. 1990. *Slow Motion.* New Brunswick: Rutgers University Press.

Stein, Arlene. 2005. "Make Room for Daddy." *Gender & Society* 19(5): 601–20.

Ward, Jane. 2008. "Dude-Sex: White Masculinities and 'Authentic' Heterosexuality among Dudes Who Have Sex with Dudes." *Sexualities* 11(4): 414–34.

Waters, Mary. 1990. *Ethnic Options.* Berkeley: University of California Press.

Wilkins, Amy. 2004. "Puerto Rican Wannabes." *Gender & Society* 18(1): 103–21.

Wilkins, Amy. 2008. *Wannabes, Goths, and Christians.* Chicago: University of Chicago Press.

Wilkins, Amy. 2009. "Masculinity Dilemmas: Sexuality and Intimacy Talk among Christians and Goths." *Signs* 34(2): 343–68.

Wolkomir, Michelle. 2001. "Wrestling with the Angels of Meaning: The Revisionist Ideological Work of Gay and Ex-Gay Christian Men." *Symbolic Interaction* 24(4): 407–25.

27

Providing Women, Kept Men: Doing Masculinity in the Wake of the African HIV/AIDS Pandemic

SANYU A. MOJOLA

Socioeconomic change has left men with a patriarchal ideology bereft of its legitimizing activities.
— *Margrethe Silberschmidt (2001, 657)*

This article draws on ethnographic and interview-based fieldwork to explore accounts of relationships between widowed women and poor young men that emerged in the wake of economic crisis and a devastating HIV epidemic among the Luo ethnic group in western Kenya. I show how the co-optation of widow inheritance practices amid the presence of an overwhelming number of widows during a period of economic crisis has resulted in widows becoming providing women and poor young men becoming kept men.[1] I argue that widows in this setting, by performing a set of practices central to what it meant to be a man in this society—pursuing and providing for their partners—were effectively doing masculinity. I also show how young men, rather than being feminized by being kept, deployed other sets of practices to prove their masculinity and live in a manner congruent with cultural ideals.

These arguments draw on literature that understands masculinity as a configuration of practices located within a historically situated and shifting system of gender relations and recognizes that multiple configurations of masculinity are at work in a given social

system (Connell 1995). Understanding gender as practice, or something that is done rather than merely an identity or something that one is, enables a decoupling of masculinity from male bodies and makes the idea of women doing masculinity possible.[2] By showing both women and men simultaneously performing masculinity in the same historically situated space, I understand multiple masculinities as not just limited to relations among (those who identify as) men but rather as encompassing relations among masculinities, which can be performed by men or women. However, I will show that women's practice of masculinity in large part seemed to serve patriarchal ends. It not only facilitated their fulfillment of patriarchal expectations of femininity—particularly the expectation that widows be inherited—but also served, in the end, to provide a material base for young men's deployment of legitimizing and culturally valued sets of masculine practices.[3]

Relationships between older women and young men are rarely the focus of scholarly attention. This is especially true in examinations of cross-generational partnerships in literature on the African HIV pandemic (briefly discussed later in the article), where the focus has been on those involving older men and young women. Indeed, the data for this article come from a larger study among the Luo, who have faced the worst HIV epidemic in Kenya. It was designed to explore

Mojola, Sanyu A., "Providing Women, Kept Men: Doing Masculinity in the Wake of the African HIV/AIDS Pandemic." *Signs* 39 (2), copyright © 2014 University of Chicago Press. Reprinted with permission by the publisher.

young women's high HIV rates by examining young people's transitions to adulthood in the context of an ongoing HIV epidemic, with perspectives from youth, the middle aged, and elderly adults. As fieldwork progressed, however, respondents both within and outside of formal interview settings would remark, often as an aside, on relationships between widowed women and young men. As I will show, these comments and discussions raise important questions about the effects of the HIV epidemic on shifting gender relations and provide an opportunity to reflect on the implications of these relationships for thinking about masculinity and the persistence of patriarchal systems.

I first begin with a discussion of the crisis of youth masculinity in Africa, examining traditional and contemporary paths to manhood and adulthood, and the way current economies and population dynamics are disrupting these pathways across the continent and among the Luo specifically. Next, I discuss the HIV pandemic, its creation of widows, and practices of widow inheritance. I then describe the study setting, data, and methods before discussing the findings. I draw on fieldwork data to focus on the dilemmas of widows who have become providing women and the benefits experienced by youth who have become kept men. I examine the evolution of widow inheritance practices, as well as how young men have co-opted them to forge new pathways to manhood. The article concludes with a discussion of the implications of these relationships for thinking about masculinity as performed by women and men.

THE CRISIS OF CONTEMPORARY AFRICAN YOUTH MASCULINITY

For many young African men in patrilineal societies, the primary practices associated with the attainment of manhood and adulthood were provision of land to a wife or wives for subsistence farming, establishing a household, and siring children, as well as gaining authority over one or more women through bridewealth-based marriage.[4] The attainment of these goals underpinned the reproduction of patriarchal systems. In a typical illustration of this process, Philip Setel describes Chagga men of northern Tanzania's transition to adulthood thus: "In the nineteenth century, undergoing

initiation, entering an age grade, establishing a new homestead, and concluding a *kihamba* [land] based bridewealth marriage were the key cultural institutions and processes through which Chagga men established adult status. . . . These social institutions surrounded the transition from youth to adulthood, shaped men's entry into reproductive life, and inculcated values of responsible manhood and adult citizenship within the stratified social schema of Chagga clans and chiefdoms" (1996, 1170). What these traditional patterns implied was not just that a man would have authority over women but also that he would have authority over his sons until they established their own households on land given to them by their father. Among the Luo of Kenya, for example, a father determined when a young man had reached a sufficient age to build his own *simba* (bachelor hut) and assigned him land on which to do so. A young man also had to ask permission from his father to be allowed to find a woman to marry. The father, along with male relatives, provided bridewealth to the woman's relatives to contract the marriage, and the young man's *simba* would subsequently become his marital home.[5]

The colonial and early postcolonial era provided an opportunity to circumvent these traditional routes to adulthood. Young men's migration outside of their home area for work, as well as their education, led to semi-skilled and white-collar jobs that enabled them to earn money to set up their own independent households and to finance their own marriages without relying on their male elders.[6] This was especially salient among the Luo of Nyanza. By the second half of the twentieth century, between a quarter and half of young Luo men were migrating out of the province for work.[7] Such large-scale male labor migration and accompanying wages enabled young Luo men to contract their own marriages with their bride's relatives and to establish their own households (Whisson 1964; Cohen and Atieno Odhiambo 1989; Shipton 2007).

However, the stalled, declined, and slow-growth economies of the past two decades, coupled with a burgeoning youth population, have had a number of consequences for young men, and these consequences have caused a disruption to contemporary practices demonstrating the attainment of adulthood and manhood. In Kenya, high fertility rates and falling infant mortality rates resulted in a large youth population. The rapid spread of mass education, however, was coupled with an economy that was not expanding at a rate that could accommodate the graduates (Buchmann 1999). A substantial increase in educational access has thus been accompanied by growing disillusionment about employment prospects among youth and adults in many countries in Africa, with male youth unemployment rates reaching as high as 40–50 percent in settings such as South Africa, and more educated youth being especially affected.[8] This may partly be because if youth reach high school, their aspirations stretch to white-collar jobs. As Thomas Owen Eisemon and John Schwille note, "Parents do not send their children to school to become better farmers or to learn vernacular languages and practical skills that will suit them for rural life. They want an education for their children that affords them an opportunity for a much better life off the farm" (1991, 26). As such, looking for wage employment often involves a more protracted search than is associated with self-employment, agriculture, or other manual labor.

A lack of jobs and subsequent income was particularly problematic because it limited young men's ability to maintain a girlfriend. Many felt there was "no romance without finance" (Mills and Ssewakiryanga 2005).[9] A small but growing body of work suggests that some young men instead engaged in transactional sex relationships with older women, or sugar mummies.[10] These are nonmarital, noncommercial sexual partnerships in which money and gifts are exchanged but in which issues of love and trust are sometimes also at stake.[11] The flow of gift giving is predominantly one way—with older, wealthier partners providing to secure partnerships with younger partners. A rather more extensive literature, however, suggests that the primary participants in these sorts of relationships are young women and older men.[12]

Unfortunately, even as contemporary routes to adulthood are beginning to falter, young men have increasingly been unable to return to traditional pathways to manhood. Large numbers of youth are becoming landless, especially because of population growth and limited land to split among sons (Setel 1996; Amuyunzu-Nyamongo and Francis 2006). Thus, even though many fathers have died prematurely from AIDS, there is little left for their sons to inherit. Having no land or limited land on which a wife could engage in subsistence farming, or having few cattle with which to finance bridewealth, greatly constrains young men's ability to set up independent households and marry. Thus, remaining "perpetually poor, perpetually youth," as Jennifer Cole (2005, 892) has noted of the young Malagasy men (*jaombilo*) she studied, they are left in social limbo, unable to transition to adulthood (Amuyunzu-Nyamongo and Francis 2006). The fact that these dilemmas have been documented in several African countries suggests the structural nature of the problem faced by young men who are unable to fulfill their end of the patriarchal bargain (Kandiyoti 1988). Indeed among many young Luo men I interviewed, these limitations in the ability to achieve manhood—as defined by a configuration in which the key legitimizing activities were the provision of money to girlfriends, bridewealth to a woman's relatives, and a home and land for a wife—have made being a young man a frustrating and in some ways debilitating experience. In order to make ends meet, many worked in itinerant or low-paying jobs, such as transportation (e.g., bicycle taxi work) or agriculture, that were not always commensurate with their education. In this article, however, I focus on a particular strategy some young Luo men pursued and how the HIV/AIDS epidemic reconfigured sexual, economic, and domestic partnerships in ways that have provided opportunities for them to forge new pathways to manhood.

THE AFRICAN HIV/AIDS PANDEMIC AND WIDOW INHERITANCE

The HIV/AIDS pandemic is now an indelible part of sub-Saharan Africa, with 69 percent (23.5 million) of the world's HIV/AIDS victims and 70 percent (1.2 million) of AIDS-related deaths (UNAIDS 2012). Thus far, a key social dynamic underlying the rapid spread and cycling of HIV across genders and generations has been cross-generational marital, extramarital, and transactional sex relationships between older men and young women. HIV rates have been particularly high among young women in their late teens and twenties and middle-aged men in their late thirties and forties (Laga et al. 2001; Clark 2004; UNAIDS and WHO 2005, 2009). A major result of these relationships, given the limited availability of antiretroviral medication to prolong the lives of people living with HIV/AIDS, has been particularly high mortality among middle-aged men and younger women. Consequently, the AIDS pandemic has produced large numbers of widows. Among the Luo of Nyanza Province, Kenya, one in six women in their thirties and one in five women in their forties were widowed. This extent of widowhood was partly the result of high rates of polygamy among Luo. About a third of Luo women (31 percent) and more than a fifth of Luo men (24 percent) over thirty years of age were involved in polygamous partnerships.[13] As such, older men who could afford multiple wives also left multiple widows upon their death.

Many patrilineal African societies, including the Luo of Nyanza Province, practiced and continue to practice widow inheritance.[14] After the death of a husband, traditional widow inheritance offered a "corporate safety net for widows and orphans" (Slater 1986, xvi). Among the Luo, a brother of the deceased husband or one of his other male relatives would inherit the widow. While widows were included in deciding who the inheritor was to be, the final decision was in the hands of male relatives of the deceased husband because they had paid bridewealth for her and therefore felt that she belonged to them and could not be inherited by a stranger or nonrelative (Nyambedha, Wandibba, and Aagaard-Hansen 2003). The main benefit of this system for women was that, by remaining within the folds of her husband's lineage, a widow could remain on her deceased husband's land and retain his property, thus enabling her to support herself and her children. Also, especially in the absence of sons, any children resulting from the widow's sexual partnership with the inheritor would be considered as belonging to the deceased, thus allowing his line to continue and providing heirs to the deceased man's property. This was especially important because a widow would otherwise have no rights to her husband's land or property.[15] The inheritor was usually a married man who continued to live in his own home with his wife while the widow stayed in her own home with her children. While the widow and inheritor typically had a sexual relationship, the inheritor had no financial responsibility for her or her children, and she in turn did not have any obligations to cook or perform other domestic services for him (Potash 1986). Women rarely had the recourse of returning to their natal home because

such a move was predicated on a return of bridewealth, which their families could rarely afford.

Many women complied with widow inheritance practices because of the immense social pressure to conform. Numerous taboos and sanctions were enforced in the event that a woman refused to be inherited. She would eventually become an outcast in her community and could be dispossessed from the land. If her house fell apart, no one would rebuild it for her.[16] A woman needed to be inherited to be allowed to plant her own farm. If she was not inherited, she would not be allowed to enter certain households, her sons could not marry, and any deaths of her children would be attributed to her refusal to be inherited (see also Luginaah et al. 2005; Geissler and Prince 2010; Dworkin et al. 2013).[17]

The HIV/AIDS epidemic, however, radically changed the practice of widow inheritance, primarily because the volume of widows began to overwhelm traditional systems. A tragic consequence of the practice was the death of one brother after another as HIV spread throughout a family. Consequently, to avoid HIV, some wives began refusing to share their husbands with widows who were being inherited. Widows were thus left with continuing social pressure to be inherited but limited men from their husband's lineage available or willing to inherit them. New and, to some, unsettling solutions emerged to deal with the problem of what widows were to do "when the obvious brother is not there," to borrow Christopher Oleke, Astrid Blystad, and Ole Bjørn Rekdal's (2005) phrase. In the accounts to follow, I will show how inheritor and transactional sex relationships between widows and young men resolved the social and economic challenges that both groups faced.[18] I first describe the study setting, data, and methods before presenting the findings. . . .

PROVIDING WOMEN:
THE EVOLUTION OF WIDOW
INHERITANCE

When your husband dies and you are not inherited, you are like a taboo woman, and so nobody will give you something even if your house is leaking. Nobody can do anything for you. They don't want to touch that house unless they remarry you. So sometimes if you are poor [and] your house is falling apart, they cannot do it for you. And they say they have to remarry you, otherwise in [the] future, no one will help you. You will have to accept so that you are helped. So this is where custom comes in. You don't want to do it. You don't feel like doing it. But here poverty comes in. [If] you were rich, you could do it by yourself by simply leaving [hiring] people to do it for you. But you have nothing to do because you have no money and so you will rely on your brother-in-law to do it for you.

This excerpt from a middle-aged woman in a focus group interview that took place at the beginning of my study was a typical complaint from the Luo widows I encountered during my fieldwork. Widows, especially in rural areas, faced continual pressure from family and community members to be inherited and often succumbed to it despite their profound reluctance. For many, the extent to which they were able to resist was related to their wealth.[19] However, in this context, where the majority of widows were poor and most lived below the poverty line, few women felt they were in a position to resist.

As my fieldwork progressed, it became clear that critical changes were occurring to the practice of widow inheritance, with brothers-in-law reluctant to inherit widows and with continued social pressure to be inherited. Widows were increasingly choosing younger unmarried men to inherit them, and young men were moving in to live with them. This represented a dramatic break with tradition in that, first, the widow rather than her husband's male relatives was choosing the inheritor, and second, the young man did not maintain his own separate residence. One middle-aged female respondent explained:

> It is like the woman is the one who has married. Because the first man paid dowry [bridewealth], came to look for you and paid dowry, you wedded, isn't that your husband? But this one, you went to look for him because you want a man in this house. *So you have to provide for him.* You are the one now marrying him actually. You are the one marrying him. And there are such that if you don't do what he wants, he disappears because he doesn't have love for you. He came for enjoyment, [to] eat and bathe and then lust. (Emphasis added.)

Widows referred to these inheritor relationships as "marriage," and the relatedness of the young men to

women's deceased husbands was not brought up as important during interviews. They used the term "marriage" because, as in marriage, the young man stayed in the widow's household. (In traditional inheritance, the inheritor stayed in his own household with his own wife.) In addition, as in marriage, widows engaged in traditional feminine roles such as cooking and caring for the men. What was striking, however, was that widows were also engaging in traditionally masculine practices by looking for the man and bringing him into her house on her land, which she was providing as a husband normally would. A widow's taking on the masculine roles of pursuing and bringing home a partner compelled her to also take on the concomitant role of provider—the final piece of what was a traditional configuration of masculine practice.

Another middle-aged respondent described her aunt's situation:

> I love my aunt. My aunt's husband died, [she is] an old woman now. She visits me here and I always feel that my aunt is starving. I give her the proper food to eat and even take her to hospital. But my brother called me recently and told me that if you visit her at home, she cooks for some man. Ei! An old woman, you are still bringing a man into your [house], my aunt, what do you want? That I want him to dig for me. And she is the one feeding the man. And this is a young man. So actually with the money I send for her, she feeds this man, so that the man cannot go away. . . . You go and borrow to give him, otherwise he will leave you.

As we can see, an interesting circulation was occurring: a woman was sending money to support her older female relative who in turn used that money to keep her younger man by providing for him so that he would not leave her. While both women were engaging in provision, it was the aunt's provision in the household, functioning in the masculine provider role for a young "husband," that was shocking for the respondent. Men were supposed to provide a house for women, not the other way round. This point can be further emphasized in examining the gendered language around particular roles. In the dhoLuo language, men marry and women are married. Indeed, "to cook" and "to get married/be married" are the same word. "Akinyi has gone to cook for Daniel" (*Akinyi odhi tedo ne Daniel*) means that Daniel married Akinyi. It is linguistically incorrect to say the opposite: one cannot say Daniel has gone to cook for Akinyi (*Daniel odhi tedo ne Akinyi*). Thus, as shown in the quotation above, a woman simultaneously performing the feminized practice of "cooking for" and the masculinized practice of "feeding" (providing for) her male partner was problematic. This was part of the improperness of the practice that respondents were trying to convey in their statements.

As highlighted in both quotations, men's motivations were clear to widows—they would stay with them as long as they were providing. Once the provision ended, the men would leave and sometimes move on to another widow. Many widows resented this evolution of widow inheritance because keeping a man was a costly exercise. In addition, they resented the economy that seemed to be at work. That is, the fear of a young man leaving reflected the reality that the large number of widows had essentially created a buyer's market for young men. There was a sense among respondents that richer widows were in a stronger position than poorer ones. They felt that young men made this distinction, preferring homes that were relatively wealthy and that would yield them a good and comfortable life, while turning down poorer widows.[20] This is illustrated, for example, in the following excerpt from a focus group among widows:

R1: Even here we can see some women who are widows and are rich, they are okay. If she wants somebody to move with, she will choose a man of her choice because she has money. She can make a choice. But if you don't have, how can you choose while you are starving?

R2: He can't even accept you.

R3: He can't. Actually the poor they don't want. They don't want. They want to come because they know at the back of their minds, they know that these things are there. They know that they are facing death and so they want to enjoy themselves. Nice food, you have to feed them, you have to treat them like kids.

I: Who?

R3: These people who come to inherit. You treat them better than your own husband.

R4: He sits like a log of wood, but you feed them, gives you another burden.

As the interview excerpt illustrates, poorer widows were decidedly less fortunate in these relationships as compared to rich widows. Interviews often revealed the lengths that poorer widows would go to, giving their inheritors the best food while splitting what was left with their children, in order to keep a man in the house for as long as possible. A key informant working in community health, for example, described the plight of widows in her community: "Another issue with the women who are widows is that they are having problems with the inheritors because when the inheritor comes they don't want to eat vegetables. They like to eat special food like meat, fish, eggs, things like that. So you find that this lady who is a widow, her children will be eating vegetables, but she will strive to give this man whatever he wants." In lakeside communities, widows described going to fish-landing beaches to engage in transactional partnerships with fishermen to get financial support to cater for their families.

The focus group excerpt above also suggests, however, that the richest widows had the most options. The few widows who were independently wealthy, making their own money from lucrative businesses or high-salary jobs (and therefore outside the purview of their deceased husband's relatives), were the most able to opt out of inheritance and engage instead in transactional relationships with young men out of choice. Accounts of these widows emerged in the course of interviews among men.

KEPT MEN: RECUPERATING MASCULINITY

Several middle-aged and older men pointed out young men's pursuit of relationships with older women in the course of my fieldwork. For example, in response to a question on changes among the Luo over time, one older male respondent, in his eighties, replied, "Education is expensive. After that expensive education there are no jobs. So the children who are educated have lost their way [and] get into different things. We have problems because they are back with us in the house. They come to disturb us parents. You had educated him or her. You have no money. [So] when they can't support themselves, they get into drugs. From drugs they go after women who are wealthy. An old but rich woman can take your son who is eighteen years old [and] live with him as her husband." Similarly, a middle-aged district official and a retired older educational official independently described the experience of attending funerals of a prominent contemporary who had likely died of AIDS. Both noted that young men were fighting in the back room over who would inherit the widow. In one case, the chief in attendance went to the back and ordered that the men be arrested, so physical and presumably disruptive was the fighting. As my field notes describe, the older man recounted, "they [the young men] were like 'this time she is mine, you are always taking them.'"

The accounts were startling not just to my respondents—men remarking on these puzzling and worrying developments among their juniors—but also to me. Why would young men in their prime be pursuing rich older women or fighting over a potentially HIV-positive widow?

My fieldwork suggested a number of ways in which young men benefited from inheritor relationships with widows. First, by co-opting tradition, young men were able to turn continued social pressure on widows to be inherited into commercial advantage. Tom Mboyo Okeyo and Ann K. Allen (1994) and Rose Ayikukwei et al. (2008) document the rise of local commercial industries around widow inheritance and other sex-related rites such as sexual cleansing (to rid the widow of her husband's ghost) among the Luo over the past decade and a half. Because there were fewer older men to go around, because wives were reluctant to share their husbands with widows, and because of the large numbers of widows, families were starting to pay men (called *joter*) to inherit widows and perform these rites. Money gained from this payment, in addition to money the widow used to provide for the man, enabled young men to attain the Luo ideal of enjoying the good life (*hero raha*). Since the widow was now responsible for feeding, clothing, and caring for her inheritor, a young man in such a relationship, especially if the widow or her deceased husband had been rich, could enjoy the high life and gain resources he otherwise would not have had access to, with few or none of the obligations a traditional husband would have. As the excerpts from my interviews with widows highlight, a young man in this position could "eat, bathe, and lust"; "sit like a log"; and experience better treatment than a husband, as a woman worked hard to satisfy her man so that he would not leave her for another widow. This experience

provided young men with a stark contrast to their original home, where, as the older man above noted, their parents were unable to provide for them and where parents felt they were disturbing them. They could essentially marry up from their parental home. This explained the attraction to richer widows, who in this setting were fewer in number than poor widows, and why they were worth fighting for.

The same financial and material benefits extended to young men in transactional relationships with rich women who wanted, as a respondent noted, "to dress well, drink, and here is a sugar mummy." In an interview among young fishermen, they noted that rich widowed fisherwomen, who used to buy fish in bulk from fishermen and then transport and sell it in other parts of the country, would often pursue them and invite them into their homes to keep them. One noted, "You have been offered a soda, you have been welcomed into a house, nice food has been cooked for you, and you have been offered a place to sleep and you find things start happening." The high male mortality rates in the fishing communities that fishermen traveled to when selling their fish had changed the gender norms around relationships: "It is now opposite—that ladies go for men, but men don't go for ladies. . . . So you find that especially with the young men, most of them are lost. They don't even come home." The fisherman went on to note that this had happened to him personally. While for itinerantly employed young fishermen, these relationships provided access to this high life above and beyond their basic needs, for other young men who were unemployed, these relationships helped them deal with the more immediate problem of poverty. For example, in a focus group interview among out-of-school youth, a young man noted:

What I can say is that AIDS is a big problem in this area because there are no jobs and many people are idle because there are no jobs. You find that you will be having an idle mind. So . . . for me I see that why we are getting AIDS is, like right now for me, I try to look for work and don't find it. So I go and find an old lady with a Pajero [SUV], with money. And maybe she is willing to give me monthly allowances. So I will be like a husband to her. And maybe she is giving me allowances, but she is infected [with HIV]. I don't go to her because she is beautiful and I admire her but because of hunger.

In the context of widespread poverty where most people lived on less than a dollar a day, older women's money provided financial support in the face of a lack of jobs and income.

Finally, young men involved in inheritor and transactional relationships with older women were able to use the monetary benefits to engage in at least one of the "legitimizing activities" (Silberschmidt 2001, 657) commonly associated with manhood: being able to provide for women. The amount of money young men earned from being a commercial cleanser or inheritor was enough to pay bridewealth and contract their own marriage (Ayiyukwei et al. 2008; see also Potash 1986). Widows thus provided a means for young men to gain resources needed to provide for a wife and set up their own household. Among the young men who had transactional relationships with fisherwomen, the fact that their older partners migrated to sell fish elsewhere provided opportunities for transactional relationships with younger women. As one fisherman described, "When they get young men like us, she will give them all the money to carry. . . . These ladies have money. From Mombasa [coastal Kenyan city], she will buy for you some clothes, shoes, your lifestyle really changes. So during the time she is in Mombasa, you look for a young lady and bring her close. So you spend this money with this young lady while she is away. When she comes back, now you kind of tell this young lady to hold on." In this way, a young man could have a concurrent relationship with an older fisherwoman and one or more younger girlfriends in the community. Schoolgirls interviewed often mentioned fishermen as attractive and ideal boyfriends because they had money. In this case, young men were able to use their widowed female partner's money as a material base with which to perform a providing masculinity with younger girlfriends.

However, this expression came with particular costs in terms of both the risk of acquiring HIV and the risk of passing it on. The danger of young men's concurrent relationships with widows and younger partners was highlighted in an interview with young out-of-school women, where an HIV-positive respondent described how she thought she had gotten infected. She said:

R: With me I think I got it from my boyfriend. Because he was unfaithful. He used to have many girlfriends and some women whose husbands had died.

I: So he had relationships with widows?

R: Yes.

I: So he used to, like, inherit?

R: Yes . . .

I: And how old was he?

R: He was twenty-five.

I: And you?

R: I was sixteen.

I: And how did you find out yourself [that you were positive]?

R: The way I saw him, with the mothers he used to go with, he is sick.

It was at this point that she decided to go for an HIV test and discovered her positive status.

In light of continued high HIV rates and AIDS-related widowhood in this setting, if these trends are demographically significant, young men, previously considered safe compared to young women, might now be facing death as they put themselves at risk of contracting HIV from the widows who are keeping them.

DISCUSSION

Economic crisis and the HIV epidemic have created significant dilemmas for Luo young men and widows. For young men, unemployment and constrained access to money have limited their ability to achieve manhood as defined by provision of money to girlfriends, bridewealth, and a home and land for a wife. Widows faced intense social pressure to be inherited but had a limited number of willing partners from their husband's lineage to inherit them. For some, relationships between widowed women and poor young men were creative solutions to the challenges both faced. These solutions have important implications for thinking about what it means to do masculinity and the persistence of patriarchal systems.

In examining the configurations of practices Luo widows and young men engaged in, I have argued that both groups were doing masculinity. Widows, by pursuing and providing for their male partners, were performing what had historically been a key configuration of masculinity in this culture. The richest widows, who were independently wealthy, were able to exercise financial and relational autonomy by initiating and engaging in relationships with younger men upon whom they could lavish money. Their relative wealth allowed them to opt out of and resist the pressure to be inherited and to engage in transactional relationships with younger men out of choice. However, in this poor setting, many widows were not independently wealthy and subsequently experienced their masculine practice as burdensome and stressful as they struggled to provide for and hang on to their partners. Young men had found a way out of remaining perpetual youth by engaging in relationships with providing widowed women. The relationships enabled them to move out of their parental home, to enjoy the good life, to have a respite from poverty, to pursue romance without laboring for the attendant finance, and, for some, to accumulate the resources to go on to contract a marriage and set up their own independent household. In addition, young men in these relationships were referred to using masculine terminology such as "husbands" as opposed to the feminizing term "wives" despite the unconventional and disturbing manner in which they had achieved this status.

Masculinity, then, was no longer in crisis. Indeed, among these young Luo men, it seemed as if rather than sacrificing their manhood by being kept by providing women, they were instead able to better achieve it. They were able to utilize economic crisis and the social changes wrought by the HIV epidemic to craft a configuration of masculine practice that culturally marked and legitimized them as men in ways that affirmed and maintained rather than destabilized their culture's patriarchal ideology. Providing women, in turn, were in complex ways propping up patriarchal systems and ways of doing manhood. Widows, rich and poor, provided young men with resources that some used to marry or pursue romance with younger women. Further, for many of these widows, the HIV epidemic did not provide them with a way to opt out of widow inheritance altogether but rather a new way to perpetuate it. By taking on young men as inheritors, they were using an unconventional method to meet social demands, but unfortunately they were also participating in the preservation of a system that ultimately burdened them. Indeed, for many widows, young men had the upper hand. Young men's leverage was enabled by the

high supply of widows and by their ability to co-opt the cultural pressure on widows to be inherited. This leverage enabled them to choose better resourced widows to inherit and to decide how long they were going to stay. The system left the poorest widows worst off, having to borrow money and struggle to entice young men, with their choice of widows, to stay.

Women's practices and young men's benefits reproduced and perpetuated this patriarchal system, with striking results. In this case, arguably, women's masculine practices enabled patriarchal expectations for femininity—to be inherited, and to be provided for by men—to be restored for the next generation of women and provided the material resources for young men to fulfill their end of the patriarchal bargain.

NOTES

1. Women in many parts of sub-Saharan Africa have been responsible for the bulk of provision of food for the family through subsistence farming and food gathering, among other things. My reference here and throughout the article to women as "providing women" refers specifically to their engaging in the kinds of provision considered the primary responsibility of men in this culture.

2. See Amadiume (1987), West and Zimmerman (1987), Oyěwùmí (1997), Lindsay and Miescher (2003), and Pascoe (2005).

3. Following the death of her husband, a Luo woman is expected to be inherited by her husband's brother or his close male relatives. I discuss this practice, and its implications in the age of AIDS, at length later in this article.

4. See, e.g., Moore (1986), Agadjanian (2002), Cornwall (2002), Hunter (2002), Barker and Ricardo (2005), Smith (2007), Wyrod (2007, 2008), and Bingenheimer (2010).

5. See Whisson (1964), Cohen and Atieno Odhiambo (1989), Malo and Achieng (1999), Mboya and Achieng (2001), and Shipton (2007).

6. See Setel (1996, 1999), Agadjanian (2002), Lindsay and Miescher (2003), Livingston (2005), and Mutongi (2007).

7. See Whisson (1964), Odinga (1967), DuPré (1968), and Shipton (1989).

8. See Setel (1996, 1999), Silberschmidt (2001, 2004), Barker and Ricardo (2005), Al-Samarrai and Bennell (2007), and World Bank (2009).

9. See Ashforth (1999), Cornwall (2002), Hunter (2002), and Mills and Ssewakiryanga (2005).

10. See Owuamanam (1995), Meekers and Calvès (1997), Izugbara (2001), Nyanzi, Pool, and Kinsman (2001), Kuate-Defo (2004), Nyanzi et al. (2004), and Cole (2005).

11. See Mojola (2011).

12. For literature reviews, see Luke and Kurz (2002), Luke (2003), and Chatterji et al. (2004); see also Poulin (2007).

13. These statistics are drawn from my analysis of 2003 data from the Kenya Demographic and Health Survey (CBS et al. 2004), calculating the extent of widowhood and polygamy among Luo residents in Nyanza Province.

14. See, e.g., Potash (1986), Cattell (2003), Lugalla et al. (2004), Oleke, Blystad, and Rekdal (2005), Shipton (2007), and Thomas (2008).

15. See Potash (1986), Cohen and Atieno Odhiambo (1989), Nyambedha, Wandibba, and Aagaard-Hansen (2003), and Shipton (2007).

16. Because many houses in rural areas are built of mud, cow dung, and thatched grass roofs, they are not permanent and are in constant need of repair. However, the work is labor intensive and was often seen as requiring male assistance.

17. Widows who resisted inheritance often turned to nongovernmental organizations (NGOs) or local churches to help them deal with the consequences. For example, churches could provide widows with labor to rebuild or repair their houses, and NGOs provided widows in some areas with material support. However, these options were not available for many widows as they were not evenly distributed across the province. See also Shipton (2007) and Geissler and Prince (2010).

18. My analysis focuses on the instrumental and material dimensions of these relationships (rather than affective dimensions), as these are what were discussed in interviews.

19. I discuss wealthy widows later in this article.

20. It is worth noting here that while there were clear disparities in wealth among widows, from a young man's point of view, the appropriate comparison may have been between his parental household and the widow's household. That is, someone coming from a poor household with unreliable meals would consider a household with regular meals a step up even if the widow considered herself poor. She was comparatively wealthier than the household he was coming from. The wealthiest women mentioned by young men were those who were independently wealthy, and these relationships were most likely to be transactional as opposed to inheritor relationships.

REFERENCES

Agadjanian, Victor. 2002. "Men Doing 'Women's Work': Masculinity and Gender Relations among Street Vendors in Maputo, Mozambique." *Journal of Men's Studies* 10(3):329–42.

Al-Samarrai, Samer, and Paul Bennell. 2007. "Where Has All the Education Gone in Sub-Saharan Africa? Employment and Other Outcomes among Secondary School and University Leavers." *Journal of Development Studies* 43(7):1270–1300.

Amadiume, Ifi. 1987. *Male Daughters, Female Husbands: Gender and Sex in an African Society.* London: Zed.

Amuyunzu-Nyamongo, Mary, and Paul Francis. 2006. "Collapsing Livelihoods and the Crisis of Masculinity in Rural Kenya." In *The Other Half of Gender: Men's Issues in Development,* ed. Ian Bannon and Maria C. Correia, 219–44. Washington, DC: World Bank.

Ashforth, Adam. 1999. "Weighing Manhood in Soweto." *Codesria Bulletin*, nos. 3–4: 51–58.

Ayikukwei, Rose, Duncan Ngare, John Sidle, David Ayuku, Joyce Baliddawa, and James Greene. 2008. "HIV/AIDS and Cultural Practices in Western Kenya: The Impact of Sexual Cleansing Rituals on Sexual Behaviours." *Culture, Health and Sexuality* 10(6):587–99.

Barker, Gary, and Christine Ricardo. 2005. "Young Men and the Construction of Masculinity in Africa: Implications for HIV/AIDS, Conflict and Violence." In *The Other Half of Gender: Men's Issues in Development*, ed. Ian Bannon and Maria C. Correia, 159–93. Washington, DC: World Bank.

Bingenheimer, Jeffrey B. 2010. "Men's Multiple Sexual Partnerships in 15 Sub-Saharan African Countries: Sociodemographic Patterns and Implications." *Studies in Family Planning* 41(1):1–17.

Buchmann, Claudia. 1999. "The State and Schooling in Kenya: Historical Developments and Current Challenges." *Africa Today* 46(1):94–117.

Cattell, Maria. 2003. "African Widows: Anthropological and Historical Perspectives." *Journal of Women and Aging* 15(2–3):49–66.

CBS (Central Bureau of Statistics), MOH (Ministry of Health), Kenya Medical Research Institute, National Council for Population and Development, ORC Macro, and Centers for Disease Control and Prevention. 2004. "Kenya Demographic and Health Survey 2003." Calverton, MD: CBS, MOH, and ORC Macro.

Chatterji, Minki, Nancy Murray, David London, and Philip Anglewicz. 2004. "The Factors Influencing Transactional Sex among Young Men and Women in 12 Sub-Saharan African Countries." Report, Policy Project, USAID. http://pdf.usaid.gov/pdf_docs/PNADA925.pdf.

Clark, Shelley. 2004. "Early Marriage and HIV Risks in Sub-Saharan Africa." *Studies in Family Planning* 35(3):149–60.

Cohen, David W., and E. S. Atieno Odhiambo. 1989. *Siaya: The Historical Anthropology of an African Landscape.* London: James Currey

Cole, Jennifer. 2005. "The Jaombilo of Tamatave (Madagascar), 1992–2004: Reflections on Youth and Globalization." *Journal of Social History* 38(4):891–914.

Connell, Raewyn. 1995. *Masculinities.* Malden, MA: Polity.

Cornwall, Andrea. 2002. "Spending Power: Love, Money, and the Reconfiguration of Gender Relations in Ado-Odo, Southwestern Nigeria." *American Ethnologist* 29(4):963–80.

DuPré, Carole E. 1968. *The Luo of Kenya: An Annotated Bibliography*. Washington, DC: Institute for Cross-Cultural Research.

Dworkin, Shari L., Shelly Grabe, Tiffany Lu, Abbey Hatcher, Zachary Kwena, Elizabeth Bukusi, and Esther Mwaura-Muiru. 2013. "Property Rights Violations as a Structural Driver of Women's HIV Risks: A Qualitative Study in Nyanza and Western Provinces, Kenya." *Archives of Sexual Behavior* 42(5):703–13.

Eisemon, Thomas Owen, and John Schwille. 1991. "Primary Schooling in Burundi and Kenya: Preparation for Secondary Education or for Self-Employment?" *Elementary School Journal* 92(1):23–39.

Geissler, Paul Wenzel, and Ruth Jane Prince. 2010. *The Land Is Dying: Contingency, Creativity and Conflict in Western Kenya*. New York: Berghahn.

Hunter, Mark. 2002. "The Materiality of Everyday Sex: Thinking beyond 'Prostitution.'" *African Studies* 61(1):99–120.

Iliffe, John. 2006. *The African AIDS Epidemic: A History*. Oxford: James Currey.

Izugbara, Chimaraoke Otutubikey. 2001. "Tasting the Forbidden Fruit: The Social Context of Debut Sexual Encounters among Young Persons in a Rural Nigerian Community." *African Journal of Reproductive Health* 5(2):22–29.

Kandiyoti, Deniz. 1988. "Bargaining with Patriarchy." *Gender and Society* 2(3): 274–90.

KNBS (Kenya National Bureau of Statistics), National AIDS Control Council, National AIDS/STD Control Programme, Ministry of Public Health and Sanitation, Kenya Medical Research Institute, National Coordinating Agency for Population and Development, and MEASURE DHS, ICF Macro et al. 2010. "Kenya Demographic and Health Survey 2008–09." Calverton, MD: KNBS and ICF Macro.

Kuate-Defo, Barthelemy. 2004. "Young People's Relationships with Sugar Daddies and Sugar Mummies: What Do We Know and What Do We Need to Know?" *African Journal of Reproductive Health* 8(2):13–37.

Laga, Marie, Bernhard Schwärtlander, Elisabeth Pisani, Papa Salif Sow, and Michel Caraël. 2001. "To Stem HIV in Africa, Prevent Transmission to Young Women." *AIDS,* no. 15:931–34.

Lindsay, Lisa A., and Stephan F. Miescher, eds. 2003. *Men and Masculinities in Modern Africa*. Portsmouth, NH: Heinemann.

Livingston, Julie. 2005. *Debility and the Moral Imagination in Botswana*. Bloomington: Indiana University Press.

Lugalla, Joe, Maria Emmelin, Aldin Mutembei, Mwiru Sima, Gideon Kwesigabo, Japhet Killewo, and Lars Dahlgren. 2004. "Social, Cultural and Sexual Behavioral Determinants of Observed Decline in HIV Infection Trends: Lessons from the Kagera Region, Tanzania." *Social Science and Medicine* 59(1):185–98.

Luginaah, Isaac, David Elkins, Eleanor Maticka-Tyndale, Tamara Landry, and Mercy Mathui. 2005. "Challenges of a Pandemic: HIV/AIDS-Related Problems Affecting Kenyan Widows." *Social Science and Medicine* 60(6):1219–28.

Luke, Nancy. 2003. "Age and Economic Asymmetries in the Sexual Relationships of Adolescent Girls in Sub-Saharan Africa." *Studies in Family Planning* 34(2): 67–86.

Luke, Nancy, and Kathleen Kurz. 2002. "Cross-Generational and Transactional Sexual Relations in Sub-Saharan Africa: Prevalence of Behavior and Implications for Negotiating Safer Sex Practices." Report, ICRW, Washington, DC. http://www.icrw.org/files/publications/Cross-generational-and-Transactional-Sexual-Relations-in-Sub-Saharan-Africa-Prevalence-of-Behavior-and-Implications-for-Negotiating-Safer-Sexual-Practices.pdf.

Malo, Shadrack, and Jane Achieng. 1999. *Luo Customs and Practices*. Nairobi: ScienceTech Network.

Mboya, Paul, and Jane Achieng. 2001. *Paul Mboya's "Luo Kitgi Gi Timbegi": A Translation into English*. Nairobi: Atai.

Meekers, Dominique, and Anne-Emmanuèle Calvès. 1997. "'Main' Girlfriends, Girlfriends, Marriage, and Money: The Social Context of HIV Risk Behavior in Sub-Saharan Africa." *Health Transition Review* 7 (Suppl.): 361–75.

Mills, David, and Richard Ssewakiryanga. 2005. "'No Romance without Finance': Commodities, Masculinities and Relationships among Kampalan Students." In *Readings in Gender in Africa*, ed. Andrea Cornwall, 90–95. Bloomington: Indiana University Press.

Mojola, Sanyu A. 2011. "Fishing in Dangerous Waters: Ecology, Gender and Economy in HIV Risk." *Social Science and Medicine* 72(2):149–56.

Moore, Sally Falk. 1986. *Social Facts and Fabrications: "Customary" Law on Kilimanjaro, 1880–1980*. New York: Cambridge University Press

Mutongi, Kenda. 2007. *Worries of the Heart: Widows, Family, and Community in Kenya*. Chicago: University of Chicago Press.

Nyambedha, Erick Otieno, Simiyu Wandibba, and Jens Aagaard-Hansen. 2003. "Changing Patterns of Orphan Care due to the HIV Epidemic in Western Kenya." *Social Science and Medicine* 57(2):301–11.

Nyanzi, Stella, Barbara Nyanzi, Bessie Kalina, and Robert Pool. 2004. "Mobility, Sexual Networks and Exchange among Bodabodamen in Southwest Uganda." *Culture, Health and Sexuality* 6(3):239–54.

Nyanzi, Stella, Robert Pool, and John Kinsman. 2001. "The Negotiation of Sexual Relationships among School Pupils in South-western Uganda." *AIDS Care* 13(1):83–98.

Odinga, Oginga. 1967. *Not Yet Uhuru: The Autobiography of Oginga Odinga*. London: Heinemann.

Okeyo, Tom Mboya, and Ann K. Allen. 1994. "Influence of Widow Inheritance on the Epidemiology of AIDS in Africa." *African Journal of Medical Practice* 1(1):20–25.

Oleke, Christopher, Astrid Blystad, and Ole Bjørn Rekdal. 2005. "'When the Obvious Brother Is Not There': Political and Cultural Contexts of the Orphan Challenge in Northern Uganda." *Social Science and Medicine* 61(12):2628–38.

Owuamanam, Donatus O. 1995. "Sexual Networking among Youth in Southwestern Nigeria." *Health Transition Review* 5 (Suppl.): 57–66.

Oyěwùmí, Oyèrónk. 1997. *The Invention of Women: Making an African Sense of Western Gender Discourses*. Minneapolis: University of Minnesota Press.

Pascoe, C. J. 2005. *Dude, You're a Fag: Masculinity and Sexuality in High School*. Berkeley: University of California Press.

Potash, Betty, ed. 1986. *Widows in African Societies: Choices and Constraints*. Stanford, CA: Stanford University Press.

Poulin, Michelle. 2007. "Sex, Money, and Premarital Partnerships in Southern Malawi." *Social Science and Medicine* 65(11):2383–93.

Republic of Kenya. n.d. "District Development Plans, Bondo, Nyando, Kisumu and Homa Bay." Report, Rural Planning Department, Nairobi.

Setel, Philip. 1996. "AIDS as a Paradox of Manhood and Development in Kilimanjaro, Tanzania." *Social Science and Medicine* 43(8):1169–78.

Setel, Philip. 1999. *A Plague of Paradoxes: AIDS, Culture, and Demography in Northern Tanzania*. Chicago: University of Chicago Press.

Shipton, Parker. 1989. *Bitter Money: Cultural Economy and Some African Meanings of Forbidden Commodities*. Washington, DC: American Anthropological Association.

Shipton, Parker. 2007. *The Nature of Entrustment: Intimacy, Exchange and the Sacred in Africa*. New Haven, CT: Yale University Press.

Silberschmidt, Margrethe. 2001. "Disempowerment of Men in Rural and Urban East Africa: Implications for Male Identity and Sexual Behavior." *World Development* 29(4):657–71.

Silberschmidt, Margrethe. 2004. "Men, Male Sexuality and HIV/AIDS: Reflections from Studies in Rural and Urban East Africa." *Transformation*, no. 54: 42–58.

Slater, Miriam K. 1986. "Foreword: Sons and Levirs." In Potash 1986, xv–xxii.

Smith, Daniel J. 2007. "Modern Marriage, Men's Extramarital Sex, and HIV Risk in Southeastern Nigeria." *American Journal of Public Health* 97(6):997–1005.

Thomas, Felicity. 2008. "Remarriage after Spousal Death: Options Facing Widows and Implications for Livelihood Security." *Gender and Development* 16(1):73–83.

UNAIDS. 2012. "Global Report: UNAIDS Report on Global AIDS Epidemic." Report, UNAIDS, Geneva. http://www.unaids.org/en/media/unaids/contentassets/documents/epidemiology/2012/gr2012/ 20121120_UNAIDS_Global_Report_2012_en.pdf.

UNAIDS and WHO (World Health Organization). 2005. "AIDS Epidemic Update: December 2005." Report, UNAIDS and WHO, Geneva. http://www.unaids.org/en/media/unaids/contentassets/dataimport/publications/irc-pub06/epi_update2005_en.pdf.

UNAIDS and WHO (World Health Organization). 2009. "AIDS Epidemic Update 2009." Report, UNAIDS and WHO, Geneva. http://www.unaids.org/en/dataanalysis/knowyourepidemic/epidemiologypublications/2009aidsepidemicupdate/.

West, Candace, and Don Zimmerman. 1987. "Doing Gender." *Gender and Society* 1(2):125–51.

Whisson, Michael. 1964. *Change and Challenge: A Study of the Social and Economic Changes among the Kenya Luo*. [Nairobi?]: Christian Council of Kenya.

World Bank. 2009. "Youth and Employment in Africa: The Potential, the Problem, the Promise." Africa Development Indicators 2008/09 report, World Bank, Washington, DC. http://siteresources.worldbank.org/INTSTATINAFR/Resources/ADI-200809-essay-EN.pdf.

Wyrod, Robert. 2007. "Bwaise Town: Masculinity in Urban Uganda in the Age of AIDS." PhD dissertation, Department of Sociology, University of Chicago.

Wyrod, Robert. 2008. "Between Women's Rights and Men's Authority: Masculinity and Shifting Discourses of Gender Difference in Urban Uganda." *Gender and Society* 22(6):799–823.

PART V

FAMILIES

In the late twentieth and early twenty-first centuries, major transformations in world economic and cultural systems have affected all families and households and given rise to new patterns of family living. Despite these changes, family life remains shrouded in myth. No matter how much families change, they remain idealized as natural or biological units based on the timeless functions of love, motherhood, and childbearing. "**Family**" evokes ideas of warmth, caring, and unconditional love in a refuge set apart from the public world. In this image, family and society are separate. Relations *inside* the family are idealized as nurturant, and those *outside* the family are seen as competitive. This ideal assumes a **gendered division of labor**: a husband/father associated with the public world and a wife/mother defined as the heart of the family. Although this image bears little resemblance to the majority of family situations, it is still recognizable in cultural ideals and public policies.

In the past four decades, feminist thought has been in the forefront of efforts to demythologize the family. Feminist thinkers have demonstrated that family forms are socially and historically constructed, not monolithic universals that exist across all times and all places or the inevitable result of unambiguous differences between women and men. Feminist thinkers have drawn attention to myths that romanticize "traditional" families in deference to male privilege and to the contradictions between idealized and real patterns of family life. They have directed attention to the close connections between families and other institutions in society. Early feminist critiques of the family characterized it as a primary site of women's oppression and argued in support of women's increased participation in the labor force as a means of attaining greater autonomy. But this analysis did not apply well to women of color or working-class women, most of whom were employed and keenly aware of inequalities in the workplace, because it falsely universalized the experiences of white upper- and middle-class women.

MOTHERHOOD AND FATHERHOOD

The first four articles explore the symbolic meanings and lived realities of motherhood and fatherhood. They uncover experiences that are not simply gendered, but also shaped by other lines of difference. First, Patricia Hill Collins takes race, class, and history into account as she investigates mother–daughter relations among African Americans. In contrast to Eurocentric views of motherhood, she describes patterns of communal and collective mothering relations.

Collins's concept of "other mothers" is adopted in the reading by Lisa J. Udel as she explains why Native American women are loyal to cultural traditions that puzzle white U.S. feminists.

A growing U.S. market for domestic and child-care workers is redefining motherhood for many Latinas. In their article, Pierrette Hondagneu-Sotelo and Ernestine Avila reveal a family arrangement in which immigrant mothers work in the United States while their children remain in Mexico or Central America. Calling this adaptation "**transnational mothering**," their study shows how global patterns of family dispersal produce variations in the meanings and priorities of motherhood.

Like that of motherhood, current scholarship on fatherhood opens the gender field to new kinds of questions. In the United Kingdom, government policies do more to support caretaking by fathers than do policies in the United States (although they do less than Northern European countries such as Sweden). In addition, British men in general have positive attitudes toward involved fatherhood, with many believing that they will reduce their work hours to share care-taking of new infants. Yet, their actual involvement is not as equitable as their attitudes would suggest. What explains the discrepancy between what British men *say* and what they *do* regarding fatherhood and parenting? Tina Miller compares British men's views of fatherhood and work. Her study finds that the men's intentions are strongly influenced by the meaning of paid work within hegemonic masculinity, the structural context of the United Kingdom, and its family-leave policies. The implications for women, their relationship to work and motherhood, and the prospects for gender-equal parenthood are also considered.

WORK AND FAMILIES

Feminist thought has explored a more complex understanding of the relationship between family and work by examining differences among women and by taking men's experiences into account. Women's and men's new employment trends are transforming family realms. Yet the worldwide entrance of women into the public sphere of employment has not resulted in gender equality, nor has it freed women from the demands of labor in the private sphere. The reading by Stephanie Coontz illustrates the connections among gender attitudes, work experiences, and family arrangements. Whereas media stories often feature contemporary women who are "opting out" of the workplace in favor of domesticity, Coontz offers a different explanation. She reveals that most people favor gender equity, but they are forced to act in ways that contradict their ideals because of social policies. Coontz examines a number of these policies in the United States, from labor standards to family-leave policies, demonstrating how they impact couples' decision making in ways that reinforce traditional family and gender arrangements.

Gender divisions of labor in families and workplaces often extend to other domains of society, as Michael A. Messner and Suzel Bozada-Deas show in the next reading, a study of youth sports organizations in which most men volunteers become coaches and most women volunteers become team moms. Their findings challenge common-sense ideas about "natural" gender divisions. Although participants say the division of labor between men and women volunteers results from individual choices, Messner and Bozada-Deas uncover informal patterns of socially structured gender disparities that reproduce the work/family divide in youth sports organizations.

By now, it is a truism that the movement of women into the workforce everywhere affects families. But work and family opportunities vary greatly because they are linked within a larger society that is structured by class, race, and gender. The next two readings address the power of larger economic forces on women's family roles. The reading by Elizabeth Higginbotham and Lynn Weber examines the role of the family in the achievements of black and white professional women. Their intersectional approach offers new understandings about race, class, and the upward mobility of women and men. Finally, Kathryn Edin addresses the connections between economic marginality and marriage in the lives of low-income single mothers. Although the mothers in this study aspire to marriage, they think it is more risky than rewarding. Their stories provide an understanding of the retreat from marriage as it is conditioned by men's employment and women's desire for marriage with a measure of trust, respectability, and control.

28

The Meaning of Motherhood in Black Culture and Black Mother–Daughter Relationships

PATRICIA HILL COLLINS

"What did your mother teach you about men?" is a question I often ask students in my courses on African-American women. "Go to school first and get a good education—don't get too serious too young," "Make sure you look around and that you can take care of yourself before you settle down," and "Don't trust them, want more for yourself than just a man," are typical responses from Black women. My students share stories of how their mothers encouraged them to cultivate satisfying relationships with Black men while anticipating disappointments, to desire marriage while planning viable alternatives, to become mothers only when fully prepared to do so. But, above all, they stress their mothers' insistence on being self-reliant and resourceful.

These daughters, of various ages and from diverse social class backgrounds, family structures and geographic regions, had somehow received strikingly similar messages about Black womanhood. Even though their mothers employed diverse teaching strategies, these Black daughters had all been exposed to common themes about the meaning of womanhood in Black culture.[1]

This essay explores the relationship between the meaning of motherhood in African-American culture and Black mother–daughter relationships by addressing three primary questions. First, how have competing perspectives about motherhood intersected to produce a distinctly Afrocentric ideology of motherhood? Second, what are the enduring themes that characterize this Afrocentric ideology of motherhood? Finally, what effect might this Afrocentric ideology of motherhood have on Black mother–daughter relationships?

"The Meaning of Motherhood in Black Culture and Black Mother–Daughter Relationships," from *Double Stitch: Black Women about Mothers and Daughters*. Edited by Patricia Bell-Scott. Copyright © 1991 Beacon Press. Reprinted by permission of the author.

COMPETING PERSPECTIVES ON MOTHERHOOD

The Dominant Perspective: Eurocentric Views of White Motherhood

The cult of true womanhood, with its emphasis on motherhood as woman's highest calling, has long held a special place in the gender symbolism of White Americans. From this perspective, women's activities should be confined to the care of children, the nurturing of a husband, and the maintenance of the household. By managing this separate domestic sphere, women gain social influence through their roles as mothers, transmitters of culture, and parents for the next generations.[2]

While substantial numbers of White women have benefited from the protections of White patriarchy provided by the dominant ideology, White women themselves have recently challenged its tenets. On one pole lies a cluster of women, the traditionalists, who aim to retain the centrality of motherhood in women's lives. For traditionalists, differentiating between the experience of motherhood, which for them has been quite satisfying, and motherhood as an institution central in reproducing gender inequality, has proved difficult. The other pole is occupied by women who advocate dismantling motherhood as an institution. They suggest that compulsory motherhood be outlawed and that the experience of motherhood can only be satisfying if women can also choose not to be mothers. Arrayed between these dichotomous positions are women who argue for an expanded, but not necessarily different, role for women—women can be mothers as long as they are not *just* mothers.[3]

Three themes implicit in White perspectives on motherhood are particularly problematic for Black women and others outside of this debate. First, the assumption that mothering occurs within the confines of a private, nuclear family household where the mother has almost total responsibility for child-rearing is less applicable to Black families. While the ideal of the cult of true womanhood has been held up to Black women for emulation, racial oppression has denied Black families sufficient resources to support private, nuclear family households. Second, strict sex-role segregation, with separate male and female spheres of influence within the family, has been less commonly found in

African-American families than in White middle-class ones. Finally, the assumption that motherhood and economic dependency on men are linked and that to be a "good" mother one must stay at home, making motherhood a full-time "occupation," is similarly uncharacteristic of African-American families.[4]

Even though selected groups of White women are challenging the cult of true womanhood and its accompanying definition of motherhood, the dominant ideology remains powerful. As long as these approaches remain prominent in scholarly and popular discourse, Eurocentric views of White motherhood will continue to affect Black women's lives.

Eurocentric Views of Black Motherhood

Eurocentric perspectives on Black motherhood revolve around two interdependent images that together define Black women's roles in White and in African-American families. The first image is that of the Mammy, the faithful, devoted domestic servant. Like one of the family, Mammy conscientiously "mothers" her White children, caring for them and loving them as if they were her own. Mammy is the ideal Black mother for she recognizes her place. She is paid next to nothing and yet cheerfully accepts her inferior status. But when she enters her own home, this same Mammy is transformed into the second image, the too-strong matriarch who raises weak sons and "unnaturally superior" daughters.[5] When she protests, she is labeled aggressive and unfeminine, yet if she remains silent, she is rendered invisible.

The task of debunking Mammy by analyzing Black women's roles as exploited domestic workers and challenging the matriarchy thesis by demonstrating that Black women do not wield disproportionate power in African-American families has long preoccupied African-American scholars.[6] But an equally telling critique concerns uncovering the functions of these images and their role in explaining Black women's subordination in systems of race, class, and gender oppression. As Mae King points out, White definitions of Black motherhood foster the dominant group's exploitation of Black women by blaming Black women for their characteristic reactions to their own subordination.[7] For example, while the stay-at-home mother has been held up to all women as the ideal, African-American women have been compelled to work outside the home, typically in a very narrow range of occupations. Even though Black women were forced to become domestic servants and be strong figures in Black households, labeling them Mammies and matriarchs denigrates Black women. Without a countervailing Afrocentric ideology of motherhood, White perspectives on both White and African-American motherhood place Black women in a no-win situation. Adhering to these standards brings the danger of the lowered self-esteem of internalized oppression, one that, if passed on from mother to daughter, provides a powerful mechanism for controlling African-American communities.

African Perspectives on Motherhood

One concept that has been constant throughout the history of African societies is the centrality of motherhood in religions, philosophies, and social institutions. As Barbara Christian points out, "There is no doubt that motherhood is for most African people symbolic of creativity and continuity."[8]

Cross-cultural research on motherhood in African societies appears to support Christian's claim.[9] West African sociologist Christine Oppong suggests that the Western notion of equating household with family be abandoned because it obscures women's family roles in African cultures.[10] While the archetypal White, middle-class nuclear family conceptualizes family life as being divided into two oppositional spheres—the "male" sphere of economic providing and the "female" sphere of affective nurturing—this type of rigid sex-role segregation was not part of the West African tradition. Mothering was not a privatized nurturing "occupation" reserved for biological mothers, and the economic support of children was not the exclusive responsibility of men. Instead, for African women, emotional care for children and providing for their physical survival were interwoven as interdependent, complementary dimensions of motherhood.

In spite of variations among societies, a strong case has been made that West African women occupy influential roles in African family networks.[11] First, since they are not dependent on males for economic support and provide much of their own and their children's economic support, women are structurally central to families.[12] Second, the image of the mother is one that is culturally

elaborated and valued across diverse West African societies. Continuing the lineage is essential in West African philosophies, and motherhood is similarly valued.[13] Finally, while the biological mother–child bond is valued, child care was a collective responsibility, a situation fostering cooperative, age-stratified, woman-centered "mothering" networks.

Recent research by Africanists suggests that much more of this African heritage was retained among African-Americans than had previously been thought. The retention of West African culture as a culture of resistance offered enslaved Africans and exploited African-Americans alternative ideologies to those advanced by dominant groups. Central to these reinterpretations of African-American institutions and culture is a re-conceptualization of Black family life and the role of women in Black family networks.[14] West African perspectives may have been combined with the changing political and economic situations framing African-American communities to produce certain enduring themes characterizing an Afrocentric ideology of motherhood.

ENDURING THEMES OF AN AFROCENTRIC IDEOLOGY OF MOTHERHOOD

An Afrocentric ideology of motherhood must reconcile the competing worldviews of these three conflicting perspectives of motherhood. An ongoing tension exists between efforts to mold the institution of Black motherhood for the benefit of the dominant group and efforts by Black women to define and value their own experiences with motherhood. This tension leads to a continuum of responses. For those women who either aspire to the cult of true womanhood without having the resources to support such a lifestyle, or who believe the stereotypical analyses of themselves as dominating matriarchs, motherhood can be oppressive. But the experience of motherhood can provide Black women with a base of self-actualization, status in the Black community, and a reason for social activism. These alleged contradictions can exist side by side in African-American communities, families, and even within individual women.

Embedded in these changing relationships are four enduring themes that I contend characterize an Afrocentric ideology of motherhood. Just as the issues facing enslaved African mothers were quite different from those currently facing poor Black women in inner cities, for any given historical moment the actual institutional forms that these themes take depend on the severity of oppression and Black women's resources for resistance.

Bloodmothers, Othermothers, and Women-Centered Networks

In African-American communities, the boundaries distinguishing biological mothers of children from other women who care for children are often fluid and changing. Biological mothers, or bloodmothers, are expected to care for their children. But African and African-American communities have also recognized that vesting one person with full responsibility for mothering a child may not be wise or possible. As a result, "othermothers," women who assist bloodmothers by sharing mothering responsibilities, traditionally have been central to the institution of Black motherhood.[15]

The centrality of women in African-American extended families is well known.[16] Organized, resilient, women-centered networks of bloodmothers and othermothers are key to this centrality. Grandmothers, sisters, aunts, or cousins acted as othermothers by taking on child care responsibilities for each other's children. When needed, temporary child care arrangements turned into long-term care or informal adoption.[17]

In African-American communities, these women-centered networks of community-based child care often extend beyond the boundaries of biologically related extended families to support "fictive kin."[18] Civil rights activist Ella Baker describes how informal adoption by othermothers functioned in the Southern, rural community of her childhood:

> My aunt who had thirteen children of her own raised three more. She had become a midwife, and a child was born who was covered with sores. Nobody was particularly wanting the child, so she took the child and raised him . . . and another mother decided she didn't want to be bothered with two children. So my aunt took one and raised him . . . they were part of the family.[19]

Even when relationships were not between kin or fictive kin, African-American community norms were such that neighbors cared for each other's children. In the following passage, Sara Brooks, a Southern domestic worker, describes the importance of the community-based child care that a neighbor offered her daughter. In doing so, she also shows how the African-American cultural value placed on cooperative child care found institutional support in the adverse conditions under which so many Black women mothered:

> She kept Vivian and she didn't charge me nothin either. You see, people used to look after each other, but now it's not that way. I reckon it's because we all was poor, and I guess they put theirself in the place of the person that they was helpin.[20]

Othermothers were key not only in supporting children but also in supporting bloodmothers who, for whatever reason, were ill-prepared or had little desire to care for their children. Given the pressures from the larger political economy, the emphasis placed on community-based child care and the respect given to othermothers who assume the responsibilities of child care have served a critical function in African-American communities. Children orphaned by sale or death of their parents under slavery, children conceived through rape, children of young mothers, children born into extreme poverty, or children who for other reasons have been rejected by their bloodmothers have all been supported by othermothers who, like Ella Baker's aunt, took in additional children, even when they had enough of their own.

Providing as Part of Mothering

The work done by African-American women in providing the economic resources essential to Black family well-being affects motherhood in a contradictory fashion. On the one hand, African-American women have long integrated their activities as economic providers into their mothering relationships. In contrast to the cult of true womanhood, in which work is defined as being in opposition to and incompatible with motherhood, work for Black women has been an important and valued dimension of Afrocentric definitions of Black motherhood. On the other hand, African-American women's experiences as mothers under oppression were such that the type and purpose of work Black women were forced to do had a great impact on the type of mothering relationships bloodmothers and othermothers had with Black children.

While slavery both disrupted West African family patterns and exposed enslaved Africans to the gender ideologies and practices of slaveowners, it simultaneously made it impossible, had they wanted to do so for enslaved Africans to implement slaveowners' ideologies. Thus, the separate spheres of providing as a male domain and affective nurturing as a female domain did not develop within African-American families.[21] Providing for Black children's physical survival and attending to their affective, emotional needs continued as interdependent dimensions of an Afrocentric ideology of motherhood. However, by changing the conditions under which Black women worked and the purpose of the work itself, slavery introduced the problem of how best to continue traditional Afrocentric values under oppressive conditions. Institutions of community-based child care, informal adoption, greater reliance on othermothers, all emerge as adaptations to the exigencies of combining exploitative work with nurturing children.

In spite of the change in political status brought on by emancipation, the majority of African-American women remained exploited agricultural workers. However, their placement in Southern political economics allowed them to combine child care with field labor. Sara Brooks describes how strong the links between providing and caring for others were for her:

> When I was about nine I was nursin my sister Sally—I'm about seven or eight years older than Sally. And when I would put her to sleep, instead of me goin somewhere and sit down and play, I'd get my little old hoe and get out there and work right in the field around the house.[22]

Black women's shift from Southern agriculture to domestic work in Southern and Northern towns and cities represented a change in the type of work done, but not in the meaning of work to women and their families. Whether they wanted to or not, the majority of African-American women had to work and could not afford the luxury of motherhood as a noneconomically productive, female "occupation."

Community Othermothers and Social Activism

Black women's experiences as othermothers have provided a foundation for Black women's social activism. Black women's feelings of responsibility for nurturing the children in their own extended family networks have stimulated a more generalized ethic of care where Black women feel accountable to all the Black community's children.

This notion of Black women as community othermothers for all Black children traditionally allowed Black women to treat biologically unrelated children as if they were members of their own families. For example, sociologist Karen Fields describes how her grandmother, Mamie Garvin Fields, draws on her power as a community othermother when dealing with unfamiliar children.

> She will say to a child on the street who looks up to no good, picking out a name at random, "Aren't you Miz Pinckney's boy?" in that same reproving tone. If the reply is, "No, ma'am, my mother is Miz Gadsden," whatever threat there was dissipates.[23]

The use of family language in referring to members of the Black community also illustrates this dimension of Black motherhood. For example, Mamie Garvin Fields describes how she became active in surveying the poor housing conditions of Black people in Charleston.

> I was one of the volunteers they got to make a survey of the places where we were paying extortious rents for indescribable property. I said "we," although it wasn't Bob and me. We had our own home, and so did many of the Federated Women. Yet we still fell like it really was "we" living in those terrible places, and it was up to us to do something about them.[24]

To take another example, while describing her increasingly successful efforts to teach a boy who had given other teachers problems, my daughter's kindergarten teacher stated, "You know how it can be—the majority of children in the learning disabled classes are *our children*. I know he didn't belong there, so I volunteered to take him." In these statements, both women invoke the language of family to describe the ties that bind them as Black women to their responsibilities to other members of the Black community as family.

Sociologist Cheryl Gilkes suggests that community othermother relationships are sometimes behind Black women's decisions to become community activists.[25] Gilkes notes that many of the Black women community activists in her study became involved in community organizing in response to the needs of their own children and of those in their communities. The following comment is typical of how many of the Black women in Gilkes' study relate to Black children: "There were a lot of summer programs springing up for kids, but they were exclusive . . . and I found that most of *our kids* (emphasis mine) were excluded."[26] For many women, what began as the daily expression of their obligations as community othermothers, as was the case for the kindergarten teacher, developed into full-fledged roles as community leaders.

Motherhood as a Symbol of Power

Motherhood, whether bloodmother, othermother, or community othermother, can be invoked by Black women as a symbol of power. A substantial portion of Black women's status in African-American communities stems not only from their roles as mothers in their own families but from their contributions as community othermothers to Black community development as well.

The specific contributions Black women make in nurturing Black community development form the basis of community-based power. Community othermothers work on behalf of the Black community by trying, in the words of late nineteenth-century Black feminists, to "uplift the race," so that vulnerable members of the community would be able to attain the self-reliance and independence so desperately needed for Black community development under oppressive conditions. This is the type of power many African-Americans have in mind when they describe the "strong, Black women" they see around them in traditional African-American communities.

When older Black women invoke this community othermother status, its results can be quite striking. Karen Fields recounts an incident described to her by her grandmother illustrating how women can exert power as community othermothers:

> One night . . . as Grandmother sat crocheting alone at about two in the morning, a young man walked into the living room carrying the portable TV from upstairs. She said, "Who are you looking for this time of night?" As Grandmother [described] the incident to me over the phone, I could hear a tone of voice that I know well. It said, "Nice boys don't do that." So I imagine the burglar heard his own mother or grandmother at that

moment. He joined in the familial game just created: "Well, he told me that I could borrow it." "Who told you?" "John." "Um um, no John lives here. You got the wrong house."[27]

After this dialogue, the teenager turned around, went back upstairs and returned the television.

In local Black communities, specific Black women are widely recognized as powerful figures, primarily because of their contributions to the community's well-being through their roles as community othermothers. Sociologist Charles Johnson describes the behavior of an elderly Black woman at a church service in rural Alabama of the 1930s. Even though she was not on the program, the woman stood up to speak. The master of ceremonies rang for her to sit down but she refused to do so claiming, "I am the mother of this church, and I will say what I please." The master of ceremonies later explained to the congregation—"Brothers, I know you all honor Sister Moore. Course our time is short but she has acted as a mother to me. . . . Any time old folks get up I give way to them."[28]

IMPLICATIONS FOR BLACK MOTHER–DAUGHTER RELATIONSHIPS

In her discussion of the sex-role socialization of Black girls, Pamela Reid identifies two complementary approaches in understanding Black mother–daughter relationships.[29] The first, psychoanalytic theory, examines the role of parents in the establishment of personality and social behavior. This theory argues that the development of feminine behavior results from the girls' identification with adult female role models. This approach emphasizes how an Afrocentric ideology of motherhood is actualized through Black mothers' activities as role models.

The second approach, social learning theory, suggests that the rewards and punishments attached to girls' childhood experiences are central in shaping women's sex-role behavior. The kinds of behaviors that Black mothers reward and punish in their daughters are seen as key in the socialization process. This approach examines specific experiences that Black girls have while growing up that encourage them to absorb an Afrocentric ideology of motherhood.

African-American Mothers as Role Models

Feminist psychoanalytic theorists suggest that the sex-role socialization process is different for boys and girls. While boys learn maleness by rejecting femaleness via separating themselves from their mothers, girls establish feminine identities by embracing the femaleness of their mothers. Girls identify with their mothers, a sense of connection that is incorporated into the female personality. However, this mother-identification is problematic because, under patriarchy, men are more highly valued than women. Thus, while daughters identify with their mothers, they also reject them, since in patriarchal families, identifying with adult women as mothers means identifying with persons deemed inferior.[30]

While Black girls learn by identifying with their mothers, the specific female role with which Black girls identify may be quite different than that modeled by middle-class White mothers. The presence of working mothers, extended family othermothers, and powerful community othermothers offers a range of role models that challenge the tenets of the cult of true womanhood.

Moreover, since Black mothers have a distinctive relationship to White patriarchy, they may be less likely to socialize their daughters into their proscribed role as subordinates. Rather, a key part of Black girls' socialization involves incorporating the critical posture that allows Black women to cope with contradictions. For example, Black girls have long had to learn how to do domestic work while rejecting definitions of themselves as Mammies. At the same time they've had to take on strong roles in Black extended families without internalizing images of themselves as matriarchs.

In raising their daughters, Black mothers face a troubling dilemma. To ensure their daughters' physical survival, they must teach their daughters to fit into systems of oppression. For example, as a young girl in Mississippi, Black activist Ann Moody questioned why she was paid so little for the domestic work she began at age nine, why Black women domestics were sexually harassed by their White male employers, and why Whites had so much more than Blacks. But her mother refused to answer her questions and actually became angry whenever Ann Moody stepped out of her "place."[31] Black daughters are raised to expect to work, to strive for an education so that they can support themselves, and to anticipate carrying heavy responsibilities in their families and communities because these skills are essential for their own survival as well as for the survival of those for whom they will eventually be responsible.[32] And yet mothers know that if daughters fit too well into the limited opportunities offered Black women, they become willing participants in their own subordination. Mothers may have ensured their daughters' physical survival at the high cost of their emotional destruction.

On the other hand, Black daughters who offer serious challenges to oppressive situations may not physically survive. When Ann Moody became involved in civil rights activities, her mother first begged her not to participate and then told her not to come home because she feared the Whites in Moody's hometown would kill her. In spite of the dangers, many Black mothers routinely encourage their daughters to develop skills to confront oppressive conditions. Thus, learning that they will work, that education is a vehicle for advancement, can also be seen as ways of preparing Black girls to resist oppression through a variety of mothering roles. The issue is to build emotional strength, but not at the cost of physical survival.

This delicate balance between conformity and resistance is described by historian Elsa Barkley Brown as the "need to socialize me one way and at the same time to give me all the tools I needed to be something else."[33] Black daughters must learn how to survive in interlocking structures of race, class, and gender oppression while rejecting and transcending those very same structures. To develop these skills in their daughters, mothers demonstrate varying combinations of behaviors devoted to ensuring their daughters' survival—such as providing them with basic necessities and ensuring their protection in dangerous environments to helping their daughters go farther than mothers themselves were allowed to go.

The presence of othermothers in Black extended families and the modeling symbolized by community othermothers offer powerful support for the task of teaching girls to resist White perceptions of Black womanhood while appearing to conform to them. In contrast to the isolation of middle-class White mother/daughter dyads, Black women-centered extended family networks foster an early identification with a much wider range of models of Black womanhood, which can lead to a greater sense of empowerment in young Black girls.

Social Learning Theory and Black Mothering Behavior

Understanding this goal of balancing the needs of ensuring their daughters' physical survival with the vision of encouraging them to transcend the boundaries confronting them sheds some light on some of the apparent contradictions in Black mother–daughter relationships. Black mothers are often described as strong disciplinarians and overly protective parents; yet these same women manage to raise daughters who are self-reliant and assertive.[34] Professor Gloria Wade-Gayles offers an explanation for this apparent contradiction by suggesting that Black mothers "do not socialize their daughters to be passive or irrational. Quite the contrary, they socialize their daughters to be independent, strong and self-confident. Black mothers are suffocatingly protective and domineering precisely because they are determined to mold their daughters into whole and self-actualizing persons in a society that devalues Black women."[35]

Black mothers emphasize protection either by trying to shield their daughters as long as possible from the penalties attached to their race, class, and gender or by teaching them how to protect themselves in such situations. Black women's autobiographies and fiction can be read as texts revealing the multiple strategies Black mothers employ in preparing their daughters for the demands of being Black women in oppressive conditions. For example, in discussing the mother–daughter relationship in Paule Marshall's *Brown Girl, Brownstones,* Rosalie Troester catalogues some of these strategies and the impact they may have on relationships themselves:

> Black mothers, particularly those with strong ties to their community, sometimes build high banks around their young daughters, isolating them from the dangers of the larger world until they are old and strong enough to function as autonomous women. Often these dikes are religious, but sometimes they are built with education, family, or the restrictions of a close-knit and homogeneous community . . . this isolation causes the currents between Black mothers and daughters to run deep and the relationship to be fraught with an emotional intensity often missing from the lives of women with more freedom.[36]

Black women's efforts to provide for their children also may affect the emotional intensity of Black mother–daughter relationships. As Gloria Wade-Gayles points out, "Mothers in Black women's fiction are strong and devoted . . . but . . . they are rarely affectionate."[37] For far too many Black mothers, the demands of providing for children are so demanding that affection often must wait until the basic needs of physical survival are satisfied.

Black daughters raised by mothers grappling with hostile environments have to confront their feelings about the difference between the idealized versions of maternal love extant in popular culture and the strict, assertive mothers so central to their lives.[38] For daughters, growing up means developing a better understanding that offering physical care and protection is an act of maternal love. Ann Moody describes her growing awareness of the personal cost her mother paid as a single mother of three children employed as a domestic worker. Watching her mother sleep after the birth of another child, Moody remembers:

> For a long time I stood there looking at her. I didn't want to wake her up. I wanted to enjoy and preserve that calm, peaceful look on her face, I wanted to think she would always be that happy . . . Adline and Junior were too young to feel the things I felt and know the things I knew about Mama. They couldn't remember when she and Daddy separated. They had never heard her cry at night as I had or worked and helped as I had done when we were starving.[39]

Renita Weems's account of coming to grips with maternal desertion provides another example of a daughter's efforts to understand her mother's behavior. In the following passage, Weems struggles with the difference between the stereotypical image of the super strong Black mother and her own alcoholic mother, who decided to leave her children:

> My mother loved us. I must believe that. She worked all day in a department store bakery to buy shoes and school tablets, came home to curse out neighbors who wrongly accused her children of any impropriety (which in an apartment complex usually meant stealing), and kept her house cleaner than most sober women.[40]

Weems concludes that her mother loved her because she provided for her to the best of her ability.

Othermothers often play central roles in defusing the emotional intensity of relationships between bloodmothers and their daughters and in helping daughters understand the Afrocentric ideology of motherhood. Weems describes the women teachers, neighbors, friends, and othermothers that she turned to for help in negotiating a difficult mother/daughter relationship. These women, she notes, "did not have the onus of providing for me, and so had the luxury of talking to me."[41]

June Jordan offers one of the most eloquent analyses of a daughter's realization of the high personal cost Black women have paid as bloodmothers and othermothers in working to provide an economic and emotional foundation for Black children. In the following passage, Jordan captures the feelings that my Black women students struggled to put into words:

> As a child I noticed the sadness of my mother as she sat alone in the kitchen at night. . . . Her woman's work never won permanent victories of any kind. It never enlarged the universe of her imagination or her power to influence what happened beyond the front door of our house. Her woman's work never tickled her to laugh or shout or dance. But she did raise me to respect her way of offering love and to believe that hard work is often the irreducible factor for survival, not something to avoid. Her woman's work produced a reliable home base where I could pursue the privileges of books and music. Her woman's work invented the potential for a completely different kind of work for us, the next generation of Black women: huge, rewarding hard work demanded by the huge, new ambitions that her perfect confidence in us engendered.[42]

Jordan's words not only capture the essence of the Afrocentric ideology of motherhood so central to the well-being of countless numbers of Black women. They simultaneously point the way into the future, one where Black women face the challenge of continuing the mothering traditions painstakingly nurtured by prior generations of African-American women.

NOTES

1. The definition of culture used in this essay is taken from Leith Mullings, "Anthropological Perspectives on the Afro-American Family," *American Journal of Social Psychiatry* 6 (1986): 11–16. According to Mullings, culture is composed of "the symbols and values that create the ideological frame of reference through which people attempt to deal with the circumstances in which they find themselves" (13).

2. For analyses of the relationship of the cult of true womanhood to Black women, see Leith Mullings, "Uneven Development: Class, Race and Gender in the United States before 1900," in *Women's Work, Development and the Division of Labor by Gender,* ed. Eleanor Leacock and Helen Safa (South Hadley, MA: Bergin & Garvey, 1986), pp. 41–57; Bonnie Thornton Dill, "Our Mothers' Grief: Racial Ethnic Women and the Maintenance of Families," Research Paper 4, Center for Research on Women (Memphis, TN: Memphis State University, 1986); and Hazel Carby, *Reconstructing Womanhood: The Emergence of the Afro-American Woman Novelist* (New York: Oxford University Press, 1987), esp. chapter 2.

3. Contrast, for example, the traditionalist analysis of Selma Fraiberg, *Every Child's Birthright: In Defense of Mothering* (New York: Basic Books, 1977) to that of Jeffner Allen, "Motherhood: The Annihilation of Women," in *Mothering, Essays in Feminist Theory,* ed. Joyce Trebilcot (Totowa, NJ: Rowan & Allanheld, 1983). See also Adrienne Rich, *Of Woman Born: Motherhood as Experience and Institution* (New York: Norton, 1976). For an overview of how traditionalists and feminists have shaped the public policy debate on abortion, see Kristin Luker, *Abortion and the Politics of Motherhood* (Berkeley, CA: University of California, 1984).

4. Mullings, "Uneven Development"; Dill, "Our Mother's Grief"; and Carby, *Reconstructing Womanhood.* Feminist scholarship is also challenging Western notions of the family. See Barrie Thorne and Marilyn Yalom, eds., *Rethinking the Family* (New York: Longman, 1982).

5. Since Black women are no longer heavily concentrated in private domestic service, the Mammy image may be fading. In contrast, the matriarch image, popularized in Daniel Patrick Moynihan's, *The Negro Family: The Case for National Action* (Washington, D.C.: U.S. Government Printing Office, 1965), is re-emerging in public debates about the feminization of poverty and the urban underclass. See Maxine Baca Zinn, "Minority Families in Crisis: The Public Discussion," Research Paper 6, Center for Research on Women (Memphis, TN: Memphis State University, 1987).

6. For an alternative analysis of the Mammy image, see Judith Rollins, *Between Women: Domestics and Their Employers* (Philadelphia: Temple University, 1985). Classic responses to the matriarchy thesis include Robert Hill, *The Strengths of Black Families* (New York: Urban League, 1972); Andrew Billingsley, *Black Families in White America* (Englewood Cliffs, NJ: Prentice Hall, 1968); and Joyce Ladner, *Tomorrow's Tomorrow* (Garden City, NY: Doubleday, 1971). For a recent analysis, see Linda Burnham, "Has Poverty Been Feminized in Black America?" *Black Scholar* 16 (1985):15–24.

7. Mae King, "The Politics of Sexual Stereotypes," *Black Scholar* 4 (1973):12–23.

8. Barbara Christian, "An Angle of Seeing: Motherhood in Buchi Emecheta's *Joys of Motherhood* and Alice Walker's *Meridian,*" in *Black Feminist Criticism,* ed. Barbara Christian (New York: Pergamon, 1985), p. 214.

9. See Christine Oppong, ed., *Female and Male in West Africa* (London: Allen & Unwin, 1983); Niara Sudarkasa, "Female Employment and Family Organization in West Africa," in *The Black Woman*

Cross-Culturally, ed. Filomina Chiamo Steady (Cambridge, MA: Schenkman, 1981), pp. 49–64; and Nancy Tanner, "Matrifocality in Indonesia and Africa and Among Black Americans," in *Woman, Culture, and Society,* ed. Michelle Rosaldo and Louise Lamphere (Stanford, CA: Stanford University Press, 1974), pp. 129–56.

10. Christine Oppong, "Family Structure and Women's Reproductive and Productive Roles: Some Conceptual and Methodological Issues," in *Women's Roles and Population Trends in the Third World,* ed. Richard Anker, Myra Buvinic, and Nadia Youssef (London: Croom Heim, 1982), pp. 133–50.

11. The key distinction here is that, unlike the matriarchy thesis, women play central roles in families and this centrality is seen as legitimate. In spite of this centrality, it is important not to idealize African women's family roles. For an analysis by a Black African feminist, see Awa Thiam, *Black Sisters, Speak Out: Feminism and Oppression in Black Africa* (London: Pluto, 1978).

12. Sudarkasa, "Female Employment."

13. John Mbiti, *African Religions and Philosophies* (New York: Anchor, 1969).

14. Niara Sudarkasa, "Interpreting the African Heritage in Afro-American Family Organization," in *Black Families,* ed. Harriette Pipes McAdoo (Beverly Hills, CA: Sage, 1981), pp. 37–53; and Deborah Gray White, *Ar'n't I a Woman? Female Slaves in the Plantation South* (New York: W. W. Norton, 1985).

15. The terms used in this section appear in Rosalie Riegle Troester's "Turbulence and Tenderness: Mothers, Daughters, and 'Othermothers' in Paule Marshall's *Brown Girl, Brownstones,*" *SAGE: A Scholarly Journal on Black Women* 1 (Fall 1984):13–16.

16. See Tanner, "Matrifocality"; see also Carrie Allen McCray, "The Black Woman and Family Roles," in *The Black Woman,* ed. LaFrances Rogers-Rose (Beverly Hills, CA: Sage, 1980), pp. 67–78; Elmer Martin and Joanne Mitchell Martin, *The Black Extended Family* (Chicago: University of Chicago Press, 1978); Joyce Aschenbrenner, *Lifelines, Black Families in Chicago* (Prospect Heights, IL: Waveland, 1975); and Carol B. Stack, *All Our Kin* (New York: Harper & Row, 1974).

17. Martin and Martin, *The Black Extended Family;* Stack, *All Our Kin;* and Virginia Young, "Family and Childhood in a Southern Negro Community," *American Anthropologist* 72 (1970):269–88.

18. Stack, *All Our Kin.*

19. Ellen Cantarow, *Moving the Mountain: Women Working for Social Change* (Old Westbury, NY: Feminist Press, 1980), p. 59.

20. Thordis Simonsen, ed., *You May Plow Here, The Narrative of Sara Brooks* (New York: Touchstone, 1986), p. 181.

21. White, *Ar'n't I a Woman?;* Dill, "Our Mothers' Grief"; Mullings, "Uneven Development."

22. Simonsen, *You May Plow Here,* p. 86.

23. Mamie Garvin Fields and Karen Fields, *Lemon Swamp and Other Places, A Carolina Memoir* (New York: Free Press, 1983), p. xvii.

24. Ibid, p. 195.

25. Cheryl Gilkes, "'Holding Back the Ocean with a Broom,' Black Women and Community Work," in *The Black Woman,* ed. Rogers-Rose, 1980, pp. 217–31, and "Going Up for the Oppressed: The Career Mobility of Black Women Community Workers," *Journal of Social Issues* 39 (1983):115–39.

26. Gilkes, "'Holding Back the Ocean,'" p. 219.

27. Fields and Fields, *Lemon Swamp,* p. xvi.

28. Charles Johnson, *Shadow of the Plantation* (Chicago: University of Chicago Press, 1934, 1979), p. 173.

29. Pamela Reid, "Socialization of Black Female Children," in *Women: A Developmental Perspective,* ed. Phyllis Berman and Estelle Ramey (Washington, DC: National Institutes of Health, 1983).

30. For works in the feminist psychoanalytic tradition, see Nancy Chodorow, "Family Structure and Feminine Personality," in *Woman, Culture, and Society,* ed. Rosaldo and Lamphere, 1974; Nancy Chodorow, *The Reproduction of Mothering* (Berkeley, CA: University of California, 1978); and Jane Flax, "The Conflict Between Nurturance and Autonomy in Mother–Daughter Relationships and within Feminism," *Feminist Studies* 4 (1978):171–89.

31. Ann Moody, *Coming of Age in Mississippi* (New York: Dell, 1968).

32. Ladner, *Tomorrow's Tomorrow;* Gloria Joseph, "Black Mothers and Daughters: Their Roles and Functions in American Society," in *Common Differences,* ed. Gloria Joseph and Jill Lewis (Garden City, NY: Anchor, 1981), pp. 75–126; Lena Wright Myers, *Black Women, Do They Cope Better?* (Englewood Cliffs, NJ: Prentice Hall, 1980).

33. Elsa Barkley Brown, "Hearing Our Mothers' Lives," paper presented at fifteenth anniversary of African-American and African Studies at Emory College, Atlanta, 1986. This essay appeared in the Black Women's Studies issue of *SAGE: A Scholarly Journal on Black Women,* vol. 6, no. 1:4–11.

34. Joseph, "Black Mothers and Daughters"; Myers, 1980.

35. Gloria Wade-Gayles, "The Truths of Our Mothers' Lives: Mother–Daughter Relationships in Black Women's Fiction," *SAGE: A Scholarly Journal on Black Women* 1 (Fall 1984):12.

36. Troester, "Turbulence and Tenderness," p. 13.

37. Wade-Gayles, "The Truths," p. 10.

38. Joseph, "Black Mothers and Daughters."

39. Moody, *Coming of Age,* p. 57.

40. Renita Weems, "'Hush. Mama's Gotta Go Bye Bye': A Personal Narrative," *SAGE: A Scholarly Journal on Black Women* 1 (Fall 1984):26.

41. Ibid, p. 27.

42. June Jordan, *On Call, Political Essays* (Boston: South End Press, 1985), p. 145.

29

Revision and Resistance

The Politics of Native Women's Motherwork

LISA J. UDEL

Contemporary Native women of the United States and Canada, politically active in Indigenous rights movements for the past thirty years, variously articulate a reluctance to affiliate with white feminist movements of North America. Despite differences in tribal affiliation, regional location, urban or reservation background, academic or community setting, and pro- or anti-feminist ideology, many Native women academics and grass-roots activists alike invoke models of preconquest, egalitarian societies to theorize contemporary social and political praxes. Such academics as Paula Gunn Allen, Rayna Green, and Patricia Monture-Angus, as well as Native activists Wilma Mankiller, Mary Brave Bird, and Yet Si Blue (Janet McCloud) have problematized the reformative role white feminism can play for Indigenous groups, arguing that non-Native women's participation in various forms of Western imperialism have often made them complicit in the oppression of Native peoples.[1] More important, Native women contend that their agendas for reform differ from those they identify with mainstream white feminist movements. The majority of contemporary Native American women featured in recent collections by Ronnie Farley, Jane Katz, and Steve Wall, for example, are careful to stress the value of traditional, precontact female and male role models in their culture.[2] One aspect of traditional culture that Native women cite as crucial to their endeavor is what Patricia Hill Collins calls "motherwork."[3] Many Native women valorize their ability to procreate and nurture their children, communities, and the earth as aspects of motherwork. "Women are sacred because we bring life into this world," states Monture-Angus. "First Nations women are respected as the centre of the nation for [this] reason."[4] Native women argue that they have devised alternate reform strategies to those advanced by Western feminism. Native women's motherwork, in its range and variety, is one form of this activism, an approach that emphasizes Native traditions of "responsibilities" as distinguished from Western feminism's notions of "rights."

Writing for an ethnically diverse feminist audience in the journal *Callaloo*, Clara Sue Kidwell (Choctaw/Chippewa) warns: "Although feminists might deny this equation of anatomy and destiny, the fact is that the female reproductive function is a crucial factor in determining a woman's social role in tribal societies. Women bear children who carry on the culture of the group."[5] Mary Gopher (Ojibway) explains the analogy of woman/Earth inherent in philosophies of many tribes: "In our religion, we look at this planet as a

Reprinted from *Frontiers: A Journal of Women Studies*, Volume 22, Number 2 (2001) by permission of the University of Nebraska Press. Copyright © 2002 by Frontiers Editorial Collective.

woman. She is the most important female to us because she keeps us alive. We are nursing off of her."[6] Carrie Dann (Western Shoshone) adds: "Indigenous women, they're supposed to look at themselves as the Earth. That is the way we were brought up. This is what I try to tell the young people, especially the young girls."[7] Gopher and Dann invest motherwork with religious and cultural authority that they, as elders, must transmit to younger women in their communities. Many contemporary Native women argue that they must also educate white women in their traditional roles as women in order to safeguard the Earth, so that they will survive. Calling upon traditions of female leadership, Blue (Tulalip) contends:

> It is going to be the job of Native women to begin teaching other women what their roles are. Women have to turn life around, because if they don't, all of future life is threatened and endangered. I don't care what kind of women they are, they are going to have to worry more about the changes that are taking place on this Mother Earth that will affect us all.[8]

Blue, like many Native women activists, links women's authority as procreators with their larger responsibilities to a personified, feminized Earth.

Several Native women condemn Western feminism for what they perceive as a devaluation of motherhood and refutation of women's traditional responsibilities.[9] Paula Gunn Allen attributes the pronatalist stance articulated by so many Native women to the high incidence of coerced sterilization in Indian Health Service (IHS) facilities. An overpowering awareness of the government's abduction of Indian children, the nonconsensual sterilization of Native women, along with the nation's highest infant mortality rates, pervades the work of Native writers and activists.[10] American Indian Movement (AIM) veteran and celebrated author Mary Brave Bird, for instance, discusses the sterilization of her mother and sister, performed without their consent.[11] Many women told Jane Katz stories of the forced abduction of their children by social welfare agencies and mission schools that were published in *Messengers of the Wind*.[12] In her autobiography *Halfbreed*, Maria Campbell (métis) tells a similar story of the Canadian government placing her siblings in foster care when her mother died, despite the fact that her father—the children's parent and legal guardian—was still alive.[13]

Native women argue that in their marital contracts with Euramerican men they lost power, autonomy, sexual freedom, and maternity and inheritance rights, which precluded their ability to accomplish motherwork. Green observes, for example, that an eighteenth-century Native woman allied to a fur trader relinquished control over her life and the lives of the children she bore from her white partner. This lack of control was compounded by the fact that Native women married to white men gave birth to more children than those partnered with Native men. Furthermore, a Native woman lost the freedom to divorce of her own free will, and the "goods and dwelling that might have been her own property in Indian society became the possession of her white husband."[14] In contrast, within many Native traditions, notes Green:

> The children belonged entirely to women, as did the property and distribution of resources. Indian men abided by the rules of society. If a couple separated, the man would leave with only that which had belonged to him when he entered the relationship; if a woman formed an alliance with a European by choice, she had every reason to imagine that her society's rules would be followed. For Indians, a white man who married an Indian was expected to acknowledge the importance and status of women. . . . In some tribes, adult women were free to seek out sexual alliances with whomever they chose.[15]

In order to do motherwork well, Native women argue, women must have power.

Euramericans held different ideas about female sexuality and inheritance. Many white men married Indian women who owned land in order to acquire their inheritance. When conflict over property rights inevitably arose, European laws dominated, Native women lost ownership rights to their land and suffered diminished economic autonomy and political status. Examples of this phenomenon occurred in the early twentieth century when oil was discovered in Oklahoma; white men married into wealthy female-centered Osage families and inherited the family's property. "Under Osage practice, the oil revenues would have been reserved for the woman's family and controlled by her. Common property laws established by white men gave the husband control," explains Green. "In a number of notorious instances in Oklahoma, women were murdered so that their husbands could inherit their wealth."[16] Certainly the concept that Indian women suffer through sexual contact with non-Native men is evident in the works of Beth Brant, Green, and Mankiller, as well as in the story of the women of Tobique, who lost their Indian status once they married white men.

Native women also experienced the loss of economic and political power through diminished reproductive freedom. Christian ideology recast women's sexuality, emphasizing procreation, virtue, and modesty. Early records show missionaries' agitation over the sexual autonomy of most unmarried Native women. As Christian-based roles were asserted, Native traditions of birth control and population control were forgotten. For example, Cherokee women traditionally held the right to limit population through infanticide. Similarly, Seneca women were able to limit their families, starting childbearing early and ending it early. Seneca society also did not mandate marriage for legitimate childbearing.[17]

The involuntary sterilization of Native women (as well as Mexican American and African American women) is common knowledge among those communities affected but remains largely unknown to those outside the communities. A federal government investigation in 1976 discovered that in the four-year period between 1973 and 1976 more than three thousand Native women were involuntarily sterilized. Of the 3,406 women sterilized, 3,001 were between the ages of fifteen and forty-four.[18] A 1979 report revealed that six out of ten hospitals routinely sterilized women under the age of twenty-one, a clear violation of the 1974 Department of Health, Education, and Welfare (DHEW) guidelines prohibiting involuntary sterilization of minors.[19] According to Bertha Medicine Bull, a leader on the Montana Lame Deer Reservation, two local fifteen-year-old girls were sterilized when they had appendectomies, without their knowledge or consent.[20] Only four out of twelve IHS facilities were investigated; therefore, the estimated number of women sterilized either coercively (often through the illegal threat of withholding government aid or the removal of existing children), or without their knowledge, during this period is estimated at twelve thousand.[21]

Green writes that because of "sterilization and experimentation abuse on Native American women and men in Indian Health Service facilities, Native American people have been warier than ever of contraceptive technologies."[22] Many Native women, responding to the involuntary sterilization cases they have encountered directly and indirectly, blame the U.S. government for genocidal policies toward Native populations. Connie Uri (Choctaw), for example, observed in 1978: "We are not like other minorities. We have no gene pool in Africa or Asia. When we are gone, that's it."[23] Activist Barbara Moore (the sister Mary Brave Bird describes) links sterilization with genocide much more explicitly: "There are plans to get rid of Indians. They actually plan different kinds of genocide. One way to do that is through alcohol, another way is birth control, and one of the most cruel ways is to sterilize Indian women by force."[24] Moore recounts the story of her child's birth, delivered by Cesarean section and reported as a still-birth, although the autopsy she demanded determined the cause of death as inconclusive. Moore states: "My child was born healthy. Besides this, they told me that I could not have any more children because they have had to sterilize me. I was sterilized during the operation without my knowledge and without my agreement."[25]

Native women thus value and argue for reproductive autonomy, which they link with empowered mother-work; but, they approach this autonomy from a perspective that they feel differs from mainstream feminism. Given the history of the IHS campaign to curtail Native women's reproductive capacity and thus Native populations, Native women emphasize women's ability, sometimes "privilege," to bear children. Within this paradigm, they argue, Native women's procreative capability becomes a powerful tool to combat Western genocide. Motherhood recovered, along with the tribal responsibility to nurture their children in a traditional manner and without non-Indigenous interference, assumes a powerful political meaning when viewed this way.[26]

WHITE FEMINISM AND REPRODUCTIVE AUTONOMY

The role of white feminism in the campaign for reproductive autonomy has been a sore point among many Native women who link the American eugenics movement with American birth control movements of the early twentieth century. Both movements, which involved the participation of white feminists of their time, began as an effort to grant women control over their fertility, and thus gain some measure of economic and political autonomy, but eventually gave way to eugenic and population control forces. The focus moved from "self determination" to the "social control" of immigrant and working classes by "the elite." As historian Linda Gordon explains, eugenics became a dominant aspect of the movement to legalize contraception and sterilization, and, eventually, "Birth controllers from the socialist-feminist revolution . . . made accommodations with eugenists."[27]

White-dominated feminism's historic failure to combat racist and classist ideologies, compounded by promotion of ideologies to gain suffrage in the past, has perpetuated the link between white mainstream feminism to eugenics. The resulting conflation of birth control movements with eugenics and population control has had a negative impact both on disadvantaged people vulnerable to external social control and also on the feminist movement. Gordon argues that feminist birth control advocates accepted racist attitudes of the eugenicists and population controllers, even sharing anti–working-class, anti-immigrant sentiment.[28] The population control and eugenics movements dominated early and mid-twentieth-century white feminism, obfuscating the latter's agenda and efficacy. This history continues to influence theories of birth control today. According to Gordon, "Planned Parenthood's use of small-family ideology and its international emphasis on sterilization rather than safe and controllable contraception have far overshadowed its feminist program for women's self-determination."[29]

The public does not distinguish between birth control "as a program of individual rights" and population control as social policy that strips the individual of those very rights. It is this blurred distinction that Native women criticize. Brave Bird, for instance, points out the irrelevance of abortion rights to Indian women who see tribal repopulation as one of their primary goals. A self-identified Indian feminist, Brave Bird recognizes the value of reproductive rights for women whose bodies have been controlled by others; however, she objects to white feminists who would dictate an Indian feminist agenda to her.[30] In 1977 the Hyde Amendment withdrew federal funding for abortions but left free-on-demand surgical sterilizations funded by the DHEW; consequently some poor women were forced to choose infertility as their method of birth control because pregnancy prevention was also not funded.

Native women employ motherist rhetoric in their critiques of Western feminism as a response to their history of enforced sterilization and also as a defensive strategy crucial to marking women's dignity and contributions to Native cultures. Speaking to a predominantly white audience of feminists at the National Women's Studies Association meeting in 1988, Green explained that "models of kinship [mother, sister, grandmother, aunt] are used by Indian women to measure their capacity for leadership and to measure the success of their leadership."[31] Such kinship models of evaluation, however, are not to be read literally. These roles are *not* biologically determined, Green emphasized; they are symbolic:

> Women like me are going to blow it in the role of mother if left to the narrow, biological role. But in Indian country, that role was never understood necessarily only as a biological role; grandma was never understood as a biological role; sister and aunt were never understood in the narrow confines of genetic kinship.[32]

As leaders, Native women must oversee the survival of Native peoples, notes Green. While Green, like Blue and Carrie Dann, sees Native people as the primary redeemers of America, she emphatically refutes the appropriation of Native traditions to "heal" mainstream American culture. "We cannot do that," she explains.

> There has been so much abuse of this role that it's frightening. . . . *All* Indigenous people have that power, because we speak from the earth. . . . But we cannot heal you; only you can heal yourselves. . . . If we have any model to give, it is an aesthetic model, a cultural model, that works for us.

Green warns that Western appropriation of Indigenous traditions, rituals, and philosophies (made popular in the New Age Movement, for example) will not provide a "quick fix" for the problems of Western culture. Green's position is an attempt to clarify the role of Native traditions in the reformative enterprise. Native activists will not perform the service-work of healing Western cultures. Green points out that such expectations are embedded in colonial histories; they keep the "sick" Western subject at the center to be tended by the Native "other."[33]

Native women's strategic use of a motherist stance is a conscious act of separation from traditional feminists.[34] The women locate their activism not in feminist struggle, but in cultural survival, identifying themselves, as Anne Snitow explains, "not as feminists but as militant mothers, fighting together for [the] survival [of their children]." Women become motherists, Snitow writes, when "men are forced to be absent (because they are migrant workers or soldiers) or in times of crisis, when the role of nurturance assigned to women has been rendered difficult or impossible."[35] A motherist position would apply to Native women living on and off reservations where employment opportunities are scarce for men, as well as for women who lose their mothering capacity to sterilization or their living children to boarding schools. The motherists Snitow describes intuitively relied upon the presence of their female community because "crisis made the idea of a separate, private identity beyond the daily struggle for survival unimportant."[36]

White feminists and Native motherists endorsed divergent strategies, notes Snitow. Her model perfectly characterizes dichotomies between Native women's collective identifications—including their loyalties to traditions that puzzle white women—and non-Native feminists' individuating theories. "Collectivist movements are powerful, but they usually don't raise questions about women's work," she explains. "Feminism has raised the questions, and claimed an individual destiny for each woman, but remains ambivalent toward older traditions of female solidarity."[37] For example, traditional dichotomies of public and private domains, characteristic of much feminist writing of the 1970s and 1980s, does not work for women of color for whom "those domains are not separate or at least not separate in the same ways as for white women."[38] This is especially true with Native cultures, which are structured along collective rather than individual dynamics characteristic of Western cultures.[39] The separation of public and private spheres, along with "the primacy of gender conflict as a feature of the family, and the gender-based assignment of reproductive labor," constitute three concepts of traditional white feminist theory that ignore the interaction of race and gender and thus fail to account for Native women's experience of motherwork.[40]

Evelyn Nakano Glenn observes that for racial ethnic women, the concept of the "domestic" extends beyond the nuclear family to include broadly defined relations of kin and community. Often living in situations of economic insecurity and assault on their culture, racially ethnic women have not been able to rely solely on the nuclear family because it is not self-sufficient, but have relied upon and contributed to an extended network of family and community. Thus, work conducted in the domestic, hence "private," sphere includes contributions to the extended "public" network, where women care for each other's children, exchange supplies, and help nurse the sick. Racial ethnic women's work has simultaneously moved into the public sphere of the ethnic community, in support of the church, political organizing, and other activities on behalf of their collective. Glenn writes that racial ethnic women are "often the core of community organizations, and their involvement is often spurred by a desire to defend their children, their families, and their ways of life."[41]

Certainly Glenn's point is relevant to contemporary Native women living on and off the reservation. Focused on strengthening Native economies and traditions, contemporary Native women may engage in traditional skills of beadwork or quilting, for example, in order to earn money and prestige to benefit, feed, and educate their children. Women may engage in activities historically associated with men in order to revise and strengthen tribal culture. Such women drum at local powwows, or are political activists, such as Mary Brave Bird of AIM and, more recently, Winona LaDuke (White Earth Ojibwa), founder of the White Earth Land Recovery Project, cochair of the Indigenous Women's Network, and vice presidential candidate for the Green Party in the last two elections. Patricia Hill Collins notes that work and family do not function as separate, dichotomous spheres for women of color, but are, in fact, often overlapping. By linking individual and collective welfare, Collins neatly articulates the philosophy underlying most Native cultures. While individual achievement is sought and recognized, it is always within the context of the collective that such endeavors are valued. It follows that Wilma Mankiller became Principal Chief of the Cherokee to benefit the Cherokee.[42]

For women of color, then, motherwork involves working for the physical survival of children and community, confronting what Collins calls the "dialectical nature of power and powerlessness in structuring mothering patterns, and the significance of self-definition in constructing individual and collective racial identity." This type of motherwork, while ensuring individual and community survival, can result in the loss of individual autonomy "or the submersion of individual growth for the benefit of the group."[43] The deemphasis on individual autonomy proves troubling to white feminists who have sought to extricate the individual woman's identity from the debilitating influences of social expectation in order to articulate and celebrate her emergence into what has generally been viewed as a more liberated individual. Once again we experience the fallout of conflicting ideas between Western liberalism and Native collectivism.

When feminist theory posits "the family" as "the locus of gender conflict," focusing on the economic dependence of women and the inequitable division of labor, it inevitably draws upon models of the white, middle-class, nuclear family. Viewed thus, marriage within the white, middle-class, nuclear family oppresses women. In order to gain liberation, white feminists have argued, women must be free from the unequal balance of power marriage has conferred. In contrast, Glenn points out, women of color often experience their families as a "source of resistance to oppression from outside institutions." Within Glenn's construct, we see that women of color engage in activities to keep their families unified and teach children survival skills. This work is viewed as a method of resistance to oppression rather than gender exploitation. Unified in struggle against colonial oppression, family members focus on individual survival, maintenance of family authority, and the transmission of cultural traditions. Economically, Glenn notes, women of color remain less dependent upon men than white women because they must earn an income to support the family. Both incomes are necessary for a family's survival. Glenn writes that because the earning gap between women and men of color is narrower than that of whites, "men and women [of color have been] mutually dependent; dependence rarely ran in one direction." Such families may be sustained by members whose relationships are characterized by interdependence and gender complementarity.[44]

Glenn's paradigm of the family can be applied in a broader context in order to consider aspects of contemporary reservation and urban life. For example, Christine Conte's study of western Navajo women examines how they employ kin ties and cooperative networks to perform tasks, obtain resources, and acquire wealth. Such cooperation typically includes the exchange of labor, commodities, subsistence goods, information, cash, and transportation.[45] Similarly, women featured in Steve Wall's collection of interviews with tribal elders describe themselves as family leaders, intent on transmitting cultural traditions to the generation that follows them.[46] AIM schools of the 1970s, typically run by women, provide one example of offering Native children an alternative value system to the mission and boarding schools that many of their parents (such as Mary Brave Bird) experienced.

Like Glenn and Collins, Patricia Monture-Angus points to the differing roles that the family plays for Native women and non-Native women. Citing Marlee Kline, Monture-Angus notes that, while women of color and white women can both experience violence in the family, women of color look to their family as a system of support against violent racism from outside the family. Thus, while the Native family may "provide a site of cultural and political resistance to White supremacy,"[47] Native women can also experience contradictory relationships within their families, requiring that they also revise their families as they go along. Drawing upon networks of kin for support, survival, and pleasure, Native women also combat trends in domestic violence and prescribed gender roles that threaten and constrain them.[48]

Collins identifies three main themes that comprise ethnic women's struggles for maternal empowerment: 1) reproductive autonomy; 2) parental privileges; and 3) the threat of cultural eradication by the dominant culture.[49] Many women of color have not known the experience of determining their own fertility. For Native women sterilized without their consent, choosing to become a mother takes on political meaning, an act that challenges, as Angela Davis has said, "institutional policies that encourage white middle-class women to reproduce and discourage low-income racial ethnic women from doing so, even penalizing them."[50] Once a woman of color becomes a parent, she is threatened with the physical and/or psychological separation from her children "designed to disempower racial ethnic individuals and undermine their communities."[51] The Indian boarding and mission schools of the nineteenth and twentieth centuries serve as an example of this disempowerment, coupled, as they were, with "the pervasive efforts by the dominant group to control their children's minds" by forbidding any use of Native languages and the denigration of "the power of mothers to raise their children as they see fit."[52] For women of color, motherwork entails the difficult tasks of "trying to foster a meaningful racial identity in children within a society that denigrates people of color" and sustaining a form of resistance.[53]

For many Native women, motherwork is linked with the authority of leadership.[54] Discussing Western imperialism's degenerate effect on female leadership, Chief Wilma Mankiller contends:

> Europeans brought with them the view that men were the absolute heads of households, and women were to be submissive to them. It was then that the role of women in Cherokee society began to decline. One of the new values Europeans brought to the Cherokees was a lack of balance and harmony between men and women. It was what we today call sexism. This was not a Cherokee concept. Sexism was borrowed from Europeans.[55]

Mankiller characterizes the resistance she encountered to her campaign for the position of Principal Chief of the Cherokee as evidence of the erosion of traditional Native political structures under the onslaught of Western influence. Although traditionally matrilineal, the Cherokee adopted Western configurations of gender that favor patriarchal structures, notes Mankiller. Among recent Cherokee accomplishments, such as addressing issues of poverty and education reform, and the revitalization of cultural traditions, Mankiller includes revised gender roles and the reclamation of women's power.

The current status of Native women—both on and off the reservations involved in tribal political, cultural, and religious revitalization—drives many contemporary writers to emphasize the richness of traditional Native women's lives as models for reform. Just as Green insists on traditions that cultivate women's leadership, Lakota anthropologist Beatrice Medicine emphasizes the importance women play in Lakota ceremonial and artistic life, along with the status their work garners. Medicine contends that "the traditional woman was greatly respected and revered," that she hosted feasts and participated in sacred ceremonies, and that women's societies held competitions in the arts of sewing, beading, and other crafts that proved economically lucrative in trade and were thus prestigious for the winner. Contemporary life on the reservations is very different, Medicine notes. Lakota women suffer diminished prestige, and they are threatened by poor economic conditions, government usurpation of the functions traditionally provided by the family (such as welfare and education), and the loss of traditional values that unify kinship roles and obligations. Where Sioux women formerly used their artistic talents to make a respectable marriage and to earn prestige and wealth, they now continue their artistic work but with diminished economic return. At one time a woman might have earned one horse in exchange for a "skillfully decorated robe"; now she will earn approximately sixty cents an hour for a quilt.[56]

Many Native women agree with Allen, who contends, "The tradition of strong, autonomous, self-defining women comes from Indians. They [Euroamericans] sure didn't get it in sixteenth-century Europe."[57] Monture-Angus explains that the term "traditional" privileges neither "static" nor regressive perspectives, but embraces holistic approaches to reform. Monture-Angus points out that "traditional perspectives include the view that the past and all its experiences inform the present reality."[58] She advocates an interpretation of traditions that is fluid and adaptive, one that will enable Native societies to confront situations of contemporary life such as domestic violence, substance addiction, and youth suicide. Because many precontact cultures did not condone abuse of women, Monture-Angus argues, a literal interpretation of traditions will fail to provide a contemporary model of social reform. "What we can reclaim is the values [sic] that created a system where the abuses did not occur. We can recover our own system of law, law that has at its centre the family and our kinship relations. . . . We must be patient with each other as we learn to live in a decolonized way."[59] Monture-Angus articulates a belief in the beauty and efficacy of Native traditions shared by many Native women writing about strategies for battling colonialism and supporting tribal survival.

Part of the reclamation of cultural traditions involves the recognition of "responsibilities," a term many Native theorists distinguish from Western notions of "rights." Native women thus articulate their responsibilities in terms of their roles as mothers and leaders, positing those roles as a form of motherwork. "Responsibility focuses attention not on what is mine, but on the relationships between people and creation (that is, both the individual and the collective)," writes Monture-Angus.[60] Native activists argue that rights-based theories predispose Western cultures to abuse the earth and to oppress other societies that value their relationship to the earth. Renee Senogles (Red Lake Chippewa) notes: "The difference between Native American women and white feminists is that the feminists talk about their rights and we talk about our responsibilities. There is a profound difference. Our responsibility is to take care of our natural place in the world."[61] Osennontion and Skonaganleh:rá concur, clarifying the emphasis of Haudenosaunee law on responsibilities within political and social realms, which include the observance of clan structure and communal ties, and a personal code of honor, integrity, compassion, and strength, linked to the maintenance of a relationship with the natural world.[62]

One primary goal of Native activists involves restructuring and reinforcing Indian families. This includes their reevaluation of both women's and men's roles. If Native women are to fulfill traditions of female leadership, they argue, Native men must reclaim their responsibilities so that the enterprise supporting Indigenous survival and prosperity can move forward. Native women repeatedly fault white feminists for the devaluation of men in their revisionary tactics. Part of a man's responsibility is to protect and provide for his family, as well as to expedite political and social duties. If a man fails in his responsibilities, it falls upon the society's women to instruct, reeducate, and remind him of his obligations. Native activists fault Western hegemony and capitalism as systems responsible for alienating so many Native men from their traditional responsibilities.

In the face of coerced agrarianism and the attending devaluation of hunting, and the consequences of forced removal and relocation, Native men have suffered a loss of status and traditional self-sufficiency even more extensive than their female counterparts, argue many Native women.[63] Women's traditional roles as procreator, parent, domestic leader, and even artisan have, to some extent, remained intact. For example, Clara Sue Kidwell observes that during early contact, women's "functions as childbearers and contributors to subsistence were not

threatening to white society and were less affected than those of Indian men."[64] In situations of contact, Kidwell points out, women often became the custodians of traditional cultural values, engaging in reproductive labor and motherwork. In contrast, men suffer from an inability to fulfill traditional roles. On the Pine Ridge reservation of the Lakota, employment opportunities for Lakota men are practically nonexistent. Federal agencies, such as the BIA and IHS provide the majority of the employment available. Very few businesses are owned by the Lakota, and, because of the land allotment, less than 10 percent of reservation land is actually owned by Native Americans. Jobs available to men, such as construction, are project-oriented and thus sporadic, whereas job opportunities for women, such as nursing, teaching, clerical, and domestic work, are more consistently available.[65] Ramona Ford observes that contemporary Native women hold down more jobs than do Native men, although they earn inadequate wages.[66] It is evident that such cash-based, gender-delimited jobs keep the majority of Native people living below the poverty line in both the United States and Canada.[67]

Part of their responsibilities then, contend many Native women, is the restoration of traditional male roles, along with the selection and training of appropriate male leaders. Once installed in leadership roles, Osennontion and Skonaganleh:rá write, the men are responsible to the women who have empowered them, and the women ensure that their leaders remain "good men," mindful of the reciprocal relationship between leader and subject.[68] The definition of their responsibilities—their attendance to clan and communal structure through an investment in male esteem—coincides with the taxonomy I discuss in reproductive labor and motherwork.

While some Western feminists might recoil from such an investment in the restoration of male psyche, seeing it as a refined form of female abjection, it is important to remember that the majority of Native women writing and speaking today—who are political activists, feminist scholars, anthropologists, law professors, and grassroots organizers—all emphasize the importance of men to the revitalization of Native communities. Obviously then, these Native women do not prescribe female subjugation, but rather the solidification of a communal, extended network of support that acts as the family. This family takes many forms and rarely resembles the Western model of the nuclear, patriarch-led unit. For example, the two collections *Women of the Native Struggle* and *Wisdom's Daughters* feature vastly extended, matrilineal and matrilocal families, often with single, pregnant women as their members and leaders.[69] Such families seek to reintegrate men into communal life, but not within Western patriarchal paradigms. Osennontion and Skonaganleh:rá argue for the necessity of women's participation on the Band Council, the governing body for many East Coast Canadian tribes, including the Haudenosaunee: "Women have a responsibility to make sure that we don't lose any more, that we don't do any more damage, while we work on getting our original government system back in good working order."[70] As Monture-Angus notes, an emphasis on Native traditions does not preclude the integration of old and new. While recognizing the value of traditional culture and practice, Native activists and feminists do not blindly embrace behavior simply because it may be called "traditional," especially if it is oppressive to women. Just who determines what is to be called "traditional" and therefore valuable is also under scrutiny.

Indigenous women activists cite the difficulties that inform their theories and praxes of activism: the widespread violence committed against Native women; the common occurrence of rape; the murder of family members (Brave Bird, Campbell, and Lee Maracle, for instance, all recount such experiences); the murder and mutilation of leaders and friends (such as activist Annie Mae Aquash); the government's abduction of Indian children; and sterilization of Native women. It is vital that Native communities retrieve lost traditions of gender complementarity, they argue. The majority of Native American women involved in women's rights point to their own brand of feminism that calls on obscured traditions of women's autonomy and power. Such efforts, which are generally grassroots, reflect Native traditions of community-based activism comparable to the paradigm Snitow outlines.

In any discussion of possible coalition between contemporary Indigenous groups and white feminist groups, Native women insist that their prospective partners recognize Indigenous traditions of female autonomy and prestige, traditions that can provide models of social reform in white, as well as Native, America. This proposed coalition suggests a move beyond idealized appropriation, to a shared vision of political and cultural reform. In their eagerness to coalesce, white feminists have been rightly accused of ignoring or eliding differences between and among women. Native women resist reductionist impulses inherent in Western feminism, insisting that we examine the varying historical contingencies of each group that continue to shape feminist discourses into the next century.

NOTES

1. Examples include Paula Gunn Allen, *Off the Reservation: Reflections on Boundary-Busting, Border-Crossing, Loose Canons* (Boston: Beacon Press, 1998), *The Sacred Hoop: Recovering the Feminine in American Indian Traditions* (Boston: Beacon Press, 1986), and *Spider Woman's Granddaughters: Traditional Tales and Contemporary Writing by Native American Women* (Boston: Beacon Press, 1989); Jane Caputi, "Interview with Paula Gunn Allen," *Trivia* 16 (1990): 50–67, and "Interview" in *Backtalk: Women Writers Speak Out*, ed. Donna Perry (New Brunswick, N.J.: Rutgers University Press, 1993); Rayna Green, "American Indian Women: Diverse Leadership for Social Change," in *Bridges of Power: Women's Multicultural Alliances*, ed. Lisa Albrecht and Rose M. Brewer (Philadelphia: New Society Publishers, 1990), "Review Essay: Native American Women," *Signs: Journal of Women in Culture and Society* 6:2 (1980): 248–67, and *Women in American Indian Society* (New York: Chelsea House Publishers, 1992); Patricia A. Monture-Angus, *Thunder in My Soul: A Mohawk Woman Speaks* (Halifax: Fernwood Publishing, 1995); Patricia A. Monture, "I Know My Name: A First Nations Woman Speaks," in *Limited Edition: Voices of Women, Voices of Feminism*, ed. Geraldine Finn (Halifax: Fernwood Publishing, 1993); Wilma Mankiller and Michael Wallis, *Mankiller: A Chief and Her People* (New York: St. Martin's Press, 1993); Mary Brave Bird and Richard Erdoes, *Ohitika Woman* (New York: Harper Collins, 1993); Mary Crow Dog and Richard Erdoes, *Lakota Woman* (New York: Harper Collins, 1991); and Janet McCloud, in *Women of the Native Struggle: Portraits and Testimony of Native American Women*, ed. Ronnie Farley (New York: Orion Books, 1993).

2. Farley, *Women of the Native Struggle*, Jane Katz, ed., *Messengers of the Wind: Native American Women Tell Their Life Stories* (New York: Ballantine Books, 1995); and Steve Wall, ed., *Wisdom's Daughters: Conversations with Women Elders of Native America* (New York: Harper Perennial, 1993).

3. Patricia Hill Collins applies the term "motherwork" to the tasks engaged in by women/mothers of color. Collins contends that women of color recognize the embattled nature of their families and

identify the most destructive forces as coming from outside their families rather than from within. Part of women's work, or mother-work, consists of maintaining "family integrity." The kind of motherwork Collins outlines, and many Native women describe, reflects the belief that "individual survival, empowerment, and identity require group survival, empowerment, and identity" ("Shifting the Center: Race, Class, and Feminist Theorizing About Motherhood," in *Representations of Motherhood,* ed. Donna Bassin, Margaret Honey, and Meryle Mahrer Kaplan [New Haven: Yale University Press, 1994], 59).

4. Monture-Angus, *Thunder in My Soul,* 49.

5. Clara Sue Kidwell, "What Would Pocahontas Think Now? Women and Cultural Persistence," *Callaloo* 17:1 (1994): 149.

6. Mary Gopher, in Farley, *Women of the Native Struggle,* 77.

7. Carrie Dann in Farley, *Women of the Native Struggle,* 77.

8. Yet Si Blue in Farley, *Women of the Native Struggle,* 83.

9. Monture-Angus, *Thunder in My Soul,* 210; Paula Gunn Allen, quoted in Caputi, "Interview," 8; and Ingrid Washinawatok-El Issa in Farley, *Women of the Native Struggle,* 48.

10. Allen, "Interview," in Perry, *Backtalk,* 17.

11. Mary Crow Dog and Richard Erdoes, *Lakota Woman* (New York: Harper-Perennial, 1991) 78–79.

12. Jane Katz, ed., *Messengers of the Wind: Native American Women Tell Their Life Stories* (New York: Ballantine Books, 1995), 35–37, 60, 80–81.

13. Maria Campbell, *Halfbreed* (Lincoln: University of Nebraska Press, 1973), 103–7.

14. Green, *Women in American Indian Society,* 37.

15. Green, *Women in American Indian Society,* 37–38.

16. Green, *Women in American Indian Society,* 38. Linda Hogan's *Mean Spirit* (New York: Ivy Books, 1990) is a fictionalized account of this gynocidal episode in Native-Euramerican history.

17. Ramona Ford, "Native American Women: Changing Statuses, Changing Interpretations," in *Writing the Range: Race, Class, and Culture in the Women's West,* ed. Elizabeth Jameson and Susan Armitage (Norman: University of Oklahoma Press, 1997), 58; and Nancy Shoemaker, "The Rise or Fall of Iroquois Women," *Journal of Women's History* 2:3 (1991): 39–57, 51. For further discussion of gender in precontact cultures, see Evelyn Blackwood's "Sexuality and Gender in Certain Native American Tribes," *Signs: Journal of Women in Culture and Society* 10:1 (1984): 27–42.

18. Janet Karsten Larson, "And Then There Were None: Is Federal Policy Endangering the American Indian Species?" *Christian Century* 94, January 26, 1977, 61–63; and Mark Miller, "Native American Peoples on the Trail of Tears Once More: Indian Health Service and Coerced Sterilization," *America* 139 (1978): 422–25.

19. R. Bogue and D. W. Segelman, "Survey Finds Seven in 10 Hospitals Violate dhew Guidelines on Informed Consent for Sterilization," *Family Planning Perspectives* 11:6 (1979): 366–67.

20. Miller, "Native American Peoples on the Trail of Tears," 424.

21. Charles R. England, "A Look at the Indian Health Service Policy of Sterilization, 1972–1976," *Native American Homepage,* October 10, 1997, 6. For a fuller discussion of this topic, see Myla F. Thyrza Carpio, "Lost Generation: The Involuntary Sterilization of American Indian Women" (master's thesis, Johns Hopkins, 1991).

22. Green, "Review Essay," 261.

23. Connie Uri, quoted in Miller, "Native American Peoples on the Trail of Tears," 423.

24. Barbara Moore quoted in Fee Podarski, "An Interview with Barbara Moore on Sterilization," *Akwesasne Notes* 11:2 (1979): 11–12.

25. Barbara Moore, quoted in Podarski, "An Interview with Barbara Moore," 11.

26. Indian status is another aspect of the eradication of Native populations. Both in Canada and the United States, entire tribes have lost their status as "Indian" or "Native" and are identified instead as "colored." For an example in early-twentieth-century Virginia see J. David Smith, *The Eugenic Assault on America: Scenes in Red, White, and Black* (Fairfax, Va.: George Mason University Press, 1993); and for a more recent example pertaining to the Tobique in Canada, see Tobique Women's Group, *Enough Is Enough: Aboriginal Women Speak Out,* as told to Janet Silman, (Toronto: The Women's Press, 1987).

27. Linda Gordon, "Why Nineteenth-Century Feminists Did Not Support 'Birth Control' and Twentieth-Century Feminists Do: Feminism, Reproduction, and the Family," in *Rethinking the Family: Some Feminist Questions,* ed. Barrie Thorne and Marilyn Yalom (Boston: Northeastern University Press, 1992), 149.

28. Linda Gordon, *Woman's Body, Woman's Right: A Social History of Birth Control in America* (New York: Grossman Publishers, 1976), 281.

29. Gordon, "Why Nineteenth-Century Feminists Did Not Support 'Birth Control,'" 150.

30. Mary Brave Bird and Richard Erdoes, *Ohitika Woman* (New York: Harper-Perennial, 1993), 58.

31. Green, "American Indian Women," 65.

32. Green, "American Indian Women," 66.

33. Green, "American Indian Women," 63, 64, 71.

34. Ironically, early feminists and advocates of "voluntary motherhood" proposed an agenda similar to Native women's. Both saw voluntary motherhood as part of a movement to empower women (Gordon, "Why Nineteenth-Century Feminists Did Not Support 'Birth Control,'" 145). Suffragists' desire to exalt motherhood was a way of creating a dignified, powerful position for women in contrast to popular notions of womanhood that connoted fragility and virtue. By evoking a powerful model, women responded to their sexual subjugation to men and created an alternate arena where they had authority (Gordon, *Woman's Body,* 133–34).

35. Ann Snitow, "A Gender Diary," in *Conflicts in Feminism,* ed. Mariann Hirsch and Evelyn Fox Keller (New York: Routledge, 1990), 20.

36. Snitow, "A Gender Diary," 20.

37. Snitow, "A Gender Diary," 22.

38. Quotation from in Bassin, Honey, and Kaplan, *Representations of Motherhood,* 5. See, for example, Jessica Benjamin, "Authority and the Family Revisted: Or, a World without Fathers," *New German Critique* 4:3 (1978): 35–57; Nancy Chodorow, "Family Structure and Feminine Personality," in *Women, Culture, and Society,* ed. Michelle Zimbalist Rosaldo and Louise Lamphere (Stanford: Stanford University Press, 1974), 43–66; and Jean Bethke Elshtain, *Public Man, Private Woman: Women in Social and Political Thought* (Princeton: Princeton University Press, 1981).

39. For more detailed critiques of the limitations of dualistic separation of private and public sectors for gender analysis generally, see Susan Himmelweit, "The Real Dualism of Sex and Class," *Review of Radical Political Economics* 16:1 (1984): 167–83. For Native women more particularly, see Patricia Albers, "Sioux Women in Transition: A Study of Their Changing Status in a Domestic and Capitalist Sector of Production," in *The Hidden Half: Studies of Plains Indian Women,* ed. Patricia Albers and Beatrice Medicine (Latham, Md. University Press of America, 1983), and Albers, "Autonomy and Dependency in the Lives of Dakota Women: A Study in Historical Change," *Review of Radical Political Economics* 17:3 (1985): 109–34.

40. Evelyn Nakano Glenn, "Racial Ethnic Women's Labor: The Intersection of Race, Gender and Class Oppression," *Review of Radical Political Economics* 17:3 (1985): 101; Patricia Hill Collins, "Shifting the Center"; and Bonnie Thornton Dill, "Our Mothers' Grief: Racial Ethnic Women and the Maintenance of Families," *Journal of Family History* 13:4 (1988): 415–31, use the term "reproductive labor" to refer to all of the work of women in the home. Dill describes reproductive labor to include "the buying and preparation of food and clothing, provision of emotional support and nurturance for all family members, bearing children, and planning, organizing, and carrying out a wide variety of tasks associated with the socialization" ("Our Mothers' Grief," 430).

I adopt Patricia Hill Collins's use of the term "motherwork," which she employs to "soften the dichotomies in feminist theorizing about motherhood that posit rigid distinctions between private and public, family and work, the individual and the collective, identity as individual autonomy and identity growing from the collective self-determination of one's group. Racial ethnic women's mothering and work experiences occur at the boundaries demarking these dualities" ("Shifting the Center," 59).

41. Glenn, "Racial Ethnic Women's Labor," 102, 103. Several recent studies of modern Native household units find that women often head extended families and kinship networks that resist capitalist models that marginalize them. See Albers, "Autonomy and Dependency in the Lives of Dakota Women," "From Illusion to Illumination: Anthropological Studies of American Indian Women," in *Gender and Anthropology. Critical Reviews for Research and Teaching,* ed. Sandra Morgan (Washington, D.C. American Anthropological Association, 1989), and "Sioux Women in Transition"; Martha C. Knack, *Life Is with People: Household Organization of*

the Contemporary Southern Paiute Indians (Socorro, N. Mex.: Ballena Press, 1980); and Loraine Littlefield, "Gender, Class and Community: The History of Sne-Nay-Muxw Women's Employment" (Ph.D. diss., University of British Columbia, 1995).

42. Collins, "Shifting the Center," 58. Obviously, personal ambition is usually seen as selfish and suspect for women generally. Women have typically couched descriptions of their ambitions in terms of altruism and collective responsibility. My point here, however, is that leadership within Native paradigms embraces collective more than individual identity.

43. Collins, "Shifting the Center," 61, 62.

44. Glenn, "Racial Ethnic Women's Labor," 103–4. The high rate of single, female-headed households undermines Glenn conclusions somewhat. As seen in Wall's *Wisdom's Daughters,* for example, contemporary Native women may not "require" the income of Native men to survive at the subsistence level; however, they argue that women require men's economic contribution to live well, or above subsistence/poverty level. More important, Native women argue, they require men's social and cultural participation in tribal life in order to ensure survival of specific collective experiences and to perpetuate their traditions.

45. Christine Conte, "Ladies, Livestock, and Land and Lucre: Women's Networks and Social Status on the Western Navajo Reservation," *American Indian Quarterly* 6:1/2 (1982): 105, 116.

46. For example, Wall, *Wisdom's Daughters,* 169–70, 224–26.

47. Marlee Kline, cited in Monture-Angus, *Thunder in My Soul,* 42.

48. Not all Native women experience capitalism equally. Conte's study shows that while most Navajo women have been adversely affected by the forces of a market economy, several are able to manipulate elements of capitalism to benefit themselves and their households, while others experience diminished wealth ("Ladies, Livestock, and Land and Lucre," 120). Albers draws similar conclusions from her research on the Devil's Lake Sioux, particularly in "Autonomy and Dependency in the Lives of Dakota Women," 124–28.

49. Collins, "Shifting the Center," 65.

50. Angela Davis, quoted by Collins in "Shifting the Center," 65.

51. Collins, "Shifting the Center," 65.

52. Collins, "Shifting the Center," 66.

53. Collins, "Shifting the Center," 68.

54. See the proceedings from the United Nations Fourth World Conference on Women, Mothers of Our Nations, *Indigenous Women Address the World: Our Future—Our Responsibility* (Rapid City, S. Dak., 1995).

55. Mankiller and Wallis, *Mankiller,* 20.

56. Beatrice Medicine, "The Hidden Half Lives," in *Cante Ohitika Win (Brave-Hearted Women): Images of Lakota Women From the Pine Ridge Reservation South Dakota,* ed. Caroline Reyer (Vermillion: University of South Dakota Press, 1991), 5; and Albers and Medicine, *The Hidden Half,* 134–35. Nonetheless, Albers and

Medicine contend that in contemporary life, star quilts remain one of the most prestigious items in the Sioux give-away system. Quilts are displayed or given at honoring ceremonies and when "Sioux return home from military service or college," at community events of importance such as memorial feasts and naming ceremonies, and during "donations of powwow officials" (Patricia Albers and Beatrice Medicine, "The Role of Sioux Women in the Production of Ceremonial Objects: The Case of the Star Quilt").

57. Allen, "Interview," in Perry, *Backtalk*, 10.

58. Monture-Angus, *Thunder in My Soul*, 244.

59. Monture-Angus, *Thunder in My Soul*, 258.

60. Monture-Angus, *Thunder in My Soul*, 28.

61. Renee Senogles, quoted in Farley, *Women of the Native Struggle*, 69.

62. Osennontion (Marlyn Kane) and Skonaganleh:rá (Sylvia Maracle), "Our World: According to Osennontion and Skonaganleh:rá," *Canadian Woman Studies/Les Cahiers de la Femme* 10:2/3 (1989): 7–19, 11.

63. Medicine, "Hidden Half Lives," 5; and Lindy Trueblood, "Interview," in Reyer, *Cante Ohitika Win*, 50.

64. Kidwell, "What Would Pocahontas Think Now?" 150.

65. Trueblood, "Interview," in Reyer, *Cante Ohitika Win*, 50.

66. Ford, "Native American Women," 59.

67. In Canada the 1986 average income for Aboriginal people was $12,899 compared to $18,188 earned by the average non-Native Canadian. The 1990 U.S. census reported the median household income of Indians living on a reservation was $19,865, compared with the U.S. median of $30,056. Thirty-five percent of U.S. Natives live below the federal poverty level (Jo Ann Kauffman and Yvette K. Joseph-Fox, "American Indian and Alaska Native Women," in *Race, Gender, and Health*, ed. Marcia Bayne-Smith [Thousand Oaks, Calif.: Sage Publications, 1996], 71).

68. Osennontion and Skonaganleh:rá, "Our World," 14.

69. Katz, *Messengers of the Wind*; and Wall, *Wisdom's Daughters*.

70. Osennontion and Skonaganleh:rá, "Our World," 14.

30

"I'm Here, but I'm There"

The Meanings of Latina Transnational Motherhood

PIERRETTE HONDAGNEU-SOTELO

ERNESTINE AVILA

While mothering is generally understood as a practice that involves the preservation, nurturance, and training of children for adult life (Ruddick 1989), there are many contemporary variants distinguished by race, class, and culture (Collins 1994; Dill 1988, 1994; Glenn 1994). Latina immigrant women who work and reside in the United States while their children remain in their countries of origin constitute one variation in the organizational arrangements, meanings, and priorities of motherhood. We call this arrangement "transnational motherhood," and we explore how the meanings of motherhood are rearranged to accommodate these spatial and temporal separations. In the United States, there is a long legacy of Caribbean women and African American women from the South, leaving their children "back home" to seek work in the North. Since the early 1980s, thousands of Central American women, and increasing numbers of Mexican women, have migrated to the United States in search of jobs, many of them leaving their children behind with grandmothers, with other female kin, with the children's fathers, and sometimes with paid caregivers. In some cases, the separations of time and distance are substantial; 10 years may elapse before women are reunited with their children. In this article we confine our analysis to Latina transnational mothers currently employed in Los Angeles in paid domestic work, one of the most gendered and racialized occupations.[1] We examine how their meanings of motherhood shift in relation to the structures of late-20th-century global capitalism.

Motherhood is not biologically predetermined in any fixed way but is historically and socially constructed. Many factors set the stage for transnational motherhood. These factors include labor demand for Latina immigrant women in the United States, particularly in paid domestic work; civil war, national economic crises, and particular development strategies, along with tenuous and scarce job opportunities for women and men in Mexico and Central America; and the subsequent increasing numbers of female-headed households (although many transnational mothers are married). More interesting to us than the macro determinants of transnational motherhood, however, is the forging of new arrangements and meanings of motherhood.

Central American and Mexican women who leave their young children "back home" and come to the United States in search of employment are in the process

Pierrette Hondagneu-Sotelo and Ernestine Avila, "'I'm Here, but I'm There': The Meanings of Latina Transnational Motherhood," from *Gender & Society* 11, 548–571. Copyright 1997. Sage Publications. Reprinted by permission.

of actively, if not voluntarily, building alternative constructions of motherhood. Transnational motherhood contradicts both dominant U.S., White, middle-class models of motherhood, and most Latina ideological notions of motherhood. On the cusp of the millennium, transnational mothers and their families are blazing new terrain, spanning national borders, and improvising strategies for mothering. It is a brave odyssey, but one with deep costs. . . .

RETHINKING MOTHERHOOD

Feminist scholarship has long challenged monolithic notions of family and motherhood that relegate women to the domestic arena of private/public dichotomies and that rely on the ideological conflation of family, woman, reproduction, and nurturance (Collier and Yanagisako 1987, 36).[2] "Rethinking the family" prompts the rethinking of motherhood (Glenn 1994; Thorne and Yalom 1992), allowing us to see that the glorification and exaltation of isolationist, privatized mothering is historically and culturally specific.

The "cult of domesticity" is a cultural variant of motherhood, one made possible by the industrial revolution, by breadwinner husbands who have access to employers who pay a "family wage," and by particular configurations of global and national socioeconomic and racial inequalities. Working-class women of color in the United States have rarely had access to the economic security that permits a biological mother to be the only one exclusively involved with mothering during the children's early years (Collins 1994; Dill 1988, 1994; Glenn 1994). As Evelyn Nakano Glenn puts it, "Mothering is not just gendered, but also racialized" (1994, 7) and differentiated by class. Both historically and in the contemporary period, women lacking the resources that allow for exclusive, full-time, round-the-clock mothering rely on various arrangements to care for children. Sharing mothering responsibilities with female kin and friends as "other mothers" (Collins 1991), by "kin-scription" (Stack and Burton 1994), or by hiring child care (Uttal 1996) are widely used alternatives.

Women of color have always worked. Yet, many working women—including Latina women—hold the cultural prescription of solo mothering in the home as

an ideal. We believe this ideal is disseminated through cultural institutions of industrialization and urbanization, as well as from preindustrial, rural peasant arrangements that allow for women to work while tending to their children. It is not only White, middle-class ideology but also strong Latina/o traditions, cultural practices, and ideals—Catholicism, and the Virgin Madonna figure—that cast employment as oppositional to mothering. Cultural symbols that model maternal femininity, such as *La Virgen de Guadalupe*, and negative femininity, such as *La Llorona* and *La Malinche*, serve to control Mexican and Chicana women's conduct by prescribing idealized visions of motherhood.[3]

Culture, however, does not deterministically dictate what people do.[4] Many Latina women must work for pay, and many Latinas innovate income-earning strategies that allow them to simultaneously earn money and care for their children. They sew garments on industrial sewing machines at home (Fernández Kelly and Garcia 1990) and incorporate their children into informal vending to friends and neighbors, at swap meets, or on the sidewalks (Chinchilla and Hamilton 1996). They may perform agricultural work alongside their children or engage in seasonal work (Zavella 1987); or they may clean houses when their children are at school or alternatively, incorporate their daughters into paid house cleaning (Romero 1992, 1997). Engagement in "invisible employment" allows for urgently needed income and the maintenance of the ideal of privatized mothering. The middle-class model of mothering is predicated on mother–child isolation in the home, while women of color have often worked with their children in close proximity (Collins 1994), as in some of the examples listed above. In both cases, however, mothers are with their children. The long distances of time and space that separate transnational mothers from their children contrast sharply to both mother–child isolation in the home or mother–child integration in the workplace.

Performing domestic work for pay, especially in a live-in job, is often incompatible with providing primary care for one's own family and home (Glenn 1986; Rollins 1985; Romero 1992, 1997).[5] Transnational mothering, however, is neither exclusive to live-in domestic workers nor to single mothers. Many women continue with transnational mothering after they move into live-out paid domestic work, or into other jobs.

Women with income-earning husbands may also become transnational mothers.[6] The women we interviewed do not necessarily divert their mothering to the children and homes of their employers but instead reformulate their own mothering to accommodate spatial and temporal gulfs.

Like other immigrant workers, most transnational mothers came to the United States with the intention to stay for a finite period of time. But as time passes and economic need remains, prolonged stays evolve. Marxist-informed theory maintains that the separation of work life and family life constitutes the separation of labor maintenance costs from the labor reproduction costs (Burawoy 1976; Glenn 1986). According to this framework, Latina transnational mothers work to maintain themselves in the United States and to support their children—and reproduce the next generation of workers—in Mexico or Central America. One precursor to these arrangements is the mid-20th-century Bracero Program, which in effect legislatively mandated Mexican "absentee fathers" who came to work as contracted agricultural laborers in the United States. Other precursors, going back further in history, include the 18th- and 19th-centuries' coercive systems of labor, whereby African American slaves and Chinese sojourner laborers were denied the right to form residentially intact families (Dill 1988, 1994).

Transnational mothering is different from some of these other arrangements in that now women with young children are recruited for U.S. jobs that pay far less than a "family wage." When men come north and leave their families in Mexico—as they did during the Bracero Program and as many continue to do today—they are fulfilling familial obligations defined as breadwinning for the family. When women do so, they are embarking not only on an immigration journey but on a more radical gender-transformative odyssey. They are initiating separations of space and time from their communities of origin, homes, children, and—sometimes—husbands. In doing so, they must cope with stigma, guilt, and criticism from others. A second difference is that these women work primarily not in production of agricultural products or manufacturing but in reproductive labor, in paid domestic work, and/or vending. Performing paid reproductive work for pay—especially caring for other people's children—is not always compatible with taking daily care of one's own family. All of this raises questions about the meanings and variations of motherhood in the late 20th century.

TRANSNATIONAL MOTHERHOOD AND PAID DOMESTIC WORK

Just how widespread are transnational motherhood arrangements in paid domestic work? Of the 153 domestic workers surveyed, 75 percent had children. Contrary to the images of Latina immigrant women as breeders with large families—a dominant image used in the campaign to pass California's Proposition 187—about half (47 percent) of these women have only one or two children. More significant for our purposes is this finding: Forty percent of the women with children have at least one of their children "back home" in their country of origin.

Transnational motherhood arrangements are not exclusive to paid domestic work, but there are particular features about the way domestic work is organized that encourage temporal and spatial separations of a mother-employee and her children. Historically and in the contemporary period, paid domestic workers have had to limit or forfeit primary care of their families and homes to earn income by providing primary care to the families and homes of employers, who are privileged by race and class (Glenn 1986; Rollins 1985; Romero 1992). Paid domestic work is organized in various ways, and there is a clear relationship between the type of job arrangement women have and the likelihood of experiencing transnational family arrangements with their children. To understand the variations, it is necessary to explain how the employment is organized. Although there are variations within categories, we find it useful to employ a tripartite taxonomy of paid domestic work arrangements. This includes live-in and live-out nanny-housekeeper jobs and weekly housecleaning jobs.

Weekly house cleaners clean different houses on different days according to what Romero (1992) calls modernized "job work" arrangements. These contractual-like employee–employer relations often resemble those between customer and vendor, and they allow employees a degree of autonomy and scheduling flexibility. Weekly employees are generally paid a flat fee, and they work shorter hours and earn considerably higher hourly rates than do live-in or live-out domestic workers. By contrast, live-in domestic workers work and live in isolation from their own families and communities, sometimes in arrangements with feudal remnants (Glenn 1986). There are often no hourly parameters to their jobs, and as our survey results show, most live-in workers in Los Angeles earn below minimum wage. Live-out domestic workers also usually work as combination nanny-housekeepers, generally working for one household, but contrary to live-ins, they enter daily and return to their own home in the evening. Because of this, live-out workers better resemble industrial wage workers (Glenn 1986).

Live-in jobs are the least compatible with conventional mothering responsibilities. Only about half (16 out of 30) of live-ins surveyed have children, while 83 percent (53 out of 64) of live-outs and 77 percent (45 out of 59) of house cleaners do. As Table 1 shows, 82 percent of live-ins with children have at least one of their children in their country of origin. It is very difficult to work a live-in job when your children are in the United States. Employers who hire live-in workers do so because they generally want employees for jobs that may require round-the-clock service. As one owner of a domestic employment agency put it,

> They (employers) want a live-in to have somebody at their beck and call. They want the hours that are most difficult for them covered, which is like six thirty in the morning 'till eight when the kids go to school, and four to seven when the kids are home, and it's homework, bath, and dinner.

According to our survey, live-ins work an average of 64 hours per week. The best live-in worker, from an employer's perspective, is one without daily family obligations of her own. The workweek may consist of six very long workdays. These may span from dawn to midnight and may include overnight responsibilities with sleepless or sick children, making it virtually impossible for live-in workers to sustain daily contact with their own families. Although some employers do allow for their employees' children to live in as well (Romero 1996), this is rare. When it does occur, it is often fraught with special problems, and we discuss these in a subsequent section of this article. In fact, minimal family and mothering obligations are an informal job placement criterion for live-in workers.

Table 1 Domestic Workers: Wages, Hours Worked and Children's Country of Residence

	Live-ins (n = 30)	Live-outs (n = 64)	House cleaners (n = 59)
Mean hourly wage	$3.79	$5.90	$9.40
Mean hours worked per week	64	35	23
Domestic workers with children	(n = 16)	(n = 53)	(n = 45)
All children in the United States (%)	18	58	76
At least one child "back home"	82	42	24

Many of the agencies specializing in the placement of live-in nanny-housekeepers will not even refer a woman who has children in Los Angeles to interviews for live-in jobs. As one agency owner explained, "As a policy here, we will not knowingly place a nanny in a live-in job if she has young kids here." A job seeker in an employment agency waiting room acknowledged that she understood this job criterion more broadly, "You can't have a family, you can't have anyone (if you want a live-in job)."

The subminimum pay and the long hours for live-in workers also make it very difficult for these workers to have their children in the United States. Some live-in workers who have children in the same city as their place of employment hire their own nanny-housekeeper—often a much younger, female relative—to provide daily care for their children, as did Patricia, one of the interview respondents whom we discuss later in this article. Most live-ins, however, cannot afford this alternative; ninety-three percent of the live-ins surveyed earn below minimum wage (then $4.25 per hour). Many live-in workers cannot afford to bring their children to Los Angeles, but once their children are in the same city, most women try to leave live-in work to live with their children.

At the other end of the spectrum are the house cleaners that we surveyed, who earn substantially higher wages than live-ins (averaging $9.46 per hour as opposed to $3.79) and who work fewer hours per week than live-ins (23 as opposed to 64). We suspect that many house cleaners in Los Angeles make even higher earnings and work more hours per week, because we know that the survey undersampled women who drive their own cars to work and who speak English. The survey suggests that house cleaners appear to be the least likely to experience transnational spatial and temporal separations from their children.

Financial resources and job terms enhance house cleaners' abilities to bring their children to the United States. Weekly housecleaning is not a bottom-of-the-barrel job but rather an achievement. Breaking into housecleaning work is difficult because an employee needs to locate and secure several different employers. For this reason, relatively well-established women with more years of experience in the United States, who speak some English, who have a car, and who have job references predominate in weekly housecleaning. Women who are better established in the United States are also more likely to have their children here. The terms of weekly housecleaning employment—particularly the relatively fewer hours worked per week, scheduling flexibility, and relatively higher wages—allow them to live with, and care for, their children. So, it is not surprising that 76 percent of house cleaners who are mothers have their children in the United States.

Compared with live-ins and weekly cleaners, live-out nanny-housekeepers are at an intermediate level with respect to the likelihood of transnational motherhood. Forty-two percent of the live-out nanny-housekeepers who are mothers reported having at least one of their children in their country of origin. Live-out domestic workers, according to the survey, earn $5.90 per hour and work an average workweek of 35 hours. Their lower earnings, more regimented schedules, and longer workweeks than house cleaners, but higher earnings, shorter hours, and more scheduling flexibility than live-ins explain their intermediate incidence of transnational motherhood.

The Meanings of Transnational Motherhood

How do women transform the meaning of motherhood to fit immigration and employment? Being a transnational mother means more than being the mother to children raised in another country. It means forsaking deeply felt beliefs that biological mothers should raise their own children, and replacing that belief with new definitions of motherhood. The ideal of biological mothers raising their own children is widely held but is also widely broken at both ends of the class spectrum.

Wealthy elites have always relied on others—nannies, governesses, and boarding schools—to raise their children (Wrigley 1995), while poor, urban families often rely on kin and "othermother" (Collins 1991).

In Latin America, in large, peasant families, the eldest daughters are often in charge of the daily care of the younger children, and in situations of extreme poverty, children as young as five or six may be loaned or hired out to well-to-do families as "child-servants," sometimes called *criadas* (Gill 1994).[7] A middle-aged Mexican woman that we interviewed, now a weekly house cleaner, homeowner, and mother of five children, recalled her own experience as a child-servant in Mexico: "I started working in a house when I was 8 . . . they hardly let me eat any food. . . . It was terrible, but I had to work to help my mother with the rent." This recollection of her childhood experiences reminds us how our contemporary notions of motherhood are historically and socially circumscribed, and also correspond to the meanings we assign to childhood (Zelizer 1994).

This example also underlines how the expectation on the child to help financially support her mother required daily spatial and temporal separations of mother and child. There are, in fact, many transgressions of the mother–child symbiosis in practice—large families where older daughters care for younger siblings, child-servants who at an early age leave their mothers, children raised by paid nannies and other caregivers, and mothers who leave young children to seek employment—but these are fluid enough to sustain ideological adherence to the prescription that children should be raised exclusively by biological mothers. Long-term physical and temporal separation disrupts this notion. Transnational mothering radically rearranges mother–child interactions and requires a concomitant radical reshaping of the meanings and definitions of appropriate mothering.

Transnational mothers distinguish their version of motherhood from estrangement, child abandonment, or disowning. A youthful Salvadoran woman at the domestic employment waiting room reported that she had not seen her two eldest boys, now ages 14 and 15 and under the care of her own mother in El Salvador, since they were toddlers. Yet, she made it clear that this was different from putting a child up for adoption, a practice that she viewed negatively, as a form of child abandonment. Although she had been physically separated from her boys for more than a decade, she maintained her mothering ties and financial obligations to them by regularly sending home money. The exchange of letters, photos, and phone calls also helped to sustain the connection. Her physical absence did not signify emotional absence from her children. Another woman who remains intimately involved in the lives of her two daughters, now ages 17 and 21 in El Salvador, succinctly summed up this stance when she said, "I'm here, but I'm there." Over the phone, and through letters, she regularly reminds her daughters to take their vitamins, to never go to bed or to school on an empty stomach, and to use protection from pregnancy and sexually transmitted diseases if they engage in sexual relations with their boyfriends.

Transnational mothers fully understand and explain the conditions that prompt their situations. In particular, many Central American women recognize that the gendered employment demand in Los Angeles has produced transnational motherhood arrangements. These new mothering arrangements, they acknowledge, take shape despite strong beliefs that biological mothers should care for their own children. Emelia, a 49-year-old woman who left her five children in Guatemala nine years ago to join her husband in Los Angeles explained this changing relationship between family arrangements, migration, and job demand:

> One supposes that the mother must care for the children. A mother cannot so easily throw her children aside. So, in all families, the decision is that the man comes (to the U.S.) first. But now, since the man cannot find work here so easily, the woman comes first. Recently, women have been coming and the men staying.

A steady demand for live-in housekeepers means that Central American women may arrive in Los Angeles on a Friday and begin working Monday at a live-in job that provides at least some minimal accommodations. Meanwhile, her male counterpart may spend weeks or months before securing even casual day laborer jobs. While Emelia, formerly a homemaker who previously earned income in Guatemala by baking cakes and pastries in her home, expressed pain and sadness at not being with her children as they grew, she was also proud of her accomplishments. "My children," she stated, "recognize what I have been able to do for them."

Most transnational mothers, like many other immigrant workers, come to the United States with the intention to stay for a finite period of time, until they can pay off bills or raise the money for an investment in a house, their children's education, or a small business. Some of these women return to their countries of origin, but many stay. As time passes, and as their stays grow longer, some of the women eventually bring some or all of their children. Other women who stay at their U.S. jobs are adamant that they do not wish for their children to traverse the multiple hazards of adolescence in U.S. cities or to repeat the job experiences they themselves have had in the United States. One Salvadoran woman in the waiting room at the domestic employment agency—whose children had been raised on earnings predicated on her separation from them—put it this way:

> I've been here 19 years, I've got my legal papers and everything. But I'd have to be crazy to bring my children here. All of them have studied for a career, so why would I bring them here? To bus tables and earn minimum wage? So they won't have enough money for bus fare or food?

Who Is Taking Care of the Nanny's Children?

Transnational Central American and Mexican mothers may rely on various people to care for their children's daily, round-the-clock needs, but they prefer a close relative. The "other mothers" on which Latinas rely include their own mothers, *comadres* (co-godmothers) and other female kin, the children's fathers, and paid caregivers. Reliance on grandmothers and *comadres* for shared mothering is well established in Latina culture, and it is a practice that signifies a more collectivist, shared approach to mothering in contrast to a more individualistic, Anglo-American approach (Griswold del Castillo 1984; Segura and Pierce 1993). Perhaps this cultural legacy facilitates the emergence of transnational motherhood.

Transnational mothers express a strong preference for their own biological mother to serve as the primary caregiver. Here, the violation of the cultural preference for the biological mother is rehabilitated by reliance on the biological grandmother or by reliance on the ceremonially bound *comadres*. Clemencia, for example, left her three young children behind in Mexico, each with their respective *madrina,* or godmother.

Emelia left her five children, then ranging in ages from 6 to 16, under the care of her mother and sister in

Guatemala. As she spoke of the hardships faced by transnational mothers, she counted herself among the fortunate ones who did not need to leave the children alone with paid caregivers:

> One's mother is the only one who can really and truly care for your children. No one else can. . . . Women who aren't able to leave their children with their mother or with someone very special, they'll wire money to Guatemala and the people (caregivers) don't feed the children well. They don't buy the children clothes the mother would want. They take the money and the children suffer a lot.

Both Central American and Mexican women stated preferences for grandmothers as the ideal caregivers in situations that mandated the absence of the children's biological mother. These preferences seem to grow out of strategic availability, but these preferences assume cultural mandates. Velia, a Mexicana who hailed from the border town of Mexicali, improvised an employment strategy whereby she annually sent her three elementary school-age children to her mother in Mexicali for the summer vacation months. This allowed Velia, a single mother, to intensify her housecleaning jobs and save money on day care. But she also insisted that "if my children were with the woman next door (who babysits), I'd worry if they were eating well, or about men (coming to harass the girls). Having them with my mother allows me to work in peace." Another woman specified more narrowly, insisting that only maternal grandmothers could provide adequate caregiving. In a conversation in a park, a Salvadoran woman offered that a biological mother's mother was the one best suited to truly love and care for a child in the biological mother's absence. According to her, not even the paternal grandmother could be trusted to provide proper nurturance and care. Another Salvadoran woman, Maria, left her two daughters, then 14 and 17, at their paternal grandmother's home, but before departing for the United States, she trained her daughters to become self-sufficient in cooking, marketing, and budgeting money. Although she believes the paternal grandmother loves the girls, she did not trust the paternal grandmother enough to cook or administer the money that she would send her daughters.

Another variation in the preference for a biological relative as a caregiver is captured by the arrangement of Patricia, a 30-year-old Mexicana who came to the United States as a child and was working as a live-in, caring for an infant in one of southern California's affluent coastal residential areas. Her arrangement was different, as her daughters were all born, raised, and residing in the United States, but she lived apart from them during weekdays because of her live-in job. Her three daughters, ages 1 1/2, 6, and 11, stayed at their apartment near downtown Los Angeles under the care of their father and a paid nanny-housekeeper, Patricia's teenage cousin. Her paid caregiver was not an especially close relative, but she rationalized this arrangement by emphasizing that her husband, the girls' father, and therefore a biological relative, was with them during the week.

> Whenever I've worked like this, I've always had a person in charge of them also working as a live-in. She sleeps here the five days, but when my husband arrives he takes responsibility for them . . . When my husband arrives (from work) she (cousin/paid caregiver) goes to English class and he takes charge of the girls.

And another woman who did not have children of her own but who had worked as a nanny for her aunt stated that "as Hispanas, we don't believe bringing someone else in to care for our children." Again, the biological ties help sanction the shared child care arrangement.

New family fissures emerge for the transnational mother as she negotiates various aspects of the arrangement with her children, and with the "other mother" who provides daily care and supervision for the children. Any impulse to romanticize transnational motherhood is tempered by the sadness with which the women related their experiences and by the problems they sometimes encounter with their children and caregivers. A primary worry among transnational mothers is that their children are being neglected or abused in their absence. While there is a long legacy of child-servants being mistreated and physically beaten in Latin America, transnational mothers also worry that their own paid caregivers will harm or neglect their children. They worry that their children may not receive proper nourishment, schooling and educational support, and moral guidance. They may remain unsure as to whether their children are receiving the full financial support they send home. In some cases, their concerns are intensified by the eldest child or a nearby relative who is able to monitor and report the caregiver's transgression to the transnational mother.

Transnational mothers engage in emotion work and financial compensation to maintain a smoothly functioning relationship with the children's daily caregiver. Their efforts are not always successful, and when problems arise, they may return to visit if they can afford to do so. After not seeing her four children for seven years, Carolina abruptly quit her nanny job and returned to Guatemala in the spring of 1996 because she was concerned about one adolescent daughter's rebelliousness and about her mother-in-law's failing health. Carolina's husband remained in Los Angeles, and she was expected to return. Emelia, whose children were cared for by her mother and sister with the assistance of paid caregivers, regularly responded to her sister's reminders to send gifts, clothing, and small amounts of money to the paid caregivers. "If they are taking care of my children," she explained, "then I have to show my gratitude."

Some of these actions are instrumental. Transnational mothers know that they may increase the likelihood of their children receiving adequate care if they appropriately remunerate the caregivers and treat them with the consideration their work requires. In fact, they often express astonishment that their own Anglo employers fail to recognize this in relation to the nanny-housekeeper work that they perform. Some of the expressions of gratitude and gifts that they send to their children's caregivers appear to be genuinely disinterested and enhanced by the transnational mothers' empathy arising out of their own similar job circumstances. A Honduran woman, a former biology teacher, who had left her four sons with a paid caregiver, maintained that the treatment of nannies and housekeepers was much better in Honduras than in the United States, in part, because of different approaches to mothering:

> We're very different back there . . . We treat them (domestic workers) with a lot of affection and respect, and when they are taking care of our kids, even more so. The Americana, she is very egotistical. When the nanny loves her children, she gets jealous. Not us. We are appreciative when someone loves our children, and bathes, dresses, and feeds them as though they were their own.

These comments are clearly informed by the respondent's prior class status, as well as her simultaneous position as the employer of a paid nanny-housekeeper in Honduras and as a temporarily unemployed nanny-housekeeper in the United States. (She had been fired from her nanny-housekeeper job for not showing up on Memorial Day, which she erroneously believed was a work holiday.) Still, her comments underline the importance of showing appreciation and gratitude to the caregiver, in part, for the sake of the children's well-being.

Transnational mothers also worry about whether their children will get into trouble during adolescence or if they will transfer their allegiance and affection to the "other mother." In general, transnational mothers, like African American mothers who leave their children in the South to work up North (Stack and Burton 1994), believe that the person who cares for the children has the right to discipline. But when adolescent youths are paired with elderly grandmothers, or ineffective disciplinary figures, the mothers may need to intervene. Preadolescent and adolescent children who show signs of rebelliousness may be brought north because they are deemed unmanageable by their grandmothers or paid caregivers. Alternatively, teens who are in California may be sent back in hope that it will straighten them out, a practice that has resulted in the migration of Los Angeles–based delinquent youth gangs to Mexican and Central American towns. Another danger is that the child who has grown up without the transnational mother's presence may no longer respond to her authority. One woman at the domestic employment agency, who had recently brought her adolescent son to join her in California, reported that she had seen him at a bus stop, headed for the beach. When she demanded to know where he was going, he said something to the effect of "and who are you to tell me what to do?" After a verbal confrontation at the bus kiosk, she handed him $10. Perhaps the mother hoped that money will be a way to show caring and to advance a claim to parental authority.

Motherhood and Breadwinning

Milk, shoes, and schooling—these are the currency of transnational motherhood. Providing for children's sustenance, protecting their current well-being, and preparing them for the future are widely shared concerns of motherhood. Central American and Mexican women involved in transnational mothering attempt to ensure the present and future well-being of their children through U.S.

wage earning, and as we have seen, this requires long-term physical separation from their children.

For these women, the meanings of motherhood do not appear to be in a liminal stage. That is, they do not appear to be making a linear progression from a way of motherhood that involves daily, face-to-face caregiving toward one that is defined primarily through breadwinning. Rather than replacing caregiving with breadwinning definitions of motherhood, they appear to be expanding their definitions of motherhood to encompass breadwinning that may require long-term physical separations. For these women, a core belief is that they can best fulfill traditional caregiving responsibilities through income earning in the United States while their children remain "back home."

Transnational mothers continue to state that caregiving is a defining feature of their mothering experiences. They wish to provide their children with better nutrition, clothing, and schooling, and most of them are able to purchase these items with dollars earned in the United States. They recognize, however, that their transnational relationships incur painful costs. Transnational mothers worry about some of the negative effects on their children, but they also experience the absence of domestic family life as a deeply personal loss. Transnational mothers who primarily identified as homemakers before coming to the United States identified the loss of daily contact with family as a sacrifice ventured to financially support the children. As Emelia, who had previously earned some income by baking pastries and doing catering from her home in Guatemala, reflected,

> The money (earned in the U.S.) is worth five times more in Guatemala. My oldest daughter was then 16, and my youngest was 6 (when I left). Ay, it's terrible, terrible, but that's what happens to most women (transnational mothers) who are here. You sacrifice your family life (for labor migration).

Similarly, Carolina used the word *sacrifice* when discussing her family arrangement, claiming that her children "tell me that they appreciate us (parents), and the sacrifice that their papa and mama make for them. That is what they say."

The daily indignities of paid domestic work—low pay, subtle humiliations, not enough food to eat, invisibility (Glenn 1986; Rollins 1985; Romero 1992)—means that transnational mothers are not only stretching their

U.S.-earned dollars further by sending the money back home but also by leaving the children behind, they are providing special protection from the discrimination the children might receive in the United States. Gladys, who had four of her five children in El Salvador, acknowledged that her U.S. dollars went further in El Salvador. Although she missed seeing those four children grow up, she felt that in some ways, she had spared them the indignities to which she had exposed her youngest daughter, whom she brought to the United States at age 4 in 1988. Although her live-in employer had allowed the four-year-old to join the family residence, Gladys tearfully recalled how that employer had initially quarantined her daughter, insisting on seeing vaccination papers before allowing the girl to play with the employer's children. "I had to battle, really struggle," she recalled, "just to get enough food for her (to eat)." For Gladys, being together with her youngest daughter in the employer's home had entailed new emotional costs.

Patricia, the mother who was apart from her children only during the weekdays when she lived in with her employer, put forth an elastic definition of motherhood, one that included both meeting financial obligations and spending time with the children. Although her job involves different scheduling than most employed mothers, she shares views similar to those held by many working mothers:

> It's something you have to do, because you can't just stay seated at home because the bills accumulate and you have to find a way . . . I applied at many different places for work, like hospitals, as a receptionist—due to the experience I've had with computers working in shipping and receiving, things like that, but they never called me . . . One person can't pay all the bills.

Patricia emphasized that she believes motherhood also involves making an effort to spend time with the children. According to this criterion, she explained, most employers were deficient, while she was compliant. During the middle of the week, she explained, "I invent something, some excuse for her (the employer) to let me come home, even if I have to bring the (employer's) baby here with me . . . just to spend time with my kids."

Transnational mothers echoed these sentiments. Maria Elena, for example, whose 13-year-old son resided with his father in Mexico after she lost a custody battle, insisted that motherhood did not consist of only breadwinning: "You can't give love through money." According to Maria Elena, motherhood required an emotional presence and communication with a child. Like other transnational mothers, she explained how she maintained this connection despite the long-term geographic distance: "I came here, but we're not apart. We talk (by telephone) . . . I know (through telephone conversations) when my son is fine. I can tell when he is sad by the way he speaks." Like employed mothers everywhere, she insisted on a definition of motherhood that emphasized quality rather than quantity of time spent with the child: "I don't think that a good mother is one who is with her children at all times . . . It's the quality of time spent with the child." She spoke these words tearfully, reflecting the trauma of losing a custody battle with her ex-husband. Gladys also stated that being a mother involves both breadwinning and providing direction and guidance. "It's not just feeding them, or buying clothes for them. It's also educating them, preparing them to make good choices so they'll have a better future."

Transnational mothers seek to mesh caregiving and guidance with breadwinning. While breadwinning may require their long-term and long-distance separations from their children, they attempt to sustain family connections by showing emotional ties through letters, phone calls, and money sent home. If at all financially and logistically possible, they try to travel home to visit their children. They maintain their mothering responsibilities not only by earning money for their children's livelihood but also by communicating and advising across national borders, and across the boundaries that separate their children's place of residence from their own places of employment and residence.

Bonding with the Employers' Kids and Critiques of "Americana" Mothers

Some nanny-housekeepers develop very strong ties of affection with the children they care for during long workweeks. It is not unusual for nanny-housekeepers to be alone with these children during the workweek, with no one else with whom to talk or interact. The nannies, however, develop close emotional ties selectively, with some children, but not with others. For nanny-housekeepers who are transnational mothers, the loving daily caregiving that they cannot express

for their own children is sometimes transferred to their employers' children. Carolina, a Guatemalan woman with four children between the ages of 10 and 14 back home, maintained that she tried to treat the employers' children with the same affection that she had for her own children "because if you do not feel affection for children, you are not able to care for them well." When interviewed, however, she was caring for two-year-old triplets—for whom she expressed very little affection—but she recalled very longingly her fond feelings for a child at her last job, a child who vividly reminded her of her daughter, who was about the same age:

> When I saw that the young girl was lacking in affection, I began to get close to her and I saw that she appreciated that I would touch her, give her a kiss on the cheek . . . And then I felt consoled too, because I had someone to give love to. But, I would imagine that she was my daughter, ah? And then I would give pure love to her, and that brought her closer to me.

Another nanny-housekeeper recalled a little girl for whom she had developed strong bonds of affection, laughingly imitating how the preschooler, who could not pronounce the "f" sound, would say "you hurt my peelings, but I don't want to pight."

Other nanny-housekeepers reflected that painful experiences with abrupt job terminations had taught them not to transfer mother love to the children of their employers. Some of these women reported that they now remained very measured and guarded in their emotional closeness with the employers' children, so that they could protect themselves for the moment when that relationship might be abruptly severed.

> I love these children, but now I stop myself from becoming too close. Before, when my own children weren't here (in the United States), I gave all my love to the children I cared for (then toddler twins). That was my recompensation (for not being with my children). When the job ended, I hurt so much. I can't let that happen again.
>
> I love them, but not like they were my own children because they are not! They are not my kids! Because if I get to love them, and then I go, then I'm going to suffer like I did the last time. I don't want that.

Not all nanny-housekeepers bond tightly with the employers' children, but most of them are critical of what they perceive as the employers' neglectful parenting and mothering. Typically, they blame biological mothers (their employers) for substandard parenting. Carolina recalled advising the mother of the above-mentioned little girl, who reminded her of her own child, that the girl needed to receive more affection from her mother, whom she perceived as self-absorbed with physical fitness regimes. Carolina had also advised other employers on disciplining their children. Patricia also spoke adamantly on this topic, and she recalled with satisfaction that when she had advised her current employer to spend more than 15 minutes a day with the baby, the employer had been reduced to tears. By comparison to her employer's mothering, Patricia cited her own perseverance in going out of her way to visit her children during the week:

> If you really love your kids, you look for the time, you make time to spend with your kids . . . I work all week and for some reason I make excuses for her (employer) to let me come (home) . . . just to spend time with my kids.

Her rhetoric of comparative mothering is also inspired by the critique that many nanny-housekeepers have of female employers who may be out of the labor force but who employ nannies and hence do not spend time with their children.

> I love my kids, they don't. It's just like, excuse the word, shitting kids . . . What they prefer is to go to the salon, get their nails done, you know, go shopping, things like that. Even if they're home all day, they don't want to spend time with the kids because they're paying somebody to do that for them.

Curiously, she spoke as though her female employer is a wealthy woman of leisure, but in fact, both her current and past female employers are wealthy business executives who work long hours. Perhaps at this distance on the class spectrum, all class and racially privileged mothers look alike. "I work my butt off to get what I have," she observed, "and they don't have to work that much."

In some ways, transnational mothers who work as nanny-housekeepers cling to a more sentimentalized view of the employers' children than of their own. This strategy allows them to critique their employers, especially homemakers of privilege who are occupied with neither employment nor daily caregiving for their children. The Latina nannies appear to endorse motherhood as a full-time vocation in contexts of sufficient financial resources, but in contexts of financial hardship such as their own, they advocate more elastic definitions of motherhood, including forms that may include long spatial and temporal separations of mother and children.

As observers of late-20th-century U.S. families (Skolnick 1991; Stacey 1996) have noted, we live in an era wherein no one normative family arrangement predominates. Just as no one type of mothering unequivocally prevails in the White middle class, no singular mothering arrangement prevails among Latina immigrant women. In fact, the exigencies of contemporary immigration seem to multiply the variety of mothering arrangements. Through our research with Latina immigrant women who work as nannies, housekeepers, and house cleaners, we have encountered a broad range of mothering arrangements. Some Latinas migrate to the United States without their children to establish employment, and after some stability has been achieved, they may send for their children or they may work for a while to save money, and then return to their countries of origin. Other Latinas migrate and may postpone having children until they are financially established. Still others arrive with their children and may search for employment that allows them to live together with their children, and other Latinas may have sufficient financial support—from their husbands or kin—to stay home full-time with their children.

In the absence of a universal or at least widely shared mothering arrangement, there is tremendous uncertainty about what constitutes "good mothering," and transnational mothers must work hard to defend their choices. Some Latina nannies who have their children with them in the United States condemn transnational mothers as "bad women." One interview respondent, who was able to take her young daughter to work with her, claimed that she could never leave her daughter. For this woman, transnational mothers were not only bad mothers but also nannies who could not be trusted to adequately care for other people's children. As she said of an acquaintance, "This woman left her children (in Honduras) . . . she was taking care (of other people's children), and I said, 'Lord, who are they (the employers) leaving their children with if she did that with her own children!'"

Given the uncertainty of what is "good mothering," and to defend their integrity as mothers when others may criticize them, transnational mothers construct new scales for gauging the quality of mothering. By favorably comparing themselves with the negative models of mothering that they see in others—especially those that they are able to closely scrutinize in their employers' homes—transnational mothers create new definitions of good-mothering standards. At the same time, selectively developing motherlike ties with other people's children allows them to enjoy affectionate, face-to-face interactions that they cannot experience on a daily basis with their own children.

DISCUSSION: TRANSNATIONAL MOTHERHOOD

In California, with few exceptions, paid domestic work has become a Latina immigrant women's job. One observer has referred to these Latinas as "the new employable mothers" (Chang 1994), but taking on these wage labor duties often requires Latina workers to expand the frontiers of motherhood by leaving their own children for several years. While today there is a greater openness to accepting a plurality of mothering arrangements—single mothers, employed mothers, stay-at-home mothers, lesbian mothers, surrogate mothers, to name a few—even feminist discussions generally assume that mothers, by definition, will reside with their children.

Transnational mothering situations disrupt the notion of family in one place and break distinctively with what some commentators have referred to as the "epoxy glue" view of motherhood (Blum and Deussen 1996; Scheper-Hughes 1992). Latina transnational mothers are improvising new mothering arrangements that are borne out of women's financial struggles, played out in a new global arena, to provide the best future for themselves and their children. Like many other women of color and employed mothers, transnational mothers rely on an expanded and sometimes fluid number of family members and paid caregivers. Their caring circuits, however, span stretches of geography and time that are much wider than typical joint custody or "other mother" arrangements that are more closely bound, both spatially and temporally.

... Although not addressed directly in this article, the experiences of these mothers resonate with current major political issues. For example, transnational mothering resembles precisely what immigration restrictionists have advocated through California's Proposition 187 (Hondagneu-Sotelo 1995).[8] While proponents of Proposition 187 have never questioned California's reliance on low-waged Latino immigrant workers, this restrictionist policy calls for fully dehumanized immigrant workers, not workers with families and family needs (such as education and health services for children). In this respect, transnational mothering's externalization of the cost of labor reproduction to Mexico and Central America is a dream come true for the proponents of Proposition 187.

Contemporary transnational motherhood continues a long historical legacy of people of color being incorporated into the United States through coercive systems of labor that do not recognize family rights. As Bonnie Thornton Dill (1988), Evelyn Nakano Glenn (1986), and others have pointed out, slavery and contract labor systems were organized to maximize economic productivity and offered few supports to sustain family life. The job characteristics of paid domestic work, especially live-in work, virtually impose transnational motherhood for many Mexican and Central American women who have children of their own.

The ties of transnational motherhood suggest simultaneously the relative permeability of borders, as witnessed by the maintenance of family ties and the new meanings of motherhood, and the impermeability of nation-state borders. Ironically, just at the moment when free trade proponents and pundits celebrate globalization and transnationalism, and when "borderlands" and "border crossings" have become the metaphors of preference for describing a mind-boggling range of conditions, nation-state borders prove to be very real obstacles for many Mexican and Central American women who work in the United States and who, given the appropriate circumstances, wish to be with their children. While demanding the right for women workers to live with their children may provoke critiques of sentimentality, essentialism, and the glorification of motherhood, demanding the right for women workers to choose their own motherhood arrangements would be the beginning of truly just family and work policies, policies that address not only inequalities of gender but also inequalities of race, class, and citizenship status.

NOTES

1. No one knows the precise figures on the prevalence of transnational motherhood just as no one knows the myriad consequences for both mothers and their children. However, one indicator that hints at both the complex outcomes and the frequencies of these arrangements is that teachers and social workers in Los Angeles are becoming increasingly concerned about some of the deleterious effects of these mother–child separations and reunions. Many Central American women who made their way to Los Angeles in the early 1980s, fleeing civil wars and economic upheaval, pioneered transnational mothering, and some of them are now financially able to bring the children whom they left behind. These children, now in their early teen years, are confronting the triple trauma of simultaneously entering adolescence—with its own psychological upheavals; a new society—often in an inner-city environment that requires learning to navigate a new language, place and culture; and they are also entering families that do not look like the ones they knew before their mothers' departure, families with new siblings born in the United States, and new step-fathers or mothers' boyfriends.

2. Acknowledgment of the varieties of family and mothering has been fueled, in part, by research on the growing numbers of women-headed families, involving families of all races and socioeconomic levels—including Latina families in the United States and elsewhere (Baca Zinn 1989; Fernández Kelly and Garcia 1990), and by recognition that biological ties do not necessarily constitute family (Weston 1991).

3. *La Virgen de Guadalupe*, the indigenous virgin who appeared in 1531 to a young Indian boy and for whom a major basilica is built, provides the exemplary maternal model, *la mujer abnegada* (the self-effacing woman), who sacrifices all for her children and religious faith. *La Malinche*, the Aztec woman that served Cortes as a translator, a diplomat, and a mistress, and *La Llorona* (the weeping one), a legendary solitary, ghostlike figure reputed either to have been violently murdered by a jealous husband or to have herself murdered her children by drowning them, are the negative and despised models of femininity. Both are failed women because they have failed at motherhood. *La Malinche* is stigmatized as a traitor and a whore who collaborated with the Spanish conquerors, and *La Llorona* is the archetypal evil woman condemned to eternally suffer and weep for violating her role as a wife and a mother (Soto 1986).

4. A study comparing Mexicanas and Chicanas found that the latter are more favorably disposed to homemaker ideals than are Mexican-born women. This difference is explained by Chicanas' greater exposure to U.S. ideology that promotes the opposition of mothering and employment and to Mexicanas' integration of household and economy in Mexico (Segura 1994). While this dynamic may be partially responsible for this pattern, we suspect that Mexicanas may have higher rates of labor force participation because

they are also a self-selected group of Latinas; by and large, they come to the United States to work.

5. See Romero (1997) for a study focusing on the perspective of domestic workers' children. Although most respondents in this particular study were children of day workers, and none appear to have been children of transnational mothers, they still recall significant costs stemming from their mothers' occupation.

6. This seems to be more common among Central American women than Mexican women. Central American women may be more likely than are Mexican women to have their children in their country of origin, even if their husbands are living with them in the United States because of the multiple dangers and costs associated with undocumented travel from Central America to the United States. The civil wars of the 1980s, continuing violence and economic uncertainty, greater difficulties and costs associated with crossing multiple national borders, and stronger cultural legacies of socially sanctioned consensual unions may also contribute to this pattern for Central Americans.

7. According to interviews conducted with domestic workers in La Paz, Bolivia, in the late 1980s, 41 percent got their first job between the ages of 11 and 15, and one-third got their first job between the ages of 6 and 8. Some parents received half of the child-servant's salary (Gill 1994, 64). Similar arrangements prevailed in preindustrial, rural areas of the United States and Europe.

8. In November 1994, California voters passed Proposition 187, which legislates the denial of public school education, health care, and other public benefits to undocumented immigrants and their children. Although currently held up in the courts, the facility with which Proposition 187 passed in the California ballots rejuvenated anti-immigrant politics at a national level. It opened the door to new legislative measures in 1997 to deny public assistance to legal immigrants.

REFERENCES

Blum, Linda, and Theresa Deussen. 1996. Negotiating independent motherhood: Working-class African American women talk about marriage and motherhood. *Gender & Society* 10:199–211.

Burawoy, Michael. 1976. The functions and reproduction of migrant labor: Comparative material from Southern Africa and the United States. *American Journal of Sociology* 81:1050–87.

Chang, Grace. 1994. Undocumented Latinas: Welfare burdens or beasts of burden? *Socialist Review* 23:151–85.

Chinchilla, Norma Stoltz, and Nora Hamilton. 1996. Negotiating urban space: Latina workers in domestic work and street vending in Los Angeles. *Humboldt Journal of Social Relations* 22:25–35.

Collier, Jane Fishburne, and Sylvia Junko Yanagisako. 1987. *Gender and kinship: Essays toward a unified analysis.* Stanford, CA: Stanford University Press.

Collins, Patricia Hill. 1991. *Black feminist thought. Knowledge, consciousness, and the politics of empowerment.* New York: Routledge.

Collins, Patricia Hill. 1994. Shifting the center: Race, class, and feminist theorizing about motherhood. In *Mothering: Ideology, experience, and agency,* edited by Evelyn Nakano Glenn, Grace Chang, and Linda Rennie Forcey. New York: Routledge.

Dill, Bonnie Thornton. 1988. Our mothers' grief. Racial ethnic women and the maintenance of families. *Journal of Family History* 13:415–31.

Dill, Bonnie Thornton. 1994. Fictive kin, paper sons and compadrazgo: Women of color and the struggle for family survival. In *Women of color in U.S. society,* edited by Maxine Baca Zinn and Bonnie Thornton Dill. Philadelphia: Temple University Press.

Fernández Kelly, M. Patricia, and Anna Garcia. 1990. Power surrendered, power restored: The politics of work and family among Hispanic garment workers in California and Florida. In *Women, politics & change,* edited by Louise A. Tilly and Patricia Gurin. New York: Russell Sage.

Gill, Lesley. 1994. *Precarious dependencies: Gender-class and domestic service in Bolivia.* New York: Columbia University Press.

Glenn, Evelyn Nakano. 1986. *Issei, Nisei, warbride: Three generations of Japanese American women in domestic service.* Philadelphia: Temple University Press.

Glenn, Evelyn Nakano. 1994. Social constructions of mothering: A thematic overview. In *Mothering: Ideology, experience, and agency,* edited by Evelyn Nakano Glenn, Grace Chang, and Linda Rennie Forcey. New York: Routledge.

Griswold del Castillo, Richard. 1984. *La Familia: Chicano families in the urban Southwest, 1848 to the present.* Notre Dame, IN: University of Notre Dame Press.

Hondagneu-Sotelo, Pierrette. 1995. Women and children first: New directions in anti-immigrant politics. *Socialist Review* 25:169–90.

Rollins, Judith. 1985. *Between women: Domestics and their employers.* Philadelphia: Temple University Press.

Romero, Mary. 1992. *Maid in the U.S.A.* New York: Routledge.

Romero, Mary. 1996. Life as the maid's daughter: An exploration of the everyday boundaries of race, class and gender. In *Feminisms in the academy: Rethinking the disciplines,* edited by Abigail J. Steward and Donna Stanon. Ann Arbor: University of Michigan Press.

Romero, Mary. 1997. Who takes care of the maid's children? Exploring the costs of domestic service. In *Feminism*

and families, edited by Hilde L. Nelson. New York: Routledge.

Ruddick, Sara. 1989. *Maternal thinking: Toward a politics of peace.* Boston: Beacon.

Scheper-Hughes, Nancy. 1992. *Death without weeping: The violence of everyday life in Brazil.* Berkeley: University of California Press.

Segura, Denise A. 1994. Working at motherhood: Chicana and Mexican immigrant mothers and employment. In *Mothering: Ideology, experience, and agency,* edited by Evelyn Nakano Glenn, Grace Chang, and Linda Rennie Forcey. New York: Routledge.

Segura, Denise A., and Jennifer L. Pierce. 1993. Chicana/o family structure and gender personality: Chodorow, familism, and psychoanalytic sociology revisited. *Signs: Journal of Women in Culture and Society* 19:62–79.

Skolnick, Arlene S. 1991. *Embattled paradise: The American family in an age of uncertainty.* New York: Basic Books.

Soto, Shirlene. 1986. Tres modelos culturales: La Virgin de Guadalupe, la Malinche, y la Llorona. *Fem* (Mexico City), no. 48:13–16.

Stacey, Judith. 1996. *In the name of the family: Retaining family values in the postmodern age.* Boston: Beacon.

Stack, Carol B., and Linda M. Burton. 1994. Kinscripts: Reflections on family, generation, and culture. In *Mothering: Ideology, experience, and agency,* edited by Evelyn Nakano Glenn, Grace Chang, and Linda Rennie Forcey. New York: Routledge.

Thorne, Barrie, and Marilyn Yalom. 1992. *Rethinking the family: Some feminist questions.* Boston: Northeastern University Press.

Uttal, Lynet. 1996. Custodial care, surrogate care, and coordinated care: Employed mothers and the meaning of child care. *Gender & Society* 10:291–311.

Weston, Kath. 1991. *Families we choose: Lesbians, gays, kinship.* New York: Columbia University Press.

Wrigley. 1995. *Other people's children.* New York: Basic Books.

Zavella, Patricia. 1987. *Women's work and Chicano families: Cannery workers of the Santa Clara Valley.* Ithaca, NY: Cornell University Press.

Zelizer, Viviana. 1994. *Pricing the priceless child: The social value of children.* Princeton, NJ: Princeton University Press.

Zinn, Maxine Baca. 1989. Family, race and poverty in the eighties. *Signs: Journal of Women in Culture and Society* 14:856–69.

31

Falling Back into Gender?

Men's Narratives and Practices around First-time Fatherhood

TINA MILLER

BACKGROUND

A recurrent theme across scholarship on gender, equality and family lives is that new questions need to be asked or old ones reframed. This is as a consequence of the "stalled" and "slow processes of change" that continue to pattern the organization of paid work, domestic tasks and caring for children, discernible in gendered and unequal ways across western societies (Björnberg and Kollind, 2005: 139; Coltrane, 1996; Thébaud, 2010; Townsend, 2002). More particularly, in order to better understand how men as fathers occupy these spaces, the need to "open a conversation" and "talk about fathers differently" has been urged (Ruddick, 1997: 217). Similarly, the need to take account of "how and under what circumstances women and men reproduce, break or transgress gender norms" around the division of labour and family life has also been noted (Björnberg and Kollind, 2005: 126). These various calls are informed by, and emanate from, theoretical debates around "doing" and "undoing gender" and how these are practised in everyday life (West and Zimmerman, 1987). The need to focus in more *precise* ways on daily practices, which either reproduce or

reduce and so could be claimed to undo or dismantle gender differences, has become a more recent concern (Deutsch, 2007: 107; Risman, 2009). So too has the need to more critically engage with "issues of conflict, power and control" in social relations so as to move beyond explanations of doing and undoing gender only at the level of individual practices of agency (Fox, 2009: 32–3). Drawing on these calls for an analytic shift in explorations of gender, family contexts and individual practices, this article examines the "micro politics" of men's intentions and practices of anticipating and then doing early fathering, set against a slowly shifting societal landscape (Hearn and Pringle, 2006).

The data in this article are taken from a qualitative longitudinal study on transition to first-time fatherhood in the UK carried out between 2005 and 2009. Using interview schedules similar to those used in an earlier study on transition to motherhood (Miller, 2005, 2007), this study explores how a group of men make sense of their transition through a focus on the strands of discourse they draw on in narrating transition experiences. This longitudinal focus and juxtaposing of rich, qualitative data illuminates the dynamic relationship between intention, experience, masculine choices and

Reproduced by permission of SAGE Publications Ltd., London, Los Angeles, New Delhi, Singapore, and Washington DC, from Miller, Tina "Falling Back into Gender? Men's Narratives and Practices around First-Time Fatherhood." *Sociology* 45, Copyright © SAGE Publications 2011.

everyday practices. It enables glimpses of new possibilities to be discerned (undoing gender?) in the early
weeks following the birth as men become involved in
caring practices, but all too soon circumstances can
lead the new fathers (and so the new mothers) to fall
back into normative gendered behaviours. The unfolding data illuminate how a more precise focus on behaviours which constitute doing and undoing gender, over
time, can reveal men's *simultaneous* engagement in
such practices and also how masculine choices are constructed in this historically maternal arena. Although
the obduracy of "patriarchal habits" (Ruddick, 1997:
213) remains in evidence, so too are new possibilities
gleaned across the men's unfolding narratives. . . .

Contemporary western representations of involved
fatherhood emphasize greater emotional closeness in
men's "relationships with their children" and men's
sharing of "the joys and work of caregiving with mothers" (Wall and Arnold, 2007: 509). But at the outset it
is important to note the gendered and patriarchal struggles which have implicitly and explicitly configured
women's "historical connection to care giving" and
men's absence from it (Doucet, 2006: 29). Clearly, this
is not uncontested terrain. Choices and constraints in
relation to practices of agency across caring and paid
work are etched through with historical precedent and
behaviours which have been shaped in relation to patriarchy (Ruddick, 1997). In stark contrast to constructions of motherhood and women's lives, where much
has been simplistically universalized and taken for
granted, the relationship between men and fatherhood
is much less clear. It is little surprise then that even
where discourses of equality and policies to facilitate
shared caring exist (e.g. in Nordic countries), men are
still more able to determine "the terms for their engagement and participation" and caring continues to be
more generally viewed as a female practice: but change
and even "dissolution" of these arrangements are discernible too (Björnberg and Kollind, 2005: 128).

The shifting structural context invoked above refers
in the UK to the introduction in 2003 of two weeks'
paid paternity leave and the right for fathers to request
"flexible working." UK employers now have a "duty" to
consider parental leave requests and further consultation on the division of parental leave is currently underway.[1] Whilst the UK is many years behind other
northern European countries in relation to policies

focusing on gender equality in family life (e.g. Sweden),
it is ahead of other industrialized countries (e.g.
Ireland and the USA), where economic fatherhood—
"breadwinning"—continues to be more singularly emphasized (Townsend, 2002: 157). These policy changes
across Europe (coined the "Nordic turn") have coin-
cided with and/or prompted other shifts which make
more emotionally involved, hands-on fathering seem
both possible and plausible (Wall and Arnold, 2007:
509). For example, understandings of masculinity as
multiple and fluid and visions "of a new care-oriented
masculinity" and the "nurturing man" are discernible
in promotions of father involvement in caring (Johansson and Klinth, 2007: 2; Vuori, 2007). Related discourses have also provided (some) men with the
"discursive resources" to articulate new demands in
both public and private spheres (Hobson and Morgan,
2002: 14). Nevertheless, it is important to note the diversity which patterns men's lives as fathers and family
variability, and to note that just because policies which
can facilitate fathering involvement exist does not ensure
their take up (Deutsch, 2007: Duncan et al., 2010; Featherstone, 2009; Henwood and Proctor, 2003; Lupton and
Barclay, 1997).

Changes in men's lives as fathers clearly have implications for women's lives too. Mothering and fathering
are supremely gendered, contingent practices in which
parents can "struggle against their own patriarchal
habits" (Ruddick, 1997: 213). Ambiguity and ambivalence also inflect understandings and experiences of
maternal—and paternal—subjectivities and agency: so
too essentialist discourses which can be drawn upon in
sometimes perturbing ways to underscore and reinforce
gendered positions and/or inhibit change. Research
over many years has also concluded that men have
greater powers to choose the parameters of their involvement in family life (Gatrell, 2007; Lamb et al.,
1987; Townsend, 2002). Yet others have more recently
claimed that involvement in fatherhood is more a consequence of structural circumstances that are not of
men's choosing (Featherstone, 2009; Williams, 2008).
These apparently competing positions on masculine
practices of agency and power underpin fathering involvement and in practice both positions are tenable:
that men do have more power than women in many
areas that shape family lives, and that these have
become embedded and durable, within contexts and

discourses which for contemporary fathers may not be of their choosing (McNay, 2000; Marsiglio and Pleck, 2005). Moving to a context in which "creating equality in everyday life" becomes a possibility is then largely about "doing gender" differently according to Björn-berg and Kollind (2005: 131), or conversely can be indicative of "undoing gender" using Deutsch's definition of behaviours that *reduce* gender inequality with the potential to become "genderless" (2007: 122).

In this article I focus on the experiences of men who appear to conform to normative visions and associated discourses of those who constitute the good "involved" father. They are employed in skilled jobs that mostly position them as middle class and appear to afford them some job security. They are partnered (some are married) and they are becoming fathers at a culturally appropriate stage in an adult life-course and are the biological father of their (unborn) child(ren). They are white (several are in ethnically mixed partnerships or marriages) and heterosexual. The pregnancies are mostly planned and the men are eligible for statutory paternity leave and some talk of the possibility of "flexible working" and "family-friendly work place policies." Indeed, the men could be described as living and working in circumstances which more readily facilitate father involvement and opportunities to disrupt traditional normative behaviours around caring and paid work. But what can and do their accounts of intentions and subsequent practices of first-time fathering enable us to say about individual, masculinist practices of agency, caring and theorizations of doing and undoing gender? . . .

THE FINDINGS

Anticipating Fatherhood: Intentions and Imaginings

The data collected in the antenatal interviews largely centred on the men imagining what fathering might be like and their intentions to 'be there' for their child(ren)[2] in ways they envisage will be qualitatively different to their own fathers. All the men produce culturally recognizable accounts which resonate with ideals of the good, involved father. These include intentions to be involved in hands-on and emotional aspects of caring for their new babies, sharing (sometimes) equally all facets of caring except where breastfeeding is planned.

The men all talk about "sharing care," "caring," "supporting," "hoping to reduce work hours" and striking "a decent balance" between caring and paid work. Men can occupy a novel space at this time ("I mean it's such a new world for me" Stephen, aged 29 years), in which societal assumptions of them possessing any pre-existing, essentialist instincts are largely absent. Consequently, the "good" father-to-be is expected to avail himself of relevant information and attend birth preparation classes in order to demonstrate a commitment to being involved (Draper, 2002). The participants engage in these activities to a greater or lesser extent, usually orchestrated through their partner or wife. Reassurance is drawn from a belief that the mother of their child will instinctively know how to care for the baby once born, but anticipation of their own natural instincts—"a fantastic bond"—emerging at the birth is also evident across some of the antenatal narratives. Interestingly, here the men invoke recognizable elements of discourses of nature and biological predisposition more usually associated with maternal bodies. Mike, who is 32 years old and employed in car sales, draws upon these as he alludes to his novice status in this antenatal phase, "I don't know, I think I am only going to find out when it (the birth) happens and hopefully all the instincts, urges and so on kick in."

All the men planned to take either statutory paternity leave of two weeks and/or saved annual holiday. Yet, more fundamental change of work patterns, which might enable the "equal" or similar sharing that is envisaged, is not planned. From the outset, a false correlation is made which involves imagining that a physically small baby will make similarly small demands, which will only take up a small part of a 24-hour day. Imagining fathering involvement in this way makes it appear possible to equally share caring alongside other work commitments. Like all the fathers in the study, Sean, who is 33 years old, envisages being significantly involved in "everything really" related to caring for the baby:

> Initially the only thing that I think that I probably can't do is breastfeed [but] I don't see myself as not doing anything and in real terms Ella wanted to express (breast milk) anyway, so at some point I'll be able to feed . . . But I don't see that there's going to be anything particularly that I won't do. Obviously Ella hopefully will be having nine months (maternity

leave), so there will be far more that she'll be doing anyway, *just because of time*. [But] changing nappies and bathing, I'll try and have a go and get involved and do these things. (emphasis added)

Mike too talks of wanting to "be a part of it as much as I can" and expects to "wash it, bath it, change its nappy, feed it, wind it, burp it [and] whatever else kind of comes." But like other fathers his involvement will occur around his job:

I just want to be a part of it as much as I can, as I say I only work 10 minutes away so it's an ideal situation if something should happen, work is quite flexible in that you know I can go home and build up flexi time and those kind of things so I expect to be rolling my sleeves up.

Nick, aged 33 years, also anticipates being significantly involved in caring for his child. He thinks men's involvement has "changed hugely" with men now expected to be "a primary carer rather than a breadwinner." In the following extract Nick, who works in education, draws upon ideas of caring masculinities and uses language more readily associated with mothers to narrate his intentions: at some level these imply doing gender differently:

I've enjoyed looking after her (wife) and I think there's something about preparing for that primary care role . . . I think there's something there about preparing myself for that primary care, that actually it's going to be up to me to prepare a bottle or a meal or a feed or whatever for our child.

However, Nick is not actually planning to take on the "primary role" as in primary responsibility for the baby once it arrives as the term might imply, but rather primary responsibility is related to undertaking particular tasks, which correspond to those used to describe caring involvement by the other men. Ben, who is 32 years old and an artist, like Sean in an earlier extract, points to breastfeeding as one reason why caring for the baby cannot initially be completely equal, but he too talks of "sharing" the responsibility of care and "doing his bit":

Well obviously it is not equal because at first Hannah is going to have to take responsibility for feeding . . . [but] there is a sort of sense of shared, a very shared or a quality of kind of share in that responsibility so I will expect to be up in the night as well and just being

there for them both and hopefully doing my bit, doing whatever I can . . . I will have to be glad to do whatever needs doing.

What soon becomes clear from the men's antenatal accounts is how differently responsibilities of caring for a child are constructed and understood in relation to fathers and mothers, even though all imply at some level an intention to disrupt traditional patterns of caring. Hands-on caring is always described through supportive, and so secondary, task-based acts ("doing my bit"). The men can only imagine and articulate their caring involvement in this way *because* their wife or partner is already implicitly positioned (by them and in normative ideals of "good" mothering *and* parenting) as having primary responsibility. This leaves space for Dylan, a 33-year-old agricultural worker, to envisage fathering in the following way:

But right from the start I would like to negotiate work so that I have, you know, sort of a day off work a week to be a father and to do child care and to be involved and I would really like to be able to maintain that throughout my working life if possible.

It is almost unthinkable that a woman could articulate her anticipated mothering in this partial and episodic way (Miller, 2005, 2007). But masculine identities and associated practices of agency are not subsumed within paternal identities as men anticipate doing fathering, as is the case for women becoming mothers. It remains acceptable for men to talk of "fitting fathering in" and for work to remain dominant even where "priorities" are said to be shifting. But, consequently, men can feel marginalized if they want to take on the primary caring role as a full-time father (Doucet, 2006).

Across the antenatal interviews the men position themselves as wanting to be involved fathers and doing things differently; for example, being "more involved in doing tasks that would have been associated with a female role" (Mike). Although the participants engage a language more associated with maternal subjectivities— "instincts," "primary role," "bonding"—and acknowledge a changing cultural backdrop, deeply embedded ways of doing gender and performing masculinities remain powerful in how caring and child rearing is, or can be, contemplated and so articulated. The dilemma in attempting to do gender differently in a sphere infused with "pseudoscientific directives" and essentialist claims is to first overcome the legacy of these constructs and their continued impact on the binary categories of motherhood and fatherhood (Duden, 1993: 4). These categorizations both invoke particular constructions of masculine subjectivities and enable corresponding practices of agency. Involved fatherhood then assumes more emotional and hands-on care but economic provision is also a necessary dimension of being a good father. As William, who is 36 years old and employed in defence, acknowledges:

> What I'm trying to say is when I'm around the house I think I'll be quite sort of hands on but there'll be lots of time because of my job that I won't be around the house. I'll be making the money to kind of look after them.

Hegemonic constructions of worker identity as a prized dimension of masculinities and achievement sit at odds with constructions of more involved, emotional fatherhood that the men have also envisaged and which apparently herald new possibilities. Indeed, Nick inadvertently alludes to these alternative possibilities when asked how he thinks he will be involved in caring for his child:

> At this stage I want to say in everything. I want to take the baby [to] do the weekly shop, I want to be doing the bath and staying at home so that Shelley can go out and all that. I want everything to be divided down the middle. How much of that is a fantasy . . . in six months' time I might be very grateful that I'm the one who is going out to work.

What becomes clear through the antenatal interviews is that the men are aware of, and invoke, strands of discourse of involved fatherhood but in a context which is framed by an anticipated return to paid work. The men are able to discursively frame their intentions across a wider repertoire of masculine storylines than those available to women anticipating motherhood.

Early Fathering Experiences: The Early Postnatal Interviews

The birth of their first child(ren) provides the men with a different perspective from which to narrate their experiences as intentions are supplanted by experiences. The men are all present at the hospital births[3] and subsequently take between two and seven weeks' paternity

and/or holiday leave. Across all the men's early fathering narratives, recognizable aspects of involved fatherhood are prominently drawn upon. Additionally, some of the new fathers talk of having an "immediate bond" with their child and a "father instinct" kicking in, as aspects of caring are felt to have come "naturally." Emerging paternal identities are made visible and narrated through particular practices which are cited by the men. These include involvement in various hands-on activities across these very early weeks. Essentialist language (bonding and instincts) more traditionally assumed of mothers is also discursively invoked by the fathers, signalling a sense of more caring masculinities and the discursive resources (more emotional language) through which to narrate their feelings. There is a real sense of sharing and learning together through these early days and weeks following the birth and glimpses of the men engaged in caring relationships, which imply that traditional gendered patterns are being undone. Apart from breastfeeding, most of the men describe sharing "evenly"—which does not necessarily mean equally—in caring for the baby. Chris, a 28-year-old administrator, is surprised by how "kind of instinctive" he has found it:

> I thought also I wouldn't settle into it as quickly as I have . . . because I see babies as so delicate I thought I wouldn't necessarily know what to do with it. But it's kind of instinctive . . . Yeah I think we take it pretty evenly, I mean until Susan starts expressing (milk) then I can't do the feeding but I do everything else.

But economic necessity coupled with very different lengths of paternity and maternity leave in the UK means that the men's resumption of paid work lurks ominously—and inevitably—over this period. All the men either say, or imply, that the very early weeks together at home have been important in helping them to become "far more involved" with their new baby. For example, Ben describes these early weeks as having been a "special time," but:

> . . . then you go back to work and it is like you kind of have to sort of not withdraw from it, but I needed to get more sleep so Hannah dealt with the night a bit more and then whole days and then suddenly you become a bit more secondary [now] Hannah is kind of doing most of the care . . . Then when you go back [to work] suddenly the routine is continually changing so just when you think you have got it he is changing

because he is growing so quickly but I don't think I quite know all of the issues now . . . and quite quickly you can feel out of it.

Ben, like the other fathers, moves from a very intense period of shared involvement and establishing a caring relationship with the new baby, to quite quickly being back in the familiar world of paid work.

As the men resume their place in the public sphere and so spend less time enmeshed in the detail of their baby's (changing) needs, they can soon feel and become out of touch with "all of the issues" as "every time you think you're in a rhythm, the baby then changes" (Richard, a 39-year-old teacher). Importantly, becoming proficient at recognizing and meeting a growing baby's needs is a continually changing enterprise and so the men can feel they never (quite) become "expert" and/or primary in this relationship. Aspects of involvement are now much more mediated through their wife or partner who remains at home (on statutory maternity leave) as the primary carer and who, as Richard observes, are "immersed in the minutiae" of everyday caring. A consequence of this is that the mothers become more practised at recognizing and responding to their baby's needs. This in turn can be interpreted as evidence of "natural" maternal instincts and very soon the glimpses of engaged, involved masculine practices of caring, which signalled undoing gender, become a dim memory. Competing paternal and workplace demands lead the men to revise their earlier intentions.

Different constructions of maternity and paternity leave in the UK, shaped through policy and discourse, alongside the hard and exhausting work in the early weeks of new parenting, do not provide ideal conditions in which to try to disrupt or transgress normative parenting patterns: at times the path of least resistance may be to fall back upon these. By the time of the early postnatal interviews (between six and 12 weeks) most of the men have spent more time back at work than at home. Across the unfolding narratives, elements of the breadwinner discourse are more evident as they describe their inability to do caring in any way that approximates to "sharing evenly," as envisaged earlier. The men's narratives across the early postnatal period conclude with greater emphasis placed upon rationalizing their involvement in relation to economic provision and protection ("I've got to make sure there is food in the cupboard" and "the reason you work changes . . .

in some ways work becomes more important"). As Joe, a 28-year-old computer programmer, says "I'd like to think I'd want to look after her all the time, but going to work is quite nice, you get that break and, like I say, it's great for me." But even though antenatal intentions do not map out in the *sustained* ways anticipated in the early weeks, the men still participate in emotionally attuned, hands-on caring in the spaces around paid work in ways that, at times, undo aspects of traditionally gendered caring.

Returning to a New Normal: Later Fathering Episodes

The later postnatal interviews were carried out with the participants at between nine and 12 months and a further nine interviews were carried out at two years. The data collected across these interviews show that men have continued to be more involved in practical caring tasks than they recall their own fathers to have been. Some describe being more involved now that breastfeeding has mostly ceased and they can participate in feeding their older and more responsive baby. Some of the fathers now take on regular solo caring for their baby during evenings and weekends as wives and partners return to or take on part-time, paid work. This requires debriefing and "routines" are described by all the men as an essential aspect of being able to manage pockets of childcare. Two of the fathers have concentrated their regular working hours into a shorter working week in order to accommodate more childcare. Work outside the home remains a dominant theme, but one father, Nick, says he has tried to think differently about the hours spent at home and work: "There are forty hours of the week that I'm not here but there's however many hours that I am here and I'm trying to work more on that."

By the time of these later interviews, masculinist practices of gender and paternal subjectivities together with discursive and practical "choices" have become clearer. The mismatch between earlier antenatal intentions and how fathering has become practised on a daily basis is now apparent. Lack of time as a consequence of full-time work is clearly one factor, but there are other factors too. In the following extracts, Gus, a 28-year-old cook, and Richard reflect on the dimensions of their involvement at home and, in doing so, crucially illuminate a key variable in how gender is done—having choices. This is illustrated in the following extract as Gus talks about food preparation for his baby, which is something he says he should "probably do," but never does:

Because one of the roles that Anna, one of the things that she does regularly is she gets his food ready for the next day. So (she) goes into the freezer, gets out a cube of whatever, puts it all into pots . . . it's something she does every night. I should probably do it but I never do . . . I think you know it's always said to me that blokes can switch off a little bit more. I'm sure scientists have done tests on our brains which says you know blokes can just sort of switch off, whereas women when they go to bed, a million things can be going around their head.

Richard also alludes to what he sees as the practical differences between masculine and feminine caring behaviours:

I'm doing plenty of childcare [but] Ros is taking responsibility for her [the baby's] future orientation of where we will be going next . . . It's not that I couldn't do that but I'm not doing that . . . men can't do it because men can't do practical things, actually it is easy to feed the baby but knowing what to feed her tomorrow is difficult.

In these extracts the two fathers rationalize differences they have encountered in relation to caring practices, knowledge and responsibilities when compared to their wives or partners: and there were many examples across the data. Gus invokes a discourse of science ("tests") to support his actions, whilst implicitly alluding to his own agency. Differences in how gendered behaviours are conceptualized and how consequent choices operate and can be articulated and indeed accomplished—"It's not that I couldn't do that, but I'm not doing that"—are crystallized here.

Although the men are more involved in childcare activities than in their own fathers' generation, they are also able to exercise agency as fathers in ways not so readily available to women as mothers (especially in relation to the work place) and so have greater choices available to them (Miller, 2005, 2011). They also very quickly realize that paid work is more highly valued than the largely invisible ("feminine") work of child care at home ("it's more difficult to feel that this is something that is really important and good," Graham, a civil servant aged 32 years) and they have a wider range of discourses through which to narrate and situate their choices around work and home life. Research over many years has shown that "the importance of being a breadwinner to men's identities remains strong" (Thébaud, 2010: 334) and the men confirm this in these later interviews. Capturing these interconnected themes, Dylan confides:

. . . all sorts of issues have come up that I never dreamed, you know, the male pride thing, that is very important now, more so than ever . . . that my existence is justified . . . that I sort of still feel the need to prove myself perhaps in my job more than anything else and perhaps it's not valid or recognized to prove yourself as a father.

Dylan's concern about "the male pride thing" is culturally recognizable within hegemonic masculinities discourse and associated gendered behaviours. In the earlier study on motherhood, women also recognized and missed the "status thing" of paid work and many eventually returned to work, combining paid work and child care in a range of ways (Miller, 2005). But unlike the men, the new mothers could not invoke so acceptably "the female pride thing" and/or discourse of the breadwinner. They carefully constructed narratives to demonstrate an accomplishment of gender that showed they were not bad or negligent mothers just because they also worked.

FALLING BACK INTO GENDER?

The aim at the outset of this article was to more precisely explore and theorize dimensions of doing—and undoing—gender. The unfolding narratives have shown that whilst there has been a move away from "a single model of unified masculinities" and evidence of more emotional engagement in fathering practices, elements of hegemonic masculinity and associated subjectivities, agency and power endure (Connell, 1995; Morgan, 2002: 280). The *legacy* of patriarchal and structural arrangements, men's power and "choices" cannot be erased from contemporary debates or experiences even if there is a desire to do so. The men's intentions of doing gender differently, and so caring in ways that are described as "shared," "even" and sometimes "equal," is only partially realized. During the early weeks following the birth there are clear examples of "undoing gender" according to Deutsch's definition— "social interactions that reduce gender difference" (2007: 122). But the practices of undoing gender that are glimpsed do not occur in a vacuum. Both individual ("male pride thing") and structural ("then you go back to work") elements of patriarchal histories and habits, which have denoted accomplished performances of hegemonic masculinities, provide a potent backdrop against which new fathering is experienced, and which is different in significant ways to normative assumptions and associated practices around motherhood (Miller, 2011). The physical ("I never expected a child to be so much, to need so much attention or work or time," Dylan) and emotional ("it is more emotionally draining than I thought," Nick) aspects of becoming a father for the first time do not produce the circumstances in which more than partial and/or temporary disruptions of normative gendered behaviours are achieved. In spite of the best of intentions, returning to performances of selves which are recognizable, familiar and so also gendered can be a path of least resistance in this new world of parenthood. For example, Stephen, who is a 29-year-old IT worker, talks of having "got into a really nice relaxed routine" in which his wife "looks after the baby all day" so that he "can bring in [economic] support for the family" and also meet the payments on their "100% mortgage." Nevertheless, around this apparently traditionally configured arrangement, Stephen, like the other fathers, is also engaged in hands-on caring for his young son which is "quite a lot of hard work . . . not something . . . you can teach to somebody [but] something they'd have to pick up" and concludes by affirming that he has "got quite a strong bond with [his] son." Interestingly, Stephen here positions himself as both breadwinner and father who has learnt the skills of caring and has a "strong bond" with his child: a description of fathering which demonstrates doing gender in traditional ways and at times simultaneously doing—and discursively narrating— gender differently.

What the data show then is new fathers undoing and doing gender in partial and sometimes temporary ways that are also contingent and at times accomplished, simultaneously. Optimistically, caring involvement and practices which can reduce gender differences are both possible and evident in the data. But parenting contexts are complex because of how gender *has been* done and the persistence of patriarchal legacies and associated practices of agency. These continue to enable men to construct and justify caring responsibilities and obligations alongside work choices through the wider array of discourses available to them as men, fathers and workers. It "is no mean feat" then, as Björnberg and Kollind have observed, to overcome "fixed gender norms" or the "informal mechanisms that lead to different conditions or possibilities" for both men and women (2005: 131). The data show that opportunities to transgress normative ways of doing caring can also be refused or avoided ("I should probably do it but I never do"), and/or explained through apparent incompetence ("they're with each other all the time, Sophie's much better at picking up on cues and knowing when baby is needing food or tired"), and so normative patterns of gendered behaviours continue.

CONCLUSION

This article has explored the experiences of a predominately middle-class group of men as they become fathers for the first time. It has done so as policy on parental leave has become a key focus in political and popular debate. The longitudinal data show that whilst sharing, equality and sameness in caring for the unborn child is anticipated and narrated, there is a naivety about how this will be practically managed and *sustained* alongside full-time paid work. In part, the introduction of two weeks' paid paternity leave in the UK enables these men to envisage significant sharing in hands-on caring.

However, without any previous knowledge of the often hard, time-consuming and relational work of caring, their hopes and intentions turn out to have been overstated. Following the birth the men are indeed more actively and emotionally involved in caring for their child than they recall their own fathers to have been. But a return to paid work reveals the temporary nature of any intentions—or possibilities—to significantly disrupt normative gender behaviours. The fathers' caring practices are not forgotten, however, but rather are developed more slowly as they are squeezed into evenings and weekends: and their wives or partners quite quickly become more "expert" through practice. Importantly, the relational dimensions of caring and being continually attuned to a baby/child's changing needs are revealed across the data—and yet are currently absent from policy debates. Even though paternity leave is embraced, more durable elements of hegemonic masculinities in relation to (the value of) paid work and associated choices are eventually drawn upon as intentions and responsibilities are discursively reframed. Although the structural context in the UK in which fathering is accomplished is undergoing some change for some fathers, the pace and extent of change is slow and does not reflect the significant changes which have occurred in women's lives as mothers *and* workers. Whilst taking turns in aspects of caring, and glimpses of doing gender differently, are discernible across the data, for the most part it remains the mother who is left holding the baby.

NOTES

1. This consultation process has resulted in changes to maternity/paternity leave being introduced (April 2011). These changes allow fathers to share paid maternity leave up to a total of six months if certain criteria are met. http://www.direct.gov.uk/en/Parents/Moneyandworkentitlements/WorkAndFamilies/Paternityrightsintheworkplace/DG_190788

2. Two of the participants knew from antenatal ultrasound scans that their partners had conceived twins.

3. One of the 17 births was a planned home delivery.

REFERENCES

Björnberg U. and Kollind A. 2005. *Individualism and Families*. Abingdon: Routledge.

Bray I, Gunnell D. and Davey Smith D. 2006. Advanced paternal age: how old is too old? *Journal of Epidemiological Community Health* 60(10): 851–53.

Coltrane S. 1996. *Family Man*. New York: Oxford University Press.

Connell RW. 1995. *Masculinities*. Cambridge: Polity.

Dermott E. 2008. *Intimate Fatherhood*. London: Routledge.

Deutsch FM. 2007. Undoing gender. *Gender & Society* 21(1): 106–26.

Doucet A. 2006. *Do Men Mother?* Toronto: University of Toronto Press.

Draper J. 2002. 'It was a real good show': the ultrasound scan, fathers and the power of visual knowledge. *Sociology of Health and Illness* 24(6): 771–59.

Duden B. 1993. *Disembodying Women: Perspectives on Pregnancy and the Unborn*. Cambridge, MA: Harvard University Press.

Duncan S, Edwards R. and Alexander C. 2010. *Teenage Parenthood: What's the Problem?* London: Tufnell Press.

Featherstone B. 2009. *Contemporary Fathering*. Bristol: Policy Press.

Fox B 2009. *When Couples Become Parents. The Creation of Gender in the Transition to Parenthood*. Toronto: Toronto University Press.

Gatrell C. 2007. Whose child is it anyway? The negotiation of paternal entitlements within marriage. *The Sociological Review* 55(2): 352–72.

Gillies V. 2009. Understandings and experiences of involved fathering in the United Kingdom: exploring classed dimensions. *The Annals of the American Academy of Political and Social Science* 624(1): 49–60.

Hearn J. and Pringle K. 2006. *European Perspectives on Men and Masculinities: National and Transnational Approaches*. Basingstoke: Palgrave Macmillan.

Henwood K. and Proctor J. 2003. The "good father": reading men's accounts of paternal involvement during the transition to first-time fatherhood. *British Journal of Social Psychology* 42: 337–55.

Hobson B. and Morgan DHJ. 2002. Introduction. In: Hobson B. (ed.) *Making Men into Fathers: Men, Masculinities and the Social Politics of Fatherhood*. Cambridge: Cambridge University Press.

Johansson T. and Klinth R. 2007. Caring fathers. The ideology of gender and equality and masculine positions. *Men and Masculinities* 11(1): 42–62.

Jurik N.C. and Siemsen C. 2009. "Doing gender" as canon or agenda: a symposium on West and Zimmerman. *Gender & Society* 23(1): 72–5.

Knijn T. and Selten P. 2002. Transformations of fatherhoods: The Netherlands. In: Hobson B (ed.) *Making Men into Fathers: Men, Masculinities and the Social Politics of Fatherhood*. Cambridge: Cambridge University Press.

Lamb ME, Pleck JH, Charnov EL. and Levine JA. 1987. A biosocial perspective on paternal involvement. In: Lancaster J, Altmann J, Rossi A. and Sherrod L. (eds) *Parenting across the Lifespan: Biosocial Dimensions*. New York: Aldine de Gruyter.

Lupton D. and Barclay L. 1997. *Constructing Fatherhood: Discourses and Experiences*. London: SAGE.

McNay L. 2000. *Gender and Agency*. Cambridge: Polity.

Marsiglio W. and Pleck J. 2005. Fatherhood and masculinities. In: Kimmel S, Hearn J. and Connell RW. (eds) *Handbook of Studies on Men and Masculinities*. London: Sage.

Miller T. 2005. *Making Sense of Motherhood: A Narrative Approach*. Cambridge: Cambridge University Press.

Miller T. 2007. "Is this what motherhood is all about?" Weaving experiences and discourse through transition to first-time motherhood. *Gender & Society* 21(3): 337–58.

Miller T. 2011. *Making Sense of Fatherhood: Gender, Caring and Work*. Cambridge: Cambridge University Press.

Morgan DHJ. 2002. Epilogue. In: Hobson B (ed.) *Making Men into Fathers: Men, Masculinities and the Social Politics of Fatherhood*. Cambridge: Cambridge University Press.

O'Brien M. 2005. *Shared Caring: Bringing Fathers into the Frame*. Working Paper 18. Norwich: University of East Anglia.

Risman B. 2009. From doing to undoing: gender as we know it. *Gender & Society* 23: 81–4.

Ruddick S. 1997. The idea of fatherhood. In: Nelson HL (ed.) *Feminism and Families*. London: Routledge.

Shirani F. and Henwood K. 2011. Continuity and change in a qualitative longitudinal study of fatherhood: relevance without responsibility. *International Journal of Social Research Methodology* 14(1): 17–29.

Thébaud S. 2010. Masculinity, bargaining, and breadwinning: understanding men's housework in the cultural context of paid work. *Gender & Society* 24(3): 330–54.

Townsend N.W. 2002. *The Package Deal: Marriage, Work and Fatherhood in Men's Lives*. Philadelphia, PA: Temple University Press.

Vuori J. 2007. Men's choices and masculine duties. Fathers in expert discussions. *Men and Masculinities* 12(1): 45–72.

Wall G. and Arnold S. 2007. How involved is involved fathering? An exploration of the contemporary culture of fatherhood. *Gender & Society* 21(4): 508–26.

West C. and Zimmerman D. 1987. Doing gender. *Gender & Society* 1(2): 125–51.

Williams S. 2008. What is fatherhood? Searching for the reflexive father. *Sociology* 42(3): 487–502.

32

Why Gender Equality Stalled

By Stephanie Coontz

This week is the 50th anniversary of the publication of Betty Friedan's international best seller, "The Feminine Mystique," which has been widely credited with igniting the women's movement of the 1960s. Readers who return to this feminist classic today are often puzzled by the absence of concrete political proposals to change the status of women. But "The Feminine Mystique" had the impact it did because it focused on transforming women's personal consciousness.

In 1963, most Americans did not yet believe that gender equality was possible or even desirable. Conventional wisdom held that a woman could not pursue a career and still be a fulfilled wife or successful mother. Normal women, psychiatrists proclaimed, renounced all aspirations outside the home to meet their feminine need for dependence. In 1962, more than two-thirds of the women surveyed by University of Michigan researchers agreed that most important family decisions "should be made by the man of the house."

It was in this context that Friedan set out to transform the attitudes of women. Arguing that "the personal is political," feminists urged women to challenge the assumption, at work and at home, that women should always be the ones who make the coffee, watch over the children, pick up after men and serve the meals.

Over the next 30 years this emphasis on equalizing gender roles at home as well as at work produced a revolutionary transformation in Americans' attitudes. It was not instant. As late as 1977, two-thirds of Americans believed that it was "much better for everyone involved if the man is the achiever outside the home and the woman takes care of the home and family." By 1994, two-thirds of Americans rejected this notion.

But during the second half of the 1990s and first few years of the 2000s, the equality revolution seemed to stall. Between 1994 and 2004, the percentage of Americans preferring the male breadwinner/female homemaker family model actually rose to 40 percent from 34 percent. Between 1997 and 2007, the number of full-time working mothers who said they would prefer to work part time increased to 60 percent from 48 percent. In 1997, a quarter of stay-at-home mothers said full-time work would be ideal. By 2007, only 16 percent of stay-at-home mothers wanted to work full time.

Women's labor-force participation in the United States also leveled off in the second half of the 1990s, in contrast to its continued increase in most other countries. Gender desegregation of college majors and occupations slowed. And although single mothers continued to increase their hours of paid labor, there was a significant jump in the percentage of married women, especially married women with infants, who left the labor force. By 2004, a smaller percentage of

From *The New York Times*, February 16, 2013. © 2013 The New York Times Company. All rights reserved. Used by permission and protected by the Copyright Laws of the United States. The printing, copying, redistribution, or retransmission of the Content without express written permission is prohibited.

married women with children under 3 were in the labor force than in 1993.

Some people began to argue that feminism was not about furthering the equal involvement of men and women at home and work but simply about giving women the right to choose between pursuing a career and devoting themselves to full-time motherhood. A new emphasis on intensive mothering and attachment parenting helped justify the latter choice.

Anti-feminists welcomed this shift as a sign that most Americans did not want to push gender equality too far. And feminists, worried that they were seeing a resurgence of traditional gender roles and beliefs, embarked on a new round of consciousness-raising. Books with titles like "The Feminine Mistake" and "Get to Work" warned of the stiff penalties women paid for dropping out of the labor force, even for relatively brief periods. Cultural critics questioned the "Perfect Madness" of intensive mothering and helicopter parenting, noting the problems that resulted when, as Ms. Friedan had remarked about "housewifery," mothering "expands to fill the time available."

One study cautioned that nearly 30 percent of opt-out moms who wanted to rejoin the labor force were unable to do so, and of those who did return, only 40 percent landed full-time professional jobs. In "The Price of Motherhood," the journalist Ann Crittenden estimated that the typical college-educated woman lost more than $1 million dollars in lifetime earnings and forgone retirement benefits after she opted out.

Other feminists worried that the equation of feminism with an individual woman's choice to opt out of the work force undermined the movement's commitment to a larger vision of gender equity and justice. Joan Williams, the founding director of the Center for WorkLife Law at the University of California's Hastings College of the Law, argued that defining feminism as giving mothers the choice to stay home assumes that their partners have the responsibility to support them, and thus denies choice to fathers. The political theorist Lori Marso noted that emphasizing personal choice ignores the millions of women without a partner who can support them.

These are all important points. But they can sound pretty abstract to men and women who are stuck between a rock and a hard place when it comes to arranging their work and family lives. For more than two decades the demands and hours of work have been intensifying. Yet progress in adopting family-friendly work practices and social policies has proceeded at a glacial pace.

Today the main barriers to further progress toward gender equity no longer lie in people's personal attitudes and relationships. Instead, structural impediments prevent people from acting on their egalitarian values, forcing men and women into personal accommodations and rationalizations that do not reflect their preferences. The gender revolution is not in a stall. It has hit a wall.

In today's political climate, it's startling to remember that 80 years ago, in 1933, the Senate overwhelmingly voted to establish a 30-hour workweek. The bill failed in the House, but five years later the Fair Labor Standards Act of 1938 gave Americans a statutory 40-hour workweek. By the 1960s, American workers spent less time on the job than their counterparts in Europe and Japan.

Between 1990 and 2000, however, average annual work hours for employed Americans increased. By 2000, the United States had outstripped Japan—the former leader of the work pack—in the hours devoted to paid work. Today, almost 40 percent of men in professional jobs work 50 or more hours a week, as do almost a quarter of men in middle-income occupations. Individuals in lower-income and less-skilled jobs work fewer hours, but they are more likely to experience frequent changes in shifts, mandatory overtime on short notice, and nonstandard hours. And many low-income workers are forced to work two jobs to get by. When we look at dual-earner couples, the workload becomes even more daunting. As of 2000, the average dual-earner couple worked a combined 82 hours a week, while almost 15 percent of married couples had a joint workweek of 100 hours or more.

Astonishingly, despite the increased workload of families, and even though 70 percent of American children now live in households where every adult in the home is employed, in the past 20 years the United States has not passed any major federal initiative to help workers accommodate their family and work demands. The Family and Medical Leave Act of 1993 guaranteed covered workers up to 12 weeks unpaid leave after a child's birth or adoption or in case of a family illness. Although only about half the total work force was eligible, it seemed a promising start. But aside from the belated requirement of the new Affordable Care Act that nursing mothers be given a private space at work to pump breast milk, the F.M.L.A. turned out to be the inadequate end.

Meanwhile, since 1990 other nations with comparable resources have implemented a comprehensive agenda of "work–family reconciliation" acts. As a result, when the United States' work–family policies are compared with those of countries at similar levels of economic and political development, the United States comes in dead last.

Out of nearly 200 countries studied by Jody Heymann, dean of the school of public health at the University of California, Los Angeles, and her team of researchers for their new book, "Children's Chances," 180 now offer guaranteed paid leave to new mothers, and 81 offer paid leave to fathers. They found that 175 mandate paid annual leave for workers, and 162 limit the maximum length of the workweek. The United States offers none of these protections.

A 1997 European Union directive prohibits employers from paying part-time workers lower hourly rates than full-time workers, excluding them from pension plans or limiting paid leaves to full-time workers. By contrast, American workers who reduce hours for family reasons typically lose their benefits and take an hourly wage cut.

Is it any surprise that American workers express higher levels of work–family conflict than workers in any of our European counterparts? Or that women's labor-force participation has been overtaken? In 1990, the United States ranked sixth in female labor participation among 22 countries in the Organization for Economic Cooperation and Development, which is made up of most of the globe's wealthier countries. By 2010, according to an economic research paper by Cornell researchers Francine Blau and Lawrence Kahn, released last month, we had fallen to 17th place, with about 30 percent of that decline a direct result of our failure to keep pace with other countries' family-friendly work policies. American women have not abandoned the desire to combine work and family. Far from it. According to the Pew Research Center, in 1997, 56 percent of women ages 18 to 34 and 26 percent of middle-aged and older women said that, in addition to having a family, being successful in a high-paying career or profession was "very important" or "one of the most important things" in their lives. By 2011, fully two-thirds of the younger women and 42 percent of the older ones expressed that sentiment.

Nor have men given up the ideal of gender equity. A 2011 study by the Center for Work and Family at Boston College found that 65 percent of the fathers they interviewed felt that mothers and fathers should provide equal amounts of caregiving for their children. And in a 2010 Pew poll, 72 percent of both women and men between 18 and 29 agreed that the best marriage is one in which husband and wife both work and both take care of the house.

But when people are caught between the hard place of bad working conditions and the rock wall of politicians' resistance to family-friendly reforms, it is hard to live up to such aspirations. The Boston College study found that only 30 percent of the fathers who wanted to share child care equally with their wives actually did so, a gap that helps explain why American men today report higher levels of work–family conflict than women. Under the circumstances, how likely is it that the young adults surveyed by Pew will meet their goal of sharing breadwinning and caregiving?

The answer is suggested by the findings of the New York University sociologist Kathleen Gerson in the interviews she did for her 2010 book, "The Unfinished Revolution: Coming of Age in a New Era of Gender, Work, and Family." Eighty percent of the women and 70 percent of the men Ms. Gerson interviewed said they wanted an egalitarian relationship that allowed them to share breadwinning and family care. But when asked what they would do if this was not possible, they described a variety of "fallback" positions. While most of the women wanted to continue paid employment, the majority of men said that if they could not achieve their egalitarian ideal they expected their partner to assume primary responsibility for parenting so they could focus on work.

And that is how it usually works out. When family and work obligations collide, mothers remain much more likely than fathers to cut back or drop out of work. But unlike the situation in the 1960s, this is not because most people believe this is the preferable order of things. Rather, it is often a reasonable response to the fact that our political and economic institutions lag way behind our personal ideals.

Women are still paid less than men at every educational level and in every job category. They are less likely than men to hold jobs that offer flexibility or family-friendly benefits. When they become mothers, they face more scrutiny and prejudice on the job than fathers do.

So, especially when women are married to men who work long hours, it often seems to both partners that they have no choice. Female professionals are twice as likely to quit work as other married mothers when their husbands work 50 hours or more a week and more than three times more likely to quit when their husbands work 60 hours or more.

The sociologist Pamela Stone studied a group of mothers who had made these decisions. Typically, she found, they phrased their decision in terms of a preference. But when they explained their "decision-making process," it became clear that most had made the "choice" to quit work only as a last resort—when they could not get the flexible hours or part-time work they wanted, when their husbands would not or could not cut back their hours, and when they began to feel that their employers were hostile to their concerns. Under those conditions, Professor Stone notes, what was really a workplace problem for families became a private problem for women.

This is where the political gets really personal. When people are forced to behave in ways that contradict their ideals, they often undergo what sociologists call a "values stretch"—watering down their original expectations and goals to accommodate the things they have to do to get by. This behavior is especially likely if holding on to the original values would exacerbate tensions in the relationships they depend on.

In their years of helping couples make the transition from partners to parents, the psychologists Philip and Carolyn Cowan have found that tensions increase when a couple backslide into more traditional roles than they originally desired. The woman resents that she is not getting the shared child care she expected and envies her husband's social networks outside the home. The husband feels hurt that his wife isn't more grateful for the sacrifices he is making by working more hours so she can stay home. When you can't change what's bothering you, one typical response is to convince yourself that it doesn't actually bother you. So couples often create a family myth about why they made these choices, why it has turned out for the best, and why they are still equal in their hearts even if they are not sharing the kind of life they first envisioned.

Under present conditions, the intense consciousness raising about the "rightness" of personal choices that worked so well in the early days of the women's movement will end up escalating the divisive finger-pointing that stands in the way of political reform.

Our goal should be to develop work–life policies that enable people to put their gender values into practice. So let's stop arguing about the hard choices women make and help more women and men avoid such hard choices. To do that, we must stop seeing work–family policy as a women's issue and start seeing it as a human rights issue that affects parents, children, partners, singles and elders. Feminists should certainly support this campaign. But they don't need to own it.

33

Separating the Men from the Moms

The Making of Adult Gender Segregation in Youth Sports

Michael A. Messner

Suzel Bozada-Deas

In volunteer work, just as in many families and workplaces, gender divisions are pervasive and persistent. Women are often expected to do the work of caring for others' emotions and daily needs. Women's volunteer labor is routinely devalued in much the same ways that housework and childcare are devalued in the home and women's clerical and other support work is devalued in the professions (Hook 2004). Similarly, men tend to do the instrumental work of public leadership, just as they do in the family and the workplace, and their informal work is valued accordingly.

This article examines the social construction of adult gender divisions of labor in a community volunteer activity, youth sports. A few scholars have examined women's invisible labor in sports (Boyle & McKay 1995). In her study of a Little League Baseball league, Grasmuck (2005) estimates that the 111 league administrators, head coaches, and assistant coaches (mostly men) contribute a total of 33,330 hours of volunteer labor in a season—an average of about 300 hours per person. Much of the work women do in youth sports is behind-the-scenes support that is less visible than coaching (Thompson 1999). In a study of Little League Baseball in Texas, Chafetz and Kotarba (1999, 48–49)

observed that "team mothers" in this "upper middle class, 'Yuppie' Texas community" do gender in ways that result in "the re-creation and strengthening of the community's collective identity as a place where, among other things, women are primarily mothers to their sons." As yet, no study has focused on how this gender divide among adults in youth sports happens. How do most men become coaches, while most women become "team moms"? How do adult gender divisions of labor in youth sports connect with commonsense notions about divisions between women and men in families and workplaces? This is important: Millions of children play community-based youth sports every year, and these athletic activities are a key part of the daily lives of many families. It is also important for scholars of gender—studying segregation in this context can reveal much about how gender divisions are created and sustained in the course of everyday life.

COACHES AND "TEAM MOMS"

In 1995, when we (the first author, Mike, and his family) arrived at our six-year-old son's first soccer practice, we

Michael A. Messner & Suzel Bozada-Deas, *Gender & Society 23*. Copyright © 2009 Sage Publications. Reprinted by permission of Sage Publications.

were delighted to learn that his coach was a woman. Coach Karen, a mother in her mid-30s, had grown up playing lots of sports. She was tall, confident, and athletic, and the kids responded well to her leadership. It seemed to be a new and different world than the one we grew up in. But during the next decade, as our two sons played a few more seasons of soccer, two years of youth basketball, and more than a decade of baseball, they never had another woman head coach. It is not that women were not contributing to the kids' teams. All of the "team parents" (often called "team moms")—parent volunteers who did the behind-the-scenes work of phone-calling, organizing weekly snack schedules and team parties, collecting money for gifts for the coaches, and so on—were women. And occasionally, a team had a woman assistant coach. But women head coaches were few and far between.

In 1999, we started keeping track of the numbers of women and men head coaches in Roseville's[1] annual American Youth Soccer Organization (AYSO) and Little League Baseball/Softball (LLB/S) yearbooks we received at the end of each season. The yearbooks revealed that from 1999 to 2007, only 13.4 percent of 1,490 AYSO teams had women head coaches. The numbers were even lower for Little League Baseball and Softball; only 5.9 percent of 538 teams were managed by women. In both AYSO and LLB/S, women coaches were clustered in the younger kids' teams (ages five to eight) and in coaching girls. Boys—and especially boys older than age 10—almost never had women coaches. These low numbers are surprising for several reasons. First, unlike during the 1950s and 1960s, when there were almost no opportunities for girls to play sports, today, millions of girls participate in organized soccer, baseball, softball, basketball, and other sports. With this demographic shift in youth sports, we expected that the gender division of labor among parents would have shifted as well. Second, today's mothers in the United States came of age during and after the 1972 institution of Title IX and are part of the generation that ignited the booming growth of female athletic participation. We wondered how it happened that these women did not make a neat transition from their own active sports participation into coaching their own kids. Third, women in Roseville outnumber men significantly in every volunteer activity having to do with kids, such as the Parent and Teacher

Association (PTA), Scouts, and school special events. Coaching youth sports is the great exception to this rule. Sport has changed over the past 30 years, from a world set up almost exclusively by and for boys and men to one that is moving substantially (although incompletely) toward gender equity (Messner 2002). Yet, men dominate the very public on-field volunteer leadership positions in community youth sports.

This article is part of a larger study of gender in adult volunteering in two youth sports programs in a small independent suburb of Los Angeles that we call Roseville. Both of the sports leagues are local affiliates of massive national and international organizations. LLB/S and AYSO offer an interesting contrast in youth sports organizations, especially with respect to gender. Little League Baseball began in 1938 and for its first 36 years was an organization set up exclusively for boys. When forced against its will by a court decision in 1974 to include girls, Little League responded by creating a separate softball league into which girls continue to be tracked. Today, LLB/S is an organization that boasts 2.7 million child participants worldwide, 2.1 million of them in the United States. There are 176,786 teams in the program, 153,422 of them in baseball and 23,364 in softball. Little League stays afloat through the labor of approximately 1 million volunteers.

When AYSO started in 1964, it was exclusively for boys, but by 1971, girls' teams had been introduced, Thus, over the years, the vast majority of people who have participated in AYSO have experienced it as an organization set up for boys *and* girls. AYSO remains today mostly a U.S. organization, with more than 650,000 players on more than 50,000 teams. The national AYSO office employs 50 paid staff members, but like LLB/S, AYSO is an organization largely driven by the labor of volunteers, with roughly 250,000 volunteer coaches, team parents, and referees.

The differently gendered history of these two organizations offers hints as to the origins of the differences we see; there are more women head coaches in soccer than in baseball. Connell (1987) argues that every social institution—including the economy, the military, schools, families, or sport—has a "gender regime," which is defined as the current state of play of gender relations in the institution. We can begin to understand an institution's gender regime by measuring and analyzing the gender divisions of labor and power in the organization (i.e., what kinds of jobs are done by women and men, who has the authority, etc.). The idea that a gender regime is characterized by a "state of play" is a way to get beyond static measurements that result from a quick snapshot of an organizational pyramid and understanding instead that organizations are always being created by people's actions and discourse (Britton 2000). These actions often result in an organizational inertia that reproduces gender divisions and hierarchies; however, organizations are also subject to gradual—or occasionally even rapid—change.

Institutional gender regimes are connected with other gender regimes. Put another way, people in their daily lives routinely move in, out, and across different gender regimes—families, workplaces, schools, places of worship, and community activities such as youth sports. Their actions within a particular gender regime—for instance, the choice to volunteer to coach a youth soccer team—and the meanings they construct around these actions are constrained and enabled by their positions, responsibilities, and experiences in other institutional contexts. We will show how individual decisions to coach or to serve as team parents occur largely through nonreflexive, patterned interactions that are infused with an ascendant gender ideology that we call "soft essentialism." These interactions occur at the nexus of the three gender regimes of community youth sports, families, and workplaces.

RESEARCH METHODS

The low numbers of women coaches in Roseville AYSO and LLB/S and the fact that nearly all of the team parents are women gave us a statistical picture of persistent gender segregation. But simply trotting out these numbers couldn't tell us *how* this picture is drawn. We wanted to understand the current state of play of the adult gender regime of youth sports, so we developed a study based on the following question: What are the social processes that sustain this gender segregation? And by extension, we wanted to explore another question: What is happening that might serve to destabilize and possibly change this gender segregation? In other words, are there ways to see and understand the internal mechanisms—the face-to-face interactions as well as the meaning-making

processes—that constitute the "state of play" of the gender regime of community youth sports?

Questions about social processes—how people, in their routine daily interactions, reproduce (and occasionally challenge) patterned social relations—are best addressed using a combination of qualitative methods. Between 2003 and 2007, we systematically explored the gender dynamics of volunteer coaches in Roseville by deploying several methods of data collection. First, we conducted a content analysis of nine years (1999–2007) of Roseville's AYSO and LLB/S yearbooks (magazine-length documents compiled annually by the leagues, containing team photos as well as names and photos of coaches and managers). The yearbook data on the numbers and placement of women and men coaches provides the statistical backdrop for our study of the social processes of gender and coaching that we summarized above.

Second, we conducted field observations of numerous girls' and boys' soccer, baseball, and softball practices and games. We participated in clinics that were set up to train soccer and baseball coaches and a clinic to train soccer referees. We observed annual baseball and softball tryouts, a managers' baseball "draft," and several annual opening ceremonies for AYSO and LLB/S.

Third, Mike conducted several seasons of participant observation—as a volunteer assistant coach or as scorekeeper—of his son's Little League Baseball teams, ranging from six- and seven-year old co-ed T-ball teams to 13- and 14-year-old boys' baseball teams. These positions gave him observational vantage points near the coaches from which he could jot down short notes that he would later develop into longer field notes. Mike's "insider" role as a community member and a father of kids in these sports leagues allowed him easy access. He always informed the coaches of his sons' teams that he was doing a study, but like many who conduct participant observation, it seemed that his role as researcher was frequently "forgotten" by others and that he was most often seen as a father, an assistant coach, or a scorekeeper.

Fourth, we conducted 50 in-depth interviews with women and men volunteers—mostly head soccer coaches and baseball or softball managers of both boys' and girls' teams but also a small number of assistant coaches and team parents. The interviewees were selected through a snowball sampling method.

All but three of those interviewed were parents of children playing in the Roseville soccer, baseball, or softball leagues. Although there were far more men coaches than women coaches from whom to choose, we purposely interviewed roughly equal numbers of women (24) and men (26) coaches. Two of the women coaches were single with no children, one was a divorced single mother, one was a mother living with her female partner, and the rest were mothers living with a male spouse. One of the men coaches was single with no children, two were divorced fathers, and the rest were fathers living with a female spouse. Most of the men interviewed were in their 40s, with an average age of 45. The women were, on average, 39 years old. Nearly all of the interviewees were college educated, living in professional-class families. They self-identified ethnically as 68 percent white, 18 percent Hispanic, 4 percent Asian American, and 10 percent biracial or other. This ethnic breakdown of our interviewees reflects roughly the apparent ethnic composition of coaches in the annual yearbooks. However, since whites are only 44 percent and Asian Americans are 27 percent of the population of Roseville, it is apparent that whites are overrepresented as coaches and Asian Americans are underrepresented (Roseville is 16 percent Hispanic).

We conducted the first three interviews together. Suzel then conducted 38 of the subsequent interviews, while Mike did nine. Mike used his insider status as a member of the community and as a parent of kids who had played in the local youth sports leagues to establish trust and rapport with interviewees. No doubt his status as a white male college professor with a deep background in sports also gave him instant credibility with some interviewees. Suzel, by contrast, was an outsider in most ways. She was a Latina graduate student, not a resident of Roseville, and her own two daughters did not play local youth sports. Moreover, she had almost no sports background. Suzel closed the social distance with her interviewees by enrolling in a coaching clinic and a refereeing clinic and by observing several practices and games to better understand the role that coaches play with the kids. In the interviews, Suzel judiciously used her knowledge from these clinics and her observations of practices and games to ask knowledgeable questions and sharp follow-up probes. This strategy created rapport and it also allowed Suzel to demonstrate knowledge of sports and coaching, thus bridging what might otherwise have been a credibility gap between her and some of those with deep athletic experience and knowledge. At times, Suzel used her outsider status as a benefit, asking naïve questions about the particularities of Roseville that might have sounded disingenuous coming from an insider.

THE COACHES' STORIES

When we asked a longtime Little League Softball manager why he thinks most head coaches are men while nearly all team parents are women, he said with a shrug, "They give opportunities to everybody to manage or coach and it just so happens that no women volunteer, you know?" This man's statement was typical of head coaches and league officials who generally offered up explanations grounded in individual choice: Faced with equal opportunities to volunteer, men just *choose* to be coaches, while women *choose* to be team parents.

But our research shows that the gendered division of labor among men and women volunteers in youth coaching results not simply from an accumulation of individual choices; rather, it is produced through a profoundly *social* process. We will first draw from our interviews with head coaches to illustrate how gender divisions of labor among adult volunteers in youth sports are shaped by gendered language and belief systems and are seen by many coaches as natural extensions of gendered divisions of labor in families and workplaces. We next draw observations from our field notes to illustrate how everyday interactions within the gendered organizational context of youth sports shapes peoples' choices about men's and women's roles as coaches or team parents. Our main focus here will be on reproductive agency—the patterns of action that reproduce the gender division of labor. But we will also discuss moments of resistance and disruption that create possibilities for change.

Gendered Pipelines

When we asked coaches to describe how they had decided to become coaches, most spoke of having first served as assistant coaches—sometimes for just one season, sometimes for several seasons—before moving into head coaching positions. Drawing from language used by those who study gender in occupations, we can describe the assistant coach position as an essential part of the "pipeline" to the head coach position (England 2006). One of the reasons for this is obvious: many parents—women and men—believe that as a head coach, they will be under tremendous critical scrutiny by other parents in the community. Without previous youth coaching experience, many lack the confidence that they feel they need to take on such a public leadership task. A year or two of assistant coaching affords one the experience and builds the confidence that can lead to the conclusion that "I can do that" and the decision to take on the responsibility of a head coaching position.

But the pipeline from assistant coaches to head coaches does not operate in a purely individual voluntarist manner. A male longtime Little League manager and a member of the league's governing board gave us a glimpse of how the pipeline works when there is a shortage of volunteers:

> One time we had 10 teams and only like six or seven applicants that wanted to be strictly manager. So you kinda eyeball the yearbook from the year before, maybe a couple of years [before], and see if the same dad is still listed as a[n assistant] coach, and maybe now it's time he wants his own team. So you make a lot of phone calls. You might make 20 phone calls and hopefully you are going to get two or three guys that say, "Yes, I'll be a manager."

The assistant coach position is a key part of the pipeline to head coaching positions both because it makes people more confident about volunteering to be a head coach and, as the quote above illustrates, because it gives them visibility in ways that make them more likely to be actively recruited by the league to be a head coach. To understand how it is that most head coaches are men, we need to understand how the pipeline operates—how it is that, at the entry level, women's and men's choices to become assistant coaches and/or team parents are constrained or enabled by the social context.

Recruiting Dads and Moms to Help

There is a lot of work involved in organizing a successful youth soccer, baseball, or softball season. A head coach needs help from two, three, even four other parents who will serve as assistant coaches during practices and games. Parents also have to take responsibility for numerous support tasks like organizing snacks, making team banners, working in the snack bar during games, collecting donations for year-end gifts for the coaches, and organizing team events and year-end parties. In AYSO, parents also serve as volunteer referees. When we asked head coaches how they determined who would help them with these assistant coaching and other support tasks, a very common storyline developed: the coach would call a beginning-of-the-season team meeting, sometimes preceded by a letter or e-mail to parents, and ask for volunteers. Nearly always, they ended up with dads volunteering to help as assistant coaches and moms volunteering to be team parents. A woman soccer coach told a typical story:

> At the beginning of the season I sent a little introductory letter [that said] I really badly need an assistant coach and referee and a "team mom." You know anyone that is keen on that, let's talk about it at the First practice. And this year one guy picked up the phone and said. "Please, can I be your assistant coach?" And I spoke to another one of the mums who I happen to know through school and she said, "Oh, I can do the team mum if you find someone to help me." And by the first practice, they'd already discussed it and it was up and running.

We can see from this coach's statement how the assistant coach and team parent positions are sometimes informally set up even before the first team meeting and how a coach's assumption that the team parent will be a "team *mom*" might make it more likely that women end up in these positions. But even coaches—such as the woman soccer coach quoted below—who try to emphasize that team parent is not necessarily a woman's job find that only women end up volunteering:

> Before the season started, we had a team meeting and I let the parents know that I would need a team parent and I strongly stressed *parent*, because I don't think it should always be a mother. But we did end up with the mom doing it and she assigns snacks and stuff like that.

None of the head coaches we interviewed said that they currently had a man as the team parent. Four coaches recalled that they had once had a man as a team parent (although one of these four coaches said, "Now that I think about it, that guy actually volunteered his wife do it"). When we asked if they had ever had a team parent who was a man, nearly all of the coaches said never. Many of them laughed at the very thought. A woman soccer coach exclaimed with a chuckle, "I just can't imagine! I wonder if they've *ever* had a 'team mom' who's a dad. I don't know [laughs]." A man soccer coach stammered his way through his response, punctuating his words with sarcastic laughter: "Ha! In fact, that whole concept—I don't think I've ever *heard* of a team dad [laughs]. Uh—there *is* no team dad, I've never heard of a team dad. But I don't know why that would be." A few coaches, such as the following woman softball coach, resorted to family metaphors to explain why they think there are few if any men volunteering to be team parents: "Oh, it's always a mom [laughs]. 'Team mom.' That's why it's called 'team *mom*.' You know, the coach is a male. And the mom—I mean, that's the *housekeeping*—*you* know: Assign the snack."

There are gendered assumptions in the language commonly linked to certain professions, so much so that often, when the person holding the position is in the statistical minority, people attach a modifier, such as *male* nurse, *male* secretary, *woman* judge, *woman* doctor. Or *woman* head coach. Over and over, in interviews with coaches, during team meetings, and in interactions during games, practices, and team parties, we noticed this gendered language. Most obvious was the frequent slippage from official term *team parent* to commonly used term *"team mom."* But we also noticed that a man coach was normally just called a coach, while a woman coach was often gender marked as a woman coach. As feminist linguists have shown, language is a powerful element of social life—it not only reflects social realities such as gender divisions of labor, it also helps to construct our notions of what is normal and what is an aberration (Thorne, Kramarae, and Henley 1983). One statement from a woman soccer coach, "I wonder if they've *ever* had a 'team mom' who's a dad," illustrates how gendered language makes the idea of a man team parent seem incongruous, even laughable. In youth sports, this gendered language supports the notion that a team is structured very much like a "traditional" heterosexual family: The head coach—nearly always a man—is the leader and the public face of the team; the team parent—nearly always

a woman—is working behind the scenes, doing support work; assistant coaches—mostly men, but including the occasional woman—help the coach on the field during practices and games.

Teams are even talked about sometimes as "families," and while we never heard a head coach referred to as a team's "dad," we did often and consistently hear the team parent referred to as the "team mom." This gendered language, drawn from family relations, gives us some good initial hints as to how coach and team parent roles remain so gender segregated. In their study of self-managing teams, which was intended to break down gender divisions in workplaces, Ollilainen and Calasanti (2007) show how team members' use of family metaphors serves to maintain the salience of gender, and thus, helps to reproduce a gendered division of labor. Similarly, in youth sports contexts, gendered language structures people's conversations in ways that shape and constrain their actions. Is a man who volunteers to be a team parent now a "team mom"?

Gender Ideology and Work/Family Analogies

When we asked the coaches to consider why it is nearly always women who volunteer to be the team parent, many seemed never to have considered this question before. Some of the men coaches seemed especially befuddled and appeared to assume that women's team-parenting work is a result of an almost "natural" decision on the part of the woman. Some men, such as the following soccer coach, made sense of this volunteer division of labor by referring to the ways that it reflected divisions of labor in men's own families and in their community: "In this area we have a lot of stay-at-home moms, so it seems to kind of fall to them to take over those roles." Similarly, a man baseball coach whose wife served as the team parent explained, "I think it's because they probably do it at home. You know, I mean my wife—even though she can't really commit the time to coach, I don't think she would *want* to coach—uh, she's very good with that [team parent] stuff." A man soccer coach explained the gender divisions on youth sports teams in terms of people's comfort with a nostalgic notion of a "traditional family":

> That's sort of the classical family, you know, it's like the Donna Reed family is AYSO, right? . . . They have these assigned gender roles . . . and people in

Roseville, probably all over the United States, they're fairly comfortable with them, right? It's, uh, maybe insidious, maybe not, [but] framed in the sort of traditional family role of dad, mom, kids. . . . people are going to be comfortable with that.

Another man baseball coach broadened the explanation, drawing connections to divisions of labor in his workplace:

It's kinda like in business. I work in real estate, and most of your deal makers that are out there on the front lines, so to speak, making the deals, doing the shuckin' and jivin', doing the selling, are men. It's a very Good Ol' Boys network on the real estate brokerage side. There are a ton a females who are on the property management side, because it's *housekeeping*, it's *managing*, it's like running the *household*, it's behind the scenes, it's like cooking in the kitchen—[laughs]—I mean, I hate to say that, but it's that kind of role that's secondary. Coach is out in the front leading the squad, mom sitting behind making sure that the snacks are in order and all that. You know—just the way it is.

Having a male coach and a "team mom" just seemed normal to this man, "You know, just the way it is," because it seemed to flow naturally from divisions of labor in his household and in his workplace—gendered divisions of labor that have the "the Good Ol' Boys" operating publicly as the leaders "on the front lines . . . shuckin' and jivin'," while the women are offering support "behind the scenes . . . like cooking in the kitchen." Echoing this view, a man soccer coach said, "I hate to use the analogy, but it's like a secretary: You got a boss and you've got a secretary, and I think that's where most of the opportunities for women to be active in the sports is, as the secretary."

When explaining why it is that team parents are almost exclusively women, a small number of women coaches also seemed to see it in essentialist terms—like most of the men coaches saw it.

Many women coaches, however, saw the gendering of the team parent position as a problem and made sense of its persistence, as did many of the men, by referring to the ways that it reflects family- and work-related divisions of labor. But several of the women coaches added an additional dimension to their explanations by focusing on why they think the men don't or won't consider doing team parent work. A woman soccer coach said, "I think it's because the dads want to be involved with the action. And they are not interested in doing paperwork and collecting money for photos or whatever it is. They are not interested in doing that sort of stuff." Another woman soccer coach extended this point: "I think it's probably, well, identity, which is probably why not many men do it. You know, they think that is a woman's job, like secretary or nurse or, you know." In short, many of the women coaches were cognizant of the ways that the team parent job was viewed by men, like all "women's work," as nonmasculine and thus undesirable. A woman Little League coach found it ironically funny that her husband, in fact, does most of the cooking and housework at home but will not take on the role of team parent for his daughter's team. When asked if changing the name to "team dad" might get more men to volunteer, she replied with a sigh,

I don't know. I wish my husband would be a team dad because he's just very much more domesticated than I am [laughs]. You know, "Bring all the snacks, honey, hook us up," you know. I think there's a lot of men out there, but they don't want to be perceived as being domesticated.

This coach's comment illustrates how—even for a man who does a substantial amount of the family labor at home—publicly taking on a job that is defined as "feminine" threatens to saddle him with a "domesticated" public image that would be embarrassing or even humiliating. In sum, most coaches—both women and men—believe that men become coaches and women become team parents largely because these public roles fit with their domestic proclivities and skills. But the women add an important dimension to this explanation: women do the team parent work because it has to be done . . . and because they know that the men will not do it.

Finding a "Team Mom"

The interview data give us a window into how people make sense of decisions that they have made as youth sports volunteers and provide insights into how gendered language and beliefs about men's and women's work and family roles help to shape these decisions. Yet, asking people to explain how (and especially why) things such as gendered divisions of labor persist is not by itself the most reliable basis for building an explanation. Rather, watching *how* things happen gives us a deeper understanding of the social construction of gender (Thorne 1993). Our observations from team meetings and early season practices reveal deeper social processes at work—processes that shaped people's apparently individual decisions to volunteer for assistant coach or team parent positions. This excerpt from field notes from the first team meeting of a boys' baseball team illustrates how men's apparent resistance to even consider taking on the team parent position ultimately leaves the job in the hands of a woman (who might also have been reluctant to do it):

> Coach Bill stands facing the parents, as we sit in the grandstands. He doesn't ask for volunteers for assistant coaches; instead, he announces that he has "invited" two of the fathers "who probably know more about baseball than I do" to serve as his assistants. He then asks for someone to volunteer as the "team mom." He adds, "Now, 'team mom' is not a gendered job: it can be done by a mom or a dad. But we really need a 'team mom.'" Nobody volunteers immediately. One mom sitting near me mutters to another mom, "I've done this two years in a row, and I'm not gonna do it this year." Coach Bill goes on to ask for a volunteer for scorekeeper. Meanwhile, two other moms have been whispering, and one of them suddenly bursts out with "Okay! She's volunteered to be 'team mom!'" People applaud. The volunteer seems a bit sheepish; her body-language suggests someone who has just reluctantly agreed to do something. But she affirms that, yes, she'll do it.

This first practice of the year is often the moment at which the division of labor—who will be the assistant coaches, who will be the team parent—is publicly solidified. In this case, the men assistant coaches had been selected before the meeting by the head coach, but it apparently took some cajoling from a mother during the team meeting to convince another mother to volunteer to be the "team mom." We observed two occasions when a woman who did not volunteer was drafted by the head coach to be the "team mom." In one case, the reluctant volunteer was clearly more oriented toward assistant coaching, as the following composite story from field notes from the beginning of the season of a seven-year-old boys' baseball team illustrates:

> At the first practice, Coach George takes charge, asks for volunteers. I tell him that I am happy to help out at

practice and games and that he should just let me know what he'd like me to do. He appoints me Assistant Coach. This happens with another dad, too. We get team hats. Elena, a mother, offers to help out in any way she can. She's appointed "co-team mom" (the coach's wife is the other "team mom"). She shrugs and says okay, fine. Unlike most "team moms," Elena continues to attend all practices. At the fifth practice. Coach George is pitching batting practice to the kids; I'm assigned to first base, the other dad is working with the catcher. Elena (the "team mom") is standing alone on the sidelines, idly tossing a ball up in the air to herself. Coach George's son suddenly has to pee, so as George hustles the boy off to the bathroom, Elena jumps in and starts pitching. She's good, it turns out, and can groove the pitch right where the kids want it. (By contrast, George has recently been plunking the kids with wild pitches.) Things move along well. At one point, when Coach George has returned from the bathroom, with Elena still pitching to the kids, a boy picks up a ball near second base and doesn't know what to do with it. Coach George yells at the kid: "Throw it! Throw it to the 'team mom!'" The kid, confused, says, "Where is she?" I say, "The pitcher, throw it to the pitcher." Coach George says, "Yeah, the 'team mom.'"

A couple of years later, we interviewed Elena and asked her how it was that she became a team parent and continued in that capacity for five straight years. Her response illuminated the informal constraints that channel many women away from coaching and toward being team parents:

> The first year, when [my son] was in kindergarten, he was on a T-ball team, and I volunteered to be manager, and of course the league didn't choose me, but they did allow me to be assistant coach. And I was so excited, and [laughs] of course I showed up in heels for the first practice, because it was right after work, and the coach looked at me, and I informed him that "I'm your new assistant." And he looked at me—and I don't know if *distraught* is the correct word, but he seemed slightly *disappointed,* and he went out of his way to ask the parents who were there watching their children if there was anyone who wanted to volunteer, even though I was there. So there was this male who did kind of rise to the occasion, and so that was the end. He demoted me without informing me of his decision [laughs]—I was *really* enthused, because [my son] was in kindergarten, so I *really* wanted to be coach—or assistant coach at least—and it didn't

happen. So after that I didn't feel comfortable to volunteer to coach. I just thought, okay, then I can do "team mom."

As this story illustrates, women who have the background, skills, and desire to work as on-field assistant coaches are sometimes assigned by head coaches to be "team mom." Some baseball teams even have a niche for such moms: a "dugout coach" (or "dugout mom") is usually a mom who may help out with on-field instruction during practices, but on game days, she is assigned the "indoors" space of the dugout, where it is her responsibility to keep track of the line-up and to be sure that the boy who is on-deck (next up to bat) is ready with his batting gloves and helmet on. The dugout coach also—especially with younger kids' teams—might be assigned to keep kids focused on the game, to keep equipment orderly, to help with occasional first aid, and to help see that the dugout is cleaned of empty water bottles and snack containers after the game is over. In short, the baseball, softball, and soccer fields on which the children play are gendered spaces (Dworkin 2001; Montez de Oca 2005). The playing field is the public space where the (usually male) coach exerts his authority and command. The dugout is like the home—a place of domestic safety from which one emerges to do one's job. Work happens in the indoor space of the dugout, but it is like family labor, behind-the-scenes, supporting the "real" work of leadership that is done on the field.

CHALLENGES AND RESISTANCE

The head coach's common assumption that fathers will volunteer to be assistant coaches and mothers to be "team moms" creates a context that powerfully channels men and women in these directions. Backed by these commonsense understandings of gendered divisions of labor, most men and women just "go with the flow" of this channeling process. Their choices and actions help to reproduce the existing gendered patterns of the organization. But some do not; some choose to swim against the tide. A mother who had several seasons of experience as a head soccer coach described the first team meeting for her youngest child's team:

At our first team meeting, the coach announced, "I'm looking for a couple of you to help me out as assistant coaches," and he looked directly at the men, and *only* at the men. None of them volunteered. And it was really amazing because he didn't even *look* at me or at any of the other women. So after the meeting, I went up to him and said, "Hey, I've coached soccer for like 10 seasons; I can help you out, okay?" And he agreed, so I'm the assistant coach for him.

This first team meeting is an example of a normal gendered interaction that, if it had gone unchallenged, would have reproduced the usual gender divisions of labor on the team. It is likely that many women in these situations notice the ways that men are, to adopt Martin's (2001) term, informally (and probably unconsciously) "mobilizing masculinities" in ways that reproduce men's positions of centrality. But this woman's 10 years of coaching experience gave her the confidence and the athletic "capital" that allowed her not only to see and understand but also to challenge the very gendered selection process that was taking place at this meeting. Most mothers do not have this background, and when faced with this sort of moment, they go with the flow.

On another occasion, as the following composite story from field notes describes, Mike observed a highly athletic and coaching-inclined woman assertively use her abilities in a way that initially *seemed* to transcend the gender segregation process, only to be relegated symbolically at season's end to the position of "team mom":

A new baseball season, the first team meeting of the year; a slew of dads volunteer to be assistant coaches. Coach George combs the women for a "team mom" and gets some resistance; at first, nobody will do it, but then he finds a volunteer. At the first few practices, few assistant coaches actually show up. Isabel, a mom, clearly is into baseball, very knowledgeable and athletic, and takes the field. She pitches to the kids, gives them good advice. On the day when George is passing out forms for assistant coaches to sign, he hands her one too. She accepts it, in a matter-of-fact way. Isabel continues to attend practices, working with the kids on the field.

Though few dads show up for many of the practices, there never seems to be a shortage of dads to serve as assistant coaches at the games. At one game, Coach George invites Isabel to coach third base, but beyond that, she is never included in an on-field coaching role during a game.

End of season, team party. Coach George hands out awards to all the kids. He hands out gift certificates to all the assistant coaches but does not include Isabel. Then he hands out gift certificates to the "team moms," and includes Isabel, even though I don't recall her doing any team parent tasks. She had clearly been acting as an assistant coach all season long.

This story illustrates how, on one hand, a woman volunteer can informally circumvent the sorting process that pushes her toward the "team mom" role by persistently showing up to practices and assertively doing the work of a coach. As Thorne (1993, 133) points out, individual incidences of gender crossing are often handled informally in ways that affirm, rather than challenge, gender boundaries: An individual girl who joins the boys' game gets defined "as a token, a kind of 'fictive boy,' not unlike many women tokens in predominantly men settings, whose presence does little to challenge the existing arrangements." Similarly, Isabel's successful "crossing" led to her becoming accepted as an assistant coach during practices but rarely recognized as a "real" coach during games. She was a kind of "token" or "fictive" coach whose gender transgression was probably unknown to the many adults who never attended practices. So, in the final moment of the season, when adults and children alike were being publicly recognized for their contributions to the team, she was labeled and rewarded for being a "team mom," reaffirming gender boundaries.

A few coaches whom we interviewed consciously attempted to resist or change this gendered sorting system. Some of the women coaches, especially, saw it as a problem that the team parent job was always done by a woman. A woman softball coach was concerned that the "team mom" amounted to negative role-modeling for kids and fed into the disrespect that women coaches experienced:

The kids think that the moms should just be "team moms." Which means that they don't take the mothers seriously, and I think that's a bad thing. I mean it's a *bad thing.* I think that's a lack of respect to women, to mothers.

Another woman Little League coach said that most team parents are women because too many people assume

that's all the women are good for. I think that's what the mentality is. I made it very clear to our parents that it did not have to be a mother, that it could be a father

and that I encourage any dad out there that had time to do what team parents are supposed to do, to sign up and do it. But it didn't happen.

Such coaches find that simply degendering the language by calling this role *team parent* and even stressing that this is not a gendered job is unlikely to yield men volunteers. So what some women coaches do is simply refuse to have a team parent. A woman soccer coach said, "I do it all. I don't have a team parent." Another said, "I think in general, compared to the men who coach, I do more of that [team parent work]." This resistance by women coaches is understandable, especially from those who see the phenomenon of "team mom" as contributing to a climate of disrespect for women coaches. However, this form of resistance ends up creating extra work for women coaches—work that most men coaches relegate to a "team mom."

The very few occasions when a father does volunteer—or is recruited by the coach—to be the team parent are moments of gender "crossing" that hold the potential to disrupt the normal operation of the gender-category sorting process. But ironically, a team parent who is a man can also reinforce gender stereotypes. One man soccer coach told me that the previous season a father had volunteered to be the team parent, but that

he was a disaster [laughs]. He didn't do *anything,* you know, and what little he did it was late; it was ineffective assistance. He didn't come, he didn't make phone calls, I mean he was just like a black hole. And so that—that was an unfortunate disaster. This year it's a woman again.

The idea that a man volunteered—and then failed miserably to do the team parent job—may serve ultimately to reinforce the taken-for-granted assumption that women are naturally better suited to do this kind of work.

THE DEVALUATION OF WOMEN'S INVISIBLE LABOR

The Roseville "team moms" we observed were similar to those studied by Chafetz and Kotarba (1999) in terms of their education, professional-class status, and family structure. The Texasville and Roseville "team moms" are doing the same kinds of activities, simultaneously contributing to the "concerted cultivation" of their own children (Lareau 2003) while helping to enhance the social cohesion of the team, the league, and the community.

Despite the importance of the work team parents are doing, it is not often recognized as equivalent to the work done by coaches. Of course, the team parent typically puts in far fewer hours of labor than does the head coach. However, in some cases, the team parents put in more time than some assistant coaches (dads, for instance, whose work schedules don't allow them to get to many practices but who can be seen on the field during a Saturday game, coaching third base). Yet, the team parent's work remains largely invisible, and coaches sometimes talk about team parents' contributions as trivial or unimportant. Several coaches, when asked about the team parent job, disparaged it as "not very hard to do," "an easy job." But our interviews suggest that the women team parents are often doing this job as one of many community volunteer jobs, while most of the men who coach are engaged in this and only this volunteer activity. A field note from a boys' baseball game illustrates this:

> It is the second to last game of the season. During the first inning, Dora, the "team mom," shows up and immediately starts circulating among the parents in the stands, talking and handing out a flier. The flier announces the "year end party," to be held in a couple of weeks. She announces that she will supply ice cream and other makings for sundaes. Everyone else can just bring some drinks. She also announces (and it's on the flier) that she's collecting $20 from each family to pay for a "thank you gift . . . for all their hard work" for the head coach and for each of the three assistant coaches (all men). People start shelling out money, and Dora starts a list of who has donated. By the start of the next inning, she announces that she's got to go saying "I have a Webelos [Cub Scouts] parents meeting." She's obviously multitasking as a parent volunteer. By the fourth inning, near the end of the game, she is back, collecting more money, and informing parents on details concerning the party and the upcoming playoffs. Finally, during the last inning, she sits and watches the end of the game with the rest of us.

Dora, like other "team moms," doing work before, during, and after the game—making fliers, communicating with parents, collecting money, keeping lists and records, organizing parties, making sure everyone knows the schedule of upcoming events. And she is sandwiching this work around other volunteer activities with another youth organization. This kind of labor keeps organizations running, and it helps to create and sustain the kind of vibrant community "for the kids" that people imagine when they move to a town like Roseville (Daniels 1985).

SORTING AND SOFT ESSENTIALISM

In this article, we have revealed the workings of a gender-category sorting process that reflects the interactional "doing" of gender discussed by West and Zimmerman (1987). Through this sorting process, the vast majority of women volunteers are channeled into a team parent position, and the vast majority of men volunteers become coaches. To say that people are "sorted" is not to deny their active agency in this process. Rather, it is to underline that organizations are characterized by self-perpetuating "inequality regimes" (Acker 2006). What people often think of as "free individual choices" are actually choices that are shaped by social contexts. We have shown how women's choices to become team parents are constrained by the fact that few, if any, men will volunteer to do this less visible and less honored job. Women's choices are enabled by their being actively recruited—"volunteered"—by head coaches or by other parents to become the "team mom." Moreover, men's choices to volunteer as assistant coaches and not as team parents are shaped by the gendered assumptions of head coaches, enacted through active recruiting and informal interactions at the initial team meeting.

This gender-category sorting system is at the heart of the current state of play of the gender regime of adult volunteer work in youth sports in Roseville. There are several ways we can see the sorting system at work. First, our research points to the role of gendered language and meanings in this process. The term *coach* and the term *"team mom"* are saturated with gendered assumptions that are consistent with most people's universe of meanings. These gendered meanings mesh with—and mutually reinforce—the conventional gendered divisions of labor and power in the organization in ways that make decisions to "go with the flow" appear natural. Second, we have shown how having women do the background support work while men do the visible leadership work on the team is also made to appear natural to the extent that it reiterates the gender divisions of labor that many parents experience in their families and in their workplaces. Roseville is a diverse community that is dominated culturally by white, professional-class families, who—partly through the language and practice of youth sports—create a culturally hegemonic (though not a numerical majority) family form in which educated mothers have "opted out" of professional careers to engage in community volunteer work and "intensive mothering," of their own children (Hays 1996; Stone 2007).

The women we interviewed who had opted out of professional careers narrated their decisions to do so in language of personal choice, rather than constraint. The husbands of these women say that they support their wives' choices. This language of (women's) personal choice also saturates coaches' discussions of why women become "team moms." By contrast, when people talk about men, they are far less likely to do so using a language of choice. Men seem to end up in public careers or as youth sports coaches as a matter of destiny. Grounded in the strains and tensions of contemporary professional-class work–family life, this discourse on gender recasts feminist beliefs in a woman's "right to choose" as her responsibility to straddle work and family life, while the man continues "naturally" to be viewed as the main family breadwinner. We call this ascendant gender ideology "soft essentialism."

Youth sports is a powerful institution into which children are initiated into a gender-segregated world with its attendant ideology of soft essentialism (Messner forthcoming).

In the past, sport tended to construct a categorical "hard" essentialism—boys and men, it was believed, were naturally suited to the aggressive, competitive world of sport, while girls and women were not. Today, with girls' and women's massive influx into sport, these kinds of categorical assumptions of natural difference can no longer stand up to even the most cursory examination. Soft essentialism, as an ascendant professional-class gender ideology, frames sport as a realm in which girls are empowered to exercise individual choice (rehearsing choices they will later face in straddling the demands of careers and family labor), while continuing

to view boys as naturally "hard wired" to play sports (and ultimately, to have public careers). Girls are viewed as flexibly facing a future of choices; boys as inflexible, facing a linear path toward public careers. Soft essentialism, in short, initiates kids into an adult world that has been only partially transformed by feminism, where many of the burdens of bridging and balancing work and family strains are still primarily on women's shoulders. Men coaches and "team moms" symbolize and exemplify these tensions.

Time after time, we heard leaders of leagues and some women coaches say that the league leadership works hard to recruit more women coaches but just cannot get them to volunteer. The *formal agency* here is to "recruit more women coaches." But what Martin (2001) calls the *informal practicing of gender* (revealed most clearly in our field-note vignettes) amounts to a collective and (mostly) nonreflexive sorting system that, at the entry level, puts most women and men on separate paths. Martin's work has been foundational in showing how gender works in organizations in informal, nonreflexive ways that rely on peoples' "tacit knowledge" about gender. In particular, she points out "how and why well-intentioned, 'good people' practise gender in ways that do harm" (Martin 2006, 255).

Our study shows a similar lack of "bad guys" engaged in overt acts of sexism and discrimination. Instead, we see a systemic reproduction of gender categorization, created nonreflexively by "well intentioned, good people." The mechanisms of this nonreflexive informal practicing of gender are made to seem normal through their congruence with the "tacit knowledge" of soft essentialism that is itself embedded in hegemonic professional-class family and workplace gender divisions of labor. The fact that soft essentialism emerges from the intersections of these different social contexts means that any attempt to move toward greater equality for women and men in youth sports presupposes simultaneous movements toward equality in workplaces and families.

NOTE

1. Roseville is a pseudonym for the town we studied, and all names of people interviewed or observed for this study are also pseudonyms.

REFERENCES

Acker, Joan. 2006. Inequality regimes: Gender, class and race in organizations. *Gender & Society* 20:441–64.

Boyle, Maree, and Jim McKay. 1995. You leave your troubles at the gate: A case study of the exploitation of older women's labor and "leisure" in sport. *Gender & Society* 9:556–76.

Britton, Dana. 2000. The epistemology of the gendered organization. *Gender & Society* 14:418–34.

Chafetz, Janet Saltzman, and Joseph A. Kotarba. 1999. Little League mothers and the reproduction of gender. In *Inside sports,* edited by Jay Coakley and Peter Donnelly. London and New York: Routledge.

Connell, R. W. 1987. *Gender and power.* Stanford, CA: Stanford University Press.

Daniels, Arlene Kaplan. 1985. Invisible work. *Social Problems* 34:363–74.

Dworkin, Shari L. 2001. Holding back: Negotiating a glass ceiling on women's muscular strength. *Sociological Perspectives* 44:333–50.

England, Paula. 2006. Toward gender equality: Progress and bottlenecks. In *The declining significance of gender?* edited by Francine D. Blau, Mary C. Brinlon, and David B. Grusky. New York: Russell Sage.

Grasmuck, Sherri. 2005. *Protecting home: Class, race, and masculinity in boys' baseball.* Piscataway, NJ: Rutgers University Press.

Hays, Sharon. 1996. *The cultural contradictions of motherhood.* New Haven, CT: Yale University Press.

Hook, Jennifer L. 2004. Reconsidering the division of household labor: Incorporating volunteer work and informal support. *Journal of Marriage and Family* 66:101–17.

Lareau, Annette. 2003. *Unequal childhoods: Class, race, and family life.* Berkeley: University of California Press.

Martin, Patricia Yancy. 2001. Mobilizing masculinities: Women's experiences of men at work. *Organization* 8:587–618.

Martin, Patricia Yancy. 2006. Practicing gender at work: Further thoughts on reflexivity. *Gender, Work and Organization* 13:254–76.

Messner, Michael A. 2002. *Taking the field: Women, men, and sports.* Minneapolis: University of Minnesota Press.

Messner, Michael A. Forthcoming. *It's all for the kids: Gender, families and youth sports.* Berkeley: University of California Press.

Montez de Oca, Jeffrey. 2005. As our muscles get softer, our missile race becomes harder: Cultural citizenship and the "muscle gap." *Journal of Historical Sociology* 18:145–71.

Ollilainen, Marjukka, and Toni Calasanti. 2007. Metaphors at work: Maintaining the salience of gender in self-managing teams. *Gender & Society* 21:5–27.

Stone, Pamela. 2007. *Opting out: Why women really quit careers and head home.* Berkeley: University of California Press.

Thompson, Shona. 1999. The game begins at home: Women's labor in the service of sport. In *Inside sports,* edited by Jay Coakley and Peter Donnelly. London and New York: Routledge.

Thorne, Barrie. 1993. *Gender play: Girls and boys in school.* New Brunswick, NJ: Rutgers University Press.

Thorne, Barrie, Cheris Kramarae, and Nancy Henley. 1983. *Language, gender and society.* Rowley, MA: Newbury House.

West, Candace, and Don Zimmerman. 1987. Doing gender. *Gender & Society* 1:125–51.

34

Moving Up with Kin and Community

Upward Social Mobility for Black and White Women

ELIZABETH HIGGINBOTHAM

LYNN WEBER

. . . When women and people of color experience upward mobility in America, they scale steep structural as well as psychological barriers. The long process of moving from a working-class family of origin to the professional–managerial class is full of twists and turns: choices made with varying degrees of information and varying options; critical junctures faced with support and encouragement or disinterest, rejection, or active discouragement; and interpersonal relationships in which basic understandings are continuously negotiated and renegotiated. It is a fascinating process that profoundly shapes the lives of those who experience it, as well as the lives of those around them. Social mobility is also a process engulfed in myth. One need only pick up any newspaper or turn on the television to see that the myth of upward mobility remains firmly entrenched in American culture: With hard work, talent, determination, and some luck, just about anyone can "make it." . . .

The image of the isolated and detached experience of mobility that we have inherited from past scholarship is problematic for anyone seeking to understand the process for women or people of color. Twenty years of scholarship in the study of both race and gender has taught us the importance of interpersonal attachments to the lives of women and a commitment to racial uplift among people of color . . .

. . . Lacking wealth, the greatest gift a Black family has been able to give to its children has been the motivation and skills to succeed in school. Aspirations for college attendance and professional positions are stressed as *family* goals, and the entire family may make sacrifices and provide support . . . Black women have long seen the activist potential of education and have sought it as a cornerstone of community development—a means of uplifting the race. When women of color or White women are put at the center of the analysis of upward mobility, it is clear that different questions will be raised about social mobility and different descriptions of the process will ensue. . . .

RESEARCH DESIGN

These data are from a study of full-time employed middle-class women in the Memphis metropolitan area. This research is designed to explore the processes of upward social mobility for Black and White women by

Elizabeth Higginbotham and Lynn Weber, "Moving Up with Kin and Community: Upward Social Mobility for Black and White Women," from *Gender & Society,* Volume 6/1992, p. 416–440. Copyright © 1992. Reprinted by permission.

examining differences between women professionals, managers, and administrators who are from working- and middle-class backgrounds—that is, upwardly mobile and middle-class stable women. In this way, we isolate subjective processes shared among women who have been upwardly mobile from those common to women who have reproduced their family's professional–managerial class standing. Likewise, we identify common experiences in the attainment process that are shared by women of the same race, be they upwardly mobile or stable middle class. Finally, we specify some ways in which the attainment process is unique for each race–class group . . .

. . . We rely on a model of social class basically derived from the work of Poulantzas (1974), Braverman (1974), Ehrenreich and Ehrenreich (1979), and elaborated in Vanneman and Cannon (1987). These works explicate a basic distinction between social class and social status. Classes represent bounded categories of the population, groups set in a relation of opposition to one another by their roles in the capitalist system. The middle class, or professional–managerial class, is set off from the working class by the power and control it exerts over workers in three realms: economic (power through ownership), political (power through direct supervisory authority), and ideological (power to plan and organize work; Poulantzas 1974; Vanneman and Cannon 1987).

In contrast, education, prestige, and income represent social statuses—hierarchically structured relative rankings along a ladder of economic success and social prestige. Positions along these dimensions are not established by social relations of dominance and subordination but, rather, as rankings on scales representing resources and desirability. In some respects, they represent both the justification for power differentials vested in classes and the rewards for the role that the middle class plays in controlling labor.

Our interest is in the process of upward social class mobility, moving from a working-class family of origin to a middle-class destination—from a position of working-class subordination to a position of control over the working class. Lacking inherited wealth or other resources, those working-class people who attain middle-class standing do so primarily by obtaining a college education and entering a professional, managerial, or administrative occupation. Thus we examine carefully

the process of educational attainment not as evidence of middle-class standing but as a necessary part of the mobility process for most working-class people.

Likewise, occupation alone does not define the middle class, but professional, managerial, and administrative occupations capture many of the supervisory and ideologically based positions whose function is to control workers' lives. Consequently, we defined subjects as *middle class* by virtue of their employment in either a professional, managerial, or administrative occupation. . . . Classification of subjects as either professional or managerial–administrative was made on the basis of the designation of occupations in the U.S. Bureau of the Census's (1983) "Detailed Population Characteristics: Tennessee." Managerial occupations were defined as those in the census categories of managers and administrators; professionals were defined as those occupations in the professional category, excluding technicians, whom Braverman (1974) contends are working class.

Upwardly mobile women were defined as those women raised in families where neither parent was employed as a professional, manager, or administrator. Typical occupations for working-class fathers were postal clerk, craftsman, semiskilled manufacturing worker, janitor, and laborer. Some working-class mothers had clerical and sales positions, but many of the Black mothers also worked as private household workers. *Middle-class stable* women were defined as those women raised in families where *either* parent was employed as a professional, manager, or administrator. Typical occupations of middle-class parents were social worker, teacher, and school administrator as well as high-status professionals such as attorneys, physicians, and dentists. . . .

FAMILY EXPECTATIONS FOR EDUCATIONAL ATTAINMENT

Four questions assess the expectations and support among family members for the educational attainment of the subjects. First, "Do you recall your father or mother stressing that you attain an education?" Yes was the response of 190 of the 200 women. Each of the women in this study had obtained a college degree, and many have graduate degrees. It is clear that for Black and White women, education was an important concern in their families. . . .

The comments of Laura Lee,[1] a 39-year-old Black woman who was raised middle class, were typical:

> Going to school, that was never a discussable issue. Just like you were born to live and die, you were going to go to school. You were going to prepare yourself to do something.

It should be noted, however, that only 86 percent of the White working-class women answered yes, compared to 98 percent of all other groups. Although this difference is small, it foreshadows a pattern where White women raised in working-class families received the least support and encouragement for educational and career attainment.

"When you were growing up, how far did your father expect you to go in school?" While most fathers expected college attendance from their daughters, differences also exist by class of origin. Only 70 percent of the working-class fathers, both Black and White, expected their daughters to attend college. In contrast, 94 percent of the Black middle-class and 88 percent of the White middle-class women's fathers had college expectations for their daughters.

When asked the same question about mother's expectations, 88 percent to 92 percent of each group's mothers expected their daughters to get a college education, except the White working-class women, for whom only 66 percent of mothers held such expectations. In short, only among the White working-class women did a fairly substantial proportion (about one-third) of both mothers and fathers expect less than a college education from their daughters. About 30 percent of Black working-class fathers held lower expectations for their daughters, but not the mothers; virtually all middle-class parents expected a college education for their daughters.

Sara Marx is a White, 33-year-old director of counseling raised in a rural working-class family. She is among those whose parents did not expect a college education for her. She was vague about the roots of attending college:

> It seems like we had a guest speaker who talked to us. Maybe before our exams somebody talked to us. I really can't put my finger on anything. I don't know where the information came from exactly.

"Who provided emotional support for you to make the transition from high school to college?" While 86 percent of the Black middle-class women indicated that family provided that support, 70 percent of the White middle-class, 64 percent of the Black working class, and only 56 percent of the White working class received emotional support from family.

"Who paid your college tuition and fees?" Beyond emotional support, financial support is critical to college attendance. There are clear class differences in financial support for college. Roughly 90 percent of the middle-class respondents and only 56 percent and 62 percent of the Black and White working-class women, respectively, were financially supported by their families. These data also suggest that working-class parents were less able to give emotional or financial support for college than they were to hold out the expectation that their daughters should attend.

FAMILY EXPECTATIONS FOR OCCUPATION OR CAREER

When asked, "Do you recall your father or mother stressing that you should have an occupation to succeed in life?" racial differences appear: Ninety-four percent of all Black respondents said yes. In the words of Julie Bird, a Black woman raised-middle-class junior high school teacher:

> My father would always say, "You see how good I'm doing? Each generation should do more than the generation before." He expects me to accomplish more than he has.

Ann Right, a 36-year-old Black attorney whose father was a janitor, said:

> They wanted me to have a better life than they had. For all of us. And that's why they emphasized education and emphasized working relationships and how you get along with people and that kind of thing.

Ruby James, a Black teacher from a working-class family, said:

> They expected me to have a good-paying job and to have a family and be married. Go to work every day. Buy a home. That's about it. Be happy.

In contrast, only 70 percent of the White middle-class and 56 percent of the White working-class women indicated that their parents stressed that an occupation was needed for success. Nina Pentel, a 26-year-old white medical social worker, expressed a common response: "They said 'You're going to get married but get a degree, you never know what's going to happen to you.' They were pretty laid back about goals."

When the question focuses on a career rather than an occupation, the family encouragement is lower and differences were not significant, but similar patterns emerged. We asked respondents, "Who, if anyone, encouraged you to think about a career?" Among Black respondents, 60 percent of the middle-class and 56 percent of the working-class women answered that family encouraged them. Only 40 percent of the White working-class women indicated that their family encouraged them in their thinking about a career, while 52 percent of the White middle-class women did so. . . .

When working-class White women seek to be mobile through their own attainments, they face conflicts. Their parents encourage educational attainment, but when young women develop professional career goals, these same parents sometimes become ambivalent. This was the case with Elizabeth Marlow, who is currently a public interest attorney—a position her parents never intended her to hold. She described her parents' traditional expectations and their reluctance to support her career goals fully.

> My parents assumed that I would go to college and meet some nice man and finish, but not necessarily work after. I would be a good mother for my children. I don't think that they ever thought I would go to law school. Their attitude about my interest in law school was, "You can do it if you want to, but we don't think it is a particularly practical thing for a woman to do."

Elizabeth is married and has three children, but she is not the traditional housewife of her parents' dreams. She received more support outside the family for her chosen lifestyle.

Although Black families are indeed more likely than White families to encourage their daughters to prepare for careers, like White families, they frequently steer them toward highly visible traditionally female occupations, such as teacher, nurse, and social worker. Thus many mobile Black women are directed toward the same gender-segregated occupations as White women. . . .

MARRIAGE

Although working-class families may encourage daughters to marry, they recognize the need for working-class women to contribute to family income or to support themselves economically. To achieve these aims, many working-class girls are encouraged to pursue an education as preparation for work in gender-segregated occupations. Work in these fields presumably allows women to keep marriage, family, and child rearing as life goals while contributing to the family income and to have "something to fall back on" if the marriage does not work out. This interplay among marriage, education, financial need, and class mobility is complex (Joslin 1979).

We asked, "Do you recall your mother or father emphasizing that marriage should be your primary life goal?" While the majority of all respondents did not get the message that marriage was the *primary* life goal, Black and White women's parents clearly saw this differently. Virtually no Black parents stressed marriage as the primary life goal (6 percent of the working class and 4 percent of the middle class), but significantly more White parents did (22 percent of the working class and 18 percent of the middle class).

Some White women said their families expressed active opposition to marriage, such as Clare Baron, a raised-working-class nursing supervisor, who said, "My mother always said, 'Don't get married and don't have children!'"

More common responses recognized the fragility of marriage and the need to support oneself. For example, Alice Page, a 31-year-old White raised-middle-class librarian, put it this way:

> I feel like I am really part of a generation that for the first time is thinking, "I don't want to have to depend on somebody to take care of me because what if they say they are going to take care of me and then they are not there? They die, or they leave me or whatever." I feel very much that I've got to be able to support myself and I don't know that single women in other eras have had to deal with that to the same degree.

While White working-class women are often raised to prepare for work roles so that they can contribute to family income and, if necessary, support themselves, Black women face a different reality. Unlike White women, Black women are typically socialized to view marriage separately from economic security, because it is not expected that marriage will ever remove them from the labor market. As a result, Black families socialize all their children—girls and boys—for self-sufficiency (Clark 1986; Higginbotham and Cannon 1988). . . .

. . . Fairly substantial numbers of each group had never married by the time of the interview, ranging from 20 percent of the White working-class to 34 percent of the Black working-class and White middle-class respondents. Some of the women were pleased with their singlehood, like Alice Page, who said:

> I am single by choice. That is how I see myself. I have purposely avoided getting into any kind of romantic situation with men. I have enjoyed going out but never wanted to get serious. If anyone wants to get serious, I quit going out with him.

Other women expressed disappointment and some shock that they were not yet married. When asked about her feeling about being single, Sally Ford, a 32-year-old White manager, said:

> That's what I always wanted to do: to be married and have children. To me, that is the ideal. I want a happy, good marriage with children. I do not like being single at all. It is very, very lonesome. I don't see any advantages to being single. None!

SUBJECTIVE SENSE OF DEBT TO KIN AND FRIENDS

McAdoo (1978) reports that upwardly mobile Black Americans receive more requests to share resources from their working-class kin than do middle-class Black Americans. Many mobile Black Americans feel a "social debt" because their families aided them in the mobility process and provided emotional support. When we asked the White women in the study the following question: "Generally, do you feel you owe a lot for the help given to you by your family and relatives?" many were perplexed and asked what the question meant. In contrast, both the working- and middle-class Black women tended to respond immediately that they felt a sense of obligation to family and friends in return for the support they had received. Black women, from both the working class and the middle class, expressed the strongest sense of debt to family, with 86 percent and 74 percent, respectively, so indicating. White working-class women were

least likely to feel that they owed family (46 percent), while 68 percent of white middle-class women so indicated. In short, upwardly mobile Black women were almost twice as likely as upwardly mobile White women to express a sense of debt to family.

Linda Brown, an upwardly mobile Black women, gave a typical response, "Yes, they are there when you need them." Similar were the words of Jean Marsh, "Yes, because they have been supportive. They're dependable. If I need them I can depend upon them."

One of the most significant ways in which Black working-class families aided their daughters and left them with a sense of debt related to care for their children. Dawn March expressed it thus:

> They have been there more so during my adult years than a lot of other families that I know about. My mother kept all of my children until they were old enough to go to day care. And she not only kept them, she'd give them a bath for me during the daytime and feed them before I got home from work. Very, very supportive people. So, I really would say I owe them for that.

Carole Washington, an upwardly mobile Black woman occupational therapist, also felt she owed her family. She reported:

> I know the struggle that my parents have had to get me where I am. I know the energy they no longer have to put into the rest of the family even though they want to put it there and they're willing. I feel it is my responsibility to give back some of that energy they have given to me. It's self-directed, not required.

White working-class women, in contrast, were unlikely to feel a sense of debt and expressed their feelings in similar ways. Irma Cox, part owner of a computer business, said, "I am appreciative of the values my parents instilled in me. But I for the most part feel like I have done it on my own." Carey Mink, a 35-year-old psychiatric social worker, said, "No, they pointed me in a direction and they were supportive, but I've done a lot of the work myself." Debra Beck, a judge, responded, "No, I feel that I've gotten most places on my own." . . .

COMMITMENT TO COMMUNITY

The mainstream "model of community stresses the rights of individuals to make decisions in their own self-interest, regardless of the impact on the larger society" (Collins 1990, 52). This model may explain relations to community of origin for mobile White males but cannot be generalized to other racial and gender groups. In the context of well-recognized structures of racial oppression, America's racial-ethnic communities develop collective survival strategies that contrast with the individualism of the dominant culture but ensure the community's survival (Collins 1990; McAdoo 1978; Stack 1974; Valentine 1978). McAdoo (1978) argues that Black people have *only* been able to advance in education and attain higher status and higher paying jobs with the support of the wider Black community, teachers in segregated schools, extended family networks, and Black mentors already in those positions. This widespread community involvement enables mobile people of color to confront and challenge racist obstacles in credentialing institutions, and it distinguishes the mobility process in racial-ethnic communities from mobility in the dominant culture. For example, Lou Nelson, now a librarian, described the support she felt in her southern segregated inner-city school. She said:

> There was a closeness between people and that had a lot to do with neighborhood schools. I went to Tubman High School with people that lived in the Tubman area. I think that there was a bond, a bond between parents, the PTA . . . I think that it was just that everybody felt that everybody knew everybody. And that was special.

Family and community involvement and support in the mobility process means that many Black professionals and managers continue to feel linked to their communities of origin. Lillian King, a high-ranking city official who was raised working class, discussed her current commitment to the Black community. She said:

> Because I have more opportunities, I've got an obligation to give more back and to set a positive example for Black people and especially for Black women. I think we've got to do a tremendous job in building self-esteem and giving people the desire to achieve.

Judith Moore is a 34-year-old single parent employed as a health investigator. She has been able to maintain her connection with her community, and that is a source of pride.

> I'm proud that I still have a sense of who I am in terms of Black people. That's very important to me. No matter how much education or professional status I get, I do not want to lose touch with where I've come from. I think that you need to look back and that kind of pushes you forward. I think the degree and other things can make you lose sight of that, especially us Black folks, but I'm glad that I haven't and I try to teach that [commitment] to my son.

For some Black women, their mobility has enabled them to give to an even broader community. This is the case with Sammi Lewis, a raised-working-class woman who is a director of a social service agency. She said, "I owe a responsibility to the entire community, and not to any particular group." . . .

CROSSING THE COLOR LINE

Mobility for people of color is complex because in addition to crossing class lines, mobility often means crossing racial and cultural ones as well. Since the 1960s, people of color have increasingly attended either integrated or predominantly White schools. Only mobile White ethnics have a comparable experience of simultaneously crossing class and cultural barriers, yet even this experience is qualitatively different from that of Blacks and other people of color. White ethnicity can be practically invisible to White middle-class school peers and co-workers, but people of color are more visible and are subjected to harsher treatment. Our research indicates that no matter when people of color first encounter integrated or predominantly White settings, it is always a shock. The experience of racial exclusion cannot prepare people of color to deal with the racism in daily face-to-face encounters with White people.

For example, Lynn Johnson was in the first cohort of Black students at Regional College, a small private college in Memphis. The self-confidence and stamina Lynn developed in her supportive segregated high school helped her withstand the racism she faced as the first female and the first Black to graduate in economics at Regional College. Lynn described her treatment:

> I would come into class and Dr. Simpson (the Economics professor) would alphabetically call the roll. When he came to my name, he would just jump over it. He would not ask me any questions, he would not do anything. I stayed in that class. I struggled through. When it was my turn, I'd start talking. He would say,

"Johnson, I wasn't talking to you" [because he never said Miss Johnson]. I'd say, "That's all right, Dr. Simpson, it was my turn. I figured you just overlooked me. I'm just the littlest person in here. Wasn't that the right answer?" He would say, "Yes, that was the right answer." I drove him mad, I really did. He finally got used to me and started to help me.

In southern cities, where previous interaction between Black and White people followed a rigid code, adjustments were necessary on both sides. It was clear to Lynn Johnson and others that college faculty and students had to adapt to her small Black cohort at Regional College.

Wendy Jones attended a formerly predominantly White state university that had just merged with a formerly predominantly Black college. This new institution meant many adjustments for faculty and students. As a working-class person majoring in engineering, she had a rough transition. She recalled:

I had never gone to school with White kids. I'd always gone to all Black schools all my life and the Black kids there [at the university] were snooty. Only one friend from high school went there and she flunked out. The courses were harder and all my teachers were men and White. Most of the kids were White. I was in classes where I'd be the only Black and woman. There were no similarities to grasp for. I had to adjust to being in that situation. In about a year I was comfortable where I could walk up to people in my class and have conversations.

For some Black people, their first significant interaction with White people did not come until graduate school. Janice Freeman described her experiences:

I went to a Black high school, a Black college and then worked for a Black man who was a former teacher. Everything was comfortable until I had to go to State University for graduate school. I felt very insecure. I was thrown into an environment that was very different— during the 1960s and 1970s there was so much unrest anyway—so it was extremely difficult for me.

It was not in graduate school but on her first job as a social worker that Janice had to learn to work *with* White people. She said, "After I realized that I could hang in school, working at the social work agency allowed me to learn how to work *with* White people. I had never done that before and now I do it better than anybody."

Learning to live in a White world was an additional hurdle for all Black women in this age cohort. Previous generations of Black people were more likely to be educated in segregated colleges and to work within the confines of the established Black community. They taught in segregated schools, provided dental and medical care to the Black communities, and provided social services and other comforts to members of their own communities. They also lived in the Black community and worshiped on Sunday with many of the people they saw in different settings. As the comments of our respondents reveal, both Black and White people had to adjust to integrated settings, but it was more stressful for the newcomers.

SUMMARY AND CONCLUSION

Our major aim in this research was to reopen the study of the subjective experience of upward social mobility and to begin to incorporate race and gender into our vision of the process. In this exploratory work, we hope to raise issues and questions that will cast a new light on taken-for-granted assumptions about the process and the people who engage in it. The experiences of these women have certainly painted a different picture from the one we were left some twenty years ago. First and foremost, these women are not detached, isolated, or driven solely by career goals. Relationships with family of origin, partners, children, friends, and the wider community loom large in the way they envision and accomplish mobility and the way they sustain themselves as professional and managerial women.

Several of our findings suggest ways that race and gender shape the mobility process for baby boom Black and White women. Education was stressed as important in virtually all of the families of these women; however, they differed in how it was viewed and how much was desired. The upwardly mobile women, both Black and White, shared some obstacles to attainment. More mobile women had parents who never expected them to achieve a college education. They also received less emotional and financial support for college attendance from their families than the women in middle-class families received. Black women also faced the unique problem of crossing racial barriers simultaneously with class barriers.

There were fairly dramatic race differences in the messages that the Black and White women received from family about what their lives should be like as adults. Black women clearly received the message that they needed an occupation to succeed in life and that marriage was a secondary concern. Many Black women also expressed a sense that their mobility was connected to an entire racial uplift process, not merely an individual journey.

White upwardly mobile women received less clear messages. Only one-half of these women said that their parents stressed the need for an occupation to succeed, and 20 percent said that marriage was stressed as the primary life goal. The most common message seemed to suggest that an occupation was necessary, because marriage could not be counted on to provide economic survival. Having a career, on the other hand, could even be seen as detrimental to adult happiness.

Upward mobility is a process that requires sustained effort and emotional and cognitive, as well as financial, support. The legacy of the image of mobility that was built on the White male experience focuses on credentialing institutions, especially the schools, as the primary place where talent is recognized and support is given to ensure that the talented among the working class are mobile. Family and friends are virtually invisible in this portrayal of the mobility process.

Although there is a good deal of variation in the roles that family and friends play for these women, they are certainly not invisible in the process. Especially among many of the Black women, there is a sense that they owe a great debt to their families for the help they have received. Black upwardly mobile women were also much more likely to feel that they give more than they receive from kin. Once they have achieved professional managerial employment, the sense of debt combines with their greater access to resources to put them in the position of being asked to give and of giving more to both family and friends. Carrington (1980) identifies some potential mental health hazards of such a sense of debt in upwardly mobile Black women's lives.

White upwardly mobile women are less likely to feel indebted to kin and to feel that they have accomplished alone. Yet even among this group, connections to spouses and children played significant roles in defining how women were mobile, their goals, and their sense of satisfaction with their life in the middle class.

These data are suggestive of a mobility process that is motivated by a desire for personal, but also collective, gain and that is shaped by interpersonal commitments to family, partners and children, community, and the race. Social mobility involves competition, but also cooperation, community support, and personal obligations. Further research is needed to explore fully this new image of mobility and to examine the relevance of these issues for White male mobility as well.

NOTE

1. This and all the names used in this article are pseudonyms.

REFERENCES

Braverman, Harry. 1974. *Labor and monopoly capital*. New York: Monthly Review Press.

Carrington, Christine. 1980. Depression in Black women: A theoretical appraisal. In *The Black women*, edited by La Frances Rodgers Rose. Beverly Hills, CA: Sage.

Clark, Reginald. 1986. *Family life and school achievement*. Chicago: University of Chicago Press.

Collins, Patricia Hill. 1990. *Black feminist thought: knowledge, consciousness, and the politics of empowerment*. Boston: Routledge.

Ehrenreich, Barbara, and John Ehrenreich. 1979. The professional-managerial class. In *Between labor and capital*, edited by Pat Walker. Boston: South End Press.

Higginbotham, Elizabeth, and Lynn Weber Cannon. 1988. *Rethinking mobility: Towards a race and gender inclusive theory*. Research Paper no. 8. Center for Research on Women, Memphis State University.

Joslin, Daphne. 1979. Working-class daughters, middle-class wives: Social identity and self-esteem among women upwardly mobile through marriage. Ph.D. diss., New York University, New York.

McAdoo, Harriette Pipes. 1978. Factors related to stability in upwardly mobile Black families. *Journal of Marriage and the Family* 40:761–76.

Poulantzas, Nicos. 1974. *Classes in contemporary capitalism*. London: New Left Books.

U.S. Bureau of the Census. 1983. Detailed population characteristics: Tennessee. Census of the Population, 1980. Washington, DC: GPO.

Vanneman, Reeve, and Lynn Weber Cannon. 1987. *The American perception of class*. Philadelphia: Temple University Press.

35

What Do Low-Income Single Mothers Say about Marriage?

KATHRYN EDIN

When marriage rates among the poor plunged during the 1970s and 1980s, the American public began to blame welfare. During that time, an unmarried mother who had little or no income or assets could claim welfare until her youngest child aged out of the program (this was the case until 1996, when welfare became time-limited). If she were to marry, her access to welfare would be restricted. Up until the late 1980s, only about half of the states offered any benefits to married couples. By 1990, all states were required to offer welfare benefits to married couples with children who met certain income and eligibility criteria. Yet these benefits were hard to claim because the husband's income and assets were counted in determining the family's ongoing eligibility for the program (all of his income if he was the children's father, and a portion of his income if he was not), and the couple had to prove the principal wage earner had a recent history of work. One study indicates that few welfare recipients understood these complex rules regarding marriage; they generally assumed that marrying would mean the loss of welfare, food stamp, and Medicaid benefits (Edin and Lein 1997).

Not surprisingly, the public viewed the program as one that discouraged the poor from marrying. The Personal Responsibility and Work Opportunity Reconciliation Act of 1996 (PRWORA) has many aims, but one is to increase the costs of non-marriage by decreasing the resources an unmarried mother can claim from the state (see Corbett 1998). To accomplish this goal, PRWORA mandates states to ensure that recipients comply with certain requirements and offers them new flexibility to go beyond these mandates and impose further requirements. At minimum, PRWORA requires that states limit cash benefit receipt to no more than five years in an adult recipient's lifetime. A second minimum requirement is that states must impose a 20-hour work requirement after two years of receipt. States can opt for other requirements such as school attendance for minor children and participation in "work-related activities" like job search or short-term training. Violations of these requirements can result in a full cut-off or a partial reduction of benefits (these are referred to as "sanctions"). These new time limits and participation requirements sharply limit (or make more costly) the resources that single mothers can claim from the state. Meanwhile, the welfare rolls have fallen to nearly half their early 1990s levels. Though some of the decline is a response to improving economic conditions, the decline is much greater than the improvement in the economy would lead us to expect. Some scholars have claimed that the remainder is due to the "signaling effect" of welfare reform (e.g., that PRWORA has signaled to current and prospective

Kathryn Edin, "What Do Low-Income Single Mothers Say about Marriage?" from *Social Problems,* Volume 47, Number 1, pp. 112–133. Copyright © 2000 by the Society for the Study of Social Problems. All rights reserved.

clients that the rules have changed and that welfare is no longer an acceptable or feasible way of life), though there is little clear evidence in this regard.

. . . Yet despite this new world of welfare that confronts low-income adults, an analysis of ethnographic data from two cities suggests that the large majority of welfare recipients who are experiencing the changes with regard to welfare reform, are not planning on marrying in the near future. Furthermore, these recipients report that welfare reform has not changed their views on marriage. This is the case even though recipients said they believed welfare reform was "real" and would indeed be implemented (Edin, Scott, London, and Mazelis 1999).

. . . I utilize data drawn from in-depth, repeated ethnographic interviews with 292 low-income African American and white single mothers in three U.S. cities, to add qualitative grounding to our understanding of these trends. I seek to explicate the social role that marriage plays in the lives of low-income single mothers more fully. Drawing from these data, I show that though most low-income single mothers aspire to marriage, they believe that, in the short term, marriage usually entails more risks than potential rewards. Mothers say these risks may be worth taking if they can find the "right" man—and they define "rightness" in both economic and non-economic terms. They say they are willing, and even eager, to marry if the marriage represents an increase in their class standing and if, over a substantial period of time, their prospective husband's behavior indicates he won't beat them, abuse their children, refuse to share in household tasks, insist on making all the decisions, be sexually unfaithful, or abuse alcohol or drugs. However, many women also believe they can mitigate against these risks if they forgo marriage until the tasks of early child rearing are completed and they can concentrate more fully on labor market activities (e.g., holding a stable job). These women believe that by forgoing marriage until they can make regular and substantial contributions to the household economy, they can purchase the right to share more equally in economic and household decision-making within marriage. Additionally, an income of their own insures them against destitution if the marriage should fail. Mothers often say that they are hesitant to enter into marriage unless they have enough resources to legitimately threaten to leave the marriage if the previously

mentioned behavioral criteria are violated. In this way, they believe they will have more control over a prospective husband's behavior and insurance against financial disaster should the marriage ultimately fail.

LITERATURE REVIEW

The median age at a first marriage is the highest it has been since the United States began keeping reliable statistics: twenty-four for women and twenty-six for men (U.S. Bureau of the Census 1991b). The propensity to remarry has also declined (Cherlin 1992). Furthermore, more women and men are choosing not to marry during the prime family-building years, and thus, more children are living with a single parent. Both non-marriage and single parenthood are particularly common among the poorest segments of American society (U.S. Bureau of the Census 1991a; Schoen and Owens 1992:116). . . .

Both rates of entry into first marriage and remarriage are far lower for poor women than for their more advantaged counterparts (Bumpass and Sweet 1989). Once a woman has children, her chances of marrying are also lower than a childless woman's (Bennett, Bloom, and Craig 1991). There are also large differences by race (Bennett, Bloom and Craig 1990, 1989; Staples 1988). Yet it is poor women with children, a disproportionate share of whom are African Americans, on whom social welfare policy has focused.

Current theories that attempt to explain the decline in marriage have generally focused on four areas: women's economic independence; the inability of men (particularly minority men) to obtain stable family-wage employment; the role that welfare has played in creating marriage disincentives among the poor; and on what might be called cultural factors, such as the stalled revolution in gender roles (see Luker 1996:158–160).

Many scholars argue that women's prospects for economic independence through work make it possible for them to raise their children apart from fathers who are wife beaters, child abusers, or otherwise difficult to live with (Becker 1981; South and Trent 1988; Teachman, Polonko, and Leigh 1987; Trent and South 1989). In the classic version of this argument (Becker 1981), women who specialize in child rearing and household management, while their spouses specialize in market work, will find marriage very attractive. Women who combine such tasks with work will be less dependent on men to fulfill the bread-winning role. As wages rise, women's employment also rises, and the attractiveness of marriage declines. . . .

A second argument is that there is a shortage of marriageable men among some groups. Most work in this area has focused on African Americans, since it is among blacks that marriage rates are lowest. Some have addressed the question of whether this is due to an insufficient supply of marriageable black men, either because of rising unemployment and incarceration (Wilson 1996, 1987), declining earnings (Oppen-heimer 1993), or sex-ratio imbalances (South and Lloyd 1992; Tucker and Mitchell-Kernan 1996). Most analyses show there is some evidence to support each of these variations on the male marriageable pool hypothesis, but the proportion of families headed by a single mother is simply much greater than this approach would predict (Fossett and Kielcolt 1993; Lichter, LeClere and McLaughlin 1991; South and Lloyd 1992).

Third, some have argued that the government may keep poor parents apart by making it more rewarding for the mother to collect welfare benefits than to marry a father with a menial job (Becker 1991; Murray 1984). According to this theory, welfare, rather than work, provides the economic independence that makes it possible, and even profitable, for mothers to eschew marriage. There is little evidence that out-of-wedlock birth rates are affected by either state variations in welfare levels or by changes in state benefits over time, though there is a modest negative effect for remarriage (Bane and Ellwood 1994; Hoffman 1997; Moffitt 1995).

Finally, some scholars argue that marriage decisions are influenced by what are generally termed "cultural" factors, even though these factors can sometimes be traced back to material realities. One argument points to the stalled revolution in sex roles. Although many men are earning less money than previously, and although wives are much more likely to work, few men truly share the household labor and childcare tasks (Hochs-child 1989). Kristen Luker argues that when "men are increasingly less able to contribute financially to the household and when they show little willingness to do more work around the house, women will inevitably revise their thinking about marriage, work, and the raising of children" (1996:132). The gender gap in sex-role

expectations has grown in recent decades. Scanzoni (1970:148) found that the divergence between husbands and wives over what constitutes legitimate male authority is widest at the lowest class levels. He also found that low status husbands exercised more power in conflict resolution than higher status husbands (1970:156). White women's views tend to be more egalitarian than white men's, both in terms of work and household duties. Black men and women both hold egalitarian views in terms of women's work, but black men lag behind their female counterparts (and white males) in their view of gender roles (Blee and Tickameyer 1995; Collins 1987). No study I know of estimates the strength of the relationship between the gender gap in sex-role expectations and marriage rates. . . .

METHOD

I chose to study the social role of marriage among low-income single mothers for three reasons. First, they are the targets of recent legislation that attempts to encourage marriage. Second, the majority of low-income adult women, for whom the costs of non-marriage and child bearing are presumably the highest, are neither childless nor married (either because they never married or they divorced), and this trend appears to be growing stronger over time (U.S. Bureau of the Census 1993). . . . Third, it is most appropriate for the method I employ. Qualitative research designs typically focus on a single group or "case" and involve an in-depth investigation of the rich interplay of factors involved in some aspect of that group's shared experience (Becker 1992:209–210). . . .

These data consist of transcripts and field notes from in-depth, repeated, qualitative interviews with 292 low-income single mothers in three U.S. cities. In each city, my collaborators and I interviewed roughly 100 low-income single mothers: 87 in Charleston, South Carolina, 105 in Chicago, and 100 in Camden, New Jersey/Philadelphia, Pennsylvania. In Chicago and Charleston, the sample was evenly divided between African Americans and whites. Interviews were conducted between 1989 and 1992. In Camden/Philadelphia, the sample is also predominately African American and white. These interviews were conducted between 1996 and 1999. About half of the respondents in each city and racial group relied on welfare, and about half worked at low-wage jobs (they earned less than $7.50 per hour).

The cities vary in a number of interesting ways. Chicago offered average welfare benefits ($376 for a three-person family) and had an average labor market in the early 1990s, when we did most of our interviewing there. Charleston, South Carolina had very modest welfare benefits ($205 for a family of three) and a tight labor market. Camden, New Jersey is an industrial suburb of Philadelphia, Pennsylvania. In both states, residents received better-than-average welfare benefits in the mid-1990s (roughly $420 for three persons) but the labor market in the Philadelphia region was quite slack. . . .

In all three cities, we scheduled conversations with each respondent at least twice to ensure that there was sufficient time to develop adequate rapport. Within the context of these conversations, we addressed a predetermined set of topics, as well as additional topics brought up by the respondents. The order and precise wording of the questions regarding each topic was not prescribed, but followed the natural flow of conversation.

The primary goal of this analysis is to show what a relatively large, heterogeneous group of low-income single mothers say about the declining propensity of poor mothers and fathers to marry. The analysis is not meant to prove or disprove existing theories of family formation among the poor, but rather to give an in-depth account of the social role marriage plays in the lives of a relatively heterogeneous (in terms of city and race) group of mothers within a single social category. The analysis will show that much of what poor mothers say supports existing theory, though mothers' accounts show a greater degree of complexity than these theories recognize. The reader will also see that poor mothers' accounts reveal motivations that existing approaches generally neglect. The result is a complex set of personal accounts that can lend crucial qualitative grounding to other representative studies of the retreat from marriage among the poor.

RESULTS

Analysis of the Chicago and Charleston low-income single mothers' accounts reveals five primary reasons why poor parents do not form or reform a legal union with a man (see Table 1). The first line of Table 1 shows the percentage of mothers whose transcripts revealed positive views toward marriage and hoped to marry in the future. As is true in nationally representative surveys (South 1993), whites are somewhat more positively oriented toward marriage than are African Americans, particularly in our Southern site. There are no differences by city. Lines two through six show the five motivations the Chicago and Charleston women most often discussed when they talked about these views in depth. Since we asked all of the Camden/Philadelphia mothers about each of these motivations, all talked about them, and nearly all felt they were relevant in mothers' decisions regarding marriage (even if they were not relevant to them personally).

Table 1 Percent of Low-Income Single Mothers with Positive Views Regarding Marriage, Plans to Marry, and the Percent Who Discussed the Importance of Various Factors on Marriage Attitudes by City and Race

	Chicago African American	Chicago White	Charleston African American	Charleston White	Sig. of F Race	Sig. of F City
Positive Orientation toward	46	60	41	62	*	
Marriage						
Affordability	79	66	55	39	*	***
Respectability	62	50	69	52	*	
Control	79	54	55	36	*	
Trust	66	94	44	60	**	***
Domestic violence	21	54	16	48	***	

Notes: *p < .10 **p < .05 ***p < .001

Affordability

Men's income is an issue that matters enormously in poor parents' willingness and ability to stay together. Though the *total* earnings a father can generate is clearly the most important dimension for mothers, so is the *regularity* of those earnings, the *effort* men expend finding and keeping work, and the *source* of his income.

One African American mother in Chicago summed her views about contemporary marriage this way: "Men simply don't earn enough to support a family. This leads to couples breaking up." When we asked mothers specifically about their criteria for marriage, nearly every one told us the father would have to have a "good job." One reason was their recognition that the couple would probably not be able to sustain an independent household unless the father made a "decent" living. One African American Camden respondent told us:

> You can't get married and go on living with your mother. That's just like playing house. She expects your husband to be able to provide for you and if he can't, what is he doing marrying you in the first place! She's not going to put up with having him under her roof.

When mothers judge the merits of marriage, they worry a lot about the stability of men's earnings simply because they have to. At the bottom of the income distribution, single mothers who must choose between welfare or low-wage employment to pay their bills face a constant budget shortfall and thus, must continually find ways of getting extra money to pay their bills (Edin and Lein 1997). To generate extra cash, mothers must either find a side job or another adult who can provide regular and substantial economic support. Meanwhile, any given father or boyfriend is likely to have limited skills and a troubled employment history. In sum, while mothers have constant income needs, the men who father their children often cannot consistently meet these needs.

Mothers said their men often complained that women did not understand how difficult it was for men to find steady work. Yet, even mothers who were inclined to sympathize with men's employment difficulties were in a bind: they simply could not afford to keep an economically unproductive man around the house. Because of this, almost all of the low-income single mothers we interviewed told us that rather than marry the father of their children, they preferred to live separately or to cohabit. In cohabiting situations, mothers nearly always said they enforced a "pay and stay" rule. If a father quit his job or lost his job and did not (in the mother's view) try very hard to find another one, or drank or smoked up his paycheck, he lost his right to co-reside in the household. Since her name, not his, was generally on the lease, she had the power to evict him. A black mother from the Philadelphia area explained her practices in this regard:

> We were [thinking about marriage] for a while, but he was real irresponsible. I didn't want to be mean or anything, [but when he didn't work] I didn't let him eat my food. I would tell him, "If you can't put any food here, you can't eat here. These are your kids, and you should want to help your kids, so if you come here, you can't eat their food." Finally, I told him he couldn't stay here either. Right now, I think I would never [get tied to] a[nother] man who is irresponsible and without a job.

Keeping an unemployed man in the house puts a strain on a mother's, already overstrained, budget. It also precludes a woman's ability to offer co-residence to an alternative man who is employed. One African American mother from Charleston told us:

> I've been with my baby's father for almost 10 years, since high school graduation. He's talking marriage, but what I'm trying to do now is get away from him. He just lost his job [at the Naval base]. He worked there for 18 years. [Now] he's in work, out of work, then in work again. Right now he's just working part-time at McDonalds. I can do bad by myself, I don't need no one helping me [do bad]. I want somebody better, somebody [who can bring home] a regular paycheck. [So] I'm trying to get away from him right now.

If they are not married, she has the flexibility to lower her household costs by getting rid of him, and the possibility of replacing him with another more economically productive man (or at least one who is working at the time).

Women whose male partners couldn't, or wouldn't, find work, often lost respect for them and "just couldn't stand" to keep them around. A white Chicago divorcee told us:

> I couldn't get him to stay working. [T]he kids would be hungry and I'd throw a fit and he'd have a nerve to tell me, "Who cares? You're always over [at your mother's], why can't you ask her for some food?" Talk

about a way [to lose someone's respect]. It's hard to love somebody if you lose respect. . . . [Finally, I couldn't take it and I made him leave].

As one can well imagine, men in this situation knew they were purchasing their place in the household and, to some extent, their hold on the woman's affections. The women we interviewed said this made men feel that their girlfriends "only want me for my money." They told us their children's fathers resented their girl-friends' "materialistic" attitudes. Holding fathers to these standards was often emotionally wrenching for mothers. One African American Camden mother expressed her emotional dilemma as follows:

> It was like there was a struggle going on inside of me. I mean, he lost his job at the auto body shop when they went [bankrupt] and closed down. Then he couldn't find another one. But it was months and months. I was trying to live on my welfare check and it just wasn't enough. Finally, I couldn't do it any more [because] it was just too much pressure on me [even though] he is the love of my life. I told him he had to leave, even though I knew it wasn't really his fault that [he wasn't working]. But I had nothing in the house to feed the kids, no money to pay the bills. Nothing. And he was just sitting there, not working. I couldn't take it, so I made him leave.

An African American mother from Charleston emphasized the fact that women not only value earnings, but respect a man who is making his best effort to support his family. She said, "Am I gonna marry him? Of course! If he didn't have a steady job? No, no. [But] If he's helping out the best he can, yeah, I would. He drives a truck [right now]." According to these mothers, a man who could not find work in the formal sector had two choices: he could stay home and wait for the children's mother to kick him out, or he could try to maintain his place in the family by finding work in the underground economy. Sometimes this technique worked, but more often, it backfired. Work in criminal trades was generally easier to get, but mothers said that fathers who engaged in crime for any length of time, generally lost their place in the family as well. When a father began to earn his living by selling drugs, a mother feared that he would bring danger into the household. Mothers worried that fathers' criminal companions might "come for them" at the house, or that fathers might store drugs, drug proceeds, or weapons in the

house. Even worse, mothers feared that a father might start "using his product." Mothers also felt that a drug-dealing father would be a very poor role model for their children. Thus, mothers did not generally consider earnings from crime as legitimate earnings (they said they wouldn't marry such a man no matter how much he earned from crime).

Chicago respondents were more likely to discuss economic factors than Charleston mothers were. This difference could be due to the fact that, when the interviews took place, Chicago's unemployment rate was higher than Charleston's, or possibly due to more traditional values among Southerners regarding marriage. Blacks also discussed economic factors more often than whites. This is presumably because black men's earnings are lower than those of whites with similar skill levels.

Respectability

Even within very poor communities, residents make class-based distinctions among themselves. Most of our mothers' eventual goal was to become "respect-able," and they believed that respectability was greatly enhanced by a marriage tie to a routinely employed partner earning wages significantly above the legal minimum. However, mothers said that they could not achieve respectability by marrying someone who was frequently out of work, otherwise underemployed, supplemented his income through criminal activity, and had little chance of improving his situation over time. Mothers believed that marriage to such a man would diminish their respectability, rather than enhance it.

Mothers seldom romanticized a father's economic prospects when it came to marriage (though they sometimes did so when conceiving the man's child [see Kefalas and Edin 2000]). They generally knew that if they entered into marriage with a lower-class man, the marriage was unlikely to last because the economic pressures on the relationship would simply be too great. Even if they had contemplated marriage to their children's father "for love" or "romantic feelings," their family members and friends generally convinced poor parents that such a marriage would collapse under economic strain (see also Stack 1974). For these mothers, marriage meant tying oneself to the class position of one's partner "for life." Even if a woman could afford to marry a man whose economic prospects were bleak, her decision would have signaled to her kin and neighbors that he was the best she could do. Mothers expected that marriage should pull them up the class ladder. Community notions of respectability help to explain sentiments like the one revealed by this African American mother in Charleston:

> I want to get married. I've always wanted to get married and have a family. [My baby's father,] he is doing pretty good, but I am not going to marry him until . . . we get some land. [We'll] start off with a trailer, live in that for about 10 years, and then build a dream house. But I am not going to get married and pay rent to someone else. When we save up enough money to [buy] an acre of land and [can finance] a trailer, then we'll marry.

Many mothers told us that their children's fathers also said that they planned to marry them, but wanted to "wait 'till we can afford a church wedding, not just a justice of the peace thing." Marriage made a statement to the larger community about each partner's current and prospective class standing. Thus, marriage could either confer respectability or deny it. If a low-income woman had a child with an erratically employed and unskilled man to whom she was not married, she had not tied herself in any permanent way to him or his class position. Most mothers weren't willing to sign an apartment lease with the man they were with, much less a marriage license. Mothers who remained unmarried were able to maintain their dream of upward mobility. "Marrying up" guaranteed the woman the respect of her community, while marrying at her own class level only made her look foolish in the eyes of her family and neighbors. When we asked mothers whether they would marry the erratic or low earners that had fathered their children, the most common response was "I can do bad by myself."

In addition to the importance women placed on respectability, they also had strong moral (and oftentimes religious) objections to marrying men whose economic situation would, in their view, practically guarantee eventual marital dissolution. Mothers often talked about the "sacred" nature of marriage, and believed that no "respectable" woman would marry under these circumstances (some spoke of such a marriage as a "sacrilege"). In interview after interview, mothers stressed the seriousness of the marriage commitment and their belief

that "it should last forever." Thus, it is not that mothers held marriage in low esteem, but rather the fact that they held it in such high esteem that convinced them to forgo marriage, at least until their prospective marriage partner could prove himself worthy economically or they could find another partner who could. To these mothers, marriage was a powerful symbol of respectability, and should not be diluted by foolish unions.

Respectability was equally important for respondents in Chicago and Charleston, though it was somewhat more important for African Americans than for whites (and probably for the same reasons that affordability concerns were). Respondents' discourse in regard to respectability, however, varied quite dramatically by race (Bulcroft and Bulcroft 1993). Many African American respondents who claimed they wanted to marry "up or not at all" knew that holding to such standards might well mean not marrying at all. Whites had less of these anxieties. White respondents typically had sisters, other kin, and friends who had married men who earned a "decent" wage, and were somewhat more sanguine about their own chances of finding such a man than were blacks. A handful of white respondents even told us they planned to "marry out of poverty" so they could become housewives. Only one black respondent reported such plans.

Control and the Stalled Sex Role Revolution at Home

In a non-marital relationship, women often felt they had more control than they would have had if they married. Even if the couple cohabited, they nearly always lived with her mother or in an apartment with her name on the lease. Thus, mothers had the power to evict fathers if they interfered with child rearing, or tried to take control over financial decision-making. Mothers said that fathers who knew they were "on trial" could do little about this state of affairs, especially since they needed a place to live and could not generally afford one on their own. One African American Philadelphia-area respondent's partner quipped, "her attitude is like, 'it's either my way or the highway.'"

Why was control, not power, such an important issue for these women? Most mothers said they thought their children's fathers had very traditional notions of sex roles—notions that clashed with their more egalitarian views. One white cohabiting mother from Charleston said, "If we were to marry, I don't think it would be so ideal. [Husbands] want to be in charge, and I can't deal with that." Regardless of whether or not the prospective wife worked, mothers feared that prospective husbands would expect to be "head of the house," and make the "final" decisions about child rearing, finances, and other matters. Women, on the other hand, felt that since they had held the primary responsibility for both raising and supporting their children, they should have an equal say.

When we asked single mothers what they liked best about being a single parent, their most frequent response was "I am in charge," or "I am in control." Mothers seemed willing to take on the responsibilities of child rearing if they were also able to make and enforce the rules. In most mothers' views, the presence of fathers often interfered with their parental control, particularly if the couple married. Most women also felt that the presence of a husband might impede their efforts to discipline and spend time with their children. Mothers criticized men for being "too demanding" of their time and attention. A white Chicago mother answered the question, "What is it like being a single mother?" as follows: "It's great in terms of being independent. I'm just thrilled being away from my ex-husband. The joy of that hasn't worn off. I feel more freedom to be a parent how I want [to be]. We did not agree on parenting at all." A white Charleston respondent said, "[Marriage isn't an option] right now. I don't want any man thinking that he has any claim on my kids or on how I raise them."

Mothers were also concerned about losing control of the family's financial situation. One African American Chicago mother told us, "[I won't marry because] the men take over the money. I'm too afraid to lose control of my money again." Still another said, "I'm the head of the household right now, and I make the [financial] decisions. I [don't want to give that up]."

Finally, mothers often expressed the view that if they married, their men would expect them to do all of the household chores, plus "cook and clean" and otherwise "take care of" them. Some described their relationships with their ex-partners as "like having one more kid to take care of." We asked another divorced white Charleston mother whether she would ever consider marriage again. She answered,

I don't know, I can't think that far ahead. I can't see it. This guy I'm with right now, I don't know. I like being by myself. The thought of having to cook and clean for somebody else? I'm like, "No." I'm looking for somebody who is going to cook and clean for me!

Concerns over control did not, however, mean that most women had abandoned their plans to marry. But they felt their own situations had to be such as to maximize their chances of exerting control in the marriage relationship. The primary way mothers who wanted to marry thought they could maintain power in a marriage relationship was by working and contributing to the family budget. One African American mother living in Charleston told me,

One thing my mom did teach me is that you must work some and bring some money into the household so you can have a say in what happens. If you completely live off a man, you are helpless. That is why I don't want to get married until I get my own [career] and get off of welfare.

Mothers also wanted to get established economically prior to marriage because men had failed them in the past. This is why they often told us that if they did get married, they would make sure "the car is in my name, the house is in my name" and so on. They wanted to "get myself established first, and then get married" so if the marriage broke up, they wouldn't be "left with nothing." One African American Camden mother commented, "[I will consider marriage] one day when I get myself together. When I have my own everything, so I won't be left depending on a man."

The experience of breakup or divorce and the resulting financial hardship and emotional pain fundamentally transformed these women's relational views. I heard dozens of stories of women who had held traditional views regarding sex roles while they were younger and still in a relationship with their children's fathers. When the men for whom they sacrificed so much gave them nothing but pain and anguish, they felt they had been "duped." Their childhood fantasy of marriage was gone, as was their willingness to be dependent on or subservient to men.

Because of these painful experiences, formerly married white mothers generally placed as high priority on increasing their labor market skills and experience as their black never-married counterparts. They felt that a hasty remarriage might distract them from this goal (possibly because their husbands' income would make them too comfortable and tempt them to quit school or work). Like the African American mothers who had seldom been married, whites also said that once they remarried, they would keep working no matter what. The "little money of my own" both African American and white mothers spoke of was valued, not only for its contribution to the household economy, per se, but for the power it purchased them within the relationship, as well as its insurance value against destitution if the marriage should fail.

Mothers told us that the more established they became economically, the more bargaining power they believed they would have in a marital relationship. The mothers they knew who were economically dependent on men had to "put up with all kinds of behavior" because they could not legitimately threaten to leave without serious financial repercussions (due to the fact that they could not translate their homemaking skills into wages). Mothers felt that if they became more economically independent (had the car in their name, the house in their name, no common debts, etc.), they could legitimately threaten to leave their husbands if certain conditions (i.e., sexual fidelity) weren't met. These threats would, in turn they believed, keep a husband on his best behavior.

Taking on these attitudes of self-reliance and independence wasn't always easy. Some formerly married women whose partner failed them had never lived alone before, having gone straight from their parents' household to their husband's. In addition, some hadn't held a job in years, had no marketable skills, and had no idea about how to make their way in the world of employed women. One white Chicago resident was a full-time homemaker until her divorce. After getting no child support from her ex-husband for several months, this mother decided she had better get a job, but the best job she could find paid only minimum wage at the time. Her journey from her first job to her current position (which paid $7 an hour) was a painful one. Giving up this hard-won self-sufficiency for dependence on a man was simply too great a risk for her to take. She said, "I don't want to depend on nobody. It's too scary."

The often difficult life experiences of these mothers had convinced them of competencies they might not have known they had before single motherhood.

Because of these experiences, their roles expanded to encompass more traditionally male responsibilities than before. The men, in their view, weren't respectful of these competencies. Instead, they expected them to revert to more traditional female roles. When we asked a white Chicago mother whether there were any advantages to being apart from the father of her children, she replied:

You're the one in control. The good thing is that I feel good about myself. I feel more independent. Whereas when I was with Brian, I didn't. I had never been out on my own, but I took that step to move out and, since I did, I feel much better about myself as a person, that I can do it.

While it was true that some women were poorer financially than before their relationships ended, the increased pride they felt in being able to provide for themselves and their children partially compensated for economic hardship. Another white Chicago mother said "You know, I feel better [being alone] because I am the provider, I'm getting the things that I want and I'm getting them for myself, little by little."

Concerns about power might explain why childbearing and marriage have become separated from one another, particularly among the low-income population. Though we did not ask our Chicago and Charleston mothers questions about the ideal time to bear children and to marry, we did ask our Camden/Philadelphia mothers these questions. Most felt childbearing should ideally occur in a woman's early 20s, but that marriage should ideally occur in a woman's late 20s or early 30s. These answers are somewhat suspect because respondents might simply have been rationalizing past behavior (most hadn't been married when they had had their children, and half had never married). Even more confusing is the fact that these same respondents generally said that one should be married before having children. When interviewers probed deeper, respondents revealed that, though the goal of getting married first and having children second was indeed their ideal, it was hardly a practical choice given their economic situations and those of their partners.

Respondents' explanations of their views also revealed that many felt that childbearing required at least a temporary or partial withdrawal from the labor market. Childbearing within marriage and the labor market withdrawal it required, made women "dependent" and "vulnerable" and weakened their control. When mothers told us they wanted to wait to marry or remarry until their late 20s or early 30s, most assumed that, at this point, their youngest child would be in school. Thus, they would be free to more fully pursue labor market activities and, in this way, enhance their potential bargaining and decision-making role in any subsequent marital relationship. One African American Camden mother said:

> One guy was like, "marry me, I want a baby." I don't want to have to depend on anybody. No way. I [would rather] work. [If I married him and had his baby], I'd [have to quit work and] be dependent again. It's too scary.

There was no significant difference between cities in the salience of sex roles and power. Blacks were more concerned about these issues than whites, yet the differences are probably smaller than other studies of racial differences in sex-role attitudes would suggest. Many of the white women we interviewed had been married in the past and most of them reported that they had begun their marriages thinking that they would stay at home or work part-time (at least while their children were young). Their husbands, they assumed, would be the primary breadwinners, while they specialized in household management and parenting. After the breakup of these relationships, white mothers were often shocked by how vulnerable their withdrawal from the labor market had made them. It was after learning these hard lessons that most white mothers developed the conviction that it was foolish to marry unless they had "established themselves" first.

Trust

For some mothers, the reaction of their partner to an unplanned pregnancy became their first hard lesson in "the way men are." Mothers said that fathers' responses ran the gamut from strong negative responses to strong positive ones, but some men were clearly panicked by the prospect of being responsible for a child—particularly those who feared a child support order. Some fathers denied paternity even when they had encouraged the mother to get pregnant and/or carry the child to term. In these situations, fathers often claimed that the child was not theirs because the mother was "a whore." One partner of a pregnant Camden mother told the interviewer (in the mother's presence), "how do I know the baby's mine? Who knows if she hasn't been stepping out on me with some other man and now she wants me to support another man's child!"

Subsequent hard lessons were learned when mothers' boyfriends or husbands proved unfaithful. This experience was so common among respondents that many simply did not believe men "could be faithful to only one woman." This "men will be men" belief did not mean that women were willing to simply accept infidelity as part of the natural course of a marriage. Most said they would rather never marry than to "let him make a fool out of me." One black Chicago resident just couldn't conceive of finding a marriageable man.

> All those reliable guys, they are gone, they are gone. They're either thinking about one of three things: another woman, another man, or dope. . . . [M]y motto is "there is not a man on this planet that is faithful." It's a man thing. I don't care, you can love your wife 'til she turns three shades of avocado green. A man is gonna be a man and it's not a point of a woman getting upset about it. It's a point of a woman accepting it. 'Cause a man's gonna do what a man's gonna do. . . . [Other] black women, they say "once you find a man that's gonna be faithful, you go ahead and get married to him." [They] got it all wrong. Then they gonna [be surprised when they find out] he ain't faithful. And the wife gonna end up in a nut house. It's better not to get married, so you don't get your expectations up.

A white mother from Charleston said, "I was married for three years before I threw him out after discovering that he had another woman. I loved my husband, but I don't [want another one]. This is a wicked world we are living in." A black Charlestonian said,

> I would like to find a nice man to marry, but I know that men cannot be trusted. That's why I treat them the way I do—like the dogs they are. I think that all men will cheat on their wives regardless of how much he loves her. And you don't ever want to be in that position.

Mother after mother told us cautionary tales of married couples they knew where either the man or the woman was "stepping out" on their spouse. They viewed the wounded spouse as either hopelessly naive (if they did not know) or without self-respect (if they did know). They did not want to place themselves in a similar position. Demands for sexual fidelity within marriage had a practical, as well as an emotional dimension. Women often gave examples of married men they knew who "spen[t] all his money on the little woman he [had] on the side." Mothers often feared that men would promise them and their children "the world" and then abandon them. One African American Camden mother summed up her views as follows: "Either they leave or they die. The first thing is, don't get close to them, 'cause they ain't no good from the beginning. When that man ain't doing right for me, I learn to dump [him]." A white mother from Chicago said: "I've been a single parent since the day my husband walked out on me. He tried to come back, but I am not one to let someone hurt me and my children twice. I am living on welfare [rather than living with him]."

Even the most mistrustful of our respondents generally held out some hope that they would find a man who could be trusted and who would stay around. One white Chicago mother said, "I want to meet a man who will love me and my son and want us to grow together. I just don't know if he exists." An African American mother living in Chicago said,

> Maybe I'll find a good person to get married to, someone to be a stepfather to my son. They're not all the same; they're not all bad. There are three things in my life: my school, my work, and my son. Not men. At first they love you, they think you're beautiful, and then they leave. When I got pregnant, he just left. My father is like that. He has kids by several different women. I hate him for it. I say, "I hate you. Why do you do that? Why?"

A white divorcee from Chicago explained her views of the differences between the sexes in this regard as follows:

> Men can say. "Well honey, I'm going out for the night." And then they disappear for two months. Whereas, the mother has a deeper commitment, conscience, or compassion. . . . If [women] acted like men, our kids would be in the park, left. We'd say "Oh, somebody else is going to take care of it." Everybody would be orphaned.

An African American mother from the Philadelphia area told us,

> I'm frustrated with men, period. They bring drugs and guns into the house, you take care of their kids, feed them, and then they steal your rent money out of your purse. They screw you if you put your self out for them. So now, I don't put myself out there any more.

Because their own experiences and the experiences of their friends, relatives, and neighbors has been so overwhelmingly negative, many women reduced the expressive value they placed on their relationships over time. Some instrumentalized their relationships with men to the point that they didn't "give it away anymore," meaning they no longer had sex without expecting something, generally something material, in return. A white Chicago mother put it this way: "Love is blind. You fall in love with the wrong one sometimes. It's easy to do. [Now] I am so mean . . . [when] I sleep with a guy I am like, 'Give me the money and leave me alone.'" Nonetheless, many of *these same women* often held out hope of finding a man who was "different," one who could be trusted.

Chicago mothers were significantly more likely to voice trust issues than their Charleston counterparts. This difference may reflect regional differences (Southerners may be more trusting than Northerners). It may also be true that trust issues are least salient in a tight labor market where jobs for unskilled men are more plentiful. Whites talked about the issue more than African Americans and could reflect differences in spontaneous self-reports of domestic abuse (discussed below).

Domestic Violence

In Chicago and Charleston, we did not ask directly about domestic abuse, yet, a surprisingly high number spontaneously spoke of some history of domestic violence in their childhood or adult lives. In Table 1, we include only those mothers for which the abuse had some bearing on marriage attitudes. We see no important differences across cities, but rather startling differences by race. One white mother living in Chicago decided to have her child with the assumption that she would marry the father, but after a series of physically abusive episodes triggered by arguments about his drinking and drug use, she changed her mind.

> The person I was with wasn't quite what I thought he was. We were going to get married, [but] I don't believe in making two mistakes. [There were about] four [big] blowouts before I finally actually [ended it]. The last one was probably the worst. We went to a friend's

house [and] he started drinking, [doing] drugs, and stuff. I said, "please take me home now." So [we got in the car] and we started arguing about why he had to hang around people like that [who do] drugs and all that sort of stuff. One thing led to another and he kind of tossed me right out of the car.

Many women reported physical abuse during pregnancy. Several mothers reported having miscarriages because of such abuse. For others, the physical abuse began after the child was born. It was not uncommon for women to report injuries serious enough to warrant trips to the hospital emergency room. Two African American women from Charleston ended up in the emergency room following beatings from their boyfriends. One recounted:

My daughter's father, we used to fight. I got to where nobody be punching on me because love is not that serious. And I figure somebody is beating on you and the only thing they love is watching you go the emergency room. That's what they love. A lot of these chicks, they think "he [hitting] me because [he loves me and] he don't want me looking at nobody [else]." Honey, he need help, and you need a little more help than he do because you stand there [and take it].

The other interjected: "Just leave him [if he abuses you], you get over [him]. You will be over [him eventually]."

The fact that women tended to experience repeated abuse from their children's fathers before they decided to leave attests to their strong desire to make things work with their children's fathers. Many women finally left when they saw the abuse beginning to affect their children's well-being. One white Charleston mother explained:

... it was an abusive situation. It was physical. . . . [My daughter] saw us fighting a lot. The minute she would see us fighting, she would go into hysterics. It would turn into an all-out brawl. She was terrified. And this was what that did to her and I thought. "I've got to get out of here."

But the economic pressures associated with leaving sometimes propelled mothers into another harmful relationship. One white Chicago mother explained:

I married [my first husband] a month after I had [our son]. And I married him because I couldn't afford [to live alone]. Boy, was that stupid. And I left him [two

years after that] when our daughter was five months old. I got scared. I was afraid because my kids were starting to get in the middle. [My son] still to this day, when he thinks someone is hurting me, he'll start screaming and crying and beating on him. He had seen his father [beat me up]. I didn't want him to see that. I remarried six months later because I couldn't make it [financially]. And I got into another abusive marriage. And we got separated before the year was even up. He would burn me [with cigarettes]. He was an alcoholic. He was a physical abuser, mental [too]. I think he would have killed me [if I had stayed].

Another white Chicagoan said, "after being abused, physically abused, by him the whole time we were married, I was ready to [kill him]. He put me in the hospital three times. I was carrying our child four and a half months, he beat me and I miscarried." A white Charlestonian said, "I was terrified to leave because I knew it would mean going on welfare. . . . But that is okay. I can handle that. The thing I couldn't deal with is being beat up." When we asked one black Charleston woman if there were any advantages to being a single mom, she replied, "not living with someone there to abuse you. I'm not scared anymore. I'm scared of my bills and I'm scared of I get sick, what's going to happen to my kids, but I'm not afraid for my life."

We are not sure why there is so much domestic violence among poor parents, but our interviews with mothers give us a few clues. First, mothers sometimes linked episodes of violence to fathers' fears about their ability to provide, especially in light of increased state efforts toward child support enforcement. This explanation was most often invoked in reference to the beatings women received when they were pregnant. Second, some mothers living in crime-ridden, inner-city neighborhoods talked about family violence as a carryover from street violence. The Camden/Philadelphia mothers talked at length about the effect this exposure had had on their children's fathers' lives (and their own), and some even described the emotional aftermath of this exposure as "Post-Traumatic Stress Syndrome."

DISCUSSION

Since the 1970s, a sharply declining proportion of unskilled men have been able to earn enough to support a family (U.S. House of Representatives 1997). These trends clearly have had a profound influence on marriage among low-income men and women. But even when a marriage might be affordable, mothers might judge the risks marriage entails as too great for other reasons, some of which reflect changes in the economy, but are not economic *per se*.

In these mothers' view, wives still borrow their class standing from their husbands. Since a respectable marriage is one that lasts "forever," mothers who marry low-skilled males must themselves give up their dreams of upward mobility. In the interim, single motherhood holds a somewhat higher status than a "foolish" marriage to a low-status man. . . .

Beyond affordability and respectability concerns, these interviews offer powerful evidence that there has been a dramatic revolution in sex-role expectations among women at the low end of the income distribution, and that the gap between low-income men's and women's expectations in regard to gender roles is wide. Women who have proven their competencies through the hard lessons of single parenthood aren't generally willing to enter subservient roles—they want to have substantial control and bargaining power in subsequent relationships. Some mothers learned the dangers of economic dependence upon men through the pain and financial devastation that accompanied a separation and divorce. Others were schooled by their profound disappointment at their baby's father's reaction to the pregnancy and his failure to live up to the economic and emotional commitments of fatherhood. Both groups of mothers equate marital power with economic power, and believe that the emotional and financial risk that marriage entails is only sustainable when they themselves have reached some level of economic self-sufficiency.

The data also show that, though a small number of women want to marry and become housewives, the overwhelming majority want to continue working during any subsequent marriage. Since these mothers generally believe that childbearing and rearing young children necessitate a temporary withdrawal from the labor market, many place the ideal age at which to marry in the late 20s (when their youngest child is school age) and the ideal age to bear children in the early 20s—the age they say is the "normal" time for women to have children. Delaying marriage until they can concentrate more fully on labor market activity maximizes their chances of having a marriage where

they can have equal bargaining power. The income from work also allows them to legitimately threaten to leave the husband if certain behavioral standards are not met and many women believe that such threats will serve to keep husbands in line. These data suggest that the bargaining perspective, which many studies of housework currently employ, may be useful in understanding marriage attitudes and non-marital relational dynamics, as well.

Mothers believe that marital power is crucial, at least partially, because of their low trust of men. I know of no data that demonstrate that gender mistrust has grown over time, but certainly the risk of divorce, and the economic destitution for women that so often accompanies it, has grown. Trust issues are exacerbated by the experience of domestic violence. Many mothers told interviewers that it was these experiences that taught them "not to have any feeling for men." National-level data show that violence is more frequent among those with less income (Ptacek 1998). Presumably, such violence, along with the substance abuse that frequently accompanies it, is a way of "doing gender" for men who cannot adequately fulfill the breadwinner role. Though women's accounts did not always allow me to establish the sequence of events leading up to episodes of violence, many of those that did showed that violence followed job loss or revelation of a pregnancy. Both are sources of economic stress.

These data also reveal some interesting differences by city and by race, though the sample size is small. Charleston mothers worried less about affordability and trust issues than Chicago mothers. The first difference could result from the differences in local labor markets (tight versus somewhat slack) which disproportionately affect the employment of unskilled and minority men (Jencks 1992), or regional differences (Southerners might be more traditional than Northerners). The second difference is harder to explain, though regional differences and economic differences between the cities may also play a role. If men behave in an untrustworthy manner (i.e., "unfaithful") in order to compensate for their inability to fulfil the provider role, we would expect that women in tight labor markets might find it easier to trust male partners than women in slack labor markets. The impact of labor market conditions and regional variations on the marriage attitudes and rates for low-skilled men and women would be fruitful topics for further study across a wider range of labor markets and regions.

The analysis also revealed some interesting race difference. In both Charleston and Chicago, African Americans were more likely to name affordability, respectability, and control concerns, while whites mentioned trust and domestic violence more often. Affordability and respectability might be more salient for blacks because their chances of finding a marriage partner with sufficient economic resources to satisfy such concerns are lower than for whites. The salience of trust for whites might reflect higher rates of domestic violence, though these figures reflect spontaneous comments and probably underestimate the actual rate of violence for women in the sample. They may also reflect the fact that whites who elaborated on these experiences generally stayed with the violent partner (to whom they were often married) longer than African Americans. Whites' living arrangements might also have afforded less protection from violent men than blacks' in that whites were more likely to cohabit with their partner, while blacks were more likely to live in an extended-kin household. Nationally representative data also show that low-income whites cohabit significantly more often than comparable African Americans (Harris and Edin 1996).

In relation to theories of the retreat from marriage, there is no doubt that economic factors are necessary, though not sufficient, criteria for marriage among most low-income women interviewed. Theories that posit the importance of the stalled revolution of sex roles and Wilson's argument that non-marriage among blacks results from very low levels of trust, were both strongly supported, though our analysis revealed that trust was even more important for whites. Drake and Cayton and Rainwater's notions of instrumentality in male–female relationships also received support. I will say more about the economic independence and welfare disincentives arguments below.

In sum, the mothers we spoke to were quite forthcoming about the fact that the men who had fathered their children often weren't "worth a lifetime commitment" given their general lack of trustworthiness, the traditional nature of their sex-role views, the potential loss of control over parental and household decisions, and their risky and sometimes violent behavior. While mothers maintained hopes of eventual marriage, they viewed such hopes with some level of skepticism. Thus, they devoted most of their time and energy toward raising their children and "getting it together financially" rather than "waiting on a man." Those that planned on marrying generally assumed they would put off marriage until their children were in school and they were able to be fully engaged in labor market activity. By waiting to marry until the tasks associated with early child rearing and the required temporary withdrawal from the labor market were completed, mothers felt they could enhance their bargaining power within marriage.

This complex set of motivations to delay marriage or remarriage (or less frequently, to avoid them altogether) has interesting implications for welfare reform. The authors of PRWORA explicitly sought to encourage marriage among the poor by increasing the cost of non-marriage (e.g., reducing the amount of resources an unmarried mother can claim from the state). Put in the language of the welfare disincentives argument, PRWORA decreases the disincentives to marry, or, according to the economic independence theory, limits one source of financial independence for women who forgo marriage. If single mothers have fewer resources from the state, it is reasonable to argue that they might become more dependent on men and men's income. This may seem particularly likely given the fact that unskilled and semiskilled ex-welfare recipients will probably not be able to make enough money in the low-wage sector to meet their monthly expenses (Edin and Lein 1997) and that the gap between their income and expenses is likely to grow as they move from welfare to work (at least after the increased earned-income disregards some states offer elapse at the five year point or sooner). To make matters worse, unless the labor market remains extremely tight, low-skilled mothers' wages are not likely to increase over time because of a lack of premium on experience in the low-wage sector (Blank 1995; Burtless 1995; Harris and Edin 1996).

If PRWORA is fully implemented, these new financial realities might well encourage some couples to marry. However, if men's employment opportunities and wages do not increase dramatically, these data suggest that mothers might continue to opt for boyfriends (cohabiting or not), who can be replaced if they do not contribute, rather than husbands who cannot be so easily traded for a more economically productive man.

Even if mothers believed that they would be no worse off, or even slightly better off, by marrying than by remaining single, these data show that marriage is far more complicated than a simple economic cost–benefit assessment. The women's movement has clearly influenced what behaviors (i.e., infidelity) women are willing to accept within a marital relationship, and the level of power they expect to be able to exert within the relationship. Given the low level of trust these mothers have of men—oftentimes rooted in the experience of domestic violence—and given their view that husbands want more control than the women are willing to give them, women recognize that any marriage that is also economically precarious might well be conflict-ridden and short lived. Interestingly, mothers say they reject entering into economically risky marital unions out of respect for the institution of marriage, rather than because of a rejection of the marriage norm.

In the light of PRWORA and the new set of financial incentives and disincentives it provides, it is likely that cohabitation will increase, given the fact that cohabitation nearly always allowed the mothers interviewed to make a substantial claim on the male cohabiter's income. However, increased cohabitation might put women and children at greater risk if their partner is violent. In these situations, a separate residence may be a protective factor, as the race differences in the experience of domestic abuse I report here may indicate.

CONCLUSION

In short, the mothers interviewed here believe that marriage will probably make their lives more difficult than they are currently. They do not, by and large, perceive any special stigma to remaining single, so they are not motivated to marry for that reason. If they are to marry, they want to get something out of it. If they cannot enjoy economic stability and gain upward mobility from marriage, they see little reason to risk the loss of control and other costs they fear marriage might exact from them. Unless low-skilled men's economic situations improve and they begin to change their behaviors toward women, it is quite likely that most low-income women will continue to resist marriage even in the context of welfare reform. Substantially enhanced labor market opportunities for low-skilled men would address both the

affordability and respectability concerns of the mothers interviewed. But other factors, such as the stalled sex-role revolution at home (control), the pervasive mistrust of men, and the high probability of domestic abuse, probably mean that marriage rates are unlikely to increase dramatically.

REFERENCES

Bane, Mary Jo, and David T. Ellwood. 1994. *Welfare Realities.* Cambridge, MA: Harvard University Press.

Becker, Gary S. 1981. *A Treatise on the Family.* Cambridge, MA: Harvard University Press.

Becker, Howard S. 1992. "Cases, causes, conjectures, stories, and imagery." In *What is a case?*, eds. Charles C. Ragin and Howard S. Becker, 205–216. New York: Cambridge University Press.

Bennett, N. C., D. E. Bloom, and P. H. Craig. 1990. "American marriage patterns in transition." Paper presented at the Conference on Demographic Perspective on the American Family, April, Albany, New York.

Blank, Rebecca M. 1995. "Outlook for the U.S. labor market and prospects for low-wage entry jobs." In *The Work Alternative,* eds. Demetra Smith Nightingale and Robert H. Haveman. Washington, DC: The Urban Institute Press; Cambridge, MA: Harvard University Press.

Blee, Kathleen M., and Ann R. Tickameyer. 1995. "Racial differences in men's attitudes about women's gender roles." *Journal of Marriage and the Family* 57:21–30.

Bulcroft, Richard A., and Kris A. Bulcroft. 1993. "Race differences in attitudinal and motivational factors in the decision to marry." *Journal of Marriage and the Family* 55:338–355.

Bumpass, Larry, and James A. Sweet. 1989. "Children's experience in single parent families: Implications of cohabitation and marital transitions." *Family Planning Perspectives* 61(6):256–260.

Burtless, Gary. 1995. "Employment prospects of welfare recipients." In *The Work Alternative,* eds. Demetra Smith Nightingale and Robert H. Haveman. Washington, DC: The Urban Institute Press; Cambridge, MA: Harvard University Press.

Cherlin, Andrew. 1992. *Marriage, Divorce, Remarriage.* Cambridge, MA: Harvard University Press.

Collins, Patricia H. 1987. "The meaning of motherhood in black culture and black mother/daughter relationships." *Signs* 4:3–10.

Corbett, Thomas. 1998. "Reallocation, redirection, and reinvention: Assessing welfare reform in an era of discontinuity." Unpublished manuscript.

Edin, Kathryn, and Laura Lein. 1997. *Making Ends Meet: How Single Mothers Survive Welfare and Low Wage Work*. New York: Russell Sage Foundation.

Fossett, Mark A., and K. Jill Kielcolt. 1993. "Mate availability and family structure among African Americans in U.S. metropolitan areas." *Journal of Marriage and the Family* 55:302–331.

Harris, Kathleen Mullan, and Kathryn Edin. 1996. "From welfare to work and back again." Unpublished manuscript.

Hochschild, Arlie. 1989. *The Second Shift*. New York: Viking.

Hoffman, Saul. 1997. "Could it be true after all? AFDC benefits and non-marital births to young women." *Poverty Research News*. Chicago: Joint Center for Poverty Research, 1(2):1–3.

Hoffman, Saul D., and Greg Duncan. 1994. "The role of incomes, wages, and AFDC benefits on marital disruption." *The Journal of Human Resources* 30(10):19–41.

Jencks, Christopher. 1992. *Rethinking Social Policy*. Cambridge, MA: Harvard University Press, 120–142.

Kefalas, Maria, and Kathryn Edin. 2000. "The meaning of motherhood." Unpublished manuscript.

Lichter, Daniel T., F. B. LeClere, and Diane K. McLaughlin. 1991. "Local marriage market conditions and the marital behavior of black and white women." *American Journal of Sociology* 96:843–867.

Luker, Kristin. 1996. *Dubious Conceptions: The Politics of Teenage Pregnancy*. Cambridge. MA: Harvard University Press.

Moffitt, Robert A. 1995. "The effect of the welfare system on non-marital childbearing." *Report to Congress on Out of Wedlock Childbearing*. Department of Health and Human Services. Washington, DC: U.S. Government Printing Office, 167–173.

Murray, Charles. 1984. *Losing Ground*. New York: Basic Books.

Nelson, Timothy, Kathryn Edin, and Susan Clampet-Lundquist. 1999. "Doing the best I can: How low-income non-custodial fathers talk about their families." Unpublished manuscript.

Oppenheimer, Valerie K. 1993. "Women's rising employment and the future of the family in industrial societies." *Population and Development Review* 20(2):293–342.

Ptacek, James. 1988. "Why do men batter wives." In *Feminist Perspectives on Wife Abuse*, eds. K. Yllo and M. Bograd. Thousand Oaks: Sage Publications.

Raphael, Jody, and Richard D. Tolman. 1997. *Trapped by Poverty, Trapped by Abuse*. Chicago, IL: The Taylor Institute.

Scanzoni, John H. 1970. *Opportunity and the Family*. New York: Free Press.

Schoen, Robert, and Dawn Owens. 1992. "A further look at first unions and fist marriages," In *The Changing American Family*, eds. Scott J. South and Steward E. Tolnay. Boulder, CO: Westview Press.

South, Scott J. 1992. "For love or money? Socio-demographic determinants of the expected benefits from marriage." In *The Changing American Family: Sociological and Demographic Perspectives*, eds. S. J. South and S. E. Tolnay, 171–194. Boulder, CO: Westview.

South, Scott J. 1993. "Racial and ethnic differences in the desire to marry." *Journal of Marriage and the Family* 55:357–370.

South, Scott J., and Kim M. Lloyd. 1992. "Marriage opportunities and family formation: Further implications of imbalanced sex ratios." *Journal of Marriage and the Family* 54:440–451.

Stack, Carol B. 1974. *All Our Kin*. New York: Harper and Row.

Staples, Robert. 1988. "An overview of race and marital status." In *Black Families*, ed. H. P. McAdoo, 187–189. Newbury Park, CA: Sage.

Teachman, Jay D., Karen A. Polonko, and Geoffrey K. Leigh. 1987. "Marital timing: Race and sex comparisons." *Social Forces* 66:239–268.

Trent, Katherine, and Scott J. South. 1989. "Structural determinants of the divorce rate: A cross-societal comparison." *Journal of Marriage and the Family* 51:391–404.

Tucker, Belinda B., and Claudia Mitchell-Kernan. 1996. *The Decline in Marriage among African Americans: Causes, Consequences, and Policy Implications*. New York: Russell Sage Foundation.

U.S. Bureau of the Census. 1993. *Poverty in the United States: 1992. Current Population Reports*, Series P60, No. 185, Washington, DC: U.S. Government Printing Office.

U.S. Bureau of the Census. 1991a. "Marital status and living arrangements, 1990." *Current Population Reports*, Series P-20, No. 450:1, Table A. Washington DC: U.S. Government Printing Office.

U.S. Bureau of the Census. 1991b. "Marital status and living arrangements, 1990." *Current Population Reports*, Series P-20, No. 461. Washington DC: U.S. Government Printing Office.

U.S. House of Representatives, Committee on Ways and Means. 1997. *Overview of Entitlement Programs (Greenbook)*. Washington DC: U.S. Government Printing Office.

Wilson, William J. 1996. *When Work Disappears*. New York: Alfred A. Knopf.

Wilson, William J. 1987. *The Truly Disadvantaged*. Chicago: University of Chicago Press.

PART VI

CONSTRUCTING GENDER
IN THE WORKPLACE

How much does gender influence one's status at work? Does the feminization of paid labor around the world place women on a more equal footing with men? Or is paid labor another arena that intensifies women's disadvantages? Is it an arena that intensifies *some* women's disadvantages more than others? *Why* is gender inequality such a pervasive feature of work? Is it built into the workplace, or is it the outcome of differences in women and men themselves, their socialization, their behaviors, and their interactions? The readings in this part rely on studies of women and men in different work settings to address these questions. They show how the societal patterns of gender, race, class, sexuality, and immigrant status shape the work experiences of different groups.

Paid workers are increasingly diverse. Today's average worker in the global economy may be either a man or a woman and of any age, race, class, sexual orientation, or nationality. The average worker in the global economy may labor virtually unseen inside the home or may work in a public workplace as an assembler, teacher, secretary, or restaurant worker. Yet whatever the average worker does for a living, she or he is likely to work at a job assigned on the basis of gender. Everywhere, gender organizes workplaces. Even five-year-olds can readily identify what is a "man's job" and what is a "woman's job." Women's jobs and men's jobs are structured with different characteristics and different rewards. Seldom do women and men do the same jobs in the same place for the same pay. In every society we find a familiar pattern: women earn less than men, even when they work in similar occupations and have the same level of education.

In the United States, the level of **occupational gender segregation**, as measured by the index of dissimilarity, was .32 in 2012, meaning that approximately one-third (32%) of all men (or all women) would have to change jobs to achieve gender integration. Occupational gender segregation is a significant contributor to the **gender wage gap** where women make 77 cents for every dollar their male counterparts make. This represents an average gender pay gap of 19%, although the gap varies across industries from nearly zero to 35% (Tomaskovic-Devey et al. 2012). The gender pay gap is one measure of the devaluation of women's work and it exists even in female-dominated occupations like babysitting, teaching, nursing, and administrative work where men are paid more. However, much of the pay gap is due to gender segregation and the devaluing of "women's" occupations. Consider, for example, the median wages for a female-dominated occupation, childcare workers ($19,510) in comparison to a male-dominated occupation, refuse material collectors ($32,780) (Occupational Outlook Handbook 2012). Both groups do important and valuable work, but the pay disparity (approximately $400,000 over a 30-year career) raises questions about the value assigned to the forms of work typically performed by women and men. In addition to the average pay gap between all men and women, greater pay disparities exist when taking race into account: black men earn 73% of what white men earn, black women 68%, Hispanic men 61%, and Hispanic women 59% (National Women's Law Center 2013). Other studies show that gay men earn less than heterosexual men (Sears and Mallory 2011).

What causes occupational gender segregation and the gender pay gap? Whereas some point to women's preferences or women's disproportionate responsibility for children and family, a substantial body of research demonstrates that employer discrimination is the main cause. For example, one revealing area of research involves experiments where researchers send identical application materials for an employee who is randomly assigned either a male or a female name (similar studies vary the racial-ethnic identity, parental status, or criminal record). These studies found that male applicants are judged to be significantly more competent and hirable than female applicants, and the male applicants are offered significantly higher salaries than female applicants (Moss-Racusin et al. 2012). Importantly, male and female employers are equally likely to exhibit this gender bias in hiring. Similarly, mothers are penalized on their perceived competence and starting salary although fathers are not penalized, and some even benefit from being a parent (Correll et al. 2007). Yet, not all men benefit from this gender disparity. In a matched pairing of black and white job applicants, Pager (2003) found not only that white male applicants are more likely to receive a callback than black male applicants, but also that white male applicants with a felony record are more likely to receive a callback than black male nonoffenders.

In addition to discrimination in hiring, how else does work become so dramatically divided? How is workplace inequality maintained? Can gender boundaries be dismantled? All of the readings in this section speak to these questions. Further, the readings show how the experience of workers is complicated by the interplay of gender and other power systems. Women and men of different races, national origins, and immigrant groups become clustered in certain kinds of work. Job opportunities are shaped by *who* people are—by their being women or men, educated or uneducated, of a certain race, sexual orientation, and residents of specific geopolitical settings—rather than their skills, talents, and interests.

For example, many women who work in men's occupations experience a **glass ceiling** that blocks their upward mobility, whereas many men who work in women's professions experience a **glass escalator** that facilitates their upward mobility within these fields. But many other workers, particularly racial-ethnic minorities and the working class, face altogether different working conditions. In the first reading, Christine Williams revisits the glass escalator and provides new insights on how it is racialized, classed, and gendered. In addition to reviewing studies showing that racial-ethnic minority and gay men do not benefit from the glass escalator as professional white men do, Williams describes how transformations in the workplace are creating widespread class disparities where there is no opportunity for upward mobility for either women or men, and all but the economic elite suffer job and financial insecurity.

Amy Denissen and Abigail Saguy further the intersectional analysis of gender in the workplace by looking at the experiences of lesbian and straight tradeswomen in the construction industry. Despite the gains that women have made in many male-dominated occupations, such as in medicine and the law, women account for less than 2% of construction workers. Denissen and Saguy explain that **gendered homophobia** in the workplace harms all women, but it does so in different ways depending on race, gender presentation, and sexual orientation. For example, tradeswomen who are perceived as feminine by their coworkers are more likely to be sexually harassed or treated as incompetent, whereas those perceived as masculine are more likely to be ostracized or subjected to a misogynist work culture. In addition, Denissen and Saguy show how the threat of being labeled a lesbian and becoming a target of homophobia is a mechanism that isolates tradeswomen from each other and limits any collective response to harassment and discrimination.

In her study of African American professionals, Adia Harvey Wingfield explores how racism is gendered for black women and men professionals. She analyzes the controlling images that black professionals encounter at work. Although some of these images are similar for black men and women, such as racist assumptions that they are less intelligent and less capable, other controlling images differ along gender lines such as the "modern mammy," the "educated black bitch," and the "angry black man." Wingfield shows how gendered racism makes it difficult for black professionals to confront racism and sexism at work.

The last reading, by Miliann Kang, illustrates one of the central arguments of intersectional analysis—the relational nature of dominance and subordination—in her study of Korean nail salons in New York City. Kang examines the emotional and symbolic labor that manicurists perform in response to customer expectations that their "bodies get pampered" and "their feelings [get] massaged as well." Kang explores how grooming is implicated in the production of "docile bodies," both in disciplining the customer's body to meet standards of beauty and in disciplining the worker's body to meet expectations for service. Further, she examines the disciplining of women's bodies as it reproduces relationships of dominance and subordination through "model minority" stereotypes and expectations of deference that are imposed on Korean manicurists by their white, middle-class customers. Korean manicurists have a variety of ways of responding to these expectations, including status by association, strategic acquiescence, and subtle forms of resistance. Yet, Kang finds that unequal power relationships in the workplace limit the women's resistance while creating strong pressures to assimilate.

REFERENCES

Correll, Shelley J., Stephen Benard, and In Paik. 2007. "Getting a Job: Is There a Motherhood Penalty?" *American Journal of Sociology* 112(5): 1297–1338.

Moss-Racusin, Corinne A., et al. 2012. "Science Faculty's Subtle Gender Biases Favor Male Students." *Proceedings of the National Academy of Sciences of the United States of America* 109(41): 16474–16479.

National Women's Law Center. 2013. "Closing the Wage Gap Is Crucial for Women of Color and Their Families." http://www.nwlc.org/sites/default/files/pdfs/2013.11.13_closing_the_wage_gap_is_crucial_for_woc_and_their_families.pdf.

Occupational Outlook Handbook. 2012. United States Department of Labor, Bureau of Labor Statistics. www.bls.gov/ooh/

Pager, Devah. 2003. "The Mark of a Criminal Record." *American Journal of Sociology* 108(5): 937–975.

Sears, Brad, and Christy Mallory. July 2011. "Documented Evidence of Employment Discrimination and Its Effects on LGBT People." Los Angeles: The Williams Institute.

Stainback, Kevin and Donald Tomaskovic-Devey. 2012. Documenting Desegregation: Racial and Gender Segregation in Private-Sector Employment Since the Civil Rights Act. Russell Sage Foundation.

36

The Glass Escalator, Revisited

Gender Inequality in Neoliberal Times, SWS Feminist Lecturer

CHRISTINE L. WILLIAMS

In 1992, I published an article titled "The Glass Escalator" about the "hidden advantages" that men receive in predominately female professions. This article has been reprinted in dozens of textbooks and cited over 500 times in scholarly articles, and there are even flashcards about it.[1] Although I am proud of this acclaim, receiving the SWS Feminist Lecturer Award gives me the opportunity to revisit that work. The world of work has changed considerably in the past twenty years, and so has my understanding of gender inequality. Thanks largely to the scholarship of a new generation of gender sociologists, I now believe that the concept is of limited use in explaining men's economic advantages over women. In this article, I attempt to further specify the contexts in which the glass escalator applies.

I will begin my discussion by defining the glass escalator and summarizing my original argument. Then I will focus on two major limitations of the concept as I see it today. First, I will argue that the concept lacks an analysis of intersectionality. The glass escalator was based on the experiences of straight, white, middle-class men. I will review three studies that demonstrate the importance of race, sexuality, and class for understanding gender inequality in the workplace, and that

have transformed the way I think about the glass escalator. Second, I will argue that the concept is limited because it is based on traditional assumptions about work organizations, such as the expectation of stable employment, bureaucratic hierarchies, and widespread support for public institutions. These are no longer taken-for-granted features of work organizations. Jobs have become increasingly flexible, project-based, and temporary. The metaphor of the glass escalator may no longer apply in this new economic context. I argue that new concepts are needed to understand gender inequality in the 21st century. I will conclude with some thoughts for a new feminist agenda for the sociology of work.

THE GLASS ESCALATOR

When women work in male-dominated professions, they encounter a "glass ceiling" that prevents their ascension into the top jobs. Twenty years ago, I introduced the concept of the "glass escalator," my term for the advantages that men receive in the so-called women's professions (nursing, teaching, librarianship, and social work).

Williams, Christine L., "The Glass Escalator, Revisited: Gender Inequality in Neoliberal Times, SWS Feminist Lecturer." *Gender & Society* 27 (5) pp. 609–29. Copyright © 2013 SAGE Publications Ltd. Reprinted by permission of SAGE Publications Ltd.

When I was working on that project (that culminated in my 1995 book *Still a Man's World*), many sociologists argued that women's disadvantages in the workplace were the result of their token status. Very few women occupied top positions, and those who did experienced increased visibility, role encapsulation, and boundary heightening, which marginalized them and excluded them from positions of power and responsibility. The major hurdle facing women aspiring to leadership positions, according to this perspective, was numerical rarity, not gender discrimination.

The experiences of men in the so-called women's professions offered a powerful critique of this theory of tokenism. I showed that numerical rarity does not have negative consequences for men in these fields. Because men and qualities associated with masculinity are more highly valued than qualities associated with women and femininity, men in nursing, teaching, librarianship, and social work tend to benefit from their token status.

Although I was focusing on men in predominantly female professions, my goal was to understand men's advantages in the workplace in general, regardless of where they worked. In my opinion, too much attention had been paid to addressing questions like "What are the deficiencies of women?" and "What are the barriers to women?"; not enough attention was being paid to questions like "What is so great about men?" and "What are the advantages that men receive?" I argued that the mechanisms that privileged men in the workplace would be more apparent in these jobs, but that they would be common throughout the labor market.

My research showed that in predominantly female professions, men were assumed to be more competent and better leaders than women. As a result, many were drawn into higher-paying specialties and administrative positions. Supervisors, coworkers, clients, and the men themselves colluded in this reproduction of masculine privilege. I labeled this pattern the "glass escalator" (to contrast it with the "glass ceiling" experienced by women in male-dominated occupations).[2]

Some men did encounter discrimination in these professions, especially if they were employed in specialties closely associated with children, such as kindergarten teaching or children's librarianship. Negative stereotypes about male sexuality aroused suspicions about their possible motives, including pedophilia. Such discrimination is harmful, I argued, but since these job specialties tended to be lower paying, the consequence was to push men up to higher-paying and more prestigious specialties. Those men who wanted to stay in the most feminine-identified specialties had to struggle to stay in place—hence the metaphor of the moving glass escalator.

The overall patterns of gender inequality in the four professions I studied have not changed much in the intervening twenty years. Table 1 shows the distribution

Table 1 Men in the "Women's Professions": Number (in Thousands) and Distribution of Men Employed in the Occupations, Selected Years

Profession	1975	1980	1990	2002	2011
Registered nurses					
No. of men	28	46	92	164	208
% men	3.0	3.5	5.5	7.1	8.9
Elementary school teachers					
No. of men	194	225	223	398	463*
% men	14.6	16.3	14.8	17.0	18.3
Librarians					
No. of men	34	27	32	38	21
% men	18.9	14.8	16.7	18.3	13.8
Social workers					
No. of men	116	134	179	220	141
% men	39.2	35.0	31.8	26.0	18.4

Note: Year 1975, 1980, and 1990 data from C. L. Williams (1995). Year 2002 data from Bureau of Labor Statistics (2004). Year 2011 data from http://www.bls.gov/cps/cpsaat39.pdf (accessed July 2012).

*2011 data on elementary school teachers includes middle school teachers.

of men in nursing, teaching, librarianship, and social work from 1975 to 2011.

As Table 1 indicates, the percentage of men in nursing has increased, from 5.5 percent in 1990 to 8.9 percent in 2011. Although this increase represents a doubling in the number of men in the profession—the topic of a front-page *New York Times* article (Dewan and Gebeloff 2012)—the percentage of men today is, in fact, similar to what it was in 1890 (9%). Nursing remains a highly gender-segregated profession. Regarding the other three professions I studied, Table 1 shows that the percentage of men in librarianship and social work has declined over the past 20 years. It is unclear if the representation of men has changed in elementary school teaching, since middle school teachers are now included in the statistics.

Just as gender segregation persists, so does the wage gap, with men enjoying an income advantage over women in each of these professions (see Table 2). The income difference is not large, but that there is a difference at all is notable. (Information for male librarians is missing because the Bureau of Labor Statistics (BLS) does not report income for jobs with fewer than 50,000 workers; nevertheless, one can deduce from the numbers that men make more than women.) Thus, the general patterns of gender inequality in these professions are similar to what I observed when I first explored the issue.

Since the original article was published, the concept of the glass escalator has been evaluated and analyzed by several other researchers. The basic mechanism has been verified with quantitative studies, and qualitative work has shown that workplace interactions in a variety of occupations are consistent with what I found (e.g., Budig 2002; Hultin 2003; Maume 1999; Snyder and Green 2008). To say the least, I am extremely gratified by this scholarly confirmation.

However, a number of studies have re-oriented and refined my thinking about the glass escalator, and to these studies I now turn. The first set of challenges emerged from research on intersectionality.

INTERSECTIONALITY AND THE GLASS ESCALATOR

When I originally formulated the concept of the glass escalator, I realized that it did not apply to all men. Gay men and racial/ethnic minority men, in particular, seemed to be excluded from the benefits of the glass escalator. But I didn't theorize that exclusion—I merely mentioned that the experiences of gay men and non-white men were "different" and left it at that. This is an example of what Adrienne Rich (1979) would have called "white solipsism," the notion that white experience is the norm, the average, and the model for all other groups. To the extent that others vary from the white norm, they are considered "exceptions" that require separate studies to understand their "differences." Clearly, the concept of intersectionality had yet to influence my thinking on workplace inequality.

Intersectionality is an approach to studying gender that takes race/ethnicity, class, and sexuality into account. Many versions of intersectionality have been developed in the past twenty years (Cho, Crenshaw, and McCall 2013; Choo and Ferree 2010; Collins 2000; Ridgeway and Kricheli-Katz 2013). Common to all is the notion that gender is not an abstract and timeless essence, but an embodied and historical practice that is structured by other forms of inequality. Applying an intersectional framework involves at least two steps: first, sociologists who study gender are encouraged to investigate the experiences of groups who are marginalized

Table 2 Median Weekly Earnings of Full-Time Professional Workers by Sex and Ratio of Female–Male Earnings, 1990 and 2011, in 2011 Dollars[a]

Occupation	Both	Men	Women	Ratio
Registered nurses				
1990	$1057	$1070	$1057	0.99
2011	$1039	$1081	$1034	0.96
Elementary school teachers				
1990	$902	$999	$892	0.89
2011[b]	$974	$1022	$933	0.91
Librarians				
1990	$850	—[c]	$833	—[c]
2011	$850	—[c]	$813	—[c]
Social workers				
1990	$773	$840	$746	0.88
2011	$817	$902	$798	0.88

Source: C. L. Williams (1995, 82); http://www.bls.gov/cps/cpsaat39.pdf, accessed July 3, 2012.

a. 1990 dollars were converted to 2011 dollars via www.dollartimes.com/calculators/inflation.htm

b. Includes middle school.

c. The Labor Department does not report income averages for base sample sizes consisting of fewer than 50,000 individuals.

by race, sexuality, and class in order to avoid the "unwarranted universalizing of white, middle-class American women's experiences" (Choo and Ferree 2010, 132). Second, we are called upon to explain how the experiences of marginality are produced by the same institutional forces that privilege those in the center. In other words, we must show how social privilege is gained at the expense of social marginality. As Cho, Crenshaw, and McCall write, "what makes an analysis intersectional . . . is its adoption of an intersectional way of thinking about the problem of sameness and difference and its relation to power" (2013, 11). Our task, then, is to explain how power operates through socially constructed and historically specific binary oppositions.

Practicing intersectionality is hard. It requires sociologists to overcome our "ingrained habits of reductionism" (Choo and Ferree 2010, 147). The second step is especially difficult: as Choo and Ferree (2010, 145) point out, it is "easier to include multiply-marginalized groups than to analyze the relationships that affect them intersectionally." A further complication is the fact that scholarship on race, class, sexuality, and gender developed as separate literatures with unique histories and politics, and dominant cultural beliefs treat them as "distinct systems of difference and inequality" even though they intersect in social relations (Ridgeway and Kricheli-Katz 2013, 3). Consequently, intersectionality scholars may feel trapped into utilizing the language of separate systems to analyze essentially intertwined processes.

My discussion of intersectionality and the glass escalator reflects but does not resolve these conundrums, as I discuss race, sexuality, and class separately. This is not a failure of the studies I reference; each is lodged in an intersectional framework. My goal in separating the discussion into these analytic categories is to illuminate how the experiences of specifically marginalized groups (black men in nursing, gay and lesbian teachers, working-class transmen) can further refine the study of the glass escalator. I do so not to reify these identity categories, which are "fluid and changing, always in the process of creating and being created by dynamics of power" (Cho, Crenshaw, and McCall 2013, 11). Rather, my goal is to show how the glass escalator depends not only on gender inequality but on the exclusion and marginalization of those oppressed on the basis of race, sexuality, and class. This exercise of bringing the

marginalized into the center, I hope, will illustrate the power of an intersectional analysis and specify the limitations of the glass escalator concept.

Black Men in Nursing

Perhaps the best example of the power of the intersectional perspective is the work of Adia Harvey Wingfield. In her article "Racializing the Glass Escalator" (2009), Harvey Wingfield examined the experiences of black men in nursing. She found no evidence of the glass escalator in their careers. Unlike white men, black men nurses are often seen as less skilled than women nurses. Many of the white men I interviewed said that patients confused them with doctors, but few black men encountered this assumption; they were often mistaken for orderlies or janitors. Even patients who understood that they were registered nurses treated these men with suspicion. She describes one white man who prevented his wife from receiving an injection from a black male nurse—an example that reflects sexual stereotypes about black men. Furthermore, Harvey Wingfield found that behaviors that denote "leadership" ability in white men are interpreted as "menacing" behavior from black men. Evidently, black men in nursing do not experience warm and congenial relationships with their white women colleagues, nor do they share gendered bonds with their male supervisors that ease their mobility into higher status positions. Instead, they face discrimination in the nursing profession that stymies their career development. In the predominantly white institutions where her respondents worked, they are not pressured to move up into higher-paid and more prestigious specialties.

Harvey Wingfield's work demonstrates that we cannot fully understand the mechanism of the glass escalator without an understanding of racism. The experience of black men nurses is not simply "different" from that of white men—they are two sides of the same coin. Masculine hegemony is based on white privilege. As Harvey Wingfield concludes, the glass escalator relies on the existence of racial inequality, and will persist as long as racism persists.

Gay and Lesbian Teachers

The same is true for homophobia: The exclusion of gay men from the glass escalator is not merely an exception to the rule; it is part of the process of reproducing hegemonic masculinity.

For this insight, I am indebted to Catherine Connell (2012), whose work on gay and lesbian teachers reveals how the glass escalator depends on homophobia. I did my research on men in nontraditional occupations from the early 1980s to the early 1990s. During this decade, there were very few legal protections for LGBT workers. These were the years of the Reagan/Bush presidencies; it was the height of the AIDS epidemic in the United States; and gays and lesbians were banned from many jobs, including those in the military (it wasn't until December 1993 that the U.S. military permitted *closeted* gays and lesbians to serve). Thus the concept of the glass escalator was developed during the heyday of the closet, and its very existence may depend upon it.

To reveal the impact of homophobia on professional careers, Connell studied gay and lesbian teachers in two settings—in California and in Texas. These two states have vastly different levels of legal protection, political activism, and cultural acceptance of LGBT workers. She found that in contexts where homophobia is rife and institutionalized, LGBT teachers face immense pressure to engage in "passing" strategies so as not to draw attention to their sexuality. This means conforming to heteronormative appearance standards and behavior—all of which support the glass escalator. For example, lesbians may feel compelled to wear make-up to work and to defer to male authority; gay men may try to avoid the use of certain mannerisms and expressions identified as gay in the classroom or feign an interest in masculine activities like sports. Conforming to these heteronormative practices can easily push men into leadership positions and women into support roles.

What happens in a context where there are legal protections for LGBT workers? Connell shows that individual teachers may be more willing to enact and disclose their sexual identities as LGBT. Granted, gay-friendly workplaces can exact a new "homonormativity." In a study with Patti Giuffre and Kirsten Dellinger (Williams, Giuffre, and Dellinger 2009), we found that "gay friendly" workplaces may accept gay and lesbian workers only if they conform to conventional gender practices. So legal protections are not enough. Connell's work demonstrates that antidiscrimination laws in the teaching profession must be accompanied by cultural acceptance made possible through political organizing,

union support, and curricular changes that are LGBT confirming. Under these conditions, I would expect the glass escalator to break down. When men and women are not expected or compelled to conform to stereotypically masculine and feminine behavior, a central pillar of the glass escalator is shaken.[3]

Working-Class Transmen

The four occupations I studied were middle-class jobs; consequently the glass escalator reflects that particular class location. This insight comes from Kristen Schilt (2011). Her study brings an intersectional perspective to bear on the experiences of transmen in the workplace.

The transmen that Schilt interviewed had lived and worked as women before they transitioned to living as men. Many assumed that when they made the switch they would be fired, ridiculed, and harassed. Instead, Schilt found that many transmen actually benefited at work. They experienced more authority, they were assumed to be more competent, and they received greater rewards, recognition, and economic opportunities compared to when they were women. Transwomen, in contrast, do not experience these benefits. All of this is consistent with the glass escalator.

However, not all transmen ride the glass escalator. Those who enjoyed the most workplace benefits were white and achieved the most masculine presentation of self. Other transmen either experienced no changes or else more negative treatment at their workplaces. Thus, Schilt draws our attention to the importance of embodiment in the experience of the glass escalator. Those who are unable to achieve a masculine appearance are not as accepted and may face more discrimination in the workplace.

Schilt doesn't tie this observation to social class, but following Bourdieu, I would argue that class and appearance are linked. Many middle-class occupations privilege a particular habitus—workers have to look right and sound right for the job (Williams and Connell 2010). The aesthetic requirements in these jobs can include physical attributes—such as height—as well as specific mannerisms, styles, and dispositions associated with professional work. Only those who embody the appropriate class-based aesthetic can ride the glass escalator.

Schilt also discovered that occupational context determines whether or not transmen benefit after transitioning. Those employed in retail jobs, for example, didn't accrue benefits. In this case, there was no escalator; in fact, there was no career ladder at all. These dead-end jobs offered no opportunities for advancement, status, or authority to anyone, regardless of gender. Although she did find evidence of gender segregation in these jobs—transmen were relocated from front-of-house positions to the back room stocking jobs, for example—for the most part there was "gender equity" in the treatment of employees. Not a good kind of equality, either: Everyone was treated like crap.

The glass escalator, then, applies to only certain kinds of jobs—those that contain built-in opportunities for advancement. The concept was developed based on the experiences of middle-class professionals whose jobs offered the possibility of increasing rewards. It is grounded by class just as it is by race/ethnicity and sexuality. Intersectionality enhances our understanding of gender inequality in the workplace. Without this framework, research isn't necessarily wrong, but it is partial. That's what I see today when I revisit my work on the glass escalator.

WORK TRANSFORMATION
AND THE GLASS ESCALATOR

In addition to being based on the experiences of middle-class, straight, white men, the glass escalator concept is based on a historically specific form of work organization. As I have noted, built into the concept are assumptions about stable employment, job hierarchies, and career ladders. Furthermore, the concept was developed during a period of widespread support for public institutions. These features no longer characterize many jobs in the labor market today—not even middle-class jobs. This raises the question of whether the glass escalator is still relevant in workplaces of the 21st century, and whether new concepts are needed to analyze gender inequality.

In traditional work organizations, workers can look forward to a lifetime of loyal service to a single employer. They are rewarded for this loyalty with promotions, raises, increased benefits, and retirement pensions. Traditional work organizations are hierarchical, with entry-level positions at the bottom. Job descriptions, organizational charts, and the labor process

are set in advance and controlled by managers. The image of the traditional corporation is the massive skyscraper; inside is a rational bureaucracy (as described by Weber), with power, prestige, and income increasing at each level, up to the executive offices at the top.

This traditional model of work organizations was still very much in place when I conducted my research on the glass escalator. Workers in these four professions were expected to gain their appropriate credential (through state-subsidized higher education), obtain an entry-level position, and acquire on-the-job training. Through loyal service, hard work, and long hours, individuals could prove their value to their organization and get rewarded with higher pay, status, and positions of authority. In some cases, public unions supported job security and ensured that those with the most seniority would receive the most rewards.

Although these features of jobs and careers appear gender-neutral on the surface, we know that this traditional organizational form is biased in favor of men (Acker 1990; Williams 2001). Rewarding uninterrupted devotion to work implicitly discriminates against women, who typically have competing family obligations that they are forced to accommodate. Furthermore, managers draw on gendered stereotypes when developing organizational charts and job descriptions, which reward characteristics associated with men and masculinity, and devalue ones associated with femininity. The result is the glass ceiling for women and the glass escalator for men. These metaphors are successful because they can be easily imagined inside that sturdy skyscraper.

This traditional model of work is increasingly anachronistic. In the past thirty years or so, organizations have undergone downsizing, restructuring, globalization, and computerization (DiMaggio 2001; Kalleberg 2000). Referred to under the heading of "work transformation," this general and vast process of change has impacted the work lives of almost everyone. Figure 1 describes the major features of 21st-century work transformation.

Workers today expect to switch employers frequently in search of better opportunities, and in response to outsourcing, mergers, and downsizing. Employers increasingly turn to part-time or temporary workers—or "consultants"—to perform tasks that were previously carried out by workers in-house, in full-time, permanent positions. Instead of loyalty and

Traditional Work Organization	"Neoliberal" Work Organization
Loyalty and seniority rewarded	Flexibility and adaptability rewarded
Full-time jobs with benefits	Temporary and contingent contracts
Lifetime career	Boundary-less career
Specialized job descriptions	Project based requirements
Hierarchically organized departments	Horizontal interdisciplinary teams
Career ladders	Career maps or "I-deals"

Figure 1. Major Features of 21st-Century Work Transformation

seniority, employers seek flexibility and adaptability in ideal employees. The result is what human relations (HR) and management literatures call the "protean" or "boundaryless" career (Arthur 1994; Hall 2004).

The nature of jobs is changing, too. Under the traditional system, workers carried out narrow and specific tasks identified by their job descriptions and they were evaluated and compensated by managers who controlled the labor process. Today, work organizations are flatter and less hierarchical. Layers of management have been removed, and work is increasingly organized into self-managed teams. Teams typically work with considerable discretion on time-bounded projects, and are judged on results and outcomes, often by peers. Career "ladders"—with clearly demarcated rungs that lead to higher-paying and more responsible positions—are being eliminated or replaced by career maps or "I-deals," which are individualized programs of career development (Babcock and Laschever 2003; DiMaggio 2001; Powell 2001).[4]

I refer to this new model of work organization as "neoliberal." Neoliberalism is a world view that advocates minimal government regulation of the economy, privatization of state resources, distribution of social services through the market, and exaltation of the autonomous, self-serving individual (Campbell and Pedersen 2001; Eisenstein 2010). The new organization of work is compatible with this ideological agenda. Corporations designed this new structure with minimal input from workers to shift their economic risks and responsibilities onto employees, while undercutting the protections of labor law and unions.

This new model has its advocates. The literature in management and HR celebrates these changes for heralding unprecedented opportunities for professional growth, technological innovation, and personal fulfillment. Even some feminists applaud the new model of work, as its built-in flexibility is considered more compatible with women's nonlinear career paths (Hewlett 2007; see also Xie and Shauman 2005). But in my view, the major beneficiaries of work transformation are executives, the financial industry, and shareholders. Although a few workers do benefit from this new career model—especially high-tech professionals with specialized skills—for most the result is staggering college debt, job insecurity, increased stress and responsibility at work, and salary stagnation (Kalleberg 2000, 2009).

We can see the impact of neoliberalism on the four professions I analyzed. Each of them is dependent on the government for support. Public schools, hospitals, libraries, and welfare services are funded by taxes. In keeping with the neoliberal agenda, their budgets have all been slashed in recent years, while the power of their unions has come under attack (e.g., Gabriel and Dillon 2011). As Table 2 demonstrates, the incomes of workers in these professions have barely kept pace with inflation. Today, college students pay exorbitant tuition to obtain credentials in these fields; gone are the days of generous state subsidies for higher education. Those in fields requiring master's degrees (social work and librarianship, but increasingly teaching and nursing as well) typically take out loans to fund their education, accumulating an average of more than $17,000 per year in debt (College Board 2012, 21). Some evidence suggests that women have a higher debt load than men after graduation, which may be due in part to women's concentration in these professional disciplines (Dwyer, Hodson, and McCloud 2013). Newly minted graduates in some of these fields can no longer count on obtaining jobs in state institutions; they increasingly seek employment in private settings, including corporations and nonprofits, often on a contract basis.

If the old model of work organization is the sturdy high-rise filled with grey-suited bureaucrats, the new model is more like a ship at sea filled with mercenaries seeking adventure and fortune. In my more pessimistic moments, I imagine the ship buffeted by a powerful storm and in danger of sinking, with workers desperately trying to stay on board, or else grasping for life jackets (which they have to pay for themselves), while the executives get first crack at the lifeboats.

Gender inequality characterizes both the traditional and the neoliberal models of work organization. Women are not calling the shots either in the high-rise or on the ship. But I believe we need new metaphors to capture the workings of gender inequality in the neoliberal context. The glass ceiling and the glass escalator seem far too static to capture what is going on in our current era of flexible, project-based, horizontal, and contingent employment.

In a recent article I published with Chandra Muller and Kristine Kilanski (Williams, Muller, and Kilanski 2012), we identified new mechanisms that reproduce gender inequality in the neoliberal context. That article is based on our research on women geoscientists in the extremely lucrative oil and gas industry. We identified the gender, race, and sexual dynamics of the team structure, career maps, and networking as keys to understanding men's continued advantages over women in that industry.

To give one example, career maps, which have replaced career ladders in many industries, are individually negotiated—they are sometimes called "I-deals." Geoscientists plan out long- and short-term goals with their team supervisors, who are supposed to supply them with the tools and resources needed to achieve their goals. Workers do not know the details of each other's "I-deals"; in fact, it is against corporate policy to even discuss salary and bonuses with others. In this context, where the "rules of the game" are both variable and unknown, biases can freely proliferate. Meanwhile, a corporate embrace of "diversity" hides the systematic privileging of heterosexual white men occurring in the industry (Williams, Kilanski, and Muller, n.d.).

The case of women geoscientists in the oil and gas industry is especially interesting to us because women are graduating with master's degrees in numbers equal to men, and anecdotal evidence suggests that they are being hired in numbers equal to men in the major companies. These jobs are highly paid and the hours are reasonable, especially at the midcareer level. But after ten years or so, the women are virtually all gone. Instead of hitting their heads on a glass ceiling, they seem to be disappearing through a *trap door* (or, in keeping with the ship metaphor, perhaps they are *walking the plank*). (In contrast, conservatives have been using the term "opting out" to describe what is happening to these women.) My colleagues and I are trying to ascertain the forces that are pushing and pulling these women scientists out of the industry altogether.

Scientists in the oil and gas industry are among society's most privileged workers; the women scientists we interviewed are in the top one percent of all women income earners. I am also interested in exploring the consequences of work transformation for women at the bottom of the employment spectrum. Over the past decade, I have been studying low-wage workers in the retail industry, an industry that has exploded in size in recent decades (Williams 2006). Today, the number of retail workers *exceeds* the number of manufacturing workers in the United States (Jordan 2011).

In low-wage retail work, there are no glass ceilings or glass escalators, only *revolving doors*. Employers routinely hire part-time and temporary "at will" workers whom they "let go" the minute their store staffing needs change. Retail workers are required to work weekends and to change their hours from one week to another, exemplifying the meaning of the word "flexible" in retail. One week you might be scheduled to work 10 hours; the next week, 30. This is exactly the kind of job that is incompatible with doing anything else, such as caring for family members. Note that the problem is not the standard 40-hour work week, which has been identified as biased against women (Acker 1990; Williams 2001). "Flexible" schedules are even worse, because workers have to be available at any time, and erratic hours mean that income fluctuates from week to week (Lambert 2008). As a result of this work organization, the retail industry has one of the highest turnover rates in the economy. At the toy stores where I worked, for example, few employees lasted through the three-month probationary period. Employers know this and expect and even cultivate it because churning the labor force prevents worker solidarity from forming and keeps wages low (Williams 2006).

I really like my image of the sinking ship, but all kidding aside, the true "role model" for the U.S. economy today is Wal-Mart (Lichtenstein 2006, 2009). Today, Wal-Mart is the single largest private employer in the United States, Canada, and Mexico. In addition to demanding "flexibility" from its workers, Wal-Mart pays workers as little as possible, encourages high turnover, fights off all unionizing efforts, offers few, if any, benefits, and externalizes employees' health care costs. Meanwhile it touts its commitment to "diversity" and to equal opportunity for women, racial/ethnic minorities, and LGBT workers (Wal-Mart has been "gay friendly" since 2003). Its organizational model is taught in business schools and copied by high-end retailers (such as Whole Foods and Apple Computers). Even organizations not involved in the retail industry emulate the Wal-Mart model (including the hospitality and tourism industry, as represented by that ill-fated cruise ship at sea).

Wal-Mart is notorious for its sexism, despite its commitment to "diversity." It recently fought off the largest-ever class-action lawsuit brought by women charging gender discrimination in promotions and pay (for updates on the suit, see www.walmartclass.com). But in this regard, the company is hardly unique. Gender inequality is rampant throughout the retail industry. Among retail salespersons employed full time—which is rare—women earn 75 percent of what men earn.[5] This is partly the result of stores placing men and women in different jobs. Job-level segregation is just as extreme in low-wage occupations as in the higher-wage labor market (Lovell, Hartmann, and Werschkul 2007), and it helps to account for the gender disparities in pay. Not that men are raking in the dough. At one of the toy stores where I worked, for example, only men were hired in bicycle assembly jobs, which paid $8 to $9 an hour, compared to the $7.50 that I earned as a cashier. This is an advantage, but it is not an escalator. It is more like *a higher ring in hell*.

In sum, the concept of the glass escalator was developed based on the traditional work organization. It assumes the existence of job security, full-time schedules, the availability of career ladders, and the expectation that workers will be rewarded for loyal service. These assumptions can no longer be taken for granted in our neoliberal economy. As Steve Vallas (2011) argues, the very concept of a "job" is fast becoming a thing of the past. We need new concepts and metaphors to explain gender inequality in neoliberal times.

CONCLUSION

It has been a true honor to have this opportunity to revisit my work on the glass escalator. Since that work was first published, I have learned a great deal from the community of gender scholars. In this article, I explained how the intersectionality framework has enhanced and deepened my understanding of gender inequality in the workplace. I now believe that any discussion of the glass escalator must be attuned to how racism, homophobia, and class inequality advantage some groups of men, and exclude and discriminate against others.

I also argued that my original analysis of the glass escalator failed to take into account the economic context of the era in which it was developed. The concept was based on the assumptions of traditional work organizations, which have been fundamentally altered by work transformation. As our study of geoscientists suggests, the concept of the glass escalator may be of limited use in explaining gender inequality in workplaces today. We need new metaphors to understand the persistence of male privilege in the flexible, project-based, and flatter neoliberal organization.[6]

In the case of low-wage jobs, I believe we need a new feminist agenda altogether. Gender inequality is stubbornly persistent at the top and the bottom of the labor market, but class inequality has exploded (Cobble 2007; McCall 2007). Using the paradigmatic case of retail work, I argued that work transformation degrades the quality and pay of jobs in this ever-growing sector of the economy. These jobs are precarious, lack benefits, and do not pay a living wage.

Workers in low-wage service sector jobs need a new employment contract, one that offers security, opportunities for advancement, and a decent living standard for everyone, women and men. Employers can be forced to treat workers better. Although the shrinking number of well-paid manufacturing jobs in our economy is lamentable, it is important to remember that those jobs did not start off as good jobs. At the turn of the 20th century, manufacturing jobs were appallingly dangerous, exploitative, and dehumanizing. They became good jobs only because workers organized, fought, and bled to make them so. That same militancy is needed to upgrade jobs in the retail industry and other low-wage sectors of the economy. Nothing inherent in these jobs makes them low paid. In Sweden, for example, retail jobs pay good wages and are not considered "bleak" jobs at all (Andersson et al. 2011).

However, upgrading these jobs may not be in the interests of all women. I do not assume that the women at the top of the occupational pyramid share common cause with the women at the bottom any more than men do. At ExxonMobil corporate headquarters in Houston, for example, janitors, who currently earn $8.35 an hour, are fighting for a pay raise. Of course, because of the neoliberal work organization, they don't actually work for ExxonMobil; they work for cleaning subcontractors who bid on temporary contracts to provide cleaning services, and who employ legions of women workers on an "as needed" basis. Consequently, the spokesperson for ExxonMobil can claim that his company doesn't "have anything to do with" the low wages paid to janitors who clean their offices.[7] But there is no question that the immense profits of the oil and gas industry and the high pay of the geoscientists who work for it come from squeezing the workers on the bottom. Outsourcing, temporalizing, and shifting risk onto workers is the essence of the neoliberal business model.

For these reasons, I believe that feminist demands for gender equality in the workplace are not enough. Do women janitors deserve to be treated the same as men janitors? Yes, of course they do. But they also deserve more than $8.35 an hour, which will not happen unless their employers are forced to pay them more. That is why a critique of capitalism must accompany our critique of gender inequality. This is my "new" feminist agenda for the sociology of work.

This "new" agenda is in fact at least 40 years old, harkening back to the "socialist feminism" of the 1970s. That agenda has been lost in recent years, overcome by what Nancy Fraser has called the "feminist romance with capitalism" (2009, 110). This is the idea that women's emancipation requires their entry into paid work. This idea has been used to motivate women around the world to seek dignity and equality in the labor market— even though, for the vast majority of women, paid work is synonymous with extreme exploitation and family hardship. Feminist scholars rightly criticize women's economic dependency on men and the devaluation of women's caring labor in the home. But we must not ignore the fact that the alternative can be just as bad. Capitalists rely on women's unpaid work in the home to reproduce the labor force AND they exploit women's labor to generate enormous profits. In effect, they have harnessed the dream of women's liberation to the engine of capitalist accumulation. Feminists have been complicit with this insofar as we endorse the model of competitive individualism in the marketplace for women (Collins and Mayer 2010; Eisenstein 2010). I now believe that a feminism that is divorced from a critique of capitalism will only make things worse for most women.

The glass escalator explains the advantages that straight white men receive in professional jobs in traditional work organizations. Because it analyzes male privilege without critiquing capitalist exploitation, it loses sight of the diminishing rewards available to most workers. It may be time to retire the concept. We need new metaphors to explain gender inequality in our neoliberal age.

NOTES

1. http://quizlet.com/2729873/sociology-flash-cards.

2. The mechanisms that reproduce the glass ceiling might also be subject to further specification, a topic beyond the scope of this article.

3. Work organizations do exist today that celebrate and encourage expressions of nonnormative gender and queer sexuality. However, in a recent review of the literature (Williams and Giuffre 2011), we found that most are located in the entertainment and sex work industries. "Respectably queer" organizations are still very rare, even in California (Ward 2008).

4. These categories describe organizational trends that in practice overlap considerably. It is best to treat them as "ideal types" in the Weberian sense.

5. http://www.bls.gov/cps/cpsaat39.pdf, p. 5.

6. Additional intriguing suggestions include the "glass obstacle course" (De Welde and Larson 2011) and the "glass cliff" (Ryan and Haslam 2005).

7. http://www.marketplace.org/topics/wealth-poverty/houston-janitors-fight-fair-pay-economic-boom (accessed August 7, 2012).

REFERENCES

Acker, Joan. 1990. Hierarchies, jobs, bodies: A theory of gendered organizations. *Gender & Society* 4:139–58.

Andersson, Thomas, Ali Kazemi, Stefan Tengblad, and Mikael Wickelgren. 2011. Not the inevitable bleak house?: The positive experiences of workers and managers in retail work in Sweden. In *Retail work,* edited by I. Grugulis and O. Bozkurt. Hampshire, UK: Palgrave Macmillan.

Arthur, Michael B. 1994. The boundaryless career: A new perspective for organizational inquiry. *Journal of Organizational Behavior* 15:295–306.

Babcock, Linda, and Sara Laschever. 2003. *Women don't ask: Negotiation and the gender divide.* Princeton, NJ: Princeton University Press.

Budig, Michelle. 2002. Male advantage and the gender composition of jobs: Who rides the glass escalator? *Social Problems* 49:258–77.

Bureau of Labor Statistics. 2004. Women in the labor force: A databook. Bureau of Labor Statistics Report 973 (February), Table 11, p. 27, http://www.bls.gov/cps/wlf-databook.pdf.

Campbell, John Lorne, and Ove Kaj Pedersen. 2001. *The rise of neoliberalism and institutional analysis.* Princeton, NJ: Princeton University Press.

Cho, Sumi, Kimberle Williams Crenshaw, and Leslie McCall. 2013. Toward a field of intersectionality studies: Theory, applications, and praxis. *Signs* 38:1–26.

Choo, Hae Yeon, and Myra Marx Ferree. 2010. Practicing intersectionality in sociological research: A critical analysis of inclusions, interactions, and institutions in the study of inequalities. *Sociological Theory* 28:129–48.

Cobble, Dorothy Sue. 2007. *The sex of class: Women transforming American labor.* Ithaca, NY: Cornell University Press.

College Board. 2012. Trends in student aid. http://trends.collegeboard.org/sites/default/files/student-aid-2012-full-report.pdf. Accessed January 7, 2013.

Collins, Jane, and Victoria Mayer. 2010. *Both hands tied: Welfare reform and the race to the bottom in the low-wage labor market.* Chicago: University of Chicago Press.

Collins, Patricia Hill. 2000. *Black feminist thought: Knowledge, consciousness and politics of empowerment.* New York: Routledge.

Connell, Catherine. 2012. Dangerous disclosures. *Sexuality Research and Social Policy* 9:168–77.

De Welde, Kris, and Sandra Larsen. 2011. The glass obstacle course: Formal and informal barriers for STEM Ph.D. students. *International Journal of Gender, Science and Technology* 3:547–70.

Dewan, Shaila, and Robert Gebeloff. 2012. More men enter fields dominated by women. *The New York Times,* 21 May.

DiMaggio, Paul. 2001. *The twenty-first century firm.* Princeton, NJ: Princeton University Press.

Dwyer, Rachel E., Randy Hodson, and Laura McCloud. 2013. Gender, debt, and dropping out of college. *Gender & Society* 27:30–55.

Eisenstein, Hester. 2010. *Feminism seduced: How global elites use women's labor and ideas to exploit the world.* Boulder, CO: Paradigm.

Fraser, Nancy. 2009. Feminism, capitalism, and the cunning of history. *New Left Review* 56:97–117.

Gabriel, Trip, and Sam Dillon. 2011. GOP governors take aim at teacher tenure. *The New York Times,* 1 February.

Hall, Douglas. 2004. The protean career: A quarter-century journey. *Journal of Vocational Behavior* 65:1–13.

Harvey Wingfield, Adia. 2009. Racializing the glass escalator: Reconsidering men's experiences with women's work. *Gender & Society* 23:5–26.

Hewlett, Sylvia A. 2007. *Off-ramps and on-ramps: Keeping talented women on the road to success.* Boston: Harvard Business School.

Hultin, Mia. 2003. Some take the glass escalator, some hit the glass ceiling: Career consequences of occupational sex segregation. *Work and Occupations* 30:30–61.

Jordan, Laura. 2011. Avoid the trap: Discursive framing as a means of coping with working poverty. In *Retail work,* edited by I. Grugulis and O. Bozkurt. Hampshire, UK: Palgrave Macmillan.

Kalleberg, Arne. 2000. Nonstandard employment relations. *Annual Review of Sociology* 26:341–65.

Kalleberg, Arne. 2009. Precarious work, insecure workers: Employment relations in transition. *American Sociological Review* 74:1–22.

Lambert, Susan. 2008. Passing the buck: Labor flexibility practices that transfer risk onto hourly workers. *Human Relations* 61:1203–27.

Lichtenstein, Nelson, ed. 2006. *Wal-Mart: The face of twenty-first-century capitalism.* New York: New Press.

Lichtenstein, Nelson. 2009. *The retail revolution: How Wal-Mart created a brave new world of business.* New York: Metropolitan Books.

Lovell, Vicky, Heidi Hartmann, and Misha Werschkul. 2007. More than raising the floor: The persistence of gender inequalities in the low-wage labor market. In *The sex of class: Women transforming American labor,* edited by Dorothy Sue Cobble. Ithaca, NY: Cornell University Press.

Maume, David. 1999. Glass ceilings and glass escalators: Occupational segregation and race and sex differences in managerial promotions. *Work and Occupations* 26:483–509.

McCall, Leslie. 2007. Increasing class disparities among women and the politics of gender equity. In *The sex of class: Women transforming American labor,* edited by Dorothy Sue Cobble. Ithaca, NY: Cornell University Press.

Powell, Walter W. 2001. The capitalist firm in the 21st century: Emerging patterns in Western enterprise. In *The twenty-first century firm,* edited by Paul DiMaggio. Princeton, NJ: Princeton University Press.

Rich, Adrienne. 1979. Disloyal to civilization: Feminism, racism, gynephobia. In *On lies, secrets, and silence,* by Adrienne Rich. New York: Norton.

Ridgeway, Cecilia, and Tamar Kricheli-Katz. 2013. Intersecting cultural beliefs in social relations: Gender, race, and class binds and freedoms. *Gender & Society.* 27: 294–318.

Ryan, Michelle, and Alexander Haslam. 2005. The glass cliff: Evidence that women are overrepresented in precarious leadership positions. *British Journal of Management* 16:81–90.

Schilt, Kristen. 2011. *Just one of the guys?* Chicago: University of Chicago Press.

Snyder, Karrie Ann, and Adam Isaiah Green. 2008. Revisiting the glass escalator: The case of gender segregation in a female-dominated occupation. *Social Problems* 55:271–99.

Vallas, Steven. 2011. *Work: A critique.* Boston: Polity Books.

Ward, Jane. 2008. *Respectably Queer: Diversity culture in LGBT activist organizations.* Nashville, TN: Vanderbilt University Press.

Williams, Christine L. 1992. The glass escalator: Hidden advantages for men in the "female" professions. *Social Problems* 39:253–67.

Williams, Christine L. 1995. *Still a man's world: Men who do "women's work."* Berkeley: University of California Press.

Williams, Christine L. 2006. *Inside Toyland: Working, shopping, and social inequality.* Berkeley: University of California Press.

Williams, Christine L., and Catherine Connell. 2010. Looking good and sounding right: Aesthetic labor and social inequality in the retail industry. *Work and Occupations* 37:349–77.

Williams, Christine L., and Patti Giuffre. 2011. From organizational sexuality to queer organizations: Research on homosexuality and the workplace. *Sociology Compass* 5/7:551–63.

Williams, Christine L., Patti Giuffre, and Kirsten Dellinger. 2009. The gay-friendly closet. *Sexuality Research & Social Policy* 6:29–45.

Williams, Christine L., Kristine Kilanski, and Chandra Muller. n.d. The problem with corporate diversity.

Williams, Christine L., Chandra Muller, and Kristine Kilanski. 2012. Gendered organizations in the new economy. *Gender & Society* 26:549–73.

Williams, Joan. 2001. *Unbending gender: Why family and work conflict and what to do about it.* New York: Oxford University Press.

Xie, Yue, and Kimberlee A. Shauman. 2005. *Women in science: Career processes and outcomes.* Cambridge, MA: Harvard University Press.

37

Gendered Homophobia and the Contradictions of Workplace Discrimination for Women in the Building Trades

Amy M. Denissen

Abigail C. Saguy

The effects of double binds, in which femininity and competence are seen as mutually exclusive, are well documented in male-dominated workplaces (Jamieson 1995; Valian 1998). Previous research shows that women resist double binds in part by "finding a variety of ways to do gender" (Pierce 1995, 13–14) that trouble boundaries of gender difference. Women may directly challenge gender dualities by, for instance, demanding respectful recognition as women while performing masculinity (Denissen 2010b). They may also invoke shared identities based on race, class, occupational hierarchy, or culture to deemphasize gender difference (Denissen 2010b; Janssens, Cappellen, and Zanoni 2006). Women workers thereby participate in "gender maneuvering" (Schippers 2002; see also Finley 2010), or the manipulation of gender rules to redefine the relationship between femininity and masculinity.

We still know very little, however, about how sexual identity and gender presentation—such as femme, gender-blenders/blending (Devor 1987; Moore 2011), and butch/dyke—shape how dominant groups seek to control women and how the latter respond. Kazyak's

(2012) work suggests that gender presentation—and gender more broadly—shapes the experiences of lesbians and heterosexual women alike. And yet, the gender literature is characterized by an undertheorization of "the relationship between heterosexuality and gender oppression" (Schilt and Westbrook 2009, 441), or what Chrys Ingraham calls heterogender (Ingraham 1994). Following Valentine's (2007) critique of the fusing of gender and sexual categories (e.g., conflating homosexuality and gender variance), as well as attempts to ontologically separate these categories, we conceptualize gender and sexuality as co-constructed and relational features of social organization whose meanings vary across time and context.

Drawing on interviews with a diverse sample of lesbian and straight women in the construction trades, such as electricians and sheet metal workers, of which women comprise less than 2 percent of the workforce nationwide (Bilginsoy 2009), this article extends our understanding of gender maneuvering by exploring how the meaning of race, body size, and seniority impact the constraints tradeswomen face and the

Denissen, Amy M., and Abigail C. Saguy. "Gendered Homophobia and the Contradictions of Workplace Discrimination for Women in the Building Trades." from *Gender & Society*, 28(3) Copyright © 2014. Reprinted by permission.

cultural resources available to them for resisting gender boundaries. We argue that the presence of women in male-dominated jobs threatens the perception of this work as inherently masculine (Collinson 2010; Epstein 1992; Paap 2006). We further argue that branding all tradeswomen lesbians, and thus—in the popular imagination—as not fully women, can partly be understood as an attempt to neutralize this threat. While the lesbian label (whether or not women personally identify as such) offers some degree of acceptance and freedom from performing emphasized femininity, it can place demands on tradeswomen to perform a subordinate blue-collar masculinity that may include participating in a misogynistic work culture (Connell 1987; West and Zimmerman 1987).

Moreover, the presence of lesbians (and sexually autonomous straight women whose sexuality is not directed toward tradesmen) threatens heteronormativity and men's sexual subordination of women, or what Ingraham calls "patriarchal heterosexuality" (Ingraham 1994). By sexually objectifying tradeswomen, tradesmen, in effect, attempt to neutralize this threat. While tradeswomen, in turn, are sometimes able to deploy femininity to manage men's conduct and gain some measure of acceptance as women, it often comes at the cost of their perceived professional competence and sexual autonomy and—in the case of lesbians—sexual identity.

Those who refuse to be sexually objectified may subsequently find themselves the target of open hostility. Certain women—including lesbians and those who present as butch, large, or black—may be less able to access emphasized femininity as a resource and thus more subject to open hostility. We show that tradeswomen navigate among imperfect strategies and engage in complex risk assessments (McDermott 2006). Extending Denissen (2010b), we highlight how tradeswomen reflexively manipulate gender meanings, adding a new emphasis on the intersection between sexuality, gender representation, race, and body size. Ultimately, however, we argue that individual strategies are insufficient and show how tradesmen deploy the stigma of lesbianism to discourage solidarity and collective action among tradeswomen. We consider the implications of these findings within the larger debate about the efficacy of interactional forms of resistance for challenging patriarchy and the dominant gender order.

FINDINGS

Previous work shows that men working in male-dominated blue-collar occupations accentuate their manliness by distinguishing their work from women's work (Epstein 1992; Schrock and Schwalbe 2009) and how managers manipulate gender ideology to control workers (Collinson 2010; Epstein 1992; Paap 2006). For instance, in a coal miner's protest about being asked to lift too much weight, the foreman asked, "What's the matter? Aren't you man enough?" (Epstein 1992, 243). By encouraging workers to identify with their gender and, also, their race, national, and class identities, employers divide workers and distract them from working conditions in order to enhance labor control (Hossfeld 1990). Generalizing from Ramirez (2010), many "macho" masculinities can be understood as working-class men's "compensatory reactions" to subordination when other sources of masculine identity are blocked (Zinn 1982) or become insecure because of declining wages, job security, union power, and social regard (Paap 2006). When men derive psychic and social rewards and managers derive economic benefits from these identifications, both groups can be expected to resist the entrance of women workers, which undermines the sense that it is, in fact, "men's work" (Epstein 1992).

We analytically disentangle two related threats that arise when women work on job sites: the masculine definition of the building trades as "men's work" and individual tradesmen's heteromasculinity. In the first instance, we show how tradesmen reinforce the idea of the construction trades as men's work by assuming that tradeswomen must be lesbians. Thus, the lesbian label offers some freedom from gender expectations.

However, we show how the presence of lesbians violates the dictates of compulsory heterosexuality. The idea of an autonomous female sexuality that is not directed at men also undermines understandings of masculinity as involving sexual control over women. In an attempt to neutralize this threat, some men sexualize lesbians and straight tradeswomen, especially if they are more feminine in their presentation. While providing some degree of integration, such objectification can be unpleasant and even dangerous and reaffirms tradeswomen's femininity over their competence. Those tradeswomen whose threat to masculinity is not so easily neutralized by heterosexualization, including many lesbians, may avoid the traps of objectification only to find themselves the objects of direct hostility. We discuss how tradeswomen respond to these constraints, often in creative and artful ways, and how their strategies are constrained and enabled by sexual orientation, gender presentation, body size, and race. We then discuss how tradesmen deploy homophobia to stymie the expression of solidarity among women, gay or straight.

NEGOTIATING THREATS TO THE MASCULINE DEFINITION OF THE WORK

Tradeswomen report that homophobic comments, jokes, and graffiti are pervasive and that tradesmen regularly use terms like "gay" and "faggot" to publicly establish hetero-masculine identities and to reinforce the masculine definition of the work. For example, Monique says her male coworkers "pick on each other, [saying things] like: 'The electricians are faggots,' 'The carpenters are faggots,' 'Because he walks a certain way, he's gay.'" In this example, tradesmen use homophobic comments to assert dominance over "rival" groups of men (such as men from other trades) and to regulate the gender and sexual behavior of men. Yet, unlike the high school boys studied by Pascoe who claim not to direct fag discourse at boys known to be gay (Pascoe 2005), tradesmen unapologetically use homophobic slurs to repudiate both homosexuality and femininity (in men). This was not lost on the tradeswomen interviewed, who attributed the fact that they did not know any openly gay men to their sense that the trades are dangerous for openly gay men.

Similarly, the presence of women on job sites threatens the definition of the construction trades as "men's work." One way that tradesmen make sense of tradeswomen's presence and neutralize this threat is to label them lesbians or likely lesbians. Lynne, an Asian American lesbian, explains, "People think if you're a tradeswoman, you're a lesbian. You want to do a man's job, so you want to be a man, so you're a lesbian." Stephanie, a straight white woman, says, "People think I'm gay a lot of the time because . . . I don't look real feminine." Holly, another straight white woman, says a fellow apprentice "never discussed her love life at work, and she [then] mentioned having a boyfriend.

Everybody looked at her like 'You have a boyfriend?' They thought she was gay." Imagining tradeswomen as lesbians, that is, not fully female, preserves the idea of the trades as "men's work."

This opens up the possibility that straight tradeswomen may be perceived as more of a threat to the masculine definition of the work than lesbian tradeswomen. Indeed, Loretta, a black lesbian, says that her male coworkers do not "want any women at all," but that "somebody like me is safer for them because they can ignore me like a guy they don't like":

> They're, like, "There's a chick here, but there's not really a chick here. It's Loretta, she's not really a chick." But [with] a chick, they're hitting on them, they're getting in trouble. They've got to be a little bit more on the Ps and Qs about what they say and the way they act. They can be a little freer [with me] because I'm not going to beat them up about their language and scratching their balls and acting like assholes.

Loretta notes that while some tradesmen resent the presence of all women in the trades, straight or lesbian, that she, as a lesbian, is "not really a chick" and her presence does not limit tradesmen's freedom to perform masculinity as they please. This may be especially true for lesbians like Loretta who present as butch. Indeed, Vicky, a lesbian tradeswoman who describes herself as "a bit girlier" notes that tradesmen are more likely to treat a woman who "doesn't look as feminine on the outside" as "one of the guys," while they are more likely to "watch their potty mouth" around more "girly"-presenting lesbians. We also find some evidence that butch lesbians are somewhat less likely to be targeted by sexual advances.

A few tradeswomen claim that, as lesbians, they are fully accepted as "one of the guys." For example, Toni, a white lesbian, who describes herself as someone who "used to be extremely feminine" but no longer bothers because "it required too much maintenance," describes how she is incorporated into the men's sex talk:

> [My coworker] tells his girlfriend, "She's like one of the guys, you know, I can tell her anything." That's how most of the guys think of me anyways. They just talk about whatever they want to. It's, like, [I'll tell the men,] "You should do this [sexual maneuver] or you should try that [sexual position]." [And, later they'll tell me,] "Oh, that worked! Thanks a lot, Toni." So it's all good.

For Toni, offering advice on women's sexuality is a "good" form of inclusion because it takes place within a supportive working relationship with coworkers.

At the same time, finding acceptance as "one of the guys" can be fraught with danger. Lori, the Jewish butch lesbian introduced earlier, describes a lunchtime interaction she had as an apprentice, when she was especially vulnerable:

> They're sitting around talking about the Mike Tyson case when he sexually assaulted this woman. For me, rape is no joking matter. So here's nine of 'em, a foreman, journeymen, apprentices, and one shop steward, and I'm the only woman in this discussion. They're all sitting there talking about it and joking about it, and I'm, like, "Whoa. I'm feeling really, really violent." So I said, "The next person who says anything, I'm gonna get really violent." They all shut the fuck up. Then there was another situation where they were talking about wife beating. I got mad, but sometimes it's not worth it 'cause it's, like, "Oh, she's got no sense of humor." So then I just don't eat lunch with them anymore.

As her words illustrate, being "one of the guys" may involve participating in a misogynistic work culture. Lori tells of not being able to tolerate such expectations, becoming angry and removing herself from the work group. She explains how she censured her own responses out of fear that resistance to the sexist work culture would jeopardize her insider status by stigmatizing her as lacking a "sense of humor." Several of the tradeswomen, including Lori, say that, after completing apprenticeships and becoming certified, they felt less at risk and, as a result, used more assertive and visible— as opposed to accommodative or subtle—strategies.

While lesbians may be more likely than straight women to be accepted as "one of the guys," and while this can provide some camaraderie and acceptance as a serious worker, they rarely experience full acceptance. Rather, tradeswomen typically emphasize that acceptance as one of the guys is incomplete and conditional. Many tradeswomen say their male coworkers hold them to an exaggerated standard of masculinity, making them carry heavier materials and do dirtier and more dangerous work, in order to prove they can work "like a guy." Further, as we discuss ahead, acceptance as one of the guys in some contexts does not exempt them from the ideals of emphasized femininity in others.

Managing Perceived Threats to the Heterogendered Order

While the presumption that tradeswomen are likely lesbians neutralizes threats to the masculine definition of the work, it threatens heteronormativity and the sexual and economic subordination of women to men. In response, tradesmen sometimes direct gendered homophobic comments at lesbian tradeswomen. In other instances, they sexually objectify (lesbian and straight) tradeswomen. We examine tradeswomen's accounts of this behavior and how they respond to it.

Keeping Them Guessing, Keeping It Private, and Other Responses to Gendered Homophobia. Just as they use fag discourse to police gender noncomformity among men, so tradesmen use the lesbian label to control the gendered conduct of tradeswomen. For example, Elena (a Latina heterosexual) says tradesmen single out lesbian tradeswomen as deviant "freaks": "The guys talk about them really bad, like, she's trying to play a man role, she likes it rough, men can't satisfy her, she must be freaky and have freaky needs." Lauren, a white lesbian who describes herself as tomboyish but not butch, says that she has heard her coworkers make disparaging comments about "hardcore dyke lesbians." She recounts how one tradesman exclaimed, "Damn, I'm working with this guy and next thing I know she turns around and, shit, she's got tits!" When Lauren asked him if she was a good worker, he responded, "I don't know, I couldn't work with her."

Racial minority status and body size can intersect with sexual identity and gender presentation to heighten stigmatization and otherness. Loretta, the black butch lesbian, is large and has a shaved head. An electrician, a trade that historically has had among the lowest number of minority workers (Bilginsoy 2005), Loretta describes job sites as "bastions of white male supremacy." She notes that, in recent years, an influx of Latino workers has heightened racial tensions and that the prevailing message conveyed to women, "queers," and people of color is "You shouldn't be here." She tells of hearing tradesmen say, "Now they're letting animals in the trade." When asked to whom they were referring, Loretta exclaims, "Me! Or my crewmember who [was] a person of color." Loretta speaks of how she is threatening, not just as a woman, but as a large, black, butch lesbian woman with an aggressive personality, a composite that "messes with the whole expectation of what your gender, what your behavior's supposed to be."

Loretta says that tradesmen sometimes "picked on" her about her large size, saying things like, "You're fat" or that her size "ain't cool for chicks." Similarly, Lori, who describes herself as a "big butch dyke" (a "three-part package"), says that her coworkers' negative comments about her size are gendered: "They'll accommodate a big guy where they won't accommodate a big woman."

Sometimes the label "lesbian" is decoupled from women's own sexual identity, as when tradesmen target tradeswomen for gendered homophobia because their appearance or behavior does not conform to tradesmen's gender expectations. For instance, Cheryl, a white heterosexual, explains how one of her coworkers "was mad because I'd showed him up that day," performing better than he in a workplace task. He asked her, "What's the matter with you? Are you one of those lesbian women, you know, and you're not interested in me?" In this example, Cheryl's coworker accuses her of being a lesbian, and thus unfeminine, because she outperforms him. He thereby conflates her occupational competence and sexual orientation, considering both as signs of gender nonconformity.

In response to gendered homophobia, lesbian tradeswomen engage in complex risk assessments and employ a variety of disclosure options. For example, Anna, a Latina lesbian who describes herself as tomboyish and "not real girly but not real butchy," remarks about a coworker, "I've heard him make comments about fags and queers and I didn't want to go there. When he said, 'Are you married?' I said, 'No' and I didn't say I have a partner." Here, Anna speaks a "half-truth to power" (Sullivan 2001). It is true that she is not married, but she conceals the full truth—that she has a same-sex romantic partner—from this coworker because his homophobic comments make that revelation feel unsafe. Further, Anna says that in situations that feel safer, she selectively discloses her sexual identity:

> I don't totally come out and say, "Okay, I'm gay." I just ease into it, kind of feel it out. . . . They say, "What's your boyfriend do?" I'll say, "I don't have a boyfriend." If it's somebody that I know that I can trust I'll say, "I've got a girlfriend." As long as I think that it wouldn't be a bad situation. It's a judgment call.

Racial minority status often heightens othering and perceived risk, further limiting tradeswomen's disclosure options. For example, Lori, a self-described Jewish butch lesbian, says she did not disclose her sexual orientation on one job site early in her career because she had heard "a bunch of sexist, racist, and homophobic speech" that made disclosure feel unsafe. While her coworkers were specifically "targeting the Hispanics," their behavior "really frightened" her "because they had swastikas and Nazi and KKK-type talk." Yet, later in her career and on less racist job sites, she developed a strategy of singling out one man with whom she would be more open:

> What I do generally is I'd make allies with one dude who I felt was more open-minded or we have a connection. I would be honest with him about who I was. As long as I had one person I could be myself with, then I felt okay. Now I'm pretty much out. I decided that I'm out in the union as a whole, but I pick and choose how much I say.

Several of the respondents similarly spoke about becoming more open, but still guarded, regarding their sexuality as they gained more occupational seniority.

Sometimes tradeswomen conceal their sexual identity not simply out of fear of retaliation but also to resist the salience of their sexual identity in workplace interactions. We call this strategy "keeping it private." Vanesa, a white lesbian, explains that she brought her best friend, rather than her girlfriend, to union picnics both because she wants to keep her "personal life private" and also because she hopes to "keep away from the stigma" and does not "want a guy not to teach me because of who I am." Anita, a Native American lesbian, similarly evokes a concern with both privacy and homophobia, explaining that she was not initially out because "it's nobody's business, and then going into a man's field I figured it's probably not a good idea to advertise." Yet, she says that "if it came up, I didn't deny it," akin to what others have labeled an "open closet door policy" (Reimann 2001). Similarly, Lauren, a white lesbian, says, "There's some guys that don't know. Maybe that's my way of blending in without any confrontation. I like to get in there, get my job done, and get out. I've had a couple of guys ask me, and if they got the balls to ask me, I'll tell them."

Gina, a large, black, straight, married woman, evokes a "keep them guessing" strategy that entails sending mixed messages about sexual identity as part of an attempt to "break that stereotype":

> I had them so fooled there were people that didn't have any idea what my sexual orientation was. If somebody questioned me, [I'd say,] "I'm gay, leave me alone, I'm a lesbian." Or [I'd say,] "I'm single," or "I have two kids," or "I have a husband." People would be running around, [saying,] "No, she told me she was gay." Or "Gina, you're not gay, I met your husband." So you'd keep them guessing because the point was that your sexual orientation didn't matter.

While keeping the men guessing may function partially as an expression of solidarity with lesbian tradeswomen, a sort of reverse passing intended to challenge stereotypes about lesbians, Gina herself says it is also a way of resisting the salience of women's sexual identities at work.

Similarly, Alex, a white lesbian, talks about mixing displays of subordinated feminine heterosexuality with more stereotypically masculine behavior in order to resist homophobia and sexism. She explains that while she used to be mistaken for a man because she "looked completely androgynous," she has grown her hair since joining the trades because short hair "would be such a red flag" that she is a "dyke" or is "so manly":

> I'd rather act feminine and friendly and cute than get harassed, ignored, or treated worse. But at the same time it's like I have to be careful that I don't act overly feminine because they'll think I can't work. Sometimes I'll say something that will totally throw them for a spin [or] make them raise an eyebrow because I'll say it in a masculine way. I'll say something that's really clear, concise, and to the point, and they don't expect that of me. They think I'm a bubbly person; they stereotype me as a female.

Alex is managing a classic double bind where she is held accountable to conflicting expectations for gendered conduct. She is aware that her coworkers may mark (raised eyebrow) and sanction (harassment, isolation) masculine conduct. Alex says she flirts with men and acts "feminine" in an effort to forestall certain forms of harassment and exclusion, but fears that overdoing it may detract from her perceived competence. She performs an intricate gender maneuvering in trying to strike a balance by varying heterofeminine displays with more assertive (masculine) actions to transgress dualistic sexual

and gender boundaries. While white respondents, straight and gay, were more likely to speak of incorporating displays of emphasized femininity into their gender maneuvering, black, butch, and large tradeswomen were more likely to emphasize their ability to "hold their own" with the heaviest, dirtiest, and most dangerous tasks.

Turning the Tables: Resistance to Compulsory Heterosexuality. Another way that tradesmen neutralize the threat of lesbian/female autonomy is by recasting them as objects of men's sexual desire. Some lesbian tradeswomen say tradesmen embrace them through the heterosexual male fantasy of having "fancy sex" with multiple women. For instance, when asked if she ever was directly targeted by homophobia, Anna, the Latina lesbian introduced earlier, responds, "No, because I'm a female. Some guys say, 'I don't care about the women. I think that's great! That's fancy for me! I just can't stand the guys.'" Yet, Toni, a white lesbian, suggests that this form of acceptance has its costs: "They'll make innuendos like 'You should hook up with her and then hook up with me later.' They know I'm not interested in them. They just continue to do it because they know it bugs me." In this instance, Toni's coworkers impose heterosexual expectations and meanings onto her and intentionally "bug" her. By redefining lesbian relationships as serving male heterosexual desire, tradesmen neutralize the perceived threat of lesbian desire to heterosexism.

Out lesbian tradeswomen use various strategies to resist their coworkers' efforts to heterosexualize them and, sometimes, to reaffirm their sexual identity as lesbians. Jan, a lesbian of white and Native American descent, who is slim and has long blonde hair, and says she "doesn't go out of her way to be feminine" but "doesn't seem butch to the guys," complains about how she has to tell her coworkers that she is not "free porn." Others speak of resisting traditional gender dynamics by showing a sexually assertive interest in their coworker's women partners. Anna, the Latina lesbian, explains:

> [My coworkers] accept me for who I am. [He'll say,] "That's cool, girl. Can we get some?" [laughs] I'll be, like, "Can I get some of yours? I'll let you talk to my girl if you let me talk to your wife." And he'll be, like, "Fuck you." Guys are cool with me. [They'll say,] "How's your girl? She's pretty hot." I go, "Yeah, thank you. So is your wife." [Laughs.]

While Anna describes her interactions with her co-workers as playful and respectful ("They accept me for who I am"), she also experiences counterresistance from her coworker ("Fuck you"). Indeed, it seems that she gets respect, in large part, because she can give as good as she gets, using masculine displays of dominance to neutralize efforts to sexually dominate her. We call this strategy "turning the tables."

Similarly, Lynne, an Asian American lesbian whom we would describe as gender-blending but who is sometimes mistaken for a man, explains how she responded to a coworker who constantly asked her if he could watch her have sex with another woman:

> I said, "Why don't you talk to your girlfriend about it? Bring me a picture; I want to see what she looks like." He got all defensive: "Who, wait, what'd you mean? I don't have a picture. She ain't going for that shit." He backed off that whole line of conversation after that.

Like Anna, Lynne successfully wards off her coworker's efforts to sexualize her by turning the tables and sexualizing his girlfriend. While this interaction seems to have been successful in curtailing demands to watch Lynne have sex with other women, later in the interview Lynne says this incident led to a strained working relationship with this particular coworker.

Moreover, tradeswomen are not equally able to resist their coworker's efforts to sexualize them. Julia, a Latina lesbian apprentice who described herself as "looking like a little dude," describes an extreme case in which a coworker attempted to sexually force himself on her:

> Every day he would bug me, "Hey, you should come over to my house. We should hang out and you should be my girlfriend." I'm, like, "No, dude. I don't like guys." He started telling me sexual stuff like "We should have a threesome." Every day for, like, three weeks he would tell me, "Watch, I'm going to get you. I always get what I want." I never said anything because I didn't believe he would because there were always people around. One day he started getting in my face and walking me back into a unit. He picked me up and took me in there and then, that fool, he turned me around and hugged me from the waist like [he was] kissing his girlfriend. He went down to kiss me and I was laughing because I was scared. I was, like, "Man, what's wrong with you?" And at that moment one of my coworkers was passing by and they

saw each other and this guy let go. I got scared; he could have done anything, you know.

This tradesman disregards Julia's identity as a lesbian, as well as her resistance to his sexual advances, trying to force himself on her. He responds to her defiance with threats to "get her," culminating with a sexual assault on the job site. Fearing for her job, she initially refused to report the incident but ultimately did so, upon the urging of the superintendent and the coworker who witnessed the assault. Julia says she never saw the assailant again.

Other tradeswomen also report being targeted with overt hostility and violence after refusing to engage in sexual banter or feminine displays. Some of the more egregious examples include having electrical wires turned on while they were working on them, having tools dropped on them, or finding feces in their hard hat. These sorts of incidents highlight the risks and limitations of individual-level resistance.

How Gendered Homophobia Limits Collective Resistance. While individual strategies have subversive potential, successful "contestation of gender hierarchy is fundamentally a collective process" (Connell 2009, 109). With typically few allies at work, one might expect tradeswomen to seek each other out for safety and support. Yet many of our respondents say they avoid other women both on and off the construction site. In some cases, this stems from their own homophobia, but it is more often described as an effort to protect themselves from homophobic stigma and sexist stereotypes. Vanesa, a white lesbian, explains, "Women will tell me they don't want to be seen with other women or belonging to a women's group because a lot of the guys say, '[If] you women want to be just like us men so much, then why do you have this little women's group?'" Some tradesmen pressure her and other tradeswomen to avoid associating with other women. Vanesa further describes how tradesmen reframe women's efforts to support each other as attempts to gain special privileges. For example, her foreman remarked, after seeing her in a tradeswomen's convention T-shirt, "I don't think there should be separate organizations, you guys need to be treated the same."

Loretta, the black butch lesbian, says that she "would never hang out with the girls" and that "the girls on the crew wouldn't want to hang out with me, because they wouldn't want the other guys to think that they were gay. Because of that guilt by association thing it's, like, 'Well, if we're nice to you, they might think we're like you.'" Loretta's comments speak to how lesbian stigma is attached not only to joining women's associations but also to socializing with other women on the job. Similarly, Lori, a Jewish butch lesbian, says, "I wanted to start a lesbian tradeswomen group but not even the lesbians want to start it with me." Moreover, she says, "Sometimes even other women in the trades are afraid to be seen with me because I'm an out lesbian. Like it'll spill off on them and the guys will see it." At a conference for women in the trades, the women became particularly animated when they heard that tradesmen were referring to the conference as a "big lesbian orgy" in what seemed like an attempt to discredit the conference and keep both straight and lesbian tradeswomen away.

As Lori describes it, tradesmen effectively use the specter of lesbianism to stymie gender solidarity and political activism: "Sometimes there's solidarity, sometimes not, because the lesbians think they have to align themselves with the men for power and that means turning against other women or a more out lesbian. They'll be more closeted or they're afraid to be seen as lesbian whether they're lesbian or not." In distancing themselves from other women in order to protect themselves from the gendered homophobia of their coworkers, both straight and lesbian tradeswomen are made more vulnerable as they become isolated from each other. Yet, there is also evidence of resistance and change. For example, the tradeswomen conference has grown steadily over time from a state to an international event and active tradeswomen's groups have formed online, demonstrating organizational success despite these challenges.

CONCLUSION

Drawing on interviews with a diverse sample of lesbian and straight women in the construction trades, this article examines how the cultural meanings of sexual identity, gender presentation, race, and, more tentatively, body size and seniority, inform how men seek to control tradeswomen and how the latter respond to these efforts. We show that labeling tradeswomen as lesbians, and thus—in the popular imagination—as not fully women,

both makes sense of their presence and reaffirms the perception of the trades as "men's work." Some lesbian tradeswomen report being more accepted than their straight women coworkers and claim that the lesbian label offers them some freedom from performing emphasized femininity. This acceptance is limited, however, and can place them in uncomfortable situations where they are expected to perform misogynist versions of masculinity. Moreover, while lesbians may be less threatening to the notion of the trades as men's work, their presence threatens heteronormativity and assumptions about the sexual subordination of women. We explain how tradesmen's efforts to sexually objectify tradeswomen can be understood as attempts to neutralize threats to heteronormativity and male privilege.

We demonstrate that in response to these constraints, tradeswomen use gender maneuvering (Schippers 2002) to combine performances of femininity and masculinity, to gain some measure of acceptance as women, and to maintain their perceived competence as workers. While tradeswomen strategically draw upon multiple strategies, we further show how the meanings attributed to tradeswomen's sexuality, gender presentation, race, body size, and seniority influence their preferred strategies. For instance, lesbian tradeswomen who are perceived as "like one of the guys" are more likely than straight tradeswomen to report using sexual banter to find commonality with their male coworkers. White respondents, straight and gay, are most likely to incorporate elements of emphasized femininity in their gender maneuvering. In contrast, black, butch, and large tradeswomen are more likely to emphasize that they can "hold their own" with the heaviest, dirtiest, and most dangerous tasks.

Straight and lesbian tradeswomen alike invoke a "keeping them guessing" strategy, which involves giving varying and contradictory cues about sexual identity over time. This strategy is structurally equivalent to the gender maneuvering strategies of varying masculine and feminine gender displays (see also Denissen 2010b). In addition, lesbians use various strategies to manage the stigma related to their sexual orientation, including telling half-truths to power, selectively disclosing, and employing an open closet door policy (Reimann 2001; Sullivan 2001). Lesbians also invoke a strategy we call "keeping it private," in which they conceal their sexual identity on the basis that it is not relevant. This strategy parallels tradeswomen's efforts to suppress the salience of gender by emphasizing other commonalities such as race, class, and occupation (Denissen 2010b).

We provide evidence that experienced tradeswomen are somewhat more comfortable with assertive and visible—as opposed to deferential and covert—strategies, such as "turning the tables," in which tradeswomen sexualize tradesmen's girlfriends or wives. Future work should examine the extent to which tradesmen's behavior systematically varies by their age/generation as well. One might expect younger generations to be more inclusive of women and minorities, but this merits systematic examination. More broadly, since men's cooperation and training is crucial for women's success in male-dominated contexts, more research that examines men's role as allies is needed.

While individual tradeswomen are creative and sometimes successful in their efforts to resist men's attempts to marginalize and exclude them, our study suggests that individual responses may not be enough to produce widespread or lasting change. Tradeswomen's efforts to organize, however, are stymied by insinuations of lesbianism. Thus, gendered homophobia plays a crucial role in isolating and dividing tradeswomen, undermining their efforts to create solidarity, engage in collective resistance, and bring about institutional change. The risks of associating with lesbians and other women may be greatest for women of color and other especially vulnerable populations, a question that merits additional research.

We show how contradictions in the dominant heterogender order constrain tradeswomen, while opening up possibilities for—and even necessitating—more reflexive, varied, and strategic forms of gender and sexual practices (Denissen 2010b). Since gendered expectations of tradeswomen are intrinsically contradictory (e.g., sufficiently masculine to be deemed competent but sufficiently feminine to be socially acceptable), tradeswomen must constantly vary the way they "do gender" (West and Zimmerman 1987). Earlier work shows that exclusion of women in the building trades is reproduced despite women's resistance at the level of interaction and identity construction (Denissen 2010b). This article sheds light on one key mechanism whereby women's strategic agency is limited: the isolation of tradeswomen from other women. Thus, while individual tradeswomen strategically maneuver among gender and sexual meanings in ways that transgress heterogender boundaries and trouble the heterogender order, they face greater counter-resistance when they collectively organize. This study expands on previous research that documents how race, class, and gender identities can be used to divide and control workers (Hossfeld 1990) by showing how tradesmen use gendered homophobia as a means of dividing and subordinating women workers.

These findings speak to debates about the extent to which individual-level resistance disrupts patriarchy or, alternatively, unwittingly reinforces the dominant gender order (Devor 1987; Ridgeway and Correll 2004). According to Finley (2010), transformations in gender relations are more likely in women-controlled than male-dominated spaces. Finley argues that women's networks are crucial for transforming the dominant gender order and that women in male-dominated settings are too isolated from other women to be effective. Our findings regarding women's isolation from each other and limits to collective resistance are consistent with Finley's argument.

Yet, we suspect that female- and male-dominated settings each present their own set of struggles. Challenges to a large and powerful sector of the economy, such as the construction trades, are likely to meet strong resistance. Moreover, in male-dominated contexts, those who have an interest in upholding the dominant gender order have a numerical and normative advantage. In contrast, in women-centered contexts such as roller derbies (Finley 2010) or alternative hard rock scenes (Schippers 2002), women may face less resistance. However, these subcultures are themselves marginalized from sites of political and economic power, limiting the impact of women's gains. Perhaps the path toward undoing the hegemonic gender order lies in combining "micromaneuvering" and collective activism (Schippers 2002) with coalition building across contexts. The Internet offers opportunities for tradeswomen wishing to build coalitions, as exemplified by an online forum created by and for tradeswomen that announces to readers, "we encourage guys to work with us and join [name of group] to show men and women working together." Supportive women-centered spaces are important, yet working-class women and women of color also emphasize the importance of organizing alongside men.

As Paap (2006) demonstrates, employers profit from "macho" masculinities at the expense of tradesmen, who work harder, faster, and more dangerously to prove their worth, undermining working conditions for all construction workers while also marginalizing tradeswomen.

REFERENCES

Applebaum, Herbert. 1999. *Construction workers, U.S.A.* Westport, CT: Greenwood.

Bilginsoy, Cihan. 2005. Registered apprentices and apprenticeship programs in the U.S. construction industry between 1989 and 2003: An examination of the AIMS, RAIS, and California Apprenticeship Agency databases. Department of Economics Working Paper Series (Working Paper #2005–09), University of Utah, Salt Lake City.

Bilginsoy, Cihan. 2009. *Wage structure and unionization in the US construction sector.* Salt Lake City, UT: University of Utah, Department of Economics.

Burke, Marc. 1994. Homosexuality as deviance: The case of the gay police officer. *British Journal of Criminology* 34:192–203.

Collinson, David L. 2010. *Managing the shopfloor.* Boston, MA: De Gruyter.

Connell, R. W. 1987. *Gender and power: Society, the person, and sexual politics.* Stanford, CA: Stanford University Press.

Connell, Raewyn. 2009. "Doing gender" in transsexual and political retrospect. *Gender & Society* 23 (1): 94–98.

Crenshaw, Kimberle. 1989. Demarginalizing the intersection of race and sex: A Black feminist critique of antidiscrimination doctrine, feminist theory and antiracist policies. *University of Chicago Legal Forum* 139–67.

Denissen, Amy M. 2010a. Crossing the line: How women in the building trades interpret and respond to sexual conduct at work. *Journal of Contemporary Ethnography* 39:298–327.

Denissen, Amy M. 2010b. The right tools for the job: Constructing gender meanings and identities in the male-dominated building trades. *Human Relations* 63:1051–69.

Devor, Holly. 1987. Gender blending females women and sometimes men. *American Behavioral Scientist* 31:12–40.

Epstein, Cynthia Fuchs. 1992. Tinkerbells and pinups. In *Cultivating differences: Symbolic boundaries and the making of inequality*, edited by Michèle Lamont and Marcel Fournier. Chicago: University of Chicago Press.

Fikkan, Janna L., and Esther Rothblum. 2011. Is fat a feminist issue? Exploring the gendered nature of weight bias. *Sex Roles* 66:575–92.

Finley, Nancy J. 2010. Skating femininity: Gender maneuvering in women's roller derby. *Journal of Contemporary Ethnography* 39:359–87.

Frank, Miriam. 2001. Hard hats and homophobia: Lesbians in the building trades. *New Labor Forum* 8:25–36.

Goffman, Erving. 1963. *Stigma: Notes on the management of a spoiled identity.* New York: Prentice Hall.

Gruber, James E. 1998. The impact of male work environments and organizational policies on women's experiences of sexual harassment. *Gender & Society* 12:301–20.

Halberstam, Judith. 1998. *Female masculinity.* Durham, NC: Duke University Press.

Hossfeld, Karen J. 1990. "Their logic against them": Contradictions in sex, race, and class in Silicon Valley. In *Women workers and global restructuring*, edited by Kathryn B. Ward. Ithaca, NY: Cornell University Press.

Ingraham, Chrys. 1994. The heterosexual imaginary: Feminist sociology and theories of gender. *Sociological Theory* 12:203–19.

Jamieson, Kathleen H. 1995. *Beyond the double bind: Women and leadership.* New York: Oxford University Press.

Janssens, Maddy, Tineke Cappellen, and Patrizia Zanoni. 2006. Successful female expatriates as agents: Positioning oneself through gender, hierarchy, and culture. *Journal of World Business* 41:133–48.

Kanter, Rosabeth M. 1977. *Men and women of the corporation.* New York: Basic Books.

Kazyak, Emily. 2012. Midwest or lesbian? Gender, rurality, and sexuality. *Gender & Society* 26:825–48.

Lucal, Betsy. 1999. What it means to be gendered me: Life on the boundaries of a dichotomous gender system. *Gender & Society* 13:781–97.

MacKinnon, Catharine. 1982. Feminism, Marxism, method and the state: An agenda for theory. *Signs* 7:533–44.

McDermott, E. 2006. Surviving in dangerous places: Lesbian identity performances in the workplace, social class and psychological health. *Feminism and Psychology* 16:193–211.

Miller, Susan L., Kay B. Forest, and Nancy C. Jurik. 2003. Diversity in blue: Lesbian and gay police officers in a masculine occupation. *Men and Masculinities* 5:355–85.

Moore, Mignon. 2011. *Invisible families: Gay identities, relationships, and motherhood among Black women.* Berkeley: University of California Press.

Myers, Kristen A., Kay B. Forest, and Susan L. Miller. 2004. Officer friendly and the tough cop: Gays and lesbians navigate homophobia and policing. *Journal of Homosexuality* 47:17–37.

Paap, Kris. 2006. *Working construction: Why white working-class men put themselves—and the labor movement—in harm's way*. Ithaca, NY: Cornell University Press.

Pascoe, C. J. 2005. "Dude, you're a fag": Adolescent masculinity and the fag discourse. *Sexualities* 8:329–46.

Pateman, Carol. 1988. *The sexual contract*. Stanford, CA: Stanford University Press.

Pierce, Jennifer L. 1995. *Gender trials: Emotional lives in contemporary law firms*. Berkeley: University of California Press.

Ramirez, Hernan. 2010. Masculinity in the workplace: The case of Mexican immigrant gardeners. *Men and Masculinities* 14:97–116.

Reimann, Renate. 2001. Lesbian mothers at work. In *Queer families, queer politics*, edited by Mary Bernstein and Renate Reimann. New York: Columbia University Press.

Rich, Adrienne. 1993. Compulsory heterosexuality and lesbian existence. In *The lesbian and gay studies reader*, edited by Henry Abelove, Michele Aina Barale, and David Halperin. New York: Routledge.

Ridgeway, Cecilia L., and Shelley J. Correll. 2004. Unpacking the gender system: A theoretical perspective on gender beliefs and social relations. *Gender & Society* 18:510–31.

Saguy, Abigail C. 2012. Why fat is a feminist issue. *Sex Roles* 68:600–7.

Schilt, Kristen. 2011. *Just one of the guys? Transgender men and the persistence of workplace gender inequality*. Chicago: University of Chicago.

Schilt, Kristen, and Laurel Westbrook. 2009. Doing gender, doing heteronormativity: "Gender normals," transgender people, and the social maintenance of heterosexuality. *Gender & Society* 23:440–64.

Schippers, Mimi. 2002. *Rockin' out of the box: Gender maneuvering in alternative hard rock*. New Brunswick: Rutgers University Press.

Schrock, Douglas, and Michael Schwalbe. 2009. Men, masculinity, and manhood acts. *Annual Review of Sociology* 35:277–95.

Seidman, Steven. 2010. *The social construction of sexuality*. 2nd ed. New York: Norton.

Sullivan, Maureen. 2001. Alma mater: Family "outings" and the making of the Modern Other Mother (MOM). In *Queer families, queer politics*, edited by Mary Bernstein and Renate Reimann. New York: Columbia University Press.

Valentine, David. 2007. *Imagining transgender: An ethnography of a category*. Durham, NC: Duke University Press.

Valian, Virginia. 1998. *Why so slow? The advancement of women*. Cambridge: MIT Press.

West, Candace, and Don H. Zimmerman. 1987. Doing gender. *Gender and Society* 1:125–51.

Zinn, Maxine Baca. 1982. Chicano men and masculinity. *Journal of Ethnic Studies* 10:29–44.

38

The Modern Mammy and the Angry Black Man: African American Professionals' Experiences with Gendered Racism in the Workplace

ADIA HARVEY WINGFIELD

Studies of how racism affects African Americans constitute a sizable body of the sociological literature on race relations. Research in this vein has examined how racism affects African Americans at work, in the educational system, and in everyday life, as well as the overall significance (or lack thereof) of racism for Black Americans (Collins, 1998; Feagin, 1991; Feagin & Sikes, 1996; Ferguson, 2000; Wilson, 1988). The overwhelming majority of these studies suggest that racism still shapes many, if not most, facets of life for Black Americans. However, these studies often tacitly assume that race generally impacts Black men and women in the same way or fail to take gender differences into account when analyzing the manifestations and effects of racism. Feminist researchers have attempted to rectify this conceptual limitation by drawing attention to the ways that Black women's experiences with racism are also intertwined with sexism. Thus, studies of Black women in various settings—community organizations, work, public spaces—carefully delineate the intersecting effects of race and gender, noting that both of these categories interact to shape Black women's experiences (Byng, 1998; Gilkes, 1988;

Harvey, 2005; Texeira, 2002). However, among the studies of how racism affects African Americans and studies of how race and gender affect Black women, few specifically address how Blacks' experiences with racism differ by gender. In this study, I offer a comparative analysis of the ways Black professional men's and women's experiences with racism in the workplace are gendered.

THEORETICAL FRAMEWORK

Gender, Race, and Work

Studies of race in the workplace document the extent to which racism plays a role in shaping minorities' experiences in the labor force (Cose, 1993; Higginbotham & Weber, 1997; Tomaskovic-Devey, 1993). Collins (1998) argues that affirmative action policies have produced essential occupational niches that allowed many Blacks to experience social and economic mobility. Feagin and Sikes (1996) claim that in the middle class workplace Black employees experience stereotypes, discrimination, and pay inequity relative to their white

"The Modern Mammy and the Angry Black Man: African American Professionals' Experiences with Gendered Racism in the Workplace" by Adia Harvey Wingfield in *Race, Gender & Class* volume 14, number 1–2 (2007). Reprinted with permission.

colleagues. At the other end of the class hierarchy, Newman and Ellis (1999) and Neckerman and Kirschenman (1999) consider the stigmas of low wage work available to working class and poor Black inner-city residents, and the ways race affects employers' perceptions of potential Black inner-city employees, respectively. Finally, in her study of Black women workers in the hair industry, Harvey (2005) finds that among working-class Black women, the absence of occupational opportunities can push them towards entrepreneurial ventures.

In focusing on these issues of race in the labor market, few comparisons are made as to how the intersections of race and gender differently shape Black women's and Black men's work experiences. Feminist researchers discuss the concept of gendered racism, which posits that racism exists at both the institutional and individual levels, but is a phenomenon that is experienced differently by men and women (Chavetz, 1997; hooks, 1988; King, 1988; Glenn, 2000; Zinn & Dill, 1996). However, many studies based on the conceptual framework of gendered racism focus primarily on how intersections of racism and sexism impact minority women. Although researchers note that "not only Black women, but also Black men are confronted with racism structured by racist constructions of gender role, notable examples being the absent father stereotype or myth of the Black rapist," very few studies draw a comparative analysis between how Black men and Black women experience gendered racism (Essed, 1991:33).

Controlling Images and Gendered Racism

Espiritu (1997) argues that gendered racism helps to explain several predominant stereotypes of Asian Americans. The Dragon Lady and Lotus Blossom stereotypes are specifically female images of hypersexualized, deceitful women, or docile, subservient geishas, respectively. In contrast, the Fu Manchu and Chinese laundryman stereotypes depict Asian men as evil, villainous, asexual schemers or as eager, willing servants. Espiritu argues that while all of these images are founded in racist stereotypes, they are also explicitly gendered images which suggest that Asian men and women are ultimately unable to meet dominant ideals of masculinity and femininity. Ultimately, the images are manifestations of gendered racism that provide specific justification for anti-Asian biases and promote hegemonic white masculinity as a normative standard. Collins (1990; 2004) has been particularly perceptive in drawing attention to the ways racist images of Blacks are distinctly gendered. Historically, stereotypes of Black men as lustful, brutal rapists were used to justify violent repression and lynching of Black men in order to protect the chastity of white womanhood (Davis, 1984; Olsen, 2001). Like Espiritu's analysis of the effects of gendered racism, the stereotype of the lustful Black male rapist served to validate racial inequality but also to contrast Black masculinity with white masculinity as a hegemonic ideal. This image, however, was specific to Black men. In contrast, the "controlling images" of Black womanhood described by Collins (1990) include the asexual Mammy and the castrating matriarch. These racist stereotypes are also gendered in their portrayal of Black women's inability to fit the dominant ideal of motherhood, and in their implicit messages that as unfit mothers, Black women fall short of the larger ideal of appropriate womanhood.

In a contemporary analysis of a "new racism" that is defined by an increasingly global economy, proliferation of mass media images and transnational states where racism is controlled less by local or regional governments, Collins (2004) suggests that the images of Black men as lazy Sambos or brutal rapists and Black women as mammies, tragic mulattos, or Jezebels have been refined and updated to reflect socio-political and cultural changes. Today, controlling images of Black men and women are class-specific and reflect a global economy, unprecedented media reach, and transnational racial inequality as well as the economic, legal, and social changes that have affected Blacks over the last 50–60 years. According to Collins, gendered racism now produces controlling images of working-class Black women in the form of the "Bad Black Mother" (often depicted as the "welfare queen") and the "Bitch" (a materialistic, hypersexual, manipulative figure prevalent in hip-hop culture), while middle-class Black women are depicted as "Black Ladies" whose potentially unrestrainable sexuality is safely confined to heterosexual marriage, "educated Black bitches" who are manipulative and controlling, or "modern-day Mammies," who uphold white-dominated structures, institutions, or bosses at the expense of their personal lives. Controlling images of Black men now exist in the form of working-class Black men as irreverent "athletes" or dangerous "criminals," while middle-class Black men are presented as effeminate "sissies" or non-threatening "sidekicks" to a white protagonist. Underlying all these images are the same old stereotypes of Black women as treacherous, hypersexual, aggressive, and/or ideal for service, and Black men as dangerous beings whose sexuality is a threat to the natural order and must be curtailed and harnessed.

Gendered Racism and Controlling Images in the Workplace

The nature of these controlling images has potentially devastating consequences for minority men and women at work. While sociologists have yet to engage in comprehensive research that examines gendered racism's effects on minority workers, some studies have acknowledged that racism in the workplace is gendered and takes on different manifestations for minority men and women (Browne & Misra 2003). Woo (1998) argues that gendered racism which emphasizes images of Asian American women as doll-like and dainty has facilitated their entry into broadcast journalism while simultaneously rendering Asian-American men undesirable for this work. Similarly, the overrepresentation of Latina women into domestic service suggests a gendered racism that presents these women as ideal for low-paying service work in the home, while gendered racism channels Latino men into construction and landscaping work outside of the home.

In their study of the combined effects of racism and sexism on Black women, St. Jean and Feagin (1998) offer a particularly insightful assessment of the mechanisms of gendered racism in the workplace. The authors argue that while Black women experience the "double burden" of racism and sexism, some white employers may view Black women as more desirable coworkers and employees than Black men because they are less threatening. According to these authors, white employers may prefer Black women because their gender makes them more easily controlled through sexist put-downs, whereas Black men's gender renders them less controllable through these means and thus more of a threat. Following this line of reasoning, in their study of the effects of racism on African Americans, Sidanius and Pratto (2001) in fact argue that gendered racism disadvantages Black men to a greater degree than Black women. While numerous other data challenges this conclusion (see Browne & Misra, 2003; Browne, 1999; Maume, 1999), these debates underscore the fact that examining racism as a gendered phenomenon reveals a complex picture of its impact on African Americans.

In this article, I examine ways Black professionals' experiences with racism in the workplace are gendered. I also address how Black workers' responses to racism are also shaped by gender. By treating racism as a gendered phenomenon, I address the different implications workplace racism has for minority men and women.

METHODOLOGY

Data for this project were collected from semi-structured, intensive interviews with 23 African American professionals employed in a variety of occupations. . . . Respondents were all college educated and ranged in age from 24–61. Fourteen had attended predominantly white institutions for undergraduate degrees, and the remaining nine attended historically Black colleges or universities. Eleven had advanced degrees, and two were in the process of completing an advanced degree. Seven were married, three were divorced, and the remainder had never married. I used a snowball sample to create the data set, beginning with respondents that I knew personally, and asking these subjects to refer me to others who fit the criteria for the study. All names were changed to ensure confidentiality.

Most respondents worked in settings where they estimated that African Americans constituted 10 percent or fewer of the company's employees. All the respondents described themselves as employed in occupations where working effectively with coworkers was an integral factor in their job success, and that interacting with coworkers comprised the majority of their jobs. In other words, these workers stated that some or all of their jobs required them to work closely with colleagues in interracial groups. As Black professionals continue to integrate predominantly white workplaces and in some cases occupations that were previously predominantly white, I expected that these workplace dynamics would be ones where Black professionals would likely be exposed to expressions of racism.

FINDINGS

Grounded theory methods revealed that Black professionals' experiences with gendered racism often took the form of combating controlling images. Interestingly, Black women's encounters with gendered racism evoked the controlling images Collins (2004) describes in her analysis of the "new racism" that characterizes contemporary American society. Specifically, gendered racism in the professional workplace often meant that Black women were expected to conform to controlling images of the modern mammy or that they were sexualized and objectified. For Black professional men, experiences with gendered racism also took the form of encounters with controlling images, though not the ones Collins (1990, 2004) describes. Instead, they faced a new controlling image—that of the "angry Black man." The existence of these controlling images also structures the ways in which Black professionals—both men and women—respond to encounters with gendered racism.

Black Women and Gendered Racism

For Black professional women, the most common controlling image they had to counter was the image Collins (2004) characterizes as the "modern Mammy." The modern Mammy is expected to sacrifice all vestiges of a personal life in order to demonstrate unshakeable loyalty to the (usually white) boss or institution. This image dovetails with St. Jean and Feagin's (1998) observation that white employers may perceive Black women, by virtue of their gender, as easily exploited. Many of the women interviewed here stated that they often encountered situations where they were expected to accept unreasonable demands, willingly accept compromising roles, or silently accept disrespectful treatment to avoid potentially disrupting the smooth inner workings of the organization. In other words, colleagues expected Black women to fit the image of the modern Mammy through a willingness to make enormous personal sacrifices for the sake of the business.

Angie is a higher education administrator who speaks directly to this issue. One of her most pronounced experiences with racism involved an unpleasant interaction with a lower-level staff member who worked in the university dining hall. The dining hall mistakenly charged a dinner to Angie's department, and when Angie called to rectify the error:

> that woman called me rude and condescending and hung up on me! She filed a complaint. So I had to meet with the dean, who arranged for mediation. When they did the mediation, everyone was trying to support this woman, even though she hung up on me and I am in a much higher position than she is. Even with everyone kissing her ass, this woman got mad, said she wasn't staying, and walked out! Now can you imagine that happening if I were a white man? There's no way that woman would have talked to me like that, and no way the other administrators would have supported her for doing it.

Angie's experience clearly reflects this aspect of gendered racism. Her treatment is that of many Black workers who are treated disrespectfully by coworkers, even those in positions with less status. However, the racism Angie experiences is also gendered, in that her status as a woman likely made her more easily disparaged. Even more important, the institutional procedures used to resolve such disputes were instrumental in pressuring Angie to conform to the image of the modern Mammy. The administrators' tacit support of the lower-level service employee in the supposedly neutral mediation session suggests that Angie is expected to conform to and accept disrespectful treatment in order to avoid causing trouble. Significantly, Angie herself implies that the discourteous treatment she received in this situation is attributable to gendered racism, when she questions whether the incident would have occurred not only if she were white, but a white man.

Similarly, Simone, a community educator for a nonprofit organization, cites experiences with racism that are not neutral but are quite gender-specific. She asserts that during her tenure in the organization, she was frequently asked to do things that she found uncomfortable and compromising. Specifically, she cites an incident where "we had a Black client who had really terrible body odor. I was solicited to deal with this person. "I had to ask, is this because I'm black? It would not look racist for me to tell this other Black person they have BO, but if you all say it, it looks like you're being racist? Is that what you think?" They all got quiet. I might be the only Black person in the organization, but I will be damned if they'll put me in situations like that! They were always trying, though."

Ostensibly, this experience is one of a Black worker being solicited to deal with a Black customer with whom they might (at least theoretically) have greater familiarity and cultural ties. However, when interpreted through the lens of gendered racism, the nature of this request suggests that it is another example of the assumption that Black women are more easily placed in compromising positions or exploited than Black men in comparable positions. Like Angie, Simone's colleagues saw nothing wrong with expecting her to perform a distasteful task on behalf of the organization, even though this task was clearly outside the bounds of her job description as a community educator. Her experiences with gendered racism reflect the struggle faced by Black women who confront colleagues who expect to interact with the modern Mammy.

Gendered racism was also reported in the form of Black women workers feeling uncomfortably sexualized and exoticized by white colleagues. Many of the women interviewed described unwelcome sexual tensions shaped by a perception that as Black women, they were exotic, sexually powerful beings. The stereotype of the uncontrollably sexual Black woman has a long history and has, in one form or another, been implicit in controlling images of Black women as welfare mothers, Jezebels, and the Black bitch (Collins, 1990; 2004). In contemporary work spaces, these images remain problematic for African American women.

Marcia, a consultant for a health care firm, describes one disturbing incident of visiting a hospital that was a client of her firm and feeling sexualized by a patient's relative. During this visit, Marcia endured listening to the patient's relative reminisce about the "good old days in the South" and how people "knew their place." At the end of the visit:

> he came over and kissed me on the cheek! I was so dumbfounded that I couldn't figure out what was going on or if I should take my knee and slam him because I've never been kissed on the cheek by a little white man who felt that women were . . . (trails off). And I'm the only person he kissed in that room, this man I had never seen before in my life. But that this man would go on and on about the days when people knew their place and then kiss me, out of all the people in the room? I bet I knew exactly what place he—I know what was on his mind.

In Marcia's role as a health care consultant visiting a client of her firm, a patient's relative taking the liberty of kissing her is unorthodox at best. However, she astutely notes that this advance came after a thinly veiled reference to Southern life when Blacks were openly subjugated and Black women were routinely subjected to—and often powerless to resist—unwelcome advances from white men. This experience with racism is specifically gendered in that Marcia was unwillingly cast in the role of the sexually available Black woman.

Georgia, an analyst for a nonprofit organization, also reports gendered racism in the form of being confronted with stereotypes of Black women as exotic sexual beings. Interestingly, this took place in the context of an interaction with a white female coworker. Georgia recounts attending a board meeting where she wore a red leather suit:

> I had no idea what buzz got created until I talked to a board member who did not participate but her husband was there. She called and said, "Georgia, I don't know what you had on, but it certainly got my husband's attention." First off, this is a man who wears white socks all the time. Second, I don't want to know that her husband is checking me out in my suit! And why would she tell me that? We don't have that kind of relationship.

Given the history of Black women as prey for more powerful white men, the convergence of race and gender here create a situation that renders Georgia particularly uncomfortable with the board member's uninvited interest.

Gendered racism structures both the nature and scope of the experiences these women recount as well as their reactions to these experiences. When confronted with expectations that they would accept unreasonable demands and/or disrespectful treatment for the sake of the organization, many of the women interviewed openly expressed their irritation, frustration, and anger. For instance, Angie recounts her reaction to the administration's support of the lower-level employee who treated her rudely:

> I'm totally disgusted and feeling totally devalued by the situation. After the session was over and she decided she wasn't going to go through it, I basically told them exactly how I felt. I said this is uncalled for, I requested mediation, and this is not a mediation . . .

[My reaction] was not a controlled thing, they heard exactly how I felt right then and there.

In the meeting with the administration, Angie unequivocally expressed the irritation, frustration, and dissatisfaction she felt in response to her experience with gendered racism. However, the availability of this response can also be interpreted as an effect of gendered racism. As St. Jean and Feagin (1998) suggest, Black women, because they are women, are generally considered less threatening than Black men. As such, Angie's vocal expression of discontent was likely less problematic to her white superiors than a similar response coming from a Black man. Gendered racism structures workplace interactions such that Black female respondents were not considered threatening and thus had more leeway to vocalize their feelings of frustration. Some women purposely adopted a more threatening, intimidating role, because they viewed this as one of few options that allowed them to be taken seriously and to avoid the awkward, uncomfortable situations that accompanied coworkers' expressions of gendered racism. Sherice, a professor of humanities, states:

I sometimes play a no-nonsense role that makes people feel intimidated but not with thinking about it. If I don't actively work to correct it will happen. People give me more credit for being on top of things and less willing to put me in positions where I feel uncomfortable. It makes people feel intimidated or overly respectful.

Sherice's statement echoes the view that because Black women are seen as more malleable and controllable because of their gender, they experience gendered racism in the form of being placed in awkward situations. As she indicates, some Black women consciously present themselves as tough and intimidating in order to avoid the gendered racism in the form of exploitation.

Black Men and Gendered Racism

Many Black men experienced gendered racism in the form of countering white colleagues' perceptions of them as threatening, menacing, or overly aggressive, or as many respondents described, the image of the "angry Black man." As respondents described it, the angry Black man image is a middle-class, educated African American male who, despite his economic and occupational successes, perceives racial discrimination everywhere and consequently is always enraged.

Many respondents perceived that white colleagues and superiors expected them to fit this image. As such, they took pains to avoid engaging in any behavior that might reflect it. Todd is a banker with a major financial institution. He asserts that a constant part of his job involves carefully constructing his demeanor, actions, and behaviors so that he does not threaten or intimidate his white colleagues:

Most of them haven't spent too much time around Black people, so what they think they know is usually from TV or some other stupid source. So if they already think most Black guys grow up in the 'hood and sell drugs and are basically like [popular rapper] 50-cent, then I have to do everything I can not to portray that. That means that if they say something to me that reflects that they think that about me, I can't ever get mad. I have to brush it off, always be the nice guy who's not too threatening, not too militant, because they'll lose it if they ever really see me in that way. And that would have serious repercussions for my job.".

As Todd describes, he is always in a battle to present himself in opposition to this particular stereotype of Black men. Note that he particularly attempts to portray himself as someone who is not too "threatening or militant," since these are the key characteristics associated with the stereotype of the angry Black man. Consequently, he experiences gendered racism at work in that he must constantly show, through his behavior, speech, mannerisms, and general demeanor, that he is in no way this threatening, angry persona often associated with Black masculinity.

Garrett, an accountant for a major sports organization, was one of the respondents who specifically evoked this controlling image by name. Here he describes how he must constantly monitor employees' treatment of him as well as their reactions to him:

I always have to tread lightly because I know I can't afford to be seen as that "angry Black man." You have to always watch how people react to you, and even then it's like, why wasn't I invited to that meeting? Or that dinner? And if I say something, I'm always watching, like, how did people take that? How did they respond to it?

Like Todd, Garrett experiences racism at work in the unspoken pressure to counter coworkers' concerns that he is uncontrollably angry and therefore threatening. Steven is a loan officer for a bank who gives another example of the tension of combating the image of the "angry Black man."

> Being a black male, you're put in a situation where you have to work twice as hard to prove yourself. Especially in the corporate world, because it's such a white male dominated field . . . I've always put myself in a position where I felt it was my job to represent the race. So I can't ever be that stereotype that others have of us—loud, angry, I can't really talk about or acknowledge race at work . . . I can't be that stereotype of that guy, because that's just perpetuating the stereotype. So I've sort of taken that on my back in my work environment to prove that whatever you may think about people who look like me, I'm going to open your eyes to a whole other perspective.

Note that Steven describes a stereotype of a loud and angry man who openly addresses racial issues as the image that he must refute through contrasting behavior. Like Todd and Garrett, Steven also locates this stereotype as one that is present among whites and one that Black men in particular must work to avoid. Gendered racism may also be implicit in the lack of close ties and exclusion from social networks that characterized many Black men's interactions at work. Of the workers interviewed for this research, many more Black men than Black women reported that they were often excluded from collegial workplace interactions and that they had fewer friends or close acquaintances (if any) among their coworkers. Garrett describes these feelings of exclusion, stating:

> A lot of the guys in the office, they usually get together after work and play poker, I believe. Poker's their thing. And I've never been invited, I don't know any other black person in the office that's ever been invited. It kind of seems like a little clique. Not that it necessarily bothers me, but it's something that I play in the back of mind. Like, I wonder why nobody's ever asked me to play? Things like that.

Garrett describes this poker group as comprised solely of white men, noting that no other Black colleagues are invited to join. Though some of the Black women in this study certainly experienced isolation from colleagues, Black men were much more likely to report being excluded from work-related events and to have few office allies.

Similarly, Ken describes a workplace where he has given up trying to forge ties with his coworkers. He states:

> the thing is, my coworkers don't speak to me. This one guy never speaks to me. I say hello to him in the morning, and the guy just looks at me. The only time he speaks to me is if it's negative or sarcastic, and we don't have that kind of relationship where he can be sarcastic with me. It's like once a week he'll mess with me. If I was off of the job I'd say something, but since I'm on the job I have to keep it to myself, because he is a manager. He's not my direct manager, he couldn't fire me, but he is a manager.

Like Garrett, Ken is not a part of the informal interactions that occur at work, and he has not been able to develop a very cordial relationship with many of his colleagues. While Black women were much more likely to state that they were often exploited or placed in uncomfortable, compromising positions, they rarely suggested that they had difficulties interacting with colleagues in general. This difference may also be a residual effect of gendered racism—that Black men experience gendered racism in the presumption that they are intimidating, fearsome people, and this perception makes them people with whom other coworkers would prefer not to regularly interact.

Gendered racism also structured Black men's responses to these affronts, revealing reactions that differed sharply from Black women's. While Black women, because they were perceived as less threatening, could speak out about the treatment they received, Black men had no such luxury. Their attempts to repudiate coworkers' assessments of them as frightening people meant that they could not afford to actually get angry or vocalize their displeasure at various offenses. They feared that colleagues would perceive such assertions as evidence of the very stereotypical traits Black men were attempting to downplay. Gendered racism, therefore, structured Black men's responses to racism such that they tended to repress any emotions, statements, or behaviors that could possibly be construed as militant, angry, or belligerent.

Roger, an analyst at a nonprofit research organization, reinforces that it is incumbent upon Black men not to reveal any sense of anger at work:

> Different black men I've seen in my office and growing up and knowing about, we focus so much on not

bringing or showing our feelings at the office, but a lot of times the office produces so much stress you bring that back home. It's difficult to keep them both separate.

Roger's account emphasizes how gendered racism leaves Black men with few outlets at work where they can express "negative" emotions, and also highlights that this lack of outlets places Black men in a predicament where repressing these behaviors and emotions affects their lives outside of work as well.

Black men were also much more likely than Black women to downplay or minimize their feelings of irritation or displeasure at their experiences with gendered racism. Recall that because gendered racism renders Black women less threatening, they often were able to immediately vocalize their feelings about being treated as the modern Mammy without serious repercussions. In contrast, because gendered racism suggests that Black men are inherently threatening, Black men interviewed here perceived a greater risk in drawing attention to their coworkers' and employers' gendered racism. Without the option to speak out, Black men frequently became emotionally detached at work and minimized their anger at the gendered racism they encountered.

Leon, a community educator, states:

I work with a woman who is a complete racist and culturally clueless. And what do I do when she tells the biracial woman on our team that her hair looks like a poodle's? Or when she assumes that because I'm Black I know people in [names a predominantly Black part of the city]? I stay calm, change the subject, and get back to work. I have to do this, because how will it look if I curse her out, even when she deserves it? I'll be the one in the fire, not her.

Leon's rhetorical question of how he will appear should he respond to his colleagues' racially insensitive remarks underscores the constant burden on these Black professional men to disprove stereotypical images of Black men as angry, out of control, or bothered by racial issues, and the importance of doing this by displaying the opposite characteristics. Leon's response is a stark contrast to those of Angie and Donette who took the opportunity to establish themselves as no-nonsense women who could be intimidating.

Nate, for example, is a mortgage loan officer who employs complicated strategies to discourage his co-workers from seeing him as an angry Black man. He describes ignoring racial slurs at work unless they are repeated frequently to him, and even then states that his policy is to "pull someone aside to quietly tell them I may not like what they're saying." However, despite the effort he exerts to avoid the possibility that his co-workers might view him as the angry Black man, he still tries to diminish his feelings of irritation at the gendered racism that creates these circumstances:

When I think about it now, I mean, definitely I'm upset but it has to be something really big and overt and serious before I could get really pissed. So you downplay it, contain it like that.

Though Nate assumes a measured, careful reaction to avoid being stereotyped as the angry Black man, he also minimizes his irritation with this situation in ways that Black women in this study did not do. Black male workers' efforts to remain calm, affable, and genial in order to rebut the image of the angry Black man sharply contrast Black women's willingness to vocalize and speak up about their colleagues' and supervisors' gendered racism.

CONCLUSION

Black men and women in this study both describe experiences with racism that are clearly shaped by gender. Black men confront gendered racism at work when they struggle to avoid manifesting any behaviors or attitudes that could possibly reinforce colleagues' perceptions of Black men as threatening or intimidating. Even when Black men attempt to portray themselves as nonthreatening, affable people, coworkers may still find them too daunting and unapproachable for the inter-office friendships and socializing that are often essential to occupational advancement. Black women deal with gendered racism in their encounters with the controlling image of the modern Mammy, and in confronting coworkers' sexualized, exoticized perceptions of them. Both Black men's and Black women's reactions to racism are also structured by gender. Black men have fewer outlets for challenging gendered racism and thus minimize their feelings about it, while Black women's responses to gendered racism are shaped by its implications that they are fundamentally unthreatening. Drawing attention to gendered racism in the workplace refines sociological understanding of exactly how racism is manifested at work. The results of this study demonstrate that it is erroneous to presume that Black men and Black women experience racism in the same way. While in some ways they experience similar manifestations of racism—assumptions that they are less intelligent and capable, the existence of glass ceilings, institutional discrimination—focusing on gendered racism provides a more nuanced understanding of the ways in which Black women may experience racism in ways that are inapplicable to Black men, and vice versa.

A particularly significant finding is that while gendered racism contributes to the perception that Black women are easily exploited, particularly for the sake of the workplace, the responses of the women here suggest that this very perception creates a space for them to demonstrate their opposition. In other words, when they know that they are seen as more easily taken advantage of than Black men, they often take the opportunity to assert themselves and demonstrate their toughness. This reaction, however, is complex and in some ways potentially problematic. While Black women who assert their refusal to conform to the stereotypes of the modern mammy may convincingly rebut that stereotype, they run the risk of being alternatively perceived as a version of the "educated Black bitch."

Collins (2004) describes the controlling image of the "educated Black bitch" as one of Black women with "money, power, and good jobs [who] control their own bodies and sexuality" (145). The Black bitch label is often assigned to Black women who fail to embody the extreme loyalty of the modern Mammy or who cannot uphold the image of the Black lady. With the women interviewed here, their assertive refusals to conform and outspoken rejection of confining workplace norms and organizational cultures that rendered them easily exploited or sexually available leave them dangerously subject to gendered racism in the form of being labeled the Black bitch. As such, while gendered racism creates confining norms for Black women, it also may create a space for opposition. Ultimately, however, this opposition can potentially reinforce controlling images like that of the Black bitch, thereby upholding yet another manifestation of gendered racism.

While Black women face the predicament of avoiding one controlling image by potentially embracing another, Black men face a different conundrum. Their struggle stems from informal workplace norms that pressure them to appear genial and cordial to undermine the controlling image of the "angry Black man." This issue highlights the fluidity of gender privilege as it intersects with race—while men, in general, receive rewards in patriarchal society, for Black men, gendered racism may function to minimize male privilege in some settings. Indeed, the Black women interviewed here did not indicate that they experienced the same sense of exclusion and social isolation as their Black male counterparts. For Black men, the dynamics of gendered racism suggest that in certain contexts the advantages of masculinity are less apparent than in others.

The results of this study do not suggest that gendered racism advantages Black women at the expense of Black men, nor that gendered racism eliminates the advantages of male privilege for Black men. Rather, this study reveals a picture of racism that is starkly complicated by gender. As a group, Black men still enjoy gender privileges relative to Black women in occupational, social, political, and economic spheres (Cole & Guy-Sheftall, 2003). However, it is important to consider this gender privilege as a fluid state that is not constant in all environments or social settings. The results of this study clearly indicate that Black men's gender privilege at work does not correlate into an ability to openly address the ways in which racism is manifested for them. Furthermore, the controlling image of the angry Black man, like the controlling images described by Espiritu (1997) and Collins (1990, 2004) should be further explored for its implications for African American men. This image, like those of the Fu Manchu, Chinese laundryman, sissy, sidekick, and others, ultimately seems to uphold hegemonic white masculinity. This image suggests that Black male rage at racism is inopportune and unfounded, and simultaneously reinforces the perception of Black men as a threat and a danger to the social order. The implications of this in the workplace are seen in many of the respondents' unwillingness to confront racial hostilities at work. Thus, this image controls Black men by presenting their anger at racism as unjustified paranoia that threatens to dismantle the social order.

Finally, it is interesting to consider what implications Black men's responses to gendered racism may have on their interactions outside of the workplace. If Black men learn at work that they should repress their aggravation with gendered racism, what effect does this emotional control have in other spheres of social life? Does downplaying feelings help Black men to achieve some of the tenets of hegemonic masculinity, specifically those that suggest that men should always control their emotions (Kimmel, 2001; Connell, 1987)? If so, does the practice of repressing emotions benefit Black men in social spheres where conforming to hegemonic masculinity is idealized?

Ultimately, this research suggests that understanding racism as a gendered phenomenon offers a more nuanced depiction of its impact on African Americans and a more intricate portrayal of their responses to it. This study furthers existing research on gendered racism by addressing the ways gendered racism produces controlling images that impact African Americans at work and the strategies Black workers utilize to counter these images.

REFERENCES

Browne, I. (1999). Latinas and African American women in the labor market. In I. Browne (ed.), *Latinas and African American women at work*, pp. 1–34. New York: Russell Sage Publications.

Browne, I. & Misra, J. (2003). The intersection of gender and race in the labor market. *Annual Review of Sociology*, 29:487–513.

Byng, M. (1998). Mediating discrimination: Resisting oppression among African American Muslim women. *Social Problems* 45(4):473–487.

Chavetz, J. S. (1997). Feminist theory and sociology: Underutilized contributions for mainstream theory. *Annual Review of Sociology*, 23:97–120.

Cole, J. & Sheftall, B. G. (2003). *Gender talk: The struggle for women's equality in African American communities*. New York: Ballantine Books.

Collins, P. H. (2004). *Black sexual politics*. New York: Routledge.

Collins, P. H. (2000). *Black feminist thought*. New York: Routledge.

Collins, S. (1997). *Black corporate executives: The making and breaking of a black middle class*. Philadelphia: Temple University Press.

Connell, R. W. (1995). *Masculinities*. Berkeley: University of California Press.

Cose, E. (1993). *The rage of a privileged class*. New York: HarperCollins.

Davis, A. (1981). *Women, race, and class*. New York: Vintage Books.

Essed, P. (1991). *Understanding everyday racism*. Newbury Park, CA: Sage.

Espiritu, Y. L. (2000). *Asian American women and men: Labor, laws, and love*. Walnut Creek, CA: Altamira Press.

Feagin, J. (1991). The continuing significance of race: Antiblack discrimination in public places. *American Sociological Review*, 56(1): 101–116.

Feagin, J. & Sikes, M. (1996). *Living with racism: The black middle class experience*. Boston: Beacon Press.

Ferguson, A. A. (2000). *Bad boys: Public schools and the making of Black masculinity*. Ann Arbor: University of Michigan Press.

Gallagher, C. (2000). White like me? Methods, meaning, and manipulation in the field of white studies. In F. Windance Twine & J. W. Warren (eds.), *Racing research, researching race: Methodological and ethical dilemmas in field research*, 67–92. New York: NYU Press.

Gilkes, C. T. (1988). If it wasn't for the women. In S. Bookman & A. Morgen (eds.), *Women and the politics of empowerment*. Philadelphia, PA: Temple University Press.

Glaser, B. & Strauss, A. (1967). *The discovery of grounded theory*. Chicago: Aldine Publishers.

Hartigan, J. (1999). *Racial situations: Class predicaments of whiteness in Detroit*. Princeton, NJ: Princeton University Press.

Harvey, A. M. (2005). Becoming entrepreneurs: Intersections of race, gender, and class in the Black beauty salon. *Gender & Society*, 19(6):789–808.

Higginbotham, E. & Weber, L. (1999). Perceptions of workplace discrimination among Black and white professional–managerial women. In I. Browne (ed.), *Latinas and African Americans at work*. New York: Sage.

hooks, b. (1988.). *Ain't I a woman?* Boston: South End Press.

Kimmel, M. (2001). Masculinity as homophobia: Fear, shame, and silence in the construction of gender identity. In T. Cohen (ed.), *Masculinities*, pp. 29–41. Belmont, CA: Wadsworth.

King, D. (1988). Multiple jeopardy, multiple consciousness: The context of a Black feminist ideology. *Signs*, 14(1):42–72.

Kirschenmen, J. & Neckerman, K. M. (2006). 'We'd Love to Hire Them But . . .' The Meaning of Race for Employers. In C. A. Gallagher (ed.), *Rethinking the color line: Readings in race and ethnicity*, pp. 306–317. NY: McGraw–Hill.

Maume, D. (1999). Glass ceilings and glass escalators: Occupational segregation and race and sex differences in managerial promotions. *Work and Occupations*, 26:483–509.

Newman, K. & Ellis, C. (2007). There's no shame in my game: Status and stigma among Harlem's working poor. In C. Gallagher (ed.), *Rethinking the color line*, 2nd ed. New York: McGraw–Hill.

Olson, L. (2001). *Freedom's daughters: The unsung heroines of the Civil Rights movement from 1830–1970*. New York: Scribner.

Sidanius, J. & Pratto, F. (2001). *Social dominance: An intergroup theory of social hierarchy and oppression*. Cambridge, UK: Cambridge University Press.

St. Jean, Y. & Feagin, J. (1998). *Double burden*. New York: Armonk.

Texeira, M. T. (2002). Who protects and serves me? A case study of sexual harassment of African American women in one U.S. law enforcement agency. *Gender and Society*, 16(4):524–545.

Tomaskovic-Devey, D. (1993). *Gender and racial inequality at work: The sources and consequences of job segregation*. Ithaca, NY: ILR Press.

Wilson, W. J. (1987). *The truly disadvantaged: The inner city, the underclass, and public policy*. Chicago: University of Chicago Press.

Woo, D. (1995). The gap between striving and achieving: The case of Asian American women. In M. Andersen & P. H. Collins (eds.), *Race, class, and gender*, 2nd ed. Thousand Oaks, CA: Wadsworth.

Zinn, M. B. & Dill, B. T. (1996). *Women of color in US society*. Philadelphia: Temple University Press.

39

"I Just Put Koreans and Nails Together"

Nail Spas and the Model Minority

MILIANN KANG

Having them done is a pleasure, a luxury. Doing them myself is tedious, having them done is a treat. It's the whole idea of going and having something nice done for myself. If I do them myself, it's just routine upkeep of my body—like washing your hair or keeping your clothes clean. . . . They do it all day long so they are better at it. The Koreans are usually very good at the massages. . . . I just put Koreans and nails together.

—*Kathy, Uptown Nails customer*

Let me tell you about you. You come in here with your fingernails gleaming and outstretched; you've just had them done next door at ajumma's beauty salon. My mother is jealous of your nails, not because she likes them, but because you have the time to do them.

—*Ishle Park, "Anatomy of a Fish Store"*

Customer satisfaction in upscale nail spas depends not only on the attractive appearance of their nails but also the enjoyment derived from being pampered, and customers regard Korean women as particularly skillful in this enterprise. Body labor transforms a hygienic process, otherwise equated with washing hair or clothes, into a richly rewarding physical and emotional experience— that is, when it meets customers' expectations. When it fails to do so, the physical and emotional intimacy of this exchange produces an equal and opposite negative reaction. Appropriate performance of this form of "pampering body labor" involves extensive physical care, along with attention to the emotional needs of customers, including engaged conversations.

The manicure takes on additional complexities when considered from the other side of the table. The poet Ishle Park depicts a Korean immigrant woman who is eyeing her customer's manicured nails. In this case the Korean woman is not the manicurist herself but the proprietor of a neighboring fish store. Nonetheless, this *ajumma* (literally, "aunt" but used generally to address middle-aged Korean women) expresses jealousy toward women who receive manicures, not necessarily because of their appearance but because they can indulge in this kind of self-care. The poem resonates with women working in nail salons, like Jean Hwang, an owner in Brooklyn, who noted, "Grooming one's feet and nails is unimaginable in Korea. It made me think how Americans enjoy themselves. With twenty dollars they treat themselves and enjoy themselves. I was jealous. . . . I don't think we have that leisure. We've experienced and are still living very rigorous lives." These women chafe at the differences between themselves and their customers that are manifested in the unequal treatment of their bodies and feelings.

Miliann Kang, *The Managed Hand: Race, Gender, and the Body in Beauty Service Work.* © 2010 by the Regents of the University of California. Published by the University of California Press.

In upscale nail spas the manicure is not simply an economic transaction. It is also a symbolic exchange that involves the buying and selling of deference and attentiveness. In accommodating the various demands of body labor, Asian immigrant women rewrite their own identities to conform to a pampering service demeanor and to the "model minority" stereotype. Customers may profess a belief in Asians as "honorary whites," but in their face-to-face interactions they do not necessarily hold Asians in high esteem. Thus the appearance of cordial intimate relations belies underlying tensions, as the gendered practices of pampering body labor uphold the race and class privilege of customers and enforce the subservience of manicurists.

The hit television sitcom *Seinfeld* provides a humorous yet revealing representation of Asian manicurists' interactions with white middle- and upper-class customers. Elaine, a regular at a Korean-owned nail salon, becomes suspicious that the conversations among the Korean-speaking manicurists include references to her that are less than admiring. To her dismay she learns that the manicurists are in fact calling her a princess and ridiculing her self-importance. Although she is upset, Elaine does not want to find another nail salon, as she sees her Korean manicurists as the best. Thus she must negotiate conflicted feelings, because she regards highly the actual physical manicure but is upset by the lack of emotional attentiveness.

In capturing Elaine's quandary, the *Seinfeld* episode underscores the complexities of the manicure for customers who patronize upscale nail spas—it is not enough that their bodies get pampered; they often want their feelings massaged as well. Conditioned by the stereotypical framing of Asians as the hardworking and accommodating model minority, many customers, like Elaine, come to Asian-owned nail salons expecting both a high-quality manicure and a subservient demeanor. They are often surprised and offended when instead they get "attitude." Their reactions to the manicuring exchange invoke not only gendered notions of beauty but also racial perceptions of Asians as the providers of these services.

This exchange is illuminated by Michel Foucault's influential work on the production of "docile bodies" through disciplinary practices. Nail salons serve as sites that discipline certain women's bodies to conform to

beauty regimens while disciplining other women's bodies to provide the services necessary for these regimens. Feminist scholars have recognized Foucault's many contributions to illuminating the body as a locus for the exercise of power, but have criticized his neglect of gender. Sandra Bartky asks, "Where is the account of the disciplinary practices that engender the 'docile bodies' of women, bodies more docile than the bodies of men?" However, feminist scholars have overlooked how women's bodies are not only disciplined to be more docile than men's but also that some women's bodies are rendered more docile than others based on race, class, and other forms of difference. By bringing Foucault's scholarship on disciplinary technologies of the body into dialogue with feminist intersectional approaches to gendered work, this chapter examines how the performance of pampering body labor disciplines the bodies of Asian manicurists into docile service to other women's bodies. Interactions in nail spas such as Uptown and Exclusive Nails illuminate the general patterns of pampering service in nail spas as well as the ways that individual actors challenge and renegotiate these exchanges and how particular conditions support or undermine this resistance.

GENDER AND THE MODEL MINORITY

Service interactions between Korean service providers and white middle-class customers reinforce the model minority stereotype, described by Eric Fong, by which "Asian Americans either do not face any discrimination relative to other racial minority groups or, if they did, they have overcome them." This stereotype permeates public discourse and has been thoroughly critiqued in academic circles. Rather than a single stereotype, the model minority references a constellation of factors that frame Asians not only as a laudable racial group but as proof that the United States is open and egalitarian. The core characteristics used to describe the model minority include hard work, laudable family values, economic self-sufficiency, noncontentious politics, academic achievement, and entrepreneurial success. Thus it is not simply that Asian Americans are praiseworthy but that this praise is premised on their smooth assimilation into productive but passive citizens who validate the vision of an open meritocratic U.S. society. Academic scholarship has complicated this one-dimensional stereotype, arguing that it is far from a positive representation of Asian Americans. Instead, the stereotype enforces simplistic and idealized views not only of Asian Americans but of other racial groups and, more broadly, of race relations in the United States. As Dana Takagi writes: "The concept of the model minority was born in the midst of the tumultuous racial change of the 1960s. Against the backdrop of rioting in black ghettos, the 'long hot summers' of the late 1960s, and mass public demonstrations for civil rights, Asian-Americans appeared to be a relatively quiescent minority. . . . Angered by black criticism of the 'white establishment,' some whites pointed to Asian-American achievement as evidence that racial minorities could get ahead in America, if only they would 'try.'" The designation of one group as the "model" thus enforces a hierarchy in which other minorities are judged as lacking. While ostensibly lauding Asian Americans, this framework chastises other racial and ethnic minorities, particularly blacks, for not following in Asians' footsteps. By emphasizing the success of Asians and their commonalities with whites, the model minority concept serves the dual purpose of holding Asian Americans up as an example for other people of color while also defending the existing U.S. racial order.

The bestowing of honorary white status on Asians simultaneously denigrates other racial and ethnic groups while reinforcing white privilege—and both purposes are enacted through body politics. As David Palumbo-Liu writes, "The image of the Asian in America performs certain ideological functions that serve to secure certain racial and national identities for both Asians and whites," and these ideologies emphasize the "correlation of the raced body and the national psyche." He asserts that views of racialized Asian bodies, and foreign bodies more generally, as desirable or undesirable emerge as part of a larger project through which nonwhite immigrants and their descendants are welcomed into or excluded from the American nation based on their willingness to support U.S. capitalism and its expansion.

The embrace of Asians as the model minority thereby is premised simultaneously on their embodied demonstration of economic productivity and smooth assimilation into mainstream cultural norms, and it is quickly withdrawn when these conditions are not met. Laudatory views of Asians can be invoked to discredit the claims of other minority groups and then revoked when Asians emerge as a potential threat to whites. In addition to the fickle and contradictory ways that it is applied, the model minority framing of all Asian immigrants and their children as economically successful and upwardly mobile is itself a fiction, as the category of Asian American encompasses heterogeneous groups and experiences ranging from Hong Kong financiers to Hmong refugees to Amerasian adoptees.

How does gender matter in shaping the ideology of the Asian model minority, and what new dimensions does a gender analysis illuminate about this racial framework? The focus on the gendered work processes of body labor expands the study of the model minority beyond a U.S.-centric focus on racialized representations to focus attention on workplace interactions shaped by the restructuring forces of global capitalism. Specifically, a gendered analysis of Asian women's work in nail salons reveals new embodied and emotional dimensions of how Asian Americans are constructed as a deserving group based on their willingness to perform deferent and subservient work. As Yen Le Espiritu argues: "Because of their racial ambiguity, Asian Americans have been constructed historically to be both 'like black' and 'like white,' as well as *neither* black *nor* white. Similarly, Asian women have been both hyperfeminized and masculinized, and Asian men have been both hypermasculinized and feminized. And in social class and cultural terms, Asian Americans have been cast as the 'unassimilable alien,' and the 'model minority' (Okihiro 1994). Their ambiguous, middling positions maintain systems of privilege and power but also threaten and destabilize these constructs of hierarchies."

Drawing on Espiritu's analysis, I bring a gender perspective to the critique of the ideology of the Asian model minority as an erroneous and politically motivated myth. Specifically, nail salons uncover forms of interaction that reproduce racialized, classed, and gendered discourses of the Asian model minority, through representations but even more so through material embodied exchanges. Customers, owners, and workers all participate in this reproduction, even as they offer limited forms of resistance.

MANICURING THE MODEL MINORITY

The model minority stereotype of Asians, and Koreans in particular, as successful, servile, and industrious takes on specifically gendered dimensions in the niche of nail services. Pampering body labor intersects with racial discourses in ways that valorize the work ethic of Korean and other Asian immigrants and construct a specifically gendered version of this discourse. The comments and behavior of customers demonstrate that while many adhere ideologically to the laudatory view of Asians as the model minority, their interactions with Asian women belie this rhetoric.

Like many customers in this study, Kathy, the white personal trainer whom I quoted earlier in this chapter, attributed a particular skillfulness in service, especially in the giving of massages, to Asian women, even elevating this understanding to the level of urban lore:

> I assume they're Korean. That's interesting—I wonder how I first came to know they are Korean. I think it's one of those urban myth kind of things you just pick up on it when you're living in New York. . . . Like the delis—everyone says, "I'm going to the Korean deli." Now that I think about it, they could be Chinese or Japanese or Vietnamese, but I just heard the people who did the nail salons were Korean, and then I see someone who looks Korean enough, so I just assume they're Korean. It's like if I had a massage and the person doing it were tall and blond and blue-eyed, I would just assume they were Swedish. . . . [The stereotype of Koreans is] willing to work very hard, interested in their children's education. Like, a friend of my husband's [is] Korean, and his parents worked for thirty years in a Dunkin' Donuts and sent their kid to Columbia. That kind of captures it. . . . [Regarding nail salons] I agree that they work hard.

Kathy frames Korean women's skillfulness in manicures as similar to equating "Swedish" with massage. However, Swedish massage is a type of massage characterized by specific techniques rather than simply an ethnic designation. In contrast, Kathy references cultural stereotypes, not specific techniques, to explain why she regards manicuring work as the distinct purview of Korean women. Ignoring the forces of immigration, racialization, and economic restructuring, she holds to a simplistic gendered version of the model minority stereotype that essentializes Korean women, or women who look "Korean enough," as possessing intrinsic manicuring skills.

Similarly, many white middle-class respondents explain Asian women's clustering in nail salon work by invoking their natural ability and innate sense of service. Thus gendered Orientalist tropes of Asian women's inborn affinity for body services naturalizes their work in nail salons as somehow deriving from inherent biological or cultural traits. As this customer described it, having an Asian manicurist imbues these services with an exoticized quality that enhances their appeal: "The quality of the massage here is much better. I like to go to the Japanese beauty salons for the same reason, they do shiatsu on your head, it's amazing. Culturally, there are things Asians can bring to [this] service that I don't think others are as sensitive to. . . . This [American] culture doesn't understand a service. It's not subservience or being a doormat. It's just the level to which you are willing to accommodate the needs of another, to go out of your way." Thus Orientalist framings reinforce the notion that Asian women not only are well suited to this work but that they enjoy it.

According to the sociologist Christine Williams, this belief that people end up in certain jobs because they like them is a distinctly "middle-class conceit." In her study of retail employees in toy stores, she debunks the myth that workers select their jobs based on their interests, skills, or preferences—"In the world of low-wage retail work, no one assumes that people choose their occupations or that their jobs reflect who they are." However, with regard to Asian women in nail salon work, the assumption that they somehow choose this work because they like it and are good at it is strangely persistent. Yet customers do not apply this same logic of natural affinity to other racial and ethnic women in nail salons. For example, Barbara, an Uptown Nails customer, commented, "I think it's because they [Asian women] specialize in making the manicure a nice experience, but they also seem to enjoy it and know what they are doing. I used to have my hair, facial, and nails all done at the same place; it was women from Russia or Poland. But they didn't really want to do manicures." Thus Barbara regards women from Eastern Europe as quickly moving in and out of the salon industry because they are not well suited to it. In contrast, her racial construction of Asian women in nail salons positions them not simply as having expertise in this work but as finding the work enjoyable and something they "want to do."

Consistent with Barbara's observations, many Russian immigrant women initially worked in the nail salon niche but then moved into other work. However, contrary to Barbara's assertion that they simply do not enjoy it, the explanation for Russian women's departure does not lie solely in their individual proclivities for this work or lack thereof. A trade magazine article suggests one explanation: although Russian immigrants dominated nail salons before the 1970s, "their education level suggests that once they mastered English, they moved on to other opportunities." While this explanation is somewhat plausible, it fails to address why Korean women, many of whom also have high levels of education and similar mastery of English, have not been able to move on to other opportunities.

Furthermore, although Russians dominated the niche at one point, the association of Russian women and manicurist did not become a widespread cultural stereotype. Why not? The answer lies not only in individual human capital, such as language ability or education, but in racial categorization. Once they acquire basic language fluency, Russians and other recent immigrants from Eastern Europe are able to quickly assimilate as whites—not as "honorary whites" or as a "model minority" but simply as whites. Even with heavily accented English, this racial status then gives them greater ability to enter into the U.S. mainstream and gain access to wider employment opportunities. In contrast, Koreans and other Asian immigrants, even those who conform to the stereotype of the upwardly mobile, hardworking model minority, still occupy a marginalized status in which nail salon work remains among the best of the options available to them.

These racial and gender constructions of Asian women as gentle, hardworking, and eager to please normalize their position as willing and able providers of service to higher-status groups. This gendered version of the model minority further disciplines other racial and ethnic women who do not meet the same standards of industrious deferential service. Elizabeth, a social worker in her midfifties whose Russian parents fled the former Soviet Union, lauded the industriousness of Koreans while chiding other groups, particularly blacks, for their supposed animosity toward Koreans. Referring to the boycotts of Korean grocery stores in the early

1990s (see chapter 5), she said: "You know, I'm a Russian Jew—so I have a special feeling toward people coming and trying to make a new life in a new country. To attack people based on their ethnicity because they're trying to earn a living—they [blacks] could have done that too [started small businesses] . . . I admire the ability of you Koreans to pull together group resources, to help each other. I'm always open to people who work hard and take care of themselves." Interestingly, many of the white respondents in the study who invoked a sense of affinity with Koreans were Jewish. Thus Jews, who may be considered white but also have a history of oppression, as well as fairly recent immigration, may feel a sense of connection with Asian immigrants that mainstream whites do not necessarily share. In addition, customers like Elizabeth not only emphasize similarities between Asian immigrants and their own Russian Jewish ancestors but also chastise blacks, whom they regard as unfairly blaming Koreans for blacks' own lack of resourcefulness. Thus Elizabeth attributes the paucity of black women in the ranks of nail salon owners (and owners of other small business enterprises) to African Americans' own failures, rather than questioning whether Elizabeth or her friends would patronize these businesses if they were black owned. In the post–civil rights era, the employment of blacks in service jobs can evoke feelings of guilt or fear on the part of white customers. Thus white customers' enthusiasm for Asian manicurists not only reproduces gendered model minority constructions of Asians but also enforces less desirable views of black and other minority women.

These racial constructions also draw distinctions and hierarchies among different Asian ethnicities. In contrast to the black working-class customers in chapter 5 who tended to lump Koreans into a broad category of Asians or "Orientals," most middle-class white customers specifically identified the nail salons as Korean owned and attached favorable ethnic-specific meanings to Koreans as opposed to other Asians. Clara, a high school teacher in her early forties, identified most nail salons in her affluent neighborhood as specifically Korean run and invoked the model minority framework to describe them:

> I know they're Korean. Different ethnic groups go into different fields—the Chinese have laundries, the Koreans have produce stands and nail salons. . . . I

know the stereotypes about hardworking students and close families. Although I took an aerobics class with this young woman who was doing research about the boycott of the Korean stores. She was an ultra, ultra-liberal. . . . Anyway, she completely disabused me of those success story stereotypes—but then again, she got her BA from Harvard, and I think she was going to Yale, and now she's teaching college somewhere.

While Clara claims that she has been disabused of the narrow "success story stereotype" of Koreans, in the end this encounter validates her belief in the model minority. In her mind the Korean American aerobics student's attendance at Ivy League institutions stands out more than the woman's arguments refuting the stereotype.

While these ethnic-specific views of Koreans are significant, overall they feed into generalized model minority views of Asian Americans as a group. Some customers, particularly the descendants of white ethnic immigrants such as Jews, assert a sense of affinity with Asians while still asserting their own white privilege. Ignoring the historically and culturally heterogeneous experiences that shape Asian Americans as a diverse racial group, the model minority stereotype lumps them all together into a single collective autobiography. In this monolithic story line the much-touted upward mobility of the second generation deflects attention from the difficulties confronted by the first generation, as well as from inequalities in U.S. society.

Gendered service interactions in upscale nail spas reflect large-scale social forces, but these forces are often concealed behind racial and gender stereotypes of Asian women as naturally doting and deprecatory. In line with customers' expectations, upscale nail spas place great importance on physical and emotional attentiveness as crucial components of the service interaction. Rarely do customers, or manicurists themselves, recognize the influence of discrimination or other structural barriers as pushing these women into this niche. Even less do customers acknowledge how they benefit from and participate in the truncated opportunity structures that relegate Asian women to working as their manicurists. In nail spas such as Uptown and Exclusive Nails, the gendered expectations of beauty service work combine with the racial stereotype of the model minority to produce a style of pampering body labor that is not natural but imposed.

UPTOWN NAILS

The concentrated faces of six Korean immigrant women sitting in a row of small manicuring tables are visible from the right side of the storefront window beneath the neon cursive letters spelling out "Uptown Nails." The women are identically attired in matching pink smocks and white pants resembling the uniforms of dental assistants and deftly wield emery boards, cuticle pushers, quick-dry sprays, and assorted polishes. From the left side of the window the customers sitting across the manicure tables are visible—five professionally dressed white women and one white man in suit and tie—all with their hands languidly extended before them in a posture suggestive of concert pianists or praying mantises.

"Tuesday is my salon day," explained Gwen, who was in her eighties and regularly patronized this salon. Her statement was not an exaggeration, as her regular visits were nearly half-day affairs. Dropped off by her professionally dressed daughter in the morning, Gwen would remain for two or three hours before being picked up by a private home healthcare provider. During her stay in the salon this customer received, in addition to a manicure and a pedicure, various caregiving services that were taken for granted yet unremunerated. Removing Gwen's shoes and knee-high panty hose and helping her climb up to the thronelike pedicure chair required two manicurists. For the next hour these women stooped at Gwen's feet, preparing a fragrant foot bath, massaging her arthritic feet and legs, clipping her cracked yellow toenails, placing cotton balls between her toes, polishing her nails in pastel pink, sliding on brown paper slippers to prevent smudges, and escorting her as she walked ducklike to the manicuring station. These elaborate processes were then repeated on her hands.

While the degree of care that Gwen demands is beyond what the average customer receives, she nonetheless illustrates the intense emotional and physical attention that is common in pampering body labor. Gwen usually needed to go to the bathroom at least twice during her visits, requiring at least two manicurists to virtually lift her out of her chair and walk her gingerly to the restroom. After settling her at the drying table, manicurists brought her a magazine and cup of coffee. On one occasion Gwen drifted off to sleep and began to slump sideways in her chair. A manicurist spotted her and carefully slid Gwen's chair next to the wall to prevent her from falling. When she awakened, Gwen prattled happily about the weather, the comings and goings of her children and grandchildren, and her various ailments and medications. The manicurists attended to her smilingly as they indulged her in conversation. "Your grandson is graduating from college already!" "Are you wearing a new dress?" While they were clearly fond of her, the exacting toll of her visits was evident. As Gwen approached the front door one day, Stacey, the manager, sighed and asked, "OK, who wants the 'famous grandmother' today?"

Steeped in the discourse of Asians as the model minority, many middle- and upper-class whites like Gwen extol the virtues of their manicurists and exhibit comfort with and even a measure of gratitude toward them. At the same time the customers are mostly oblivious to the hardships involved in manicuring work and are even less aware of the ways that they participate in the maintenance of subtle and not-so-subtle practices of privilege and subordination. For example, Gwen appreciated the care she received at Uptown Nails but seemed blind to the demands she placed on the women who provided this care. Instead, she claimed, "We have fun together. I like to talk, keep it lively. Some of them don't understand, which can be frustrating, but I know they try hard. They are very kind, hardworking people and they are very good at what they do. . . . I think this is a good job for them. I've heard some of them even get rich doing this." Glossing over the demanding work that her manicurists performed before her eyes, or rather at her feet and on her hands, Gwen described this as a good, "fun" job and a vehicle for upward mobility. Overlooking the physical and emotional effort of the women who perform this work, she suggested instead that she accommodates them by tolerating their limited language ability.

When her caregiver arrived, Gwen thanked her manicurists for their help and left what seemed like a generous tip. But what did this tip cover? How much would it cost to pay her home-care provider for the two hours of assistance that her manicurists provide for free as an extension of their manicuring services? How much pay would her daughter forgo if she had to take a morning off from work to care for her mother herself or assist her at the nail salon? None of these hidden costs was reflected in the price of Gwen's mani–pedi.

Instead, the physical and emotional care conferred in addition to the actual nail services was invisible, as was the toll of this work on the women who do it.

DISCREPANCIES IN THE VALUATION OF BODY LABOR

The disjuncture in the valuing of a manicure by customers versus the work invested by manicurists often shows up in the customers' assessment of tips. Sheila, a white woman in her late twenties who works in advertising, saw herself as a generous and appreciative customer, especially toward Esther, whom Sheila saw often. A seasoned Korean manicurist who had worked at Uptown Nails for nearly ten years, Esther was in high demand for her relaxing and invigorating hand massages. She energetically kneaded, stroked, and pushed pressure points, finishing off the massage by holding each of Sheila's hands between her own and alternately rubbing, slapping, and gently pounding them with a flare that had wooed many a customer into a regular nail salon habit. Sheila appreciated Esther's efforts and said, "I think I'm a good tipper. I usually tip 20 percent regardless, just like in a restaurant." After she left, Esther commented, "I can't believe she thinks she's a good tipper. We should get more than what they tip at a restaurant. This takes more skill, and we are making them look pretty, not just putting food on the table like a waitress. I don't expect her to tip a lot because she looks like she doesn't make much money, but I can't believe she thinks she's a good tipper."

Clearly, two different standards for tipping, and for assessing the value of a service, were operating in this exchange. Sheila calculated what she regarded as a big tip, in accordance with the protocols of other service occupations, such as waiting tables. Esther, on the other hand, made a different assessment based on the unique nature of *this* service and the particular skills and effort it entails. From her perspective a manicure is not comparable to serving food. In terms of the benefit to the customer, it enables the highly valued accomplishment of looking pretty. In terms of the output by the manicurist, it requires more skill, not only in the physical manicure itself but in attending to the feelings of customers.

Many customers did show appreciation for Esther's hard work. Margie, a white accountant in her midthirties who was single, squeezed Esther's hand at the end of a hand massage and said, "I swear, I couldn't stay in my job without this!" Esther reciprocated with a warm, somewhat shy, smile. This customer's compliment acknowledged the benefits she received but did not take into account the wear and tear on Esther's own hands. In chapter 6, I address the occupational health risks involved in manicuring work in more detail, but these include exposure to toxic chemicals, allergies, rashes, carpal tunnel syndrome, and repetitive strain injury. These common health complaints of long-time manicurists like Esther, let alone the effort it takes for manicurists to discipline their own bodies to perform this work, rarely appear on the radar of customers.

DISCIPLINARY TECHNOLOGIES OF BODY LABOR

From the gentle removal of undernail dirt to the careful trimming of cuticles and buffing of calluses to the massaging of hands and feet, Korean manicurists literally rub up against their customers, who are mostly white middle-class and upper-class women. In their efforts to pamper other women's bodies, the manicurists must discipline their own. Like many manicurists at upscale salons, thirty-four-year-old Judy Cha, who emigrated in 1993, told me that attentive body labor was not something that came naturally to her. Instead, her ability to conform to the pampering service expectations of her elite clientele was hard won over time. Furthermore, these were not simply voluntary adaptations but were dictated by the feeling and body rules of her workplace. She explained:

> Three years ago we didn't give a lot of massages but now customers ask more and more. It makes me weak and really tired . . . I guess because I don't have the right training to do it in a way that doesn't tire my body. Some manicurists give massage all the time to get tips, but sometimes I don't even ask [clients if they want a massage] if I'm tired. Owners keep asking you to ask them, but on days I'm not feeling well, I don't ask. . . . One of my biggest fears working in the salon is, what if I don't understand what the customer is saying? They don't really talk in detail, just say, "How is the weather?" But in order to have a deeper relationship, I need to get past that and to improve my English. It makes it very stressful.

Judy had learned not only to give manicures and massages but also to attend to customers' emotions, especially by engaging in conversation to make customers feel comfortable and relaxed. Learning to perform body labor thus includes both physical and emotional dimensions and the integration of the two.

The physical dimensions of pampering body labor encompass a range of service practices, including the use of high-end salon products and equipment, massages, and creation of a soothing and relaxing atmosphere, as well as management of the workers' own bodies as they perform these services. The attention devoted to creating a pampering environment at Uptown Nails is impressive and included hot cotton towels, bowls of warm soaking solution, and calming background music. The salon also offered specialized services, such as hot stone massages, lactol and paraffin wax soaks, aromatherapy, and skin refiners. The salon boasted high-end equipment, such as special drying tables with ultraviolet lights and pedicure chairs with hydrotherapy and massage features. These are big-ticket investments—high-end equipment costs thousands of dollars—and they are indicative of the substantial capital outlay that is necessary to open and sustain an upscale salon. However, while the products and tools are important, the effective delivery of pampering body labor depends mainly upon the performance of the manicurist herself.

Manicurists' efforts to adapt their bodies to this work are evident in their changed comportment during break times. During lulls in customer flows, manicurists often slip off their shoes and assume relaxed postures. Some women comfortably assume squatting positions, knees together, feet apart, while others sit casually with one leg bent and the foot tucked under the opposite thigh. The moment a customer walks in, however, they immediately assume upright positions. These dynamics are certainly not unique to nail salons, as it is not uncommon for service workers in a range of industries to adopt what Erving Goffman calls "frontstage" and "backstage" bodily self-presentations, relaxing when customers are not around, then snapping to attention when someone appears. However, when a customer walks in, manicurists quickly both abandon their off-duty postures and avoid any bodily arrangements that suggest premodernity and ethnic otherness. Furthermore, they do not choose their postures—these are mandated by customers' expectations and labor management practices in the salons. For example, Grace Lee, a new worker and recent immigrant who was employed at Uptown Nails, prepared for a pedicure by assuming a squatting position at her customer's feet. Stacey, the manager, slid a stool over to Grace and chastised her, saying, "It doesn't look good to squat. Sit on this." At another salon I heard one owner hiss, "Don't take your shoes off while you're with a customer," after spying a manicurist who had slipped her shoes off under the table. Nail salon owners and managers thus pick up on cues from their customers' embodied norms and then impose these bodily controls on workers.

THE BODY POLITICS OF FOOD

Practices of bodily control not only target manicurists' physical postures but extend to the management of the foods, particularly the strong-smelling ethnic dishes, that the manicurists eat. Cara Park, the owner of a nail spa in Brooklyn, actively discouraged certain pungent Korean foods in her salon, especially kimchi, the Korean national dish of pickled cabbage with hot red pepper. "We don't eat kimchi or other smelly foods here because the customers don't like it—they think we're low class if our food and breath smells." Whereas this owner imposed an explicit policy prohibiting certain foods, other salon owners implemented indirect measures to control workers' meals and the body odors they produced. Esther, the manicurist at Uptown Nails, told me, "In another salon where I worked the owner gave us gum after meals. Once I heard her say to a manicurist that she should go brush her teeth. We all brought different dishes and shared our meals, and sometimes [the owner] would look unhappy and make comments that something had a strong smell."

Manicurists themselves also regulate their food at work so as not to offend customers. Nancy at Uptown Nails expounded on the politics of smell, acknowledging customers' concerns but countering that while she vigilantly regulated her food-induced ethnic body odors, her customers were oblivious to their own emissions. "They [customers] are very sensitive about the smell of Korean foods. I know kimchi has a strong smell even for those that are used to it, so I understand that we shouldn't eat it right before sitting so close to

someone for a manicure. . . . But those people don't realize that they also have a strong American smell." When I asked her to elaborate on what constitutes an "American smell," she reacted with surprise:

> You don't know the American smell? It's not exactly like milk, it's sort of like milk and grease together [laughs]. I remember the first time I arrived here from Korea at JFK, and I walked off the plane and it was like—aigu [wow]! I could tell we were in America because of the way the people smelled, but they don't think they smell. One time I went into the waxing room, and there was a woman lying down for a bikini wax. She must have just eaten a hamburger and French fries for lunch and she smelled so bad, but she didn't seem to notice or care.

Nancy's comments reveal her understanding that she must control her own body odors while not reacting to her customers'. Although certain practices are imposed by management, the workers internalize these expectations and conform to them, as they recognize that the embodied protocols of service work are one-sidedly focused on regulating foreign bodies.

What do the micropolitics of smell reveal about the performance of body labor by Asian immigrant women? As the American studies professor Robert Lee writes in his book *Orientals*, "Food habits, customs, and rules are central symbolic structures through which societies articulate identity; you are, symbolically at least, what you eat." Evaluations of food smells—from both the food itself and the clothes or breath of those who have eaten it—are thus culturally relative and context specific, yet they carry great weight in everyday interactions. It could be argued that avoiding emitting unpleasant body odors is simply good manners. However, pleasant and unpleasant are subjective categories. Nearly a century after the large wave of Italian immigrants moved into lower Manhattan, the strong smell of garlic on the breath of customers at high-end restaurants in Little Italy is no longer a signal of low class and ethnic otherness but rather of gourmet dining. In contrast, the strong smell of garlic in Korean food and on those who have consumed it often elicits strong negative reactions.

Exhortations to abstain from eating strong-smelling ethnic foods emerge in the social context of the nail salons, not simply as proper etiquette pointers from Miss Manners or Emily Post but rather as labor management practices. The regulation of body odor through the control of ethnic food consumption in nail salons does not arise simply out of individual adjustments to new cultural norms but as a by-product of body-service work. Immigrant manicurists learn to conform their bodies to white middle-class American expectations because the manicurists' jobs demand this. These demands are communicated both through the direct labor control of owners and managers and through the indirect disapproval of customers. Such disapproval also is directed at manicurists' uses of language.

THE LANGUAGE OF SERVICE

"Your nails look awesome!" Angela Shin, a perky twenty-seven-year-old receptionist at Uptown Nails, would tell customers, peppering her speech with colloquial phrases such as "How's it going?" and "Why don't you hang out and read some magazines?" While somewhat comical, her conversational style succeeded at putting customers at ease, even though her actual language ability was less advanced than that of some of the other Korean women who worked in the salon. Angela's conversational ability was the hard-earned outcome of an intensive "accent reduction" class, a cottage-industry that has sprung up to serve recent immigrants. Later, when I interviewed her, I was surprised that her seeming fluency was mostly artifice, as she did not understand when I ventured outside the vocabulary of salon services and asked her questions in English that were related to my research.

While a friendly, chatty receptionist can certainly be an asset in a business predicated on making customers feel good, Angela's conversational practices reveal more than just a talkative personality. They reflect the communicative demands of what Robin Leidner in her book *Fast Food, Fast Talk* refers to as "interactive service work." While Leidner notes a general expectation of pleasant conversation in service interactions, this dimension of service work is heightened when the service provider and customer do not speak the same language. Korean manicurists thus must learn two new languages—basic English and the language of pampering service. More important than general fluency are the particular language skills related to the provision of nail services that manicurists must also learn. Customers expect conversational attentiveness, owners and managers dictate it, and manicurists develop skills to provide it.

Despite the manicurists' efforts, many customers complain, not only about the manicurists' limited English ability but also their communication among themselves in Korean. Like Elaine in the *Seinfeld* episode, many white middle-class customers have strong reactions to their manicurists' practice of speaking in Korean and are suspicious that clients are the topic of these conversations. Customers are often unaware of the demands that they impose on their manicurists for proper and unaccented English and attentive conversation. In addition, clients often become upset when they perceive that service providers are intentionally ignoring their requests or talking about them. Many express feelings like those to which this customer attested: "To tell you the truth, I don't think they really listen, they just do what they want to do. It's not because they don't understand me." Thus some white middle-class customers interpret the lack of response to their service requests, as well as the Korean women's use of their native language, as signs of willfulness, manipulation, or subversion, and in some cases the customers are right.

EVERYDAY RESISTANCE TO BODY LABOR

Even to maximize their earnings or job security, manicurists are not solely committed to meeting customers' needs. Instead, they balance meeting customers' demands with maintaining a sense of dignity in accommodating this work. While the manicurists may recognize the value of English fluency as a way of conforming to model minority expectations in their work, they also develop ways of resisting what they see as excessive demands. The ambivalence that some Korean manicurists express toward improving their language ability hints at the benefits that accrue from the inability or perceived inability to understand English. While most manicurists are intent on improving their language ability and want to communicate effectively with customers, some, like Sandy, avoided conversations and requests as a way of rejecting the role of subservient model minority member. Unfortunately, this strategy often was double edged, as it both shielded against and increased tensions with customers. Upon completion of her manicure, a customer frowned disapprovingly at the color and asked Sandy, "Since it's not dry yet, do you think you can just change the color?" Refusing to pick up on the obvious cues of a dissatisfied customer, Sandy responded, "Oh, dry, you want dry, go over there," pointing to the dryers against the opposite wall and briskly escorting the customer from her seat. In addition to buffering Sandy from dissatisfied or derogatory comments and allowing her to respond in kind, her language strategies enable her to have a modicum of control over the work she performs. However, these strategies also undercut her ability to earn higher tips and acquire skills that could enable her to move into other kinds of work, let alone to feel more at ease in her new country.

Unlike Sandy, most manicurists recognize customers' high expectations with regard to standards for communication, and they largely conform to these expectations. At the same time they find ways to subvert these demands, and language can serve as an effective, albeit limited, tool of resistance. The ability to communicate in Korean makes their working conditions more tolerable and serves as a form of resistance to cultural domination. Nancy, who was usually easygoing and soft-spoken, had raised hackles as she recounted an instance of talking about a customer as a means of retribution for the woman's insensitive comments:

> Once I was with a customer, and she hadn't said anything to me, not even, "Hi, how are you?" but all of a sudden she asks me, "Is it true that you eat dogs in Korea?" I didn't know what to say, so I just acted like I didn't understand her. Later, when she was drying, I told Esther what she had said. So right in front of her, Esther says in Korean, "Yes, we eat dogs but only raw!" You know how funny Esther can be, she went on and on. I was laughing so hard I can't remember everything she said, something like we only eat the fat ones that are other people's pets! I know it's not right, but I have to admit, I really enjoyed making fun of her.

Whether the customer's question about eating dogs indicates derision or insensitivity, it taps into a familiar motif that placed Nancy in the position of having to defend her culture. The title of Jessica Hagedorn's novel *Dogeaters* illustrates the pejorative ways that the consumption of dog meat in particular has been used as a way of denigrating Asian cultures. Such comments call into question the acceptance of Asians as a model minority. With Esther's help and their ability to talk about the customer, Nancy used humor and camaraderie to neutralize the sting of the customer's query. Thus manicurists use language practices both to fend off work requests and to release negative feelings aroused by

insensitive or upsetting customer comments. However, these uses of language as resistance are largely symbolic. They help to vent frustrations, but they do not fundamentally challenge relations of power and privilege. Customers' discomfort with manicurists' speaking to each other in Korean signals clients' recognition of this act as subversive, whether intentional or not. In some cases manicurists use Korean to talk about customers, but more often they are simply communicating about work-related issues or conversing with coworkers. These practices allow them to reestablish a sense of identity independent of their work, but they carry a high cost.

Some would argue that speaking in another language in front of others who do not understand it is simply rude and should be discouraged in all situations. However, this understanding of rudeness is unevenly applied in different contexts. Many English speakers regularly use English in front of those who do not understand it, adopting an "English-only" mentality even in foreign countries or communities that speak another language. Acknowledging these tendencies, Jiwon Cho, a manicurist at another upscale nail salon in Manhattan, voiced sympathy for the customers and urged her colleagues to learn English and abstain from speaking in Korean. She said:

> When you don't understand and speak English, your job becomes so pitiful. I didn't realize this in the beginning. For example, if a nervous and difficult customer comes, there is no one who can take care of that customer. When she complains about something, even though it might be a very simple and basic problem, since no one understands, the customer leaves very upset. . . . Some customers tell me, "Before making money, learn English." In the beginning I thought that it was just a friendly advice, but then as time went on I realized that they really meant what they said. . . . They are frustrated, and they look down on us. I get angry when they say these things, but sometimes I wonder if they are right. If a foreigner was living in Korea and did not speak Korean, I would pity them and look down on them, too.

While Jiwon conjectured that she too would harbor negative feelings toward foreigners in her country who do not learn the native language, the reality is that many foreigners go to South Korea for business or travel and never learn a word of Korean yet usually are treated well or at least are not denigrated. In fact, many U.S. citizens, even when they are visiting or working in another country, expect that others should speak English, rather than that Americans should make an effort to learn the culture and language of the country they are visiting. Given these language dynamics, manicurists like Jiwon are more likely to see themselves as pitiful for resorting to the use of Korean rather than questioning the customers' strong reactions to hearing a foreign language.

Similarly, manicurists who remain in nail salon work for the long term mostly conform to customer demands in terms of embodied expectations. At the same time, as with language, the manicurists engage in limited acts of embodied resistance that may ameliorate but do not change the demands of pampering body labor. At Uptown Nails one form that this takes is poking fun at customers' serious investment in their nails. One day, close to Halloween, I entered the salon during a slow time to find the manicurists festively, and somewhat conspiratorially, painting each other's nails the colors of M&M candies. They revealed that they also painted hearts on their nails around Valentine's Day and green clovers for St. Patrick's Day. In their gleefulness they seemed aware that they were doing something mildly subversive by bestowing on each other a semblance of the pampering treatment that they usually reserve for their customers. At the same time they were doting on each other in a way that undermined the seriousness of the enterprise and instead made it both playful and somewhat ridiculous. However, when the women left the salon at the end of the day, they had removed the candy-colored polish from their nails. Thus these seeds of resistance did not flower into any sustained collective consciousness or action inside, let alone outside, the salon.

Resistance to body labor is further undermined by manicurists' identification with the needs and status of their customers, wherein they claim status by association with their customers' racial and class privilege. Some manicurists gain satisfaction and a vicarious sense of status by performing skillful work for customers of a higher social position and earning their appreciation. For example, as the owner of an upscale salon in Manhattan, Lisa Park has a well-established clientele and is in high demand. She is the only manicurist at the salon who schedules appointments, and these are reserved for elaborate silk or linen wraps. The painstaking process of layering nails with thin strands of delicate fabric to strengthen, lengthen, and smooth them can

take well over an hour and generally costs more than $50. After Lisa completed a flawless silk wrap one day, her regular customer exclaimed, "Lisa, you're the best in the city!" and supplemented her appreciation with an exceptionally generous $20 tip. Lisa beamed and proudly displayed her $20 to her workers and customers. Later, when asked about her relationship with this high-tipping customer, Lisa did not acknowledge any particular fondness for her, saying, "I think maybe she's a lawyer. Anyway, she's a very rich and high [status] person, and she only trusts me, so I feel good." Even when they do not become personally close to their customers, some owners and manicurists, like Lisa, enjoy helping their well-heeled clients to look good, in addition to realizing the monetary rewards that may accrue as a result. In many salons the more skillful manicurists perform difficult and expensive procedures and mainly attend to regular patrons, thus putting themselves in a position to receive the biggest tips and most appreciation.

Manicurists thus exhibit a range of responses to the demands of pampering body labor. Some internalize the service ethic and identify with the higher status of their customers, at times deriving a sense of status by association. Others engage in strategic acquiescence, outwardly fulfilling service expectations but inwardly rejecting positions of subservience. Finally, some manicurists are able to engage in subtle forms of resistance, by talking about customers or refusing to perform certain tasks. These responses demonstrate their assertion of agency but also reveal the circumscribed parameters in which the manicurists exercise resistance. At another upscale salon, Exclusive Nails, customers and service providers were able to express genuine caring and connection, but underlying power relations persisted.

EXCLUSIVE NAILS: THE LIMITS OF PERSONAL TIES

Charlie, the owner of Exclusive Nails (see chapter 2), is a generous and proud woman who regarded her relations with customers as based not on servility or economic necessity but on friendship. Her position as owner, the prosperity of her salon, as well as the receptivity of her customers allowed her to validate this more empowering framing of her work. At the same time this alternative framework was subject to cracks, as even a well-liked and successful owner like Charlie is not immune to the demands that she acquiesce to a position of subservience as she supplies pampering body labor. Despite the absence of overt discrimination or exploitation, inequalities persist, as does the discourse of the model minority and the expectations that accompany it.

As she had with many of her customers, Charlie had developed a special relationship with Patti, a hospital social worker and chronic nail biter. These two women had forged a relationship as customer and manicurist that was mutually supportive and humanizing, and they attempted to rewrite the dynamics of service as a story of genuine friendship. However, this alternative narrative did not hold up against structural forces that overrode the terms of their connection. Patti, who was plagued by her nail biting habit, did not take for granted the care that she received. "I always get very anxious and this is my habit. I don't smoke or overeat, I don't drink or do drugs, but I bite my nails. . . . So, it is important that [the manicurists] take care of me. They would hurt me unless they are very careful. See? You see what I did to my nails. You see the bottom of the thumb? . . . I would not go anywhere else. It is nice here compared to other places where they are not as careful and they do not care. . . . I trust her [Charlie]." Patti frames the intensive body labor that she receives at Exclusive Nails not as a commercialized exchange or as an exercise in racial and class privilege but as a relationship with another woman based on trust, intimacy, and reciprocity. She was eager to help Charlie with English-language documents and often stepped in as an intermediary with new or disgruntled customers. Poignantly, Patti told me, "There have been times when the only way I celebrated my birthday was to come here to get a manicure from Charlie."

In return, Charlie expressed appreciation for Patti and also referred to her as a friend. At the same time Charlie acknowledged the multiple challenges of negotiating their relationship within the constraints of their roles as customer and service provider. Charlie said of Patti, "She is my friend, we help, each other. . . . Really, her nails are in terrible shape—I have to be so careful not to hurt her because all the skin under the nail is exposed." As Charlie acknowledged, although she appreciated Patti's patronage and various forms of assistance, working on her gnawed nails was highly stressful. Despite both women's insistence that they were friends,

ultimately, the work of maintaining their relationship fell on Charlie. Patti often refers to Charlie as her "therapist," which attests to the level of emotional labor that Charlie invested. I noticed that if Charlie was working on another customer when Patti arrived, she hurried to finish or asked another manicurist to take over so that she could attend to Patti promptly. On one occasion Patti had waited for a few minutes, then apologetically but impatiently pointed to her watch, pressuring Charlie to finish quickly. These interactions do not suggest the equal footing of friends but rather the dictates of a generous but nonetheless demanding customer toward a beholden service provider. Furthermore, while Charlie and Patti were able to forge some semblance of a friendship within the salon, this relationship did not extend into their lives outside the service setting. When I asked Charlie whether they ever saw each other outside the salon, she took the question literally—"Oh, yes, she always waves when she walks by."

All this is not to say that the kind of genuinely caring service relationship that Charlie and Patti had nurtured is not meaningful or worth developing. What it does say is that while these positive microinteractions can take the sting out of the subservience associated with body labor, they do not fundamentally alter the terms of these exchanges and the relative status and power of the actors involved. These relationships coexist with systemic inequalities, including the hierarchies of service provision and the racial discourses of white privilege and the Asian model minority. They do not erase them. Furthermore, these embodied and emotional dimensions of service provision shape particular patterns of assimilation.

EMOTIONAL AND EMBODIED ASSIMILATION

Through the performance of pampering body labor, immigrant women service providers like Charlie undergo processes of emotional and embodied assimilation in order to conform to customers' expectations, the protocols of their workplace, and racial and gender stereotypes of Asian Americans. I ran into Charlie one day as she was leaving a gourmet deli with a bag of groceries and a bouquet of rainbow tulips. Pointing to the flowers, I asked if she was going to visit someone, and unlike many immigrant women, who might feel self-conscious or indulgent about such a purchase, she answered unapologetically, "No, I just bought them for myself." Charlie often brought fresh-cut flowers into the salon, earning customers' approving comments, and it appears that the attention she put into pampering body labor had rubbed off on the ways she now pampered herself. As a successful nail salon owner, Charlie rewarded herself for a hard day's work in quintessentially American style—through the conspicuous consumption of high-end goods. These small purchases reveal that the day-in, day-out work of conforming to the physical and emotional register of customers reconfigures manicurists' own identities in small but unalterable increments. The performance of pampering body labor fosters emotional and embodied forms of assimilation that draw upon both the racial rhetoric of Asians as the model minority and the gendered framing of Asian women as attentive to service and aesthetics. These frameworks extend beyond the nail salon into other areas of women's lives.

At the same time Charlie had not yet internalized the service expectations of her customers to the point that she herself would purchase the same kind of high-end manicures that she so expertly provided. When I asked her about this, she curtly replied, "No, that's what I do for work." In other words, although Charlie had absorbed certain elements of the ethic of pampering self-care, she drew the line at actually shifting from the seat of the beauty service provider to that of the consumer. Her assimilation into the ethos of pampering body labor redefined her identity and relationships in ways that complemented but did not alter her social position as a manicurist and nail salon owner performing pampering body labor. In the end she conformed to the discourse of the model minority and to the gendered norms of spa-level beauty service.

Sadly, even with this high level of assimilation, Charlie is still viewed and treated by many customers as someone outside the American mainstream. In the following exchange, Alexandra, a regular customer, revealed both her high standards for body labor as well as her sense of privilege over Charlie as a provider of these services. When I asked Alexandra what improvements she might like to see at the salon, she first directed her comments to me, then made a revealing shift in tone as she addressed Charlie in broken English:

Make it more like a spa. Have aromatherapy when you get a pedicure. It is not that expensive, and you can do probably forty–fifty pedicures and use that one same bottle before you run out. I don't think it is going to be a lot of added cost. . . . They are going to remodel the place which they really need. The place is so outdated. *[She notices that Charlie is listening and directs her next comments to her, conspicuously switching her tone and grammar.]* People come in and see old decoration, they think old store, dirty, not good. So they are more likely to leave. When you have fresh new appearance, people think fresh new look, good stuff!

Later, when I asked Charlie, who had lived in the United States for more than ten years by then and was quite conversant in English, how she felt about Alexandra's way of speaking to her, she shrugged and said, "They all do it. Maybe they think they are making it easier for us to understand, but it shows how they think we are stupid."

Alexandra was not intentionally disrespectful of Charlie or the other Korean women in the salon—on the contrary, she prided herself on her knowledge and appreciation of Korean culture and she proudly shared how she taught a unit on the "Asian model minority" in her social studies class. Nonetheless, her social position as a white middle-class customer gave her the prerogative to make recommendations to the salon owner about how to run her business and to do so in language that replicated stereotypical notions of Asians as foreigners who cannot speak English. Far from elevating Charlie to a position as an equal, or even as a member of a model minority group, Alexandra spoke to Charlie as if chastising a child. In so doing, she exercised her own racial and class privilege while diminishing Charlie's social position. Even as a successful, highly assimilated salon owner, Charlie was vulnerable to such service exchanges, which reveal to her that customers like Alexandra "think we are stupid." In addition, such exchanges undermine claims that Asians have triumphed over discrimination and exclusion.

CONCLUSION

Manicuring exchanges in Asian-owned nail spas serving mostly middle- and upper-class whites call into question the "model minority" representation of passive and industrious Asians who easily assimilate into the mainstream and enjoy high socioeconomic and racial status comparable to whites'. Instead, interactions in upscale nail spas reveal that derogatory stereotypes and unequal power continue to infuse these exchanges. The mundane exchanges in Asian-owned nail salons demonstrate that racialized representations, combined with gendered stereotypes of Asian women as subservient and well suited to detailed handiwork, naturalize their concentration in this work. Different patterns of service emerge at different sites, refuting the one-dimensional stereotype. The dominant, albeit not exclusive, pattern in nail spas serving white middle- and upper-class customers is one in which gendered work practices, as enacted through pampering body services, reinforce existing racial and class hierarchies.

At upscale salons such as Uptown Nails, the servicing of some women's bodies entails the disciplining of other women's bodies. Manicurists not only must enact embodied practices directly associated with the manicure, such as clipping, polishing, touching, and massaging, but they also must regulate their own bodily comportment and contact, including the ways they sit and the foods they eat. In responding to customers' feelings about these embodied exchanges, manicurists must learn to speak not one, but two new languages. First, they must acquire basic English-language fluency, and second, they must develop fluency in the language of complimenting, coddling, and capitulating to their customers' needs. Language skills are an essential element of the emotional management involved in body labor, but language skills can also carry the price of increased vulnerability to negative comments and excessive customer demands. At the same time manicurists can use their language skills to resist these demands and unsettle customers by conversing in Korean. However, such subtle acts of resistance carry costs in terms of negative responses from owners and customers, and they do not fundamentally alter the power dynamics of these exchanges.

At Exclusive Nails the manicurists engaged in fewer of these attempts at resistance because relations with customers were genuinely more authentic and therefore required less ostentatious displays of deference. However, this did not mean that the inequalities in these relations disappeared. Just because women are genuinely nice to each other and treat each other with dignity does not

change the vast differences in their lives and resources. At the same time the real measures of caring and respect expressed between them are not insignificant. They enable women who work in these salons to maintain their self-respect while doing this work. However, the modicum of genuine connection that they forge can easily disappear in the face of customer dissatisfaction or insensitivity, or simply the pressures of a busy day.

The forms of emotional and embodied assimilation that Asian manicurists undergo in performing gendered service work ultimately reinforce dominant racial and gender framings of Asian women as docile, subservient, and well suited to detailed work. At the same time, while the structures of the global service economy channel Asian immigrants into this niche, these women are not mere cogs in the machine of global capitalism. They make choices and give meaning to this work, either by embracing their customers and the work itself or by asserting limits on how they perform it. Nonetheless, as Carol Wolkowitz writes in her book *Bodies at Work*, such "intra-psychic" forms of resistance rarely challenge the "emotional order" of organizations but instead "enable individual workers to distance themselves psychologically without necessarily encouraging more collective efforts directed towards transformation rather than survival." Similarly, customers are not bound to the enacting of scripts of pampering and privilege but can rewrite them, in either more oppressive or more egalitarian ways.

Some customers actively resist the idea that nail salon interactions reflect prejudices and social inequalities, insisting that their relations with their manicurists are affectionate and mutual. One customer approached me in a salon and asserted, "I really care about these women, and I think I can say the same for them. How can you not feel something for someone who has done your nails for years?" Indeed, strong emotional bonds between manicurists and customers are not uncommon. However, these bonds do not negate the often invisible inequalities of race, class, and immigrant status that shape body labor. Instead, intimate emotional and embodied contact coexists with and can even further entrench divisions between women. Thus the act of women serving women, even and especially when the purchase of pampering body labor is involved, is not a recipe for forging alliances so much as for reinscribing differences.

PART VII

EDUCATION AND SCHOOLS

In the United States, education is heralded as the great leveler of class, racial, and gender inequalities, promising social mobility to working-class and nonwhite youth and to women and girls. The reality often falls short because social inequalities are often reproduced within schools. But while holding out the promise of upward social mobility, what do schools teach about gender, race, and class? As all of the articles in this section attest, schools teach far more than the standard curriculum.

We begin by considering how schools define student achievement. The recent ascendance of high-stakes testing as the measure of achievement, as well as the focus on racial-ethnic "gaps" in test scores, has affected schools in significant ways. Gilda L. Ochoa examines how teachers and students in a Southern California high school make sense of their school's test scores and the students' differing educational outcomes. She shows how the model of high-stakes testing reinforces biological and cultural deterministic frames that attribute the achievement gap to the students' supposed biological and cultural differences. Ochoa refers to these as **power-evasive frames** because they blame individual students and their families while ignoring structural inequalities in schools and the larger society. She shows how these frames lead to confining and self-fulfilling categories that limit all students, both those perceived positively, such as the "model minority" Asian students, and those perceived negatively, such as the "troublemaker" Latino/a students.

The next article also addresses the question of what schools teach children about themselves. Popular culture and educational institutions are imbued with gendered images of "nice girls" and "naughty boys." Boys in our culture are thought of as naughty and rambunctious, but innocent. When they commit minor transgressions, they are frequently let off the hook by the idea that "boys will be boys" and that their natural development entails mischievous tumbles with "snakes and snails and puppy dog tails." This, after all, is seen as preparation for manhood. But as Ann Ferguson's research, based on a detailed ethnographic study in Oakland schools and neighborhoods, shows, boys' special dispensation for transgressive behavior comes packaged with white racial privilege. When inner-city African American boys misbehave, they do not receive the protections of childhood. African American elementary school boys are routinely perceived to be hyperdangerous and plain old bad, and this has serious repercussions in many arenas, including education.

In the last chapter, the subjects are high-achieving white and Mexican American working-class high school students. Based on ethnographic and interview research, Julie Bettie shows that these teens must not only show their mastery of classroom work, but also carefully navigate relations with the other "prep" students, and here negotiating class and racial differences is paramount. In some cases, a bicultural class identity becomes a necessary resource.

40

Framing the "Gap"

Dominant Discourses of Achievement

GILDA L. OCHOA

Joe Berk remembered, "When I was applying for [this position], I said that there were two campuses at this same school—a high-performing campus, which is predominately Asian, and a low-performing one that is predominately Hispanic . . . This is not a [Southern California High School] phenomenon. Hispanics, in general, emphasize putting food on the table over education."

—*Field notes, February 1, 2007*

While at Southern California High School (SCHS), I frequently heard about "high-performing students," "low-performing students," and the "gap"—determined largely by standardized tests and course placement. Students more commonly described themselves and their schoolmates as "smart" and "stupid." These constant distinctions were made between the two largest panethnic groups at the school—usually referred to by school officials and students as Asians and Hispanics. These two groups were cast in opposition to each other, and analyses of their academic performances were often rooted in supposed biological and cultural differences, as when administrator Joe Berk describes an emphasis among Latinas/os on working to survive rather than working toward educational goals.

For generations, politicians, academics, and educators have offered various explanations for differences in educational attainment. These explanations range from arguments that blame individuals and groups for their supposed deficiencies to ones that critique biased school officials or unequal schooling facilities. The popularity of these theories has fluctuated over time and has varied in scope. However, the biological and cultural deficiency frameworks that are so pervasive at SCHS have been the most influential in shaping schools and the overall racial, economic, political, and social order (Gonzalez 1990).

Such deficiency frameworks largely dismiss the impacts of historical, structural, and institutional inequalities as well as systems of race, class, and gender on life opportunities. They are what Ruth Frankenberg (1993) labels "power-evasive," and they are part of a neoconservative perspective. At SCHS, with the exception of a small percentage of staffulty and students, these discourses inform explanations for educational outcomes. Much of the blame is placed on students and their families, deflecting attention away from the role of schools and society in perpetuating multiple gaps.

This chapter analyzes the individual and group-level explanations or frames that are often used by SCHS's staffulty to understand differences in educational outcomes. As Susan Rosenbloom (2010) describes, "Framing

© University of Minnesota Press 2013. *Academic Profiling: Latinos, Asian Americans, and the Achievement Gap* by Gilda L. Ochoa. Published by the University of Minnesota Press.

refers to the way people label and identify their worldview by relying on interpretations or maps that organize their experiences into discrete chunks of information" (6). Given the prevalence of power-evasive frameworks in the United States that claim we are in a postracial society, assume we have free choice and equal opportunity, and tout that we live in a meritocracy, many like Berk employ biological and cultural arguments. While heard less frequently, some at SCHS adopt what I refer to as power-aware approaches to understanding educational outcomes, where they consider disparities in resources and forms of discrimination. Given the magnitude of power-evasive approaches at SCHS and in U.S. society, they are hegemonic ideologies that shape people's perceptions and structure people's lives. Thus they are centered in this chapter.

At SCHS, Asian Americans and Latinas/os are the focus of these discourses, demonstrating the relational aspects of race/ethnicity—that these categories and racialized assumptions are not fixed or naturally occurring but are given meaning in relationship to one another. In contrast, Whites and Blacks are rarely discussed, but they are not absent in the school's racial/ethnic constructions. In particular, the silence surrounding whiteness—White identity, White privilege, and cultural practices—is considered in this chapter, while the positioning of Whites and Blacks at the school is considered in more detail in chapter 5.

This chapter details four of the most common power-evasive discourses at SCHS ("the gap," biological deficiency, cultural deficiency, and the invisibility of whiteness) that set the context for understanding the disparities, divisions, and hierarchies at the school. Given their roles as institutional agents in influencing the school culture, the staffulty's perceptions take center stage. Occasionally, students' views are included, but their narratives are emphasized in subsequent chapters. Throughout this chapter, I highlight some of the factors influencing the staffulty's frameworks and the implications of such perspectives. However, these perspectives are not fixed; people may adopt multiple explanations, or their views may change. Similarly, these perspectives are not simply products of individuals. They are part of the fabric of schools and society and mirror dominant ideologies. They are so entrenched that they may become accepted knowledge that few people question. Thus analyzing the frames that the staffulty use to understand schooling

helps uncover the multiple structures and systems of belief that maintain unequal school practices and keep many Asian Americans and Latinas/os unequal and apart at schools such as SCHS.

FRAMING THE "GAP"

A common frame in today's discussions about education is that there is "an achievement gap" based on race/ethnicity. While grades and rates of high school graduation and college attendance are sometimes considered, scores on standardized tests are increasingly *the* primary measurement of achievement, and each year newspapers and school marquees across the nation announce test scores—symbolically bolstering their importance. This emphasis on standardized tests emerged during the Reagan–Bush era and intensified with the policies of the federal government's No Child Left Behind (NCLB) Act of 2001. Accountability is at the core of NCLB, and test performance is used to assess students, schools, and teachers. Among the requirements of NCLB is annual testing in math and reading of children from grades 3 to 8 and at least once in high school. To determine how different groups of students are faring, test scores are disaggregated by race/ethnicity, limited English proficiency, and special education. Schools that do not meet their targeted competency scores or make what is referred to as "adequate yearly progress" receive increasingly severe sanctions. These sanctions range from paying for transportation for students who may transfer to other schools to funding private tutoring programs to being taken over by the state or closed entirely (Wood 2004). As well as diverting public funds away from schools in need, these sanctions fuel the movement for school vouchers, school choice, and charter schools (Hursh 2005). Thus these policies are part of a neoliberal agenda to control the curriculum, evaluate teachers, and ultimately privatize public school education. They are fueled by "power-evasive" discourses because typically the extensive focus on the "gap" exists without a simultaneous interrogation of the larger factors influencing disparities and fueling the test-based movement in education.

Within the context of high-stakes testing, SCHS school officials begin each academic year by presenting data on students' performances. Second-year teacher Laura Cooper explains, "From the moment we step into our teachers' meetings three days before school starts, it's 'results from testing; results from testing!' 'We are down again; we need strategies; we need this; we need to get students involved! We need; we need, and we need!'" Each year, this hurried pace of looking at data takes a similar format. Laura Cooper continues,

> The principal and assistant principal of instruction show the teachers last year's test scores and then this year's test scores. So we see that we went down by fifteen points or whatever. Then they put up a slide and do very little explanation of the slide; [they] just assume that everybody understands it the same way. Next thing that is put up is the achievement at the different grade levels. So three bar charts right next to each other, and you have that for Hispanic, Asian, and White; no other [group is presented]: just those three. Then you go through really quickly and see how the Latinos are performing versus the Asians. [The administration] says, "We've got to close that gap."

In large, rushed meetings, data are presented as accurate, meaningful, and self-explanatory. Limited consideration is given to the various factors influencing test performance, such as the construction of the tests; school and social inequalities; and students' diverse backgrounds, skills, and experiences.

There is minimal opportunity to digest, analyze, and reflect on the test scores. According to Laura Cooper, with no chance to process the data, discussions about what is even meant by "an achievement gap" are missing:

> You understand that there is a gap [when the data are presented], and when [the idea of] an achievement gap is brought up again, you make the association to these test scores. But it hasn't necessarily been defined . . . It's glossed over because I don't think that there is a set definition. It's mentioned over and over again like it has been defined, and it is just common knowledge at this point about what it's all about.

Thus while so much emphasis is put on a supposed achievement gap, much is excluded from the presentations that open each school year. Without dialogue, all this becomes "common knowledge" and accepted as the norm.

The racialized associations of achievement also become normalized. Simply presenting data by racial categories without discussion reifies differences and stereotypes. Laura Cooper illustrates,

> You can put graphs up there all day long. But unless you are explaining what we see in the data and then come up with potential reasons why that data is the way that it is and then ultimately what can affect those things that we have identified in a positive way, nothing is going to change. You can say achievement gap all day; we know "achievement," and we know "gap." And we see the 150 points that are between our Asian population and our Latino population. I think what it is doing at least for the teachers is reaffirming their stereotypes. It is saying, "Well you know we are going to teach to the Asians."

When I asked Laura if she hears explicit stereotypes or if there are more subtle messages and beliefs, she clarifies:

> No teacher here would say that [they teach to the Asians], and it is not because they don't want to [say it], but I don't think that they really consciously think that way. It's what they internalize. I think most teachers here feel that this is an equal opportunity education and they're not picking out certain students to teach to, but it is just [done] subconsciously.

When school administrators impart decontextualized and unanalyzed data that supports stereotypes, the internalization of the subconscious beliefs that Laura Cooper describes is facilitated. Similarly, presenting panethnic categories may reinforce the conception that Asian Americans and Latinas/os are diametrically opposed and that these categories are biologically and culturally natural instead of socially constructed as products of human social systems.

Just as there is no definition of the achievement gap or an interrogation of race/ethnicity, there is limited discussion of whether standardized tests are complete measurements of student learning. In fact, decades of research have demonstrated the many biases in standardized tests (see Gonzalez 1990; de Leon and Holman 2002). Students who have middle- and upper-class experiences are more likely to perform well on standardized tests because they often share the reference points and cultural backgrounds of those constructing the tests (Ochoa 2007, 176).

Not only may such biases skew test results, but also some teachers fear that the extensive emphasis on test performance and school rankings based on test scores is actually overshadowing student learning and personal growth. According to Laura Cooper, with a focus on improving the school's Academic Performance Index (API), a summary measurement used to evaluate school performance and progress on statewide assessments, the message within SCHS is as follows:

> We have this achievement gap. We need to close it so we can bring up our API. So *we* can win, not so Brian, who is sitting here, can win when he graduates from high school and that a company that hires him that assumes he can write a business letter [wins]. That's what it *needs* to be.

Seventh-year teacher Beth Hill concurs that the focus is misplaced:

> I feel like [the administration] is so focused on [test performance] because they know that if our Hispanic students raise their scores, that will raise our API. *That* is why they are concerned. I don't get the general "I care about them, and they need to do better."

Fourth-year teacher Michelle Mesa also criticizes this hyperemphasis on API scores and test-taking skills and how it deflects attention away from how students are experiencing the campus:

> We are being very blind sighted if we only look at that by test-taking strategies in the classroom. I'm wondering if we didn't start giving a little more attention to the culture that we're providing, to the messages that we're sending, and that perhaps that wouldn't be incentive enough for some of our students that are not performing to want to do better. If I am a student and I feel like I have no worth and there's nobody here that speaks to me on any level whatsoever why should I perform and give you what you want because at the end of the day you don't think I can do well anyway. As administrators and staff, we have to really look at how the subtle or not so subtle messages that we're sending are also impacting things like the API . . . It's not just all about test-taking strategies.

In such climates, the needs of students are overlooked. When test scores drive schooling, this perpetuates a type of schooling that is based on what sociologist Angela Valenzuela refers to as the "technical" or "aesthetic," where the impersonal and standardized are privileged over personal connections and human affection

(1999, 22). This type of "aesthetic" schooling is "subtractive" and often divests students from what they know and experience. As such, it can push students away from school in the manner described by teacher Michelle Mesa.

Rather than attend to the needs of students, SCHS trumpets an ethos of winning, competition, and rivalry. Returning to her critique of how the administrators present the data to the faculty, Laura Cooper elaborates,

> And then the last slide that they put up is our scores in the content areas for the three different groups: Hispanic, Asian, and White for our school against [another school in the district] . . . and the principal [says], "I just wanted to put that up there to see fairly comparable schools. I just wanted to let you know. It is not necessarily a rivalry thing." Of course it is a rivalry thing, of course it is! It is supposed to get us all fired up.

This emphasis on competition may even push students away from one another as they are encouraged to vie for higher scores against other students and schools. In the context of school rivalries fueled by sports, competition on standardized tests may also perpetuate divisions between schools. This overall focus on competition is antithetical to building collaborative and trusting relationships (Johnson and Johnson 2000).

Illustrating the normalization of test scores, their association with racial/ethnic groups, and how they foster divisions is the way that some students, typically Asian Americans enrolled in honors and advanced placement (AP) courses, comment on the school's API. Without prompting, students explain how teachers' remarks, administrators' announcements, posters around campus, and public rankings of schools have made them aware of the value the school places on doing well on standardized tests. Junior Carmen Chu details,

> We know about our API scores because we have video bulletins every Monday, and sometimes they'll talk about how the API scores are going down. [They tell us,] "We want to bring them up. This is our goal to have this certain amount when it comes to STAR [Standardized Testing and Reporting] testing."

Similar to their teachers, students also feel the pressure to do well for the school, and they hear racial/ethnic correlations on test performance and which groups are supposedly hurting the school's ranking.

Senior Patty Song explains how some of her teachers even joke in class that "the Asian kids help us have a high API." She believes that "teachers and the administration kind of have it in their heads that the Asians are the smart ones, like they are the ones that make our API go high." In conjunction, students like junior Tommy Huie are "hearing from people outside our school that our API is kind of low because the Mexican people are dragging it down." Drawing on racist assumptions of academic ability, some teachers, administrators, and community members blame the school's perceived declining prestige to falling test scores supposedly caused by Mexican American students, and they put undue pressure on Asian American students.

Overall, the nationally imposed culture surrounding assessment and the excessive focus on the "gap" are detrimental to schooling and students' experiences. They reduce the attention on students' well-being and foster assumptions that standardized tests are fair and precise assessments of student learning. In addition, posting test performances by panethnic categories and without analyses of within-group heterogeneity and the role of larger factors on test performance perpetuates the power-evasive framework that something must be wrong with those groups who are thought to be responsible for lowering scores. As Claude Steele (1997) has documented in his work on "stereotype threat," it could even become self-fulfilling so that Asian Americans rise to others' expectations and Latinas/os may underperform on tests in accordance with dominant assumptions. Finally, the narrow emphasis on an achievement gap that leaves unquestioned standardized test results also positions Asian Americans against Latinas/os and fosters the invisibility of Whites and Blacks, who at SCHS are left out of the data or barely discussed. Given the relatively small percentage of Whites and Blacks at the school, their scores may not impact the overall ranking of the school. Thus their performances and such students are largely dismissed. As detailed next, this focus on standardized tests and decontextualized presentations of students' performance work in tandem with the prevalence of individual and group-level frameworks on educational success. Together, they reinforce the legacy of biological and cultural deficiency arguments that further hierarchical constructions of Latinas/os and Asian Americans.

INDIVIDUAL AND GROUP-LEVEL ARGUMENTS FOR EDUCATIONAL OUTCOMES

The approach to education might be like an Asian tradition. Since back for thousands of years, education has been *the* thing for like millions of years. Chinese dinosaurs probably took school seriously.

—*Sandra Wu, International Baccalaureate (IB) senior*

Student Sandra Wu's comments rooting Asian educational success in the time of the dinosaurs capture other dominant frameworks. Such arguments posit that some groups possess and others lack the supposed biological or cultural attributes for progress and achievement. These arguments assume that racism and discrimination are passé and that the United States is a meritocracy. So the roles of class inequality and individual, institutional, and structural discrimination on educational experiences and life chances are largely dismissed. Furthermore, both biological and cultural arguments are essentialist and are used to profile students since all members of particular races/ethnicities, classes, and genders are perceived to possess defining traits. Within-group heterogeneity and the ways that race/ethnicity, class, and gender are sociopolitical, economic constructs are overlooked. Such perspectives have shaped popular discourse, and at SCHS, they are apparent in (1) biological determinist arguments that naturalize gender and race/ethnicity and assert that some groups are inherently more mature, more disciplined, or smarter than other groups; (2) cultural determinist beliefs that assume, for example, that Asian Americans and the middle and upper classes, in comparison to Latinas/os and the poor, come from families and traditions that are more likely to value schooling and hard work; and (3) the invisibility of whiteness. By glossing over student differences and ignoring macro-meso-micro factors fostering disparities in schools, broad categorizations of Asian American and Latina/o students and general designations of "high performing" and "low performing" reproduce dominant structures, maintain hegemonic gendered and racialized assumptions, pit groups against each other, and hinder the possibilities of change. Cultural determinist beliefs are also connected to assimilationist arguments and the "model minority" myth discussed in more detail in chapter 5. For now, we turn to the perspectives of the staffulty and the reinforcement of dominant ideologies.

The Belief That Biology Is Destiny: Naturalizing Sex, Gender, and Race

Ninth-grade girls do well until they get the two Bs—boobs and boyfriends.

—*Tom O'Brien, teacher*

You grow up in a world where some people are just stupid and some people are smart. You assume that Asians are smart and that Mexicans are always stupid.

—*Monique Martínez, student*

The comments made by Tom O'Brien before a faculty meeting and the reflections from junior Monique Martínez during an interview reveal the naturalizing of both gender and race/ethnicity as biological entities. Although some might interpret Tom O'Brien's remarks as a statement of students' changing interests over the life course, his specific reference to breasts implies anatomical differences and hormonal fluctuations that supposedly disrupt the academic performance of all ninth-grade girls, who he assumes are distracted by boys. Just as O'Brien claims that girls' academic performance dips with the onset of puberty, Monique Martínez's explanations of intelligence also suggest that biology is destiny. In this case, she has come to believe that Asians are naturally smarter than Mexicans. While such biological determinist arguments have long been disproved and replaced by theories of race/ethnicity and gender as socially constructed, some at SCHS reduce academic performance to biology and use assumed biological traits to profile students.

ROOTING SEX AND GENDER IN BIOLOGY

Although national statistics reveal an overall gender gap where women across all racial/ethnic groups have higher rates of school achievement and college attendance (Lopez 2003; Gándara and Contreras 2009), gender and educational outcomes were rarely discussed during the interviews. Similarly, school personnel reported that little was said at the school about their salience. Many did not seem to question this silence

because as some indicated, they did not notice the significance of gender in their classrooms, or they figured that standardized test scores are presented by race/ethnicity. So they believed that the school simply draws on available data when trying to understand educational outcomes, and with the mandates of No Child Left Behind, test performance by race/ethnicity is emphasized.

Several of the school officials who described noticing gendered patterns in school performance naturalized them with comments such as "we all know that girls tend to perform better in school." A couple explicitly adopted a biological explanation by stressing differences in maturation. Teacher Jane King's comments are illustrative:

> English has a tendency to be a class that girls do better in because it's a linguistic-based class and, you know, the boys are not quite as talkative and not quite as social . . . I think honestly they're not ready for it yet, you know. They are when they're seniors; maturity-wise, they're where the girls are when they were freshman. You know, they're just not ready for it yet.

Believing that it is common knowledge that as two distinct groups all boys and all girls differ in terms of maturation, Jane King thrice uses the phrase "you know" to express her point. She is not alone in accepting this sentiment. Coach Jim Scott echoes her as he reflects on the students who have assisted him:

> The girls perform higher than the boys because of the maturation; girls usually mature faster than guys. There's like a five-year gap between the girls and the guys, maturity-wise . . . The people that help me in my office, the good ones are the girls that are really good on the computer and are able to handle the things I need done. I don't think I've ever had a male office aide that was good on the computer, so it's always been a female student.

Not only is sex and maturation conflated with gender identities, but such biological determinist perspectives often foster unequal treatment. In this case, young women are given the opportunity to work with Coach Scott. This provides them with capital such as computer skills and social networks that young men may be denied. Similarly, just as young men are restricted by this biological categorization, it may also reinforce gender expectations of women's labor and the assumption that women are effective assistants and good with data entry.

Longtime teacher Margaret Albert extends this perception that there are natural variations in maturation by sex and gender. As she explains, in comparison to girls, boys have more energy, and this accounts for their higher representation in remedial courses:

> When I had the remedial English [class], the majority were guys. We know that there are some differences in maturation . . . [I]t's pretty difficult with their energy level for them to have to keep still for as long as they have to.

According to Margaret Albert, these supposed differences make it hard to force boys to sit in class for long periods of time. So she alters her teaching strategies to accommodate for their perceived differences:

> [Guys are] more active. I'd need to have some of them run around the building a few times [to] get rid of that energy. And I need to have more hands on and moving around. It's cruelty to them to have to sit still that long.

Many people find it difficult to remain seated for hours each day in a traditional classroom. However, rather than critique a lecture-based classroom structure that requires students to quietly sit next to other students as they listen to the teacher and take notes, some such as Margaret Albert instead locate the problem in males' supposed unique biological composition. Also underlying this teacher's comments is an assumption that women are naturally more adept at sitting passively. Although Margaret Albert tries to accommodate the presumed high energy of males in her remedial classes by changing her pedagogy, this does not address the larger factors that lead to the unequal placement of young men in remedial classes, such as the transitional English class described in the preface, that funnel students away from college. It also does little to disrupt the traditional one-way transfer of knowledge in the classroom that expects students to inactively receive information from teachers.

Similar to their teachers, students only occasionally considered gender as a factor influencing schooling. Nonetheless, a couple of students repeated a biological determinist argument that they learned in class. Eleventh-grader Margaret Kang explains, "Recently, we heard in English that girls excel in English and liberal arts and then guys are more logical thinkers."

Several students labeled girls as "hard workers" and guys as "lazy." Sometimes, guys were characterized as "chill"—which seems to contradict teacher Margaret Albert's description of boys having a lot of energy. For junior Summer Reyes, this apparent relaxed demeanor in comparison to girls' "more emotional" state is genetic:

> I think the girls are harder on themselves. I guess because girls are weaker or more emotional, so they get really stressed, so they work themselves really hard. The guys, they're chill about everything . . . I think it's just in their genes. Girls are just more caring about things.

Senior Jean Kim concurs with Summer that "guys are more laid back; just naturally they're laid back. Even if they're smart, they're laid back." She adds that girls "take [more] initiative and actually try to work harder than guys, but then sometimes guys are smarter. They don't even need to try; they just are smarter," The assumption in such comments is that in comparison to men, women are not inherently smart; they are just harder workers.

Remarks such as these reveal how some at SCHS equate sex with gender. Such conflating ignores the ways that gender is not natural. Instead, gender is a sociopolitical economic construction that is influenced by socialization from family members, peers, schools, the media, and others, Gender is also performed in everyday interactions and embedded in cultural expectations and institutional disparities (Risman 1998). Furthermore, such comments assume that one's biological sex always matches one's gender identity and that genders are genetically distinct from each other. In spite of research demonstrating that the two-sex (male–female) and two-gender (man–woman) system is constructed and that there are more variations *within* the categories of males and females than between males and females (Epstein 1988), such conflating of sex with gender persists. This discourse perpetuates the belief that both sex *and* gender are biological and that variations between sexes and genders are normal. It is alleged that girls and boys differ biologically and that these differences produce fundamentally distinct people. Expecting changes in academic performances is thus futile because the assumption is that boys and girls are just naturally different. Such sentiments may then become self-fulfilling to the extent that students are profiled based on these assumptions and encounter unequal treatment and expectations.

EMPLOYING BIOLOGICAL CONSTRUCTS OF RACE/ETHNICITY AND INTELLIGENCE

In comparison to discussions surrounding sex and gender, school officials were much less likely to provide such explicit biological arguments when explaining academic differences by race/ethnicity. Instead, they were merged with cultural deficiency arguments or their language was racially coded. For example, coach Marilyn Garcia combined biological and cultural explanations in her assessment of students' coordination:

> Asians, they're more oriented to academics, to their studies. They'd rather not play softball or hit the ball, or they don't have the coordination. But then, the Mexican kids are a lot more fun in terms of sports because they're not studying hard at home. There's no one really to beat them up to do the school work because the focus seems to be different.

Although few school officials adopted such traditional racist beliefs linking race, biology, and performance—in this case that Asian Americans lack coordination—there were indications that some school officials still accept the belief that intelligence is biological and that select people are innately more inclined to certain subjects. For instance, during an IB meeting with students, a school official instructed "natural-born mathematicians" to enroll in an additional calculus class, while those who are "not the brightest light as math is concerned" should take statistics.

Teacher Manuel Cadena also reinforces conceptions that intelligence is biological:

> If you're lucky enough, you are on this side of the tracks. You're given students that are unbelievably bright. You've got three people [at SCHS] that scored perfect on the SATs. Here, if you get something below 1200, something's wrong with you. We've got all this raw talent, but then you get these kids from the other side of the train tracks that are not prepared. So you can only do so much.

While unstated, race/ethnicity and socioeconomic status are embedded in Manuel Cadena's train tracks metaphor. In comparison to the primarily poor and working-class Latina/o neighborhood on "the other side of the train tracks," SCHS is situated in a more socioeconomically privileged and racially diverse area—factors that, according to Manuel Cadena, result in students with "raw talent" in comparison to other students who he believes "can only do so much." Such references to talent and brightness in this context reinforce assumptions that intelligence is not only innate but also correlated with class and race/ethnicity. His equation of SAT scores with talent also overlooks years of hard work studying for the test and unequal resources such as differential access to tutors and paid preparation courses.

Whereas during their interviews most school officials tended not to equate race/ethnicity to biology, students frequently used phrases such as "smart" and "stupid" to refer to different racial/ethnic groups, as in Monique Martinez's opening quote. It was not always clear if such labels and racial/ethnic associations were linked to an underlying belief in biological differences, but the associations are made so frequently that some students start to deduce, as Monique does, that "Asians are smart and that Mexicans are always stupid." According to at least one group of friends, such comments are as frequent as saying "Hi" at school.

Some of what students hear emanates from their teachers. Sophomores Jenn Vanderhol and Fran Padilla reflect on the power of teacher's comments:

JENN: He would just talk about how Asians are smarter. How we are not smart 'cause "you're not Asian."

FRAN: He was always joking around, but it's like even if you're joking around there is always some form of truth to it. It has to come from somewhere.

As Fran suggests, even though her teacher may be joking, these racialized messages from authority figures may be internalized and reproduced. After all, Fran believes that such so-called jokes must bear some "truth."

Mexican Americans Rebecca Ramos and Gloria Camacho accept similar beliefs, and they too draw upon a teacher's lesson to prove their points. When asked why one of the two middle schools that many SCHS students attend is perceived as better than the middle school they attended, Rebecca and Gloria offer the following explanation:

REBECCA: They're all Asians over there . . .

GLORIA: They're probably just born smart.

REBECCA: Yeah, and well, our first period teacher was showing us how many people go to college, and Mexicans were last. First, it was Asians and then it was White people, then it was Black people, then it was Mexicans.

While their teacher's intent in sharing current demographic information on educational attainment was not clear, if the data were presented without interrogation as the standardized test results are presented to teachers, a phenomenon similar to the one teacher Laura Cooper described earlier may occur for students. That is, like some teachers, students may also interpret such statistics as confirmation of a racial/ethnic hierarchy where Asian American students are positioned as smarter than other students.

These biological arguments from some school officials and students are not isolated. For much of history, biological deficiency perspectives dominated academic and public discourse, and they have bolstered school practices. Through the 1950s, White middle- and upper-class researchers and educators often used biological arguments to justify de jure segregation, Americanization programs, and vocational courses for students of color. For example, proponents of biological determinism believed that Mexican American students were naturally inclined toward sex rather than education, were predisposed physically to perform agricultural labor, and lacked the mental capabilities to excel in academically rigorous courses (see Gonzalez 1990). These theories justified separate and unequal schools that punished those who spoke languages other than English, emphasized U.S. patriotism, and prepared students for low-wage and gender-specific occupations. Meanwhile, Euro-American students were largely schooled to fill higher-paying occupations in accordance with their gender and class positions.

More recently, there have been several high-profile cases illustrating the endurance of biological arguments, including in 2005 when, at an economics conference, then–Harvard University president Lawrence Summers attributed the underrepresentation of women scientists in senior positions to genetics (Goldenberg 2005). In 2009, a Harvard PhD student completed a dissertation arguing that immigrants have lower IQs

than White Americans. The content of the dissertation was made public when a well-known conservative think tank aimed to use it to bolster their argument against immigration reform (Wessler 2013).

Even though the idea of superior and inferior sexes, genders, and races/ethnicities has long been disproved scientifically, biological arguments persist. They seep into dominant ideologies, people's imaginations, and even our language. Furthermore, along with some of the cultural determinist arguments detailed in the following section, they have maintained and reproduced a race-based capitalist and gendered labor system that divides and ranks students.

Cultural Determinism: Fostering Homogenization and Hierarchies

The Asians seem to be motivated and driven. The Latinos don't seem to value education in the same way. [Their] parents don't seem to be as involved the way the Asian parents are.

—Anthony Castro, teacher

Notwithstanding the existence of some biological assumptions, cultural explanations such as those presented by fifth-year teacher Anthony Castro were more commonly provided during the interviews. These arguments emphasize supposed differences in values, parental expectations, and work ethics. As in the biological arguments surrounding race, in most cases, Asian Americans—believed to possess the preferred cultural and familial predispositions necessary to excel—are positioned in opposition to Latinas/os. However, at times, Asian Americans are judged just as harshly as Latinas/os but still in binary ways, with Asian Americans characterized as being overly involved or demanding too much academically of their children and Latinas/os as being too lax when it comes to school. Similarly, some teachers also use a "culture of poverty" explanation when they argue that the poor and working classes are "apathetic" toward education (see Lewis 1966). Thus, just as these cultural determinist arguments homogenize groups and overlook systems of power and inequality, they also foster racial/ethnic and class hierarchies.

The assumption that Latinas/os and Asian Americans are diametrically opposed in their support for and involvement in education is ubiquitous. Comments such as the following by school official Jackie Towne are typical: "The achievement gap is going to be there because the mind-set of the Asian culture and the mind-set of the Hispanic culture are different. They're just different." Teacher Jane King, who earlier attributed supposed biological differences in maturation to gendered performances in English language courses, agrees with Jackie Towne that "culture" and "family life" are preeminent factors in influencing educational outcomes:

> Whether or not somebody is academically successful? What influences that? Oh, first and foremost, their family life, how they were raised, the culture of the family, what the family believes—100 percent, and that's why we have a gap at this school between the Asian population, Hispanic . . . You're going to see the number one difference is what's going on in the home, not what's going on in the classroom.

Along with referring generally to the undefined but apparently understood "gap" at SCHS, Jane King is quick to dismiss any role that the school may have in creating and perpetuating inequalities. According to her and many of the staffulty, "the culture of the family" is 100 percent liable for student performance. This discourse of the family is pervasive; it reinforces assumptions of good and bad families, and it ignores the multiple economic and political contexts infringing on household resources and opportunities. The implication is that educational outcomes cannot be changed unless families and cultures are altered. Schools and society are held unaccountable.

FRAMING LATINAS/OS

Even when the staffulty do not explicitly compare Latinas/os with Asian Americans, these assumptions of cultural difference and a cultural hierarchy are rampant. Teacher Manuel Cadena, whose views span biological, cultural, and power-aware arguments, is one among several school personnel to offer a scathing critique of what he refers to as "the attitude" of Latina/o parents:

> Latino parents have no involvement in what their kids are doing . . . The attitude of the village needs to change. The entire Latino village needs to change the way it raises kids to understand the value of being educated and realize they're a big population that can be heard.

While study after study reveals that Latina/o students have higher aspirations to go to college than do students from the general population and that 94 percent of Latina/o parents say they expect their own children to go to college (Delgado-Gaitan 1992; Kao 2000; Pew Hispanic Foundation/Kaiser Family Foundation 2004), sweeping generalizations are made about Latinas/os not valuing education. Incidentally, earlier in his interview, as described in the section on biological determinism, Manuel Cadena argued that students on "the other side of the train tracks" (read: Latina/o and poor or working class) are "not prepared. So you can only do so much." In this current example, he criticizes Latina/o parents for not valuing education. Yet members of the same Latina/o community that he castigates across the tracks who attend SCHS are actually "choice students." These students and their families made the decision to leave their home schools to attend the more highly ranked school in the district with the hopes of increasing their educational opportunities. One such student, sophomore Daniela Gutierrez, explains her parents' decision: "My brother was coming here, and I guess they thought that [SCHS] was a better school . . . They have higher test scores or something like that." Thus while some working-class and Latina/o families are actually investing significant time to enroll their children in SCHS and then driving them several miles each day to and from school, Manuel Cadena dismisses these efforts by assuming that parents do not value education. Instead, he seems to equate valuing education to attending school meetings:

> If you look at the parents of these kids in [my non–college prep. course], you'll see a difference in their parental attitude compared to the parents of kids in [my college prep, course]. Parent conference night, for example, I'll see one or two sets of parents from two kids from [my non–college prep, course]. The rest of the fifty-some parents that I see are from my [other class].

This belief that attendance at school meetings is a crucial indication of parent caring is a fallacy accepted by many who possess stereotyped perceptions of Latina/o families and narrow conceptions of parent participation (Lareau 1989; Quijada and Alvarez 2006).

Not only do parents believe that all forms of raising children are critical, including providing food, clothing, and verbal encouragement (Williams and Stallworth

1983; Gándara 1995), but working-class, immigrant, or Latina/o parents may also be more likely to expect that schools and teachers are responsible for student learning since they are officially trained for this undertaking (Lareau 1987). However, given the hegemony of middle-class and upper-middle-class frameworks of parent participation, these broader views may be ignored by the staff fully. Likewise, by blaming parents' cultures, the responsibilities of schools in creating spaces inclusive of all parents—including working-class, immigrant, and non-English-speaking—are overlooked.

Also overlooked in cultural deficiency frameworks are the ways that class position and previous experiences with institutions of higher education may influence families' cultural and social capital. In particular, low-income and Latina/o families may not have the same forms of school-expected cultural capital (knowledge of how the school system works and what it values) and social capital (access to institutional agents) than middle- and upper-class students who are often White and Asian American (Lareau 1989; Gándara and Contreras 2009, 68). However, rather than examining how schools may assume that all possess the same forms of capital or that schools bear no responsibility for providing information and access that may be taken for granted by more privileged parents, Latina/o families are blamed.

While only mentioned in regard to Latinas/os, a couple of school officials drew on classic cultural deterministic arguments that blame what has been referred to as a "language handicap" for hindering academic success (see Chavez 1991). Fourth-year teacher Mike Williams expounds,

> There's a huge language issue because they're taught Spanish first and then they come to an American school where everything is done in English. So they're already behind because they don't have that language acquisition. They don't have the language to function academically, so that already is an enormous setback for most.

Rather than seeing bilingualism as an asset or faulting schools for the elimination of bilingual education, Mike Williams assumes that Spanish-speaking students are deficient—that they lack "language acquisition." This sentiment was common, especially through the 1960s when much of the academic scholarship on bilingualism was premised on the belief that English-language learners

experience impairment in speech, intellect, confidence, and originality of thought (Soto 1997, 3). Disproving such biased assumptions, more recent studies indicate that when students are provided the opportunity to acquire two languages through dual-immersion programs, they demonstrate superiority in concept formation, mental flexibility, and verbal problem-solving abilities relative to their monolingual peers (Lindholm 1995, 247).

By only focusing on Latinas/os and the Spanish language, teacher Mike Williams assumes that Latinas/os are the group most held back by language or that they are more likely to come from non-English-speaking households. However, as documented by the California Department of Education, equal numbers of Latina/o and Asian American students (about one hundred each) are designated English-language learners at SCHS. Although no group should be the target of such a fallacious statement that they lack "language acquisition," this sentiment is also unequally applied.

FRAMING ASIAN AMERICANS

In contrast to Latina/o parents, who are typically described as not valuing education, Asian American parents are often characterized as just the opposite. Second-year teacher Alison Adams's comments capture this sentiment: "I see honors/AP as your high achievers, and that tends to be your Asian kids. I think it's cultural. I took a class once, and we talked about that, and culturally Asian parents tend to push more. They're very involved in education." Dominant representations of Asian Americans as a so-called model minority who are believed to really "push" education prevail, and in the case of Alison Adams, she learned this in her teacher education program. Teacher Mike Williams bases his assessment on his observations:

> Education, from what I've seen in most Asian families, is something that is held in the highest regard. If you want to get anywhere in your life and become successful and prosper and be a professional, education is that key. What I've noticed even with little, little Asian American children is, "School, school, school, work work, work. Study your butt off." And because knowledge and education is so revered in so many Asian American families, that's quite naturally what a lot of Asian American students bring to school with them.

While his qualifying language of "most" and "a lot" tempers Mike William's simplifications, he nonetheless casts a broad stroke in describing Asian Americans. Likewise, he conveys his assumption that "education is that key" to success, "to get[ing] anywhere in life." Such a sentiment supposes that there is just one path and one conception of success, that everyone has equal access to education, and that education necessarily results in prosperity. In contrast to these assumptions, relative to Whites, Asian Americans do not receive comparable returns on their education, and they often face blocked opportunities to career advancement, especially in managerial positions (Woo 2000; Chen 2006). Some suggest that it is precisely these *structural* barriers that are a product of racial discrimination that lead some families to do all they can to encourage education for their children in hopes of reducing the impacts of racism (Louie 2004). Like their Latina/o immigrant counterparts, studies suggest that Asian American parents place much hope in their children's education. However, at SCHS, the financial resources and knowledge of educational institutions of Asian American and Latina/o parents often differ because of parents' variations in class-based resources and educational backgrounds.

While school officials tend to praise Asian American families for what they believe is a strong emphasis on education, underlying some of these cultural arguments is that Asian Americans might just "push" their children too much. Veteran teacher Margaret Albert reflects,

> The bad side of that is that some Asian parents have, and again I'm lumping all Asians and it's very different being wherever you're from, but sometimes, it's so unrealistic that their parents are pushing them that that creates a lot of problems. You know, it's unrealistic that everyone's going to go to UC [University of California] Berkeley.

Softening her generalization of Asian Americans by mentioning geographic and ethnic differences, Margaret Albert cautions Asian American parents from being "unrealistic" and "pushing" too hard. However, like many, she does not challenge the structure of society and schools that are based on competition and driven by hierarchies that rank schools and individuals. The push to achieve greater and more rewards is embedded in society and schools. As described earlier, SCHS's emphasis on its API score is just one of many examples

of this culture of competition in schools. Rather than critique this culture, the supposed culture of Asian Americans is targeted.

The image that Asian American parents are not just "unrealistic" but even downright abusive has, according to teacher Beth Hill, become part of the student lore. She shares, "The students always joke, 'You have no idea what beating I would get if I get a B.' That's like a big joke, but I don't know if it really is." While Asian American students may be playing with stereotypes of their parents when they make these comments to their teachers, Beth Hill hears such comments so often that she is even beginning to believe them.

Just as some critique Asian Americans for "pushing" their children in what they perceive as too much, a few such as Beth Hill belittle families for being insistent with teachers:

> I have a student that was absent a lot and his mom has been e-mailing me. Since he got a C for the semester and a B– [overall], and I didn't advise him to go on to AP because I feel like the absences are really going to [hurt him], she e-mailed me, "Please."

Parents have the right to request that their children be placed in advanced courses. However, Beth Hill believes that this request was too demanding and emblematic of some of her exchanges with Asian American parents. To punctuate her point, she continues with a second example:

> One [family member] I had asked to change a grade. [The student] took my sophomore class as a junior for honors because he was in IB and he needed a better grade than a D. He still got a D in my class his junior year. That aunt [said], "Please, can you just change it?" I'm like, "No." They come, and they push.

While it is unclear how often teachers encounter this second example, where they are asked to change a grade, some teachers may equate these two interactions with Asian Americans parents only. However, middle-class and upper-middle-class children and parents in high curriculum tracks such as the International Baccalaureate program or those with high socioeconomic status may be more likely to make such requests because of their own privileged positions and sense of entitlement in school and society (Lareau 1989). As education scholar Lisa Delpit (1995) has documented, they may possess a variation of the "culture of power" in knowing what to expect and what to ask of the school to best serve their interests.

. . .

GENDERED AND RACIALIZED ASSUMPTIONS

Just as some acknowledge class variation among Latinas/os, a small number of school officials link gender and race/ethnicity to argue that there are more gender differences between Latinas and Latinos than between Asian American women and men. As teacher Anthony Castro proclaims, for the Hispanic group, the guys are less motivated to do well. For Asians, "guys and girls are equally motivated." In making such assessments, the emphasis is again on allegedly different values between Latinas/os and Asian Americans.

In fact, a few staffuly, such as teacher Margaret Albert, drew on hegemonic constructions of race and teen pregnancy to characterize Latinas as more sexually active and desirous of children in comparison to other groups of students on campus:

> I've felt there was a marked difference between the Hispanic female, and I remember reading a very interesting article on how it was a status symbol practically, you know, you're proud that you're pregnant at an early age . . . If you're in one part of the subculture, it's kind of cute for the girl to walk around pregnant. And she's young and then he's young and then there's the limit to how much education you can get.

Despite research indicating that Latina adolescents are less likely to be sexually active than European American and African American girls (Blum et al. 2000, as referenced in Denner and Guzmán 2006, 4) and that having a child as a teenager is linked to class resources, the assumption is that Latinas/os as a group favor young mothers. Teacher Margaret Albert expounds on her essentializing of Latina hypersexuality and young parenthood in comparison with her beliefs of Asian Americans:

> Among the Asian population, generally dating and really getting involved in boyfriend–girlfriend relationships is something that is delayed a great deal. And therefore they have more time to do other things.

Such categorizations are also pervasive in the media, and they position Latinas and Asian American women into racialized and gendered binaries. During various historical periods, Latinas and Asian Americans have been cast as sexually promiscuous and flaunting their sexuality or as asexual and virgins until marriage. In contrast, Latino men are often stereotyped as "Latin lovers" or hypermasculine, whereas Asian American men may be feminized (Ramírez-Berg 1997; Espiritu 1997). These representations are confining. They divide groups into whore/virgin and masculine/feminine dichotomies; they do not allow for the individual agency of Asian Americans and Latinas/os in determining their own sexualities, and they assume that education is necessarily sidelined by relationships and pregnancy. The few studies centering the perspectives of Latina teens actually suggest that motherhood increases educational aspirations for some teens (Russell and Lee 1994, as referenced by Trejos-Castillo and Frederick 2011). With so much focus on the supposed values of racial/ethnic groups, young Latinas are derogatorily cast as "at risk" and seen as the source of the believed problem of teen pregnancy (Garcia 2012). Meanwhile, sex education remains absent in most schools, limiting students' opportunities to learn more about their bodies, relationships, and sexual health (Fields 2008).

Several school officials noted that they believe Latinos in particular have more "behavioral" problems than other students, and Latinos were typically named as the root of the problem. Teacher John Alvarez, who at first faulted the school for eliminating vocational classes that might appeal to some students, reverted to a cultural explanation by clarifying that "within the Hispanic culture, [boys] like to get involved with their hands. They like to work with cars." Even Alvarez, who believes that SCHS needs to provide more course options for students, reverts to an underlying assumption that Latinos, in comparison to other students, have a predilection for working with their hands. Arguments such as these permeated rationales used through the 1950s to confine Mexicans to manual labor in the agricultural fields, brickyards, and mines (Gonzalez 1990).

In spite of the variations in people's emphasis on supposed cultural differences, such explanations prevail in the dominant representations of Asian Americans as an assumed "model minority" in comparison to Latinas/os. These beliefs divide Latinas/os from Asian Americans, and as history teaches us, these same frameworks are used to justify differences in academic achievement and to shape school practices. With groups of color defined as the "problem," attention is also diverted from Whites and White privilege.

"THE WHITE ELEPHANT": WHITENESS IS LARGELY UNMARKED

Early during my research, a member of the staffulty referred to the achievement gap between Asian Americans and Latinas/os as the "white elephant" because few people actually discuss it. As previously described, staffulty mention the "gap" constantly but only look superficially at the quantitative data. They do not delve into the complexities behind the numbers. When I heard this "white elephant" phrase, I understood it as a mistaken reference to the popular idiom of "an elephant in the room" used in reference to a taboo topic that people ignore. The addition of the word "white" is apropos given the overall silence regarding Whites, White privilege, and the normative cultural practices sustaining the racial/ethnic hierarchies at the school. As part of the power-evasive discourse at SCHS, whiteness is one of the elephants in the school. Few White staffulty reflected on their own identities or the manifestations of White privilege. These silences are as significant as the biological and cultural arguments for maintaining disparities and for illustrating the dominance of power-evasive thinking.

. . .

Ignoring and Asserting White Privilege

In a society steeped in racism and where race and ethnicity influence opportunities, a few staffulty who ignore their identities also overlook the multiple forms of White privilege—what Beverley Daniel Tatum describes as "the systematically conferred advantages they receive simply because they are White" (1997, 95). Ranging from the ability to shop without being treated as suspect by clerks to being seen as an individual rather than as a representative of her race, in her now classic piece, Peggy McIntosh (1995) lists forty-six daily benefits of White privilege. Sociologists Oliver and Shapiro (1995) document the state policies

fostering a cumulative legacy of White privilege and white supremacy that has resulted in vast wealth differentials between Whites and African Americans. These include unequal access to loans, a history of restrictive housing covenants, contemporary residential segregation, and differential rates of home appreciation based on the racial composition of communities. A lack of awareness of such everyday, institutional, and structural advantages granted to Whites relative to people of color reproduces the racial order. It also maintains the idea that individuals are solely responsible for their positions in society (McIntosh 1995).

This limited consciousness of privilege was most apparent in Joe Berk's retelling of his schooling and career trajectory. Raised in Southern California in the 1960s and 1970s, Joe attended a Catholic high school with a majority of White and Latina/o students. For him, school was "easy," and he "got along well" with his teachers, who were virtually all White. As has been the pattern in the racial skewing of course placement, he was placed in the top classes away from his Latino friends, who were put into courses that were several levels below his. This practice of being pushed up the educational pipeline continued throughout his life: after he became a teacher, he was selected to be a counselor, a director, and eventually an administrator. Recounting his experiences, Joe piped, "Everything I did, I always got pushed into some leadership role." This experience of what Williams (1995) describes as the "glass elevator effect" contrasts with the "glass ceiling" often encountered by women and people of color who face multiple barriers to academic and career advancement. Nevertheless, Joe did not initially understand his experiences as an example of White and male privilege. Instead, he stumbles to explain why he was pushed up the career ladder:

> I don't know why. I, I just, I don't know why. Ummm, it's like even when I was finishing up at high school umm and I was asked by the coaches to come out and help coach in the spring of my senior year. Why they asked me, I don't know. Then when I was, when I first started teaching umm, I was pulled into a role as a counselor . . . I was just being pulled into those roles. Ummm, one of the things I remember that was written on my observation when I was doing my student teaching was that they felt that I would eventually be suitable for an administrative position.

Joe Berk's multiple false starts, repetition, and lengthy pauses suggest that he is uncomfortable or even nervous answering the question. Such "rhetorical incoherence" increases when people discuss sensitive topics (Bonilla-Silva 2006, 68). This difficulty contrasts with the ease at which Joe characterized Asian Americans and Latinas/os at the beginning of this chapter.

As Joe explains his current position, he continues in a similar manner of rhetorical incoherence and without an analysis of the advantages his race/ethnicity and gender have had on his promotions:

> I've always been kind of trusted with these leadership roles. Umm, I was thrust into uhh the role at [a private high school] as a counselor. And, before I left there, they, they were thrusting me into a disciplinary position as a leader. Then when I started teaching at the public school, after my second year there, I got pushed into department chairmanship. I got pushed, kind of, uhh into taking the athletic director's role.

Flustered to understand why he was so trusted and promoted, Joe eventually attributes his advancement to "showing an interest" and people being "happy to give" him high status roles. However, at the end of our two interviews spanning multiple weeks, Joe shared an epiphany: after the first interview, he started considering how he might have been pushed up in curriculum tracks and in job promotions because he is White.

While Joe Berk's narrative illustrates how people's perspectives can change, it also highlights how the invisibility of whiteness is similar to biological and cultural arguments in that it shifts attention away from structural and institutional causes of inequality and the salience of race/ethnicity, gender, and class. For staff member Nancy Gardiner, her ignorance of White privilege— including, as described in the previous section, her unawareness of her own identity—leads her to invert the reality of power differentials and to blame immigrants for "ruin[ing]" the United States:

NANCY GARDINER: Sometimes I resent it. It's like, "Wait a minute. You came in and you think this is all about you. Excuse me." You just sometimes feel run over. I mean, some of my more defensive emotions might be, "Well, you came here to America for the good that America has to offer, but then in so many ways, a lot of people seem to ruin it."

GILDA OCHOA: What do you mean? Are there any examples you can think of?

NANCY GARDINER: I feel that a lot of people take advantage of what's given to them and do not respond in an appreciative way. In some ways, things have been made too easy for people who have needs or people who come illegally. I might be wrong, but a lot of my perception of poverty and crime for example are from a lot of people who are here illegally and take advantage of the system in America like free medical, free public education, communicating in your primary language.

By failing to note power and privilege, Nancy Gardiner overlooks the many hardships immigrants encounter living and working in a new country. She also inaccurately reverses who is really advantaged within the United States and who benefits from our current system. Rather than critique the role of U.S. economic and military policies that impel people to migrate and that are also impacting the livelihoods of working people within the United States, she faults undocumented immigrants. This framework allows her to ignore how immigrant labor forms the base of the U.S. economy so that the low wages paid to immigrants advantage capitalists and consumers. These low wages and immigrant labor subsidize the food, clothing, electronics, and services that many people in the United States consume, and the economic policies and military actions of the power elite—primarily upper class White men—serve elite interests.

Psychologically, Nancy Gardiner's anti-immigrant perspective also provides her with a scapegoat for her difficulties finding a job:

> In my own [experience] seeking employment, I was becoming very concerned and frustrated that so many of the schools were looking for someone who could speak Spanish. That was upsetting to me. And a lot of the job positions were bilingual. It changed from desirable or preferred to desired, to required.

Instead of considering the possibility that others are more qualified than she is and that bilingual staff/ty are assets in schools, she exerts a sense of entitlement that she deserves to be hired:

> It became very discouraging and upsetting. It's like, "My God, here I am an intelligent adult. I just paid for

a master's degree. I have the qualifications, the credentials to be hired . . . just being more mature, having been a parent and my work in schools, a lot of other things in my background that were very desirable to be hired, even in schools where I knew people." But I felt I was not getting hired because I could not speak Spanish.

When she was not immediately hired and she could not benefit from her social connections, Nancy Gardiner claimed discrimination and reconstructed the history of the area to suit her interests:

I was being discriminated against. And that brought various thoughts and feelings like, "Wait a minute, this is America and our primary language, our national language—whether by default or whatever has been English. Why can't I get hired and all these people who didn't even have an education could get hired just like that?" And here I went and invested in a master's degree, and I felt like I was being discriminated against. So that made me angry at the whole system.

Conceiving of the region as English speaking, Nancy Gardiner adopts mainstream ideas that selectively forget that the area where Los Angeles was founded in 1781 started as a Mexican pueblo. Similarly, even when Southern California and the rest of the Southwest were forcefully incorporated by the United States in 1848, cultural rights were to be protected under the Treaty of Guadalupe Hidalgo. As Vigil notes, "Mexican cultural customs and patterns were to be given equal consideration with Anglo culture; this meant recognition and accommodation of the Spanish language and Catholic religion" (1980, 127). By overlooking this history and contemporary demographics, she accepts an image of Southern California and the United States as White and English speaking. Furthermore, Gardiner speaks in generalities about "all these people" who were being hired over her. She does not name their racial/ethnic backgrounds, but the implications are that they are less qualified, do not have an education, and are not from the United States. Her focus on the Spanish language appears to be a code word for Latinas/os and her belief that unqualified Latinas/os are taking these jobs. Nancy Gardiner assumes that she has more of a right—an entitlement—to be hired, possibly because "this is America," and she is White. In spite of the privilege Whites receive in a racially stratified society and the

legacy of discrimination against people of color, this example of claiming discrimination or "reverse racism" is a noted strategy employed by some Whites who believe people of color are responsible for taking college slots, jobs, and promotions from Whites. As Eduardo Bonilla-Silva explains, such "racial stories" of not getting jobs because of people of color help "make sense of the world but in ways that reinforce the status quo, serving particular interests without appearing to do so" (2006, 75). Despite such racial stories, the number of reverse discrimination cases actually filed with the Equal Employment Opportunity Commission is small and the majority of the cases are rejected for lack of any foundation (83).

Nancy Gardiner's description of applying to a tutoring center reflects her framework of ignoring and asserting White privilege:

I found it very interesting that when I went into the interview, everybody was Asian. People at the reception desk were speaking Chinese to the parents coming in. Again, I thought, "Oh my gosh." It's like I grew up and moved to another country. I thought, "Oh boy, it's not going to work here either."

Although this is a private tutoring business run by members of the Chinese community, Nancy was enraged when she saw who participated in the center and that Chinese was being spoken to parents. This space did not fit her white image of the United States, even though there has been a long Chinese presence in this country, especially in California. As she did throughout her interview, Gardiner defends White privilege by proclaiming an exclusionary definition of America and Americanness belonging to and populated by Whites and English speakers.

When Nancy Gardiner's assumptions that she would not be hired at the center were disproved, she celebrates what she perceives as her niche—inverting the reality that the English language is hegemonic:

But in the interview with the president of the company, she was very complimentary; she was very impressed. She wanted to hire me . . . One of the things she said was that they were interested in me being a teacher because I was a native English speaker. I am going, "Wow!" There is a market for me somewhere . . . I finally decided there are so many languages around me that my strength is on the native English speaker.

While a cultural hierarchy within the United States positions the English language over other languages, Gardiner seems to believe that the power of the English language and her role in education is threatened. She resolves this concern by embracing a belief that she has a value that others have somehow not yet realized—she is a "native English speaker."

Gardiner is unique in the amount of time she devoted during her interview to revealing her White privilege and concurrent sense of entitlement. Most staffuly said nothing about white advantage individually or institutionally. At SCHS, where Asian Americans and Latinas/os are consistently talked about, this silence surrounding whiteness and White privilege are obvious. As Frankenberg writes, "Whites are the nondefined definers of other people" (1993, 197). Such silences surrounding whiteness and White privilege are damaging. They lead to the overlooking of the macro-meso-micro factors perpetuating white supremacist practices such as assimilationist expectations. Likewise, they simultaneously advantage those who fit dominant constructions of whiteness—such as being light skinned, speaking English, being born in the United States—and disadvantage those outside of this socially constructed norm.

Silences Surrounding the School Culture

Along with not recognizing their own positionalities, most White staffuly said little about the school culture and the multiple factors influencing it. Absent was a critique of the power structure and the racial/ethnic gap between the staffuly and students. At SCHS, three-quarters of the administrators and half of the teachers are White. In contrast, 90 percent of the students are of color (California Department of Education 2008). As illustrated throughout this chapter, this racial/ethnic gap between the staffuly and students may be one of the factors fueling the school culture with deficiency and assimilationist perspectives. These perspectives are known to inhibit understanding of students and to impede more inclusionary approaches in schools (Sleeter 1993). As Valenzuela also found when analyzing the gaps between teachers and students in her Texas high school study, "Teachers see the differences in culture and language between themselves and their students from a culturally chauvinistic perspective that permits them to dismiss the possibility of a more culturally relevant approach in dealing with this population" (1999, 66). While changing the racial/ethnic demographics of school officials is not the answer to altering perspectives and the campus climate, studies suggest that increasing the percentage of teachers of color may have a positive effect on race/ethnic relations in schools by better addressing inequalities (Goldsmith 2004; Ochoa 2007). As will become apparent in the forthcoming chapters, the silences surrounding the school culture at SCHS compounded with an acceptance of power-evasive perspectives allow for the continuance of Eurocentric course curriculum and school activities.

Overall, power-evasive frameworks such as these biological and cultural arguments and the absence of an interrogation of whiteness are dangerous for what they expose, justify, and camouflage. They reveal deep-seated biases that are rooted in larger ideologies that dichotomize, homogenize, and perpetuate hierarchies. Biological and cultural deficiencies justify inequality and shape everyday perceptions and interactions, including how staffuly perceive students. They can become self-fulfilling, especially when the focus in education is on standardized tests and students' worth is simply defined by quantitative measurements. Similarly, the absence of a discussion of standardized tests and whiteness prevent an analysis of their impacts on student learning and the campus dynamics. As detailed in the upcoming chapters, students experience the power of these constructs to the point that most Asian American participants reference the limiting expectation that they be "model minorities" while Latina/o students often discuss being seen as "troublemakers." As long as such confining categorizations persist and remain uncontested, dominant discourses will inhibit the discussions necessary for dismantling larger injustices. The causes and justifications of disparities and divisions will remain intact.

To more thoroughly understand the factors influencing students' educational experiences, chapters 2 through 5 focus on the school structures, practices, and everyday dynamics that work in conjunction with the dominant discourses presented in this chapter to influence students' opportunities and peer relations. By interrogating dominant discourses and educational practices, we are better positioned to reconstruct paradigms and rebuild institutions in the movement to change exclusionary perceptions and create more equitable realities.

41

Naughty by Nature

ANN ARNETT FERGUSON

Two representations of black masculinity are widespread in society and school today. They are the images of the African American male as a criminal and as an endangered species. These images are routinely used as resources to interpret and explain behavior by teachers at Rosa Parks School when they make punishment decisions. An ensemble of historical meanings and their social effects is contained within these images.

The image of the black male criminal is more familiar because of its prevalence in the print and electronic media as well as in scholarly work. The headlines of newspaper articles and magazines sound the alarm dramatically as the presence of black males in public space has come to signify danger and a threat to personal safety. But this is not just media hype. Bleak statistics give substance to the figure of the criminal. Black males are disproportionately in jails: they make up 6 percent of the population of the United States, but 45 percent of the inmates in state and federal prisons; they are imprisoned at six times the rate of whites.[1] In the state of California, one-third of African American men in their twenties are in prison, on parole, or on probation, in contrast to 5 percent of white males in the same age group. This is nearly five times the number who attend four-year colleges in the state.[2] The mortality rate for African American boys fourteen years of age and under is approximately 50 percent higher than for the comparable group of white male youth, with the leading cause of death being homicide.[3]

The second image, that of the black male as an endangered species, is one which has largely emanated from African American social scientists and journalists who are deeply concerned about the criminalization and high mortality rate among African American youth.[4] It represents him as being marginalized to the point of oblivion. While this discourse emanates from a sympathetic perspective, in the final analysis the focus is all too often on individual maladaptive behavior and black mothering practices as the problem rather than on the social structure in which this endangerment occurs.

These two cultural representations are rooted in actual material conditions and reflect existing social conditions and relations that they appear to sum up for us. They are lodged in theories, in commonsense understandings of self in relation to others in the world as well as in popular culture and the media. But they are condensations, extrapolations, that emphasize certain elements and gloss over others. They represent a narrow selection from the multiplicity, the heterogeneity of actual relations in society.

Since both of these images come to be used for identifying, classification, and decision making by teachers at Rosa Parks School, it is necessary to analyze the

Ann Arnett Ferguson, "Naughty by Nature," from *Bad Boys: Public Schools and the Making of Black Masculinity.* Copyright © 2000, The University of Michigan Press. Reprinted with permission.

manner in which these images, or cultural representations of difference, are produced through a racial discursive formation. Then we can explain how they are utilized by teachers in the exercise of school rules to produce a context in which African American boys become more visible, more culpable as "rulebreakers."

A central element of a racist discursive formation is the production of subjects as essentially different by virtue of their "race." Historically, the circulation of images that represent this difference has been a powerful technique in this production.[5] Specifically, blacks have been represented as essentially different from whites, as the constitutive Other that regulates and confirms "whiteness." Images of Africans as savage, animalistic, subhuman without history or culture—the diametric opposite of that of Europeans—rationalized and perpetuated a system of slavery. After slavery was abolished, images of people of African descent as hypersexual, shiftless, lazy, and of inferior intellect, legitimated a system that continued to deny right of citizenship to blacks on the basis of race difference. This regime of truth about race was articulated through scientific experiments and "discoveries," law, social custom, popular culture, folklore, and common sense. And for three hundred years, from the seventeenth century to the middle of the twentieth century, this racial distinction was policed through open and unrestrained physical violence. The enforcement of race difference was conscious, overt, and institutionalized.

In the contemporary period, the production of a racial Other and the constitution and regulation of racial difference has worked increasingly through mass-produced images that are omnipresent in our lives. At this moment in time it is through culture—or culturalism[6]—that difference is primarily asserted. This modern-day form for producing racism specifically operates through symbolic violence and representations of Blackness that circulate through the mass media, cinematic images and popular music, rather than through the legal forms of the past. The representational becomes a potent vehicle for the transmission of racial meanings that reproduce relations of difference, of division, and of power. These "controlling images" make "racism, sexism, and poverty appear to be natural, normal, and an inevitable part of everyday life."[7]

CULTURAL REPRESENTATIONS OF "DIFFERENCE"

The behavior of African American boys in school is perceived by adults at Rosa Parks School through a filter of overlapping representations of three socially invented categories of "difference": age, gender, and race. These are grounded in the commonsense, taken-for-granted notion that existing social divisions reflect biological and natural dispositional differences among humans: so children are essentially different from adults, males from females, blacks from whites.[8] At the intersection of this complex of subject positions are African American boys who are doubly displaced: as black children, they are not seen as childlike but adultified; as black males, they are denied the masculine dispensation constituting white males as being "naturally naughty" and are discerned as willfully bad. Let us look more closely at this displacement.

The dominant cultural representation of childhood is as closer to nature, as less social, less human. Childhood is assumed to be a stage of development: culture, morality, sociability is written on children in an unfolding process by adults (who are seen as fully "developed," made by culture not nature) in institutions like family and school. On the one hand, children are assumed to be dissembling, devious, because they are more egocentric. On the other hand, there is an attribution of innocence to their wrongdoing. In both cases, this is understood to be a temporary condition, a stage prior to maturity. So they must be socialized to fully understand the meaning of their acts.

The language used to describe "children in general" by educators illustrates this paradox. At one districtwide workshop for adult school volunteers that I attended, children were described by the classroom teacher running the workshop as being "like little plants, they need attention, they gobble it up." Later in the session, the same presenter invoked the other dominant representation of children as devious, manipulative, and powerful. "They'll run a number on you. They're little lawyers, con artists, manipulators—and they usually win. They're good at it. Their strategy is to get you off task. They pull you into their whirlwind."

These two versions of childhood express the contradictory qualities that adults map onto their interactions with children in general. The first description of children as "little plants," childhood as identical with nature, is embedded in the ideology of childhood. The second version that presents children as powerful, as self-centered, with an agenda and purpose of their own, arises out of the experience adults have exercising authority over children. In actual relations of power, in a twist, as children become the objects of control, they become devious "con artists" and adults become innocent, pristine in relation to them. In both instances, childhood has been constructed as different in essence from adulthood, as a phase of biological, psychological, and social development with predictable attributes.

Even though we treat it this way, the category "child" does not describe and contain a homogeneous and naturally occurring group of individuals at a certain stage of human development. The social meaning of childhood has changed profoundly over time.[9] What it means to be a child varies dramatically by virtue of location in cross-cutting categories of class, gender, and race.[10]

Historically, the existence of African American children has been constituted differently through economic practices, the law, social policy, and visual imagery. This difference has been projected in an ensemble of images of black youth as not childlike. In the early decades of this century, representations of black children as pickaninnies depicted them as verminlike, voracious, dirty, grinning, animal-like savages. They were also depicted as the laugh-provoking butt of aggressive, predatory behavior; natural victims, therefore victimizable. An example of this was their depiction in popular lore as "alligator bait." Objects such as postcards, souvenir spoons, letter-openers and cigar-box labels were decorated with figures of half-naked black children vainly attempting to escape the open toothy jaws of hungry alligators.[11]

Today's representations of black children still bear traces of these earlier depictions. The media demonization of very young black boys who are charged with committing serious crimes is one example. In these cases there is rarely the collective soul-searching for answers to the question of how "kids like this" could have committed these acts that occurs when white kids are involved. Rather, the answer to the question seems to be inherent in the disposition of the kids themselves.[12] The image of the young black male as an endangered species revitalizes the animalistic trope. Positioned as part of nature, his essence is described through

language otherwise reserved for wildlife that has been decimated to the point of extinction. Characterized as a "species," they are cut off from other members of family and community and isolated as a form of prey.

There is continuity, but there is a significant new twist to the images. The endangered species and the criminal are mirror images. Either as criminal perpetrator or as endangered victim, contemporary imagery proclaims black males to be responsible for their fate. The discourse of individual choice and responsibility elides the social and economic context and locates predation as coming from within. It is their own maladaptive and inappropriate behavior that causes African Americans to self-destruct. As an endangered species, they are stuck in an obsolete stage of social evolution, unable to adapt to the present. As criminals, they are a threat to themselves, to each other, as well as to society in general.

As black children's behavior is refracted through the lens of these two cultural images, it is "adultified." By this I mean their transgressions are made to take on a sinister, intentional, fully conscious tone that is stripped of any element of childish naïveté. The discourse of childhood as an unfolding developmental stage in the life cycle is displaced in this mode of framing school trouble. Adultification is visible in the way African American elementary school pupils are talked about by school adults.

One of the teachers, a white woman who prided herself on the multicultural emphasis in her classroom, invoked the image of African American children as "looters" in lamenting the disappearance of books from the class library. This characterization is especially meaningful because her statement, which was made at the end of the school year that had included the riots in Los Angeles, invoked that event as a framework for making children's behavior intelligible.

> I've lost so many library books this term. There are quite a few kids who don't have any books at home, so I let them borrow them. I didn't sign them out because I thought I could trust the kids. I sent a letter home to parents asking them to look for them and turn them in. But none have come in. I just don't feel the same. *It's just like the looting in Los Angeles.*

By identifying those who don't have books at home as "looters," the teacher has excluded the white children in the class, who all come from more middle-class backgrounds so, it is assumed, "have books at home." In the case of the African American kids, what might be interpreted as the careless behavior of children is displaced by images of adult acts of theft that conjure up violence and mayhem. The African American children in this teacher's classroom and their families are seen not in relation to images of childhood, but in relation to the television images of crowds rampaging through South Central Los Angeles in the aftermath of the verdict of the police officers who beat Rodney King. Through this frame, the children embody a willful, destructive, and irrational disregard for property rather than simple carelessness. Racial difference is mediated through culturalism: blacks are understood as a group undifferentiated by age or status with the proclivity and values to disregard the rights and welfare of others.

Adultification is a central mechanism in the interpretive framing of gender roles. African American girls are constituted as different through this process. A notion of sexual passivity and innocence that prevails for white female children is displaced by the image of African American females as sexual beings: as immanent mothers, girlfriends, and sexual partners of the boys in the room.[13] Though these girls may be strong, assertive, or troublesome, teachers evaluate their potential in ways that attribute to them an inevitable, potent sexuality that flares up early and that, according to one teacher, lets them permit men to run all over them, to take advantage of them. An incident in the Punishing Room that I recorded in my field notes made visible the way that adult perceptions of youthful behavior were filtered through racial representations. African American boys and girls who misbehaved were not just breaking a rule out of high spirits and needing to be chastised for the act, but were adultified, gendered figures whose futures were already inscribed and foreclosed within a racial order:

> Two girls, Adila and a friend, burst into the room followed by Miss Benton a black sixth-grade teacher and a group of five African American boys from her class. Miss Benton is yelling at the girls because they have been jumping in the hallway and one has knocked down part of a display on the bulletin board which she and her class put up the day before. She is yelling at the two girls about how they're wasting time. This is what she says: "You're doing exactly what they want

you to do. You're playing into their hands. Look at me! Next going to be tracking you."

> One of the girls asks her rather sullenly who "they" is.

> Miss Benton is furious. "Society, that's who. You should be leading the class, not fooling around jumping around in the hallway. Someone has to give pride to the community. All the black men are on drugs, or in jail, or killing each other. Someone has got to hold it together. And the women have to do it. And you're jumping up and down in the hallway."

I wonder what the black boys who have followed in the wake of the drama make of this assessment of their future, seemingly already etched in stone. The teacher's words to the girls are supposed to inspire them to leadership. The message for the boys is a dispiriting one.

Tracks have already been laid down for sixth-grade girls toward a specifically feminized responsibility (and, what is more prevalent, blame) for the welfare of the community, while males are bound for jail as a consequence of their own socially and self-destructive acts.

There is a second displacement from the norm in the representation of black males. The hegemonic, cultural image of the essential "nature" of males is that they are different from females in the meaning of their acts. Boys will be boys: they are mischievous, they get into trouble, they can stand up for themselves. This vision of masculinity is rooted in the notion of an essential sex difference based on biology, hormones, uncontrollable urges, true personalities. Boys are naturally more physical, more active. Boys are naughty by *nature*. There is something suspect about the boy who is "too docile," "like a girl." As a result, rule breaking on the part of boys is looked at as something-they-can't-help, a natural expression of masculinity in a civilizing process.

This incitement of boys to be "boylike" is deeply inscribed in our mainstream culture, winning hearts and stirring imaginations in the way that the pale counterpart, the obedient boy, does not. . . .

African American boys are not accorded the masculine dispensation of being "naturally" naughty. Instead the school reads their expression and display of masculine naughtiness as a sign of an inherent vicious, insubordinate nature that as a threat to order must be controlled. Consequently, school adults view any display of masculine mettle on the part of these boys through body language or verbal rejoinders as a sign of insubordination. In confrontation with adults, what is required from them is a performance of absolute docility that goes against the grain of masculinity. Black boys are expected to internalize a ritual obeisance in such exchanges so that the performance of docility appears to come naturally. According to the vice principal, "These children have to learn not to talk back. They must know that if the adult says you're wrong, then you're wrong. They must not resist, must go along with it, and take their punishment," he says.

This is not a lesson that all children are required to learn, however. The disciplining of the body within school rules has specific race and gender overtones. For black boys, the enactment of docility is a preparation for adult racialized survival rituals of which the African American adults in the school are especially cognizant. For African American boys bodily forms of expressiveness have repercussions in the world outside the chain-link fence of the school. The body must be taught to endure humiliation in preparation for future enactments of submission. The vice principal articulated the racialized texture of decorum when he deplored one of the Troublemakers', Lamar's, propensity to talk back and argue with teachers.

Lamar had been late getting into line at the end of recess, and the teacher had taken away his football. Lamar argued and so the teacher gave him detention. Mr. Russell spelled out what an African American male needed to learn about confrontations with power.

> Look, I've told him before about getting into these show-down situations—where he either has to show off to save face, then if he doesn't get his way then he goes wild. He won't get away with it in this school. Not with me, not with Mr. Harmon. But I know he's going to try it somewhere outside and it's going to get him in *real* trouble. He has to learn to ignore, to walk away, not to get into power struggles.

Mr. Russell's objective is to hammer into Lamar's head what he believes is the essential lesson for young black males to learn if they are to get anywhere in life: to act out obeisance is to survive. The specter of the Rodney King beating by the Los Angeles Police Department provided the backdrop for this conversation, as the trial of the police officers had just begun. The defense lawyer for the LAPD was arguing that Rodney King could have stopped the beating at any time if he had chosen.

This apprehension of black boys as inherently different both in terms of character and of their place in the social order is a crucial factor in teacher disciplinary practices. . . .

Let us examine now more closely some widespread modes of categorizing African American boys, the normalizing judgments that they circulate, and the consequences these have on disciplinary intervention and punishment.

BEING "AT-RISK": IDENTIFYING PRACTICE

The range of normalizing judgments for African American males is bounded by the image of the ideal pupil at one end of the spectrum and the unsalvageable student who is criminally inclined at the other end. The ideal type of student is characterized here by a white sixth-grade teacher:

> Well, it consists of, first of all, to be able to follow directions. Any direction that I give. Whether it's get this out, whether it's put this away, whether it's turn to this page or whatever, they follow it, and they come in and they're ready to work. It doesn't matter high skill or low skill, they're ready to work and they know that's what they're here for. Behaviorally, they're appropriate all day long. When it's time for them to listen, they listen. The way I see it, by sixth grade, the ideal student is one that can sit and listen and learn from me—work with their peers, and take responsibility on themselves and understand what is next, what is expected of them.

This teacher, however, drew on the image of the Good Bad Boy when she described the qualities of her "ideal" male student, a white boy in her class. Here the docility of the generic ideal student becomes the essentially naughty-by-nature male:

> He's not really Goody Two-shoes, you know. He's not quiet and perfect. He'll take risks. He'll say the wrong answer. He'll fool around and have to be reprimanded in class. There's a nice balance to him.

The modal category for African American boys is "at-risk" of failure. The concept of "at-riskness" is central to a discourse about the contemporary crisis in urban schools in America that explains children's failure as largely the consequence of their attitudes and behaviors as well as those of their families. In early stages of schooling they are identified as "at-risk" of failing, as "at-risk" of being school drop-outs. The category has been invested with enormous power to identify, explain, and predict futures. For example, a white fifth-grade teacher told me with sincere concern that as she looked around at her class, she could feel certain that about only four out of the twenty-one students would eventually graduate from high school. Each year, she said, it seemed to get worse.

Images of family play a strong role in teacher assessments and decisions about at-risk children. These enter into the evaluative process to confirm an original judgment. Families of at-risk children are said to lack parental skills; they do not give their children the kind of support that would build "self-esteem" necessary for school achievement. But this knowledge of family is superficial, inflamed by cultural representations and distorted through a rumor mill.

The children themselves are supposed to betray the lack of love and attention at home through their own "needy" behavior in the classroom. According to the teachers, these are pupils who are always demanding attention and will work well only in one-to-one or small-group situations because of this neglect at home. They take up more than their share of time and space. Donel, one of the African American boys who has been identified as at-risk by the school, is described by his teacher:

> He's a boy with a lot of energy and usually uncontrolled energy. He's very loud in the classroom, very inappropriate in the class. He has a great sense of humor, but again it's inappropriate. I would say most of the time that his mouth is open, it's inappropriate, it's too loud, it's disrupting. But other than that [dry laugh] he's a great kid. You know if I didn't have to teach him, if it was a recreational setting, it would be fine.

So Donel is marked as "inappropriate" through the very configuration of self that school rules regulate: bodies, language, presentation of self. The stringent exercise of what is deemed appropriate as an instrument of assessment of at-riskness governs how the behavior of a child is understood. The notion of appropriate behavior in describing the ideal pupil earlier, and here as a way of characterizing a Troublemaker, reveals the broad latitude for interpretation and cultural framing of events. For one boy, "fooling around" behavior provides the balance between being a "real" boy and

being a "goody-goody," while for the other, the conduct is seen through a different lens as "inappropriate," "loud," "disruptive."

Once a child is labeled "at-risk," he becomes more visible within the classroom, more likely to be singled out and punished for rule-breaking activity. An outburst by an African American boy already labeled as "at-risk" was the occasion for him to be singled out and made an example of the consequences of bad behavior before an audience of his peers; this was an occasion for a teacher to (re)mark the identity of a boy as disruptive. . . .

. . . Once a reputation has been established, the boy's behavior is usually refigured within a framework that is no longer about childish misdemeanors but comes to be an ominous portent of things to come. They are tagged with futures: "He's on the fast track to San Quentin Prison," and "That one has a jail-cell with his name on it." For several reasons, these boys are more likely to be singled out and punished than other children. They are more closely watched. They are more likely to be seen as intentionally doing wrong than a boy who is considered to be a Good Bad Boy. Teachers are more likely to use the "moral principle" in determining whether to call attention to misdemeanors because "at-risk" children need discipline, but also as an example to the group, especially to other African American boys who are "endangered." The possibility of contagion must be eliminated. Those with reputations must be isolated, kept away from the others. Kids are told to stay away from them: "You know what will happen if you go over there." In the case of boys with reputations, minor infractions are more likely to escalate into major punishments.

UNSALVAGEABLE STUDENTS

In the range of normalizing judgments, there is a group of African American boys identified by school personnel as, in the words of a teacher, "insalvageable." This term and the condition it speaks to is specifically about masculinity. School personnel argue over whether these unsalvageable boys should be given access even to the special programs designed for those who are failing in school. Should resources, defined as scarce, be wasted on these boys for whom there is no hope? Should energy and money be put instead into children who can be saved? I have heard teachers argue on both sides of the question. These "boys for whom there is no hope" get caught up in the school's punishment system: surveillance, isolation, detention, and ever more severe punishment.

These are children who are not children. These are boys who are already men. So a discourse that positions masculinity as "naturally" naughty is reframed for African American boys around racialized representations of gendered subjects. They come to stand as if already adult, bearers of adult fates inscribed within a racial order.

NOTES

1. *New York Times*, September 13, 1994, 1.

2. *Los Angeles Times*, November 2, 1990, 3.

3. G. Jaynes and R. Williams Jr., eds., *A Common Destiny: Blacks in American Society* (Washington, D.C.: National Academic Press, 1989), 405, 498.

4. See, for example, Jewelle Taylor Gibbs, "Young Black Males in America: Endangered, Embittered, and Embattled," in Jewelle Taylor Gibbs et al., *Young, Black, and Male in America: An Endangered Species* (New York: Auburn House, 1988); Richard Majors and Janer Mancini Billson, *Cool Pose: The Dilemmas of Black Manhood in America* (New York: Lexington Press, 1992); Jawanza Kunjufu, *Countering the Conspiracy to Destroy Black Boys,* 2 vols. (Chicago: African American Images, 1985).

5. See, for example, W. E. B. Du Bois, *Souls of Black Folk* (1903); reprint, New York: Bantam, 1989): Frantz Fanon, *Black Skins, White Masks,* trans. Charles Lam Markmann (New York: Grove Press, 1967): Stuart Hall, "The Rediscovery of 'Ideology': Return of the Repressed in Media Studies," in *Culture, Society, and the Media,* ed. Michael Gurevitch et al. (New York: Methuen, 1982); Leith Mullings, "Images, Ideology, and Women of Color," in *Women of Color in U.S. Society,* ed. Maxine Baca Zinn and Bonnie Thornton Dill (Philadelphia: Temple University Press, 1994); Edward Said, *Orientalism* (New York: Vintage, 1978).

6. Gilroy, *Small Acts,* 24, argues that "the culturalism of the new racism has gone hand in hand with a definition of race as a matter of difference rather than a question of hierarchy."

7. Collins, *Black Feminist Thought,* 68.

8. While many of the staff at Rosa Parks School would agree at an abstract level that social divisions of gender and race are culturally and historically produced, their actual talk about these social distinctions as well as their everyday expectations, perceptions, and interactions affirm the notion that these categories reflect intrinsic, *real* differences.

9. See, for example, Phillipe Ariès, *Centuries of Childhood: A Social History of Family Life* (New York: Vintage, 1962).

10. Thorne, *Gender Play;* and Valerie Polakow, *Lives on the Edge: Single Mothers and Their Children in the Other America* (Chicago: University of Chicago Press, 1993).

11. Patricia Turner, *Ceramic Uncles and Celluloid Mammies: Black Images and Their Influence on Culture* (New York: Anchor, 1994), 36.

12. A particularly racist and pernicious example of this was the statement by the administrator of the Alcohol, Drug Abuse, and Mental Health Administration. Dr. Frederick K. Goodwin, who stated without any qualms: "If you look, for example, at male monkeys, especially in the wild, roughly half of them survive to adulthood. The other half die by violence. That is the natural way of it for males, to knock each other off and, in fact, there are some interesting evolutionary implications. . . . The same hyper aggressive monkeys who kill each other are also hyper sexual, so they copulate more and therefore they reproduce more to offset the fact that half of them are dying." He then drew an analogy with the "high impact [of] inner city areas with the loss of some of the civilizing evolutionary things that we have built up. . . . Maybe it isn't just the careless use of the word when people call certain areas of certain cities, jungles." Quoted in Jerome G. Miller, *Search and Destroy: African American Males in the Criminal Justice System* (New York: Cambridge University Press, 1996), 212–13.

13. The consensus among teachers in the school about educational inequity focuses on sexism. Many of the teachers speak seriously and openly about their concern that girls are being treated differently than boys in school: girls are neglected in the curriculum, overlooked in classrooms, underencouraged academically, and harassed by boys. A number of recent studies support the concern that even the well-intentioned teacher tends to spend less classroom time with girls because boys demand so much of their attention. These studies generally gloss over racial difference as well as make the assumption that *quantity* rather than *quality* of attention is the key factor in fostering positive sense of self in academic setting. See, for example, Myra Sadker and David Sadker, *Failing at Fairness: How America's Schools Cheat Girls* (New York: C. Scribner's Sons, 1994). Linda Grant looks at both race and gender as she examines the roles that first- and second-grade African American girls play in desegregated classrooms. She finds that African American girls and white girls are positioned quite differently vis-à-vis teachers. In the classrooms she observed, white girls were called upon to play an academic role in comparison with African American girls, who were cast in the role of teacher's helpers, in monitoring and controlling other kids in the room, and as intermediaries between peers. She concluded that black girls were encouraged in stereotypical female adult roles that stress service and nurture, while white girls were encouraged to press toward high academic achievement. Most important for this study, Grant mentions in passing that black boys in the room receive the most consistent negative attention and were assessed as having a lower academic ability than any other group by teachers. See Linda Grant, "Helpers, Enforcers, and Go-Betweens: Black Females in Elementary School Classrooms," in *Women of Color in U.S. Society,* ed. Maxine Baca Zinn and Bonnie Thornton Dill (Philadelphia: University of Pennsylvania Press, 1994).

42

Girls, Race, and Identity

Border Work between Classes

Many school ethnographies are comparative studies of students across class categories and make generalizations about the experiences of middle-class students and of working-class students. In order to speak about these class categories as if they are two clearly distinct peer groupings, one must ignore many students who are exceptions to the rule that class origin equates to class future. While the correlation is strong between parents' socioeconomic status and a student's membership in a middle- or working-class peer group, tracking experience, academic achievement, and consequent class future, it is imperfect, and there are always at least a handful of working-class students who are college-prep and upwardly mobile and a handful of middle-class students who are on the vocational track and downwardly mobile. Nonetheless, because research generally tends to highlight patterns, such cases are typically ignored, precisely because they are exceptions to the rule. . . .

In this chapter I want to focus on those few girls, both white and Mexican-American, who were from working-class origins but who were upwardly mobile middle-class performers in high school, en route to achieving a university education, and to ask what we might learn from their exceptionalism. Foregrounding these exceptions to the rule, I explore what their experience might reveal about the way in which race ethnicity and gender, as autonomous axes of social inequality, intersect with class. . . .

The . . . question is *how* they do it. How do they negotiate the disparity between the working-class identity acquired from home and the performance of a middle-class identity at school, the disparity between their family lives and the family lives of their middle-class peers? What is the subjective experience of class passing, of "choosing" upward mobility and all that comes with it? . . .

WHITE GIRLS: CONTINGENT ROUTES TO MOBILITY

I met Staci during a slow day in the yearbook class. Most of the students were working on various aspects of pulling that year's annual together, but Staci felt she needed to put her energy elsewhere on this day and was headed to the library to look up some information for a history paper due at the end of the week. Staci's membership in the prep crowd was unusual, given her parents' economic and cultural capital. Her father worked "doing maintenance" at a retirement community. But the fact that her mother worked for a time in the kitchen at the private elementary school in town enabled Staci to receive a subsidized private school education,

In Julie Bettie, *Women without Class: Girls, Race, and Identity.* Copyright © 2003 University of California Press. Reprinted by permission.

and she ran with the most academically elite crowd of girls at the school.

Like Staci, Heather had also attended private school but not with a subsidy, and it was difficult to understand how her parents could have afforded it. Her father worked as a mechanic and her mother as a nurse's aide. Between them they were nearing middle-income, but most Waretown families in this category were not sending their kids to private schools. As I pushed for a clearer explanation, she indicated that her parents experienced great financial sacrifice in order to send her to school, even borrowing money from relatives, but they felt it was worth it. According to her, her parents wanted to segregate her from "bad influences." This turned out to be a euphemism for Mexican-American students.

Likewise, Jennifer told me that while her parents had been able to afford to send her to private elementary school, they could not afford to send her brother too. Instead, they arranged for him to attend school in a neighboring town, and, once again, the reason was to avoid "bad influences." . . .

Mandy was also college-prep, although her membership among these girls was even more difficult to explain. She had not attended private elementary school yet did reasonably well academically in junior high and managed to get in with the prep crowd by high school. . . .

At times, . . . an individual girls academic motivation seemed to come from defining herself in opposition to older brothers who were labeled delinquent and who, as the girls had witnessed, caused their parent(s) angst. It seemed that feminine norms sometimes allowed girls to forgo the delinquent paths their brothers might have felt compelled to follow as working-class boys, the need to engage in rituals of proving masculinity. I heard this story frequently enough, among both white and Mexican-American girls, that I began to suspect that working-class girls might experience a certain advantage over their male counterparts as a consequence of being girls. The social pressure for girls to conform and follow rules as part of the definition of femininity makes it a possibility that they might do better in school than working-class boys, for whom defining manhood includes more pressure to engage in risk-taking behavior and overt resistance to control. Girls may not only be less likely to engage in such activities but are relatively less likely to be labeled and punished as delinquents if they do (although this was somewhat less true for Mexican-American girls). That working-class girls might actually do better academically than working-class boys is a possibility easily missed by those taking an additive analytical approach to race, class, and gender as social forces. Such an approach would simply presume that girls' educational experiences and opportunities are in all cases "worse" than boys', rather than exploring the unique set of challenges girls face. . . .

Liz articulated yet another route to mobility. When I asked how it was that she came to be a part of her college-prep friendship circle, she explained that early on she discovered that she was good at basketball, and it was through this sport that she met and began to spend time with girls who were far more privileged than she was. Through association with high achievers, she was exposed to information that helped her get ahead. Overhearing conversations about college requirements and college-prep courses made her aware of the existence of two tracks of schooling and what she was missing out on. She clung to a middle-class girl, Amber, her best friend, hoping, it seemed, that she might "catch" the middle-classness Amber took for granted. Unable to name her desire as class envy, she simply said, "I'd like to be in a situation like that." . . .

WHITE GIRLS: BECOMING UPWARDLY MOBILE

Common among those girls whose families were much more working-class than the families of their closest friends was their nascent awareness of the difference between these class cultures. Class is a relational identity; awareness of class difference is dependent upon the class and race geography of the environment in which one lives and moves. While the community of one's formative years and schooling experiences, in particular, may be key shapers of one's perceptions of class difference, awareness of one's location in a class hierarchy is an ongoing and context-specific process. Beverley Skeggs (1997), in her semi-autobiographical book, explains that because her childhood was spent in a class-segregated community, "My first real recognition that I could be categorized by others as working-class happened when I went to university. . . . For the first time in my life I started to feel insecure. All the prior cultural knowledge [capital] in which I had taken pride lost its value, and I entered a world where I knew little and felt I could communicate even less." The working-class, upwardly mobile girls I met, by virtue of their location in mixed-class peer groups, had an earlier awareness of class distinctions, although they did not often name those differences as such.

In other words, upward mobility might occur at various points in life. As they acquire cultural and economic capital at different ages, upwardly mobiles begin passing in middle-class contexts at different times. Where Skeggs only began passing upon entry into college, some of the girls I knew began in junior high, and those with private school educations, in elementary school. Given that Staci has been part of a middle-class peer group since her private elementary school education, even though she is from a working-class family, her experience of college will likely be far different than the one Skeggs describes for herself. . . .

Geographic variability shapes the likelihood of class mobility. Being working-class and attending a well-funded school with a middle-class clientele where a curriculum of knowledge that is highly valued by society is made available is a far different experience than attending school in an isolated working-class community where the mere exposure to a college-prep curriculum is limited. Upwardly mobile girls from Waretown will likely develop an even greater awareness of class difference when they leave this agricultural community behind.

Due to their location in a college-prep rather than a vocational curriculum, these upwardly mobile working-class girls at times showed a clearer understanding of the fact of class differences than did their vocational counterparts. Liz was one of very few students I met who actually named herself as "working-class."

JULIE: You said you were "working-class" earlier. Where did you get that term, what does it mean?

LIZ: I learned it in a social science class or maybe in history. Working-class is like the serfs you know, the working-class are the majority, blue-collar versus the college-educated. . . .

Unlike working-class girls who were segregated in vocational tracks and so were rarely in mixed-class settings or peer groups, those working-class girls who were middle-class performers were not *as* mystified by the success of preps. By virtue of crossing, they could see the advantages and privileges their middle-class friends experienced. They were more acutely aware of the cultural differences based on class, as they found themselves exposed to the children of middle-class professionals in the college-prep curriculum, on the basketball court, in student government, and in middle-class homes. They could see the reasons why they had to work harder, and they were less likely to attribute friends' success to some innate difference between them. . . .

These girls also perceived that they had to work exceptionally hard to earn their high school diploma and to get into college relative to their middle-class friends. As Staci said,

> They've always been kind of handed everything, that they've never really had to think about their future, and I was always, like, I don't want my future to be like my parents. And, I mean, that was like a big influence on me, I mean, my goal is I don't ever want to have to worry about money, like we have all my life. My friends never had to deal with that or anything and, it's just like everything has always been handed to them, and they, I mean, they never knew anything else.
>
> I want to go to college and get a good education so I can have a better life, and they have always had a good life. I work my butt off, but it just seems easier for them. It's just always everything has always kinda been there for them. . . .

Moreover, these girls were aware of the fact that they exceeded their parents' educational level early on, and they perceived the fact that their parents were unable to help them with school as a handicap. As Mandy explained,

> Ever since I've been in honors classes, I've always been around these people, you know, their parents have advanced degrees and everything else. My parents were never able to help me out with math. Once I entered algebra, that was it, that was as far as they could help me. I remember one time in this one class we had this project, we had to build something. One girl's father was an architect, and her father designed and basically built the entire project for her. We all had these dinky little things, and she's got this palace!

Later, however, she attempted to define her parents' lack of education as an asset.

I mean, I was never mad at my parents because they couldn't help me. I was actually happy, because once we get to college, you're not gonna call your parents up and say "Hey, Dad, can you design this for me?" You're on your own then. And so I've always had to work on my own with my schoolwork, it was always on my own, whereas other students, they always had their parents standing right there, you know? . . .

These middle-class-performing working-class girls were . . . readily able to see the differences between their own parents and those of their friends. They were painfully aware of the fact that their friends' parents viewed their own parents with indifference at best, disdain at worst.

. . . I sat next to Heather at a girls' basketball game one evening. She was sitting on the bleachers with the rest of her prep friends, front and center, cheering on the team, many of whom were part of their peer group. She kept glancing at the corner of the gym where several adults were standing, people who had come after halftime (when admission was free) to watch for a few minutes but weren't committed enough to staying to take a spot on the bleachers. I asked her if she was expecting someone, and she whispered, "My dad said he might stop by and check the score. I hope he doesn't." . . .

Where I first thought the idea of her father attending the game represented the standard embarrassment teens experience in relationship to having their parents near them at social events, I recognized later that its meaning went beyond this for her. In the middle-class milieu of the school, some parents are more embarrassing than others.

MEXICAN-AMERICAN GIRLS: CONTINGENT ROUTES TO MOBILITY

There was a small group of Mexican-American girls, mostly second generation but also including two girls who had immigrated, who were from poor and working-class families and who were exceptional in that they did not identify with the [vocational students] but rather were middle-class performers on the college-prep track. . . .

As with the white girls, it is difficult to account for upwardly mobile Mexican-American girls' exceptional

status, but there are a variety of enabling conditions for each of these individual girls' mobility. Although the experience of exceptionalism that these girls articulated in some ways paralleled white working-class girls' accounts, in other ways the two groups' experiences diverged, revealing the racial/ethnic specificity of their early mobility experiences.

Like Liz, Adriana's location in the college-prep curriculum seemed in part to be linked to organized sports. She showed a talent for soccer early on and received much support for it from home, because her father was a big fan. ("Soccer is always on our TV," she said. "He gets cable just for the soccer.") Adriana's friendship group in junior high thus included many of the college-prep girls who tend to dominate organized sports. Like Liz, through association with preps, she experienced the benefit of the privileged treatment by teachers and counselors that is often reserved for college-prep students. But while she was friendly with these girls in the classroom and on the playing field, she primarily located herself in a peer group of other working-class Mexican-American girls who were middle-class performers.

Like the white working-class girls, these girls at times told stories of defining self in opposition to delinquent brothers. . . .

But more often they told stories of older siblings as the source of help and inspiration to go to college. Usually, but not always, these older siblings were sisters, generally an older sister who had finally managed, through a long and circuitous route that included junior college and many part-time and full-time jobs, to attend a four-year school. The older sisters sought to help their younger siblings manage more easily by advising them on the importance of getting the courses required for state university or UC admission done in high school (rather than in junior college), on taking SAT tests, and on filling out applications for financial aid and admissions on time. Luisa had two older sisters attending state schools, and she had been accepted to three university campuses. . . .

When I asked her if she had understood the differences between attending a junior college versus a state university or UC school, she said,

Yeah, just from my sister. She always taught me what, you know, she's the one who told me what the differences were, and she helped me figure out that I wanted to go to UC, because I didn't want to go spend two yews at a JC and [then] like go for four more years, because I thought that was like a waste of two years.

Although Angela did not have older siblings guiding her, she clearly saw it as her job to help her five younger siblings. When I asked her about her social life, she said,

> Well, I don't spend time like I used to, with friends so much. My family, my little brothers and sister are more important than friends. They need to get ahead. And I don't want them to get behind or something. I want to help them do well.

Because she had so many younger siblings to help, who took energy away from her own schooling and who would need to use the family's economic resources, I had doubts that Angela's college dream would be realized, but it seemed likely that her siblings would benefit from her sacrifices. Indeed, this was a factor for Victoria, whose mobility was fostered by having older siblings—much older, in fact, since her mother was forty-two when Victoria was born. Not only were these older siblings able to advise her, but by the time she was ready to go to college many of them were established and could help her financially.

In short, older siblings who were the first in the family to go to college turned out to be important sources of insider information already known to students whose parents were college-educated, providing cultural and social capital not available from parents, and at times economic capital as well.

Two of the girls in this middle-class performing group were immigrants, and explaining their exceptionalism requires other considerations. These two girls were fluent enough in English to be able to complete college-prep courses. The remainder of immigrant girls in the senior class were on the vocational track. Many authors have noted the greater educational success of immigrant students compared to their second- and third-generation counterparts. It was Waretown school counselors' subjective impression that immigrant students "do better" in school. . . .

One explanation for the achievement of these two immigrant girls is that their parents had some other benefits and resources that enabled them to be more mobile than their vocational track counterparts. In her work on the educational mobility of low-income Chicana/os, Patricia

Gándara (1995) asks not why low-income Chicana/os fail, but why those who experience class mobility succeed. She suggests that "family stories" can work as a kind of cultural capital for these students. The people in her study told stories of coming from families that were well-to-do or had achieved high levels of education in Mexico, or of families that had lost their fortunes—and so their status and financial well-being—in fleeing Mexico because they were on the losing side in the Mexican revolution.

When I asked Lupita, who had immigrated at thirteen, had quickly learned English, was an academic star at the school, and had been admitted to several University of California campuses, why she was different from the other students in her neighborhood, she explained that while their families had immigrated from rural areas of Mexico, her family had come from an urban environment where there was greater access to education. In fact, she had an older sibling who had received a college degree in Mexico. . . .

The girls I studied were fully aware of the fact that the status of Mexican-Americans was not on a linear progression upward and that their lives might not be any easier, even given the Mexican-American civil rights movement. In just the past five years, they had witnessed the passage of three ballot measures in California that put clear brakes on the possibility of mobility for Mexican Americans. Proposition 187, passed in 1994, took social services such as public health care and public school education away from undocumented immigrants. Proposition 209, passed in 1996, eliminated affirmative action and thus encouraged other states to do the same. Proposition 227, passed in 1998, formally ended bilingual education in the state of California, reigniting an English-only movement that spread throughout the country.

I began to identify an "immigrant orientation" (Ogbu and Matute-Bianchi 1986) that existed among some girls, regardless of whether they were immigrants or not, meaning they employed as a mobility strategy the belief in the classical immigrant story of using education as a route to the American dream of upward mobility. . . . This group of working-class college-prep students engaged this strategy, holding out hope for education as their route to mobility, more than did vocational students . . . , who were far more cynical about their ability to achieve success via education.

However, these college-prep girls were not blind to the barriers that exist or to new ones that were currently being created by the state legislature. They were in fact, neither duped by achievement ideology or blindly assimilated, but rather were able to hold both hope and a practical cynicism in their minds simultaneously.

If . . . working-class students of color at times have higher aspirations than white working-class students, this does not mean that those higher aspirations result in higher achievement; a variety of structural barriers remain in place that inhibit their mobility. In the cases of Lupita and Angela, while family benefits, whether real or imagined, shape student aspirations, they do not dictate outcomes. Lupita did appear to come from an educated extended family in Mexico, and her college-educated sibling provided her with cultural capital that would possibly benefit her. But with five younger siblings, no health care, and a sick mother, Angela remains less likely to reap the benefits of her higher aspirations. Even though she was admitted to a UC campus, she was hoping to attend a nearby junior college:

> That's the only place I can go, because I can't afford to go away.

And when I asked Lupita about her family's income, she explained,

> Oh, you know how Mexican families are, a little bit from here, a little bit from there. My dad pays the rent, mom buys the food, my little brother pays the phone bill, and I'm responsible for the gas bill. My uncles fill in whatever else is needed.

Adriana cannot afford not to live at home, and her family cannot spare her economic contribution to the household.

MEXICAN-AMERICAN GIRLS: BECOMING UPWARDLY MOBILE

As with white working-class upwardly mobiles, these Mexican-American middle-class performers could see the differences between themselves and middle-class preps (mostly white) somewhat more clearly than their vocational counterparts could. But where whites articulated their difference from preps in veiled class term, Mexican-American girls articulated their difference clearly in terms of race. For example, Luisa commented:

> I think it is harder for Mexican-American students, because I think most white people have, like, money, like their parents, they went to college, and they have money. They have an education. But, you know, I'm not saying, well, you know, it's my mom's fault that she didn't go to college. She could have, you know, but I don't know, it's just, like, that's just what it is, kind of. The white students don't understand because, you know, their parents got to go to college, you know, had an education, they all have jobs.

Like white girls, Mexican-American girls wanted to point to the importance of mobility, yet did not want this to mean that their parents' lives were without value. They thus expressed a certain amount of ambivalence toward mobility and/or the acquisition of the middle-class cultural forms that accompany mobility. . . .

Mobility experiences can never be understood outside of their racial/ethnic specificity. Like white working-class girls, these girls were well aware of having exceeded their parents' abilities. But for them the acquisition of middle-class cultural forms also meant becoming bilingual, while their parents remained primarily Spanish speakers.

Where white working-class girls would say generally that they didn't want to struggle for money the way their parents did, Mexican-American girls were cognizant of the correlation between being Mexican-American and being poor and were more likely to name the specific occupations that the poorest people in their community worked and identified their motivation to escape these kinds of work. Angela declared:

> I don't want to be like everyone else, I want to, I want something better. I hate working in the fields, that's not for me, and I don't want to do that. It is minimum wage and I don't want to work for that. . . .

Unlike third-generation girls of middle-class origin who struggled hard in this particular context with being at once Mexican-American and middle-class and who tended at times to buy into the idea that to be authentically Mexican one must adopt working-class cultural forms, the college-prep working-class girls discussed here refused to interpret mobility as assimilation to whiteness and were not apologetic about their mobility; they did not feel any "less Mexican" for being college bound. John Ogbu and Maria Eugenia Matute-Bianchi (1986) suggest there is a difference between students who adopt an immigrant orientation toward schooling and those who adopt a caste-like orientation. A caste-like orientation equates schooling with a loss of racial/ethnic identity (i.e., "acting white") and leads to an adaptive strategy of resistance (often resulting in school failure). . . . The exact reason why some students of color equate educational mobility with acting white while others do not and instead formulate a bicultural identity is unclear. . . .

This handful of working-class college-prep girls enacted a different strategy than students who experienced or feared school success as assimilation. The former saw themselves as disproving white stereotypes about Mexican-Americans through their hard work and success, and they took pleasure from that. They adopted a strategy of "accommodation without assimilation," meaning that in the face of racial conflict and inequality, they made accommodations "for the purpose of reducing conflict," yet at the same time allowed their "separate group [identity and culture] to be maintained" (Gibson 1988, 24–25). In this formulation it is indeed possible to do well in school and not objectively be assimilated or "acting white." In short, they found ways to reject assimilation without resisting educational mobility. . . .

The correlation of race and poverty promotes the common-sense belief that middle-class and whiteness are one and the same; as a result Mexican-American students must negotiate educational mobility with the broader social perception that this mobility represents assimilation to whiteness. This assimilation is resisted and gets played out as intraethnic tension, as vocational Mexican-American students accuse college-preps of "acting white." These working-class upwardly mobiles did occasionally receive such accusations from their working-class peers, but they interpreted this as a joke, which though painful at times, was not taken as a real challenge, and their racial/ethnic identity remained unthreatened by their college-prep status. . . .

The fact that upwardly mobile students grew up working-class meant that their identity as Mexican-American was consistent with the common understanding of race and class as correlated. Their Mexican identity appeared less challenged (both internally and externally) than was the case for some middle-class Mexican-American girls, whose middle-class status made them appear to themselves and to others as acculturated. This, even though they were not so far removed from Mexican-American cultural forms. Some of their grandparents, with whom they had much contact, were immigrants; their parents were fluent in Spanish; and parents' work (as an ethnic studies professor, a labor lawyer, and a university administrator of minority programs, for example) promoted or at least made available a cultural and political racial/ethnic identity. Perhaps they were not "actually" or "really" more acculturated, but they were more middle-class, and this affected their view of themselves and others' view of them. . . .

RACE MATTERS

While all of these girls, across race/ethnicity, have not articulated their early mobility as particularly painful, it is likely to become more so as they (if they) proceed into college, which will take them much further away culturally from family and community than mere high school mobility could. Many have written of the pain that working-class upwardly mobile people experience when leaving their community behind and/or the difficulty of finding ways to reconcile the discord between class background and present status due to mobility. This experience differs, of course, for whites and people of color, as racial/ethnic groups of color are more consciously aware of themselves as a community of people because of a common history of colonization and oppression that results from being historically defined as a racial group. Alternatively, an aspect of whiteness is that whites often do not immediately experience themselves as members of the racial/ethnic category "white," but as individuals, and, without a cultural discourse of class identity, they do not readily experience themselves as members of a class community either. Evidence of this can be seen in the way white working-class college-prep girls expressed their experience of and concern over how education was distancing themselves from their parents. They did not articulate this as a distancing from their working-class *community*; their pain was more often articulated in relationship to an *individual* family, not a people. In short, these white working-class girls were not routinely accused of acting "too bourgeois" the way that middle-class performing Mexican-American girls were accused of acting "too white," because such clear language for class difference was unavailable. Their mobility appears less complicated because they are not made to feel that they are giving up racial/ethnic belonging in the process. . . . In a way, the lack of class discourse may be either a hindrance or a help for white working-class students. On the one hand, because class is unarticulated, they have only individual characteristics to blame for their class location: their status is a consequence of the fact that they and/or their parents are just "losers." On the other hand, their mobility may be made easier since they did not experience the same intra-ethnic tension or antagonism within their community over the link between mobility and assimilation that Mexican-American girls did.

As we have seen, being brown or black tends to signify working-class in the United States, given the high correlation between race and class. Consequently, for white working-class upwardly mobiles, the class referent is escapable precisely because of their whiteness. For whites, class does not as easily appear encoded onto the body (although it certainly can be and often is). White working-class upwardly mobiles can pass as middle-class more readily. At school, where no one necessarily knew where working-class white students lived or what their parents looked like, their classed identities could be invisible if they worked at it and learned how to pass, as many do. The possibility of, and perhaps ease of, upward mobility favoring white working-class students may also be greater, given that Mexican-American girls were more likely to experience

tracking as a consequence of counselors' perceptions and stereotypes. The correlation between race/ethnicity and class means that counselors are likely to assume that brown students are from low-income families (even when they are not) and therefore to make assumptions about what educational resources they need and can handle. White working-class students can escape tracking more easily because their color does not stand in for or signify lowness. . . .

The experiences of these girls reveals that, in order not to be vulnerable to tracking, a Mexican-American student has to be phenomenally good academically, perform a school-sanctioned femininity that signifies middle-classness to school personnel, and have no transgressions or slip-ups along the way. . . .

REFERENCES

Gándara, Patricia, 1995. *Over the Ivy Walls: The Educational Mobility of Low-Income Chicanos.* Albany: State University of New York Press.

Gibson, Margaret A. 1988. *Accommodation without Assimilation: Sikh Immigrants in an American High School.* Ithaca, N.Y.: Cornell University Press.

Ogbu, John V. and Maria Eugenia Matute-Bianchi, 1986. "Understanding Sociocultural Factors: Knowledge Identity and School Adjustment." In *Beyond Language: Social and Cultural Factors in Schooling Language Minority Students*, developed by the Bilingual Education Office, California State Department of Education, 73–142. Los Angeles: Evaluation Dissemination and Assessment Center, California State University, Los Angeles.

Skeggs, Beverley. 1997. *Formations of Class and Gender: Becoming Respectable.* London: Sage.

PART VIII

POPULAR CULTURE

Most of the chapters in this book have examined gender and other relations of inequality primarily in terms of people's lived experiences within social institutions such as families, workplaces, and schools. However, the arena of beliefs, symbols, and values is also of crucial importance. Take, for example, the recent debates about sexual violence in the media, sex education in schools, "family values," and gay and lesbian marriage. To be sure, these debates and their outcomes will have a real impact on people's lives within social institutions. But the terrain of these debates is largely the arena of ideas, values, and symbols. And one of the most dynamic places in which people learn, contest, and forget values and beliefs is in the vast arena of popular culture. The articles in this section encourage reflection on how the film and television we watch, the products we purchase, the radio programs we listen to, and the Internet sites and Facebook pages that we frequent are cultural creations through which dominant values are often imposed but also arenas in which these values are contested and new values forged.

Dominant cultural beliefs and media images of subordinated groups—be they women, racialized or colonized "others," working-class people, or sexual minorities—tend to obscure, and thus legitimize, the privileges of dominant groups. Widespread stereotypes of these groups in popular film and television, as well as the underrepresentation of these groups in speaking roles, are well documented in media studies. Before introducing the readings for this section, let's review a few of the key findings.

In a study of 500 popular films, Stacy L. Smith and her co-authors found that females are grossly underrepresented in speaking roles (only 28%), and they are more likely than males to be portrayed in sexy attire or partially naked, including an increase in the sexualized portrayal of teen girls. A second study of 120 films from 11 countries found that only 31% of the speaking or named characters were female and that the United States ranked near the bottom (the United Kingdom, Brazil, and Korea ranked at the top but no country reached gender parity) (Smith et al. 2014a). Further, when examining the roles that characters play in film, female characters comprised just 22.5% of workers, including a paltry 13.9% of executives, 11.6% of scientists, and less than 10% of lawyers, high-level politicians, judges, professors, sports figures, clergy, and engineers (Smith et al. 2014a). Similarly, racial-ethnic minorities are underrepresented in speaking roles, accounting for just over a quarter (25.9%) of speaking characters, although these groups comprise 37% of the U.S. population and buy 46% of all movie tickets (Smith et al. 2014b). Hispanics are the most underrepresented (4.9% of speaking roles while comprising

16.3% of the population) and were the most likely to be shown partially or fully naked (females) or in tight, alluring, or revealing clothing (males).

Media studies also document widespread inequalities in the representation of women and racial-ethnic minorities as directors and producers. In a study of more than 3,500 primetime television programs, white male directors are significantly *over*represented (69%), whereas minority males (17%), minority females (2%), and white females (12%) are *under*represented (DGA Report 2014). This is important, not only in terms of employment discrimination, but also because the underrepresentation of women and racial-ethnic minorities behind the screens is directly related to their underrepresentation and misrepresentation on screen. Smith and her coauthors (2012, 2014b), for example, found that films made by women directors have more female characters (and less sexualization of them) and that films made by black directors have more black characters. Taken together, these studies document widespread inequality in the media in terms of who is represented, how they are represented, and, perhaps most importantly, who creates the stories the media tells about us and the values and beliefs we uphold. For the readings that follow, consider how the underrepresentation of women and racial-ethnic minorities as producers of media culture might help to explain what is found.

In the first article in this section, Susan Jane Gilman draws on her own childhood memories of ambivalence while playing with Barbie dolls to level a stinging critique of the ways that for little girls, these dolls "quickly become the defining criteria" for beauty and their sense of status and worth. Gilman notes that the pain that accompanies this realization can be more acute for "other" girls like she and her friends—urban, Jewish, black, Asian, and Latina girls. But she also notes that many girls develop their own, culturally unintended modes of playing with Barbie—including decapitation! She ends with a humorous list of Barbie dolls that she would like to see—dolls that speak to a spectrum of girls' body types, sexualities, ethnicities, and religions.

Kristen Myers analyzes messages about gender, sexuality, and feminism in television programming for children. She finds that despite superficial claims to gender equality and "girl power," a media-generated backlash distorts feminism and misrepresents feminist goals and achievements. Myers describes how television shows for young girls, such as *Hannah Montana* and *iCarly*, frequently degrade and objectify femininity while valorizing mean girls and dismissing feminism as a joke. She concludes by considering the impact of these messages on the next generation of feminists and the importance of social justice for the future they envision.

Emily Rutherford examines the implications of Facebook's website design, which required users to choose identities as "male" or "female." Although the Internet is sometimes construed as a new site of gender freedom, here we see how one of the popular media sites reproduced gender binaries. LBGT groups responded by protesting these constraints, and although Facebook was initially reluctant to change its practices, it now offers custom gender identification and neutral pronouns.

The third reading examines how the media, particularly conservative commentators like Rush Limbaugh and Mike Savage, contribute to a sense of *aggrieved entitlement* among white American men. Michael Kimmel talked to white men from across the United States about their experiences of downward mobility as they watched their jobs, and the American Dream they felt entitled to, disappear. Kimmel argues that "what unites them is their belief in a certain ideal of masculinity," the self-made man, and their feelings of emasculation as they felt their authority and power erode. Although their anger is not without reason, Kimmel shows how it is misplaced and dangerously focused on vulnerable groups (such as women, people of color, immigrants, and gays and lesbians). At the same time, many white men's feelings of anger and aggrieved entitlement fail to consider the benefits that accrue to the most privileged groups as economic disparities in the United States increase. Kimmel hopes that by drawing attention to the "steady [media] diet of disinformation and misinformation," we can "break the cycle of anger that impoverishes men's lives."

REFERENCES

DGA Report. Employers Make No Improvement in Diversity Hiring in Episodic Television. September 17, 2014. http://www .dga.org/News/PressReleases/2014/140917-Episodic-Director-Diversity-Report.aspx/.

Smith, Stacy L., Marc Choueiti, Elizabeth Scofield, and Katherine Pieper. 2012. "Gender Inequality in 500 Popular Films: Examining On-Screen Portrayals and behind-the-Scenes Employment Patterns in Motion Pictures Released between 2007–2012." http://annenberg.usc.edu/pages/~/media/MDSCI/Gender_Inequality_in_500_Popular_Films_-_Smith_2013 .ashx/.

Smith, Stacy L., Marc Choueiti, and Katherine Pieper. 2014. "Gender Bias without Borders: An Investigation of Female Characters in Popular Films across 11 Countries." http://seejane.org/wp-content/uploads/gender-bias-without-borders-executive-summary.pdf/.

Smith, Stacy L., Marc Choueiti, and Katherine Pieper. 2014b. "Race/Ethnicity in 600 Popular Films: Examining On Screen Portrayals and behind the Camera Diversity." http://annenberg.usc.edu/pages/~/media/MDSCI/Racial%20Inequality% 20in%20Film%202007-2013%20Final.ashx/.

43

Klaus Barbie, and Other Dolls I'd Like to See

SUSAN JANE GILMAN

For decades, Barbie has remained torpedo-titted, open-mouthed, tippy-toed and vagina-less in her cellophane coffin—and, ever since I was little, she has threatened me.

Most women I know are nostalgic for Barbie. "Oh," they coo wistfully, "I used to *loooove* my Barbies. My girlfriends would come over, and we'd play for hours . . ."

Not me. As a child, I disliked the doll on impulse; as an adult, my feelings have actually fermented into a heady, full-blown hatred.

My friends and I never owned Barbies. When I was young, little girls in my New York City neighborhood collected "Dawns." Only seven inches high, Dawns were, in retrospect, the underdog of fashion dolls. There were four in the collection: Dawn, dirty-blond and appropriately smug; Angie, whose name and black hair allowed her to pass for Italian or Hispanic; Gloria, a redhead with bangs and green eyes (Irish, perhaps, or a Russian, Jew?); and Dale, a black doll with a real afro.

Oh, they had their share of glitzy frocks—the tiny wedding dress, the gold lamé ball gown that shredded at the hem. And they had holes punctured in the bottoms of their feet so you could impale them on the model's stand of the "Dawn Fashion Stage" (sold separately), press a button and watch them revolve jerkily around the catwalk. But they also had "mod" clothes like white go-go boots and a multicolored dashiki outfit

called "Sock It to Me" with rose-colored sunglasses. Their hair came in different lengths and—although probably only a six-year-old doll fanatic could discern this—their facial expressions and features were indeed different. They were as diverse as fashion dolls could be in 1972, and in this way, I realize now, they were slightly subversive.

Of course, at that age, my friends and I couldn't spell subversive, let alone wrap our minds around the concept. But we sensed intuitively that Dawns were more democratic than Barbies. With their different colors and equal sizes, they were closer to what we looked like. We did not find this consoling—for we hadn't yet learned that our looks were something that required consolation. Rather, our love of Dawns was an offshoot of our own healthy egocentrism. We were still at that stage in our childhood when little girls want to be everything special, glamorous and wonderful—and believe they can be.

As a six-year-old, I remember gushing, "I want to be a ballerina, and a bride, and a movie star, and a model, and a queen. . . ." To be sure, I was a disgustingly girly girl. I twirled. I skipped. I actually wore a tutu to school. (I am not kidding.) For a year, I refused to wear blue. Whenever the opportunity presented itself, I dressed up in my grandmother's pink chiffon nightgowns and rhinestone necklaces and paraded around the apartment

Susan Jane Gilman, "Klaus Barbie, and Other Dolls I'd Like to See," from Ophira Edut, ed., *Adios Barbie*. Copyright © 1998 Seal Press.

495

like the princess of the universe. I dressed like my Dawn dolls—and dressed my Dawn dolls like me. It was a silly, fabulous narcissism—but one that sprang from a crucial self-love. These dolls were part of my fantasy life and an extension of my ambitions. Tellingly, my favorite doll was Angie, who had dark brown hair, like mine.

But at some point, most of us prima ballerinas experienced a terrible turning point. I know I did. I have an achingly clear memory of myself, standing before a mirror in all my finery and jewels, feeling suddenly ridiculous and miserable. *Look at yourself*, I remember thinking acidly. *Nobody will ever like you.* I could not have been older than eight. And then later, another memory: my friend Allison confiding in me, "The kids at my school, they all hate my red hair." Somewhere, somehow, a message seeped into our consciousness telling us that we weren't good enough to be a bride or a model or a queen or anything because we weren't pretty enough. And this translated into not smart enough or likable enough, either.

Looks, girls learn early, collapse into a metaphor for everything else. They quickly become the defining criteria for our status and our worth. And somewhere along the line, we stop believing in our own beauty and its dominion. Subsequently, we also stop believing in the power of our minds and our bodies.

Barbie takes over.

Barbie dolls had been around long before I was born, but it was precisely around the time my friends and I began being evaluated on our "looks" that we became aware of the role Barbie played in our culture.

Initially, my friends and I regarded Barbies with a sort of vague disdain. With their white-blond hair, burnt orange "Malibu" skin, unblinking turquoise eyes and hot-pink convertibles, Barbie dolls represented a world utterly alien to us. They struck us as clumsy, stupid, overly obvious. They were clearly somebody else's idea of a doll—and a doll meant for vapid girls in the suburbs. Dawns, my friend Julie and I once agreed during a sleepover, were far more hip.

But eventually, the message of Barbie sunk in. Literally and metaphorically, Barbies were bigger than Dawns. They were a foot high. They merited more plastic! More height! More visibility! And unlike Dawns, which were pulled off the market in the mid-'70s, Barbies were ubiquitous and perpetual bestsellers.

We urban, Jewish, black, Asian and Latina girls began to realize slowly and painfully that if you didn't look like Barbie, you didn't fit in. Your status was diminished. You were less beautiful, less valuable, less worthy. *If you didn't look like Barbie, companies would discontinue you.* You simply couldn't compete.

I'd like to think that, two decades later, my anger about this would have cooled off—not heated up. (I mean, it's a *doll* for chrissake. Get over it.) The problem, however, is that despite all the flag-waving about multiculturalism and girls' self-esteem these days, I see a new generation of little girls receiving the same message I did twenty-five years ago, courtesy of Mattel. I'm currently a "big sister" to a little girl who recently moved here from Mexico. When I first began spending time with her, she drew pictures of herself as she is: a beautiful seven-year-old with café au lait skin and short black hair. Then she began playing with Barbies. Now she draws pictures of both herself and her mother with long, blond hair. "I want long hair," she sighs, looking woefully at her drawing.

A coincidence? Maybe, but Barbie is the only toy in the Western world that human beings actively try to mimic. Barbie is not just a children's doll; it's an adult cult and an aesthetic obsession. We've all seen the evidence. During Barbie's thirty-fifth anniversary, a fashion magazine ran a "tribute to Barbie," using live models posing as dolls. A New York museum held a "Barbie retrospective," enshrining Barbie as a pop artifact—at a time when most human female pop artists continue to work in obscurity. Then there's Pamela Lee. The Barbie Halls of Fame. The websites, the newsletters, the collectors clubs. The woman whose goal is to transform herself, via plastic surgery, into a real Barbie. Is it any wonder then that little girls have been longing for generations to "look like Barbie"— and that the irony of this goes unchallenged?

For this reason, I've started calling Barbie dolls "Klaus Barbie dolls" after the infamous Gestapo commander. For I now clearly recognize what I only sensed as a child. This "pop artifact" is an icon of Aryanism. Introduced after the second world war, in the conservatism of the Eisenhower era (and rumored to be modeled after a German prostitute by a man who designed nuclear warheads), Barbies, in their "innocent," "apolitical" cutesiness, propagate the ideals of the Third Reich. They ultimately succeed where Hitler failed: They instill in legions of little girls a preference for whiteness, for blond hair, blue eyes and delicate features, for an impossible *über* figure, perched eternally and submissively in high heels. In the Cult of the Blond, Barbies are a cornerstone. They reach the young, and they reach them quickly. *Barbie, Barbie!* The Aqua song throbs. *I'm a Barbie girl!*

It's true that, in the past few years, Mattel has made an effort to create a few slightly more p.c. versions of its best-selling blond. Walk down the aisle at Toys-R-Us (and they wonder why kids today can't spell), and you can see a few boxes of American Indian Barbie, Jamaican Barbie, Cowgirl Barbie. Their skin tone is darker and their outfits ethnicized, but they have the same Aryan features and the same "tell-me-anything-and-I'll-believe-it" expressions on their plastic faces. Ultimately, their packaging reinforces their status as "Other." These are "special" and "limited" edition Barbies, the labels announce: clearly *not* the standard.

And, Barbie's head still pops off with ease. Granted, this makes life a little sweeter for the sadists on the playground (there's always one girl who gets more pleasure out of destroying Barbie than dressing her), but the real purpose is to make it easier to swap your Barbies' Lilliputian ball gowns. Look at the literal message of this: Hey, girls, a head is simply a neck plug, easily disposed of in the name of fashion. Lest anyone think I'm nit-picking here, a few years ago, a "new, improved" Talking Barbie hit the shelves and created a brouhaha because one of the phrases it parroted was *Math is hard.* Once again, the cerebrum took a backseat to "style." Similarly, the latest "new, improved" Barbie simply trades in one impossible aesthetic for another: The bombshell has now become the waif. Why? According to a Mattel spokesperson, a Kate Moss figure is better suited for today's fashions. Ah, such an improvement.

Now, I am not, as a rule, anti-doll. Remember, I once wore a tutu and collected the entire Dawn family myself. I know better than to claim that dolls are nothing but sexist gender propaganda. Dolls can be a lightning rod for the imagination, for companionship, for learning. And they're *fun*—something that must never be undervalued.

But dolls often give children their first lessons in what a society considers valuable—and beautiful. And so I'd like to see dolls that teach little girls something more than fashion-consciousness and self-consciousness. I'd like to see dolls that expand girls' ideas about what is beautiful instead of constricting them. And how about a few role models instead of runway models as playmates? If you can make a Talking Barbie, surely you can make a Working Barbie. If you can have a Barbie Townhouse, surely you can have a Barbie business. And if you can construct an entire Barbie world out of pink and purple plastic, surely you can construct some "regular" Barbies that are more than white and blond. And remember, Barbie's only a doll! So give it a little more inspired goofiness, some real *pizzazz!*

Along with Barbies of all shapes and colors, here are some Barbies I'd personally like to see:

Dinner Roll Barbie. A Barbie with multiple love handles, double chin, a real, curvy belly, generous tits and ass and voluminous thighs to show girls that voluptuousness is also beautiful. Comes with miniature basket of dinner rolls, bucket o'fried chicken, tiny Entenmann's walnut ring, a brick of Sealtest ice cream, three packs of potato chips, a T-shirt reading "Only the Weak Don't Eat" and, of course, an appetite.

Birkenstock Barbie. Finally, a doll made with horizontal feet and comfortable sandals. Made from recycled materials.

Bisexual Barbie. Comes in a package with Skipper and Ken.

Butch Barbie. Comes with short hair, leather jacket, "Silence = Death" T-shirt, pink triangle buttons, Doc Martens, pool cue and dental dams. Packaged in cardboard closet with doors flung wide open. Barbie Carpentry Business sold separately.

Our Barbies, Ourselves. Anatomically correct Barbie, both inside and out, comes with spreadable legs, her own speculum, magnifying glass and detailed diagrams of female anatomy so that little girls can learn about their bodies in a friendly, nonthreatening way. Also included: tiny Kotex, booklets on sexual responsibility. Accessories such as contraceptives, sex toys, expanding uterus with fetus at various stages of development and breast pump are all optional, underscoring that each young women has the right to choose what she does with her own Barbie.

Harley Barbie. Equipped with motorcycle, helmet, shades. Tattoos are non-toxic and can be removed with baby oil.

Body Piercings Barbie. Why should Earring Ken have all the fun? Body Piercings Barbie comes with changeable multiple earrings, nose ring, nipple rings, lip ring, navel ring and tiny piercing gun. Enables girls to rebel, express alienation and gross out elders without actually having to puncture themselves.

Blue Collar Barbie. Comes with overalls, protective goggles, lunch pail, UAW membership, pamphlet on union organizing and pay scales for women as compared to men. Waitressing outfits and cashier's register may be purchased separately for Barbies who are holding down second jobs to make ends meet.

Rebbe Barbie. So why not? Women rabbis are on the cutting edge in Judaism. Rebbe Barbie comes with tiny satin *yarmulke*, prayer shawl, *tefillin*, silver *kaddish* cup, Torah scrolls. Optional: tiny *mezuzah* for doorway of Barbie Dreamhouse.

B-Girl Barbie. Truly fly Barbie in midriff-baring shirt and baggy jeans. Comes with skateboard, hip hop accessories and plenty of attitude. Pull her cord, and she says things like, "I don't *think* so," "Dang, get outta my face" and "You go, girl." Teaches girls not to take shit from men and condescending white people.

The Barbie Dream Team. Featuring Quadratic Equation Barbie (a Nobel Prize–winning mathematician with her own tiny books and calculator), Microbiologist Barbie (comes with petri dishes, computer and Barbie Laboratory) and Bite-the-Bullet Barbie, an anthropologist with pith helmet, camera, detachable limbs, fake blood and kit for performing surgery on herself in the outback.

Transgender Barbie. Formerly known as G. I. Joe.

44

Choose One

EMILY RUTHERFORD

Miles Wilcox, a sophomore at Bard College at Simon's Rock, is an avid Facebook user, but he's disgruntled with the website's design. "I have serious issues with how Facebook is so heterosexist," he says. Wilcox, who identifies as a queer transman, objects to the very first field in the Facebook profile: a drop-down box asking users to select a sex from the options "male" and "female." He continues, "Facebook needs to get a grip on reality and acknowledge that not everyone feels comfortable with explicitly identifying as one gender or the other . . . I see no need for Facebook to know what is in my pants, but that's what they ask everyone that signs up."

When the Facebook's creators and designers decided how to structure the website's profile, they placed strict limits on users' choices. Users must rank sex and relationship status above political and religious views, and those above favorite books and movies due to the design of Facebook's profile page. Furthermore, Facebook rigidly reinforces a gender binary, offering only "male" and "female" as options in the "sex" drop-down box, and only allowing users to check "men" and "women" under "interested in." The world around us is increasingly accepting of a spectrum of sexual orientations and gender identities, but Facebook is still sticking to outdated, problematic paradigms.

In July 2008, Facebook took the rigidity beyond the male/female binary in the "sex" information box, citing issues with translating the website into other languages. The company asked users to select a gender-specific pronoun, "he" or "she," so that the News Feed would know which pronoun to use instead of the ungrammatical single "they"—as in, "John added *The Great Gatsby* to **his** favorite books" or "Jane updated **her** political views" (emphasis added). All this is distinctly marginalizing for transgender or gender-nonconforming people like Wilcox who are less able to shelve themselves or the recipients of their interest into one of only two categories.

Ironically, groups that object to Facebook's practices are protesting and raising awareness using Facebook itself. For example, Moriya Vanderhoef, a student at University of Wisconsin Milwaukee, created a group called "Expand Gender Options on Facebook Petition," which currently has 2,326 members. Vanderhoef, who studies LGBT history, says that she started the group "because there are far more genders and sexes in the world than just 'male' and 'female' . . . I do not appreciate Facebook giving me the option to name my religious [affiliations], but restricting my gender and sexuality to the ultra narrow 'male' or 'female.'" However, the petition has not achieved its goal of bringing this problem

Emily Rutherford, *Campus Progress* (June 16, 2009). Copyright © 2009 Center for American Progress. Reprinted by permission.

to Facebook's attention: Vanderhoef has "never once heard from anyone in power about [the] group or the possibility of changing this problem."

Rebecca Bettencourt is another Facebook user who was frustrated by the company's lack of response to user concerns about the "sex" field, believing that "Facebook's limited set of options is not only problematic but grossly misrepresentative and insulting to thousands— maybe even millions—of people." She tried addressing the problem in a different way: when Facebook first allowed users to design their own applications, Bettencourt says, "I immediately knew what my mission was. If Facebook wasn't going to fix this error, I was going to have to take matters into my own hands. As soon as the Facebook API was available, I created the SGO application."

SGO, which stands for "sex/gender/orientation," provides more options than Facebook's own, including fill-in fields so that users can describe their gender and sexuality however they wish. SGO has had a modest amount of success among Facebook's LGBT population, but users cannot accord its content the same level of importance as the official Facebook fields.

Bettencourt would like to see a change. "I do believe that Facebook, as well as other websites, should standardize their gender and orientation options along the lines of my app," she says. "Not all the fields my app offers would be necessary, of course; I'd just like to see the fields for Gender Identity and Sexual Orientation that offered these additional options and/or a text field."

Wilcox, who uses the application, agrees: "The SGO app is a really awesome tool, but essentially what it is, is an addition to supplement where people feel Facebook is lacking or failing them. Right now it's helping, but I do think that Facebook should identify these issues and try to fix them," he says.

However, Facebook has done little to address these concerns. The company attempted to mollify those who disagreed with its gender-specific pronouns decision with a June 27 blog post last summer: "We've received pushback in the past from groups that find the male/female distinction too limiting. We have a lot of respect for these communities, which is why it will still be possible to remove gender entirely from your account, including how we refer to you in Mini-Feed."

That is not an adequate solution, however, for those who actually want to display a gender option outside of the male–female binary. Bettencourt, who has followed the issue closely, observed, "This is the only peep ever heard from Facebook regarding this issue, and it only confirms my suspicions of transphobia among the people running Facebook." (Facebook did not respond to requests for further comment on the policy.)

Other efforts to organize on Facebook as a means of changing its available options have been successful in the past. A few years ago, a different group of concerned Facebook users was able to successfully expand the options available in the "political views" field beyond a spectrum from "very liberal" to "very conservative." In 2007 and early 2008, as Facebook became increasingly popular in countries outside of the United States, a series of groups and petitions with titles like "By 'Libertarian' I mean Anarchist" generated a fair amount of attention from the Facebook user base. In contrast to the company's unresponsiveness on the gender issue, Facebook seemed to have taken notice of this campaign. As of March 2008, users are now allowed a fill-in-the-blank political views field.

Of course, the political views movement had numbers on its side. Demographically speaking, far more people desire to label themselves as "socialist" or "libertarian" than, say, "genderqueer" or "pansexual." The minority of gender-variant individuals who feel limited by Facebook's gender binary—unable to sustain a critical mass or to impress upon Facebook's staff the importance of their cause—has been unable to lobby successfully for the change it wants to see.

Figure 1. Facebook still excludes those that don't accept gender binaries. (Illustration: Brett Marler)

Some might argue that Facebook is not doing anything particularly shocking—after all, we are asked to choose from "male" or "female" just about every time we fill out a job application, complete a silly online quiz, or use a public restroom. But a policy is not the right choice simply because it is the status quo. Because of its ubiquity among our generation, Facebook plays as important a role in shaping cultural norms and expectations as it does in reflecting them. Facebook has done much to revolutionize the way we present ourselves and communicate with one another, but it could be even more revolutionary if it were to embrace the diversity of its user base.

45

Manufacturing Rage: The Cultural Construction of Aggrieved Entitlement

MICHAEL KIMMEL

"Tom," from Wichita, Kansas, has been waiting on hold, he tells us, for two hours and twenty minutes. An army veteran, he lost his job earlier this year. For months, he's been looking for work, sending out hundreds of résumés. A few interviews, no offers. What will happen to his family when his unemployment insurance runs out? "We're into the red zone," he explains. "We're cutting essentials: food, laundry, clothing, shoes." He's worried, he says, "scared to death." Repeatedly, he insists he is "not a whiner."

What he wants to know, he asks Rush Limbaugh on his nationally syndicated radio show, is what President Obama is doing to turn the economy around. Why was he spending all this energy on health care when people are out of work? What has the stimulus plan done to create jobs for people like him, with families to support? Fortunately, he says, his wife has a job that provides health care for the family. But if he doesn't find something soon, he's considering reenlisting. He lost his own father in Vietnam, he says, softly, and he's afraid that at forty-three, he might leave his own children fatherless. "My self-esteem is right now at its lowest that I've ever had it," Tom says. "I'm getting choked up."

"I know," replies Limbaugh empathetically. "I've been there." Limbaugh recounts his own history of unemployment. But then, he transforms Tom's experience.

"I don't hear you as whining," says Rush. "I hear you as mad."

Wait a second. Did you hear Tom as mad? I'm no expert in auditory interpretation, but what I heard was anxiety, vulnerability, and more than just a slight tremor of fear. I heard someone asking for help. In a revealing analysis of Limbaugh's radio persona, anti-violence activist Jackson Katz carefully parses this particular exchange as emblematic—how the talk-show host transforms this plaintive emotional expression into something else. What starts as sadness, anxiety, grief, worry is carefully manipulated into political rage.

Rush Limbaugh is a master at this translation of emotional vulnerability or insecurity into anger. All that he needs is that shared sense of aggrieved entitlement—that sense that "we," the rightful heirs of America's bounty, have had what is "rightfully ours" taken away from us by "them," faceless, feckless government bureaucrats, and given to "them," undeserving minorities, immigrants, women, gays, and their ilk. If your despair can be massaged into this Manichaean struggle between Us and Them, you, too, can be mobilized into the army of Angry White Men.

Limbaugh is one of hundreds of talk-show hosts on radio dials across the nation—indeed, the AM radio dial seems to have nothing but sports talk, Spanish-language stations, and vitriolic white men hosting radio

From *Angry White Men* by Michael Kimmel, copyright © 2013. Reprinted by permission of Nation Books, a member of the Perseus Books Group.

shows. Talk radio is the most vibrant part of the radio dial—thirty-five hundred all-talk or all-news stations in the United States—up from about five hundred two decades ago. According to the Pew Research Center for the People and the Press, while the majority of radio, newspaper, and magazine consumers are female (51 percent), Limbaugh (59 percent), Sean Hannity (57 percent), and Stephen Colbert (58 percent) skew most heavily toward men. (So, incidentally, does Rachel Maddow, at 52 percent.) Limbaugh's audiences skew slightly older, less educated (only 29 percent are college graduates, compared to 39 percent and 35 percent for liberals Colbert and Maddow, respectively). Their income tends to be squarely in the middle—30 percent make more than seventy-five thousand dollars, 37 percent between thirty and seventy-five thousand dollars, and 21 percent below thirty thousand dollars a year. Obviously, more than seven in ten identify as conservative.

Visitors to Limbaugh's website tilt even more rightward. It's visited by 1.1 million people a month—more than 94 percent white and 85 percent male, most are between thirty-five and sixty-five, with the biggest bulge at forty-five to fifty-four. Most (54 percent) do not have kids. Two-thirds have incomes below one hundred thousand dollars a year, though two-thirds also have at least a college, if not a graduate, degree. (That's an index of downward mobility; their educational achievements haven't paid off in better jobs.) This would make the typical Limbaugh fan (enough to view his website) a downwardly mobile white male, whose career never really panned out (college or grad school but only modest income) and whose family life didn't either (majority childless). That is a recipe for aggrieved entitlement. Everything was in place to partake of the American Dream, and it didn't quite work out. Just whose fault is that?

Sociologist Sarah Sobieraj and political scientist Jeffrey Berry call it "outrage media"—talk-radio, blog, and cable news designed "to provoke a visceral response from the audience, usually in the form of anger, fear, or moral righteousness through the use of overgeneralizations, sensationalism, misleading or patently inaccurate information, ad hominem attacks, and partial truths about opponents." Sobieraj and Berry trace this development through the technological shifts from radio and TV to cable news, the blogosphere, and talk radio as the news vehicles of choices and to the incredible consolidation of media companies, so that only a handful of companies control virtually all of America's airwaves. (Women own about three of ten businesses in America but own only 6 percent of radio stations. Racial minorities own 18 percent of all businesses, but only 7.7 percent of radio stations. Clearly, white men are being squeezed out, right?)

But it's also linked to the displacement of white men from every single position of power in the country. Talk radio is the last locker room, juiced not on steroids but on megahertz. It's the circled wagons keeping out the barbarian hordes, who may be just a millimeter away on that dial. It's the Alamo on AM frequency.

The rise of outrage media is coincident with the erosion of white male entitlement. Outrage media generally begins with Peter Finch in the film *Network* (1976), exhorting his audience to go to their windows and scream, "I'm mad as hell, and I'm not going to take it anymore!" Finch's impotent outburst provides a heroic riposte to a film about the steamroller of corporate takeovers, the ethically rudderless drive for ratings trumping all other criteria, including quality. Like the tabloid newspaper or local newscast—whose motto is "If it bleeds, it leads"—the motto of outrage radio is closer to "If he yells, it sells."

Of course, one needn't be some academic postmodernist to understand how the catharsis of the experience is what enables us to take more of it. We feel outrage, and we're told it's not our fault and that we have plenty of company.

But it's more than just the cheerleaders of the angry mobs. Anger sells. It's become part of marketing strategies for products ranging from regular-guy cars and beer to defiantly politically incorrect items like Hummers and cigars. Anger, after all, implies some degree of hope, of "aspiration," which is a core element in advertising strategy. Anger implies commitment; if you're angry, you feel yourself to be a stakeholder. Anger is emotion seeking an outlet, an excited politicized electron seeking to connect with other atoms. (Contrast it with what happens to the anger that does not find a means of expression: it can become nihilistic, despondent, or resigned bitterness. The resigned and despondent do not buy products. They sulk. They give up.)

You could hear that anger, the aggrieved entitlement, on election night 2012, as President Obama handily defeated Mitt Romney for president. Romney, the unfathomably wealthy corporate plutocrat, was unable to transform himself into a populist firebrand. Even though white men were the only demographic who went for Romney (although not decisively), it was too close in all those battleground states to offset the huge margins Obama racked up with African Americans, women, union workers, and Latinos.

The fact that white men are not a monolithic group—and that enough voted Democratic, especially in blue states—is, of course, an important empirical counterweight to the claims of many of the Angry White Male choirmasters on talk radio and Fox News who say that they speak for all of "us."

But it hardly deters them. Do you recall the commentary on election night 2012? Rush Limbaugh said that he went to bed thinking "we'd lost the country." Bill O'Reilly quoted one of his listeners, mourning that "we have lost our American way of life." "I liked it the way it was," former Saturday Night Live news anchor Dennis Miller (now more of a self-parodying talk-show host) said about the country. "It's not going to be like that anymore." And what was the single unifying campaign slogan the Tea Party had to offer? "We want to take back our country."

When I read these comments, I was reminded of a joke from my childhood. It seems that the Lone Ranger and Tonto were riding across the plains when suddenly they were surrounded by ten thousand angry Indian warriors. (The word savages would likely have been used in those days.)

"We're in trouble, Tonto," says the Lone Ranger.

"What do you mean 'we,' kemosabe?" is Tonto's reply.

Tonto was right. Just what *do* they mean by "we"? Whose country is it?

One has to feel a sense of proprietorship, of entitlement, to call it "our" country. That sense has led millions of Americans, male and female, white and nonwhite, to feel like stakeholders in the American system and motivated millions to lay down their lives for that way of life. It's prompted some of the most moving stories of sacrifice, the most heroic and touching moments of connectedness with neighbors and strangers during crises. But it has its costs. That sense of holding on to what's "ours" can be turned into something ugly, sowing division where unity should be. Just as religiosity can motivate the most self-sacrificing charity and loving devotion, it can also be expressed as sanctimonious

self-righteousness, as if a privileged access to revealed truth grants permission to unspeakable cruelties.

It's not the depth of those collective feelings that is troubling—obviously, love of country can inspire us to great sacrifice; rather, it's their direction. When threatened, that sense of entitlement, of proprietorship, can be manipulated into an enraged protectionism, a sense that the threat to "us" is internal, those undeserving others who want to take for themselves what we have rightfully earned. "We" were willing to share, we might say, totally inverting the reality that "they" ask only for a seat at the table, not to overturn the table itself; "they" want it all for themselves. According to these angry white men, "they" not only want a seat, but now they got a guy sitting at the head of the table itself.

Note, also, that I said "can be manipulated." The expression of emotion often leaves one also vulnerable, susceptible to manipulation. There's little empirical evidence for some biologically driven or evolutionarily mandated tribalism—at least a tribalism based on such phony us-versus-them characteristics. Sure, it's true that when threatened, we have an instinctive reaction to circle the wagons and protect ourselves against whatever threatens us. So, for example, the fierce patriotism that emerged after the 9/11 attacks was a natural, collective response to invasion, just as the mobilization of the entire nation's sympathies after Hurricane Katrina or Sandy; few Americans were inured to the outpouring of collective grief, anguish, and shared purpose.

But to fixate on Saddam Hussein and the invasion of Iraq? That had to be manipulated: Iraq had not invaded us; indeed, Saddam Hussein was antipathetic to al-Qaeda. There were no weapons of mass destruction—but even had there been, why was it necessary to try to divert the outpouring of grief and desire for revenge to a different enemy? That we feel collective sentiments tells us nothing about how those sentiments can be mobilized and manipulated. In the case of the Iraq War, there was no threat, just the raw sentiments ripe for exploitation by cynical politicians.

Angry white men are genuinely floundering—confused and often demoralized, they experience that wide range of emotions. But their anger is often constructed from those emotional materials, given shape and directed at targets that serve other interests. Angry white men are angry, all right, but their anger needs to be channeled toward some groups—and away from others.

OUTRAGEOUS RADIO

As an emotion, anger has a fairly short shelf life. It's a "hot" emotion, like sexual desire, not a cooler emotion like devotion to a loved one, or abiding love of country, or pride in one's child. Anger must be fed, its embers constantly stoked—either personally, by holding a grudge, or collectively, by having sustained the sense that you have been injured, wounded, and that those who did it must pay. Feeling like the wronged victim is a way to channel hurt into a self-fueling sense of outrage; a personal sense of injury becomes "politicized" as an illustration of a general theme.

The politicization of the countless injuries, hurts, and injustices is the job of the self-appointed pundits in the media. It is they who offer a political framework for the anguish that you might feel, suggest how it represents a larger pattern of victimization of "people like you," and then urge collective action to redress it. (The collective action can be simply tuning in to the same radio show every day, knowing that you are among friends and allies.)

As a result, Angry White Men are a virtual social movement. I don't mean that they are "virtually" a movement—as in "almost, but not quite." I mean that they organize virtually, that their social-movement organization is a virtual organization. They sit alone, listening to the radio, listening to Rush Limbaugh and Mike Savage and Sean Hannity. They meet online, in chat rooms and on websites, whether promoting anti-feminist men's rights or the re-Aryanization of America. They troll cyberspace, the anti-PC police, ready to attack any blogger, columnist, or quasi liberal who dares to say something with which they disagree.

It is the task of the Angry White Male pundits in the media to act as the choirmasters of the Angry White Male chorus, to direct and redirect that rage, to orchestrate it so that the disparate howls of despair or anguish, the whimpers of pain, or the mumblings of confusion can sound unified. They are the conductors; they believe that we are their instruments. It's their job to take the anger that might, in fact, be quite legitimate and direct it elsewhere, onto other targets.

Say, for example, you are an autoworker, and you've seen your wages cut, your benefits dismantled, and your control over your hours steadily compromised. You may well be a bit miffed. But at whom? Left to your own

devices—and conversations with your friends—you might conclude that it is the fault of rapacious corporate moguls, who line their pockets and pay themselves fat bonuses and who squeeze every drop they can from America's working man. You might even list to the Left and make common cause with others in similar situations and try to get the government to regulate the industry, raise wages, protect benefits, and institute national health care. You might even work with your union.

So, if I were to try to channel Rush Limbaugh or Mike Savage, my task would be to redirect that anger onto others, those even less fortunate than you. Perhaps the reason you are so unhappy is because of all those immigrants who are streaming into America, driving the costs of labor lower and threatening "American" jobs. Or perhaps it's because women—even, perhaps, your own wife—want to enter the labor force, and that's what is driving down labor costs, as corporations no longer need to pay men a "family" wage, since they no longer support a family. Your grievances are not with the corporations, but with those just below you. In other words, as Thomas Frank points out in *What's the Matter with Kansas?*, it's the task of the pundits to create "a French Revolution in reverse—one in which the sans-culottes pour down the streets demanding more power for the aristocracy."

Limbaugh and Savage are only two of the hundreds of angry white men who have staked out an angry white male club on radio waves. I'll focus on them briefly here not because they are any worse than any of the others, but rather because they are so similar—in that masculinity is so central in their radio ratings. They're among the most popular: The Savage Nation is heard on 350 radio stations and reaches 8.25 million listeners each week, ranking third behind only Rush Limbaugh and Sean Hannity. Limbaugh outpaces everyone else, heard on more than 600 stations, with a weekly audience of more than 20 million.

Angry White Men dominate the American airwaves (even though their claim that the media tilt leftward enables them to both claim dominance and victimhood); their goal is to protect and preserve the dominance of American white men, even at the moment when white men, in real life, are actually accommodating themselves to greater and greater gender equality—and, actually, liking it very much.

What, though, are they actually so angry about?

Angry White Men exhibit what French social theorist Georges Sorel called "ressentiment"—a personal sense of self that is defined always in relationship to some perceived injury and whose collective politics mixes hatred and envy of those who we believe have injured us. That "creative hatred," Sorel argues, is anathema to serious collective action because it is so easily manipulated; it is more likely to spawn sporadic spasmodic violent eruptions than a serious social movement.

This sense of self, grounded in victimhood, both hating and envying others, can be a brilliant strategy, generating an audience of consumers. And it's not only these angry white men. Indeed, Oprah Winfrey's early television success involved constructing her audience as victims. In the early 1990s, I entered a discussion to appear on her show following the publication of my book *Men Confront Pornography*. When I spoke to the producer, she suggested that I appear alongside several women whose "husbands or boyfriends had forced them to do degrading sexual things after they'd seen them in pornography." I said no, that my book was a serious effort to invite men to take on the political debate that was, at the time, roiling feminism. I proposed being on with a few men who took the issues seriously. We went back and forth, up the ladder of increasingly senior producers. Finally, the very seniormost producer of the show, the one who talks directly with Oprah, admitted she didn't understand how my idea would work or what was wrong with her idea. "I just don't see it," she said. "I don't see who the victim is. You can't have an Oprah show without a victim."

What a revealing statement! As the producer saw it, the world was divided into two groups, viewers and victims. Viewers would tune in each day, perhaps feeling that their lives were miserable. And then they'd watch the show and exhale, and say, "Well, at least my husband doesn't force me to do degrading sexual things after he sees them in pornography! Maybe my life isn't so bad after all." And the next day, as the effects wear off, and viewers feel crappy again, they tune in to see someone who has it far worse, and they feel, temporarily, better. It's like *Queen for a Day*, a show I watched assiduously as a young child, in which three different women would tell of the terrible fates that had befallen them (husband injured on the job and unable to work,

debilitating illnesses, and so on), and the studio audience would vote (by the loudness of their applause, registering on an "Applause-o-Meter") which one of the women would be crowned queen and receive gifts like a new refrigerator and other household appliances. (I ended up going on *The Phil Donahue Show* instead.)

Oprah's shows in her last years on the air were more inspirational—not necessarily a parade of victims, but more about people who had triumphed over adversity, who had fallen down seven times and gotten up eight. But the theme of viewers and victims resonates more now on talk radio. It's but a short hop from dichotomous viewers and victims to a more unified community of viewers as victims. The genius of Rush Limbaugh and the others is that they have appropriated a more commonly "feminine" trope of perpetual victimhood and successfully masculinized it. In fact, they claim, it's your very manhood that is constantly under threat!

As befits an industry leader, Rush Limbaugh's politics of ressentiment has been amply parsed for its racism and sexism—he's popped into national consciousness usually when he strays over a line already drawn far to the other side of decency and respect.

He defends white people against what Lothrop Stoddard and Madison Grant, early-twentieth-century racialists, called "the rising tide of color." Limbaugh's racism is as transparent as his nativism and sexism. Here's what he said after Obama was elected the first time: "It's Obama's America, is it not? Obama's America, white kids getting beat up on school buses now. You put your kids on a school bus, you expect safety, but in Obama's America, the white kids now get beat up with the black kids cheering, 'Yeah, right on, right on, right on,' and, of course, everybody says the white kid deserved it: he was born a racist; he's white."

And how does one get ahead in Obama's America? "By hating white people. Or even saying you do. . . . Make white people the new oppressed minority. . . . They're moving to the back of the bus. . . . That's the modern day Republican Party, the equivalent of the Old South: the new oppressed minority."

Poor white people, the victims of government-sponsored racial discrimination. And poor men, victims of reverse sexism as well. For example, when Sandra Fluke, a graduate student at Georgetown, testified in support of requiring all institutions receiving federal funds to actually obey the law and provide contraception,

Limbaugh launched into a vicious ad feminam attack against Fluke personally, calling her a slut and a whore for having so much sex, and demanded, as a taxpayer, that she provide high-quality videos of her sexual escapades. "If we are going to pay for your contraceptives and thus pay for you to have sex, we want something. We want you to post the videos online so we can all watch."

It's easy to understand the sense of entitlement that this sixth-generation upper-class heir to a Missouri family of lawyers and politicians might feel. And it's not so very hard to understand how so many of his white male listeners might identify with him, even if they're more recent arrivals, and they've always held jobs for which you shower after work, not before it.

What binds this bilious martinet to his listeners, though, is that they are men, at least the overwhelming majority of them, and their sense of entitlement comes from their deep-seated feeling that they are the heirs to the American Dream that, as Woody Guthrie should have sung, this land was really made for them. Note that he assumes that his listeners are male—that "we" are entitled to see videos of Sandra Fluke or that it's a little white boy who is being harassed. "We" is white and male. Indeed, a cover story in *Newsweek* on talk radio called it "group therapy for mostly white males who feel politically challenged."

Rarely, though, have commentators gone much further than noticing how these shows resonate with white men. It's as if noting the demographics explains the sociology. So they rarely discuss gender, discuss how masculinity is implicated. Nor do they see Limbaugh's rage as a particularly masculine rage, the "gender" of the pain he claims to channel into outrage. On the one hand, he's a real man, a man's man—"a cigar-smoking, NFL-watching, red-meat right winger who's offended by the 'feminization' of American society." His sense of aggrieved entitlement is to restore not the reality but the possibility of dominance. It is simultaneously aspirational and nostalgic—he looks back to a time when it was all there, unchallenged, and forward to its restoration. Limbaugh's own public struggles with his weight, his failed childless marriages, his avoidance of military service, his addiction to OxyContin (surely the wimpiest addiction possible; real men smoke crack or shoot heroin), and his well-known need for Viagra all testify to a masculinity in need of propping up, in need of

reconfirmation. In Limbaugh's case, right-wing racist and sexist politics is the conduit for the restoration of his manhood—and for the manhood of other fellow sufferers of aggrieved entitlement. Limbaugh offers a prescription for political Viagra, designed to get that blood flowing, reenergize a flagging sense of white American manhood.

But if the elite-born Limbaugh plays in the populist sandbox, Mike Savage is both the real deal and even more a poseur. At least he's a working-class guy—born Michael Alan Weiner, the son of Russian Jewish immigrants who settled in the Bronx during World War II. But then, why would such a nice Jewish boy, whose own mother and father were the beneficiaries of the American Dream of immigration, now want to slam the door on the faces of everyone else?

Limbaugh is positively tame compared to Savage, who seems to believe that the higher the decibels of his denunciations, the more persuasive they will be. And like Limbaugh, he's interested in reversing the very multicultural trends that he represents. Like Limbaugh, he's immensely popular, and like Limbaugh, he engages in a conspiratorial Us–Them framing, in which "we" are the enlightened few and "they" are the dupes of the government-inspired hijacking of freedom. He calls illegal immigrants and their allies "brown supremacists" and accuses activists for sexual equality of "raping" children through media campaigns for tolerance.

But ultimately, it all has to do with masculinity. Savage alternates between Limbaugh's conspiratorial outrage—can you believe what they are doing to us?—and chastising his audience for allowing this all to happen under their very noses. The campaign for so-called civil rights is a "con," and affirmative action stole his "birthright." What you have now, he claims, is "the wholesale replacement of competent white men." And what has been our reaction? We've become a "sissified nation," a "sheocracy." Part of "the de-balling of America," "true red-blooded American types have been thrown out of the—out of the government."

Part of this is women's fault, of course—feminist women who have become more masculine. Here's what he said on his show: "Particularly today, the women are not, you know, what they were thirty years ago. The women have become more like guys, thanks to the hags in the women's movement, and the white race is dying. That's why they won't reproduce, because the women want to be men. They want to behave like men, they want to act like men, they've been encouraged to think like men, act like men, be like men. Consequently, they don't want to be women, and they don't want to be mothers."

Were you to ask Limbaugh and Savage, and the others who aspire to their seats of influence, they'd likely tell you that they aren't really antiwomen but antifeminist, and specifically promale, more about legitimizing the anger of white men. Feminism comes under attack—after all, it was Limbaugh who popularized the term feminazi—phantasmagorically linking campaigns for wage equality, or safety from battery and rape, to the organized, methodical genocide in the Third Reich.

Now, why has this resonated? Because the defensiveness of white men is so narcissistic that any criticism of masculinity and male entitlement is seen as the effort to leverage the apparatus of the state in the service of the destruction of an entire biological sex. But these guys aren't really interested in women. They're interested in promoting the interests of white men.

In a particularly revealing rant, Savage links racism, sexism, and anti-immigrant nativism in his pitch to fellow angry white men:

> Many of you have been hoodwinked into believing that we are a multicultural nation, which we are not. We're a nation of many races and many cultures, that is true, it has been true from the beginning, but in the past people would come over and become Americans. Now they come over, and they want you to become them. . . . We're going to have a revolution in this country if this keeps up. These people are pushing the wrong people around. . . . If they keep pushing us around and if we keep having these schmucks running for office, catering to the multicultural people who are destroying the culture in this country, guaranteed the people, the white male in particular . . . the one without connections, the one without money, has nothing to lose, and you haven't seen him yet. You haven't seen him explode in this country. And he's still the majority, by the way, in case you don't know it. He is still the majority, and no one speaks for him, everyone craps on him . . . and he has no voice whatsoever. . . . And you're going to find out that if you keep pushing this country around, you'll find out that there's an ugly side to the white male.

Outrage media is not, however, a one-way street. The audience is an active participant; together with the host, they produce the rage of the day and direct it toward the issues on which the free-floating rage will land. Each day offers no shortage of the horrors of what "they" are doing to "us"—"they" being government bureaucrats in thrall to the feminist cabal, implementing the gay agenda, illegals, and minorities guided by sinister Marxian forces. (They often come perilously close to denouncing their Zionist puppeteers of the International Jewish Conspiracy. Indeed, were it not for the convenience of stoking anti-Muslim sentiment since 9/11, we'd hear quite a bit more anti-Semitism from some of these hosts. Generally, the right wing loves Israel, but hates Jews.)

Angry White Male Radio is the New England town meeting of the twenty-first century. The participatory experience, with its steady stream of callers, ups the emotional ante. Sure, there's plenty of defensive anger to go around. But the tone expresses a sense of aggrieved entitlement. Rush's followers call themselves "dittoheads," echoing every sentiment. "What Rush does on his shows is take frustration and rage and rearticulate and confirm them as ideology," writes Sherri Paris, after listening nonstop for several weeks. "Limbaugh's skill lies in weaving political alienation and anger into the illusion of common political ground." He's creating a community out of people's individual frustrations, giving them a sense of "we-ness."

"I love it," says Jay, a twenty-six-year-old Nebraskan with obvious self-consciousness. Jay was one of several dittoheads I talked with around the country. Actually, he drove the taxi from the university where I'd been lecturing to the airport. Rush was on in the cab. "I mean, all day long, all I get is multicultural this and diversity that. I love it because I can let off steam at how stupid the whole thing is. I can't stop it—there's no way. But I get all these other guys who remind me that it's not right, it's not fair, and the system's out of control. And I'm the one getting screwed!"

Jay was among the more articulate when it came to discussing substantive issues like affirmative action or race and gender preferences in admissions. Most of the guys I spoke with whose analysis came from Limbaugh and Fox News merely mouthed platitudes they took directly from the shows, without so much as actually thinking if they applied to their situations. I cannot count the number of times I heard lines like "It's not the government's money, it's the people's money" in response to tax policy.

You'd think that after nearly a half century of sustained critique of racial and gender bias in the media, of the most convincing empirical social and behavioral science research imaginable, of civil rights, women's, and gay and lesbian movements, white guys would have finally understood how bias works and would have accommodated themselves to a new, more egalitarian, more democratic, and more representative media. Or at least you'd think they'd be less vocal in their resistance. But as far as they're concerned, the world hasn't merely changed—it's been upended, turned upside down into its perverse mirror image. "It's completely crazy," says Matt. "The inmates are running the asylum. They're completely in power, and they get anything they want. And us regular, normal white guys—we're like nothing. We don't count for shit anymore."

Outrage media offers a case of what Frankfurt School philosopher Herbert Marcuse called "repressive desublimation." Although not exactly the catchiest of phrase makers, Marcuse was on to something that, as a refugee from Hitler's Germany, he found so scary: how the ability to sound off angrily, to express all your pent-up rage (the "desublimation" part), could actually serve the interests of those in power. Being able to rebel in these impotent ways actually enables the system to continue (hence, the "repressive" part). You think you're rebelling by listening to jazz, or punk rock, or even angry rap music, having a lot of sex, drinking and screaming your heads off about how the system is oppressing you. You find common cause with others who are doing the same thing: instant community. And, after desublimating, you go back to work, a docile, sated drone, willing to conform to what the "system" asks of you because the system also lets you blow off steam. Bread and circuses. Participatory entertainment. (Instead of worrying, for example, that an excessive diet of violent video games would make a young guy more likely to commit an act of violence, the Frankfurt School would have been more worried that he'd be more docile, that he'd never rebel socially, collectively, because he got all that rebellion out of his

system on a machine created by one of the world's largest corporations.)

Yet, ironically, the very medium that provides the false sense of community of Limbaugh's dittoheads can also be, simultaneously, isolating. "People tend to be less angry when they have to interact with each other," writes journalist and media commentator Joe Klein; they become afflicted with "Information Age disorder"—the "product of our tendency to stew alone, staring into computer screens at work, blobbing in front of the television at home." Perhaps we're not bowling alone, but fuming alone. Together.

So American white men, still among the most privileged group of people on the face of the earth—if you discount hereditary aristocracies and sheikdoms—feel that they are the put-upon victims of a society that grows more equal every day. It's hard if you've been used to 100 percent of all the positions of power and privilege in the world to wake up one morning and find people like you in only 80 percent of those positions. Equality sucks if you've grown so accustomed to inequality that it feels normal.

Listen to the words of one leader, defending the rights of those disempowered white men: "Heaven help the God-fearing, law-abiding Caucasian middle class, Protestant or even worse evangelical Christian, Midwest or Southern or even worse rural, apparently straight or even worse admittedly [heterosexual], gun-owning or even worse NRA card-carrying average working stiff, or even worst of all, male working stiff . Because not only don't you count, you're a downright obstacle to social progress." That leader was, incidentally, Charlton Heston, acting less like Moses and more like an angry Pharaoh, feeling powerless as he watches his slaves disappear.

These are not the voices of power but the voices of entitlement to power. The positions of authority, of power, have been stolen from them—handed over to undeserving "others" by a government bureaucracy that has utterly abandoned them. If listening to Guy Radio and watching Guy TV is about blowing off steam, this is what that steam smells like.

Far from fomenting a reactionary revolution, Limbaugh and his ilk are the Peter Finches of the twenty-first century, screaming about how they are mad as hell and not going to take it anymore—which is the very thing that enables them to take far more of it.

A GLANCE BACK: A BRIEF HISTORY OF AMERICAN ANGRY WHITE MEN

Of course, this isn't the first time that Americans have been treated to a chorus of complainers that rail against the "masculinization" of women and the "feminization" of men. A century ago, pundits across America bemoaned what they saw as a crisis of masculinity. They bemoaned the loss of the hardy manly virtues that had settled the country, harnessed its natural resources toward amazing industrial breakthroughs, "tamed" a restive native population, and fended off external threats. Men were becoming soft, effeminate. Ironically, it was the somewhat effete novelist Henry James who captured this sentiment most eloquently in the character of Basil Ransome, the dashing southern gentleman in *The Bostonians* (1885):

> The whole generation is womanized; the masculine tone is passing out of the world; it's a feminine, nervous, hysterical, chattering, canting age, an age of hollow phrases and false delicacy and exaggerated solicitudes and coddled sensibilities, which, if we don't soon look out, will usher in the reign of mediocrity, of the feeblest and flattest and most pretentious that has ever been. The masculine character, the ability to dare and endure, to know and yet not fear reality, to look the world in the face and take it for what it is . . . that is what I want to preserve, or, rather, recover; and I must tell you that I don't in the least care what becomes of you ladies while I make the attempt!

Where these critics disagreed was over the source of this emasculation—and, therefore, of course, what solutions might be helpful to restore American men's manly virtues. Most agreed that modern urban civilization had a feminizing effect: instead of working in the fields, or in factories, or as artisanal craft workers, American men now sat in stuffy offices, in white-collared shirts, pushing paper around desks. Instead of being apprenticed to older, seasoned male workers, young boys were now taught by female teachers, by female Sunday-school teachers, and, most of all, by their mothers, as fathers were away all day at work. (The separation of work and home may have meant that women were "imprisoned" in the home, as Betty Friedan would later argue, but it also meant that men were exiled from it, away all day, and returning to an increasingly feminized Victorian living space.) Even religion had become "feminized,"

as Protestant ministers spoke of a beatific and compassionate Christ, who loved his enemies and turned the other cheek.

Not only were women demanding entry into the public sphere—going to work, joining unions, demanding the right to vote and go to college—but native-born white men were facing increasing competition from freed slaves migrating to northern industrial cities and waves of immigrants from Asia and southern and eastern Europe, moving into tenement slums and creating a vast pool of cheap labor.

Everywhere men looked, the playing field had grown increasingly competitive and uncertain. Just as Horatio Alger was celebrating the "luck and pluck" that would enable young men of modest means to make their way to the top, native-born American white men were becoming far less concerned with how to make it to the top and far more anxious about sinking to the bottom. Restoring or retrieving a lost heroic manhood was less about the thrill of victory, as television announcers might have said, had there been *ABC's Wide World of Sports* in 1900, and far more about forestalling or preventing the agony of defeat.

Actually, there was the equivalent of Jim McKay, host of that iconic TV show. Or, rather, a lot of equivalents. It was at the turn of the last century that all the modern sports we know and love today—hockey, football, baseball, basketball—were organized into leagues and prescribed, especially, for schoolboys to promote a healthy, hardy manliness. Following on the heels of the British elite private schools and the success of Tom Brown's School Days, American reformers were quick to point out the restorative qualities of athletic prowess and the tonic virtues of the outdoors. Baseball, for example, was trumpeted by Theodore Roosevelt, himself the epitome of manly triumph over aristocratic weakness, as a "true sport for a manly race." "All boys love baseball," wrote the western novelist Zane Grey in 1909. "If they don't, they're not real boys."

Getting in shape was a manly preoccupation at the turn of the last century, as urban men fretted about the loss of manly vigor. In studying the late nineteenth and early twentieth centuries, I discerned three patterns of response to this mounting crisis, three avenues in which American men were counseled to restore the manhood that seemed so threatened.

First, they sought self-control. Believing that American men had grown soft and indolent, they sought to demonstrate greater amounts of self-control. Believing that the body was an instrument of their will, American men at the turn of the twentieth century bulked up, pumped up, and worked out as never before. As famed psychologist G. Stanley Hall put it, "You can't have a firm will without firm muscles." Gyms sprouted up all over the country, especially in large cities where middle-class white-collar office workers followed athletic regimens offered by scions of "physical culture" (like Bernarr Macfadden) and admired the physique of bodybuilders like Eugen Sandow. By the 1920s, they'd begun to follow a young, scrawny, Italian American immigrant who'd been unsuccessful at picking up a girl at the beach at Coney Island, Brooklyn. Ashamed of his physique—he called himself a "97 Pound runt . . . skinny, pale, nervous and weak"—young Angelo Siciliano developed a muscle-building regime that became the most successful body-transforming regimen in US history. Along the way, Siciliano changed more than his physique, becoming the "world's most perfect man." He also changed his name, to Charles Atlas.

The biceps weren't the only muscles over which American men felt they needed to exert greater control. They were equally concerned that they'd grown soft and weak because of their sexual profligacy. Masturbation not only threatened a man's healthy development, but was also a moral threat to the nation. Reformers utilized what one historian labeled the language of a "spermatic economy" to discourage it. Sperm were a resource, not to be squandered or "spent," but rather "saved" and "invested" in the future. Other health reformers like Sylvester Graham, C. W. Post, and J. H. Kellogg experimented with different whole grains and flours in their crackers and cereals to help keep men regular and thus prevent the blockages that pollute the body, and thus the mind, and lead to solitary vices. It's one thing to prescribe graham crackers or Post Toasties, or even Corn Flakes, and quite another to prescribe suturing the foreskin closed without anesthesia as a way for parents to ensure that their sons didn't masturbate. But that is what Kellogg did in his efforts to treat all sorts of male malaise in his sanitarium in Battle Creek, Michigan (Kellogg's own hysteria was held up to hilarious ridicule by novelist T. Coraghessan Boyle in *The Road to Wellville*).

These efforts represented only one of the three major patterns of solutions to the "crisis" of masculinity that were offered to American men at the turn of the last century. A second strategy was "escape." Boys needed to escape the feminizing clutches of women; they had to run away, ship out on the Pequod, join Henry Fleming in the army, or otherwise be "lighting out for the territory," in the immortal last words of Huckleberry Finn, "because Aunt Sally she's gonna adopt me and sivilize me, and I can't stand it." Modern society had turned "robust, hardy self-reliant boyhood into a lot of flat-chested cigarette smokers with shaky nerves and doubtful vitality," according to Ernest Thompson Seton, who founded the Boy Scouts of America in 1910 to turn the tide of feminization. Other clubs and organizations followed, including the Boone and Crockett Club, and later the YMCA (Young Men's Christian Association) itself, proclaiming itself a "man factory," providing a homosocial haven in an increasingly coeducational world.

Just as their sons needed to be rescued from the feminizing clutches of mothers and teachers, American men, too, set off to retrieve their deep manhood. And while the boys were busy with Boy Scouts and the Boone and Crockett Club, college guys were joining Greek-letter fraternities and rowing and boxing. Middle-aged men were joining fraternal lodges (nearly one in four American men belonged to a lodge in 1900) or heading off on safaris and treks and military-inspired adventures in search of the ever-receding frontier, or creating the frontier itself at newly invented "dude ranches" where urban gentlemen could get their hands dirty learning to rope and ride and play cowboy. "The wilderness will take hold on you," wrote western naturalist George Evans. "It will give you good red blood; it will turn you from a weakling into a man." Or they could always read westerns, like *The Virginian* (1902), by Owen Wister, the story of an urban dude who encounters a real man of the West and devotes his life to recounting his exploits (written by a Harvard-educated upper-class dandy who, himself, was a convert to the vigorous virtue of the West).

Or they were attending men-only religious revivals with itinerant preacher Billy Sunday (a former Chicago Cubs baseball player-turned-evangelist) whose "Muscular Christianity" was a riposte to the "dainty, sissified, lily-livered piety" of mainstream Protestantism. Jesus,

Sunday thundered, was a scrapper, who kicked the money changers out of the Temple; Christianity was "hard muscled, pick-axed religion, a religion from the gut, tough and resilient."

Finally, and most germane to our purposes here, men saw "exclusion" as a strategy to protect their ability to sustain themselves as men. If the playing field had now grown more crowded, and the cries for leveling it had grown more insistent, then one strategy was to kick them out. One can read American nativism, racism, anti-immigrant sentiment, and, of course, anti-feminism through this lens; movements to restrict immigration, to keep women out of college or the labor market, to maintain racial segregation were all efforts by white men to make the playing field smaller and therefore minimize the competition and maintain the opportunities that white men had earlier enjoyed. Then, as now, social Darwinism and the "natural" hierarchies of race and nation were useful fictions on which to base this exclusion. "How long before the manly warlike people of Ohio of fair hair and blue eyes," asked Ohio congressman Samuel Sullivan Cox, "would become, in spite of Bibles and morals, degenerate under the wholesale emancipation and immigration [of black slaves]?"

Racists, nativists, and anti-Semites all made common cause: protecting the pure white race from degeneracy required keeping "them" out, away from "our" women, and from competing for "our" jobs. Anti-immigrant sentiment from the Know-Nothings of the 1840s to the present day has seen border closings as a win–win: we don't have to deal with "their" ways and accommodate ourselves to their needs for health care or education in their own languages, and we can eliminate the additional competition for jobs.

Interestingly, the grounds for exclusion were often gendered—that is, the "other" was simply not appropriately masculine. In what I have come to call the "Goldilocks Dilemma," the masculinity of the other was like the porridge—either "too hot" or "too cold," but never "just right." They were either "hypermasculine" (violent, out-of-control, rapacious animals) or "hypomasculine" (weak, effeminate, irresponsible, and dependent). We, by contrast, had just the right mixture of hardy self-reliance and community spirit: we had tamed our animal nature into civilized gentlemen, but not so much that we lost sight of our rugged side.

Jews were imagined as weak, effete, and bookish nerds, who were also so avariciously greedy that they controlled the economy of the entire world. Blacks were lazy, irresponsible, dependent, and also rapacious predatory sexual animals. Feminist women, for that matter, were more masculine than their men. Chinese men were slight, frail, and effeminate, were nonviolent, and wore women's clothing, and, at the same time, they were part of a yellow peril that was maniacally sweeping over California ports. One critic wanted it both ways; the Chinese were, he wrote, "a barbarous race, devoid of energy." This constant jumping between hyper- and hypomasculine, often in the same utterances, would be echoed by today's white supremacists, as we will see later in this book.

Of course, these strategies for manly restoration are broad, and not mutually exclusive. For example, many of the fraternal orders were not only for men only, but also racially exclusionary. The Loyal Order of the Moose, Modern Woodmen, and the Order of the United American Mechanics were all white by charter; the latter could be relied on as a racist goon squad. And, of course, the resurgence of the fraternal order of the Ku Klux Klan in the first decades of the twentieth century, in border regions like southern Indiana, was dedicated to expunging "aliens" as well as resisting racial equality.

Several best sellers at the turn of the last century sounded an alarm that has echoed across the century into the voice of today's angry white men. Then, Lothrop Stoddard's *The Rising Tide of Color* (1920), Homer Lea's *The Day of the Saxon* (1912), and Madison Grant's *The Passing of the Great Race* (1916) prefigured contemporary warnings about the dangers of immigration, miscegenation, and interracial sex. At the turn of the last century, it bordered on hysteria. "The whole white race is exposed to the possibility of social sterilization and final replacement or absorption by the teeming colored races," wrote Stoddard; that would be "an unspeakable catastrophe." "The white man is being rapidly bred out by negroes," echoed Grant, resulting in an "ever thinning veneer of white culture." Grant was convinced that "the cross between a white man and a Negro is a Negro," and "the cross between a European and a Jew is a Jew." Race mixing was race destroying. (This last is a revealing insight into the fears of angry white men: that the sexuality of the other is imagined as both more predatory and rapacious, but also that the other is far more sexually capable, whether in stereotypes about black men's penis size, hot-blooded Italian ardor, Filipino alacrity, or Latino suaveness. Of course, such projections are far less about the feared and far more about the anxieties and insecurities of the fearful and their insecurities about their ability to satisfy increasingly sexually entitled women.)

Women's and men's missions were clear. Women had to have babies—white babies—and a lot of them to avoid "race suicide" and ensure the perpetuation of the purity of the race. Men had to stand tall and determined against the rising tide of color, providing steadfast resistance to the promise of the Statue of Liberty. If the promise of America would be a welcome mat to new opportunities for the world's "huddled masses," angry white men would make sure they felt utterly unwelcome. There was no way they would let the welcome mat to others turn them, the Americans who were entitled to be here, into a doormat. It's a fine line, and they would not let it be crossed.

At the turn of the last century, that's how it sounded, how racism and nativism blended together in fears of loss and downward mobility and rage at a government that would so casually erode the inalienable rights of native-born white folk. And that's pretty much how it sounds today, along the fences that anti-immigrant groups patrol to make sure "they" stay out.

BORDER PATROLS

Old habits die hard. At the turn of the twentieth century, those angry white men sought to seal the borders and make sure that aliens did not overrun the country. Today, their grievances are no less palpable. Perhaps these are the great-grandsons of the Lothrop Stoddards and Madison Grants of the 1920s—still protecting their women from those bestial hordes, still furious at a government too enthralled with the ideals of multiculturalism, and beholden to corporations who like the wage suppression that invariably accompanies immigration, and terrified that the country they knew, "their" country, was becoming unrecognizable. They don't ride horses along those borders very much; now it's mostly pickup trucks with gun racks and high-beam lights. But their anger echoes their forebears, and their sense that "their"

country is being taken away from them is no less tangible.

The sense of aggrieved entitlement is evident in the language of these contemporary nativists. It's not "immigration" but an "invasion" of "illegals" who are "alien" and unsuited for our way of life. "An invasion is spreading across America like wildfire, bringing gangs, drugs, and an alien culture into the very heartland of America" is how a video from the Voice of Citizens Together put it in 1999. Anti-immigration activists use the same language as Nazis or Hutus and others who promote genocide. They are a "cancer" threatening the healthy body from within, a foreign invading army, threatening from outside—often both. Immigrants are a "hostile force on our border" and a "cultural cancer . . . eating at the very heart of our nation."

They come because they want what we have—which has always been one of the reasons for immigration to the United States, after all, the promise of a better life, of starting over in the land of the do over. The founding fathers remembered that America had been founded by illegal immigrants who had been hounded out of their own country for being too religiously rigid; they created an open society where, by the turn of the twentieth century, the world's "huddled masses, yearning to breathe free," came by the boatloads. Today's nativists have forgotten their own origins in another country and want to deny to others what they, themselves, found.

The mobilization to repel this invasion of illegals is justified by gender. "Their" women are hypersexual, reproductive machines, cranking out babies with utter disregard for propriety. They're unwashed, unclean, and unpleasant. Their men are sexually irresponsible, equally unwashed, and predatory. Listen to Joe Arpaio, America's nativist in chief, the racist, self-proclaimed "America's toughest sheriff," sheriff of Maricopa County, Arizona: "All these people that come over, they could come with disease. There's no control, no health checks or anything. They check fruits and vegetables, how come they don't check people? No one talks about that! They're all dirty. I sent out 200 inmates into the desert, they picked up 18 tons of garbage that they bring in—the baby diapers and all that. Where's everybody who wants to preserve the desert?"

Arpaio is hardly an environmentalist, seeking to preserve the desert. He's far more interested in preserving white native-born entitlement to the desert. Perhaps the most visible public figure seeking to close the border to Mexican immigration, he seems to revel in accusations of racism (he is said to have found it "an honor" to be compared to the KKK, since "it means we're doing something"). He's been under federal indictment for racial profiling (which he admits), for setting up some of the most miserable jail conditions in America, including a tent city for overflow inmates (which he calls a "concentration camp"), feeding inmates surplus food, limiting meals to twice a day, and forcing inmates to wear pink underwear as a sign of their humiliation.

But Arpaio is also a figurehead in the anti-immigration movement and one of the more willing to see the battle as between "real men" and poseurs. While Mexican men are lazy, dependent on welfare, dirty, and clearly unable to maintain the necessary self-control to be real Americans, they're also bloodthirsty soldiers in a war of reconquest. "My parents did not regard any inch of American soil as somehow belonging to Italy, so their arrival here never constituted a 'reconquest' of that land. A growing movement among not only Mexican nationals, but also some Mexican-Americans contends that the United States stole the territory that is now California, Arizona and Texas, for a start, and that massive immigration over the border will speed and guarantee the reconquista of these lands, returning them to Mexico."

Arpaio is hardly alone. Take Harley Brown, a perennial candidate for office in Idaho. (He ran unsuccessfully for Congress in 2010.) In his campaign for the state's sole congressional seat, Brown, who bills himself as "A Real Man for Congress," outlined his policy positions:

THE MIDDLE EAST: "Nuke Their Ass, Take Their Gas"

GUN CONTROL: "Hitting Your Target"

GAYS IN THE MILITARY: "Keep the Queens Out of the Marines"

IMMIGRATION POLICY: "Adios, Amigos"

Sure, Brown is a life-size cartoon, a caricature of the crazed armchair warrior, a Duke Nukem who has never been to actual war. But Brown expresses the epigrammatic anger of a wide band of American men who are joining the Tea Parties, rural militias, Minutemen, and

Patriot groups to patrol our borders. "The Zoo has an African lion and the White House has a lyin' African," commented one Tea Party placard.

As with Limbaugh's legions, it was difficult to get any of the Tea Party protesters I met at any of the sparsely attended rallies I observed to say anything of more substance than the aphorisms that were already on their placards. I'd ask what I thought was an innocent question, and I usually got puzzled looks, as though I might have been speaking a different language. For example, at one rally, I asked a nicely dressed older guy named Ralph, a former sales rep perhaps in his late sixties, who was wearing khakis, a plaid shirt, and a three-cornered hat, what about the original Boston Tea Party had proved so inspiring to him. "They revolted against taxation from an illegitimate government," he said flatly, as if he were reciting a catechism. "They were revolting against a government takeover." When I asked what he meant, he said—as did every single Tea Partier with whom I spoke—that Obamacare was socialized medicine that would raise taxes on the middle class. "It's part of the plan. They want to take over everything. But America was founded on the idea that the government couldn't tell you what to do. We need to get back to that."

Such contentless statements are what often passes for political discourse in America in 2013. When I tried, foolishly, as it turned out, to ask exactly how universal health care would raise taxes, or raise the cost of care, or how government spending on such things as education, highways, or the GI Bill augured a government takeover, or how government regulations to rein in corporate greed somehow hurt middle-class Americans—well, I got initially puzzled looks, followed pretty quickly by more hostile glares and a simple shrug as they walked off. Slogans are the Tea Party's version of political theory; oft-repeated falsehoods gradually become self-evident truths.

I heard the same thing when I talked with anti-immigrant groups. These groups see illegal immigration as an "alien invasion," as the Minutemen do. And most see the repulsion of this invading horde as akin to the colonials kicking out the British colonists in 1776. (It's one of the great ironies of the current nativist movement that it cloaks itself in the language of the founding fathers, but its politics are far more reminiscent of those of King George III. Well, except for that fact that he taxed the colonials to further his own ambition.) The Minutemen, another private paramilitary band of white middle- and working-class guys in border states who patrol the borders, doing the job that they believe our own immigration police fail to do, are most explicit in calling for a second American Revolution against a tyrannical King Barack. "Do the citizens of the United States view the Federal Government as an oppressive force occupying Washington? There came a point in American history—April 19, 1775—that the colonists could no longer tolerate oppression of the occupying forces that consumed their rights and led to the revolution. It was a moment in history, which not only shocked the Kingdom of Great Britain, but also set off a cascade effect that is still felt today."

And these sentiments are not limited only to the southwestern border states. I talked to people who were demonstrating against the building of an interfaith Islamic community center in Lower Manhattan, who seemed to think that establishing a place for dialogue and day care was establishing a beachhead on Normandy Beach in preparation for the full-on assault on the capital of the world economy. (These are the same people who complain that the "legitimate" Muslim world did not immediately condemn the terrorist attacks of 9/11. When a group actually does want to build a bridge, they're accused of refusing to design it properly.)

One of the most horrific cases happened, in fact, right around the corner from my campus on Long Island. Long Island is the quintessential American suburb—one of the first suburbs in the nation. Its demographic profile—largely white and middle class, with a significant influx of immigrants and minorities in recent decades—makes it a cauldron in which anti-immigrant sentiment bubbles up to unify disparate levels of discontent. Here, in those split-level houses atop those leafy front lawns, breathes the same rage that drives pickup trucks along the Texas–Mexico border, patrolling illegal immigrants and attacking their families.

Farmingville is a "typical" middle-class Long Island suburb. But in 2004 it erupted when two Mexican day laborers were attacked and nearly murdered by a gang of white male suburbanites. Not far away, in 2008 an Ecuadoran immigrant named Marcelo Lucero was attacked by seven white teenagers and stabbed to death simply because of his ethnicity. Lucero had been walking with a friend near the Long Island Rail Road station around midnight in November 2008 when they were confronted by the white teenagers who had gone out specifically looking for a Hispanic to attack. "Let's go beat up some Mexican guys," they had said. They found one, and they killed him. Four of the teenage boys pleaded guilty to the hate crime and testified against the other three.

Although we northerners are used to feeling horror, revulsion, and more than a little contempt for the white South when we hear about racist lynchings in the Jim Crow South, we don't really know how to absorb that such things are happening all over our country. The siege mentality, the defense against invasion—these are themes that echo across all classes and in every region.

This notion that America is under siege contains several layers of anxiety among white American men. The fear that "they" are taking over is an insult to "our" manhood—for they will take our jobs, our homes, and our women if we are not vigilant. The fear that they are taking what is rightfully ours—a government that serves our needs to be left alone, as opposed to their need to have everything handed to them on a silver platter. The fear that we are being emasculated—by these less than fully manly hordes and by a feckless government utterly in their thrall.

In a sense, the government that is imagined by Angry White Men embodies the same hyper- and hypomasculine qualities that the "other" embodies. On the one hand, the government is weak, having been invaded by all these special interests (like women or unions or minorities or gays and lesbians) and unable to resist being taken over by them. The "others" are the real men, more masculine than the government, which has become weak, a "nanny state," feminized.

On the other hand, the government is voracious, taxing and regulating, greedy beyond measure. Hypermasculine, it subdues the raw, noble masculinity of the heroic American white man and subordinates it to the ignoble, undeserving, unmanly hordes clamoring for what we have. This is a government that doesn't "permit" others to learn in their native language and thus become integrated; it's a government that will pretty soon require that everyone speak Spanish. Thus, "English only" is not arrogant and entitled but protectionist, just holding on to what we have.

Angry White Men are thus stuck—between a voracious state and the hypermasculine invading army, or between a feminized nanny state and these dependent, weak, and irresponsible masses. Or perhaps it's more of a mix and match: a hypermasculine alien force capturing the weakened state, or a greedy nanny state taking from us, from real men, and giving to those whining, victim-mongering wimps. The permutations are far less important than the result of the equation: we, we once-happy few, we American men, who built this country with our own hands, are now having it wrenched from us and given to these undeserving others. Right under our noses.

The thread that ties together these disparate and often contradictory strands is gender—masculinity. These tropes float, collide, contradict, but they fit together in an ever-shifting cosmology because they are bound together by codes of gender. "They" emasculate "us"—both by being more primally masculine than we are (and thus in need of control) and, simultaneously, by being dependent and weak (and thus needing the state to control "us" from succeeding). Only from the position of aggrieved entitlement can these various images be reconciled—irrationally, but viscerally.

. . .

ANGRY WHITE WOMEN

Of course, by now most of you are ready to remind me that it's not just white men who are angry. Quite true. There are plenty of angry people of color—both male and female. And plenty of them feel some amount of aggrieved entitlement—feeling "entitled" to an even playing field in education, employment, or housing, to health care, to the right to vote without some arcane new law that throws up obstacles. And, to be fair, many poor and working people, of all races, feel entitled to government support for health care, for food and financial support if they are unemployed, for support to raise their children. That is, they tend to feel entitled while looking "up," looking at what their country tells them they are entitled to—equality, fairness, an equal chance at making it.

Angry White Men feel entitled while looking "down"—at the hordes of "others" who are threatening to take what they believe is rightfully theirs and are being aided in their illegitimate quest by a government that is in their thrall. It's ironic that the Angry White

Men I am discussing in this book feel they can actually get what they are entitled to only if the government shrinks—nearly to the point of disappearing. By contrast, poor people should—I emphasize the normative—understand that they can get what they want only if the government expands to stimulate growth, promote consumer spending, and provide a social safety net.

This irony is resolved not by some abstract analysis of entitlement, but by a sense of historical context. Angry White Men tend to feel their sense of aggrieved entitlement because of the past; they want to restore what they once had. Their entitlement is not aspirational; it's nostalgic. Poor people and people of color, by contrast, feel entitled to what they should have, what others in fact do have. Angry white men feel entitled to restrict equality; people of color want to expand it.

And, of course, there are legions of angry white women. Since 2008 they've been mobilized through the Tea Party and its standard-bearers, former Alaska governor Sarah Palin and Minnesota congresswoman Michele Bachman. Angry white women are decidedly not upper-middle-class, Volvo-station-wagon-driving, Chardonnay-sipping soccer moms. They're hockey moms, drinking beer and driving Chevy pickups. (Palin famously explained the difference between a hockey mom and a pit bull: lipstick.) Now they've declared themselves "mama grizzlies."

At first glance, the presence of so many women in the Tea Party—surely, one of the angriest white people's organizations this side of the Klan—would tend to undermine my argument that the current political rage is such a gendered phenomenon. In addition to their femme fatale standard-bearers, many of the most visible leaders of the movement are also women, like Jenny Beth Martin of the Tea Party Patriots, Amy Kremer of the Tea Party Express, and Tabitha Hale of Freedom-Works. Keli Carender, then a thirty-year-old Seattle woman, is often credited with initiating the whole movement, even before CNBC host Rick Santelli famously used the phrase on the air (although his utterance was what mobilized the well-publicized and well-financed and male-backed events). According to *Slate* writer Hanna Rosin, six of the eight board members of Tea Party Patriots, their national coordinators, are women; fifteen of the twenty-five state coordinators are women.

That's not, of course, to say that the Tea Party is a "women's movement." Its rank and file tend to be male: the typical Tea Partier, according to a *New York Times/CBS* poll, is white, male, married, and older than forty-five—similar to the typical Limbaugh listener. But that is illusive, since nearly half of the Tea Party members are female. And yes, it's also true that the big money behind all these spontaneous eruptions of populist sentiment is male—in fact, the overwhelming amount of funding comes from the billionaire Koch brothers, fabulously wealthy right-wingers who want to foment the illusion of a populist groundswell.

As a result, it's been easy for some to write off the Tea Party as internally incoherent—epitomized by the "Keep the Government Out of My Medicare" placard—and often contradictory, with members perfectly happy with their benefits, but unwilling to extend them to anyone else. The Tea Party's been castigated as a fake populism, manipulated from outside by powerful corporate interests (which is, itself, ironic, since so much of their message is also tending toward the anticorporate). The male money financing the movement also leads many to dismiss the gender of so many of its followers. That's also a mistake. The Tea Party is a populist movement, a movement from below—it just happens to be directed at those even further below them (minorities, immigrants) and those in the government who are seen as supporting them.

Populism is an emotion, not a political ideology. And its dominant emotion is outrage at what is being done to "us," the little guy. This is true of populisms of the Left, like the American populists of the turn of the last century or the Spanish anarchists or even the Parisian mob so lovingly portrayed in *Les Miserables*, just as it is true of populisms of the Right, like the Italian Fascists or the violent anti-immigrant Know-Nothings of mid-nineteenth-century America (and equally lovingly portrayed in *Gangs of New York*).

So let's acknowledge that the anger of the Tea Party is real. It's just not true. That distinction is important for us: Tea Partiers are right to be angry. There is a lot to be angry about. But like all the other groups I describe in the book, they are delivering their mail to the wrong address.

So, what of the women of the Tea Party? What is the particularly gendered source of their anger?

In some cases, these angry white women of the Right are living lives very much like their leaders, who are making a career out of telling women they shouldn't pursue careers. But in other cases, as historian Ruth Rosen points out, the Tea Party acknowledges that these women need to work, that some even choose to work. Excluded from the Republican Party (GOP standing for Grand Old Patriarchs), these working women do not—*cannot*—embrace the traditional roles that the party might have envisioned for them.

What Rosen misses, I think, is that they want to. The women of the Tea Party believe themselves entitled to live in a traditional, conservative household. Their sense of aggrieved entitlement runs parallel to the men's: they *want* their men to be the traditional heads of households, able to support their families. They want to be *moms*, not "women."

Look at how they describe themselves: hockey moms and mama grizzlies. "It seems like it's kind of a mom awakening," said Sarah Palin in a 2012 speech. It's "a lot of mama bears worried about their families," says spokeswoman Rebecca Wales.

Listen to Debbie, a thirty-eight-year-old mother of three, whom I met at a Tea Party rally in Harrisburg, Pennsylvania. "I'm afraid. You know, I think I'm angry because I'm so afraid. I'm afraid that we're bankrupting our children. We're spending so much, in debt up to our eyeballs, and who's going to have to pay for that? My kids. Their kids. We're going to leave them a complete mess—a debt-ridden country where immigrants feed off our taxes like we're goddamned breast-feeding them. It's just wrong. It's all upside down."

Debbie's sentiments were echoed by pretty much every one of the Tea Party women with whom I spoke. Again, their statements were largely aphoristic and contentless. But their fears and their anger were real. In their view, the government is a misguided sponge, slurping up all the resources from hardworking "real" Americans and then squeezing it out all over the undeserving, unwashed, undocumented. "I can't believe we've gone so wrong," says Lucy, a forty-one-year-old bookkeeper and mother of two. "The way we tax and spend, we will have nothing left for our children. We're breaking open their piggy bank, instead of putting money into it!"

Tea Party women speak as mothers, not as women. Their language is more reminiscent of another "women's" movement at the turn of the last century: the temperance movement. They speak of caregiving, of mothering, of fixing the mess that men have made of things. They are going to clean up the national household—since women, the bearers of morality and sobriety, are better at cleaning up the messes in their own homes.

Feminist in practice, antifeminist in theory, conservative feminism hopes to secure the economy so that women can return to their families and their homes and leave the labor force. If liberal feminists are housewives who want to be working, these conservative feminists are working women who want to be housewives.

Of course, there are class differences: when those liberal feminists are eager to enter the labor force, they're thinking not of being cashiers or secretaries or waitresses, but of being accountants and lawyers. Even in the labor force, Tea Party women think as women, not as workers. When they campaign against higher taxes or government intervention, it's less about the rights of entrepreneurs to keep their profits and more about balancing household accounts, shrinking family budgets, unsustainable spending. They're concerned about the economy this generation is leaving for its children. As one sign at a Tea Party rally put it, "My Kid Isn't Your ATM."

That seems to be the particular genius of the Tea Party. Alongside traditionally libertarian slogans about smaller government and lower taxes—words like *autonomy*, *individual*, and *freedom*—the Tea Party has added words like *family*, *community*, *children*, and *mother*. The Tea Party mobilizes angry white women alongside angry white men, wannabe stay-at-home moms alongside wannabe domestic patriarchs, looking back to a long-gone era in which white men went to work, supported their wives and families, and all the government programs that enabled and supported that—the roads, the bridges, the schools, the training sites, the military—were paid for invisibly, so it appeared that they had built it all by themselves.

The future of the Tea Party is unclear. But one thing that is clear is that it's going to have fewer women. Women flocked to the Tea Party as a populist movement because the Republican Party had so long ignored them, especially as mothers. But the Tea Party has done little to address distinctively *mothers'* needs, either. Republican corporatist economic policies don't hold much appeal; corporations would prefer to staunch any trickle-down economics; they'd like tax policies and regulation to better turn the faucets upward in a reverse waterfall. The very programs that mothers need to have the lives they actually say they want—the *option* to work; with well-fed and -clothed children, who go to good schools, and remain healthy—require massive government expenditures.

Support among white women is waning; according to a *Washington Post* poll, white women were less interested in and less positive about the Tea Party in 2012 than they were in 2011, whereas rates of approval among white men have remained relatively stable. The Tea Party will, most likely, come increasingly to resemble all the other populist iterations of aggrieved entitlement: white, southern, midwestern and rural, lower middle class, overeducated, or underemployed—that is, downwardly mobile, if not from their family of origin, then at least downwardly mobile from the expectations they had about where they'd end up. And male. For women, aggrieved entitlement may be more of a fleeting emotional response to setbacks; for men, it may become more of a way of life.

46

Anti-feminist Messages in American Television Programming for Young Girls

KRISTEN MYERS

From 2008 to 2011 there was a popular show on the Disney Channel in the US called Suite Life on Deck, aimed at an audience of preadolescent girls. On this program, teenagers attended high school on a cruise ship that traveled around the world. In one episode, their teacher, Miss Tutwiler, lectured about fairy-tales in preparation for their visit to Germany. Miss Tutwiler said, "Before we read the fairy-tales, we need to understand the context of the patriarchal society in which they originated." She made a time-line illustrating how women were systematically disenfranchised for hundreds of years. One by one, the kids fell asleep. With her back to the class, Miss Tutwiler explained: "Now by the end of the eighteenth century, after years of women being treated like cattle, we finally saw the birth of feminism." Meanwhile, the kids dreamed about the fairy-tales. . .

One girl dreamed that she was the queen in Snow White. She asked the magic mirror, "Mirror, mirror in the woods, now who's really got the goods?" When the mirror answered, "Snow White," the enraged queen summoned the hunter, telling him, "I want you to find a girl." The hunter groaned, "You sound like my mother." Although he was told to kill Snow White, the hunter secretly warned her to flee into the woods, where she stumbled upon the dwarves' slovenly cabin. The dwarves asked Snow White to stay to "do a little cooking and cleaning." She protested, "What do I look like, the maid?" One dwarf held up a tiny French maid's costume and said, "You will when you wear the uniform." Another dwarf handed her a broom, and she began cleaning.

Throughout the episode, several students' dreams similarly revised other fairy-tales. Eventually Miss Tutwiler noticed her sleeping students: "Well. I put my whole class to sleep." She looked at her watch: "That gives me 20 minutes to get a pedicure. My feet are getting kinda gnarly!" She stepped over her prone students and left.

This episode began with the promise of a feminist critique of fairy-tales. On the surface, the kids' dreams could be interpreted as an extension of that critique, humorously highlighting the sexism inherent in the tales. At the same time, however, their dreams were riddled with decidedly non-feminist messages. The lecture on feminism literally put everyone to sleep. And even the ostensibly passionate Miss Tutwiler—rather than waking them—abandoned her efforts in favor of a pedicure. The messages about feminism, gender stereotypes, and sexuality were muddied. Programs like this one are broadcast in the US several times a day, every day, where they are consumed by millions of young girls.

"Anti-Feminist Messages in American Television Programming for Young Girls" by Kristen Myers (abridged) in *Journal of Gender Studies* 22(2), 2013, Routledge. Reprinted by permission of the publisher Taylor & Francis Ltd, www.tandfonline. com. Abridged with permission of the author.

Western girls today are supposedly growing up in a society where feminist progress is an everyday, taken-for-granted reality (Baumgardner and Richards 1999, 2004). Feminism has taught girls that they do not have to be docile, passive, and obedient, but can instead protest and act out. "Misbehaving women" have helped shift the traditional gender order (Ulrich 2008), and new feminisms are developing to meet the changing lives of Western girls (Aapola et al. 2005).

But despite these inroads—or perhaps because of them—a media-generated backlash against "girl power" has emerged. McRobbie (2004) has argued that the media discourage girls' misbehavior and encourage, instead, "bad" behavior disguised as feminism. "Bad" behavior is antisocial, selfish, and anti-feminist. Threatened by the changing gender order, "post-feminist" media are distorting and undoing feminism. What do these distorted messages about feminism look like? How are they marketed to young girls—the future feminists of society?

In this paper, I analyze messages about gender, sexuality, and feminism that are made available to young girls through television programming on two major cable networks in the US. Through qualitative textual analysis of 45 episodes of four television series aimed at young girls, I find that the prevailing messages were anti-feminist. Despite the successes of feminist movement, there is evidence of the media backlash described by McRobbie (2004).

YOUNG FEMINISMS

Feminism takes myriad forms and is defined in various ways across time and place (Lorber 2009). At its heart, feminism problematizes inequality between men and women, boys and girls. Conventional wisdom associates feminism with adults rather than children. However, thanks to the development of the field of Girls' Studies, feminism has been targeted at and applied to children. According to Kearney (2009), Girls' Studies developed in response to two trends in the literature: researchers' treatment of boys' experiences as the standard for all kids; and Women's Studies' marginalization of girlhood in its attempt to separate women from girls. Girls' Studies re-centered girls'[1] experiences as worthy of study, revealing unique problems faced by girls and empowering them (see also Harris 2004).

Aapola et al. (2005) describe two new "young feminisms" that emerged from this discourse on girls. First is "girl power feminism," which eschews traditional femininity. It rejects the idea that "proper girls" must be "heterosexual, chaste, submissive, attentive to their 'looks,' family-oriented, professionally unambitious and compliant" (2005, p. 6). In contrast, the girl power image is heroic: "feisty, sassy, attractive and assertive young women who are protagonists of TV shows, pop culture icons, and media idols" (p. 8). Girl power is a "sassy, don't-mess-with-me adolescent spirit" (p. 28). These girls are sexual actors, neither objects nor victims (Thorpe 2008).

The second is "third-wave feminism," or "girly feminism." Baumgardner and Richards (1999, p. 83) argue that third-wave feminists were "born with feminism simply in the water," which acted as an invisible "political fluoride" protecting against the "decay" of patriarchy. Feminism and its critics have always been part of these girls' lives (Baumgardner and Richards 2004). Many of these girls repudiate "feminist" identity, even while espousing feminist rhetoric. They expect to be treated as equals to boys, despite the persistence of long-standing structural gender inequalities, such as the pay gap. They feel entitled to gender and sexual equity, without feeling compelled to take a stand.

Girls' Studies has spawned feminist analyses of contemporary girls' experiences and struggles, engendering some anxiety. For example, parents and teachers worry that girls are becoming too sexual too soon, mostly because of the media's hypersexualization of girlhood (Pipher 1994, Durham 2009, Levin and Kilbourne 2009). Others fear that girl power encourages girls to act "like boys," leading them to adopt bullying and antisocial behaviors (Chesney-Lind and Irwin 2004). Aapola et al. (2005) argue that confusion over girls' sexual empowerment has led people to conclude, erroneously, that society no longer needs feminism. McRobbie agrees:

> My argument is that "postfeminism" actively draws on and invokes feminism as that which can be taken into account in order to suggest that equality is achieved, in order to install a whole repertoire of meanings which emphasize that it is no longer needed, a spent force. (McRobbie 2004, p. 4)

Similarly, Ringrose (2007) conceptualizes post-feminism as "part backlash, part cultural diffusion, part repressed anxiety over shifting gender orders" (p. 473). Girl power has threatened the dominant gender order, and post-feminism is a persuasive conservative orthodoxy (Bourdieu 1977) for repositioning girls into a subordinate status.

CHILDREN'S TELEVISION AND THE DEPLOYMENT OF POST-FEMINISM

McRobbie (2004, 2008) sees the media as driving post-feminism, eroding feminist inroads. She writes that the media, ". . . a complex array of machinations . . . are perniciously effective in regard to the undoing of feminism" (2004, p. 3). She argues, "The media have become the critical site for defining emergent sexual codes of conduct. They pass judgment and establish the rules of play" (2004, p. 7). The media have distorted girl power by valorizing "emancipated female subjects" who glorify self-expression above political consciousness, thereby giving them "license to behave badly" (2004, p. 9).

Kids easily absorb messages communicated through popular media, because "young children are immersed in media-rich worlds" (Martin and Kazyak 2009, p. 317). McAllister and Giglio (2005) explain that the media have an especially great impact on children, who consume it while their identities are being formed (see also Corsaro 1997, Baker-Sperry 2007). Television media have been shown to impact children's early gendered behavior (Powell and Abels 2002). Indeed, the media might have a greater impact on children today than ever before, given the nearly ubiquitous nature of television programming directed at them in the US (McAllister and Giglio 2005). McAllister and Giglio explain that cable television has produced entire networks—"kidnets"—aimed at children. Recognized for their buying potential, and for their influence over parents' buying practices, children have become an important audience for advertisers. Children's programming is broadcast 24 hours a day, every day, and the number of kids' channels grows each year. The two largest kidnets are Disney and Nickelodeon. On 14 March 2011, Disney channel ranked as the number one network in the US among tweens for the sixteenth week in a row, according to Tvbythenumbers.com. Even during the National Basketball Association playoffs in spring 2011,

Disney ranked as the third most watched network during prime time, among all viewers. When rating all-day programming between November 2010 and May 2011, Nickelodeon consistently topped the charts at about 2.1 million viewers, with Disney coming in second at 1.6 million. Hannah Montana's final episode garnered a monster 6+ million viewers. Adults and children watch these networks. They also buy T-shirts, dolls, CDs, and DVDs. These shows are entire industries (McAllister and Giglio 2005).

Nickelodeon has several channels: Nick Jr, Nick, Teennick, Nick at Nite, and Nicktoons. Programming on these channels often overlaps. Similarly, Disney broadcasts on three channels: Disney Channel, Disney XD, and Playhouse Disney. Both Disney and Nickelodeon are broadcast in the US, Latin America, Central and Southeast Asia, Europe, the Middle East, Australia, India, and Taiwan. Although I only examine US programming, programs of this sort are broadcast internationally.

To fill air time, episodes from a single series are re-broadcast five to six times daily, with a single episode often airing twice a day. Thus, the opportunity for children to consume the same program repeatedly is substantial. And, as Crawley et al. (1999) have shown, repeated viewing leads to greater comprehension by child viewers.

Much programming on both Disney and Nickelodeon is aimed specifically at young girls. Banet-Weiser (2004), in her analysis of Nickelodeon's programming, says that "Nickelodeon is one of the most influential producers of children's programming and media in the U.S., and it attracts a large audience of pre-adolescent and adolescent girls" (2004, p. 120). She says that Nickelodeon "produces girl culture," and I argue that Disney does as well.

Disney, which began making movies in the 1930s, has long been criticized for their heteronormative, misogynist, and racist messages (Bell et al. 1995, Best and Lowney 2009). Martin and Kazyak (2009), for example, have shown that even G-rated, animated Disney movies are riddled with heterosexualized imagery. Similarly, Martin's (2009) study of mothers shows that girls learn Disney's story-lines about princesses, falling in love, and marriage, and that mothers use these themes as they interpret their children's interactions and identities. Disney's animators continue to hypersexualize young female characters and demonize sexually mature females, despite criticism (Giroux 1999). Disney's enormous corporate reach and creative public relations department have protected their "squeaky clean" image (Giroux 1999, Best and Lowney 2009).

A relative newcomer, 30-year-old Nickelodeon has been less thoroughly studied in regard to gendered messages. According to Banet-Weiser (2004), Nickelodeon has enjoyed critical acclaim for its pro-girl programming. In 2000, the Museums of Television and Radio in both New York and Los Angeles heralded Nickelodeon for 20 years of positive programming, for challenging gender stereotypes, and for featuring girls as protagonists. Banet-Weiser credits Nickelodeon with helping to make "girl power" a mainstream concept: "In the contemporary cultural climate, the empowerment of girls is now something that is more or less taken for granted by both children and parents, and has certainly been incorporated into commodity culture" (Banet-Weiser 2004, p. 120). Interestingly, none of Nickelodeon's pro-girl programming analyzed by Banet-Weiser is still on the air, even in re-runs. Girl power series, like *Wild Thornberries*, *As Told by Ginger*, and *Rocket Power*, are gone. Despite critical acclaim, Nickelodeon has begun to produce a form of girl culture similar to Disney's, neither of which, I argue, is feminist.

In this paper, I analyze the content of television programming by Disney and Nickelodeon that is aimed at young girls. I recognize that, although children consume a great deal of television on a weekly basis, they do not passively absorb larger cultural messages. Children are actors in their own right, negotiating meanings among themselves (Thorne 1993, Van Ausdale and Feagin 2002, Myers and Raymond 2010), with adults (Baraldi 2008, DeMol and Buysse 2008), and with the media itself (Fingerson 1999, Bragg and Buckingham 2004). However, children are affected by and grapple with cultural frames (Myers and Raymond 2010, Neitzel and Chafel 2010). Martin and Kazyak (2009) have argued that it is therefore important to understand the messages that are available to the children who consume them.

Using qualitative textual analysis of popular programming aimed at young girls, I find that anti-feminist messages are aggressively marketed to young girls.

These media messages help to foment a context in which everyday girls make real-life choices (Bjornstrom et al. 2010).

METHODS

In an earlier phase of this project (2008–2010), I conducted focus group interviews with elementary-school-aged girls (n = 62), to find out their interests, hobbies, and activities (Myers and Raymond 2010). The focus groups provided information about the kinds of media consumed by these girls. Primarily, these girls regularly watched Disney shows *Hannah Montana*, *Suite Life on Deck*, and *Wizards of Waverly Place*, as well as Nickelodeon's *iCarly*. They quoted lines from the shows, discussed the actors' biographies and romantic exploits, and argued about which show was the best. Girls in my study used these programs as references for how boys and girls should interact in "real life."

Because of the salience of these shows in everyday girls' lives, I conducted qualitative textual analysis of them, which I report here. . . .

In total, I analyzed 13 episodes of *Suite Life on Deck*, 10 episodes of *Hannah Montana*, 10 episodes of *Wizards of Waverly Place*, and 12 episodes of *iCarly* (45 total episodes). Table I describes each program.

My analysis centered on the meanings constructed through the plots lines, dialogue, costuming, and physical representations/embodiment of characters in these programs. Because these programs were literally scripted, every message was carefully planned, practiced, edited, and finally communicated to viewers. My analytic strategy draws upon critical discourse analysis (CDA), whose goal is to examine the social construction of reality through language, both spoken and textual (Fairclough 1992, van Dijk 1993, Halliday 1994, Galasinski 2011). CDA reveals meanings beyond simple dichotomies (Wodak 1999), focusing on contradictions (Billig et al. 1988). CDA recognizes that there are multiple interpretations to most messages and that analyses must be on-going, subject to change over time and in different contexts (Wodak 1999). I follow those tenets here. However, I do not employ a strict critical discourse analysis. I analyze more than dialogue: I include additional forms of communication such as costuming, characters' embodiment, and elements of physical comedy.

. . .

FINDINGS

In my analysis, I found that the prevailing messages in the television programs were anti-feminist, operationalized as such: programs celebrated beauty and heterosexual coupling, demonized strong and unattractive women, and valorized antisocial girls. They "took feminism into account," while simultaneously dismissing it. These messages were overt, integrated into main plot lines, episode after episode, across all four series.

Although this analysis is largely qualitative, I did note the frequency of anti-feminist incidents. Of all of the shows, *iCarly* was the most thoroughly saturated with anti-feminist messages, with an average of 11.4 incidents per 22-minute episode. *Hannah Montana* contained the fewest messages (6.4 per episode), but their content was no less problematic than other shows' messages. *Suite Life* was the most traditionally sexist show, concentrating primarily on valorizing beauty, heterosexism, and degrading women/girls. They also "took feminism into account" most often. *Wizards* and *iCarly* centered on badly behaved girls. Anti-feminist messages were broadcast every 2–3 minutes on these shows, making them hard to avoid.

BEAUTY AND BOYS

Similar to Martin and Kazyak's (2009) argument about G-rated films, a major message across programs was that girls were more valuable if they were beautiful. Plot lines on episodes of two shows centered on beauty pageants (twice on *Suite Life* and once on *iCarly*). For example, on *Suite Life*, the boys staged a beauty pageant to meet girls. London saw the announcement and squealed: "A beauty pageant. And I'm beauty-ful!" She cleared off a shelf in her cabin to make room for her tiaras. Her room-mate, Bailey, protested when London moved her things. London said, "What do you need a tiara shelf for? If you enter a beauty contest, the only thing they'll put on your head is a paper bag." To London, beauty was

a girl's most important attribute, and imperfection should be hidden from view, under a "paper bag."

In these television programs, girls were more valuable if they were desired by boys. Plot lines focused on finding and keeping boyfriends (on all shows) and getting dates for the prom (*Hannah*, *Wizards*, and *Suite Life*). Heterosexual coupling enhanced the status of both boys and girls. For example on *Hannah Montana*, Oliver and Lilly bragged about going to the prom together:

Oliver and Lilly walked through school, arms around each others' shoulders. To a group of girls, Oliver said, "Oh I am so sorry, ladies, it's too late, but don't hate, Ollie's already got a prom date." As he spoke, Lilly mouthed his words, and waved at the girls, tauntingly. They went up to a group of guys, and Lilly said, "You can have your eggs, and you can have your bacon, but you can't have Lilly, 'cause she's taken."

It was not enough for Oliver and Lilly to be a couple; they made a spectacle of themselves, broadcasting to single girls and boys that they had missed their chance to date one of them. They asserted that being date-less was problematic. Lilly said, "You know it's so great not having to sit around praying that the one guy you really want to go with will ask you. That feeling of being so desperate, so needy, so, so, so . . ." They walked closer to Miley, who was staring at a guy and whispering, "Ask me. Ask me. Ask me." Lilly said, "So, that," pointing at Miley. Miley mewled, "Ask me nooooow!" Oliver shook his head, saying, "Single people." Lilly stroked Miley's hair and said, "So sad." Oliver and Lilly called each other, "Olliepop" and "Lillipop," and gazed at each other longingly.

Heteronormative messages such as these are readily available in children's media (Bell et al. 1995, Giroux 1999, Martin and Kazyak 2009): girls must attract and attach themselves to boys so as to achieve status and satisfaction. Television programming allows these messages to be repackaged daily, even hourly, for children's viewing.

DEGRADING AND OBJECTIFYING FEMININITY

The television programs degraded femininity at least once per episode. For example, on *Suite Life*, femininity was frequently associated with weakness. In one episode, Zack complimented an old man on his athleticism. The man asked, "What do you think, I'm a little girl?" In another episode, Woody arm-wrestled a female classmate, who slammed his arm down so hard that he fell out of his desk. She held up her arms and yelled, "In your face! Eighty-three pounds of pure power!" Cody said, "Dude, you just got beat by a girl who can fit in a keyhole." Their teacher asked Woody what he was doing on the floor. Zack said, "Looking for his pride." Woody called, "Can't find it! 00, but I found a piece of gum!" which he took from beneath the desk and ate. Although a girl won the match, the over-arching message in this scene was not girl power. Instead, the focus was on Woody's losing the match, which feminized and devalued him.

Television programs also objectified girls for male consumption. For example, in one episode of *Hannah*, Miley tried to convince Oliver and Lilly that she did not want a boyfriend. Oliver stood up on the crowded beach and said, "Yo! Single dudes! Listen up! I got a perfectly good girl here, good height-to-weight ratio, not hard to look at. Let's start the bidding at uh . . ."

Miley knocked him down. He continued, from the ground, "She's got a temperament issue, but the right guy could tame her." Miley grabbed him by the nose. He said, "You're blowing the sales pitch." Miley said, "I can get a boyfriend on my own." Oliver said, "You might want to speed it up, because you're starting to look a little pathetic." Oliver tried to auction off Miley, but she did not passively accept his efforts. She physically interrupted him. Yet, he had the last word, reminding her that girls should have boyfriends in order to fit in.

On these programs, teenagers openly demeaned adult women in positions of authority. For example, on *iCarly*, Freddy's mom—Mrs Benson, the only parent on the series—was depicted as a shrill, unstable harpy, and the kids openly disrespected her. In one episode, Freddy pushed Carly out of the way of an on-coming truck, but he got hit instead, breaking his leg. Mrs Benson repeatedly hissed at Carly, "It should have been you!" Carly brought Freddy flowers, and his mother soaked them in bleach and pounded them with a mallet to "protect Freddy from allergens." In another episode, Mrs Benson forbade Freddy to attend a mixed martial arts match. She explained, "Exposure to violence is very bad for a teenaged boy's development." Sam snarled, "Says who?" Mrs Benson shrieked: "I read it on aggressiveparenting.com!" Sam groaned, "Why you gotta always irritate everybody?" Mrs Benson was portrayed as pathologically overprotective, even when her concerns were valid.

On *Wizards*, even fantasy creatures were demeaned if they were strong women. In one episode, Mother Nature punished Justin for using magic to alter the weather. She arrived dressed in black spandex and leather, with a black floral garland in her hair and an Earth decal on her biker vest. Justin said, "I thought you were supposed to be all natural, like sandals with birds flying around you." She said, "Yeah, yeah, I used to dress like that, but nobody took me seriously. What I wear to work is my business. I don't want to talk about this." To punish Justin, Mother Nature assigned him his own rain cloud, drenching him incessantly. Later, Mother Nature admitted that she had over-reacted, saying, "I've had a lot to deal with lately." Alex asked, "Is it dating trouble? Because I can help you with that." Justin said, "No, Alex, she's talking about the environment." Mother Nature said, "You people have to understand this is a delicate system. Every time you mess with the weather, it affects somewhere else." Alex said, "I think I found your dating problem: it's that non-stop talking about the weather, isn't it?" Mother Nature dressed tough to be taken seriously, and she wielded power over the elements, but she was casually dismissed and reduced to a heterosexual failure by a teenaged girl.

GIRLS BEHAVING BADLY

Each series had strong girl characters. On the surface, these seemed like "grrrls," who eschewed passive femininity to get ahead in a "man's world." However, on closer inspection, they resembled McRobbie's (2004) "badly behaved" girls: they bullied and cheated. Two characters stood out for their bad behavior: Sam from *iCarly* and Alex from *Wizards*. Both were portrayed as tomboys—they even had boys' names—but they were more complicated than that.

Sam was not the official protagonist in *iCarly*, but she was a central character, appearing in every episode. Many episodes centered on her character flaws: she hated school, cheated on tests, and refused to do homework. She lied easily and frequently. She stole lunches from kids at school. She had been in "juvie." She once suggested that her mobster uncle, Carmine, could be hired to hurt Freddy's mom. Another time, she offered to have Uncle Carmine make the school superintendent "disappear." Sam wanted to go to the mixed martial arts match "to learn a shoulder-crushing move." Carly patted Sam, saying, "I bet you can learn all kinds of new ways to hurt people." Sam, excited, yelled "I know!" In a paintball war, Sam shot several of her classmates between the eyes, like an assassin. Another time, she put sticks of butter in a sock and "got swingy with it," smacking the faces of television writers who had stolen ideas from the *iCarly* webshow. She threw herself onto a couch and pitched a screaming fit to persuade Carly to enter a beauty pageant. Her mother appeared only once,[2] but Sam described her as a "dead-beat," and she spent time at Carly's apartment to avoid her. Sam terrorized most people, but Carly always affectionately tolerated her, like a child.

Wizards' Alex was more clever than thuggish, more manipulative than violent. Like Sam, she was sarcastic, selfish, and lazy, failing at school and wizarding. She lied and cheated. Even the program's theme song, sung by Alex, stated that you could use magic to "write a report on a book you never read." Being bad was a central part of Alex's identity. The school principal wanted Alex's help in catching rule-breakers at school, explaining, "You are an evil genius, not just evil." Flattered, she helped. But she was so good at catching rule-breakers that someone put a "good citizenship" award on her locker.

Alex said,

That's low! Harper, you have to help me. If I don't stop being good, one day I'm going to wake up as a doctor. Or worse! One of those guys who drives the back end of the fire truck!

Alex's parents were suspicious of her when she was nice, and they pretended not to know her when she misbehaved. Harper repeatedly asked her to stop being bad, but she kept being her friend and acquiesced to her bullying.

Both Sam and Alex were heterosexually desirable, despite their "bad girl" nature. Sam looked femme: she had almost-waist-length blond hair, curled in ringlets.

She dressed in tight T-shirts and skater shorts, like the other girls. She practiced an in-your-face heterosexuality. She stole a boy's basketball because she thought he was cute. She bragged about boys she'd kissed and competed with Carly for boys' attention. Alex was portrayed as a tomboy who hated dresses, yet she always wore high heels, tight jeans, and lots of jewelry. She flirted with boys skillfully. For example, in one episode Alex agreed to help Harper set up the school's Quizbowl. She approached a tough boy, asking, "Do you want to thumb wrestle for jobs?" He said, "Cute." She flipped her hair and said, "Oh, I know. Get used to it." Charmed, he followed her around for the rest of the episode.

These girls represented the media-warped version of strong girls described by McRobbie (2004). Their characters valorized some elements of grrrl power, such as femininity, self-confidence, and sexual assertiveness. But their power was amped up into antisocial, self-interested aggression. These characters were heterosexy bullies, not feminists.

POST-FEMINISM

Applying McRobbie's (2004, 2008) definition, I find that these programs were not only anti-feminist but also post-feminist: they ostensibly supported tenets of feminism, but usually undermined them in the end. Sometimes, the post-feminist messages were subtle. For example, both *Hannah* and *Suite Life* featured smart, goal-oriented girl characters: Miley and Bailey, respectively. Miley adroitly juggled a career as a popstar, her school work, and her friends. Bailey excelled at all subjects in school, spoke Japanese, and earned an academic scholarship. Both came from small towns and succeeded at big challenges. These characters sent feminist messages. Yet both girls turned to jelly around cute boys. On *Hannah*, after Miley repeatedly assured Oliver and Lilly that she did not want a boyfriend, she was taken aback by a blind date they had arranged. He was so cute that Miley batted her lashes at him and spoke in a baby voice. He said, "You have the cutest accent." Miley said, "Well fiddle-dee-dee, I do believe I am a-blushing." Miley's feminist resolve dissolved under his gaze. Similarly, on one episode of *Suite Life*, the kids toured a museum in Greece. Bailey admired the artifacts, saying, "What a magnificent vase."

London said, "What a hot guy!" Bailey chastised London, telling her how lucky she was to be surrounded by ancient art. London turned Bailey's head to see the "hot guy," and Bailey said, "Sweet potato pie! I wouldn't mind looking for a penny in a haystack with him." She instantly abandoned her scholarly appreciation of antiquities so as to objectify a living Adonis—indeed, that was his actual name. So even though Bailey and Miley were strong, they went weak around "hot guys." Heterosexual desire drowned out competing messages about independence and intellect.

Most of the post-feminist messages were overt. Many characters actually invoked feminism, and then acted in ways that negated it, as in the fairy-tale episode of *Suite Life*, discussed in the opening of this paper. Similarly, on *Wizards*, Justin was assigned to catch monsters for wizarding school. Misreading his instruments, he almost turned in his vampire girlfriend, Juliet, and her parents to the wizarding authorities. He diverted the authorities but was disappointed in the end: "I kind of wish I had caught three monsters. I would have gotten a trophy." He gestured to Juliet, saying, "Well, I guess my trophy's right here." Juliet flinched: "Justin, as a woman of the twenty-first century, do not objectify me. But . . . as a woman who's been alive for thousands and thousands of years before that . . . come here!' She smiled, pulled him into a hug, and he looked relieved. In effect, Juliet dismissed feminism as a fad.

On *Suite Life*, Bailey entered that beauty pageant to try to beat London. Cody, her boyfriend, thought she was kidding. Bailey showed him the gingham dress she planned to wear. He said, "Ahh, and to protest [the pageant], you're going to undermine the event by wearing an ugly dress and avoiding all the trappings of conventional female beauty?" She was offended, and he realized that she really meant to compete. He said, "I thought you'd find beauty pageants sexist and demeaning to women." Bailey said, "Pageants are about more than beauty. You can win scholarships." During the interview part of the pageant, Bailey showed her intellect: "Thus, by balancing classic Keynesian economics with the best of Malthusian theory, we can decrease Third World debt by increasing our gross domestic product." Zack called out: "Boring!" Noticing the audience glazing over, Bailey announced, "I love puppies!" Everyone cheered, and she won. Bailey mimicked the nonintellectual contestants strategically, but she did so to beat them at their own game, not to rise above the competition itself.

On *Hannah*, Miley hoped that Gabe would ask her to the prom, but she made light of it to Lilly and Oliver: "I mean either way is fine with me. I'm an independent, mature, strooong woman." But when Gabe walked toward her, she launched herself into his path and muttered "Ask me to prom!" He kept walking. When she finally got up the nerve to ask him herself, he already had a date, Theresa. Miley said she didn't mind that Gabe was going with Theresa. But when Theresa walked by her at lunch, Miley stuck out her leg and tripped her. When Theresa fell down, Miley laughed and said, "Now I feel much better!" These girl characters tried to "talk the feminist talk." They invoked feminist concepts. They understood and seemingly problematized sexism and objectification. They recognized that beauty pageants demean women and that strong women don't need boyfriends. And yet, their behavior ultimately undermined girl power within the same episode: Juliet rewarded Justin with a hug; Bailey acted puerile to win the pageant; and Miley first begged a boy to ask her out and then physically attacked his date. Rather than rejecting the tenets of traditional femininity, these girls acquiesced to heteronormative pressure so as to fit in. They all "took feminism into account," and then dismissed it. These programs portrayed feminism as unnecessary, as actually interfering with the girls' true goals. Ironically, these characters were most heroic when they yielded their independence and embraced heterosexualized fantasies about girlhood.

CONCLUSION

I began this paper by exploring the content of distorted messages about feminism and how they were marketed to young girls. In examining television programming aimed at young girls, I discovered pervasive anti-feminist messages. These messages distorted feminism by objectifying and demeaning femininity, while ostensibly celebrating girls' sexuality and strength. They perverted girl power into a cut-throat "bad girl" archetype. They "took feminism into account," and then dismissed it as unnecessary if not problematic.

These series aggressively marketed anti- and post-feminist messages to young girls, broadcasting them about every two minutes per 26-minute episode. These messages were virtually inescapable for viewers. Based on my earlier research (Myers and Raymond 2010), I know that everyday girls avidly consumed these messages, applying them to their real lives.

Baumgardner and Richards (1999, p. 83) have argued that young girls today are growing up with "feminism simply in the water," like invisible "political fluoride" protecting them from patriarchal decay. If they are correct, I would expect that anti-feminist messages would be few and far between. I found the opposite. Most girls today are immersed in "media-rich worlds" (Martin and Kazyak 2009). Perhaps, for them, their "water" is the media. If so, resisting anti-feminism will be especially challenging. One wonders how long feminist inoculation can last given the content of girls' favorite television shows. Although I analyzed US programming only, both Disney and Nickelodeon are international companies, broadcasting similar messages world-wide.

In this analysis, I found evidence of a media backlash against young feminisms, consistent with McRobbie's (2008) argument. The media's repackaging and distortion of feminism subtly reinscribes gender and re-subordinates girls to boys and to each other based on a hierarchy of heterosexualized capital. Instead of promoting sisterhood in these shows, girl protagonists policed older women and each other, to the raucous amusement of the pre-recorded laugh-track in the background. The take-away message: feminism is a joke.

If we continue on this trajectory, the effectiveness of young feminism to empower and politicize girls will be eroded. The consequences are great: the larger feminist project—which seeks to eradicate social inequalities (Lorber 2006)—depends upon future generations of feminists. Young girls benefit psychically, physically, and materially from feminist progress (Manago et al. 2009). Young feminists must recognize the ways that the media distort and undo girl power even for very young girls, and reclaim the voice of authority so as to ensure that girls today continue to benefit from the positive effects of feminism.

NOTES

1. Children, tweens, teens, young women, and middle-aged women are called "girls" or "girlie" in this literature (Harris 2004).

2. That episode garnered the most cable viewers for that week, with 5.9 million viewers.

REFERENCES

Aapola, S., Gonick, M., and Harris, A., 2005. *Young femininity: girlhood, power and social change*. Palgrave: New York.

Baker-Sperry, L., 2007. The production of meaning through peer interaction. *Sex Roles*, 56, 717–727.

Banet-Weiser, S., 2004. Girls rule! Gender, feminism, and Nickelodeon. *Critical Studies in Media Communication*, 21, 119–139.

Baraldi, C., 2008. Promoting self-expression in classroom interactions. *Childhood*, 15, 238–257.

Baumgardner, J. and Richards, A., 1999. *Manifesta*. New York: Farrar, Straus and Giroux.

Baumgardner, J. and Richards, A., 2004. Feminism and femininity. In: A. Harris, ed. *All about the girl*. New York: Routledge, 59–68.

Bell, E., Haas, L., and Sells, L., eds., 1995. *From mouse to mermaid*. Bloomington: Indiana University Press.

Best, J. and Lowney, K., 2009. The disadvantage of a good reputation. *The Sociological Quarterly*, 50, 431–449.

Billig, M., et al., 1988. *Ideological dilemmas*. London: Sage.

Bjornstrom, E., et al., 2010. Race and ethnic representations of lawbreakers and victims in crime news. *Social Problems*, 57, 269–293.

Bourdieu, P., 1977. *Outline of a theory of practice*. Oxford: Cambridge University Press.

Bragg, S. and Buckingham, D., 2004. Embarrassment, education, and erotics. *European Journal of Cultural Studies*, 7, 441–459.

Chesney-Lind, M. and Irwin, K., 2004. From badness to meanness. In: A. Harris, ed. *All about the girl*. New York: Routledge, 45–58.

Corsaro, W., 1997. *The sociology of childhood*. Berkeley, CA: Pine Forge Press.

Crawley, A., et al., 1999. Effects of repeated exposures to a single episode of the television program *Blue's Clues* on the viewing behaviors and comprehension of preschool children. *Journal of Educational Psychology*, 91, 630–637.

DeMol, J. and Buysse, A., 2008. Understanding children's influence in parent–child relationships. *Journal of Social and Personal Relationships*, 25, 359–379.

Durham, G., 2009. *The effect*. New York: Overlook.

Fairclough, N., 1992. *Discourse and social change*. Oxford: Polity Press.

Fingerson, L., 1999. Active viewing. *Journal of Contemporary Ethnography*, 28, 389–418.

Galasinski, D., 2011. The patient's world: discourse analysis and ethnography. *Critical Discourse Studies*, 8, 253–265.

Giroux, H., 1999. *The mouse that roared*. New York: Rowman and Littlefield.

Glaser, B. and Strauss, A., 1967. *The discovery of grounded theory*. New York: Aldine–Transaction.

Halliday, M.A.K., 1994. *An introduction to functional grammar*. 2nd ed. London: Edward Arnold.

Harris, A., ed., 2004. *All about the girl*. New York: Routledge.

Kearney, M. C., 2009. Coalescing: the development of girls' studies. *NWSA Journal*, 21, 1–28.

Levin, D. and Kilbourne, J., 2009. *So sexy so soon*. New York: Ballantine.

Lofland, J., et al., 2005. *Analyzing social settings*. New York: Wadsworth.

Lorber, J., 2006. Shifting paradigms and challenging categories. *Social Problems*, 53, 448–453.

Lorber, J., 2009. *Gender inequality*. New York: Oxford.

Manago, A., Brown, C., and Leaper, C., 2009. Feminist identity among Latina adolescents. *Journal of Adolescent Research*, 24, 750–776.

Martin, K., 2009. Normalizing heterosexuality: mothers' assumptions, talk, and strategies with young children. *American Sociological Review*, 74, 190–207.

Martin, K. and Kazyak, E., 2009. Hetero-romantic love and heterosexiness in children's G-rated films. *Gender & Society*, 23, 315–336.

McAllister, M. and Giglio, M., 2005. The commodity flow of U.S. children's television. *Critical Studies in Media Communication*, 22, 26–44.

McRobbie, A., 2004. Notes on postfeminism and popular culture. In: A. Harris, ed. *All about the girl*. New York: Routledge, 3–14.

McRobbie, A., 2008. Young women and consumer culture. *Cultural Studies*, 22, 531–550.

Myers, K. and Raymond, L., 2010. Elementary school girls and heteronormativity: The girl project. *Gender and Society*, 24, 167–188.

Neitzel, C. and Chafel, J., 2010. And no flowers grow there and stuff. *Sociological Studies of Children and Youth*, 13, 33–59.

Pipher, M., 1994. *Reviving Ophelia*. New York: Grosset/Putnam.

Powell, K. and Abels, L., 2002. Sex role stereotypes in TV programs aimed at the preschool audience. *Women and Language*, 25, 14–22.

Ringrose, J., 2007. Successful girls? *Gender and Education*, 19, 471–489.

Thorne, B., 1993. *Gender play*. Rutgers University Press.

Thorpe, H., 2008. Foucault, technologies of self, and the media discourses of femininity in snowboarding culture. *Journal of Sport & Social Issues*, 32, 199–229.

Ulrich, L., 2008. *Well behaved women seldom make history*. New York: Vintage.

Van Ausdale, D. and Feagin, J., 2002. *The first R*. New York: Rowman and Littlefield.

van Dijk, T.A., 1993. Principles of critical discourse analysis. *Discourse & Society*, 4, 249–283.

Warren, C. and Karner, T., 2009. *Discovering qualitative methods*. New York: Oxford.

Wodak, R., 1999. Critical discourse analysis at the end of the 20th century. *Research on Language and Social Interaction*, 32, 185–193.

PART IX

CHANGE AND POLITICS

Lesbians and gays flock to San Francisco to participate in marriage, an institution once denounced as a bastion of sexism by the early feminist and gay liberation movements. Disability rights activists criticize the discriminatory ableism of pro-choice feminists who use prenatal disability diagnosis as a justification for access to late-term abortion. Meanwhile, a multiracial group of men from different nations gather to issue a declaration on gender rights. The chapters in this section examine how social change is emerging in the daily practices of individuals and communities, through social movement organizations, in renegotiated institutions, and in the forward-looking visions of the future. Change is multifaceted and it often comes from unlikely candidates and in unlikely places. The following chapters are a diverse set of examples of social change from the United States and around the world and from the micro level of personal transformation to large-scale social movements. Together, the authors in this final section of the book show us that embracing the prism of difference is a vital step toward building a more democratic future.

First, Thomas Rogers focuses our attention on the micro level, specifically chromosomes and the reality that people are born neither fully female nor fully male. As he puts it, "everyone's a little bit of both," and this acknowledgment must be followed with social recognition of intersex persons. The next two chapters, by the Delhi collective and Kevin Powell, raise equally important questions: Is sexism a static, permanent, and unyielding characteristic? Are men so committed to retaining patriarchal privileges that they are unable to change and support justice and equality in gender relations? According to Powell and the Delhi collective, the answer is a resounding no. In Powell's poignant and candid confession of the dilemmas he has faced as a recovering misogynist, he opens the door to a world based on new consciousness and newly negotiated relations of race and gender. This is preceded by a short but powerful declaration from a global symposium on men, boys, and gender equality that occurred in Delhi in 2014. Here we hear the voices of a diverse group of men from 94 nations, mostly from the global South, speaking out against continued gender oppression of women and girls and the violence and self-destruction that gendered systems of inequality pose for men and boys. The Delhi Call to Action calls for change from the bottom to the top. This includes changes in men's gender attitudes and practices, as well as programmatic efforts of community-based organizations, employers, nonprofit organizations, and state agencies to eradicate gender oppressions and inequalities.

The next two articles ask whether intersectionality and the recognition of differences create division or serve as a powerful tool for social change. For example, can white women use their privileged positions and resources to promote social change for poor, incarcerated women of color? Based on a study of a white women's antiracist, antiprison organization that works on behalf of incarcerated women, Jodie Michelle Lawston finds that sisterhood across class and race can bridge differences and promote progressive social change. Along the way, complex negotiations of "sisterhood" and solidarity are forged, and the author argues that ultimately, white feminist organizations pursing social change cannot veil differences of race and class, but must be willing to recognize, name, and understand those differences. Similarly, Dorothy Roberts and Sujatha Jesudason worked with women's groups whose different experiences of reproductive and genetic technologies created divisions between the women's rights, racial justice, and disability rights movements. They show how intersectionality became the basis for overcoming these divisions and defining a shared set of inclusive values. Roberts and Jesudason learned that the key to doing intersectionality is the willingness of groups to openly acknowledge differences while actively recognizing connections among systems of oppression.

The last reading takes us inside the Occupy Movement as it first developed in New York City's Zuccotti Park in early September 2011. In response to the economic crisis of 2007–2008 and inspired by the Arab Spring (a protest movement that spread through the Middle East and Northern Africa beginning in 2010), Occupy became a global movement against economic and social inequality. Manissa McCleave Maharawal shares her firsthand account of the early days of Occupy as people developed a consensus model of governance and drafted the Occupy Declaration. In a Facebook post she titled "So Real It Hurts," Maharawal describes the discomfort she felt as a South Asian woman in a movement largely led by white men. She shares the pain she felt when those leaders failed to acknowledge racial-ethnic injustice in the Occupy Declaration and the strength it took for her to explain privilege to the white male leaders and to insist on changes to the Declaration. Maharawal provides a poignant account of the reality of social justice work—the fear and frustration as well as the joy and gratification of becoming an active part of social change.

47

We're All Intersex

Thomas Rogers

In the fall of 1998, Lisa May Stevens, a 32-year-old from Idaho, went on a camping trip. Stevens had been told for most of her life that she was a boy, but in her 20s had discovered the truth about her sex—that she had been born a hermaphrodite, and that doctors had conducted surgeries on her genitalia as an infant. After learning the news, she consulted her priest, who said that while God usually condemns suicides, for her he might make an exception. A decade later, on the third day of her camping trip, she put a pistol under her jaw and pulled the trigger.

Gerald N. Callahan, an associate professor in the microbiology, immunology and pathology department at Colorado State University, uses this heart-wrenching anecdote to open *Between XX and XY*, his new book about people who are born neither male nor female (at least in the traditional sense of those words). They are better known as "intersex," an umbrella term that includes people with a tremendous number of genetic conditions, from those born with an extra X chromosome to those with overdeveloped adrenal glands.

Stories about intersex people have had some cultural currency—from Jeffrey Eugenides' "Middlesex" to urban legends about Jamie Lee Curtis's hermaphroditism—but their experiences have yet to attain widespread recognition or become widely understood, something that Callahan hopes to change. As he describes in the book, many children born with these conditions have been surgically (and often arbitrarily) assigned a gender shortly after their birth—but as his interviews with intersex people and doctors show, early surgical intervention has often had disastrous repercussions on patients' later lives. Many never fully fit into their assigned gender and don't learn about their reassignment until well into adulthood, with understandably traumatic results.

Between XX and XY combines the personal narratives of intersex people, semi-lyrical (and occasionally overdramatic) descriptions of the sexual development process, and examples from the natural world to argue for a less invasive approach to sexual reassignment for intersex children. More boldly, Callahan also attacks the "myth of the two sexes," arguing that most humans don't exist as purely "male" or "female," but somewhere in between.

Salon spoke with Callahan by phone about the diversity of the intersex world, what hyenas can teach us about gender, and why we shouldn't forget that sex ought to be fun.

S: Given that you work in the field of pathology, intersexuality isn't exactly your immediate area of expertise. How did you end up writing this book?

C: The area I'm most involved with within pathology is immunology, which on one level is the study of how we manage to distinguish ourselves from the

---

Thomas Rogers, *Salon.com* (July 7, 2009). Copyright © 2009 Salon Media Group Inc. Reprinted by permission.

rest of the universe. I was preparing for a course when I came across an article that mentioned that 65,000 children are born of indeterminate sex each year. I thought that was amazing—because that was a much higher number of individuals than those afflicted by many diseases I was very aware of—and I began to wonder why I hadn't heard about them.

S: Given that transgender issues have been getting so much more attention in the past few years, why haven't we heard about intersex people?

C: They haven't had movies like *Transamerica* to bring their issues to the fore. But I also think that intersex is something that makes people a little more uneasy [than gender dysphoria], because it makes us question these things we like to take more or less as God given, which is the sanctity and the gravity of sex.

S: Then you think that this polarized distinction—between men and women—isn't accurate?

C: There's no other place where we so quickly divide humans into two categories as sex. When I started doing research on the biology of sex development, one of the things that I realized is that the process is controlled by a series of enzymes and the reaction may be more or less complete. It's not just two poles where that whole process can end up. In between what we call the ideal biological male or ideal biological female, there's a whole range of other possibilities that don't differ from our basic preconceptions to the extent that we have names for them or call them a disorder. Just like with every other human trait, there are an infinite number of possibilities.

S: So in essence you'd like for people to think of sex in the same way that we think of hair color, or eye color, or other sorts of physiological traits.

C: Exactly. We might say two people have brown eyes but that doesn't mean that they're brown in exactly the same way, or what is seen through those eyes is the same.

S: Before reading the book, I was familiar with a few intersex conditions, like Turner Syndrome, in which people are missing an X chromosome, but I was honestly shocked by the sheer diversity of what you described.

C: The more I looked into it, the more I was amazed by the range of possibilities. My sampling of it is small at this point—otherwise my book would have been encyclopedic. There's XO, XY. There's non-disjunction during fetal development, so someone loses an X chromosome. Sometimes they get lost later on during cell division, so people can end up being mosaics, in which some of their cells have XO or XY or XX and their body can contain two or three different chromosomal cell types—and whether they appear physically as a man or a woman depends on which of those cells ends up in the developing gonads.

S: One of the people you speak with in the book claims that *Will & Grace* was good for intersex people, which I find interesting because I don't think many people think of them when they think of gay and lesbian culture, much less *Will & Grace*. Do you think the community should be lumped in with the gay and lesbian movement?

C: I don't claim to speak for intersex people, but I think no. I think that they have a different sense of their world than people who are gay or lesbian. Sexual preference is completely different in my mind from biological sex. Gay and lesbian people can fairly easily identify with the classic binary of male and female, and intersex people for the most part cannot. They have to me a much more complex and graduated series of events they need to deal with [than do gay and lesbian people]. I think that people have a tendency to group all of that together—sexual preference, gender dysphoria, transgender, intersex—and they're really in my mind very separate sorts of things.

S: In the book you argue that we need to think of sex as being fun—and not just for reproduction. What does that have to do with the intersex?

C: We have mutilated thousands of children a year [through genital surgery], and parents and physicians have felt the drive to do that because their No. 1 goal is to maintain reproductive function. If we think the sole function of genitalia is reproduction, then nonreproductive genitalia is, in some sense, a bad thing and something needs to be done about it. If we think that genitals serve a lot of functions beyond reproduction, maybe we wouldn't feel like it was so necessary to try to make people look alike.

S: But don't these doctors also do these procedures to allow their patients to have a normal sex life?

C: I realize that on behalf of parents and physicians there's an enormous motivation to try to offer to this child as many opportunities as possible. But Dr. Alice Domurat Dreger [an associate professor at the Feinberg School of Medicine], whom I quote in the book, had interacted with an enormous number of intersex people, and she had met only one person who was pleased with the surgery—most thought they had lost, not gained, something.

S: So how do you think these decisions about surgery should be made?

C: This idea was introduced to me by Joel Frader [professor at Northwestern's Feinberg School of Medicine], but I think the best situation now is for the parents to be involved, for there to be a team of physicians—a surgeon, an endocrinologist, a psychiatrist—to be involved and for them to try to explain to the parents the most they can do in the most realistic way. In this world it may not be possible to raise a child without a gender, but that doesn't mean that surgery has to be performed. The ideal situation would be that, at a later date, the child could participate directly in the decision that might involve irreversible surgery.

S: You spoke with a number of intersex people in the book, most of whom have very moving stories. I imagine many of them were uncomfortable talking about their experience. How did you get them to open up to you?

C: It took me months to establish relationships where people finally acquired enough trust and were willing to share with me. I'm amazed in hindsight that it came together as well as it did, because my own stupidity at the outset alienated nearly everyone.

At first I put out an ad saying I was doing research for a book, without establishing my credentials, and I got several negative comments from people saying, "Here it goes again." A couple of people remained hostile to me after that—I think they'd just been burned. One of them had participated with an author before, and the author had ended up writing a book claiming, "Here's what intersex people think, and this is what it feels like to be intersex" based on a fairly small amount of information. Another person had been involved with someone who'd basically written something about how "weird" these people are.

S: You also go to great lengths describing how some other animals, like hyenas (whose females have penislike appendages) and fish (some of which can spontaneously change sex) reproduce in unconventional ways. It seemed like an arbitrary comparison to me, given that the natural world has such a diversity of reproductive strategies. Why do you think that it's helpful to look at other species' sexual reproduction?

C: Many species have evolved different ways of dealing with sex. It suggests the classic relationship of the male–female binary just doesn't fit very well with the real world. If that female–male division is true of humans, which as you know I don't believe it is, that would make us the biological exception rather than the rule.

S: But those adaptations you described have an evolutionary purpose, while most intersex conditions don't—at least to an immediate observer.

C: I didn't mean to suggest that intersex is a biological adaptation that will somehow further the species. The persistence of intersex reminds me that there's a continuum, that we isolate people in the middle and say they have a problem because they're reproductively incompetent or don't look right or whatever. None of us meet the criterion of being the perfect male or the perfect female. We are all intersex.

48

Men and Boys for Gender Justice: Delhi Declaration and Call to Action

We live in a world of profound inequalities and unbalanced power relations, where rigid norms and values about how people should behave fuel and exacerbate injustices. We have to change that. This is why more than 1200 activists/professionals coming from 94 countries, and with a broad variety of organisational backgrounds, convened the second MenEngage Global Symposium in New Delhi, India, November 10–13, 2014.

Gender equality is an essential component of human rights, as upheld by international standards articulated, including the *Universal Declaration of Human Rights*; the Convention on the Elimination of All Forms of Discrimination Against Women, the *International Covenant on Civil and Political Rights*, and the Convention on the Rights of the Child. We reiterate our commitment to implementing the International Conference on Population and Development Programme of Action (1994), the Beijing Declaration and Platform for Action (1995), the outcomes of the annual United Nations Commission on the Status of Women (including at its 48th Session in 2004), and all other relevant agreements. We reaffirm our commitment to implementing the MenEngage Rio and Johannesburg Calls to Action (2009). We look forward to future agreements, including the development agenda beyond 2015, and to continue to uphold boys' and men's engagement as key to the achievement of gender equality and gender justice for all.

This Symposium reflected the full complexity and diversity of gender justice issues. It challenged us to reflect, think strategically, reach out across socially-constructed boundaries, and strengthen partnerships. There are gaps. As an outcome of this historic event, and as a shared commitment and **Call to Action**, we offer the following concerns and affirmations:

1. **Patriarchy and gender injustice remain defining characteristics of societies around the world, with devastating effects on everyone's daily life.** No matter who we are, and no matter where we are in the world, these forces make our relationships less fulfilling, less healthy and less safe. From an early age, they introduce suffering, violence, illness, hate and death within our families and communities. They strip us of our fundamental human rights and hinder our ability to live a life with love, dignity, intimacy and mutual respect. They hamper the development of our economies and keep our global society from flourishing. These are the root causes of many barriers to sustainable development around the world.

Men and Boys for Gender Justice. 2014. "Delhi Declaration and Call to Action." 2ⁿᵈ MenEngage Global Symposium, November 10–13, 2014. New Delhi. http://www.menengagedilli2014.net/delhi-declaration-and-call-to-action.html Courtesy MenEngage, www.menengage.org

We urgently need to overcome these immense threats to human well-being.

2. **Patriarchy affects everyone, but in different ways.** Women and girls continue to face significant, disproportionately high levels of gender injustice and human rights violation. Men and boys are both privileged and damaged by patriarchy, but are rarely aware of that fact. Men and boys are also gendered beings. Gender equality brings benefits to women, men and other genders.

We urgently need to acknowledge that gender inequalities are unacceptable no matter who is affected.

3. **We build on a precious heritage.** We owe our awareness of gender injustices, our efforts to promote equality, and the occurrence of this Symposium itself to the pioneering courage and vision of feminist and women's rights movements. We align with the work of women's rights organisations and recognise all achievements in the transformation of the social, cultural, legal, financial and political structures that sustain patriarchy.

Keeping its historical context in view, we shall continue our work with men and boys towards gender equality informed by feminist and human rights principles, organisations, and movements and in a spirit of solidarity.

4. **We believe in an inclusive approach to realise gender justice.** We are men, women and transgender persons calling for *everyone* to participate in the gender justice movement. The importance of engaging men and boys in such efforts has often been overlooked.

We seek to make visible the most effective ways in which men and boys can contribute to gender equality, without being used as mere instruments.

5. **Patriarchal power, expressed through dominant masculinities, is among the major forces driving structural injustices and exploitation.** We are particularly concerned about the many manifestations of militarism and neoliberal globalisation, including war; the proliferation of weapons; global and local economic inequality; violent manifestations of political and religious fundamentalisms; state violence;

violence against civil society; human trafficking; and the destruction of natural resources.

We urgently need to expose the link between patriarchy and the exploitation of people and the environment, and to help boys and men change their behaviour from "power over" to "power with."

6. **Gender inequalities are related to inequalities based on race, age, class, caste, ethnicity, nationality, sexual orientation, gender identity, religion, ability and other factors.** We value the diversity of our world, and cannot continue to address these intersecting injustices in isolation.

We commit to promoting social and economic inclusion through meaningful participation, deepened partnerships, and joint actions among social justice movements.

7. **It is essential that each of us live the values of gender justice.** This requires men and boys in particular to reflect critically on their own power and privilege, and to develop personal visions of how to be gender-just men. It requires all of us to base our work on deep personal and political convictions. Whenever and wherever any of us says one thing but behaves differently, it fundamentally undermines our cause. We must speak out both in private and in public when we see others acting unjustly; being a silent bystander to an unjust act means being complicit in that act.

Our beliefs, behaviours, relationships, and organisational structures must reflect those we want to see in the world. To this end we must hold ourselves, as well as our friends, relatives, colleagues and allies accountable.

8. **Investment in engaging men and boys in gender-justice work makes this work more comprehensive. It should not detract from investing in other effective strategies, especially those undertaken by women's rights organisations.** We reject attempts to weaken our alliances or to put complementary gender justice approaches in competition with one another. We are representatives of diverse organisations, pursuing multiple complementary approaches. We stand in solidarity with each other and commit to strengthening our shared vision of comprehensive gender justice work.

We call on policy makers and donors to dramatically increase the resources available for all gender justice work and to include effective gender justice strategies in all development programmes.

9. **Priorities for specific policy areas and actions for engaging men and boys in gender justice work include:** gender-based violence; violence against women; violence against girls, boys and trans-children; violence among men and boys; violence in armed conflict; violence against human rights defenders; caregiving and fatherhood; gender and the global political economy; sexual and reproductive health and rights; sexual and gender diversities and sexual rights (LGBTIQ); men's and boys' gender vulnerabilities and health needs; sexual exploitation; HIV and AIDS; youth and adolescents; the education sector; work with religious and other leaders; environment and sustainability; and strengthening the evidence base.

10. **The Post-2015 Development Agenda must embrace a human rights approach and transform unequal power relations.** We believe that achieving gender justice requires the engagement of men and boys—for the benefit of women and girls, for men and boys themselves, for people of all sexual orientations and gender identities. For a world that is just, safe and sustainable. **We advocate for all activists, civil society organisations, private sector partners, governments and UN agencies to actively promote these principles and ensure that the new international development agenda is just and inclusive.**

DELHI CALL TO ACTION

EXAMPLES OF HOW TO ADDRESS GAPS

Bring Work with Men and Boys from the Programme and Project Level into Policies and Institutions

The personal is political, and vice-versa. Accelerating change, moving from the personal to the structural, requires reaching larger numbers of men and boys. We have to put systems in place which ensure that

institutions and individuals are held accountable for gender equality. We must change systems and institutions, including government, schools, families, the health sector, and the workplace, because they play a critical role in creating and maintaining gender norms and have the potential to reach large numbers of individuals.

We call for the reexamination of systems and institutions, including education and training, workplace behaviours and policies, legislation, management of public spaces, operation of faith-based institutions, and prevailing social norms.

Policies and legal reform can institutionalise more gender-equitable relations in homes and offices, factories and fields, in government and on the street. Therefore we must:

- Develop, implement and monitor policies to engage men and boys in gender equality, and build state capacity to implement those policies.
- Actively advance institutional and governmental policies that address the social and structural determinants of gender inequalities, including through advocacy work.
- Train staff to implement these policies.
- Create public awareness campaigns to transform men's and boys' perceptions of gender roles.

Promote Gender Equitable Socialisation

We are deeply concerned about the gender socialisation of girls and boys that begins at a very early age, hindering the achievement of their full potential and inhibiting full realisation of their rights. We strongly believe that all parents—especially fathers—must demonstrate sensitivity and equitable and just behaviour, especially to boys, starting at home and school.

Reaching out to boys during their critically important formative stages will contribute to realising a new generation of men with more positive behaviours toward women, children, men and trans-people. It is vital to sensitise and involve boys and girls from early childhood and continue involving them as adolescents, preparing them to become gender sensitive, equitable and caring adults.

Examples of specific policy areas and actions for engaging boys and men in gender justice include:

- Empowering children and young people to develop and foster gender transformative behaviour to help break the cycle of violence; and mobilise them as agents of change.

- Developing comprehensive sexuality education and primary prevention of gender-based violence (GBV) as an integral part of school curricula, including human rights, gender equality, and sexual and reproductive health and rights.
- Creating curricula that challenge gender stereotypes and encourage critical thinking.
- Training teachers and administrators to provide gender-sensitive learning environments.
- Utilising life-cycle and socioecological based strategies, beginning in early childhood and continuing with adolescents, to prepare them to be gender sensitive, equal and caring adults.

Engage Boys and Men in the Prevention of Gender-Based Violence (GBV)

Men and boys perpetuate the majority of GBV, even as they themselves are harmed by it. Rigid gender norms socialise boys and men to respond to conflict with violence and to dominate their partners. Men and boys are simultaneously victims of violence and perpetrators. A frequent contributing factor to men's perpetration of GBV is having experienced or witnessed violence while growing up; the effects of this on men and boys must be addressed. Moreover, it is essential to work with men and boys to transform the social norms that perpetuate GBV, and to understand and address the root causes of gender inequality. These include unequal power relations, practices and stereotypes that perpetuate discrimination against women and girls, sexual minorities and non-gender conforming people, and promoting alternative role models for boys.

Examples of specific policy areas and actions for engaging men and boys in the prevention of GBV include:

- Engaging men and boys to be more equitable in their own lives and to reject all forms of violence, including domestic violence and harmful practices such as child marriage and forced marriage, gender-biased sex selection, and female genital mutilation.
- Encouraging men and boys to question pervasive and structural inequalities.
- Promoting policies that integrate engaging men and boys into primary prevention of GBV.

- Developing policies to engage men and boys in making public spaces free of violence for women and girls.
- Designing progammes for male perpetrators that are integrated with the judicial sector and victim advocacy and provide legal, financial and psychosocial support for survivors and witnesses of violence.
- Implementing gun control.

Engage Men as Fathers and Caregivers and in Taking Equal Responsibility for Unpaid Care Work Evidence shows that when fathers are involved with their children at an early stage, including in the prenatal period, the likelihood is greater that they will remain connected to their children throughout their lives. Given that women and girls carry out two to ten times more care work than men and boys, there is a need to achieve men's and boys' equal participation in care work; and women's participation in the paid work force with equal pay. This can only be accomplished when care work is fully shared.

Examples of specific policy areas and actions for engaging men in taking equal responsibility for unpaid care work include:

- Promoting shared responsibility within the household and families, and via public services and social protection policies that support families.
- Reducing and redistributing unpaid care work, to allow women, in particular, more time for other pursuits such as self-care, education, political participation and paid work; redistributing care-work from poorer households to the state by financing, providing and regulating care services.
- Promoting the equal sharing of unpaid care work between men and women and to change the attitudes that reinforce the gendered division of labour, to reduce the disproportionate share of unpaid care work for women and girls.
- Promoting more progressive paternity leave policies.
- Implementing public awareness campaigns and education to transform men's perceptions of caregiving roles.
- Supporting fatherhood preparation courses and campaigns that focus on men's roles in the lives of children can address fathers' reported feelings of being unprepared for caregiving and help them see the benefits of greater participation.

Engage Men as Supportive Partners, Clients and Positive Agents of Change in Sexual and Reproductive Health and Rights (SRHR)

Throughout the world, SRHR are largely considered the sole responsibility of women. At the same time, many men neglect their own SRHR needs and those of their partners and their families. Men's lower use of SRH services, such as HIV testing and treatment, is a result of rigid gender norms as well as structural barriers, such as clinics that are ill-prepared to address male-specific health issues. As a result, not only are women and girls left to bear much of the burden of their own and their families' SRHR, but men's lack of involvement places expensive and unnecessary burdens on health-care systems. Interventions with men and boys around SRHR have been effective at increasing men's use of services, as well as their support and respect for their partner's SRHR. This involvement, in turn, improves the health of women, children and men themselves.

Examples of specific policy areas and actions for engaging men as supportive partners, clients and positive agents of change in SRHR include:

- Promoting accessible sexual and reproductive health services and rights for women.
- Engaging men and boys in the transformation of rigid norms that shape sexual and reproductive health outcomes, and enabling them to seek information and services that address their own sexual and reproductive health needs.
- Providing comprehensive sexuality education that promotes critical reflection about gender norms, healthy relations, and power inequalities.
- Promoting men's and boys' shared responsibilities around sexual and reproductive behaviour and rights.
- Expanding the availability and use of male contraceptive methods and STI-prevention.
- Creating spaces for men to take their share of responsibility in prenatal and child health services.

49

Confessions of a Recovering Misogynist

KEVIN POWELL

I Am a Sexist Male

I take no great pride in saying this. I am merely stating a fact. It is not that I was born this way; rather, I was born into this male-dominated society, and, consequently, from the very moment I began forming thoughts, they formed in a decidedly male-centered way. My "education" at home with my mother, at school, on my neighborhood playgrounds, and at church all placed males at the center of the universe. My digestion of 1970s American popular culture in the form of television, film, ads, and music only added to my training, so that by as early as age nine or ten I saw females, including my mother, as nothing more than the servants of males. Indeed, like the Fonz on that TV sitcom *Happy Days*, I thought I could snap my fingers and girls would come running.

My mother, working poor and a product of the conservative and patriarchal South, simply raised me as most women are taught to raise boys: The world was mine, there were no chores to speak of, and my aggressions were considered somewhat normal, something that we boys carry out as a rite of passage. Those "rites" included me routinely squeezing girls' butts on the playground. And at school boys were encouraged to do "boy" things: work and build with our hands, fight each other, and participate in the most daring activities during our gym time. Meanwhile, the girls were relegated to

home economics, drawing cute pictures, and singing in the school choir. Now that I think about it, school was the place that spearheaded the omission of women from my worldview. Save Betsy Ross (whom I remember chiefly for sewing a flag) and a stoic Rosa Parks (she was unfurled every year as an example of Black achievement), I recall virtually no women making appearances in my American history classes.

The church my mother and I attended, like most Black churches, was peopled mainly by Black women, most of them single parents, who dragged their children along for the ride. Not once did I see a preacher who was anything other than an articulate, emotionally charged, well-coiffed, impeccably suited Black man running this church and, truly, these women. And behind the pulpit of this Black man, where he convinced us we were doomed to hell if we did not get right with God, was the image of our savior, a male, always White, named Jesus Christ.

Not surprisingly the "savior" I wanted in my life was my father. Ten years her senior, my father met my mother, my father wooed my mother, my father impregnated my mother, and then my father—as per *his* socialization—moved on to the next mating call. Responsibility was about as real to him as a three-dollar bill. When I was eight, my father flatly told my mother,

Kevin Powell, "Confessions of a Recovering Misogynist," from *Who's Gonna Take the Weight?: Manhood, Race, and Power in America*. Copyright © 2003 Crown Publishing Group.

via a pay phone, that he felt she had lied, that I was not his child, and that he would never give her money for me again. The one remotely tangible image of maleness in my life was gone for good. Both my mother and I were devastated, albeit for different reasons. I longed for my father's affections. And my mother longed to be married. Silently I began to blame my mother for my father's disappearance. Reacting to my increasingly bad behavior, my mother turned resentful and her beatings became more frequent, more charged. I grew to hate her and all females, for I felt it was women who made men act as we do.

At the same time, my mother, a fiercely independent and outspoken woman despite having only a grade-school education and being poor, planted within me the seeds of self-criticism, of shame for wrongful behavior—and, ultimately, of feminism. Clear that she alone would have to shape me, my mother spoke pointedly about my father for many years after that call, demanding that I not grow up to "be like him." And I noted the number of times my mother rejected low-life male suitors, particularly the ones who wanted to live with us free of charge. I can see now that my mother is a feminist, although she is not readily familiar with the term. Like many women before and since, she fell hard for my father, and only through enduring immense pain did she realize the power she had within herself.

I Once Hated Women, and I Take No Pride in This Confession

I entered Rutgers University in the mid-1980s, and my mama's-boy demeanor advanced to that of pimp. I learned quickly that most males in college are some variety of pimp. Today I lecture regularly, from campus to campus, all over the country, and I see that not much has changed. For college is simply a place where we men, irrespective of race or class, can—and do—act out the sexist attitudes entrenched since boyhood. Rape, infidelity, girlfriend beat-downs, and emotional abuse are common, and pimpdom reigns supreme. There is the athlete pimp, the frat boy pimp, the independent pimp, and the college professor pimp. Buoyed by the antiapartheid movement and the presidential bids of Jesse Jackson, my social consciousness blossomed along racial lines, and behold— the student leader pimp was born.

Blessed with a gift for gab, a poet's sensibility, and an acute memory for historical facts, I baited women

with my self-righteousness by quoting Malcolm X, Frantz Fanon, Machiavelli, and any other figure I was sure they had not studied. It was a polite form of sexism, for I was always certain to say "my sister" when I addressed women at Rutgers. But my politeness did not lend me tolerance for women's issues, nor did my affiliation with a variety of Black nationalist organizations, especially the Nation of Islam. Indeed, whenever women in our African Student Congress would question the behavior and attitudes of men, I would scream, "We don't have time for them damn lesbian issues!" My scream was violent, mean-spirited, made with the intention to wound. I don't think it is any coincidence that during my four years in college I did not have one relationship with a woman that lasted more than three or four months. For every friend or girlfriend who would dare question my deeds, there were literally hundreds of others who acquiesced to the ways of us men, making it easy for me to ignore the legitimate cries of the feminists. Besides, I had taken on the demanding role of pimp, of conqueror, of campus revolutionary—there was little time or room for real intimacy, and even less time for self-reflection.

Confessions Are Difficult Because They Force Me to Visit Ghettos in the Mind I Thought I Had Long Escaped

I was kicked out of college at the end of my fourth year because I drew a knife on a female student. We were both members of the African Student Congress, and she was one of the many "subversive" female leaders I had sought to purge from the organization. She *had* left but for some reason was in our office a few days after we had brought Louis Farrakhan to speak at Rutgers. Made tense by her presence, I ignored her and turned to a male student, asking him, as she stood there, to ask her to jet. As she was leaving, she turned and charged toward me. My instincts, nurtured by my inner-city upbringing and several months of receiving anonymous threats as the Farrakhan talk neared, caused me to reach into my pocket and pull out a knife I had been carrying.

My intent was to scare her into submission. The male student panicked and knocked the knife from my hand, believing I was going to stab this woman. I would like to believe that that was not the case. It did not matter. This woman pressed charges on and off campus, and my college career, the one I'd taken on for myself, my undereducated mother, and my illiterate grandparents, came to a screeching halt.

It Is Not Easy for Me to Admit I Have a Problem

Before I could be readmitted to school I had to see a therapist. I went, grudgingly, and agonized over my violent childhood, my hatred of my mother, my many problems with women, and the nauseating torment of poverty and instability. But then it was done. I did not bother to try to return to college, and I found myself again using women for money, for sex, for entertainment. When I moved to New York City in August 1990, my predator mentality was still in full effect. I met a woman, persuaded her to allow me to live with her, and then mentally abused her for nearly a year, cutting her off from some of her friends, shredding her peace of mind and her spirit. Eventually I pushed her into the bathroom door when she blew up my spot, challenging me and my manhood.

I do not want to recount the details of the incident here. What I will say is that I, like most Black men I know, have spent much of my life living in fear: fear of White racism, fear of the circumstances that gave birth to me, fear of walking out my door wondering what humiliation will be mine today. Fear of Black women—of their mouths, of their bodies, of their attitudes, of their hurts, of their fear of us Black men. I felt fragile, as fragile as a bird with clipped wings that day when my ex-girlfriend stepped up her game and spoke back to me. Nothing in my world, nothing in my self-definition prepared me for dealing with a woman as an equal. My world said women were inferior, that they must at all costs be put in their place, and my instant reaction was to do that. When it was over, I found myself dripping with sweat, staring at her back as she ran barefoot out of the apartment.

Guilt consumed me after the incident. The women I knew through my circle of poet and writer friends begged me to talk through what I had done, to get counseling, to read the books of bell hooks, Pearl Cleage's tiny tome *Mad at Miles*, the poetry of Audre Lorde, the many meditations of Gloria Steinem. I resisted at first, but eventually I began to listen and read, feeling electric shocks running through my body when I realized that these women, in describing abusive, oppressive men, were talking about me. Me, who thought I was progressive. Me, who claimed to be a leader. Me,

who still felt women were on the planet to take care of men.

During this time I did restart therapy sessions. I also spent a good deal of time talking with young feminist women—some friends, some not. Some were soothing and understanding, some berated me and all men. I also spent a great deal of time alone, replaying my life in my mind: my relationship with my mother, how my mother had responded to my father's actions, how I had responded to my mother's response to my father. I thought of my education, of the absence of women in it. How I'd managed to attend a major university affiliated with one of the oldest women's colleges in America, Douglas College, and visited that campus only in pursuit of sex. I thought of the older men I had encountered in my life—the ministers, the high school track coach, the street hustlers, the local businessmen, the college professors, the political and community leaders—and realized that many of the ways I learned to relate to women came from listening to and observing those men. Yeah, I grew up after women's studies classes had appeared in most of the colleges in America, but that doesn't mean feminism actually reached the people it really needed to reach: average, everyday American males.

The incident, and the remorse that followed, brought about something akin to a spiritual epiphany. I struggled mightily to rethink the context that had created my mother. And my aunts. And my grandmother. And all the women I had been intimate with, either physically or emotionally or both. I struggled to understand terms like *patriarchy, misogyny, gender oppression*. A year after the incident I penned a short essay for *Essence* magazine called, simply, "The Sexist in Me," because I wanted to be honest in the most public forum possible, and because I wanted to reach some men, some young Black men, who needed to hear from another male that sexism is as oppressive as racism. And at times worse.

I Am No Hero. I Am No Saint. I Remain a Sexist Male

But one who is now conscious of it and who has been waging an internal war for several years. Some days I am incredibly progressive; other days I regress. It is very lonesome to swim against the stream of American male-centeredness, of Black male bravado and nut grabbing. It is how I was molded, it is what I know, and in rejecting it I often feel mad naked and isolated. For example, when I publicly opposed the blatantly sexist and patriarchal rhetoric and atmosphere of the Million Man March, I was attacked by Black men, some questioning my sanity, some accusing me of being a dupe for the White man, and some wondering if I was just "trying to get some pussy from Black women."

Likewise, I am a hip-hop head. Since adolescence I have been involved in this culture, this lifestyle, as a dancer, a graffiti writer, an activist, a concert organizer, and most prominently a hip-hop journalist. Indeed, as a reporter at *Vibe* magazine, I found myself interviewing rap icons like Dr. Dre, Snoop Dogg, and the late Tupac Shakur. And although I did ask Snoop and Tupac some pointed questions about *their* sexism, I still feel I dropped the ball. We Black men often feel so powerless, so sure the world—politically, economically, spiritually, and psychologically—is aligned against us. The last thing any of us wants is for another man to question how we treat women. Aren't we, Black men, the endangered species anyhow? This is how many of us think.

While I do not think hip-hop is any more sexist or misogynist than other forms of American culture, I do think it is the most explicit form of misogyny around today. It is also a form of sexism that gets more than its share of attention, because hip-hop—now a billion-dollar industry—is the sound track for young America, regardless of race, of class. What folks don't understand is that hip-hop was created on the heels of the Civil Rights era by impoverished Blacks and Latinos, who literally made something out of nothing. But in making that something out of nothing, many of us men of color have held tightly to White patriarchal notions of manhood—that is, the way to be a man is to have power. Within hip-hop culture, in our lyrics, in our videos, and on our tours, that power translates into material possessions, provocative and often foul language, flashes of violence, and blatant objectification of and disrespect for women. Patriarchy, as manifested in hip-hop, is where we can have our version of power within this very oppressive society. Who would want to even consider giving that up?

Well, I have, to a large extent, and these days I am a hip-hopper in exile. I dress, talk, and walk like a hip-hopper, yet I cannot listen to rap radio or digest music videos without commenting on the pervasive sexism.

Moreover, I try to drop seeds, as we say, about sexism, whenever and wherever I can, be it at a community forum or on a college campus. Some men, young and old alike, simply cannot deal with it and walk out. Or there is the nervous shifting in seats, the uneasy comments during the question-and-answer sessions, generally in the form of "Why you gotta pick on the men, man?" I constantly "pick on the men" and myself because I truly wonder how many men actually listen to the concerns of women. Just as I feel it is Whites who need to be more vociferous about racism in their communities, I feel it is men who need to speak long and loud about sexism among ourselves.

I Am a Recovering Misogynist

I do not say this with pride. Like a recovering alcoholic or a crack fiend who has righted her or his ways, I am merely cognizant of the fact that I have had some serious problems in my life with and in regard to women. I am also aware of the fact that I can lapse at any time. My relationship with my mother is better than it has ever been, though there are days when speaking with her turns me back into that little boy cowering beneath the belt and tongue of a woman deeply wounded by my father, by poverty, by her childhood, by the sexism that has dominated her life. My relationships since the incident with my ex-girlfriend have been better, no doubt, but not the bomb.

But I am at least proud of the fact I have not reverted back to violence against women—and don't ever plan to, which is why I regularly go to therapy, why I listen to and absorb the stories of women, and why I talk about sexism with any men, young and old, who are down to rethink the definitions we've accepted so uncritically. Few of us men actually believe there is a problem, or we are quick to point fingers at women, instead of acknowledging that healing is a necessary and ongoing process, that women *and* men need to be a part of this process, and that we all must be willing to engage in this dialogue and work if sexism is to ever disappear.

So I fly solo, and have done so for some time. For sure, today I count among my friends, peers, and mentors older feminist women like bell hooks and Johnnetta B. Cole, and young feminists like Nikki Stewart, a girls' rights advocate in Washington, D.C., and Aishah Simmons, who is currently putting together a documentary on rape within the Black community. I do not always agree with these women, but I also know that if I do not struggle, hard and constantly, backsliding is likely. This is made worse by the fact that outside of a handful of male friends, there are no young men I know whom I can speak with regarding sexism as easily as I do with women.

The fact is, there was a blueprint handed to us in childhood telling us this is the way a man should behave, and we unwittingly followed the script verbatim. There was no blueprint handed to us about how to begin to wind ourselves out of sexism as an adult, but maybe there should have been. Every day I struggle within myself not to use the language of gender oppression, to see the sexism inherent in every aspect of America, to challenge all injustices, not just those that are convenient for me. I am ashamed of my ridiculously sexist life, of raising my hand to my girlfriend, and of two other ugly and hateful moments in college, one where I hit a female student in the head with a stapler during the course of an argument, and the other where I got into a punch-throwing exchange with a female student I had sexed then discarded like an old pair of shoes. I am also ashamed of all the lies and manipulations, the verbal abuse and reckless disregard for the views and lives of women. But with that shame has come a consciousness and, as the activists said during the Civil Rights Movement, this consciousness, this knowing, is a river of no return. I have finally learned how to swim. I have finally learned how to push forward. I may become tired, I may lose my breath, I may hit a rock from time to time and become cynical, but I am not going to drown this time around.

50

"We're All Sisters"

Bridging and Legitimacy in the Women's Antiprison Movement

JODIE MICHELLE LAWSTON

In both waves of the feminist movement, white middle-class feminists have drawn on notions of "sisterhood" to create and sustain solidarity. Their claims to sisterhood have largely been premised on women's experiences with gender oppression (Dill 1983; hooks 1984; Lorde 1984), ignoring differences among women, particularly in terms of race and class (Dill 1983; hooks 1984; Lorde 1984; Moraga and Anzaldua 1981; Romero 1988). Many white feminists insisted on the "universality and over-riding importance of patriarchy," a claim that put womanhood above race and class (Dill 1983, 136). Critiques of the use of sisterhood and the corresponding failure of women's organizations to address multiple forms of oppression highlighted the failure to interrogate differences among women and led many researchers to dismiss sisterhood as a legitimate claim to solidarity. In dismissing this concept, however, scholarship has not fully examined the ways that sisterhood may continue to be utilized by feminist activists.

This article examines the complex functions of sisterhood in an ethnographic study of a white, middle-class, feminist, antiracist organization that uses the language of sisterhood in its work on behalf of incarcerated women, who are predominantly of color and poor. I find that sisterhood is rooted in women's experiences with oppression and in women's experiences with pride and pleasure and that sisterhood serves complex functions. Beyond creating and sustaining solidarity in feminist organizations that seek to work across difference, claims to sisterhood that are sensitive to differences influence an organization's stated intentions. I also offer insights into how structural inequality persists despite attention to difference.

SISTERHOOD

Prior research on the language of sisterhood has defined the concept (Dill 1983; hooks 1984), described who has used it and for what purposes (Dill 1983; Fox-Genovese 1979; Freedman 1981; hooks 1984; Shrom Dye 1975), and, especially, identified its shortcomings (Dill 1983; hooks 1984; Lorde 1984; Moraga and Anzaldua 1981; Romero 1988). Sisterhood has been defined as "a nurturant, supportive feeling of attachment and loyalty to other women" (Dill 1983, 132). It has been used in organizations—particularly those that were white and middle class—in an attempt to engender solidarity among women. Both Dill (1983) and Fox-Genovese (1979) point out that the promotion of solidarity has served two purposes: to maintain a separation between

Jodie Michelle Lawston, *Gender & Society 23*, pp. 639–664. Copyright © 2009 Sage Publications. Reprinted by permission of Sage Publications.

the public, political sphere of men and the private, domestic sphere of women and to inspire sociopolitical action based upon the shared needs and experiences of women (Dill 1983, 132).

For example, Freedman's (1981) research on the women's prison reform movement of the nineteenth century shows that the language of sisterhood was used to uphold separate spheres between men and women. Between 1840 and 1900, groups of white, middle-class, Quaker and other Protestant women located mostly in the Northeast began to visit and work with white, working-class, incarcerated women. Women were originally housed in men's prisons (Dodge 2006; Freedman 1981); however, women prison reformers ardently supported the division of labor and separate sexual spheres and believed that women were intrinsically nurturing and domestic. Reformers' belief in separate spheres propelled them to establish women's prisons—termed "reformatories"—where "fallen women" could be reformed into the nineteenth-century ideal: obedient wives and mothers relegated to the home (Dodge 2006; Freedman 1981). Interestingly, Rafter (1990) argues that the language of sisterhood meant that women prison reformers extended middle-class control over women who did not fit that ideal. In addition to class, what placed reformers in a dominant position relative to imprisoned women were institutional arrangements in which imprisoned women were required to be submissive to reformers in order to be released. Because those who were white and young were most likely to be sent to reformatories, women of color, especially Black women, remained in men's custodial institutions and were omitted from the sisterhood equation (Freedman 1981; Rafter 1990).

The use of sisterhood for the purpose of inspiring sociopolitical action is best exemplified by feminist activism in the 1960s and 1970s, during which time sisterhood was largely based on the contention that women are universally oppressed by virtue of their "secondary social and economic positions in all societies and in the family" (Dill 1983, 132). The women who used this language were largely white, heterosexual, and middle class. It quickly became apparent that all women are not oppressed in the same ways, however. For example, because they had a history of being tied to childrearing and the home—and experienced this as oppressive—white, middle-class, heterosexual women conceptualized work *outside* of the home as liberation. In contrast, working-class women and women of color

worked out of necessity in jobs that offered little autonomy and economic stability; as such, many conceptualized work outside of the home as a source of oppression (Nadasen 2002).

Critiques of sisterhood came from Black and Latina women in the late 1970s and 1980s, and from third-world feminists during the 1990s, who criticized white, middle-class, heterosexual feminists for, "organizing along the binary gender division male/female alone" (Sandoval 2000, 44.5; see also Dill 1983; hooks 1984; Lorde 1984; Moraga and Anzaldua 1981; Romero 1988). Critics argued that white feminists focused on analyzing women's experiences with patriarchal oppression and ignored inequalities based on race, class, and sexuality. hooks (1984, 46) argues that because this use of sisterhood focused on women's experiences as victims of oppression rather than their shared strengths and resources, white women were able to "abdicate responsibility for their role in the maintenance and perpetuation of sexism, racism, and classism, which they did by insisting that only men were the enemy."[1]

IMPLICATIONS FOR CURRENT RESEARCH

The language of sisterhood has historically assumed "homogeneity of experience" (Lorde 1984, 116) among women and has failed to consider the ways that race, class, and gender interact to produce inequality. Manifestations of this history can be seen in the contemporary women's prison movement, where some organizations adhere to the idea that women in prison and women on the outside of prison are united in a sisterhood of common gender experiences. While researchers have explored definitions and uses of sisterhood, the majority of this literature has critiqued this concept for not addressing differences among women and has not done enough to illustrate the complexities of a concept that continues to be fundamental to some organizations that are engaged in "on-the-ground" feminist work. Research has not pinpointed the varied functions that sisterhood may serve, beyond attempts at unity, maintenance of a distinction between the public and the private spheres, or inspiration of sociopolitical action.

Through an analysis of a white, middle-class, feminist, antiprison organization that uses the language of sisterhood in its work with incarcerated women—who are predominantly of color and poor—this article extends and complicates our understanding of this language. I ask the following questions: First, how is sisterhood conceptualized by white feminist activists? Second, beyond the uses enumerated thus far in the feminist literature and in light of the criticisms waged against it, what functions may sisterhood serve? In answering these questions, this article pushes the literature forward in four ways. First, it identifies the ways that contemporary white feminist activists define sisterhood. Building upon arguments that understand sisterhood as emerging from common experiences with oppression, I show that sisterhood is simultaneously predicated on oppression and women's experiences with pride and pleasure. Second, this article identifies the complex functions of a concept that has historic and continuing significance in feminist organizations. I find that sisterhood is used by white feminists in an attempt to bridge differences between women, particularly in regard to race, class, and life experiences, and that it functions to legitimate activists' work to one another.[2] Third, this article underscores the ways that sisterhood—through its functions of bridging and establishing legitimacy—influences an organization's stated intentions. Fourth, this article enumerates the ways that structural inequality persists in feminist organizations, despite attention to difference.

DATA AND METHODS

This study is based on an ethnographic research project that I conducted from 2002 to early 2005 on an organization that I refer to as Network for Prisoners (NP). NP is part of a women's prison movement that has emerged in the United States to contest the conditions of incarceration and, in some cases, the existence of prisons themselves. This movement includes a variety of organizations, some of which include former prisoners, current prisoners, family members and friends of prisoners, lawyers, and academics.[3]

Description of the Organization

At the time of this study, NP was small, with fewer than twenty members, all of whom were women. The activists identified as white and middle class. They were highly educated, and none had been incarcerated. Like other

segments of the contemporary prison movement (see McCorkel and Rodriquez 2009), activists realized that communities of color are targeted by the criminal justice system—therefore they believed NP should be led by the people most affected by the system. However, activists experienced difficulty in recruiting women of color and former prisoners. They explained that former prisoners wanted to put prison experiences behind them or were overwhelmed by difficulties in transitioning back into society, while communities of color that are connected in some way to the criminal justice system often struggle with the day-to-day of work, raising families, and visiting loved ones in prison, leaving little time for activism. While activists connected with other, more diverse prison groups in a spirit of support and collaboration, the organization's own racial and class privilege was of paramount importance for activists to analyze as they sought to work with incarcerated women.

During the study, activists met with fifteen prisoners to determine what issues are most important to them.[4] These fifteen women formed the core of the prisoners with whom activists were meeting; activists interacted with dozens of other prisoners on a less permanent basis. The prison restricted the number of prisoners with whom activists could meet during visits; one or two could meet with one prisoner for an hour or two at a time over a period of five hours; the more activists who could attend, the more prisoners they could see on a given afternoon. Prisoners explained that they initially heard about NP through "word of mouth" and contacted the group when they wanted to connect with activists on an issue, such as aid with parole. Activists met with prisoners with a range of sentences, from women serving a few months to those on death row.

One prisoner with whom activists worked was white, middle class, and educated; a second was white and working class. The remaining women had few resources; were African American, Latina, or First Nation; and were poor and undereducated: none had attended college, and few had finished high school. All but one of the prisoners reported experiencing physical and/or sexual violence before incarceration.

Interviews, Participant Observation, and Archival Research

This study draws from semistructured interviews, participant observation, and archival materials. I conducted fifteen semistructured interviews with activists. While I requested interviews with all members of the group, a few indicated reluctance to participate because of a perceived vulnerability to outsiders (Lofland and Lofland 1995). Questions on the interview guide covered activists' backgrounds and experiences with movement activities; identification in terms of race, class, and ideology; the ways gender did or did not connect them in a "sisterhood" to incarcerated women; and the ways that differences in race, class, and prison experience complicated this relationship. Interviews lasted from one and a half to two hours.

To interview women in prison, I was fortunate that NP invited me to join them on their prison visits. In total, I interviewed fifteen prisoners. Visits lasted five hours, during which time I conducted three to four interviews with prisoners and observed two to four discussions between activists and prisoners. The interview guide included questions about prisoners' lives, daily struggles in prison, and conceptions of NP. I spoke with prisoners about what the organization did for them and about their perceptions of the goals of the organization. To understand whether prisoners saw activists as "sisters," I asked them whether they felt that gender connected them to activists and how they felt about differences in race, class, and prison experience between themselves and members of the organization. Interviews lasted forty-five minutes to one hour.

Participant observation consisted of attending monthly meetings and events. During prison visits I was able to observe activist–prisoner interactions to further understand how the sisterhood frame was used. To cross-reference my data with organizational information, I examined the group's archival material, including Web site material and the mission statement. I used the program ATLAS/ti to code and analyze interview and archival material and field notes.

The Positionality of the Researcher   I am a white, middle-class woman, and I shared high levels of formal education, gender, and race with the NP activists. All of the activists I interviewed talked openly about the ways gender connects them to women in prison and how, simultaneously, differences in race, class, and prison experience impede their efforts to connect. I suspect that our shared race, gender, and class facilitated these conversations and provided activists with comfort during interviews.

With prisoners, I occupied an "insider" status insofar as I was raised in a working-class family that, like many prisoners' families, saw and continues to see drug and alcohol abuse, violence, and intervention by the police; my father also continues to be in and out of prison. Because I spoke openly about my life, these experiences helped me to relate to many of the imprisoned women. However, there still remained several differences between us—particularly my whiteness, my level of formal education, my current class status, and my having never been incarcerated—which contributed to my "outsider" position. While prisoners did not indicate that they *defined* me as an activist (I identified as a researcher during the project), I was like the activists in that I was a "free person" who was not subject to the same regulations and humiliating procedures (such as strip searches) to which prisoners are subject (see also McCorkel and Myers 2003). Because I could easily communicate with activists, prisoners may have feared that I would share their responses with the group. I report in this article the responses and observations that I received and made during the course of this project, while keeping in mind the influence that aspects of my identity had on the research process. I have changed the names of all respondents to respect their privacy and do not use any information that would identify the group.

THE EMERGENCE OF NP

NP can be situated in a rich tradition of women's prison activism, beginning with the women's prison reform movement of the nineteenth century and including women's prison activism of the 1970s. White, middle-class women reformers of the nineteenth century sought to "reform" imprisoned women to behave in ways that upheld a strict gender dichotomy (Dodge 2006; Freedman 1981). Prison reform in that era was initially more about upholding separate sexual spheres and reforming individual women rather than contesting the basis of imprisonment. While some women undoubtedly continued to visit and work with incarcerated women, organized efforts again emerged in the 1970s.[5] These organizations did not seek to uphold gender norms or to reform individual women. Some were reformist in that they worked to alleviate harsh conditions in women's prisons, while other radical groups sought to abolish prisons as part of a commitment to transforming American institutions and values (Resources for Community Change 1975).

Prison activism for women again increased in the 1990s, when incarcerated women began to draw attention to prison conditions. Women complained about medical neglect and abusive treatment by correctional officers (Amnesty International 1999). Women on the outside of prison organized NP to support women inside and to educate the public about prison conditions. They banded together to become, as activists put it, "a voice and a presence" for incarcerated women, whom they referred to as their "sisters." Such phrasing was typical of activists during interviews, meetings, and in organizational publications.

Like prison reformers of the nineteenth century, activists were white and middle class. Unlike prison reformers of the nineteenth century, activists did not aim to uphold gender norms, blame women's incarceration on moral failing, or seek to reform prisoners. On the contrary—given that close to 70 percent of imprisoned women are Black, Latina, First Nation, or Asian and that most are poor or working class—activists maintained that the process of incarceration is "shaped by racial and economic status rather than by criminal or criminalized acts" (James 2005, xxxvi). Activists argued that prisons, which serve to maintain white supremacy and economic injustice, are sites where the poor and people of color are warehoused. They explained that prisons are a space in which racial and class oppression are intensely magnified.

Given their ideological base, NP activists identify as prison abolitionists. The abolition of the prison system "is a long-range goal that . . . requires an analysis of 'crime' that links it with social structures, as opposed to individual pathology, as well as 'anticrime' strategies that focus on the provision of social resources" (Davis and Rodriguez 2000, 215). Abolitionist activists argue that rather than relying on imprisonment, resources such as education, food, housing, jobs, health care, substance abuse treatment, and mental health services should be prioritized to create safe communities. NP members spent a considerable amount of time talking about abolition during meetings and with other activists.

At the same time, activists articulated that a critical role of their organization is to work on behalf of imprisoned women. As they explained, given the difficulty in access to prisoners—with prison administration determining when they can visit, for how long, what items can be sent to prisoners, and sometimes the substance of conversations during visits—the direct ideological work they can engage in with imprisoned women is limited. Hence, a significant portion of activists' sociopolitical action was support work rather than talks with prisoners about abolition. This included writing letters in support of parole and to demand health care for individual women, writing to the governor to demand improvements in the prison system, helping to find lawyers for incarcerated women, and providing resources to individual prisoners. This type of action is extremely important, as prisoners are constrained in the actions they can take on their own behalf. For instance, when incarcerated women file grievances, it is not unusual for the staff and administration to retaliate through write-ups, withholding of mail, or refusal of visitation. Activists could engage in support work from the outside of prison with limited threat of retaliation.[6] In practice, then, the organization's role was bifurcated. Activists engaged in support work on behalf of individual prisoners with whom they had direct contact. Largely outside prison, activists promoted their primary goal of abolition, which they saw as on behalf of all imprisoned people and communities disproportionately affected by the criminal justice system.

NP activists identify as feminist and antiracist. They believe women occupy a collective position of subordination in relation to men and that women must come together to fight for equality (Martin 1990). However, they are also ideologically "committed to challenging racism as systemic in institutions and everyday life" (Srivastava 2005, 36). NP activists are committed to fighting for a society in which race is no longer attached to differences in access to resources and power.

Despite activists' social change goals, they were faced with a quandary. Given glaring differences in race, class, and prison experience, on what basis could activists—as they hoped—authentically be "a voice and a presence" for incarcerated women?

MAKING SENSE OF DIFFERENCE

Activists knew that their differences from prisoners called into question their ability to adequately work on behalf of incarcerated women. Sandra explains,

As a white middle-class woman I've benefited from a white supremacist society in many ways. Just being white means that I am not racially profiled and am not overrepresented in the prison system. My family benefited from programs that excluded people of color, like FHA loans, so I have more wealth, could go to college, and have access to good lawyers if I ever got arrested. It really brings into question whether we as white women can actually speak on behalf of prisoners.

Activists' lives have been shaped very differently through race and class than those of incarcerated women. Activists understand that gender is constructed by interlocking inequalities, or what Patricia Hill Collins (1990) has referred to as a "matrix of domination." White middle-class activists experience gender oppression differently than incarcerated women. While activists understand that differences in race, class, and prison experience influence their work, they feel that race especially poses a barrier and repeatedly made reference to the fact that they do not know what it is like to experience racial discrimination.

The differences between activists and prisoners cast doubt on activists' claim that they are "a voice and a presence" for imprisoned women. Their awareness of the racial and class privileges afforded them by the system that oppresses prisoners created discomfort for activists because their capacity to help prisoners stems from their privileges. Activists made comments like, "I question whether I should do this work," suggesting that they doubt their legitimacy in engaging in anti-prison work.

Despite these obstacles, activists did not abandon NP; they felt strongly that they had a responsibility to remain politically active on behalf of imprisoned women. Walking away, they maintained, would be a stronger indication of privilege as it would mean turning their back on structural inequality. How, then, did activists attempt to "bridge the gap" between themselves and prisoners, and legitimate their work? I use the term "bridge" to refer to the ways that activists connected to imprisoned women so that they had a working relationship and could more accurately represent their needs.

Activists drew on sisterhood as a collective action frame during prison visits. Collective action frames are "action oriented sets of beliefs that inspire meaning and legitimate social movement activities and campaigns" (Benford 1997, 416). Frames are used to produce and maintain meaning and provide a rationale for collective action. As I show, the sisterhood frame produced meaning for both activists and prisoners and was used by activists to bridge differences in racial, class, and prison experience and to legitimate their work.

CONCEPTUALIZING SISTERHOOD

During prison visits, activists employed a sisterhood frame to converse with incarcerated women. This frame focused on similar gender experiences under patriarchy, but unlike the women's prison reform movement of the nineteenth century, activists did not essentialize gender. Rather, they argued that in our current patriarchal system, women have experiences that have been socially constructed similarly. "Sisterhood" as used in NP is conceptualized as simultaneously rooted in oppression and in pride and pleasure and, as such, does not merely emerge from victimization (hooks 1984).

The sisterhood frame includes two components: a focus on gendered abuse, understood as oppressive; and a focus on women's experiences as caregivers, understood as both oppressive and pleasurable. Phrases like "we've all experienced abuse as women" and "we have a lot of similarities in that we have children" were used by activists to explain how they connect to women in prison despite differences in race, class, and prison experience. Statements such as "I can really relate to the abuse you suffered; I was abused" were used by activists during visits with prisoners to stress their connection to imprisoned women.

Abuse suffered at the hands of men was used most often as a common ground of discussion. This is a very salient component of sisterhood, and while feminists often identify experiences of gendered interpersonal violence as a shared experience among women (Dworkin 1997; MacKinnon 1988), prior research has not examined how white, middle-class activists deploy this shared experience in an attempt to bridge differences.

Half of the activists experienced abuse, witnessed domestic abuse in a family context, or knew women who had; and all but one of the incarcerated women had experienced physical or sexual abuse. Some research shows that 43 percent of women in the general population have reported physical or sexual abuse at some point in their lives (Walker et al. 1999), while between

57 percent (Bureau of Justice Statistics 1999) and 75 percent (Browne, Miller, and Maguin 1999) of women prisoners have histories of such violence. Abuse is therefore a gendered experience that cuts across race, class, and prison lines and was particularly salient for incarcerated women. The following is an excerpt from a conversation between Sandra and a prisoner named Barbara:

SANDRA: How are you dealing about the abuse you suffered?

BARBARA: The other day we were in group and I talked about it, and how terrified I was to leave him, and all the beatings. I cried for three days after that.

SANDRA: I know how you feel. Every time I talk about the abuse I went through I have meltdowns. It's something we as women have to constantly deal with.

Sandra relates with Barbara in terms of the domestic violence they both experienced but takes the connection a step further by stating, "It's something we *as women* have to constantly deal with." This suggests that experiences with abuse are a common point of reflection for women, cross race and class lines, and emerge from structural inequality between men and women.

Activists who did not experience abuse listened to incarcerated women and related to them by talking about larger trends of gender violence. The following excerpt comes from a conversation between an activist named Tanya and a prisoner named Jeni:

JENI: I continue to struggle with the abuse I went through, and not feeling like I could get out. I was talking to some other women and we all have the same problem of the violence coming back in our minds.

TANYA: Violence against women is common. It unites women because it's all around us. Either we experience it or see it in the media, or we have friends or family who have gone through it. It's enraging that women continue to be oppressed by it.

JENI: What helps is being able to talk to others about it—to talk to people who can understand, like you and the women in here who went through it.

Tanya connects Jeni's experiences to larger trends of violence against women. She alludes to a general experience of being controlled under a patriarchal system that oppresses women through violence or the threat of violence. What appears to be more important than Tanya's experiencing abuse herself is that she is able to understand Jeni's experiences.

Activists also established common ground with prisoners through discussions about their caregiving experiences. While some respondents defined caregiving broadly to include caring for other women, family, or friends, most activists and prisoners focused on caregiving experiences with children. Women have historically been the primary caretakers of children, and at least two-thirds of incarcerated women are mothers to children under age eighteen (Mumola 2000). Eight of the fifteen prisoners reported having children, whereas only four of the activists reported having children. This may help to explain why caretaking experiences were used less often to establish common ground between activists and prisoners. It was commonly activists with children who used caretaking experiences as part of a larger sisterhood frame. They spoke of the difficulty in rearing children and serving as primary caretakers (the "oppressive" aspect of caretaking) and also of the pride and pleasure that comes from it; activists who did not have children listened to prisoners as they spoke about their children. An activist named Linda and a prisoner named Mara discussed the accomplishments of their children:

LINDA: My daughter is graduating high school, I'm so proud of my baby.

MARA: That's wonderful news. They get big so fast, don't they? My kids have grown so fast, and I'm proud of them, especially given that I'm in here. They are the best things that happened to me.

LINDA: Kids can really change our lives for the better. They bring me so much happiness. We can feel like we have accomplished something through our kids.

While in some instances activists and prisoners focused on the difficulty in being the primary caretaker for children, conceptualizing mothering roles as oppressive through statements such as "men have it easy; we still end up doing most of the childrearing," in most cases they conceptualized childrearing as a source of satisfaction. Activists and prisoners related that caretaking has brought them pleasure and that they look at their children with pride and delight. The sisterhood frame therefore originates in experiences with both op-pression in the form of abuse (and sometimes caretak-ing) *and* shared pleasure that emerges from caretaking, and as such it cannot be reduced to only focusing on women's victimization. Sisterhood moves beyond vic-timization and begins to focus on the complexities of women's experiences as they relate to both subordina-tion and joy.

Taking Direction from Prisoners

In addition to discussing abuse and caretaking, activists also asked prisoners to enumerate their needs. This pro-cess was important as activists recognized that prison-ers had different needs, given their structural positions in relation to activists, from their own. The following is a discussion between Linda and a prisoner named Mara:

MARA: This place is sick. The food is awful, the guards don't give a shit about us. They refused to take a woman to the doctor the other day, she needs re-fills for her thyroid meds and they don't do a damn thing about it.

LINDA: What do you need from us? How can we sup-port you?

MARA: You can start to send parole letters in for me. The more letters the better. If you can also send in a care package of food, I can share it with the other women.

A fundamental part of prison visits and in establishing sisterhood is learning from incarcerated women about their needs. While activists did not have prolonged discussions with incarcerated women about their lack of prison experience, some activists made statements to prisoners such as, "You're the one experiencing this, you should tell us what you need." A key distinction between earlier and more contemporary uses of sister-hood, then, is that rather than basing their work on shared needs *and* experiences (Dill 1983), NP activists recognized the differing needs of women in varying racial and sociostructural positions. While rejecting the notion of shared needs, activists strategically deployed a rhetoric of shared experience. The difference between earlier and more contemporary uses of sisterhood is that NP activists abandoned assumptions of shared needs and engaged in ideological work to construct a basis for shared experience.

FUNCTIONS OF SISTERHOOD

Bridging

The sociopolitical action that prisoners can take on their own behalf is limited due to their confinement in a "total institution" (Goffman 1961) in which staff may retaliate against women. Activists can take actions on behalf of, but cannot easily organize large-scale actions together with, imprisoned women. Given the institu-tional difficulty and risk of organizing women in prison, coupled with differences in race, class, and prison ex-perience between activists and incarcerated women, the sisterhood frame was used primarily to bridge activists to prisoners and, as I demonstrate, to legitimate activist work, rather than to promote sociopolitical action.

While frames are used to "inspire and legitimate" collective action, they are also used to recruit new mem-bers and to mobilize potential adherents and constituents (Snow et al. 1986). Efforts by social movement organi-zations to link their interests with those of prospective constituents are conceptualized as "frame alignment processes," which include the processes of frame bridg-ing, frame amplification, frame extension, and frame transformation (Snow et al. 1986). Although these con-cepts have generally been used to understand how new recruits are added to movements, frame bridging is useful for understanding the ways that sisterhood functions to establish relationships with incarcerated women.

Frame bridging refers to the process of "linking two or more ideologically similar but unconnected frames regarding a specific issue or problem" (Snow et al. 1986, 467). It is used to induce groups or individuals with similar interests as one's own to join a movement and is achieved through organizational outreach (Snow et al. 1986). In NP, activists bridged to incarcerated women by using a sisterhood frame that is based on experiences with interpersonal violence and caretaking. Indeed, the frame that activists also received from prisoners was based on abuse and caretaking. The two groups of women connected around experiences of vi-olence and caretaking, and activists in turn provided resources and support (what prisoners identified as needs) to imprisoned women. This process does more than create and sustain solidarity. Sharing experiences with abuse and caretaking bridges activists to prisoners so that the two groups have a working relationship and so that activists can represent and fulfill prisoner needs.

That experiences with abuse and caretaking bridge activists to prisoners is a strong contention among activists. For example, Sandra states, "These experiences connect us to women inside; men could not relate in the same way." Activists contend that they understand many of incarcerated women's experiences because they too experience gender oppression and violence, and they too serve in caretaking roles that a patriarchal society has defined for them. Activists' experiential knowledge with gender replaces their lack of experiential knowledge with racial and class oppression and imprisonment.

Prisoners reported that the sisterhood frame resonates with them and provides them with the opportunity to share their own stories. Barbara states,

> As women I feel like we all have a lot in common. We have histories of abuse, for example, that women better understand because we have that direct experience with it, and then we can tell each other those stories. Men are less likely to be victims of domestic abuse so they wouldn't quite understand it the way a woman would.

Prisoners shared the belief with activists that women have particular experiences with gender oppression. The sisterhood frame worked to create a point of reciprocal identification for activists and prisoners. The exchanges between these groups of women provided an important opportunity for incarcerated women to overcome the prison system's silencing effects, as they were able to speak with individuals on the outside of prison walls who could understand their struggles as women.

However, prisoners' responses should be interpreted with caution. I have no doubt that prisoners felt connected with activists, as they had sustained relationships with them. But women prisoners are in a vulnerable position: they are silenced in the larger society, more often than not have few visitors, and are in need of resources. Prisoners' desire for outside contact and need for continued advocacy may have affected their responses.

In addition to understanding one another as connected by common gender experiences, another piece of the bridging puzzle relates to the question of agenda setting. Activists worked to build bridges across race, class, and prison experience, but who set the agenda for the group? While activists, like bridge leaders (Robnett 1997), worked to take direction from incarcerated women, their efforts were impeded by the prison system itself. For example, incarcerated women repeatedly asked that activists exert pressure on their behalf to improve their health care. Activists found, however, that prison officials were unresponsive to their efforts to create large scale changes. The institution itself is resistant to change, which has resulted in *activists'* changing their focus to provide more manageable services to prisoners, such as writing letters for parole. The prison, to a large extent, defines the type of work that activists can successfully engage in on behalf of prisoners.

Legitimacy

Legitimacy is a crucial issue in any movement organization. Robnett (1997, 13) argues that "constituents must be convinced of the credibility and legitimacy of their participation." NP activists, as constituents of an organization that works on behalf of women in prison, must be convinced of the legitimacy of their work, especially given their feelings of doubt in their ability to work on behalf of imprisoned women.

Activists reported that their ability to bridge to incarcerated women based on gendered experiences with abuse and caretaking inspires feelings of legitimacy. Sandra states,

> I'm a woman and I have had some of the same experiences prisoners have. I may not be inside, but I know what they have gone through. I don't think a man can relate in the same way. Our experiences as women connect us to women inside and therefore validate us and the work we are doing.

Activists feel more legitimate engaging in prison work because they have similar experiences as women. Activists never explicitly told prisoners that their work is legitimate because they are women—they implied it by talking with prisoners about the ways that they all connect based on abuse and caretaking. Activists did, however, speak in meetings of their gender experiences as legitimating their work. This suggests that activists are particularly concerned with negotiating their feelings of doubt amongst one another.

Incarcerated women—who are on the receiving end of the sisterhood framework—also conceptualized activists as credible because they are women. With the exception of one prisoner, who indicated that gender does not matter as long as someone helps her, prisoners explained that they feel more comfortable talking to women about their problems, as women "have keen insight into one another's needs" (Barbara). They explained that given the abuse they endured from male friends, acquaintances, or loved ones, and due to ongoing surveillance from male guards, they find it difficult to trust or relate to men.

All of the prisoners also reported that activists are credible because they have access to—and provide prisoners with—resources to which the prisoners do not have access. Stacy states,

> They have a lot of information that we don't have access to. These women know how everything works, so they can help us with what we need. I don't always know how the system works, how to get a lawyer, things like that.

Activists also reported feeling credible because of the information to which they have access. Sandra states, "We have information and resources that prisoners don't have access to, and I think this validates our work. We use our resources to give prisoners what they need." Interestingly, imprisoned women reported that receiving information and help from NP actually improved their status in the prison; they explained that if they did not have the information that NP gave them, other incarcerated women would ask, "Why should we listen to you, since you're still here?"

Prisoners acknowledged that activists have not experienced prison or racial discrimination and also differ in terms of class and educational backgrounds. Even so, all of the prisoners I interviewed said that they have strong relationships with activists. One incarcerated woman, Ruby, states,

> I don't care what race they are, the women are important to me because they care about me, as a person . . . they help us with the things we need, and we can relate on many levels about our lives. They feel like sisters.

Sisterhood, here, is interestingly conceptualized as common gender experiences *and* activists' ability to provide prisoners with resources.

While a sisterhood connection between "giver" and "receiver" is not required for work with prisoners (NP could potentially do the same work it is doing without using a sisterhood frame), activists grounded their support work and resource provision in claims to sisterhood. Because activists want the relationship between them and prisoners to be egalitarian, it is important that they not view themselves as simply providing charity, as this would reproduce the hierarchal paradigm that they seek to eradicate. For activists, claims to sisterhood inscribe a sense of egalitarianism between them and prisoners as they engage in resource provision, which, to activists, legitimates their work.

It is important to analyze the arbiters of, and audiences for, legitimizing discourse. Legitimacy or credibility construction in framing theory is based on the ways that *constituents* legitimate their work. In this case, credibility depends greatly on activists' perceptions, so that the arbiters of and audience for discourses of legitimacy are activists themselves. The focus on how sisterhood legitimates activists—through statements such as "we can just understand women prisoner's experiences better than men, which validates our work"—occurred during meetings and interviews, but not with prisoners and not with public audiences. This suggests that activists used the sisterhood frame as a legitimizing device *for themselves*. Sisterhood helps activists make sense of and justify why they are involved with NP despite difference vis-à-vis prisoners, which sustains their participation in the organization.

While activists are the primary audience for legitimizing discourse in that they determine whether their work on behalf of women prisoners is justified, prisoners are at the receiving end of the sisterhood frame and are also an audience for such language. Activists use language such as "we're all sisters" and "we can work to get you the resources you need." Prisoners construct activists as credible based on their gender *and* their ability to provide them with support. Some of NP's credibility, as understood by prisoners, is therefore received by virtue of its status as an outside organization and activists' positions of privilege relative to prisoners.

SISTERHOOD, NONDISCLOSURE OF ABOLITION, AND ORGANIZATIONAL INTENTIONS

While visits with prisoners are crucial, a significant portion of NP's organizational and ideological work is focused on abolition. Many of the discussions amongst activists centered on pathways to abolition, such as moving away from policing and instead using community-based models that hold people accountable for their actions. Activists also fought against prison expansion by contesting the construction of new prisons through methods such as letter-writing campaigns. But while activists identified prison abolition as a main goal of the organization, the language of abolition was absent from the sisterhood frame and activist–prisoner discussions. Activists explained this omission in three ways.

First, discussing abolition in a prison poses threats to activists and prisoners. Activists could potentially lose their access to prisoners as they may be construed as supporting nonconformity to institutional regulations that demand that prisoners be docile and compliant. Additionally, if such a discussion is broached and correctional officers overhear it, those officers may retaliate against prisoners for alleged malevolent intentions.

Second, activists have found that prisoners' goals differ from their own. Sandra states,

> As we got involved in this work and connected more and more to incarcerated women, we found that they have needs that must be addressed and are not necessarily focused on prison abolition. Admittedly, we have time to devote to abolition but prisoners are living in this oppressive system and just need to survive. If we are to say we are representing prisoners' needs, we really need to represent those needs. That means taking direction from those women, not merely following our own agenda. This tends to get away from our goal of abolishing the prison system as women inside are more focused on service provision and really, reform keeps the prison going.

Sandra identifies a key class- and race-based tension found in many social movements, based on the fact that the beneficiaries of a movement often want their lives to be improved in the short term, while more privileged constituents often focus on Utopian notions of revolution. For example, in contemporary transnational movements such as those that have organized to prevent child labor in Bangladesh and to stop gender discrimination in the workplace in Mexico (Hertel 2006), beneficiaries "put forward alternative understandings of human rights norms" (Hertel 2006, 3) that addressed the issues they were most concerned about, not necessarily what constituents or outside observers would consider most important. In organizations within the anti–violence against women (Scott 2000) and reproductive justice

movements (Nelson 2003), both white women and women of color worked to incorporate the needs and perspectives of women of color and poor women, with more privileged activists being challenged to reconceptualize their goals in the name of antiracism and social justice. In such movements, constituents ended up adapting, reformulating, and forgoing their own objectives to meet the needs and demands of beneficiaries. Similarly, NP activists adapted their agenda during visits with prisoners so that they could learn from and fulfill the needs of incarcerated women. In using the sisterhood frame to bridge to prisoners and legitimate their work, activists found that their organizational practices must focus on the urgent needs that weigh heavily on incarcerated women. Their intentions changed in light of the needs of prisoners.

Sandra interestingly explains that activists feel there is a tension between abolitionist and reformist work. Activists reported that their engagement in service-delivery work fails to challenge the basis of the prison system and only contests certain conditions within it. Since NP activists believe that the penal system is the chronotope that most poignantly embodies the material contradictions of U.S. capitalism, it is illogical to them to turn to a corrupt system to be the guarantor of civil rights when in fact the system is predicated upon maintaining inequality.

Finally, activists reported that they do not speak about abolition with prisoners because prisoners do not subscribe to such an ideology. Tanya states, "We don't talk about abolition. The language of punishment is internalized, so they believe they should be there." As a result, incarcerated women reported that NP is a service and resource organization. In explaining this discrepancy, activists made the case that prisoners are entrenched in a criminal justice system that repeatedly tells them they are "bad" or "pathological." This system denies the social patterns of racism and classism that channel certain groups of women into it. Activists argued that prisoners may not support abolition because they blame themselves for their imprisonment.

To be sure, prisoners explained their incarceration in terms of individual failings. Mara states, "I've made a lot of mistakes in my life, I take responsibility for my actions and it took prison to realize my mistakes." This statement exemplifies how prisoners use the language of individual responsibility." Prisoners must, if they go up for parole, express a *mea culpa* and prove to the parole board that they have been rehabilitated. Arguments for the structural reasons behind mass incarceration, from prisoners or their supporters, will not likely lead to parole. Moreover, the majority of the prisoners resisted the discourse of abolition, albeit indirectly. While one white, middle-class prisoner identified herself as an abolitionist, and one Black, working-class prisoner stated that abolition "would be wonderful but probably won't happen soon," the rest of the prisoners asserted that people who commit crimes need to be held responsible and incarcerated. Ruby states, "Most people deserve to be here, I would not want these people on the streets." Abolition, then, is not a realistic or immediate concern of the majority of prisoners. Still, the fact that activists chose not to disclose an integral organizational goal indicates a power relation: activists are in control of what information to divulge about themselves and their organization, which problematizes a sisterhood frame that implies both activists and prisoners are on equal footing.

DISCUSSION

NP activists have taken steps to address inequality in ways that some earlier feminist organizations have not, particularly in not assuming one overarching women's experience and in taking direction from marginalized women. This distinction is especially true when comparing contemporary prison activists to their predecessors of the nineteenth century. While nineteenth-century reformers sought to uphold patriarchal norms and prisons themselves, NP activists possess a radically different vision of a post-prison, egalitarian society. Nineteenth-century prison activists did not allow prisoners to define their needs and instead spoke for them. These reformers did not address the class privilege they held over incarcerated women or their failure to work with Black women (Rafter 1990). In contrast, contemporary activists take direction from and urge imprisoned women, both of color and poor, to define their needs. But while NP activists are sensitive to and have instated some strategies for addressing difference, inequality persists in this organization in four important ways.

First, the institutional barriers that the prison poses mean that NP activists have a freedom of movement to

which prisoners are not privy. Activists are able to move in and out of the prison relatively easily, whereas prisoners are subject to rigid institutional rules that dictate their movement. The fact that prisoners are confined and cannot engage in day-to-day organizational work with activists means that they are omitted from important organizational work and decisions. Second, prisoners do not have the same access to resources as activists. This relationship makes prisoners continually dependent on activists, with the possibility that prisoners do not feel safe critiquing the group.

Third, activists control information, which complicates the sisterhood frame. Activists exercise the option to disclose or not disclose debates about differences in race, class, and prison experience, as well as abolitionism, which are intrinsic to the organization's work. This consolidates power for activists, as they possess information that is relevant to the relationship between the two groups. The fact that activists do not share their feelings about differences in race, class, and prison experience, which provoke discomfort for them, forecloses prisoners' abilities to participate in and contribute to an important discussion, one that dictates the creation of the sisterhood frame. With its silence around race and class, the sisterhood frame fails to contest power hierarchies between activists and prisoners. Activists frame the terms of their relationships with incarcerated women.

Fourth, the sisterhood frame's function of legitimizing activists' work is complicated by the fact that its basis depends on prisoners' not contesting activist claims. If prisoners contest the sisterhood frame—as women of color and working-class women have done in other arenas—activists could not use this frame to legitimate their work *or* bridge to imprisoned women. Thus, the use of sisterhood depends largely on prisoners' silence around differences in race, class, and prison experience, which could be present because of a potential fear that in raising such issues—to me or activists—activists will stop visiting prisoners. While activists may be able to create some common ground, structures of race and class, combined with the institutional boundaries of prison, create hierarchies that are not easily overcome.

The relationship between bridging and legitimacy can also be looked at another way. Bridging can be understood as a conduit for flows in two directions: in one direction flows support, information, and resources for incarcerated women; in another, legitimacy. The bridge does little to contest the unequal relationship between activists and prisoners, which serves both sides, to an extent: prisoners receive support, while activists feel legitimate in their work. Inequality remains, limiting the effectiveness of the bridge in creating an egalitarian relationship between the two groups.

This article also has important implications for social movement theory. First, prison activism problematizes the idea of movement legitimacy, as beneficiary involvement is limited due to institutional constraints, difficulty in access to imprisoned women, and the dangers of incarcerated women's involvement in political activity. As McCarthy and Zald (1977) have noted, an organization's legitimacy may be compromised when it includes constituents—racially and economically privileged actors who do not stand to benefit from movement success—sans beneficiaries—marginalized groups and individuals who benefit directly from movement success—in its ranks. Second, frames are useful not only for producing and maintaining meaning but for bridging differences and legitimating an organization's collective action. Third, frames potentially affect an organization's stated intentions, especially when dominant and more marginalized groups work together. In NP, for privileged activists to use the sisterhood frame and work on behalf of imprisoned women meant that they had to foreground incarcerated women's experiences, needs, voices, and goals, which, for activists, overshadows their abolitionist work.

In thinking through the ways in which feminist organizations may better address difference, dialogue is necessary. As Lorde (1984) noted more than two decades ago, it is not differences between women that separate them, but the refusal to recognize those differences. In a society that continues to be predicated upon inequality, feminist activists must continue to find ways to productively discuss race and class, as well as sexuality, age, and other differences that may divide women. Feelings of illegitimacy or doubt, as experienced by many well-meaning activists, will not dissipate without productive dialogue amongst not just the women experiencing such feelings but also the women who experience the inequality that makes many white feminists doubt their organizational positions. Given structural inequality, white feminist organizations must identify the

silence—*together with* women of color, working-class women, and women from all walks of life—that enshrouds differences (Lorde 1984).

NOTES

1. Feminists have responded to these criticisms by attempting to implement racially diverse organizations (Scott 1998) that meet the needs of women of color and working-class women. However, research shows that most feminist organizations have failed in this endeavor. This failure has been attributed to ongoing splits between white women and women of color over definitions of racism (Simonds 1996; Zajicek 2002); feelings of anger, fear, or betrayal that result from addressing racial difference in organizational contexts (Morgen 2002; Srivastava 2005); and the difficulty in bridging the stratified positions that women occupy in the social order (Poster 1995; Smith 1995).

2. While this article examines a white feminist group and its use of sisterhood, feminists of color, particularly Black feminists, may use sisterhood in a different way. Black women, who have drawn on "sisterhood" and have called each other "sister" for some time, mark race and gender rather than erasing it.

3. Several antiprison organizations have emerged that are composed of women of color (see James 1999; Sudbury 2004). Organizing has also occurred by prisoners, especially those who are of color (see Cummins 1994; Diaz-Cotto 1996), and by the larger Black community (see McCorkel and Rodriquez 2009). NP should therefore be situated among a rich trajectory of activism in which women of color are also engaging.

4. Activists spoke of prisoners' "membership" in the group as complicated, given that prisoners could not engage in regular meetings and that access to them is strictly monitored by prison staff.

5. There was a radical men's prison movement that emerged, particularly in California, during the 1960s (see Cummins 1994).

6. There is always the chance that the prison could refuse activists visitation with prisoners, but at the time of study that had not occurred.

REFERENCES

Amnesty International. 1999. Not part of my sentence: Violations in the human rights of women in custody, www.amnestyusa.org/women/womeninprison.html (accessed April 5, 2008).

Benford, Robert. 1997. An insider's critique of the social movement framing perspective. *Sociological Inquiry* 67:409–30.

Browne, A., B. Miller, and E. Maguin. 1999. Prevalence and severity of lifetime physical and sexual victimization among incarcerated women. *International Journal of Law and Psychiatry* 22 (3–4): 301–22.

Bureau of Justice Statistics. 1999. *Women offenders*. Washington, DC: Government Printing Office.

Collins, Patricia Hill. 1990. *Black feminist thought: Knowledge, consciousness, and the politics of empowerment*. Boston: Unwin Hyman.

Cummins, Eric. 1994. *The rise and fall of California's radical prison movement*. Stanford, CA: Stanford University Press.

Davis, Angela, and Dylan Rodriguez. 2000. The challenge of prison abolition: A conversation. *Social Justice* 27 (3): 212–18.

Diaz-Cotto, Juanita. 1996. *Gender, ethnicity, and the state: Latino and Latina prison politics*. Albany: State University of New York Press.

Dill, Bonnie Thornton. 1983. Race, class and gender: Prospects for an all-inclusive sisterhood. *Feminist Studies* 9:131–50.

Dodge, L. Lara. 2006. *Whores and thieves of the worst kind: A study of women, crime, and prisons, 1835–2000*. DeKalb: Northern Illinois University Press.

Dworkin, Andrea. 1997. *Life and death*. New York: Free Press.

Fox-Genovese, Elizabeth. 1979. The personal is not political enough. *Marxist Perspectives* 8:94–113.

Freedman, Estelle B. 1981. *Their sister's keepers: Women's prison reform in America, 1830–1930*. Ann Arbor: University of Michigan Press.

Goffman, Erving. 1961. *Asylums: Essays on the social situation of mental patients and other inmates*. New York: Anchor.

Hertel, Shareen. 2006. *Unexpected power: Conflict and change among transnational activists*. Ithaca, NY: Cornell University Press.

hooks, bell. 1984. *Feminist theory: From margin to center*. Boston: South End.

James, Joy. 1999. Resting in gardens, battling in deserts: Black women's activism. *The Black Scholar* 29 (4): 2–7.

James, Joy. 2005. *The new abolitionists: (Neo) slave narratives and contemporary prison writings*. Albany: State University of New York Press.

Lofland, John, and Lyn Lofland. 1995. *Analyzing social settings: A guide to qualitative observation and analysis*. Belmont, CA: Wadsworth.

Lorde, Audre. 1984. *Sister outsider*. Trumansburg, NY: Crossing Press.

MacKinnon, Catherine. 1988. *Feminism unmodified: Discourses on life and law*. Boston: Harvard University Press.

Martin, Patricia Yancy. 1990. Rethinking feminist organizations. *Gender & Society* 4; 182–206.

McCarthy, John D., and Mayer Zald. 1977. Resource mobilization and social movements: A partial theory. *American Journal of Sociology* 82 (6): 1212–41.

McCorkel, Jill, and Kristen Myers. 2003. What difference does difference make? Position and privilege in the field. *Qualitative Sociology* 26 (2): 199–31.

McCorkel, Jill, and Jason Rodriquez. 2009. "Are you an African?" The politics of self construction in status-based social movement. *Social Problems* 56 (2): 357–84.

Moraga, Cherrie, and Gloria Anzaldua, eds. 1981. *This bridge called my back: Writings by radical women of color*. New York: Kitchen Table Women of Color Press.

Morgen, Sandra. 2002. *Into our own hands: The women's health movement in the United States, 1969–1990*. New Brunswick, NJ: Rutgers University Press.

Mumola, Christopher. 2000. *Incarcerated parents and their children*. Washington, DC: Bureau of Justice Statistics.

Nadasen, Premilla. 2002. Expanding the boundaries of the women's movement: Black feminism and the struggle for welfare rights. *Feminist Studies* 28 (2): 271–301.

Nelson, Jennifer. 2003. *Women of color and the reproductive rights movement*. New York: New York University Press.

Poster, Winifred. 1995. The challenges and promises of class and racial diversity in the women's movement: A study of two women's organizations. *Gender & Society* 9 (6): 659–79.

Rafter, Nicole H. 1990. *Partial justice: Women, prisons, and social control*. New Brunswick, NJ: Transaction Publishers.

Resources for Community Change. 1975. Women behind bars: An organizing tool. Barnard Center for Research on Women, http://www.barnard.edu/bcrw/archive/prison.htm (accessed April 2, 2009).

Robnett, Belinda. 1997. *How long? How long? African-American women in the struggle for civil rights*. New York: Oxford University Press.

Romero, Mary. 1988. Sisterhood and domestic service: Race, class, and gender in the mistress–maid relationship. *Humanity and Society* 12 (4): 318–46.

Sandoval, Chela. 2000. *Methodology of the oppressed*. Minneapolis: University of Minnesota Press.

Scott, Ellen. 1998. Creating partnerships for change: Alliances and betrayals in the racial politics in two feminist organizations. *Gender & Society* 12 (4): 400–23.

Scott, Ellen. 2000. Everyone against racism: Agency and the production of meaning in the anti-racism practices of two feminist organizations. *Theory and Society* 29:785–818.

Shrom Dye, Nancy. 1975. Creating a feminist alliance: Sisterhood and class conflict in the New York Women's Trade Union League, 1903–1914. *Feminist Studies* 2 (2–3): 24–38.

Simonds, Wendy. 1996. *Abortion at work: Ideology and practice in a feminist clinic.* Philadelphia: Temple University Press.

Smith, Barbara Ellen. 1995. Crossing the great divides: Race, class and gender in southern women's organizing, 1979–1991. *Gender & Society* 9:680–96.

Snow, David, E. Burke Rochford, Steven K. Worden, and Robert D. Benford. 1986. Frame alignment processes, micromobilization, and movement participation. *American Sociological Review* 51:464–81.

Srivastava, Sarita. 2005. You're calling me a racist? The moral and emotional regulation of antiracism and feminism. *Signs: Journal of Women in Culture and Society* 31 (1): 29–62.

Sudbury, Julia. 2004. A world without prisons: Resisting militarism, globalized punishment, and empire. *Social Justice* 30 (3): 134–40.

Walker, E., J. Unutzer, C. Rutter, A. Gelfand, K. Saunders, M. VonKorff, M. Koss, and W Katon. 1999. Costs of health care use by women HMO members with a history of childhood abuse and neglect. *Archive of General Psychiatry* 56:609–13.

Zajicek, Anna. 2002. Race discourses and antiracist practices in a local women's movement. *Gender & Society* 16 (2): 155–74.

51

Movement Intersectionality

The Case of Race, Gender, Disability, and Genetic Technologies

DOROTHY ROBERTS[1]

SUJATHA JESUDASON

INTRODUCTION

Intersectional analysis does not apply only to the ways identity categories or systems of power intersect in individuals' lives. Nor must an intersectional approach focus solely on differences within or between identity-based groups. It can also be a powerful tool to build more effective alliances between movements to make them more effective at organizing for social change. Using intersectionality for cross movement mobilization reveals that, contrary to criticism for being divisive, attention to intersecting identities has the potential to create solidarity and cohesion. In this article, we elaborate this argument with a case study of the intersection of race, gender, and disability in genetic technologies as well as in organizing to promote a social justice approach to the use of these technologies. We show how organizing based on an intersectional analysis can help forge alliances between reproductive justice, racial justice, women's rights, and disability rights activists to develop strategies to address reproductive genetic technologies. We use the work of Generations

Ahead to illuminate how intersectionality applied at the movement-building level can identify genuine common ground, create authentic alliances, and more effectively advocate for share policy priorities.

Founded in 2008, Generations Ahead is a social justice organization that brings diverse communities together to expand the public debate on genetic technologies and promote policies that protect human rights and affirm a shared humanity. Dorothy Roberts is one of the founding board members of Generations Ahead, and Sujatha Jesudason is the Executive Director.

Since its inception, Generations Ahead has utilized an intersectional analysis approach to its social justice organizing on reproductive genetics. Throughout 2008–2010, the organization conducted a series of meetings among reproductive justice, women's rights, and disability rights advocates to develop a shared analysis of genetic technologies across movements with the goals of creating common ground and advancing coordinated solutions and strategies. This cross-movement relationship- and analysis-building effort laid the foundation for successfully resisting historical divisions

---

Roberts, Dorothy and Sujatha Jesudason. "Movement Intersectionality: The Case of Race, Gender, and Disability and Genetic Technologies", abridged, *Du Bois Review: Social Science Research on Race* 10(2). Copyright © 2013 W.E.B. Du Bois Institute for African and African American Research. Reprinted with the permission of Cambridge University Press.

between reproductive rights, racial justice, and disability rights issues in several important campaigns. In examining the ways in which the theory and practice of intersectionality are used here we hope to demonstrate the kinds of new alliances that now become possible—alliances that can be both more inclusive and effective in the long term.

FROM DIFFERENCE TO RADICAL RELATEDNESS

In her classic article, "Demarginalizing the Intersection of Race and Sex," Kimberlé Crenshaw (1989) focused on Black women to show that the "single-axis" framework of discrimination analysis not only ignores the way in which identities intersect in people's lives, but also erases the experiences of some people. As a result, she argued, "[b]lack women are sometimes excluded from feminist theory and antiracist policy discourse because both are predicated on a discrete set of experiences that often does not accurately reflect the interaction of race and gender" (p. 140). The intersectional framework revealed that Black women suffer the combined effects of racism and sexism and therefore have experiences that are different from those of both White women and Black men, experiences which were neglected by dominant antidiscrimination doctrine (Crenshaw 1989). Extending from the example of Black women, an intersectional perspective enables us to analyze how structures of privilege and disadvantage, such as gender, race, and class, interact in the lives of all people, depending on their particular identities and social positions.[2] Furthermore, intersectionality analyzes the ways in which these structures of power inextricably connect with and shape each other to create a system of interlocking oppressions, which Patricia Hill Collins (2000) termed a "matrix of domination" (p. 18).

The value of intersectional analysis, however, is not confined to understanding individual experiences or the ways systems of power intersect in individuals' lives. Over the last two decades, feminist scholars have discussed and debated the potential applications of intersectionality. As a "framework of analysis" or "analytic paradigm," intersectionality has been applied to theory, empirical research, and political activism; it provides a lens to criticize dominant legal discourse as well

as being "integrated into mainstream social science ways of conducting research and building knowledge" (Dhamoon 2011, p. 230).[3]

In addition to supporting these differing methodologies, intersectionality can be marshaled to achieve varying goals. Many legal scholars have used an intersectional analysis to reveal the weaknesses in dominant legal approaches that confine discrimination to a single axis of race or gender or class, thereby ignoring people who are harmed by a combination of inequities (Crenshaw 1989). Social scientists have conducted multigroup studies to analyze and compare the complexities of advantage and disadvantage experienced by various intersecting categories, such as wage inequality by gender, race, and class (McCall 2005). Should intersectionality "be deployed primarily for uncovering vulnerabilities or exclusions or should we be examining it as a resource, a source of empowerment?" asks Kathy Davis (2008, p. 75). The answer is both, because uncovering how dominant discourses and systems marginalize certain groups in intersecting ways and at specific sites can be a basis for solidarity, and action. An intersectional framework can be used in a positive way to reveal and create commonalities among people who are affected by the same matrix of domination. Although she focused on the erasure of Black women from dominant discourses, Crenshaw concluded that, by categorizing struggles as singular issues, the single-axis framework "undermine[s] potential collective action." Intersectionality, in turn, allows us to develop tools not only to critique the dominant view of discrimination but also to forge "some basis for unifying activity" (1989, p. 167).

By highlighting the differences in experiences among women, it might seem that an intersectional approach would make coalition building harder. Some scholars have criticized its attention to identity categories for hindering both intra- and cross-movement mobilization by splintering groups, such as women, into smaller categories, and accentuating the significance of separate identities (Brown 1997). As Andrea Canaan (1983) observed in *This Bridge Called My Back*, the singular focus on identity can lead us to "close off avenues of communication and vision so that individual and communal trust, responsibility, loving and knowing are impossible" (p. 236).

Yet intersectionality presents an exciting paradox: attending to categorical differences *enhances* the potential to build coalitions between movements and makes them more effective at organizing for social change.

How can illuminating differences build solidarity? First, it is only by acknowledging the lived experiences and power differentials that keep us apart that we can effectively grapple with the "matrix of domination" and develop strategies to eliminate power inequities. This is not a matter of *transcending* differences. To the contrary, activists interested in coalition building must confront their differences openly and honestly. "Our goal is not to use differences to separate us from others, but neither is it to gloss over them," writes Gloria Anzaldua and AnaLouise Keaton (2002, p. 3). Intersectionality avoids the trap of downplaying differences to reach a false universalism and superficial consensus—a ploy that always benefits the most privileged within the group and erases the needs, interests, and perspectives of others. An intersectional approach should not create "homogenous 'safe spaces'" where we are cordoned off from others according to our separate identities (Cole 2008, p. 443). Rather, it can force us into a risky place of radical self-reflection, willingness to relinquish privilege, engagement with others, and movement toward change.

Second, once differences are acknowledged, an intersectional framework enables discussion among groups that illuminates their similarities and common values. In her chapter celebrating *The Bridge Called My Back*, AnaLouise Keating (2009) explores the methodology the anthology's contributors used to build a radical vision for transforming feminist theorizing. Their tool of "making connections through differences" used the honest, self-exposing exploration of differences among women to "forge commonalities without assuming that their experiences, histories, ideas, or traits are *identical* with those of the others" (p. 85). Commonality is not the same thing as sameness. Searching for and creating commonalities among people with differing identities through active engagement with each other is one of intersectionality's most important methodologies not only for feminist theorizing but also for political activism.

Third, analysis of our commonalities reveals ways in which structures of oppression are related and therefore highlights the notion that our struggles are linked. Despite our distinct social positions, we discover that "we are all in the same boat" (Morales 1983, p. 93). Not only does intersectionality apply to everyone in the sense that all human beings live within the matrix of power inequities, but also that the specific intersections of multiple oppressions affect each and every one of us.

Of course, these intersecting systems affect individuals differently, depending on the specific context and their specific political positions. This is why engagement between groups with differing perspectives is critical to understanding the dynamics of inequality and to organizing for social change. Rather than erasing our identities for the sake of coalition, we learn from each other's perspective to understand how systems of privilege and disadvantage operate together and, therefore, to be better equipped to dismantle them. An intersectional approach is particularly effective because, as Ann Russo (2009) observed in her epilogue to *The Intersectional Approach*, alliances and coalitions forged from such an analysis "do not require anyone to choose one's oppression over another nor to sacrifice some needs over others" (pp. 309, 315). Rabab Abdulhadi similarly recognized the challenge to build alliances based on shared oppressions, values, and vision "while always acknowledging the specificity of each group . . . and the context in which particular forms come up, without thinking that one form should dominate another" (quoted in Cole 2008, p. 447).

Far from building walls around identity categories, then, intersectionality forces us to break through these categories to examine how they are related to each other and how they make certain identities invisible. This shift from seeing our differences to seeing our relatedness requires that we understand identity categories in terms of matrices of power that are connected rather than solely as features of individuals that separate us (Cole 2008; Dhamoon 2011).[4] "While analytically we must carefully examine the structures that differentiate us, politically we must fight the segmentation of oppression into categories such as 'racial issues,' 'feminist issues,' and 'class issues,'" writes Bonnie Thornton Dill (1983, p. 148). Indeed, our radical *interrelatedness* is equally as important as our differences. To us, the radical potential for intersectionality lies in moving beyond its recognition of difference to build political coalitions based on the recognition of connections among systems of oppression as well as on a shared vision of social justice. The process of grappling with differences, discovering and creating commonalities, and revealing interactive mechanisms of oppression itself provides a model for alternative social relationships.

AN INTERSECTIONAL ANALYSIS OF RACE, GENDER, DISABILITY, AND REPRODUCTIVE GENETIC TECHNOLOGIES

Our scholarly and activist work on reproductive justice illustrates the potential for an intersectional approach to forge radical connections between movements for social justice. Reproductive justice is a prime example of applying an intersectional framework to both political theorizing and political action. Women of color developed a reproductive justice theory and movement to challenge the barriers to their reproductive freedom stemming from sex, race, and class inequalities (Nelson 2003; Roberts 1997, 2004; Silliman et al., 2004). Reproductive justice addresses the inadequacies of the dominant reproductive rights discourse espoused by organizations led by White women that was based on the concept of choice and on the experiences of the most privileged women. Thus, women of color contributed to the understanding of and advocacy for reproductive freedom by recognizing the intersection of race, class, and gender in the social control of women's bodies.

What if we complicated the matrix even more by including disability as an identity and political category in theorizing and organizing by women of color? Far from being a marginal social division because it affects fewer people, disability helps to shape reproductive and genetic technologies and policies that affect everyone.[5] Like intersectionality's central claim that "representations of gender that are 'race-less' are not by that fact alone more universal than those that are race-specific" (Crenshaw 2011, p. 224), representations of race and gender that neglect disability are no more universal than those that are based solely on able bodies.[6] It was only when we engaged with disability rights activists that we began to grapple with their perspectives on reproductive politics and changed our own perspectives in concrete ways.

Just as the dominant conception of discrimination imposed by courts erases Black women, organizing for social change along certain categories can obscure the importance of other perspectives and opportunities for building coalitions to achieve common social justice goals. Disability rights discourse largely has failed to encompass racism, and anti-racism discourse largely has failed to encompass disability. The disability rights

and civil rights movements are often compared as two separate struggles that run parallel to each other, rather than struggles that have constituents and issues in common,[7] even as both people of color and people with disabilities share a similar experience of marginalization and "othering" and even though there are people of color with disabilities (Pokempner and Roberts, 2001).

Race, gender, and disability do not simply intersect in the identities of women of color with disabilities, however. Rather, racism, sexism, and ableism work together in reproductive politics to maintain a reproductive hierarchy and enlist support for policies that perpetuate it (Roberts 2009, 2011). In her past work, Roberts (1997) has contrasted policies that punish poor women of color for bearing children with advanced technologies that assist mainly middle- and upper-class White women not only to have genetically-related children, but to also have children with preferred genetic traits. While welfare reform laws aim to deter women receiving public assistance from having even one additional healthy baby, largely unregulated fertility clinics regularly implant privileged women with multiple embryos, knowing the high risk multiple births pose for premature delivery and low birth weight that requires a fortune in publicly-supported hospital care. Rather than place these policies in opposition, however, Roberts argued in "Privatization and Punishment in the New Age of Reprogenetics" (2005) and "Race, Gender, and Genetic Technologies: A New Reproductive Dystopia?" (2009) that they are tied together. Policies supporting both population control programs and genetic selection technologies reinforce biological explanations for social problems and place reproductive duties on women that privatize remedies for illness and social inequities.

Advances in reproduction-assisting technologies that create embryos in a laboratory have converged with advances in genetic testing to produce increasingly sophisticated methods to select for preferred genetic traits, and de-select for disability. Liberal notions of reproductive choice obscure the potential for genetic selection technologies to intensify both discrimination against disabled people and the regulation of women's childbearing decisions. These technologies stem from a medical model that attributes problems caused by the social inequities of disability to each individual's genetic make up and that holds individuals, rather than the public, responsible for fixing these inequities. Disability rights activists have pointed out that prenatal and pre-implantation genetic diagnosis reinforce the view that "disability itself, not societal discrimination against people with disabilities, is the problem to be solved" (Parens and Asch, 1999, p. s13). This medicalized approach to disability assumes that difficulties experienced by disabled people are caused by physiological limitations that prevent them from functioning normally in society, rather than the physical and social limitation enforced by society on individuals with disabilities (Saxton 2007). Although disabilities cause various degrees of impairment, the main hardship experienced by most people with disabilities stems from pervasive discrimination and the unwillingness to accept and embrace differing needs to function fully in society.

Locating the problem inside the disabled body rather than in the social oppression of disabled people leads to the elimination of these bodies becoming the chief solution to impairment. By selecting out disabling traits, these technologies can divert attention away from social arrangements, government policies, and cultural norms that help to define disability and make having disabled children undesirable (Wendell 1996). Genetic selection is also discriminatory in that it reduces individual children to certain genetic traits that by themselves are deemed sufficient reasons to terminate an otherwise wanted pregnancy or discard an embryo that might otherwise have been implanted (Asch 2007).

The expectation of genetic self-regulation may fall especially harshly on Black and Latina women, who are stereotypically defined as hyperfertile and lacking the capacity for self-control (Gutierrez 2008; Roberts 1997). In an ironic twist, it may be poor women of color, not affluent White women, who are most compelled to use prenatal genetic screening technologies. This paradox is revealed only by a political analysis that examines the interlocking systems of inequity based on gender, race, and disability that work together to support policies that rely on women's management of genetic risk rather than social change. This intersectional analysis also reveals that reproductive justice, women's rights, and disability rights activists share a common interest in challenging unjust reprogenetics policies and in forging an alternative vision of social welfare.

THE DYNAMICS OF INTER- AND INTRA-MOVEMENT MOBILIZATION ROOTED IN AN INTERSECTIONAL FRAMEWORK

Sociologists, social psychologists, and historians have extensively investigated solidarity within political organizations and collaborations within movements where political organizations with similar causes come together for collective action, including the women's, labor, civil rights, and environmental movements (Beamish and Luebbers, 2009; Greenwood 2008). Surprisingly, scholars have devoted relatively little attention to coalitions *across* movements where political organizations focused on different causes, often rooted in differing identity categories, engage in collective action to achieve shared goals (Beamish and Luebbers, 2009). Sociologists Thomas D. Beamish and Amy J. Luebbers contend that cross-movement alliances "pose special problems for collaboration that cannot be sufficiently addressed through within-movement studies," because they must "reconcile distinctive, sometimes competing explanations as well as remedies for the social problems they jointly seek to stem" (p. 648).

An intersectional approach provides a method for overcoming these barriers to collaboration and even using differences between identity categories and causes as a tool for more effective strategizing and action. As Bonnie Thornton Dill (1983) contends, "Through joint work on specific issues, we may come to a better understanding of one another's needs and perceptions and begin to overcome some of the suspicions and mistrust that continue to haunt us" (p. 146). Engaged in this intersectional praxis, movements organized around separate identity categories can reach a more effective level of political struggle "where the differences between us ENRICH our political and social action rather than divide it . . . " (p. 148).

Based on this model, Generations Ahead organized a series of meetings among reproductive rights and justice, women of color and Indigenous women, and disability rights advocates to dig deeper into the areas of tension between movements and to develop a shared analysis of genetic technologies across movements, with the goals of creating common ground and advancing coordinated solutions and strategies.

In September 2008, Generations Ahead hosted its first national convening of women of color and Indigenous women to talk about reproductive and genetic technologies. With the support of seven reproductive rights and justice organizations, Generation Ahead convened twenty-one women of color and Indigenous women leaders from across the United States for two days to discuss specific concerns about the relationships between genetic technologies and different racialized communities (Generations Ahead 2008). Because disability and LGBTQ rights were deemed to be central intersecting identities for this group, the convening was also designed to include these identities, in addition to race and gender.

In order to openly and honestly identify the distinctive ways in which reproductive and genetic technologies affected different constituencies, the participants were asked to divide themselves up into self-identified constituency groups. It was clearly acknowledged that participants were not being asked to privilege or prioritize any one identity over others, but rather that they were being asked to share the unique and distinguishing perspectives of different constituencies. The twenty-one participants divided up into the following groups: Indigenous women, Asian women, women of African descent, women (of color) with disabilities, and Latinas living in the United States. Queer identified people agreed to raise their specific concerns within all of the other groups. Each group's members then spent time identifying the particular benefits and concerns genetic technologies raised for their group, and the values that they wanted to see integrated into any advocacy on this issue.

Rather than starting the discussion about the benefits and risks of genetic technologies based on a universal and generic human being, these constituency groups were able to do several interesting things simultaneously. First, when asked to consider these technologies from the standpoint of their identity-specific perspective, these issues became more relevant for all participants. None of the participants were users of these technologies, and, up until that moment, most felt that they were not relevant to their lives and social justice advocacy. But once they were able to connect what felt like an abstract, futuristic, and privileged issue to their lives and communities, their investment in the issue shifted. Most participants were now able to reflect on and attach genetic technologies to issues that they deeply cared about: sex selection and son preference for Asian women; genetic determinism and eugenics for women of African

descent; prenatal disability de-selection for women with disabilities; blood quantum and tribal identity for Indigenous women; and family formation and fertility for Latinas. By the end of the discussion, all participants were able to understand the issues raised by genetic technologies as an extension of their existing social justice commitments and concerns (Generations Ahead 2008).

Second, the participants were able to make these linkages as a part of a larger, shared "matrix of domination," rather than as a hierarchical analysis of oppression. Because everybody was able to speak to the intersections with their lived experiences, and since all identities were equally valued, the discussion quickly and easily transitioned to shared struggles and solidarity, rather than a debate over who was more or less oppressed or privileged in the development and use of genetic technologies. Shared concerns were quickly visible in the similar histories of reproductive oppression and genetic determinism, and the ways in which biology, bodies, and reproduction have been historically categorized, regulated, stigmatized, and controlled for some groups. . . .

This convening laid the groundwork for future, more challenging conversations and collaborations between reproductive justice and disability rights leaders. The lessons and praxis of using an intersectional approach were then applied to a series of five roundtable conversations between two groups that have a long history of tension, mistrust, and aversion to working together—reproductive rights and disability rights advocates. These roundtable discussions started with the most difficult area of disagreement between these two movements—their differing approaches to genetic testing technologies and abortion:

> While reproductive rights advocates have supported the idea of "fetal anomalies" as an argument for abortion rights, disability rights advocates have argued that this reinforces negative views of disability. And while the reproductive rights movement is fighting to restrict the legal definition of personhood to protect abortion, the disability rights movement is fighting to expand a perceptual definition of personhood to increase the social inclusion of people with disabilities. (Generations Ahead 2009, p. 1)

These discussions were started with an open acknowledgment of this third rail of disagreement, and recognition that there was a mutual history of hurt and fear, where each movement felt that the other did not appreciate its perspective or deep concerns about the other movement's perspective. Generations Ahead used an intersectional framework to begin the discussion with storytelling that highlighted the other identities of all fifteen participants, such as race, sexual orientation, class, and immigration. This ensured that, even though this was a conversation between women about reproductive rights and disability, any one person or group could not cling to a victim–oppressor binary (Generations Ahead 2009). This created much more emotional and political space to candidly discuss the apparently oppositional positions and find a way toward better understanding of the difference, if not necessarily come to agreement.

For example, when White women with disabilities charged the reproductive rights and justice advocates without disabilities with not truly understanding what it was like to live with disability in this society, women of color were able to respond, "And that is ok, because you can't truly understand what it is like to live as a person of color in this society." So instead of participants feeling guilty and immobilized around their privilege, everybody was able to create connection around shared experiences of discrimination, marginalization, and privilege. This created the possibility of then identifying common values and mutual areas of advocacy interest. In addition, the women of color with disabilities who participated in the conversations embodied the intersection of race and disability and reinforced the impossibility of privileging one identity over another. As members of both groups, they spoke directly to their multiple experiences of racism amongst White people with disabilities, and ableism amongst people of color, all mixed in with classism, homophobia, and zenophobia—two of them were raised poor, one was an immigrant, and another identified as Queer. They reminded the whole group throughout the conversations that neither race nor disability was the sole meaningful axis of oppression.

Once the participants established everyone's shared multiple and intersecting interests in genetic technologies and abortion, they worked to discover and develop a set of common values, including the recognition and support of people's right to independent decision making, resources that allow them to control their own lives,

and respectful and dignified treatment. Their discussion of shared values enabled them to identify bridging frameworks that linked their movements. They found commonality between the social model of disability ("the notion that it is the negative social attitudes toward disability rather than the disability itself that are the source of oppression for those with disabilities") and the reproductive justice framework ("the understanding that multiple, intersecting structural factors influence both women's ability to not have, but also to have children and parent them with dignity") (Generations Ahead 2009, p. 2). As a result of their engagement over conflicts and common values, the advocates were able to agree on a shared alternative paradigm for addressing genetic technologies based on "long-term, comprehensive, intersectional policies that create structural changes in social inequality" (Generations Ahead 2009, p. 6).

Instead of these two groups being at loggerheads over whether to regulate abortion and prenatal screening to prevent the de-selection of people with disabilities or allow unfettered reproductive freedom that could lead to the eugenic elimination of disability, participants were able to define a set of shared values. These include:

- Reproductive autonomy should include support for people making the choice to have children, including children with disabilities, and support to raise their children with dignity.
- All women who choose to parent should be valued as parents and all children should be valued as human beings, including children with disabilities.
- Policy advocacy should focus on providing social and material supports to women, families, and communities, not on when life begins, whose life is more valued, or who can be a parent.
- Both movements should broaden their agendas to fight to improve the social, political, physical, and economic contexts within which women and people with disabilities make decisions about their lives. The focus should be on changing society, not on individual decision-making (Generations Ahead 2009, p. 2).

Through these shared values all participants were able to affirm women's self-determination and the value of people with disabilities, so that one was not pitted against the other. And they were able to include an analysis that encompassed concerns about race, class, immigration, and sexual orientation. Their values were about all women, all parents, and all children, not just the White, middle-class, able-bodied, and heteronormative U.S. citizen. In working together in an intersectional framework, they were able to define shared values that made each movement both more inclusive and focused. Highlighting the multiple axes of differences in the room, rather than splintering the group, then became a resource for radical relatedness and unifying action.

Based on these discussions and relationships, the two movements then worked together on three different collaborative projects, projects that probably would not have been possible without having articulated these shared values to guide their advocacy. In October 2008, Congress worked to pass the Prenatally and Postnatally Diagnosed Conditions Awareness Act, a bill that called for comprehensive information and support for women who receive a prenatal or postnatal diagnosis of Down syndrome or any other conditions. Initially Beltway reproductive rights groups and lobbyists were suspicious and dismissive of this legislation, in large part because it was authored by then Senator Sam Brownback (R-Kansas), an ardent anti-choice advocate.

Based on the cross-movement discussions facilitated by Generations Ahead, reproductive rights advocates reached out to disability rights advocates and vice versa. A collaboration of five organizations (World Institute on Disability, Disability Rights Education and Defense Fund, National Women's Health Network, Reproductive Health Technologies Project, and Generations Ahead) authored a joint statement, with each trusting its own movement to educate its members about how this legislation was good for both women and people with disability and had the support of both movements (The Prenatally and Postnatally Diagnosed Conditions Awareness Act Fact Sheet 2012). This collaboration then set the stage for disability rights advocates welcoming reproductive rights advocates to join in designing the implementation of the Act in such a way as to not demonize women and their reproductive decision-making. Additionally, reproductive rights advocates were able to use this as a moment to affirm their support for disability rights and highlight shared areas of interest. This joint statement was sent out to a board network of allies and advocates in both movements.

In the spring of 2010, anti-choice advocates enacted legislation in Nebraska making later abortion more difficult to obtain by replacing the twenty-four-week viability concept with one based on the fetus' ability to experience pain at twenty weeks. In the mad scramble to defeat the legislation, prochoice groups were increasingly using messaging and storytelling that relied on pre-natal disability diagnosis as a justification for access to late abortion. This political and rhetorical strategy that described any potential disability as a "painful tragedy" to be avoided at all costs was viewed by disability rights advocates as ignorant and disrespectful of the lives of people with disability, and experienced as ableist and discriminatory.

Advocates who had participated in the previous roundtable discussions quickly mobilized and brought a small, but respected group of reproductive justice and disability rights advocates together from across the country for a day-long strategy session. Together they developed five concrete recommendations for reproductive rights advocates to defend access to abortion without demonizing disability. The recommendations included a pivot away from a "pain" framework that asks policymakers to choose between the suffering of parents and the pain of the fetus, advocating instead for the government to provide the enabling conditions for families to make the best decisions for themselves, and increasing investment in the Prenatally and Postnatally Diagnosed Conditions Awareness Act (Jesudason and Epstein, 2012). These recommendations were shared with all the major prochoice advocacy groups involved nationally and locally in the Nebraska legislative fight. In response, several organizations intentionally changed their messaging and language with regards to disability, although not completely eliminating it from their strategy.

In October of 2010 this network of disability and reproductive rights/justice advocates mobilized again in response to Dr. Robert Edwards winning the Nobel Prize. Edwards was recognized for his pioneering work in assisted reproductive technologies, but this group objected to his promotion of these technologies to prevent the birth of children with disabilities. At the same time, Virginia Ironside, a British columnist, in defense of abortion, was arguing that it was immoral, selfish, and cruel to knowingly give birth to a child with a disability (Fireandreamitchell.com 2010). Several of these advocates collectively issued a sign-on statement titled, "The Unnecessary Opposition of Rights," in which they stated:

> As people committed to both disability rights and reproductive rights, we believe that respecting women and families in their reproductive decisions requires simultaneously challenging discriminatory attitudes toward people with disabilities. We refuse to accept the bifurcation of women's rights from disability rights, or the belief that protecting reproductive rights requires accepting ableist assumptions about the supposed tragedy of disability. On the contrary, we assert that reproductive rights includes attention to disability rights, and that disability rights requires attention to human rights, including reproductive rights (Generations Ahead 2010).

Within a few weeks of circulating this letter through advocacy networks, more than 150 individuals and organizations internationally had signed the statement in support of the values it expressed.

While these have not been major policy victories, they have been important and noteworthy steps toward building a cross-movement alliance where before there had been only mistrust and oppositional politics. Using intersectionality to analyze the interlocking systems of race, gender, and disability; discover and create shared values related to genetic technologies; and implement joint strategies in practice was critical to building this new alliance.

CONCLUSION

As the work of Generations Ahead illustrates, the radical potential for intersectionality lies in moving beyond its acknowledgement of categorical differences to build political coalitions based on the recognition of connections among systems of oppression as well as on a shared vision of social justice. We used an analysis of the interlocking systems of race, gender, and disability in conjunction with a radical practice of coalition building between reproductive rights and justice, antiracist, and disability rights activists to demonstrate the use of an intersectional paradigm as a positive tool for social change. In the process we have learned several important lessons for how to "do" intersectionality in organizing and advocacy.

First, a good process for radical relationship- and alliance-building requires forthrightly acknowledging the multiple intersecting lived experiences of all participants. Radical alliances can only be built on the basis of being honest about differences and disagreements. This honesty is what creates the potential for new solidarities based on shared but different experiences. Second, trust must be developed through the process. Alliance building is a progressive, developmental process where trust is built through repeated contact, connection, conversation, and collective action. Identifying multiple and intersecting interests is crucial to creating repeated opportunities for collaboration. The third lesson is related to a willingness on the part of all participants to change their perspectives and politics. An intersectional framework is a critical tool for disrupting oppressed–oppressor binaries, and opening up the possibilities for discovering values and experiences in common. And the final lesson is to keep the focus on shared values. While scholars and advocates for social change might disagree on general strategy and tactics, they can more easily agree on shared values that can form the basis for a common vision, as well as for joint action on specific campaigns. Here again, an intersectional approach is useful in deconstructing disagreements and reconstructing similar experiences and hopes.

Using this approach can have interesting and unintended consequences. In this case of genetic technologies, Generations Ahead used intersectionality to create a cohort of women of color leaders on an issue that is traditionally presumed to be a White, mostly affluent women's issue. When Generations Ahead first began engaging women of color activists in conversations about reproductive genetic technologies there was a significant amount of pushback that this was not a priority issue since White women who could afford it were the primary users of these technologies. Issues of class and privilege were a constant implicit and explicit aspect of these conversations and actions. Without using an intersectional approach, it would have been impossible to engage activists who often argued that they did not have time for this discussion when there were other more pressing issues to focus on, such as access to basic reproductive health care. Now, through intersectionality, a cohort of women of color has emerged who speak and act authoritatively on these issues and make the connections between policies on genetic technologies and inequities based on race, gender, disability, and class, perspectives that are rarely acknowledged in mainstream discussions. While the actions the women organized seemed to focus on the intersection of gender and disability, race was an embedded and important element, as it was women of color who were visible leaders in the organizing. Through their presence and leadership they disrupted the assumptions that reproduction and disability are "White issues" and reminded others that there was more at stake for social justice. Through their activism they have started conversations that are critically important now and will only become more so in the future as the use of genetic technologies increases.

In acknowledging that all of us have multiple identities and by including all of those identities in the organizing process, intersectionality in practice can be a powerful tool for grappling with differences and uncovering shared values and bridging frameworks. This process provides a basis for collective action and a model for alternative social relationships rooted in our common humanity. Instead of separating groups, as some have argued, using an intersectional framework can create new and authentic alliances even among historically oppositional groups that can lead to more inclusive, focused, and effective efforts for social change. Intersectionality as a theory and practice for social change can, and should, be used as a critical tool in struggles for social justice that seek to include us all.

NOTES

1. I thank Alexius Cruz O'Malley for excellent research assistance and the Kirkland & Ellis Fund and the Dorothy Ann and Clarence L. Ver Steeg Distinguished Research Fellowship for generous research support.

2. See Thornton Dill (1983), "Just as the gender-class literature tends to omit race, the race-class literature gives little attention to women" (p. 137).

3. Delineating "a wide range of methodological approaches to the study of multiple, intersecting, and complex social relations" as anticategorical, intercategorical, and intracategorical complexity (McCall 2005, pp. 1772–1773).

4. Dhamoon (2011) distinguishes among *"identities* of an individual or set of individuals or social group that are marked as different (e.g., a Muslim woman or Black women), the *categories of difference* (e.g., race and gender), the *processes of differentiation* (e.g., racialization and gendering), and the *systems of domination* (e.g., racism, colonialism, sexism, and patriarchy)" (p. 233, emphasis in original).

Dhamoon further argues identities and categories of difference "are ideally examined by contextualizing the processes and systems that constitute, govern, and counter difference" (p. 234).

5. Comparing social divisions such as gender which "tend to shape most people's lives in most social locations" to social divisions such as disability, which "tend to affect fewer people globally" (Yuval-Davis 2011, pp. 155, 160). Indeed, we have heard disability rights activists note that disability is the one identity that everyone will share if they live long enough. "The biggest difference between disability and the other stigmatized statuses we have considered here is that on the other cases the non-stigmatized have little fear of suddenly joining the ranks of the stigmatized" (Gordon and Rosenblum, 2005, p. 16).

6. Arguing that "disability as a category of analysis, an historical community, a set of material practices, a social identity, a political position, and a representational system" should be integrated in feminist theory (Garland-Thomson 2002, p. 28).

7. "We know something of how the history of disability rights activism owes something to the civil rights movements of Blacks in this and other countries, but we know only relatively little about how Whiteness and racism is played out in concrete terms on the bodies of people with disabilities as they struggle to move from the margins to the center" (Smith 2004, p. 21).

REFERENCES

Anzaldua, Gloria and AnaLouise Keating (Eds.) (2002). *This Bridge We Call Home: Radical Visions for Transformation.* New York: Routledge.

Asch, Adrienne (2007). Why I Haven't Changed by Mind about Prenatal Diagnosis: Reflections and Refinements. In Erik Parens and Adrienne Asch (Eds.), *Prenatal Testing and Disability Rights,* pp. 234–258. Washington, DC: Georgetown University Press.

Beamish, Thomas D. and Amy J. Luebbers (2009). Alliance Building across Social Movements: Bridging Difference in a Peace and Justice Coalition. *Social Problems,* 56(4): 647–676.

Brown, Wendy (1997). The Impossibility of Women's Studies. *Difference: A Journal of Feminist Cultural Studies,* 9(3): 79–101.

Canaan, Andrea (1983). Brownness. In Cherrie Moraga and Gloria Anzaldua (Eds.), *This Bridge Called My Back: Writings by Radical Women of Color,* pp. 232–237. New York: Kitchen Table, Women of Color Press.

Cole, Elizabeth (2008). Coalitions as a Model for Intersectionality: From Practice to Theory. *Sex Roles,* 59: 443–453.

Crenshaw, Kimberlé (1989). Demarginalizing the Intersection of Race and Sex: A Black Feminist Critique of Antidiscrimination Doctrine, Feminist Theory and Antiracist Politics. *University of Chicago Legal Forum,* pp. 139–167.

Crenshaw, Kimberlé (2011). Postscript. In Helma Lutz, Maria Teresa Herrera Vivar, and Linda Supik (Eds.), *Framing Intersectionality: Debates on a Multi-Faceted Concept in Gender Studies*, pp. 221–233. Surrey, England: Ashgate Publishing Limited.

Davis, Kathy (2008). Intersectionality as Buzzword: A Sociology of Science Perspective on What Makes a Feminist Theory Successful. *Feminist Theory*, 9(1): 67–85.

Dhamoon, Rita Kaur (2011). Considerations on Mainstreaming Intersectionality. *Political Research Quarterly*, 64(1): 230–243.

Fireandreamitchell.com (2010). British Progressive Liberal Virginia Ironside Says Would Put a Pillow over the Head of Her Baby If It Was Suffering from a Disability. October 4. (http://www.fireandreamitchell.com/2010/10/04/british-progressive-liberal-virginia-ironside-says-would-put-a-pillow-over-the-head-of-her-baby-if-it-was-suffering-from-a-disability/) (accessed May 17, 2012).

Garland-Thomson, Rosmarie (2002). Integrating Disability, Transforming Feminist Theory. *NWSA Journal*, 14(3): 1–32.

Generations Ahead (2008). A Reproductive Justice Analysis of Genetic Technologies: Report on a National Convening of Women of Color and Indigenous Women. (http://www.generations-ahead.org/files-for-download/articles/GenAheadReport_ReproductiveJustice.pdf) (accessed May 17, 2012).

Generations Ahead (2009). Bridging the Divide: Disability Rights and Reproductive Rights and Justice Advocates Discussing Genetic Technologies, convened by Generations Ahead 2007–2008. (http://www.generations-ahead.org/files-for-download/articles/GenAheadReport_BridgingTheDivide.pdf) (accessed May 21, 2012).

Generations Ahead (2010). Robert Edwards, Virginia Ironside, and the Unnecessary Opposition of Rights. (http://www.generations-ahead.org/resources/the-unnecessary-opposition-of-rights) (accessed May 17, 2012).

Gordon, Beth Omansky and Karen E. Rosenblum (2005). Bringing Disability into the Sociological Frame: A Comparison of Disability with Race, Sex, and Sexual Orientation Statuses. *Disability & Society*, 16(1): 5–19.

Greenwood, Ronni Michelle (2008). Intersectional Political Consciousness: Appreciation for Intragroup Differences and Solidarity in Diverse Groups. *Psychology of Women Quarterly*, 32: 36–47.

Gutierrez, Elena R (2008). *Fertile Matters: The Politics of Mexican Origin Women's Reproduction*. Austin, TX: University of Texas Press.

Hill Collins, Patricia (2000). *Black Feminist Thought: Knowledge, Consciousness and the Politics of Empowerment*, 2ed. New York: Routledge.

Jesudason, Sujatha A. (2009). In the Hot Tub: The Praxis of Building New Alliances in Reprogenetics. *Signs: Journal of Women in Culture and Society*, 34(Summer): 901–924.

Jesudason, Sujatha and Julia Epstein (2012). The Paradox of Disability in Abortion Debates. (http://www.generations-ahead.org/files-for-download/success-stories/Paradox_of_Disability_in_Abortion_Debates_FINAL.pdf) (accessed May 17, 2012).

Keating, AnaLouise (2009). From Intersections to Interconnections, *Lessons for Transformation from* This Bridge Called my Back: Radical Writings by Women of Color. In Michele Tracy Berger and Kathleen Guidroz (Eds.), *The Intersectional Approach: Transforming the Academy through Race, Class, and Gender*, pp. 81–99. Chapel Hill, NC: University of North Carolina Press.

McCall, Leslie (2005). The Complexity of Intersectionality. *Signs*, 30(3): 1771–1800.

Morales, Rosario (1983). We're All in The Same Boat. In Cherrie Moraga and Gloria Anzaldua (Eds.), *This Bridge Called My Back: Writings by Radical Women of Color*, pp. 91–93. New York: Kitchen Table, Women of Color Press.

Nelson, Jennifer (2003). *Women of Color and the Reproductive Rights Movement*. New York: NYU Press.

Parens, Erik and Adrienne Asch (1999). The Disability Rights Critique of Prenatal Genetic Testing: Reflections and Recommendations. *The Hastings Center Report*, 29(5): s1–s22. The Hastings Center.

Pokempner, Jennifer and Dorothy E. Roberts (2001). Poverty, Welfare Reform, and the Meaning of Disability. *Ohio State Law Journal*, 62: 425–463.

The Prenatally and Postnatally Diagnosed Conditions Awareness Act Fact Sheet. (http://www.generations-ahead.org/files-for-download/success-stories/InfoSheet-BrownbackKennedyLegislation_final.pdf) (accessed May 17, 2012).

Roberts, Dorothy (1997). *Killing the Black Body: Race, Reproduction, and the Meaning of Liberty*. New York: Pantheon.

Roberts, Dorothy E. (2004). Women of Color and the Reproductive Rights Movement. *Journal of the History of Sexuality*, 13: 535–539.

Roberts, Dorothy E. (2005). Privatization and Punishment in the New Age of Reprogenetics. *Emory Law Journal*, 54: 1343–1360.

Roberts, Dorothy (2009). Race, Gender, and Genetic Technologies: A New Reproductive Dystopia? *Signs*, 34: 783–804.

Roberts, Dorothy (2011). *Fatal Invention: How Science, Politics, and Big Business Re-create Race in the Twenty-first Century*. New York: The New Press.

Russo, Ann (2009). Epilogue: The Future of Intersectionality: What's at Stake. In Michele Tracy Berger and Kathleen Guidroz (Eds.), *The Intersectional Approach: Transforming the Academy through Race, Class, and Gender,* pp. 309–318. Chapel Hill, NC: University of North Carolina Press.

Saxton, Marsha (2007). Why Members of the Disability Community Oppose Prenatal Diagnosis and Selective Abortion. In Erik Parens and Adrienne Asch (Eds.), *Prenatal Testing and Disability Rights,* pp. 147–164. Washington, DC: Georgetown University Press.

Silliman, Jael, Marlene Gerber Fried, Loretta Ross, and Elena R. Guttierez (2004). *Undivided Rights: Women of Color Organize for Reproductive Justice.* Boston, MA: South End Press.

Smith, Phil (2004). Whiteness, Normal Theory, and Disability Studies. *Disability Studies Quarterly,* 24(2): 1–30.

Thornton Dill, Bonnie (1983). Race, Class, and Gender: Prospects for an All-Inclusive Sisterhood. *Feminist Studies,* 9(1): 131–150.

Wendell, Susan (1996). *The Rejected Body: Feminist Philosophical Reflections on Disability.* New York: Routledge.

Yuval-Davis, Nira (2011). Beyond the Recognition and Re-distribution Dichotomy: Intersectionality and Stratification. In Helma Lutz, Maria Teresa Herrera Vivar, and Linda Supik (Eds.), *Framing Intersectionality: Debates on a Multi-Faceted Concept in Gender Studies,* pp. 155–169. Surrey, England: Ashgate Publishing Limited.

52

So Real It Hurts: Notes on Occupy Wall Street

MANISSA MCCLEAVE MAHARAWAL

I first went down to Occupy Wall Street last Sunday, almost a week after it had started. I didn't go down before because I, like many of my other brown friends, were wary of what we had heard or just intuited that it was mostly a young white male scene. When I asked friends about it they said different things: that it was really white, that it was all people they didn't know, that they weren't sure what was going on. But after hearing about the arrests and police brutality on Saturday and after hearing that thousands of people had turned up for their march I decided I needed to see this thing for myself.

So I went down for the first time on Sunday September 25th with my friend Sam. At first we couldn't even find Occupy Wall Street. We biked over the Brooklyn Bridge around noon on Sunday, dodging the tourists and then the cars on Chambers Street. We ended up at Ground Zero and I felt the deep sense of sadness that that place now gives me: sadness over how, what is now in essence, just a construction site changed the world so much for the worse. A deep sense of sadness for all the tourists taking pictures around this construction site that is now a testament to capitalism, imperialism, torture, oppression but what is also a place where many people died ten years ago.

. . .

We get to Liberty Plaza and at first it is almost unassuming. We didn't entirely know what to do. We wandered around. We made posters and laid them on the ground (our posters read: "We are all Troy Davis" "Whose streets? Our streets!" and "Tired of Racism" "Tired of Capitalism").

And I didn't know anyone down there. Not one person. And there were a lot of young white kids. But there weren't only young white kids. There were older people, there were mothers with kids, and there were a lot more people of color than I expected, something that made me relieved. We sat on the stairs and watched everyone mill around us. There was the normal protest feeling of people moving around in different directions, not sure what to do with themselves, but within this there was also order: a food table, a library, a busy media area. There was order and disorder and organization and confusion, I watched as a man carefully changed each piece of his clothing folding each piece he took off and folding his shirt, his socks, his pants and placing them carefully under a tarp. I used the bathroom at the McDonalds up Broadway and there were two booths of people from the protest carrying out meetings, eating food from Liberty Plaza, sipping water out of water bottles, their laptops out. They seemed obvious yet also just part of the normal financial district hustle and bustle.

October 3, 2011 Racialicious – the intersection of race and pop culture (www.racialicious.com) by Guest Contributor Manissa McCleave Maharawal, originally published on her Facebook page. Reprinted by permission of the author.

But even though at first I didn't know what to do while I was at Liberty Plaza I stayed there for a few hours. I was generally impressed and energized by what I saw: people seemed to be taking care of each other. There seemed to be a general feeling of solidarity, good ways of communicating with each other, less disorganization than I expected and everyone was very very friendly. The whole thing was bizarre yes, the confused tourists not knowing what was going on, the police officers lining the perimeter, the mixture of young white kids with dredlocks, anarchist punks, mainstream looking college kids, but also the awesome black women who were organizing the food station, the older man who walked around with his peace sign stopping and talking to everyone, a young black man named Chris from New Jersey who told me he had been there all week and he was tired but that he had come not knowing anyone, had made friends and now he didn't want to leave.

And when I left, walking my bike back through the streets of the financial district, fighting the crowds of tourists and men in suits, I felt something pulling me back to that space. It was that it felt like a space of possibility, a space of radical imagination. And it was energizing to feel like such a space existed.

And so I started telling my friends to go down there and check it out. I started telling people that it was a pretty awesome thing, that just having a space to have these conversations mattered, that it was more diverse than I expected. And I went back.

On Wednesday night I attended my first General Assembly. Seeing 300 people using consensus method was powerful. Knowing that a lot of people there had never been part of a consensus process and were learning about it for the first time was powerful. We conferred about using the money that was being donated to the movement for bail for the people who had been arrested. I was impressed that such a large group made a financial decision in a relatively painless way.

After the General Assembly that night there was both a Talent Show ("this is what a talent show looks like!") on one side of the Plaza and an anti-patriarchy working group meeting (which became the safer-spaces working group) on the other. (In some ways the juxtaposition of both these events happening at once feels emblematic of one of the splits going on down there: talent shows across the square from anti-patriarchy meetings, an announcement for a zombie party right after an announcement

about the killing of Troy Davis followed by an announcement that someone had lost their phone. Maybe this is how movements need to maintain themselves, through a recognition that political change is also fundamentally about everyday life and that everyday life needs to encompass all of this: there needs to be a space for a talent show, across from anti-patriarchy meetings, there needs to be a food table and medics, a library, everyone needs to stop for a second and look around for someone's phone. That within this we will keep centrally talking about Troy Davis and how everyone is affected by a broken, racist, oppressive system. Maybe, maybe this is the way?)

I went to the anti-patriarchy meeting because even though I was impressed by the General Assembly and its process I also noticed that it was mostly white men who were in charge of the committees and making announcements and that I had only seen one women of color get up in front of everyone and talk. A lot was said at the anti-patriarchy meeting about in what ways the space of the occupation was a safe space and also not. Women talked about not feeling comfortable in the drum circle because of men dancing up on them and how to change this, about how to feel safe sleeping out in the open with a lot of men that they didn't know, about not-assuming gender pronouns and asking people which pronouns they would prefer.

Here is the thing though: I've had these conversations before, I'm sure a lot of us in activist spaces have had these conversations before, the ones that we need to keep having about how to make sure everyone feels comfortable, how to not assume gender pronouns and gender roles. But there were plenty of people in this meeting who didn't know what we were doing when we went around and asked for people's names and preferred gender pronoun. A lot of people who looked taken aback by this. Who stumbled through it, but also who looked interested when we explained what we were doing. Who listened to the discussion and then joined the conversation about what to do to make sure that Occupy Wall Street felt like a space safe for everyone. Who said that they had similar experiences and were glad that we were talking about it.

This is important because I think this is what Occupy Wall Street is right now: less of a movement and more of a space. It is a space in which people who feel a similar frustration with the world as it is and as it has been, are coming together and thinking about ways to re-create this world. For some people this is the first time they have thought about how the world needs to be re-created. But some of us have been thinking about this for a while now. Does this mean that those of us who have been thinking about it for a while now should discredit this movement? No. It just means that there is a lot of learning going on down there and that there is a lot of teaching to be done.

On Thursday night I showed up at Occupy Wall Street with a bunch of other South Asians coming from a South Asians for Justice meeting. Sonny joked that he should have brought his dhol so we could enter like it was a baarat. When we got there they were passing around and reading a sheet of paper that had the Declaration of the Occupation of Wall Street on it. I had heard the "Declaration of the Occupation" read at the General Assembly the night before but I didn't realize that it was going to be finalized as THE declaration of the movement right then and there. When I heard it the night before with Sonny we had looked at each other and noted that the line about "being one race, the human race, formally divided by race, class . . ." was a weird line, one that hit me in the stomach with its naivety and the way it made me feel alienated. But Sonny and I had shrugged it off as the ramblings of one of the many working groups at Occupy Wall Street.

But now we were realizing that this was actually a really important document and that it was going to be sent into the world and read by thousands of people. And that if we let it go into the world written the way it was then it would mean that people like me would shrug this movement off, it would stop people like me and my friends and my community from joining this movement, one that I already felt a part of. So this was urgent. This movement was about to send a document into the world about who and what it was that included a line that erased all power relations and decades of history of oppression. A line that would de-legitimize the movement, this would alienate me and people like me, this would not be able to be something I could get behind. And I was already behind it this movement and somehow I didn't want to walk away from this. I couldn't walk away from this.

And that night I was with people who also couldn't walk away. Our amazing, impromptu, radical South Asian contingency, a contingency which stood out in that crowd for sure, did not back down. We did not back down when we were told the first time that Hena spoke that our concerns could be emailed and didn't need to be dealt with then, we didn't back down when we were told that again a second time and we didn't back down when we were told that to "block" the declaration from going forward was a serious serious thing to do. When we threatened that this might mean leaving the movement, being willing to walk away, I knew it was a serious action to take, we all knew it was a serious action to take, and that is why we did it.

I have never blocked something before actually. And the only reason I was able to do so was because there were 5 of us standing there and because Hena had already put herself out there and started shouting "mic check" until they paid attention. And the only reason that I could in that moment was because I felt so urgently that this was something that needed to be said. There is something intense about speaking in front of hundreds of people, but there is something even more intense about speaking in front of hundreds of people with whom you feel aligned and you are saying something that they do not want to hear. And then it is even more intense when that crowd is repeating everything you say—which is the way the General Assemblies or any announcements at Occupy Wall Street work. But hearing yourself in an echo chamber means that you make sure your words mean something because they are being said back to you as you say them.

And so when we finally got everyone's attention I carefully said what we felt was the problem: that we wanted a small change in language but that this change represented a larger ethical concern of ours. That to erase a history of oppression in this document was not something that we would be able to let happen. That we knew they had been working on this document for a week, that we appreciated the process and that it was in respect to this process that we wouldn't be silenced. That we demanded a change in the language. And they accepted our change and we withdrew our block as long as the document was published with our change and they said "find us after and we will go through it" and then it was over and everyone was looking somewhere else. I stepped down from the ledge I was standing on and Sonny looked me in the eye and said "you did good" and I've never needed to hear that so much as then.

Which is how after the meeting ended we ended up finding the man who had written the document and telling him that he needed to take out the part about us all being "one race, the human race." But its "scientifically true" he told us. He thought that maybe we were advocating for there being different races? No we needed to tell him about privilege and racism and oppression and how these things still existed, both in the world and someplace like Occupy Wall Street.

Let me tell you what it feels like to stand in front of a white man and explain privilege to him. It hurts. It makes you tired. Sometimes it makes you want to cry. Sometimes it is exhilarating. Every single time it is hard. Every single time I get angry that I have to do this, that this is my job, that this shouldn't be my job. Every single time I am proud of myself that I've been able to say these things because I used to not be able to and because some days I just don't want to.

This all has been said by many many strong women of color before me but every time, every single time these levels of power are confronted I think it needs to be written about, talked about, gone through over and over again.

And this is the thing: that there in that circle, on that street-corner we did a crash course on racism, white privilege, structural racism, oppression. We did a course on history and the declaration of independence and colonialism and slavery. It was hard. It was real. It hurt. But people listened. We had to fight for it. I'm going to say that again: we had to fight for it. But it felt worth it. It felt worth it to sit down on a street corner in the Financial District at 11:30 pm on a Thursday night, after working all day long and argue for the changing of the first line of Occupy Wall Street's official Declaration of the Occupation of New York City. It felt worth it not only because we got the line changed but also because while standing in a circle of 20, mostly white men, and explaining racism in front of them: carefully and slowly spelling out that I as a women of color experience the world way differently than the author of the Declaration, a white man, that this was not about him being personally racist but about relations of power, that he needed to, he urgently needed to listen and believe me about this, this moment felt like a victory for the movement on its own.

And this is the other thing. It was hard, and it was fucked up that we had to fight for it in the way we did but we did fight for it and we won. The line was changed, they listened, we sat down and re-wrote it and it has been published with our re-write. And when we walked away, I felt like something important had just happened, that we had just pushed a movement a little bit closer to the movement I would like to see—one that takes into account historical and current inequalities, oppressions, racisms, relations of power, one that doesn't just re-create liberal white privilege but confronts it head on. And if I have to fight to make that happen I will. As long as my people are there standing next to me while I do that.

Later that night I biked home over the Brooklyn Bridge and I somehow felt like the world was, just maybe, at least in that moment, mine, as well as everyone dear to me and everyone who needed and wanted more from the world. I somehow felt like maybe the world could be all of ours.

Much love (and rage)
Manissa

GLOSSARY

Ableism System of oppression that privileges the able-bodied (or those perceived as able-bodied) through everyday practices, attitudes, assumptions, behaviors, and institutional rules; includes the belief that able bodies are the norm; encompasses prejudice, stereotyping, and discrimination against those perceived by themselves or others as disabled.

Ageism System of oppression that privileges some people over others based on age through everyday practices, attitudes, assumptions, behaviors, and institutional rules; encompasses prejudice, stereotyping, and discrimination.

Agency The ability to act within and upon a social context, including the power to think about social expectations and structural constraints and to make decisions about a course of action. Individual and collective agency may reaffirm the social order by following social norms or challenge it by resisting the status quo or creating new norms.

Androgynous (1) A self-ascribed state of embodiment among individuals rejecting the binary structure of woman and man; similar to genderqueer and neutrois. (2) Also used as an adjective to describe others.

Asexual A self-ascribed state of being among individuals not interested in sexual expression or practice.

Bisexual A self-ascribed state of embodiment among people who desire emotional, physical, and/or sexual relations with persons of both sexes and genders.

Bullying Any type of repeated verbal harassment, physical assault, intimidation, or coercion that targets a person based on perceived and/or real social statuses.

Care Work A category of work that involves care activities done in service of others. Care work may be paid or unpaid and involves a wide range of activities including teaching, health care, domestic work, and raising children. Because of gender-based bias, care work is performed disproportionately by women and it is widely devalued in terms of remuneration (care work is low paid or unpaid) and the lack of recognition of its contribution to the economy and wealth creation (particularly in the development of children).

Chromosomes DNA that socially is defined to categorically represent females as XX, males as XY, and intersex as a myriad of possibilities.

Cisgender Latin prefix *cis* means "same"; refers to people who embody the gender associated with their birth-assigned sex.

Classism System of oppression that privileges some people over others based on socioeconomic status through everyday practices, attitudes, assumptions, behaviors, and institutional rules; it encompasses prejudice, stereotyping, and discrimination.

Coming Out (1) A continual and selective narrative speech act among individuals who choose to publicly affirm their state of embodiment, which may also reject assumed heterosexual and/or gender identities. (2) Also used by individuals who choose to publicly reject assumptions about their person (i.e. race membership, religious membership, etc.). (3) Allies may also come out to publicly announce their commitments.

Comparative Feminist Studies Model A curricular strategy that emphasizes a comparative model for gender and women's studies classes. The model explicitly attends to power and relations of domination and resistance by focusing on the interconnectedness between global/local, One Third/Two Thirds or North/South, white women/women of color, and so on. It rejects additive, relativist (different but equal), and dualistic (oppositional categories) perspectives.

Cross-Dresser (CD) A self-ascribed state of embodiment among individuals who wear clothing and accessories associated with a different gender and may be inspired for both sexual and nonsexual reasons. Although antiquated and stigmatized, cross-dresser is sometimes synonymous with "transvestite."

Determining Gender The social practices of placing others in gender categories; occurs at multiple levels including everyday interactions, legal cases, policy decisions, and *the imaginary* or the hypothetical situations people imagine.

Disablism A social oppression that restricts people with impairments and undermines their well-being.

Discrimination The unequal allocation of valued goods and resources based on one's social position and group membership, which includes limiting the access of some groups to full benefits, privileges, and rights.

Domestic Violence (Intimate Partner Violence) Various forms of violence within partner and familial relationships, ranging from emotional (intimidation, isolation, threats) to physical, financial, and sexual abuse.

Drag Artists People who perform entertaining acts by wearing clothing and accessories associated with the different sex and gender of the performer.

Drag King A self-ascribed state of embodiment among female-bodied people who dress and perform as men, at times in a subversive way to expose some expressions of masculinity.

Drag Queen A self-ascribed state of embodiment among males who dress and perform as women.

Dyke (1) A self-ascribed identity term among female-bodied people who desire emotional, physical, and/or sexual relations with women. (2) May also be used as an epithet.

Emotion Work The management of one's own or another's emotions or feelings such as the evocation or suppression of emotion. This term typically refers to unpaid emotion work that occurs outside of work settings such as with friends and family (see also emotional labor).

Emotional Labor Emotion work that is performed for pay, as part of required or expected duties, in a work setting.

Essentialism (Essentialist) A theoretical perspective that naturalizes differences between social groups (such as gender differences, racial differences, etc.), often positing their origins in biology (i.e., genes, chromosomes, DNA, etc.).

Estrogen Hormone most often associated with females; however, estrogen is present in all bodies.

Ethnicity A socially constructed category based on characteristics such as national origin or heritage, geography, language, customs, or cultural practices (i.e., Italian, Puerto Rican, Cuban, Kurdish, Serbian, etc.).

Ethnocentrism The practice of judging another culture using the standards of one's own culture.

Family A socially constructed group whose members perceive themselves as linked by birth, marriage, adoption, cohabitation, or other means. Families come in a plurality of forms.

Female to Male (FtM/F2M) (1) A self-ascribed state of embodiment among individuals labeled female at birth who identify as men and/or present in a masculine expression. (2) Also used as an adjective to describe a transition process.

Feminism A wide range of theoretical and political perspectives that assert gender equality and that value the experiences of marginalized groups such as women and girls. Feminism is committed to activism, social change, and equality.

Gay (1) A self-ascribed state of embodiment among men who desire emotional, physical, and/or sexual relations with men. (2) Also used to refer to all gay men and lesbians. (3) Commonly used to describe something as stupid or dumb.

Gender Socially constructed categories that, in many societies, are based on a binary system that differentiates between masculinity and femininity and men and women. Recently, new gender identities such as transgender, androgynous, and genderqueer categories have been embraced and advanced.

Gender Authenticity Refers to the pursuit of full recognition as a "real" woman or man, particularly for transgender persons (see Jenness and Fenstermaker in this volume).

Gender-Bender or Gender-Blender A person who chooses to "bend" or "blend" gender roles and expressions by combining gender displays that are associated with both masculinity and femininity or that cut across sex categories and boundaries.

Gender Ideology A set of culturally and historically specific meanings that shape the social expectations for bodies, behaviors, emotions, and family and work roles, based on gender classifications.

Gender Image/Display The presentation of oneself through social interaction using culturally recognized gender symbols and markers.

Gender Reassignment Surgery (GRS) Various types of surgical procedures that some transgender individuals undergo to medically and physically align their bodies with their gender identity.

Gender Violence or Gender-Based Violence Violence that is directed against a person on the basis of gender. Gender violence reflects and reinforces gender inequalities and the larger gender order (of sex/gender system). As such, women and girls are the primary targets of gender violence although boys and men are affected as well, particularly in the enforcement of dominant masculinities. See also *sex trafficking*, *rape*, *sexual assault*, and *sexual harassment*.

Gender Wage Gap (or Gender Pay Gap) The difference between men's and women's earnings expressed as a percentage of men's earnings. The wage gap is the result of a variety of causes, including employment discrimination, occupational gender segregation (differences in the pay of positions predominantly held by men and women), and other factors. See also *occupational gender segregation*.

Gendered Division of Labor The division and assignment of tasks on the basis of gender such as the assignment of women to domestic tasks in the home and family and men to nondomestic tasks in the economy and polity. The gender division of labor is an important basis for gender inequality where men's work is systematically better rewarded with pay, power, and prestige. See also *occupational gender segregation.*

Gendered Homophobia Refers to homophobia that is used to enforce gender boundaries and gender conduct. C. J. Pascoe describes, for example, the use of the homophobic slur "fag" by high school boys to regulate and stigmatize the behavior of other boys as not masculine. Denissen and Saguy (this volume) show how men in the construction trades use the label "lesbian," as well as the associated threat of marginalization and harassment, to sanction the gender conduct of women coworkers.

Genderqueer A self-ascribed state of embodiment among individuals who reject the binary gender structure of woman and man; similar to androgynous and neutrois.

Glass Ceiling The unseen yet unbreachable barrier that keeps women and racial-ethnic minorities from rising to the upper rungs of a corporation, regardless of qualifications and achievements.

Glass Escalator The advantages that men receive in female-dominated occupations such as nursing, teaching, and social work because of preferences for men and the higher value placed on qualities associated with masculinity.

Globalization The flow of goods, technology, services, and cultures across national boundaries as economic activities (production and consumption) and networks become globally dispersed yet highly interwoven.

Globalization of Women's Work The increasing migration of women from poor countries in the global south to rich countries in the global north to perform "women's work" or care work such as child care, domestic work, and sex work. This pattern of migration benefits affluent career women, affluent men (who continue to avoid the second shift), and wealthy corporations and wealthy countries. However, it comes at great cost to women migrants and their families, in part because children must often be left behind (see *transnational motherhood*).

Hate Crime Crimes that are motivated by bias and hate against an individual based on perceived or actual social status membership (i.e., race, ethnicity, gender, sexuality, ability, religion, etc.).

Hegemonic Dominant beliefs or ideals that are taken for granted and thus "naturalized" in a culture at any given time.

Hegemonic Masculinity Refers to the dominant form of masculinity in any sociohistorical context. See also transnational business masculinity.

Hermaphrodite An antiquated and stigmatizing scientific term that was used to describe individuals with varying and/or multiple sex characteristics (i.e., chromosomes, genitalia, reproductive organs, hormones, etc.) that challenge sex determinations of "female" or "male."

Heteronormativity A system that institutionalizes heterosexuality as the standard for legitimate and expected social and sexual relations (Chrys Ingraham).

Heterosexism System of oppression that privileges heterosexual people through everyday practices, attitudes, behaviors, and institutional rules through the promotion of heterosexuality as natural and normal.

Heterosexual (1) A self-ascribed state of embodiment among individuals who desire emotional, physical, and/or sexual relations with people of their "opposite" sex and gender. (2) Also used as an adjective to describe others.

Homophobia The fear, hatred, or disapproval of and discrimination against lesbian, gay, and bisexual people.

Homosexual A self-ascribed state of embodiment among individuals who desire emotional, physical, and/or sexual relations with people of the same sex and/or gender. Some consider this an antiquated term linked to a medicalized history of stigma and shame.

Hormone Replacement Therapy (HRT) A medical process sometimes prescribed for or requested by women in menopause and transgender persons.

Hybrid Masculinities Men's selective incorporation of performance and identity elements associated with marginalized and subordinated masculinities and femininities (Bridges and Pascoe 2014).

Hypermasculinity The exaggerated exhibition of characteristics associated with masculinity such as strength, aggression, and physical or sexual domination of others, often in response to perceived threats to gender identity.

Ideology A belief system that shapes interpretations of the world and guides actions and behaviors. Ideologies often provide justification for inequality and oppression.

Intersectional (Intersectional Theory) An approach to studying various systems of inequality by thinking about difference in relational terms.

Intersex (Intersexuality) A broad term that describes individuals medically labeled outside of "typical" or "standard" sex categories (i.e., female or male). There are many causes and varieties of intersex expression. For more information, visit *Intersex Society of North America* (http://www.isna.org).

Lesbian A self-ascribed state of embodiment among women who desire emotional, physical, and/or sexual relations with women.

Male to Female (MtF/M2F) (1) A self-ascribed state of embodiment among individuals labeled male at birth who identify as women and/or in a feminine expression. (2) Also used as an adjective to describe a transition process.

Matriarchy (1) Government or rule by women or mothers, (2) a system of inequality in which women and girls hold greater power and status in society and are dominant or privileged over men and boys, the opposite of patriarchy, (3) an egalitarian, nonpatriarchal system that emphasizes maternal and feminine cultural meanings and may be governed by mothers or women. Anthropologists hold that while there are matrilineal, matrilocal, and matrifocal societies (where family descent and residence is located or traced through the mother), there are no known matriarchal societies.

Misogyny The hatred of women.

Naturalization (Naturalizing) The claim that inequalities based in biology are natural, irreversible, or difficult to change.

Nature/Nurture Dichotomy A long-standing debate over the relative importance of biology and innate traits versus environment and social learning in explaining human behavior.

Neutrois A new term of self-description embraced by individuals who reject the binary structure of woman and man; similar to androgynous and genderqueer.

Non-op A popular colloquialism used in transgender communities to describe a transgender person's current embodiment and/or decision to not undergo surgical transition.

Occupational Gender Segregation The distribution of people across and within occupations on the basis of gender. Gender segregation may also occur in specific jobs within occupations as well as across types of establishments (such as the greater share of men as wait staff in expensive restaurants). Women and men are segregated *horizontally* into "women's jobs" and "men's jobs" as well as *vertically* into high- and low-status positions. Occupational gender segregation is caused in large part by gender-based discrimination and it contributes to the gender wage gap. See also *gendered division of labor*.

Oppression The systematic denial of access to cultural, material, and institutional resources based on perceived or actual social status membership (i.e., race, ethnicity, gender, sexuality, ability, religion, etc.).

Outted Describes a nonconsensual public speech act or written announcement concerning an individual's identity or status that s/he wants to keep private (i.e., sexual identity, gender history, rape survivor, living with AIDS, etc.).

Pansexual A self-ascribed state of embodiment among individuals who recognize multiple sexes and genders and desire emotional, physical, and/or sexual relations with individuals, regardless of sex membership or gender embodiment.

Passing Describes a process whereby individuals are perceived in ways that afford keeping private an identity or status (i.e., sexual identity, gender history, rape survivor, living with AIDS, etc.).

Patriarchy (1) Government or rule by men. (2) A system of inequality in which men hold primary power in political leadership, moral authority, social privilege, and control of property and that entails the subordination of women and girls. (3) An ideological system based on the belief that men are inherently dominant or superior to women that can be believed or acted upon by either men or women (hooks 2004).

Post-op A popular colloquialism used in transgender communities to describe a transgender person's current embodiment after surgical procedures to medically or physically transition.

Power Evasive Frames Refers to explanations of social inequalities that blame individuals and groups for their supposed deficiencies and that dismiss the impact of historical, structural, and institutional causes.

Pre-op A popular colloquialism used in transgender communities to describe a transgender person's current embodiment prior to undergoing elective surgical procedures to transition (assumes decision has already been made).

Prism of Difference A way of thinking about gender that uses the image of a prism that refracts light into an ordered rainbow of colors to illustrate how gender relations are ordered when refracted through sexual, racial, class, age, and other social differences.

Privilege The systematic access to valued cultural and institutional resources that are denied to others based on social status membership (i.e., race, ethnicity, gender, sexuality, ability, religion, etc.).

Privileged Identities (see Privilege above)

Queer (1) A self-ascribed state of embodiment among individuals who reject and live outside of heteronormative structures; (2) a broad umbrella term used in place of the "LGBT" acronym.

Race Socially constructed categories that group people together based on physical features, such as phenotypic expression, skin tone, and hair textures; may also include ethnic characteristics (i.e. socially constructed cultural and economic characteristics).

Racism System of oppression that privileges people over others based on constructed racial classifications. Racism privileges those with greater social power and oppresses others through everyday practices, attitudes, assumptions, behaviors, and institutional rules and structures.

Rape A type of sexual assault that typically includes sexual penetration or intercourse without consent carried out by physical force, coercion, or abuse of authority or against a person who is incapable of valid consent.

Second Shift, the Refers to the labor performed at home in addition to paid work performed in the formal sector. Arlie Hochschild and Anne Machung described the double burden experienced by late-20th-centruy employed mothers in their 1989 book, *The Second Shift: Working Parents and the Revolution at Home.*

Secondary Sex Characteristics Biological attributes that most often, but not always, emerge during puberty and have social meaning related to gender and sexuality.

Sex Socially constructed categories based on culturally accepted biological attributes. In Western culture, females and males are categorized on the basis of chromosomes, genitalia, reproductive organs, and hormones.

Sex Reassignment Surgery (SRS) Various types of surgical procedures that some transgender individuals undergo to medically and physically align their bodies with their identity.

Sex Trafficking The process by which a person is recruited to be controlled and held captive for the purpose of sexual exploitation; includes the use of force, fraud, deception, abuse of power, and abuse of the vulnerable social or economic status of the victim.

Sexism System of oppression that privileges men over women through everyday practices, attitudes, assumptions, behaviors, and institutional rules and structures.

Sexual Assault Any involuntary or nonconsensual sexual act (such as sexual penetration, groping, kissing, sexual touching, sexual torture).

Sexual Harassment Bullying or coercion of a sexual nature including unwelcome sexual advances or attention, promise of rewards in exchange for sexual favors, or actions that create a hostile or offensive environment based on sexual threat or innuendo.

Sexual Identity (1) Sexual desire, attraction, and practice based on sexual object choice; similar to sexual orientation. (2) Category that encompasses identity terms including lesbian, gay, bisexual, pansexual, queer, or asexual.

Sexual Orientation A self-ascribed state of embodiment that describes sexual desires and practices; also implies an essential, unchanging orientation.

Sexual Scripts Socially learned norms for sexual situations, similar to a theatrical script that names the actors (which sexual partners are appropriate often based on race, gender, and age), defines the situation (when and where sexual acts are appropriate), and plots the behavior (what acts are appropriate). Sexual scripts are learned early on and typically provide for flexibility in shaping sexual behavior.

Sexuality A broad term that encompasses a range of concepts, ideologies, identities, behaviors, and expressions related to sexual personhood and desire.

Significant Other (SO) A popular colloquialism used by queer and allied communities to refer to an intimate partner.

Social Construction See social constructionism (below).

Social Constructionism A theoretical approach that emphasizes the role of social interaction and culture in meaning-making practices, including those that shape social statuses (i.e., race, ethnicity, gender, sexuality, ability, religion, etc.) and produce inequality.

Social Institution An organized system that has a set of rules and relationships that govern social interactions and activities in which people participate to meet basic needs.

Social Stratification A system by which individuals are divided into social positions that are ranked hierarchically and tied to institutional inequality.

Stealth A popular colloquialism used in transgender communities to describe individuals who have chosen to keep private various identities or statuses.

Testosterone Hormone most often associated with masculinity; however, testosterone is present in all bodies.

Tranny/Trannie (1) A self-ascribed state of embodiment among some transgender people. (2) Extremely contextual and depends on the user's intentions and tone; may be offensive and considered an epithet.

Transgender (TG) (1) An umbrella term that includes individuals who change, cross, and/or go beyond or through the culturally defined binary gender categories (woman/man). (2) A self-ascribed state of embodiment.

Transition A process of social and/or medical gender transition.

Transman A self-ascribed state of embodiment among female-bodied people who identify as men and/or masculine.

Transnational Business Masculinity The hegemonic form of masculinity in the current postcolonial and neoliberal period. It is associated with the business executives and political leaders who control the dominant economic and political institutions. Transnational business masculinity is characterized by egocentrism, conditional loyalties, wealth and accumulation, and a declining sense of responsibility toward others.

Transnational Motherhood Refers to a specific variation in the organizational arrangements, meanings, and priorities of motherhood by migrant women who work and reside in a country different from the one where their children remain.

Transphobia/Transphobic A system of oppression that privileges non-trans-gender or cisgender people through everyday practices, attitudes, assumptions, behaviors, and institutional rules; encompasses prejudice, stereotyping, and discrimination.

Transsexual (TS) Rooted in the medical and sexological development of "trans" knowledge that regards people who desire to live differently than their assigned sex at birth. Historically, this term has implied medical (i.e., surgical and hormonal) transition.

Transvestite An antiquated medicalized term that describes individuals who cross-dress for sexual and/or nonsexual reasons.

Transwoman A self-ascribed embodiment among male-bodied people who identify as women and/or feminine.

Two-sex System The social construction of dichotomous sex categories, male and female, and their assignment to individuals.

World Gender Order The structure of relationships that interconnect the gender regimes of institutions, and the gender orders of local society, on a world scale.

REFERENCES

Bridges, Tristan and C.J. Pascoe. 2014. "Hybrid Masculinities: New Directions in the Sociology of Men and Masculinities." *Sociology Compass* 8(3): 246-258.

Federal Glass Ceiling Commission. *Solid Investments: Making Full Use of the Nation's Human Capital.* Washington, D.C.: U.S. Department of Labor, November 1995, p. 4.

hooks, bell (2004). "Understanding Patriarchy." *The Will to Change: Men, Masculinity, and Love.* Washington Square Press. pp. 17–25.

Intersex Society of North America (ISNA). Available online at http://www.isna.org/.

Johnson, Allan G. 2006. *Privilege, Power and Difference*, 2nd ed. Boston: McGraw–Hill.

Lober, Judith, and Lisa Jean Moore. 2006. *Gendered Bodies: Feminist Perspectives.* Roxbury.

Transsexual Road Map Glossary. 2006. Available online at http://www.tsroadmap.com/index.html/.

Yoder, Janice D. 2007. *Women & Gender: Making a Difference*, 3rd ed. Cornwall-on-Hudson, NY: Sloan Educational.